D1279830

WITH SOFTWARE LABORATORIES

COMPUTERS

THE USER PERSPECTIVE

WITH SOFTWARE LABORATORIES

COMPUTERS

THE USER PERSPECTIVE

THIRD EDITION

SARAH E. HUTCHINSON

STACEY C. SAWYER

IRWIN

Homewood, IL 60430
Boston, MA 02116

Dedicated to B.K.W. and
to the memory of Peter Laurence Schmidt
and Henry Jacques Schmidt.—S.C.S.

For Mary and Bob Henderson.—S.E.H.

Sponsoring editor:	Larry Alexander
Developmental editor:	Rebecca Johnson
Project editor:	Gladys True
Production manager:	Carma W. Fazio
Designer:	Maureen McCutcheon
Cover and part illustrator:	Kathleen Kinkopf
Artist:	Rolin Graphics
Compositor:	Progressive Typographers, Inc.
Typeface:	10½/12 Electra
Printer:	Von Hoffmann Press, Inc.

Library of Congress Cataloging-in-Publication Data

Hutchinson, Sarah E.
Computers: the user perspective: with software laboratories / Sarah E. Hutchinson, Stacey C. Sawyer.—3rd ed.
p. cm.
Includes index.
ISBN 0-256-09372-5
1. Computers. 2. End-user computing. 3. Applications software.
I. Sawyer, Stacey C. II. Title.
QA76.5.H872 1992
004—dc20 91-4058

Printed in the United States of America
2 3 4 5 6 7 8 9 0 VH 8 7 6 5 4 3 2

SUPPLEMENTS

For the Student

Laboratory Manual (software laboratories version only)

For the Instructor

Instructor's Manual with Transparency Masters and Study Guide Disk
Color Transparencies
Lecture Guide
Test Bank
Computest

Preface

Why We Wrote This Book: The Needs of the Users

Computers: The User Perspective, third edition, is oriented toward future computer *users*, not future computer specialists. Users—also called *end-users*—treat the computer as a tool for working with reports, spreadsheets, databases, and the like. They are not the specialists who will write programs for computers or who will design computer systems.

Too many introductory texts, we believe, try to please both users and specialists and, as a result, fail both. They don't provide enough technical detail for the specialist, but they offer too much detail and not enough practical, business-related information for the user.

Why We Believe You Should Consider This Book

We believe that our book offers many of the features desired by today's instructors of the introductory course. We wrote our book to provide instructors and students with:

A User Orientation Our book is directly relevant to the user. It prepares students to use computers in business and to communicate effectively with computer specialists, such as programmers and systems designers. Everything in this book—every topic, illustration, case, and so on—is geared to the user, providing what he or she needs to know to use a computer in a business or a professional career. For example, in Chapter 10, "Systems Development Life Cycle," we explain the phases of the cycle so that students can see where they'll be involved in the process as users and thus be better able to communicate with analysts and programmers to get their needs met.

A Straightforward Look and Approach We conducted market research to learn what instructors really want from an introductory book. We learned that many instructors have become disgruntled with the overdone, confusing look and style of typical introductory texts. The instructors are concerned about the numerous boxed features, margin notes, cartoons, crossword puzzles, and the haphazard use of colors. We've taken these concerns to heart and provided solid, meaningful, and practical coverage that is not obscured by margin notes, boxed features, and other elements that compete for students' attention.

Also, we use color *meaningfully* to enhance content, not overpower it. We use four specific colors to indicate input, storage, processing, and output. As Figure 1.3 shows, *red* is used for input, *blue/green* for storage, *rust* for processing, and *gold* for output.

Flexibility Our market research has shown that some instructors teach only concepts in this course; others offer exposure to software packages; still others want students to learn packages plus some BASIC programming. In an attempt to keep up-to-date and meet employers' needs, instructors end up frequently changing books.

Thus, we've designed our book to allow you to teach the course the way you want. The first four parts of our book cover fundamentals: introduction, hardware, software, and systems concepts. Part V of the textbook with software laboratories is a "Microcomputer Laboratory." It contains five modules that cover microcomputer operating systems, word processing, spreadsheets, database management, and graphics. The "Introduction to the Modules" gives students detailed information about using a microcomputer keyboard. Each module concludes with a tutorial, "In the Lab," which introduces the student to a popular commercial software package — DOS, WordPerfect, Lotus 1-2-3, and dBASE IV. (dBASE III Plus is offered in

FIGURE 1.3

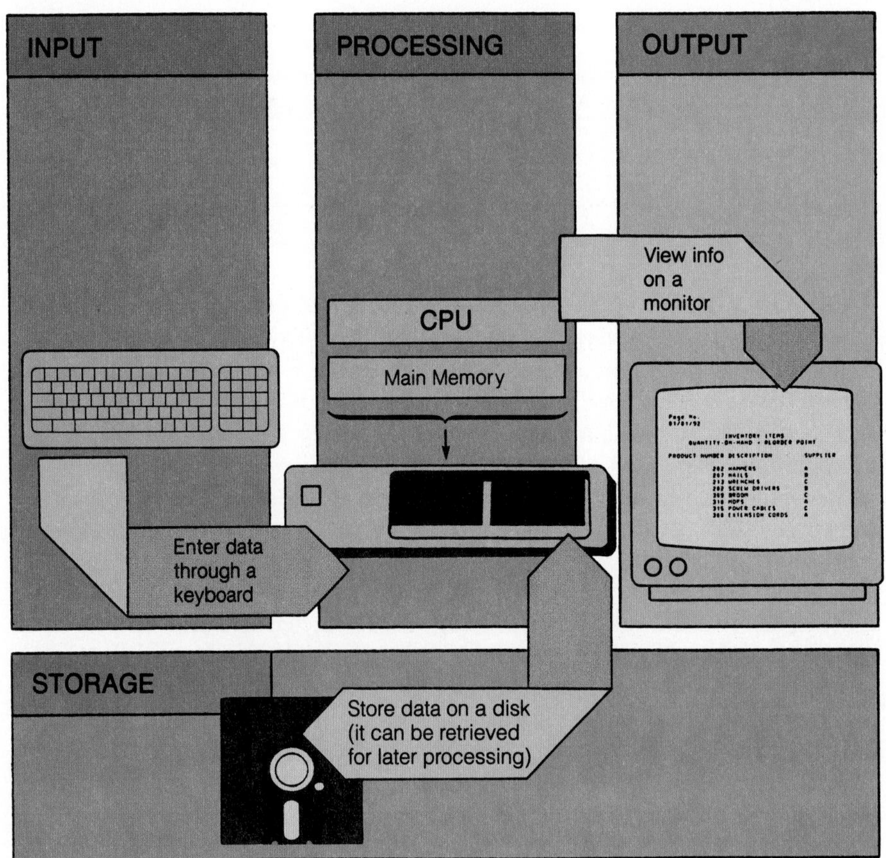

the Instructor's Manual.) Because each module is self-contained, you can choose the applications you want to cover and teach them in the order you like.

Part V of the nonmodular (concepts) version of the text contains the same introduction as the modular version, with detailed information about using a microcomputer keyboard; however, instead of hands-on tutorials, it offers detailed generic information about the functions of word processing, desktop publishing, database management, spreadsheet, and graphics software packages.

A new appendix provides the student with information about purchasing and maintaining a microcomputer system, and the appendix on BASIC has been updated. This appendix is included to allow users to take that extra step—to try some programming—and thus learn to communicate better with programmers.

A Microcomputer Orientation This book covers all types of computers—supercomputers, mainframes, minicomputers, and microcomputers. When the topic lends itself, particular focus is given to microcomputers. For examples, see the following sections:

Chapter 4	"Direct Access Storage for Microcomputers," pp. 140–152
Chapter 5	"Main Memory (RAM) for Microcomputers," pp. 176–178.
Chapter 7	"Additional Systems Software Information for Microcomputer Users," pp. 282–286.
Sporting Life, Episode 3	"What Are the Guidelines for Buying a Microcomputer?" pp. 386–390.

Microcomputer use is also the theme of Part V. For instructors who prefer a text that focuses *exclusively* on microcomputers, we have prepared the first edition of *Microcomputers: The User Perspective*.

A Continuing Business Case—"Sporting Life" Sporting Life is the name of the sporting goods store featured in our ongoing case. The four episodes are intended to be thought provoking rather than hands-on exercises. Students at this stage need real-life examples to put the concepts they've learned into perspective, but they don't yet have the background to, for example, actually choose the hardware and the software for a company. By putting themselves in the shoes of Sporting Life's owner, they gain insight into the trials and tribulations of computerizing a business.

An Interesting Writing Style Reviewers and users of this book have consistently praised our writing style. Our primary goal is to reach students—to make all the explanations as clear, relevant, and interesting as possible.

Pedagogy We've carefully developed our learning aids to maximize students' comprehension:

- *The User Perspective* opens each chapter, explaining why the user needs to know the material in that chapter.
- *History* is covered as it naturally arises in the discussion of each topic, making it more immediately relevant than if it were isolated within a separate chapter. Also, history is covered in only enough detail to provide a context for the

topic under discussion — the level of historical detail does not overwhelm the currency of the topic.

- *Great Expectations* sections briefly discuss what the future may hold for the areas covered in each chapter from Chapter 3 through Chapter 12.
- *Computers and Careers* boxes — a new feature — discuss the uses of computers in many different professions and businesses, from casting actors in films to running a restaurant or caring for zoo animals. This feature appears in Chapters 3 through 12.
- *Summary* sections that students can use for review conclude each chapter.
- *Key Terms* sections list all the important terms covered in the chapter and the number of the page where each term is defined. All key terms are also listed and defined in the glossary in the back of the book.
- *Exercises* — matching, multiple choice, short answer, and projects — test students' comprehension and encourage them to learn more about computers on their own.

WHAT'S NEW IN THIS EDITION

In addition to the career boxes, the third edition includes many additions and changes. First, at the request of users and reviewers of the second edition, we have prepared *two* versions of the third edition. The *modular version* (with software laboratories) contains the hands-on "In the Lab" tutorials in the modules in Part V, with fairly detailed sections on generic software functions in Chapter 7. The *nonmodular (concepts) version* does not include hands-on tutorials; instead, in this version, Part V consists of two new chapters, Chapters 13 and 14, which provide detailed coverage of the generic functions of commonly used software packages — word processing, database management, spreadsheet, desktop publishing, and graphics. Correspondingly, Chapter 7 in the nonmodular (concepts) version of the text includes less detailed coverage of software package functions than does Chapter 7 in the modular version. The appendix on buying and maintaining a microcomputer system — including how to install software — appears after Chapter 7 in the nonmodular version and at the back of the book in the modular version.

Second, because the topic of communications has become so important, the chapter on connectivity is now Chapter 9 instead of Chapter 12. Also, the database chapter now precedes the MIS chapter, so Part IV now consists of systems design and development (Chapter 10), database (Chapter 11), and management information systems (Chapter 12).

Of course, all hardware and software coverage has been updated, and more material has been added on the topic of the ethics of computer use. (The Instructor's Manual also includes a special expanded section on workplace issues, security, and ethics that can be used as the topic of an entire class session or copied and distributed to the students to read on their own.) The coverage of software utilities, public information services, and fax has been expanded, and new material on ISDN, hypertext, and multimedia has been added. Database terminology has been updated, and new trends in information management are discussed.

SUPPLEMENTS

Our market research showed that it's not important how *many* supplements a book has; what's important is what they are, how useful they are, and whether they're of high quality. We offer a number of supplements that we believe you'll find especially beneficial. You'll also find them to be of high quality; to ensure that they're truly useful and accurate, we've had them reviewed by instructors teaching this course.

INSTRUCTOR'S MANUAL WITH TRANSPARENCY MASTERS

This supplement contains:

Student profile sheet.

Course planning guidelines.

Chapter/module outlines.

Teaching tips.

Suggestions for using the transparency masters and full-color overhead transparencies.

Suggestions for using the Lab Manual and the Study Guide.

73 transparency masters.

COLOR TRANSPARENCIES

Seventy-five full-color transparencies of key illustrations and tables are available to qualified adopters.

TEST BANK

For each chapter/module, this supplement contains:

True/false, multiple choice, and fill-in-the-blank questions, graded in difficulty and tied to the preview objectives that begin each chapter of text.

Two forms of a reading quiz to test students' comprehension of the material.

Sample final exam of the entire text.

All answers.

COMPUTEST

This computer-based test bank is available to qualified adopters.

LABORATORY MANUAL (software laboratories version only)

This manual includes additional software lessons that go beyond the "In the Lab" sections in the modular version of the text. These lessons center on the Sporting Life sporting goods store presented in the running case episodes of the text.

STUDY GUIDE

This supplement, stored on disk, is included with the Instructor's Manual and contains, for each chapter and module:

An outline.

A summary of why coverage is important to the user.

Study tips.

Self-test questions (fill-in-the-blank, true/false, matching, and multiple choice) with answers.

LECTURE GUIDE

This guide outlines every chapter of the text and provides synopses of all main sections. It also provides guidelines for using the color transparencies and the transparency masters.

QUALITY

We are pleased to publish the third edition of this book with Irwin. Their developmental model helped ensure that we have published a book to meet your needs.

ACQUISITION AND DEVELOPMENTAL EDITORS

Our acquisition and developmental editors served in an invaluable on-line, quality control capacity to guarantee that the Hutchinson-Sawyer texts approach, as closely as possible, the ideal textbooks of potential adopters. These editors worked on a weekly, and often daily, basis with us. Few, if any, publishers offer this high degree of editorial assistance and attention to detail.

REVISION PROCESS

The first edition of the text was created as the result of extensive market research, a word-by-word developmental edit of three drafts of the manuscript, reviews by 58 instructors and 13 computer specialists, and class testing.

The second edition was developed with the assistance of diary reviewers. These instructors submitted detailed chapter comments as they taught from the book. In addition, we solicited comments from other instructors. To ensure quality and accuracy, specialists were enlisted to review in the seven areas of programming, systems, database, management information systems, communications, trends, and BASIC. Once the first draft of the second edition was completed, we again had the manuscript reviewed for currency, accuracy, organization, level of detail, user orientation, microcomputer coverage, writing style, and pedagogical effectiveness.

Both versions of the third edition — modular and nonmodular — were developed on the basis of diary reviewers' comments as well as reviews from instructors who have not used the book.

Photo and Illustration Research

Professional photo researchers, illustrators, and photographers have worked closely with us and our editors to craft the illustration program for the third edition. This art program, highly praised by first and second edition adopters and reviewers, continues to directly reinforce the text and remains a visually distinctive feature of our book.

Development of the Supplements Package

As with the text itself, the supplements package was thoroughly reviewed. The Laboratory Manual, Study Guide, Instructor's Manual, and overhead transparencies were prepared by Sarah Hutchinson. The test bank was prepared by Patricia L. Wermers of North Shore Community College. Much attention has been given to the development of these supplements to provide features that have been requested by the marketplace.

Acknowledgments

We wish to thank the reviewers, who contributed greatly to the content, organization, and focus of this book and its supplements.

Marlene Campbell, Murray State University
Tom Cannon, Danville Community College
Ken Conway, Barnes Business College
John Dinsmore, Southern Illinois University, Carbondale
Karen Forcht, James Madison University
Jerry Fottral, Kirkwood Community College
Connie Fox, West Virginia Institute of Technology
Molly Hay, Mississippi County Community College
Linda Kieffer, Eastern Washington University
John Landon, University of La Verne
Eng-Ming Lin, Eastern Kentucky University
Barbara Maccarone, North Shore Community College
John Pharr, Cedar Valley College

Ron Robison, Arkansas Technical University
Vann Spivey, Wayne University
Terry Urbine, Eastern New Mexico University
Eileen Zisk, Community College of Rhode Island

Other Contributors

We also wish to thank Karen M. Gardner, Golden Gate University, for her contribution on artificial intelligence and expert systems in Chapter 12; Russell L. Breslauer, Chabot College, Hayward, California, for his helpful list of information on p. 480; Rose M. Laird, Annandale North Virginia Community College, Silver Spring, Maryland, for her "10 commandments" of programming (Figure 8.21); Eli Boyd Cohen and Elizabeth Cohen Boyd of Bradley University for writing the BASIC appendix; Scott McIntyre of the University of Colorado, Colorado Springs, for updating the BASIC appendix to meet industry standards; and Donald B. Hutchinson for his help with the programming chapter.

The complexities and difficulties of preparing and producing a textbook like this one can be overwhelming at times—and insurmountable without the help of good people and organizations such as those whose names are listed on the copyright page. These people —highly talented professionals—have all helped establish this book's high level of quality, and we are very grateful for their help. Special appreciation goes to Larry Alexander and Rebecca Johnson for editorial assistance above and beyond the call of duty and excellent reasons to visit Chicago, Boston, and Maine, to Laurel Anderson for her diligent photo research, and to Gladys True for her excellent work and for surviving the production schedules and harassments of *two* editions!

Finally, we need to know: Was this book truly *useful* to students? We'd like to hear from you about any misstatements we might correct or improvements we could make. Write to us in care of our publisher, Richard D. Irwin.

Sarah E. Hutchinson
Stacey C. Sawyer

Contents in Brief

Contents

Part I

The Beginning: Becoming a Computer User

1

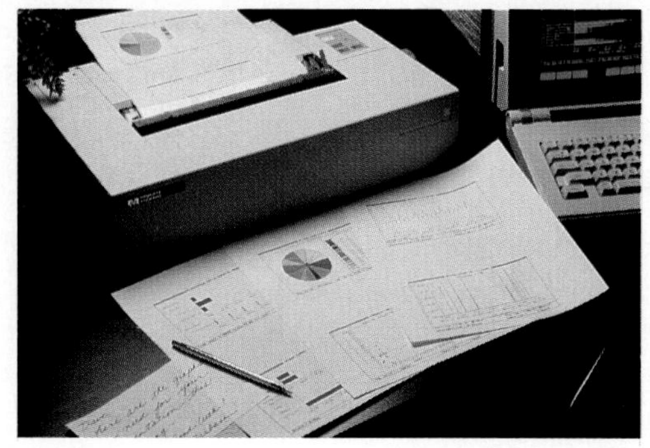

Part II

Hardware

75

CHAPTER 5

PROCESSING HARDWARE 165

CHAPTER 6

OUTPUT HARDWARE 192

SPORTING LIFE EPISODE 2:

WHAT DO YOU WANT THE COMPUTER TO DO FOR YOU? 237

Part III

Software and Connectivity

CHAPTER 9

DATA COMMUNICATIONS 338

SPORTING LIFE EPISODE 3:

WHAT ARE THE GUIDELINES FOR BUYING A MICROCOMPUTER SYSTEM? 386

Part IV

Systems Concepts and Applications

391

Part V

Microcomputer Laboratory

505

MODULE B
WORD PROCESSING: WORDPERFECT 557

MODULE C
ELECTRONIC SPREADSHEETS: LOTUS 1-2-3 591

WITH SOFTWARE LABORATORIES

COMPUTERS

THE USER PERSPECTIVE

Part I

The Beginning: Becoming a Computer User

The *end-user*, or simply the *user*—this is a term no longer heard only in computer and data processing circles. The user is *you*—the person at the end of the data and information processing chain who receives the computer's services. However, being a computer *user* does not require being a computer *expert*, as you will see.

In this first part of the book, we describe what computer systems are and their critical role in business and society—and where you, as the user, fit in.

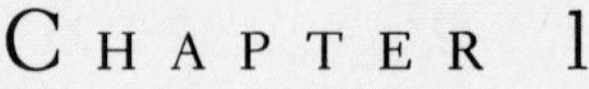

Chapter 1

Computers: Power Tools for an Information Age

The job interview can be a stressful experience for many people. But would you believe that some people actually *enjoy* interviewing for jobs? The secret, perhaps, lies in being prepared — knowing the company and the job for which you are applying, being certain of your accomplishments, and knowing which questions to ask.

Although most employers do not expect job seekers to be computer experts, they do expect their potential employees to be prepared to use computers as *tools* in whatever field or business they choose. Two questions apt to be asked today are "What do you know about computers?" and "What kind of software are you familiar with?" The more you know about how to use the computer as a resource, the more prepared you will be to handle such questions — and to enhance your effectiveness in and enjoyment of whatever activities you choose to pursue.

Preview

When you have completed this chapter you will be able to:

- Define who the user is.
- Explain what a computer system is by focusing on hardware, software, data/information, procedures, and people.
- Describe the four main types of computer systems and how each might be used in business.
- Define what it means to be computer literate and describe some of the major events in the development of computers.
- Name the three main hardware parts of a microcomputer system.
- Discuss some of the social implications of computerization.
- List some ways computers are used professionally.

The User Perspective

The automatic teller machine. The supermarket price scanner. The magic "wand" used in department stores to "read" clothing price tags. A voice on the phone that told you to "Please hang up and dial your call again."

Did you come in contact with one of these special-purpose computer devices today? If not, then you probably encountered something similar because the average person interacts — directly or indirectly — with a computer several times a day (Figure 1.1). You, then, are already a *user* of computer-processed information.

But you want to become more than that. You want to go beyond push buttons and digitized voices and become a trained user, someone who can join a business and use the computer as a problem-solving tool.

Who Is the User?

To help you better understand who the computer user is, consider the following distinction:

- A **computer professional** is a person in the field of computers — for example, a programmer, a systems analyst, or a computer operator — who has had formal education in the technical aspects of computers and who is concerned mainly with supporting the computer's physical functions in producing information for the user.
- The **user** is a person perhaps like yourself — someone without much technical knowledge of computers but who makes the decisions based on reports and other results that computers produce. The user is not necessarily a computer expert and may never need to become one. Most companies prefer to train new employees in the specific computer uses applicable to their business — and these applications may never require the user to have much technical knowledge.

Keep in mind, however, that the modern computer user is becoming more and more directly involved in the production of reports and other information through the hands-on use of *microcomputers*, often referred to as *personal*, or *desktop*, *computers*. Later in this chapter we describe the microcomputer in more detail.

As a person living in what is now often called "The Information Age," you know that computers aren't just a passing fad. Business depends on computers, and you will use computers in your job, as well as in the pursuit of private interests. To use them efficiently, you must become computer literate.

Computer Literacy: Why You're Reading This Book

Computer literacy has been a rapidly changing term. In the early 1980s, most computer professionals thought of it simply as "technical knowledge"; to users it usually meant only "computer awareness." Today, however, to be considered computer literate you must have a basic understanding of what a computer is and how it can be used as a resource. You are certainly considered computer literate if you can use a computer, probably a microcomputer, as a business tool to assist in producing the information necessary to make intelligent decisions. This change of definition is a direct result of the greatly increased use of microcomputers in business in the past decade. Because many management professionals already know how to use microcomputers, success in the business or professional world—*your* success—depends on mastering this skill, too.

Being computer literate means not only acknowledging the importance of computers and determining to overcome any fears about them, but also actively involving yourself with them. As a computer literate person you should:

- Master the terminology used to talk about what a computer is and how to use one.
- Learn to identify and describe the functions of the various components of a computer and an information system.
- Learn to use a computer to produce the information you need—that is, have some hands-on experience using word processing, spreadsheet, and database software packages (we discuss these software packages in detail later).

The objective of this book is to show you what a computer system is and how to use it—to help you achieve a level of computer literacy that will give you valuable

FIGURE 1.1

Computers in daily life. As these commonplace examples show, today it is almost impossible to avoid using a computer. (a) Users in some post offices can use a computer to find ZIP codes; (b) mass transit agencies are using computer technology and magnetic card readers to improve operations; (c) computers are being used in stores of all types to check out items; (d) students can use computers to retrieve data at the library.

(a)

(b)

(c)

(d)

skills in business and in your creative life. But don't be intimidated by the words *computer literacy*, and, by all means, don't be afraid to learn to use a computer! Computers were designed by people, built by people, programmed by people, and do only what people tell them to do.

WHAT IS A COMPUTER SYSTEM?

The term **computer** is used to describe a device made up of a combination of electronic and electromechanical (part electronic and part mechanical) components. By itself, a computer has no intelligence and is referred to as **hardware.** A computer doesn't come to life until it is connected to other parts of a computer system. A **computer system** (Figure 1.2) is a combination of five elements (listed here in the order of how expensive it would be to replace them in a system, from least to most expensive):

- Hardware.
- Software.
- Data/information.
- Procedures.
- People.

When one computer system is set up to communicate with another computer system, **connectivity** becomes a sixth system element. In other words, the manner in which the various individual systems are connected—for example, by phone lines, microwave transmission, or satellite—is an element of the total computer system.

Software is the term used to describe the instructions that tell the hardware how to perform a task; without software instructions, the hardware doesn't know what to do. People, however, constitute the most important component of the computer system. People operate the computer hardware; they create the computer software instructions and respond to the procedures that those instructions present. You will learn more about software and procedures later. Right now we want to discuss the importance of data and information.

The purpose of a computer system is to convert data into information. **Data** is raw, *unevaluated* facts and figures, concepts, or instructions. This raw material is processed into useful **information.** In other words, information is the product of **data processing.** This **processing** includes refining, summarizing, categorizing, and otherwise manipulating the data into a useful form for decision making. For example, the facts and figures contained in a stack of customer orders waiting to be entered into a computer-based order entry system are *data;* after the data is entered and processed, an output report about how that data affected product inventory would be *information*.

People "capture" data in a variety of ways—for example, by reading, listening, or seeing. Then they may record the data on a document. For instance, Roger Shu records his name on an employee timecard by first entering the letter *R*. This letter, and each of the remaining letters in his name, is an element of data, as are the numbers 12/22 and 5, used to indicate the date and the number of overtime hours worked. By themselves, these data elements are useless; we must process them to make them mean something. The report produced when Roger's data is run through a computer-based employee records system gives us information — for example, the amount of money due Roger for his overtime work.

Now we'll discuss the basics about the hardware devices that convert data into information in a typical computer-based system.

COMPUTER HARDWARE

If, at a job interview, you are asked about what kind of computer equipment you've used before or what you know about hardware, and you don't have an answer, your interviewer will probably perceive you as a person who doesn't take an active role in what's going on around you — a perception that could dramatically hurt your chances of getting the job you want. In today's business world, not knowing what computer hardware is and what typical hardware components do is similar to being a taxi driver and not knowing what a car is and that it has components such as an engine, doors, windows, and so on.

In Chapters 3 through 6 we talk in detail about the different categories of computer hardware. In this section, however, we provide a brief description of the components found in each category of hardware so that you can see how they relate

FIGURE 1.2

Recipe for a computer system. A computer system combines five elements: hardware, software, data/information, procedures, and people. Connectivity is a sixth element when two or more separate computer systems are set up to communicate.

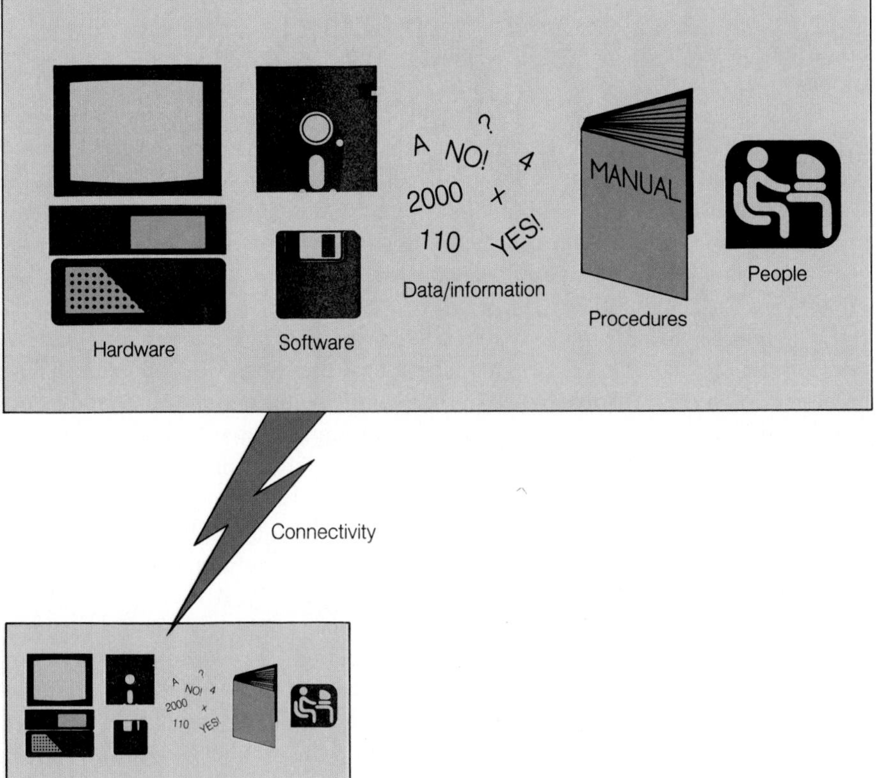

to one another and how they fit into the larger picture of computers in business. (Don't try to memorize a lot of details now; focus on the large concepts.)

Computer hardware can be divided into four categories: (1) input hardware, (2) storage hardware, (3) processing hardware, and (4) output hardware. Figure 1.3 shows the typical configuration of computer hardware.

INPUT HARDWARE

The purpose of input hardware is to collect data and convert it into a form suitable for computer processing. The most common input device is a **keyboard.** It looks very much like a typewriter keyboard with rows of keys arranged in the typical typewriter layout, as well as a number of additional keys used to enter special computer-related codes. Although it isn't the only type of input device available, the computer keyboard is the one most generally used by the business community. We will describe keyboard functions and other types of input devices in Chapter 3.

STORAGE HARDWARE

The purpose of storage hardware is to provide a means of storing computer instructions and data in a form that is relatively permanent, or **nonvolatile**—that is, the data is not lost when the power is turned off—and easy to retrieve when needed for

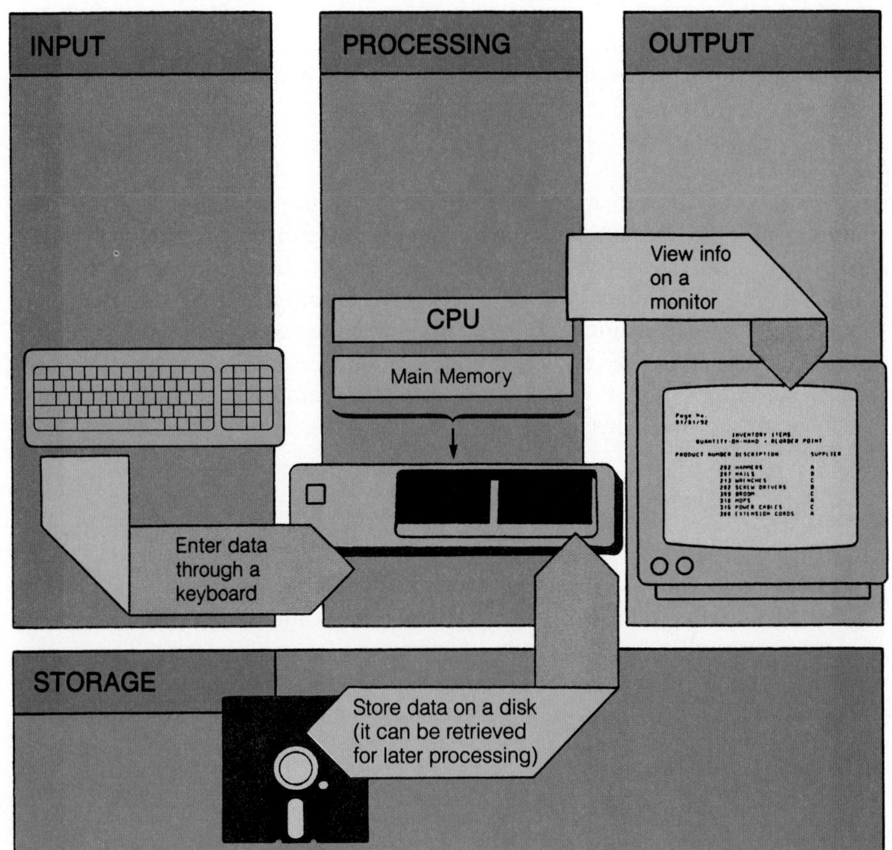

FIGURE 1.3

Typical hardware components. The four categories of computer hardware are input, storage, processing, and output.

processing. Storage hardware serves the same basic functions as do office filing systems except that it stores data as electromagnetic signals or laser-etched spots, commonly on disk or tape, rather than on paper. Storage devices are discussed in Chapter 4.

Processing Hardware

The purpose of processing hardware is to retrieve, interpret, and direct the execution of software instructions provided to the computer. The most common components of processing hardware are the central processing unit and main memory.

The **central processing unit (CPU)** is the brain of the computer. It reads and interprets software instructions and coordinates the processing activities that must take place. The design of the CPU affects the processing power and the speed of the computer, as well as the amount of main memory it can use effectively. With a well-designed CPU in your computer, you can perform highly sophisticated tasks in a very short time.

Main memory (also called *internal memory*, *primary storage*, or just *memory*) can be thought of as an electronic desktop. The more desk surface you have in front of you, the more you can place on it. Similarly, if your computer has a lot of memory, you can place more software instructions in it. The amount of memory available determines whether you can run simple or sophisticated software; a computer with a large memory is more capable of holding the thousands of instructions that are contained in the more sophisticated software programs. A large memory also allows you to work with and manipulate great amounts of data and information at one time. Quite simply, the more main memory you have in your computer, the more you can accomplish.

In Chapter 5, we describe computer processing and main memory in much more detail.

Output Hardware

The purpose of output hardware is to provide the user with the means to view information produced by the computer system. Information is output in either **hardcopy** or **softcopy** form. Hardcopy output can be held in your hand—examples are paper with text (words or numbers) or graphics printed on it. Softcopy output is displayed on a **monitor,** a television-like screen on which you can read text and graphics. We describe other types of output devices in Chapter 6. Communications hardware, which is used to transmit output among and receive input from different computer systems, is discussed in Chapter 9.

Computer Software

A computer is an inanimate device that has no intelligence of its own and must be supplied with instructions so that it knows what to do and how and when to do it. These instructions are called *software*. The importance of software can't be overestimated. You might have what most people consider the "best" computer sitting on your desk in front of you; however, without software to "feed" it, the computer will do nothing more than take up space.

Software is made up of a group of related **programs,** each of which is a group of related instructions that perform very specific processing tasks. Software acquired to perform a general business function is often referred to as a **software package.**

Software packages, which are usually created by professional software writers, are accompanied by **documentation**—users' manuals—that explains how to use the software.

Software can generally be divided into two categories: (1) systems software and (2) applications software. Chapter 7 explores each of these categories in detail, and Part V gives you even more information about microcomputer software. For now, some basic information will suffice.

SYSTEMS SOFTWARE

Programs designed to allow the computer to manage its own resources are called **systems software.** This software runs the basic operations; it tells the hardware what to do and how and when to do it. However, it does not solve specific problems relating to a business or a profession. For example, systems software will not process a prediction of what your company's tax bill will be next year, but it will tell the computer where to store the data used during processing; systems software will not process the creation of the animation strip for your next film, but it will manage how it is output.

APPLICATIONS SOFTWARE

Any instructions or collection of related programs designed to be carried out by a computer to satisfy a user's *specific* needs are **applications software.** A group of programs written to perform payroll processing is one type of applications software, as are programs written to maintain personnel records, update an inventory system, help you calculate a budget, or monitor the incubation temperatures at your poultry farm.

Applications software can be purchased "off the shelf," or packaged—that is, already programmed, or written—or it can be written to order by qualified programmers. If, for example, a company's payroll processing requirements are fairly routine, it can probably purchase one or more payroll applications software programs off the shelf to handle the job. However, if a company has unique payroll requirements, such as a need to handle the records of hourly employees, salaried employees, and commissioned employees, then off-the-shelf software may not be satisfactory. It may be more cost-effective to have the payroll programs written to exact specifications than to try to modify off-the-shelf programs to do something they were never intended to do.

Figure 1.4 shows a variety of packaged applications software available at computer stores. Many of these products are also available through vendors and mail-order sources.

WE THE PEOPLE

People, computer professionals and users, are the most important component in the computer system. Although our role may seem rather obvious, it is often underestimated. Here are some of the ways people can affect computer operations.

1. Computer professionals design computer hardware and related equipment.
2. Computer professionals design, create, and develop computer software.
3. Professional computer operators run the computer systems and monitor their activities during processing.

4. Professional data entry clerks and users key in vast amounts of data every day in computer-usable form for storage and processing at a later time.
5. Users also input data to be processed right away, depending on the design of the computer system.
6. In some cases, users create their own specialized applications software.
7. Users review information produced by the computer for use in making business and professional decisions.
8. Users and computer professionals make decisions and use and operate computer systems in ways that can affect our security, comfort, and well-being in daily life.

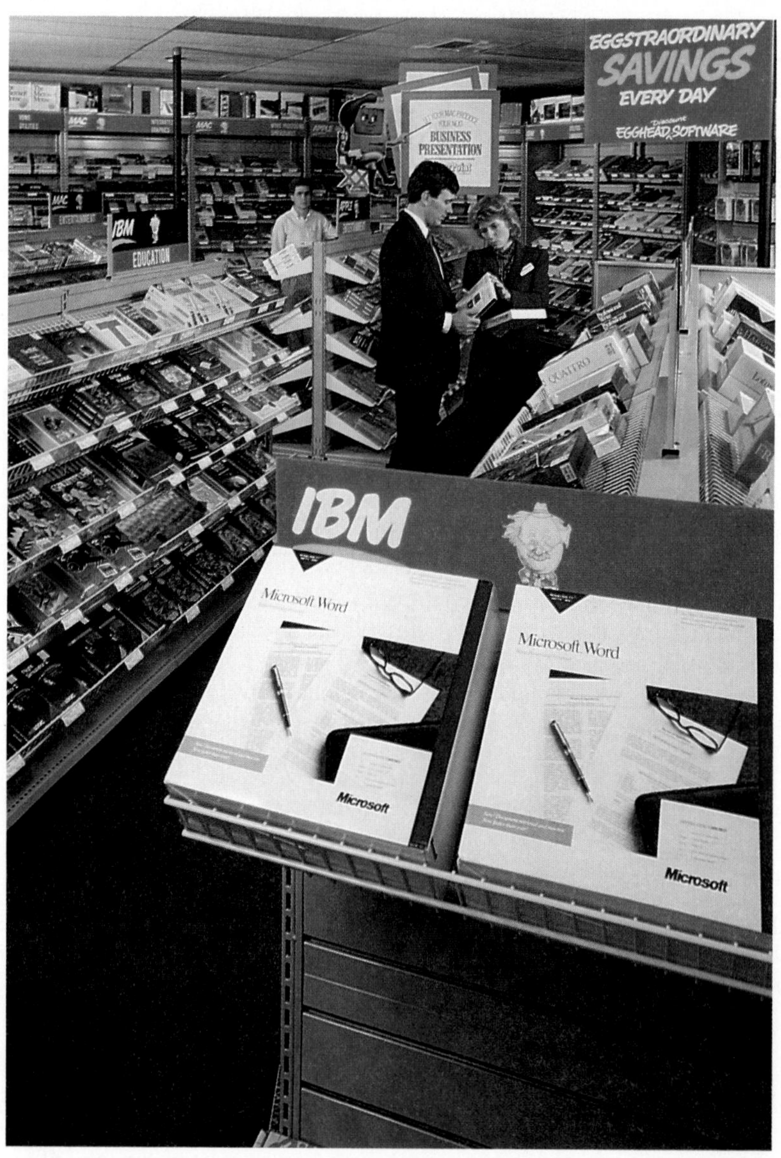

FIGURE 1.4

Software supermarket. Need help with your budget? Want to design and print some greeting cards or your own newsletter? Want to set up a large bank of cross-referenced, business-related data? Buying software is almost like buying records, tapes, and CDs. Most computer stores offer a wide variety of applications software packages. But be sure you know what you want to accomplish before you make your selection.

TYPES OF COMPUTER SYSTEMS: WHAT'S THE DIFFERENCE?

You should be familiar with the differences among computer systems if you want to show a potential employer that you have a fundamental knowledge of computers. Computers come in a variety of sizes and shapes and with a variety of processing capabilities. The earliest computers were quite large because of the crude technologies used; as technological improvements were made in computer components, the overall size of computers began to shrink. Today, the complete CPU of a computer can be smaller than a postage stamp.

To provide a basis for comparing their capabilities, computers are generally grouped into four basic categories:

1. Supercomputers, which are the powerful giants of the computer world;
2. Mainframe computers, which are large, extremely powerful computers used by many large companies;
3. Minicomputers, which are the next most powerful;
4. Microcomputers, which are the least powerful—but which you most likely will be required to use in business.

It's hard to assign a worthwhile definition to each type of computer because definitions can get bogged down in potentially confusing technical jargon. Nevertheless, the following definitions can suffice:

- A **supercomputer** (Figure 1.5) can handle gigantic amounts of scientific computation. It's maintained in a special room or environment, may be about 50,000 times faster than a microcomputer, and may cost as much as $20 million. As a user in business, you probably would not have contact with a supercomputer. However, you might if you worked in the areas of defense and weaponry, weather forecasting, scientific research, at one of several large universities, or for the National Aeronautics and Space Administration. For example, two American computer scientists, Gregory and David Chudnovsky, recently broke the world record for pi* calculations by using two supercomputers to calculate pi to 480 million decimal places (the printout would run 600 miles). And, of course, in the next few years, more and more large industries will start using supercomputers. (A new type of supercomputer, called the ***massively parallel computer***, has recently been introduced. This type of computer has hundreds or even thousands of processors.)
- A **mainframe computer** (Figure 1.6) is a large computer, usually housed in a controlled environment, that can support the processing requirements of hundreds and often thousands of users and computer professionals. It may cost from several hundred thousand dollars up to $10 million. If you go to work for an airline, a bank, a large insurance company, a large accounting company, a large university, or the Social Security Administration, you will

---

* Pi is a commonly used mathematical constant that is based on the relationship of a circle's circumference to its diameter.

likely have contact—through your individual workstation—with a mainframe computer.

- A **minicomputer,** also known as a *midsized* or *low-end mainframe computer* (Figure 1.7), is similar to but less powerful than a mainframe computer. It can support 2 to about 50 users and computer professionals. Minicomputers and mainframe computers can work much faster than microcomputers and have many more storage locations in main memory. Minicomputers cost from about $10,000 to several hundred thousand dollars. Many small and

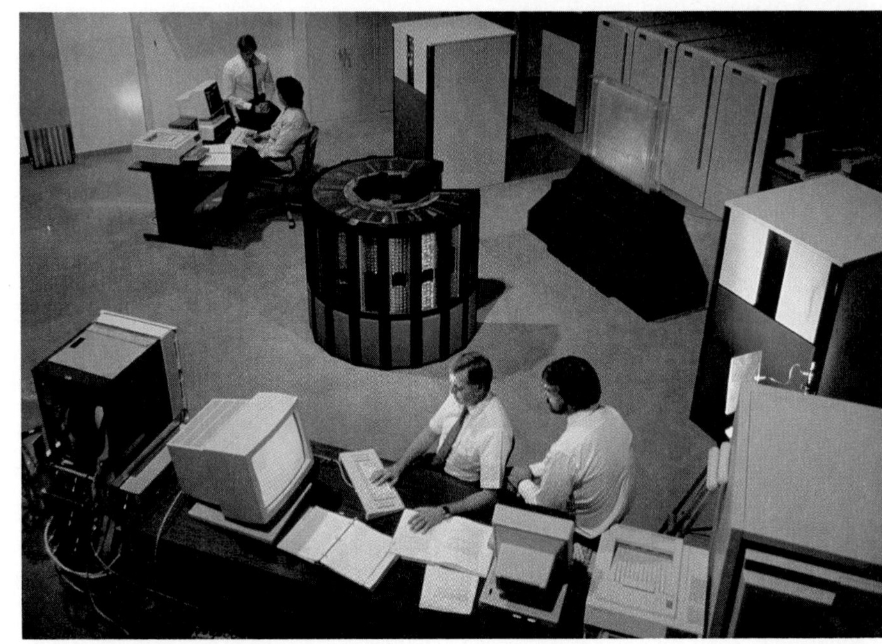

FIGURE 1.5

Supercomputer. This supercomputer (center), capable of performing 1.8 billion calculations a second, is the centerpiece of the National Test Bed. It was installed in mid-1988 at Colorado Springs for the Strategic Defense Initiative.

FIGURE 1.6

Mainframe computer. The main computer unit is front left, between two printers. At the back left are disk-drive units; tape storage units are at the back and back right.

medium-sized companies today use minicomputers, so if you go into the business world, chances are good that you will have contact with a minicomputer.

- The **microcomputer** (Figure 1.8) is the type of computer that you undoubtedly will be dealing with as a user. Many readers are probably already familiar with the microcomputer, also known as a *personal computer* (PC). Microcomputers cost between $500 and about $15,000. They vary in size from small portables, such as *laptop computers* that you can carry around like a briefcase, to powerful desktop *workstations*, such as those used by engineers and scientists. A microcomputer—generally used by only one person at a time—uses a microprocessor **chip** as its CPU. As small as one quarter of an inch square (Figure 1.9), a chip is made of silicon, a material made from sand. Silicon is referred to as a **semiconductor** because it sometimes conducts electricity and sometimes does not (*semi* means "partly"), depending on applied voltages and added chemical impurities ("dopants").

Table 1.1 compares the four basic types of computers. In general, a computer's type is determined by the following seven factors:

1. *The type of CPU.* As noted, microcomputers use microprocessors. The larger computers tend to use CPUs made up of separate, high-speed, sophisticated components.
2. *The amount of main memory the CPU can use.* A computer equipped with a large amount of main memory can support more sophisticated programs and can even hold several different programs in memory at the same time.

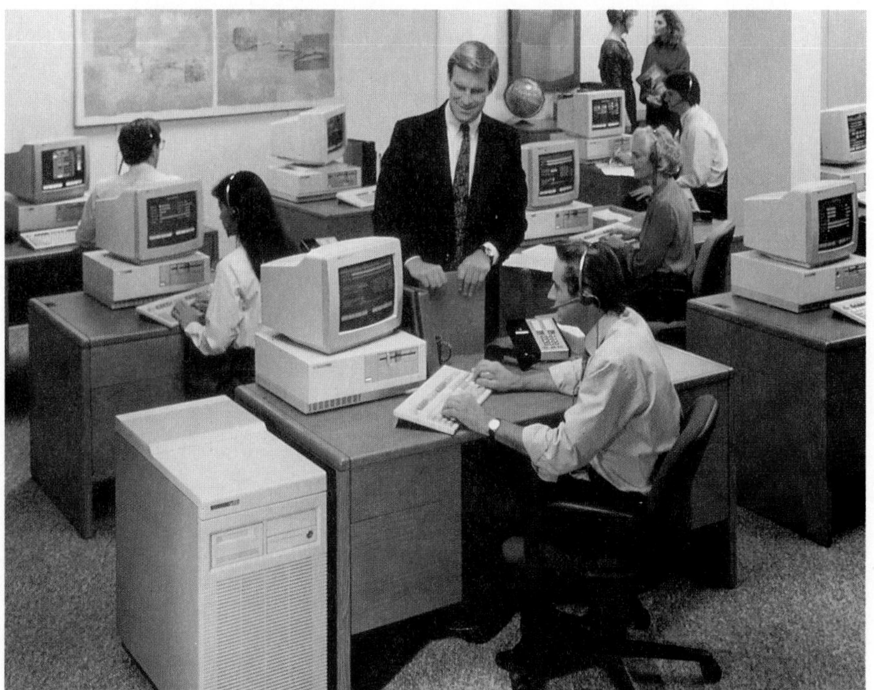

FIGURE 1.7

Minicomputer. Four to more than 100 personal computers (workstations) can be linked to a minicomputer (front left).

FIGURE 1.8

Microcomputer. This photo shows an IBM PS/2 Model 30 microcomputer; the three main components are the monitor, the system unit, and the keyboard. This unit also has a mouse.

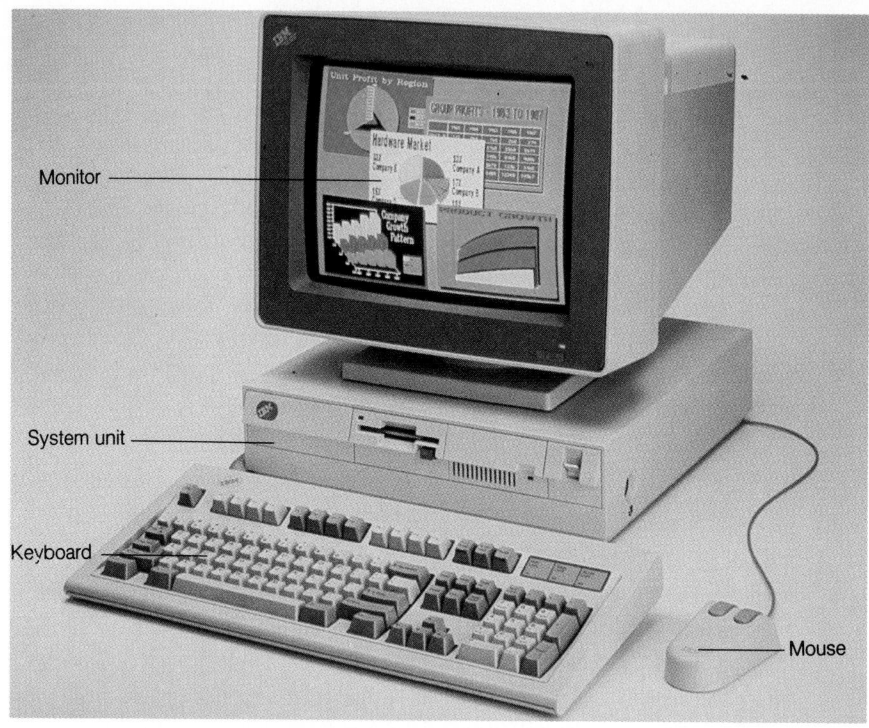

FIGURE 1.9

A chip off what kind of block? This gives you an idea of how small a chip is.

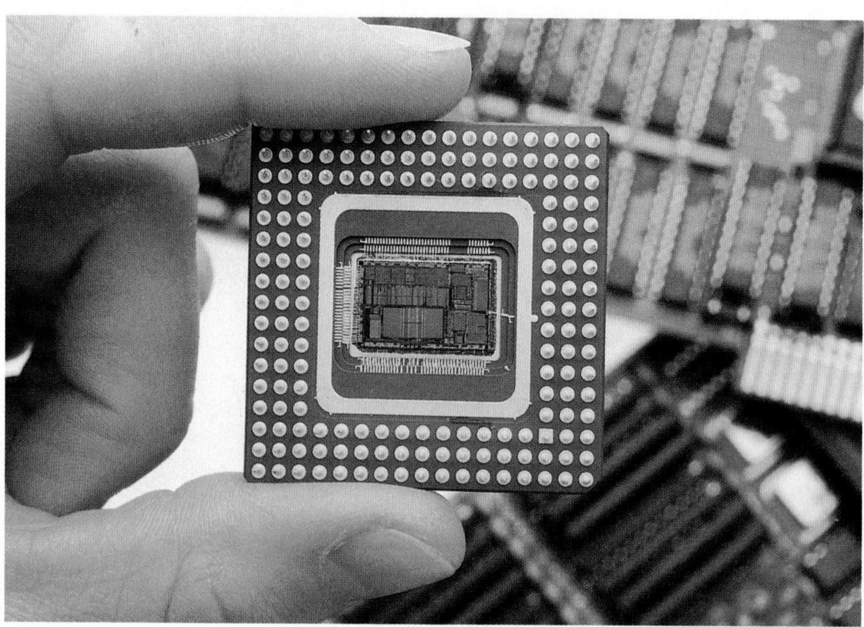

3. *The capacity of the storage devices.* The larger computer systems tend to be equipped with higher capacity storage devices (covered in Chapter 4).
4. *The speed of the output devices.* The speed of microcomputer output devices tends to be rated in terms of the number of **characters per second (cps)** that can be printed—usually in tens and hundreds of cps. Larger computers' output devices are faster and are usually rated at speeds of hundreds or thousands of *lines* that can be printed per minute.
5. *The processing speed in* ***millions of instructions per second (mips).*** The term *instruction* is used here to describe a basic task the software asks the computer to perform while also identifying the data to be affected. The processing speed of the smaller computers ranges from .7 to 40 mips. The speed of large computers can be 30 to 150 mips or more, and supercomputers can process more than 200 mips. In other words, a mainframe computer can process your data a great deal faster than a microcomputer can.
6. *The number of users that can access the computer at one time.* Most small computers can support only a single user; some can support as many as two or three at a time. Large computers can support hundreds of users simultaneously.
7. *The cost of the computer system.* Business systems can cost as little as $500 (for a microcomputer) or as much as $10 million (for a mainframe)—and much more for a supercomputer.

It's difficult to say exactly what kind of computer you'll be using in the business environment. Some companies use a combination of computers. For instance, a company with branch offices around the country might use a mainframe computer to manage companywide customer data. To access information from the mainframe, the user might use a microcomputer that sits on his or her desktop. In

The Four Kinds of Computers* **TABLE 1.1**

Component	Microcomputer	Minicomputer	Mainframe	Supercomputer
Main memory	512,000–16,000,000 characters	8,000,000–50,000,000 characters	32,000,000–200,000,000 characters	100,000,000–2,000,000,000 characters
Storage capacity	360,000–300,000,000 characters	120,000,000–1,000,000,000+ characters	500,000,000+ characters	No limitation
Processing speed	700,000–10,000,000 instructions per second	8–40 mips	30–150 mips and up	150 mips and up
Cost	$500–$15,000	$12,000–$475,000	$250,000–$10,000,000	$10,000,000 and up

* The figures in this table are average approximations: These numbers change rapidly as changing technology blurs the distinctions between categories.

addition to accessing information from the mainframe computer, the microcomputer can be used to perform specialized tasks such as generating invoices or drafting letters to customers. Although it is still relatively easy to find a company that doesn't use a supercomputer, a mainframe, or a minicomputer to process data, it is difficult to locate a company that doesn't use a microcomputer for some of its processing.

You'll be learning more later about the parts of a computer system, including equipment and software. Right now we'll concentrate a bit more on the microcomputer, since this is the machine that an employer will expect you to know the most about.

THE ANATOMY OF A MICROCOMPUTER

Chances are that when you enter the business environment you will be required to know how to use a microcomputer to perform many of your job-related functions. It is therefore critical that you understand the typical components of a microcomputer system in order to use it effectively and talk about it intelligently. The more you know about it, the more valuable you will be to a current or potential employer. To understand the tremendous role microcomputers now play in business, it's helpful to look at how that role has developed.

With the introduction of the Apple II and the Radio Shack Model I and II systems in the late 1970s, the business community began to adopt microcomputers. Then a number of additional vendors, including Atari, Commodore, Osborne, and Kaypro, entered the marketplace with computers designed to be used in the office or in the home. The interest in microcomputers grew rather slowly at first for several reasons: (1) The initial cost for some microcomputer systems was quite high, ranging up to $6,000; (2) only a limited amount of software was commercially available, and the average person was not able to write his or her own software; and (3) there were no industrywide standards to ensure the **compatibility**—that is, the usability—of data and software on different types of microcomputer systems.

However, when IBM introduced the IBM PC in 1981, so many businesses adopted the product that an industry standard was set. Most vendors now design their products to be compatible with this standard. The only other relatively successful microcomputer product lines today that have maintained their own unique standards are the Apple II and the Macintosh. The Apple II retains a fiercely loyal group of users who have supported it since its introduction in the late 1970s. Although the Apple II has been overshadowed in the business world by IBM-compatible products, Apple introduced a much more powerful version of its system—the Apple II GS—in June 1986. The powerful and versatile Apple Macintosh SE, Macintosh Plus, and Macintosh II models are now commonly used in desktop publishing operations. We'll discuss desktop publishing in more detail later.

The large number of different types of microcomputer systems in the marketplace makes it difficult to select one "best system." As a result, our discussion of the microcomputer will center on the three basic hardware devices found in most desktop microcomputer systems used in business today: the keyboard, the monitor, and the system unit (the main computer system cabinet) (Figure 1.10).

KEYBOARD

The microcomputer input device that you will use the most—the keyboard—is made up of a circuit board and related electronic components that generate a unique electronic code when each key is pressed. The code is passed along the keyboard cord to the computer system unit, where it is translated into a usable form for processing. The number of keys and their positions on the keyboard vary among machines. You should select a keyboard that is comfortable for you to use. (A mouse is also frequently used to input data, but we will describe the mouse later.)

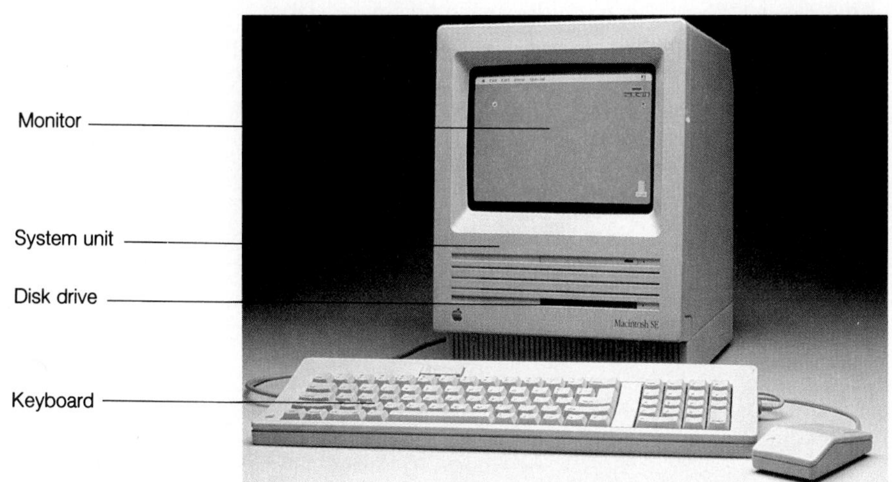

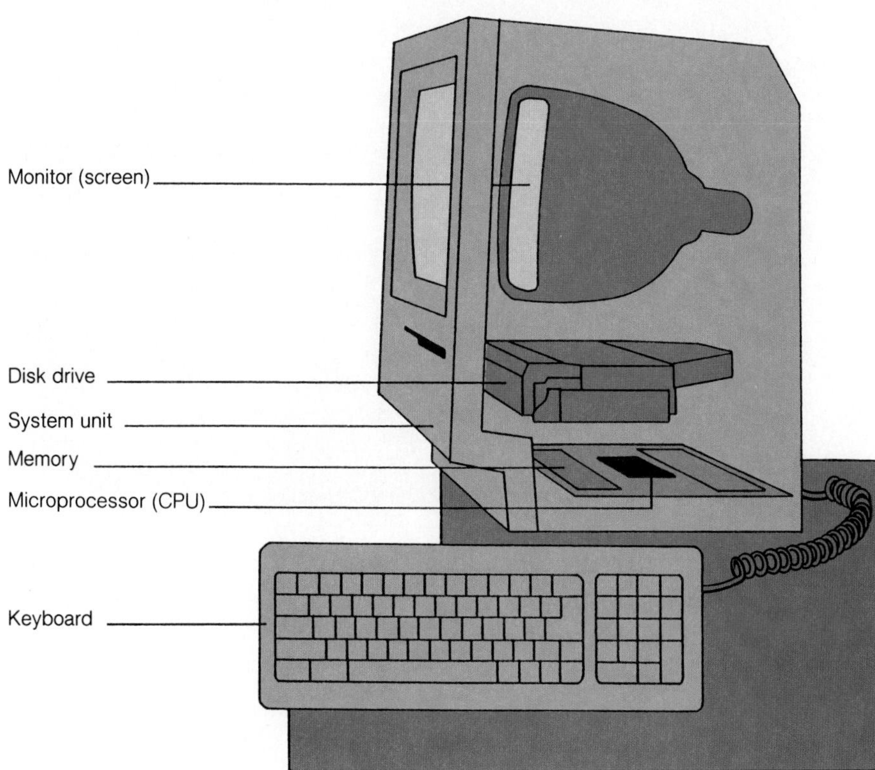

FIGURE 1.10

Basic anatomy of a microcomputer. The top part of the illustration shows a Macintosh microcomputer with monitor, keyboard, and system unit with disk drive; on the bottom is a cutaway drawing of the same basic setup.

MONITOR

The term *monitor* is used interchangeably with *screen, video display screen,* and *cathode-ray tube (CRT)*. This output device provides your principal visual contact with the microcomputer system. When you enter commands or data from the keyboard, you see the results on the monitor. A **monochrome monitor** displays text and, in some cases, graphics in a single color—commonly green or amber—usually on a dark background. A **color monitor,** often referred to as an **RGB monitor** (for red, green, blue), can display text and graphics in various colors. Most of the capabilities of the monitor, including image clarity and the ability to do graphics, are determined by the sophistication of the video display circuit board, if any, contained within the system unit. In any case, the user needs the appropriate software to take advantage of a monitor's capabilities—including the ability to display graphics.

FIGURE 1.11

Systematic. This illustration shows the basic parts of the microcomputer's system unit.

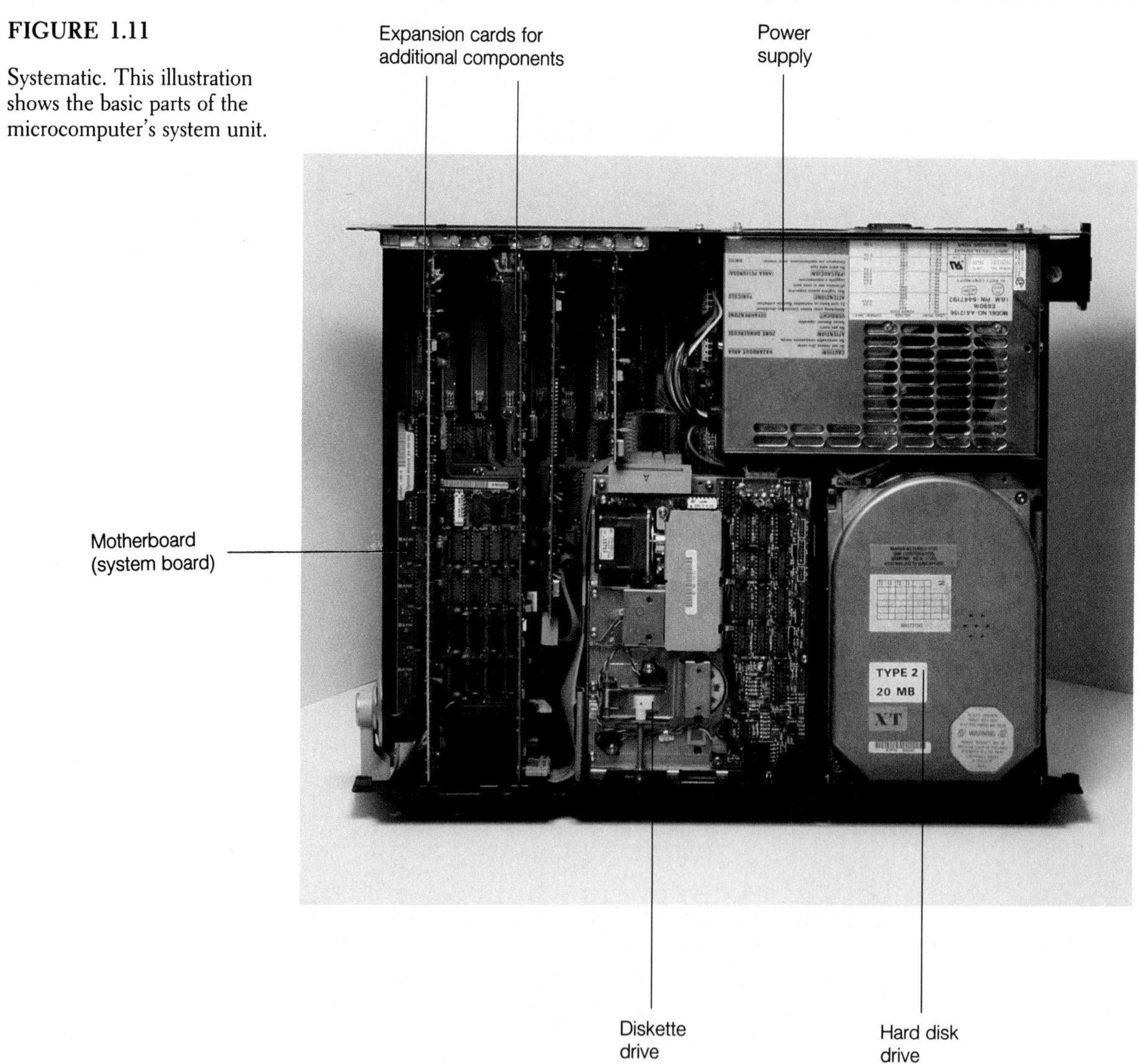

SYSTEM UNIT

The main computer system cabinet, called the **system unit** (Figure 1.11), usually houses the power supply, the system board, and the storage devices (although some storage devices—disk drives, for example—are often housed in cabinets outside the system unit). These elements can be defined as follows:

1. The **power supply** provides electrical power to all components housed in the system unit. In some microcomputers—such as the Macintosh—it also provides power to the monitor.
2. The **system board,** also known as the **motherboard,** is the main circuit board of the microcomputer system. It normally includes (1) the microprocessor chip (or CPU), (2) main memory chips, (3) all related support circuitry, and (4) the expansion slots where additional components can be plugged in.
3. The **storage devices** are usually one or more floppy disk drives and usually a high-capacity hard disk drive. A **floppy disk,** or **diskette,** is a thin plastic disk enclosed in a paper or plastic covering that can be magnetically encoded with data. **Hard disks** are rigid disks capable of storing much more data than a floppy disk. (And hard disk drives access data faster than do floppy disk drives.) Hard disks are more expensive than floppy disks. Whereas a typical floppy disk costs between $.50 and $2, depending on size and storage capacity, hard disks range in price from $200 to $1,200 or more. Since most hard disks are permanently installed in the system unit, floppy disks, which can be carried around, are often used to move data from one computer to another.
4. **Additional components:** The expansion slots on the system board allow users to add new components to their computer systems. The most popular add-on components include: (1) a memory card containing main memory chips that give you additional main memory; (2) an internal modem to facilitate data communications between computers over phone lines and similar cables; (3) a battery-powered clock and calendar mechanism; (4) additional printer ports (hook-ups) that allow you to communicate with several types of output devices; and (5) video display boards.

Don't worry about remembering what all these components are right now. They will be explained in detail later in the book. Just remember that microcomputers are likely to become an important part of your career. Pay attention to them and focus on what they can do for you. Turn their power on—to your advantage.

THE HISTORY OF COMPUTER PROCESSING

In the last section, we gave you some historical information about the use of microcomputers in business since the early 1980s so that you could put into perspective their role in business today. In this section, we go back a little farther—almost 5,000 years—to show the tremendous effect that computers have had on data processing in general, which in turn has profoundly affected the society of which you are a part.

DATA PROCESSING BEFORE COMPUTERS

To record and communicate data and information, prehistoric cave dwellers painted pictures on the walls of their caves, and the ancient Egyptians wrote on a crude form of paper called *papyrus*. Around 3000 B.C., the Sumerians created a device for representing numbers that consisted of a box containing stones. About 2,000 years later, in 1000 B.C., the Chinese took that idea one step further when they strung stones on threads in a wooden frame. The Chinese device was named after their name for box, *baccus*. The *abacus*, as we know it, remains in wide use even

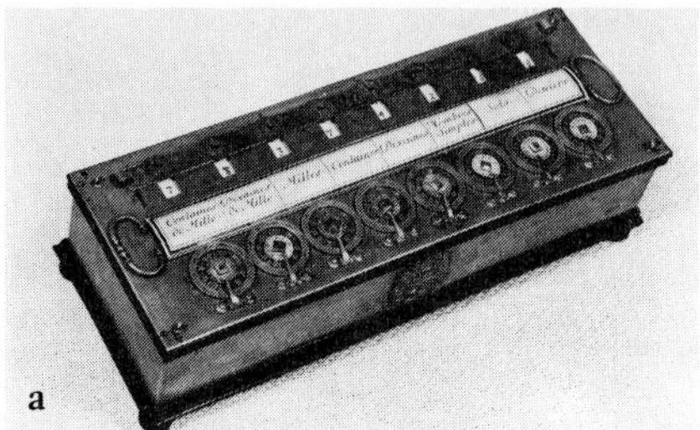

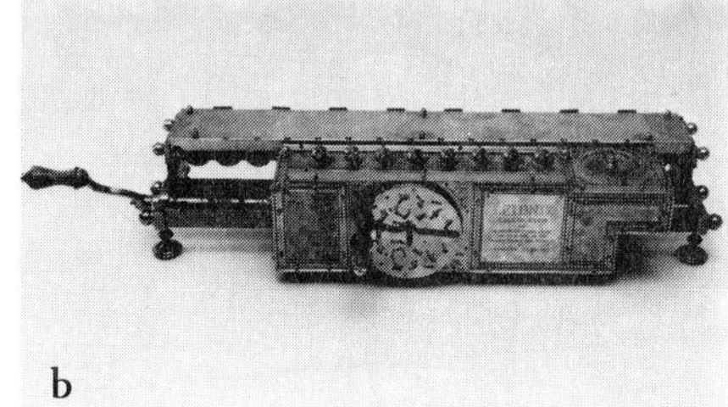

FIGURE 1.12

Which came first—computers or data processing? Many people think that we have been turning data into information only since computers came into use. The truth is that people have been processing data since prehistoric times. This illustration shows a few of the data processing methods used between the mid-1600s and the early 1900s. (a) Pascaline calculator (mid-1600s), the first automatic adding and subtracting machine; (b) Leibniz Wheel (early 1700s), the first general-purpose calculating machine; (c) Jacquard loom (1801), run by punched cards; (d) Thomas's arithnometer (1860), the first commercially successful adding and subtracting machine; (e) Hollerith's tabulating machine, used in the 1890 U.S. census; and (f) early IBM calculating machine (c. 1930).

today and is still considered a powerful tool for performing mathematical computations.

Over the centuries, people have developed an amazing variety of data processing tools and techniques. The most notable tools in use between the mid-1600s and the early 1900s are described in Figure 1.12.

THE EVOLUTION OF COMPUTERS

The first large-scale electronic computer, the Electronic Numerical Integrator and Computer (ENIAC) (Figure 1.13), became operational in 1946. It contained approximately 18,000 electronic vacuum tubes—tubes the size of light bulbs that controlled the flow of electric current. The ENIAC, which weighed 30 tons and occupied about 1,500 square feet of floor space—a huge machine compared to today's standards—was able to perform a scientific calculation involving the multiplication of four numbers in approximately 9 milliseconds (9/1,000ths of a second). Since that time, the technology used in the design and production of computers has accelerated at a remarkable pace.

The term **computer generation** helps delineate the major technological developments in hardware and software. To date, computer technology has evolved through four distinct generations and is currently developing into a fifth generation. As you read about each generation, you should be thinking about how each has affected data processing, because each development has had (and in the case of the later generations, will continue to have) an effect on you—on the job and in society in general. The major characteristics of each generation follow.

FIGURE 1.13

ENIAC. The first large-scale electronic computer. ENIAC weighed 30 tons, filled 1,500 square feet, included 18,000 vacuum tubes—and it failed about every 7 minutes!

First Generation (1944–1958)

These are the earliest general-purpose computers. Most input and output media were punched cards and magnetic tape, and main memory was almost exclusively made up of hundreds of vacuum tubes—although one computer used a magnetic drum for main memory. These computers were slow and large and produced a tremendous amount of heat. They could run only one program at a time. ENIAC and UNIVAC I—the UNIVersal Automatic Computer, which was used by the U.S. Bureau of the Census from 1951 to 1963—are examples of first-generation computers.

Second Generation (1959–1963)

By the early 1960s, transistors and some other solid-state devices that were much smaller than vacuum tubes were being used for much of the computer circuitry. Magnetic cores, which looked like very small metal washers strung together by wires that carried electricity, became the most widely used type of main memory. Removable magnetic disk packs—stacks of disks connected by a common spindle (like a stack of records)—were introduced as storage devices. Second-generation machines tended to be smaller, more reliable, and significantly faster than first-generation computers.

Third Generation (1964–1970)

During this period, the **integrated circuit**—a complete electronic circuit on a silicon chip—replaced transistorized circuitry. The use of magnetic disks became widespread, and computers began to support such capabilities as multiprogramming (processing several programs simultaneously) and timesharing (people using the same computer simultaneously). Minicomputers were being widely used by the early 1970s. The production of operating systems—a type of systems software—and applications software packages increased rapidly. The size of computers continued to decrease.

Fourth Generation (1971–Now)

In 1971, the first electronic computers were introduced that used Large-Scale Integration (LSI) circuits—thousands of integrated circuits on a chip—for main memory and logic circuitry (the circuitry that performs the logical operations of the CPU; different types of chips had different functions). These computers had a much larger capacity to support main memory. This period has also seen increased use of input and output devices that allow data and instructions to be entered directly through the keyboard. The microprocessor, introduced in 1971, combined all of the circuitry for the central processing unit on a single chip. LSI and the microprocessor enabled the development of the supercomputer.

Fifth Generation (Now and in the Future)

Definitions of what constitutes fifth-generation computers do not always agree. Some people think that the new microcomputers with faster operating speeds, greater processing capacity, and virtually unlimited memory should be included. Other people believe that fifth-generation computers will have circuitry based on gallium arsenide. Gallium arsenide offers a fivefold speed increase and uses only one tenth of the power that silicon uses. Scientists have also tried to develop new **superconductors** that can conduct electricity with *no* resistance, thus generating no heat but great speed.

Many fifth-generation computers will also incorporate hundreds or thousands of processors that operate in parallel—that is, simultaneously. Traditional computers act on only one problem at a time; **parallel processing** means that many processors will work on the problem at the same time. As you will see later on, this concept promises to provide tremendously more efficient processing than the traditional kind, as will the use of optical "circuitry" that transmits data with light rather than electricity.

What Does All This Mean to the User?

Don't worry if you don't understand all the terms used to describe the sequence of computer generations. As you work through the book, the differences between them will become more clear, and you will gain an understanding of what the general user does *not* need to know.

The net effect of the tremendous increase in processing power provided by the computer is that more data can be processed faster than ever before. This means that all the information you need in your job to make decisions will be quickly available —a necessity in today's rapidly changing business environment.

The catch to all this, however, is that the power of the computer has grown so much that it can often generate more information than we can effectively deal with at one time. As a result, we must be selective about the type of data and information we process. It must be concise, relevant, and accurate so that we avoid getting buried under an avalanche of unnecessary information. And we need to start thinking about the difference between data and information we *really need* and what we *think* we need—especially in our professional lives. Being bogged down by unnecessary details and inaccurate information is frustrating and time-consuming. The problem of being overloaded with information is being discussed more and more in business and computer publications.

The Effect of Computers on Processing Data and Information

New generations of computer technology will continue to affect the processing of data and information. Data collection continues to become easier and easier, data processing is getting faster and faster, mathematical calculations continue to be performed with increased precision, and information is being provided to users in generally more useful forms. And one of the best improvements that new technology brings us is that computers continue to become easier to use.

Data Collection: Hard Labor to Easy Time

Before computers were invented, data was collected and processed by hand in a variety of tedious ways. The data often had to be copied and recopied more than once before it could be processed into information. Data collection for early computers was often done by transcribing hardcopy data into computer-usable forms such as punched cards or paper tape (Figure 1.14). The data was recorded by punching a series of holes according to a standardized coding scheme. Technological advancements in data collection have made this cumbersome collection method almost obsolete. Chapter 3 discusses modern data collection devices in detail.

THE PRODUCTION OF INFORMATION: FASTER, EASIER, BETTER (USUALLY)

It's no wonder that so many businesses have adopted computers so readily. Quick and easy production of accurate information has become a reality to businesspeople who used to dream about it. The U.S. government was one of the first institutions to benefit from increased data processing speed. In the last century, census taking was one of the most arduous processing tasks ever undertaken in this country. Almost 50,000 people collected data by hand, completing forms for approximately 13 million households. Processing this data by hand usually took more than eight years; no sooner would the population be tallied than the new census would begin. As a result, in 1890, the U.S. Congress authorized the Bureau of the Census to hold a competition to select the most efficient new method for recording and tabulating the census. Herman Hollerith won the contest with his system for electric tabulating using data input on punched cards. Although at the time the speed of this data processing method was a major break-through—it took Hollerith six weeks to compute an unofficial census—a modern personal computer can process the same amount of data in about half the time, after capturing it in a computer-usable form.

Thanks to the science of **ergonomics** (also called *human engineering*), which designs things to be easily used by people, the convenience of computer use has also improved over the years. Many people have been afraid of computers, but great strides have been made in transforming the computer into a friendlier, less mysterious tool. Input devices have become easier to use (see Figure 1.15), and software is easier to understand than ever before (Figure 1.16). (Certain ergonomic developments will be discussed throughout the book.)

In addition to being fast and easy to use, the computer also brings us a math facility that many of us thought was eternally beyond our reach. Have you ever had difficulty balancing your checkbook or creating a budget? Or is your life overshadowed by math anxiety? Many of us find it difficult to consistently perform mathe-

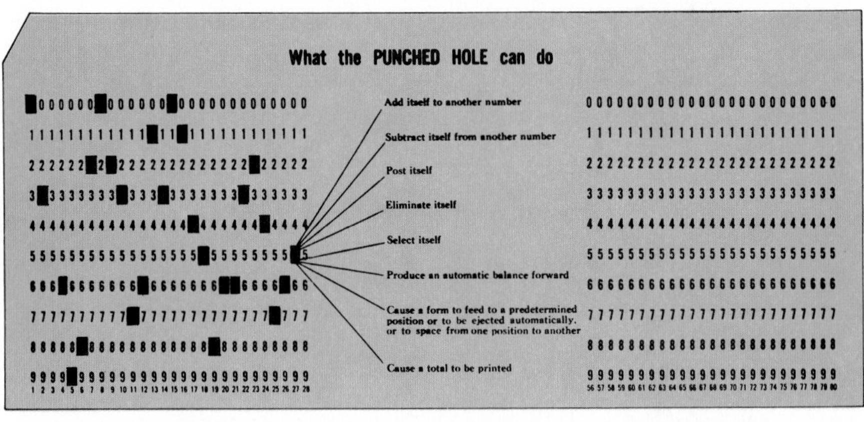

FIGURE 1.14

Taking a collection. An early method of collecting data for the computer involved the transforming of data into computer-usable form on punched cards and paper tape. Fortunately, the technology for data collection has advanced to the point where such methods have become extremely rare.

matical calculations accurately by hand. Sooner or later we make a mistake. One of the major advantages of a computer is that, with the proper software, it will perform calculations quickly and accurately, with much greater precision and speed than would be possible manually. Thus, math anxiety will not prevent you from providing your employer with, for example, complicated statistical or financial reports.

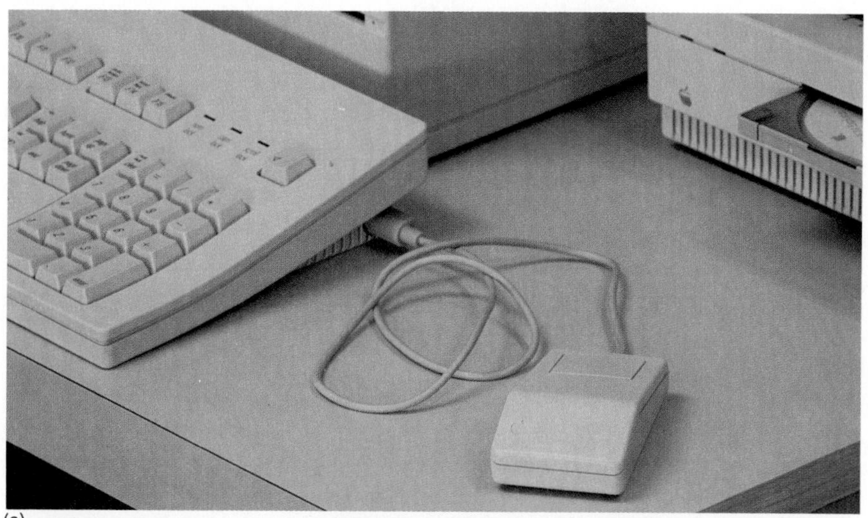

(a)

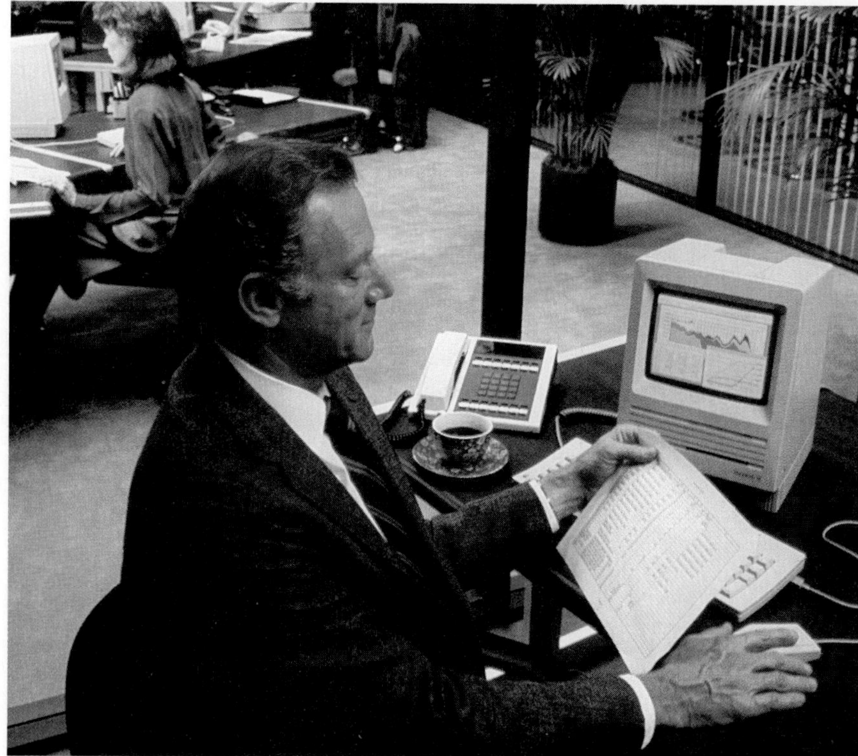

(b)

FIGURE 1.15

An ergonomic input device. In addition to the keyboard, a popular input device is the mouse (a), a hand-held device that the user moves around the desktop (b). The mouse is connected to the computer, and it transmits signals that control the position of the indicator (cursor) on the screen. It can also be used to make selections of options offered by the software and to create graphics. The keyboard is still used to type characters.

Information in Usable Forms: For the Computer and for the User

The need for business-related data to be retrieved, manipulated, and analyzed is constant. As we mentioned, in the past data was collected by hand and analyzed manually to produce a report. Then people had to go through the same procedure again if they wanted to use the same data to produce a different report. The computer allows us to capture data in *computer-usable form*—for example, on disk. Once the data is available in this form, the computer can *repeatedly* retrieve and manipulate it to produce information tailored—in people-usable form—to meet specific needs. This flexibility has been welcomed by many people in data-heavy professions such as accounting and banking. However, before we discuss some of the specific professional uses of computers, let's examine some of the general social implications of computerization.

Social and Ethical Implications of Computerization

Everything is connected to everything else. A change in one area will cause changes in other areas, even if they aren't readily apparent to us. Implementing an apparent solution to a problem often causes other, unanticipated problems. We are learning this lesson, for example, in the area of ecology. Are we also learning it in relation to the computer's growing role in business and society?

As information technology replaces energy as society's main resource, many people are concerned that too much emphasis has been put on what the computer can do to streamline business and too little on how it may be affecting the quality of our lives. For example, is it distorting the meaning of thought? That is, is it absurd

FIGURE 1.16

What will you have? Some computers and software use menus (a series of choices presented on the screen) and icons (pictures representing options) to make it easier for people to run the system.

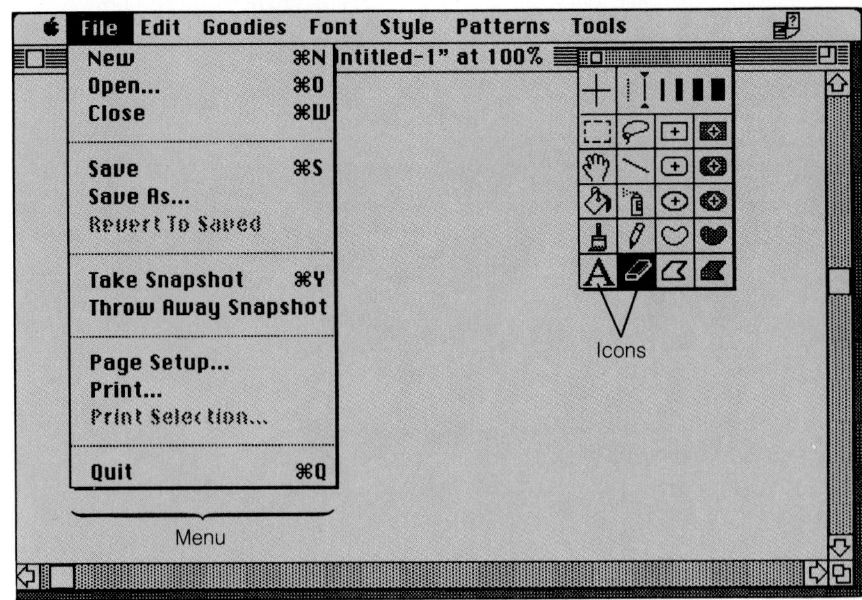

and dangerous to attribute the capabilities of thinking and creativity to a computer? People have experience, convictions, and cultural traditions. Are these qualities being devalued? If so, perhaps we are heading into an era in which machine-like qualities of speed and problem solving will be valued more highly than what used to be called *humane* qualities.

Many people assert that the computer's level of "thinking" is strictly mechanical and lacks a real capacity for judgment and that too many computer enthusiasts are confusing data with ideas. After all, nothing is information until a *person* interprets it. And information is not the same as knowledge, which is gained by thinking. Further, knowledge can be gained without new information being received by the thinker. Can a machine do this? Do you want strictly mechanical processes in control of a weapons system? Society must guard against the creation of inhumane projects thought up only because a computer made them possible, and it must develop standard checking systems to ensure the integrity of data used to make strategic decisions in government as well as business.

In addition to the problems of computer-controlled nuclear weapons, the potential for abuse of power concerns many people. On the one hand, the computer could lead to equalization — that is, a democratic situation in which all people have access to the same information. On the other hand, this possibility could lead to the opposite situation; the existence of huge banks of data and information, electronic communications, and inexpensive portable computers has led some totalitarian countries to outlaw personal possession of computers to avoid the free dissemination of information. Also, the existence of huge central data banks that contain essentially all data related to everyone's public and private life can be frightening to consider.

Many people focus on the freedom from routine and boring work that computers give. This is certainly welcome in many situations, but we must remember that what is boring and routine work to one person may be life-saving employment to another. Traditionally, in the United States, many low-level jobs are held by young people and immigrants with language problems. Therefore, what at first seems like an advantage of computerization may really be a disadvantage. McDonald's restaurants came to this conclusion not too long ago when they decided not to eliminate the order-cashier positions at the front counters staffed by people and replace them with machines that customers would use to key in their own orders. And maintaining human contact is still better for business.

One more problem to consider is the potential for computer-based systems in business to be used to monitor employees. What if terminals were programmed (and some already are) to check your speed, the pauses you make, the breaks you take, the rate of keying errors? Would it be fair for the company to do this to make sure it retains only the most efficient workers and thus increases the value of goods and services it has to sell? Or would this detract from your dignity as a human being — your right to do some things better than you do others? Would this type of company get high-quality decisions from its employees, or would the employees be too dissatisfied and afraid to work creatively? In addition, a growing percentage of the workforce is working at home. Workers can communicate with their offices via a microcomputer and communications equipment and software. But how does working at home affect employee morale, efficiency, and motivation? How does the employer maintain control of the employee? Is the employee who works at home as productive as the employee who doesn't?

Another important issue relates to the disabled and the handicapped. For most of us, computers make our lives more convenient, but for some people, computers play a much greater role. Computers have the potential for equalizing the workplace by enabling people with mobility, vision, and/or hearing impairments to do the same work as someone who isn't handicapped. Some disabled workers have difficulty holding down more than one or two keys at once or using a mouse. Blind workers need special translator hardware so they can "read" text and numbers. Fortunately, many add-on products are available to adapt standard microcomputers to the needs of the handicapped, including voice translators for the blind and software that modifies the way the keyboard and the mouse are used. However, products like these vary in sophistication and are usually quite expensive. As a result, few companies make these purchases. Aren't these companies discriminating against the handicapped? Many legislators are working to pass a bill that would make this kind of discrimination illegal.

And, before we close this section, consider the issue of software piracy, or theft, which has become a major concern of software writers and manufacturers. The act of piracy is not as dramatic as it sounds; in most cases, it simply means illegally copying private-domain (copyrighted) software onto blank disks. Because some of this software—from games to heavy-duty business publishing programs—is expensive, it's tempting to avoid purchasing an off-the-shelf package by accepting a friend's offer to supply free copies. But, according to the Copyright Act of 1976 and the Computer Software Piracy and Counterfeiting Amendment of 1983, this practice is illegal. It is also unethical. Computer programmers and software companies often spend years developing, writing, testing, and marketing software programs only to lose many royalty dollars to software "pirates." If you spent several years writing a book, only to lose royalties through the distribution of illegally copied volumes, how would you feel? The issue is the same.

Some software manufacturers write copy-protect programs into their software to prevent illegal copying; other software authors offer free (or inexpensive) copies of their programs (called "shareware") through computer-user clubs and publications. Just remember: Before you consider making a copy or accepting a copy of a software program, make sure it's legal. Its theft can result in severe penalties.

Many universities today incorporate into their computer science curriculum a course on ethics. Such courses teach students that people in the computing profession have a responsibility to act in an ethical manner. Especially in network environments, where many different computers are connected, professionals maintaining the network have a serious responsibility to hundreds or thousands of people they will never see—a responsibility to maintain privacy and accuracy of data, among other things. Interestingly, although other disciplines have long followed codes of ethics—for example, the goal of a civil engineer is to build public structures that are *safe*, and the first rule for a physician is to "do no harm"—strict codes of ethical standards have not been defined in the world of computing. Industry observers predict that users and computer professionals alike will be faced with many ethical dilemmas, or "gray areas," in the future.

The Effect of Computers on Employment Opportunities

We have seen that computers have essentially revolutionized data and information processing. Computers have also changed some industries and actually created others. The design and manufacture of computer hardware have become an enormous industry, and the need for software by all sorts of businesses—from apple growers to zoo managers—has led to the development of the applications software industry. Major retail sales and wholesale distribution operations have developed to sell these hardware and software products, as well as related products.

All these industries have one thing in common: They need workers. In fact, the growth of the computer information industry has created a vast and varied number of jobs, both for computer professionals and computer-literate users. No matter what type of business you go into, you will probably be using computers. Figure 1.17 shows a few examples of current job opportunities that involve some computer knowledge and/or experience. Starting in Chapter 3, each chapter contains a "Computers and Careers" box that will give you detailed information about how computers are used in various professions that are not directly related to computer

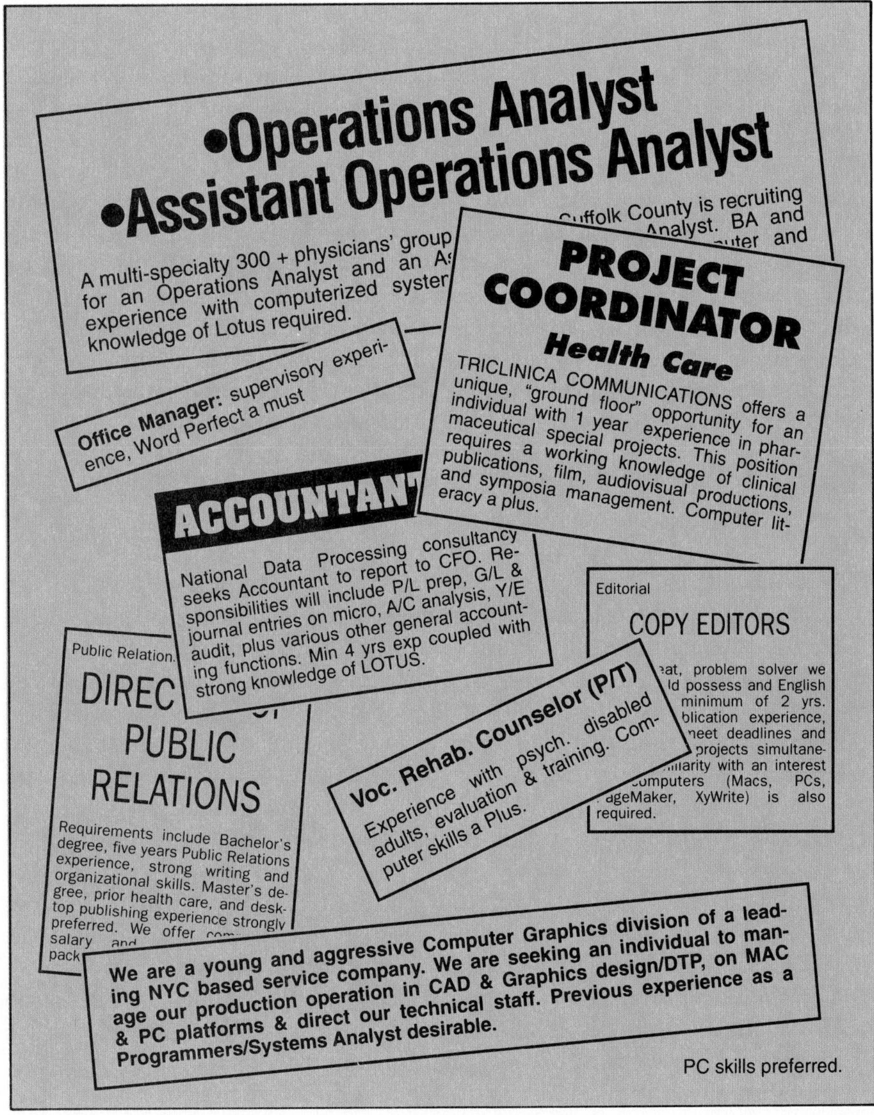

FIGURE 1.17

Write when you find work. These assorted newspaper ads give only a small sampling of the types of jobs whose requirements include some experience with computers.

hardware, software, and systems businesses. Although the following general career information may not be essential to the understanding of the main topics presented in this chapter, many students find it useful.

OPPORTUNITIES FOR COMPUTER PROFESSIONALS

The employment picture for computer professionals looks good and is getting better. Several million people are employed as computer programmers, computer operators, information managers, systems analysts, data entry clerks, database managers, and other more technical workers. The growth of the microcomputer hardware and software industries in recent years has created a large number of new jobs in the retail sales and marketing of computers as well. Many jobs have also been created by companies that manufacture the various computer components and by companies that specialize in computer repair.

In general, computer programmers design, write, test, and implement the programs that process the data in the computer system (Chapter 8 covers programming). Systems analysts know programming basics but have broader responsibilities than do programmers. They plan and design not just individual programs but entire systems of programs, including the procedures that users must follow when using the system (Chapter 10 covers systems design and analysis). The database administrator (DBA) works with systems analysts on issues relating to the database. He or she must resolve conflicts among users and among technical people working on the database and database management software and administer the use, maintenance, and security of the database. (Databases are covered in Chapter 11.) The chief information officer coordinates and gives direction to the database managers, systems analysts, programmers, and various office systems managers. He or she helps people cope with changes in technology and solves problems relating to information needs. (Information management is discussed in Chapter 12.)

OPPORTUNITIES FOR USERS

The employment picture for users (you) is good if you have had some experience actually using computers. As we've mentioned, many employers now require some degree of computer competency as a prerequisite for employment. Computers are becoming standard business tools for all employees, from the president of the company to the clerks in the typing pool. For example, accounting departments and public accounting firms now seek college graduates who have substantial hands-on microcomputer experience. Many administrative and managerial employees are also using microcomputers or computer terminals in their offices. To meet the demand for computer literacy, many schools offer extension courses or seminars in computer skills.

The most popular courses cover word processing programs (designed to output professional documents in a short amount of time), database management system programs (designed to easily store, update, and manipulate large amounts of data), and electronic spreadsheet programs (designed to handle calculations and update complex financial forms). Enrollment in these courses by working professionals has increased dramatically in the past few years. An informal survey of several universities has shown that people enroll for training for three reasons:

- *To satisfy job requirements.* Some of those surveyed stated that they were strongly encouraged or required by their employers to learn more computer skills.
- *To increase job skills and marketability.* Others surveyed said that because microcomputers and related software have become so popular, they felt they needed some additional skills to keep their jobs, to be considered for advancement, or to change to a more desirable job.
- *To learn to use a computer as a personal resource.* The remaining people indicated that they wanted to learn to use the computer as a personal resource on the job and at home. These people were not required to use computers on the job but felt computers could help them perform their jobs more efficiently.

But what are some of the specific jobs and activities that involve computer use?

COMPUTERS IN BUSINESS

Different types of businesses commonly use computers to assist with such day-to-day operating activities as:

- *Sales Order Entry:* procedures for handling customer orders, including receipt of the order and verification of availability of ordered stock.
- *Inventory Management and Control:* procedures for tracking, counting, and reordering stock items.
- *Personnel Management:* procedures for maintaining employee information (such as hire date, salary, performance rating, and date of last review) for both development and reporting purposes.
- *Payroll:* procedures for producing paychecks and reports on employee compensation.
- *Accounting:* procedures for maintaining the company's financial records.
- *Security:* procedures for controlling who has access to what data and information at what times and where, and who may enter data to a computer-based information system.
- *Investment and General Financial Management:* procedures a company institutes, follows, and reviews to guarantee profit and growth.

Computers are also being used in business to collect and analyze data, to produce concise information for management in a clear format suitable for making decisions, and to help managers avoid being overloaded with unnecessary information.

To keep up to date with detailed information about how computers are being used in the various sections of the business and banking world, consult well-known business publications such as *BusinessWeek*, *Fortune*, and *The Wall Street Journal*, as well as computer publications such as *PC World* and *Macworld*.

COMPUTERS IN GOVERNMENT

Government agencies are among the largest computer users in the world today. It would almost be impossible to collect, tabulate, and categorize the colossal amount of data the U.S. government must deal with daily without the aid of computers. For example, the Internal Revenue Service has 10 huge data centers throughout the country solely dedicated to processing income tax returns (Figure 1.18). Even so, it takes most of the year to process the prior year's tax returns.

To a large extent, the U.S. defense system, among other defense systems, is based on computer technology. Vast networks of computers work together to coordinate and disseminate strategic information relating to the management and deployment of the armed forces. Satellites are used to collect and communicate data and information, and the weapons systems have computerized components. Many weapons are now considered "smart" weapons because they can collect data, process it into information, and use it in military strategies. Of course, whether or not *people* are smart enough to use these weapons responsibly remains to be seen.

COMPUTERS IN THE LEGAL PROFESSION

Law enforcement agencies use computers to collect and analyze evidence. Many agencies are now equipped with data processing facilities that enable them to connect with large, countrywide law enforcement computer systems from which they can obtain and with which they can share information on criminal activities, as well as missing persons. As shown in Figure 1.19, many police cars are now equipped with computer terminals so that an officer can access immediate information about a suspect or a vehicle.

FIGURE 1.18

A taxing situation. The Internal Revenue Service uses computers to process the massive amounts of data included in our tax returns.

The criminal justice system uses computers to help manage large amounts of information. The documentation created when a suspect is arrested and tried can easily take up several hundred pages. Without computer-based information processing, it would be next to impossible today to collect the data, process it, and keep track of the status of cases. In addition, lawyers can save documents such as wills in a computer system for easy updating in the future.

COMPUTERS IN MEDICINE

The use of computers in the health-care industry has grown tremendously in the past 10 years. The computer has become a valuable resource in the management of records for physicians, nurses, pharmacists, nutritionists, hospitals, and medical insurance companies, as well as in patient diagnosis and physiological monitoring. Computers are used to process mountains of medical administrative paperwork, including millions of patient insurance claims, patient billing forms, inventory control accounts to track the availability and use of beds, and extensive patient records and histories of test results, treatments, and medicines.

Recent computer-related developments in the medical profession involve the use of computer systems to assist in patient diagnosis. CAT (computerized axial tomography) and PET (positron emission tomography) scanners can take computerized "pictures" of the interior of the brain and other parts of the body (Figure 1.20). Many of the devices found in intensive care units are also computerized—such as the electrocardiograph system used to record the pulses that cause a patient's heartbeat.

COMPUTERS IN EDUCATION

In recent years, educators have been involved with computers in three ways: (1) they teach students about computers; (2) they teach students about a variety of subjects such as math, language skills, reading, and grammar using computers (*computer-assisted instruction*); and (3) they use computers as classroom manage-

FIGURE 1.19 Sherlock Holmes takes on a new look. (a) Computers in police cars can be used to check out license plates, drivers' licenses, and registration papers. (b) Communications center for the Los Angeles Police Department.

(a)

(b)

ment tools (*computer-managed instruction*). Computer classes have been offered at the college level since the mid-1950s. Today many schools at all levels offer students some exposure to computers. Many colleges and universities now have their own microcomputer training labs. In addition, their libraries may use computers to aid in library searches and in management, and their special education departments are probably instructing students in the use of custom-developed programs and hardware to aid in the education of handicapped children and adults. And "electronic universities" are being established to offer all sorts of courses to people who use computers and communications technology to earn educational degrees at home.

COMPUTERS IN INDUSTRY

Many industries are being transformed by the use of computers. You probably already know that automobile and other product manufacturers use computer-based robots to do much of the routine work. People are involved not only in operating the robots, but designing them and the systems of which they are a part. Engineers and designers are using computer-aided design (discussed in more detail later) to design items from airplanes to zippers (Figure 1.21).

Publishing is a good example of one industry that has changed dramatically because of computerization. Editing, typesetting, page makeup, photo treatments,

FIGURE 1.20 Computers in medicine. (a) Genetic research; (b) studying skull anatomy.

(a)

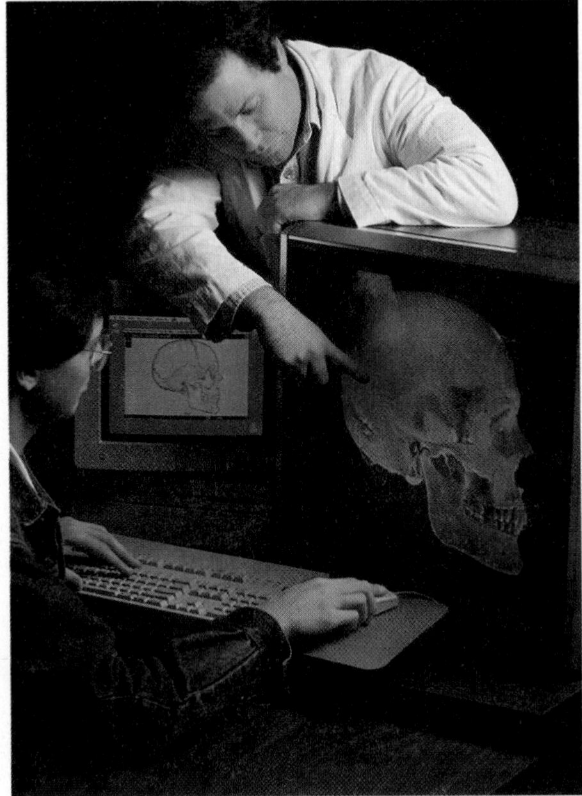

(b)

creation of illustrations, and color work can all be done electronically now—and much faster than ever before. This means that new types of jobs are being created for people who can combine publishing know-how and/or language expertise with computer experience. Also, computerization has enabled more and more publishing people to work as freelancers, because they can work with almost all the other people in the publishing cycle electronically.

(a)

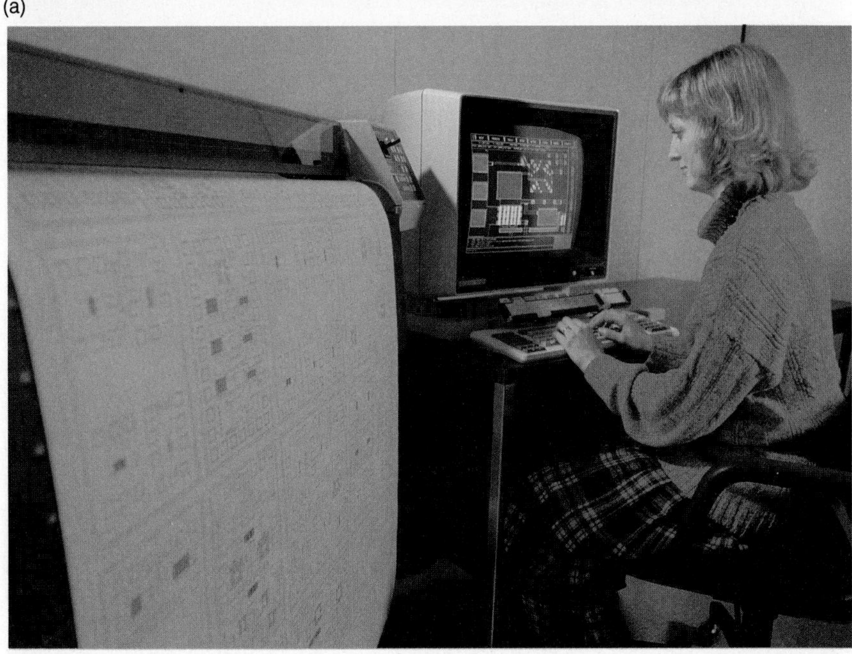

(b)

FIGURE 1.21

Computers in industry. (a) The Orchard Corporation applies its state-of-the-art computer design skills to wall covering design projects; (b) a custom microwave integrated circuit is being designed using a modern workstation.

COMPUTERS IN ENTERTAINMENT AND SPORTS

Hardly anyone living in the United States or Canada today is not aware of the effect computers have had on such entertainment businesses as moviemaking and music production (Figure 1.22). Special effects experts are in demand, as are those who combine musical talent with the ability to operate computer-based musical equipment. People who are trained in video production and modern communications can find work in broadcasting, journalism, advertising, and a number of other fields. And, of course, game companies and software companies are in need of people to develop computerized games.

In sports, athletes' performances are being analyzed and improved by the use of computers. Sports medicine has also become much more effective through the use of computer systems to analyze and treat injuries.

COMPUTERS IN AGRICULTURE

Computers are also used professionally by people who choose to go into animal husbandry — such as raising poultry, dairy cattle, or beef cattle — to monitor breeding conditions, diet, and environment, and also to manage accounting and other clerical procedures. New types of disease-resistant plants are being produced through computer-based plant engineering, and computers are being used in farming (Figure 1.23) to monitor weather, water supplies, climate, soil composition, and so on.

COMPUTERS IN THE HOME

Computers are such versatile tools that people are bringing them into their homes in increasing numbers. A wide variety of software is available for home use, including (1) educational software for young children, (2) personal financial management software, and (3) entertainment software. Many professionals also use their home computers to do some work-related tasks at home or even run their businesses from

FIGURE 1.22

Computers in entertainment. More and more of the music we hear is created on, modified by, and output by computer.

the home, using typical business software packages and modern communications technology (Chapter 9 covers communications).

Of course, many more interesting professions exist that involve the use of computers. The scientific applications alone are astounding—but we can't list all the applications here. To keep up-to-date with changing computer uses in a particular profession, consult the professional publications. Your department chairperson or a librarian will be able to help you discover those publications.

Onward: Making Use of Information

Chapter 2 focuses on the activities that normally take place in computer-based information systems (when data is processed into information using a computer). You need to understand where you will fit into this system before you can learn to use a computer efficiently. Chapter 2 also describes the different ways companies may use computers, as well as the different kinds of computer facilities you may come in contact with when working in a business that uses computers.

Summary

Why are you studying this book? Because computers are the backbone of modern business and you want to become a success in the job or profession of your choice, as well as experience new and exciting learning opportunities. The need to know how

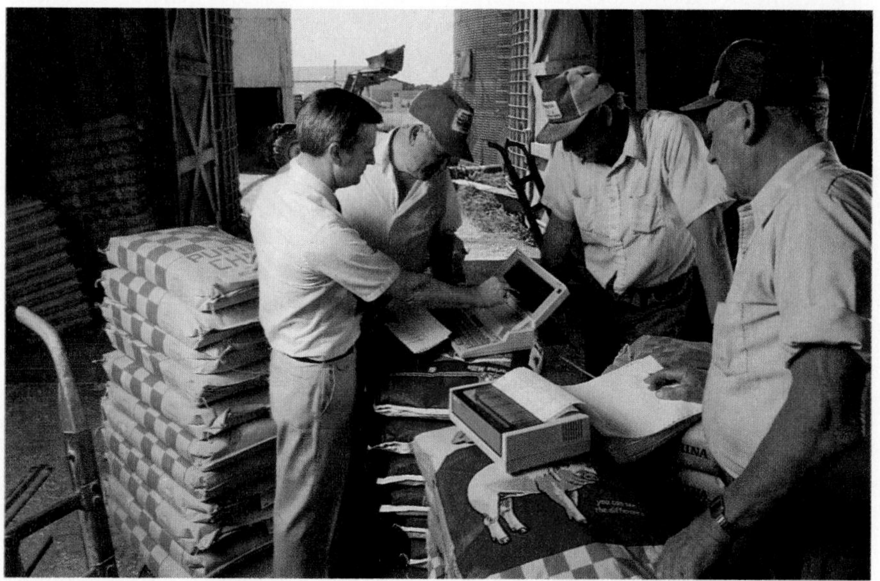

FIGURE 1.23

Computers in agriculture. Farmers learning to use computers to manage feed inventory.

to input, process, store, and output data and information has become increasingly relevant to anyone who plans to enter a business or a professional environment. Your survival in the business world of today and tomorrow depends more and more on how well you understand what a computer is, how it works, and what it can be used for.

A computer system has five components:

1. Hardware.
2. Software.
3. Data/information.
4. Procedures.
5. People.

Hardware is the actual computer equipment; it has no capabilities of its own. The equipment must be used with software, the instructions that tell the computer what to do. Software is written by people. Systems software comprises the general instructions that tell the computer how to operate; applications software comprises the specific business-task-related instructions that help a user get his or her job done. Procedures are represented by documentation such as users' manuals, which tell users how to proceed.

Data comprises the raw, unevaluated facts, concepts, or instructions processed by the computer to output *information*, the useful product of processing. Information is used to make decisions.

People have always been extremely important to the functioning of a computer system. In the past, when computers weren't so commonplace in business, many people were able to ignore them. Today, however, it is much more difficult to avoid becoming part of a computer system.

Connectivity—how separate computer systems are connected—can become a sixth component of a computer system.

The term *computer generation* was applied to different types of computers to help delineate the major technological developments in hardware and software. To date, computer technology has evolved through four distinct generations and is currently developing into a fifth generation.

1. *First Generation* (1944–1958). These are the earliest general-purpose computers. Most input and output media were punched cards and magnetic tape, and main memory was almost exclusively made up of hundreds of vacuum tubes. These computers were slow and large and produced a tremendous amount of heat. They could run only one program at a time.
2. *Second Generation* (1959–1963). By the early 1960s, transistors and some other solid-state devices that were much smaller than vacuum tubes were being used for much of the computer circuitry. Magnetic cores became the most widely used type of main memory. Removable magnetic disk packs—stacks of disks connected by a common spindle (like a stack of records)—were introduced as storage devices. Second-generation machines tended to be smaller, more reliable, and significantly faster than first-generation computers.
3. *Third Generation* (1964–1970). During this period, the integrated circuit—a complete electronic circuit on a silicon chip—replaced transistorized circuitry. The use of magnetic disks became widespread, and computers

began to support such capabilities as multiprogramming (processing several programs simultaneously) and timesharing (people using the same computer simultaneously). The size of computers continued to decrease.

4. *Fourth Generation* (1971–Now). In 1971, the first electronic computers were introduced that used Large-Scale Integration (LSI) circuits—thousands of integrated circuits on a chip—for main memory and logic circuitry. These computers had a much larger capacity to support main memory. The microprocessor, introduced in 1971, combined all of the circuitry for the central processing unit on a single chip. LSI and the microprocessor enabled the development of the supercomputer.
5. *Fifth Generation* (Now and in the Future). Some people think that the new microcomputers with faster operating speeds, greater processing capacity, and virtually unlimited memory should be included. Other people believe that fifth-generation computers will have circuitry based on gallium arsenide or other new superconductors. Many fifth-generation computers will support parallel processing—that is, many processors will work on a problem at the same time.

Computers are generally classified into one of four categories, based on seven factors:

1. Type of CPU.
2. Amount of main memory the CPU can use.
3. Storage capacity.
4. Speed of output devices.
5. Processing speed.
6. Number of users that can access the computer at one time.
7. Cost.

The smallest, slowest, and least expensive computer is the microcomputer, followed by the minicomputer, the mainframe computer, and the supercomputer.

Knowledge of a microcomputer is especially relevant for people in business today. The microcomputer's three basic hardware components are the keyboard, the monitor, and the system unit. The system unit comprises the power supply, the system board, and some storage devices such as diskette (floppy disk) drives and a hard disk drive.

Business has seen many improvements in the area of data processing since the introduction of computers:

1. Data can be collected more easily.
2. Data can be processed with much greater speed.
3. Data can be manipulated over and over again with ease.
4. Calculations are performed not only faster but usually with greater accuracy.
5. Output can be produced in more usable forms.

Significant progress has been made in making the computer easier to use by everyone. The effect of the computer on society can be felt in every area, including business, government, law, medicine, sports, entertainment, industry, agriculture, science, and the home.

The social and ethical implications of computerization are complex, and they concern all of us. Some of the concerns include:

- Potential for abuse of power and invasion of our privacy by those people/organizations owning or running large computer systems.
- Loss of security of governmental data/information.
- Elimination of entry-level jobs through computer-based automation.
- Electronic monitoring of employees.
- Maintaining and improving work opportunities for the disabled and the handicapped.
- Software piracy and violation of copyright.
- Estblishment of universal standards for use of computer systems and their data/information.

KEY TERMS

applications software, p. 9
central processing unit (CPU), p. 8
characters per second (cps), p. 15
chip, p. 13
compatibility, p. 16
computer, p. 5
computer generation, p. 21
computer literacy, p. 3
computer professional, p. 3
computer system, p. 5
connectivity, p. 5
data, p. 5
data processing, p. 5
diskette, p. 19
documentation, p. 9
ergonomics, p. 24
floppy disk, p. 19
hardcopy, p. 8
hard disk, p. 19
hardware, p. 5
information, p. 5
integrated circuit, p. 22
keyboard, p. 7
mainframe computer, p. 11
main memory, p. 8
microcomputer, p. 13
millions of instructions per second (mips), p. 15
minicomputer, p. 11
monitor, p. 8
monochrome monitor, p. 18
motherboard, p. 19
nonvolatile, p. 7
parallel processing, p. 23
power supply, p. 19
processing, p. 5
program, p. 8
RGB (color) monitor, p. 18
semiconductor, p. 13
softcopy, p. 8
software, p. 5
software package, p. 8
storage devices (hardware), p. 19
supercomputer, p. 11
superconductor, p. 22
system board, p. 19
systems software, p. 9
system unit, p. 19
user, p. 3

EXERCISES

MATCHING

Match each of the following terms to the phrase that is the most closely related.

1. ____ computer professional
2. ____ data processing
3. ____ connectivity
4. ____ keyboard

5. ____ integrated circuit
6. ____ software package
7. ____ applications software
8. ____ documentation
9. ____ information
10. ____ system unit
11. ____ compatibility
12. ____ computer (hardware)
13. ____ RGB monitor
14. ____ ergonomics
15. ____ user
16. ____ nonvolatile
17. ____ monochrome monitor
18. ____ data
19. ____ computer literacy
20. ____ parallel processing

a. Someone who does not necessarily have much technical knowledge about computers but who makes decisions based on information processed by the computer
b. Equipment made up of a combination of electronic and electromechanical components that uses software to process data
c. Raw, unevaluated facts
d. The product of data processing
e. Most common type of input device used with computers
f. A person in the field of computers who has had formal education in the technical aspects of using computers
g. This term relates to two or more computer systems being able to communicate; sixth element of a computer system
h. Refers to the usability of data and software on different types of computer systems
i. Said of data that is not lost when the power is turned off
j. A basic understanding of what a computer is and how it can be used as a resource
k. Complete electronic circuit on a chip
l. Output device that displays one color on a solid background
m. Processing of data into information
n. Many processors working on a problem at the same time
o. Explains to users how to use software
p. Output device that can display text and graphics in a variety of colors
q. Main computer system cabinet where the power supply, system board, and some storage devices are housed
r. Any collection of related programs to be carried out by the computer to satisfy a user's specific needs
s. Term often used to describe software acquired to perform a general business function
t. Science of human engineering, which designs things to be easily used by people

MULTIPLE CHOICE

1. ____ is the product of data processing.
   a. Data
   b. Information
   c. Software
   d. A computer
   e. CPU

2. The most common input device used today is the ____.
   a. motherboard
   b. central processing unit
   c. keyboard
   d. system unit
   e. semiconductor
3. Software instructions intended to satisfy a user's specific processing needs are called ____.
   a. systems software
   b. a microcomputer
   c. documentation
   d. applications software
   e. user's manual
4. Which of the following factors are used to categorize a computer?
   a. amount of main memory the CPU can use
   b. capacity of the storage devices
   c. cost of the system
   d. where it was purchased
   e. speed of the output devices
5. Which of the following is the most powerful type of computer?
   a. supermicro
   b. superconductor
   c. microcomputer
   d. supercomputer
   e. megaframe
6. Which of the following terms is related to a monitor?
   a. screen
   b. monochrome monitor
   c. RGB monitor
   d. video display
   e. all the above
7. Which kind of storage device can be carried around?
   a. hard disk
   b. system cabinet
   c. diskette
   d. main memory
   e. motherboard
8. Which of the following people probably has the least amount of technical computer knowledge?
   a. programmer
   b. user
   c. systems analyst
   d. computer operator
   e. computer professional
9. Which of the following devices allows the user to add components and capabilities to a computer system?
   a. storage devices
   b. keyboards
   c. system boards
   d. diskettes
   e. expansion slots
10. Which of the following terms applies to communication between separate computer systems?
    a. computer literacy
    b. power supply
    c. applications software
    d. connectivity
    e. none of the above

SHORT ANSWER

1. What does it mean to be computer literate? Why is computer literacy, or competency, important?
2. What does it mean to be a computer professional?

3. What are three factors used to categorize a computer (as a microcomputer, minicomputer, mainframe, supercomputer)?
4. Why do you think many companies spend a lot of money training their employees how to use computers?
5. What are the five main components of a computer system?
6. What is the meaning of the term *connectivity?*
7. What are the main characteristics of the first generation of computers?
8. Why is it better to have more main memory rather than less?
9. Briefly define *hardware* and *software.*
10. What is the main difference between systems software and applications software?
11. What is the purpose of output hardware?
12. What are a few ways that people affect computer operations?
13. Name three or four jobs that computer professionals could fill.

PROJECTS

1. Determine what types of computers are being used where you work or go to school. Are microcomputers being used? Minicomputers? Mainframes? All types? What are they being used for?
2. Look in the job opportunities section of a newspaper to see if many jobs require applicants to be familiar with using computers. What types of experience are required? If you were now looking for a job, which types of experience would you want to have?
3. Most people interact with a computer several times a day. Write a short report about how computers (all types) are being used around you. For example, have you ever used an automatic teller machine? Have you seen someone use a supermarket scanner? Clothing price tag scanner? During the course of a few days, take note of how you see computers being used. In the examples you give, describe *why* you think a computer is used.
4. How are computers used in the job or profession that you intend to pursue? Devise a questionnaire that you or someone in your chosen profession could use to determine what the uses are. Do you have any ideas for future uses?
5. Many people are afraid of or resistant to learning about computers. Are you one of them? If so, make a list of all the factors that you think are affecting your attitude, then list reasons to refute each point. Keep your list and review it again after you have finished the course. What do you still agree with? Have you changed your mind about computers?
6. Research an ethical issue you are interested in that involves the use of computers—for example, the use of computer programs to monitor employee performance. Or, what is the U.S. or Canadian government doing to protect the privacy of its citizens?

2

CHAPTER 2

THE COMPUTER-BASED INFORMATION SYSTEM

Now that we have discussed the general development of computers and covered some basic concepts, let us move on to some specific information about how you can use the computer to turn data into useful information.

The goal of this book is to provide you with tools that you can take with you into your career right away. With that goal in mind, we have devised a series of episodes that shows you how to use a computer in your own business. The first such episode immediately follows this chapter.

PREVIEW

When you have completed this chapter, you will be able to:

State what your role might be in a computer-based information system.

Describe the four phases of activity of the computer-based information system: input, processing, storage, output.

Discuss two basic approaches to inputting and processing data: batch and on-line.

Name three methods a company can use to organize its computer-based data processing facility: centralized, decentralized, distributed.

THE USER PERSPECTIVE

Can data be turned into information *without* the use of a computer? Of course—and it has been, for all the centuries of human history. Whether fingers or pebbles or coins are used to represent quantities, they may be manipulated in all sorts of ways. The main difference between then and now is speed; the computer enormously enhances the rapidity of converting data into information. The invention of computers (and the later enhancement of their speed), however, has created another important difference: what people have to do to data—and to the computer—in order to get information.

Not all your business information problems will be best solved using a computer. Right now you may not be in a position to judge when to use the computer, but you will be when you understand what is known as a *computer-based information system*—the input and processing of data and the storage and output of information. In the following pages, we will describe exactly what this system is, how it fits into a typical business organization, and what you need to know. But first let's determine where you fit in the overall picture.

WHERE DO YOU, THE USER, FIT IN?

Perhaps a secret anxiety of many users like you is the knowledge that computers don't run by themselves—a human presence, *your* presence, is required to make things happen. Indeed, you *are* a critical part of a computer-based information system, but we will lead you through it step by step so that it won't look quite so fearsome by the time you reach the end of the chapter.

As Figure 2.1 shows, during normal business activities users interact with the computer system at three points: (1) at the beginning, users *input* data in a computer-usable form; (2) during *processing*, users may be required to give the computer some direction about how to process the data; and (3) at the end, users review *output* information. This information is used as a basis for decision making and problem solving. How users direct the computer during processing depends on the applications software being used. Companies generally train users how to use their software, and software users' manuals also give guidance. (We'll get into software use in more detail later.)

The user may also interact with the computer-based information system at yet another point—the development of business software. This doesn't mean that you, the user, have to *write* the software; it means that you may have to help define your business-related requirements in enough detail so that the computer professionals assigned to develop the software understand what is to happen, when it is to happen, and how. For example, if you want the computer to prepare reports on budgeted versus actual sales of bridge paint, your requirements for how the report is to be produced must be carefully thought out. What level of detail do you require? Should reports cover information only on orange bridge paint, or should purple be included? How often do you want reports? When? In what form? and so on. During systems development it often happens that users don't communicate their needs well to the computer professionals who are writing the software for the new system, and so the users end up with a system they dislike—for which they blame the professionals.

Some type of computer hardware is required at every stage of processing. The larger the computer system is, the more removed the users are from the computer hardware. If your company uses a mainframe or a minicomputer system, you may work only with a **terminal** (usually a monitor and a keyboard) connected to the system and never even see the computer. In this case, you will need to learn how to establish communication with the central computer system and to follow the established procedures for requesting that certain programs be run in your behalf. However, if your company has only microcomputers for staff use, you will need to know a great deal more about the hardware.

WHAT IS A COMPUTER-BASED INFORMATION SYSTEM?

For our purposes, a system is a method of turning data into information. A system in which a computer is used to perform some of the processing is called a **computer-based information system.** As you know, such a system has five components:

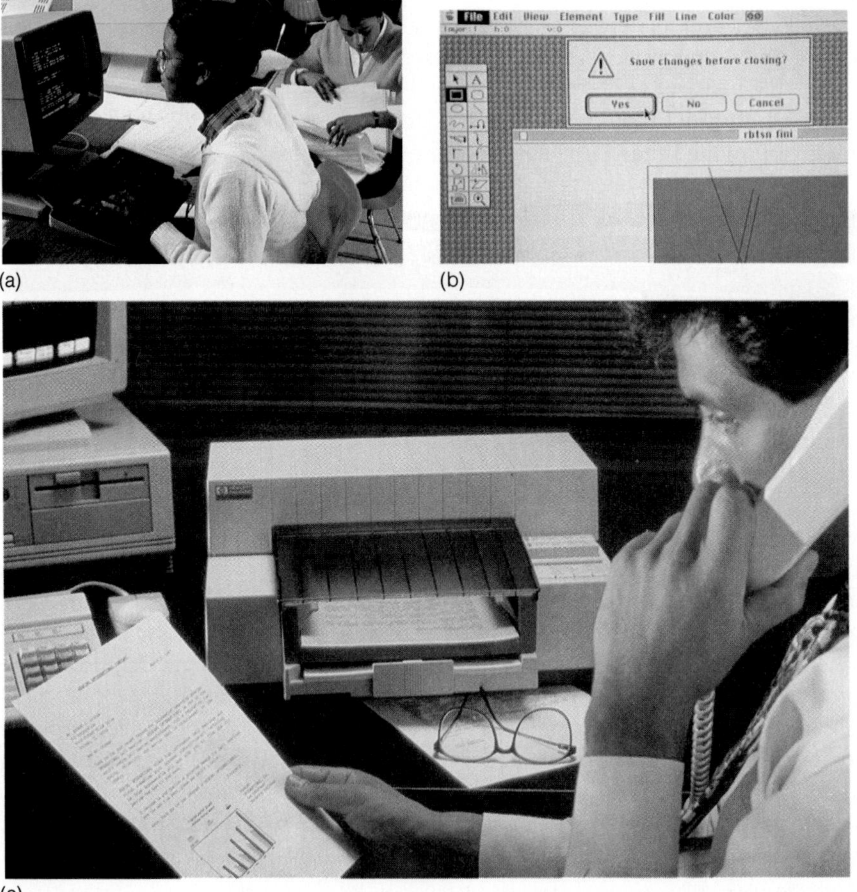

FIGURE 2.1

The systematic user. At the system's starting point (a), the user inputs data to the computer. During processing (b), the user may be asked to direct the computer. At the system's endpoint (c), the user reviews output information.

hardware, software, data/information, procedures, and people. However, it also has four phases of activity: input, processing, output, and storage (Figure 2.2). To help you understand how a computer-based information system works, we will examine how these four activity phases relate to the five components of the system. And, again, don't worry if you don't understand everything right away; you'll cover these topics in more detail as you progress through the book and as you start using the labs to gain hands-on experience.

Input Phase

During the **input phase** of a computer-based information system, business-related data is "captured" and converted to a form that can be processed by a computer. In this phase people will:

- Collect the data, either in document form or verbally.
- Instruct the computer to begin data input activities (how you do this varies according to the software package used).

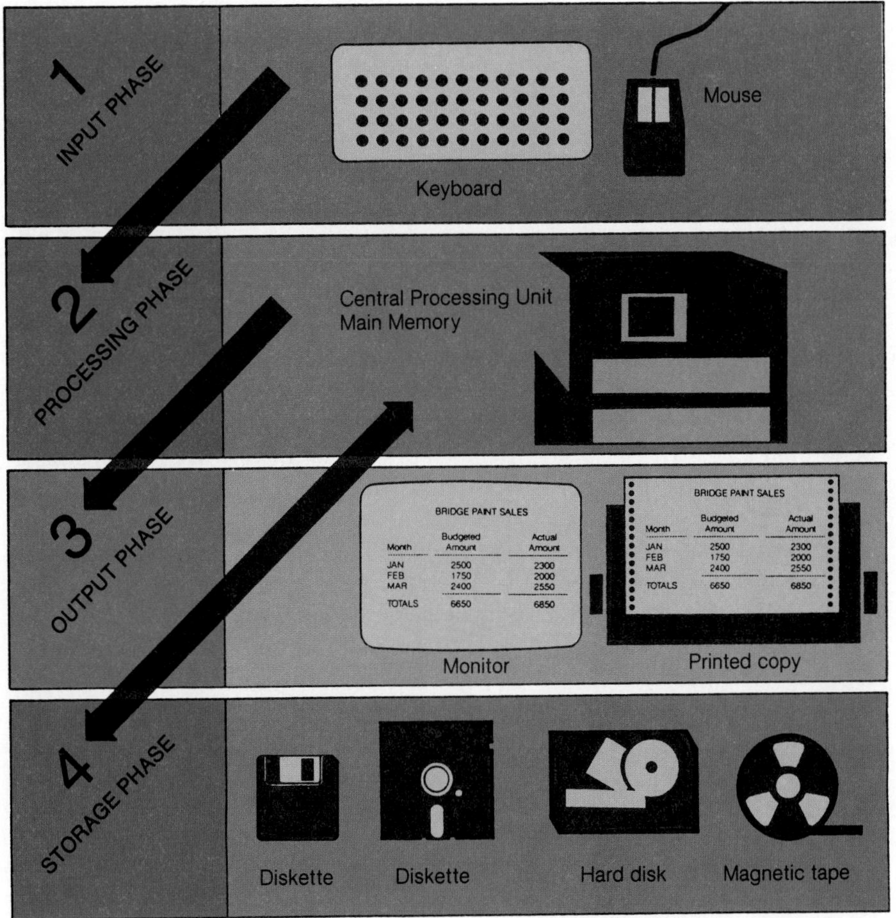

FIGURE 2.2

The four phases of a computer-based information system: (1) input, (2) processing, (3) output, and (4) storage. Note that the processing phase can lead to immediate output or to short- or long-term storage for future processing and/or output.

- Input data (using a keyboard or a mouse, for example) into a device (such as a computer terminal) that captures the data in a computer-usable form — that is, in electronic form and in a code that the computer can "understand" (codes and data representation will be discussed in Chapter 4).
- Supervise the data collection and input process.

Manual procedures — done by people but sometimes used together with computerized procedures — direct and control each activity in terms of who is supposed to do what, when, and how. For example, when data from sales receipts is being entered, someone must check to see that the sales records from which the data is being taken have been properly filled out. All the documents must be accounted for, and — after the data is input — someone must make sure that all the data has been entered. And, of course, the collection of documents and inputting of data must be scheduled. Manual procedures are recorded, not surprisingly, in a company's **procedures manual** or in memos.

Computerized procedures are required for:

- Coordinating the keying and processing of the data into the system.
- Checking the validity of the data. (Was the product number you entered a valid one? Was the data keyed in without errors? Most software will alert the user to errors.)
- Storing the data in computer-usable form for processing.
- Producing a control report that both summarizes the amount of data keyed in and provides totals on selected data elements (such as gallons of purple bridge paint sold yesterday) to ensure accurate entry.

The computer hardware devices used most often during the input phase are the keyboard, video display screen, disk storage units, and printer (to produce a control report). The software used depends on the needs of the organization that is using it.

PROCESSING PHASE

In the **processing phase** of a computer-based information system, all the number and character manipulation activities are done that are necessary to convert the data into an appropriate form of information. As shown in Figure 2.3, this includes performing calculations, classifying the input data, sorting the data, summarizing the data, and performing logical processing activities (such as listing information in a particular order).

In a well-designed computer-based information system, people rarely need to do more than issue instructions (by responding to the software's questions and directions) that tell the computer what procedures to perform. The manual procedures focus on how to begin, then how to monitor the computer processing procedures. The hardware components used most during this phase of activity are the central processing unit (CPU) and main memory.

OUTPUT PHASE

The **output phase** of the system provides the user with all the necessary information to perform and manage day-to-day business activities, as well as tactical planning (monitoring current company operations) and strategic planning (planning long-range goals for the company). Output can be provided for immediate use or for storage by the computer system for future use—either for additional processing or simply for output at a later date.

The form in which information is produced as output will vary according to needs. For example, some information can be output in *hardcopy* form (generally meaning you can touch the copy)—for example, printed on paper or output on microfilm. Other information may be more useful if displayed immediately in *softcopy* form (generally meaning that you can't actually touch it), such as on a video display screen. Hardcopy is commonly used for reports. Softcopy output is best for information that needs to be viewed only occasionally or only for a few moments.

Technological improvements have made it relatively easy and practical to produce both hardcopy and softcopy output that incorporates graphics with text. Sometimes information is also produced in an audio form, such as a telephone number given over the phone by directory assistance.

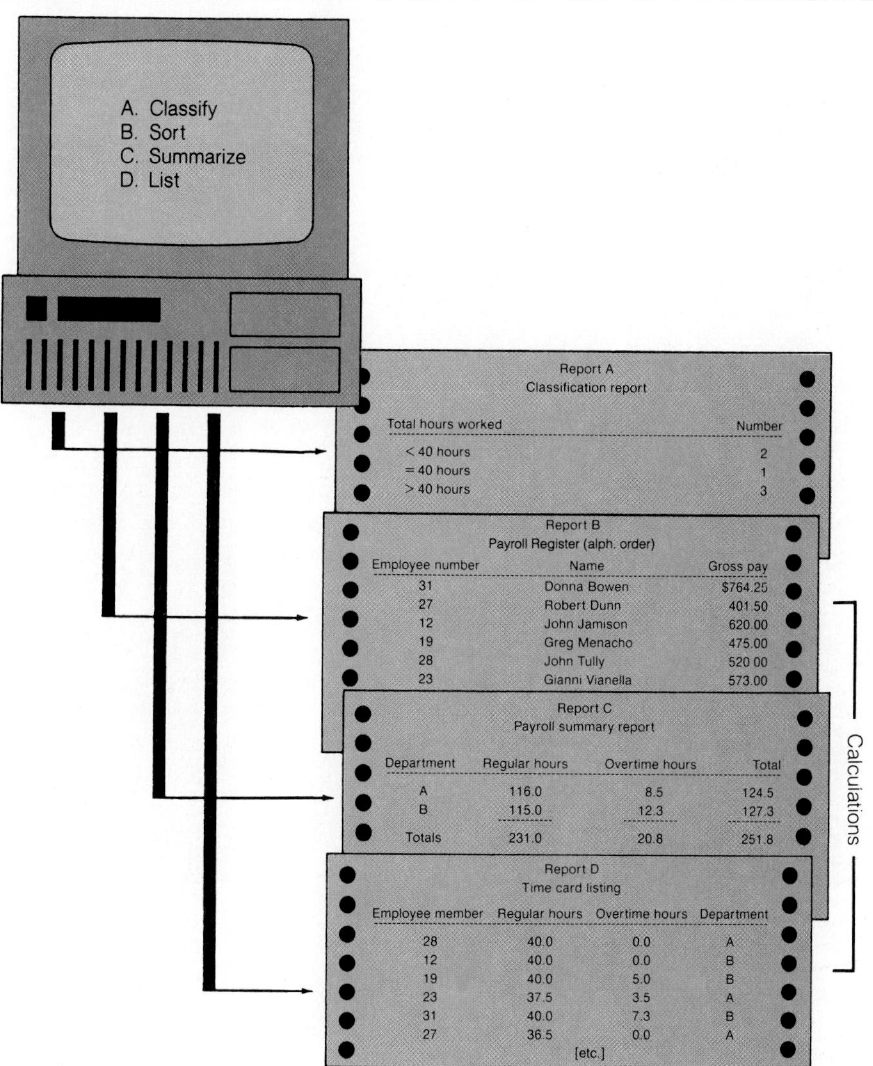

FIGURE 2.3

Examples of processing activities. Computer processing is useful for organizing different forms of output. For instance, information may be classified, sorted, summarized, or listed in a particular order. Calculations and logical manipulation are often done during such processing.

In the output phase, people usually:

- Prepare the output for distribution.
- Distribute the output to the intended recipients.
- Review the output by analyzing the information, then write reports and make decisions based on the results of the analysis.

The preparation and distribution of the output (manual procedures) would normally be controlled by a company's established standards and procedures. However,

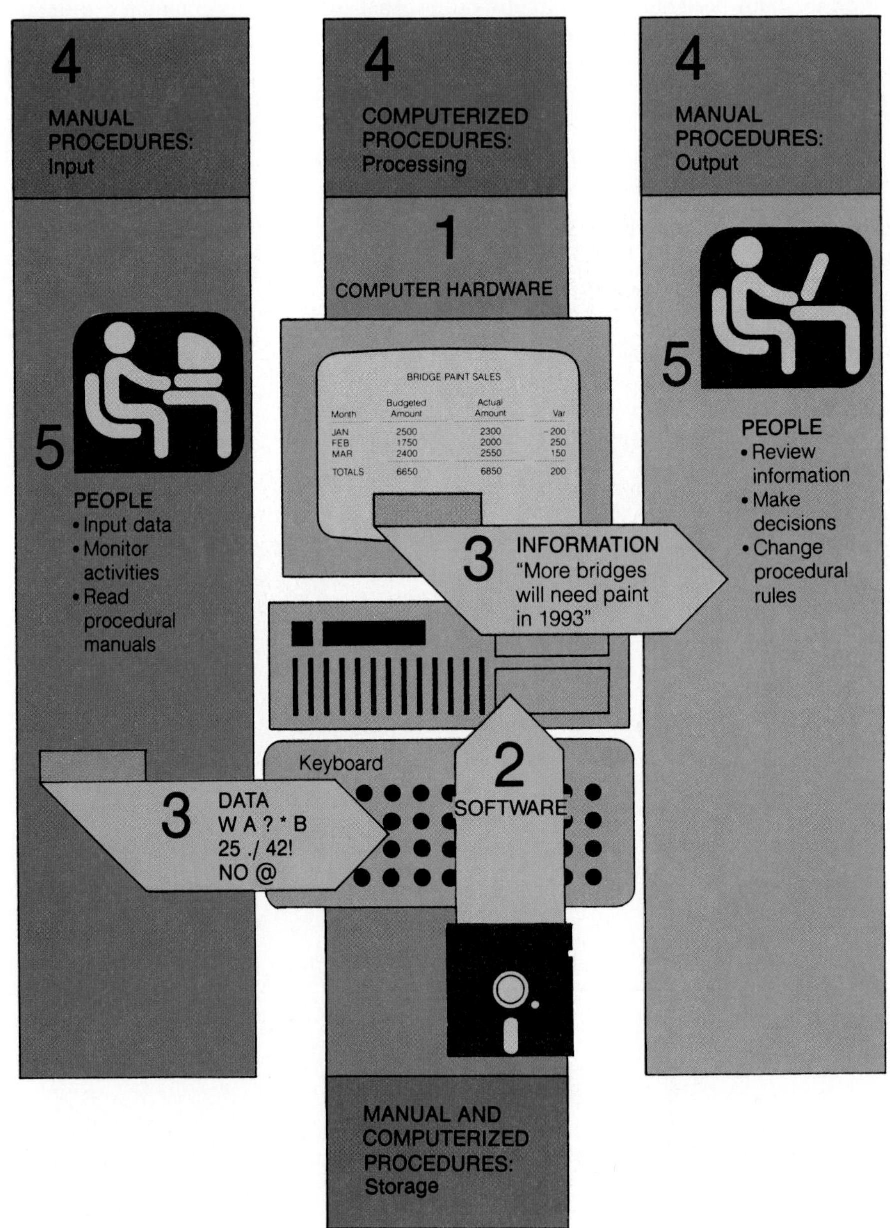

FIGURE 2.4

The systematic approach. This illustration shows the basic relationship between the five components of the computer-based information system—(1) hardware, (2) software, (3) data/information, (4) procedures, (5) people—and its four phases of activity—input, processing, storage, and output.

procedures for output review, analysis, and decision-making activities are rarely documented formally. (Computerized procedures for reviewing information involve highly sophisticated software that we'll discuss later.)

STORAGE PHASE

The **storage phase** of a computer-based information system involves storing data, information, and certain processing instructions in computer-usable form for retrieval. There is little need for human involvement in the computerized storage of data. The computer software program directs the computer to store the data in computer-usable form on disks or tapes designated by the user. People do get involved, however, in the maintenance of computer-based files. (Files are logically related data grouped together into named categories — such as all of a store's data on one customer. The user generally determines which category data belongs to and how to name each category, or file.) Files stored, for example, on disk or tape can be retrieved, updated, printed out, stored again, communicated to other computers, or erased. (Chapter 4 covers the formation and storage of files in more detail.) Someone has to monitor how long data should be retained, decide whether backup copies (duplicate disks or tapes kept elsewhere for security reasons) are required, and determine when data should be removed from the system. These activities are normally directed by formal policies and procedures relating to file retention. Indeed, much of the information stored on computers — medical records, for example — must be maintained by law for specified periods of time.

Figure 2.4 (left) gives you a basic idea of how the five components of the computer-based information system relate to the four phases of activity.

THE FOUR PHASES OF ACTIVITY AT INTOUCH OFFICE SUPPLIES, INC.

In almost every business it's easy to identify the four phases of activity in the computer-based information system. The user procedures may differ slightly, as may the hardware components; however, the general flow of activities — from the input of data into computer-usable form and the processing of data into information to the output or storage of information — remains the same.

In this section we use sales order entry — necessary to many businesses — to illustrate each phase of activity (Figure 2.5 shows the process described in this section).

INTOUCH SALES ORDER ENTRY: INPUT PHASE

Suppose you were running an office supply store named Intouch Office Supplies, Inc. One of the first things you would need to do in the input phase of the sales order entry process is identify the different *types* of input required for processing. Obviously, you have to input data that has to do with the price and amount of goods ordered by and sold to customers on a daily basis. In addition, the stock within the store must be replenished, so data about the receipt of goods into stock must also be entered into the computer.

Data related to customer orders can be received in at least three ways: (1) a customer may telephone and place an order; (2) a customer may send an order in the mail; or (3) a customer may stop by the store, pick out the needed items from the shelves, and bring them to the cash register. The input procedures might differ slightly for each circumstance.

When a customer calls on the phone, you might record the order data on an order form (**source document**) for later entry into the computer. As an alternative,

FIGURE 2.5(a)

Sales order entry. At Intouch Office Supplies, customer order data is taken by phone, mail, and in the store. The data (product numbers plus prices and amount of items sold) is input to the computer and processed. Processed data is used to update stored inventory master file, customer files, and sales order files and to output information in the form of invoices and reports.

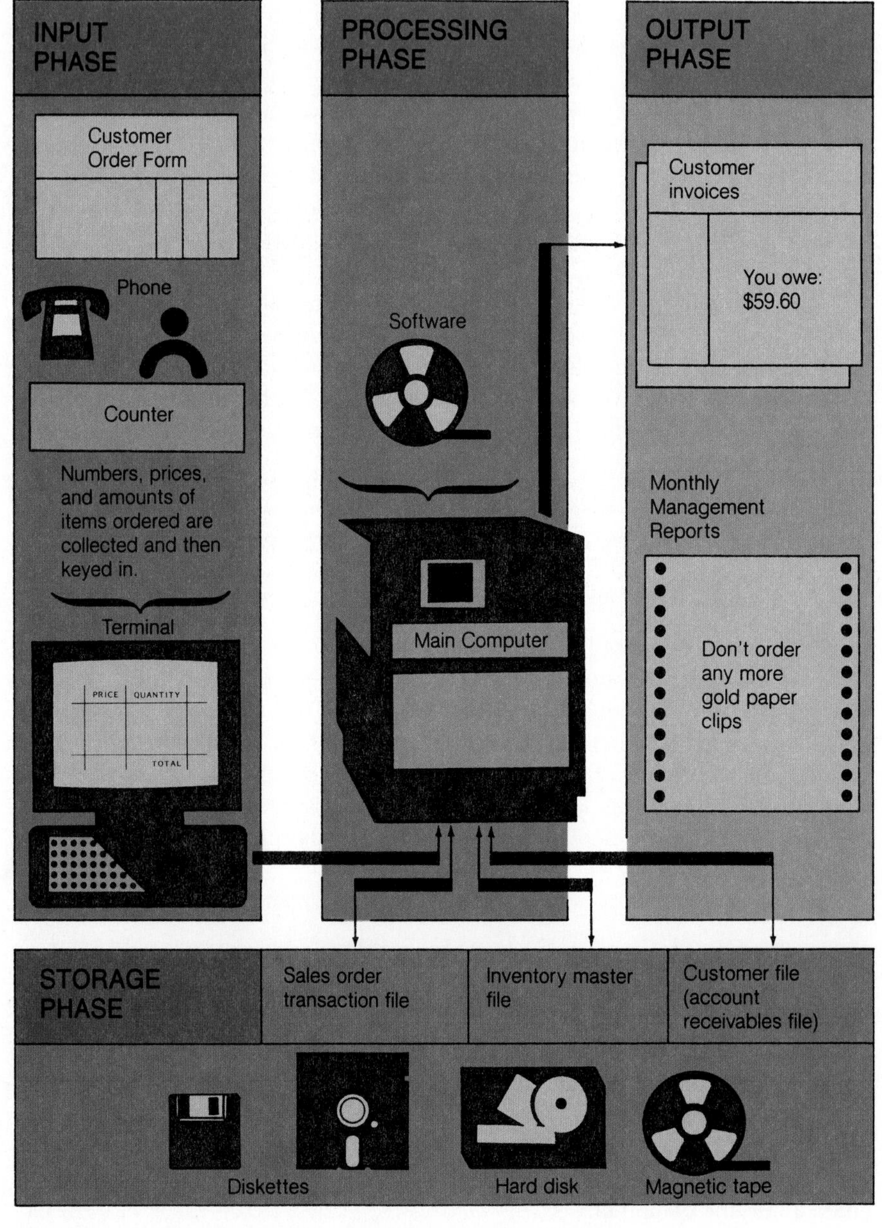

if your store is equipped with modern computer processing facilities, you might enter the data immediately into the computer through a keyboard and monitor (called a *point-of-sale terminal*) located near the cash register.

The orders received in the mail would probably be collected, grouped into small batches (a **batch** is a group of documents intended for input to the computer in a controlled fashion), and entered all at once into the system.

Customer orders placed at the store could be handled in several ways. If all the

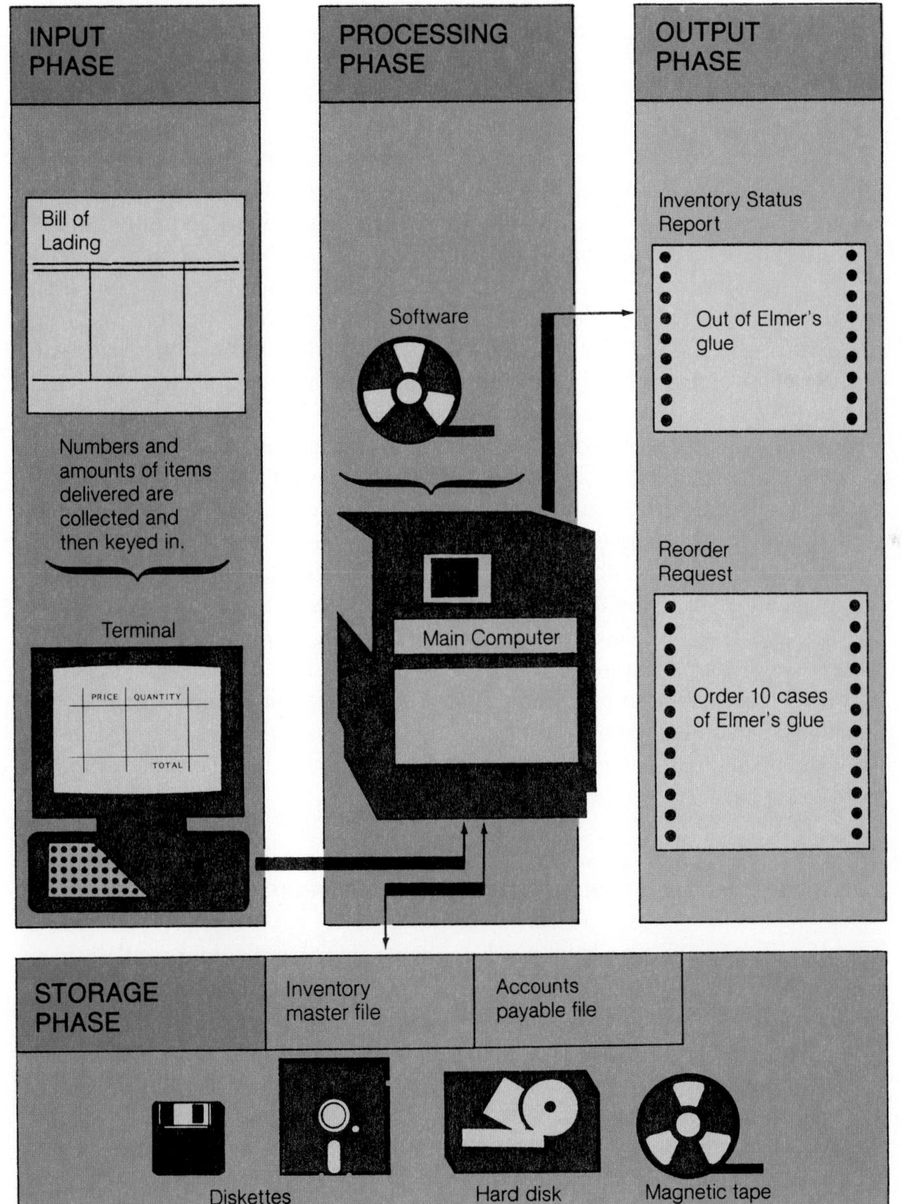

FIGURE 2.5(b)

To fill orders effectively, Intouch also needs to process data relating to the receipt of product shipments to replenish inventory. Data (numbers and amounts of items delivered, plus their cost) taken from the bills of lading is input to the computer and used to update stored inventory files and to output information in the form of inventory status reports and reorder requests.

items in the store have the bar coded tags we often see at the supermarket, you could use a bar code reading device to automatically scan the product data into computer-usable form. You could also simply use the keyboard on a terminal at the counter to enter the data on the items ordered.

To keep track of the number of items in stock, the data relating to goods ordered and received must also be entered into the computer. The product numbers and number of items received can be taken from the vendor's *bill of lading* (a document identifying the contents of a shipment) and entered directly into the computer.

INTOUCH SALES ORDER ENTRY: PROCESSING PHASE

During the processing phase, the data (now in computer-usable form) is transformed into information. Processing includes performing calculations, classifying the input data, sorting the data, summarizing the data, and performing logical processing activities such as updating files.

At Intouch, Inc., your system probably processes the customer order data in the following fashion. First, the system processes the data relating to the items ordered. The product number for each item is verified by comparing it with the number contained in the inventory master file (stored on disk or tape). Each item's price is retrieved from the master file, as well as the detailed item description. The inventory master file is updated to reflect the number of items ordered and removed from stock. Then all the order data is processed to produce the information necessary to produce an *invoice* — the bill for the customer. In the invoice, the quantity of each item ordered is multiplied by its *unit price* (the price of one item) to produce a line total. All the line totals are added to produce an invoice subtotal. The subtotal, as well as the customer's status, is analyzed to determine what type of *discount*, if any, should be allowed. (For example, customers who owe no money and who order more than 20 gold paper clips at one time get a 5 percent reduction in price.) The discount amount is computed, as well as any state and local taxes that apply. Finally, the invoice total is computed. The last step in processing customer order data involves updating the file of unpaid customer invoices (*accounts receivable*, or money owed) with a summary of the invoice-related data.

The processing of the bill of lading data (incoming product shipments) involves updating the master inventory file to reflect the number of additional items placed in stock and updating the *accounts payable* file — that is, the file that shows amounts owed to suppliers for what shipments.

INTOUCH SALES ORDER ENTRY: OUTPUT PHASE

Intouch Office Supplies probably produces two main types of output regularly in its sales order entry system: (1) customer invoices, printed out and sent to customers for payment, and (2) management reports, produced monthly to summarize and categorize the products sold and the products ordered.

In addition, **status reports** of all goods in stock are produced periodically; in other words, the number of items actually on the shelves is compared with the number indicated by the computer-based records. **Exception reports** are produced whenever the quantity of an item on hand falls below the minimum stocking level (sometimes referred to as the *reorder point*).

Intouch Sales Order Entry: Storage Phase

Your office supply company is involved with computer-based storage in three ways. First, the order data and the data on goods received (to restock inventory) are entered into a temporary storage file (called a **transaction file**) and stored until needed for processing. Second, during processing, information stored in a permanent customer file and an inventory master file is retrieved for use in performing calculations and other processing activities. Third, information stored in the inventory master file, the accounts receivable file, and the accounts payable file is updated.

In addition, all processing instructions are stored in a permanent form for easy retrieval.

Methods of Input and Processing: If Not Now, When?

We used the sales order entry process of Intouch Office Supplies to illustrate the activities that might take place in each phase of a computer-based information system; but the activities we described were specific to that example. Any organization that uses computers to process data into information has a computer-based information system. However, the activities of each phase will be different depending on what overall input and processing approach, or combination of approaches, is used.

People in the information management field disagree somewhat about the specific definitions of some input and processing methods. However, for our purposes, we can focus on the two basic approaches an organization might take to input and process data:

1. Batch
2. On-line

In batch processing, a group of data is usually entered first to temporary transaction files, and processing to update the master files is done later. In on-line processing, master files are updated as soon as data from individual transactions becomes available. Deciding which approach or combination of approaches is best depends on the input, processing, and output needs of the organization. We will use Intouch Office Supplies to illustrate the activities that might take place using the two basic approaches.

Batch Approach: Do It Later

An organization that uses batch data collection and batch processing collects data in the form of source documents (for example, customer sales orders) and places them into groups (batches). Once all the data has been collected and batched, it is forwarded to a data entry person or group responsible for keying it into computer-usable form (**batch entry**). As the data is keyed in, it may be processed immediately to update master files or stored temporarily in a transaction file for later processing.

(In some cases source documents are not used, and the data is keyed in as needed and stored in a transaction file.) Data in a transaction file may be stored for only a few hours, but in other cases it may be stored for a week or a month before the regular processing activities are scheduled. At this time each transaction in the batch is processed, one after another, until all related output has been produced and appropriate files have been updated. Figure 2.6 illustrates the batch approach to a computer-based information system.

FIGURE 2.6

Batching it. Source documents are collected over a period of time. Then their data is entered into the computer in batches (batch entry). This data can be processed immediately (on-line processing) or stored temporarily in transaction files for later processing (batch processing). Processed data is output as information (reports) and is used to update permanent master files on disk and tape.

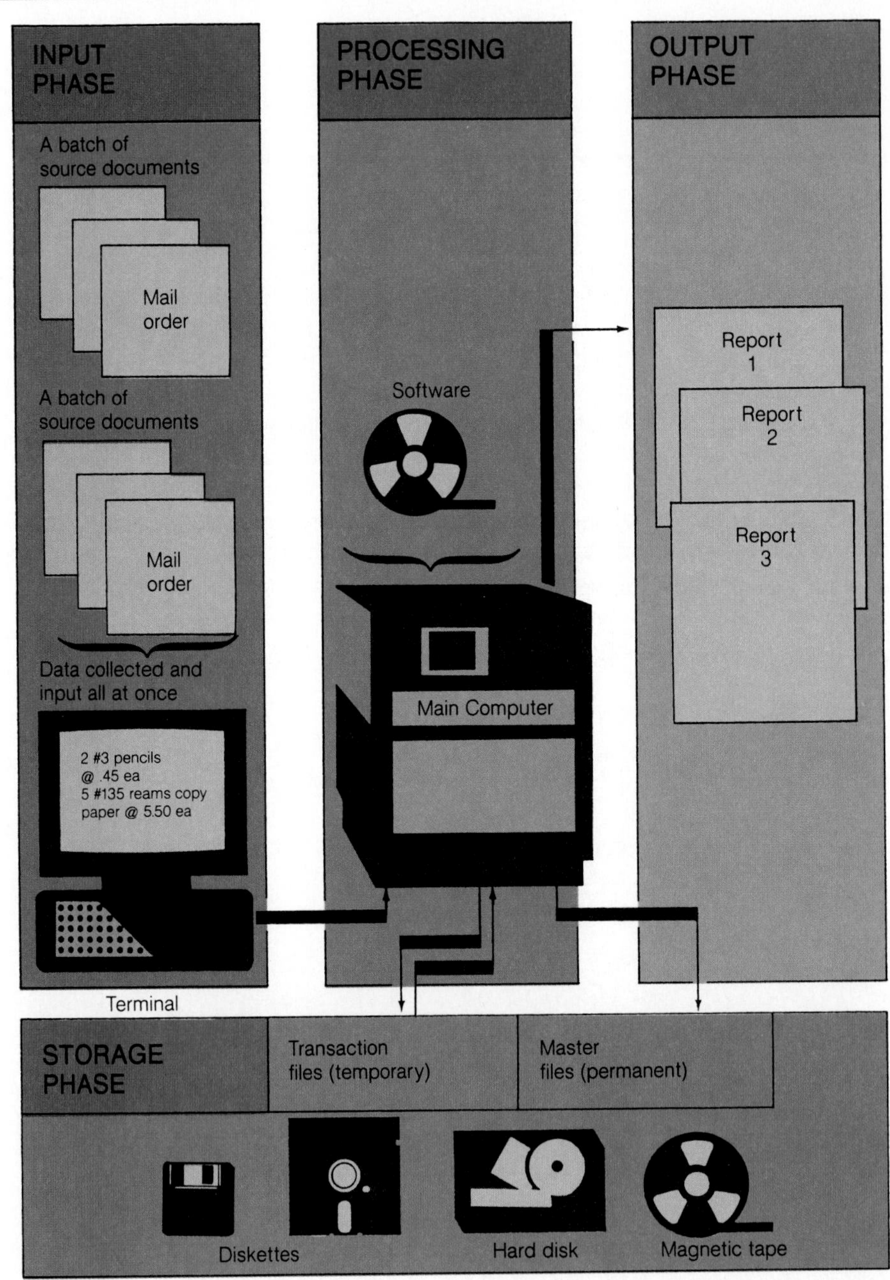

Intouch Office Supplies would probably use the batch approach to handle pertinent transaction data from mailed customer orders and bills of lading from suppliers. After collecting the data into batches, a clerk would be assigned the task of entering the data into the computer for temporary storage. (Sometimes the data is transcribed onto some other type of form or source document before it is input to the computer.) The processing activities would probably take place at the end of the workday or in the evening so as not to tie up the computer during the day.

Heavy-Duty Batch Input and Processing

Many large organizations that use batch input perform a great number of large-volume, repetitious tasks that would unnecessarily tie up the processing power of a mainframe computer system. This processing, done after regular business transactions have been taken care of, may involve, for example, printing huge numbers of output reports or invoices. For instance, a typical large corporate data processing center may produce 250,000 pages or more per month, and a public utility such as the phone company could easily produce 20 million pages per month of output reports and bills. The input data is stored on disk or tape and then output later—perhaps at night—by special high-speed printers. In some cases, specialized computers "oversee" the output process, thereby freeing up the main computer for other uses.

On-Line Approach: Do It Now

On-line equipment communicates directly with the processing computer. Off-line equipment does not communicate directly. In **on-line processing,** also known as **interactive processing,** data is input immediately as each business transaction occurs, using on-line equipment that allows immediate processing. In other words, instead of collecting manually recorded customer order data into batches for later input, the clerk at Intouch would enter order data immediately, as it came in (Figure 2.7). The data would be processed right away for output and updating of master files. It would not be temporarily stored in a transaction file.

If Intouch Office Supplies uses the batch approach for entering and processing order data received by mail, it would probably use the on-line approach for order data taken over the phone or in person at the counter.

The key characteristics of Intouch's on-line system would be:

- Customer data is acted on immediately.
- The inventory master file is updated immediately to reflect the number of items removed from inventory.
- The customer invoice is either produced on the spot or stored in a temporary print file for later output.
- The accounts receivable file (money owed to Intouch) is updated immediately to include the new invoice data.

When on-line processing occurs particularly quickly—fast enough to affect the user's activities right away—it is often called **real-time processing.** This approach is used for the most time-sensitive applications to allow decision making to occur as quickly as possible. An airline reservation system is one example of a system that requires real-time processing of transactions; airlines need to use the on-line real-time approach to keep an accurate, up-to-date record of reservations, cancellations, and scheduled flights and flight changes. Some automatic teller transactions are also handled on a real-time basis; when you withdraw your money, your balance is immediately updated and printed on your receipt. Real-time data access is critical to any Wall Street stockbroker. The data that moves across the screen represents stock market factors on which the next decision is made. Any seconds lost in decision-making time could be measured in millions of dollars.

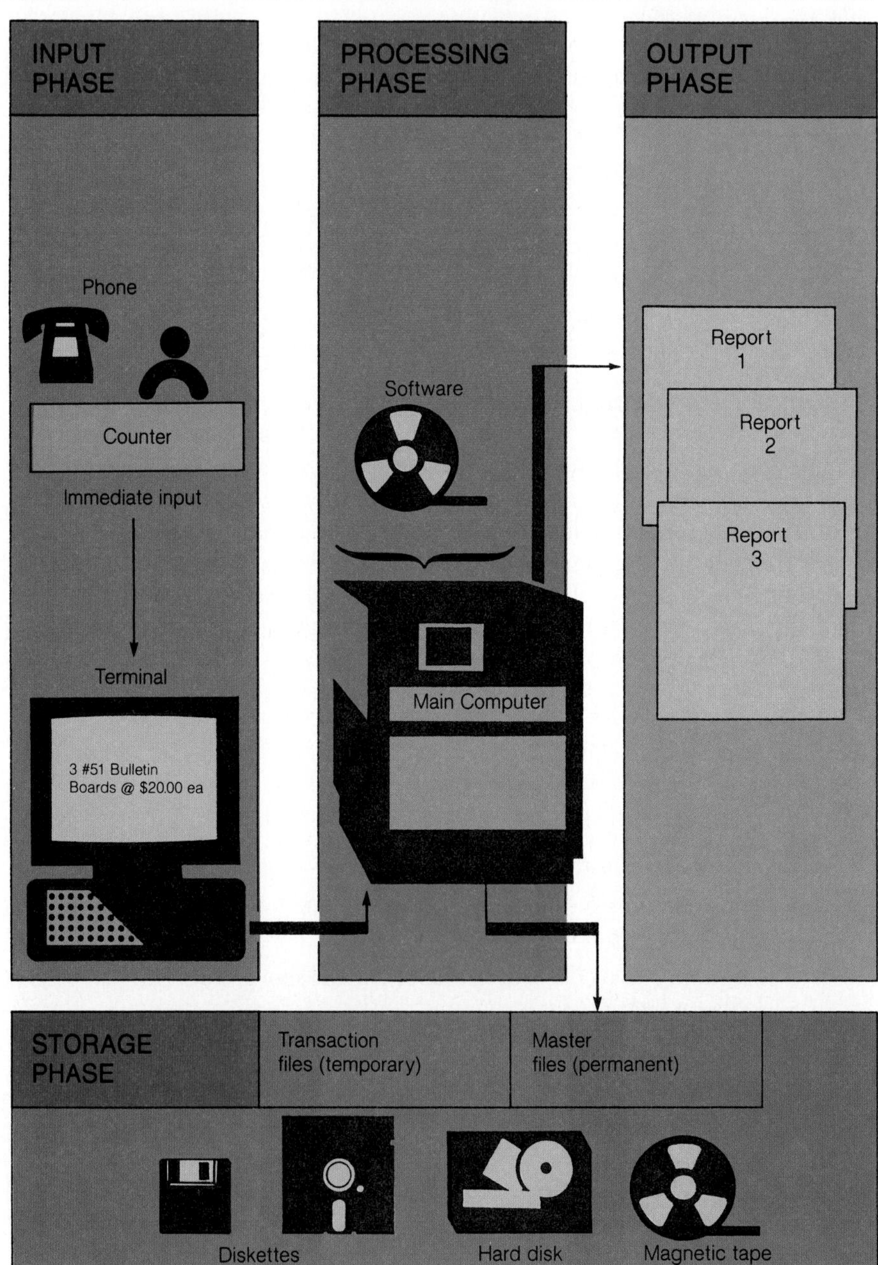

FIGURE 2.7

On-line. This approach uses no source documents with manually recorded data. Instead, data is input immediately and usually processed immediately.

Some organizations use a combination of batch and on-line input and immediate or delayed processing at different points in their operations, depending on whether processing needs are routine or time sensitive. For example, even though your ATM (automatic teller machine) receipt may have been provided on a real-time processing basis, any paper transactions you made *in* the bank during the same day are probably being batched for after-hours processing. Thus your ATM receipt may not reflect your most current balance.

ORGANIZING COMPUTER FACILITIES

When a company acquires a minicomputer or a mainframe computer system, it also usually sets up a special organizational unit, or department, to operate it. (Because microcomputers are still generally used by only one user at a time, a special department does not need to be set up to operate them — unless, of course, they are hooked up to the larger mini- or mainframe computer system.) The name of this unit may vary: Data Processing Department, Information Systems Department, or Computer Information Systems Department are common names. The computer system and related equipment plus the area set aside for the employees who staff the department are often called the *computer facility*. How a computer facility functions and how it is used within an organization tend to reflect management's organizational philosophy. You, as a user, should know how your company's computer facility is organized so that you can efficiently perform your job-related activities. Figure 2.8 diagrams the characteristics of the three types of facilities: centralized, decentralized, and distributed.

CENTRALIZED COMPUTER FACILITY: ONE FOR ALL

When an organization has established a single computer department to provide data processing and information systems services, this department is often referred to as a **centralized computer facility.** It is called *centralized* because it alone supplies data processing support to all other departments in the company. Entry and retrieval of data can occur either at the central facility or at terminals connected to the central facility through communications lines. The position of a centralized facility in the organizational structure varies. However, it often reports to one of the following: (1) the controller, who is in charge of all accounting procedures, (2) the vice president of Finance, or (3) directly to top management through a vice president of Information Systems.

When computer-based information processing was first introduced to business, it was most often used in the areas of accounting and finance. To have the computer facility staff report to the head of the department to which it provided services seemed only natural. Because many organizations computerized their accounting activities first, the data processing facility usually reported to the head of accounting.

As businesses gained experience with computer-based information processing, more departments began to recognize the value of the computer. This led to competition for the use of the computer resource, which in turn led to problems in establishing priorities. To resolve this problem, many organizations established the computer facility as a separate functional unit, or department, that reported to upper management. The management set up an independent management steering committee to objectively consider all requests for computer support and establish priorities, which were then followed by the staff of the computer facility.

The principal advantages of the centralized processing approach are:

- *Cost effectiveness.* The cost effectiveness of computer hardware resources is increased because equipment is not duplicated at difference locations.

FIGURE 2.8

Use your facilities. Companies may organize their computer facilities so that they are centralized, decentralized, or distributed. In the centralized facility, terminals in various departments are hooked up to one main computer system. In the decentralized system, each department has its own computer system, whether microcomputer based or based on a larger computer. The distributed system has independent processing functions in each department but also connects each department to a larger computer system.

CENTRALIZED COMPUTER FACILITY

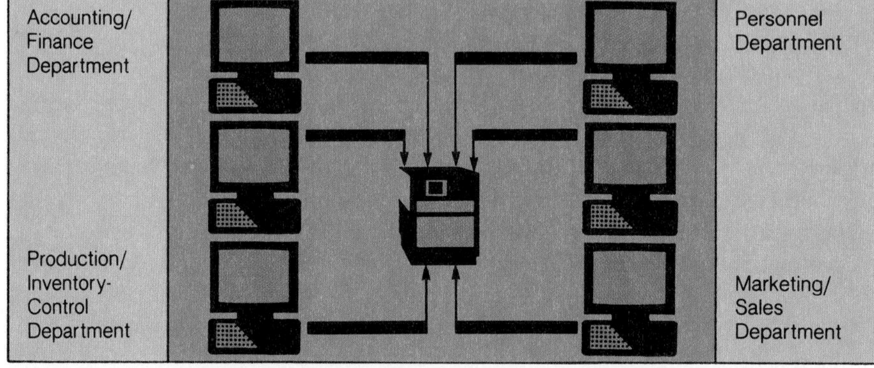

DECENTRALIZED COMPUTER FACILITY

DISTRIBUTED COMPUTER FACILITY

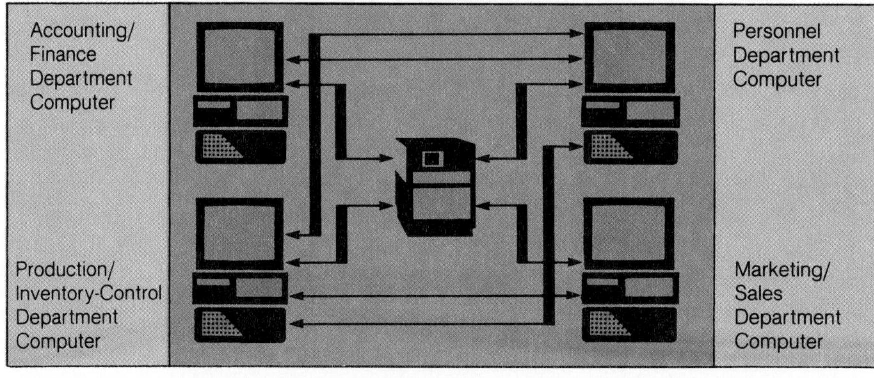

- *Coordination and control*. Processing activities are easier to coordinate and control in a centralized facility.
- *Standards*. The ability to impose and enforce processing standards is easier in a centralized facility.
- *Support of users*. Professional data processing personnel are located near users and so can develop a good working relationship with those they support.

In some cases, the centralized approach proved unsatisfactory because of:

- *Lack of accountability*. In a large company, it is difficult to track and fairly allocate the costs of the computer processing facility to the many different departments based on individual departmental use. Also, departments at remote locations may feel that their information needs are not being met.
- *Unfamiliarity*. The computer specialists responsible for the design of computer applications software ended up being responsible for working in many areas of the company with which they were unfamiliar. As a result, the specialists often took a lot of time to understand the processing requirements of a new department. This problem often caused delays in a project and sometimes led to misunderstandings — in other words, some of the software developed failed to meet the needs of the department, or failed to meet them in time.
- *Delays*.In many cases the data processing staff in centralized computer facilities had so many demands placed on their time that users had to wait for months (or even years) for their projects to be completed.
- *Costs*. Communications hardware and software costs can become high when a company's departments are spread over many distant locations.

Concerns with problems such as these led some organizations to organize their computer facility differently.

Decentralized Computer Facilities: All for One

An organization that uses a separate computer facility to service the needs of each major organizational unit has **decentralized computer facilities.** The size of each facility is determined by the processing requirements of the department it serves. Smaller departments may have a decentralized processing facility that is staffed with only one or two computer operators to initiate and control processing activities on a minicomputer. Other organizational units may have a large data processing facility with computer operators, data entry personnel, programmers, and systems analysts. (Systems analysts determine users' computer-related processing requirements and then design a computer-based applications system to meet those requirements.)

The advantages of using decentralized computer facilities are:

- They are better able to meet local departmental information needs than are centralized facilities.
- They are better able to match hardware and software to local departmental needs.
- They use less sophisticated and less expensive communications hardware and software.

Although this approach solves some problems created by centralized facilities, it also creates new ones.

- The decentralized approach makes it difficult to obtain consolidated, companywide management information because each organizational unit has its own key data and information stored on its own computer system, and the various systems are not electronically linked. Because the format and content of data and information are not consistent between organizational units, the data can't be easily accessed or subjected to a simple consolidation procedure.

  For example, suppose one company uses six different types of microcomputers: Accounting has an IBM PS/2 Model 80; the vice president of Finance uses an Apple IIe; Personnel, a Compaq Deskpro; Marketing, a Macintosh; Production, a Tandy Model 5000 (with three terminals); and the controller has a Wang system. Each computer is unable to exchange data or software easily with the others—the computers are not *compatible*. This eliminates the ability to share data in a form that can immediately be processed by a computer. As a result, the only way to share data (without using special hardware and software) is in printed form, and the only way to process combined data is to re-input it into a form compatible with the computer intended to process it.
- The duplication of hardware, software, and personnel to run decentralized computer facilities can become an unmanageable expense.

DISTRIBUTED COMPUTER FACILITY: SOMETHING FOR EVERYONE

A combination of centralized and decentralized computer facilities has been used to try to capture the advantages of both while minimizing their weaknesses. In this system, called a **distributed computer facility,** users have their own computer equipment, and one or more computer terminals are connected to a bigger system—a few microcomputers, a minicomputer, or in some cases a mainframe computer—depending on processing requirements. With the growth of powerful communications networks and the decline in computer system costs, distributed systems are becoming more common.

To illustrate, let's consider a company with four divisions located in different cities throughout the country with its corporate headquarters on the West Coast. Headquarters has a large mainframe computer system, and each division has a smaller minicomputer to handle its own local processing needs. Some individual users in various departments at the division level have microcomputers to increase their productivity. The mainframe computer performs all corporate-level processing and passes pertinent data and information to each division as needed through a communications facility built into the computer systems at all locations. The greatest processing needs at the division level are handled by the division's minicomputer system. In many cases, several departments have microcomputer terminals connected to the minicomputer system. These personal computers may be used for a variety of processing requirements. The more sophisticated personal computers are able to exchange data with the division-level computer system.

In a distributed data processing environment, the corporate-level computer facility is ultimately responsible for the control and coordination of processing activities at all company levels. This is usually accomplished through corporate-level policies and procedures, as well as by direct support from the corporate data processing department, which oversees equipment selection and systems design to maintain compatibility.

Without careful planning, the compatibility of data files can become a problem when users capture data on a microcomputer and then wish to transfer it to the central computer system. The reverse is also often true. Microcomputers use a different coding scheme for data than many larger computers do. Unless special steps are taken — adding special hardware components and using special software — data cannot be exchanged in either direction. However, when the proper steps are taken, the problem of data file compatibility is eliminated. Then the microcomputer can be a significant tool in distributing computer processing power to the users.

The principal advantages of the distributed processing approach are:

- *User involvement.* The users are more directly involved in the processing activities than they would be in a centralized structure.
- *Cost allocation.* Computer processing costs are easier to allocate to different departments than they are in a centralized computer facility.
- *Familiarity.* The computer staff is more familiar with the activities and needs of the specific organizational unit they support than they are in a centralized setup.
- *Corporate processing needs.* The central computer facility can focus more on corporate processing needs than it can when the organization uses only a centralized facility to support all its departments.
- *Fewer personnel.* There is less duplication of hardware, software, and personnel than with the decentralized approach.
- *Coordination.* There is more coordination between the corporate computer facility and the division-level computer facilities than with other approaches.

A company that has many widely dispersed units is likely to have a decentralized or a distributed computer facility. Of the two, the decentralized approach will work better when the different units are involved in unrelated activities that require little overall coordination and control. Distributed computer facilities are often found in companies where the organizational units are separate but still closely related and where corporate coordination is very important. Companies with one large headquarters are likely to have a centralized computer facility.

Onward: Applying What You've Learned

Part I has offered you an overview of many of the basic concepts that provide a foundation for understanding how computers are used in business. You should now have a general sense of what a computer system is, how it has affected the processing of data into information, and what basic phases are involved in a computer-based information system.

Now we proceed to Episode 1 of establishing your own business — a chance for you to start applying what you've learned.

SUMMARY

A computer-based information system involves collecting data (input), processing it into information, and storing the information for future reference and output. The system has five basic components — hardware, software, data/information, procedures, and people — and four major phases of activity — input, processing, output, and storage. People are most directly involved during the input and output phases.

Each organization has different processing requirements, depending on the nature of its business and activities and how quickly the data needs to be processed. To accommodate these differing needs the computer-based information system can be designed to use one or both of two basic types of processing approaches: batch and on-line. These approaches differ in terms of the methods for collecting the data for input, the amount of time that passes between data input and actual processing, and the speed with which the output is produced. In the batch approach, data recorded manually on source documents is gathered together in batches and input all at one time. In the on-line approach, data is input immediately, on a case-by-case basis, and is processed immediately. On-line processing used for immediate decision making is often called real-time processing.

In many organizations, we can see a direct relationship between computer-related functions and management's organizational philosophy. As a result, organizations set up their computer facilities differently, using either a centralized, decentralized, or distributed computer facility. A centralized computer facility has all its equipment in one location. This equipment serves all the company's departments. A decentralized facility has separate computer equipment for each department in the company. A distributed facility combines aspects of both the centralized and the decentralized facilities: Users have microcomputers with communication programs so that they may switch to the main computer from time to time. They have the choice of working independently or with the central computer.

KEY TERMS

batch, p. 53
batch entry, p. 55
centralized computer facility, p. 59
computer-based information system, p. 46
decentralized computer facilities, p. 61
distributed computer facility, p. 62
exception report, p. 54
input phase, p. 47
interactive processing, p. 57
on-line processing, p. 57
output phase, p. 48
procedures manual, p. 48
processing phase, p. 48
real-time processing, p. 57
source document, p. 52
status report, p. 54
storage phase, p. 51
terminal, p. 46
transaction file, p. 55

EXERCISES

MATCHING

Match each of the following terms to the phrase that is the most closely related.

1. C processing phase
2. K source document
3. J on-line processing
4. H computer-based information system
5. A centralized computer facility
6. G output phase
7. B input phase
8. n transaction file
9. M batch
10. I decentralized computer facility
11. L batch entry and processing
12. D distributed facility
13. F real-time processing
14. E terminal

a. This type of computer facility provides support to all departments in a company.
b. Data is "captured" and converted to a form that can be processed by a computer.
c. All the number and character manipulation activities are done that are necessary to convert data into an appropriate form of information.
d. A combination of centralized and decentralized computer facilities
e. Keyboard and monitor (with no independent processing capabilities) hooked up to a computer system
f. On-line processing used for immediate decision making
g. The user is provided with all the necessary information to perform and manage day-to-day business activities as well as tactical and strategic planning.
h. A system in which the computer user is typically concerned with collecting data, processing it into information, and storing it for future reference
i. Each department has a separate computer facility to satisfy its processing needs.
j. With this approach to processing, data is input and processed immediately, on a case-by-case basis.
k. An order form from which input data is collected
l. Data is collected from source documents into groups and then forwarded to a data-entry person or group who is responsible for keying it into computer-usable form and placing it in temporary storage for later processing.
m. A group
n. Temporary storage file

MULTIPLE CHOICE

1. People typically interface with a computer-based system when:
   a. information must be output
   b. data must be input
   c. information must be reviewed
   d. the computer needs a direction (or instruction) in order to process data
   e. all the above
2. The following typically happens in the output phase of a computer-based information system:
   a. Data is put into the computer for processing.
   b. Information is produced in hardcopy and/or softcopy form.
   c. Mathematical calculations are performed.
   d. The computer is turned off.
   e. none of the above
3. Which of the following best describes a computer-based information system?
   a. a system in which a computer is used to turn data into information
   b. inputting data
   c. processing data
   d. performing complex mathematical calculations
   e. data is entered into the computer for processing
4. Which of the following is an example of processing activities?
   a. classifying
   b. summarizing
   c. performing calculations
   d. sorting
   e. all the above
5. Which of the following pieces of hardware is used the most in the input phase of a computer-based information system?
   a. printer
   b. diskette
   c. monitor
   d. keyboard
   e. main memory
6. Which of the following statements best describes the batch method of input and processing?
   a. Regardless of whether data is input immediately or collected in batches of source documents and input later, processing is done immediately for immediate updating of master files.
   b. Data is collected in batches of source documents and input later, when it is stored temporarily in a transaction file for later processing and updating of master files.
   c. Data is input immediately and used for immediate decision making.
   d. Source documents are never used.
   e. none of the above
7. Which of the following might occur when an organization uses on-line processing?
   a. Master files are updated immediately.
   b. Output can be produced without delay.

c. All related files are updated.
d. A customer receipt can be produced right away.
e. all the above

8. The principal advantage of the centralized approach to organizing a computer facility is:
a. cost effectiveness
b. processing activities are easier to coordinate and control
c. professional data processing personnel are housed near users and so can develop a good working relationship with those they support
d. processing standards can be enforced
e. all the above

9. "Computer-usable form" means:
a. a disk or diskette
b. hardware
c. electronically encoded data that a computer can process and store
d. source documents
e. on-line processing

10. Which of the following are used in the storage phase of a computer-based information system?
a. magnetic tape
b. keyboard
c. diskette
d. hard disk
e. monitor

SHORT ANSWER

1. Are companies always required to turn data into information? Explain.
2. During which phases of a computer-based information system are users typically involved?
3. Why do you think users are more removed from the computer hardware when using a mainframe computer versus a microcomputer?
4. What are the five components of a computer-based information system? The four phases of activity?
5. What are the advantages of the distributed approach to organizing a computer facility?
6. What are some of the different activities computers enable users to perform easily? Can these same tasks be performed without a computer? If so, why do you think computers are often used?
7. How does batch processing differ from on-line processing?
8. What is the function of a computer facility within an organization? Describe briefly three different methods of organizing a computer facility.
9. When might the delayed input and processing method be used?
10. What is the purpose of a computer-based transaction file?

PROJECTS

1. Determine how the computer facility at your school, work, or other business is organized. Who decided how to organize it? Does it meet the needs of the users? How does it use batch and/or on-line data entry and processing? Are there differing opinions relating to the effectiveness of the facility? Why? Why not? Conduct a minimum of two informal interviews.
2. Interview a systems analyst (a computer professional who specializes in setting up computer-based information systems) or a student majoring in systems analysis and design. Find out the many ways users' needs and ability to communicate affect the system they end up with. Report your findings to your class.
3. Based on what you have learned so far, how do you think the four phases of activity in a computer-based system would be represented in your chosen profession? For example, how would data be input? Output? Under what circumstances? What kind of processing activities would take place? What kind of professional computer-related jobs would be necessary to support the users? Would a centralized computer facility be used?

Episode 1

Sporting Life

Do You Really Need a Computer?

The Beginning

There is no point in having computer skills unless you are going to use them. Let us, therefore, help you to do that. The four episodes in this book will help you think both critically and creatively about factors involved in purchasing and using a computer system. These episodes are not "hands-on" tutorials; instead, they are meant to be thought provoking—to be the basis of discussion.

Suppose we encourage you to start your own business. "What? Not me," you say. "I wouldn't know the first thing about it." That's how we're going to help.

Obviously, you should go into a business that you are interested in; motivation is important. Because we have no idea what your motivation might be, let us suggest one. Taking advantage of the national interest in health and fitness and your location near a college campus, let us suggest you open a store—perhaps the first of many—that carries a full line of health, sports, aerobic, free weight, and dance equipment and clothing. You can make up your own name for it, but we will suggest one: Sporting Life.

After borrowing the money to buy the initial stock of goods, you spend the first year doing the day-to-day work of running the store yourself: identifying what goods are to be sold, keeping the shelves stocked, and doing the bookkeeping. By the end of one year, you're on a roll. Business is so good that you are able to expand the store and add to the stock. That means you also need to add to the staff. You've built quite an organization, one that could be represented by the chart shown in Figure E1.1. The most important members of your staff are you; Luis, who is in charge of inventory control; and Kim, who is the company's controller and is in charge of accounting.

Kim has a full-time staff of four to assist her, including two cashiers, one accountant, and a clerk to handle personnel and payroll activities. In addition, you employ six part-timers from the local high schools and the university.

At the end of its first year of business, Sporting Life is carrying 600 items in stock and occupies 4,500 square feet. Gross sales topped $1.6 million.

HOW TO TRACK INVENTORY

Since Sporting Life was founded, you've kept your inventory records in a ledger book, one page for each item carried in inventory. Inventory information includes a description of the item, its product number, the name of the supplier, an entry including date for each sale and delivery, and a running balance of the number of items on hand. When one page gets full, you take it out and replace it with a new blank page with the balance (final item count) from the last page carried over to the top of the new page. Figure E1.2 shows a page from the inventory record ledger. Luis's job is to keep an accurate count of all items on hand, to advise you when items need to be reordered, and to restock the shelves with items from the storeroom when necessary. The procedure for maintaining inventory records can be broken down into five separate steps, as shown in Figure E1.3. Let us explain each step:

1. The inventory ledger is reviewed for accuracy once each quarter (every three months) when a physical inventory is conducted, meaning that each

FIGURE E1.1 Your organization at Sporting Life. At the end of one year, your store's organizational chart looks like this. Connecting lines between the boxes indicate who supervises whom.

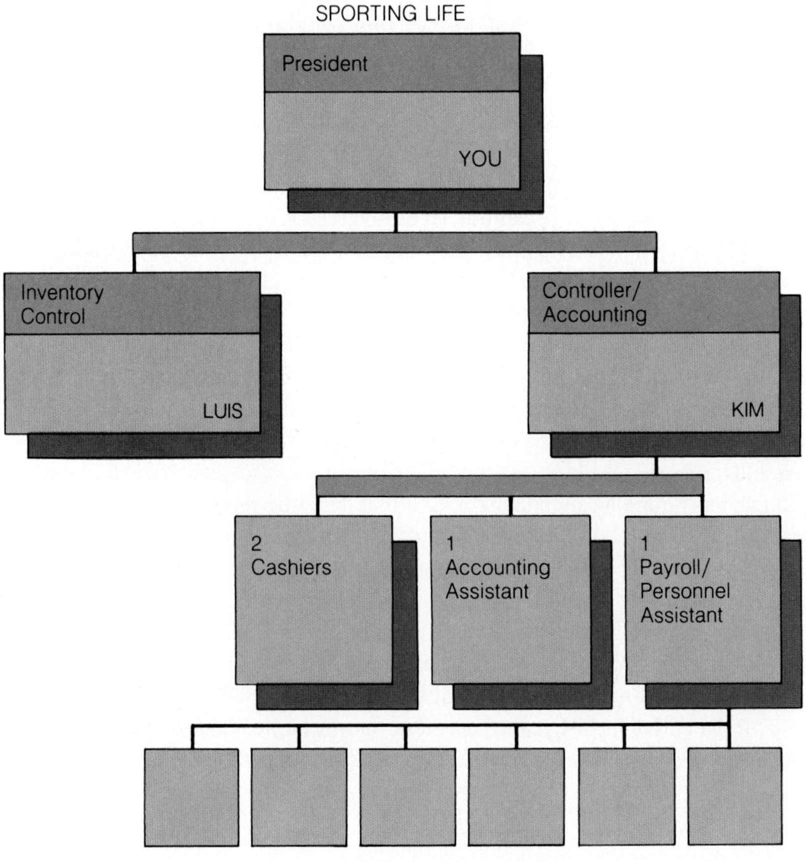

FIGURE E1.2 Track record. This shows a page from the traditional inventory record ledger that you and Luis use in your business (INV# = invoice number; P.O. = purchase order).

GENERAL JOURNAL

Inventory Record Ledger — Head Tennis Rackets   Product No. 298

Date	Description	Sold	Received	Balance on hand
1/4	Physical Inventory Count			114.
1/9	Sold INV #4014	1		113.
1/10	Sold INV #4027	2		111.
1/14	Received P.O. 2877		12	123.

FIGURE E1.3 Keeping in step. These are the five basic steps you would take to keep track of the inventory (or movement of stock) in your store.

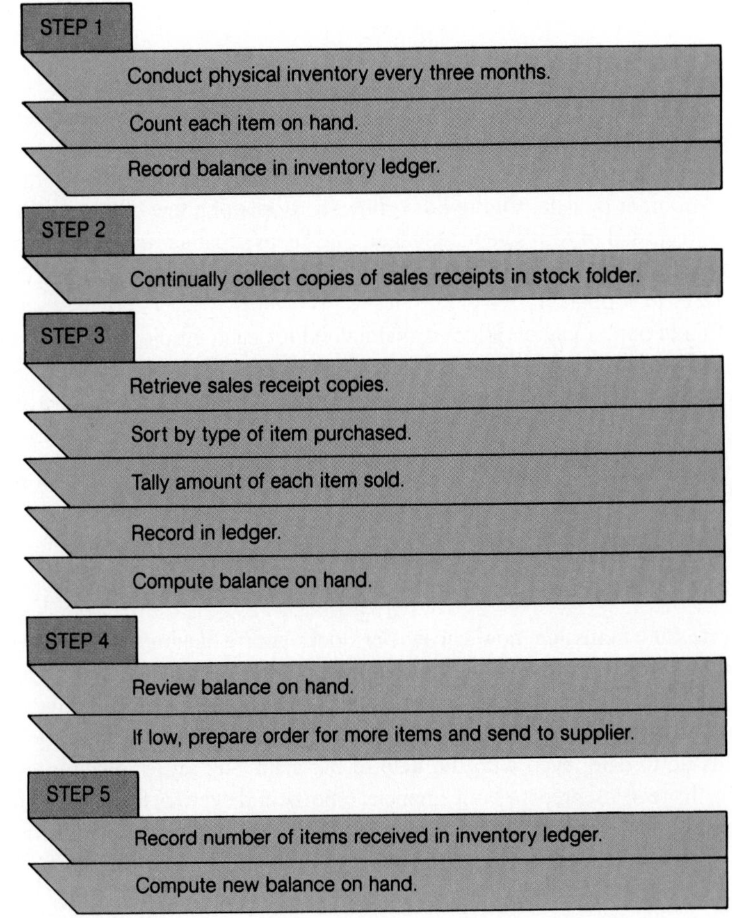
STEP 1
Conduct physical inventory every three months.
Count each item on hand.
Record balance in inventory ledger.
STEP 2
Continually collect copies of sales receipts in stock folder.
STEP 3
Retrieve sales receipt copies.
Sort by type of item purchased.
Tally amount of each item sold.
Record in ledger.
Compute balance on hand.
STEP 4
Review balance on hand.
If low, prepare order for more items and send to supplier.
STEP 5
Record number of items received in inventory ledger.
Compute new balance on hand.

item in inventory is counted by hand. The balance on hand (number counted) for each item is compared to the total in the inventory ledger. Discrepancies are researched and resolved, and any necessary adjustments are made in the ledger.

2. Copies of all sales receipts are continually collected in a stock folder.
3. Once every two weeks, you take all the sales receipts from the stock folder and do the following:
   a. Sort them into order by type of purchase—for example, tennis racquets, hockey pucks, dance leotards, and so on.
   b. Tally the amount of each item purchased (how many).
   c. Record on each item's ledger page the amount sold and the current balance of items in stock (the current balance is computed by subtracting the items sold from the balance on hand).
4. When the balance on hand for an item is relatively low, you need to restock that item (buy more). You prepare a purchase order and send it out to your supplier.
5. When the ordered goods are received, you take the bill of lading (the document identifying the contents of the shipment received) and record the information in the inventory ledger. The number of items just received is added to the prior balance to give the updated balance on hand.

How Kim Handles Finances

Kim's methods for handling her accounting record-keeping responsibilities at Sporting Life have remained basically the same since the business began. She has maintained financial records in a general ledger book where all activities are posted in order by date. Figure E1.4 shows a sample of a few of the accounting entries recorded in Kim's general ledger. She keeps separate records of accounts receivable (money owed to Sporting Life) and accounts payable (money Sporting Life owes to suppliers).

In addition, a payroll folder is maintained for each employee that contains such information as the employee's pay rate, number of tax deductions, amount of insurance deductions, payment history, and so forth. In addition, a single checking account for the company is maintained in a local bank. All payroll and tax forms are prepared manually. Employees are paid twice a month. This is quite a bit of paperwork!

Sizing Up the Situation: You Can't Go On Like This!

Because 600 items are now carried in stock, you're having trouble keeping inventory records current using the traditional manual ledger method. Far too many slow-selling items are being kept in stock, whereas some very popular items are almost always out of stock. Kim is having difficulties keeping her accounting records up to date, even with the help of her staff. She says she would like to review the records, prepare some financial reports, and even try to do some simple forecasting about Sporting Life's projected growth. But there simply isn't enough time. Besides, although she's excellent at basic math, Kim admits that she's not entirely comfortable with the idea of reports and financial projections because, even if she had the time to do them, she isn't sure what procedures she should follow.

WHAT DO YOU THINK?

You've considered buying a microcomputer to help track inventory and automate the accounting records. However, your employees are a bit anxious about computerizing the business. On the basis of what you know about the subject, discuss the following:

1. Because buying a computer is a big investment, Kim wants to do some research before you make any decisions about hardware and software. Which processing approach should she investigate for cashier and inventory purposes—that is, for collecting and processing data at the sales counter and the order receiving point? Batch? On-line? Both? Why?
2. List the activities in the five basic steps for tracking inventory that you envision the computer taking care of (see Figure E1.3). Focus on each user's needs and be as detailed as possible.
   a. What must be done? When? How fast? How often? Before or after what else?

FIGURE E1.4 General ledger. These are some of the accounting entries Kim or you might make in the general ledger, which is used to record all the financial activities of a business. Other records are kept too—such as accounts receivable and accounts payable—but first all transactions must be recorded in the general ledger. This manual activity is labor intensive and very time-consuming!

GENERAL LEDGER

Date	Description	Post Ref.	Debit	Credit
1/14 92	PAID INVOICE #AQ 459			
	CASH (CHK 1049)	101		
	OFFICE SUPPLIES	508	175.50	175.50
1/14 92	DAILY SALES TICKETS			
	CASH	101	1419.23	
	INCOME	401		
1/14 92	PAID INVOICE # 73914			1419.23
	CASH (CHK 1050)	101		
	RENT	5013	1575.00	1575.00
	RECEIVED INVOICE # 1183			
1/14 92	A/P	201		
	TELEPHONE	506	107.75	107.75

b. What forms do you want output by the computer system and who should get them?

c. Who is in charge of recording (inputting) what data?

And so on. This activity — the beginning of developing a computer-based information system — will help you later when you have to decide what software is available to meet users' needs and purchase the software and hardware for your organization. Without identifying users' needs first, you won't know what you want your software to do. (Of course, in a real situation, you or the person in charge of developing the computer-based information system would ask users to describe their own needs in detail.)

3. The staff is worried that the computer will have a negative effect on the family atmosphere of the company. Do you agree? What kinds of business activities do you think the staff would have time for if they were freed from many of the repetitious, time-consuming tasks a computer could take over?

Part II

Hardware

We can certainly make any computer user one promise: The hardware — the equipment — will change dramatically in the next decade. The processing power contained in a refrigerator-sized minicomputer is already available on a desktop machine (can we still call it a "microcomputer"?), and the power of upcoming supercomputers will be truly awesome, perhaps a thousand times more powerful than the machines used by research scientists today. Data will be input not only through the keyboard, that time-honored device, but also through more exotic equipment — for example, devices that understand human voices and electronic pencils with which users can write directly on the computer screen. Output will be on printers capable of extraordinary speeds and clarity. However, the new hardware will still support the four basic phases of the computer-based information system: input, storage, processing, and output.

3

CHAPTER 3

INPUT HARDWARE

Do you know how to type?

Some people say that it may not be necessary to learn. Methods already exist of inputting data and software instructions to a computer system that do not require a keyboard. We believe, however, that if you *do* know how to type, you are much better off. No matter what organization you join after reading this book, it will most likely want to hire people who can handle a computer keyboard—not just clerks and typists, but managers and executives as well.

PREVIEW

When you have completed this chapter, you will be able to:

■

Identify the most widely used types of input hardware and methods.

■

List the three different types of terminals used for data input and describe some of the ways they are used.

■

Describe the importance of input controls in today's computerized society.

As a computer user, you will not be able to avoid entering data of some sort. The more you understand about input hardware and methods, the better you will be able to do your job. If you find a typewriter or computer keyboard somewhat cumbersome, be glad you are entering the field now rather than back in the '60s. Then, the principal means of inputting data to a computer system was on punched cards — the so-called IBM cards that a generation of college students were admonished never to "fold, spindle, or mutilate." Although these cards are still in use in some quarters, their numbers are very few compared to the 150,000 tons of them that were used every year in the 1960s — enough, put end to end, to stretch 8 million miles.

Computers by their very nature can deal only with instructions and data that have been converted into a computer-usable form — that is, a form the central processing unit can directly access from main memory or retrieve from a storage device and put into main memory. For more than 20 years the physical activity required to convert an organization's data into computer-usable form was the largest single personnel expense in operating a computer facility. Fortunately, great technological progress has been made in terms of input hardware devices and input methods. Because sometime during your career you may well have to decide which devices and methods are best for you or your organization — including handicapped employees — in this chapter we will teach you the basic information you'll need to make such a decision.

CATEGORIZING INPUT HARDWARE

As we discussed in Chapters 1 and 2, the term ***input*** is generally used to describe the process of capturing or collecting raw data — at the beginning of a computer-based information system — in a form that is usable by the computer for processing. The objective of the input phase of a computer-based information system is to capture raw data and convert it into computer-usable form as quickly and efficiently as possible. Sometimes the data is processed right away (on-line processing), sometimes hours or days later, or even longer (batch processing). As a result, data is often stored in a computer-usable form, where it can be quickly retrieved at the time of processing with little or no human intervention (storage will be discussed in detail in Chapter 4).

When you start work, chances are that your company will have already purchased input hardware. However, if it has not yet been acquired, you may find yourself in the position of helping to decide which input hardware is best suited to your needs. In this section we describe the different types of input devices that you will typically find in a business environment.

One of the easiest ways to categorize input hardware is according to whether or not it uses a keyboard to initially capture data (see Figure 3.1). Many commonly used input devices do rely on a keyboard, and these devices generally fall into two groups: (1) terminals connected to general-purpose computer systems (microcomputers fall into this group also) and (2) dedicated data entry systems, which are specialized, single-purpose systems used for nothing else but entering data.

The nonkeyboard input devices, called ***direct-entry devices***, include optical scanners, mice, light pens, touch screens, and voice recognition equipment, among others (these devices will be discussed later in the chapter).

KEYBOARD ENTRY

A computer **keyboard** (Figure 3.2) is a sophisticated electromechanical component designed to create special standardized electronic codes when a key is pressed. The codes are transmitted along the cable that connects the keyboard to the computer system unit or terminal, where the incoming code is analyzed and converted into the appropriate computer-usable code.

Keyboards come in a variety of sizes and shapes, but most keyboards used with computer systems have a certain number of features in common: (1) standard typewriter keys, (2) function keys, (3) special-purpose keys, (4) cursor-movement keys, and (5) numeric keys.

In general, the typewriter-like keys are used to type in text and other data.

The **function keys,** labeled F1, F2, F3, and so on are used to issue commands. (Function keys are also called *programmable keys*.) The software program you are using determines how the function keys are used. The user's manual that comes with the software tells you how to use the function keys.

Computer keyboards also have some special-purpose keys such as Ctrl (Control), Del (Delete), Ins (Insert), and Alt (Alternate). **Cursor-movement keys** are used to move the **cursor** around the screen. (The cursor is the symbol on the video screen that shows where the next character or space that is input will be positioned; see Figure 3.3.) Cursor-movement keys have directional arrows on them. **Numeric keys** are used to enter numbers for mathematical manipulation.

FIGURE 3.1

To key or not to key. . . . Input hardware can be categorized according to whether or not it uses a keyboard.

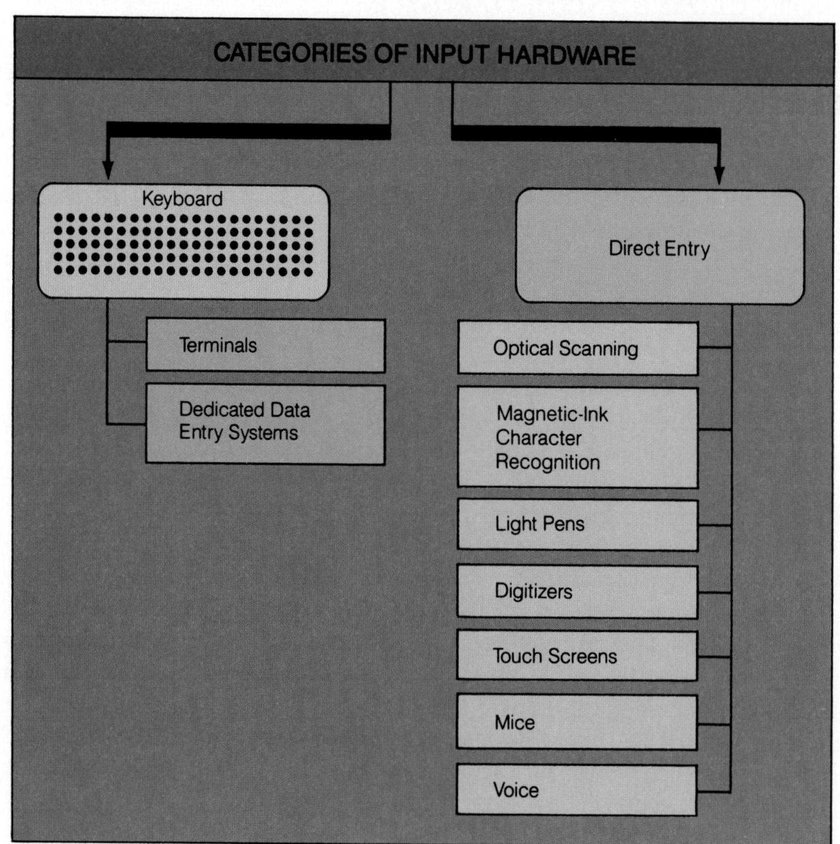

If you have used a typewriter keyboard, you should find it easy to learn to work with a computer keyboard. However, since some of the keys are different, you may want to experiment with some of the keyboard familiarization software programs on the market today (Figure 3.4). These packages provide computer users with the

(a)

(b)

FIGURE 3.2

The keyboard. (a) The keyboard of the IBM PS/2 Model 80. The function keys go across the top center of the keyboard, and the cursor-movement keys (with arrows) are on the right; (b) the Omnikey keyboard; the function keys are on the left.

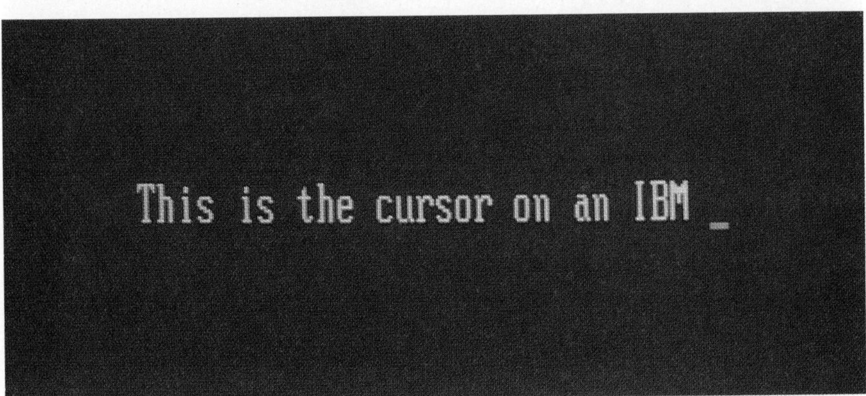

FIGURE 3.3

Cursory view. The cursor shows the position on the screen where the next character will be positioned.

opportunity to become familiar with the layout of the keyboard, which may differ according to what kind of computer you are using, and to develop typing proficiency. Also, to help you learn to use a computer keyboard quickly, *we have provided an introduction to the keyboard at the back of the book, in the beginning of Part* V.

TERMINALS

The **terminal**—typically consisting of a video display screen, a keyboard, and a communications link to hook the terminal up with the main computer system—is used for inputting data to and retrieving data from a remotely located main system. Most terminals are desktop size and are not meant to be carried around; however, some are small enough to be easily portable. Terminals can be "dumb," "smart," or "intelligent" and are used mainly by those who do their work on mini- or mainframe computers (or supercomputers).

- The low-cost **dumb terminal** is entirely dependent for all its capabilities on the computer system to which it is connected. It cannot do any processing of its own or store any data and is used only for data input (by keyboard) and retrieval (data is displayed on the monitor). An airline reservation clerk might use a dumb terminal at a customer check-in station to check flight information stored in the mainframe computer system.
- A **smart terminal** can input and retrieve data and also do some limited processing on its own—such as editing or verifying data. However, it cannot be used for programming (that is, to create new instructions). A bank loan officer might use a smart terminal on his or her desk to input data, do some calculations, and retrieve some data before approving a loan. The data is stored in the mainframe system.
- An **intelligent terminal,** also called a *programmable terminal,* can input and receive data as well as do its own processing, which means that it can be used as a *stand-alone* device. In addition to the keyboard, monitor, and

FIGURE 3.4

Type right. This illustration shows some of the software packages available to teach you how to type on a computer keyboard.

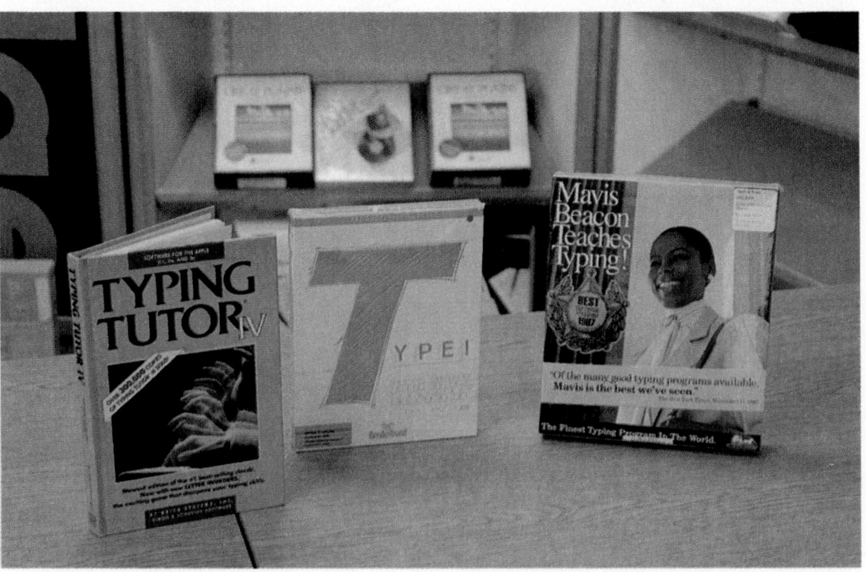

communications link, an intelligent terminal also includes a processing unit, storage capabilities, and software. This type of terminal is actually a microcomputer. Indeed, microcomputers — although much more expensive than dumb or smart terminals — are being used more and more in business as intelligent terminals because they reduce the processing and storage load on the main computer system.

A variety of computer terminals are used to enter data, including the following popular types:

- Point-of-sale (POS) terminals.
- Financial transaction terminals.
- Executive workstations.
- Portable terminals.
- Microcomputers used as terminals.

A **point-of-sale (POS) terminal** (Figure 3.5) is a smart terminal used very much like a cash register, but it also captures sales and inventory data at the time and

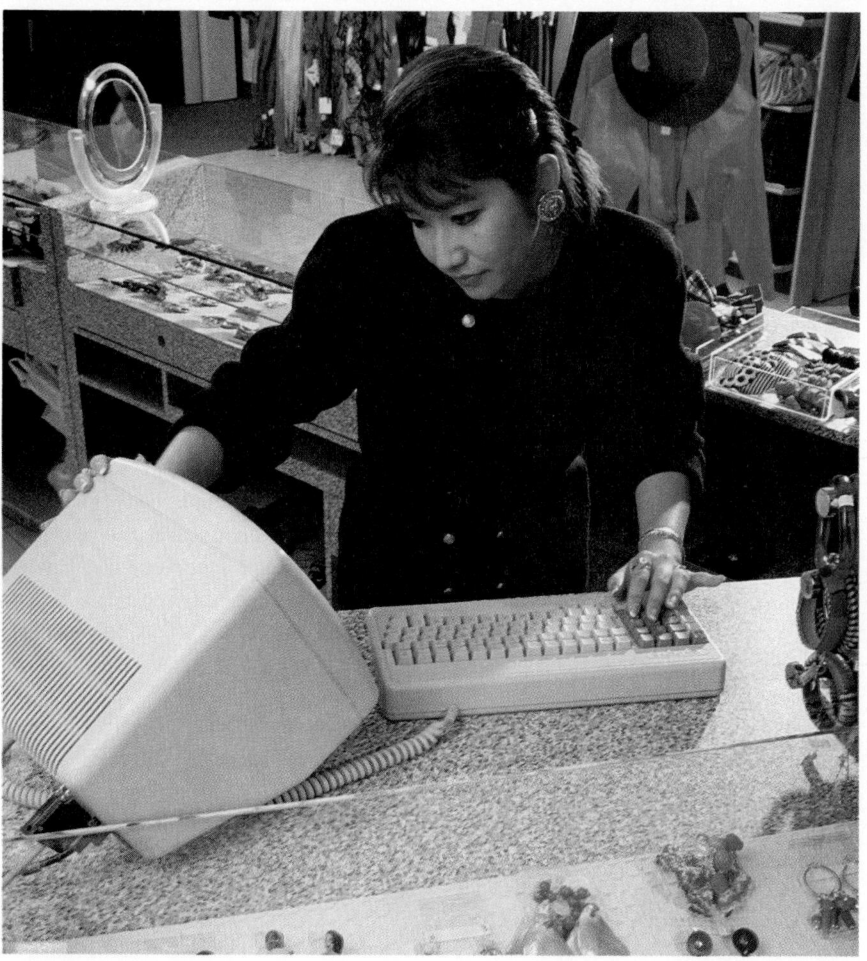

FIGURE 3.5

A smart sale. This point-of-sale terminal is being used to enter sales data at a women's clothing store. The system will also update inventory files and print out the customer's receipt.

place of a customer transaction (point of sale) and sends it to the central computer for processing. Many supermarkets have POS terminals that are connected directly to a central computer so that the sales dollars and product-sold data can be immediately recorded. This type of terminal usually displays the price, the product number, and possibly the product description. In addition, this type of terminal is equipped with a cash-register-type keyboard, a cash drawer, and a printer to print the customer's receipt.

A **financial transaction terminal** is used to store data and to retrieve data from a central computer to perform banking-related activities. The two types of financial transaction terminals we see most often are the smart automated teller machines (ATMs) located outside of many banks (Figure 3.6) and the terminals used by bank tellers to retrieve a customer's account balance when he or she withdraws or deposits money in person. The teller terminals (Figure 3.7) are usually quite small and specialized. The keyboard has special keys that allow the teller to identify which type of account is being used (savings or checking) and to enter the account number.

Executive desktop workstations, or **integrated workstations,** are intelligent terminals used by management professionals to assist them in their daily activities (Figure 3.8). These workstations can be operated by themselves as stand-alone PCs (personal computers) or in connection with a main computer. They often have voice and data communications capabilities, meaning that the terminal includes a phone for regular communication and components for special computerized communication. However, the design and features of this type of terminal tend to vary widely. Most executive terminals have built-in software (often referred to as **desktop management software**) to handle desk calendar, phone book, and desk calculator functions. Executive workstations are not used for high-volume data input. In most cases, the user enters a request for data or information to be retrieved and displayed. These terminals usually include a full-sized keyboard and a number of special function keys. Most also have some graphics capabilities (monochrome or color).

A **portable terminal** is a terminal that users can carry with them to hook up to a central computer from remote locations, often via telecommunications facilities. (The term *telecommunications* refers to communication at a distance by telephone, television, or some other means; we'll cover this topic in Chapter 9.) Most portable terminals are connected to the central computer by means of telephone lines. These terminals have components called **modems** built into them that convert the data being transmitted into a form suitable for sending and receiving over the phone. If the terminal is dumb, it can do little more than send data to and receive data from the main computer. (Some of the smallest portable terminals can only send data.) If the portable terminal is smart, some data may be entered and edited before the connection to the main computer is made.

Portable terminals are available in a wide variety of sizes and shapes. Most portable terminals include a full typewriter-like keyboard. Some specialized portable terminals are so small they are called **handheld terminals** (Figure 3.9). The handheld terminal weighs up to about 3 pounds and can be used for a variety of purposes, including checking the stock market and identifying cars with many unpaid parking tickets.

Many older-model portable terminals use only printers to display the data that has been input and the computer's response because standard video display screens are a bit cumbersome and easily damaged. However, newer portable terminals use

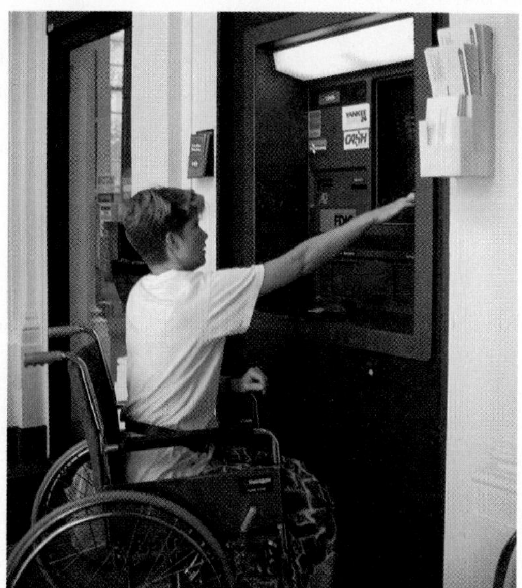

FIGURE 3.6

Midnight money. The automatic teller machine—a smart terminal—has become more than just a convenience for those who can't get to the bank during regular banking hours and for those who need cash for late-night snack attacks or unexpected emergencies. (Illustration adapted from Al Granberg, September 9, 1990.)

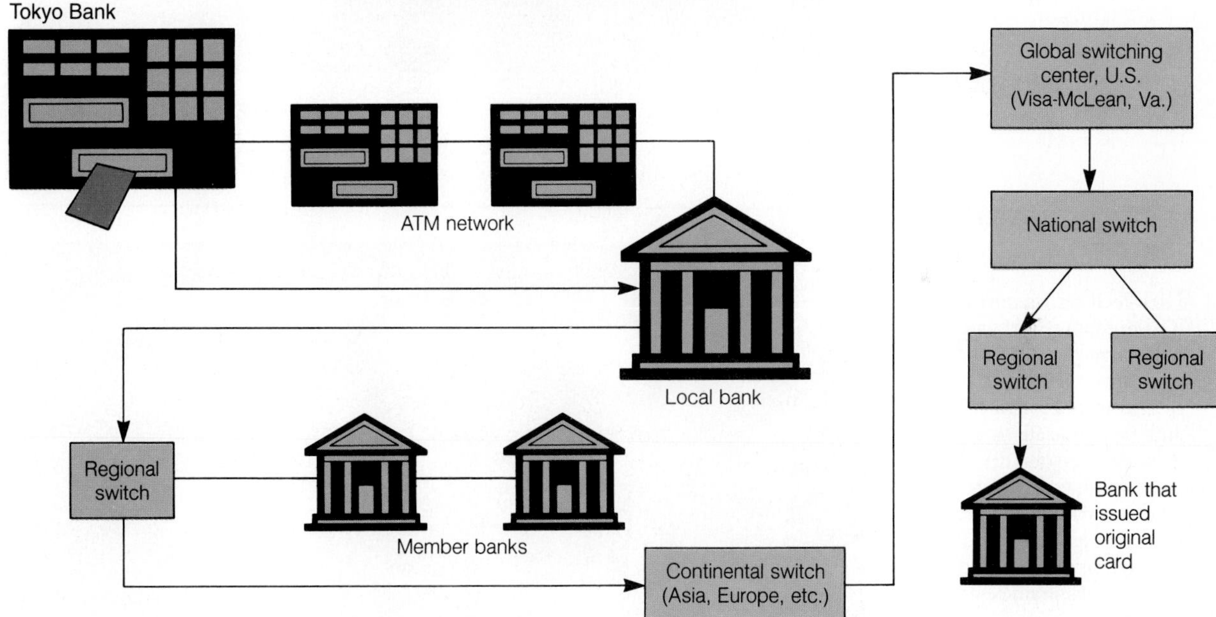

When a U.S. resident uses an ATM card in Tokyo: when a bank card is inserted at a Tokyo bank, the local bank's computer determines if that card was issued by that bank. If not, the bank sends the request to the regional switch where a computer sends it to the Cirrus or Plus network. The request then goes to the network's continental switch—in Europe, for example—then to a global switching center in the United States, next to a national switch, and finally to a regional switch. From there, the request goes to the bank that issued the card. Transaction time: 10 seconds.

FIGURE 3.7

Taking it into account. The teller terminals used in banks enable tellers to quickly identify your account and its balance.

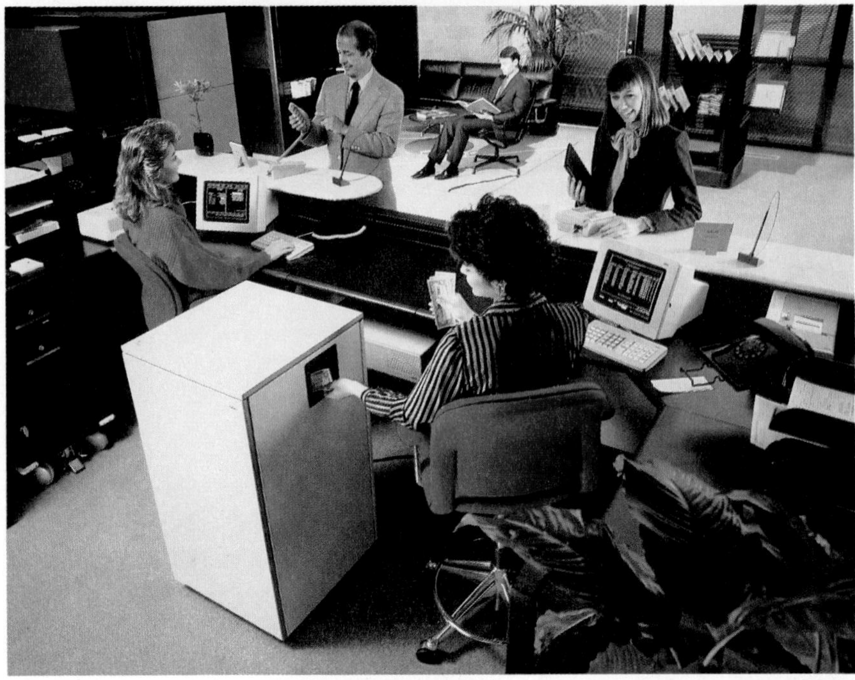

FIGURE 3.8

High-tech management tool. The executive workstation helps managers take care of daily business through the use of desk management software and communications and data processing capabilities. The workstation can operate on its own as a stand-alone personal computer as well as an intelligent terminal connected to a mini- or mainframe computer system.

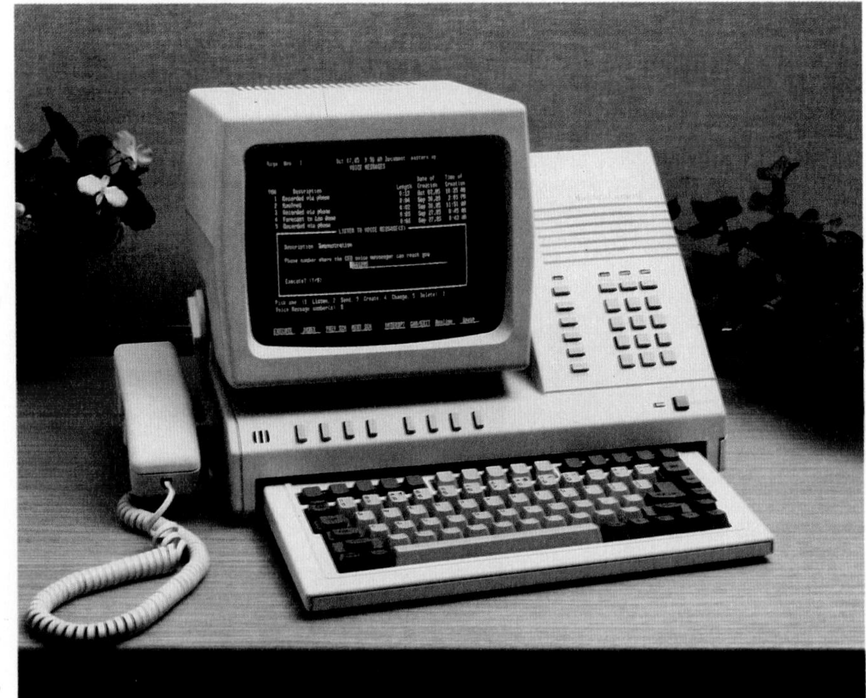

the latest technologies to provide smaller, flat screen displays that show as much text as a desktop terminal. Like executive workstations, portable terminals are rarely used for high-volume data input.

We have mentioned that **microcomputer terminals** can be used on their own for processing, as well as smart or intelligent workstations; the type of software used determines what kind of terminal the microcomputer "becomes." This flexibility is very attractive to many businesses. Data entry programs can be created for the microcomputer so that data can be input and stored locally—where the user is. When data entry is complete, the microcomputer can then be used as a terminal, and the data can be **uploaded**—transmitted from the microcomputer to the main computer—very quickly. For example, a small editorial production office in San Francisco with a microcomputer equipped with a modem and certain software can arrange with the local telephone company to have telex capabilities activated and a telex number assigned. Then the office can input data—page proof corrections, for example—that is telexed to a typesetter in Singapore, who transfers the data into the computerized typesetting system after reading it on a microcomputer screen. In turn, the typesetter can telex data back to the editorial office in San Francisco.

Some microcomputers on the market today have been designed *specifically* to be used both as stand-alone processors (that is, they operate on their own without being hooked up to a main computer) *and* as terminals. For microcomputers that were not specifically designed to fulfill both functions, manufacturers have produced special hardware that can be purchased and placed into the microcomputer to enable it to communicate with a larger computer.

DEDICATED DATA ENTRY SYSTEMS

When an organization has high-volume data input requirements, such as the Internal Revenue Service at tax time, it often uses a secondary computer—usually a minicomputer—that temporarily stores previously keyed-in data for later process-

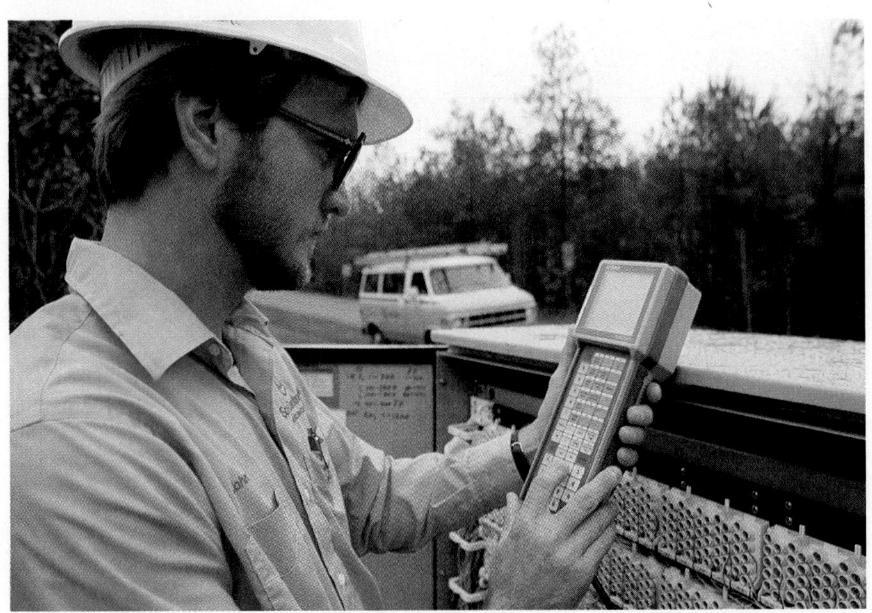

FIGURE 3.9

Handy input hardware. A telephone line worker uses a handheld terminal to call up his next repair assignment and update company records on the job just completed.

ing by the mainframe computer. This processing usually takes place at night, when the main computer's time is not taken by user requests. The group of terminals connected to the minicomputer that handle data entry and storage are called a **dedicated data entry system**—they do nothing but input and store data, using **key-to-tape, key-to-disk,** or **key-to-diskette** input systems (Figures 3.10 and 3.11). In the first case, a keyboard connected to a special recorder is used to record data onto magnetic tape reels or cassettes. The tape can then be transported to another area where a tape drive is located. The tape drive reads the data into the main computer. This procedure is similar to key-to-disk and key-to-diskette systems, except that in the latter case, data is recorded on magnetic disks, often available as portable disk packs, or on individual diskettes. (Tape, disks, and diskettes are discussed in more detail in the next chapter.) Punched-card data entry systems are also considered to be dedicated systems.

DIRECT ENTRY

Direct entry involves inputting data to a computer without the use of a keyboard. As mentioned earlier in the chapter, paper, as shown in Figure 3.12, is commonly used to record data that is to be directly input to a computer system. Indeed, for many years, the most widely used media to record input data were 80-column and 96-column punched cards and punched paper tape. Figure 3.13 shows an example of an 80-column card as well as the hardware components of a typical **keypunch machine.** The operator of a keypunch machine transcribes data from a source document by punching holes representing numbers, alphabet letters, or special characters in the cards via a keyboard according to a special code. (The 96-column card, which was developed to store 20 percent more data in a small amount of space, never found widespread use.)

FIGURE 3.10

Dedicated data entry. These warehouse employees are using a dedicated data entry system to input product delivery data into the inventory database.

We must emphasize that punched cards are rarely used today. However, you may occasionally encounter them in large companies such as public utilities, where they may still be used for billing. When the customer returns the card with payment, the keypunch operator uses the keypunch machine to record new data on the card. Then he or she runs the card through a card reader to input the data into the computer (usually a mainframe).

Paper-based input media are also used with scanners, connected to computers, that can "read" typed or handwritten data. The banking industry has long relied on paper-based input media: Our checks are printed using a special magnetic ink that can be scanned optically for magnetic retrieval of data for input to computers for processing. Optically oriented input devices are available for use with microcomputer systems, too, which puts this type of input within the reach of small businesses. For example, even a small, independently owned grocery store may have a microcomputer at the checkout and a handheld optical scanning device to read the

FIGURE 3.11 Such dedication! Key-to-tape, key-to-disk, and key-to-diskette systems are dedicated data entry systems that use special input hardware to record data on tape or disk. The tape/disk can then be transported to a drive that reads the data into the main computer. Punched card systems are also dedicated to data entry.

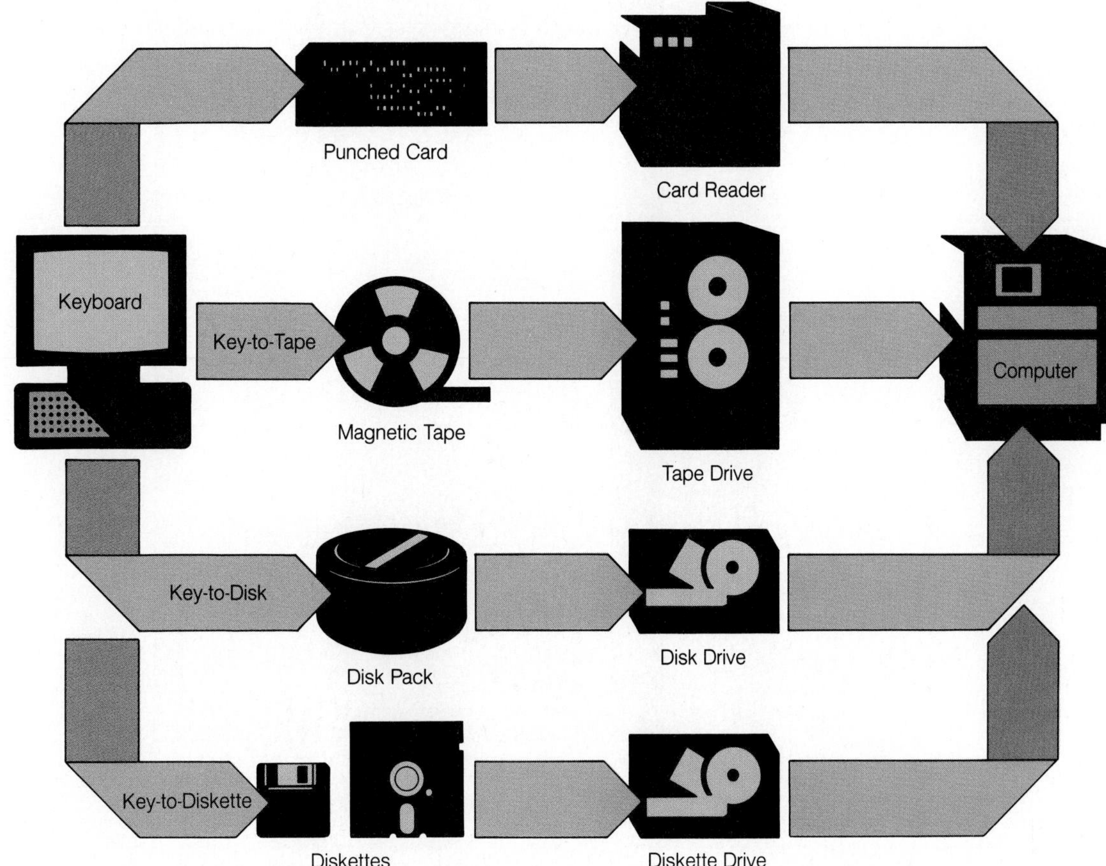

FIGURE 3.12

Paper-based direct entry. Punched cards and tape are rarely used now, but the use of scannable paper documents to input data directly is increasing.

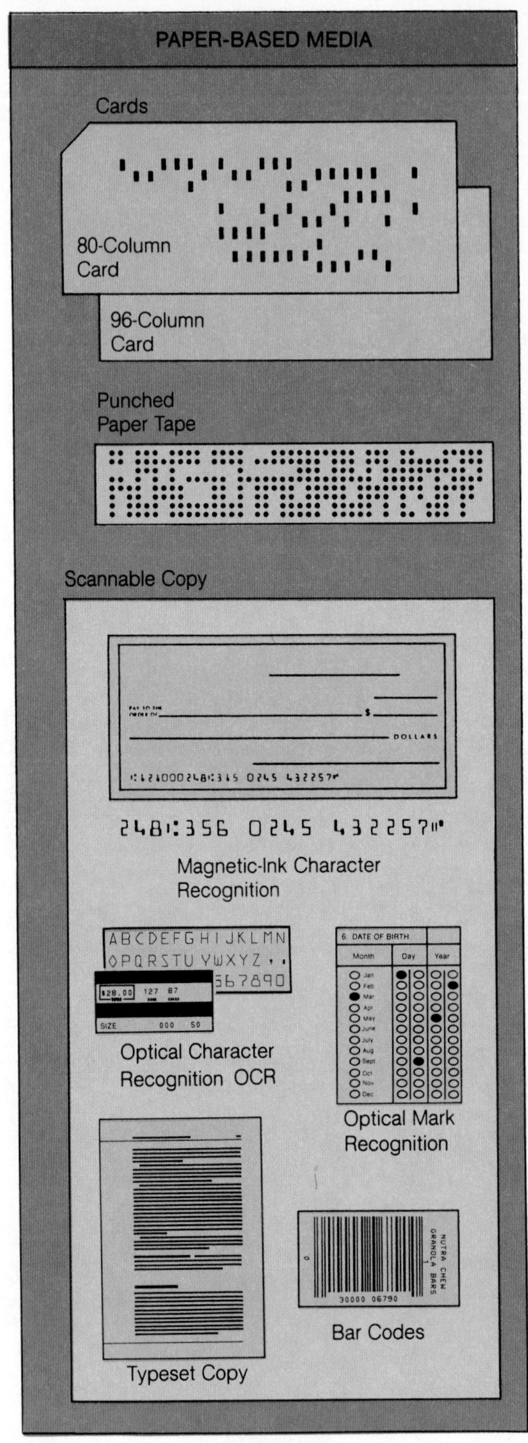

product numbers on the labels of purchased items. (The product numbers access stored computer files with the current prices, which then show on the register.)

Indeed, some of the most exciting kinds of input systems are those that use direct-entry input devices, and not all of them use paper. For example, did you know that you can touch a video display screen or use a "magic" wand to input data? Talk

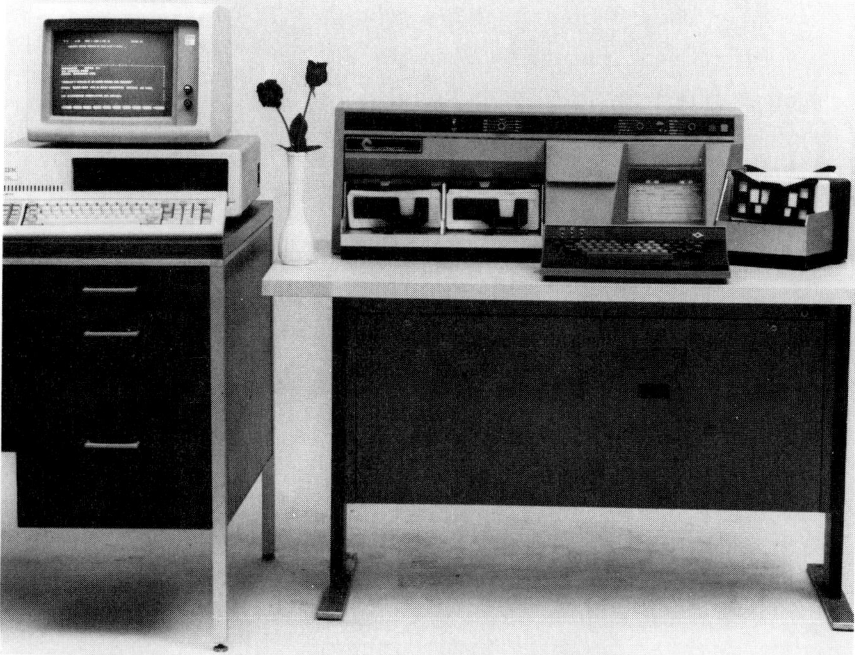

(a)

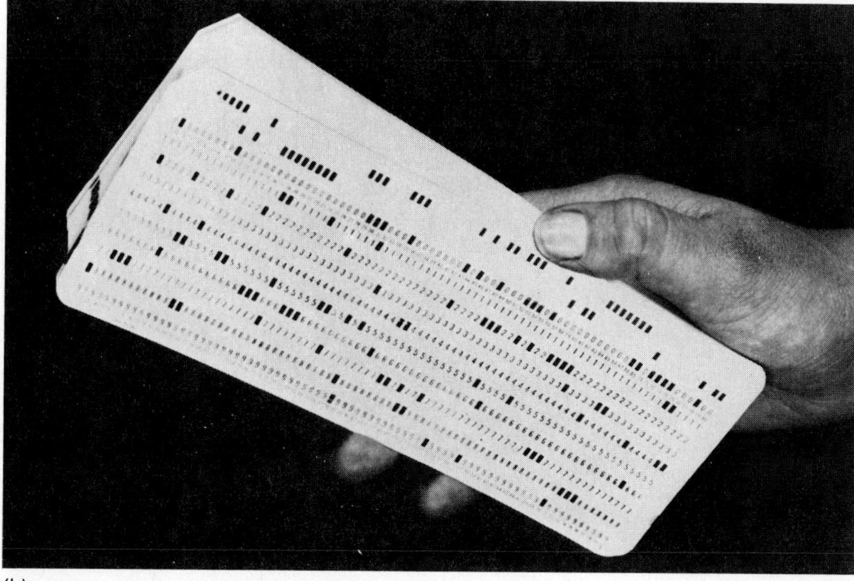

(b)

FIGURE 3.13

Getting punchy. The key-punch machine, card reader, and the 80-column card.

to the computer? Even use the movement of your eyes to tell the computer what to do? Nonkeyboard data entry systems minimize the amount of human activity required to get data into a computer-usable form. The ones receiving the most attention today are:

- Card readers.
- Scanning devices.
    - Bar code readers.
    - Optical mark readers.
    - Typewritten- and typeset-character scanners.
    - Handwritten-character readers.
    - Magnetic-ink character recognition.
- Smart cards.
- Voice input devices.
- "Pointing" devices.
    - Light pen.
    - Mouse.
    - Trackball.
    - Touch screen.
    - Digitizer.
- Touch-Tone™ device.

CARD READERS

The use of punched cards has dropped dramatically because of the speed and cost-effectiveness of the newer input devices. However, some organizations — such as the military, some government offices, utility companies, and some schools —

FIGURE 3.14

Making the grade. The Cardamation data card reader can be used with a microcomputer to read punched cards, display the input on the screen, and store the data on diskette or hard disk for later processing. Such card readers are often used in schools for grading.

still use cards. A **card reader** is used to read the holes in punched cards and transfer the appropriate electrical signals as input to the computer. Punched card readers are also available for use with microcomputers. These devices are used mostly by schools and small businesses whose data input is small. Figure 3.14 shows the Cardamation data card reader, which is often used in schools for scoring tests and tabulating daily attendance.

SCANNING DEVICES

So much business-related data and information are recorded on paper that most of us would have difficulty imagining the amount. Before many of our modern input devices and systems were available, a lot of research was devoted to eliminating the expensive and time-consuming step of inputting all this hardcopy data manually by keying it in. As a result, in the 1950s a number of **optical character recognition (OCR)** input devices were developed to read hardcopy data from source documents into computer-usable form. Today these devices use light-sensitive equipment to scan bar codes, optical marks, typewritten characters, handwriting, and magnetic ink.

BAR CODE READERS By now you have probably become familiar with bar codes similar to the one shown in Figure 3.15. They're on groceries, cosmetics, paperback novels, and so on. **Bar codes** are recorded on the products by the manufacturers and usually carry the inventory stock number (also called the *product number*). The coding scheme—called the *Universal Product Code*—for recording the data is based on the width of the bars and the space between them. Two types of input scanning devices are used to read the bar codes. The first is a handheld scanner (Figure 3.16a and b) that the clerk passes over the tag with the bar code. The wand has a scanning device that analyzes the light and dark bars for width and spacing, translating this data into electrical signals for the computer. The second is found most often in supermarkets and is built into the countertop (Figure 3.16c) along

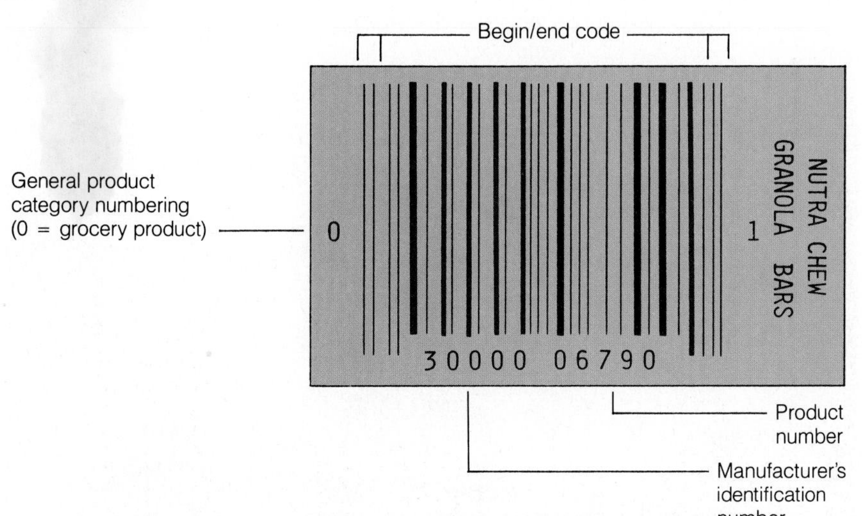

FIGURE 3.15

Bar gains. Bar codes such as this Universal Product Code used on many supermarket items contain product data that is read by a scanner and sent to the cash register display and to the main computer.

with a computerized cash register. The function of the countertop scanning device is similar to the handheld wand; however, in many cases the light source of the former may be a laser.

Bar code readers have proven to be very valuable as data entry devices for three reasons:

FIGURE 3.16

Bar hopping. Bar code reading devices can be handheld, such as this wand reader and the portable scanner used by Federal Express carriers (a) and (b), or built into the counter at the checkout stand, like this supermarket scanning equipment (c). The clerk moves the product's bar code past the bar code reader, which reads it with a light beam and sensor. The price and description of the item, which are stored in the computer system, are sent to the POS terminal, where they are printed out as a receipt for the customer. The information from the POS terminal is also used by the store, on the one hand, for accounting purposes and, on the other hand, for restocking store inventory and for analyzing which products sell better than others.

(a)

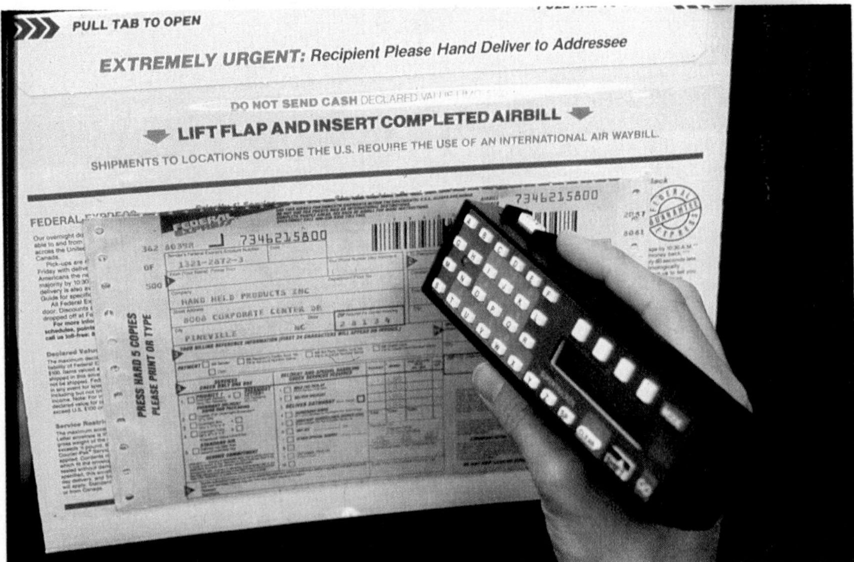

(b) Micro-Wand is a registered trademark of Hand Held Products, Inc.

- The price and the product inventory numbers do not need to be keyed in, eliminating the potential for many keying errors. (Quantities of items, however, *are* keyed in.)
- The sales data and inventory status stored on file are kept current.
- A complete history can be built and stored for each bar coded item—for delivery services such as Federal Express and UPS, this means that parcels can be traced.

However, when you're checking out at the supermarket, keep your eye on the computerized price and item description display on the register. As we mentioned earlier, the product numbers are recorded in the bar codes on the items you buy, but the corresponding price files must be updated at the supermarket. If someone forgets to enter today's special 50 percent reduction in cat food prices in the store's computer, you'll end up paying the old price.

OPTICAL MARK READERS When you took the College Board SAT (Scholastic Aptitude Test) or similar examination and marked the answers on a preprinted sheet using a no. 2 lead pencil, you worked with the simplest form of optical data recording—**optical marks** (Figure 3.17). Data recorded in this form is converted into computer-usable form by an **optical mark reader (OMR).** The OMR device has a high-intensity light inside that is directed in the form of a beam at the sheets of paper being fed through it. The beam scans the marked forms and detects the number and location of the pencil marks. The data is then converted into electrical signals for the computer. OMRs come in a variety of sizes and shapes that depend on the size of the forms to be read and the required loading and processing capacity of the reader.

The optical mark technology is used widely for scoring examinations and inputting raw data recorded on questionnaires. For OMRs to read the data accu-

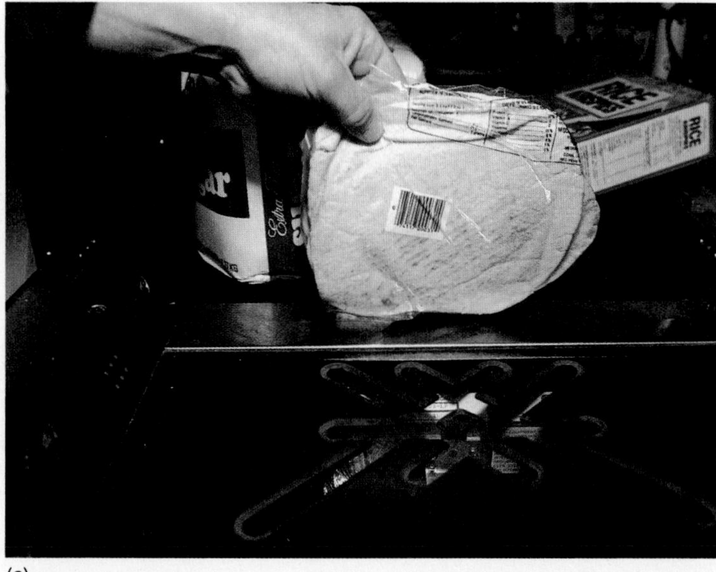

(c)

FIGURE 3.16

(continued)

rately, the forms must be carefully designed and manufactured, and the marks must be carefully recorded—which is why the College Board is so insistent on your using a no. 2 pencil. Figure 3.18 shows an OMR device that will work with both Apple and IBM-compatible personal computers.

TYPEWRITTEN- AND TYPESET-CHARACTER SCANNERS For many years, typewritten data on source documents had to be rekeyed to be entered in a computer—in some cases, it still is today. As we mentioned before, optical character recognition technology was developed to avoid this massive duplication of effort. To help speed up and reduce the cost of converting typewritten and typeset data to computer-usable form, certain manufacturers developed special type fonts (typeface styles) to be read by a **scanning device.** To assist this process the American National Standards

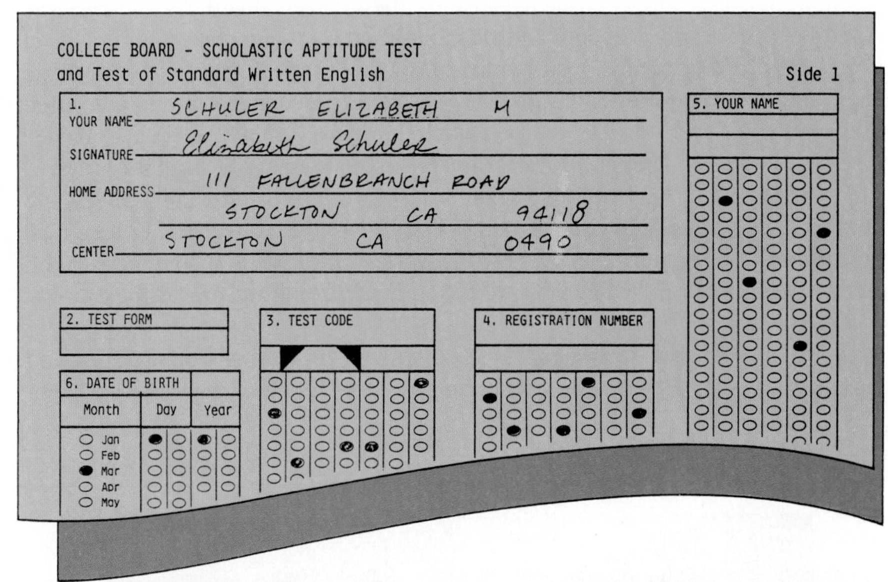

COLLEGE BOARD - SCHOLASTIC APTITUDE TEST
and Test of Standard Written English
Side 1

1. YOUR NAME SCHULER ELIZABETH M
SIGNATURE Elizabeth Schuler
HOME ADDRESS 111 FALLENBRANCH ROAD
STOCKTON CA 94118
CENTER STOCKTON CA 0490

2. TEST FORM

3. TEST CODE

4. REGISTRATION NUMBER

5. YOUR NAME

6. DATE OF BIRTH

Month	Day	Year
Jan		
Feb		
Mar		
Apr		
May		

FIGURE 3.17

On your mark . . . The College Board examination answer form requires you to mark answers—according to numbers in the test booklet—using a no. 2 lead pencil. The marks are later scanned and tabulated by an optical mark reader.

FIGURE 3.18

SCANTRON Model 1100 Optical Mark Reader. This optical mark reader can be used with Apple and IBM-compatible computers.

Computers and Careers

The Arts, Sports, and Entertainment

Not planning to make a career in computers and information processing? Think computers will have only the barest presence in your professional life? We're guessing otherwise. In every line of work, computers have become nearly as commonplace as pencil and paper, even in those fields that seem to be mostly rooted in intuition, emotions, and creativity. In this box, the first of several on computers and different career fields, we show how these instruments of logic are used in the arts, sports, and entertainment.

The casting agent is looking for an actor who can speak Spanish, owns cowboy gear, and can shoot a rifle while riding a horse. She turns to her computer and feeds her request into RoleCall, a computerized casting service for theater, film, and television. Almost instantly the computer screen produces the names of 40 actors who can fill the bill.

In rehearsals, the director uses a Macintosh computer and a program called TheaterGame to go through the process of staging ("blocking") a scene. The program offers a choice of sets, props (such as furniture, trees), and costumed characters that can be moved around on the screen by using a mouse to direct the cursor. If a chair gets in the way of the action, the director can use the mouse to push it aside. Characters can be manipulated so that they turn their heads to talk, sit, fall down, and so on. Afterward, the director can play back the staging to see how it looks.

In the television studio, there are no longer headphone-wearing operators rolling three or four cameras back and forth. Rather, there are now robotic cameras linked to a central computer, called the "cue computer" because it prompts the cameras. The cue computer is operated by an engineer, who keeps his or her eyes on several wall monitors to keep each camera in focus. Standard shots, such as an overhead view of the set, can be programmed in advance and called up on the computer as needed.

Examples of how computers can be used in nonscientific ways are found in other artistic fields. Dancers may use computers to choreograph their movements. Musicians may use them to write out musical scores while they compose them on a piano keyboard. Computer artists don't use bristles and pigments but rather metal-tipped styluses, with which they "paint" on slatelike digitizing pads, which in turn transmit their movements and colors to a computer screen. Art dealers may use the Omnivex electronic art catalogue, which stores images of artwork on videodisk and allows dealers to view them by calling them up on high-resolution computer screens.

Viewers of televised sports have become accustomed to seeing all kinds of statistics and percentages flashed on the screen. Now, however, coaches and athletes can receive this kind of computerized analysis even for sports such as tennis, using a program called Computennis. Cyclists can use computer-generated three-dimensional maps, called Terragraphics guidebooks, which give the rider a preview of a planned route. Even people who like to fish can improve their odds with the use of a computerized sonar device, called Specie Select, which, using software based on information from over 1,000 professional anglers and guides, can home in on the fish-locating information pertinent to a particular species.

Computers are an important part of all sectors of the entertainment industry. Just one example: Computerbased animation has come of age to produce spectacular new images, from glowing, flying, spinning station call letters to cartoon characters. ■

Institute (ANSI) adopted a standard type font called *OCR-A* for use with special optical character reading devices (Figure 3.19). OCR-A has become the most commonly used typeface for OCR devices. However, the more expensive OCR devices can read a variety of fonts.

In the early 1980s, small-capacity scanners were marketed for use with microcomputers. These were designed to read OCR-A, a variety of other type fonts, and also illustrations. Today the use of scanners is common, including desktop scanners that can input graphics as well as almost all types of typewritten and typeset characters (Figure 3.20a). Recently, handheld scanners (Figure 3.20b) have become available for light scanning jobs — one to a dozen pages a day; the user passes a hammer-shaped scanner, connected to the computer, horizontally across the page of printed text in order to input the text or illustration. The scanned and converted text goes into the user's software system as if he or she were typing it in at several hundred words a minute. (Take a portable computer and a handheld scanner to the library and input research notes from resource materials of all types!)

The popular **fax machine** (*fax* is short for *facsimile*, meaning *reproduction*) is a type of scanner that "reads" text and graphics and transmits them over telephone lines to a computer with a fax board or another fax machine (Figure 3.21; we'll cover fax machines in more detail in Chapter 9, on communications).

Many users think that image scanning still needs some improvement; for example, sometimes graphics need on-screen adjustment by the user after they have

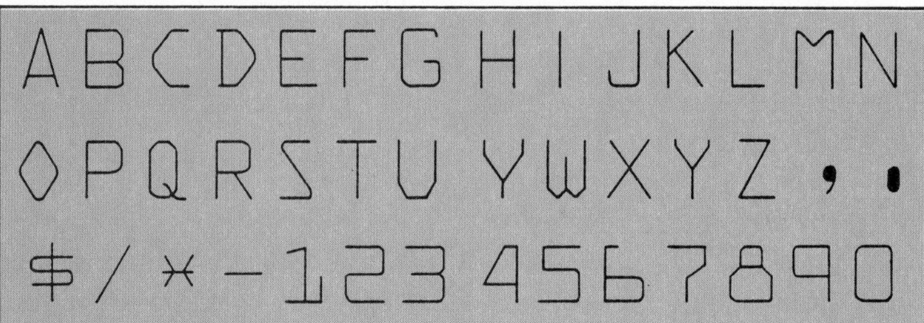

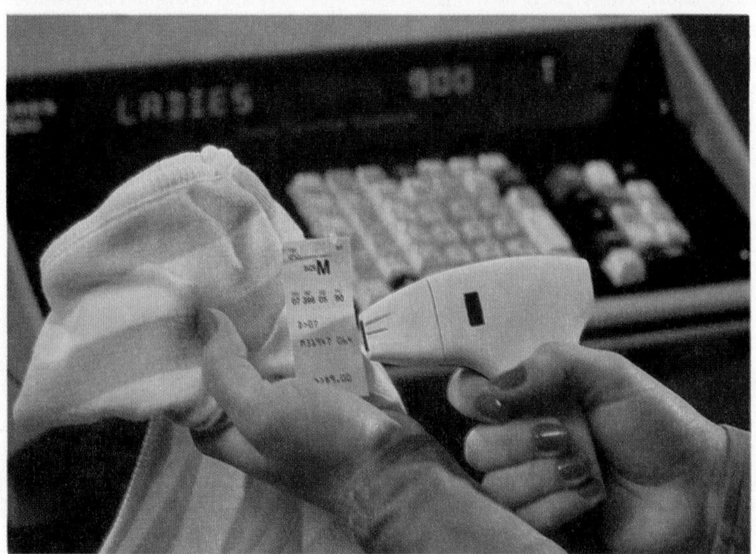

FIGURE 3.19

OCR-A typeface. The OCR-A type style was designed to be read by a special input scanning device.

(a)

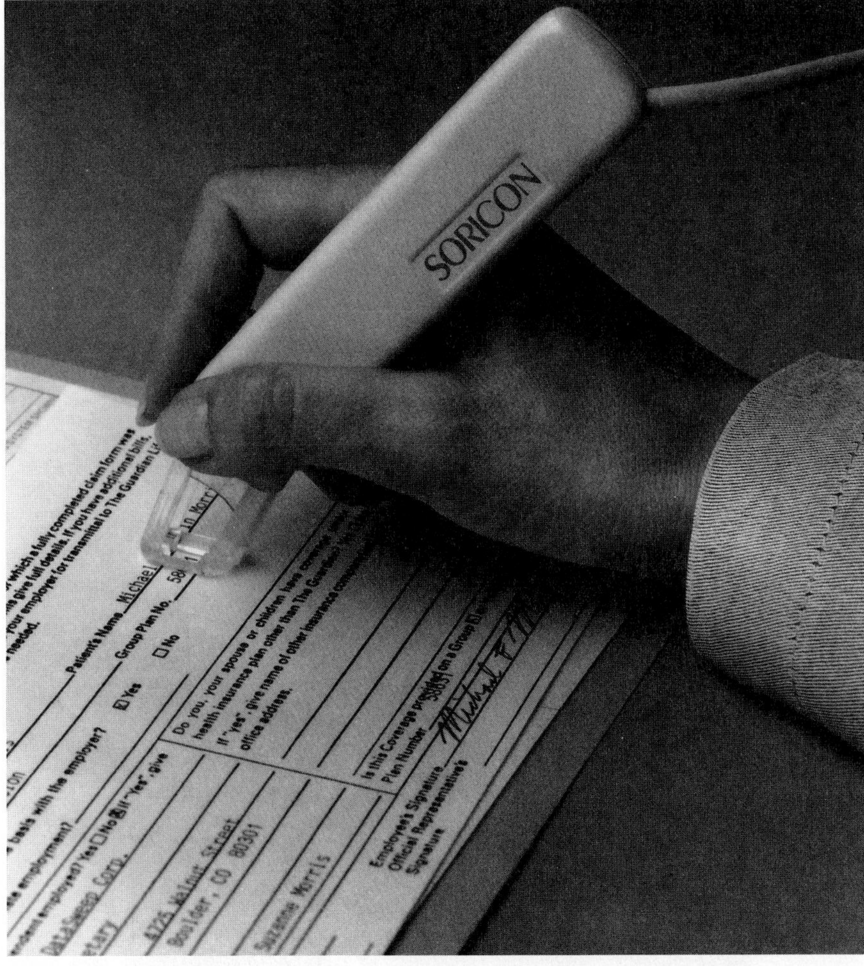

(b)

FIGURE 3.20

Scanning. (a) The Apple page scanner at left has just been used to input the photo image into computer-usable form, as shown on the Mac II display screen. (b) This hand-held text and graphics scanner (Soricon Data Sweep 2) is used for smaller scanning jobs.

been scanned into the computer. However, the time and money saved by not having to manually input data into the computer outweigh the inefficiencies of scanners.

ETHICS NOTE Copyright infringement has become an issue with graphics—photos and drawn/painted illustrations—that have been electronically manipulated after they have been scanned into a computer system. For example, software programs will allow a user to move people in a photo, take certain people out, rearrange the landscape, and so on and then output a new photo in the form of a negative. Or, the colors and composition of an artist's illustration can be changed. Such alterations of copyrighted photos and art are illegal without the permission of the copyright holder.

In addition, plagiarism—the unauthorized and uncredited use of another person's words or ideas—can inadvertently become a danger to the researcher who is scanning large amounts of printed resource material into his or her research file.

HANDWRITTEN-CHARACTER READERS Although the percentage of data recorded by hand has dropped substantially over the last 50 years, quite a bit of data is still

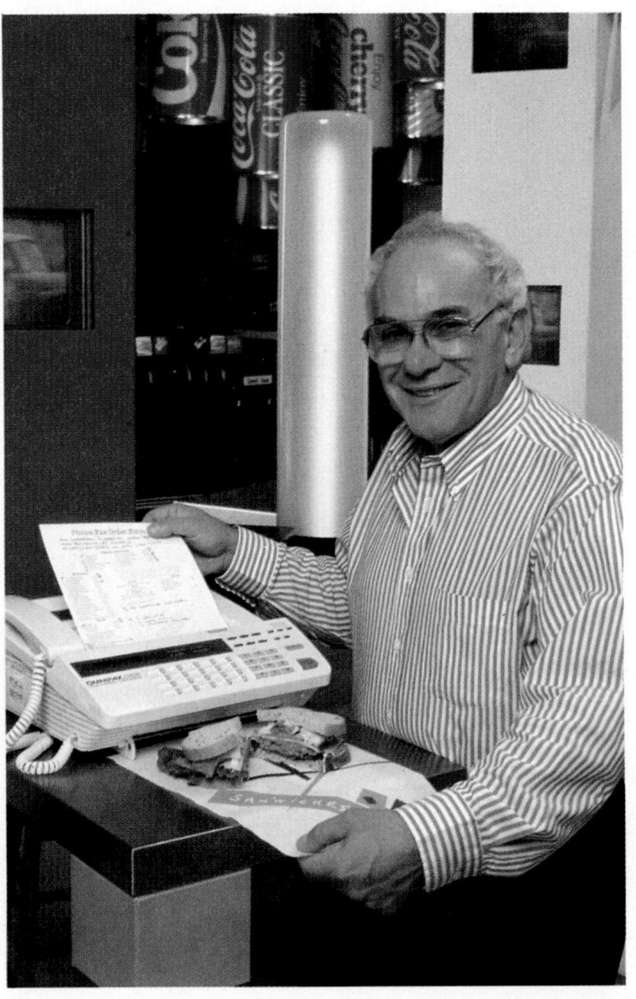

FIGURE 3.21

Fax of life. San'wiches Restaurant fills orders received via fax machine.

recorded this way. As OCR technology advanced, designers felt that it would also be possible to convert handwritten data into computer-usable form in much the same way that typewritten data is. Devices with this capability are the most sophisticated and versatile of the OCR devices. Because handwriting varies widely, specific guidelines must generally be followed so that the OCR reader will interpret the characters accurately (see Table 3.1). (A computer system that can "read" almost all handwriting in a few seconds has been patented; however, its accuracy rate remains to be tested in the general business world.)

MAGNETIC-INK CHARACTER RECOGNITION (MICR) As many as 750 million personal checks are processed each month in the United States. This number does not even include the business checks written each month, which total more than triple the number of personal checks. How does the banking industry handle this mountain of data?

The American Bankers Association (ABA), anticipating this problem in the mid-1950s, adopted the **magnetic-ink character recognition (MICR)** technology as its primary means of data entry for processing checks. This technology involves the reading of numeric characters and a few special symbols printed on checks with magnetic ink. (Alphabetic characters are not used with this technology.) Figure 3.22 shows the layout of the MICR encoding on a personal check and some MICR recording equipment.

Have you ever noticed a check, returned by your bank with your monthly statement, that had a piece of paper taped to the bottom? That piece of paper contains a duplicate of the MICR encoding on the check. What has happened is that the MICR symbols have been damaged; as a result, the MICR reader rejected your check. So one of the clerks at the bank rekeyed the MICR symbols onto a separate slip of paper and taped it to your check. In 1960, when it became apparent that some standardization was needed in the MICR type font, the ABA adopted a standard character set consisting of 14 symbols (Table 3.2).

The advantages of the MICR system are that:

- Human involvement is minimal; thus, the potential for errors is small.
- The codes can be read by both people and machines.
- It is fast, automatic, and reliable.

TABLE 3.1

Handwriting Guidelines for OCR Readers

- Print using block letters and numbers.
- Make the size of each character fairly large.
- When writing a character or letter that has a loop (like 6, 9, or *g*), carefully close the loop.
- When writing a character or letter with connecting lines (like *T*, *I*, 4, or 5), carefully connect the lines.
- Do not use script (it connects the letters), and do not connect series of zeros together in numbers.
- If necessary, use special forms that have an individual box for each handwritten character.

FIGURE 3.22

Check it out. (a) Your personal checks are encoded with magnetic ink that is read by MICR equipment. The data is then stored for processing. Note that the printed check amount in the bottom-right corner is encoded by an MICR inscriber. (b) The IBM 3890/XP check-processing system handles 2,400 checks per minute.

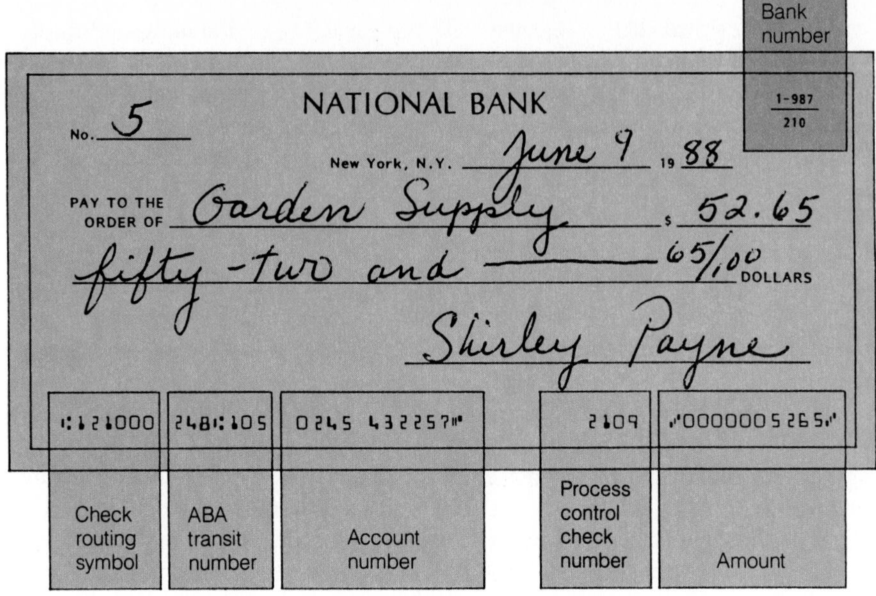

Processing Your Check

1. Checks are fed into large, high-capacity MICR reader/sorter devices.
2. MICR characters on checks are read electronically.
3. Check data is stored on tape or disk for processing.
4. Checks are sorted by bank number and returned to your bank.
5. If you wish, a bank may sort checks by account number and return them to you with the monthly statements.

(a)

(b)

However, some human involvement is still required to encode the check amount in MICR characters; thus, some room for error does remain.

Recently, the banking industry has begun to take steps to minimize the amount of paper handling necessary. That is why we are seeing more automated teller machines that use electronic "checks" instead of paper ones and why "smart cards" are becoming more common.

SMART CARDS

Smart cards (Figure 3.23), which were pioneered in the mid-1970s in France, are designed to be carried like credit cards but used like tiny transaction computers. The smart card has a computer chip that provides processing power and an electronic memory that does not lose its data when the power is turned off. To use it, the cardholder inserts the card into a special card-reading point-of-sale terminal and then enters a password on the keyboard. The cards have microchips that can keep permanent records, which are updated each time the card is used. The transaction data stored on the card can later be read into the computer for the user's bank—perhaps via an ATM—to update the user's bank records. In France and Britain smart cards are used to pay bills (while keeping current bank balances on file on the card), buy merchandise, make phone calls, buy postal money orders, get exam results from the university, store emergency medical information, and perform

TABLE 3.2

The Standard MICR Character Set

- The numbers 0–9
- An amount symbol (⑇)
- A dash symbol (⑉)
- A transit symbol (⑆)
- An "on-us" symbol (⑈) (tells who is the payer and who is the payee)

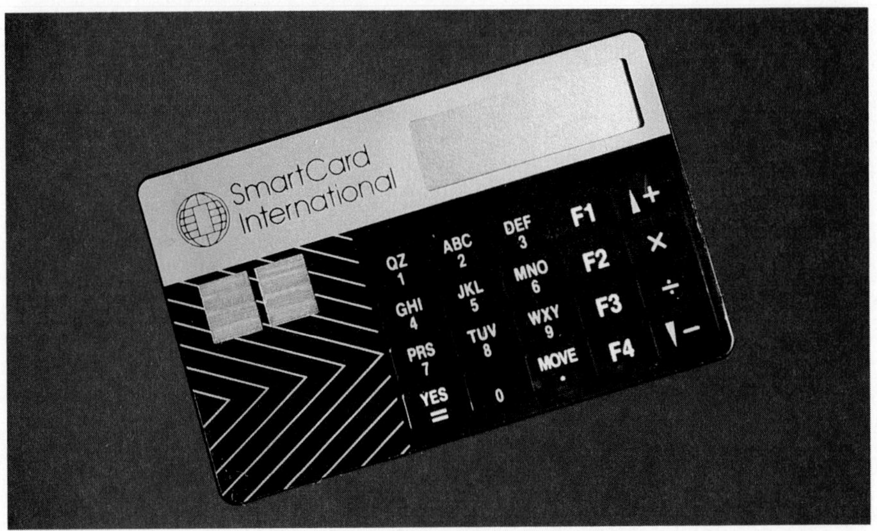

FIGURE 3.23

Get smart! The microchips on the left side of the smart card can keep permanent records, which are updated each time the card is used.

other common activities. Electronic card readers have been installed in stores, restaurants, post offices, phone booths, banks, and so on.

The cards are being used to some extent in the United States—by the U.S. Navy, for example, for purchasing procedures—and will become increasingly common. Some manufacturers are already talking about a "supersmart card" that will incorporate a keypad and a display unit along with the memory and processing capabilities. Other manufacturers are developing smart cards to use as "keys" that users must employ to gain access to certain types of computer systems. For now you can use your "unintelligent" bank card with its magnetically encoded strip to pay for gasoline and groceries at some service stations and supermarkets by electronically transferring funds; the purchase amount is automatically deducted from your bank balance, without any further action from you.

FIGURE 3.24

Voice input. The user gives voice commands or enters data through the microphone on the headset, which is connected to the computer.

(a)

(b)

VOICE INPUT DEVICES

In an effort to increase worker productivity and make computers easier to use for disabled people, a substantial amount of research is being done in voice recognition —programming the computer to recognize spoken commands. **Voice input devices** (Figure 3.24), or **voice recognition systems,** convert spoken words into electrical signals by comparing the electrical patterns produced by the speaker's voice with a set of prerecorded patterns (Figure 3.25). If a matching pattern is found, the computer accepts this pattern as a part of its standard "vocabulary."

This technology is also used by people whose jobs do not allow them to keep their hands free, as well as by disabled people who are not able to use traditional input devices. For example, NASA has developed experimental space suits that use microprocessors and storage devices to allow astronauts to view computerized displays across their helmet visors. These displays would be activated and manipulated by spoken command—convenient when you've got both hands busy on an outer space repair job!

To date, the biggest problems with this technology involve limitations on the size of the computer's vocabulary, pronunciation differences among individuals, and the computer's inability to accept continuous speech. However, research continues at a fast pace. Several voice input units are currently available for use with microcomputers. For example, the DragonDictate Voice-Typewriter system—consisting of a personal computer, special software, and a speech recognition circuit board—was billed as the first of its kind. It "knows" 30,000 words and adapts to

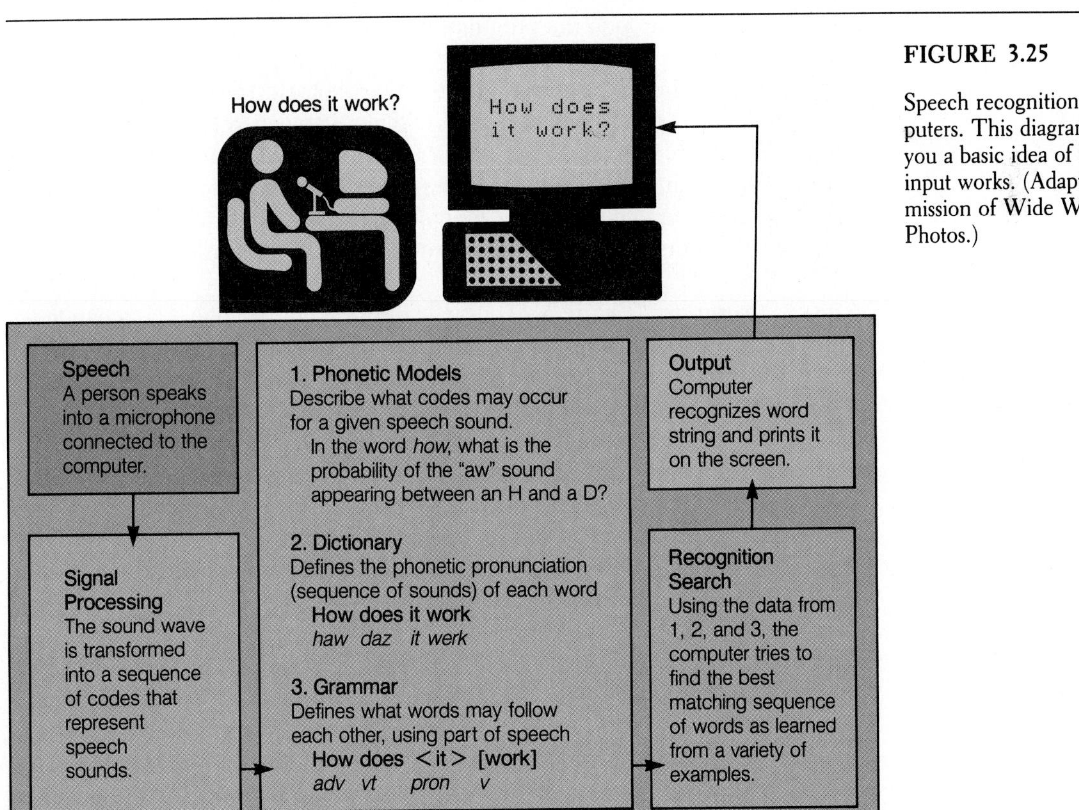
How does it work?
How does it work?
Speech
A person speaks into a microphone connected to the computer.
Signal Processing
The sound wave is transformed into a sequence of codes that represent speech sounds.
1. Phonetic Models
Describe what codes may occur for a given speech sound.
In the word how, what is the probability of the "aw" sound appearing between an H and a D?
2. Dictionary
Defines the phonetic pronunciation (sequence of sounds) of each word
How does it work
haw daz it werk
3. Grammar
Defines what words may follow each other, using part of speech
How does <it> [work]
adv vt pron v
Output
Computer recognizes word string and prints it on the screen.
Recognition Search
Using the data from 1, 2, and 3, the computer tries to find the best matching sequence of words as learned from a variety of examples.

FIGURE 3.25

Speech recognition computers. This diagram gives you a basic idea of how voice input works. (Adapted by permission of Wide World Photos.)

individual voices (previous systems could recognize no more than 5,000 words). Text appears on the video screen at the rate of 35 words a minute. A mistake can be corrected by saying "oops" and repeating the correct word. Such systems will be a boon to people who are not able to type or who cannot type well.

Voice recognition systems like DragonDictate must be "trained" to recognize the user's speech patterns, and the user must speak a bit more slowly than normal. However, speaker-independent voice recognition systems are being designed so equipment need not be tuned to the voice of any one person. For instance, Speech Systems, Inc. has developed a system that will allow radiologists to dictate reports to computer workstations without the necessity of having to train the system to recognize their voices. Verbex Voice Systems lets stocks and bonds traders pick up a phone and, without pausing between words, tell the computer the number of stocks or bonds being bought or sold, the type, and the price. Voice Technologies has developed a system that lets disabled engineers use computer-aided design software by telling the computer where to move the cursor.

"Pointing" Devices

Data input also involves entering commands and selecting options. The light pen, the mouse, the trackball, the touch screen, and the digitizer were all developed to make this easy. Each of these devices allows the user to identify and select the necessary command or option by, in effect, moving the cursor to a certain location on the screen or tablet and sending a signal to the computer. For this reason they are sometimes called **pointing devices,** and they are used in **menu-driven** programs—that is, programs that offer varying levels of menus, or choices, to the user to lead him or her through the program functions.

Light Pen The **light pen** uses a light-sensitive photoelectric cell to signal screen position to the computer (Figure 3.26). The pen is touched to the video display screen at the desired location and the switch on the pen is pushed to close the photoelectric circuit, thereby indicating the *x-y* screen coordinates to the computer. Light pens are frequently used by graphics designers, illustrators, and drafting engineers. (Of course, data may also be entered using keyboards.)

Mouse The **mouse** (Figure 3.27), briefly discussed in Chapter 1, is a handheld device connected to the computer by a small cable. As the mouse is rolled across the desktop, a ball inside the mouse that contacts the desktop moves the cursor across the screen. When the cursor reaches the desired location, the user usually pushes a button on the mouse once or twice to signal a menu selection or a command to the computer. Mouse technology is often used with graphics-oriented microcomputers like the Macintosh. With special software for graphics, the mouse can be used like a pen or a paintbrush to create figures and patterns directly on the video display screen. The keyboard, however, must still be used to type in characters and issue some commands, depending on the software.

Trackball **Trackballs** have all the functionality of a mouse, but they don't need to be rolled around on a desktop. The ball is held in a socket on top of the stationary device, and the user moves the ball with his or her fingers. Trackballs have become popular in offices where crowded desktops are the norm. Pocket-sized trackballs are available for laptop computers, eliminating the need for a flat work surface, which is required to use a mouse.

TOUCH SCREEN Limited amounts of data can be entered via a terminal or a microcomputer that has a **touch screen.** The user simply touches the screen at the desired locations, marked by labeled boxes, to "point out" choices to the computer (Figure 3.28). The software determines the kinds of choices the user has.

You may have seen touch screen terminals in, for example, airports—by touching various menu options you can get information about transportation to and from the airport, hotels, restaurants, tourist attractions, and so on. Large shopping malls often install touch screen terminals to help visitors find their way around the area and to obtain information about the various shops and services offered. Some automatic teller machines use touch screen technology, as do some lottery machines. A recent, specialized use of touch screens is to help deaf children who know American Sign Language (ASL) learn to read written English; as the child reads a story displayed on the computer screen and has trouble with a word, he or she can call up a displayed signed version of the word by touching the screen at appropriate points.

DIGITIZER An interesting method of input that is used in mapmaking is the **digitizer,** or digitizing tablet (Figure 3.29). The tablets, which come in different

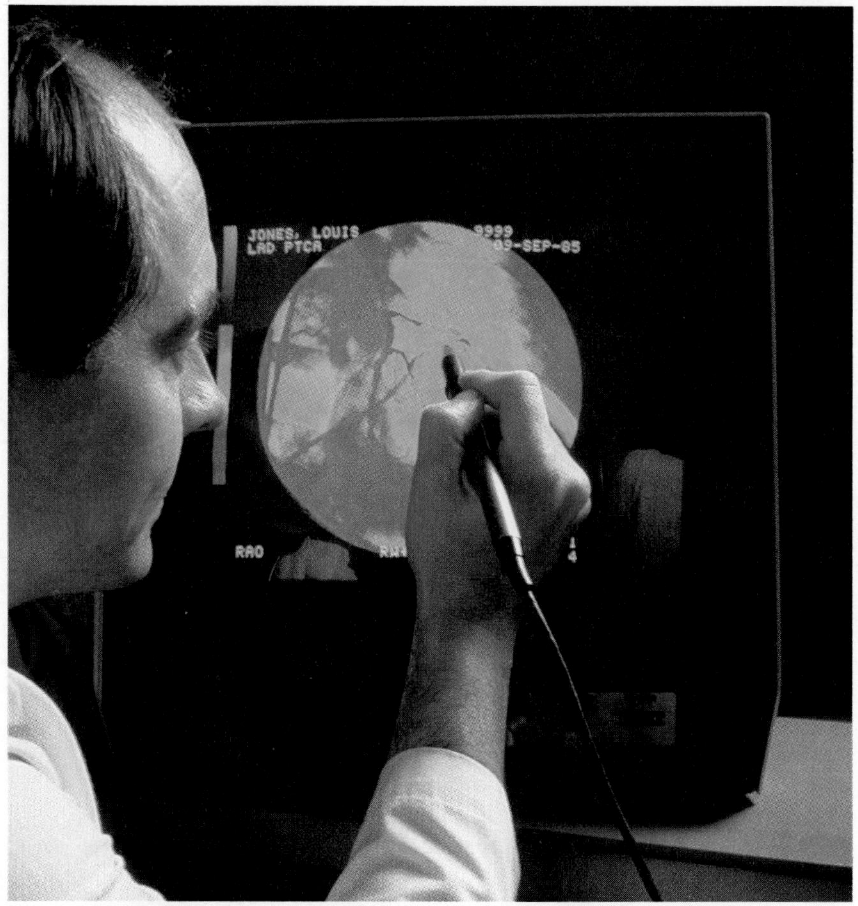

FIGURE 3.26

Light pen. This user is employing a light pen to analyze an angiogram of certain blood vessels and arteries.

sizes, are the working surface. Each is covered by a grid of many tiny wires that is connected to the computer. Drawings placed over this grid can be traced and entered into the computer by the use of a special pen or mouselike device with crosshairs that opens and closes electrical circuits in the grid and thus identifies x-y

FIGURE 3.27

Mouse. (a) When the user rolls the mouse around the desktop, the inset ball causes the cursor to move correspondingly on the screen. By rolling the mouse to move the cursor to an option—such as width of "brushstroke" on the MacPaint graphics software menu—and clicking the mouse button once or twice, the user can then proceed to draw and "paint." (b) A trackball works like a mouse, but it isn't rolled around on the desktop; instead, the user moves the ball by touch.

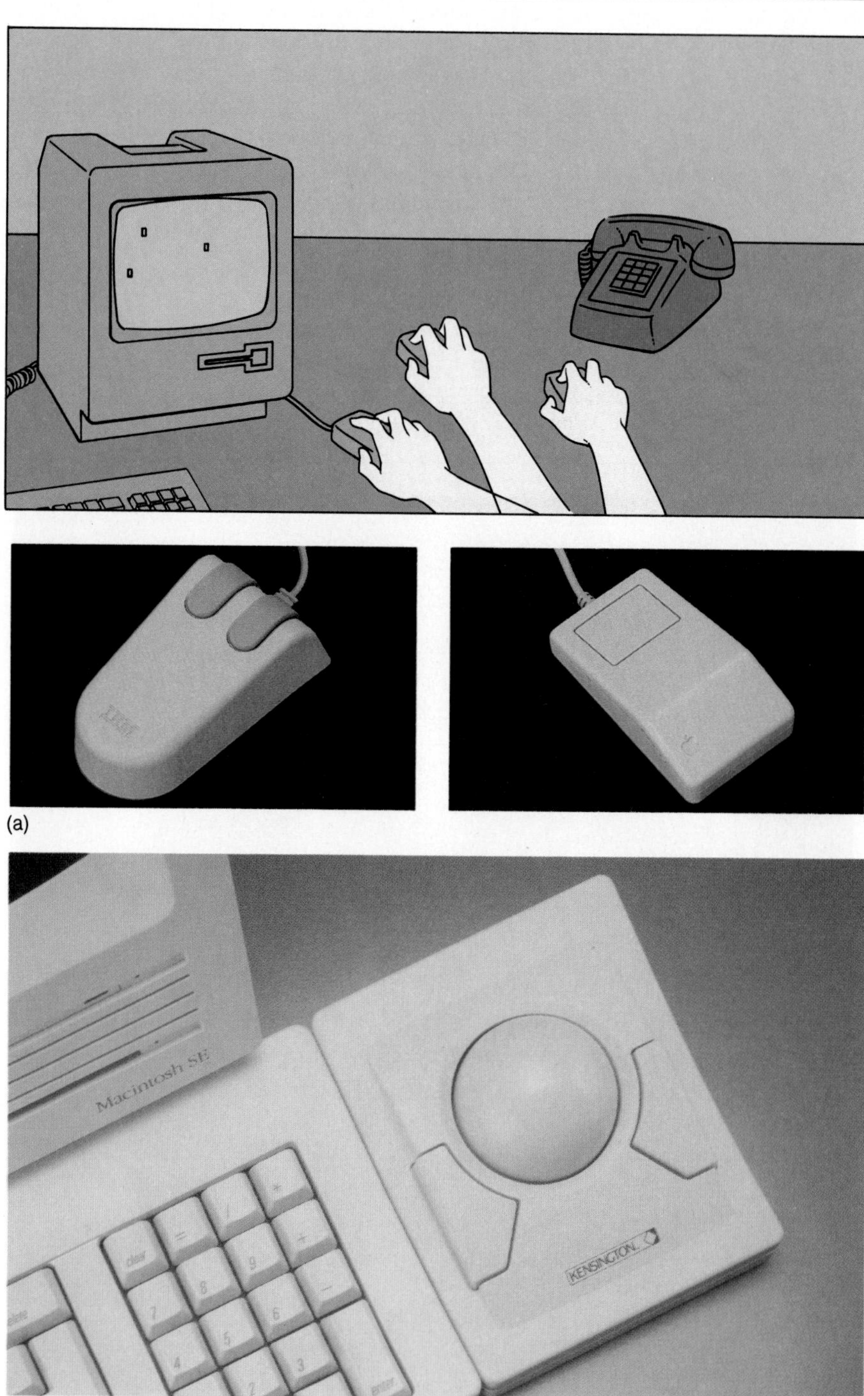

coordinates. Original drawings may also be entered. As it progresses, the drawing is displayed on the screen; it can later be stored or printed out. Digitizers are also used in design and engineering businesses — such as those that develop aircraft or computer chips.

Touch-Tone™ Device

As you probably know, you can use your **Touch-Tone™** phone to send data to a computer. For example, if you want to arrange for Federal Express to come to your home or office and pick up a package, you can call a special 800 number. A computerized voice requests that you touch the numbers for your account number, ZIP code, and number of packages being picked up. The data goes to the central computer system, is checked, and is then retrieved by the appropriate local pickup system, which sends an employee to get your package.

Touch-Tone™ devices called **card dialers** are also used to run credit card checks in retail stores (Figure 3.30). After appropriate keys are touched, the device sends data over the phone lines to a central computer, which then checks the data against its files and reports credit information back to the store.

Most specialized, nonkeyboard input devices are used in conjunction with a keyboard because the specialized devices can't be used to input all types of data and

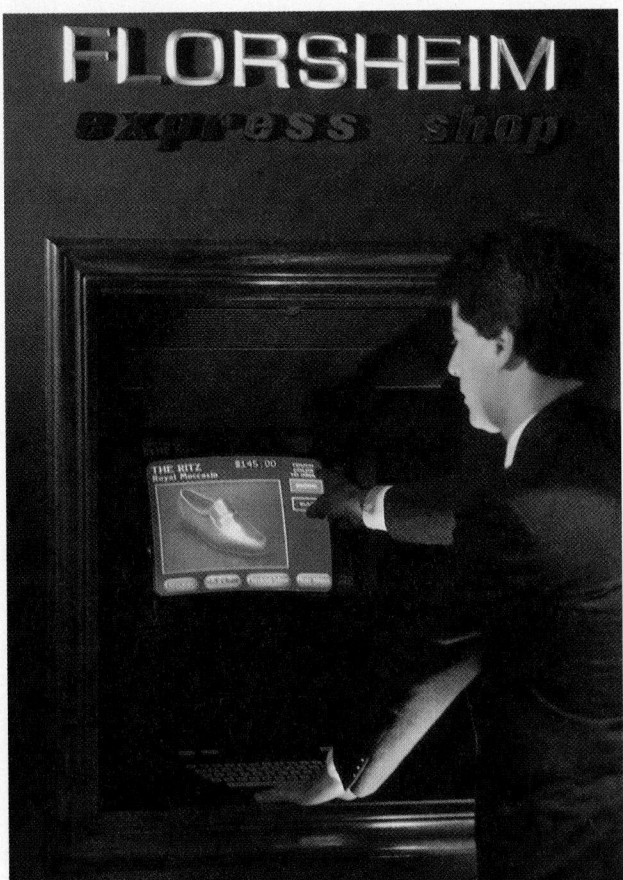

FIGURE 3.28

Touch screen. This system allows customers to order shoes quickly by touching choices on the computer screen.

instructions. An exception may be the Eyescan Communicator that translates eye movements into signals for a computer. This innovation—still being refined—allows people who cannot speak or use keyboards to communicate using a computer. The first field-tested prototype—the Eyegaze Response Interface Computer Aid, or ERICA—allows users to operate the system by focusing their eyes on screen items to choose commands and "type in" data. This process works through retinal reflection. Infrared light is emitted from the system onto the user's face, which causes the reflection. The reflection pattern moves as the person shifts his or

FIGURE 3.29

Digitizer. (a) This engineer is creating a blueprint using a mouse-like digitizer on a grid with electronic wires that is connected to the computer. (b) A student in the School of Visual Arts in New York City is using a 3-space Isotrak digitizer to draw a freehand 3-D project viewed on the monitor.

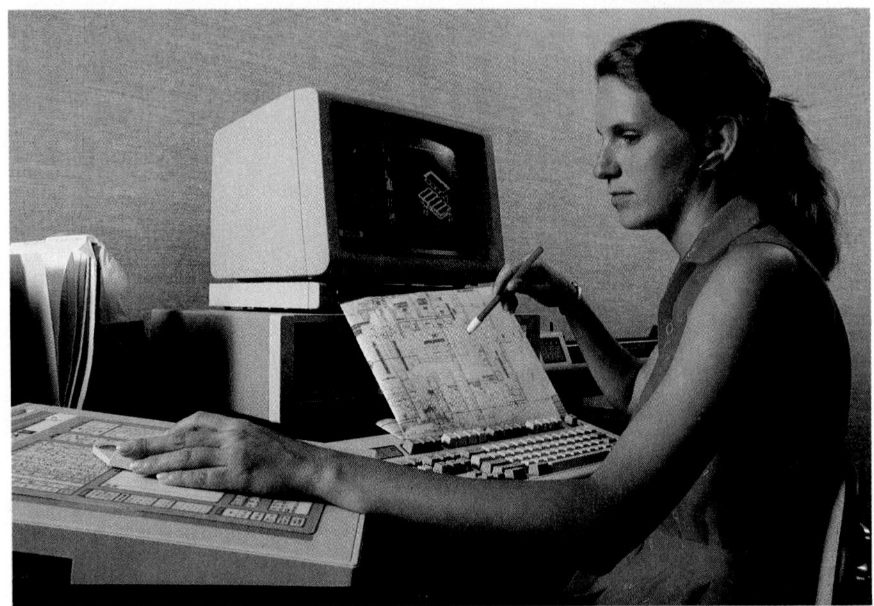

(a)

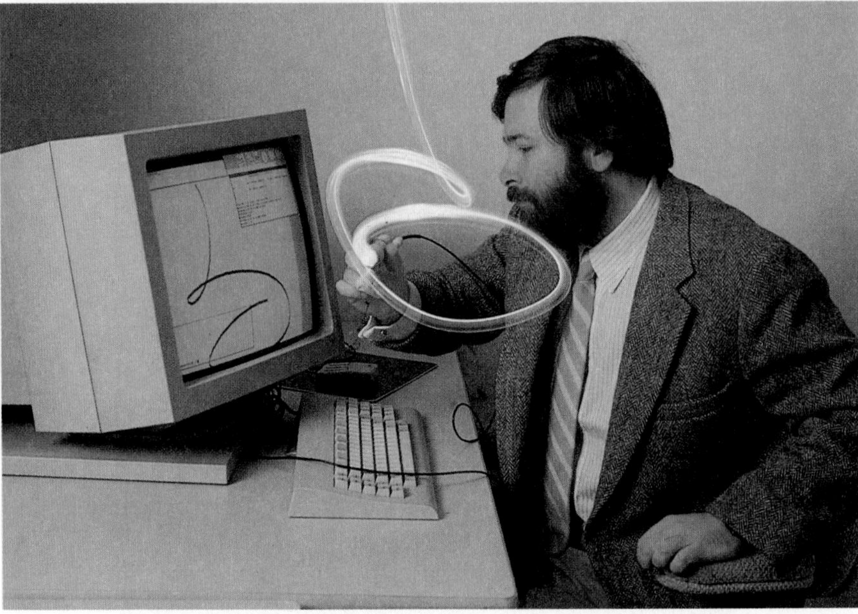

(b)

her gaze. A video camera tracks the movement and transmits the data to special hardware and software that converts the data into computer-usable form. This system is the forerunner in a new category of computers designed to transform the lives of people who cannot speak or move.

INPUT CONTROLS: PRESERVING DATA INTEGRITY

No matter how sophisticated your input hardware is and how well thought out your input methods are, you still run the risk of generating inaccurate or even useless information. The completeness and accuracy of information produced by a computer system depends to a great extent on how much care was taken in capturing the raw data that served as input to the processing procedures. An old computer-related saying summarizes this point: "Garbage In, Garbage Out" (GIGO). If you—the user—input incomplete and inaccurate data (Garbage In), then you can expect the information that is produced to be correspondingly incomplete and inaccurate (Garbage Out). How do you ensure that input data is accurate and complete?

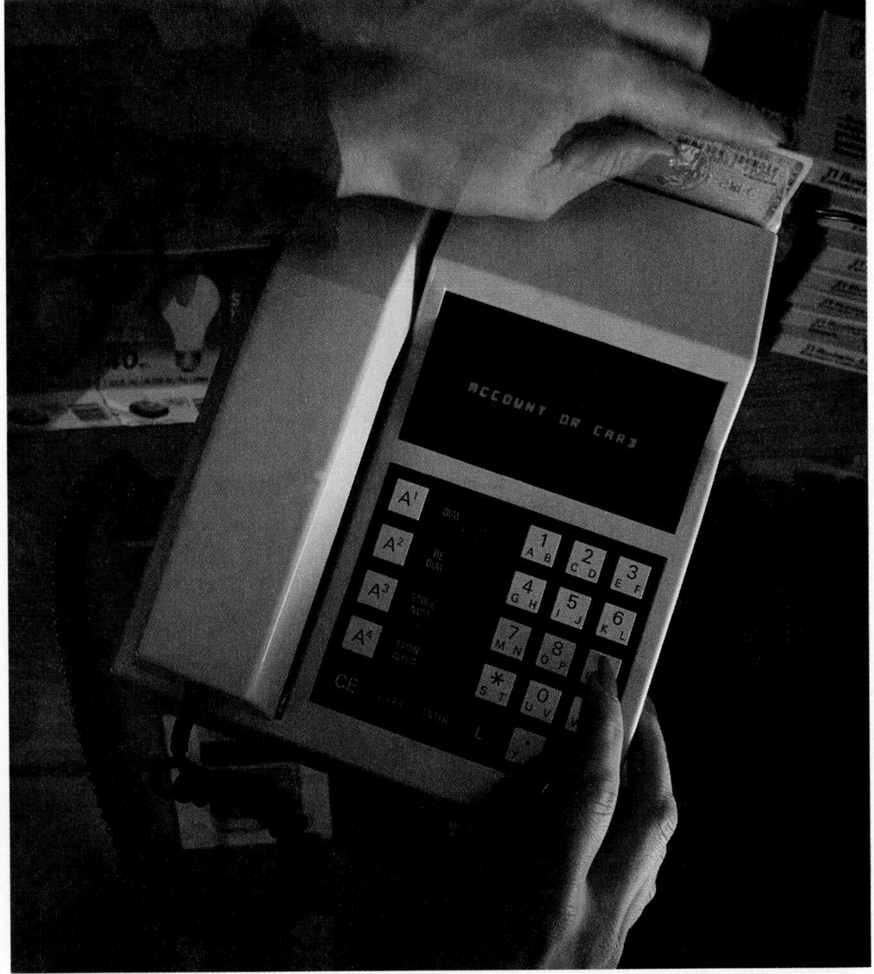

FIGURE 3.30

Card dialer. Many merchants use push-button card dialers to check customers' credit limits and ratings.

Input controls include a combination of manual and computerized control procedures designed to ensure that all input data has been accurately put into computer-usable form. A variety of control techniques can be used, depending on the design of the computer system and the nature of the processing activities taking place. When source documents (papers, forms, and so on) that contain data to be keyed into computer-usable form are used, the most commonly used control technique is the *batch control technique*, illustrated in Figure 3.31.

The input control techniques differ for on-line and on-line real-time systems — that is, when source documents aren't used and data has been keyed in through a terminal. In these cases, the user typically has a computer terminal on the desk or sales counter. As data is provided by the customer or other source, it is keyed into the computer immediately. The main computer is usually programmed to immediately verify the accuracy of the data (customer number, product number, account number, and so on) by matching it to the appropriate master computer files. In other words, the input controls in the form of editing and validation are written into the software and the user can see error messages on the screen. Corrections can generally be made immediately by the user.

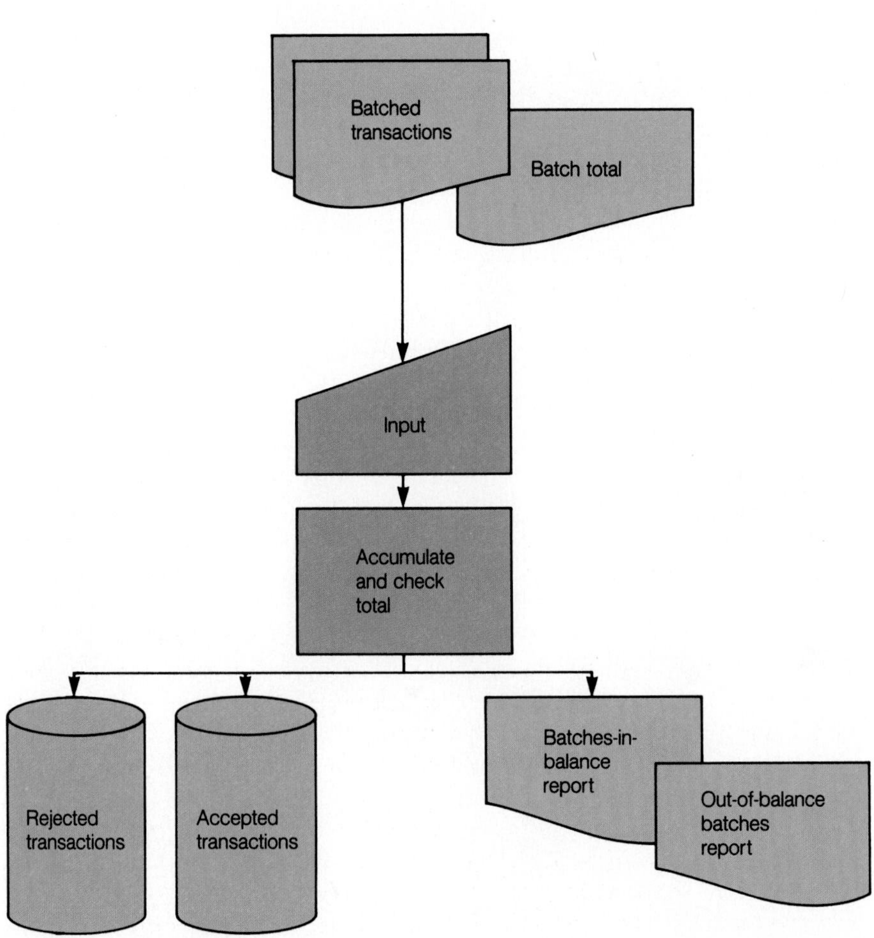

FIGURE 3.31

Waiting for GIGO? Input controls are used to ensure that data is input accurately and completely. One type of input control is *batch totaling*. Transactions are manually collected into batches, and a control total is established over each batch. The batch total can be a total document count, an item count, or a dollar amount. The batch total is calculated before processing and recorded on a special batch control record, which is input in addition to all the transactions for that particular batch. The computer accumulates that batch total itself and compares it to the control total input with the batch. If the totals do not agree, the computer rejects the batch and prints the details on the Out-of-Balance Batches Report. If the totals agree, the batch is accepted for further processing and is recorded on the Batches-in-Balance Report. Since the out-of-balance batches are held on a separate file, they can be corrected and re-entered.

How important are input controls? Consider the modest-living couple who got a phone bill for $450,000 and spent months trying to convince the company it was a mistake. The customer service personnel and the data processing staff were probably trying to identify the glitch in the input control procedures. The computer doesn't make mistakes; the people who input data and monitor input procedures do. Even software writers are not infallible. Without input controls, mistakes might be impossible to detect or correct. Imagine the consequences this could have on the level of international trade, politics, and military activities. Of course, input controls are not the only controls involving data accuracy, completeness, and security. We'll explore controls further in our discussion of systems development in Chapter 10.

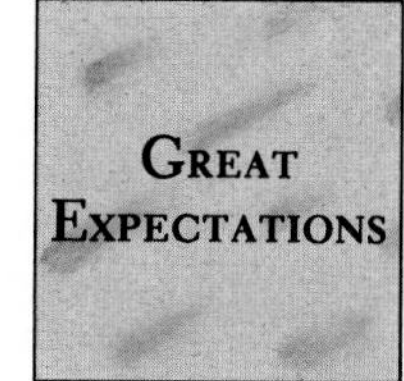

How fast is fast, how small is small, how powerful is powerful? In the world of computers, yesterday's answer is not the same as today's answer, and neither answer is tomorrow's answer. But the major trend is clear: The speeds for inputting, processing, retrieving, and outputting information will increase, and, at the same time, further miniaturization will pack more hardware and software into smaller areas. Starting with this chapter, the "Great Expectations" section will briefly examine how the specific trends in the area covered by each chapter may affect the future user.

In general, as far as input hardware is concerned, the life of the user should get easier — equipment will become simpler to use, quicker, less expensive, and more comfortable to use. Offices will become more integrated, putting the user on-line. Not only will data entry, storage, and retrieval be integrated but also mail handling, word processing, personal productivity tools, report generation, decision support, and voice/data/video communications. Complete electronic microcomputer workstations will become more common — even those that are as elaborately equipped as the one shown in Figure 3.32.

Common use of continuous-speech voice-activated computers — to which you don't . . . have . . . to . . . talk . . . like . . . this — is still a few years away but is definitely coming. This type of input system would greatly simplify the user's role and reduce the margin for error. (Can you say a "typo"?) Of course, developers may have to address the problem of a room full of users complaining that they can't hear themselves think! And another drawback is that many people will not want to spend their days talking to a machine. However, some experts think that voice recognition will become standard for controlling the computer by telephone, which could be used as a type of dictating machine for inputting data to the computer.

Scanners will continue to improve, and more and more businesses will use them, as well as fax machines, the superstars of office technology. Faxes will soon be able to give better quality output than was input (scanned). Soon there will be fax machines with built-in phones that plug into your car's lighter; hook it up to your portable microcomputer complete with fax board, and you're in business. But please don't fax and drive!

"Notebook" computers, or "stylus" computers, are also on the horizon. These notebook-size computers will allow you to input data and instructions simply by using a special pen, or stylus, to write directly on the screen in any manner you choose. These computers could be taken into the field and used independently and

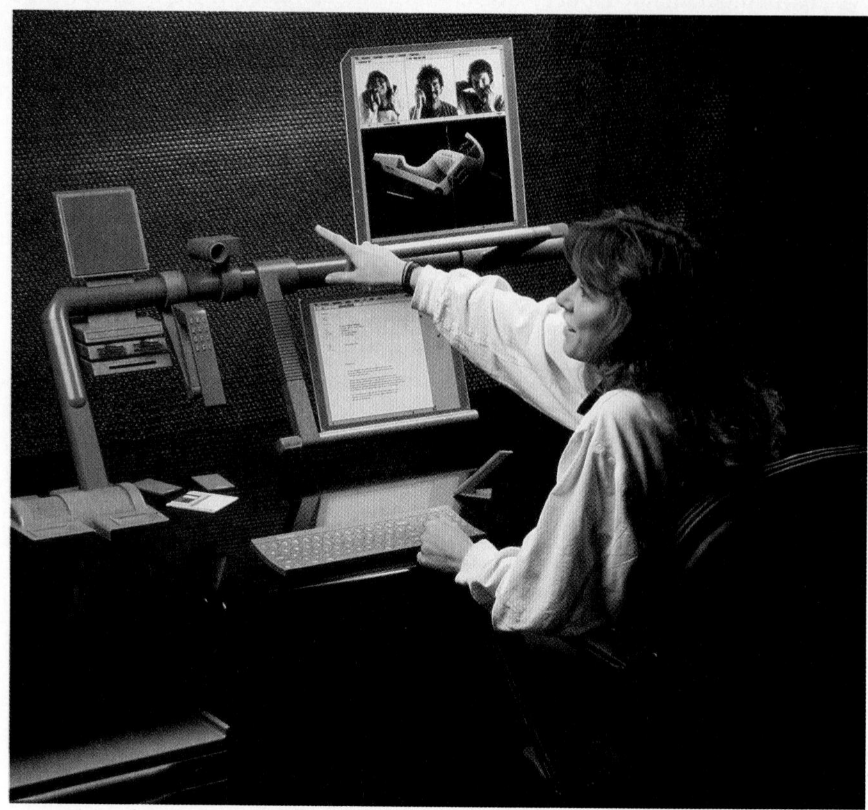

FIGURE 3.32

Modern electronic workstation. Instead of using clumsy, space-eating cabinets, system units, and disk drives, this workstation combines all computer-related elements in a single configuration. The keyboard has no cable, and the back of the keyboard acts as a scanner. The mouse is pen-shaped. The display screen's position (center) can be adjusted, and the disk drives (left) can use regular diskettes, optical disks, and cards. Video camera, microphone, speaker, and videoconference screen enable the user to participate in live conferences while displaying data and/or graphics at the same time (top right). The telephone and modem are built in.

then hooked up to telephone lines or directly to another computer to execute additional processing functions.

Whatever the developments over the next few years, one thing is sure: If you know how to use a computer keyboard, you're already ahead!

ONWARD: HOLDING ON TO WHAT YOU'VE GOT

Now that you've learned something about the hardware and the methods used to input data, it's time to move on to where and how you store the data. "On magnetic tape or disk," you say, but there's more to it than that, as the next chapter will show.

SUMMARY

Input hardware can be broken down into two main categories: keyboard-based and direct-entry. The keyboard, which comes in many shapes and sizes, is probably the most widely used mechanism for entering data in a computer-usable form. Many of its keys resemble typewriter keys; however, it also has special function keys and special-purpose keys (to issue commands, among other things), cursor-movement keys, and numeric keys (to enter numbers).

Terminals are often used for data input. They usually consist of a keyboard, video display screen, and a communications link to a main computer. Terminals can be dumb, smart, or intelligent. A dumb terminal is used only to input data; it cannot do any processing or store any data on its own. A smart computer is used to input data, but it also has some limited processing capabilities. An intelligent computer can input and receive data as well as do its own processing and storage. Common types of terminals are the point-of-sale (POS) terminal, the financial transaction terminal, the executive workstation, and the microcomputer used as a terminal.

Data is also input using dedicated data entry systems such as key-to-tape, key-to-disk, and key-to-diskette. These systems do nothing but input and store data.

Direct-entry input devices do not use a keyboard. Popular direct-entry data input devices today include: (1) card readers for microcomputer systems, (2) scanners and fax machines, (3) bar code readers, (4) optical mark readers, (5) MICR readers, (6) smart cards, (7) voice input devices, and (8) light pens, mice, trackballs, touch screens, and digitizers (this group is sometimes called *pointing devices*).

Most data that is input into a computer-usable form is not processed immediately; instead it is held on storage media until needed for processing. These media include paper and magnetic tape, disk, and diskette — magnetic media being the most widely used today. Punched cards and paper tape were the first paper-based input media, but they are not used much anymore. Today, specialized input devices are being used frequently to read data recorded by hand, typed, or typeset on paper documents.

The conversion of data into a computer-usable form is a vital part of a computer-based information system. Input control procedures are needed to safeguard the data's integrity and to ensure the production of complete and accurate information — in other words, to ensure no "garbage in" to avoid getting "garbage out."

KEY TERMS

bar code, p. 91
bar code reader, p. 92
card dialer, p. 107
card reader, p. 91
cursor, p. 78
cursor-movement keys, p. 78
dedicated data entry system, p. 86
desktop management software, p. 82
digitizer (digitizing tablet), p. 105
direct entry, p. 86
dumb terminal, p. 80
executive desktop workstation, p. 82
fax machine, p. 96
financial transaction terminal, p. 82
function keys, p. 78
handheld terminal, p. 82
input controls, p. 110
integrated workstation, p. 82
intelligent terminal, p. 80
keyboard, p. 78
keypunch machine, p. 86
key-to-disk, p. 86
key-to-diskette, p. 86
key-to-tape, p. 86
light pen, p. 104
magnetic-ink character recognition (MICR), p. 99
menu-driven, p. 104
microcomputer terminal, p. 85
modem, p. 82
mouse, p. 104
numeric keys, p. 78
optical character recognition (OCR), p. 91
optical mark, p. 93
optical mark reader (OMR), p. 93
pointing device, p. 104
point-of-sale (POS) terminal, p. 81
portable terminal, p. 82
scanning device, p. 94
smart card, p. 101
smart terminal, p. 80
terminal, p. 80
touch screen, p. 105
Touch-Tone™, p. 107
trackball, p. 104
upload, p. 85
voice input device, p. 103
voice recognition system, p. 103

EXERCISES

MATCHING

Match each of the following terms to the phrase that is the most closely related.

1. ____ bar code reader
2. ____ cursor
3. ____ keyboard
4. ____ input controls
5. ____ dumb terminal
6. ____ executive workstation
7. ____ digitizer
8. ____ fax machine
9. ____ menu-driven
10. ____ dedicated data entry system
11. ____ intelligent terminal
12. ____ card reader
13. ____ magnetic-ink character recognition
14. ____ touch screen
15. ____ mouse
16. ____ portable terminal
17. ____ upload

a. Type of scanner that "reads" text and graphics and transmits them over telephone lines
b. A user can carry this to hook up to a central computer from a remote location.
c. Terminal that can input and receive data, as well as allow users to edit, store, and process data
d. Input component entirely dependent for all of its capabilities on the computer system to which it is connected
e. Programs that offer varying levels of choices to the user to lead him or her through the program functions.
f. Group of terminals connected to a main computer that do nothing but input and store data, using tape, disk, or diskette
g. Hardware device that reads the holes in punched cards and transfers the appropriate signals as input to the computer
h. To transmit data from a smaller computer, such as a microcomputer workstation, to a main computer
i. Allows the user to touch hardware to instruct the computer to perform specialized tasks
j. Handheld input device that is rolled across the desktop to move the cursor on the screen
k. Specialized input device often used for mapmaking
l. Input device used to read the data stored in the form of magnetic bars into a computer

m. Sophisticated electromechanical component designed to create special standardized electronic codes when a key is pressed
n. This appears on the video display to mark where the next character or space will be positioned after it is typed in.
o. Safeguards used to ensure that data has been accurately input to the computer system
p. Technology used by banks to keep track of data stored on the large volumes of checks that are input daily
q. Terminal that typically includes desk-management, communications, and data processing capabilities

MULTIPLE CHOICE

1. Which of the following is considered a direct-entry input device?
   a. optical scanner
   b. mouse
   c. light pen
   d. digitizer
   e. all the above
2. Which of the following types of input media is used much less now than in the 1960s?
   a. hard disk
   b. punched cards
   c. magnetic tape
   d. floppy diskette
   e. optical disk
3. Which of the following is required when more than one person uses a central computer at the same time?
   a. terminals
   b. light pen
   c. digitizer
   d. mouse
   e. scanner
4. Which of the following typically uses a keyboard for input?
   a. desktop terminal
   b. point-of-sale terminal
   c. financial transaction terminal
   d. executive workstation
   e. all the above
5. Which of the following types of terminals is entirely dependent for all its capabilities on the computer system to which it is connected?
   a. smart terminal
   b. dumb terminal
   c. microcomputer
   d. intelligent terminal
   e. executive workstation
6. Bar code readers are valuable as data entry devices because:
   a. Price and product inventory numbers do not need to be keyed in.
   b. Many keying errors are eliminated.

c. Sales data and inventory status computer files are kept current.
d. A complete history can be built and stored for each bar coded item.
e. all the above

7. Which of the following is used only for data entry and storage, and never for processing?
   a. mouse
   b. dumb terminal
   c. microcomputer
   d. dedicated data entry system
   e. smart terminal
8. Which of the following are often used to ensure that data has been accurately input to the computer?
   a. keyboards
   b. light pens
   c. digitizers
   d. input controls
   e. scanners
9. Which of the following is not a direct-entry input device?
   a. keyboard
   b. light pen
   c. digitizer
   d. optical scanner
   e. voice recognition system
10. Which of the following would you most likely use at home as well as in the office connected to a central computer?
    a. dumb terminal
    b. point-of-sale terminal
    c. financial transaction terminal
    d. microcomputer
    e. mainframe computer

SHORT ANSWER

1. What is the difference between a dumb terminal and an intelligent terminal?
2. What is the function of a dedicated data entry system?
3. What procedures might be carried out by a company to ensure data has been input accurately?
4. What kind of input device is necessary to input bar code information to the computer?
5. What are some of the current limitations of voice input technology?
6. Describe three direct-entry input devices that are being used today.
7. Describe the different types of keys on a standard microcomputer keyboard and their functions.
8. What is the purpose of a key-to-disk system?
9. What are portable terminals? Why do many business users find it necessary to use them?
10. What capabilities do executive, or integrated, workstations typically have?

PROJECTS

1. During the next week, make a list of all the input devices you notice — in stores, on campus, at the bank, in the library, on the job, at the doctor's, and so on. At the end of the week, report on the devices you have listed and name some of the advantages you think are associated with each device.
2. Using current computer publications such as *Speech Technology*, research voice recognition input systems. Who is using them? For example, manufacturing? Government? Advertising? Travel industry? In what types of computers? Is the required hardware expensive? Do you think such systems will become very common in the near future?
3. Interview the manager of a store that uses point-of-sale terminals. Who manufactures the hardware? How expensive is it? What type of computer is connected to a series of POS terminals? Have the employees had any trouble using the terminals? What information about users' needs did the manager collect to help set up the current system in the store?

Chapter 4

Storage Hardware

A great deal of business has to do with keeping score, with record-keeping. Indeed, very few businesses can operate without keeping a running account of daily transactions: who owes what to whom, who collected what, when something is scheduled to happen, and so on. We have already described the fundamentals of the computer-based information system and how data can be converted into computer-usable form. Now let us consider how this computerized data is stored and retrieved.

Preview

When you have completed this chapter, you will be able to:

- Describe the difference between primary and secondary storage and how data is represented in each.
- Explain what is meant by the data hierarchy.
- List three data storage and retrieval methods.
- List and describe the storage devices used most often with microcomputers.
- List and describe the storage devices used most often with minicomputers and mainframes.

The User Perspective

If a business cannot store data and information, it cannot work—computerized or not. In a noncomputerized office, data is stored temporarily in in-boxes and out-boxes and semipermanently in file cabinets and on microfilm. In a computerized information processing environment, data is stored in a form that is directly usable by the computer for processing—that is, in computer-usable form (Figure 4.1). Storage can be temporary, such as in the transaction file, or semipermanent, as in the master file.

As you can imagine, the cost of managing huge amounts of paper documents and their storage areas can be overwhelming, both in a monetary sense and in a personnel management sense. Indeed, this cost is often the main reason for a

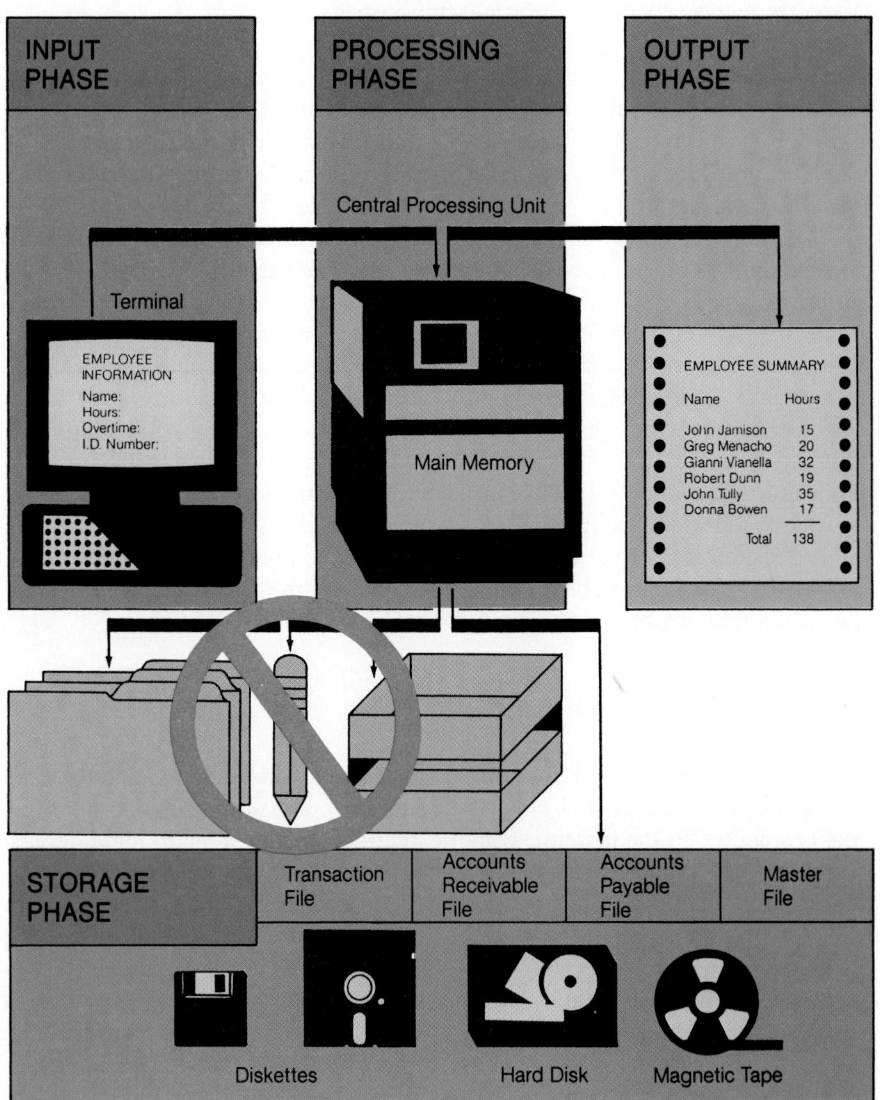

FIGURE 4.1

Out with the old. The storage phase in the computer-based information system frees people from the management of huge numbers of paper documents and their storage areas.

business to switch to a computer-based information system. Computer-based storage is:

- *Economical.* It takes up far less space than paper documents.
- *Secure.* With the use of storage controls, such as the use of passwords that must be entered into the computer system to gain access to the system's data, data is usually safe from unauthorized users, and with the use of backup systems that duplicate data for storage in a second location, data is also safe from natural and people-made disasters.
- *Almost unlimited.* There is virtually no limit to the amount of data that can be stored off-line.
- *More quickly available.* Data stored in a computer-based system is more quickly accessed than data stored in a manual system.

WHY IS STORAGE AN IMPORTANT CONCEPT?

Not understanding the concept of computer storage is like not understanding the concept of a car's gasoline tank. Without using a gasoline tank, you won't be able to get your car to go very far because, of course, without the tank, you can't use gasoline. Similarly, if you don't use a storage device with your computer, you won't have the capability to store the data that will make your computer useful.

In general, data is stored in a computer system for three principal reasons. First, current input data needs to be held for processing. For instance, the sales order data for boogie boards sold today at Sporting Life is input and stored temporarily in a transaction file until needed to produce invoices. Second, some types of data are stored on a relatively permanent basis and retrieved as required during processing. For example, to produce a customer invoice, you need the following data from the customer file: customer's name, address, billing instructions, and terms. Third, data is stored to be periodically updated. In our case, after the invoices have been produced, the accounts receivable file (reflecting what customers owe) needs to be updated to reflect the latest boogie board purchases. In addition to all this data, the computer software instructions must be stored in a computer-usable form because a copy of the software must be read into main memory from a storage device before data processing can begin.

WHAT'S IN STORE FOR YOU?

As you rise in the organizational world, you will very likely be required to write reports for your supervisor or manager. Picture yourself sitting down in front of a microcomputer for the first time with the intent of creating a report for your boss. Before you can begin, you must determine where the software that you will use to write the report is stored. Once you have written your report, you will need to save a copy of it on a storage device (particularly if you don't finish it in a single sitting). To do these things, you have to know about storage. Also, if you are going to create a very large report, the capacity of your storage medium and device may be a consideration. For example, depending on your particular computer system and the storage devices connected to it, a 100-page document may not fit on one diskette. How, then, do you write your report?

Also, to know what kind of computer system to request to buy, you need to be familiar with the differences in speed, cost, and capacity of various types of storage devices.

STORAGE FUNDAMENTALS

You know that storage hardware provides the capability to store data and program instructions — either temporarily or permanently — for quick retrieval and use during computer processing. You also know that the term *media* means the materials on which data can be recorded (magnetic media are the most popular). But to fully appreciate the storage capabilities available in computer systems, you must understand a number of storage fundamentals.

PRIMARY AND SECONDARY STORAGE

The term **primary storage** refers to the main memory of a computer, where both data and instructions are held for immediate access and use by the computer's central processing unit. Although the technology is changing, most primary storage today is considered a **volatile** form of storage, meaning that the data and instructions are lost when the computer is turned off. **Secondary storage** (or *auxiliary storage*) is any storage device designed to retain data and instructions (programs) in a more permanent form. Secondary storage is **nonvolatile,** meaning that the data and instructions remain intact when the computer is turned off.

The easiest way to differentiate between primary and secondary storage is to consider the reason data is placed in them. Data is placed in primary storage only when it is needed for immediate processing. Data in secondary storage remains there until overwritten with new data or deleted; it is accessed when needed. In very general terms, a secondary storage device can be thought of as a file cabinet. We store data there until we need it. Then we open the drawer, grab the appropriate folder (file), and place it on the top of our desk (primary storage, or main memory), where we work on it — perhaps writing a few things in it or throwing away a few papers. When we are finished with the file, we take it off the desktop (out of primary storage) and return it to the cabinet (secondary storage).

DATA REPRESENTATION: BINARY CODE

When you begin to write a report, you have quite a collection of symbols to choose from: the letters A – Z, both upper- and lowercase; the numbers 0 – 9; and numerous punctuation and other special symbols, such as ?, $, and %. People understand what these characters mean; computers cannot. Computers deal with data converted into the simplest form that can be processed magnetically or electronically — that is, binary form. The term *binary* is used to refer to two distinct states — on or off, yes or no, present or absent, 1 or 0. (The Latin prefix *bi-* means "two.") For example, a light switch can be either on or off, so it can be viewed as a binary device. When data is stored on magnetic tape or disk, it appears as the presence or absence — "on" or "off" — of magnetic spots.

To store and process data in binary form, a way of representing characters, numbers, and other symbols had to be developed. In other words, *coding schemes* had to be devised as standardized methods of encoding data for use in computer storage and processing.

A scheme for encoding data using a series of binary digits is called a **binary code.** A **binary digit (bit)** is either the character 1 (on) or the character 0 (off). It represents one of two distinct states—magnetically, electrically, or optically. You can think of a bit as a light switch. One switch—one bit—can be either on or off. However, as shown in Figure 4.2, when you have two light switches operating together, you can now set them in four different combinations: on-on, on-off, off-on, and off-off. As you can see, the number of elements of data that a series of light switches—bits—can represent is equal to the number 2 (the number of states, on or off) raised to the power of the number of light switches. In other words, if you have two states and four switches, you have 2 to the power of 4 (2^4), or 16, combinations (elements of data). It usually takes 8 bits—known as one **byte**—to form a character.

Two people contributed greatly to the coding scheme used to record and process data in computer-usable form: Herman Hollerith (1860–1929) and Samuel F. B. Morse (1791–1872). Herman Hollerith, of U.S. Census fame, developed a binary coding scheme for representing data on paper cards through patterns of punched holes. Morse is responsible for the development of the telegraph, one of

FIGURE 4.2

Every little bit counts. A bit (*b*inary dig*it*) is the smallest possible computer signal or impulse; it is used in combination with other signals or impulses to represent data (a character); it is a "1" or a "0"—that is, on or off. Different combinations of 0s and 1s are electronically translated into computerized codes.

A bit is the smallest possible unit of data; it is 1 or 0 — that is, on or off:

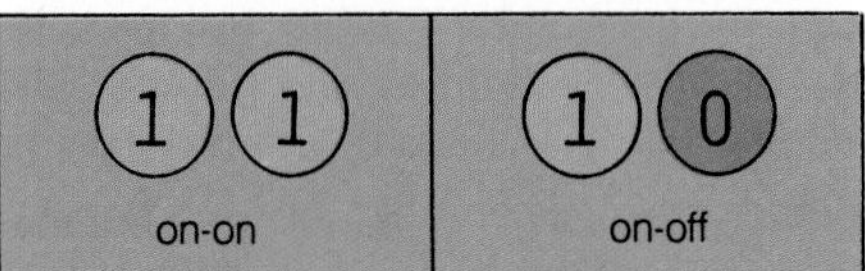

2 bits (2^2) can have four possible combinations:

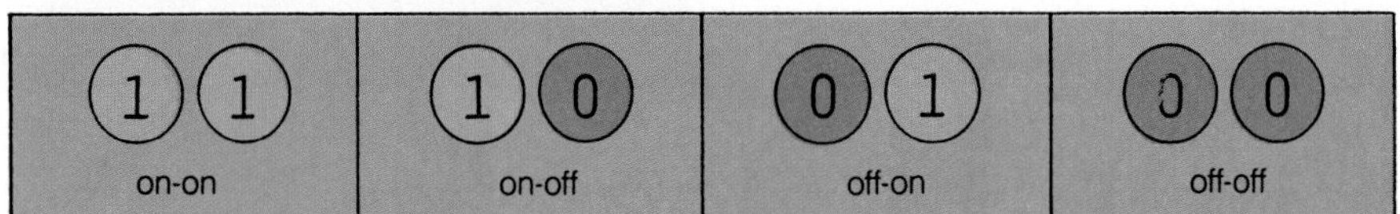

3 bits (2^3) can have 8 possible combinations:

4 bits (2^4) yield 16 possible combinations:

8 bits (2^8) yield 256 possible combinations, enough to represent all the letters of the alphabet, numbers 0–9, and special symbols.

the earliest forms of electronic data communication. His dream was to break down the information to be communicated into a coding scheme based on electrical pulses. The code for each letter and number was formed by a combination of long and short electrical pulses. A short pulse was a "dot" and a long pulse was a "dash" (Figure 4.3).

The combined contributions of Morse and Hollerith (and others) laid the foundation for the storage and processing of data in magnetic and electrical form. Several coding schemes for the computer have been adopted that rely on binary representation. Two commonly used codes are ASCII (pronounced "as-key") and EBCDIC (pronounced "eb-see-dick") (Figure 4.4). Each character's combination of bits is unique.

ASCII

The acronym **ASCII** stands for the **American Standard Code for Information Interchange,** which is widely used to represent characters in microcomputers and many minicomputers. Because microcomputers operate on data in 8-bit groups, ASCII uses 8 bits to represent a character. For example, the character A in ASCII is 01000001.

EBCDIC

The acronym **EBCDIC** refers to **Extended Binary Coded Decimal Interchange Code,** which is the most popular code used for IBM and IBM-compatible mainframe computers. In EBCDIC, A is 11000001.

As you can see in Figure 4.4, characters are coded differently in ASCII and EBCDIC. Because of these differences, transferring data between computers using different coding schemes requires special hardware and software.

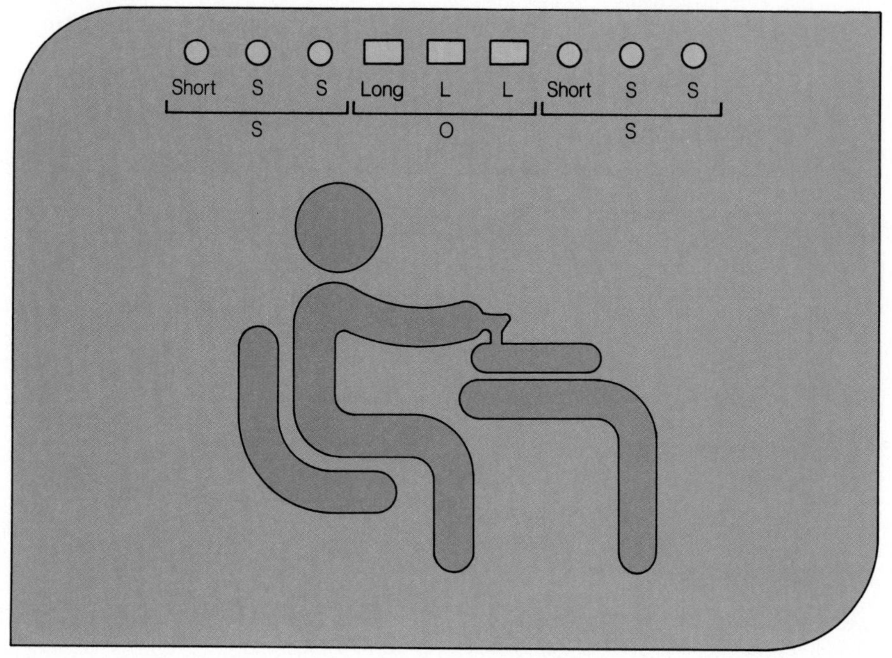

FIGURE 4.3

An early binary code. Samuel F. B. Morse, developer of the Morse code, showed that data elements (characters) could be represented by using two "states"—long and short, otherwise known as dash and dot.

PARITY BITS

The term *computer error* is often used when a mistake is caused by a person—inputting data incorrectly, for example. However, errors can be caused by other factors, such as dust, electrical disturbance, weather conditions, and improper handling of equipment. When such an error occurs, the computer may not be able to tell you exactly what and where it is, but it *can* tell you that there is an error. How does it do this? By using **parity bits,** or **check bits.** A parity bit is an extra (ninth) bit attached to the end of the byte. If you add the number of 1 bits in a byte, you will have either an odd number of ls or an even number of ls (for example, ASCII A has two ls, so it is even). Computers can be designed to use either an *odd-parity*

FIGURE 4.4

(a) ASCII and EBCDIC. This chart shows some of the printed character codes according to the two most commonly used binary coding schemes for data representation. (b) A ninth bit—the parity bit—is added to the character as part of an error-checking scheme.

Character	ASCII-8	EBCDIC	Character	ASCII-8	EBCDIC
A	0100 0001	1100 0001	N	0100 1110	1101 0101
B	0100 0010	1100 0010	O	0100 1111	1101 0110
C	0100 0011	1100 0011	P	0101 0000	1101 0111
D	0100 0100	1100 0100	Q	0101 0001	1101 1000
E	0100 0101	1100 0101	R	0101 0010	1101 1001
F	0100 0110	1100 0110	S	0101 0011	1110 0010
G	0100 0111	1100 0111	T	0101 0100	1110 0011
H	0100 1000	1100 1000	U	0101 0101	1110 0100
I	0100 1001	1100 1001	V	0101 0110	1110 0101
J	0100 1010	1101 0001	W	0101 0111	1110 0110
K	0100 1011	1101 0010	X	0101 1000	1110 0111
L	0100 1100	1101 0011	Y	0101 1001	1110 1000
M	0100 1101	1101 0100	Z	0101 1010	1110 1001
0	0011 0000	1111 0000	5	0011 0101	1111 0101
1	0011 0001	1111 0001	6	0011 0110	1111 0110
2	0011 0010	1111 0010	7	0011 0111	1111 0111
3	0011 0011	1111 0011	8	0011 1000	1111 1000
4	0011 0100	1111 0100	9	0011 1001	1111 1001
!	0010 0001	0101 1010	;	0011 1011	0101 1110

(a)

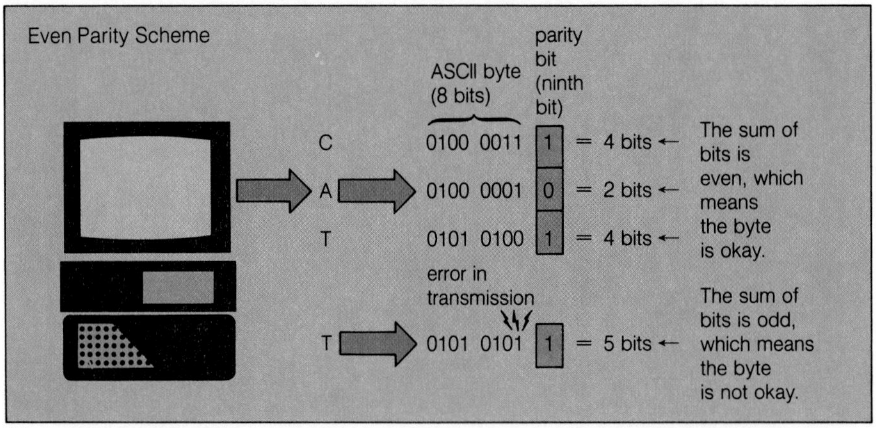

(b)

scheme or an *even-parity scheme*. In an odd-parity scheme, the ninth bit, 0 or 1, is added to make the total number of ls equal an odd number. If any byte turns up with an even number of ls in an odd-parity scheme, the computer signals an error message on the screen. Similarly, if a byte turns up with an odd number of ls in an even-parity scheme, an error message appears.

As a user, you won't have to determine whether to use an odd- or even-parity scheme. The computer manufacturer determines this, and the system software automatically checks the parity scheme. However, you will have to learn what to do when your computer signals an error. If your computer signals an error in the parity scheme, a message such as "Parity Error" will appear on the screen. If this happens to you, have your computer serviced to determine what is causing the problem.

FILES AND DATA HIERARCHY

No matter what size or type of computer you work with, you will be working with files. But before we can put data files in their proper perspective, we need to examine levels of data, known as the **data storage hierarchy**. If you look at Figure 4.5, at the top of the data hierarchy you will see the term *file*. A **file** is made up of a group of related records. A **record** is defined as a collection of related fields, and a **field** is defined as a collection of related characters, or bytes, of data. And, finally, a byte, or character, of data, as you learned in the last section, is made up of 8 bits.

To illustrate this concept, let's look at the Sporting Life inventory file (Figure 4.6). This particular inventory *file* is made up of a group of *records*, one record for each item in inventory, such as snorkels. Each record contains the same number of *fields* such as: (1) product number, (2) product description, (3) unit price, and (4)

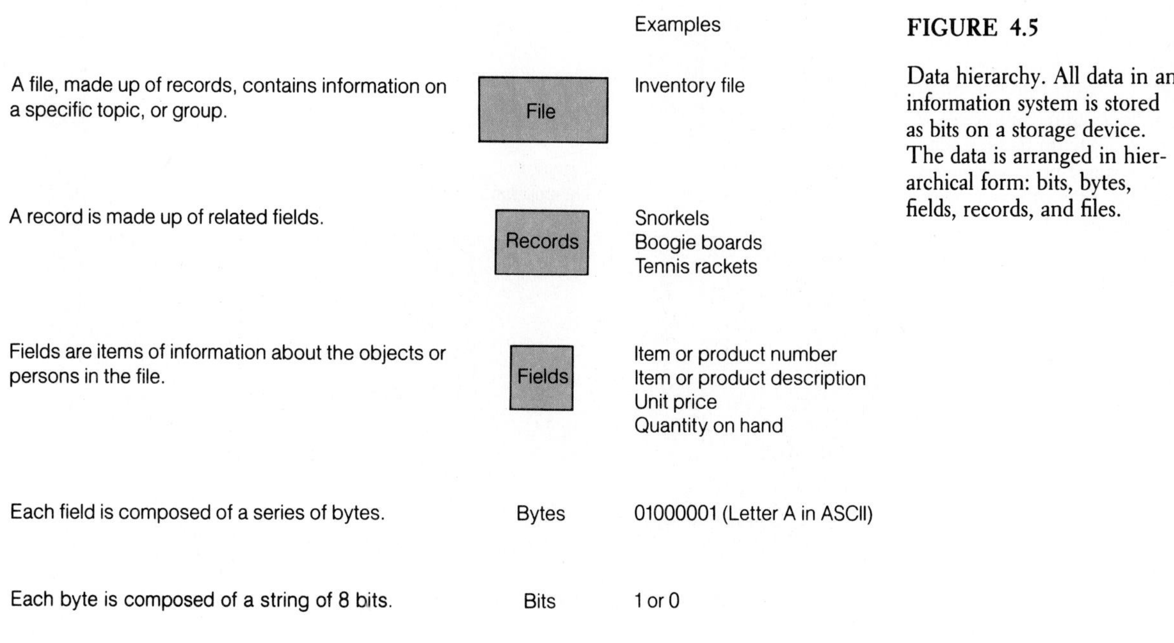
Examples
A file, made up of records, contains information on a specific topic, or group.
File
Inventory file
A record is made up of related fields.
Records
Snorkels
Boogie boards
Tennis rackets
Fields are items of information about the objects or persons in the file.
Fields
Item or product number
Item or product description
Unit price
Quantity on hand
Each field is composed of a series of bytes.
Bytes
01000001 (Letter A in ASCII)
Each byte is composed of a string of 8 bits.
Bits
1 or 0

FIGURE 4.5

Data hierarchy. All data in an information system is stored as bits on a storage device. The data is arranged in hierarchical form: bits, bytes, fields, records, and files.

quantity on hand. Each field contains a number of *characters*, such as the letter A in the product number. In turn, each character is made up of 8 bits, at the low end of the data hierarchy.

TYPES OF FILES

Up to this point, we've described various types of files in general terms, such as master files (used to permanently store data for access and updating) and transaction files (used to temporarily hold data for processing). Now that we've described how data is represented on a storage medium (with bits and bytes) and how the data hierarchy is structured, we can get a "bit" more detailed in our description of what a file is, what it does, and where it's kept.

Files generally fall into two categories: (1) files containing data (often referred to generically as *data files*) and (2) files containing software instructions (often referred to generically as ***program files***). Data files, in turn, tend to be categorized according to how they are used—as a (1) transaction file, (2) master file, (3) report file, (4) output file, (5) history file, or (6) backup file (Figure 4.7). The amount of time that data needs to be stored and the purpose of storing the data vary substantially, depending on the processing objectives. These objectives determine what type of file you'll be storing data in.

You'll recall that some data is input into computer-usable form and then retained only until it is time to process. This type of data is referred to as *transaction data*, and it is stored in an input **transaction file.**

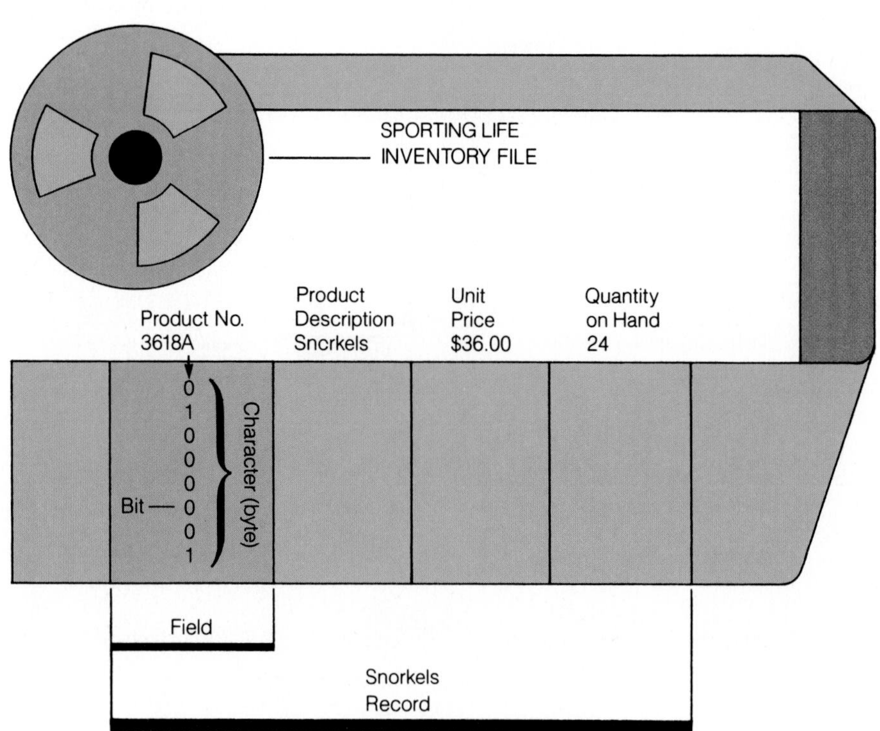

FIGURE 4.6

Example of data hierarchy at Sporting Life. The inventory file contains product records, such as the record for snorkels. Each record contains fields: product number, product description, unit price, and quantity on hand. Each field is made up of characters, or bytes, each of which comprises 8 bits.

Some data is stored in computer-usable form for lengthy periods of time, after which it is used for retrieval and is updated during processing. A file containing this type of data is referred to as a **master file.**

In large computer systems, the volume of reports to be produced is so immense that a special, smaller computer system is set up just to control and coordinate the printing of reports. This is often true of major utility companies that produce millions of customer bills and statements each month. To make this process easier, the data necessary to produce the reports is captured in a **report file,** which is then transferred to the special computer system for printing after it has been processed in the main computer.

Many computer software applications are designed to produce data as output to be used by another program or application at a later time. (An application is usually a group of related programs, such as a payroll application consisting of 14 programs.) A file created for this purpose is referred to as an **output file** at the time it is produced. However, it becomes an *input transaction file* when it is read into another program for processing.

Many organizations find it useful to produce reports that require analysis of data on past company operations. A file created to collect data for long-term reporting purposes is referred to as a **history file.**

Backup files are copies of other types of files that are made to ensure that data and programs will not be lost if the original files are damaged or destroyed. (*Users*

Types of files. How the file is used determines what type of file it is. **FIGURE 4.7**

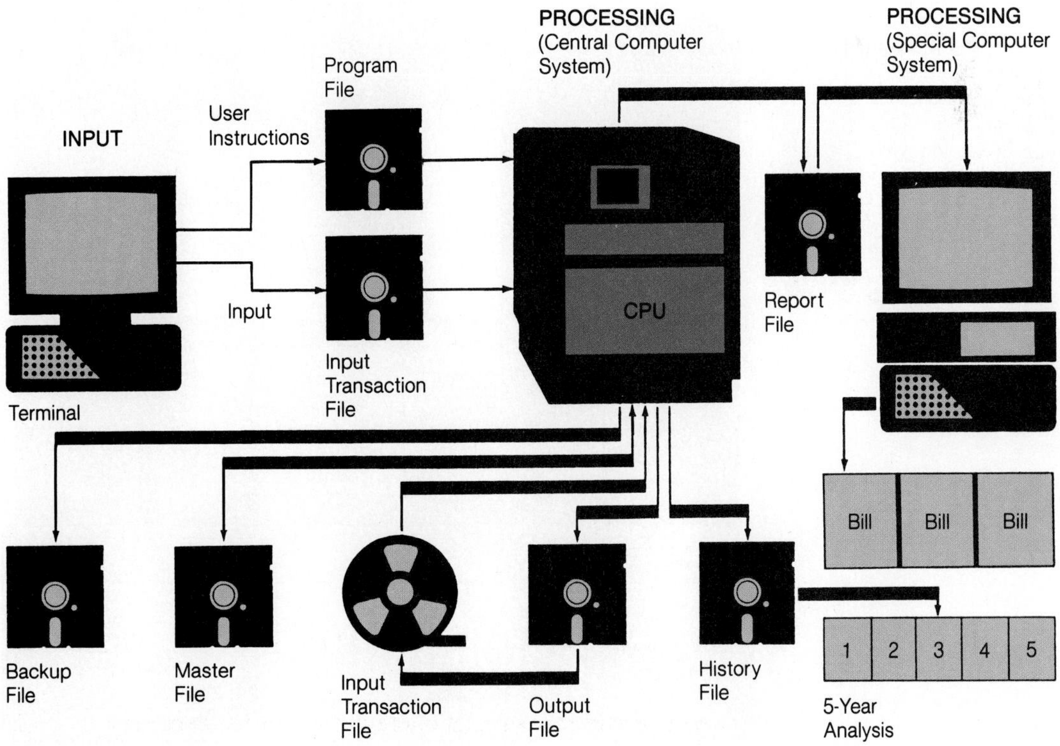

should always remember to back up their files!) Occasionally data is extracted from backup files to use in historical files.

Program files are simply instructions stored on disk or tape. They are usually controlled by the computer operations group and maintained in libraries.

HOW IS DATA STORED?

To store data for later use you need two things: a storage *medium* and a storage *device*. The storage device records the data onto the medium, where the data is held until needed. The process of recording data onto media, which is coordinated by software, involves four basic steps (Figure 4.8):

1. After input, the data to be recorded by a storage device temporarily resides, in the form of binary code, in main memory.

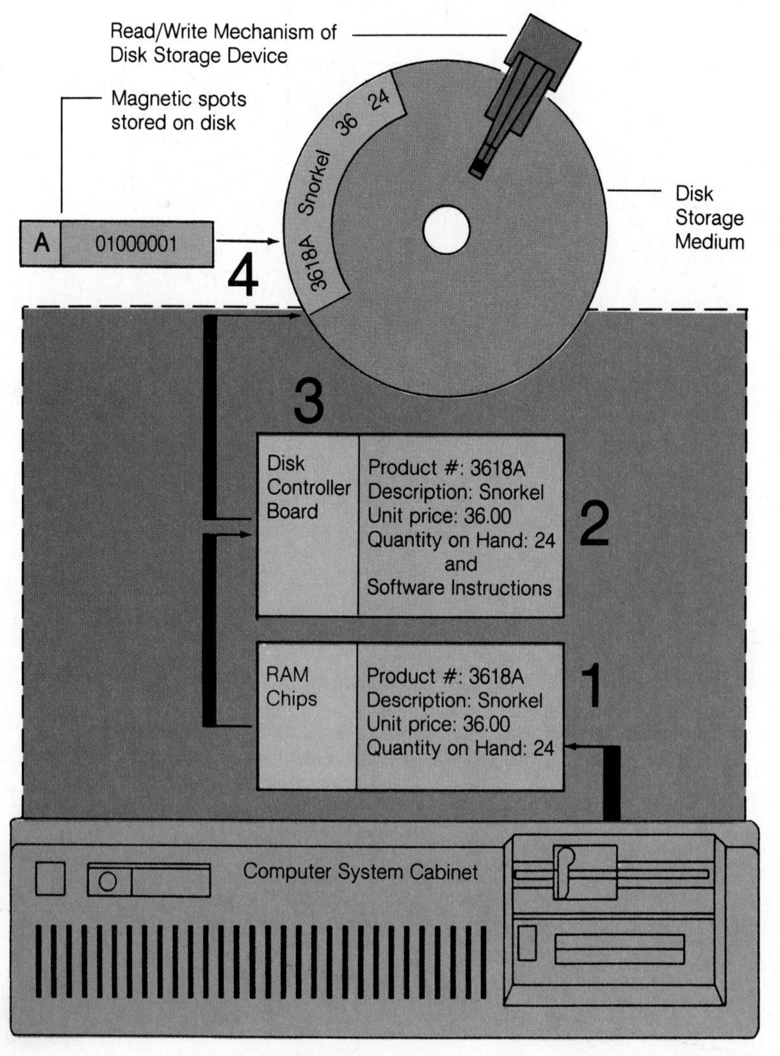

FIGURE 4.8

For the record. (1) Data enters main memory (RAM) from an external device, such as a keyboard. (2) Software instructions determine where the data is to be recorded on the disk. (3) The data goes to the disk controller board. (4) From here it flows to the read/write head in the disk storage device and is recorded on the storage medium. (Of course, from input on, data is stored in binary form. This illustration shows you what the codes would mean.)

2. Software instructions determine where the data is to be recorded on the storage medium.
3. The controller board for the storage device positions the recording mechanism over the appropriate location on the storage medium. [For storage on disk, this mechanism is referred to in most cases as a **read/write head** because it can both "read" (accept) magnetic spots and convert them to electrical impulses and "write" (enter) the spots on the disk; it can also erase the spots.]
4. The recording mechanism is activated and converts electrical impulses to magnetic spots placed on the surface of the medium as required to record the data according to the coding scheme being used (ASCII, for example).

DATA STORAGE AND RETRIEVAL METHODS

Most of us read a novel from the first page to the end of the book in sequence because we have an interest in following the story in the order that the author intended. However, in a catalog you may wish to locate the information for just a single item. It would take much more time to locate the page you desired if you started at the beginning and read all the pages instead of looking up the item in the index. The same kind of principle applies to the storage and retrieval of data in computer-usable form.

Your old filing system at Sporting Life can be used as a good example of the basic storage and retrieval concepts. In most cases, when a file cabinet is first organized, the file folders are placed in each drawer in a certain order. For a customer file, the folders are placed into drawers in sequential order by customer number or customer name. If new customers are added later, their folders are inserted into the correct location between the existing folders. When you need to retrieve data from the file cabinet, the way you get it depends on what needs to be done. For example, if you are going to prepare a report on customer status, you will probably review each folder in order. However, if a specific customer calls and asks about the status of one invoice, you will go to the file cabinet and locate and remove that one customer's folder.

In the computerized environment, a file cabinet is usually thought of as a database (a collection of interrelated files stored together); a file drawer is thought of as a file (master file, transaction file, history file, and so forth); and a folder is thought of as a record. The three principal methods of storing and retrieving the data are based on three types of file organization:

1. Sequential—meaning that records are stored and retrieved in sequential order.
2. Direct, or relative (also called *random*)—meaning that records are not stored or retrieved in any special order.
3. Indexed—a combination of the preceding two types, whereby records are stored in sequential order but with an index that allows both sequential and direct retrieval.

Each of these three approaches to computerized data storage and retrieval is suited to different applications and processing requirements. For most users, the selection of a storage method has been left up to the technical professionals involved in developing the software. However, if you find yourself involved in a project where the requirements for new software are being specified, be sure you tell the information system specialists how you need to store and retrieve data. Users' processing requirements should be used as the basis for selecting the file storage and retrieval method.

SINGLE FILE: SEQUENTIAL FILE ORGANIZATION

Sequential file organization (Figure 4.9) is ideal for situations in which most of the records in a file need to be accessed for processing—such as producing payroll (because everyone gets a check) or preparing a comprehensive inventory report by part number. In this approach, records are recorded and stored sequentially, one after the other, in ascending or descending order. Records are retrieved in the sequence in which they were recorded on the storage media. They must be accessed (retrieved) one after the other; the user cannot jump around among records.

The evolution of sequential storage and retrieval was based, at least in part, on the characteristics and limitations of the early storage media and devices. Punched

FIGURE 4.9

Sequential file organization. Records are recorded in sequence and accessed one at a time, in the order in which they were recorded. As you can see from this figure, if an airline reservations and flight information system used sequential storage on magnetic tape, it would not be able to get the information it needs very quickly, because the computer would have to read through all the records on the tape prior to the record with the needed information. Because of this disadvantage, such a system would instead use direct access on magnetic disk storage.

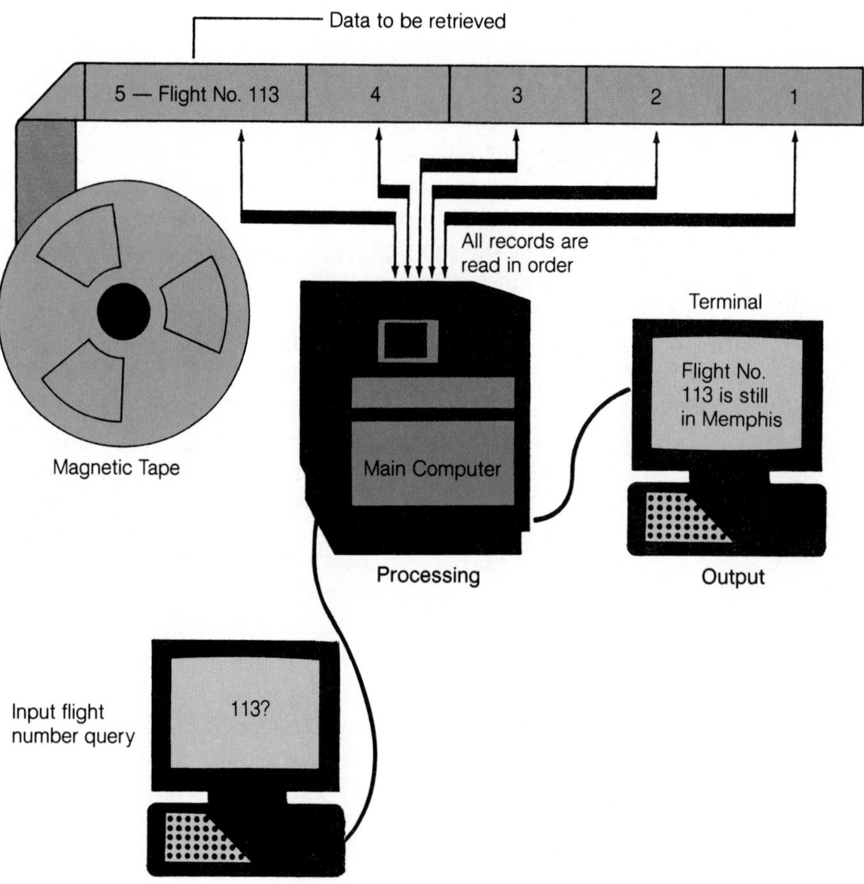

cards were used as one of the earliest types of secondary storage media. The cards were always handled in sequential order as they were read by the card reader. If the 43rd card had the data you wanted, all the preceding cards had to be read first before you could get it. To develop a mechanical device that could selectively read or extract a single card from the middle of the stack proved to be too cumbersome.

The use of new storage media such as magnetic tape, disks, and diskettes has improved the situation. However, although they can all support sequential storage and retrieval of data, they can't all be used for direct and indexed sequential storage and retrieval of data (for example, magnetic tape can be used only for sequential storage and retrieval).

ANY ORDER: DIRECT (RANDOM) OR RELATIVE FILE ORGANIZATION

Data in a **direct file** or a relative file is recorded and stored according to its disk address or to its relative position within the file. The data is retrieved by the **direct access storage and retrieval** method—also called *random access*. This data retrieval method is best suited to situations in which only a few records in a file need to be accessed in no particular sequence (Figure 4.10). Airline reservations systems rely heavily on this method, which uses on-line input/output devices. Because there is no predictable pattern in which customers call to inquire about the status of the flights, the individual records containing the status of the flights need to be stored in a fashion whereby they can be directly retrieved in any order—meaning that all the records in front of the record containing status data on your Flight No. 113 from Memphis to Cincinnati do not have to be read first.

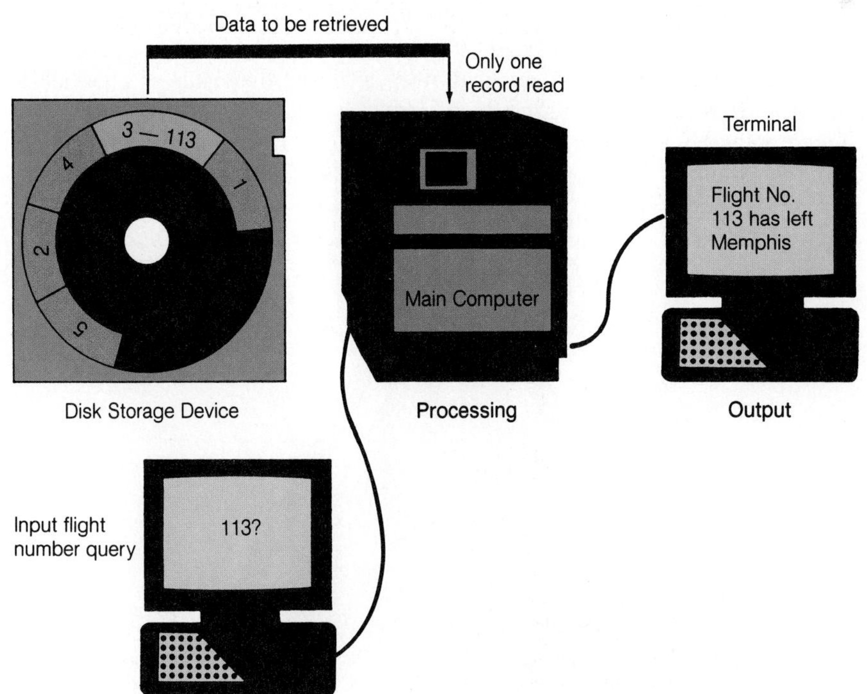

FIGURE 4.10

Direct, or relative, file organization. Records are recorded, stored, and retrieved in any order. The computer performs a mathematical operation (hashing) on each record's key field to determine where to place that record on the storage medium. A key field contains a unique number or unique group of characters.

There are a number of ways to access records directly in no particular order. The most common approach is to use a unique element of data—called a **key field** or **key**—contained in each record as a basis for identifying the record and for determining which storage location on the disk the record should be stored in or retrieved from. To determine where to store a record so it can be retrieved directly, the computer uses a formula and performs a mathematical calculation—called *hashing*—on the key field value. (Hashing is a type of **algorithm,** meaning a problem-solving rule or formula.) This computer operation translates the record's key field directly into an address or a relative location. Obviously, no two key fields should be given the same address on the disk; hashing prevents this by using a mathematical formula that (almost always) produces a unique number.

The direct access storage and retrieval method is ideal for applications such as an airline reservations system or the computerized telephone information service, where records need to be retrieved only one at a time and there is no fixed pattern or sequence to the requests for data and records. However, this method cannot be used with magnetic tape, and it is very inefficient in situations that require accessing all records in sequential order. Because the records are not stored in any particular order, following the key sequence in order to retrieve them may involve jumping back and forth around the storage medium, which takes too much time.

In general, sequential storage and retrieval is appropriate for updating master files on a regular basis, when a relatively large amount of data is input. (Sequential storage and retrieval is often used in batch input and processing.) Direct storage and retrieval is better used for irregular updates with only a small volume of input (Figure 4.11).

INDEXED FILE ORGANIZATION

In a payroll system, all records are usually accessed in order of employee number—that is, sequentially—when payroll checks are produced. However, occasionally a clerk in the payroll department may need to check the status of a particular employee. In this case, processing the records sequentially just to access data for a single employee is impractical. To be able to access stored data in *either* a sequential *or* a direct fashion, a third storage and retrieval methodology was developed that uses

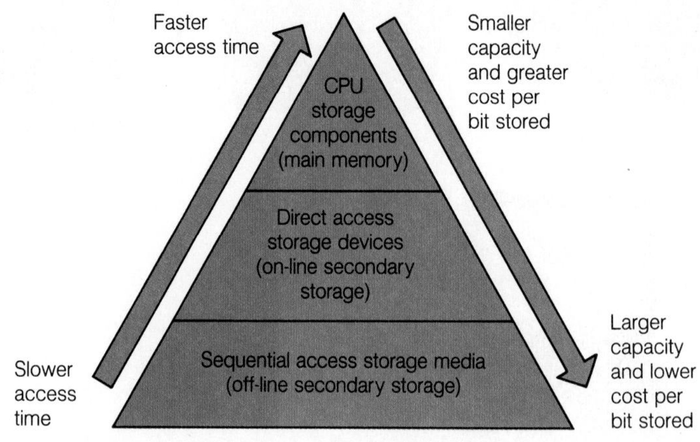

FIGURE 4.11

Storage methods: Speed and cost. CPU storage components (main memory) generally have the fastest access times, the smallest storage capacity, and the highest cost per bit stored. Secondary storage includes all direct access storage devices and sequential access storage devices.

indexed file organization (Figure 4.12). This method is used almost exclusively with direct access microcomputer storage devices to provide maximum flexibility for processing and has proven to be the most flexible for business applications.

In this approach, each file contains an index of the records stored in it. This index functions somewhat like the index at the back of a book. When you want to look something up in the book, you check the index for the item you want and locate its page number. In the case of computer file storage, the computer checks the file's index, which contains the record's address—location—on the disk. It's also possible to create more than one index for a file, which allows the file to be accessed using different key fields. For example, at least two indexes may be created for a personnel master file: an index by the primary key field (employee number) and a second index by, say, social security number. The first index could be used to provide sequential

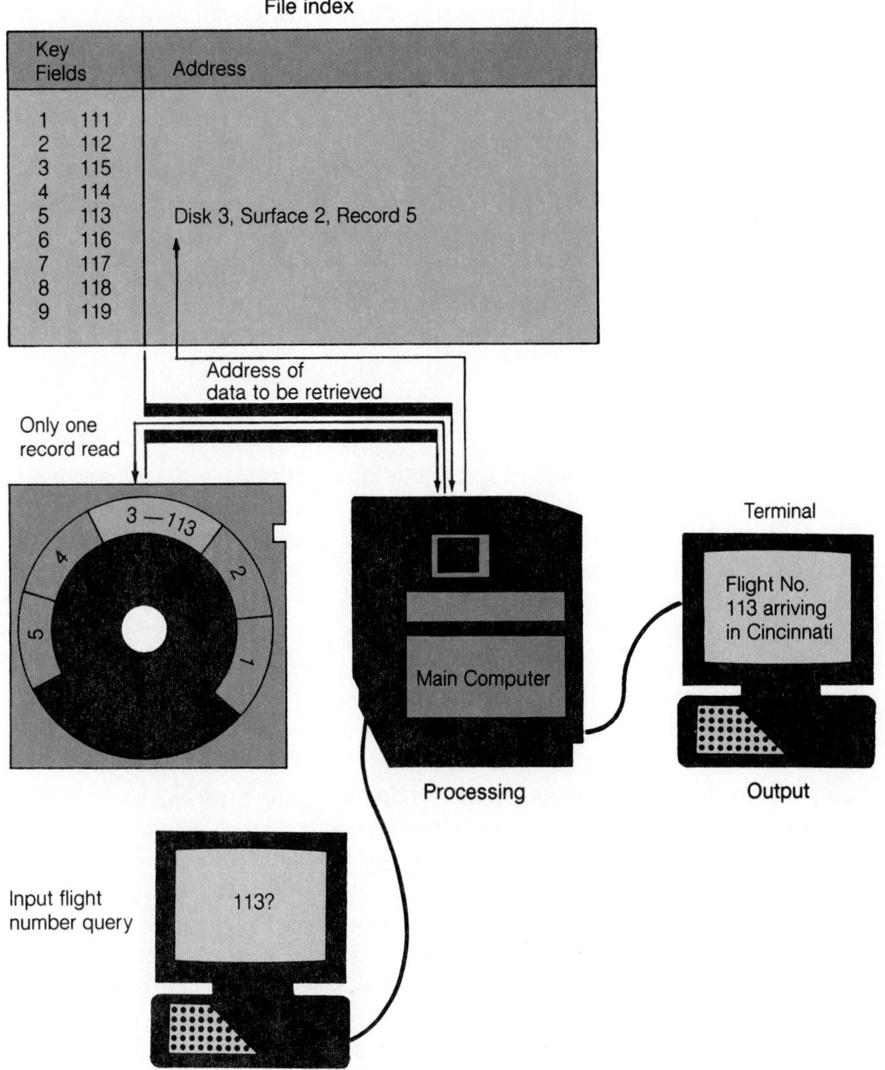

FIGURE 4.12

Indexed file organization. Records are stored sequentially but with an index that allows both sequential and direct, random access.

or direct access by employee number. The second index could be used to process the file to inquire about a specific employee by social security number.

In general, indexed file organization, which cannot be done on tape, allows efficient regularly scheduled processing of large batches of data and irregular updates with only a small amount of input. However, indexed storage and retrieval is slower than direct access, and the hardware and software needed for indexed file organization are more expensive than with sequential or direct-access organization. In addition, it makes less efficient use of storage space.

You will learn more about data and file organization in the chapter on databases (Chapter 11). Right now we want to discuss storage media and hardware in more detail.

TAPE STORAGE DEVICES

The development of magnetic tape was stimulated by the search for a faster, more convenient, and more cost-effective means than punched cards. Magnetic tape is a plastic tape (Mylar) coated with magnetizable iron oxide. The tape is ½-inch wide and is produced in a variety of lengths ranging from 200 to 3,600 feet; the latter weighs about 4 pounds and has a reel about 10 inches in diameter. A modern tape storage unit can store the equivalent of more than 2.25 million punched cards—which would weigh over 10,000 pounds and could cost over $50,000. A reel of tape typically costs less than $25. (Tape cartridges, discussed a bit later in this chapter, cost about $20.) Since tape can be carried around, it can be used to easily transport huge amounts of data.

RECORDING DATA ON MAGNETIC TAPE

Data is recorded across the width of a magnetic tape in **frames**—rows of magnetic spots; *tracks* or *channels* run the length of the tape. The computer records character codes by writing magnetic spots (1s) and leaving spaces (0s—no magnetic spots) across the frame. Among the coding schemes used on magnetic tape are ASCII and EBCDIC. EBCDIC for standard magnetic tapes involves nine tracks that run the full length of the tape (Figure 4.13). The nine positions include room for 8 character bits and 1 parity bit. The capacity, or storage density, of a magnetic tape is measured in bits per inch (bpi), or frames per inch.

Records can be recorded onto the tape one at a time or in groups referred to as **blocks.** Blocks are made up of logical records, which are defined by the user—for example, records on weightlifting products at Sporting Life. Each block is separated by a fixed length of blank tape. This section of tape is needed to compensate for the acceleration and deceleration of the tape as the individual records or blocks are positioned over or under the read/write head assembly. (You cannot stop a moving car without covering some distance slowing down; the same is true when using tape.) The blank sections are called **interrecord gaps (IRGs)** or **interblock gaps (IBGs)** (Figure 4.14). When records are blocked, space on the tape is not wasted because fewer gaps are needed. Also, records recorded in blocks can be retrieved much faster than can the same number of records individually.

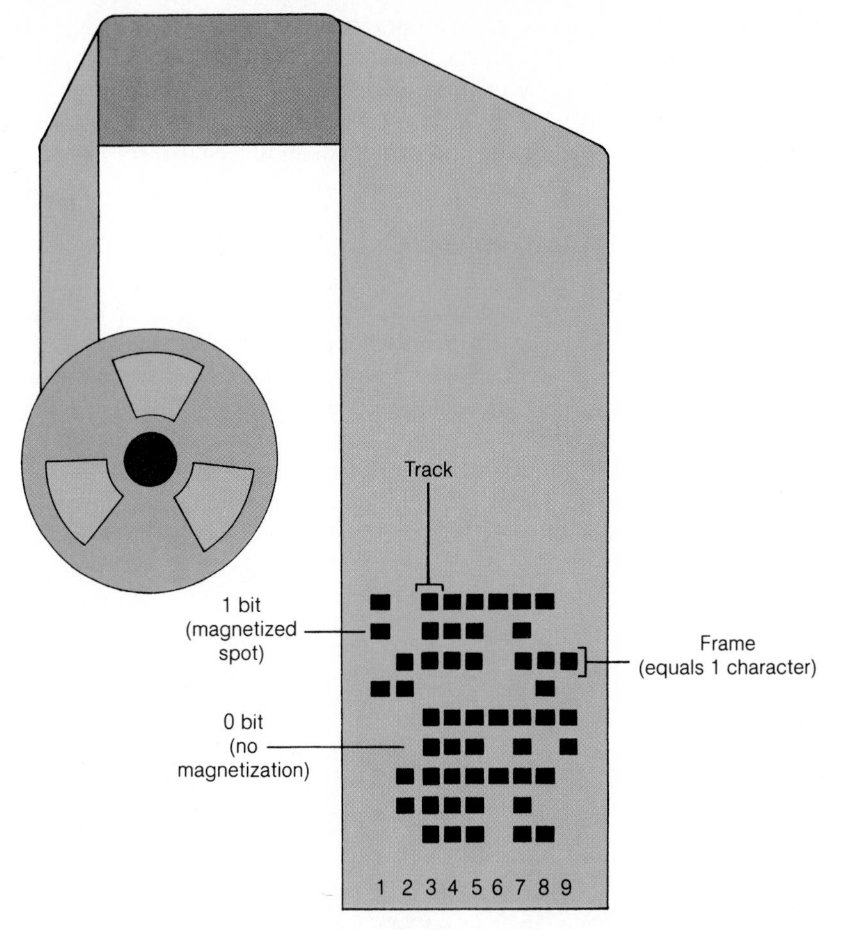

FIGURE 4.13

Tape recorder. This figure shows how characters are recorded in frames across magnetic tape using the 9-track EBCDIC code. The 9 tracks include room for 8 bits plus 1 parity bit.

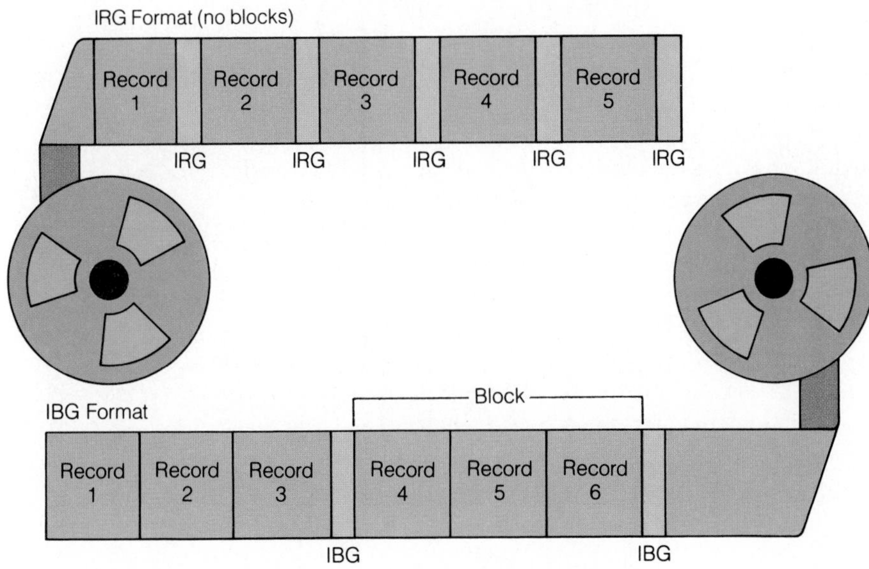

FIGURE 4.14

Communication gaps. Interrecord and interblock gaps are used on tape to compensate for varying tape speeds. The gaps allow time for the tape to accelerate or decelerate before data is recorded or retrieved. Such gaps may be as small as .3 inch in length.

As you can see, interrecord gaps and interblock gaps take up tape space, thereby decreasing the amount of space left over for actual disk storage. Because the use of magnetic disk for data storage has become more common, and tapes are now generally being used for backup of data stored on disk, "streamer" tapes have been developed that use about 1/50 of the gap space previously required. Because the streamer tape does not need to stop and start, it does not need to record large gaps.

THE TAPE DRIVE MECHANISM

Figure 4.15b shows the components of a magnetic tape storage device (Figure 4.15a). The file reel of tape is placed on the left spindle and locked in place so that it does not come loose as it spins at high speed. The tape is fed through a *drive capstan*, a small cylindrical pulley used to regulate the speed of the tape. Several feet of tape are used as slack and then the tape is run through another capstan called a *stop capstan*. Then the tape is run through the read/write head assembly and the right half of the tape mechanism, which is a mirror image of the left side. The right and left stop capstans work together to hold the tape still long enough for data to be

FIGURE 4.15

(a) Play it again, Sam. Magnetic tape storage devices are used by many large companies to provide virtually unlimited storage capacity. (b) This simplified drawing shows the workings of a magnetic tape drive.

(a)

written or read. An empty take-up tape reel is used to temporarily hold the tape after it has been read or written on. The tape moves at speeds approaching 200 inches per second. This translates into an ability to record or read data at an average speed of from 100,000 to 1,250,000 characters per second.

Magnetic Tape Processing Characteristics

Magnetic tape is ideal for applications that require only sequential access to data. Many public utilities still use magnetic tape for storing their enormous customer master files. A file with millions of customer records could easily take up close to 100 reels of magnetic tape. Because of the number of tapes to be handled, many companies hire a librarian to manage them. A special room, called a *library*, is often set aside to store the tapes, and procedures are established to control their use (Figure 4.16).

To ensure that the correct version of a tape is used for processing, an *external label* (Figure 4.17a) is placed on the tape reel and an *internal label* is recorded on

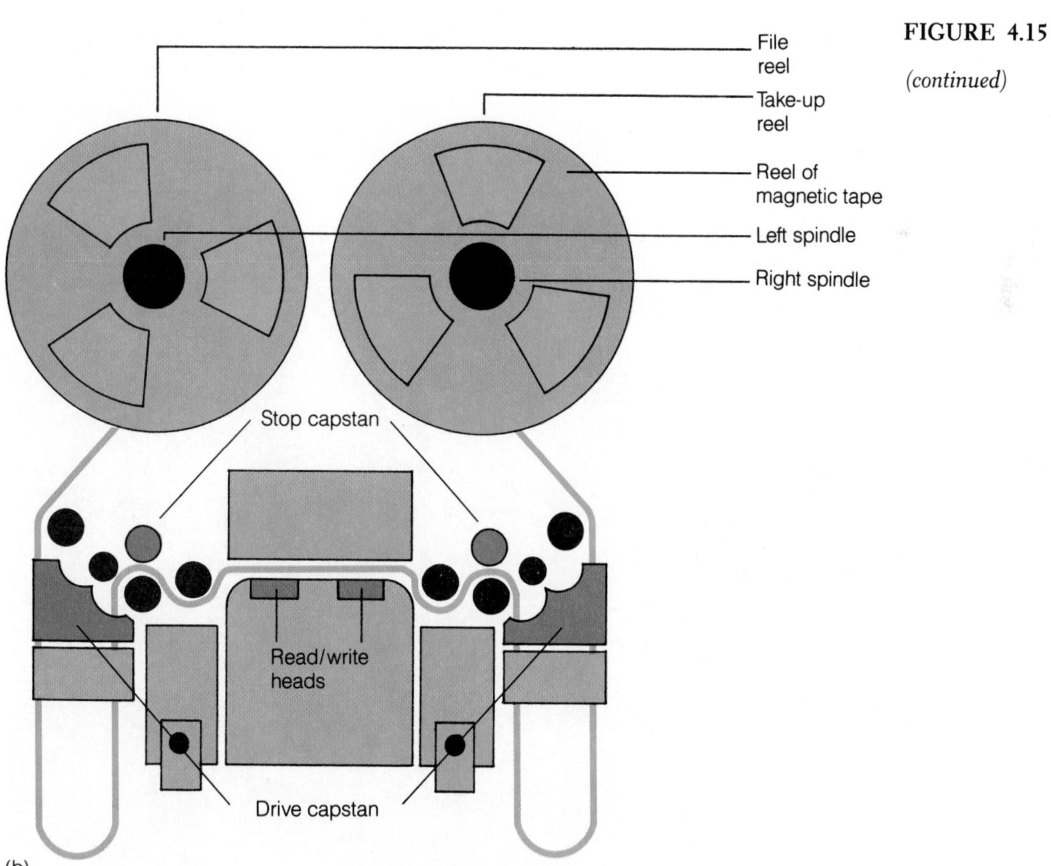

FIGURE 4.15

(continued)

the tape magnetically. The internal label is often referred to as a *header label* and is examined by a program before processing begins to ensure it is the correct tape.

Tapes are protected from being accidentally overwritten by the use of a *file protection ring*, a plastic ring inserted into the back of a tape reel (Figure 4.17b). A tape can be written on or erased only when the ring is in place, so it's the *absence* of the ring that protects the file from changes. When a new master file is created and the tape is stored in the library, the ring is immediately removed to prevent the accidental reuse of the tape.

LIMITATIONS OF MAGNETIC TAPE

Although magnetic tape provided a major improvement over punched cards in the secondary storage capabilities of computer systems, it has two major drawbacks. First, the data recorded on tape cannot be practically altered—that is, it cannot be updated or changed in place. When records need to be changed, added in sequence, or deleted, a completely new tape must be created. Second, the data is recorded on the tape sequentially and can be accessed only sequentially. These limitations make magnetic tape less attractive for applications that require an update-in-place capability and access other than sequential. As the cost of direct access storage devices (disks) dropped, magnetic tape began to lose its popularity. However, despite its limitations, magnetic tape is still used widely today in minicomputer and mainframe computer systems. It remains an ideal medium for making portable backup copies of data stored on disk to enable businesses to recover from a data center disaster.

FIGURE 4.16

In the stacks. Large organizations that use sequential storage and have high-volume data update needs often maintain extensive tape libraries.

DIRECT ACCESS STORAGE FOR MICROCOMPUTERS

The Apple II and Tandy-Radio Shack (TRS-80) Model I personal computer systems were among the first to be made available to the public (1977). These two systems—as well as many of the others that entered the marketplace shortly thereafter—initially offered only cassette-tape storage devices. These devices, which were much like a personal tape recorder, proved to be remarkably slow and awkward to use. As the microcomputer began to move from the home into the business environment, the need for fast direct access storage and retrieval became a significant issue.

This problem was solved when IBM introduced the diskette as a direct access storage medium. As a result, the microcomputer has dramatically expanded its role in information processing—and continues to do so.

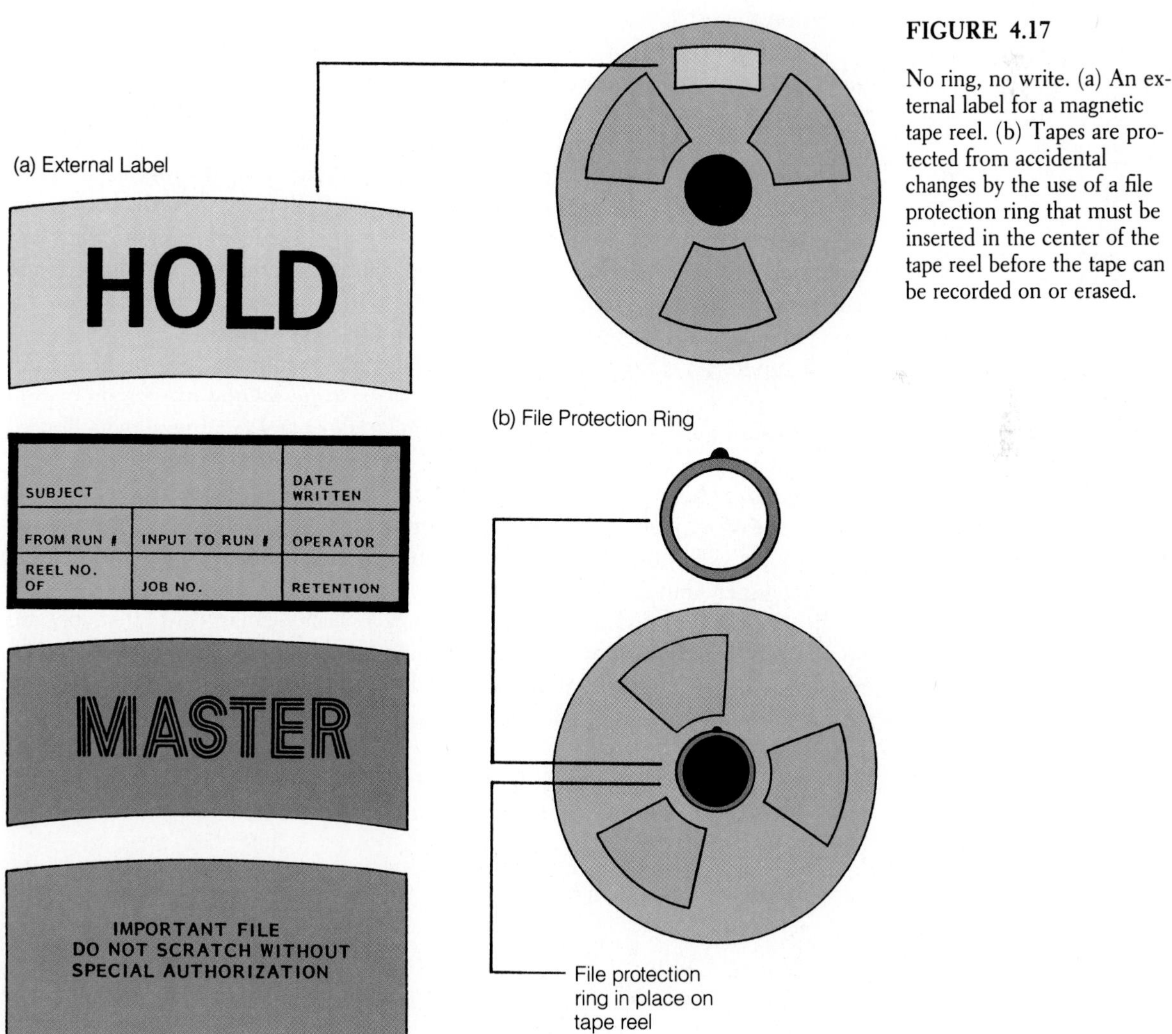

FIGURE 4.17

No ring, no write. (a) An external label for a magnetic tape reel. (b) Tapes are protected from accidental changes by the use of a file protection ring that must be inserted in the center of the tape reel before the tape can be recorded on or erased.

Computers and Careers

Health and Medicine

If medicine isn't quite like this in every locality, it probably won't be long until it is!

Every physician and hospital in town is hooked up by telephone to a medical information system, a specialized database. Doctors can admit or discharge a patient to and from the hospital without leaving their offices. They can check on how much and what kind of medication a patient has received, what kind of laboratory tests have been run, and whether the patient has been moved from one bed to another. Besides having access to patient records, physicians and other professionals concerned with the patient's health have insurance and Medicare information. When the patient leaves the hospital, the schedule of medication given on discharge will also be available to the on-line physician.

In a significant step for the future, computers are now being used to help doctors make diagnoses and keep up with rapid changes in medicine. A system called DXplain contains data on thousands of case histories and more than 2,000 diseases, including the latest on AIDS. A physician can build a clinical case description by entering patient signs, symptoms, and lab data; DXplain then presents the physician with a ranked list of diseases that should be considered possibilities. The physician can also ask the system questions, such as why a particular disease does not appear on the list.

As costs skyrocket and insurance companies switch to fixed-scale reimbursement for treatment, computerization also helps hospitals to manage their costs. Sacred Heart Hospital in Eau Claire, Wisconsin, installed a 90-terminal electronic information system and found it could save on hiring the equivalent of 50 full-time employees. It also was able to increase the speed of processing doctors' orders from 20 minutes to five. At Latter Day Saints Hospital in Salt Lake City, the computer-based system known as the Help Evaluation through Logical Processing (HELP) system can assist physicians in selecting the right medicine mix. At Moses Cone Memorial Hospital in Greensboro, North Carolina, all medical, radiology, laboratory, and pharmacy records are integrated on the same system.

Computers are beginning to find specialized uses in medicine and health not even thought of a decade ago. For instance, plastic surgeons now use computers and videos to show patients what they might look like after a face-lift, breast reduction, or other cosmetic surgery. Robots have been devised to perform tasks for those with physical disabilities. Other devices help the 13 million Americans who have some trouble speaking, reading, or writing. Computers also help children with cerebral palsy, Down's syndrome, and other problems to mitigate their disabilities by helping them to display and improve their skills.

It is possible that some day you will carry a plastic "smart card" that contains your entire medical history. Such a card could be put into a computer at hospitals, physicians' offices, and pharmacies around the country and provide details as to your chronic illnesses, allergies, and adverse reactions. ■

Diskettes: Easy Access

Like magnetic tape, **diskettes** are made of a special plastic that can be coated and easily magnetized. Diskettes are often referred to as "**floppy disks**" because they are made of flexible material. As Figure 4.18 shows, the disk is enclosed in a protective jacket—either paper or plastic—lined with a soft material specially treated to reduce friction and static. The disk jacket has four openings: (1) hub, (2) data access area, (3) write/protect notch, and (4) index hole. To store and retrieve

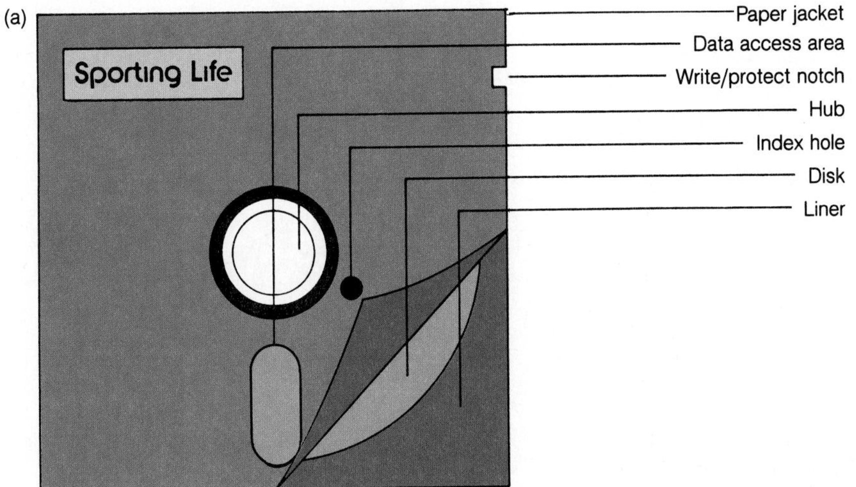

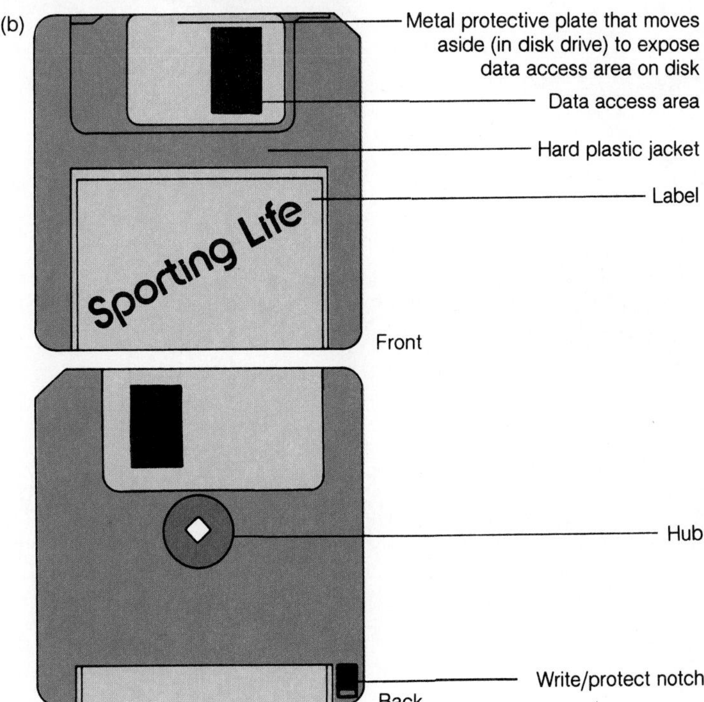

FIGURE 4.18

Diskette technology. Diskettes were developed to replace cassette tape as a data storage medium for use with microcomputers to provide fast direct access capabilities. IBM PCs and many IBM-compatible microcomputers use the 5¼-inch diskette (a); the Macintosh line of microcomputers, as well as some portable IBM-compatible computers and IBM PS/2 series microcomputers, use the 3½-inch diskette (b).

data from a diskette, you must place it into a **disk drive** (Figure 4.19), which contains special mechanical components for storing and retrieving data.

The *hub* of the diskette is the round opening in the center. When the diskette is placed into the disk drive, the hub fits over a mount, or spindle, in the drive. If you

FIGURE 4.19

Take it for a drive. (a) This cutaway illustration shows the main parts of a disk drive for diskettes. (b) IBM PC system cabinet with disk drives; inserting a 5¼-inch diskette. (c) Inserting a 3½-inch diskette. (*Note*: Not all microcomputer disk drives have gates.)

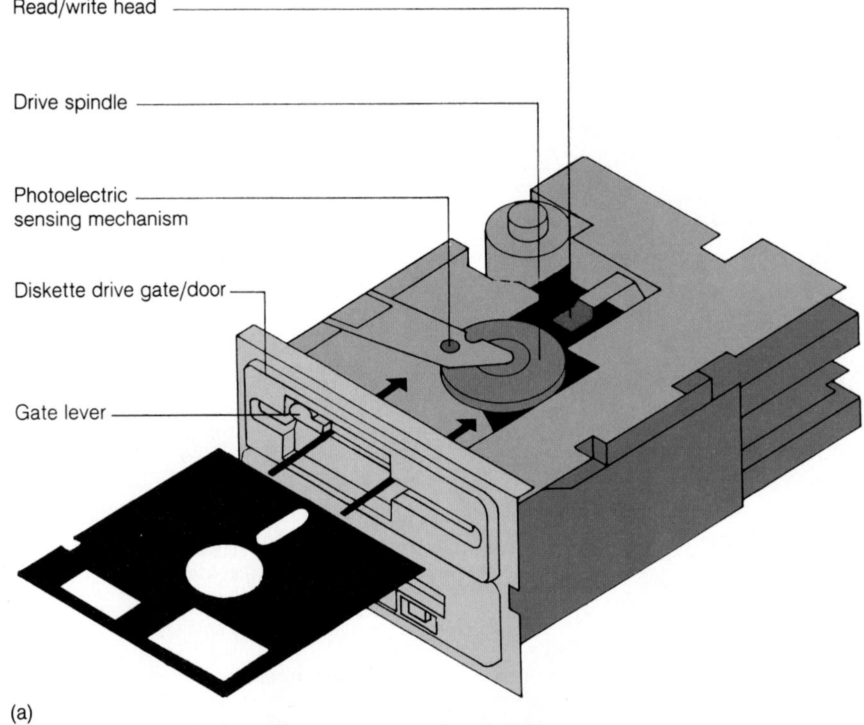

(a)

(b)

(c)

are using an IBM PC, before you can access any data on the diskette, you must close the **disk drive gate** or **door.** (Some personal computers, like the Macintosh, do not have drive doors.) The act of closing the disk drive gate moves a lever over the drive and clamps the diskette over the spindle of the drive mechanism (Figure 4.19).

When data is stored or retrieved, the diskette spins inside its jacket, and the read/write heads are clamped on the surface in the **data access area** of the disk (the exposed part of the disk). Most disk drives are equipped with two read/write heads so that the top and bottom surfaces of the diskette can be accessed simultaneously. The read/write heads are moved back and forth over the data access area in small increments to retrieve or record data as needed. Just inside the disk drive unit, a small mechanism checks to determine if the disk's **write/protect notch** is covered. If the notch is covered with tape, a switch is activated that prevents the read/write head from being able to touch the surface of the diskette, which means no data can be recorded. This is a security measure; covering the write/protect notch prevents accidental erasure or overwriting of data.

The *index hole* in the jacket is positioned over a photoelectric sensing mechanism. As the diskette spins in the jacket (when data is being recorded or retrieved), the hole (or holes—some diskettes have more than one) in the diskette passes the index hole in the jacket, is sensed, and activates a timing switch. The timing activity is critical because this is how the mechanism determines which portion of the diskette is over or under the read/write heads. The diskette spins at a fixed speed of about 300 revolutions per minute (RPM).

DISKETTE SIZES AND SHAPES

For most of the time since IBM introduced its first microcomputer—the IBM PC—in 1981, the 5¼-inch diskette was the industry standard, in spite of the fact that the popular Macintosh computer (introduced by Apple in 1984) uses a 3½-inch diskette covered with sturdy plastic. Other computer manufacturers have also used the 3½-inch diskette, including Hewlett-Packard, Grid Systems, and Toshiba in several popular laptops, but not until the introduction in 1987 of the IBM PS/2 series of microcomputers did the standard really change: IBM switched to the 3½-inch disk. Says James Porter, president of Disk/Trend, Inc., "The 3½-inch is a done deal. The only momentum for 5¼-inch drives comes from clone makers who just copy old product." However, because so much data has been recorded on 5¼-inch diskettes and because so many microcomputers that use this size diskette are sitting in offices right now, you will probably still be seeing and using the old familiar 5¼-inch diskette.

The 3½-inch diskette has several advantages over the 5¼-inch diskette:

1. It is more durable because it is covered by an inflexible plastic jacket that protects the disk from contamination and bending. (The care of diskettes is discussed later in the chapter.)
2. It can contain more data than the conventional 5¼-inch diskette—and in less space. The 3½-inch diskette can fit in your pocket.
3. The floppy disk drives that use these diskettes are smaller and lighter. Therefore, they require much less power to operate and they generate a lot less heat.
4. The 3½-inch drives are faster than the 5¼-inch drives because the read/write heads don't have to move as far to retrieve data. Because data is stored more densely, the data transfer rate is greater.

DISKETTE STORAGE CAPACITY

The byte is the unit of measure used most often to determine the capacity of a storage device used with any type of computer. (Remember, 8 bits equal 1 byte, or 1 character; *byte* and *character* are often used interchangeably.) Storage capacities are usually measured in thousands of bytes (Table 4.1). In computer terminology, 1,000 bytes is referred to as 1 **kilobyte (K).** (Technically, 1 K equals 1,024 bytes.) 1,000 K, or a million bytes, is referred to as 1 **megabyte (MB).** One billion bytes is called a **gigabyte (GB),** and a **terabyte (TB)** is 1 trillion bytes. The capacities of diskettes vary dramatically. Some disks hold as little as 360 K, and others as much as 1.44 MB, which is the equivalent of about a 500-page textbook. Diskettes are available that store more data, but they are not yet used widely. Typically, the more data the diskette is capable of storing, the more expensive it is. Diskettes range in price from less than $1 to about $5.

The capacity of a diskette does not necessarily depend only on its size. A number of factors affect how much data can be stored on a disk, including:

1. Whether the diskette stores data on only one side (single-sided) or both sides (double-sided);
2. Whether the disk drive is equipped with read/write heads for both the top and the bottom surfaces of the diskette;
3. What the data recording density is—that is, the number of bits that can be stored per inch;
4. What the track density is (the number of tracks per inch—tracks being circular bands on the disk similar to grooves on a phonograph record—in which data is recorded).

The first diskettes were **single-sided.** But as the need to store more data became a significant concern in the business community, technology produced the **double-sided disk,** which is capable of storing twice the amount of data as a comparable single-sided disk. To take advantage of a double-sided disk, however, you must have a computer with a **double-sided disk drive.** Double-sided disk drives are equipped with read/write heads for both the top and bottom surfaces of a disk. This allows data to be read from or written to both surfaces simultaneously. (The heads move together on the same mechanism so that they are positioned over corresponding locations on the surfaces of the disk.)

Disk capacity also depends on the recording density capabilities of the disk drive. **Recording density** refers to the number of bits per inch (bpi) of data that can

TABLE 4.1

Take a Byte

Bit	A binary digit; 0 or 1
Byte	8 bits, or 1 character
Kilobyte (K)	1,000 (actually 1,024) bytes
Megabyte (MB)	1,000,000 bytes
Gigabyte (GB)	1,000,000,000 bytes
Terabyte (TB)	1,000,000,000,000 bytes

be written onto the surface of the disk. Disks and drives are typically rated as having one of three recording densities:

1. **Single-density.**
2. **Double-density.**
3. **Quad-density.**

The specifications for the exact number of bits per inch (bpi) for each recording density vary from one manufacturer to another. The disk manufacturers use the recording density designation as a measure of the maximum bpi their diskettes can reliably be expected to store.

A double-sided, double-density 5¼-inch diskette (labeled "DS, DD" or "2S/2D") has a storage capacity of 360 K; a double-sided, quad-density diskette has a capacity of approximately 1.2 MB. The diskettes in the IBM PS/2 series of microcomputers hold from 720 K to 1.44 MB. As technology advances, even more data will be stored in a smaller amount of space. Table 4.2 compares the capacities of some popular diskettes.

The final factor affecting disk capacity is the track density. As pictured in Figure 4.20, data is recorded on disks in circular bands referred to as **tracks.** The read/write heads are designed to move in small increments across the data access area of the disk to find the appropriate track. As the precision of positioning the read/write head increases, the widths of the tracks become thinner. The most common **track densities** in use today are 48 tracks per inch (tpi), 96 tpi, and 135 tpi. The recording surface of a 5¼-inch disk is slightly less than 1 inch; therefore, the usable tracks per inch are 40 or 80 in most cases.

SECTORS

Typically a disk is divided up into eight or nine **sectors,** or equal, wedge-shaped areas used for storage reference purposes (Figure 4.20). The point at which a sector intersects a track is used to reference the data location; the track number indicates where to position the read/write head, and the sector number indicates when to activate the read/write head as the disk spins. Disks and drives are identified as being either hard-sectored or soft-sectored. *Hard-sectored disks* always have the same number and size of sectors, which are fixed by the manufacturer. Today most microcomputer systems use soft-sectored disks. *Soft-sectored disks* are marked

TABLE 4.2

Common Diskette Capacities

	Bytes	Tracks	Sectors/ Track	Bytes/ Sector
5¼-inch diskettes:				
Double-sided, double-density	360 K	40	9	512
Double-sided, quad-density	1.2 MB	80	15	512
3½-inch diskettes:				
Double-sided, single-density	720 K	80	9	512
Double-sided, double-density	1.44 MB	80	18	512

magnetically by the user's computer system during a process called **formatting,** or **initializing,** which determines the size and number of sectors on the disk. Since your diskettes must be adapted to the particular microcomputer and software you are using, you format your diskettes yourself with the proper number and size of factors. This is easily done using only a few simple commands on the computer.

A hard-sectored disk can be used only on the computer system for which it was created. The presence of the hard-sector marks allows data to be retrieved from the disk with less effort than from a double-sided, double-density soft-sectored disk. Hard-sectored disks have been used most often with dedicated computer systems that handle the manipulation and production of text (called *word processing*).

ACCESS TIME

The responsiveness of your computer depends to a great extent on the time it takes to locate the instructions or data being sought and then load a copy into main memory. The term **access time** refers to the average speed with which this is done. The access time of your computer's disk drive is determined by measuring the time it takes to perform each of the following activities: (1) positioning the read/write heads over the proper track (the time it takes to do this is called the *seek time*); (2) waiting for the disk to revolve until the correct sector is under or over the read/write heads (this is called *rotational delay* or *latency*); (3) placing the read/write head(s) in contact with the disks, called *setting time;* (4) transferring the data from the disk into the computer's main memory (at a speed called the *data transfer rate*).

Before you proceed to the next section, you need to know how to care for your diskettes; abuse means lost data. The accompanying chart (p. 147) refers to 5¼-inch diskettes; however, just because the 3½-inch diskettes have hard plastic jackets does not mean that they cannot be damaged, too!

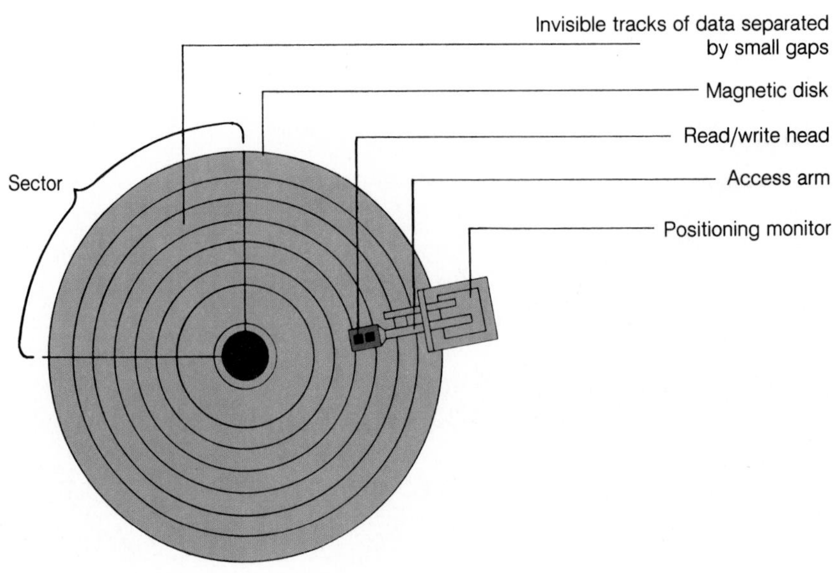

FIGURE 4.20

Staying on track. Tracks are circular bands on disks on which data is recorded. The tracks are separated by small gaps and are divided into equal areas called sectors. Tracks and sectors are used to determine addresses of fields of data.

HARD DISKS: TAKING GIANT BYTES

The introduction of high-capacity **hard disks** for microcomputer systems solved two serious problems related to the limited storage capacity of diskettes. First, as a business begins to use microcomputers extensively, the amount of software acquired and data collected tends to grow substantially. As a result, the number of

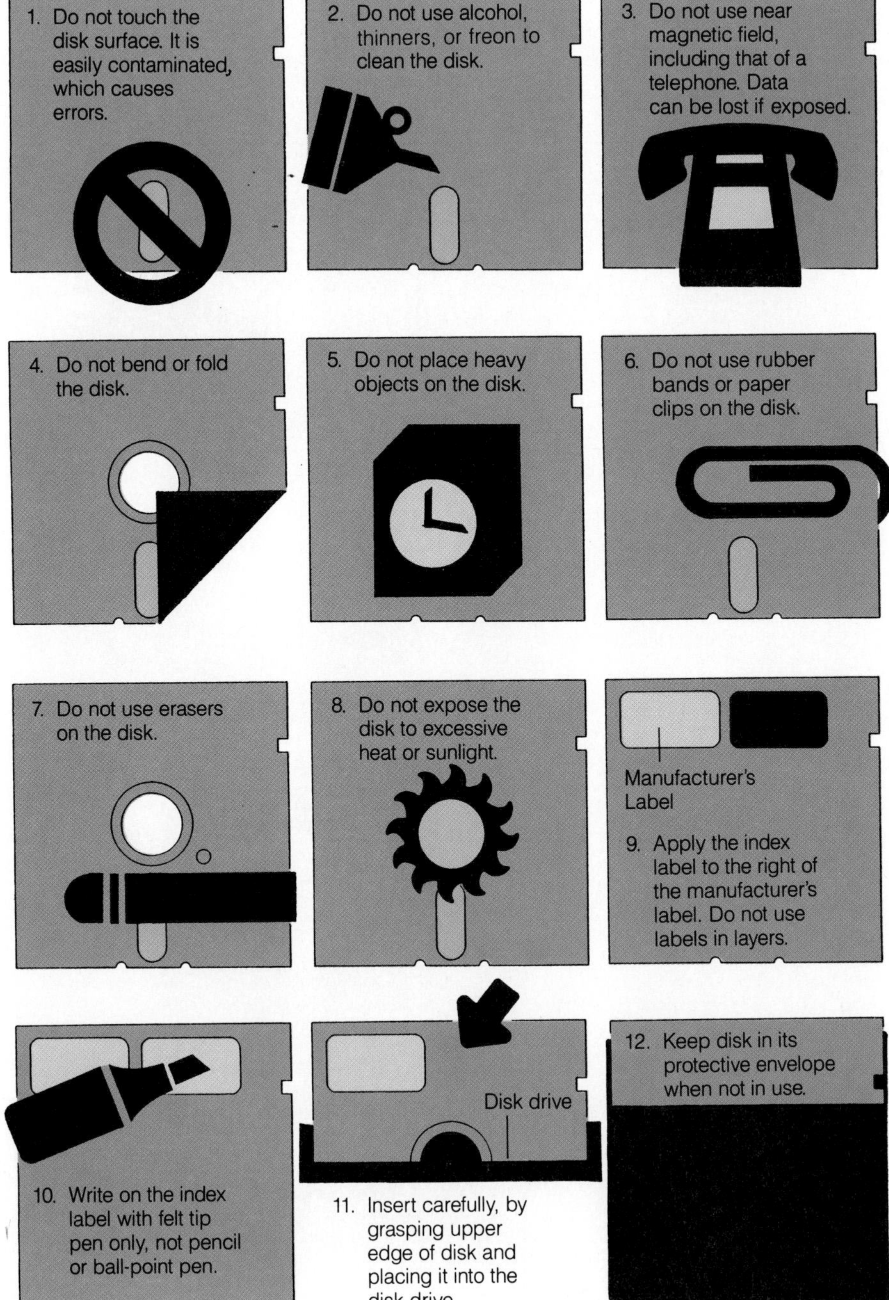

1. Do not touch the disk surface. It is easily contaminated, which causes errors.
2. Do not use alcohol, thinners, or freon to clean the disk.
3. Do not use near magnetic field, including that of a telephone. Data can be lost if exposed.
4. Do not bend or fold the disk.
5. Do not place heavy objects on the disk.
6. Do not use rubber bands or paper clips on the disk.
7. Do not use erasers on the disk.
8. Do not expose the disk to excessive heat or sunlight.
Manufacturer's Label
9. Apply the index label to the right of the manufacturer's label. Do not use labels in layers.
10. Write on the index label with felt tip pen only, not pencil or ball-point pen.
Disk drive
11. Insert carefully, by grasping upper edge of disk and placing it into the disk drive.
12. Keep disk in its protective envelope when not in use.

Handle with care! This illustration shows how to avoid disk damage.

diskettes to be handled increases dramatically. It is not uncommon for one user to have a library of 100 or more diskettes. Second, the largest file that can be accessed at one time is limited to the capacity of main memory and the storage medium. So, if the capacity of a diskette is 360 K, no files larger than that can be stored. Hard disks can store much larger files; for example, it is no longer impractical to set up an inventory system on a microcomputer that calls for working with a 45,000-item inventory master file. And the 100-page report we mentioned at the start of the chapter that didn't fit on one diskette can easily fit on a hard disk. You could have stored the report in sections in separate files on different diskettes, but that would have been very inconvenient. You would have had to continually swap diskettes,

(a)

(b)

FIGURE 4.21

Internal hard disk unit. (a) This illustration shows the main components of a hard disk unit. (b) As you can see from this photo of an IBM PS/2 computer, the hard disk does not have an exterior opening, because the disk(s) are sealed in a sterile unit inside the system cabinet. (The single drive opening you see is for a diskette.)

inserting them and ejecting them, to work on your report. The hard disk spares you that trouble.

In some hard disk systems, data is stored in the same way as it is on diskettes. A series of tracks are divided into sectors when the disk is formatted. As their name suggests, hard disks are made out of a rigid substance that is capable of storing a greater amount of data than the soft material used for diskettes. Hard disk drives for microcomputers (Figure 4.21) can be *internal* (built into the computer cabinet and nonremovable) or *external* (outside the computer cabinet and connected to it by a short cable) (Figure 4.22).

The capacity of diskettes in wide use today ranges from 360 K to 1.44 MB each. Microcomputer hard disk capacity ranges from 20 MB to 1,000 MB (1 GB) or higher. Hard disks' larger capacity allows the user to store larger files and larger programs than can be used with diskettes (Figure 4.23). Also, the access time of diskettes is longer than that of hard disks, which means that hard disks can store and retrieve data much faster than a diskette unit.

Hard disks have the following characteristics: (1) they are rigid metal platters connected to a central spindle; (2) the entire disk unit (disks and read/write heads) is placed in a permanently sealed container; (3) air that flows through the container is filtered to prevent contamination; and (4) the disks are rotated at very high speed (usually around 3,600 rpm; floppy disks rotate at about 300 rpm). These disk drives can have four or more disk platters in a sealed unit. In most of these disk units (which are often called *Winchester disk drives*), the read/write heads never touch the surfaces of the disks. Instead, they are designed to float from .5 to 1.25 millionths of an inch from the disk surface; because of this characteristic, the design is often referred to as a *flying head* design. Because the heads float so close to the sensitive disks, any contamination—such as a dust particle or a hair—can cause a *head crash*, also referred to as a *disk crash*, which destroys some or all of the data on the

FIGURE 4.22

External hard disk drive. This shot of a Mac SE shows it hooked up to a 20 MB external hard disk drive (the "box" positioned under the computer, above the keyboard). You can also see the diskette drive opening on the front of the system cabinet. Some Mac systems can also include an additional internal hard disk unit.

disk. This sensitivity is the reason why hard disk units are assembled under sterile conditions.

Sometimes adding a hard disk to your microcomputer system means either losing one of your internal diskette drives or taking up desk space with an external hard disk drive. An alternative is to buy a **hardcard** (Figure 4.24), a circuit board with a disk that plugs into an expansion slot inside the computer. Hardcards store

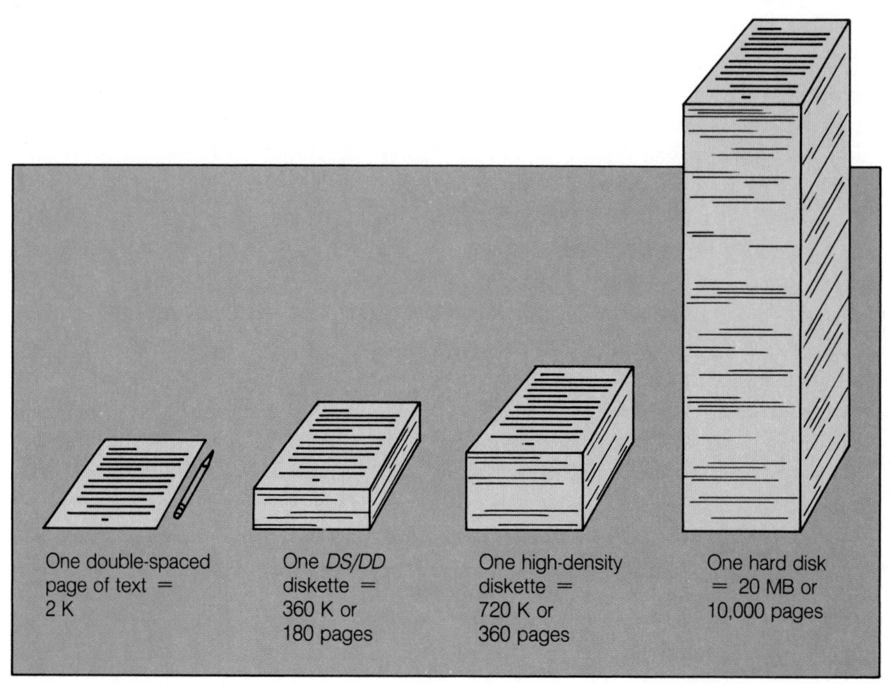

FIGURE 4.23

How to make a mountain out of a molehill. The use of hard disk units on microcomputers has greatly increased their ability to deal with large amounts of data at one time. For example, one 20 MB hard disk holds the same amount of data as 56 double-sided, double-density diskettes. (Adapted from P. G. McKeown, *Living with Computers*, 2nd ed. (Orlando, Fla.: Harcourt Brace Jovanovich, 1988), p. 183.)

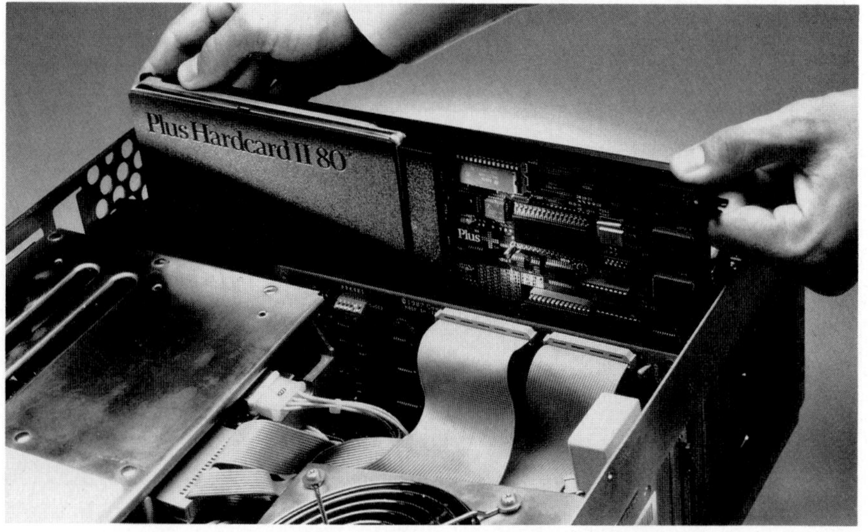

FIGURE 4.24

Hardcard. This hardcard works like a hard disk but plugs into an expansion slot inside of the microcomputer cabinet.

from 40 MB to 105 MB of data, have an access time of between 9 and 25 milliseconds, and range in price from $200 to $1,000.

Hard disk technology was first introduced by IBM in the early 1970s. Hard disks for microcomputer systems began to appear in the marketplace in 1980. Since then, hard disk units have become increasingly smaller and more necessary to handle memory-hungry software. The first units introduced for microcomputers used 8-inch-diameter disk platters. The most popular units today use 5¼-inch disks; some units use 3½-inch disks. The initial 5¼-inch disk drives were approximately 3½ inches high, whereas the newer disk drives are just over 1½ inches high; this means that you can put at least twice as much disk capacity in the same space you used before. Two diskette drives can fit where only one used to fit, and two hard disk units can occupy the space that one did. This type of configuration provides a powerful system in a small workspace. Hard disks are used widely in business microcomputers today. You'll certainly be using one soon!

Disk Cartridges

Removable **hard disk cartridges** (Figure 4.25) are an alternative to hard disk units as a form of secondary storage. The cartridges usually contain one or two platters enclosed in a hard plastic case that is inserted into the disk drive much like a music tape cassette. The capacity of these cartridges ranges from 5 to 450 MB, somewhat

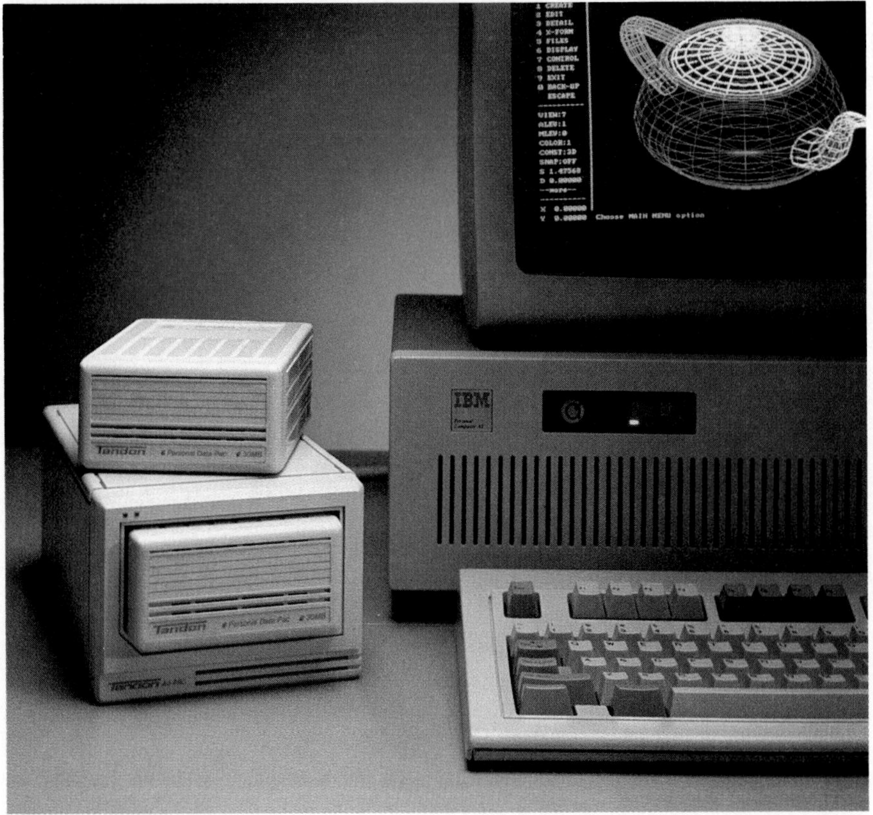

FIGURE 4.25

Hard disk cartridge. This Tandon hard disk drive has one cartridge in place; another cartridge has been placed on top of the drive.

lower than hard disk units but still substantially superior to diskettes. They are handy because they give microcomputer users access to amounts of data limited only by the number of cartridges used.

CARTRIDGE TAPE UNITS: GET YOUR BACKUP!

Although, as you know, tape is not a direct access storage medium, we discuss a type of tape storage unit here because of a particular problem microcomputer users face. As high-capacity hard disk units increased in popularity, the problem of making backup copies of disk contents became a significant concern. *Users should make backup copies of all stored data files to ensure that they don't lose their data if the hard disk is damaged or destroyed.* Many users neglect this step and live to regret it: How would you feel if your 400-page masterpiece novel was lost forever because your hard disk crashed? Or if two weeks' worth of tax computations turned to dust because your disk storage units were electrocuted by a power surge? It takes approximately 20 3½-inch diskettes to back up the contents of one 20 MB hard disk. Imagine how many diskettes would have to be used to back up a 144 MB hard disk! Something more efficient is needed.

This concern prompted the development and refinement of **cartridge tape units** (also called *tape streamers*) to back up high-capacity hard disks (Figure 4.26). Tape cartridges have a capacity (per cartridge) ranging from 20 MB to 525 MB. The copying speeds of tape backup units vary, but it would take approximately 12 minutes to copy the contents of a 60 MB hard disk.

In addition to tape units, hard disk cartridges are also used to back up hard disk units.

DIRECT ACCESS STORAGE DEVICES FOR LARGE COMPUTER SYSTEMS

The data storage requirements for large computer systems are enormous compared to the needs of microcomputer-based applications. The access time and the data transfer rate have to be much faster, and the capacity of the disk storage devices must be considerably larger. Early storage devices used with minicomputers and mainframes were limited in storage capacity and were costly. However, modern technology has overcome these problems. Today, two main types of direct access storage devices are used with large computers: (1) removable disk packs and (2) fixed disks.

REMOVABLE DISK PACKS

In large computer systems, hard disks are sometimes contained in packs that are removable (Figure 4.27), meaning that they can be removed from the computer and replaced at will. **Disk packs** typically hold 6 to 12 platters that are usually 14 inches in diameter. In disk packs, all tracks with the same track number are lined up, one above the other. All tracks with the same track number make up a **cylinder**

(Figure 4.27b). Each disk in the pack—except the top one and the bottom one—has two read/write heads so that both sides of the disk can be read. The read/write heads move together and so are always on the same cylinder at the same time. Data that needs more space than one track is continued onto the same track on another disk, so the read/write heads do not need to move. (Only one read/write head is active at one time, but the heads are very fast.) When all the tracks in a cylinder are full, the read/write heads move to another cylinder. The cylinder numbers are used by the computer operating system to determine data addresses. (The sector method is used with diskettes and single disks.)

The capacity of removable disk packs varies by manufacturer and ranges from 10 to 300 MB. A minicomputer system with four disk drives can have 1 billion characters of data on-line—that is, available—at one time for direct access. The total storage capacity could be dramatically increased by having a dozen or so extra disk packs to be interchanged with the packs in the disk drives.

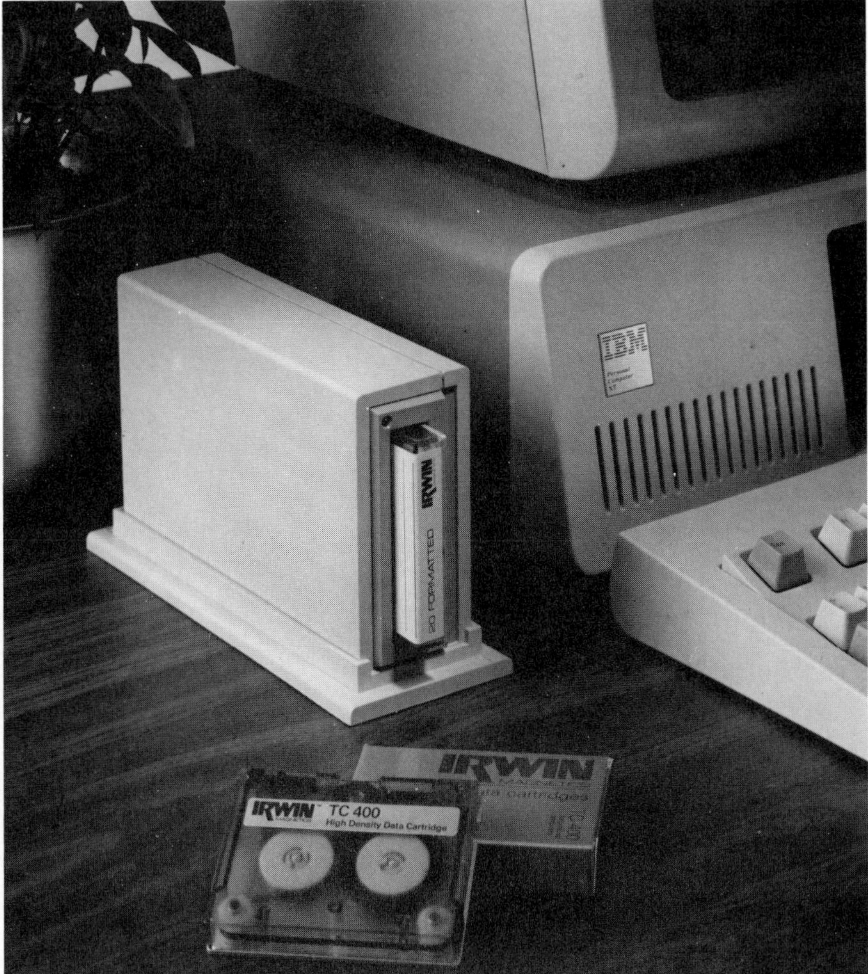

FIGURE 4.26

Cartridge tape unit. Such tape units are used with microcomputers to back up the contents of the hard disk units, so that data is not lost if the hard disk units fail.

FIGURE 4.27

Pack it in. (a) Hard disks used in large computer systems are often contained in removable packs. The spaces between the stack of disks inside the pack allow the access arms to move in and out. Each access arm has two read/write heads so that both surfaces of each disk (except the top and bottom ones) can be read and written on. The same track numbers on all the disks line up vertically—thus all tracks with the same track number form a cylinder (b).

(a)

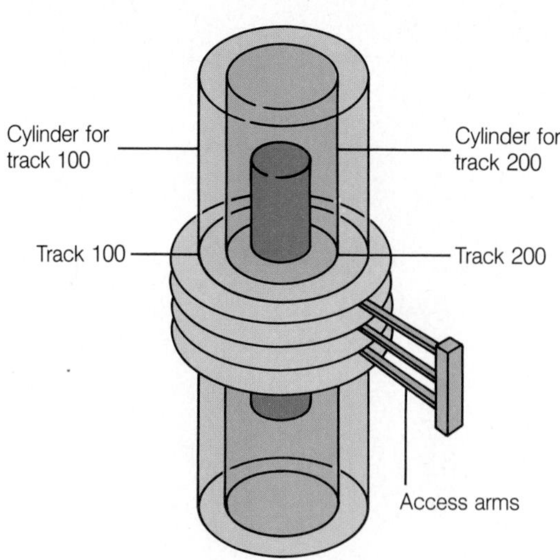

(b)

FIXED DISKS

Fixed disk units (Figure 4.28) are commonly used with medium-sized and large computers. They are either in the same cabinet as the computer or in their own cabinet. Fixed disks generally are more reliable and have higher storage capabilities than removable disks, but, of course, they are not portable.

MASS STORAGE SYSTEMS AND OPTICAL DISKS

In spite of all the improvements that have been made in magnetic disk storage technology, there still never seems to be enough capacity. Major banks, for example, each do about 600 terabytes worth of check-related processing a year. One terabyte is equivalent to the storage capacity of about 1,250 reels of high-density magnetic tape. Can you imagine trying to manage 750,000 reels of tape in your tape library?

The ability to use both multiple reels of tape and removable disk packs does extend an organization's ability to store a large amount of data. However, as you learned earlier, magnetic tape does not support direct access storage. And removable disk packs provide some flexibility, but the time required to remove a disk pack, retrieve and mount the replacement, and return the pack to the library can make its use inefficient.

FIGURE 4.28

In a fix. This IBM 9336 fixed disk unit provides storage for IBM mid-size systems. Each unit contains between two and four 5¼-inch disk drives with a storage capacity of from 942 MB to 3,428 MB, a controller, and a power supply, all in a rack-mountable unit. This rack has three units.

Mass storage systems (Figure 4.29) were developed to remedy this situation. These systems are composed of honeycomb-like "library" cells that hold as many as 2,000 data cartridges, each of which can store 50 MB of data. Each cartridge contains a strip of magnetic tape about 3 inches wide and from 150 to 770 inches long. Each bank of cartridges is serviced by a mechanical unit that retrieves the cartridges individually and positions them under a special read/write head for data transfer. IBM and Control Data Corporation both offer mass storage systems similar in capacity and capabilities. The IBM system is designed so that the data is transferred from the cartridge to a high-speed fixed disk. The Control Data System is designed so that the contents of the entire cartridge can be loaded directly into main memory, which provides much faster access to the data.

Mass storage systems are faster than regular tape-reel-based systems, but they're slower than disk-only systems because the CPU must locate the cartridge needed and transfer the data to disk or main memory before it can process the data. A faster kind of mass storage exists—optical disks.

The most promising secondary storage technology, **optical storage** (Figure 4.30), involves the use of a high-power laser beam to burn microscopic spots in a hard disk's surface coating. Data is represented by the presence (binary 1) and the absence (binary 0) of holes in the storage locations. A much lower power laser beam is used to retrieve the data. The patterns of spots detected by the laser (during a read operation) are converted into electrical signals used by the computer. To use an optical disk, you must purchase an internal or external optical drive that costs between $500 and $1,000.

The capacity of optical disk systems is enormous compared with most magnetic disk storage devices. This technology promises a storage capacity in excess of 100 GB for a single 12-inch disk. This large storage capacity is especially useful in situations where images must be stored; images take up much more storage space

FIGURE 4.29

Mass storage. Data is stored on small rolls of magnetic tape and then transferred to disk when needed for processing; afterward, the data is transferred back to the tape, which is stored in a cell. The storage capacity of such a system is in the range of 400 billion bytes. (Each tape cartridge is about 3 inches wide.)

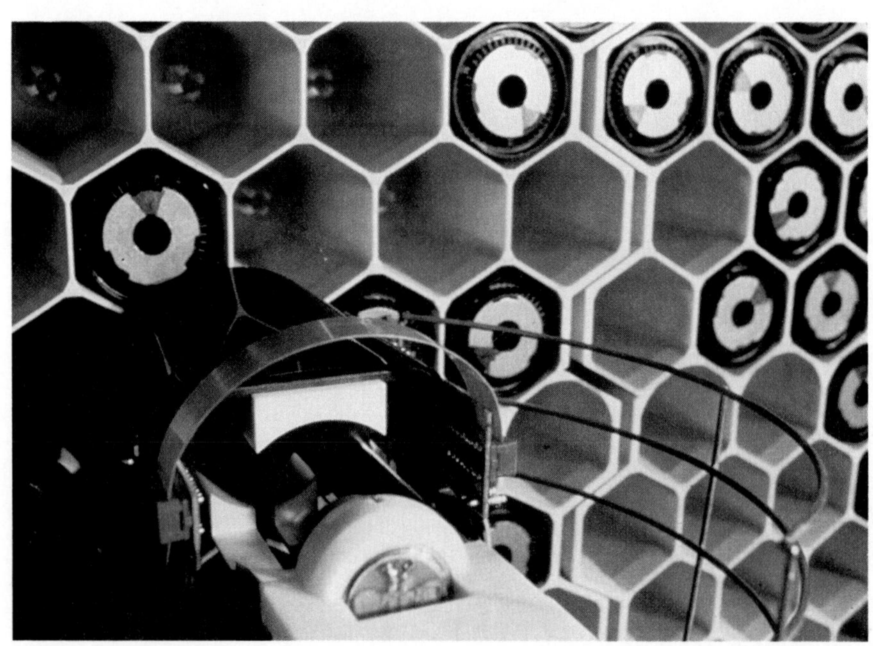

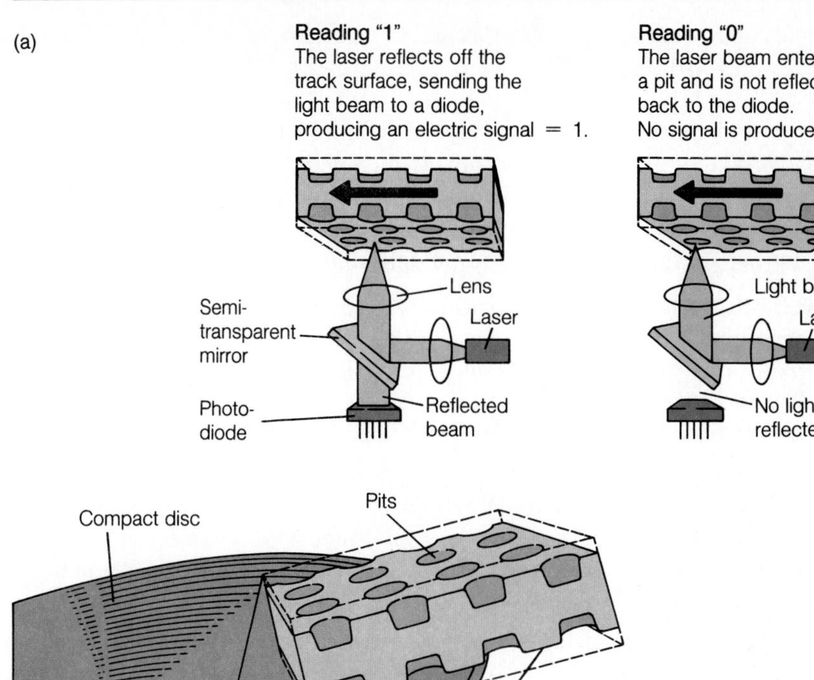

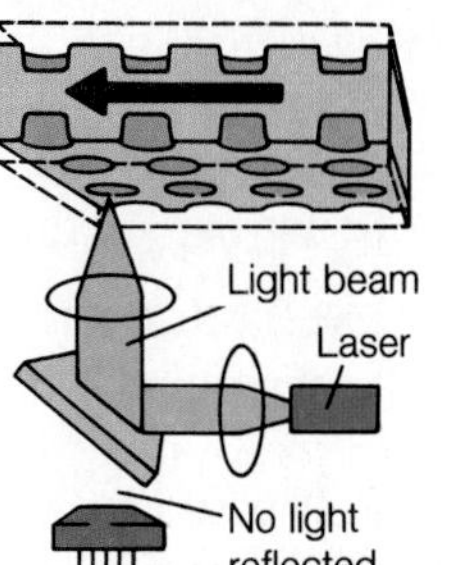

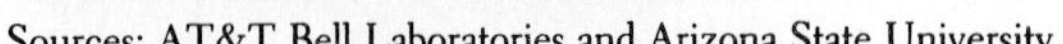
Sources: AT&T Bell Laboratories and Arizona State University.

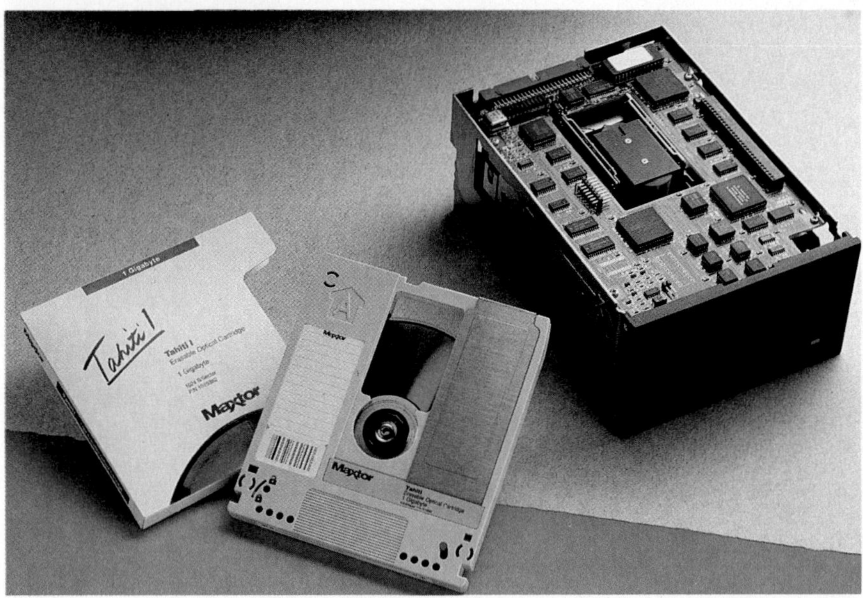

(b)

FIGURE 4.30

What you see is what you get. (a) Optical disks can store much more data than magnetic diskettes, disks, or tape can. (They offer 15,000 tracks per inch instead of the 96 tracks per inch on magnetic diskettes.) Optical storage devices are available for all sizes of computer systems. (b) This photo shows a Maxtor erasable optical disk in a cartridge along with an optical disk drive (which may be internal or external). (Adapted from Dan Foley/ *The Arizona Republic*.)

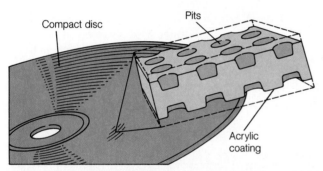

than text or numerical data. Microcomputers can use optical storage, too. A $5\frac{1}{4}$-inch optical disk—the same size as a diskette—can store between 680 MB and 1 GB! (One 800-MB optical disk = 13 60-MB tape cartridges = 40 20-MB hard disks = 111 7.2-MB diskettes.)

The cost of optical media has proven to be about $\frac{1}{10}$ that of magnetic tape and $\frac{1}{100}$ that of magnetic disk. In addition, unlike data stored on magnetic storage media, the data recorded on optical media is not damaged by stray magnetic fields and surface problems like fingerprints, dust, scratches, and so on.

Following are the three main kinds of optical disks:

1. **CD-ROM (compact disk/read-only memory).** This optical disk's data is imprinted by the disk manufacturer. The user cannot erase it, change it, or write on the disk; the user can only "read" the data. This type of optical disk is used primarily for making huge amounts of prerecorded data—such as government statistics, encyclopedias, medical reference books, dictionaries, and legal libraries—immediately available to the user (Figure 4.31).
2. **Write Once, Read Many (Worm).** WORM disks are also imprinted by the manufacturer, but the buyer can determine what is written on the disks. Once the disks have been written on, however, they can only be read from then on; again, no changes can be made.
3. **Erasable optical disks.** Erasable optical drives are an alternative to large-capacity hard disks. They store from 281 to 3200 MB of data. In contrast to

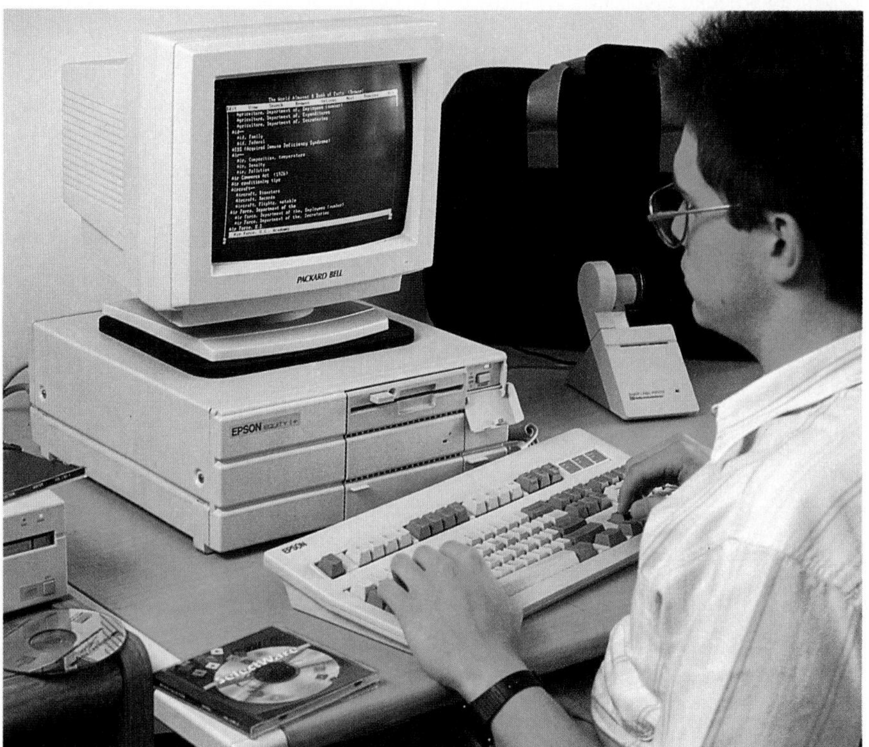

FIGURE 4.31

CD–ROM. This student is doing research using *The World Almanac and Book of Facts* stored on read-only optical disk.

CD–ROM and WORM disks, erasable disks *can* be written on and erased. The removable cartridges (about $250 each) provide convenience and security along with huge storage capacity. Optical disks can also be used to back up fixed hard disks.

Many experts think that optical disk storage will become the most efficient, inexpensive, and popular storage method. Some personal computers already have removable, erasable optical disk drives.

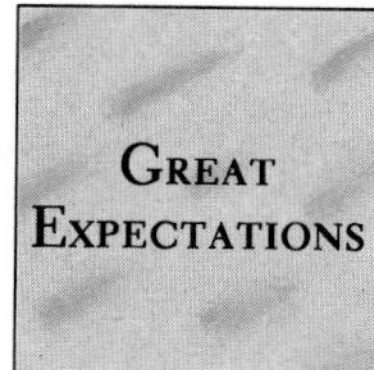

The appetite for secondary storage capacity has proven almost impossible to satisfy. The days of the personal computer with only two 360 K floppy disk drives are nearly gone. Now a typical personal computer system is equipped with a minimum of 40 MB of hard disk storage capacity. Current mass storage technologies have helped assuage the hunger to some extent; however, the general feeling is that there will never be enough storage capacity. To keep pace with the need, research and development efforts have concentrated on improving magnetic storage technology, including hard cards, and refining optical disk storage technology.

In the area of magnetic storage technology, development has focused on disks. However, new tape drives known as *digital audio tape (DAT) drives* are becoming available; these offer 1.3 gigabytes of storage on a casette the size of a credit card. Some companies are predicting the production of floppy diskettes that will be able to store from 20 MB up to 100 MB of data! Hard disks will also have greater capacity; for example, a 12-inch disk may be able to store 1 terabyte of data—the equivalent of many thousands of encyclopedias. The currently large storage capacity of optical disks will continue to expand to support the development of *multimedia*—the combination and storage of text, graphics, animation, and sound.

And don't think that 3½ inches is as small as your diskettes will be; manufacturers are working on producing diskettes that are 2.5 inches or even 1.8 inches wide (called *microfloppies*).

In spite of the improvements in diskettes, these relative storage midgets may eventually go the way of the punched card. Hard disks are common and very important, especially in microcomputer systems. Optical storage units will also become more common. At the end of the century the typical business PC will be using optical disks to manipulate *gigabytes* of data. Optical storage will also be available in card form. Although optical disk access times are currently slower than those of magnetic hard disks, their speed is expected to improve dramatically. In the meantime, the new business user can expect to continue dealing with magnetic hard disks and floppy disks, with occasional magnetic tape backup.

You can see that as storage devices become smaller and smaller and more and more efficient, the secondary storage capacities of most computer systems are becoming essentially unlimited. It's the amount of main memory and number of processors that will determine how much data can be processed during a given time (more on this in the next chapter).

What does this mean to you? As a personal computer user, you will be able to manipulate more data faster and make use of graphics software, which takes up a lot of storage space. You'll be able to build good-sized data banks (also called *databases;* we'll discuss these later) on your own PC (not to mention having access to tremendously huge data banks controlled by mainframe systems).

ONWARD: PROCESSING THE INGREDIENTS

Now that you know several ways to hold on to your data after you've input it, you need to find out what to do to it—what you *can* do to it. The third part of the computer-based information system is the processing phase, the topic of the next chapter.

SUMMARY

Storage and storage needs must be properly evaluated if a business is to run smoothly. The requirements for storage capacity, speed of data retrieval, size, cost, complexity of equipment, and so on vary from business to business.

Basically, there are two types of storage: primary storage (also called *main memory, internal memory*, or *memory*), where data is nonvolatile. If data is volatile, it is lost when the power to the computer is turned off; nonvolatile data remains intact.

In storage, data is represented using a binary code, a system of combinations of binary digits (bits). A bit is either 0, meaning "off" (no magnetic spot present), or 1, meaning "on" (magnetic spot present). Two common binary coding schemes are the American Standard Code for Information Interchange (ASCII) and the Extended Binary Coded Decimal Interchange Code (EBCDIC). ASCII is typically used to represent data on microcomputers, and EBCDIC is used on larger computers.

Data is stored in files, which can be understood by means of the data storage hierarchy. A file is a collection of records; a record is a collection of fields; fields comprise a collection of bytes. A byte, or a character, is a collection of 8 bits. A ninth bit—the parity bit—may be added as an error-checking device. Data files can be categorized as one of the following: (1) transaction file, (2) master file, (3) report file, (4) output file, (5) history file, or (6) backup file.

The three main types of file organization are (1) sequential, (2) direct, or relative, and (3) indexed. With sequential file organization—used only on tape—data can be retrieved only in the order in which it is stored. All records must be read to get to the data you want. Direct, or relative, file organization (on disk) avoids that problem by allowing you to go straight to the data you want. Key fields are used by the computer as identifiers to locate the data. Indexed file organization (on disk) allows both sequential and direct access through the use of an index set up by the computer according to key fields and locations on the storage media. Your business needs should determine the type of file organization and data retrieval method you use.

Introduced in the early 1950s, magnetic tape quickly overcame the limitations of punched cards as a storage medium. On magnetic tape, data is stored only in sequential fashion using either the ASCII or EBCDIC coding schemes. Unfortunately, data put on tape can't be reorganized or altered without creating a new tape. Because of this limitation, direct access storage media including diskettes, hard disks, hard cards, and optical disks, were developed for microcomputers. The direct access storage media used with the larger computers include removable disk packs, fixed disks, and disk cartridges.

Data is stored on disk surfaces in sectors and tracks. Higher track density (tracks per inch) and higher recording density (bits per inch) both result in the ability to store greater amounts of data per disk. Storage capacity is measured in thousands of bytes (kilobyte, or K), millions of bytes (megabyte, or MB), billions of bytes (gigabyte, or GB), and trillions of bytes (terabyte, or TB). The disk devices used on larger computers are typically capable of storing a greater amount of data in a smaller amount of space than those used for microcomputers. Microcomputer storage technology is rapidly advancing, however, so the difference in storage capacity may not last.

KEY TERMS

access time, p. 146
algorithm, p. 132
American Standard Code for Information Interchange (ASCII), p. 123
backup file, p. 127
binary code, p. 122
binary digit (bit), p. 122
block, p. 134
byte, p. 122
cartridge tape unit, p. 152
CD-ROM (compact disk/read-only memory), p. 158
check bit, p. 124
cylinder, p. 152
data access area, p. 143
data storage hierarchy, p. 125
direct access storage and retrieval, p. 131
direct file, p. 131
disk drive, p. 142
disk drive gate (door), p. 143
diskette, p. 141
disk pack, p. 152
double-density, p. 145
double-sided disk, p. 144
double-sided disk drive, p. 144
erasable optical disk, p. 158
Extended Binary Coded Decimal Interchange Code (EBCDIC), p. 123
field, p. 125
file, p. 125
fixed disk, p. 155
floppy disk, p. 141
formatting, p. 146
frame, p. 134
gigabyte (GB), p. 144
hardcard, p. 150
hard disk, p. 147
hard disk cartridge, p. 151
history file, p. 127
indexed file organization, p. 133
initializing, p. 146
interblock gap (IBG), p. 134
interrecord gap (IRG), p. 134
key field (key), p. 132
kilobyte (K), p. 144
mass storage system, p. 156
master file, p. 127
megabyte (MB), p. 144
nonvolatile, p. 121
optical storage, p. 156
output file, p. 127
parity bit, p. 124
primary storage, p. 121
quad-density, p. 145
read/write head, p. 129
record, p. 125
recording density, p. 144
report file, p. 127
secondary (auxiliary) storage, p. 121
sector, p. 145
sequential file organization, p. 130
single-density, p. 145
single-sided disk, p. 144
terabyte (TB), p. 144
track, p. 145
track density, p. 145
transaction file, p. 126
volatile, p. 121
write once, read many (WORM), p. 158
write/protect notch, p. 143

EXERCISES

MATCHING

Match each of the following terms to the phrase that is the most closely related.

1. ____ binary code
2. ____ ASCII
3. ____ backup file
4. ____ byte
5. ____ diskette drive
6. ____ write/protect notch
7. ____ read/write head
8. ____ hard disk
9. ____ EBCDIC
10. ____ sequential file organization
11. ____ removable disk pack
12. ____ optical disk drive
13. ____ gigabyte
14. ____ cartridge tape drive
15. ____ sector
16. ____ direct access

a. This hardware device is a more efficient alternative to diskettes for backing up the contents of hard disks.
b. Storage device typically used with mainframe computers that stores between 150 and 250 MB
c. Wedge shape on disk used for storage reference purposes
d. Unit of measurement approximately equal to a character
e. A billion bytes
f. Storage device that uses a laser beam to record data
g. When this is covered, data cannot be written onto a diskette.
h. Copy of an original file
i. Scheme for encoding data using a series of binary digits
j. Data retrieval method best used in situations in which only a few records in a file need to be accessed
k. Direct access storage device used with microcomputers that has a much greater storage capacity than diskettes
l. Coding scheme widely used to represent data in microcomputers
m. Inexpensive storage device used with microcomputers
n. This coding scheme is widely used to represent data in mainframe computers.
o. This component of a disk drive can convert magnetic spots to electrical impulses, and vice versa.
p. With this type of file organization, data is retrieved in the sequence in which it was recorded.

MULTIPLE CHOICE

1. Which of the following is a unit of measurement used with computer systems?
   a. byte
   b. megabyte
   c. gigabyte
   d. kilobyte
   e. all the above

2. Why do so many microcomputers today have hard disks?
   a. can be moved easily from one computer to another
   b. inexpensive
   c. very high storage capacity
   d. they are a sequential access storage device
   e. only 3½ inches in diameter
3. Hard disks and diskettes are:
   a. sequential access storage devices
   b. direct access storage devices
   c. rarely used with microcomputers
   d. capable of storing terabytes of data and information
   e. all the above
4. Which of the following terms is *not* used to refer to the recording density of a disk?
   a. mega-density
   b. single-density
   c. double-density
   d. quad-density
   e. a and d
5. Which of the following is the most appropriate unit for measuring the storage capacity of a hard disk?
   a. byte
   b. megabyte
   c. bit
   d. terabyte
   e. 2-bit
6. Which of the following statements is false?
   a. Secondary storage is nonvolatile.
   b. Primary storage is volatile.
   c. Secondary storage contains data for immediate processing.
   d. When the computer is turned off, data and instructions stored in primary storage are erased.
   e. all the above
7. Which of the following storage and retrieval methods would be well suited to your processing requirements if you need only to retrieve records one at a time and there is no fixed pattern to the requests for data and records?
   a. direct
   b. sequential
   c. indexed sectors
   d. indexed direct
   e. relative
8. Which of the following is not used for storage purposes with mainframe computers?
   a. removable disks
   b. fixed disks
   c. mass storage systems
   d. diskettes
   e. hard disks

9. Which of the following factors would you disregard when determining the storage capacity of a hard disk unit?
   a. track density
   b. height of the hard disk drive
   c. recording density
   d. number of platters
   e. diameter of the platters
10. Which of the following is true?
    a. Fields are composed of bytes.
    b. Files are composed of records.
    c. Fields are composed of characters.
    d. Records are composed of fields.
    e. all the above

PROJECTS

1. Computer shopping. Using newspapers or magazines, find ads for the following types of storage devices: (a) 5¼-inch double-sided, quad-density diskette, (b) 3½-inch double-sided, double-density diskette, (c) 40 MB hard disk, and (d) an erasable optical disk drive. For each device, describe its price, the name and address of the supplier, and why you think the device is a good purchase. Make some price comparisons.
2. What type(s) of storage hardware is currently being used in the computer you use in school or at work? What is the storage capacity of this hardware? How much storage capacity remains unused? Would you recommend alternate storage hardware? Why? Why not?
3. Research one of the newer storage technologies described in this chapter. How is this technology being applied now? Do you think its use will grow in the future? Why or why not?
4. Computer shopping. You want to purchase a hard disk for use with your microcomputer. Because you don't care how much money the hard disk costs, you are going to buy one with the highest storage capacity you can find. Using newspapers or magazines, or interviewing computer store salespeople, find a hard disk you would like to buy. What is its storage capacity? Its average access time? How much does it cost? Who is the supplier? Is it an external or an internal drive?
5. If you are already working with computers, format a diskette and watch the tracks and sectors being counted off. What do you see?
6. Talk to some computer store salespeople and find out what the main uses of CD-ROMs are. Can you think of more?

Chapter 5

Processing Hardware

When you look at a computer, you can see and even touch most of the input, output, and storage equipment — the keyboard or the mouse, the video display screen, the printer, the disk drive doors or the tape cartridge. But you cannot actually *see* the equipment that does the processing — the electronic circuitry inside the cabinet of the computer itself. Although you have no need to puzzle through wiring diagrams and the like, you should have some understanding of processing hardware, because the type of processing hardware used affects how much the computer can do for you and how quickly it can do it.

Preview

When you have completed this chapter, you will be able to:

- Identify the two main parts of the central processing unit and discuss their functions.
- Describe how the computer carries out instructions that the user gives it.
- Describe the importance of and distinguish between random access memory and the different types of read-only memory.
- Describe the factors that should be considered when evaluating the processing power of a computer.

THE USER PERSPECTIVE

You may never have to look inside a computer—although if a computer technician comes to your office to fix your microcomputer, we recommend that you look over his or her shoulder and ask the technician to identify some of the internal components, just so you can get a general idea of what's going on inside. But why, essentially, do you need to know anything about the processing hardware and activities—any more than you need to know how the engine of a car works? We think there are two reasons:

- Just as some people like to work on their own cars, you may decide it's economical for you to do some work on your microcomputer. For instance, you may find that some new software programs are too sophisticated for your computer—that your computer cannot hold enough data or instructions or process them fast enough—and that you need to add some more main memory. This may well be something you can do yourself.
- More likely, you will some day need to make a buying decision about a microcomputer, either for yourself or for an organization. And, just as when you buy a car, you should learn something about the topic first. For example, you may have to judge whether it's worth buying a machine that takes five hours to accomplish what another machine—perhaps not a microcomputer but a minicomputer or a mainframe—can accomplish in seconds. It's also important to understand processing facts and trends to avoid purchasing a machine that will be obsolete in the near future.

Before we look at processing activities, let's start our discussion of hardware components by going to the heart of the matter—the CPU.

THE CENTRAL PROCESSING UNIT

The **central processing unit (CPU)** is the heart of the computer system. Among other things, its configuration determines whether a computer is fast or slow in

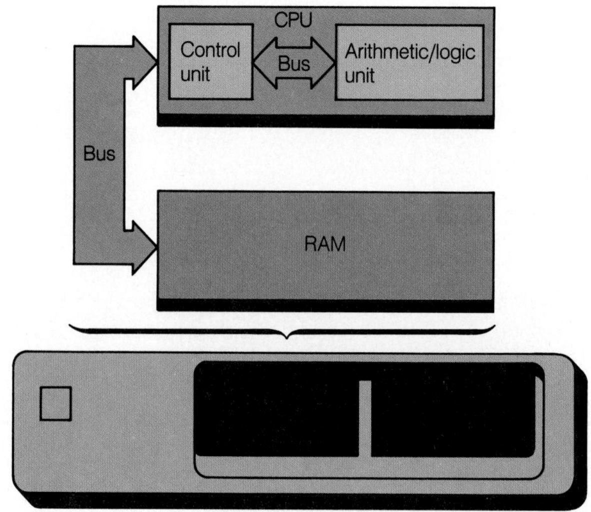

FIGURE 5.1

Travel by bus. Buses, a kind of electronic transportation system, connect the main components of the central processing unit and RAM (main memory).

relation to other computers. The CPU is the most complex computer system component, responsible for directing most of the computer system activities based on the instructions provided. As one computer generation has evolved to the next, the size of the CPU has become smaller and smaller, while its speed and capacity have increased tremendously. Indeed, these changes resulted in the microcomputer that is small enough to fit on your desk or your lap. As we mentioned earlier, the CPU circuitry of a microcomputer—called a **microprocessor**—fits on a chip about the size of your thumbnail, or even smaller.

The CPU has two main parts: (1) the control unit and (2) the arithmetic/logic unit. The parts of the CPU are usually connected by an electronic component referred to as a **bus,** which acts as an electronic highway between them (Figure 5.1). To temporarily store data and instructions, the CPU has special-purpose storage devices called **registers.**

Control Unit

The **control unit,** a maze of complex electronic circuitry, is responsible for directing and coordinating most of the computer system activities. It does not execute instructions itself; it tells other parts of the computer system what to do. It determines the movement of electronic signals between main memory and the arithmetic/logic unit, as well as the control signals between the CPU and input/output devices.

Just as a car is useless without gas, a computer is not much good without software instructions. When we use software, we are working with high-level (human language-like) instructions that are to be carried out by the control unit. These instructions are converted by a language processor into a low-level form of instructions the computer can work with—**machine language,** the only language that the CPU can understand (Figure 5.2). In machine language, data and instructions are represented in binary form (0s and 1s), and each type of computer—microcomputer, minicomputer, or mainframe—responds to a unique version. Once the instructions have been converted into this form, they can be retrieved from main memory and interpreted by the control unit (sometimes referred to as *decoding*). According to each specific instruction, the control unit issues the neces-

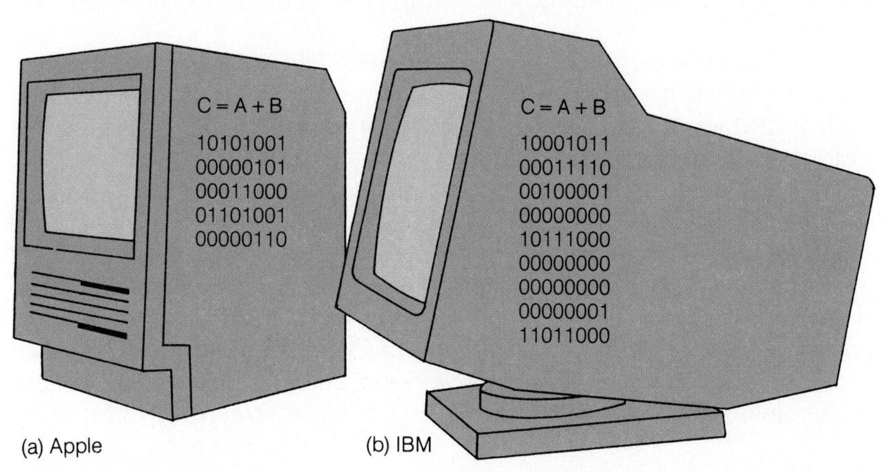

FIGURE 5.2

Machine language. This illustration shows the Apple and the IBM instructions for adding two numbers. IBM computers are incompatible with Apple computers because their processors use different versions of machine language instructions. Software written for one machine cannot be used on the other without special conversion equipment.

sary signals to other computer system components as needed to satisfy the processing requirements. This could involve, for example, directing that data be retrieved from a disk storage device, "telling" the printer to print the letter you just wrote, or simply directing the arithmetic/logic unit to add two numbers.

ARITHMETIC/LOGIC UNIT (ALU)

Without the **arithmetic/logic unit** (**ALU**), Kim would not be able to do those financial forecasts for Sporting Life on the computer, and you would not be able to use Ticketron to find out if you and your friends can get five seats at the Lemon Bowl. In fact, without the ALU, computers would not be able to do most of the tasks that we find useful. The ALU performs all the arithmetic and logical (comparison) functions—that is, it adds, subtracts, multiplies, divides, and does comparisons. These comparisons, which are basically "less than," "greater than," and "equal to," can be combined into several common expressions, such as "greater than or equal to." The objective of most instructions that use comparisons is to determine which instructions should be executed next.

The ALU controls the speed of calculations and so receives a great deal of attention from computer engineers trying to meet the needs of the fast-paced business world. Older microcomputers' speeds are usually measured in *milliseconds*—1 thousandth of a second. Newer microcomputers' speeds are measured in *microseconds*—1 millionth of a second. Larger, powerful computers' speeds are measured in *nanoseconds*—1 billionth of a second—or *picoseconds*—1 trillionth of a second. If a nanosecond were equal to one minute, then a minute would be equal to 1,900 years!

REGISTERS

Registers are special temporary storage locations within the CPU—some in the control unit and some in the ALU. Registers very quickly accept, store, and transfer data and instructions that are being used immediately. (Main memory holds data that will be used shortly; secondary storage—such as a diskette—holds data that will be used later). To execute an instruction, the control unit of the CPU retrieves it from main memory and places it into a register. The typical operations that take place in the processing of instructions are part of either the instruction cycle or the execution cycle.

The **instruction cycle,** or **I-cycle,** refers to the retrieval of an instruction from main memory and its subsequent decoding (the process of alerting the circuits in the CPU to perform the specified operation). The time it takes to go through the instruction cycle is referred to as *I-time*.

The **execution cycle,** or **E-cycle,** refers to the execution of the instruction and the subsequent storing of the result in a register. The time it takes to go through the execution cycle is referred to as *E-time*. The instruction cycle and the execution cycle together, as they apply to one instruction, are referred to as a **machine cycle** (Figure 5.3). The CPU has an internal **clock** that synchronizes all operations in the cycle. The speed is expressed in **megahertz (MHz)**; 1 MHz equals 1 million cycles per second. Generally, the faster the clock speed, the faster the computer can process information. An older IBM PC has a clock speed of 4.77 MHz; an

IBM PS/2 Model 50 has a clock speed of 10 MHz; the Mac II's clock speed is 15.7 MHz; and the Hewlett-Packard Vectra QS-16 and WYSE PC 386 have clock speeds of 16 MHz. Of course, for most users, the faster, the better . . . and the more expensive!

The number and types of registers in a CPU vary according to the CPU's design. Their size (capacity) and number can dramatically affect the processing power of a computer system. In general, the "larger" the register, the more bits can be processed at once. The size of a register is referred to as *wordsize*. Some personal computers have general-purpose registers that hold only 8 bits; others hold 16 bits; newer microcomputers have 32-bit registers. Computers that handle a 32-bit wordsize can process data twice as fast as those that handle a 16-bit wordsize. The difference in processing power due to difference in register size can be illustrated by the difference between trying to put out a fire with a small drinking glass and with a 5-gallon bucket.

Bus

The term *bus* refers to an electrical pathway through which bits are transmitted between the various computer components. Depending on the design of a system, several types of buses may be present. For the user, the most important one is the **data bus,** which carries data throughout the CPU. The wider the data bus, the more data it can carry at one time and thus the greater the processing speed of the computer. The data bus in the Intel 8088 processor is 8 bits wide, meaning that it can carry 8 bits—or one character—at a time. In contrast, the data buses in the Motorola 68020 processor (in the Macintosh II microcomputer) and the Intel

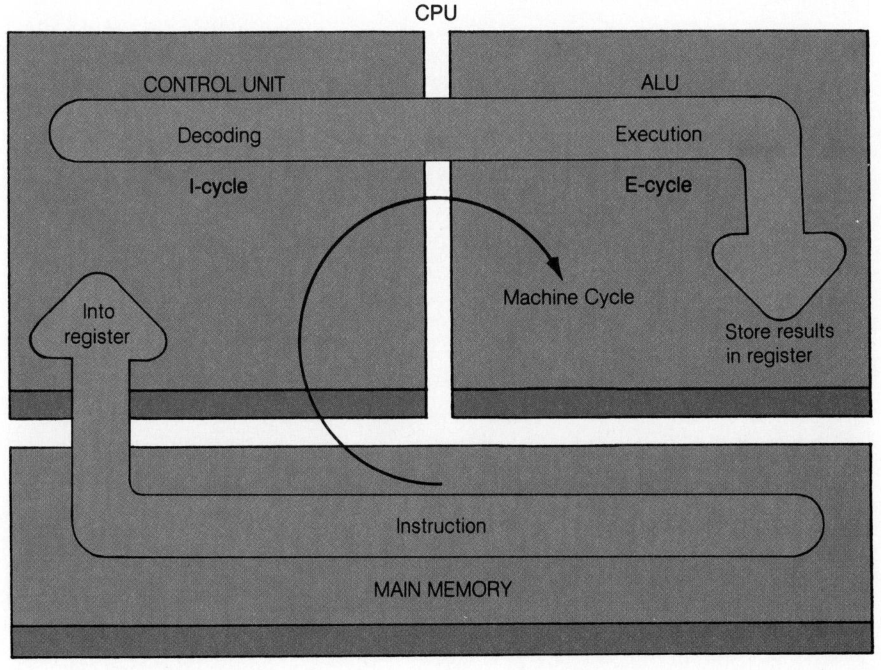

FIGURE 5.3

The machine cycle—the instruction cycle and the execution cycle as they apply to the processing of one instruction.

80386 processor (in the IBM PS/2 Model 80 microcomputer) are 32 bits wide—they can move four times more data through their data buses than the Intel 8088 bus can. Some supercomputers contain buses that are 128 bits wide. Table 5.1 shows a comparison of wordsize, bus width, and clock speed of common microprocessors.

THE MICROPROCESSOR: CONDUCTING THE SHOW

The manufacture of the CPU on a tiny chip—also called a *semiconductor* or an *integrated circuit*—revolutionized the computer industry and created the business market for microcomputers—basically providing the reason why you are reading this book now. How is this chip—the microprocessor—made?

TABLE 5.1

Comparison of Several Microprocessors

Company	Micro-processor	Word Size (bits)	Bus Width	Clock Speed (MHz)	Microcomputers Using This Chip*
Mostek	6502	8	8	4	Apple IIe Atari 800 Commodore 64
Intel	8086	16	16	8	Some IBM compatibles
Intel	8088	16	8	8	IBM PC and XT HP 150 touch screen
Intel	80286	32	16	8–12	IBM AT IBM PS/2 Model 50 Compaq Deskpro 286
Motorola	68000	32	16	16	Classic Macintosh Apple Macintosh
Motorola	68020	32	32	16–32	Macintosh LC
Motorola	68030	32	32	20–50	Macintosh IIsi NeXT computer
Motorola	68040	32	32	25+	Hewlett-Packard workstations
Intel	80386SX	32	16	16–20	NEC PowerMate SX/20 Compaq Deskpro 386s/20
Intel	80386	32	32	16–33	Compaq Deskpro 386 IBM PS/2 Model 80
Intel	80486	32	32	33–50	IBM PS/2 Model 70

* This table includes a partial list of the microcomputers using each chip.

The microprocessor contains at least a control unit and an ALU. Some of the more sophisticated microprocessor chips also include different types of memory (to be discussed shortly) and circuitry necessary to support specialized hardware devices. The microprocessor chips in early microcomputer systems weren't nearly as powerful as the CPUs in large computers, but with each technological advance—which seems to occur almost every day—microprocessors are becoming more and more powerful. Some of today's microcomputers, equipped with powerful microprocessor chips, rival the processing power found in many of today's minicomputers.

As we mentioned earlier, large wordsize and data bus width—that is, the number of bits that a computer can process at once and that a data bus can carry at once—translate directly into high processing speed. An 8-bit computer can do anything a 32-bit computer can, just slower. And an 8-bit microprocessor costs a lot less than a 32-bit microprocessor, because its circuitry is much less sophisticated.

A microprocessor's circuitry may be as small as a ¼-inch, or even ⅛-inch, square. To develop such complicated circuitry in such a small package requires a combination of technologies. Hundreds of microprocessors can be produced on a single disk—called a *wafer*—sliced from an ingot of silicon, a nonmetallic element that, after oxygen, is the most common component of the earth's crust. A wafer is about 4/1000 of an inch thick; an ingot is about 2 feet long and 6 inches in diameter (Figure 5.4). Chips are made to do different things in addition to being a CPU—for example, to expand a computer's ability to handle numeric computation (numeric coprocessor) or graphics (graphics coprocessor) and to expand a computer's memory. As a user, you will probably be interested in finding out what types of chips are available to improve your computer system.

MAIN MEMORY

CPUs, ALUs, registers, buses, instructions, input, output, storage . . . what good are they if you have no data to work with? You wouldn't have any if it weren't for **main memory** (also called *primary storage*, *memory*, and *random access memory [RAM]*), the part of the processing hardware that temporarily holds data and instructions needed shortly by the CPU. (Registers hold data and instructions that are to be used *immediately*.)

HISTORY OF MAIN MEMORY

For many years main memory was one of the most expensive computer components to manufacture. However, technology has revolutionized main memory components over the past 40 or so years; their size has been drastically reduced, and they have become less expensive as the manufacturing materials have changed from vacuum tubes to magnetic cores to transistors and finally to the chips we know today (Figure 5.5).

The earliest form of main memory was based on vacuum tubes. Today's technology can put 256 K to 4 MB on a single main memory chip; the equivalent main memory capacity would have required a shelf of vacuum tubes more than a mile long. And tubes were not reliable. Their power requirements were high, they

FIGURE 5.4

Chip off the new block. (a,b) Chips with tiny circuitry are manufactured in groups on wafers (c), which are sliced from blocks of silicon, called *ingots* (d) at places such as the Advanced Micro Devices Laboratory (e), where chips are manufactured.

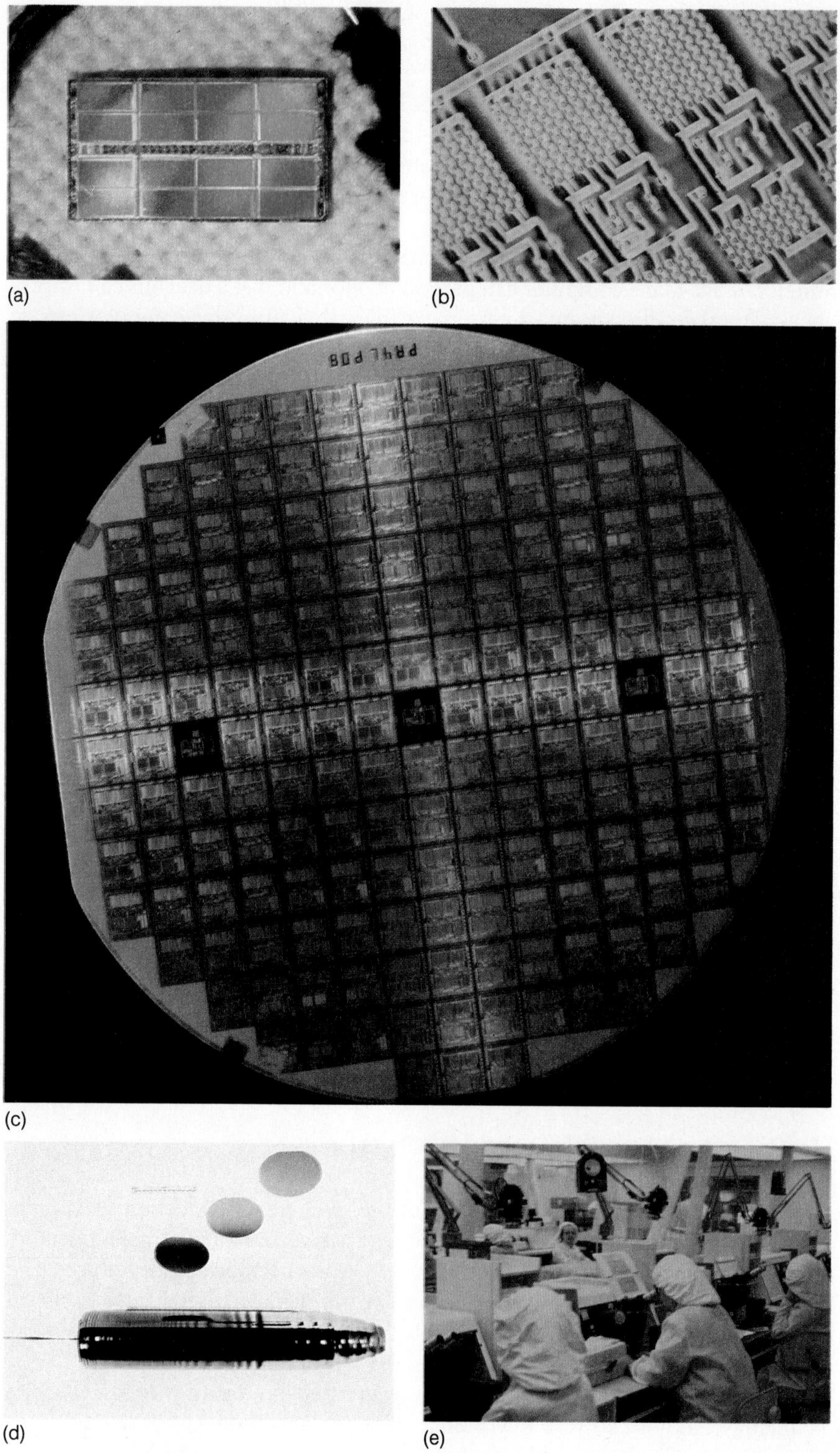

(a)

(b)

(c)

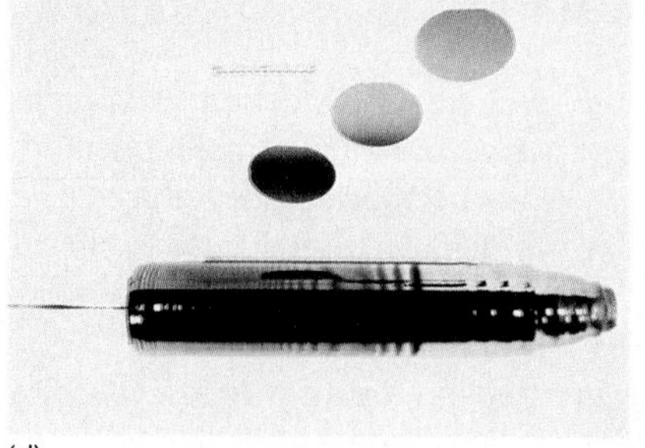

(d)

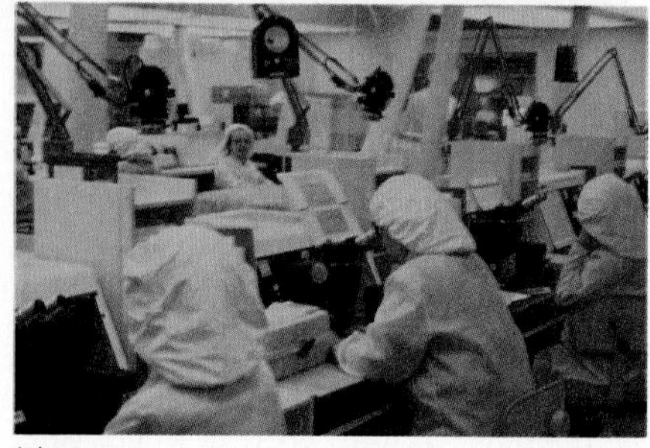

(e)

generated heat, they failed frequently, and they were slow. The transistor, invented in 1947, was a much smaller and more reliable provider of main memory. It also had smaller power requirements and failed less frequently than vacuum tubes. Magnetic cores were smaller still.

However, by the mid-1970s, work had begun on a new type of main memory technology—semiconductor memory. (A **semiconductor** is a material that conducts electricity poorly but that, when "impurities" such as arsenic and indium are added to it, can be used to form electrical circuits.) The main memory of almost all computers today is based on this technology, which involves coating a silicon chip with a material that can take on two different states once the circuits have been etched onto the surface: The material either will or will not conduct electricity. Chips are very small and relatively inexpensive to manufacture, and they do not consume as much power as older forms of main memory. The use of chips has greatly increased the memory capacity of computers. In 1979 a microcomputer with 64 K of main memory was considered to be a satisfactory system. Today a microcomputer system with less than 640 K of main memory may be considered underpowered, and many users are expanding their microcomputer's main memory to 4–8 MB.

FUNCTION OF MAIN MEMORY

The principal function of main memory is to act as a buffer between the central processing unit (CPU) and the rest of the computer system components. It functions as a sort of desktop on which you place the things with which you are about to begin to work. The CPU can utilize only those software instructions and data that are stored in main memory.

As we mentioned earlier, main memory is **random access memory,** or **RAM.** The name derives from the fact that data can be stored in and retrieved at ran-

Not totally tubular. The materials used to manufacture main memory—from large vacuum tubes (a) to transistors (b) to tiny silicon chips—have changed dramatically over the past 40 years. **FIGURE 5.5**

(a)

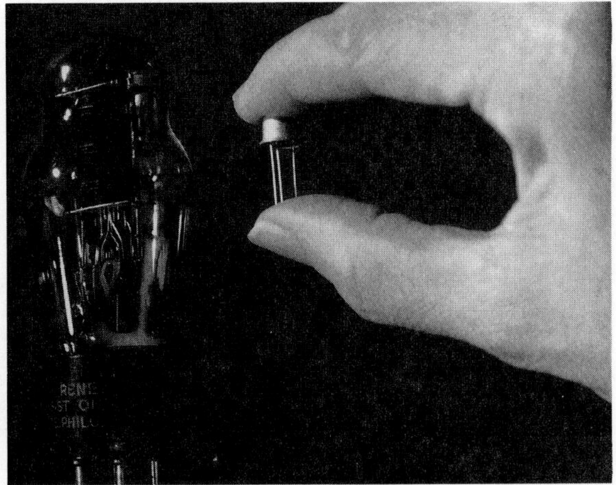
(b)

dom—from anywhere—in the electronic main memory chips in approximately the same amount of time, no matter where the data is.

Main memory is in an electronic, or volatile, state. When the computer is off, main memory is empty; when it is on, main memory is capable of receiving and holding a copy of the software instructions and data necessary for processing. Because main memory is a volatile form of storage that depends on electric power and the power can go off during processing, users often save their work frequently onto nonvolatile secondary storage devices such as diskettes or hard disks. In general, main memory is used for the following purposes:

- Storage of a copy of the main software program that controls the general operation of the computer. This copy is loaded into main memory when the computer is turned on (you'll find out how later), and it stays there as long as the computer is on.
- Temporary storage of a copy of application program instructions (the specific software you are using in your business) to be retrieved by the CPU for interpretation and execution.
- Temporary storage of data that has been input from the keyboard or other input device until instructions call for the data to be transferred into the CPU for processing.
- Temporary storage of data that has been produced as a result of processing until instructions call for the data to be used again in subsequent processing or to be transferred to an output device such as the screen, a printer, or a disk storage device.

Figure 5.6 shows the banks (a group of chips, usually nine, arranged in a row) of RAM chips found on a memory expansion card, which fits inside the system cabinet (Figure 5.7). Many people erroneously assume that a memory chip with a capacity of 64 K can hold a substantial number of characters of data; however, in main

FIGURE 5.6

Going to the bank. This photo shows banks of RAM chips (left) on a memory expansion card that will be plugged into a slot inside the system cabinet.

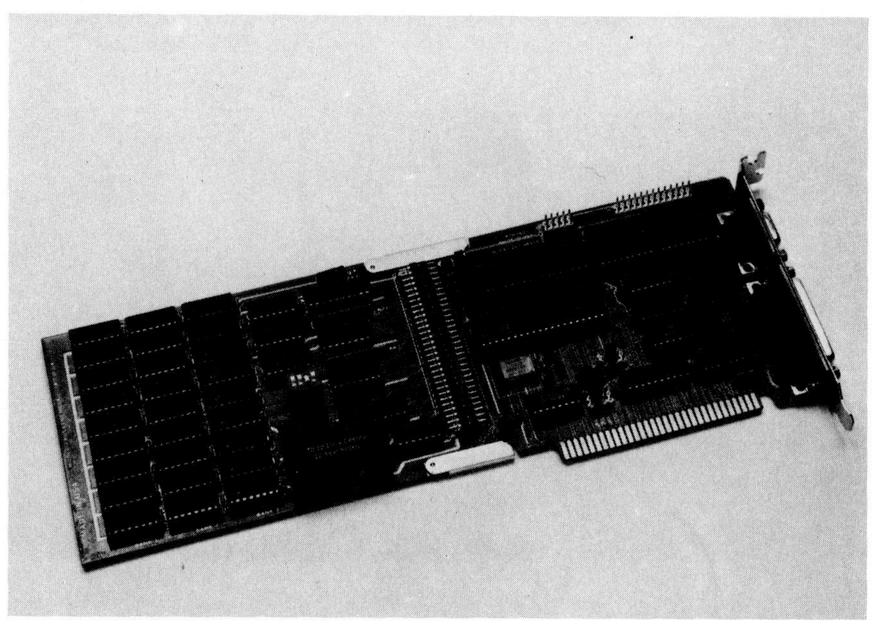

memory it takes eight chips to store one character. Each chip can be thought of as representing a column of 64 K electronic light switches that can be read one row at a time. The code for a character, such as the letter C, is stored in the same row across the entire bank of memory chips (Figure 5.8). The first 8 bits build the character;

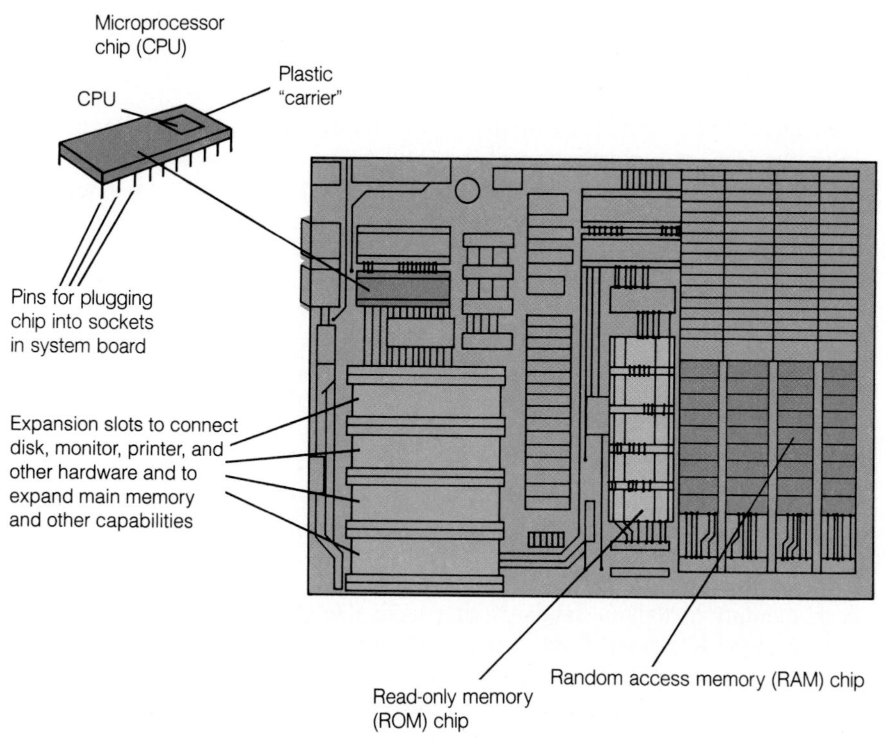

FIGURE 5.7

System board. This illustration shows the usual position of ROM and RAM chips, the CPU, and slots for expansion cards. Expansion cards are often used to increase a computer's main memory (RAM) capacity.

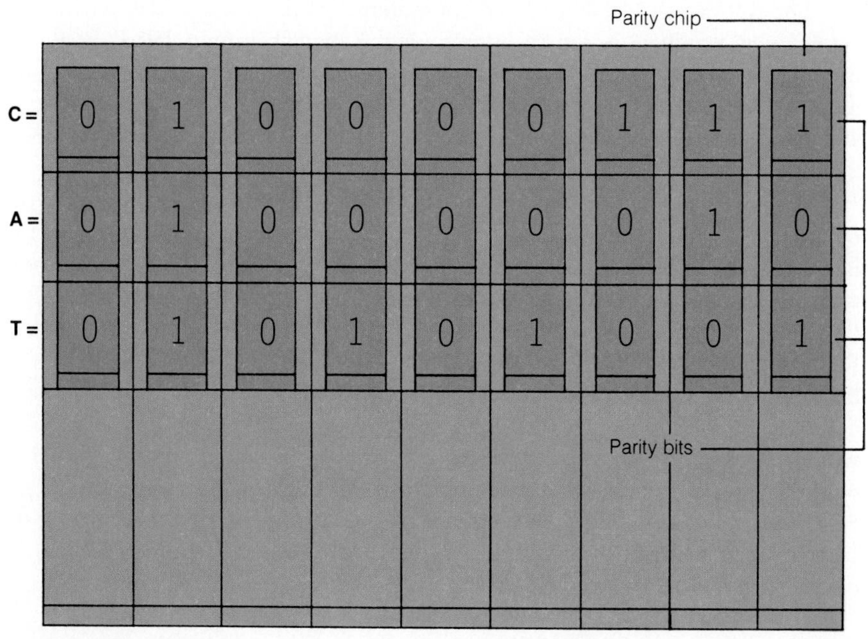

FIGURE 5.8

Chipping away at words. Many people think that a character (byte) of data can be stored in a chip, but it takes eight chips to store one character. The ninth chip is used for the parity bit. (This machine is using an even-parity scheme.)

the ninth chip, the parity chip, holds the parity bit, or check bit, that is used for error detection.

A bank of 64 K RAM chips can store 64 K, or 65,536 (1,024 × 64) bytes. Therefore, each RAM chip is capable of storing a column of 65,536 bits—each bit is *part* of the code used to represent a character.

MAIN MEMORY (RAM) FOR MICROCOMPUTERS

The amount of random access memory you have in your microcomputer directly affects the level of sophistication of the software you can use. Sophisticated, or powerful, programs take up a lot of space in RAM. Most of today's software programs require a minimum of 640 K to run. In general, the greater your machine's memory capacity, the better, because:

- It can receive and use much larger programs.
- It can hold copies of more than one program in main memory to support the sharing of the computer by more than one user at a time.
- It can operate faster and more efficiently.
- It will be able to use new, sophisticated software.
- It can hold images for creating graphics and animation.
- It can work with and manipulate more data at one time.

Early microcomputer systems were not equipped with very much random access memory by today's standards; they were able to directly access and control only up to 64 K RAM. Today users can expand memory to over 48 MB. In addition, the price of RAM chips was much higher than it is now. To upgrade the random access memory of a computer from 16 K to 48 K in 1979 could easily have cost several hundred dollars. Today that same amount can purchase several megabytes of RAM.

The software available for microcomputers did not require much RAM until certain new products began to appear on the market around 1984. With the introduction of special software called ***spreadsheets*** to handle large financial reports, the need for increased main memory grew rapidly. Now for a microcomputer to effectively use many of the newer software products, it should have at least 640 K of main memory available.

But what if you, like many users, are faced with the need to expand your computer's main memory capacity (RAM) to be able to use some new software? For instance, what if your microcomputer is not brand new and has a main memory capacity of only 256 K? This capacity would include four banks of 64 K RAM chips. Unfortunately, you cannot simply pull out two of the 64 K chips and replace them with 256 K chips to increase the amount of main memory available to 640 K because of the component referred to as the *dynamic memory access (DMA)* controller. In most older microcomputer systems, the DMA chip was designed to work with only one size of memory chip. However, in newer systems the DMA controller is designed to allow a mix of banks of 64 K, 256 K, 1 MB, 2 MB, and 4 MB memory chips. The DMA chip or module is responsible for managing the use of all main memory. It keeps track of which memory locations are in use (and by what) and which are available for use.

Two types of memory are used to increase RAM beyond the 640 K limit—expanded memory and extended memory. The type used is influenced by the sophistication of the microprocessor in your machine.

EXPANDED MEMORY

As we just described, users of early microcomputer systems couldn't increase the amount of main memory directly wired into the motherboard beyond 640 K. This situation led to the development of a wide variety of new products allowing the memory to be expanded through the use of an **add-on memory board,** or *card*, sometimes referred to as an *external memory board* (refer to Figure 5.6). This **expanded memory** board is simply pressed into an expansion slot on the motherboard. An *expansion slot* is a "plug-in" spot on the motherboard specifically meant to support add-on components (Figure 5.9). This slot connects the add-on board with the power supply for the computer and links the board with the buses for moving data and instructions. Some switch settings in the computer may need to be adjusted to account for the increased amount of memory, because the computer won't know how much main memory it has unless you tell it. Although this process may sound complicated, it really isn't; it usually takes only a screwdriver and about 10 minutes. The instructions for installing an add-on memory board come with the board.

We do need to mention here that add-on boards or cards can be inserted only in computers with **open architecture**—that is, computers built to allow users to open the system cabinet and make changes. Computers with **closed architecture**—such as some Macintosh microcomputers—do not allow the user to add expansion cards. Thus you can see that a computer's architecture becomes important to the user if he or she wants to upgrade the system—not only to increase RAM but also to add secondary storage, graphics capabilities, some communications capabilities, or

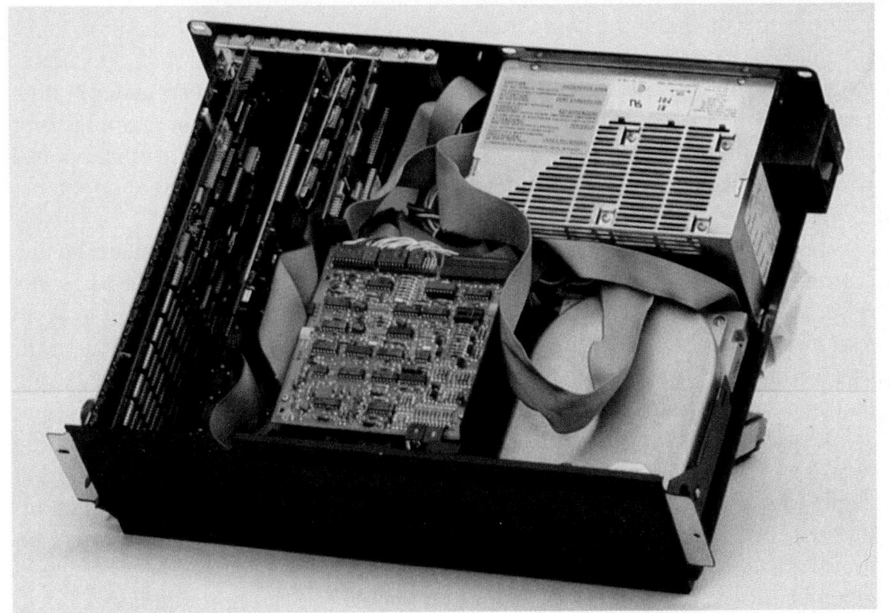

FIGURE 5.9

Feeling expansive? Buy an add-on memory board to plug in an expansion slot and increase your RAM. (The expansion card is at the far left.)

to change from a monochrome display screen to a color screen. If you are buying a computer system and think you might want to upgrade it at a later date, make sure you purchase a computer with open architecture.

Expanded memory is used in 8088, 8086, 80286, and 80386 computers (the numbers are the microprocessor model numbers).

EXTENDED MEMORY

Extended memory also refers to memory increased above 640 K. However, extended memory can be used only in 80286, 80386, and 80486 microcomputers. Extended memory is also composed of RAM chips that are either plugged directly into the motherboard or are attached to a board that is plugged into an expansion slot. With extended memory, a machine can use up to 16 MB of memory. Like expanded memory, extended memory can be used only by software that recognizes it—your applications software documentation will specify whether the software is compatible with one or both of these types of increased memory.

CACHE MEMORY

Some computers are designed with **cache memory,** to increase the speed of transfer of instructions and data from secondary storage to the processor. Like RAM, cache memory is essentially a high-speed temporary storage area for program instructions and data. However, cache memory is about 10 times faster than RAM and about 100 times more expensive. Because its storage capacity is smaller than RAM's capacity, cache memory holds only those instructions and data that the processor needs immediately.

READ–ONLY MEMORY (ROM)

How does your computer know what to do when you turn it on? How does it know to check out your hardware components (such as the keyboard or the monitor) to see that they have been connected correctly? Instructions to perform such operations, which are critical to the operation of a computer, are stored permanently on a **read-only memory (ROM)** chip (Figure 5.10) installed by the manufacturer inside the computer. This ROM chip, also called *firmware*, retains instructions in a permanently accessible, nonvolatile form. When the power in the computer is turned off, the instructions stored in ROM are not lost.

Having basic instructions permanently stored in ROM is both necessary and convenient. For example, if you are using a microcomputer with diskette drives, the more instructions in ROM, the fewer diskettes you may have to handle in order to load instructions into the computer. If you could have *all* the program instructions you'll ever need to use in ROM, you would have everything you need for processing data and information at your fingertips—always.

Unfortunately, until recently the process of manufacturing ROM chips and recording data on them was more expensive than the process of producing RAM chips. As a result, manufacturers tended to record in ROM only those instructions that were crucial to the operation of the computer. In recent years improvements in the manufacturing process of ROM chips have lowered their cost to the point where manufacturers are beginning to include additional software instructions.

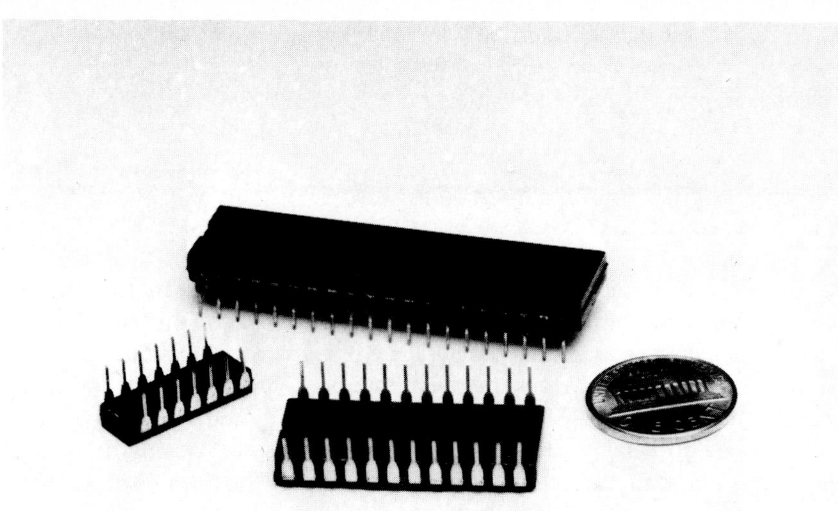

FIGURE 5.10

Thanks for the memory. ROM chips, installed by the manufacturer on the computer's system board, contain permanent instructions that are read by the computer. Since they usually cannot be rewritten, they are called *read-only*.

PROM, EPROM, EEPROM

Three additional kinds of nonvolatile memory are used in some computer systems—namely, PROMs, EPROMs, and EEPROMs. **PROM** stands for **programmable read-only memory.** This type of memory functions in the same way a regular ROM component does, with one major exception—PROM chips are custom-made for the user by the manufacturer. In other words, the user determines what data and instructions are recorded on them. The only problem with PROM chips is that, like ROM chips, once data is recorded on them, it can't be changed.

Erasable programmable read-only memory (EPROM) (Figure 5.11) chips were developed as an improvement over PROM chips. EPROM* functions exactly the same as PROM; however, with the help of a special device that uses ultraviolet light, in approximately 15 minutes the data or instructions on an EPROM chip can be erased. Then a device generically referred to as a PROM burner is used to reprogram the chip. To change instructions on an EPROM chip, the chip must be taken out of the machine and then put back when changes have been made. This task is one most computer users would prefer to avoid. The alternative to erasing and rerecording an EPROM chip is to replace it with a new EPROM that features the new program code. This is a task best performed by a trained computer professional.

Electrically erasable programmable read-only memory (EEPROM) (Figure 5.11), the latest addition to the ROM family of chips, avoids the inconvenience of having to take chips out of the computer to change data and instructions. Instead, changes can be made electrically under software control. These chips are being used in point-of-sale terminals to record price-related data for products. The

* You can tell if you have an EPROM chip by the presence of a quartz window on the top. Probably a piece of tape covers the window. Do not remove that tape; a half hour of fluorescent lamp exposure could erase the memory.

prices recorded on them can be easily updated as needed. The only disadvantage of EEPROM chips is that they currently cost substantially more than regular ROM chips and disk storage devices. However, experts expect the prices to come down substantially.

MEASURING THE PROCESSING POWER OF A COMPUTER

The proliferation of microcomputers in our society means that more and more people are becoming familiar with the processing power of computers in general. Many individuals are considering the purchase of a microcomputer on their own, with the result that more and more people are asking, "How do you determine how powerful a computer is?"

This question is fairly easy to answer. However, understanding the answer requires knowledge of a few more computer fundamentals.

ADDRESSING SCHEME

The **addressing scheme** is a computer design feature that directly determines the amount of main memory that can be controlled by the central processing unit at any one time. (Memory addresses are designed when the computer is manufactured.) The early microcomputer CPUs were limited in memory-addressing capability to 64 K. The popular IBM PC and PC-compatible computers have a memory addressing capability of 1,024 K. The IBM PS/2 Model 80 uses the 80386 microprocessor, which allows access to approximately 4 GB of main memory—equal to the addressing capability of current minicomputers. Some "super" minicomputer systems can access even more than that. Mainframes usually have an addressing scheme that allows access to between 32 and 128 MB or more of RAM.

FIGURE 5.11

Nothing to wear a corsage for. EPROM (left) and EEPROM (right).

Computers and Careers

Crime Fighting

Crime rates have increased, but they might have increased more were it not for the presence of computer technology.

Consider home security. At one time, home-security systems were expensive and notoriously unreliable, with over 90 percent of alarms triggered being false. Often the alarms were caused by user error, such as a homeowner accidentally tripping a system and forgetting how to deactivate it, but they were also caused by equipment malfunction. Today's computerized home-security systems allow one to turn off some alarms (such as those inside) and turn on others (such as door and window alarms). They can also detect and isolate malfunctioning sensors, eliminating many false alarms.

Police departments, of course, have been using computers for some time, as when an officer in a patrol car calls up on a dashboard-mounted computer the license numbers of suspicious vehicles to check whether they have been stolen. More creative uses of computers have followed. Fingerprint identification, which used to require so many hours of an officer's time that it was virtually not attempted except in the most serious cases, has proved to be extraordinarily successful in those urban police departments that have moved their fingerprint files to a computerized database. The old-fashioned police artist's pad and pencil have been replaced by a software program containing more than 100,000 facial features, allowing officers with no artistic talent to create remarkably professional composite drawings of wanted suspects.

Computers have also helped increase productivity in prosecutors' offices and make the judicial system function better. For instance, a computer system may be used to log all incoming letters and phone calls; the district attorney heading the prosecutor's office can then scan the printouts and find out which callers require return calls and which assistant D.A.s must be reminded to respond to backlogged correspondence. Confidential data can be kept on various cases, and the system can be used to create appropriate legal documents to advance cases through the court system. Weekly calendars of active cases are provided to help prosecutors avoid scheduling conflicts and alert them to necessary actions they must take.

Some prosecutors' offices have a computer system that tracks cases from arrest to disposition. For example, in the Brooklyn, N.Y., District Attorney's office, a system called FACTS (Facility for Accurate Case Tracking System) begins to pick up a case when the suspect is first brought to central booking at the police station, where the nature of the charges are keyed into a terminal. For misdemeanor cases, a terminal informs the judge about a suspect's prior record, outstanding charges, and the names of prosecuting attorneys. For felonies, the system is used to schedule the first grand jury hearing to determine if the evidence justifies an indictment. Other data includes names of witnesses, bail records, and the like.

Even the U.S. Supreme Court has acquired computer technology. The system is designed to transmit the court's opinion within minutes of its announcement. ■

REGISTER SIZE

Computers have a number of registers that are used for a variety of purposes, including arithmetic operations. The more of these registers you have and the larger they are, the more processing power you have. The registers in early microcomputers could hold only 8 bits each. The Intel 8088-type microprocessor was equipped with eight general-purpose registers, each capable of holding 16 bits. The Motorola 68000 processor, used in the Macintosh, has 16 general-purpose registers that can hold 32 bits each. Each 32-bit general-purpose register can process twice as much data in each machine cycle per register as a 16-bit register can. If you compare the size and number of registers of the Intel 8088 processor and the Motorola 68000, you can see that the 8088 has a total general-purpose register capacity of 128 bits, whereas the 68000 has a capacity of 512 bits. This means that the Motorola 68000 provides substantially more work space for data during processing.

The registers in minicomputers today are usually 32 bits. Mainframes generally have registers that are at least 64 bits in size.

DATA BUS CAPACITY

As you learned earlier, the data bus is like a pipeline used to move data and instructions among main memory, the central processing unit, and other computer system components. The size of the data bus controls the amount of data that can travel down the pipeline at one time and thus can significantly affect a computer's performance. The early computers had data buses large enough to allow 8 bits of data to pass at one time; today three basic bus designs are found in IBM and IBM-compatible microcomputer systems. The Industry Standard Architecture (ISA) passes 8 bits at a time when used with the Intel 8088 microprocessor and 16 bits with the 80286 and 80386 microprocessors. Micro Channel Architecture (MCA) and Extended Industry Standard Architecture (EISA) bus systems are used with 80386 and 80486 machines to pass 32 bits at a time through the data bus. Hardware and software must be designed specifically for the bus system that will be used. As you can imagine, the larger data bus allows data to be moved around the system much faster.

Ideally, data bus capacity should be the same as register size (see above)—but this isn't always the case. For example, although the Intel 80286 microprocessor has 32-bit processing registers, its data bus is only 16 bits wide. Therefore, the data bus isn't wide enough to utilize the registers fully. The more powerful Intel 80386 microprocessor has 32-bit processing registers and a 32-bit data bus. (The 80386SX chip is faster than the 80286 chip and less expensive than the 80386.)

CLOCK SPEED

The clock, mentioned in the section on the instruction execution cycle, is the part of the CPU that synchronizes and sets the speed of all the operations in the machine cycle. The early microcomputers operated at speeds of around 1 MHz. This means that those computers had approximately 1 million processing cycles available per second to perform useful work. The newest model personal computers are operating at speeds of 32–40 MHz.

Instruction Set

The early 8-bit microprocessors were extremely slow when performing mathematical operations. They were designed to handle only addition and subtraction; a more sophisticated operation (such as division or multiplication) had to be performed by a series of special program instructions, often called *subroutines*. For example, to multiply 6 times 2, a subroutine would add the number 2 together 6 times. The more powerful 16-bit microcomputers use additional instructions that handle mathematical operations in a single processing cycle. The 16-bit microprocessors also use single *blocks* of instructions (called *instruction sets*) that can cause whole blocks of data to be moved from one place to another. On the 8-bit microcomputers, this type of operation would also have to be handled by a number of subroutines (lots of "small," individual instructions).

How a microprocessor is designed affects how fast it can process data. Most microprocessor chips today are designed using the Complex Instruction Set Computing (CISC) approach. A multitude of software applications written for use with this chip design are being used in the business environment today. A new approach to chip design, called **Reduced Instruction Set Computing (RISC),** allows microcomputers to offer very high speed performance by simplifying the internal design and reducing the number of instruction sets needed. RISC design enables a computer to process about twice as fast as one based on CISC design. The extent to which RISC design will be employed depends on how the software industry supports it; many experts expect support to grow rapidly.

Checklist

In general, keep these points in mind when you are trying to determine the processing power of a computer:

- *Addressing scheme:* The larger the addressing capability, the more main memory the computer can control.
- *Register size:* The larger the general-purpose registers, the more data the CPU can manipulate in one machine cycle.
- *Data bus:* The larger the data bus, the more efficiently and quickly data and instructions can be moved among the processing components of the computer.
- *Clock speed:* The faster the clock speed, the more machine cycles are completed per second and the faster the computer can perform processing operations.
- *Instruction set:* The more powerful the instruction set, the fewer instructions and processing cycles it takes to perform certain tasks.

(See also Episode 3 of Sporting Life for more information about purchasing a microcomputer.)

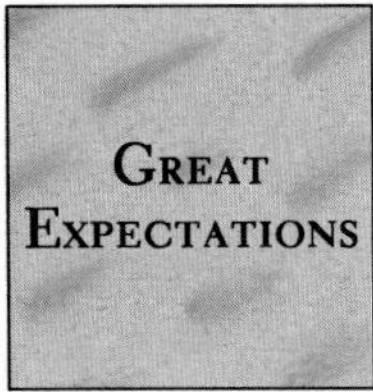

MICROPROCESSORS

A CPU of the 1940s that weighed 5 tons, took up six rooms, processed about 10,000 instructions per second, and cost about $5 million now is 5 millimeters square, about ½-inch thick, can process about 4 million instructions per second, and costs less than $5. This revolution in computer processing was caused, as you know, by the development of the microprocessor. Today a microcomputer priced at about $7,500 (such as the Compaq Deskpro 386) has essentially the same power as an IBM mainframe of more than 10 years ago—but that machine cost $3.4 million at the time. If the automobile industry had advanced this fast since 1982, said Edward Lucente, the head of IBM's Information Systems Group, "Today we'd have cars that go zero to 60 in three seconds, circle the globe on a tank of gas, and cost half as much as they did six years ago. Of course, they would be difficult to get into, because they would be only half the size."

In general, current developments in the microcomputer industry indicate that the next generation of personal computers will change not so much in the way the hardware looks but in the way the computers work; that is, main memory capacity will increase, operating systems will change, secondary storage will increase, and software will become more sophisticated and easier to use. In fact, microcomputers will have so much power that they will be able to devote 75 percent of their time to running software that improves interaction with the user and still calculate faster than current machines.

Of course, many of these improvements relate to microprocessor developments. The speed and power of microprocessors will continue to grow until the microcomputer is no longer a uniprocessor system; that is, the microcomputer will have specific processors for such functions as communications, graphics, and artificial intelligence (which we will cover later). Also, serial, or linear, processing—whereby instructions are executed one at a time—may become a thing of the past; true *parallel processing*—whereby many processors attack separate components of a problem simultaneously, which is already used to some degree with larger computers—will eventually be available on microcomputers. (Some experts regard the 80386 processor as a miniature parallel processor because it can execute one instruction while simultaneously decoding a second and fetching a third.) Gallium arsinide, which works at least three times faster than silicon as a semiconductor, may be used in combination with silicon to manufacture chips—that is, if other types of potentially cheaper and faster superconductor materials currently under research don't grab the spotlight.

Superconductor materials being examined by some scientists include special ceramic/metal compounds, bismuth- and thallium-based compounds, and a special type of plastic film that will allow chip circuits to be etched by light rays, which will greatly simplify chip production and reduce its expense. However, many of the materials under investigation are superconductive only at temperatures too low to be practical for the user, and thallium is a deadly poison! Other researchers are currently developing a neural-network computer chip with 256 processors, or "neurons," and 65,536 interconnections, or "synapses." In traditional processors, electrons travel along miniaturized metal-wire circuits engraved in silicon. However, instead of having thousands of circuits engraved onto one chip, the neural-network chip has packets of electrons injected directly into the silicon. The electrons are guided from one neuron to another, enabling each of the chip's processors to exchange data with every other processor in a continually updated circuit. Researchers suspect that neural-network chips will be useful in speech recognition, which requires high-speed processing. If future neural networks are patterned closely on the human brain, "thinking" computers may do just that.

Still other scientists are researching the use of genetically engineered organic materials to be used as *biochips* and on *optical computing*, which would use light-activated microprocessors, as well as the RISC (reduced instruction set computing) chip, which simplifies chip architecture and instruction sets, thereby enabling chips to become yet smaller and faster. AT&T has already developed the prototype of a digital optical processor that uses light (photons) instead of electricity (electrons) to process data. Optical processors hold the promise of running at clock speeds measured in gigahertz. AT&T officials hope to ready a miniaturized optical processing unit for inclusion in commercially available processors by the year 2000.

How much the user gets out of the explosion in microprocessor power and speed will depend on what the software industry does with it, because more powerful hardware will require more sophisticated programming to produce useful applications.

MINIS, MAINFRAMES, AND SUPERCOMPUTERS

In Chapter 1, we said that some mainframe computers are so powerful that they are referred to as supercomputers—"state-of-the-art" devices with such processing power and speed that ordinary computers pale by comparison. The two basic approaches to developing a supercomputer differ in terms of the number of central

FIGURE 5.12

Making the connection. The CM-2 is a member of the Connection Machine family of parallel computers. The 5-foot cube houses the system's 64,000 processors. The Data Vault mass storage system uses dozens of small disk drives to provide very rapid access to 10 GB of data.

processing units employed. In the first approach, a moderate number of very fast processors are linked together to perform linear processing—each processor typically works on a separate task. The second approach involves the use of a large number of processors to perform parallel processing; this is the direction of supercomputers of the future. Some experts say that parallel processing will be used in *all* sizes of computers by the year 2000. In supercomputer parallel processing, as many as 65,500 processors with a complexity of connectedness that begins to approach biological complexity operate simultaneously to solve problems. The Connection Machine (Figure 5.12), invented by Danny Hillis of Thinking Machines in Cambridge, Massachusetts (who once put together a working computer made entirely from Tinkertoys), is a parallel processing supercomputer.

We know that developments in supercomputer-related technologies will lead to tremendous improvements in computer processing power. Many of these improvements will filter down and be used in the minicomputers and microcomputers that are used in business and industry to manage day-to-day activities. In addition, supercomputer vendors expect to sell more of these machines to universities in the United States and to the aerospace, automotive, and oil/gas exploration industries.

ONWARD: OUT WITH IT!

Now that you have learned more hardware-related terms than you thought you'd ever need to know, we're going to give you one more hardware group to study—output hardware. The output phase of a computer-based information system is most important to the user. After all, the whole object of inputting and storing data and instructions for processing is to produce *information* that you can use to make decisions in your office or profession.

SUMMARY

If you are "tuned in" to the amount of processing power in your computer, you won't fall into the trap that many people do—namely, of buying a software program that won't run on your computer or expecting the computer to do something it isn't capable of doing.

The most important processing hardware component is the central processing unit (CPU), which comprises the control unit and the arithmetic/logic unit (ALU). CPUs used to be made of vacuum tubes, magnetic cores, and transistors, which were all relatively expensive, slow, and unreliable by today's standards. Today CPUs are manufactured from silicon; one wafer from a silicon ingot can hold hundreds of chips, also called *microprocessors*. The electric circuitry that forms the CPU is etched onto the surface of the chip.

The control unit of the CPU is responsible for directing and coordinating most of the computer system activities. It uses machine language to run the show. Unfortunately, the binary codes that make up machine language differ among machines, which creates a problem of incompatibility.

The ALU performs all arithmetic (plus, minus, times, divide by) and logical comparison (equal to, less than, greater than, not equal to) functions.

Registers are special temporary storage locations within the CPU that very quickly accept, store, and transfer data and instructions that are being used immediately. The number and types of registers in a computer vary according to the computer's design. The larger the registers, the more bits the computer can process at once. *Wordsize* is used to refer to the size of a register.

To get data and instructions moving among the various components of the system, the computer needs a data bus. The wider the bus, the more data it can move at one time.

The cycle that the computer goes through to fetch and execute one instruction is called the *machine cycle*. In the instruction cycle part of the machine cycle, an instruction is retrieved from main memory and is decoded in the CPU. The time it takes to do this is called *I-time*. In the execution cycle, the instruction is executed and the result is stored. The time this takes is called *E-time*. An internal clock in the CPU sets the speed of the machine cycle, which is measured in MHz—megahertz, or millions of cycles per second.

A computer system could not operate without main memory, also called *internal memory*, *primary memory*, *primary storage*, *random access memory (RAM)*, or simply *memory*. In general, main memory is used (1) to store a copy of the main software program that controls the general operation of the computer; (2) to store a copy of the business application software you are using; (3) to temporarily store data that has been input from the keyboard or other storage device until it is ready for processing; and (4) to temporarily store data that has been produced as a result of processing until it is ready for output or secondary storage.

In a microcomputer, main memory, or RAM, chips are usually found in banks of nine on the motherboard. A character's 8 bits are stored in a row of chips; the ninth chip holds the parity bit, which is a 1 or a 0, based on whether the parity scheme is odd or even. The parity scheme is used to check for errors produced by interferences with the electrical current.

If you have a microcomputer that needs to have its RAM expanded beyond 640 K to handle new types of software, you can purchase expanded memory or extended memory, usually in the form of an expanded memory board, to "plug in" to the motherboard.

In general, a ROM chip stores instructions necessary to tell a computer what to do when it is first turned on. These instructions are installed by the manufacturer and generally cannot be changed by the user.

Certain types of ROM chips give users added flexibility. Programmable read-only memory (PROM) chips allow you to put your own data and programs on them. Erasable programmable read-only memory (EPROM) chips can be changed by using a special ultraviolet light device; however, you have to take EPROM chips out of the computer to change the data and programs on them. Electrically erasable programmable read-only memory (EEPROM) chips can be changed without taking them out of the computer.

The processing power of a computer can be determined using the following factors: (1) addressing capability, (2) register size (wordsize), (3) data bus width, (4) clock speed, and (5) the instruction set.

KEY TERMS

add-on memory board, p. 177
addressing scheme, p. 180
arithmetic/logic unit (ALU), p. 168
bus, p. 167
cache memory, p. 178
central processing unit (CPU), p. 166
clock, p. 168
closed architecture, p. 177
control unit, p. 167
data bus, p. 188
electrically erasable programmable read-only memory (EEPROM), p. 179
erasable programmable read-only memory (EPROM), p. 179
execution cycle (E-cycle), p. 168
expanded memory, p. 177
extended memory, p. 178
instruction cycle (I-cycle), p. 168
machine cycle, p. 168
machine language, p. 167
main memory, p. 171
megahertz (MHz), p. 168
microprocessor, p. 167
open architecture, p. 177
programmable read-only memory (PROM), p. 179
random access memory (RAM), p. 173
read-only memory (ROM), p. 178
reduced instruction set computing (RISC), p. 183
register, p. 167
semiconductor, p. 173

EXERCISES

MATCHING

Match each of the following terms to the phrase that is the most closely related.

1. __A__ machine language
2. __C__ ROM
3. __G__ central processing unit
4. __I__ microprocessor
5. __H__ machine cycle
6. __E__ register
7. __F__ RAM
8. __M__ clock speed
9. __B__ open architecture
10. __K__ semiconductor
11. __J__ main memory
12. __D__ data bus
13. __L__ control unit
14. __O__ arithmetic/logic unit
15. __N__ add-on memory board

a. The only language that the CPU can understand
b. If a computer was designed using this approach, you can upgrade it with more RAM and add graphics and communications capabilities.
c. Read-only memory
d. Electronic pathway
e. Temporary storage location within the CPU
f. Random access memory
g. The "brain" of the computer
h. Instruction cycle and execution cycle together

i. Hardware component responsible for directing and coordinating most of the computer system activities
j. Storage area outside the CPU where data and instructions needed by the CPU are held temporarily
k. Material used in chips to form electric circuits
l. CPU circuitry of a microcomputer
m. Refers to the speed with which a computer performs operations
n. Technology developed so microcomputers could use more than 640 K main memory
o. Hardware component of the CPU that performs mathematical calculations and logical comparisons

MULTIPLE CHOICE

1. Which of the following holds data and processing instructions temporarily until the CPU needs them?
   a. ROM
   b. control unit
   c. main memory (RAM)
   d. coprocessor chips
   e. bus
2. Which of the following are the two main components of the CPU?
   a. control unit and registers
   b. registers and main memory
   c. control unit and ALU
   d. ALU and bus
   e. bus and registers
3. Which of the following is used for manufacturing chips?
   a. control bus
   b. control unit
   c. parity chips
   d. semiconductors
   e. transistors
4. Which of the following is a primary characteristic of ROM?
   a. It is measured in megabytes.
   b. It is volatile.
   c. It performs mathematical calculations.
   d. Instructions are stored there permanently.
   e. It is 32 bits wide.
5. Which of the following hardware components is the most volatile?
   a. ROM
   b. RAM
   c. PROM
   d. EPROM
   e. EEPROM
6. Which of the following is used to check for errors?
   a. ROM chip
   b. microprocessor chip

c. parity chip
d. EPROM chip
e. coprocessor chip

7. Which of the following are used to quickly accept, store, and transfer data and instructions that are being used immediately by the CPU?
   a. microprocessors
   b. registers
   c. ROM chips
   d. data buses
   e. RAM chips
8. Why is the width of a data bus so important to the processing speed of a computer?
   a. The narrower it is, the greater the computer's processing speed.
   b. The wider it is, the more data that can fit into main memory.
   c. The wider it is, the greater the computer's processing speed.
   d. The wider it is, the slower the computer's processing speed.
   e. The data bus isn't important to the processing speed of a computer.
9. Which of the following terms is the most closely related to main memory?
   a. nonvolatile
   b. permanent
   c. control unit
   d. temporary
   e. elephantine
10. Which of the following affects processing power and speed?
    a. data bus capacity
    b. addressing scheme
    c. clock speed
    d. register size
    e. all the above

SHORT ANSWER

1. What is the purpose of main memory?
2. What is the difference between the traditional ROM chip and some of the newer ROM-type chips (PROM, EPROM, EEPROM)?
3. What is the difference between a computer with closed architecture and one with open architecture?
4. What is the purpose of a parity chip?
5. What led to the development of add-on memory boards?
6. What is a microprocessor? A semiconductor?
7. Is data retrieval faster from main memory or from a disk storage device? Why?
8. What are the main factors affecting the processing power of a computer?
9. What would be a good indication that two computers are incompatible? Why is knowing this important to you?
10. What is the function of the control unit in a computer system? The ALU? Does every computer require one of each?

PROJECTS

1. Advances are made almost every day in microprocessor chip technology. What are some of the most recent advances? In what computers are these chips being used? How might these advances affect the way we currently use microcomputers? Research the latest advances by reviewing the most current computer magazines and periodicals.
2. Research the current uses of and the latest advances in ROM technology. How do you think ROM technology will affect the way we currently use microcomputers? Will we see a lessened need for secondary storage media?
3. Visit a well-equipped computer store, and, with the help of a salesperson, compare the advantages and disadvantages of buying and owning a popular microcomputer with closed architecture, such as the Macintosh SE, and a popular one with open architecture, such as an IBM PS/2 Model 50 or a Mac II. Decide which one *you* would buy, and explain your decision to the class.
4. If your school or university has an information department with a computer system, interview a staff member about how the factors of processing speed, capacity, and cost affected the department's decision to buy its equipment. Are they still happy with it? What would be the next step up, if the department wanted to upgrade its system?

6

Chapter 6

Output Hardware

In business, presentation is important — how you present yourself, your product, your information. Although computers may not be able to help you with your wardrobe or your public speaking skills, they *can* help you create clear and attractive informational presentations quickly. But because computers can produce beautiful, professional, seemingly error-free printouts or exciting colorful graphics on a screen, we are apt to believe that the information is more truthful than the same results scribbled on a yellow pad. In fact, the information that is output — the basis on which you and others will be making decisions — is no better than the quality of the data that was input.

Preview

When you have completed this chapter, you will be able to:

- Describe the basic forms of output and the categories of output media and hardware.
- Describe the advantages and disadvantages of the major types of hardcopy and softcopy output devices.
- Explain why it is important to implement output controls.

THE USER PERSPECTIVE

The success of a business today can depend to a large extent on the relevance and timeliness of the information the computer produces — that is, the output. Having the right information, in the right hands, in the best form, at the right time — these are the keys to effective decision making (Figure 6.1).

Output can take many forms. For instance, when you use an automated teller machine you are dealing with the following types of output: (1) the messages displayed on the video display, (2) the paper transaction receipt that is printed out, and (3) the funds dispensed. And just as forms of output vary, so do types of output devices that you can use to view computer-produced information. Different types of hardware suit different informational needs, and very few businesses use all types. Determining what type of hardware is best suited to a business takes careful consideration. If you are in charge of acquiring an output device for your office, you must first analyze your output needs — determine what *forms* of output you need and the *quantities* of these forms of output. Then you can determine what kind of output hardware will best serve those needs.

OUTPUT FUNDAMENTALS

To be effective, information must be produced in a usable form. To achieve this goal, you may need to use more than one output device and output medium, such as a display on a video screen as well as paper and a printer (as an automated teller does). Each type of output device has advantages and disadvantages. Is the hardware going to make a lot of noise? What is the quality of the output produced? Is the

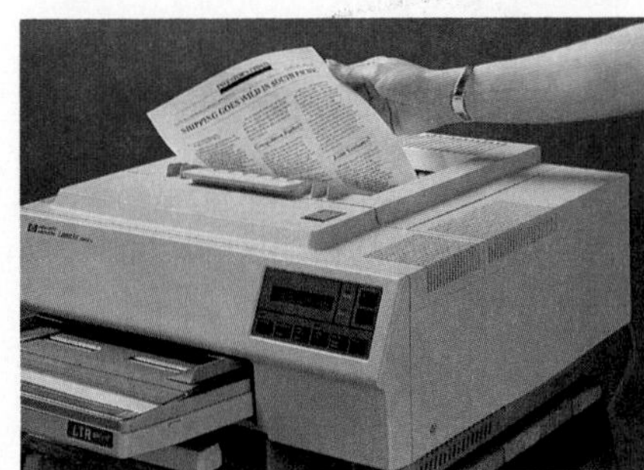

FIGURE 6.1

What form of output is best? As a computer user in the business environment, your output needs will be determined by the kind of decisions you need to make to perform your regular job duties, the type of information that will facilitate making those decisions, and the frequency with which you must make decisions.

hardware slow? Is the hardware expensive? Is it compatible with the equipment you already have? Can it handle large volumes of output? Not all types of computers work with all types of output hardware devices; neither do all software programs. How do you know which to use? To choose wisely, you must be familiar with the categories of computer output.

How Do We Categorize Output?

There are two basic categories of computer-produced output: (1) output for immediate use by people and (2) output that is stored in computer-usable form for later use by the computer (and eventually, of course, by people). Output can be in either hardcopy or softcopy form. **Hardcopy,** as defined earlier, refers to information that has been recorded on a tangible medium (generally meaning that you can touch it), such as paper or microfilm. **Softcopy** generally refers to the output displayed on a computer screen. Many people think of information recorded in computer-usable form as softcopy output because they cannot see the magnetic spots recorded on the tape or disk. However, since the recording medium is indeed tangible, this form of output could be classified as hardcopy.

In recent years, interest in the presentation of information in the form of graphic images has grown substantially, partly because of improvements in the quality of graphics hardware and advancements in the capabilities and flexibility of graphics software. Graphic output such as bar graphs and pie charts can be output in hardcopy and softcopy form. So can animation, which can be viewed on a computer screen (softcopy) or output in computer-usable form on a disk or diskette (hardcopy).

Voice output (softcopy) has recently begun to be used more often. For example, these days the telephone is used more frequently for voice output: The last time you dialed telephone information (directory assistance), the number you were given was probably provided in the form of computer-generated voice output. Some specialized computer devices are also being used to disseminate messages and marketing information automatically over the phone. The computer begins dialing a long list of telephone numbers. When the phone is answered, a message is automatically transmitted—perhaps to the annoyance of the person being called. When there is no answer or the line is busy, the computer takes note and automatically tries again later. More and more applications are being found each year that use voice as a form of computer output.

Paper is one of the most widely used hardcopy output media. Paper products come in a variety of forms including:

- Lined computer paper (11 × 14 ⅝ inches).
- Plain computer paper (8 × 11 inches).
- Special preprinted forms.
- Labels.

Individually placing these paper products in an output device (such as a printer) takes a lot of time, so they are all available in *continuous form* (Figure 6.2).

The most widely used softcopy output medium is the video display image generated on a monitor. The two types of display screen used most often are a computer terminal connected to a large computer system and a monitor attached to a microcomputer system.

The advantages and disadvantages of each output medium must be considered carefully to ensure that outputs are produced in the most usable form.

- When computer display devices are not readily available and information has some value over time, it is best produced as hardcopy.
- When computer display devices are readily available and information must be quickly accessible, it is best produced as softcopy.

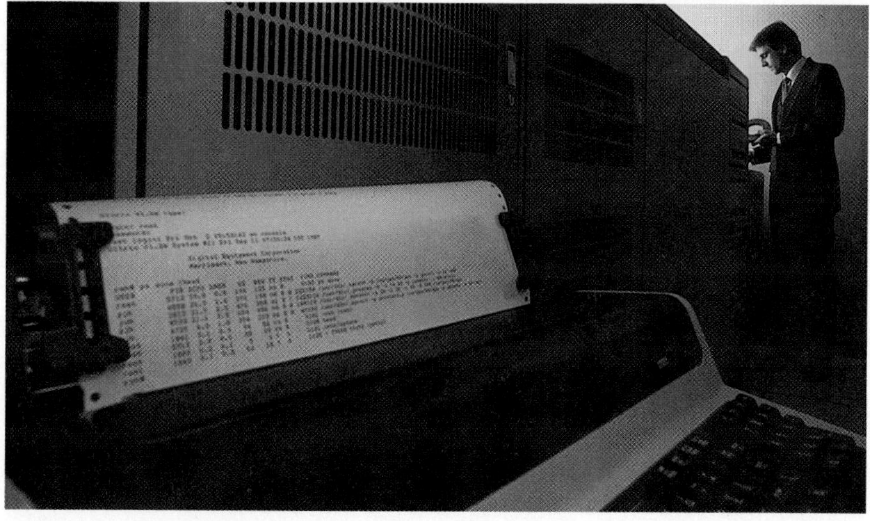

FIGURE 6.2

Feed the printer. Continuous-form paper is used to avoid having to hand-feed individual sheets of paper to the printer (called *friction feed*) when you are printing reports. The holes on both sides of the paper fit onto a *tractor-feed* mechanism attached to the printer that guides the paper and pushes it forward as directed by the software. Continuous-form paper is used more often in business than single sheets.

HARDWARE

Output hardware is categorized according to whether it produces hardcopy or softcopy (Figure 6.3). The principal hardcopy output devices are printers and plotters. The principal softcopy output devices are cathode-ray tube video screens (CRTs), flat screens, and voice output systems.

As you read the next two sections, consider which types of output hardware would best satisfy the information needs that exist in your chosen field or profession. By doing so, you'll be moving even closer to computer literacy.

HARDCOPY OUTPUT DEVICES

Of the wide variety of hardcopy output devices, printers and plotters are used the most. A **printer** is capable of printing characters, symbols, and sometimes graphics on paper. Printers are categorized according to whether or not the image produced is formed by physical contact of the print mechanism with the paper. *Impact printers* do have contact; *nonimpact printers* do not. A **plotter** is used most often for creating graphics because it can produce specialized and free-form drawings on paper. Plotters are categorized according to whether or not they use pens, how the paper is placed in them, and which of their parts move. To suit the needs of many different users, different types of printers and plotters are available with slightly different characteristics and capabilities—cost, quality, and speed.

IMPACT PRINTERS

An **impact printer** makes contact with the paper. It usually forms the print image by pressing an inked ribbon against the paper with a hammer-like mechanism. In one type of impact printer, called a *letter-quality printer*, the hammer presses images of fully formed characters against the ribbon, just like a typewriter. The print mechanism in another type of impact printer, called a *dot-matrix printer,* is made of separate pin-like hammers that strike the ribbon against the paper in computer-determined patterns of dots. Letter-quality printers and dot-matrix printers are used with microcomputer systems. Larger computer systems, which often must produce a high volume of output, use high-speed printers that fall into a separate category.

LETTER-QUALITY PRINTERS

Letter-quality printers—also called *formed character printers* or *serial printers* because they print one character at a time—produce a very high quality print image (one that is very clear and precise) because the entire character is formed with a single impact. Letter-quality output is generally used for important business letters, memos, and reports. The three principal letter-quality printers are (1) the daisy wheel printer, (2) the thimble printer, and (3) the ball printer. The **daisy wheel printer** (Figure 6.4) has a print "wheel" with a set of print characters on the outside tips of the flat spokes. To print a specific character, the wheel is spun until the appropriate spoke, or "petal," is lined up with the print hammer. The print hammer is then fired, and the print character is forced against the ribbon and paper with

Hard job, soft job? Output hardware is categorized according to whether it produces hardcopy or softcopy. Output for immediate use can be in either hardcopy form—such as paper—or softcopy form—such as on a display screen. Output in computer-usable form for later use by the computer is in hardcopy form—such as on disk or tape.

FIGURE 6.3

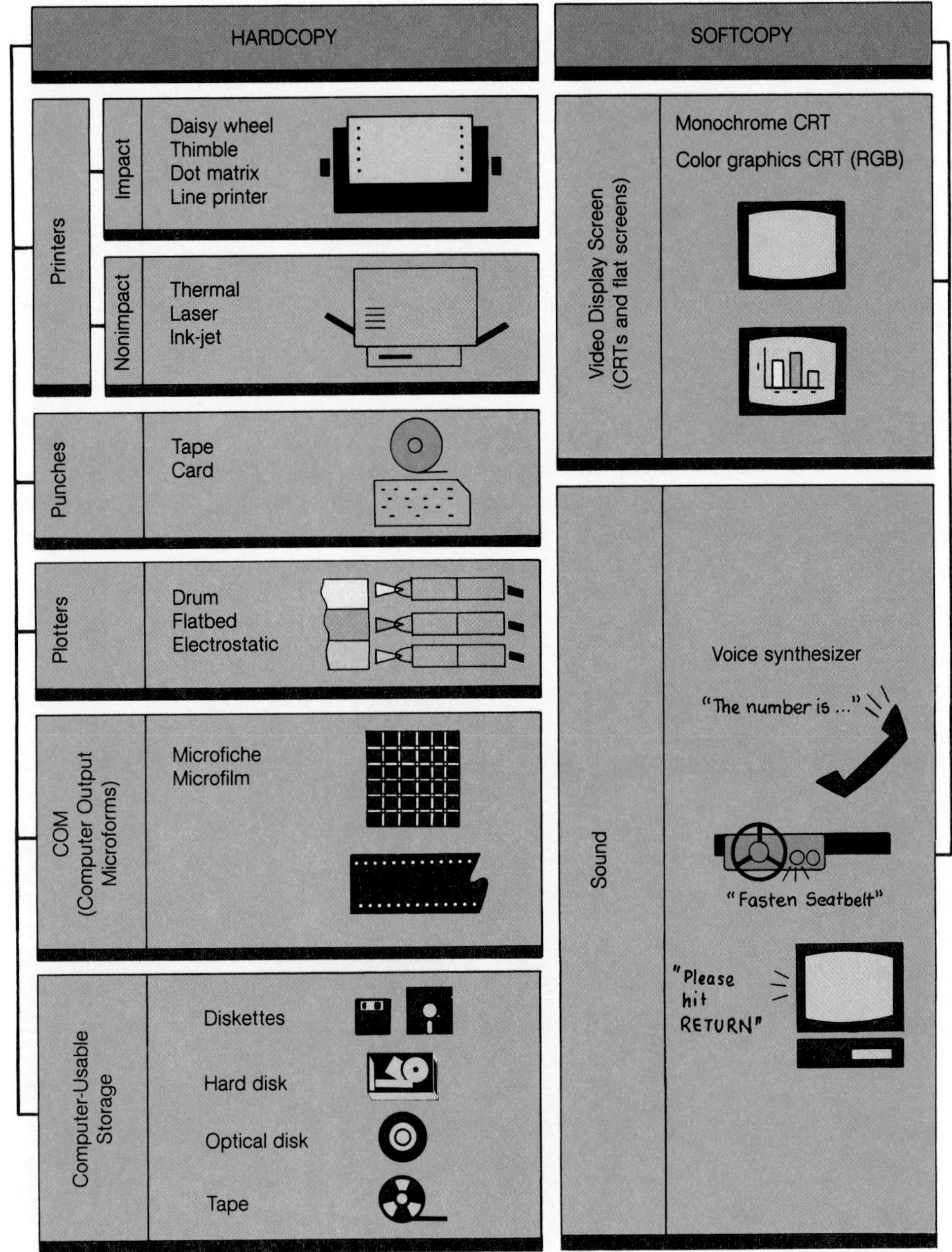

sufficient force to make a clear, crisp impression. The **thimble printer** works similarly, except that the spokes curve upward, instead of lying flat.

Some letter-quality printers have print mechanisms similar to the IBM Selectric typewriter ball and hence are referred to as **ball printers.** However, the daisy wheel and thimble printer technologies have proven superior in terms of speed. The range of speeds for letter-quality printers varies from about 60 characters per second (cps) to a maximum of about 120 cps. This speed translates into approximately 600 to 1,200 words per minute (based on an average of five characters per word). The average letter-quality printer costs approximately $500, although this type of printer is being rapidly phased out in favor of other types of printers that we will discuss shortly. The principal advantage of letter-quality printers is the excellent image produced. However, they do have some disadvantages:

- They are too slow for many large-volume output situations.
- They are very noisy.
- To change the typeface style, the operator must halt the machine and change the print wheel.
- They cannot produce graphics.

DOT-MATRIX PRINTERS

Dot-matrix printers, also called *serial printers*, were developed with two objectives in mind: greater speed and more flexibility. The images are formed by a print head that is composed of a series of little print hammers that look like the heads of pins. These print hammers strike the ribbon individually as the print mechanism moves

FIGURE 6.4

(a) Daisy wheel, (b) daisy wheel printer, and (c) drawing of how a daisy wheel mechanism works. The daisy wheel spins and brings the desired letter into position. A hammer hits the wedge, which strikes the appropriate spoke against the ribbon, which hits the paper. The daisy wheel printer is no longer as popular as it was a few years ago.

(a)

across the entire print line in both directions — that is, from left to right, then right to left, and so on. They can produce a variety of type styles and graphics without requiring an operator to stop the printer or change the print wheel.

Figure 6.5 shows how a dot-matrix print head is constructed. The print head of a dot-matrix printer usually has 9 pins. However, high-quality dot-matrix printers have print heads with as many as 24 pins, which allow a much more precise image to

FIGURE 6.4

(continued)

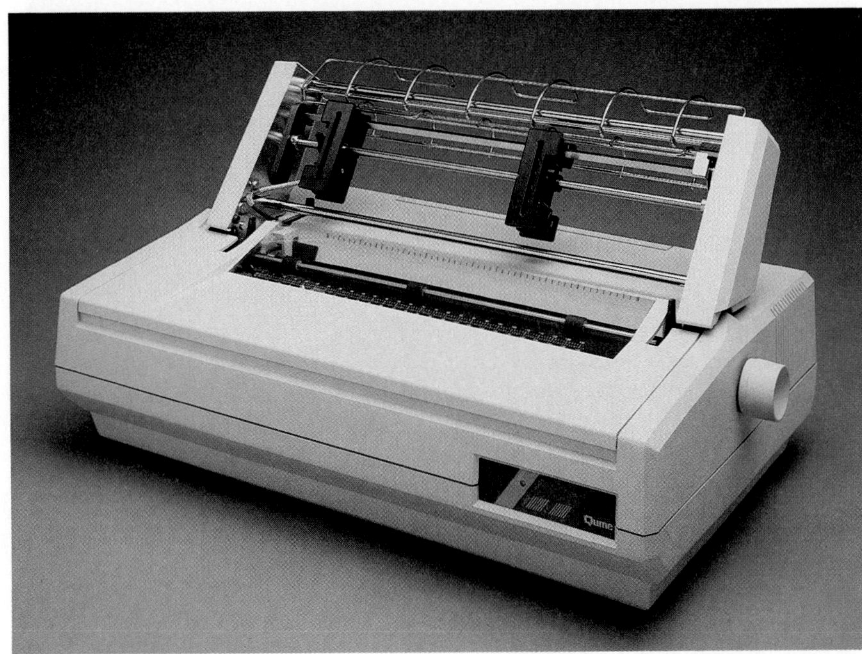

(b)

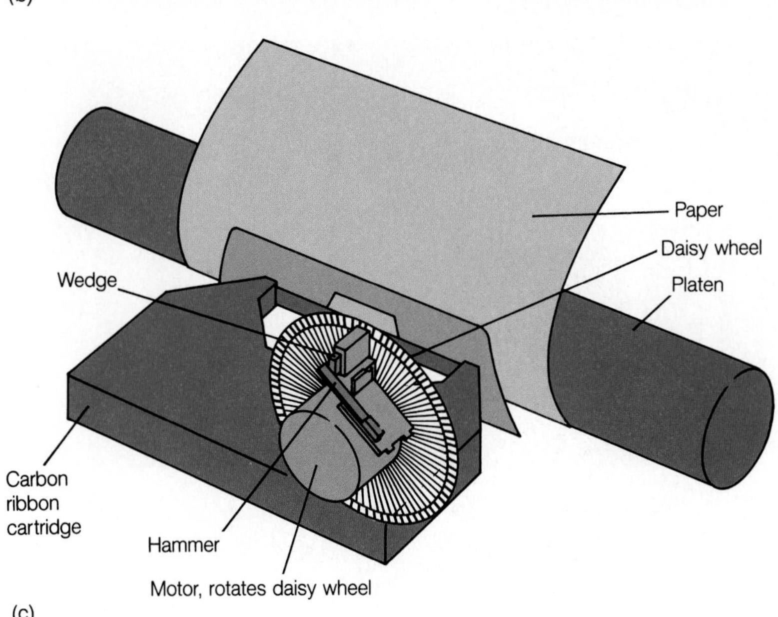

(c)

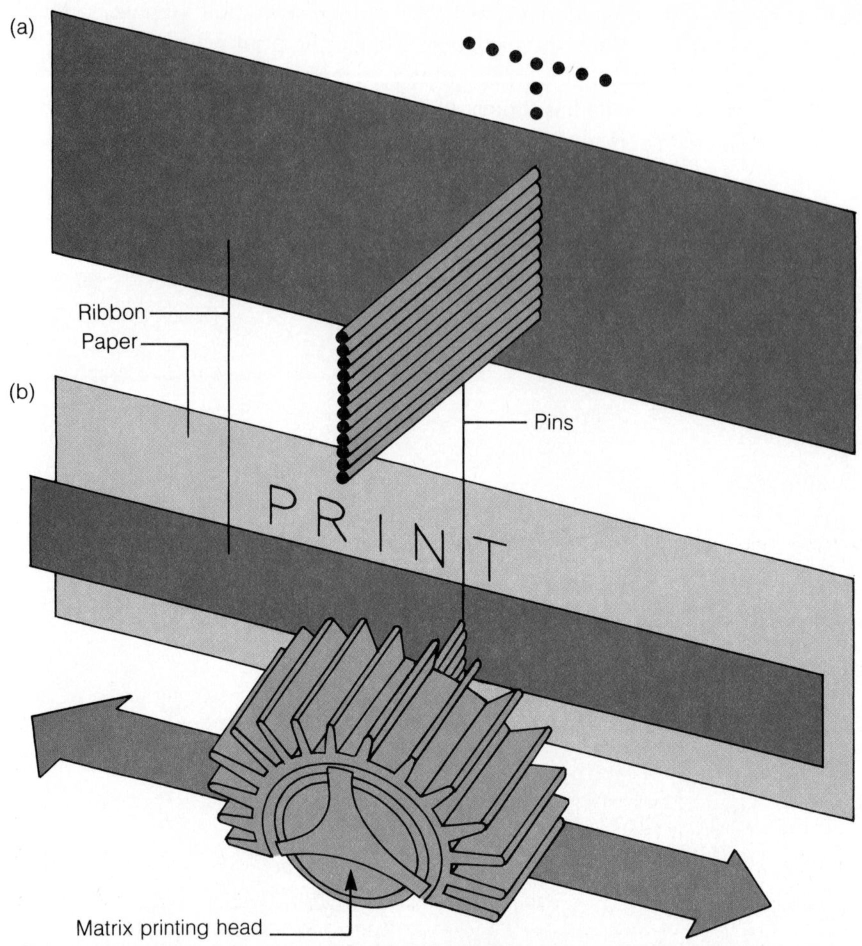

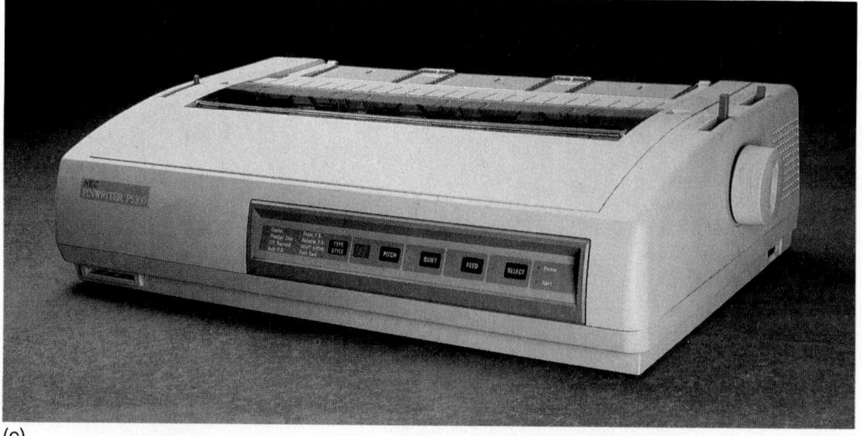

FIGURE 6.5

Dot-matrix print head. Part (a) is an enlarged view of a group of 12 pins, or print hammers, striking the printer ribbon; part (b) shows the print head. The same group of pins can be used to create a variety of characters. The photo (c) shows the NEC Pinwriter P5300, which produces color dot-matrix output.

be produced—about 360 dpi, or dots per (square) inch. Figure 6.6 gives examples of graphics produced by a 9-pin dot-matrix printer and a 24-pin printer.

In general, 9-pin printers:

- cost between $150 and $500;
- can print between 40 and 130 cps (characters per second)—between one and two pages per minute;
- are best used for quick draft printing, generating forms, and printing jobs that don't require a high-quality image.

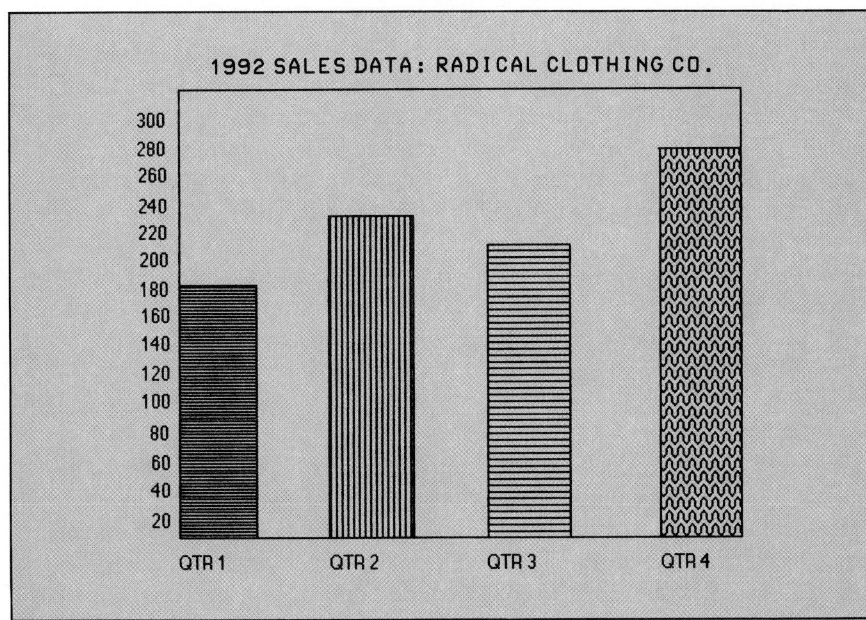

(a)

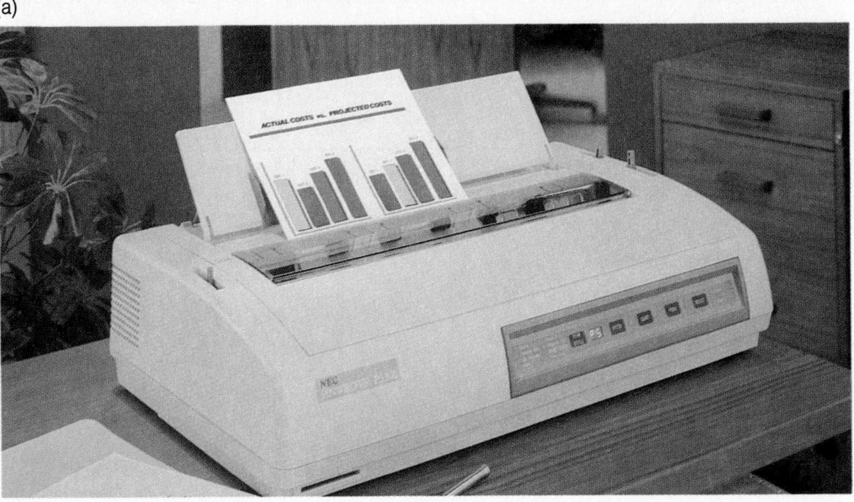

(b)

FIGURE 6.6

Dot-matrix samples. Graphics produced (a) by a 9-pin dot-matrix printer; (b) by a 24-pin color NEC Pinwriter P5300.

Most 24-pin printers:

- cost between $400 and $2,000;
- can print between 80 and 260 cps—between one and four pages per minute;
- produce a much more precise image than 9-pin printers do—about 360 dpi;
- are best used in a heavy-volume environment in which speed and quality are priorities.

If you'd like to liven up your business reports with a bit of color but can't afford a $5,000–$22,000 thermal color page printer (discussed shortly), a $500 color dot-matrix printer may be the printer for you. A color dot-matrix printer uses the same technology as a monochrome dot-matrix printer, except that it uses a color ribbon instead of a black ribbon. Color ribbons usually comprise equal bands of black, yellow, and blue. Under software control, the colors can be blended to produce up to seven colors. Color ribbons cost up to three times as much as black ribbons. To date, most color dot-matrix printers are used primarily for black printing and only occasionally for color printing. (For color printing to really take off, the software industry needs to incorporate instructions into software programs to provide the user with the capability of using color.) Color option kits for upgrading a black-only dot-matrix printer are available for $50–$100.

Dot-matrix printers generate less noise than impact letter-quality printers, and many of the dot-matrix printers can achieve a *near-letter-quality (nlq)* mode when the print head makes more than one pass for each print line, creating a darker, thicker character (Figure 6.7). (When the dot-matrix printer uses only one pass for each line, it's called *draft quality*.) Table 6.1 compares letter-quality and dot-matrix printers.

HIGH-SPEED PRINTERS

Several types of high-speed printers (nonserial printers) have been developed to satisfy the high-volume output requirements of most large computer installations, which cannot be satisfied by dot-matrix or letter-quality printers. These **line printers,** so called because they print a whole line of characters practically at once, come in several varieties, including **drum printers, band** or **belt printers,** and **chain printers** (Figure 6.8). Each of these printers has several copies of each printable character on a drum, a belt, or a print chain, with a separate print hammer for each

FIGURE 6.7

The second time around. To produce a near-letter-quality image with a dot-matrix printer, the character is printed twice; the second time the print head is positioned slightly to the right of the original image (a). (b) shows a "real" (daisy wheel) letter-quality character for comparison.

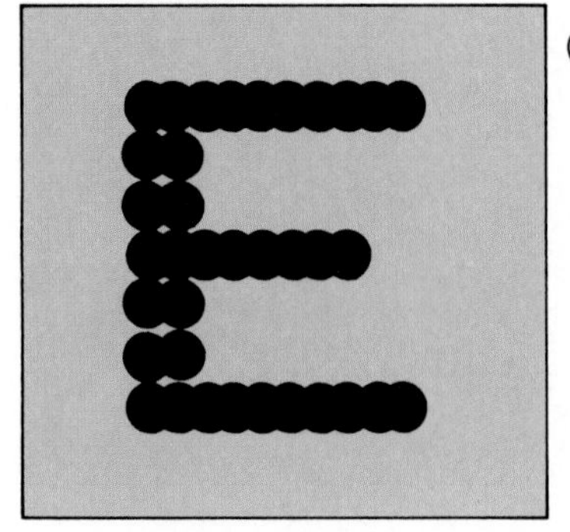

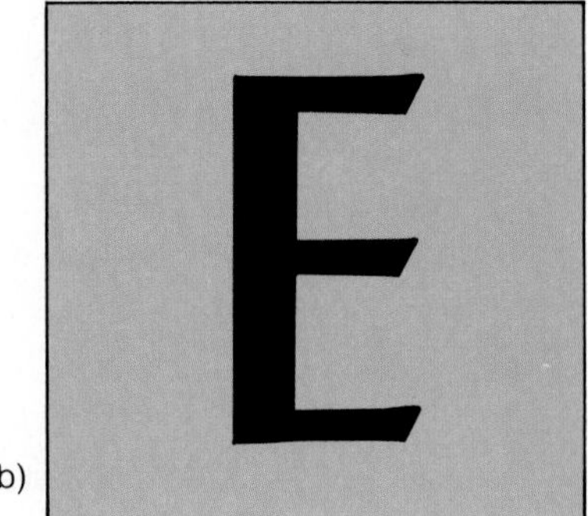

print position across the width of the paper guide. As the drum, belt, or print chain revolves, the hammers are activated as the appropriate characters pass in front of them.

Whereas speed in letter-quality and dot-matrix printers is measured in characters per second, the speed of these faster printers is measured in lines per minute (lpm). The speed achieved by this type of printer ranges from 200 to 3,000 lines per minute, which translates into about 5,280 to approximately 79,000 words per minute. Some high-speed printers can print more than 20,000 lines per minute—an astounding 528,000 words per minute! (A highly trained typist can do about 90–120 words per minute on a typewriter.) Line printers with speeds in the 200–1,000 lpm range are used with minicomputers. The faster ones are used with mainframes. (Some mainframe computer systems produce so much hardcopy output that they have a whole room full of high-speed and very-high-speed printers.)

Speed is the obvious advantage of this type of printer. Unless your business produces an extremely large volume of hardcopy output, though, you probably will not need to use one. The major disadvantages are noise and relatively poor image quality. However, these limitations are being overcome by newer printer technologies (such as laser printers, which we'll describe in the next section).

Nonimpact Printers

Printers that do not strike characters against ribbon or paper when they print are called **nonimpact printers**. The main categories of nonimpact printers are ink-jet printers, thermal printers, and laser printers. These printers generate much less noise than impact printers. However, if you're using a nonimpact printer, don't try to print on multiple-part carbon forms: Because no impact is being made on the paper, you'll end up with no copies! Believe it or not, quite a few people have purchased a nonimpact printer, put carbon forms into it, and been gravely disappointed when the carbon copies didn't materialize.

TABLE 6.1

Comparison of Impact and Dot-Matrix Printers

	Impact	Dot-Matrix
Draft-quality speed	–	80–260 cps
Letter-quality speed	60–100 cps	40–80 cps (near-letter-quality)
Image quality	Excellent	Good to very good
Cost	$500	$150–$2,000
Print mechanism	Daisy wheel, thimble, or ball	9-, 18-, 24-pin print head
Advantages	Crisp, clear characters	Fast, can do graphics
Disadvantages	Slow, noisy, can't do graphics	Noisy, characters usually less clear

FIGURE 6.8

Nonserial high-speed impact printers. (a) The mechanism of a drum printer, which can print up to 3,000 lines per minute; (b) a belt or band printer mechanism, which can print up to 2,000 lines per minute; (c) a chain printer mechanism, which can print 3,000 lines per minute. Bands and chains can be changed to use different typeface styles; drums cannot. (d) High-speed Unisys line printer.

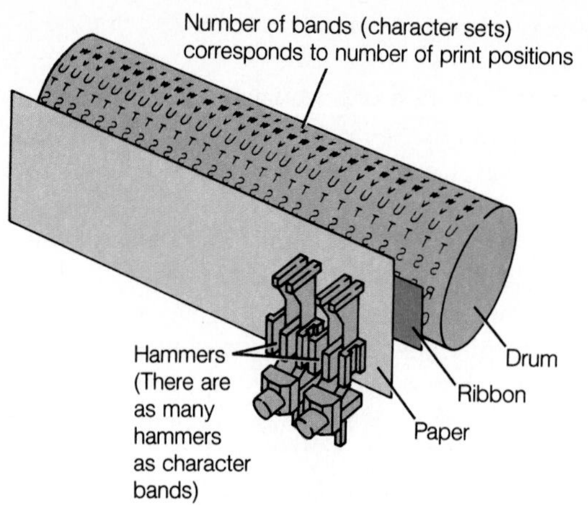

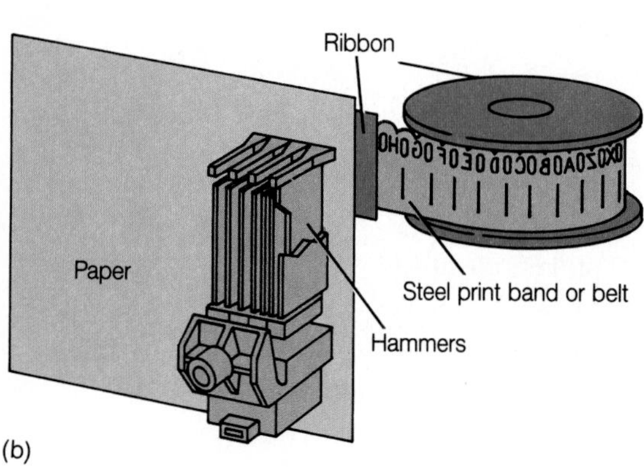

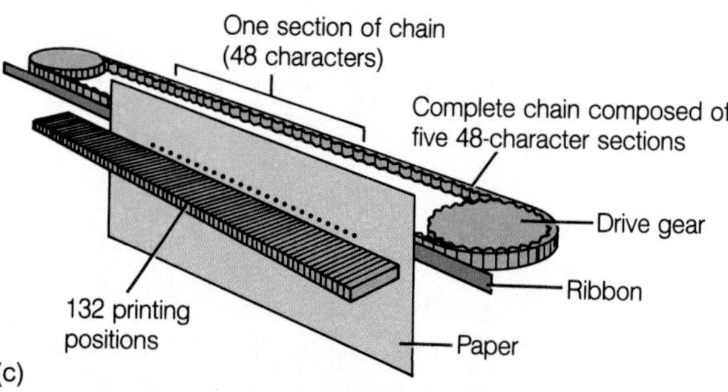

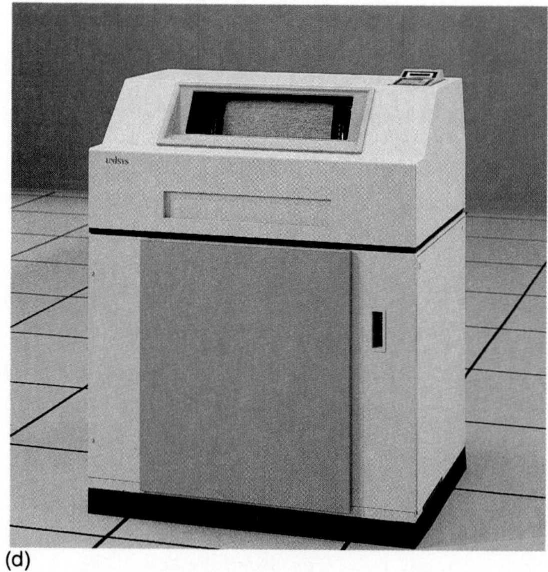

Ink-Jet Printers

Ink-jet printers (Figure 6.9) work in much the same fashion as dot-matrix printers in that they form images or characters with little dots. However, the dots are formed, not by hammer-like pins, but by tiny droplets of ink. And the text these printers produce is letter quality (rather than near-letter quality, which is produced by

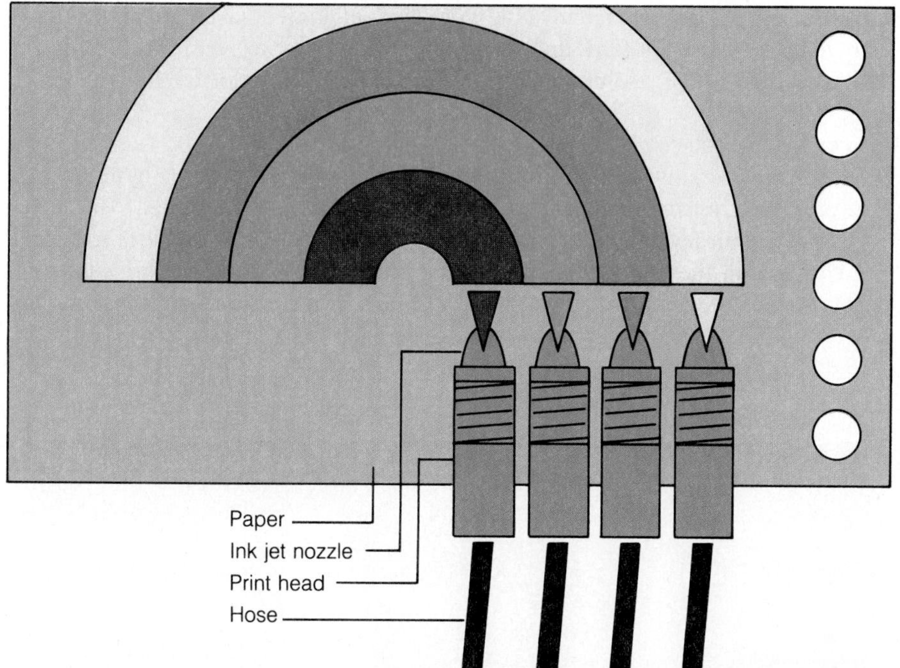

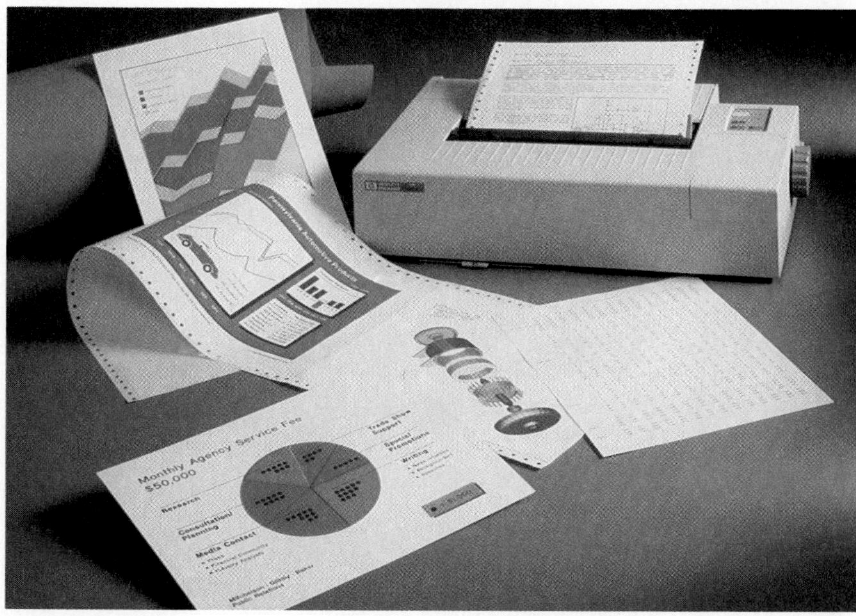

FIGURE 6.9

Jet set graphics and text. Both free-form images and text can be produced using a color ink-jet printer like this Hewlett-Packard PaintJet, which can produce a page of near-letter-quality text in 40 seconds and a page of color graphics in 4 minutes.

dot-matrix printers). These printers can almost match the speed of dot-matrix printers—between one and four pages per minute (ppm)—and they produce less noise. Hewlett-Packard's DeskJet Plus prints 2 ppm and costs around $800.

Several manufacturers produce color ink-jet printers. Some of these printers come with all their color inks in a cartridge; if you want to replace one color, you must replace all the colors. Other color ink-jet printers allow you to replace inks individually. These printers are a better choice if you use one color predominantly. Desktop color ink-jet printers can be purchased for as little as $1,300 (about 180 dpi) or as much as $8,000 for an innovative type of ink-jet printer that can generate up to 256,000 colors at once (216 dpi). Industry observers are expecting color ink-jet printers with 300 dpi resolution to appear in the near future for $3,000–$4,000.

THERMAL PRINTERS

Thermal printers use heat to produce an image on special paper (Figure 6.10). The print mechanism—rather like a dot-matrix print head—is designed to heat the surface of chemically treated paper so that a dot is produced based on the reaction of the chemical to the heat. No ribbon or ink is involved. For users who want the highest-quality desktop color printing available, thermal printers are the answer.

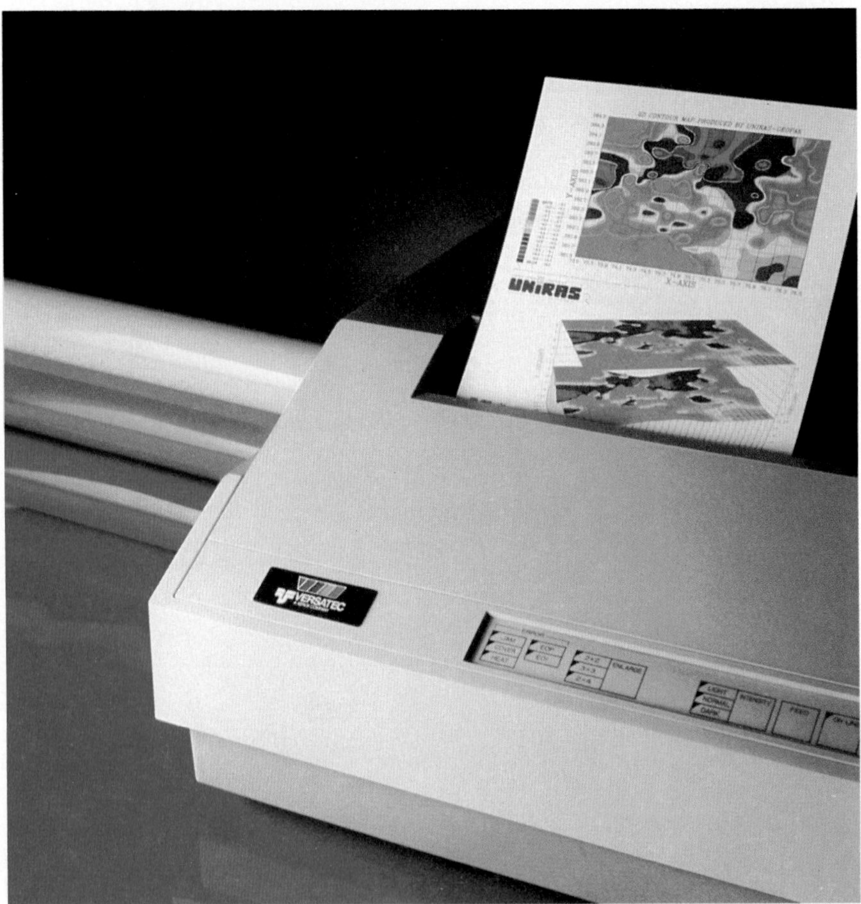

FIGURE 6.10

Hot topic. Thermal printers produce images by heating chemically treated paper until dots appear.

However, they are also expensive — $5,000 – $22,000 — and they require special, expensive paper (up to $.50 per sheet). Today, for around $10,000 you can purchase a color thermal printer that prints 300 dpi.

Of the three color printing devices available, dot-matrix remains the most complete method for standard business text and color output. It can use all types of paper, is least expensive, and, although noisier, it can produce carbon copies. Ink-jet or thermal printers are more appropriate for sophisticated business presentations and special types of graphics output.

Laser Printers

Laser printer technology is much less mechanical than impact printing (that is, no print heads move, no print hammers hit), resulting in much higher speeds and quieter operation. The process resembles the operation of a photocopy machine (Figure 6.11). A laser beam is directed across the surface of a light-sensitive drum and fired as needed to record an image in the form of a pattern of tiny dots. The image is then transferred to the paper — a page at a time — in the same fashion as a copy machine, using a special toner.

The major advantages of laser printers are:

- Very high speed.
- Low noise level.
- Low maintenance requirements.
- Very high image quality.
- Excellent graphics capabilities.
- A variety of type sizes and styles.
- On large, high-speed laser printers, forms can be printed at the same time data is recorded in them.

When high-speed laser printers (also called *page printers*) were introduced, they were very expensive. Their cost could be justified only in large data processing organizations where a print speed capability of between 10,000 and 20,000 lines (about 300 pages) per minute was required. However, recent laser printer technology has made desktop versions available at very reasonable prices. For less than $2,000, a small, desktop laser printer can be obtained that can produce between 4 and 8 ppm. With printers in this range, 300 dpi images are common. For $10,000 – $20,000, the user can purchase a high-end laser printer that is three to five times faster than a low-end laser printer and generates clearer images (400 – 600 dpi). Printing between 15 and 25 ppm, these printers are appropriate in a networked environment where many users are sharing one printer.

Most laser printers are capable of outputting a specific set of type fonts and sizes. Laser printers that include a built-in page description language on a board inside the printer provide greater flexibility by enabling users to generate fonts in any size and to produce special graphics effects. The most popular page description language is Adobe Systems' PostScript. PostScript printers generally cost $1,000 – $2,000 more than non-PostScript laser printers.

The desktop laser printer has become a very popular output device for microcomputer-based systems. Many practitioners of desktop publishing (discussed in the next chapter), which is publishing you do yourself, prefer desktop laser printers

FIGURE 6.11

Laser printing. A microprocessor controls a small laser beam that is bounced off a mirror (a) millions of times per second onto a positively charged drum. The spots where the laser beam hits become neutralized (b), enabling a special toner (containing powdered ink and powdered rosin, an adhesive) to stick to them and then print out on paper, through the use of heat and pressure. The drum is then recharged for its next cycle. (c, lower left) shows the Hewlett-Packard LaserJet for the personal computer. (d) is actual hard-copy laser output. (e) Font samples produced by a laser printer.

(a)

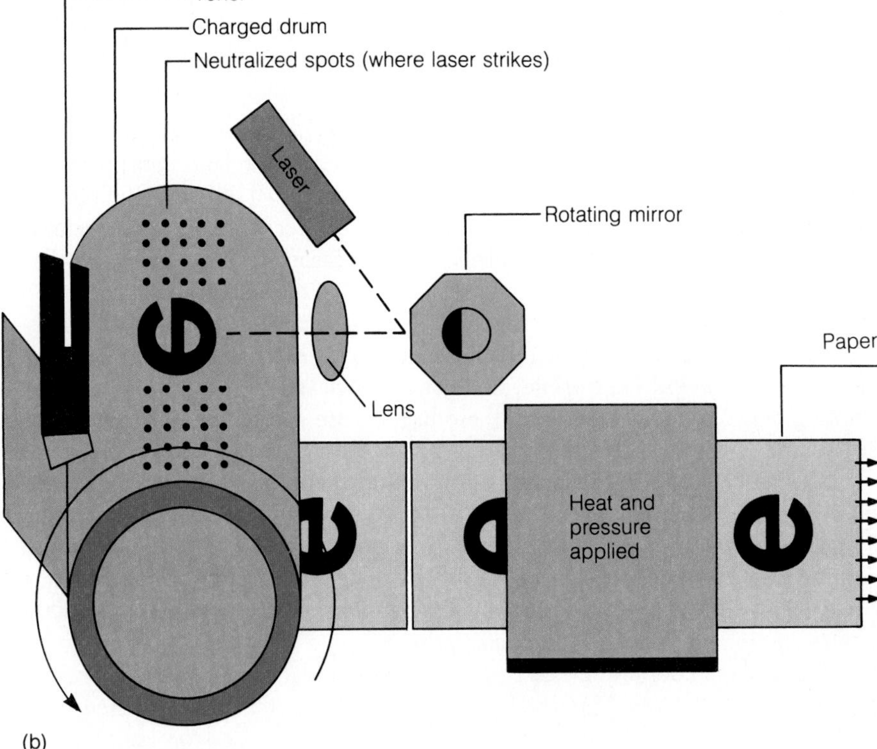

(b)

because of the high-quality images they produce. However, using laser technology to print in color is a new technology that is still quite expensive. Color laser printers cost from $10,000 to $30,000. Because this technology is still new, it remains to be seen how well these products really work.

Laser printers are very popular in the business community. To help you understand why, Table 6.2 compares the various types of nonimpact printers.

PLOTTERS

A plotter is a specialized output device designed to produce high-quality graphics in a variety of colors. There are two basic types of plotters: those that use pens and those that don't. Drum plotters and flatbed plotters both use pens. Electrostatic plotters do not.

(c)

FIGURE 6.11

(continued)

"I think there is a world market for about five computers."
—Thomas J. Watson, founder of IBM (1943)

(d)

FIGURE 6.11 *(continued)*

PORTRAIT FONTS

<table>
<tr><th>FONT ID</th><th>NAME</th><th>PITCH</th><th>POINT SIZE</th><th>SYMBOL SET</th><th>PRINT SAMPLE</th></tr>
<tr><td colspan="6">“PERMANENT” SOFT FONTS</td></tr>
<tr><td>S01</td><td>Dutch</td><td>PS</td><td>10</td><td>8U</td><td>ABCDEfghij#$@[\]^‘{|}~123
ÀÂ°ÇÑ¡¿£§êéàèëöÅØåæÄÜßÁÐÒ</td></tr>
<tr><td>S02</td><td>Dutch BOLD</td><td>PS</td><td>14</td><td>8U</td><td>ABCDEfghij#$@[\]^‘{|}~123
ÀÂ°ÇÑ¡¿£§êéàèëöÅØåæÄÜßÁÐÒ</td></tr>
<tr><td>S03</td><td>Dutch BOLD</td><td>PS</td><td>18</td><td>8U</td><td>ABCDEfghij#$@[\]^‘{|}~
ÀÂ°ÇÑ¡¿£§êéàèëöÅØåæÄÜß</td></tr>
<tr><td>S04</td><td>Dutch BOLD</td><td>PS</td><td>24</td><td>8U</td><td>ABCDEfghij#$@[\]
ÀÂ°ÇÑ¡¿£§êéàèëöÅØ</td></tr>
<tr><td colspan="6">LEFT FONT CARTRIDGE</td></tr>
<tr><td colspan="6">RIGHT FONT CARTRIDGE</td></tr>
<tr><td colspan="6">INTERNAL FONTS</td></tr>
<tr><td>I00</td><td>COURIER</td><td>10</td><td>12</td><td>8U</td><td>ABCDEfghij#$@[\]^‘{|}~123
ÀÂ°ÇÑ¡¿£§êéàèëöÅØåæÄÜßÁÐÒ</td></tr>
<tr><td>I01</td><td>COURIER</td><td>10</td><td>12</td><td>10U</td><td>ABCDEfghij#$@[\]ˆ`{|}˜123
íó│┤╢╕╣╗╜┴┼╚╔╬╩╙╥ ╘╪█▌απΦ</td></tr>
<tr><td>I02</td><td>COURIER</td><td>10</td><td>12</td><td>11U</td><td>ABCDEfghij#$@[\]ˆ`{|}˜123
íó│┤╢╕╣╗╜┴┼╚╔╬╩╙╥ ╘╪█▌απΦ</td></tr>
<tr><td>I03</td><td>COURIER</td><td>10</td><td>12</td><td>0N</td><td>ABCDEfghij#$@[\]ˆ`{|}˜123
¡¢³ ´¶¸¹»½ÁÅÈÉÍÎÐÒÔ×ØÛÞàãè</td></tr>
<tr><td>I04</td><td>COURIER BOLD</td><td>10</td><td>12</td><td>8U</td><td>ABCDEfghij#$@[\]^‘{|}~123
ÀÂ°ÇÑ¡¿£§êéàèëöÅØåæÄÜßÁÐÒ</td></tr>
<tr><td>I05</td><td>COURIER BOLD</td><td>10</td><td>12</td><td>10U</td><td>ABCDEfghij#$@[\]ˆ`{|}˜123
íó│┤╢╕╣╗╜┴┼╚╔╬╩╙╥ ╘╪█▌απΦ</td></tr>
<tr><td>I06</td><td>COURIER BOLD</td><td>10</td><td>12</td><td>11U</td><td>ABCDEfghij#$@[\]ˆ`{|}˜123
íó│┤╢╕╣╗╜┴┼╚╔╬╩╙╥ ╘╪█▌απΦ</td></tr>
<tr><td>I07</td><td>COURIER BOLD</td><td>10</td><td>12</td><td>0N</td><td>ABCDEfghij#$@[\]ˆ`{|}˜123
¡¢³ ´¶¸¹»½ÁÅÈÉÍÎÐÒÔ×ØÛÞàãè</td></tr>
<tr><td>I08</td><td>LINE_PRINTER</td><td>16.6</td><td>8.5</td><td>8U</td><td>ABCDEfghij#$@[\]^‘{|}~123
ÀÂ°ÇÑ¡¿£§êéàèëöÅØåæÄÜßÁÐÒ</td></tr>
<tr><td>I09</td><td>LINE_PRINTER</td><td>16.6</td><td>8.5</td><td>10U</td><td>ABCDEfghij#$@[\]ˆ`{|}˜123
íó│┤╢╕╣╗╜┴┼╚╔╬╩╙╥╘╪█▌απΦ</td></tr>
<tr><td>I10</td><td>LINE_PRINTER</td><td>16.6</td><td>8.5</td><td>11U</td><td>ABCDEfghij#$@[\]ˆ`{|}˜123
íó│┤╢╕╣╗╜┴┼╚╔╬╩╙╥╘╪█▌απΦ</td></tr>
<tr><td>I11</td><td>LINE_PRINTER</td><td>16.6</td><td>8.5</td><td>0N</td><td>ABCDEfghij#$@[\]ˆ`{|}˜123
¡¢³´¶¸¹»½ÁÅÈÉÍÎÐÒÔ×ØÛÞàãè</td></tr>
</table>

In a **drum plotter,** the paper is mounted on the surface of a drum. The drum revolves and the plotter pens (which are similar to felt-tip pens) are horizontally positioned over the target area. When the paper has rotated to the correct point, the pens are dropped to the surface and moved left and right under program control across the paper as the drum revolves. When the image is complete, the pens are raised from the surface. **Flatbed plotters** are designed so that the paper is placed flat and one or more pens move horizontally and vertically across the paper. **Electrostatic plotters** use electrostatic charges to create images out of very small dots on specially treated paper. The paper is run through a developer to allow the image to appear. Electrostatic plotters are faster than pen plotters and can produce images of very high resolution.

Figure 6.12 shows a drum plotter, a flatbed plotter, and an electrostatic plotter. The cost of a plotter can range from about $1,000 to more than $100,000, depending on the machine's speed and ability to generate high-resolution images. Several 2- to 8-pen flatbed plotters are available for microcomputer systems, as are some small drum plotters; large plotters, used with large computer systems, can produce drawings up to 8 feet by 8 feet, or sometimes even larger.

COMPUTER OUTPUT MICROFILM/MICROFICHE (COM) SYSTEMS

The volume of information produced by computers is staggering. If we were limited to regular hardcopy output, it is likely that most of us would be knee-deep in paper by

Comparison of Nonimpact Printers **TABLE 6.2**

Type	Technology	Advantages	Disadvantages	Typical Speed	Approximate Cost
Thermal	Temperature-sensitive; paper changes color when treated; characters are formed by selectively heating print head	Quiet; high-quality color output	Special paper required; expensive; slow	.5–4 ppm	$5,000–$22,000
Ink-jet	Electrostatically charged drops hit paper	Quiet; prints color; less expensive; fast	Relatively slow; clogged jets; lower dpi	1–4 ppm	$800–$8,000
Laser	Laser beam directed onto a drum, "etching" spots that attract toner, which is then transferred to paper	Quiet; excellent quality; very high speed	High cost; no color for desktop models	4–25 ppm	$1,000–$20,000

now. However, what do you use when you don't want to take up space with regular hardcopy output, but softcopy output on display screens is inappropriate?

Computer output systems may be an answer. The two most popular systems capture computer output on **microfilm** or **microfiche**. The principal advantages of this technology are:

- *Speed*. COM systems can easily handle output at a rate in excess of 30,000 lines per minute. This is about 50 percent faster than most large laser printers.
- *Size*. The output is condensed in size (compared to hardcopy output) by a factor ranging from 20 to 100.
- *Cost*. The cost per page of printed material is less than that of regular hardcopy output methods.

FIGURE 6.12

Not a plodder. Two commonly used pen plotters are (a) the flatbed plotter and (b) the drum plotter. The electrostatic plotter (c) uses electrostatic charges to produce images. All produce high-quality graphics output.

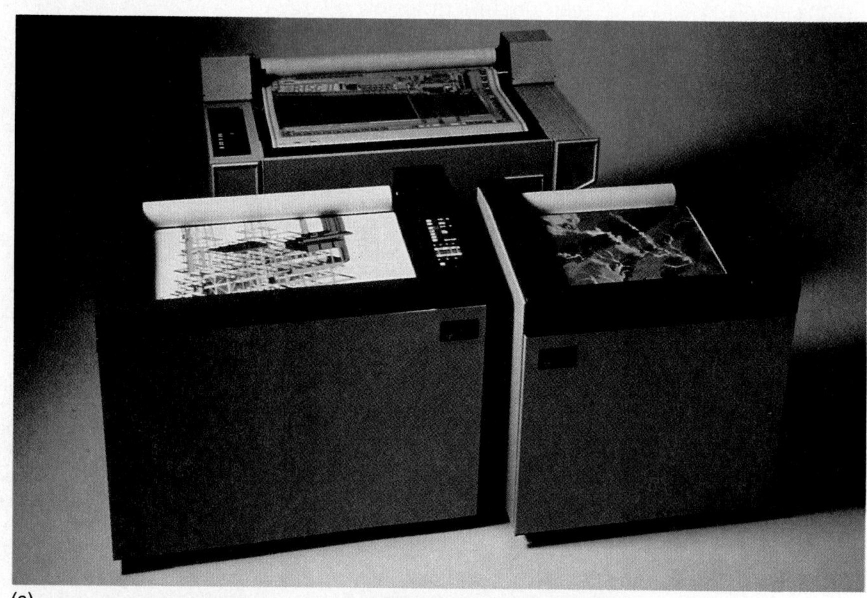

(a)

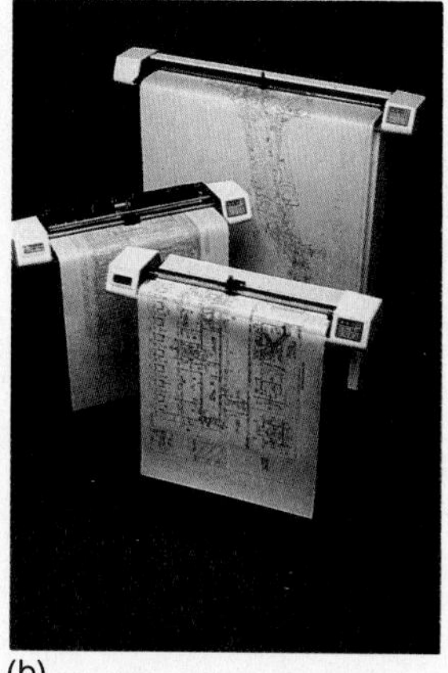

(b)

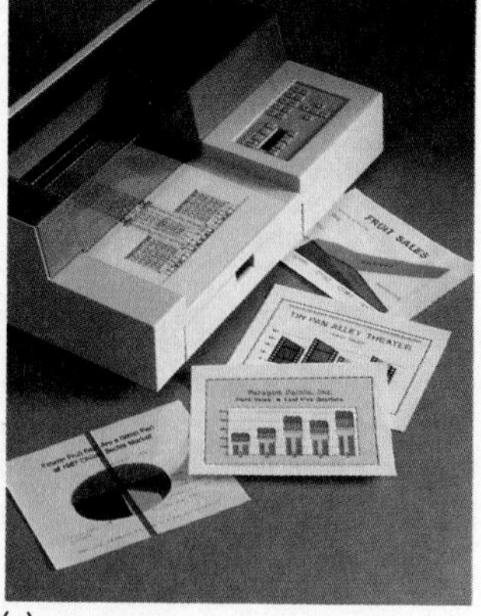

(c)

The major disadvantage of COM systems is that, because of the reduced visual size of the output, special equipment must be used to read the output that has been stored. Figure 6.13 shows microfilm/microfiche reader and output equipment. Because of the high cost of computer output systems (they can exceed $100,000), companies may not buy very many readers, so users may have to share them or go to another department to find one, which may be inconvenient. Microfilm and microfiche are most widely used by libraries for records and reference materials.

FIGURE 6.13

COMpressed. Computer output microfilm/microfiche equipment outputs information and data on microfiche sheets or microfilm rolls (a). The user needs special equipment to read the microfilm/fiche. Some COM equipment can also enlarge microfilm/fiche and print output on paper. This Minolta Integrated Information and Image Management System (b) can call up and reproduce microfilmed documents in seconds and print them out.

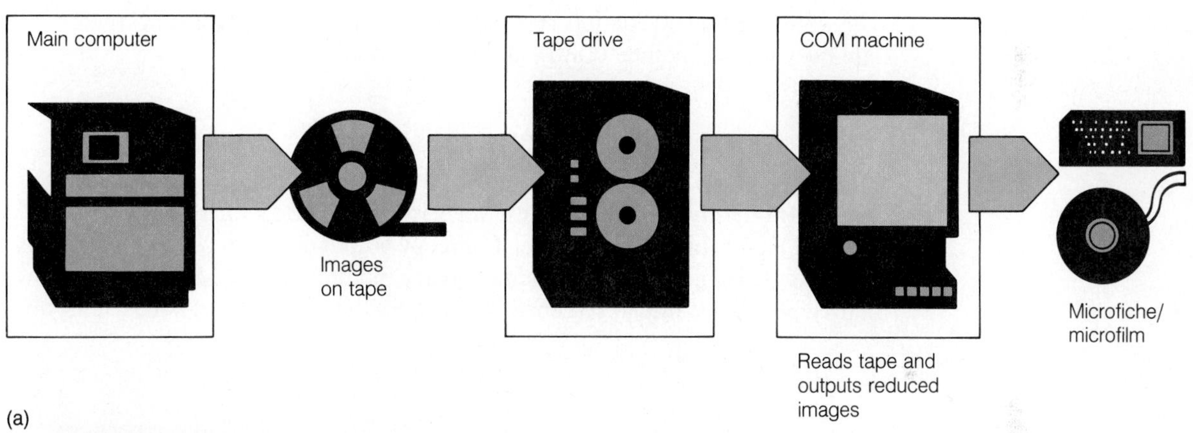

(a)

(b)

PORTABLE PRINTERS

Portable printers are becoming more and more popular as more and more business-people take their laptop computers on the road. Portable printers are compact in size and typically weigh less than 5 pounds. Nine-pin and 24-pin dot-matrix portable printers are available, as well as ink-jet and thermal printers. They each cost around $500 and can be either battery operated or plugged into a wall socket. Figure 6.14 shows the Kodak Diconix 150 Plus portable ink-jet printer, which weighs 3.75 pounds.

SOFTCOPY OUTPUT DEVICES

Eyestrain. Headaches. Neck cramps. What is a frequent cause of these complaints? The video display screen, the output device that many business users use the most. Actually, complaints have diminished as video display technology and *ergonomics*, the science of human comfort, have advanced. The two main types of video screens are the cathode-ray tube (CRT) and the flat panel.

CATHODE-RAY TUBE (CRT)

The **cathode-ray tube (CRT)** (Figure 6.15) (also called a *video display terminal*, or *VDT*), probably the most popular softcopy output device, is used with terminals connected to large computer systems and as a monitor for microcomputer systems. This type of video display screen is used to allow the operator to view data entry and

FIGURE 6.14

Portable printer. This illustration shows a Kodak Diconix 150 Plus.

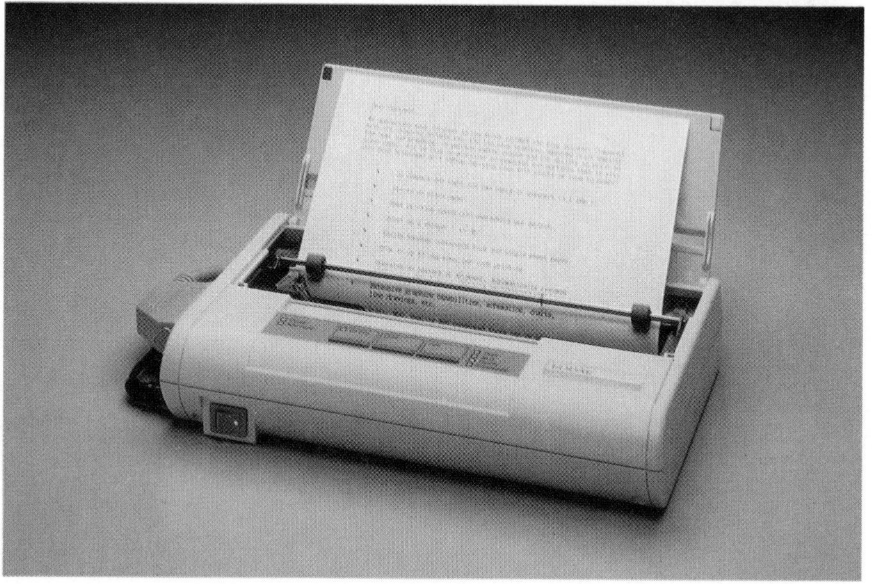

computer output. Monitors that display only letters, numbers, and special characters such as $, *, and ? are called **alphanumeric monitors** (or *alphanumeric terminals*). They look like television screens and display 80 characters per line, with 24 lines visible at one time. Screens that can display both alphanumeric data and graphics are called **graphics monitors** (or *graphics terminals*). Graphics monitors can be divided into groups that display one-, two-, and three-dimensional graphics.

The CRT's screen display is made up of small picture elements, called **pixels** for short. The smaller the pixels (the more points that can be illluminated on the screen), the better the image clarity, or **resolution.**

It takes more than one illuminated pixel to form a whole character, such as the letter *E* in the word *HELP* (Figure 6.16). And a finite number of characters can be displayed on a screen at once. The screen can be thought of as being divided into **character boxes**—fixed locations on the screen where a standard character can be placed. Most screens are capable of displaying 80 characters of data horizontally and 25 lines vertically. By multiplying the two numbers we can determine the number of character boxes that the CRT's electron gun can target—namely, 2,000. The more pixels that fit into a character box, the higher the resolution of the resulting image.

As mentioned earlier, the term *resolution* refers to the crispness of the image displayed on the screen. Three factors are used to measure resolution: lines of resolution (vertical and horizontal), raster scan rate, and bandwidth. To determine the number of lines of resolution that a video display can display vertically, simply

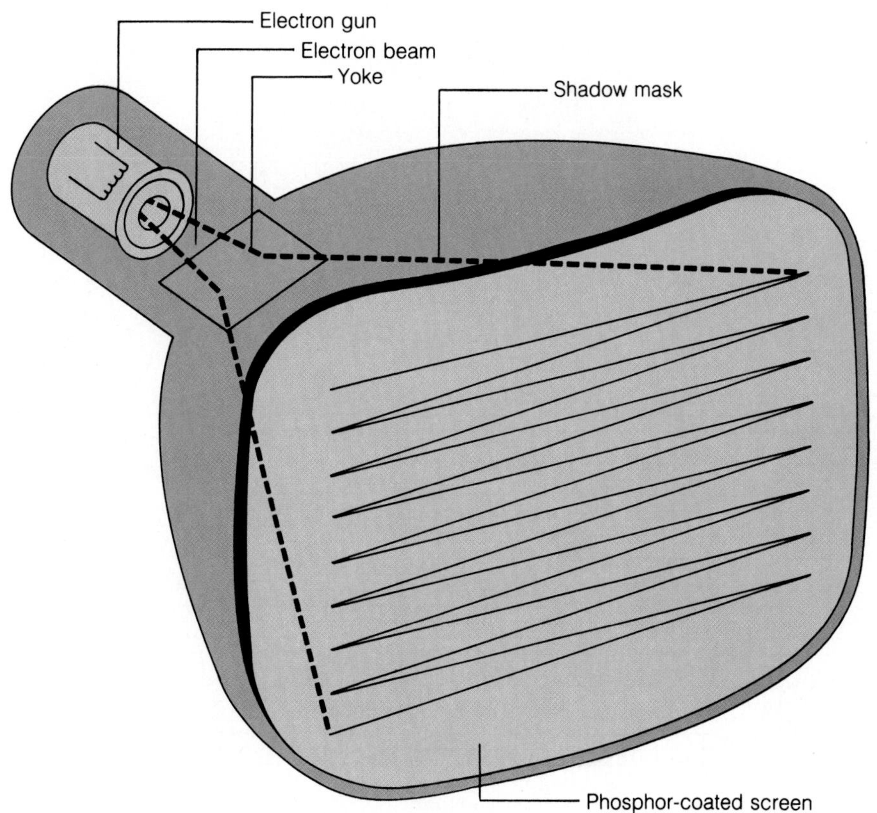

FIGURE 6.15

More than a thousand points of light. The CRT's electron gun emits a beam of electrons that moves across the interior of the phosphor-coated screen under the control of the yoke's magnetic field. The phosphors hit by the electrons emit light, which makes up the image on the screen. The distance between the points of light is fixed by the shadow mask, a shield with holes in it that is used to prevent the dispersion of the electron beam.

multiply the number of pixels in each character box vertically times the number of lines of text that can be displayed on the screen at one time—say, 25. If a character box has 14 pixels vertically, the display would have a vertical resolution of 14 × 25, which equals 350. To determine the number of lines of resolution horizontally, we simply multiply the number of pixels in each character box horizontally times the number of characters that can be displayed per line—say, 80. Thus, if a character box has 9 pixels horizontally, the horizontal resolution would be 9 × 80, or 720. For this monitor, the lines of resolution would be stated as 720 × 350. When you select a monitor, choose one with the highest possible number of lines of resolution.

The term **raster scan rate** refers to how many times per second the image on the screen can be *refreshed*—that is, "lit up" again. Because the phosphors hit by the electron beam do not glow very long, the electron beam must continuously sweep across the screen from left to right. If the raster scan rate is too low, the image will begin to fade and the screen will seem to flicker, which can be very hard on the eyes. The higher the raster scan rate, the better the image quality—and the less eyestrain.

The final factor that affects image resolution is the **bandwidth**. This term refers to the rate at which data can be sent to the electron gun to control its movement, positioning, and firing. The higher the bandwidth, the faster the electron gun can be directed to do its job.

CRTs have some disadvantages that recent technology has been trying to overcome, most notably: (1) size, (2) power consumption, and (3) fragility. The

FIGURE 6.16

Building character. Each character on the screen is made up of pixels, or picture elements.

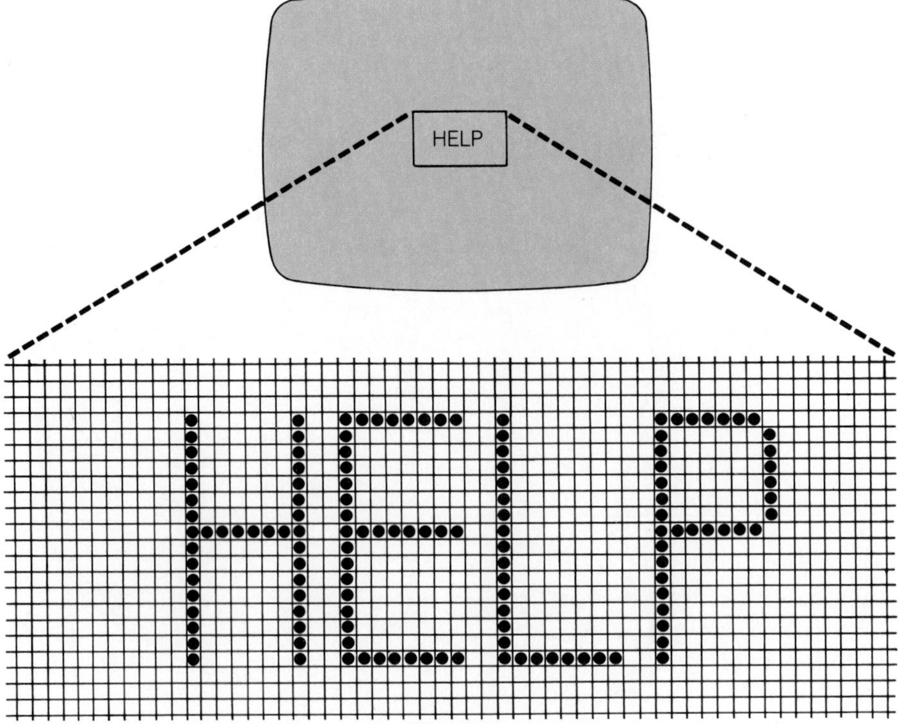

CRT is rather large and bulky because of the need to separate the electron gun from the screen by a particular distance, so it is unsuitable as a display screen for portable computers. The CRT also tends to use a substantial amount of electric power, again making it unsuitable to be used with portable computers, which occasionally need to run on batteries. Finally, as with a television, the CRT's glass tube and screen can be damaged if not handled carefully.

Monochrome and Color Monitors

A **monochrome monitor** (a monitor capable of displaying only a single-color image) and an **RGB color monitor** (RGB stands for red, green, blue) differ in two principal ways. First, they have different numbers of electron guns. A monochrome monitor has only one electron gun (Figure 6.15); however, as shown in Figure 6.17, an RGB color monitor has three electron guns. Second, the screen in an RGB color monitor is coated with three types of phosphors: red, green, and blue. The screen of a monochrome monitor is coated with only one type—or color—of phosphor, usually green or amber.

The operation principles of both monitors are almost exactly the same. However, each pixel in an RGB monitor is made up of three dots of phosphors, one of each color. The three electron guns direct their beams together. Each gun is aimed precisely so that it can hit a specific color dot in each pixel. A wide variety of colors can be created by controlling which guns fire and how long a burst they project at each dot. For example, if all three guns are fired at full intensity, a specific color is created for that pixel. If only two guns are fired at full intensity and the third gun is fired at half intensity, an entirely different color results. By varying the intensity with which the guns fire, RGB monitors are capable of displaying a large number of different colors. As you might expect, the control circuitry and software to direct the operation of an RGB monitor are somewhat more sophisticated than the corresponding components for a monochrome monitor.

Character-Mapped Display

Character-mapped display monitors, such as the IBM monochrome monitor, can display only characters. (For the character-mapped display monitor to display graphics, a video adapter card—to be discussed shortly—must be plugged into the motherboard.) The patterns of pixels used to represent the standard characters displayed on a monitor (the alphabetic characters, numbers, and special symbols) in character-mapped display are drawn from prerecorded templates (guides) stored in a video display ROM chip. When the user's software sends a request to display, for example, the letter A at a specific location, the template for that pixel pattern is looked up in the video display ROM chip. The electron gun then uses this pattern when it fires at the phosphors in the appropriate character box. In a personal computer the screen has 25 lines with 80 characters per line; this means that there are 2,000 positions on the screen where a predefined character can be placed.

Bit-Mapped Display

Character-mapped display cannot be used for extensive graphics because of the limited number of templates available. Because most software written today requires that the monitor be capable of displaying graphics, **Color Graphics Adapters (CGA), Enhanced Graphics Adapters (EGA),** and **Video Graphics Array (VGA)** cards were developed. With appropriate software, sufficient RAM, and compatible monitors, one of these cards, when plugged into the computer's motherboard, enables the monitor to display **bit-mapped graphics**. To create the variety of images necessary to produce graphics, the computer needs to be able to direct each electron beam individually at each pixel on the screen, not just superimpose a template over a character box. This approach requires more sophisticated control circuitry, software, and main memory than character-mapped display.

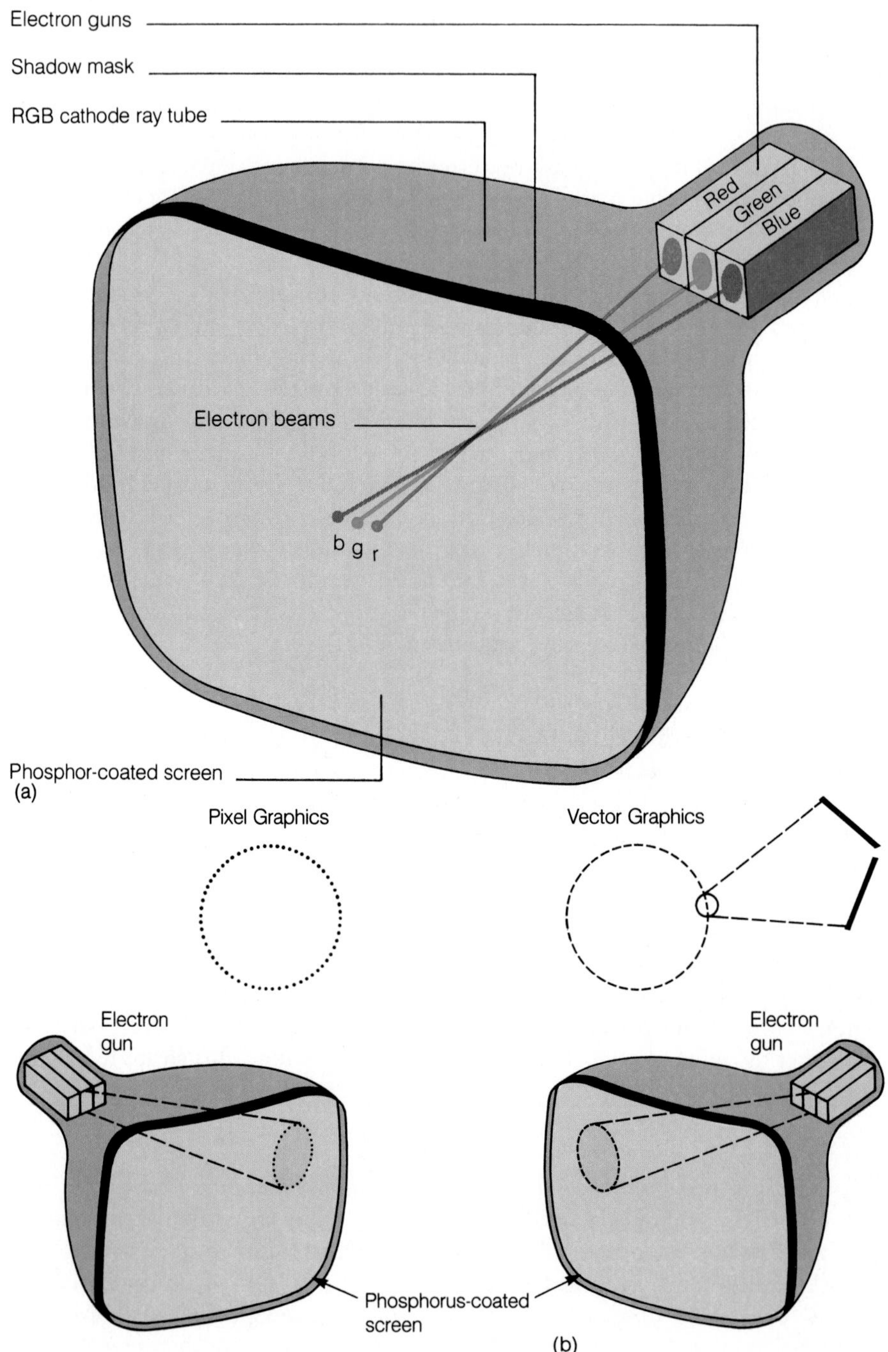

FIGURE 6.17

RGB monitor. The workings of an RGB color monitor are similar to those of a monochrome CRT, except that the types of phosphors—red, green, and blue—are hit by three electron beams (a). Each pixel has three color dots that are activated to different degrees to produce a wide range of colors. In vector graphics (b), lines instead of dots make up the image, thereby providing smoother curves than pixel graphics can produce.

In a video display with bit-mapped (also called *dot-addressable* or *all-points-addressable*) graphics capability, the entire screen is a single character box. A screen that can display 25 lines of text with 80 characters per line contains about 252,000 pixels; as a result, bit-mapped graphics-capable monitors require an ample supply of main memory to store all the image specifications before electron gun firing can begin. The more memory available, the more sophisticated the graphic image that can be created on the screen—subject to the limitations of the CRT, of course. EGA and VGA adapter boards are typically configured with 256 K or 512 K of RAM.

A CGA monitor displays four colors at a resolution of 320 × 200 when colors are displayed and 640 × 200 when monochrome images are displayed. An EGA monitor displays 16 colors at a resolution of 640 × 350. A VGA monitor also displays 16 colors but at a higher resolution (640 × 480). If one counts shades of colors, VGA monitors can display up to 256 colors simultaneously. **Super VGA (S-VGA)** monitors can display up to 256 colors with a resolution of 800 × 600. Super VGA technology is used in graphic design and engineering, as well as in animation. Figure 6.18 shows a VGA display. Figure 6.19 illustrates the difference between a high-resolution color Super VGA display and a low-resolution CGA display.

Because of their high resolution, VGA monitors are becoming more and more popular. They are also popular because, in addition to being used with software written for use with a VGA monitor, they can also be used with software written for CGA and EGA monitors. (The people who write software build assumptions into the software that determine what type(s) of monitor—CGA, EGA, VGA—the software can be used with.)

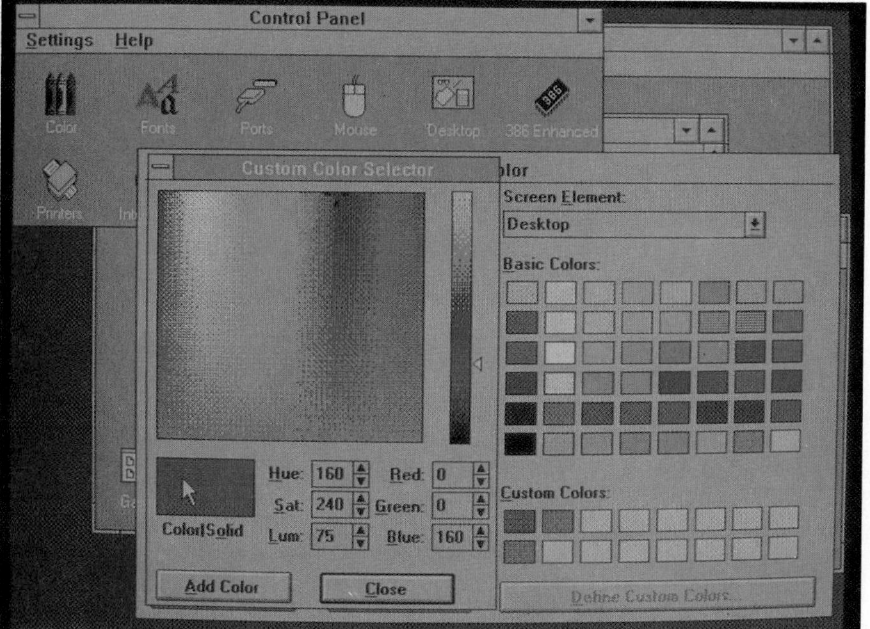

FIGURE 6.18

VGA. This screen from an IBM VGA monitor shows a wide range of colors.

Although VGA is very popular, IBM has incorporated the **Extended Graphics Array (XGA)** standard into its next-generation PS/2s. An XGA monitor can display 256 colors at a resolution of 1024 × 768. Table 6.3 summarizes the capabilities of graphics adapters.

A recent development in CRT technology called *flat tension mask* provides the user with a nonglare image that is 50–70 percent brighter than on a standard CRT tube. It can be used with any of the color cards described above. A flat tension mask color monitor produces an image of such high quality that photographs can be made directly from the screen.

ERGONOMIC CONSIDERATIONS

People often suffer physical complaints as the result of sitting, typing, and staring at the computer CRT screen for hours and hours at a time. What can you do about these complaints? Computer stores and mail-order catalogs offer many products, called computer accessories, to make the user's life easier. For example, you can purchase special desks with shelves, corners, and racks designed to hold the various components of your computer system in a comfortable manner. Special stools and

FIGURE 6.19 Low-resolution CGA display (a) and high-resolution Super VGA display (b).

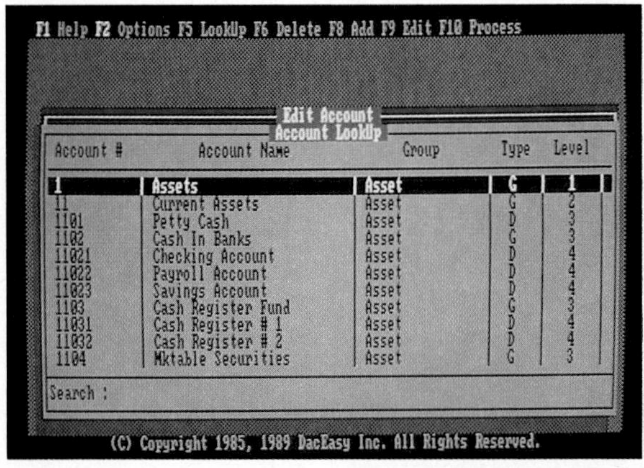

(a)

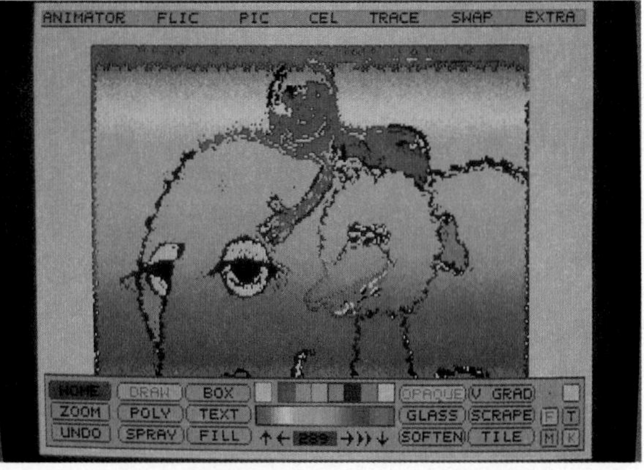

(b)

TABLE 6.3

Capabilities of Color Graphics

	Colors	Resolution
CGA (Color Graphics Adapter)	4	320 × 200
EGA (Enhanced Graphics Adapter)	16	640 × 350
VGA (Video Graphics Array)	16	640 × 480
S-VGA (Super Video Graphics Array)	256	800 × 600
XGA (Extended Graphics Array)	256	1024 × 768

Computers and Careers

Food and Beverage Service

All of us know how to eat. Some of us know how to cook. Numerous enterprising people go into the food and beverage business to try cooking for others. And computers have become as essential for restaurant operators as recipes and menus.

Many small eating and drinking establishments get by with just an electronic cash register, a calculator-like machine with a cash drawer that is not much different from the time-honored cash register. Larger foodservice operations, however, may go to a point-of-sale system. A POS system links three areas: the eating and drinking areas, the kitchen or other food-preparation areas, and the back office.

In the eating and drinking areas—what the industry calls the "front of the house"—there may be POS registers with different cash drawers for different waiters, waitresses, and bartenders. Or, if a cash drawer is shared by several servers, separate cash accountability is maintained by the software. Special-purpose software is also available that tells the host or hostess how many customers came in and when, the size of the order, and which server took the order and when. Some software can help servers be more efficient or helpful—for example, by indicating when a particular food or beverage is out of stock or by cueing servers to ask how an order of beef should be cooked.

So-called cash-taking software is important because often the person taking the order is not the cashier. Cash-taking software consolidates bar and food charges, provides information on discounts and senior-citizen specials, and indicates whether payment is by cash or credit card. Different kinds of printers are available for printing out guest checks: dot matrix or impact printers, which are commonplace but noisy; thermal printers, which require special paper; and laser printers, the most recently developed kind, which are quiet and require no special paper.

Servers in the front of the house may use flat-membrane type keyboards, touchscreen devices, and sometimes handheld terminals. Hardware in the kitchen must be of a hardier sort, capable of working amid heat, water, and grease. If orders are transmitted electronically by servers from terminals in the front of the house via cable to the kitchen, they may appear on a printer or display screen. Software may process the information sent by the server in a way to assist the preparer. For instance, similar food items might be grouped together, cooking instructions might be put in order, special cooking instructions highlighted, and instructions given on when to begin each part of an order. Software can also indicate that a kitchen is properly stocked to meet demand, based on previous experience.

Depending on the kind of eating establishment, a POS system might be hooked up to outside payment processors for credit-card charges and check clearing. Or, if the restaurant is in a hotel, it might link front-of-the-house terminals with the front desk, so that food and beverage charges may be posted to a guest's room bill.

Finally, there is the relationship of the POS system to what is called the "back office," such as the manager's office or the corporate headquarters. A manager may use the back-office terminal to collect information so that the restaurant can regulate the mix of products, adjust prices, and in general run things more efficiently. If the back-office machine is also a microcomputer, it can be used for other tasks, such as doing spreadsheets, word processing, and telecommunications. ■

chairs are also available that lessen lower back strain. Screens can be put on rotatable bases, and filters can be put on the screen to reduce glare and microwaves, infrared waves, and ultraviolet waves. You can also adjust your screen for brightness, contrast, and focus. Some experts state that green screens and amber screens are easier on the eyes than black and white screens are.

Many users are concerned that using video displays that emit very low frequency (VLF) electromagnetic radiation causes health problems—especially for pregnant women. Although no proof exists that confirms that the use of video displays is linked to pregnancy problems, no proof unequivocally dismisses this possibility. In Sweden, an agreement was made between management and labor in 1988 that had the effect of limiting VLF radiations from video displays. In response to users' concerns, IBM plans to reduce the amount of VLF radiations in future monitors.

Some people who use the computer keyboard day after day complain of aches and pains in finger, elbow, and shoulder joints. Too much typing can produce a painful hand injury known as ***repetitive strain injury (RSI)***. Specially designed keyboards can help prevent RSI. Also, the computer keyboard should be kept a level lower than regular desktop level, in order to reduce arm fatigue.

The best way to avoid aches and pains while working at a computer is to take frequent breaks, stand up, walk around, stretch, and exercise when you can. Remember: The computer is *your* tool, not the other way around.

FLAT SCREEN TECHNOLOGIES

The disadvantages of the CRT—large size, high power consumption, and fragility, plus occasional flickering images—have led to the development of **flat screen technologies.**

Flat screen technology is particularly useful for laptop computers, which can be used in the office and then taken home or on trips (Figure 6.20). Producing a truly lap-size, or laptop, computer—that is, one that is fully functional and weighing 15 pounds or less—has not been easy, and designing the video display has been the most difficult problem.

Interest in laptop computers encouraged researchers to explore different approaches to developing high-resolution, low-power-consumption flat screens with the same graphics capabilities of the traditional CRT. The most effective results to date have been achieved in three areas: liquid crystal display, electroluminescent display, and gas plasma display.

LIQUID CRYSTAL DISPLAY

The **liquid crystal display (LCD)** uses a clear liquid chemical trapped in tiny pockets between two pieces of glass. Each pocket of liquid is covered both front and back by very thin wires. In monochrome LCDs, when a small amount of current is applied to both wires, a chemical reaction turns the chemical a dark color, thereby blocking light. The point of blocked light is the pixel. In color LCDs, varying amounts of light pass through red, green, and blue filters.

LCD technology has progressed to the point that it rivals CRT technology in terms of resolution and the number of colors that can be displayed. In fact, since the LCD screen is flat, text and graphics appear crisper than on the curved surface of the

CRT, especially on the edges. In addition, images can be viewed from extreme angles with very little distortion. (Until recently, LCDs were susceptible to glare, which forced the optimum viewing angle to be very narrow.)

Many computer manufacturers are incorporating LCD technology into their laptop computers (Figure 6.21). LCDs are available today that support VGA and can display 256 colors. Color LCDs require ten times the amount of power as do monochrome LCDs, so laptops that currently incorporate this technology can't be battery-powered. However, as the production of color LCDs increases and more manufacturers develop them, technology will keep up to make them more power efficient.

The popular opinion among industry observers is that if LCDs weren't more expensive than the traditional CRT, they would not only be popular in the laptop market but would also be serious contenders in the desktop computer market.

Electroluminescent Display

Electroluminescent (EL) display (Figure 6.22) uses a thin film of solid, specially treated material that glows in response to electric current. To form a pixel on the screen, current is sent to the intersection of the appropriate row and column; the combined voltages from the row and the column cause the screen to glow at that point.

EL display provides very high image resolution and excellent graphics capability. Several manufacturers are currently working on the development of electroluminescent displays with full color capability. Most experts have predicted that this technology will come closest to matching or even surpassing all the capabilities of the traditional CRT. The major limitation of this technology has been cost.

FIGURE 6.20

CRT versus flat screen. As this photo shows, flat screen technologies have enabled manufacturers to produce personal computers small enough to be used on one's lap—the laptop computer.

GAS PLASMA DISPLAY

The oldest flat screen technology is the **gas plasma display** (Figure 6.23). This technology uses predominantly neon gas and electrodes above and below the gas. When electric current passes between the electrodes, the gas glows. Depending on the mixture of gases, the color displayed ranges from orange to red.

The principal advantages of gas plasma display are:

- The images are much brighter than on a standard CRT.
- The resolution is excellent.

FIGURE 6.21

LCDs on display. Three of the most popular laptop computers that use liquid crystal display: (a) NEC Prospeed 80386; (b) Compaq SLT/386; (c) Zenith Turbosport 386.

(a)

(b)

(c)

- Glare is not a significant problem.
- The screen does not flicker like some CRTs.

The main disadvantages are:

- Only a single color is available (reddish orange).
- The technology is expensive.
- It uses a lot of power.
- It does not show sharp contrast.

Several laptop computers use gas plasma display, including a model of the Grid Compass, the Ericsson Portable PC, the Sharp Executive PC, and the Toshiba T5100.

VOICE OUTPUT SYSTEMS

"Please close the door." "Please fasten your seatbelt." "You are now exceeding 55 miles per hour." Does your car talk to you? Many new cars have voice output devices, as do the telephone systems we've already mentioned. **Voice output systems** are relatively new and can be used in some situations where traditional display screen softcopy output is inappropriate: It is certainly more helpful to hear a warning that you are speeding than to take your eyes off the road to check a display.

Voice output technology has had to overcome many hurdles. The most difficult has been that every individual perceives speech differently; that is, the voice patterns, pitches, and inflections we can hear and understand are different for all of

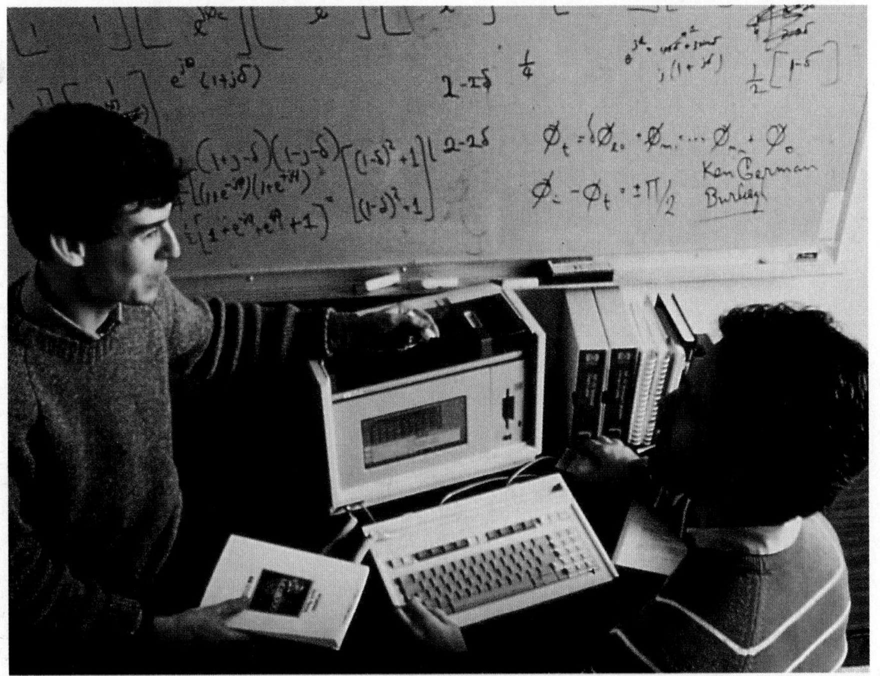

FIGURE 6.22

Electroluminescent display. This Hewlett-Packard Integral computer uses an EL flat-panel display.

us. It is not always easy to understand an unfamiliar voice pattern. At this point, two different approaches to voice output have evolved: speech coding and speech synthesis. *Speech coding* relies on human speech as a reservoir of sounds to draw from in building the words and phrases to be output. Sounds are codified and stored on disk to be retrieved and translated back as sounds. Speech coding has been used in applications such as automobiles, toys, and games. *Speech synthesis* relies on the use of a set of basic speech sounds that are created electronically without the use of a human voice.

Researchers are continuing to develop and improve voice output technologies. Many new products using voice output are expected to appear in the marketplace during the next decade. The largest application to date for the speech synthesis approach to voice output—converting text into "spoken" words—has many potential uses, including providing reading machines for the blind (Figure 6.24). And, of course, sound output does not have to be in voice form; it can be music

FIGURE 6.23

Gas plasma display. These popular laptop computers use gas plasma display: (a) GRiDCase 1500 Series, which is available with a 10 MB, a 20 MB, or a 40 MB hard disk; (b) Toshiba T5100; (c) IBM 581 plasma display.

(a)

(b)

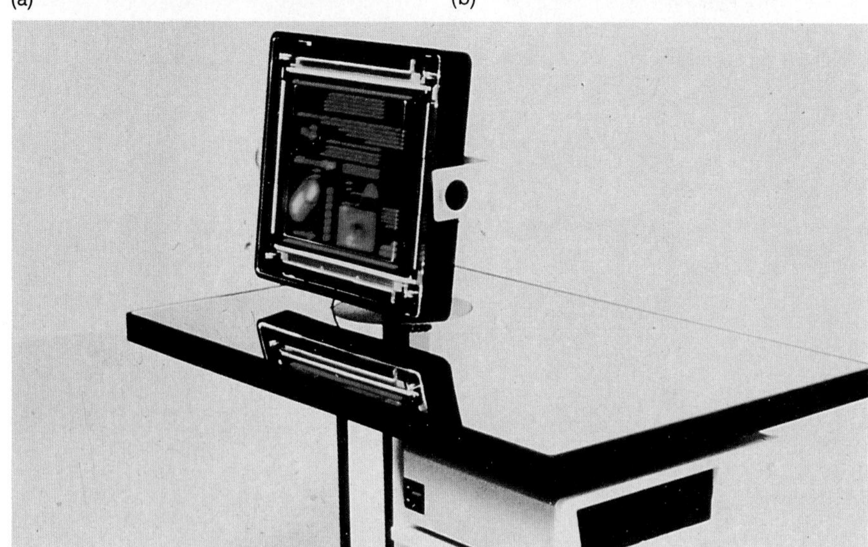

(c)

(synthesized music is, as most readers know, a booming business) or special-effects sounds, such as the sound accompaniment for computer animation.

OUTPUT CONTROLS

We have emphasized that the information a computer-based information system produces must be very reliable, because important business decisions are made on the basis of it. You have learned that data you enter must be accurate and complete and that input control methods have been designed to ensure just that. You also learned that different input and processing methods can produce information more quickly than others, thus affecting the timeliness of the information you are dealing with.

In addition, measures need to be taken to protect stored data so that not just anyone can get to it; this precaution should also be taken with sensitive output. Output information should be checked for completeness and accuracy, information should be accessible only to authorized personnel, and output that contains sensitive information should be destroyed when it is no longer needed.

Some examples of typical output controls are:

- Balancing output totals with input and processing totals.
- Auditing output reports.
- Providing distribution lists for all reports, so that only those people on the list receive the information.
- Requiring signatures on a predetermined form from those people who receive reports.

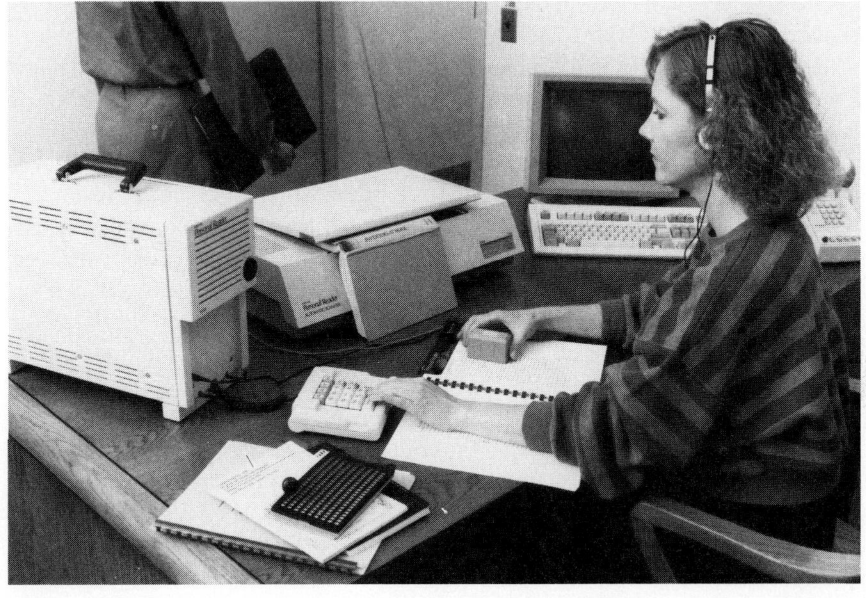

FIGURE 6.24

Xerox/Kurzweil Personal Reader, a breakthrough in technology for people who are blind, visually impaired, or dyslexic. The Personal Reader uses an optical scanner to convert typeset and typewritten material into speech. It can also be used to write and store information.

- Providing delivery schedules for reports so that people expecting them can follow up if the reports do not arrive on time.
- Requiring users to enter passwords when attempting to obtain softcopy output on the video display screen.
- Providing guidelines on how, when, and where to destroy reports after they are no longer needed.
- Securing sensitive data and information in an inaccessible location when it is not being actively reviewed.

The degree to which output control measures are taken must be determined by the needs of the business and both the people who run it and those who work there. Obviously, the extent of the controls is directly related to the value and the sensitivity of the information. In any case, the *user* has the responsibility for checking output reports for accuracy.

Although the CRT screen with improved, photograph-quality resolution will continue to be the most-used desktop monitor, flat screens will fulfill the need for microcomputer compactness and portability, as proven by the success of laptop computers. Experts expect flat screen resolution to improve so that graphics will be of high quality. Improved color flat screens will also appear in the not-too-distant future. Monochrome flat screens will be able to display 16 shades of gray, rather than just 8.

In any case, as a business user whose job involves some travel, you may expect to carry a flat screen laptop computer with you to update files, prepare reports, send information to your home company, check your company's data bank for product availability, pick up messages from your electronic mailbox, and print out reports and memos. And, on the road, your car's dashboard may include a flat screen monitor (connected to a shoe-box-sized computer hidden in the trunk) that displays road maps with your own car in position (Figure 6.25). Tape cassettes will hold the necessary data and software.

As a business user in an office, you will be jangled less and less by the loud noise of daisy wheel and dot-matrix printers. As the cost of nonimpact laser printers decreases and their capabilities improve, more and more offices will turn to these quiet printers, especially in conjunction with desktop publishing (which we will discuss later). Laser printers already output hardcopy that looks almost like traditional typeset copy; soon you won't be able to tell the difference, and you will eventually be able to print out business charts and other graphics in color on desktop laser printers. Laser printers will also get faster and smarter; that is, they will have more type fonts available and more memory, which will increase their flexibility. In the meantime, you will be able to use a sophisticated desktop nonimpact color thermal transfer printer, with many font choices and memory, to output your color graphics (Figure 6.26).

Once upon a time, it was thought the computer would lead to an all-electronic, "paperless" office. Yet all these improvements mean that computerized businesses will be generating more paper than ever!

In an effort to further increase printer speed, research is being done on other types of nonimpact printers, such as the light emitting diode (LED) printer, liquid crystal shutters, and ion-disposition printers. However, you probably will not be dealing with them for quite a while.

Something a bit farther down the road of laser printer developments is three-dimensional hardcopy—***holograms***, or three-dimensional pictures made without

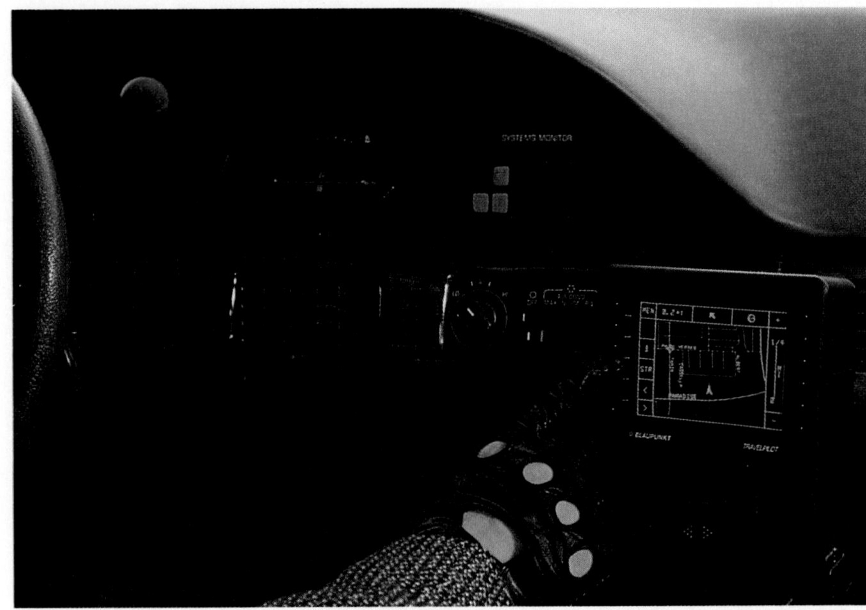

FIGURE 6.25

Dashboard electronic map.

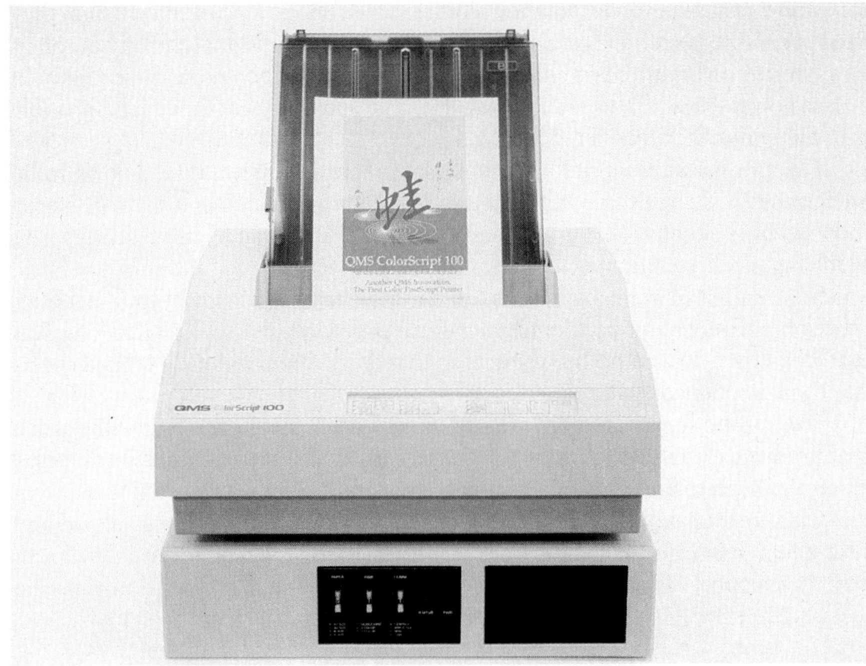

FIGURE 6.26

QMS Colorscript 100. This nonimpact color transfer printer is the industry's first color PostScript printer. (PostScript is a printer control language previously used only by laser printers.)

the use of a camera. Some experts say that the technological pieces already exist; they just have to be put together to provide this innovative type of hardcopy. If you go to work, for example, for the health industry, for an architecture firm, or for an interior design firm, perhaps you will soon be helping to prepare three-dimensional reports. For instance, surgeons could view holographic output to study organs before operating on them; architects and interior designers could show clients more accurately how a building or an office will look.

Onward: Software — Taking Care of Business

This chapter completes the section on hardware. Now that you know the basics about the hardware associated with the four parts of a computer-based information system — input, storage, processing, and output — you may wonder how you can possibly stay current with new developments after you have finished your courses or your degree and joined the work force. One of the best ways is to visit computer shows and examine the new hardware on display. Another way is to check reviews and articles in popular weekly and monthly computer newspapers and magazines — *Infoworld*, *PC Week*, *Macworld*, and *Computerworld*, to cite a few. Such publications are also good sources for staying current with the topic of our next chapter — software — as you shall see, after briefly revisiting your booming business, Sporting Life.

Summary

Before deciding which output hardware and media to use, business users must determine what *kinds* of output they require, based on the kind of information they need in order to perform regular job duties and to make decisions (and on how often they need to do both). Users should also consider how much noise the equipment makes, how fast it works, how expensive it is, and, above all, whether it is compatible with the equipment they already have.

The two basic categories of computer-produced output are (1) output to be used immediately by people and (2) output in a computer-usable form to be stored and then used later by the computer and people. Output can be in hardcopy form, which is generally thought of as being tangible, or "touchable," and softcopy form, which is thought of as intangible. Paper, the most-used hardcopy output medium, comes in a variety of forms. Continuous-form paper, which uses a tractor feed, was developed for use in computer printers so that users would not have to feed sheets into the computer one at a time.

The second most commonly used output form is a softcopy one — the video display image. The two types of display screen used most often are a computer terminal connected to a large computer system and a monitor attached to a microcomputer system. When computer display devices are not readily available and information has some value over time, it is most often produced in hardcopy form. When computer display devices are readily available and information must be accessed quickly, it is often produced in softcopy form.

The main hardcopy output devices are printers and plotters. A printer can print characters, symbols, and sometimes graphics on paper. Printers are categorized according to whether or not the image produced is formed by physical contact of the print mechanism with the paper. Impact printers make contact; nonimpact printers do not.

Impact printers usually form images by pressing an inked ribbon against the paper with a hammer-like mechanism. A letter-quality printer, like a typewriter, presses fully formed characters against the ribbon. A dot-matrix printer uses separate pin-like hammers to form characters out of dot patterns. Letter-quality printers produce higher quality images than do dot-matrix printers and are generally used for business letters, important memos, and reports. However, letter-quality printers are slower and noisier than dot-matrix printers, and they cannot produce graphics. Common types of impact letter-quality printers are the daisy wheel printer, the thimble printer, and the ball printer. Dot-matrix printers, because they do not print fully formed characters, are more flexible and can be used to print graphics in black or in colors.

The high-volume output requirements of most large computer installations cannot be satisfied by dot-matrix or letter-quality printers. Large computer systems often use special high-speed printers, called *line printers*, that print a whole line at a time. Three common types of line printers are drum printers, band or belt printers, and chain printers.

The main categories of nonimpact printers are ink-jet printers, thermal printers, and laser printers. These printers make much less noise than impact printers do, but they cannot be used to generate carbon copies.

Ink-jet printers, which are about as fast as dot-matrix printers, form images with tiny droplets of ink fired through a plate with holes drilled in it. Color ink-jet printers are used to produce graphics; however, ink jets can get clogged, and the image quality is not considered to be as good as that produced by plotters.

Thermal printers use heat to produce an image on specially treated paper. They are very quiet; however, they are slow, and the special paper is expensive.

Laser printers are nonmechanical, nonimpact printers. Because the process has no print heads that move or print hammers that fire, the result is high speed and quiet operation. Laser printers work somewhat like photocopying machines. They use laser beams to transfer images to sensitive paper that is then coated with toner—the toner sticks to the spots sensitized by the laser. Laser printers print a page at a time and can produce very high quality images, so they are often used for graphics. Laser printers used to be very expensive; however, because their prices have fallen, small laser printers are now within reach of users wanting a high-quality desktop printer. They are frequently used in desktop publishing, which uses microcomputers, special software packages, and laser printers to produce material ready to be published. However, the small, affordable desktop laser printers do not yet produce color.

A plotter is most often used for producing graphics because it can output free-form drawings on paper in color. Plotters are categorized according to whether or not they use pens, how the paper is placed into them, and which of their parts move. Drum plotters and flatbed plotters use pens; electrostatic printers do not. In a drum plotter, paper is mounted on a rotating drum onto which pens are dropped and moved left and right to create images. In flatbed plotters, the paper is flat and the pens move horizontally and vertically across the paper. Electrostatic plotters use electrostatic charges to create images out of very small dots on specially treated paper, which is then run through a developer to allow the image to appear.

The main softcopy output devices are cathode-ray tube (CRT) video screens and flat video screens. Computer output microfilm/microfiche systems and voice output systems are sometimes considered to be softcopy output systems, but we have categorized them as hardcopy.

The CRT, which is used with terminals connected to large computer systems and as a monitor for microcomputer systems, has an electron gun that fires at phosphors on the inside of the screen, causing them to glow. The glowing phosphors become the picture elements—pixels, for short. It takes a group of pixels to form one character, and there is a finite number of characters that can be displayed on the screen at once.

The three factors used to measure resolution are the lines of resolution (vertical and horizontal), the raster scan rate, and the bandwidth. Vertical resolution is found by multiplying the number of vertical pixels in the character box by the number of lines displayed on the screen; horizontal resolution is found by multiplying the number of horizontal pixels in the character box by the number of characters displayed on the line. Raster scan rate refers to how many times per second the image on the screen is refreshed—how many times the fading phosphors are relit. The higher the raster scan rate, the better the quality of the screen image and the less strain on the eyes. The bandwidth refers to the rate at which data is sent to the electron gun; the higher the bandwidth, the faster the electron gun can be directed to do its job.

CRTs can display images in one color (monochrome) or several colors. The RGB (red, green, blue) monitor uses three electron guns to illuminate red, green, and blue phosphors. CGA, EGA, and VGA color graphics cards can be plugged into the motherboards of many microcomputers in order to enable compatible monitors to display color bit-mapped graphics, whereby individual pixels are illuminated. In a character-mapped display, the display is controlled by prerecorded character templates stored in a ROM chip. Character-mapped displays cannot display graphics.

The most notable disadvantages of CRTs are their large size (to accommodate the electron gun setup), their high rate of power consumption, and their fragility. The disadvantages of the CRT and rising interest in portable and laptop computers led to the development of flat screen technology, which is becoming a favored alternative to the CRT. The three most common types of flat panel displays are liquid crystal display (LCD), electroluminescent (EL) display, and gas plasma display.

Computer output systems are often used by companies that don't want to take up space with a lot of regular hardcopy output, like paper, but have needs not met by softcopy output. These systems capture computer output on microfilm or microfiche—both approaches can be referred to as COM. COM systems are fast, produce output condensed in size, and are not particularly expensive. However, special equipment is needed to read the output that has been stored.

Voice output systems can be used in situations where hardcopy is inappropriate and commonly used softcopy output devices are inconvenient.

As with input and storage, care must be taken to ensure that output is responsibly generated, shared, and disposed of. Control methods should be established to ensure that only authorized users see sensitive output and that output is properly secured.

Key Terms

- alphanumeric monitor (terminal), p. 215
- ball printer, p. 198
- band printer, p. 202
- bandwidth, p. 216
- belt printer, p. 202
- bit-mapped (graphics) display, p. 218
- cathode-ray tube (CRT), p. 214
- chain printer, p. 202
- character box, p. 215
- character-mapped display, p. 217
- Color Graphics Adapter (CGA), p. 217
- computer output microfilm/microfiche (COM) system, p. 212
- daisy wheel printer, p. 197
- dot-matrix printer, p. 198
- drum plotter, p. 211
- drum printer, p. 202
- electroluminescent (EL) display, p. 223
- electrostatic plotter, p. 211
- Enhanced Graphics Adapter (EGA), p. 217
- Extended Graphics Array (XGA), p. 220
- flatbed plotter, p. 211
- flat screen technology, p. 222
- gas plasma display, p. 224
- graphics monitor (terminal), p. 215
- hardcopy, p. 194
- impact printer, p. 197
- ink-jet printer, p. 205
- laser printer, p. 207
- letter-quality printer, p. 197
- line printer, p. 202
- liquid crystal display (LCD), p. 222
- monochrome monitor, p. 217
- nonimpact printer, p. 203
- pixel, p. 215
- plotter, p. 197
- printer, p. 197
- raster scan rate, p. 216
- resolution, p. 215
- RGB color monitor, p. 217
- softcopy, p. 194
- Super VGA (S-VGA), p. 219
- thermal printer, p. 206
- thimble printer, p. 198
- video graphics array (VGA), p. 217
- voice output system, p. 225

Exercises

Matching

Match each of the following terms to the phrase that is the most closely related.

1. ______ plotter
2. ______ CRT
3. ______ bandwidth
4. ______ impact printers
5. ______ raster scan rate
6. ______ liquid crystal display
7. ______ RGB color monitor
8. ______ resolution
9. ______ laser printer
10. ______ alphanumeric monitor
11. ______ nonimpact printer
12. ______ monochrome monitor
13. ______ pixel
14. ______ voice output system
15. ______ output controls
16. ______ VGA

a. Rate at which data can be sent to the electron gun to control its movement, positioning, and firing
b. Specialized hardcopy output device designed to produce high-quality graphics in a variety of colors
c. Image clarity
d. The higher this is, the better the image quality will be on a video display.

e. Cathode-ray tube
f. Monitor that can display more than one color on a solid background
g. A few advantages of this type of printer are very high speed, low noise level, and high image quality.
h. Graphics card that is plugged into a microcomputer's motherboard that allows a compatible monitor to display high-resolution color graphics
i. Printers that strike characters against ribbon or paper when they print
j. A glowing phosphor, or picture element
k. This type of monitor can display only one color on a solid background.
l. Monitor that can display only letters, numbers, and special characters
m. Ink-jet, thermal, and laser printers fall into this category.
n. These are usually established within an organization to ensure that output is viewed only by authorized users.
o. Component of a computer that talks to you
p. This type of display technology is often used in laptop computers.

MULTIPLE CHOICE

1. Which of the following is used to ensure the high quality of computer output?
   a. voice output systems
   b. output controls
   c. computer output microfilm
   d. liquid crystal display
   e. ROM
2. Which of the following technologies will you likely see in laptop computers?
   a. voice output systems
   b. output controls
   c. computer output microfilm
   d. liquid crystal display
   e. RGB
3. Which of the following is the principal difference between a monochrome monitor and an RGB monitor?
   a. number of electron guns
   b. resolution
   c. size
   d. cost
   e. RAM
4. Which of the following can be output by a computer?
   a. graphics
   b. voice
   c. text
   d. computer-usable data or information
   e. all the above
5. Output hardware is often categorized according to whether it:
   a. is expensive.
   b. requires a large amount of electricity to work.
   c. produces hardcopy or softcopy.
   d. can fit on a desktop.
   e. is fast.

6. Large computer systems typically use:
   a. dot-matrix printers.
   b. daisy wheel printers.
   c. ink-jet printers.
   d. line printers.
   e. portable printers.
7. Which of the following printers will you be sure not to use if your objective is to print on multicarbon forms?
   a. daisy wheel
   b. dot-matrix
   c. laser
   d. thimble
   e. line
8. Which of the following isn't part of a CRT?
   a. phosphor screen
   b. shadow mask
   c. electron gun
   d. gas plasma
   e. pixel
9. Which of the following does not affect the resolution of a video display image?
   a. bandwidth
   b. raster scan rate
   c. vertical and horizontal lines of resolution
   d. screen size
   e. graphics adapter card
10. To produce high-quality hardcopy graphics in color, you would want to use a(n):
    a. RGB monitor.
    b. plotter.
    c. ink-jet printer.
    d. laser printer.
    e. super VGA monitor.

Short Answer

1. What is the difference between a character-mapped display and a bit-mapped display?
2. Why has there been such interest in developing flat screen technologies?
3. What advantages does the laser printer have over other printers? What is its principal limitation?
4. When might you want output to be in computer-usable form?
5. What are the principal differences between how an image is formed on a monochrome monitor and on an RGB monitor?
6. Describe four hardware devices that produce hardcopy output.
7. In what ways do letter-quality and dot-matrix printers differ?
8. If you frequently need to use a text printer in a quiet office, what type of printer would be ideal? Why?

9. Describe a situation in which an alternative to the traditional forms of hardcopy and softcopy output might be necessary.
10. Why do many people find it necessary to use a plotter to output information?

PROJECTS

1. Prepare an outline that lists all the factors a user should consider when he or she is preparing to buy a printer.
2. If you could buy any printer you want to be used with your microcomputer, what type (make, model, etc.) would you choose? Does the printer need to be small (to fit in a small space)? Does it need to print across the width of wide paper (11 × 14 inches)? In color? On multicarbon forms? Analyze what your needs might be and choose a printer (if necessary, make up what your needs might be). Review some of the current computer publications for articles or advertisements relating to printers. What is the approximate cost of the printer you would buy? Your needs should be able to justify the cost of the printer.
3. Visit a local computer store to compare the output quality of the different printers on display. Then obtain a brochure on each printer sold. After comparing output quality and price, what printer would you recommend to a friend who needs a printer that can support outputting resumés?
4. Go to a computer store and find out what software packages, microcomputers, and monitors can be used with VGA cards; report your findings.
5. At the computer store, research the hardware requirements for several graphics software packages. What kinds of monitors are required? What type of microcomputer? What kind of printer? Are any special hardware items needed to run the software?
6. Explore the state of the art of computer-generated 3-D graphics. What challenges are involved in creating photo-realistic 3-D images? What hardware and software is needed to generate 3-D graphics? Who benefits from this technology?

EPISODE 2

SPORTING LIFE

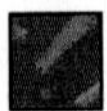

WHAT DO YOU WANT THE COMPUTER TO DO FOR YOU?

THE STORY CONTINUES . . .

When we left you at Sporting Life, you were thinking about buying a computer to help you with inventory and general ledger record-keeping. However, a lot has gone on since then, and like many people you have put off acquiring a computer until the workload and related problems have become too serious to ignore.

For example, when the company next door moved out, you acquired the space to accommodate your increasing level of business. And, to support your expanded business, you have extended your hours to seven days a week: 9:00 A.M. to 9:00 P.M. Monday through Friday and 10:00 A.M. to 6:00 P.M. on Saturday and Sunday. You now have more than 1,400 different items in stock. As a result, your sales have increased to over $2.5 million.

HELP! Luis is losing control of inventory; an increasing number of popular items are out of stock. Inventory records can't be kept up to date. In addition, the overall dollar investment in inventory has gone up substantially, and Luis feels that the money is not being properly managed. Meanwhile, Kim has run into difficulties handling the accounting workload; it's hard for her to keep up with the manual recording of all the daily sales entries to the sales journal.

All your employees now agree that your business definitely needs a computer, but what exactly do you want it to do for you? Before making *any* purchases, you must decide what you want to achieve in the areas of input, processing, storage, and output. The preceding four chapters (Part II) have taught you the basic concepts in these areas as they relate to hardware. This information is enough for you to begin to think practically about how computers are useful in business. After you have read Part III, Software, you will be able to get more specific about choosing software and compatible hardware for your business. In the meantime, to resolve the question posed above, you call a meeting to determine what the data and information needs of your staff are.

SIZING UP THE SITUATION

Kim says she expects the computer to produce a substantial amount of useful accounting information and to take over the major burden of accounting-related processing activities. She thinks that:

- She and the staff will find it useful to retrieve information—for example, the status of customers' accounts—from the files and review it on the computer's display screen.
- A large volume of hardcopy reports will have to be produced, including:
  —Accounting ledgers: single copies, 80 columns wide, about 300 pages per week.
  —Customer invoices: three copies of each, 80 columns wide, about 75 per day.
  —Special reports: single copies, 132 columns wide, about 50 pages per day.

Kim also thinks that it would be a good idea to analyze in graphic form the trends in accounts receivable and accounts payable. She is looking forward to being able to review graphs on the screen, as well as print them out occasionally.

Luis says that he needs the computer to provide assistance in tracking the status of inventory as a whole and in restocking inventory. He thinks that:

- The computer will have to allow him to quickly check on a terminal the status of any item in inventory.
- He will have to track inventory turnover.
- The following reports will have to be produced:
  —Detailed inventory listings: two copies of each, 132 columns wide, about 30 pages daily.
  —Inventory reorder report: single copies, 132 columns wide, about two pages a day.
  —Purchase orders: three copies, 80 columns wide, about 75 per week.

In addition, you, Luis, and Kim agree that you need to store the following kinds of computer files:

- Invoice files: both paid and unpaid invoices (about 5,000 invoices).
- Purchase orders: both filled and unfilled (about 500).
- Customer information: about 3,000 customers.
- Employee files: folders are kept for each employee (average 25, including part-time employees).
- Accounting files: these records currently fill six filing cabinets.
- Inventory files: all the data on items you order, store, and sell (item number, description, unit price).

SPECIFIC POINTS FOR DISCUSSION: WHAT'S YOUR OPINION?

Now that you know what your basic data and information needs are at Sporting Life, think seriously about what hardware will satisfy your business requirements for the least amount of money. Of course, you do have to keep the future in mind. You don't want to purchase something that can't be upgraded to support your steadily expanding business. Discuss the following points:

1. Which input hardware and methods would be best suited to your business?
   a. Will the volume of input activity be high enough to warrant dedicated

(special-purpose) data entry systems? Or will you be better served by a less expensive general-purpose system?
   b. Do you anticipate planning for on-line input or will batch input be satisfactory? Keep in mind that the hardware costs associated with on-line input are much greater than those associated with batch input.
   c. Do you think a bar code scanner might be useful? If so, how?
   d. How about an optical scanner?
   e. You'll probably need several types of printers. Based on your output needs, for which kinds will you research cost and limitations?

2. What factors would you consider to determine the types of computer-based storage you need?
   a. Do you think there will be a place for the use of diskettes? If so, how will they be used?
   b. Will you need a high-capacity hard disk? Why or why not?
   c. Have you considered how important making backup copies of files will be? How could this be done?

3. Will you need both hardcopy and softcopy output? Give examples. Are hardcopy or softcopy graphics going to be used? Give examples.

4. How powerful a computer system do you really need? What factors would you consider in determining whether you need a microcomputer system, minicomputer system, or mainframe computer system?

Discussing the preceding questions should help you clarify what a computer can do for your business. But don't rush out and buy anything yet. First you must learn about software—how it is developed, what forms it comes in, and what it can do. After that, in the next episode, you will learn how to choose software that will fulfill Sporting Life's needs and be compatible with the types of hardware you are interested in.

Part III

Software and Connectivity

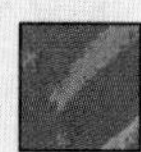

Once upon a time the term ***hardware*** described iron fittings, tools, and other things created by the village blacksmith; military jargon then expanded the definition to include machines and, still later, computer equipment. In 1962, someone used this precedent to coin a new term to describe the programs, procedures, and related documentation associated with computers—*software*. No doubt the definition of software will change as much as hardware in the coming years, but in both cases many underlying concepts will probably remain the same. In the next three chapters, we will describe applications software, such as word processing or database managers, which essentially turns the computer into the user's tool; systems software, which has more to do with the computer than the user; and communications, which involves special types of software and hardware to support networks and connectivity.

CHAPTER 7

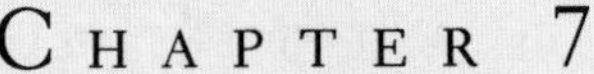

APPLICATIONS SOFTWARE AND SYSTEMS SOFTWARE

Why can't you simply buy a diskette with the software program you need, put it into your microcomputer's disk drive, start it up, and have it run? Unfortunately, it's often not that easy; buying software is not like buying an audio cassette of your favorite music and slapping it into a tape deck, or renting a movie to play on your VCR. Computer software comes in two forms: applications software and systems software. Because different systems software is made for different purposes, and some applications software is not compatible with some systems software, it is important for business users to understand the fundamental concepts and features of these two types of software and to learn to effectively evaluate software.

PREVIEW

When you have completed this chapter, you will be able to:

- Explain why you should try to evaluate your applications software requirements before your other hardware and software requirements.
- Describe what applications software is and categorize the types of applications software.
- List and describe three types of systems software.
- Explain the basic functions of an operating system and utilities.
- Name the most common operating systems available for microcomputers.
- List some points to consider when purchasing microcomputer applications or systems software.

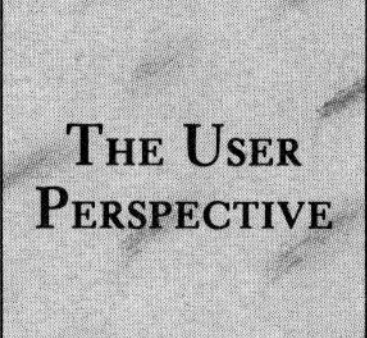

Can you use a daisy wheel letter-quality printer to print out a portrait of Abraham Lincoln? Can you use an RGB monitor to show the colors of the rainbow? With your knowledge of hardware, you know the answers to these questions. Different equipment has different uses. Likewise with software: A software program designed to handle text may not necessarily be used to draw charts and graphs or manipulate rows and columns of numbers.

To help you begin to understand the differences among types of software, let us repeat the definitions we gave back in Chapter 1 for applications and systems software.

- **Applications software** is a collection of related programs designed to perform a specific task—to solve a particular problem for the user. The task or problem may require, for example, computations for payroll processing or for maintaining different types of data in different types of files.
- **Systems software** "underlies" applications software; it starts up the computer and functions as the principal coordinator of all hardware components and applications software programs. Without systems software loaded into the main memory of your computer, your hardware and applications software will be useless.

HOW DOES SOFTWARE AFFECT YOU?

No such thing as software existed in the earliest computers. Instead, to change computer instructions, technicians would actually have to *rewire* the equipment (Figure 7.1). Then, in the 1950s, computer research, following the approach of Herman Hollerith and his census-tabulating machine, began to use punched cards to store program instructions. In the mid-1950s, high-speed storage devices that were developed for ready retrieval eliminated the need for hand-wired control panels. Since that time, the sophistication of computer hardware and software has increased exponentially.

The appearance of the microcomputer in the late 1970s made computer hardware and software accessible to many more people because it was more affordable, easier to use, and flexible enough to handle very specific job-related tasks. Because of this accessibility, a large pool of applications software has been created since then to satisfy almost any business requirement. In other words, you do not have to be a specialist to use computer software to solve complicated and tedious problems in your work. However, you will be entering the job race without your running shoes if you do not understand the uses of—and the differences among—types of software.

WHAT SOFTWARE IS AVAILABLE AND HOW GOOD IS IT?

Many people will buy an applications software program just because it was recommended by a friend. They do not bother to evaluate whether the program offers all the features and processing capabilities necessary to meet their needs. It's much easier in the short run to simply take the friend's recommendation, but, in the long

FIGURE 7.1

Progress. (a) At first only the most highly skilled specialists could use or "run" computer software, because they had to rewire the computer every time they wanted it to perform a different task. (b) Today, however, because of the current sophistication of software, people as diverse as schoolchildren and accountants are able to use computers for common tasks.

(a)

(b)

run, a lot of extra time and money will be spent. Knowing what software is available —and how to evaluate it—is vital to satisfy processing requirements.

For large computer systems, the choice of systems software tends to be made by computer specialists, and the applications software is usually custom-designed for the system. For microcomputers, the user generally receives systems software along with the computer he or she purchases or uses at work. New versions of microcomputer systems software and applications software can be bought at computer stores.

If you are starting from scratch, you should choose your applications software *first*, after you identify your processing needs. Then choose compatible hardware models and systems software that will allow you to use your applications software efficiently and to expand your system if necessary. By choosing your applications software first, you will ensure that all your processing requirements will be satisfied. You won't be forced to buy a software package that is your second choice simply because your first choice wasn't compatible with the hardware or systems software already purchased.

When you go to work in an office, chances are that the computer hardware and systems software will already be in operation, so if you have to choose anything, it will most likely be applications software to help you do your job. If you do find yourself in a position to choose applications software, make sure not only that it will satisfy the processing requirements of your job, but also that it is compatible with your company's hardware and systems software.

There is much more applications software to choose from than systems software. Applications software can be purchased off the shelf of a computer store to satisfy almost any business requirement; this software is often referred to as **off-the-shelf software.** Deciding what applications program to use therefore requires very careful analysis.

So much software is available today that even in the microcomputer software industry people need a directory or catalog of software to keep track of it. Magazines such as *Compute* (Figure 7.2) provide general users with reviews of many different kinds of software. *PC Magazine* (Figure 7.3) also provides a valuable guide to computer hardware, software, services, and related topics of interest. Figure 7.4 shows a page from *PC World*, the "business magazine of PC products and solutions." Figure 7.5 shows a typical software review found in *InfoWorld* magazine.

APPLICATIONS SOFTWARE

After the days of rewiring computers had passed, only two sources existed for basic applications software: (1) software could be purchased from a computer hardware vendor, or (2) if you were a programmer, you could develop your own. Today, computer software has become a multibillion-dollar industry. More than a thousand companies have entered the applications software industry, and they have developed a wide variety of products. As a result, the number of sources of applications software has grown. Applications software can be acquired directly from a software manufacturer or from the growing number of businesses that specialize in the sale and support of microcomputer hardware and software. Most independent and computer chain stores devote a substantial amount of shelf space to applications software programs; some businesses specialize in selling only software.

FIGURE 7.2

Compute: Your Complete Home Computer Resource. This publication contains computer-related articles and hardware and software reviews that are helpful for users of all types of microcomputers. This illustration shows part of a review of personal R:Base software, which allows users to create and manage large collections of data. (Reprinted by permission. © 1991, Compute Publications International, Ltd.)

Ease of Use . . . . ★★★★
Documentation . . . . ★★★★
Features . . . . ★★★★★
Innovation . . . . ★★★★

IBM PC and compatibles; 640K RAM for total package including tutorial and applications, 450K RAM for program alone; DOS 3.1 or higher for 5¼-inch version, DOS 3.2 or higher for 3½-inch version, DOS 3.3 for IBM PS/2; 6MB of hard disk space; color monitor recommended—$149.95

MICRORIM
15395 SE 30th Pl.
Bellevue, WA 98007
(800) 248-2001
(206) 649-9500

FIGURE 7.3

PC Magazine. This publication provides "Fact Files," concise reviews of hardware and software in each issue.

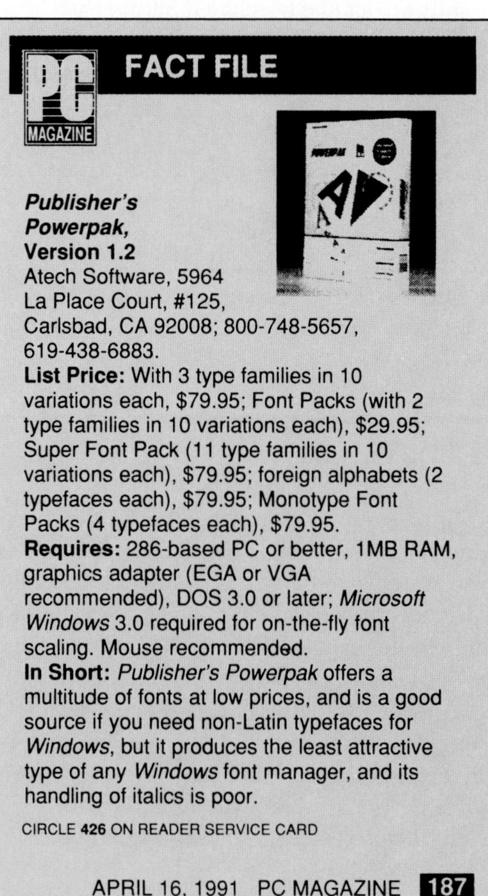

PC MAGAZINE **FACT FILE**

Publisher's Powerpak,
Version 1.2
Atech Software, 5964 La Place Court, #125, Carlsbad, CA 92008; 800-748-5657, 619-438-6883.
List Price: With 3 type families in 10 variations each, $79.95; Font Packs (with 2 type families in 10 variations each), $29.95; Super Font Pack (11 type families in 10 variations each), $79.95; foreign alphabets (2 typefaces each), $79.95; Monotype Font Packs (4 typefaces each), $79.95.
Requires: 286-based PC or better, 1MB RAM, graphics adapter (EGA or VGA recommended), DOS 3.0 or later; *Microsoft Windows* 3.0 required for on-the-fly font scaling. Mouse recommended.
In Short: *Publisher's Powerpak* offers a multitude of fonts at low prices, and is a good source if you need non-Latin typefaces for *Windows*, but it produces the least attractive type of any *Windows* font manager, and its handling of italics is poor.

CIRCLE **426** ON READER SERVICE CARD

APRIL 16, 1991 PC MAGAZINE **187**

If you can't find off-the-shelf software to meet your needs, you can develop—or have someone else develop—your own (Chapter 8). If you don't know how to do it yourself, you can have the computer professionals within your own organization develop the software, or you can hire outside consultants to do it. Unfortunately, hiring a professional to write software for you can become much more costly than the price of off-the-shelf software.

APPLICATIONS SOFTWARE VERSIONS

Many software developers sell different versions of the same software application. Each version is usually designated by a different number—generally, the higher the number, the more current the version and the more features are included with the package. In some cases, different versions are written to be used with particular microcomputer systems, such as IBM-compatibles or Macintosh microcomputers. *If you buy a software package for a microcomputer, make sure you have the version that goes with your microcomputer and systems software.*

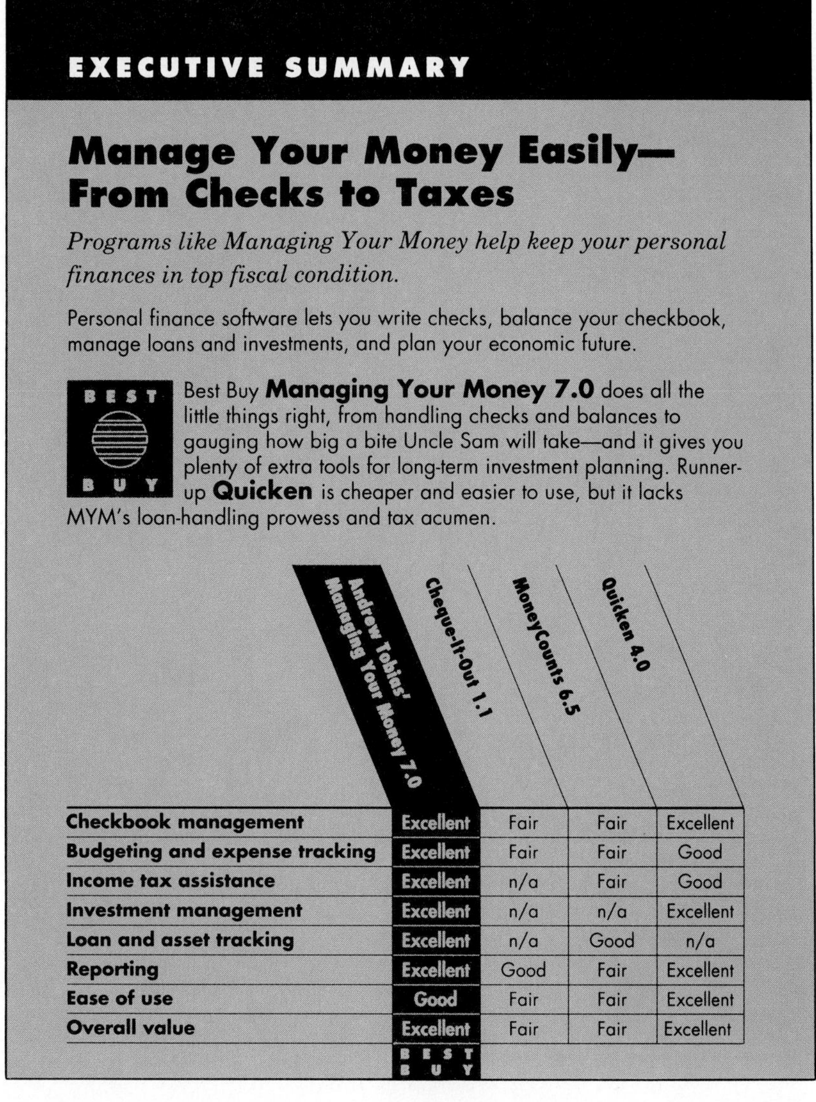

EXECUTIVE SUMMARY

Manage Your Money Easily—From Checks to Taxes

Programs like Managing Your Money help keep your personal finances in top fiscal condition.

Personal finance software lets you write checks, balance your checkbook, manage loans and investments, and plan your economic future.

BEST BUY

Best Buy **Managing Your Money 7.0** does all the little things right, from handling checks and balances to gauging how big a bite Uncle Sam will take—and it gives you plenty of extra tools for long-term investment planning. Runner-up **Quicken** is cheaper and easier to use, but it lacks MYM's loan-handling prowess and tax acumen.

	Andrew Tobias' Managing Your Money 7.0	Cheque-It-Out 1.1	MoneyCounts 6.5	Quicken 4.0
Checkbook management	Excellent	Fair	Fair	Excellent
Budgeting and expense tracking	Excellent	Fair	Fair	Good
Income tax assistance	Excellent	n/a	Fair	Good
Investment management	Excellent	n/a	n/a	Excellent
Loan and asset tracking	Excellent	n/a	Good	n/a
Reporting	Excellent	Good	Fair	Excellent
Ease of use	Good	Fair	Fair	Excellent
Overall value	Excellent	Fair	Fair	Excellent
	BEST BUY			

FIGURE 7.4

PC World review. This Executive Summary is typical of software reviews published by PCW Communications, Inc., in *PC World* magazine, available on newsstands. (Reprinted with permission of *PC World*, April 1991, PC World Communications.)

A user who buys a certain version of a software application may, after a few months, find that a later version of the application has become available. This user has two choices: either stay with the purchased version or upgrade (usually for a fee paid to the software manufacturer) to the later version.

TYPES OF POPULAR APPLICATIONS SOFTWARE

So many different types of applications software packages have come on the market that deciding which ones to buy requires some investigation. Applications software is generally expensive. You can easily spend between $200 and $700 for a single

FIGURE 7.5

InfoWorld software review. *InfoWorld* magazine publishes reviews like this in every issue. (Source: *InfoWorld*, March 4, 1991.)

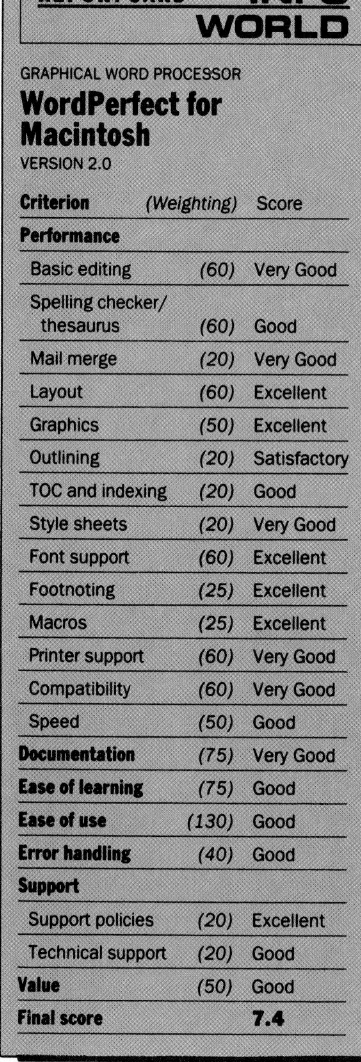

REPORT CARD INFO WORLD

GRAPHICAL WORD PROCESSOR

WordPerfect for Macintosh

VERSION 2.0

Criterion	(Weighting)	Score
Performance		
Basic editing	*(60)*	Very Good
Spelling checker/ thesaurus	*(60)*	Good
Mail merge	*(20)*	Very Good
Layout	*(60)*	Excellent
Graphics	*(50)*	Excellent
Outlining	*(20)*	Satisfactory
TOC and indexing	*(20)*	Good
Style sheets	*(20)*	Very Good
Font support	*(60)*	Excellent
Footnoting	*(25)*	Excellent
Macros	*(25)*	Excellent
Printer support	*(60)*	Very Good
Compatibility	*(60)*	Very Good
Speed	*(50)*	Good
Documentation	*(75)*	Very Good
Ease of learning	*(75)*	Good
Ease of use	*(130)*	Good
Error handling	*(40)*	Good
Support		
Support policies	*(20)*	Excellent
Technical support	*(20)*	Good
Value	*(50)*	Good
Final score		**7.4**

PRODUCT SUMMARY

Company: WordPerfect Corp., 1555 N. Technology Way, Orem, UT 84057; (801) 225-5000.
List price: $495.
Requires: Macintosh Plus, SE, or II computer; 1 megabyte of RAM; hard disk; System 6.0.3 or later.
Pros: Includes a robust drawing utility and an improved user interface.
Cons: None significant, except the bug in the Styles function.
Summary: A feature-filled program capable of handling a wide range of sophisticated word processing duties.

package. In fact, individuals and companies typically spend much more on software than on hardware.

Just as the subject matter of a book determines what literary category it falls into (such as history, gardening, cooking, or fiction), the capabilities of an applications software program determine how it is categorized. Applications software categories that are used most often include:

- General business management.
- Industry-specific.
- Special disciplines.
- Education.
- Personal/home management.
- General-purpose software for the user.

General business management software, the largest group of applications software, includes products that cover the vast majority of business software needs, including accounting, inventory control, finance and planning, personnel, office administration, project management, and many others. However, some industries have very specialized applications software requirements; special *industry-specific software* is designed to meet these needs. Typical industries requiring specific products include specialized accounting services, advertising, agriculture and farm management, architecture, banking, construction, dentistry, engineering, legal services, leasing and rental companies, personnel agencies, property management, publishing, and others.

Special discipline software is a category set aside for such hobbies and special-interest areas as amateur radio, astrology, geography, mathematics, music, sports and leisure, visual arts, and others. *Education applications software* products focus on educational administration, computer-aided instruction (CAI), and special education. *Personal/home management software* tends to group products according to whether they relate to education, entertainment, finance, or home management.

The following sections highlight the types of *general-purpose applications software* you are likely to use in the business or the professional environment. You can practice each of these types of applications software by working through the Modules that follow Chapter 12. Also, for more detailed information about these software programs, read the introductions to the corresponding modules.

WORD PROCESSING SOFTWARE

Word processing software offers capabilities that greatly enhance the user's ability to create and edit documents (Figure 7.6). It enables the user to easily insert, delete, and move words, sentences, and paragraphs without ever using an eraser. Word processing programs (Module B) also offer a number of features for "dressing up" documents with variable margins and type sizes and styles. The user can do all these manipulations on screen, before printing out hardcopy. Table 7.1 provides a list of some of the common features of word processing software packages. Figure 7.7 shows an edit menu of the WordPerfect word processing program.

Besides WordPerfect, some popular word processing packages are DisplayWrite, Microsoft Word, WordStar, PC-Write, OfficeWriter, XYWrite III Plus, AMI Professional, and MultiMate Advantage.

FIGURE 7.6

My word! With word processing software you can get (b) without having to go through (a).

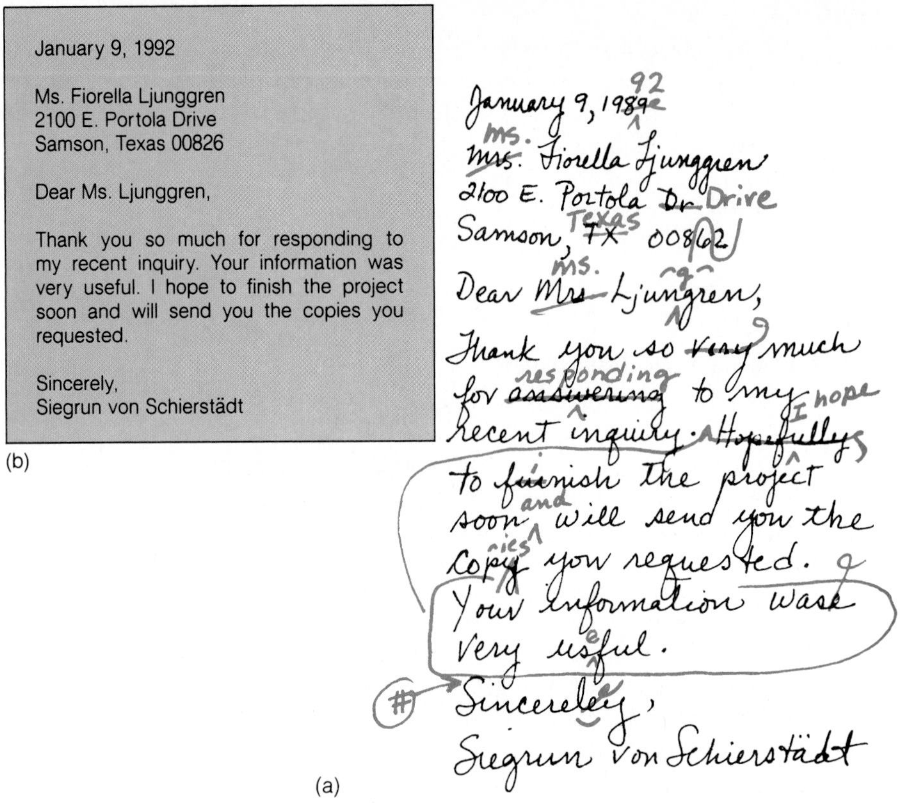

January 9, 1992

Ms. Fiorella Ljunggren
2100 E. Portola Drive
Samson, Texas 00826

Dear Ms. Ljunggren,

Thank you so much for responding to my recent inquiry. Your information was very useful. I hope to finish the project soon and will send you the copies you requested.

Sincerely,
Siegrun von Schierstädt

(b)

(a)

FIGURE 7.7

Most word processing packages provide a number of different menus to use for editing your documents. Shown here is a WordPerfect edit menu.

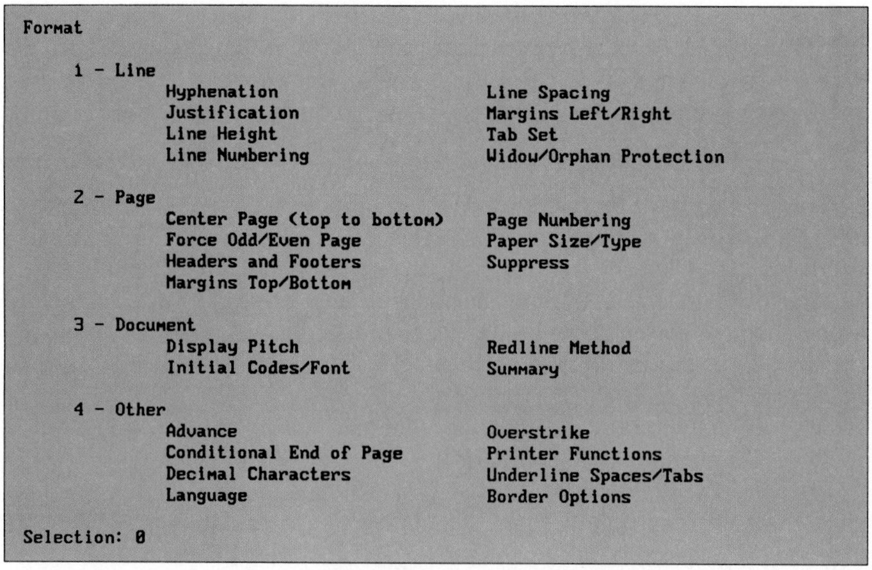

```
Format

     1 - Line
              Hyphenation                     Line Spacing
              Justification                   Margins Left/Right
              Line Height                     Tab Set
              Line Numbering                  Widow/Orphan Protection

     2 - Page
              Center Page (top to bottom)     Page Numbering
              Force Odd/Even Page             Paper Size/Type
              Headers and Footers             Suppress
              Margins Top/Bottom

     3 - Document
              Display Pitch                   Redline Method
              Initial Codes/Font              Summary

     4 - Other
              Advance                         Overstrike
              Conditional End of Page         Printer Functions
              Decimal Characters              Underline Spaces/Tabs
              Language                        Border Options

Selection: 0
```

Some Common Word Processing Software Features **TABLE 7.1**

Feature	Description
Correcting	Deleting and inserting. You simply place the cursor where you want to correct a mistake and press either the delete key or the backspace key to delete characters. You can then type in new characters. (Many packages offer shortcuts to deleting and inserting—for example, deleting lines of text at one time by hitting a special sequence of keys.)
Block and move (or cut and paste)	Marking and changing the position of a large block of text; this can be done even between different documents, not just within the same document.
Check spelling	Many packages come with a spelling checker program that, when executed, will alert you to misspelled words and offer correct versions.
Thesaurus	Thesaurus programs allow the user to pick word substitutions. For example, if you are writing a letter and want to use a more exciting word than *impressive*, you can activate your thesaurus program and ask for alternatives to that word.
Mail merge	Most word processing programs allow the user to combine different parts of different documents (files) to make the production of form letters much easier, faster, and less tedious than doing the same thing using a typewriter. For example, you can combine address files with a letter file that contains special codes where the address information is supposed to be. The program will insert the different addresses in copies of the letter and print them out.
Scrolling	This feature allows the user to "roll" text up or down across the screen; you can't see your long document all at once, but you can scroll the text to reach the point you are interested in. Most packages also allow you to "jump" over many pages at a time—for example, from the beginning of a document straight to the end.
Search and replace	You can easily search through a document for a particular word—for example, a misspelled name—and replace it with another word.
Footnote placement	This feature allows the user to build a footnote file at the same time he or she is writing a document; the program then automatically places the footnotes at appropriate page bottoms when the document is printed.
Outlining	Some packages automatically outline the document for you; you can use the outline as a table of contents.
Split screen	This feature allows you to work on two documents at once—one at the top of the screen and one at the bottom. You can scroll each document independently.
Word wrap	Words automatically break to the next line; the user does not have to press "return" or "enter."
Font choice	Many packages allow you to change your typeface and the size of the characters to improve the document's appearance.
Justify/unjustify	This feature allows you to print text aligned on both right and left margins (justified, like the main text in this book), or let the words break without aligning (unjustified, or ragged, like the text at the right side of this table).
Boldface/italic/underline	Word processing software makes it easy to emphasize text by using **bold**, *italic*, or underlining.
Sort	You can arrange text in alphabetical or numerical order.

Some word processing packages, including WordPerfect, Microsoft Word, and AMI Professional, provide *desktop publishing* features that enable users to integrate, or combine, graphics and text on a professional looking page (Figure 7.8). However, compared to dedicated desktop publishing packages (described shortly), word processing packages still do not provide the same high degree of ease and sophistication—but the line of distinction between word processing packages and desktop publishing packages is blurring.

FIGURE 7.8 Desktop publishing using a wordprocessing package. WordPerfect was used to combine text and graphics in this flyer.

LASER PRINTERS

Laser printer technology is much less mechanical than impact printing (that is, no print heads move, no print hammers hit), resulting in much higher speeds and quieter operation. The process resembles the operation of a photocopy machine: A laser beam is directed across the surface of a light-sensitive drum and fired as needed to record an image in the form of a pattern of tiny dots. The image is then transferred to the paper -- a page at a time -- in the same fashion as a copy machine, using a special toner.

Laser printers can also generate text in a variety of type sizes and styles (also called **fonts**) providing a business with the capability of outputting professional-looking typeset-quality reports. Most laser printers are capable of outputting a specific set of fonts and sizes. Laser printers that include a built-in **page description language** on a board inside the printer provide greater flexibility by enabling users to generate fonts in any size and to produce special graphics effects. The most popular page description language available is Adobe Systems' Postscript. Postscript printers are generally $1000 - $2000 more than non-Postscript printers.

A variety of laser printers, each different in terms of cost, speed, and capabilities, is available for use with microcomputers today. In general, laser printers can be viewed as falling into three categories: (1) low-end, (2) high-end, and (3) color.

The laser printers that fall into the low-end category are priced between $1000 and $3000 and can print between 4 ppm and 8 ppm. With printers in this range, 300 dpi images are common. Laser printers that are priced around $1000 are providing businesses with a low-cost alternative to the high-end 24-pin dot matrix printers.

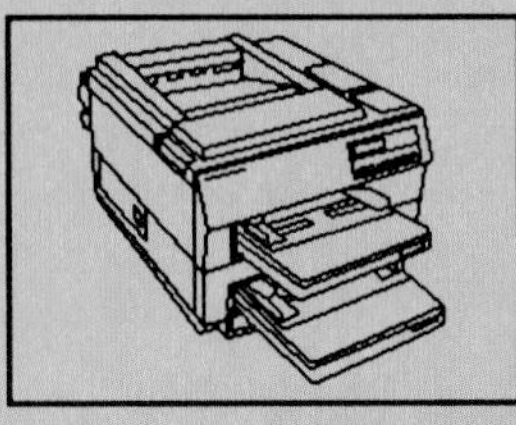

For $10,000-$20,000 a high-end laser printer can be purchased that is three to five times faster than a low-end printer and generates clearer images (400-600 dpi). Printing between 15 and 25 ppm, these printers are appropriate in a networked environment where many users are sharing one printer.

Using laser technology to print in color is a new technology and is still too expensive to be attractive to most computer users. For example, CSS Labs' color laser printer sells for around $30,000. Because this technology is still new, it remains to be seen how well these products really work.

ELECTRONIC SPREADSHEET SOFTWARE

With **spreadsheet software,** based on the traditional accounting worksheet, the user can develop personalized reports involving the use of extensive mathematical, financial, statistical, and logical processing. Its automatic calculation abilities can save the user almost a lifetime of tedious arithmetic. The spreadsheet shown in Figure 7.9 was created by a beginner in less than an hour. This spreadsheet is designed to calculate expense totals and percentages.

Some of the terms you will encounter when using spreadsheets are listed in Table 7.2. Figure 7.10 shows a window (screen-sized area) of a spreadsheet. One of the most useful functions of spreadsheet software is the performance of "What if" analyses. The user can say: "What if we changed this number? How would future income be affected?", and get an immediate answer by having the spreadsheet software recalculate *all* numbers based on the one change. Some spreadsheet packages, including versions 2.2 and 3.0 of Lotus 1-2-3, enable you to *link* spreadsheets together. Thus if a number, such as an expense amount, is changed in one spreadsheet, that change is automatically reflected in other spreadsheet files that contain the same category of expense data.

Module C introduces you to Lotus 1-2-3, the most widely used software package of any kind. Other well-known spreadsheet packages include Microsoft Excel, Quattro, SuperCalc 5, Multiplan, and PFS: Plan.

(a)

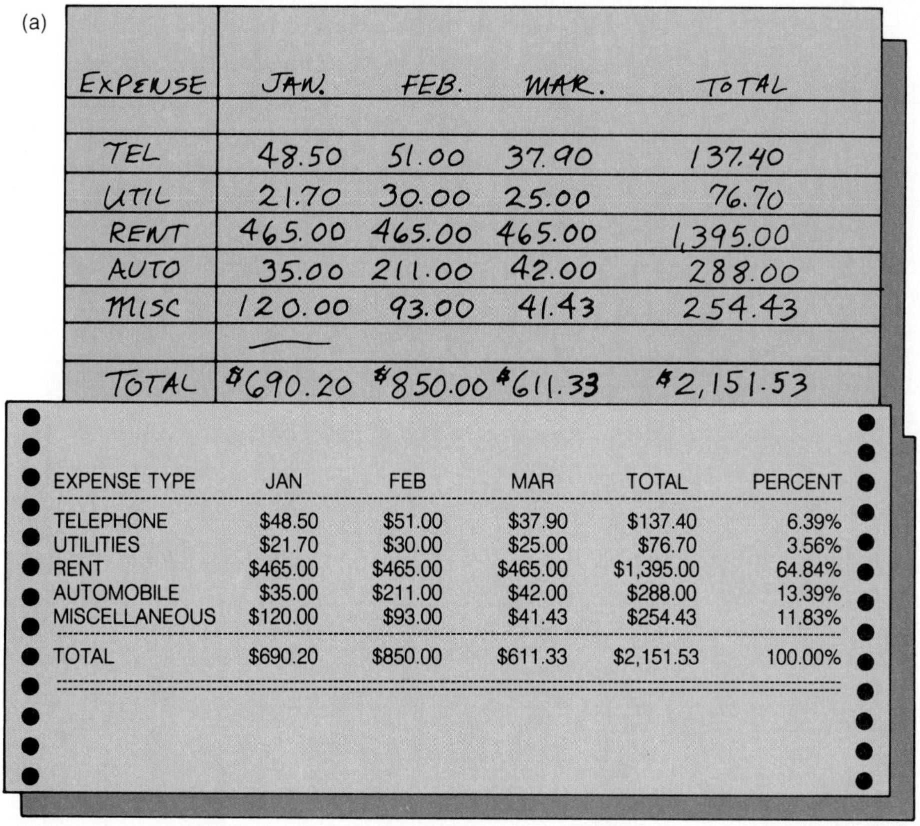

EXPENSE	JAN.	FEB.	MAR.	TOTAL
TEL	48.50	51.00	37.90	137.40
UTIL	21.70	30.00	25.00	76.70
RENT	465.00	465.00	465.00	1,395.00
AUTO	35.00	211.00	42.00	288.00
MISC	120.00	93.00	41.43	254.43
TOTAL	$690.20	$850.00	$611.33	$2,151.53

(b)

EXPENSE TYPE	JAN	FEB	MAR	TOTAL	PERCENT
TELEPHONE	$48.50	$51.00	$37.90	$137.40	6.39%
UTILITIES	$21.70	$30.00	$25.00	$76.70	3.56%
RENT	$465.00	$465.00	$465.00	$1,395.00	64.84%
AUTOMOBILE	$35.00	$211.00	$42.00	$288.00	13.39%
MISCELLANEOUS	$120.00	$93.00	$41.43	$254.43	11.83%
TOTAL	$690.20	$850.00	$611.33	$2,151.53	100.00%

FIGURE 7.9

The calculating type. Electronic spreadsheets (b) look much like spreadsheets created manually (a). However, when a number is changed in an electronic spreadsheet, all totals are automatically updated—certainly not the case when you work with a spreadsheet by hand!

DATABASE MANAGEMENT SYSTEM SOFTWARE

Database management system (DBMS) software allows the user to store large amounts of data that can be easily retrieved and manipulated with great flexibility to produce meaningful management reports. With database management system software, also called *database managers*, you can compile huge lists of data and

TABLE 7.2

Common Spreadsheet Terminology

Term	Definition
Column labels	The column headings across the top of the worksheet area.
Row labels	The row headings that go down the left side of the worksheet area.
Cell	The intersection of a column and a row; a cell holds a single unit of information.
Value	The number within a cell.
Cell address	The location of a cell. For example, "B3" is the address of the cell at the intersection of Column B and Row 3.
Cell pointer (cursor)	Indicates the position where data is to be entered or changed; the user moves the cursor around the spreadsheet using the particular software package's commands.
Window	The screen-sized area of the spreadsheet that the user can view at one time (about 8 columns and 20 rows); most spreadsheets can have up to 8,192 columns and 256 rows; some (Apple Works) have as many as 10,000 columns and more than 300 rows.
Formula	Instructions for calculations; these calculations are executed by the software based on commands issued by the user.
Recalculation	Automatic reworking of all the formulas and data according to changes the user makes in the spreadsheet.
Scrolling	"Rolling" the spreadsheet area up and down and right and left on the screen to see different parts of the spreadsheet.

FIGURE 7.10

Window (screen-sized area) of a Lotus 1-2-3 spreadsheet.

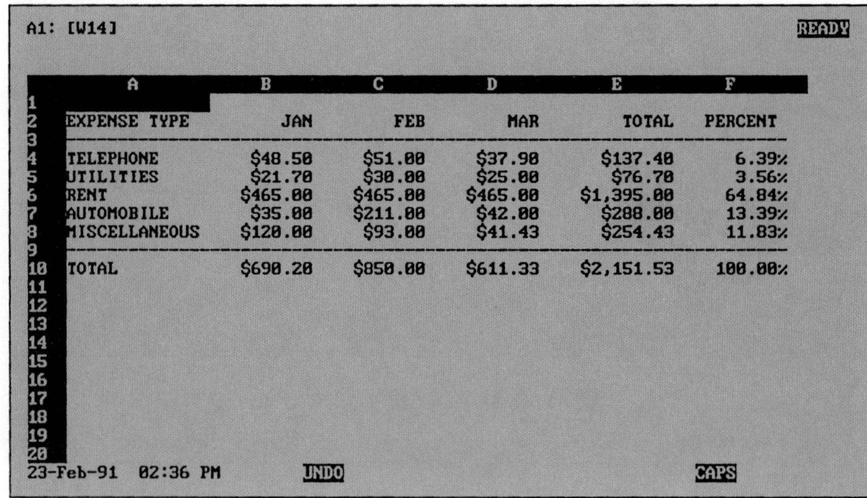

manipulate, store, and retrieve it without having to touch a single filing cabinet or folder. What would you rather have in the corner of your office—two huge filing cabinets or that nice floor-to-ceiling poster you always wanted? Table 7.3 lists some common database management software terms.

Two main categories of DBMS software exist: (1) flat-file and (2) relational. **Flat-file database management systems** (also called **file management systems**) can deal with data in only one file at a time. They can't establish relationships among data stored in different files. **Relational database management systems** can establish links by referring to fields that include that same type of data in different databases. These links enable users to update several files at once or generate a report using data from different database files. Although flat-file DBMSs are suited for generating mailing labels, most business applications require the use of a DBMS with relational capabilities.

Module D gives a practical presentation of database management systems software. Popular DBMS packages include dBASE III PLUS, dBASE IV, R:Base for DOS, Paradox, PFS: Professional File, Q&A, and Reflex.

GRAPHICS SOFTWARE

You are undoubtedly familiar with the old phrase "One picture is often worth a thousand words." Reports and presentations that include graphics can be much more effective than those that don't. **Graphics software** (Figure 7.11) enables users to produce many types of graphic creations.

In general, **analytical graphics** are basic graphical forms used to make numerical data easier to understand. The most common analytical graphic forms are bar graphs, line charts, and pie charts—or a combination of these forms (Figure 7.12). The user can view such graphics on the screen (color or monochrome) or print them out.

Common Database Management Software Terms **TABLE 7.3**

Term	Description
Record	Group of related data concerning one unit of interest—for example, one employee. A company's database would have one record for each employee.
Field	Each unit of information within a record—such as the employee's name.
Retrieve and display	When the user issues database commands (determined by the particular DBMS program) and specifies the record and field needed, the DBMS program retrieves the record and displays the appropriate section of it on the screen. The user can then change data as necessary.
Sort	Data is entered into the database in a random fashion; however, the user can use the sort function of the DBMS program to output records in a file in several different ways—for example, alphabetically by employee last name, chronologically according to date hired, or by ZIP code. The field according to which the records are ordered is the *key field*.
Calculate	Some DBMS programs include formulas that allow the user to calculate, for example, averages or highest and lowest values.
Interact	Many DBMS programs can be integrated with other types of applications software—for example, with a spreadsheet program. In other words, the data in the DBMS program can be displayed and manipulated within the spreadsheet program.

Presentation graphics are fancier and more dramatic than analytical graphics, and so the software is more sophisticated. Presentation graphics allow the user to function as an artist and combine free-form shapes and text to produce exciting output on the screen, on paper, and on transparencies and film (for slides and photos). Of course, the user can also produce output using bar graphs, line charts, and pie charts.

Module E explores the capabilities of one microcomputer graphics program. Most analytical graphics come as part of spreadsheet programs, such as Lotus 1-2-3. Popular presentation graphics programs are Harvard Graphics, Harvard Presentation Graphics, Freelance Plus, PC Paintbrush, Microsoft Chart, Chart-Master, and Adobe Illustrator.

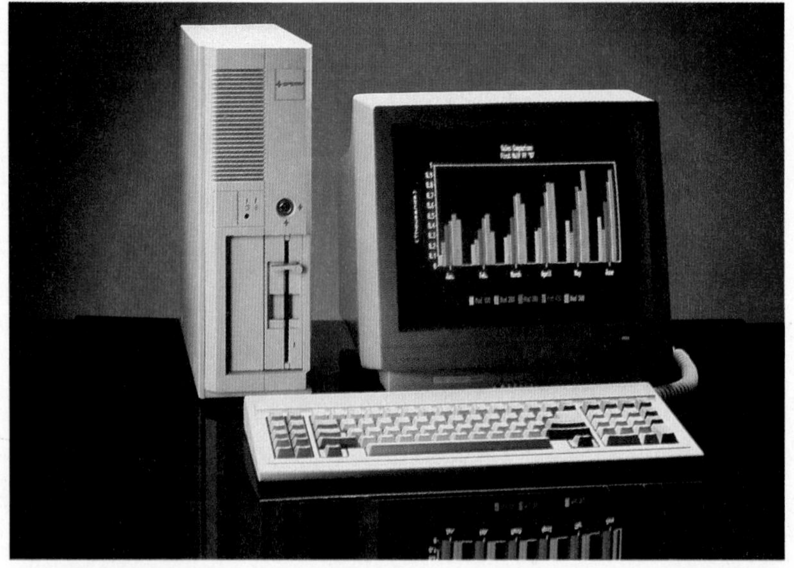

FIGURE 7.11

Graphic description. The sophistication of graphics software has increased dramatically as more and more business users have learned the value of using graphics to convey information. This illustration (top) shows several popular graphics software packages and (bottom) a common type of graphic display, the bar graph. Graphics programs can be integrated with spreadsheet software and database management software so that the data contained in those two programs can be displayed graphically.

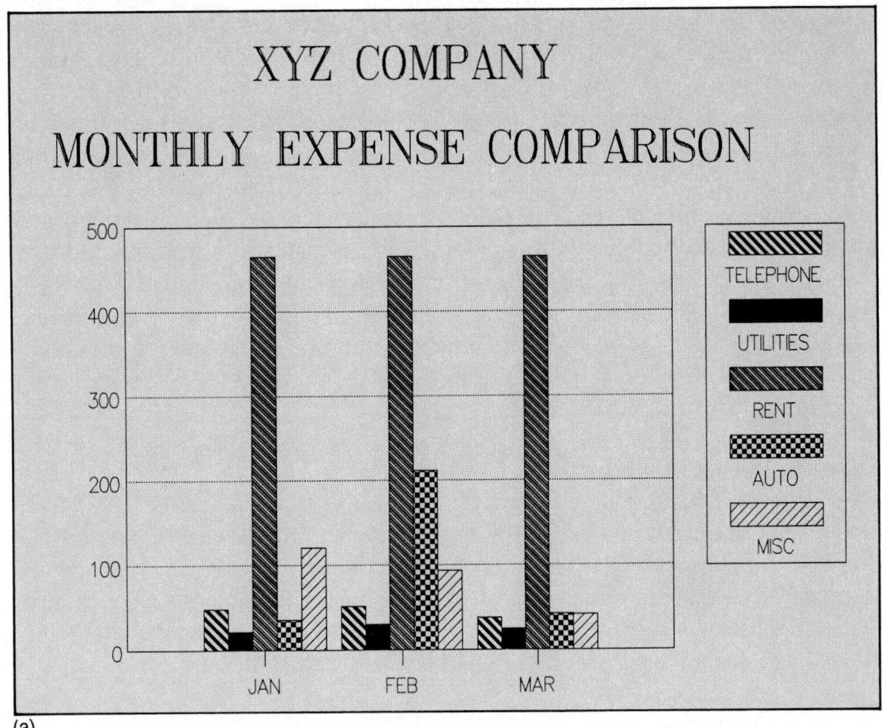

(a)

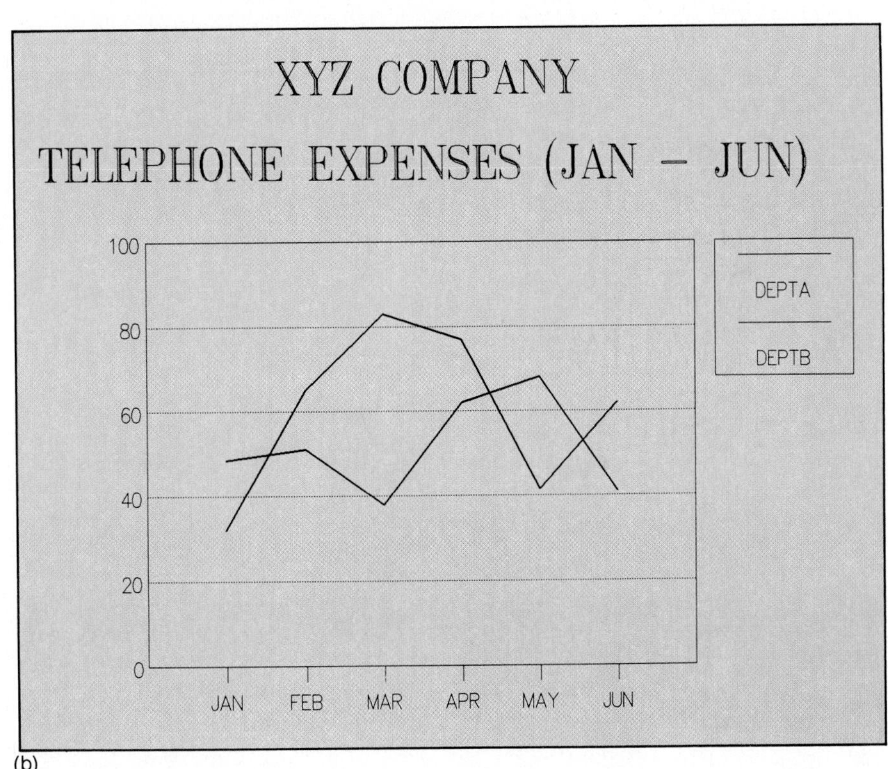

(b)

FIGURE 7.12

Bar graph (a), line chart (b), pie chart (c, next page). These three examples of hardcopy graphics output illustrate the three most common forms of analytical graphics.

INTEGRATED SOFTWARE

Integrated software represents the industry's effort to combine all the software capabilities that the typical user may need into a single package with a common set of commands and rules for its use. The objective is to allow the user to perform a variety of tasks without having to switch software programs and learn different commands and procedures to run each one. Integrated software combines the capabilities of word processing, electronic spreadsheets, database management systems, graphics, and data communications (using telephone lines, satellites, and other communications technology to transmit data and information) into one program. In Figure 7.13 the user has created a graph in one section of the screen, also called a *window*, while referring to data in another section of the screen. Symphony, by Lotus Development Corporation, is one integrated software package used in business today; others are Framework III, Microsoft Works, Enable, PFS: 1st Choice, and Smartware II.

DESKTOP PUBLISHING SOFTWARE

Desktop publishing is a combination of hardware—microcomputer, hard disk, laser printer, and scanner—and software that together provide near-typeset-quality output in a variety of sizes, styles, and type fonts (Figure 7.14). This technology can integrate, or combine, graphics and text on a professional-looking page (Figure 7.15). Well-known desktop publishing software packages are Adobe Illustrator, Aldus PageMaker, Ready-Set-Go, Quark Express, and Ventura.

FIGURE 7.12

(continued)

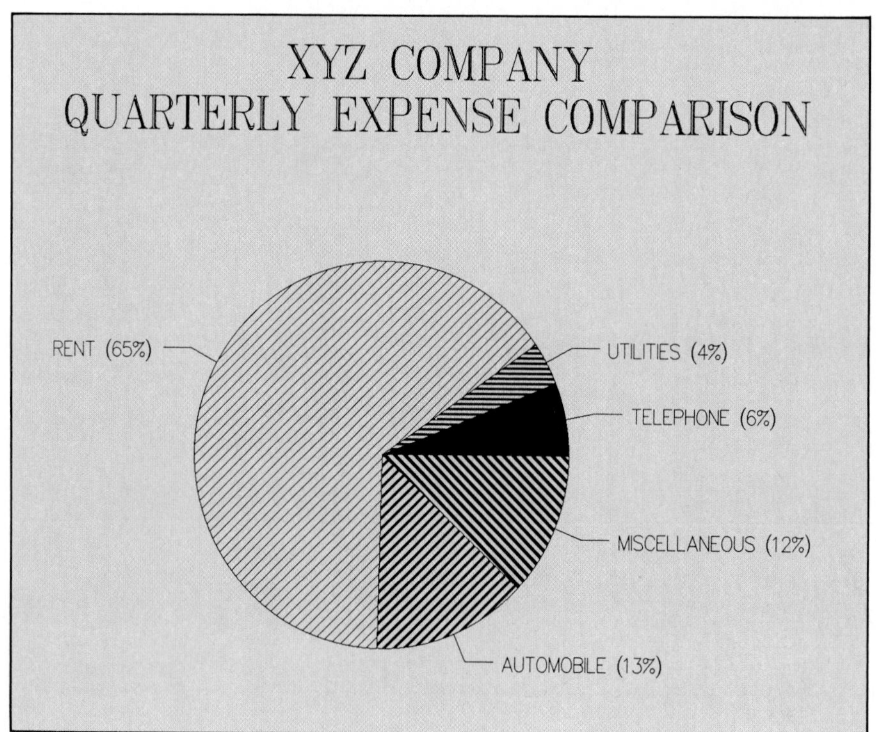

(c)

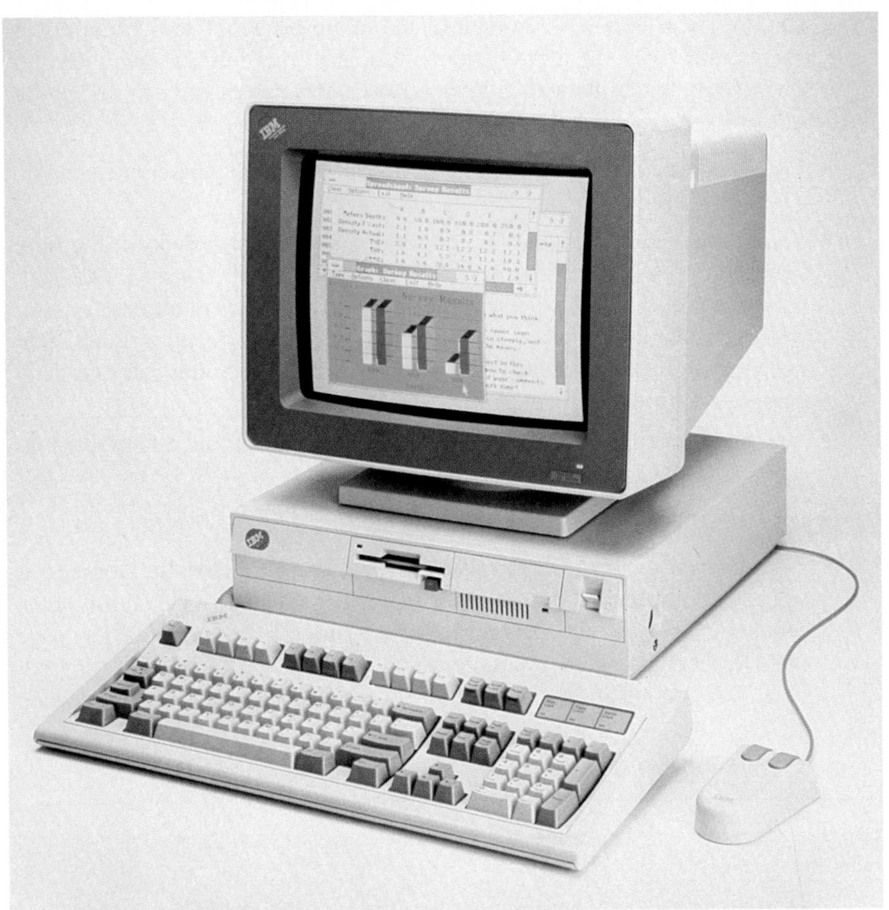

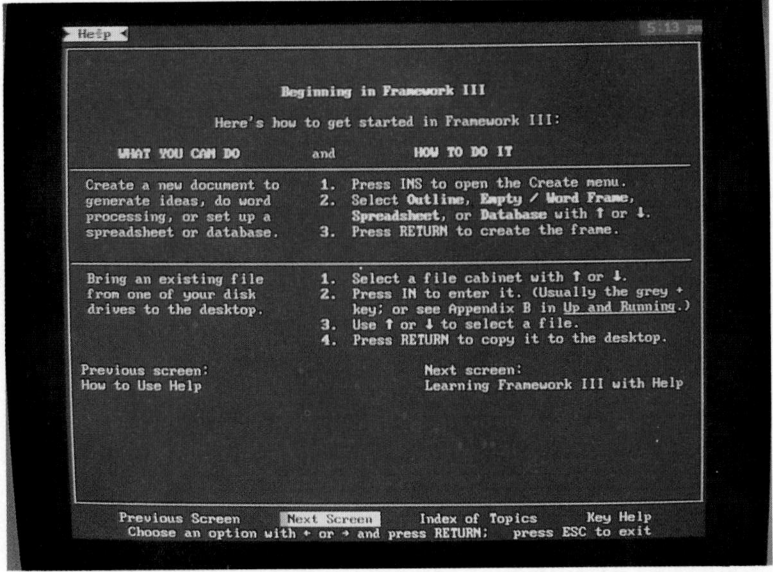

FIGURE 7.13

Using integrated software. Because integrated software combines the capabilities of several types of software programs, the user is able to create a graphic presentation in one section of the screen while referring to data in a spreadsheet—and perhaps later send the information to someone in another part of the country or the world.

Because it can lead to tremendous savings, desktop publishing can significantly affect any user who currently sends text and/or graphics out to a professional typesetter. Instead of hiring a typesetter to format documents and graphics into reports, which can be costly, with a desktop publishing system you can design the document yourself. This has the following advantages:

- *You save money*. Sending a report out to a professional typesetter can easily cost a few hundred dollars.
- *You save time*. Using a desktop publishing system can cut down the time spent on preparing documents by nearly 50 percent. Because you are preparing the report yourself electronically using a desktop publishing system, you can make any needed revisions immediately. The turnaround time necessary to make revisions when you are using a typesetter can easily add days onto a production deadline.
- *You maintain control*. You are in charge of the final output and production schedule.

The disadvantages of desktop publishing center on the following issues:

- The quality of an image that has been generated by a professional typesetter is still better. The clarity, or resolution, of an image is measured in terms of the number of dots per inch that make up the image. The resolution of an image that has been generated by a professional typesetter is around 1,200 dots per inch; in comparison, the resolution of an image generated by a desktop

FIGURE 7.14

Desktop publishing system. These newspaper layout professionals are using a desktop publishing system to make up pages. Such systems usually comprise large color monitors, a laser printer, a scanner, and several hard disks, along with a microcomputer and desktop publishing software.

publishing system is usually about 300 dots per inch. Most people, however, find it hard to tell the difference between the typeset image and the image that was desktop published (Figure 7.16). Also, the dollars saved versus lower resolution is a fair trade-off for most people.

- To produce a professional-looking report, the user needs not only the appropriate software but also some basic typesetting and design skills. You might have the best hardware and software around, but if you don't follow some specific guidelines, your output will lose its effectiveness. Desktop publishing software provides the user with hundreds of different options for formatting text and graphics. What size type should you use in the headings? How many columns of text should you have on this page? Where should the bar chart be

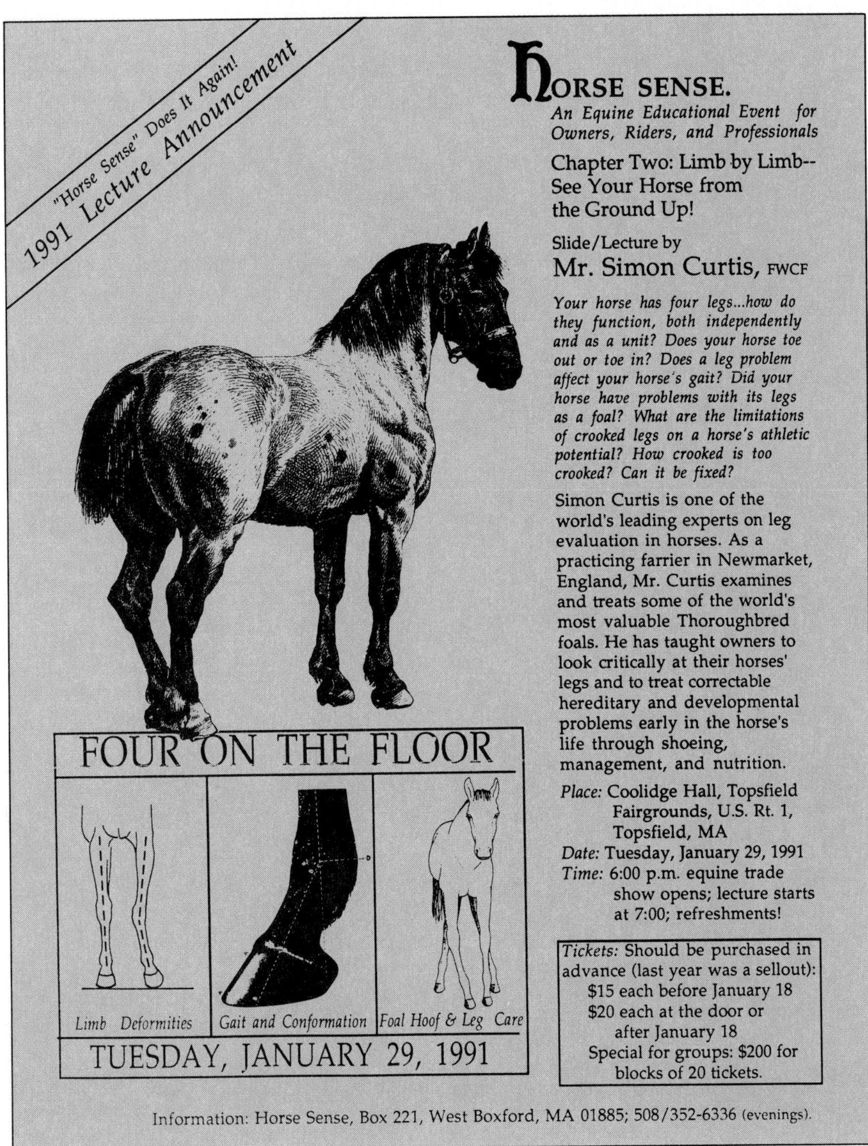

FIGURE 7.15

Do it yourself! This ad was done in a short time using a microcomputer-based desktop publishing system.

positioned on the page? How big should it be? Many people spend so much time dealing with questions such as these that time is wasted. Before attempting to generate a report using a desktop publishing system, the user should read at least one of the many articles available in computer magazines or a book on desktop publishing that provides simple guidelines for generating effective reports. Courses and seminars on the use of popular desktop publishing software are also useful.

Desktop publishing is the result of technological advances in three areas: microprocessors, laser printers with memory, and sophisticated publishing software. First, because of improvements in the processing power of microcomputers, they are now capable of satisfying the processing requirements necessary to calculate character widths and to draw special fonts and images. Also, with the current high-capacity storage devices available for use with microcomputers, such as hard disks, microcomputers can satisfy the tremendous storage requirements imposed by desktop publishing. The storage requirements for one page that combines text and graphics can be as much as 1 megabyte. Included in many desktop publishing systems is an external hard disk that is dedicated to storing the text and graphics outputs resulting from processing.

Second, desktop publishing requires that a laser printer be specially configured with a large amount of memory. For a laser printer to effectively combine text and graphics on a single page, a ***page description language (PDL)***, such as Adobe's PostScript, must be stored in the printer's memory. This special language can take up to half a megabyte of memory. Often this language is stored in a read-only

FIGURE 7.16 Typeset versus desktop-generated copy. As you can see, the typeset copy on the left does not look much different from the copy on the right, which was produced by a desktop laser printer. (T. Bove, C. Rhodes, and W. Thomas, *The Art of Desktop Publishing* [New York: Bantam Books, 1987].)

Remember the last time you prepared some text to be typeset? Did you spend a lot of time on the preparation and proofreading, and also a lot of money on a vendor's service, without much control over the schedule? Would you prefer to do the typesetting in your office, see the results immediately, and make corrections at no extra charge? Wouldn't you rather use an inexpensive personal computer so that you only have to type the text once, and have the computer do all the proofreading?

Remember the last time you prepared some text to be typeset? Did you spend a lot of time on the preparation and proofreading, and also a lot of money on a vendor's service, without much control over the schedule? Would you prefer to do the typesetting in your office, see the results immediately, and make corrections at no extra charge? Wouldn't you rather use an inexpensive personal computer so that you only have to type the text once, and have the computer do all the proofreading?

memory (ROM) chip in the printer. Fortunately, laser printer technology has kept up with desktop publishing demands and can satisfy the memory requirements imposed by desktop publishing.

Third, sophisticated software allows the user to combine text and graphics in an organized format on a single page. This software, referred to as **page description software** (such as Aldus PageMaker), takes advantage of both the increased processing power and storage capacities of a microcomputer and the flexibility in terms of output that a laser printer provides. When a business user prepares a report, the text and graphics typically included in the report have been generated using a number of different software programs. Perhaps a word processing program was used to generate the text, an electronic spreadsheet program was used to generate the tables, and business graphics were used for the illustrations. Page description software allows the user to combine the elements from different files that have been generated using different software programs into one file, or output report. Page description software falls into two categories—code-oriented and "what-you-see-is-what-you-get" (WYSIWYG).

With **code-oriented** page description software (Figure 7.17), formatting instructions are embedded (keyed) into a document in the form of codes. Code-oriented packages provide the user with more sophisticated desktop publishing options, compared to the WYSIWYG packages, and are based on traditional typesetting techniques, which also use formatting codes. There are two disadvantages to using this type of package. First, because of its high degree of sophistication, the user should have some typesetting experience before attempting to use the package. Second, the user can't see the final output until it's printed out. A user unfamiliar with how certain codes will affect the report may have to perform countless revisions. However, these programs usually require less RAM, processing power, and storage requirements than the WYSIWYG programs. Among the code-oriented packages being used today are SC Laserplus from Graham Software Corporation and Deskset from G. O. Graphics.

WYSIWYG programs (for example, PageMaker from Aldus Corporation and Ventura Publisher Edition from Xerox Corporation) allow the user to see the report on the screen as it will appear when it is printed out (Figure 7.18). Many people prefer the WYSIWYG programs over the code-oriented programs for this very reason, because they don't have to wait until they print to see what a report or a brochure will look like. With this type of program, the user chooses from menu options to format the text. This type of software is more power-, memory-, and storage-hungry than code-oriented software.

A typical desktop publishing system, including a microcomputer, laser printer, and page description software, costs around $10,000. This may sound like a lot of money, but when you consider that you might easily spend that much having just a few reports or projects professionally designed and typeset, the cost doesn't look so bad. For businesses that might easily spend over $100,000 per year for publishable items, the $10,000 figure is something to celebrate. The cost of a desktop publishing system increases when certain other peripherals are included in the overall system; for example, an optical scanner for inserting drawings and photos into a report and a mouse and graphics tablet for drawing specialized images. Just remember—if you have the opportunity to choose a desktop publishing system, examine the features of the software programs you are most interested in *first* and then determine what microcomputers and peripheral devices the software is compatible with.

FIGURE 7.17 Code-oriented page description software. The top two lines (a bumpersticker) were printed according to the codes shown below, which is what the user would have seen on the screen. The actual output was not displayed before it was printed.

DR. SCIENCE

He's not a real comedian

```
%!
/paperheight 11 72 mul def
/paperwidth 8.5 72 mul def
/width paperheight def
/height paperwidth 2 div def
/margin .375 72 mul def
/xcenter paperwidth 2 div def
/ycenter paperheight 2 div def

%xcenter ycenter translate
%.25 .25 scale
%xcenter neg ycenter neg translate

90 rotate
0 0 moveto paperheight 0 rlineto 0 paperwidth neg rlineto
paperheight neg 0 rlineto closepath 0 setlinewidth stroke

/bumpersticker
{
   /AvantGarde-Demi findfont setfont
   (ASS, DR. SCIENCE) dup stringwidth pop
   width margin sub margin sub exch div /points exch def
   /AvantGarde-Demi findfont
   [points 0 0 points 1.5 mul 0 0 ] makefont setfont
   margin margin 135 add moveto show

   /AvantGarde-DemiOblique findfont setfont
   (He's not a real comedian) dup stringwidth pop
   width margin sub margin sub exch div /points exch def
   /AvantGarde-DemiOblique findfont
   [points 0 0 points 1.5 mul 0 0 ] makefont setfont
   margin margin 20 add moveto show
} def

0 height neg translate
0 0 moveto width 0 rlineto stroke
bumpersticker
0 height neg translate
bumpersticker

showpage
```

Computer-Aided Design, Engineering, and Manufacturing

Industry, especially manufacturing, has probably experienced the greatest economic impact of computer graphics. Mechanical drawings that used to take days or weeks to complete can now be done in less than a day. Among other things, the drawings can be three-dimensional, rotated, shown in detailed sections or as a whole, automatically rendered on a different scale, and easily corrected and revised. But the use of computer graphics has evolved beyond the simple rendering of drawings; it is now used to help design, engineer, and manufacture products of all kinds, from nuts and bolts to computer chips to boats and airplanes.

Computer-aided design (CAD) shortens the design cycle by allowing manufacturers to shape new products on the screen without having to first build expensive models (Figure 7.19). The final design data and images can be sent to a **computer-aided engineering (CAE)** system, which subjects the design to extensive analysis and testing that might be too expensive to do in the real world (Figure 7.20). From there, the data may be sent to a **computer-aided manufacturing**

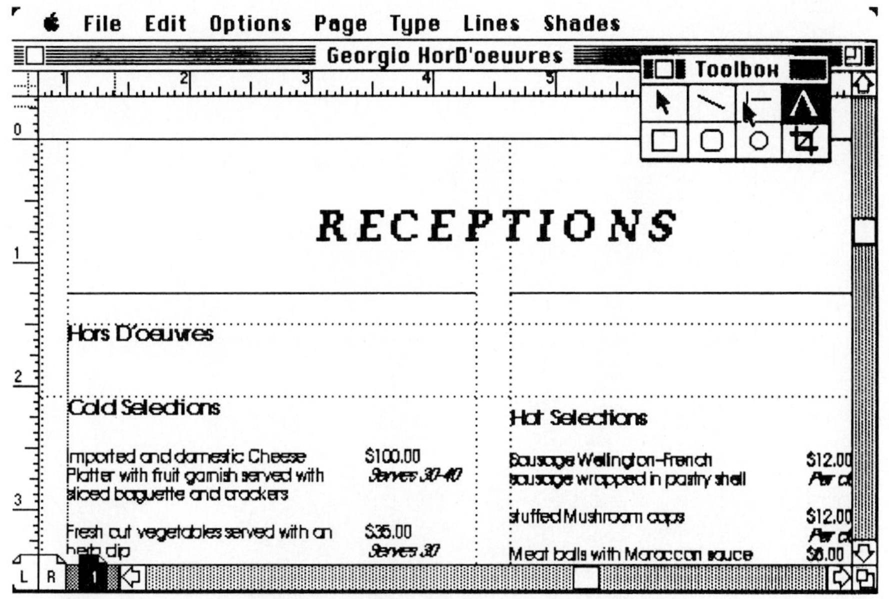

RECEPTIONS

Hors D'oeuvres

Cold Selections

Imported and domestic Cheese Platter with fruit garnish served with sliced baguette and crackers	$100.00 *Serves 30-40*
Fresh cut vegetables served with an herb dip	$35.00 *Serves 30*
Selection of duck, pork and chicken truffles pate	$40.00 *Serves 20*

Hot Selections

Sausage Wellington–French sausage wrapped in pastry shell	$12.00 *Per dozen*
stuffed Mushroom caps	$12.00 *Per dozen*
Meat balls with Moroccan sauce	$8.00 *Per dozen*
Onion Quiche	$12.00 *Serves 15*

FIGURE 7.18

WYSIWYG document. The printed restaurant menu shown at the bottom was displayed on the computer screen (top) before it was printed out. The screen illustration here is typical of an Apple Macintosh screen, with a pull-down option menu (Toolbox). The software documentation explains what the option symbols mean; the user points the cursor to the desired option and clicks the mouse button. For example, the highlighted letter A in the toolbox means the user has just chosen the option to type text into the document.

(CAM) system, which makes use of the stored computer images in automating the machines (unintelligent robots) that manufacture the finished products (Figure 7.21). Computer simulation in industry has increased productivity enormously and made previously expensive procedures affordable.

Until recently CAD/CAM systems cost about $100,000; however, microcomputer CAD systems—using CAD software such as VersaCAD and AutoCAD—are now available for about $6,000. CAM software was once used only with mainframes; now, however, CAM microcomputer workstations are showing up on factory floors in many types of manufacturing businesses.

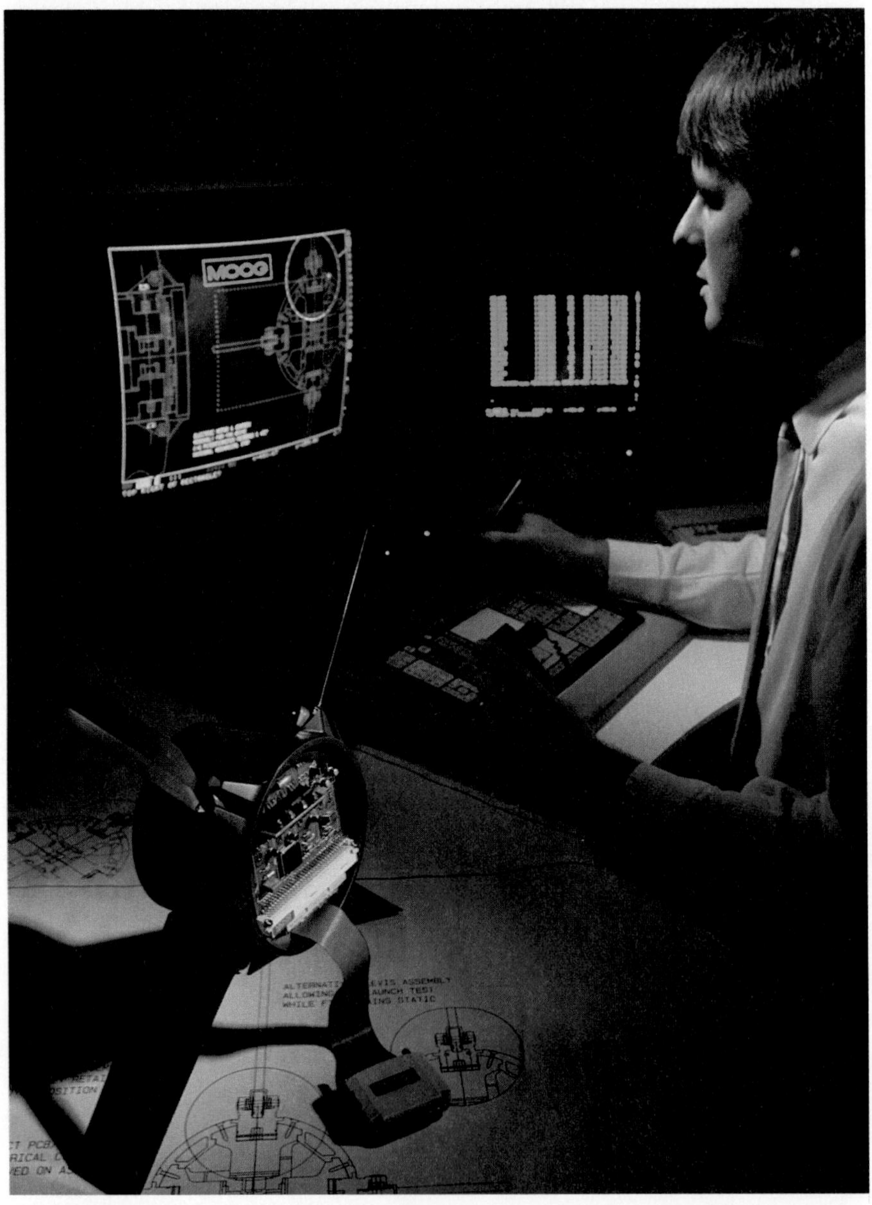

FIGURE 7.19

CAD. This designer is using CAD software to design a valve to control missiles.

Communications Software

Communications software allows users to access software and data from a computer in a remote location and to transmit data to a computer in a remote location —in other words, to establish *connectivity*. For example, the traveling business professional in Seattle, Washington, who needs to access client information daily from the company's main computer in San Diego, California, needs some communications software and a certain unit of hardware (a modem, covered in Chapter 9) to enable his or her laptop computer to communicate long-distance. Popular microcomputer communications programs are ProComm, Smartcom II, Smartcom III, and Crosstalk XVI.

Because communications software and hardware have become so important to the computer user—through systems connectivity the microcomputer is now able to share resources and services previously available only to users of large computer systems—we devote Chapter 9 to this topic.

FIGURE 7.20

CAE. This national test facility is using a computer system to simulate and test space technology.

APPLICATIONS SOFTWARE UTILITIES

Many types of **applications software utilities**—inexpensive programs that perform some basic "office management" functions for microcomputer users—are available for purchase. These programs range in price from $20 to $120 and can be categorized as follows:

- Desktop management utilities.
- Add-on utilities.
- Disk utilities.
- Keyboard and screen utilities.

Depending on their function, the instructions in utility programs reside in RAM or on disk. A **RAM-resident utility** is designed to be available at any time to the user because it resides in RAM at all times while the computer is on, even when not in use. In other words, once such a program is loaded into your computer (for example,

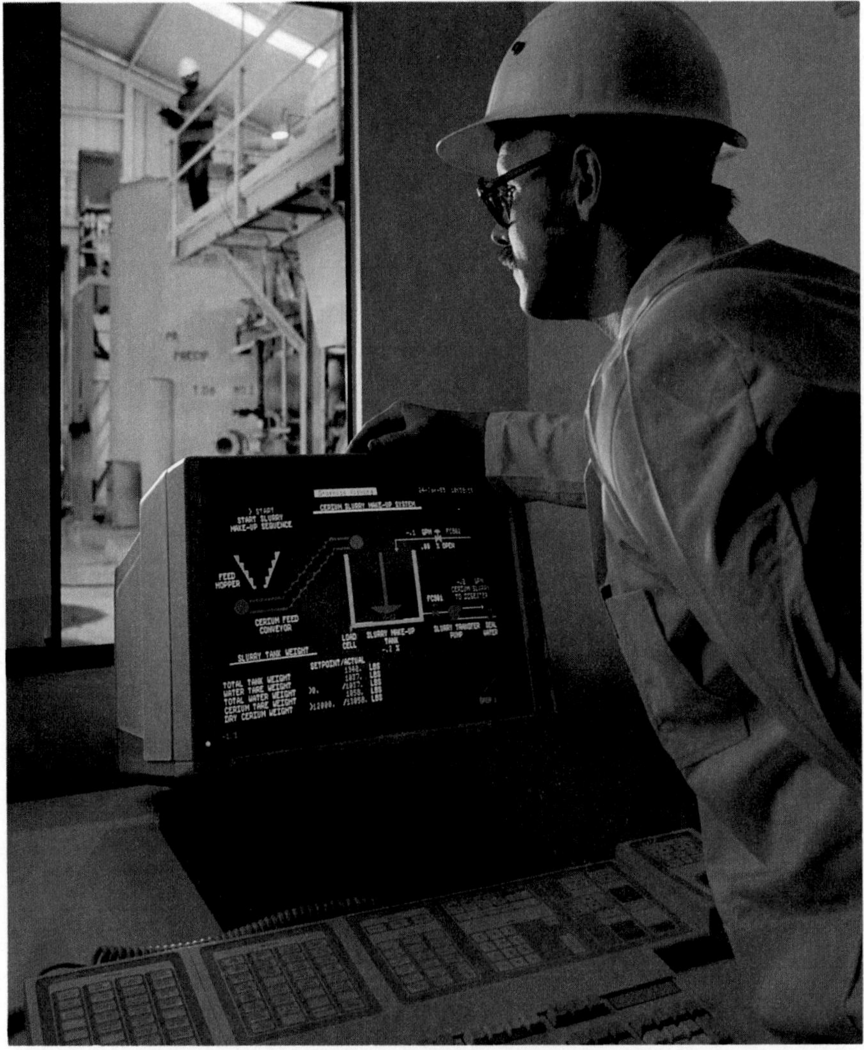

FIGURE 7.21

CAM. This computerized manufacturing plant produces high-quality cerium used in auto-exhaust catalysts, to help keep the air clean.

from a diskette), a copy stays in RAM, "underneath" any applications software programs you may be using, until you turn the power off. As long as the power is on, you do not have to put the software diskette back in the drive to use the utility program—you simply access it from RAM using certain keystrokes described in the utility software's documentation.

A **desktop management utility,** which is usually RAM-resident, allows the user to computerize many routine activities, including using a calculator, organizing an appointment calendar, taking notes, looking up words in a dictionary to make sure they are spelled correctly, and many more. The bottom line is that desktop management software can save the user time. Sidekick (Figure 7.22) and Pop-Up Windows are two popular desktop management applications utilities.

Add-on utilities are usually RAM-resident and are used in conjunction with popular microcomputer applications software packages. For example, to print wide electronic spreadsheets lengthwise on continuous-form paper (instead of across the width of the paper), many users use a program called Sideways. Allways, from Funk Software, is an add-on utility that is now sold with versions 2.2 and 3.0 of Lotus 1-2-3. This utility greatly enhances the appearance of printed spreadsheets through the use of stylized fonts in different sizes. (If you are using an earlier version of Lotus 1-2-3, you must purchase the Allways program separately.)

Disk utilities are usually stored on disk and provide users with a number of special capabilities, including: (1) recovering files that have been accidentally erased, (2) making backup copies of a hard disk, and (3) organizing a hard disk by means of a menu system—that is, by menu choices instead of by keystrokes.

Keyboard utilities are usually RAM-resident and enable you to change the way the cursor appears on the screen—usually by making it larger—so it is easier to see. **Screen utilities** are used to increase the life of your screen. If your microcomputer is turned on and you don't use it for a few minutes or more, a screen utility will automatically make the screen go blank. This saves your screen from having an

Sidekick. This desktop management applications utility software allows the user to computerize many routine activities, such as keeping track of appointments. **FIGURE 7.22**

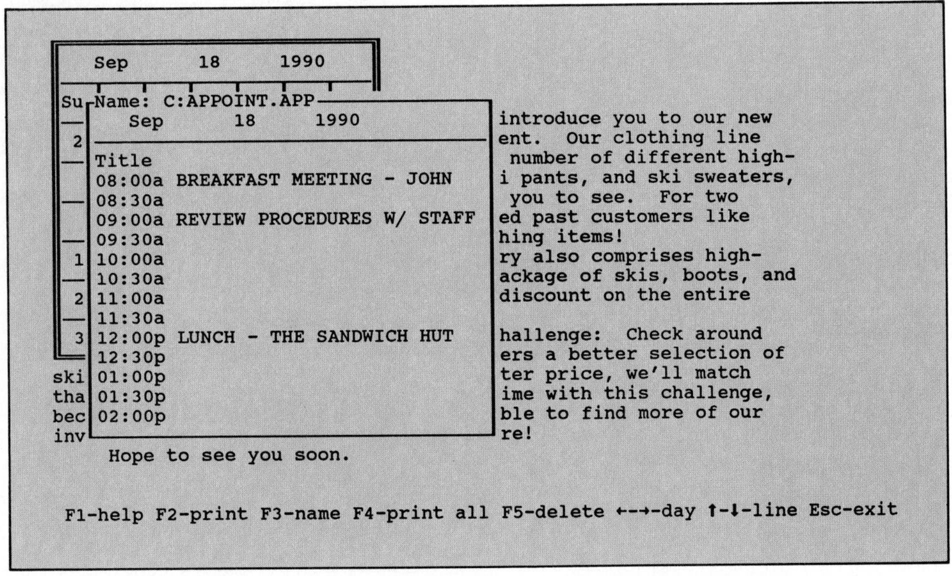

image permanently burned onto the screen. When you press a key, the screen will again display the image that was showing previously. (Many newer microcomputers have this screen-saving feature built in; check your documentation.)

We have mentioned only a few of the many utilities that can be purchased for a microcomputer. If your applications software package can't do something that you want it to, a utility program probably exists that will. You can find out by phoning a computer store that specializes in selling software.

HYPERTEXT AND MULTIMEDIA

Two new kinds of sophisticated applications software that do not easily fit into any of the preceding categories are hypertext and multimedia. **Hypertext** software — such as HyperCard, used on the Macintosh microcomputer — links basic file units comprising text and/or graphics with one another in creative ways. In HyperCard (Figure 7.23), a screen of information forms a record called a *card*; related groups of cards are organized into files called *stacks*. The user can work with the cards and stacks provided by the software program (for example, all the information in an encyclopedia) or create cards and stacks of text and graphics at will and combine them in all sorts of ways by using a mouse to click on "buttons" on the screen that move the user from card to card and stack to stack. The user can program the sequences used to connect and combine cards and stacks, thereby discovering, sorting through, using, and presenting information in convenient or unusual ways. Stackware, software packages that are collections of information created and used

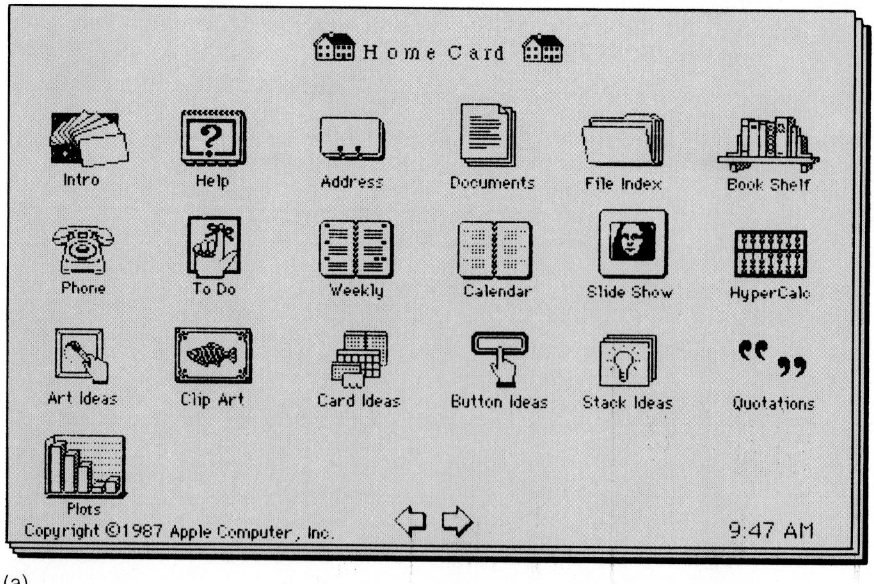

(a)

FIGURE 7.23

HyperCard software provides a new kind of "information environment" for the Apple Macintosh microcomputer. It stores information in the form of words, charts, sounds, pictures, and digitized photography — about any subject. Any "card" (piece of information) in any "stack" (related cards) can connect to any other piece of information. (a) The Home Card is the starting place for moving around in HyperCard. The various icons represent stacks for the user to click on with a mouse button. (b) An example of how HyperCard works. (Adapted from T. J. O'Leary, B. K. Williams, and L. I. O'Leary, *McGraw-Hill Microcomputing, Annual Edition 1990/1991* [Watsonville, Calif.: Mitchell Publishing, Inc., 1990], p. 194.)

with HyperCard, is available at computer stores. For example, users can purchase "Research Stacks" consisting of five 800 K disks on selected subject areas—such as "scientific Stacks," which include card stacks on amino acids, chemical elements, periodic table, vitamin structures, galaxies, the ear, laws of physics, DNA structures, and the moons of Jupiter.

Multimedia is even more sophisticated than hypertext because it combines not only text and graphics but animation, video, music, and voice as well. In creating and presenting a multimedia product, one might, for example, use a Macintosh and HyperCard to create software programs that could integrate input data. The data could be input in the form of text and graphics through a scanner, animation through a special video camera, and sound through the use of a sound digitizer. The integrated data could be stored on CD-ROM disk and then presented later on a television monitor and speaker that can run an optical disk or stored on tape and then run on a VCR. Text could also be printed out or stored on diskette or tape.

Multimedia sounds are already available on disk for users with a Macintosh microcomputer, 2 MB of RAM, HyperCard, and applications software for sound management (such as HyperComposer). For example, Desktop Sounds v.1 include the following sound effects: aircraft, animals, automotive, combat, comedy, crowds, household—and more.

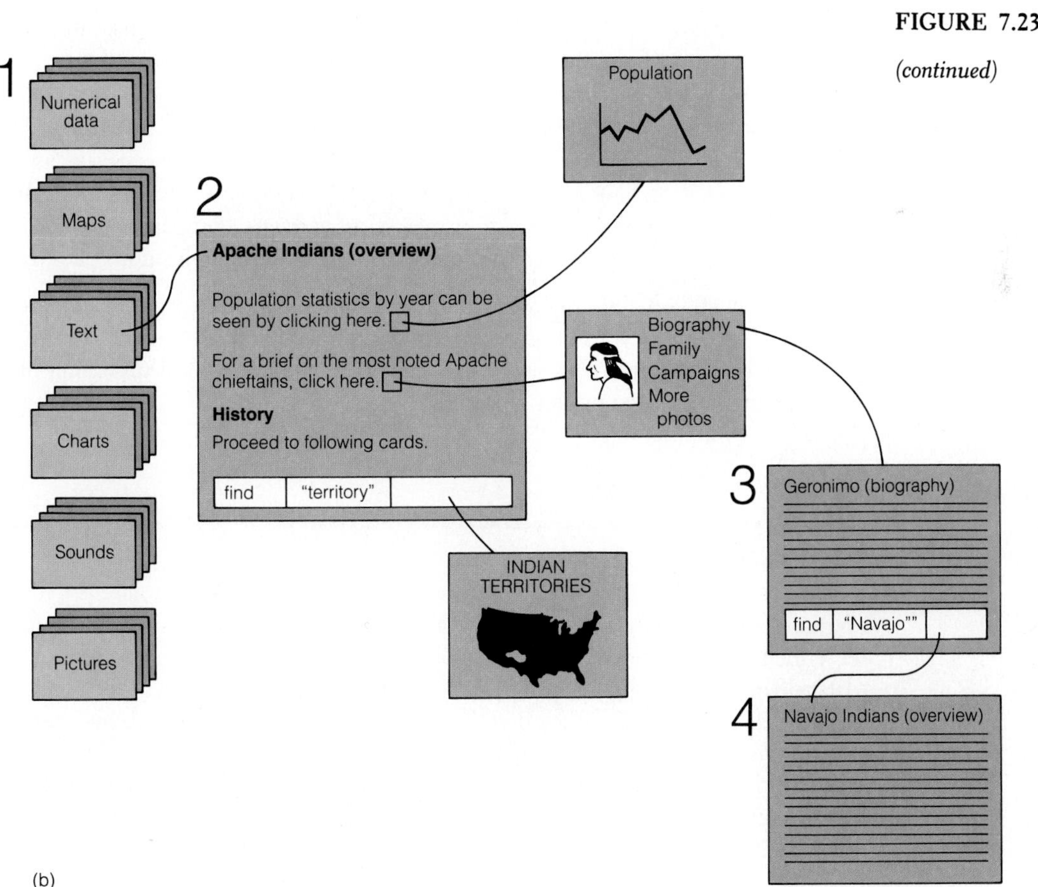

FIGURE 7.23

(continued)

USER GUIDELINES FOR PURCHASING MICROCOMPUTER APPLICATIONS SOFTWARE

Because there is so much to choose from, deciding what applications package — and then what version — to use requires careful analysis. You should evaluate applications software by focusing on the following:

- *Quality of the documentation* — Using documentation that isn't written clearly and thoroughly can be extremely frustrating. Before purchasing an applications package, leaf through the documentation material that comes with the package to see if the instructions and the reference information are clearly written and presented.
- *Ease of learning* — Even if the documentation for a particular program is good, the program still may not be easy to learn. Because training can cost thousands of dollars, companies should evaluate how easy an application is to learn before purchasing it. A good way for the user to determine how easy a program is to learn is to ask friends and colleagues who are currently using it.
- *Ease of use* — Some programs aren't easy to use on an ongoing basis. Before purchasing a package, ask people who are using the program if they enjoy using it frequently. Are some procedures difficult to perform using this application?
- *Error handling* — It's human nature to make mistakes, and we don't want to go through tortuous procedures to correct them. When we make mistakes using applications software, we want the software to provide some helpful information on the screen that tells us what we did wrong and how to fix it. The package's documentation should tell you what "help" procedures are available.
- *Support* — Is there a phone number you can call if you have questions that relate to the software you are using? Most software companies provide an 800 number that you can use to get help using their applications packages.

Note: when you buy a microcomputer applications software package, you must *install* it to work with your microcomputer system. This procedure is usually quite simple; for your convenience, we describe it in Appendix A: Purchasing and Maintaining a Microcomputer System.

SYSTEMS SOFTWARE

Without systems software you won't be able to use any of the sophisticated software described in the last section. Systems software tells the computer how to interpret data and instructions, how to run peripheral equipment like printers, keyboards, and disk drives, and how to use the hardware in general; and it allows you, the user, to interact with the computer (Figure 7.24). Systems software comprises (1) internal command instructions, (2) external command instructions, and (3) language processors. Internal and external command instructions are often referred to collectively as the **operating system,** or operating systems software.

Internal Command Instructions

Internal command instructions, often called *resident commands*, can be thought of as the innermost layer of software. These instructions direct and coordinate other types of software and the computer hardware. They are loaded into main memory (RAM) from disk as part of turning on the microcomputer — called **booting** — and they reside in main memory until the computer is turned off. (In the case of mainframes, starting the system is not called booting, but **IPL,** for **initial program load.** Booting can be done in one step; IPL may take several steps.) Without these instructions in main memory, a computer can be likened to a race car without fuel for the engine and without a driver to decide where to go and how fast. That is why the primary purpose of the procedures followed in starting up a computer is to load a copy of these special operating system instructions into main memory. These instructions are referred to as *internal command instructions* because in order to be usable, they are stored on an internal storage device (namely, main memory, or RAM). Operating instructions stored on an external storage device (such as a diskette or hard disk) are referred to as *external command instructions*. Internal command instructions are so important to the functioning of your computer that they must be directly accessible to the CPU in main memory at all times.

The "captain" of the portion of the operating system that is stored in main memory is often referred to as the **supervisor,** or the **control program.** The supervisor calls in other parts of the operating system (external command instruc-

Systems software. This type of software coordinates hardware and applications software functions. **FIGURE 7.24**

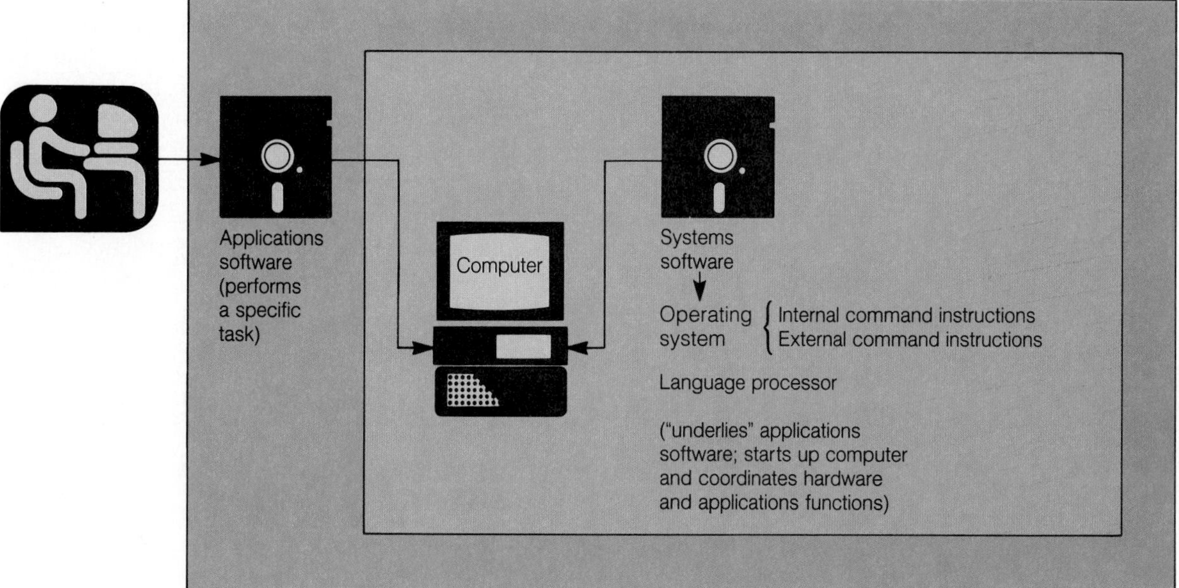

tions) and language processors as needed from secondary storage. The supervisor controls all other programs in the computer. For example, it:

- Coordinates processing.
- Manages the use of RAM.
- Allocates use of peripheral devices.
- Does parity checking for data errors.
- Checks equipment malfunction and displays error messages.
- Manages file storage.

The operating systems used on minicomputers and mainframes are more sophisticated and much larger in terms of the number of programs and routines they comprise and the amount of main memory space taken up by the supervisor. Microcomputer operating systems can sometimes allow the execution of more than one program at a time. Minicomputers can execute dozens of programs at a time, and mainframes can execute hundreds of programs at a time.

Fortunately, you probably will not have to become familiar with the technical intricacies of communicating with the operating systems of larger computer systems. Many of these systems are **proprietary operating systems,** developed for only one brand of computer. As we mentioned earlier, microcomputer operating systems usually come with the microcomputer (usually on diskettes, although sometimes the operating system is wired into the computer's ROM chips). If you have decided to use certain applications software packages, you must make sure to choose a computer whose systems software is compatible with those software packages—or be prepared to buy special hardware and software to make them compatible. We'll give you some more information about microcomputer systems software at the end of the chapter.

EXTERNAL COMMAND INSTRUCTIONS

External command instructions are general-purpose operating systems instructions that take care of what many people call "housekeeping tasks." External command instructions are not needed to run applications software; for this reason, they reside in secondary storage, instead of main memory, until needed. These instructions are generally provided by the computer manufacturer when you purchase a microcomputer. However, some software firms specialize in developing high-performance systems software utilities that can be acquired when needed. Systems software utility programs are available to assist in a wide variety of areas, including:

- Sorting and merging large files with great speed and flexibility.
- Keeping track of computer system activity—identifying who is using the computer system, what the computer is being used for, and what users should be charged.
- Monitoring the operating characteristics of computer hardware and software to ensure they are being used effectively and efficiently.
- Backing up and restoring data from disk storage devices.
- Encrypting (or coding) and decrypting (or decoding) files to prevent unauthorized disclosure of sensitive data.

- Formatting, or initializing, new disks.
- Converting data from a microcomputer-based ASCII coding scheme to a mainframe-based EBCDIC scheme.
- Converting files from one storage medium to another (for example, from tape to disk).

LANGUAGE PROCESSORS

You will recall that computers understand only one language — machine language, "written" using the digits 1 and 0. Because it is too time consuming to write programs in machine language, **high-level programming languages** were developed that are easier to learn and use. With high-level languages, programmers — the people who create software programs — don't have to use 1s and 0s to represent computer instructions. Instead they use everyday text and mathematical formulas in sentence-like *program statements*.

But how, then, does the computer "understand" the instructions written in a high-level language? Programmers use a type of systems software called a **language processor,** or **translator,** to convert high-level instructions into a specific machine language that the CPU can understand — for example, the one used by an IBM microcomputer. You will need to use a language processor only if you create a program using a high-level language, such as BASIC (*B*eginner's *A*ll-purpose *S*ymbolic *I*nstruction *C*ode), which is commonly taught in university-level courses. When you purchase an applications software package, the software instructions have already been converted by a language processor into machine language.

The first step in the development of language processors was the creation of programming languages that used symbolic abbreviations to represent machine-language instructions. These languages, which somewhat simplified the programmer's job, are called **assembly languages,** and they are machine-specific, or machine-dependent, meaning they are written to be understood only by specific makes and models of computers. This, of course, means that an assembly language is compatible only with one brand of machine. Because of this problem, applications software programs are not normally written in assembly language.

To overcome the problem of incompatibility of programs written in assembly language, high-level programming languages were developed whose structure was less machine-dependent. These languages are easier to learn and use than assembly language, are less time consuming, and can be used on more than one type of machine. However, like assembly language, high-level language programs must still be converted into machine-language instructions before they can be carried out by the computer. Today two types of language processors are used to carry out the conversion process: *compilers* and *interpreters*.

The **compiler** (Figure 7.25) is a language processor that translates an *entire* high-level language program, referred to as the **source code,** into a machine-language version of the program, called the **object code,** in a single process. If no programming errors exist in the source code, the program becomes operative. The **interpreter** (Figure 7.26) is a language processor that converts and executes high-level language instructions one instruction statement at a time. If an error is detected in the source code, the interpreter displays immediate feedback on the screen. For this reason, interpreters are commonly used with small and simple programs and in educational settings.

The most important difference between using a compiler and an interpreter is speed. Programs that are compiled tend to execute up to five times faster than interpreted programs (such as programs written in BASIC). Also, when a program is interpreted, no object code version of the program is created that can be saved. For this reason, almost all commercially available software has been compiled. Because different computers use different versions of machine language, different compilers must be used for different brands of microcomputers and for different types of computers (micros, minis, mainframes).

If you are working with microcomputers at home or in the office, you won't have to worry about compiling or interpreting — the software packages have already been compiled, and you will not even be able to look at the machine-level language the computer uses. The same situation is true for users who access mainframe data and programs in general business applications.

OTHER SYSTEMS SOFTWARE CAPABILITIES

Since the appearance of the first business computer, advances in hardware technology have increased the power of computers 100,000-fold or more. These hardware advances have made even more powerful systems software capabilities available to

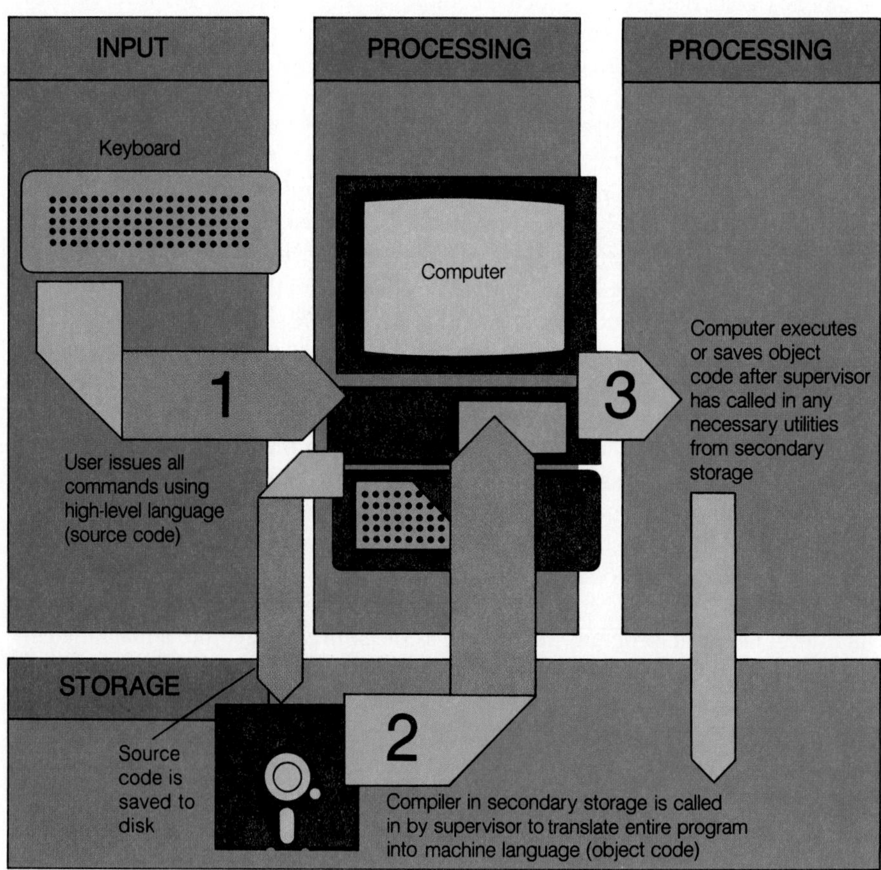

FIGURE 7.25

The compiler. This type of language processor translates an entire high-level language program into a machine-language version of the program before the program is executed.

users. In the business environment, you are likely to be using systems software that supports one or more of these capabilities.

MULTITASKING

As we have mentioned, the first operating systems were designed for computers with limited processing speed and limited main memory (RAM) and storage capacity. These early operating systems were referred to as *single-user operating systems* because they could accept commands from only a single terminal or other input source and could manage only a single program in RAM at one time. Modern large computer systems are designed to be shared by many users, so very few, if any, have single-user operating systems. In other words, they can support **multitasking,** also known as **multiprogramming.** Although most operating systems for microcomputers are considered single-user/single-program operating systems, some microcomputer operating systems are single-user but can also do multitasking—that is, they can execute more than one task or program at a time.

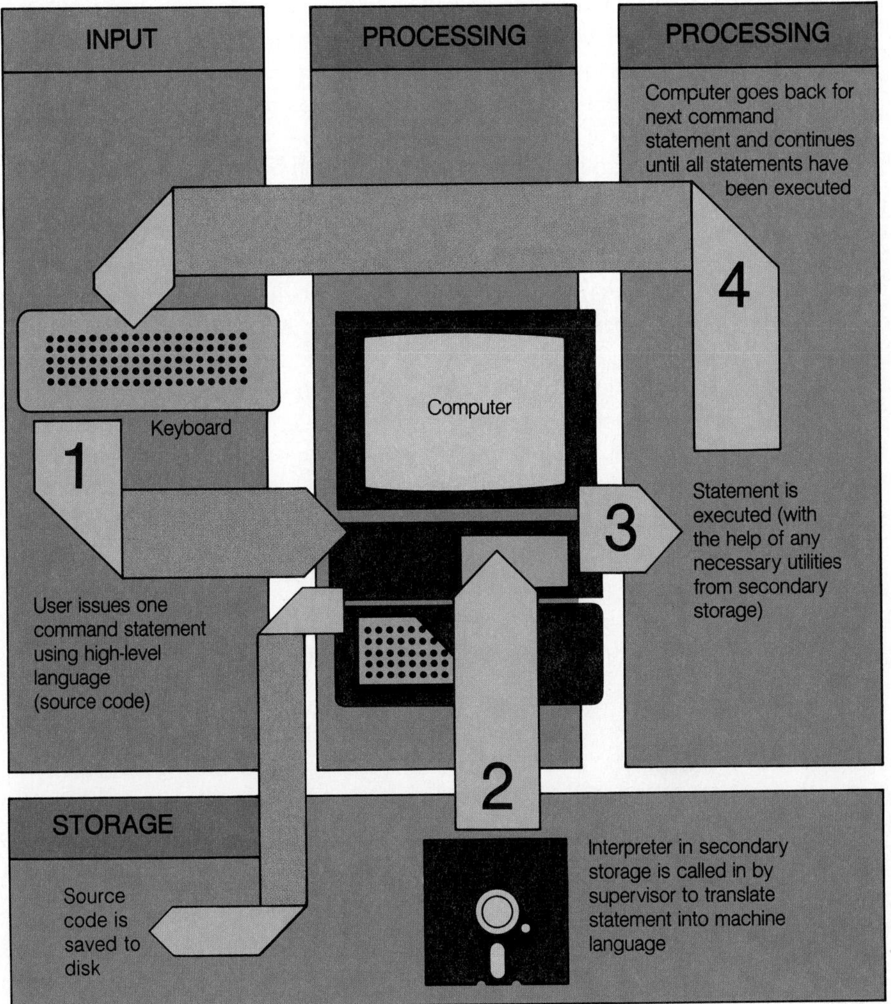
INPUT
PROCESSING
PROCESSING
Computer goes back for next command statement and continues until all statements have been executed
4
Keyboard
Computer
1
3
Statement is executed (with the help of any necessary utilities from secondary storage)
User issues one command statement using high-level language (source code)
2
STORAGE
Source code is saved to disk
Interpreter in secondary storage is called in by supervisor to translate statement into machine language

FIGURE 7.26

The interpreter. This type of language processor converts and executes high-level language instructions one statement at a time.

Computers and Careers

Politics and Government

Using 70 Macintosh SE terminals located at nine campus polling places, Stanford University's student government in April 1989 held the first totally computerized election in California history. Some 6,500 students cast ballots for the next year's Council of Presidents. Ironically, when none of the three slates won the top office, students returned to the polls a few weeks later and made their final choice using old-fashioned paper ballots.

Nevertheless, the first election was so revolutionary that it drew observers from local county registrars of voters and from the state capital. County election officials were concerned about possible fraud in electronic voting systems, but Stanford's terminals were not linked into a network, and buzzer alarms were written into the software to deter prospective hackers. To tally the results, election officials transferred the data voters recorded on the Macintosh hard disks onto floppy disks; the data was then tabulated at a single location. The biggest advantages of computerized balloting were the reduced costs of printing paper ballots (only a few were on hand for computerphobes) and the increased speed in tabulating returns.

Electronic voting may be the wave of the future, but computers are already being used extensively in politics and government. Political parties have long used computers for campaign purposes, primarily for fund-raising. Anyone who has ever contributed to a candidate or political party is sure to be in some database. Computers are also used to aim direct mail pieces at selective audiences with very specific messages. Another use is to identify certain voter groups, such as those who tend to vote in Presidential elections but not in off-year congressional elections, in order to urge them to the polls.

Computers also came in for heavy use following the 1990 census, when state legislators used them to redraw boundaries of new election districts in ways that would most favor the party in power. For instance, in one system, a legislator could use computer graphics to call up his or her district on a screen, then shift the boundaries and get instant numbers of what the voting behavior, racial composition, and other population characteristics would be in the new district.

Census Bureau data is not available only to politicians, however. The bureau developed a computer map system called TIGER (for *T*opologically *I*ntegrated *G*eographic *E*ncoding and *R*eferencing system) that, when used with a database such as the 1990 census results or a company's own customer files, provides a detailed cartographic profile. TIGER can produce a map with 25 million street intersections and every city block, river, railroad line, or governmental entity in the country. The entire map comprises 16 billion lines. ■

In multitasking, a copy of each program to be executed is placed in a reserved portion of RAM, usually called a *partition* (Figure 7.27). The supervisor is more sophisticated in an operating system with multitasking capabilities because it coordinates the execution of each program. It directs the central processing unit to spend a predetermined amount of time (according to programmed priorities) executing the instructions for each program, one at a time. In essence, a small amount of each program is processed, and then the CPU moves to the remaining programs, one at a time, processing small parts of each. This cycle is repeated until processing is complete. The processing speed of the CPU is usually so fast that it may seem as if all the programs are being executed at the same time. However, the CPU is still executing only one instruction at a time, no matter how it may appear to users. (Sometimes a user working on a mainframe terminal may be interrupted while the processor turns to a higher-priority program.)

MULTIPROCESSING

A multitasking operating system works with only one CPU. However, the computer is so fast that, if it spends a little bit of time working on each of several programs in turn, it can allow a number of programs to run at the same time. The key is that the operating system can keep track of the status of each program so that it knows where it left off and where to continue processing. The **multiprocessing** operating system is much more sophisticated; it manages the *simultaneous* execution of programs

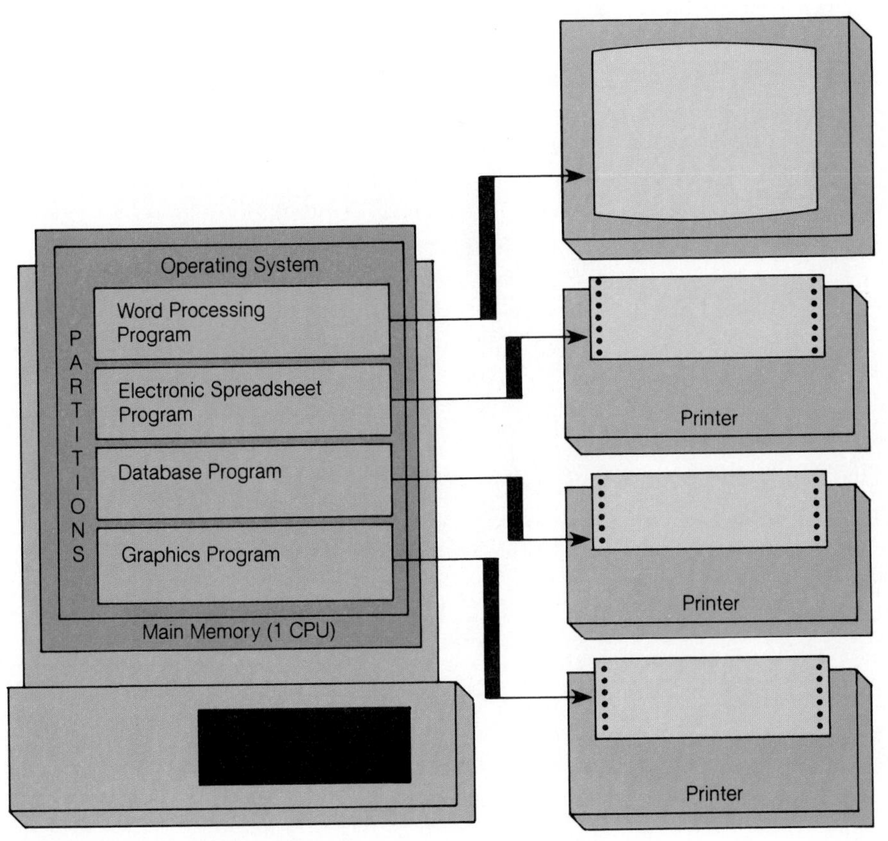

FIGURE 7.27

Multitasking. An operating system that can execute more than one program at a time (concurrently) is capable of multitasking—in other words, the user can run several different application programs at the same time. Although it may seem as if the programs are being processed exactly at the same time, they are actually being processed one after the other, extremely quickly.

with two or more CPUs (Figure 7.28). This can entail processing instructions from different programs or different instructions from the same program. Multiprocessing configurations are very popular in large computing systems and are becoming practical on powerful UNIX-based microcomputers. (We'll discuss the UNIX operating system shortly.)

TIMESHARING

A **timesharing** computer system supports many user stations or terminals simultaneously; in other words, the users share time on the computer based on assigned *time slices*. Timesharing is like multitasking, except that multitasking computers shift tasks based on program *priorities*, whereas timesharing systems assign each program a slice of time and then process the programs in small increments of time, one after the other. The processing requirements of an operating system with timesharing capabilities are great. As a result, in some cases a computer called a **front-end processor,** which is smaller than the main computer, is used to schedule and control all the user requests entering the system from the terminals. (A front-end processor functions somewhat like a receptionist in a large, busy front office—accepting calls and receiving visitors and then channeling them to the proper place

FIGURE 7.28 Multiprocessing. Some computers use two or more CPUs and sophisticated operating system software to process different programs simultaneously.

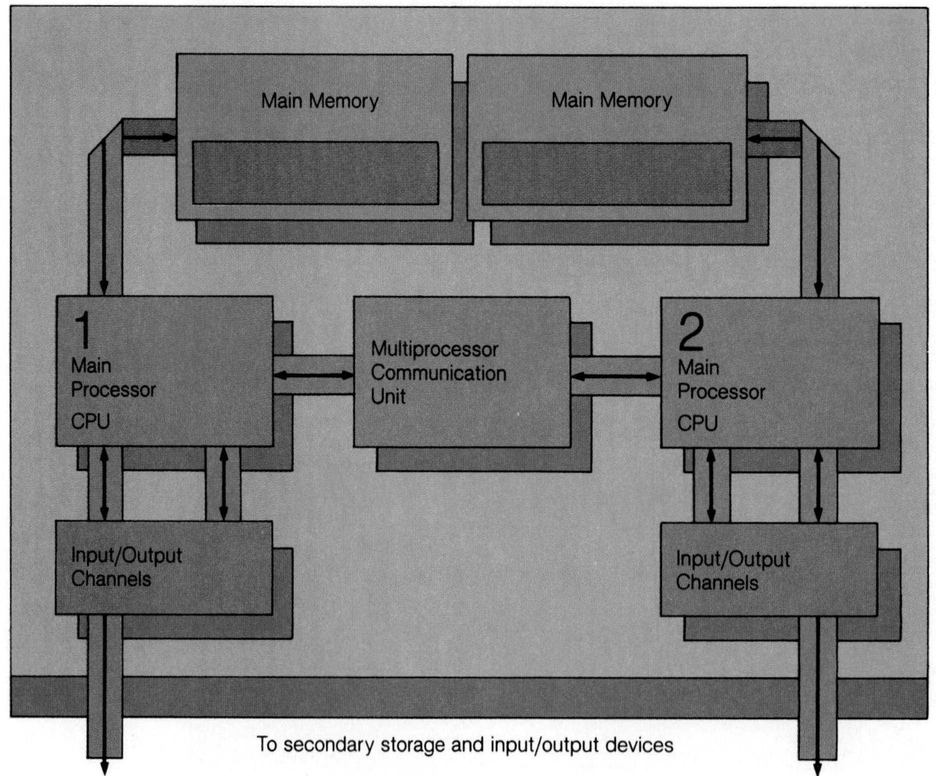

at the appropriate time.) The use of a front-end processor allows the main computer to concentrate solely on processing applications as quickly as possible (Figure 7.29).

Timesharing systems are most often used for three purposes:

1. As general-purpose systems, they enable users to create and run their own applications software using a variety of programming languages.
2. As a commercial service to other companies, they access the system with terminals to run a wide variety of existing programs that the companies would otherwise have to buy or write themselves.
3. As a service bureau, they offer companies without their own computer access to the software and hardware required to do all of their processing. The service bureau has the computer, the computer operators, and all of the support staff. The users enter only the data required by the programs and submit requests for the reports that need to be produced. One typical use of such a service is payroll processing. The obvious advantage of using a service bureau is that users do not have to purchase the computer or the software. Several companies can use the computer's time in batch mode and pay only for that time.

FIGURE 7.29 Do you have the time? In a timesharing environment, the front-end processor schedules and controls users' processing requests. The main computer is thus freed up for processing.

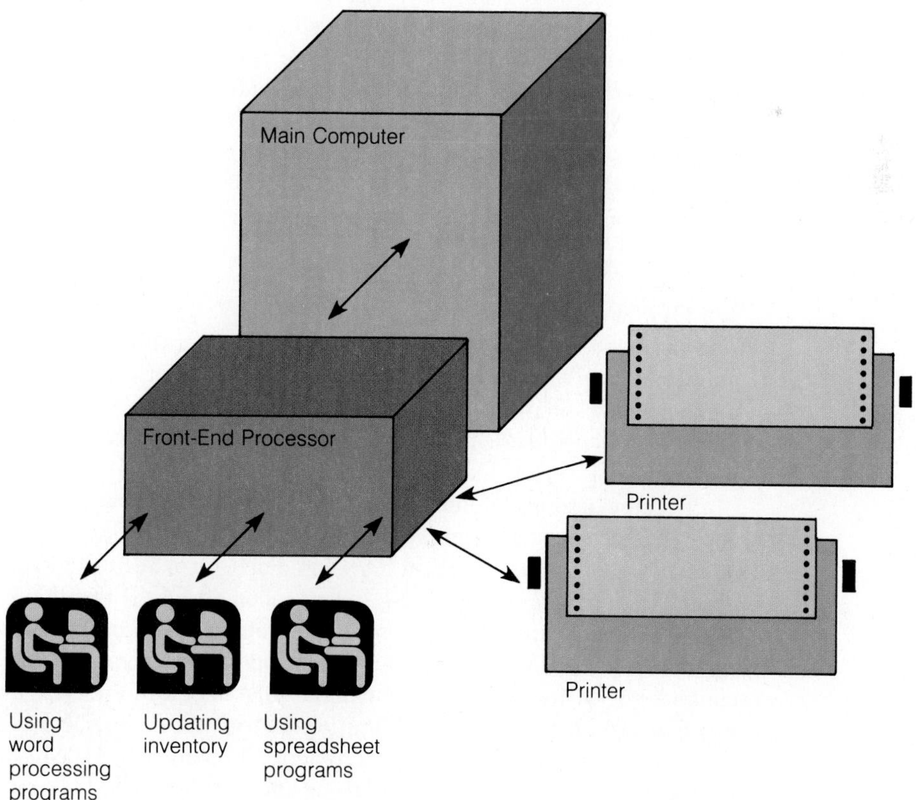

VIRTUAL MEMORY

Virtual memory, or **virtual storage,** is an operating system element that enables the computer to process as if it contained an almost unlimited supply of RAM. One of the major tasks of all operating systems is to manage the use of main memory carefully. Virtual storage enables a program to be broken into modules, or small sections, that can be loaded into main memory when needed. Modules not currently in use are stored on a very-high-speed disk (secondary storage) and retrieved one at a time when the operating system determines that the current module has completed executing. In the past, all computer operating systems were designed so that an entire program had to be loaded into main memory before it could begin execution. As a result, the size and sophistication of a program were limited by the amount of main memory available. As you may guess, the use of virtual memory facilitates multitasking.

ADDITIONAL SYSTEMS SOFTWARE INFORMATION FOR MICROCOMPUTER USERS

Because more readers of this book will be using microcomputers than minicomputers and mainframe computers, we have chosen to give you a few more details about the systems software available for microcomputers. Although problems of compatibility between operating systems and applications software packages are becoming less significant as computer technology advances, they still deserve your attention.

In the late 1970s and early 1980s, a number of microcomputer hardware vendors introduced products that included their own individual, machine-specific operating systems. This created a software compatibility problem because each software package was written for specific operating systems and machines—if it worked with one type, it couldn't be used with another. A few operating systems became more popular than others because more software applications were written to be used with them. Software vendors decided to concentrate on developing software for these operating systems—namely, MS-DOS/PC-DOS, OS/2, UNIX, and Macintosh DOS.

MS-DOS/PC-DOS

The development of this microcomputer **disk operating system (DOS)** (pronounced "doss") began in 1978 when Intel Corporation announced the development of a new and much more powerful microprocessor, the Intel 8088 chip. The new processor could use much more main memory and was substantially faster than the older 8080 series of processors.

Because of some differences between the old and the new processors, it became apparent that a new operating system would have to be developed to take advantage of the power of the new chips. In 1979 Tim Paterson of Seattle Computer Products began developing a new operating system called 80-DOS. The rights to distribute 80-DOS were acquired by Microsoft Corporation; Microsoft then entered into an agreement with IBM to make 80-DOS the operating system for the new personal computer IBM had under development. IBM added further program enhancements to 80-DOS and released the product in 1981 as IBM **PC-DOS** (IBM Personal Computer Disk Operating System). The impact of IBM's entry into the microcomputer marketplace was so strong that users and vendors began to indicate a preference for PC-DOS and its generic equivalent, **MS-DOS** (Microsoft Disk Operating System). The main reason for the popularity was that so many high-quality software applications were being written to be used with PC-DOS. Today, many of the microcomputers manufactured by IBM still use PC-DOS (some IBM microcomputers use OS/2, which we'll describe shortly). PC-DOS/MS-DOS became so common that in 1987 Apple released new versions of its popular Macintosh computer (using Macintosh DOS) that can run PC-DOS/MS-DOS-compatible software by means of an add-on board.

Many hardware manufacturers package systems software with their microcomputer systems. To package MS-DOS, the hardware manufacturer must enter into an agreement with Microsoft. Microsoft owns the source code for MS-DOS and licenses it to hardware manufacturers for a large fee. The hardware manufacturer makes slight adaptations to the code so it will run on their system, gives it a new name, and then supplies the necessary documentation. For example, Compaq licenses MS-DOS from Microsoft and names it COMPAQ-DOS. AT&T, Zenith, AST, Toshiba, and NEC also license MS-DOS from Microsoft and call their versions AT&T DOS, Zenith DOS, AST DOS, Toshiba DOS, and NEC DOS, respectively. The modifications these manufacturers make to MS-DOS are slight, so that software written for MS-DOS will run on any of these machines.

Every year or so, Microsoft releases an updated version of MS-DOS that includes the same capabilities of the previous version plus a few new ones. Version 4.0 was a major improvement over previous versions in terms of ease of use because it allows users to issue commands by choosing options from a menu (Figure 7.30). Previous versions required the user to know more of the rules associated with using each command. The latest version of MS-DOS is 5.0.

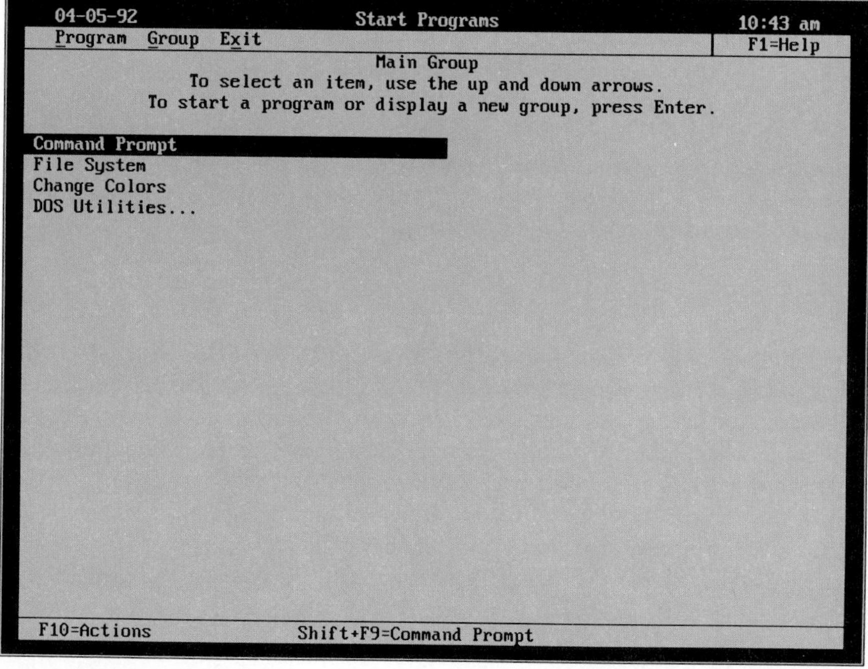

FIGURE 7.30

MS-DOS 4.0 menus. One menu extends across the top of the screen: "Program," "Group," "Exit." A second menu extends down the left side of the screen: "Command Prompt," "File System," "Change Colors," "DOS Utilities."

When Microsoft releases an updated version, the hardware manufacturers usually upgrade the version of MS-DOS they are selling with their microcomputers. *When you purchase an applications software package, make sure it is compatible with the version of DOS you are using.* Some software applications are compatible only with later versions of DOS. The versions of MS-DOS that an application is compatible with are usually listed on the front of the applications software package—for example, "DOS version 2.0 or higher."

MS-DOS AND WINDOWS

Despite its popularity, the MS-DOS operating system has its limitations. MS-DOS was designed principally to perform a single task for a single user. Although it is well suited for microprocessors that have been around for a while (Intel 8088, 8086), it can't fully utilize the capabilities of the more sophisticated microprocessors (Intel 80286, 80386, 80486). In addition, although the 80286 chip is capable of addressing, or using, up to 16 MB of RAM, MS-DOS can use only 640 K. And, finally, users often complain that MS-DOS is difficult to use. As a result, Microsoft developed **Microsoft Windows,** which is used in conjunction with MS-DOS to make it easier to use and more powerful. Most industry observers agree that Microsoft Windows will stop people from readily switching to more powerful operating systems such as UNIX and OS/2.

Windows supports multitasking, which enables users to run more than one application at a time, to easily switch between them, and to move data between applications. Windows also enables users to use 640 K of conventional RAM and up to 16 MB of extended memory (described in Chapter 4). Windows also provides users with a **graphic user interface** (Figure 7.31). Such an interface enables users to select menu options by choosing a picture, called an **icon,** that corresponds to the appropriate processing option. Graphic user interfaces are intended to make software easier to use. Using software that includes a graphic user interface is typically easier with a mouse rather than a keyboard, because using a mouse to choose menu options requires fewer steps.

To use Windows you need an 80286 or 80386 PC, 640 K of RAM, and 4–6 MB of free disk space. Windows can be used with software applications that were written for MS-DOS as well as applications written specifically for Windows. All applications written for Windows have a similar graphic user interface that makes it easier to learn how to use an application—that is, they all provide the user with a similar structure for choosing commands.

OS/2

In 1988, IBM and Microsoft introduced **Operating System/2 (OS/2),** which, like Microsoft Windows, is designed to get around some of the limitations imposed by MS-DOS and to take advantage of today's more sophisticated microprocessors, including those in the IBM PS/2 series of microcomputers. OS/2 supports multitasking and will allow new software applications to directly address up to 16 MB of RAM. OS/2 is packaged with **Presentation Manager** (Figure 7.32), also developed by Microsoft and IBM, which provides users with a graphic user interface that is similar to that used in Microsoft Windows.

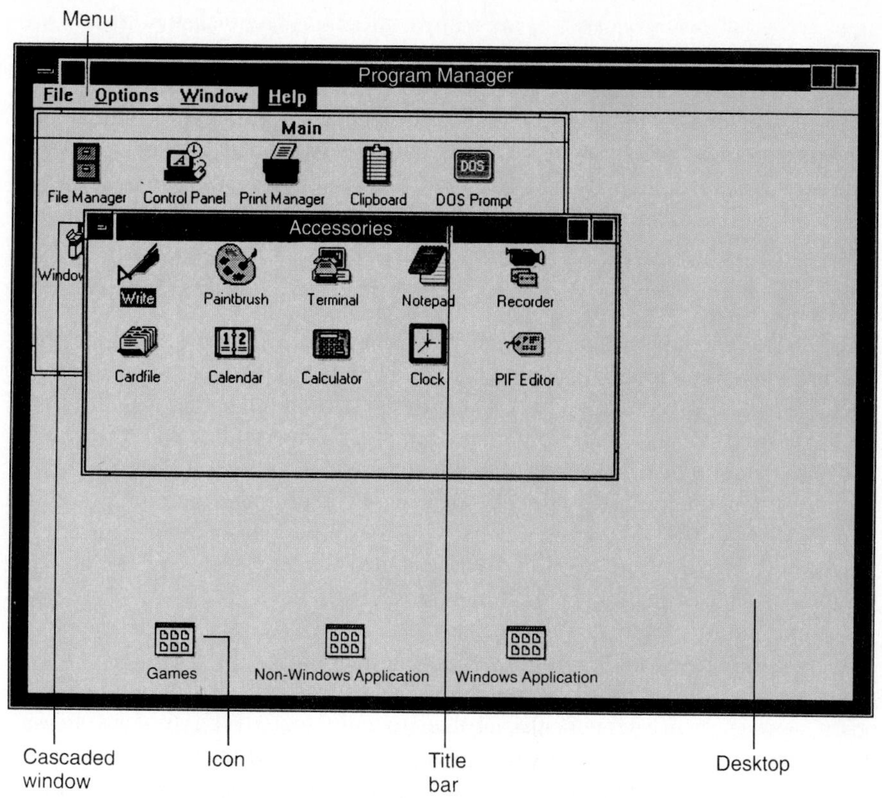

FIGURE 7.31

Microsoft Windows' Graphic User Interface. Most software developed now and in the future will incorporate a graphic user interface that uses many of the components labeled here.

FIGURE 7.32

(a) Presentation Manager screen; (b) Microsoft Windows screen.

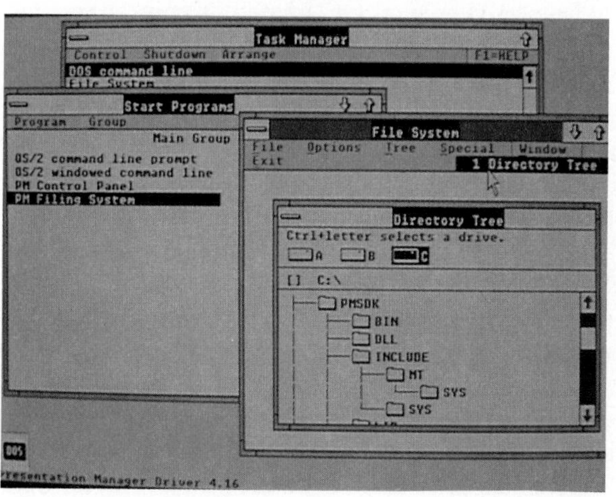

(a)

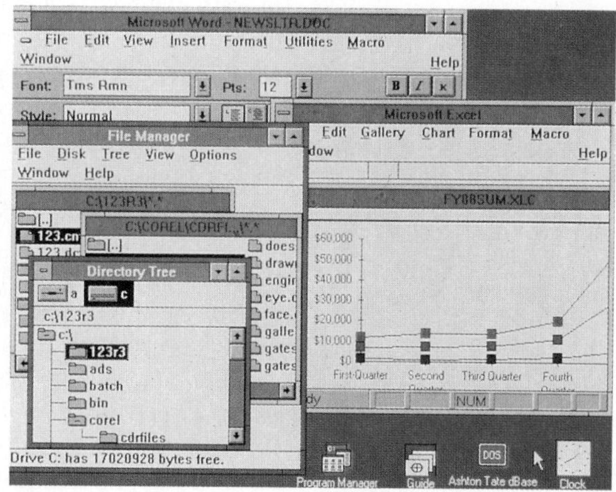

(b)

Compared with MS-DOS and Windows, OS/2 and Presentation Manager are much more powerful. Because of the many instructions that make up OS/2 (over 1.5 million bytes' worth), the hardware requirements to support it are greater than those required to support MS-DOS. To run efficiently, the typical Presentation Manager machine should have an 80386 microprocessor, run at 20 MHz, and be configured with at least 4 MB of RAM and a 60 MB hard disk. The average cost for such a system is around $3,000. OS/2 and Presentation Manager can be found in large companies that need to support processing tasks with powerful applications written for OS/2.

UNIX

The **UNIX** operating system was developed by Kenneth Thompson at Bell Laboratories, where the earliest version was released in 1971. This operating system was initially created for minicomputers and provides a wide range of capabilities, including virtual storage, multiprogramming, and timesharing. In 1973, the system was rewritten in a high-level language, called C, which allowed it to be used on a wider variety of computers, ranging from the largest mainframe computers to some of the more powerful microcomputers. UNIX is a popular operating system in universities where a multiuser (networked) environment is needed to support computer science students, programmers, and researchers.

Some industry observers agree that OS/2 and UNIX will be the operating systems to supercede DOS. In the multiuser environment, UNIX offers a major advantage over DOS and OS/2: Because UNIX terminals (a monitor and a keyboard) can be used in a network instead of microcomputers, UNIX is cheaper to use. The terminals can be connected to a high-powered central microcomputer. The U.S government and large companies use UNIX in networks because of its cost-effectiveness and its ability to support software applications on many different types of computers.

Although the cost of UNIX-specific applications software is higher than DOS- and OS/2-based software, a company still saves money when it establishes a multiuser environment based on UNIX. Realizing that UNIX might well be the operating system of the future, software vendors are developing UNIX versions of software that has traditionally been used only on DOS-based machines. You will soon see UNIX versions of such microcomputer applications software packages as WordPerfect, Microsoft Word, FoxBase, AutoCAD, Lotus 1-2-3, and dBASE.

MACINTOSH DOS

Apple Computer Corporation introduced its popular Apple II personal computer system in the late 1970s. Because the Apple machines were based on entirely different microprocessors than those used in the IBM microcomputers, their operating systems were incompatible and unable to share data and instructions. The disk operating system used on many Apple computers is called **Apple DOS** and is designed to perform a single task for a single user.

A more powerful disk operating system—often referred to as **Macintosh DOS**—was designed to be used on the Apple Macintosh computer (based on the 68030 microprocessor), which supports multitasking and virtual memory. The latest version of Macintosh DOS is called System 7. Special hardware and software must be purchased to allow Apple computers to share data with PC-DOS/MS-DOS-based microcomputers and OS/2-based microcomputers.

USER GUIDELINES FOR PURCHASING MICROCOMPUTER SYSTEMS SOFTWARE

If you ever have to choose a microcomputer, consider carefully the systems software choices available in light of your specific processing needs. There is no right choice for everyone. The choice you make should be determined by:

- Type and quantity of compatible applications software you are interested in.
- Ease of use by both users and programmers.
- Speed of operation.
- Capability to support multitasking and multiuser needs.
- Types of compatible hardware you will need.
- Availability of trained technical support personnel and manufacturer's hot-line support available to help you solve problems using your equipment and software.
- Expected practical life of the microcomputer. For example, a computer with an 8088 processor may do what you want it to do this year, but can it handle any expansion/update needs you think you may have in the near future?

Table 7.4 reviews the main systems software used with microcomputers. For detailed information about the features of MS-DOS and how to load it into your microcomputer, see the introduction to the Modules at the back of the book. Also, Appendix A provides more detailed information about purchasing and maintaining a microcomputer system, including software.

Table 7.5 lists some common systems software for IBM mainframes.

TABLE 7.4

Microcomputer Operating Systems

Processor	Apple DOS	Macintosh DOS	MS-/PC-DOS	OS/2	UNIX
M6502	X				
M68030		X			
Intel 8088			X		
8086			X		X
80286			X	X	X
80386			X	X	X
80486			X	X	X
Single-user	X		X		
Multitask		X		X	X
Multiuser					X
Virtual memory		X		X	

TABLE 7.5

Mainframe Systems Software

CICS	Customer Information Control System. Connects user terminals to computer
CMS	Conversational Monitor System. Connects user terminals to computer
DOS	Disk Operating System
MVS	Multiprogramming with Virtual Storage. Operating system
OS	Operating System
TSO	Time-Sharing Option. Connects user terminals to computer
VM/370	Virtual Machine. Operating system for IBM model 370 computers
VM/XA	Virtual Machine/Extended Architecture. Operating system

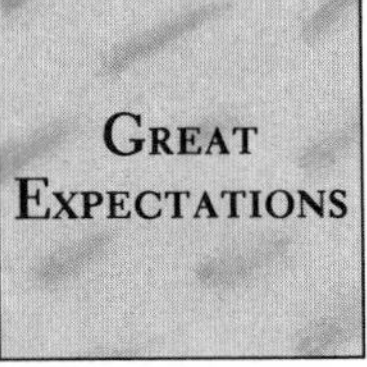

It's hard to say exactly what the future holds for systems and applications software, but one thing is certain: Software in general will be much more intuitive in nature. In other words, instead of having to read pages and pages of documentation before doing anything useful on your computer, you will be able to simply view graphics and text on your screen to be able to begin and continue processing. Graphic user interfaces will be the force that makes microcomputers a more effective cultural tool, rather than simply a business tool. Industry observers note that once an easy-to-use interface is established, the use of computers will spread much like the use of VCRs has. Apple Macintosh computers are already based on a standard graphical interface that has been praised for its ease of use. However, a major segment of society is currently using microcomputers that aren't compatible with Apple computers (in other words, data can't be shared unless special hardware and software are purchased), such as the computers manufactured by IBM, which is a latecomer in developing a standard graphical interface.

Many experts expect that by the mid-1990s, an improved OS/2 will be the dominant operating system with IBM-compatible microcomputers. The standard graphical interface that will insulate users from the cumbersome system command line will likely be Presentation Manager. So that IBM users' applications software will run with Presentation Manager, applications software developers will have to create packages that conform to this strict and uniform programming environment. As a result, the look and feel of different IBM-based software applications will be just about the same. In addition, because the applications will be written according to the rules and syntax of Presentation Manager, it will be possible to easily transfer data from one program to another. Presentation Manager interface will also make it easier for users to learn to use both systems and applications software.

Because MS-DOS/PC-DOS already has so many users, new DOS versions will probably still be developed—6.0 and perhaps 7.0.

ONWARD: WRITING SOFTWARE

Chapter 7 described what is available for you in the way of software—systems software and applications software—or what you may find in place when you start your job. But how is software actually written? The next chapter describes the tools available for creating software.

SUMMARY

Software plays a critical role in computer-based information systems because our hardware would be useless without it. Software comprises the instructions that tell the hardware what to do. If possible, you should first select the software that meets your information needs, then choose compatible hardware.

Software can be divided into two major categories: systems software and applications software. Applications software is a collection of related programs designed to perform a specific task—to solve a particular problem for the user. Systems software, which "underlies" applications software, starts up (boots) the computer and functions as the principal coordinator of all the hardware components and applications software programs.

Many off-the-shelf applications software packages are available to the user, and reviews of these packages can be found in several types of publications, including popular computer magazines. The six major categories of applications software are:

1. General business management.
2. Industry-specific.
3. Special disciplines.
4. Education.
5. Personal/home management.
6. General-purpose for the user.

In the category of general-purpose software, the main types of software you will encounter in an average business are:

1. Word processing software, which enables the user to easily insert, delete, and move words, sentences, and paragraphs automatically and also to change the appearance of the written material.
2. Electronic spreadsheet software, with which the user can conveniently develop reports involving the use of extensive mathematical, financial, statistical, and logical processing.
3. Database management systems (DBMS) software, which allows the user to store large amounts of data that can be easily retrieved and manipulated with great flexibility to produce reports.
4. Graphics software, which gives the user the ability to make reports and presentations even more effective through the use of graphs and other types of drawings.

5. Integrated software, which combines the software capabilities of several types of software programs to enable the user to perform different types of tasks without having to change software and to transmit data and information to other computers through the use of telephone lines, satellites, and other communications technology.
6. Applications software utilities, which are often RAM-resident, staying "underneath" other software, until the power is turned off. The user can interrupt one task, switch over to the RAM-resident software, perform another task, and switch back to the original applications package. This category includes: desktop management, add-on, disk, screen, and keyboard utilities.
7. Desktop publishing software, which allows the user to take advantage of particular text and graphics software and use laser printers to produce material of publishable quality.
8. Computer-aided design (CAD), computer-aided engineering (CAE), and computer-aided manufacturing (CAM) programs, which allow manufacturers to more easily design, engineer, and produce finished products.

Hypertext and multimedia involve the use of very sophisticated software that can combine text and graphics, and text, graphics, animation, music, and voice, respectively, in unusual and creative ways.

Table 7.6 lists some questions to ask when you are choosing applications software.

Systems software is composed of (1) internal command instructions, (2) external command instructions, and (3) language processors, or translators. The part of the operating system that resides in main memory (internal instructions) is most important; without these instructions, the computer cannot operate. These instructions must be loaded from secondary storage when the computer is first turned on (called *booting* for microcomputers and *initial program load* for mainframes); otherwise, none of the hardware components will function. Internal instructions must reside in main memory (RAM) at all times while the computer is on.

External command instructions perform so-called housekeeping tasks, which frequently have to do with file and storage management.

TABLE 7.6

Selecting Applications Software (Source: Adapted from T. J. O'Leary and B. K. Williams, *Computers and Information Systems*, 2nd ed. [Redwood City, Calif.: Benjamin/Cummings, 1989], p. 93. Reprinted by permission.)

Key questions you should ask the seller about each software package before you buy are the following:

1. How much does it cost?
2. What specific problems does it solve?
3. What are its key features?
4. What kind of hardware, operating system, and main memory (RAM) is required?
5. What kind of documentation and self-paced training, if any, is available?
6. If problems arise, what kind of field or store support and telephone support is available?
7. What kind of warranty is offered, if any?
8. Can you give me the names of users with needs like mine who are using this software?

Language processors, or translators, convert the high-level language of the user's software into the only language the computer can understand—machine language. Some low-level languages, called *assembly languages*, were created using abbreviations to help programmers avoid the tedious and time-consuming task of writing programs in machine language (0s and 1s). High-level languages were developed to make the job even easier. However, both high-level and assembly languages must be translated into machine language for the CPU to use them. The translation can be done by interpreters, which convert software instructions (source code) one line at a time and thus allow for on-the-spot error correction, or by compilers, which convert the whole source program at once and create a program in object code that the computer can understand (called an *object program*) and save. The average business user will not have to interact directly with language translators.

The level of sophistication of systems software depends on the size of the computer it operates and the tasks it is intended to perform. When operating systems were first developed, they could support only single users; many mainframe operating systems and some microcomputer operating systems can now support multitasking (performing several tasks so fast that it appears they are being done at once), multiprocessing (using two or more CPUs to process two or more programs simultaneously), timesharing (allowing several users to work at the computer at the same time using assigned time slices), and virtual storage (employing a piecemeal procedure for using secondary storage that increases the efficiency of main memory use).

The most popular disk operating systems for microcomputers are MS-DOS/PC-DOS (now often used with Microsoft Windows), OS/2 (used with Presentation Manager), UNIX, and Macintosh DOS. Operating systems were originally developed to support single users and single tasks. However, as microcomputer hardware became more powerful, it was capable of supporting more sophisticated operating systems. For example, OS/2 and UNIX can support multiusers and multitasking on microcomputers.

Systems software is written to work with a particular type of microprocessor and is incompatible with machines that do not use that type of processor. Applications software is written to be used with particular systems software and is incompatible with others. Thus, the user who is in the position of acquiring a microcomputer should consider the availability of applications software needed and then pick systems software and hardware that are mutually compatible and compatible with the applications software. Users who pick hardware first may find themselves unable to use the software best qualified to do the job at hand.

Determining what operating system to use on a microcomputer depends on a number of factors, including:

1. Type and quantity of compatible applications software you are interested in.
2. Ease of use.
3. Speed of operation.
4. Capability of supporting multitasking and multiuser needs.
5. Capability of being used with other hardware (compatibility).
6. Availability of technical and hot-line support.
7. Expected practical life of the microcomputer.

KEY TERMS

add-on utility, p. 269
analytical graphics, p. 255
Apple DOS, p. 286
applications software, p. 243
applications software utility, p. 268
assembly language, p. 275
booting, p. 273
code-oriented, p. 263
communications software, p. 267
compiler, p. 275
computer-aided design (CAD), p. 265
computer-aided engineering (CAE), p. 265
computer-aided manufacturing (CAM), p. 265
control program, p. 273
database management system (DBMS) software, p. 254
desktop management utility, p. 269
desktop publishing, p. 258
disk operating system (DOS), p. 282
disk utility, p. 269
external command instructions, p. 274
file management system, p. 255
flat-file database management system, p. 255
front-end processor, p. 270
graphics software, p. 255
graphic user interface, p. 284
high-level programming language, p. 275
hypertext, p. 270
icon, p. 284
initial program load (IPL), p. 271
integrated software, p. 258
internal command instructions, p. 273
interpreter, p. 275
keyboard utility, p. 269
language processor, p. 275
Macintosh DOS, p. 286
Microsoft Windows, p. 284
MS-DOS, p. 283
multimedia, p. 271
multiprocessing, p. 279
multiprogramming, p. 277
multitasking, p. 277
object code, p. 275
off-the-shelf software, p. 245
operating system, p. 272
Operating System/2 (OS/2), p. 284
page description software, p. 263
PC-DOS, p. 282
presentation graphics, p. 256.
Presentation Manager, p. 284
proprietary operating system, p. 274
RAM-resident utility, p. 268
relational database management system (DBMS), p. 255
screen utility, p. 269
source code, p. 275
spreadsheet software, p. 253
supervisor, p. 273
systems software, p. 243
timesharing, p. 280
translator, p. 275
UNIX, p. 286
virtual memory (storage), p. 282
word processing software, p. 249
WYSIWYG, p. 263

EXERCISES

MATCHING

Match each of the following terms to the phrase that is the most closely related.

1. _____ desktop publishing software
2. _____ integrated software
3. _____ interpreter

4. _____ systems software
5. _____ applications software
6. _____ timesharing
7. _____ word processing software
8. _____ front-end processor
9. _____ external command instructions
10. _____ virtual memory
11. _____ multitasking
12. _____ database management systems software
13. _____ booting
14. _____ spreadsheet software
15. _____ internal command instructions
16. _____ applications software utility

a. Computer that schedules and controls users' processing requests
b. Program, usually RAM-resident, that performs basic "office management" functions for the user when he or she is using an applications software package
c. Software used to easily store large amounts of data, sort it into order, and retrieve and manipulate information
d. Software used to develop personalized reports involving the use of mathematical, financial, statistical, and logical processing
e. This refers to many terminals or user stations connected to (sharing) one computer.
f. With this, the computer can process as though it has an almost unlimited supply of main memory.
g. This involves turning a computer on and loading a copy of important systems software instructions into main memory.
h. Systems software that supports this capability can execute more than one program at a time.
i. Instructions automatically loaded into main memory when the computer is turned on
j. Software that allows you to easily create, edit, and print documents
k. This type of language processor converts high-level program instructions into machine-language instructions one instruction at a time.
l. These types of systems software instructions are stored on disk because they are not needed to run applications programs; instead, they perform "housekeeping" tasks.
m. Software that allows you to combine text and graphics to create near-typeset-quality newsletters, documentation manuals, and forms on a laser printer
n. Software intended to satisfy your particular business or personal processing requirements
o. Software that combines word processing, spreadsheet, database, graphics, and communications capabilities
p. Software that tells the computer how to interpret data and instructions, how to run peripheral equipment, and how to use hardware in general

MULTIPLE CHOICE

1. Which of the following types of software must you have in main memory in order to use your keyboard?
   a. word processing
   b. systems
   c. spreadsheet
   d. applications
   e. CAD/CAM
2. If you want to execute more than one program at a time, the systems software you are using must be capable of:
   a. word processing
   b. virtual memory
   c. compiling
   d. multitasking
   e. interpreting
3. Which of the following is a type of systems software used on microcomputers?
   a. Apple DOS
   b. MS-DOS
   c. PC-DOS
   d. UNIX
   e. all the above
4. Which of the following is helpful in evaluating what applications software will best suit your needs?
   a. recommendations by other users
   b. computer magazines
   c. objective software reviews
   d. computer periodicals
   e. all the above
5. Which of the following are loaded into main memory when the computer is booted?
   a. internal command instructions
   b. external command instructions
   c. disk utilities
   d. word processing instructions
   e. multiusers
6. Which of the following tasks does the operating system supervisor perform?
   a. coordinates processing and checks equipment malfunction
   b. manages RAM
   c. manages files stored on disk
   d. allocates use of peripheral devices
   e. all the above
7. Which of the following is not applications software?
   a. word processing
   b. spreadsheet
   c. UNIX
   d. desktop publishing
   e. DBMS
8. Which of the following types of software should you use if you often need to create, edit, and print documents?
   a. word processing
   b. spreadsheet
   c. Presentation Manager
   d. CAD/CAM
   e. applications utility
9. Which of the following will determine your choice of systems software for your computer?
   a. Is the applications software you want to use compatible with it?
   b. Is it expensive?
   c. Is it compatible with your hardware?
   d. (a) and (c)
   e. (b) and (c)

10. Which of the following might be used by programmers to convert high-level language instructions into machine language?
    a. systems software
    b. applications software
    c. Microsoft Windows
    d. compiler
    e. integrated software

SHORT ANSWER

1. What is the difference between applications software and systems software?
2. Why is systems software so important to a computer system?
3. How are interpreters and compilers different?
4. What is the difference between internal and external command instructions?
5. What is an icon, and why is it relevant to operating systems?
6. What are some factors to consider when choosing systems software?
7. What is the difference between multiprogramming and multiprocessing?
8. If you are in charge of acquiring microcomputer hardware and software, which should you select first—the hardware or the software? Why?
9. What is spreadsheet software used for? How is it different from database software? From word processing software?
10. What should you consider before buying a microcomputer applications software package?
11. What do the abbreviations CAD, CAE, and CAM mean?
12. What are applications software utilities?
13. What does the term *booting* mean?

PROJECTS

1. Compare MS-DOS and Microsoft Windows with OS/2 and Presentation Manager. Which combination do you think is currently more popular, and which do you think will be more popular in five years? Why? Base your report on articles in computer publications and interviews with computer store salespeople, as well as any users you can find.
2. Attend a computer user group meeting in your area. What is the overall purpose of the group? Software support? Hardware support? In what ways? Does it cost money to be a member? How many members are there? How does the group get new members? Do you think this group is useful? Why/why not?
3. Locate a department at your school or a company that is using some custom-written software. What does the software do? Who uses it? Why couldn't it have been purchased off the shelf? How much did it cost? Can it be updated? Do you think custom-written software will be required in your chosen profession? Why or why not?
4. Go to a large computer store and find out how many microcomputers (and what types) run on which operating systems—PC-DOS (or other MS-DOS-based operating systems), OS/2, UNIX, Macintosh DOS. Which use Microsoft Windows? Ask the salesperson's opinion on which disk operating system is the most powerful and flexible. Why?

CHAPTER 8

DEVELOPING SOFTWARE

At this point, just learning how to use computer hardware and software may seem challenging enough. Yet there often comes a day when users suddenly discover that the ready-made, off-the-shelf programs available to them won't do everything they want. People renovate their houses or modify their clothes for the same reasons that software users fiddle with their programs. Would you ever be able to create applications software yourself? Or be able to help someone else do so? And are you curious about where software comes from—how it is created? In this chapter, we describe ways to develop or modify applications software through the use of programming languages and techniques and through existing software.

PREVIEW

When you have completed this chapter, you will be able to:

- Describe what software development tools exist and which ones you are most likely to use.
- Describe some of the advantages and disadvantages of using some of the most popular high-level programming languages.
- Explain how a user could use existing microcomputer software to customize software programs.
- Identify the responsibilities of the user in the programming process.
- Name the five basic steps in developing a computer program.
- Identify some structured programming tools and techniques.
- Identify the three logic structures used in structured programming.
- Explain the importance of program testing and documentation.

One day at work you are tinkering with your database management program on your microcomputer when you suddenly realize you can't make it produce a sales report in just the right format. Or perhaps your spreadsheet won't automatically extract all the right data for a particularly useful analysis of an investment strategy. As new computer users gain more experience, they find it easier to identify areas where software can be modified or created to provide more useful and sophisticated processing capabilities above and beyond those of a purchased package. As we mentioned earlier, to obtain custom-made software the user can (1) hire an outside computer specialist to develop it; (2) ask the firm's computer specialists to do it; or (3) go it alone. Regardless of the approach you take, you need to understand the process by which software is developed and be familiar with the tools available for you to use.

In addition, users need to understand the programming process so that they can effectively communicate with the programmers who are creating software for them. If users can't specify their requirements effectively, they may end up with software they are not happy with.

WHAT TOOLS ARE AVAILABLE FOR DEVELOPING SOFTWARE?

Just as many tools exist for building a house, many tools are available for creating, or writing, software. These tools comprise different types of programming languages, each of which consists of a number of different commands that are used to describe the type of processing to be done, such as multiplying two numbers together. In short, programming languages are used to write detailed sets of instructions that enable the user to process data into information in an appropriate manner.

Software development tools can best be categorized as falling into one of five generations of programming languages (Figure 8.1). The languages in each successive generation represent an improvement over those of the prior generation—just as the electric saw was an improvement over the manual one. Languages of later generations are easier to learn than earlier ones, and they can produce results (software) more quickly and more reliably. But just as a builder might need to use a manual saw occasionally to cut a tricky corner, professional programmers still need to use early generation languages (except machine language, which we'll explain shortly) to create software. Each of the five language generations will be described in detail in this chapter.

Compared with later generations, the early-generation programming languages (first, second, and third) require the use of more complex vocabulary and syntax to write software; they are therefore used primarily by computer professionals. The term **syntax** refers to the precise rules and patterns required for the formation of the programming language sentences, or statements, that tell the computer what to do and how to do it. Programmers must use a language's syntax—just as you would use the rules of German, not French, grammar to communicate in German—to write a program in that language. Because more efficient software development tools are available, programmers don't create software using machine language anymore, and few use assembly language, except for programs with special processing requirements. However, third-generation languages are still in wide use today.

Fourth-generation languages still require the user to employ a specific syntax, but the syntax is easy to learn. In fact, fourth-generation programming languages are so much easier to use than those in prior generations that the noncomputer professional can create software after about a day of training.

Natural languages—currently under development—will constitute the fifth generation of languages. With this type of language, the user will be able to specify processing procedures using statements similar to idiomatic human speech—simple statements in English (or French, German, Japanese, and so on). The use of natural language will not require the user to learn a specific syntax.

In addition to the five generations of programming languages, some microcomputer software packages (such as electronic spreadsheet and database management software) are widely used for creating software. Although these packages generally cannot be categorized into one of the five generations, many people consider some of the database management systems software used on microcomputers, such as dBASE IV, as belonging to the fourth-generation category.

FIGURE 8.1

The five generations of programming languages.

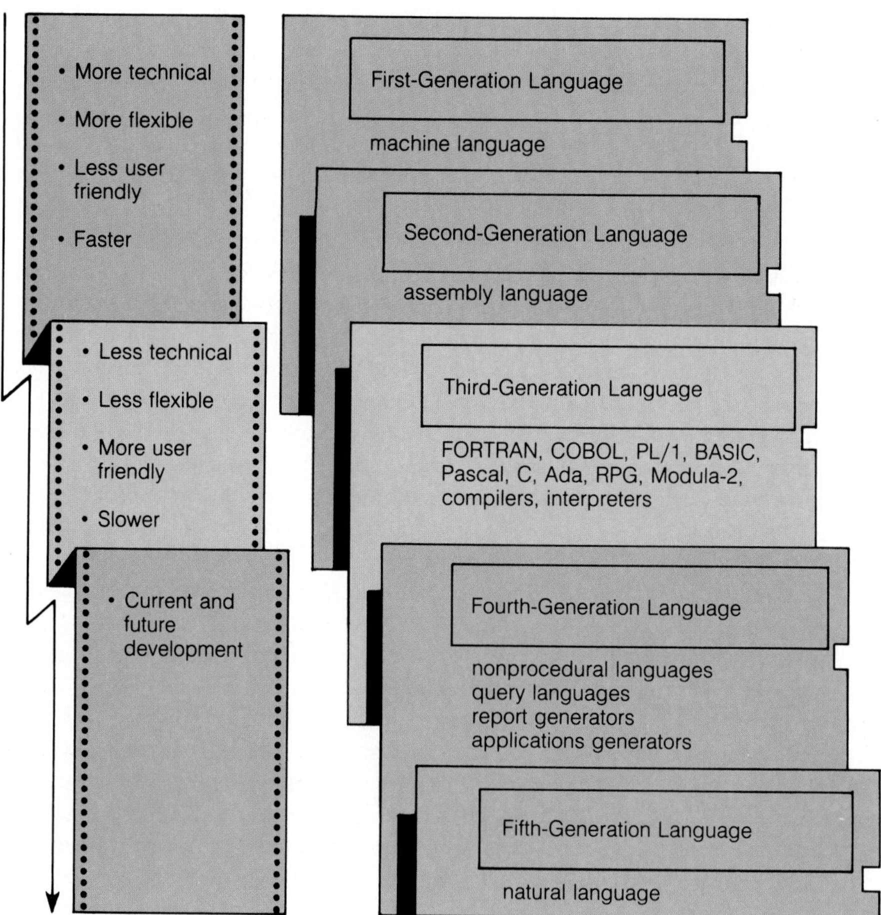

WHICH TOOLS ARE YOU MOST LIKELY TO USE?

The decision about which software development tool to use depends on what processing procedures you need to perform. Developing software is like building a house: The work will go much faster if you have a plan and the right tools. However, the tools have little value if you don't know how to use them; consequently, one of the most important steps toward effective and efficient software development is the selection of the right development tool.

If you become a computer specialist, you will need to learn to use the most popular of the third-generation programming languages because much of the available applications software is based on them. In other words, the software that you buy off the shelf of a computer store has been created by a computer specialist using one of these languages. Also, computer specialists need to know how to use these languages in order to update, or maintain, this existing software to accommodate new processing and output requirements.

For the user who is not a computer specialist, the most popular tools for developing software will be the fourth-generation programming languages and existing off-the-shelf software packages such as electronic spreadsheets and database management systems software, because one does not have to be an experienced computer professional to use them. The user who is working with these tools can create specialized software applications, such as keeping track of a company's expenses by department (a good application for a spreadsheet package), or maintaining a comprehensive customer file used in a clothing store for billing, marketing, and checking customer credit status (a good application for a database package).

GENERATIONS OF SOFTWARE DEVELOPMENT TOOLS

Over the past 40 years, the programming languages used to develop software have been steadily improving in terms of ease of use, the time it takes to develop software, and the reliability of the finished product. In the following pages we describe the major characteristics of each generation of languages, or software development tools, and pay special attention to the tools you will likely be using in the business environment.

FIRST AND SECOND GENERATIONS

As you learned in Chapter 7, all higher-level language instructions are converted into machine-language form—**first-generation language**—before they can be carried out by the computer. As you learned in Chapter 4, machine-language instructions and data are represented by binary digits (a series of 1s and 0s corresponding to on and off electrical states). Because the specific format and content of the instructions vary according to the architecture of each type of computer, machine-language programs can be run only on the type of computer for which they were designed; that is, they are machine-dependent.

The first step in making software development easier and more efficient was the creation of **assembly languages**, also known as **second-generation languages**. (Some people consider them to be the first low-level languages and place machine language in a separate category.) You'll recall from the last chapter that assembly languages use symbols as abbreviations for major instructions instead of a long combination of binary digits. This means a programmer can use abbreviations instead of having to remember lengthy binary instruction codes. For example, it is much easier to remember L for Load, A for Add, B for Branch, and C for Compare than the binary equivalents—strings of different combinations of 0s and 1s.

Although assembly languages represented an improvement, they had obvious limitations. They can be used only by computer specialists familiar with the architecture of the computer being used. And because they are also machine-dependent, assembly languages are not easily converted to run on other types of computers. Assembly-language programs are still written today, but only when storage must be minimized or processing speed increased, results that can be achieved only by tailoring instructions to the architecture of the specific computer. For example, many small businesses have captured large amounts of data with a microcomputer using database management system (DBMS) software. However, when a business attempts to sort stored data into a particular sequence for a certain job, the sorting activity may take as long as several hours. To drastically reduce this time, a "sort program" can be purchased that has been written in assembly language for the business's specific computer.

THIRD GENERATION

Third-generation languages, also known as *high-level languages*, are very much like everyday text and mathematical formulas in appearance. They are designed to run on a number of different computers with few or no changes. Unlike machine and assembly languages, then, many high-level languages are *machine-independent*. Among the most commonly used high-level programming languages are COBOL, FORTRAN, and BASIC. A large number of additional languages have been developed, each with its own strengths. The objectives of high-level languages are:

- To relieve the programmer of the detailed and tedious task of writing programs in machine language and assembly language.
- To provide programs that can be used on more than one type of machine with very few changes.
- To allow the programmer more time to focus on understanding the user's needs and designing the software required to meet those needs.

Most high-level languages are considered to be procedure-oriented languages, or **procedural languages**, because the program instructions comprise lists of steps, or procedures, that tell the computer not only *what* to do but *how* to do it. High-level language statements generate, when translated, a comparatively greater number of assembly-language instructions and even more machine-language instructions (Figure 8.2). The programmer spends less time developing software with a high-level language than with assembly or machine language because fewer instructions have to be created.

A language processor is still required to convert (translate) a high-level language program into machine language. As described in Chapter 7, two types of language processors are used with high-level languages: compilers and interpreters.

Compilers convert the high-level (procedural) language program (source code) into a machine language code (object code) that can be saved and run later. Interpreters convert the high-level language program one statement at a time into machine language code just before the program is executed. No object code is saved.

The importance of high-level languages was quickly recognized by the computer industry, and substantial human and financial resources were dedicated to their development. By the early 1960s, most computer manufacturers were working on a version of FORTRAN, the first widely used high-level language, for their computers. Various manufacturers' versions of FORTRAN were similar; however, their efforts to make one package better than the others resulted in a number of small differences. The problems associated with resolving these differences led to the realization that industry standards were needed to ensure complete compatibility of high-level language programs with different computers. The task of establishing such standards was turned over to the American Standards Association, and in 1966 the association released the first FORTRAN standards.

Since the late 1960s, the association—now known as the **American National Standards Institute (ANSI)**—worked with the **International Standards Organization (ISO)** to develop, among other things, standards for all high-level programming languages. All versions of programming languages that developers wish to have designated as meeting the standards must accommodate all the commands, syntax, and processing requirements formulated by the ANSI and the ISO. We'll now describe some popular standard high-level programming languages.

FORTRAN

The **FORTRAN**—short for **FORmula TRANslator**—programming language was first made available in 1957 by IBM. One of the very first high-level languages (Figure 8.3), FORTRAN was designed for technical and scientific applications. Its popularity grew rapidly, and by the 1960s a version of the language was available for almost all types of computers; however, it is used primarily on minicomputers and

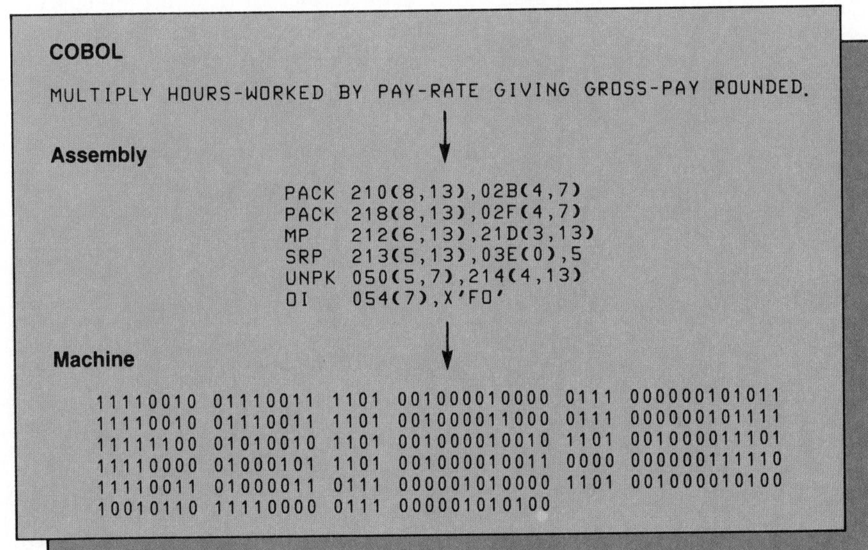

FIGURE 8.2

Down through the generations. An example of a statement in COBOL, part of which is converted first to assembly language and then to machine language. As you can see, the high-level (third-generation) language requires few statements to create a large number of machine-language (first-generation) instructions. (T. J. O'Leary and B. K. Williams, *Computers and Information Systems*, 2nd ed. [Redwood City, Calif.: Benjamin/Cummings, 1989].)

mainframes. Because the language was designed to handle research and analytical problems definable in terms of mathematical formulas and relationships, the majority of people using FORTRAN are mathematicians, scientists, and engineers.

The primary advantages of FORTRAN are:

- It can handle complex mathematical and logical expressions.
- Its statements are relatively short and simple.
- Programs developed in FORTRAN on one type of computer can often be easily modified to work on other types.

The main disadvantages are:

- It does not handle input and output operations to storage devices as efficiently as some other high-level languages.
- It has only a limited ability to express and process nonnumeric data.
- It is not as easy to read and understand as some other high-level languages.

COBOL

COmmon Business Oriented Language, or **COBOL** for short, was released in 1960. The U.S. Department of Defense, which is one of the world's largest buyers of data processing equipment, no longer wanted to commission the development of software in unalterable assembly language, so it funded the development of this programming language for business. The leader of the team that developed COBOL was naval officer Grace Hopper. The concern over the differences among versions of FORTRAN—all machine-dependent—led the developers of COBOL to adopt machine independence as one of the primary objectives. The U.S. government then adopted a policy that required a computer to have the COBOL programming language available if the vendor wanted to sell or lease the equipment to the government. In 1968, COBOL was approved as the standard business programming language in the United States; the latest ANSI standards for COBOL were released in 1985.

The commands and syntax of COBOL's instruction statements are like English. As a result, it is much easier for a programmer to read and understand COBOL than FORTRAN. A COBOL program has four divisions: the *identification division*, which contains reference information such as program name and programmer's name; the *environment division*, which describes the type of com-

FIGURE 8.3

FORTRAN. Here, a FORTRAN statement calculates a discount (7 percent of the invoice amount) if the invoice is greater than $500. Otherwise, no discount is given to the customer.

```
IF (XINVO .GT. 500.00) THEN
   DISCNT = 0.07 * XINVO
ELSE
   DISCNT = 0.0
ENDIF
XINVO = XINVO - DISCNT
```

puter to be used; the *data division*, which describes the data to be processed; and the *procedure division*, which contains the programming logic. Figure 8.4 shows an extract from the procedure division of a typical COBOL program.

COBOL is used primarily on minicomputers and mainframes but is also available for microcomputer use, and it is the language most used for business applications. Its major advantages are as follows:

- It is machine-independent.
- Its English-like statements are easy to understand, even for a nonprogrammer.
- It can handle many files, records, and fields.
- It easily handles input-output operations.

The main disadvantages are as follows:

- Because it is so readable, it is wordy, and thus even simple programs become long, and programmer productivity is slowed.
- It cannot handle mathematical processing as well as FORTRAN.

In spite of the drawbacks, many programmers believe that COBOL will remain the most widely used language for writing business applications.

PL/1

The intended uses of FORTRAN and COBOL were always very clear. However, as the complexity and sophistication of the applications being developed for business increased, a language was needed that would be capable of dealing with computation *and* heavy-duty file handling. For this reason, IBM and two international organizations of computer users began to develop a general-purpose programming language, which was designated **Programming Language 1**, or **PL/1**. PL/1 was released in the mid-1960s for use on the IBM System 360 series of computers and has since been used primarily on mainframe computer systems. Figure 8.5 shows an extract from a PL/1 program.

```
OPEN-INVOICE-FILE.
     OPEN I-O INVOICE-FILE.

READ-INVOICE-PROCESS.
     PERFORM READ-NEXT-REC THROUGH READ-NEXT-REC-EXIT UNTIL END-OF-FILE.
     STOP RUN.

READ-NEXT-REC.
     READ INVOICE-REC
          INVALID KEY
               DISPLAY 'ERROR READING INVOICE FILE'
               MOVE 'Y' TO EOF-FLAG
               GOTO READ-NEXT-REC-EXIT.
     IF INVOICE-AMT > 500
          COMPUTE INVOICE-AMT = INVOICE-AMT - (INVOICE-AMT * .07)
          REWRITE INVOICE-REC.

READ-NEXT-REC-EXIT.
     EXIT.
```

FIGURE 8.4

COBOL. This COBOL statement shows the same discount calculation given in Figure 8.3.

The primary advantages of PL/1, which is used mostly on mainframes, are as follows:

- It combines text and mathematical processing capabilities.
- It is very flexible—the programmer using it has few coding restrictions.
- It automatically identifies and corrects common programming errors.

PL/1's main disadvantages are:

- It requires a substantial amount of main memory (usually requires a mainframe).
- Its list of options is long and difficult to memorize.
- It is harder to learn than COBOL.

BASIC

Beginner's All-purpose Symbolic Instruction Code, or **BASIC**, was developed in the mid-1960s at Dartmouth College, where the large computer timesharing system that supported many student terminals allowed interactive testing of the new computer language. BASIC was intended to be a programming language that was easy to learn and flexible enough to solve a variety of simple problems. It was used primarily to teach people how to program. BASIC is an *interactive* language—user and computer can communicate with each other during the writing and running of programs.

By the late 1970s and early 1980s, BASIC had become so popular that it was selected as the primary language for implementation on microcomputers, although it can be used on all types of computers. Because of its popularity, a number of extensions have been added to the language to facilitate file creation and handling and the creation of graphics. Figure 8.6 shows an excerpt from a BASIC program.

The primary advantage of BASIC has been its ease of use. The primary limitation, aside from its normally slow processing speed, used to be a lack of official standardization, although Microsoft's version of BASIC, called MS-BASIC, was accepted as a de facto standard. Each implementation of the language for a particular machine had a few subtle differences that required specific attention when a program was run on a different machine. However, in 1987 the ANSI adopted a new standard for the BASIC language that eliminated portability problems. New versions of BASIC for use on microcomputers, such as Microsoft QuickBASIC, can be compiled as well as interpreted and so are much faster than previous versions. See the appendix for more detailed coverage of BASIC.

FIGURE 8.5

PL/1. The discount calculation of Figures 8.3 and 8.4 shown in PL/1.

```
/*CALCULATE DISCOUNT*/
GET LIST (INVOICE);
IF INVOICE > 500 THEN DISCOUNT = INVOICE * .07;
ELSE DISCOUNT = 0;
END;
```

RPG

The **Report Program Generator**, or **RPG**, language was introduced by IBM in 1964 to help small businesses generate reports and update files easily. RPG is not as procedure-oriented as other third-generation languages but is still often referred to as a programming language. The programmer fills out a number of very detailed coding forms that are easy to learn to use; however, because RPG is designed to be used to solve clear-cut and relatively simple problems, it is much more limited than FORTRAN, COBOL, BASIC, and some other programming languages. RPG is used on a variety of IBM computers and has been *enhanced*, or improved, several times. The first revision, RPG II, was released in the early 1970s and provided enhanced capabilities for handling tape and disk files. The latest version of the language, RPG III (released in 1979), added the capabilities necessary to extract reports from data stored in a database system. Figure 8.7 shows an RPG form with data entered (other forms exist for input, output, and file description specifications). After the data is entered on the form, it is typed into the computer.

The major advantages of RPG are the ease with which reports can be produced with minimal time and effort on the part of the programmer or user and the low number of formal rules for syntax and grammar compared to other high-level

BASIC. Our discount calculation in BASIC. **FIGURE 8.6**

```
10  REM   This Program Calculates a Discount Based on the Invoice Amount
20  REM         If Invoice Amount is Greater Than 500, Discount is 7%
30  REM         Otherwise Discount is 0
40  REM
50  INPUT "What is the Invoice Amount"; INV.AMT
60  IF INV.AMT > 500 THEN LET DISCOUNT = .07 ELSE LET DISCOUNT = 0
70  REM         Display results
80  PRINT "Original Amt", "Discount", "Amt after Discount"
90  PRINT INV.AMT, INV.AMT * DISCOUNT, INV.AMT - INV.AMT * DISCOUNT
100 END
```

RPG. The discount calculation. **FIGURE 8.7**

GX21-9093-2 UM/050* Printed in U.S.A.
*No. of forms per pad may vary slightly

IBM International Business Machine Corporation

RPG CALCULATION SPECIFICATIONS

Program | Programmer | Date | Punching Instruction | Graphic | Punch | Card Electro Number | Page 1 2 of | Program Identification 75 76 77 78 79 80

Line (3–5)	Form Type (6)	Control Level (L0–L9, LR, SR, AN/OR) (7–8)	Indicators (9–17)	Factor 1 (18–27)	Operation (28–32)	Factor 2 (33–42)	Result Field Name (43–48)	Length (49–51)	Decimal Positions (52)	Half Adjust (H) (53)	Resulting Indicators High (54–55)	Low (56–57)	Equal (58–59)	Comments (60–74)
01	C			INVAMT	COMP	500					15			
02	C		15	INVAMT	MULT	.07	DISCNT	5	2					
03	C		N15	INVAMT	MULT	.00	DISCNT							
04	C			INVAMT	SUB	DISCNT	INVAMT							
05	C													

languages. However, the first version of RPG had limited computational capabilities and could not be used effectively in scientific or other applications requiring extensive mathematical processing. RPG II and RPG III substantially corrected some of these limitations. However, no formal RPG standards have yet been introduced by the industry.

C

This programming language, invented after the languages "A" and "B" had been developed, was introduced by Brian Kernighan and Dennis Ritchie at Bell Laboratories in the early 1970s for use in writing systems software. **C**, which is quite sophisticated, was used to create most of the UNIX operating system (assembly language was used to create the rest). The recent interest in UNIX as a powerful operating system for microcomputers has sparked interest in converting existing applications software to run with UNIX and in writing new software using C. The primary advantages of C are:

- It can be used on different types of computers, including microcomputers.
- It is fast and efficient.
- Its compiler is easily written.
- It is useful for writing operating systems software, database management software, and a few scientific applications.

Its disadvantages include:

- It has no input/output routines; these must be imported (brought in) from other programs.
- It is not good for checking *types* of data—whether it is numeric, characters, etc.

Figure 8.8 shows an example of the C programming language.

PASCAL

The **Pascal** language, named after the 17th-century French mathematician Blaise Pascal, was developed by Swiss scientist Niklaus Wirth and introduced in the early 1970s. Available for both large and small computer systems (Turbo Pascal, among other packages, is available for microcomputers), it was developed to teach programming as a systematic and structured activity. Pascal classes are offered at most universities and colleges because of its superior structured programming format.

FIGURE 8.8

C. The C version of the 7 percent discount. C has many characteristics of both assembly and high-level programming languages, and, although it is a complex language to learn, it can be used on a variety of machines.

```
if (invoice_amount > 500.00)

   discount = 0.07 * invoice_amount;

else

   discount = 0.00;

invoice_amount = invoice_amount - discount;
```

Structured programming, which we describe later in this chapter, is based on the principle that any desired programming procedures can be broken into three parts:

1. Logic that allows a series of operations to be performed in sequence.
2. Logic that allows data elements to be compared and decisions to be made that determine the direction of subsequent processing.
3. Logic that allows procedures to be repeated a controlled number of times (looping).

The major advantages of Pascal are as follows:

- It can be used for mathematical and scientific processing.
- It has extensive capabilities for graphics programming.
- It is easy to learn.

The major disadvantage of Pascal is its limited input/output programming capability, which, in turn, limits its business applications. Figure 8.9 is an excerpt from a Pascal program.

MODULA-2

Developed by Niklaus Wirth as an improvement of Pascal and introduced in 1980, **Modula-2** is better suited for business use than Pascal, and, although it's used primarily to write systems software, it can be used as an applications software development tool. Many experts believe that it may become a popular business programming language.

ADA

In 1975, the U.S. Department of Defense began to encourage the creation of a language that would facilitate the development and maintenance of large programs that could be used for any type of application—from business to missile launching—and that could be used and modified over a long period of time. This decision was prompted by the results of a study that showed that lack of uniformity in the use of languages resulted in yearly software costs of billions of dollars. These costs were necessary to pay for the large staff of programmers required to support all the different languages used.

The programming language **Ada** was derived from Pascal and named after Augusta Ada, Countess of Lovelace, the daughter of the famous English poet Lord Byron. The Countess of Lovelace worked with the mathematician Charles Babbage

```
if INVOICEAMOUNT > 500.00 then
   DISCOUNT := 0.07 * INVOICEAMOUNT
else
   DISCOUNT := 0.0;
INVOICEAMOUNT := INVOICEAMOUNT - DISCOUNT
```

FIGURE 8.9

Pascal. The customer discount calculation shown in Pascal.

in the mid-1800s to develop mechanical computing devices and is considered to be the world's first programmer. This language is intended primarily for use in computer systems that are an integral part of another system for which they act as the control mechanism; that is, they are *embedded* systems. Many military weapons systems and equipment, for example, have embedded computer systems. However, the language can be used for commercial as well as military applications. Ada combines the good qualities of Pascal with improved input/output capabilities. Figure 8.10 is a sample excerpt of an Ada program.

Ada's main advantages include:

- Extensive support of real-time processing.
- Automatic error recovery.
- Flexible input/output operation.
- Structured and modular design—sections, or "modules," of the program can be created and tested before the entire program is put together.

Among its disadvantages are:

- High level of complexity and difficulty.
- Large storage requirements.
- Not as efficient as some other languages.

Although Ada has great potential, it is not yet widely used outside of the U.S. Department of Defense.

HOW DOES A PROGRAMMER KNOW WHICH LANGUAGE TO USE?

We have discussed only a few of the most popular high-level programming languages; more than 500 programming languages exist for programmers to choose from. However, if a programmer has a good understanding of what a program needs to accomplish—and it is the *users* who must communicate this information to the programmer—then deciding what language to use may not be difficult. The following factors are usually considered when a decision is made:

- Does the company already have a standard language that the programmers use?

FIGURE 8.10

Ada. The 7 percent solution in Ada.

```
if INVOICE_AMOUNT > 500.00 then
   DISCOUNT := 0.07 * INVOICE_AMOUNT
else
   DISCOUNT := 0.00
endif;
INVOICE_AMOUNT := INVOICE_AMOUNT - DISCOUNT
```

- How easy is it to learn the language?
- What other languages are supported on the computer system? How do they need to interface?
- Do the processing requirements match the capabilities of the language? For example, FORTRAN is very effective for computations, whereas COBOL is very good for handling large volumes of business information.
- Will the program need to run on more than one type of computer system? If so, transportability becomes a consideration; that is, the degree of a language's machine dependence needs to be evaluated. And not all languages are available for all machines.
- Are the intended applications using the high-level language oriented toward a batch or an on-line environment?
- What are the maintenance requirements? If the program needs to be updated frequently, will that be easy to do in the chosen language?

In general, the use of third-generation languages to write applications software is inconvenient for the ordinary user because:

- Users require special training to use these languages — thus they need to hire programmers, who may be booked up for a long time in advance. Users may have to wait quite a long time before they can get their applications programs written.
- Programmers and other computer specialists, such as systems designers, are expensive.
- Users may think they know what they want but after testing the program discover they didn't. Modifications can be costly and expensive — and the programmers might not be immediately available to make them.

How can users sometimes avoid these inconveniences? By creating their own customized applications software using fourth-generation languages and applications generators. However, we are not suggesting that the ordinary user can undertake complicated programming without training and experience.

Fourth Generation

Also known as very-high-level languages, **fourth generation languages (4GLs)** are as yet difficult to define, because they are defined differently by different vendors; sometimes these languages are tied to a software package produced by the vendor, such as a database management system. Basically 4GLs are easier for programmers — and users — to handle than third-generation languages. Fourth-generation languages are **nonprocedural languages**, so named because they allow programmers and users to specify *what* the computer is supposed to do without having to specify *how* the computer is supposed to do it, which, as you recall, must be done with third-generation, high-level (procedural) languages. Consequently, fourth-generation languages need approximately one tenth the number of statements that a high-level language needs to achieve the same result.

Because they are so much easier to use than third-generation languages, fourth-generation languages allow users, or noncomputer professionals, to develop certain types of applications software. It is likely that, in the business environment, you will at some time use a fourth-generation language. Five basic types of language tools fall into the fourth-generation language category: (1) query languages, (2) report generators, (3) applications generators, (4) decision support systems and financial planning languages, and (5) some microcomputer applications software.

Query languages allow the user to ask questions about, or retrieve information from, database files by forming requests in normal human-language statements (such as English). Query languages do have a specific grammar, vocabulary, and syntax that must be mastered (like third-generation languages), but this is usually a simple task for both users and programmers. For example, a manager in charge of inventory may key in the following question of a database:

```
How many items in inventory have a quantity-on-hand that
is less than the reorder point?
```

The query language will do the following to retrieve the information:

1. Copy the data for items with quantity-on-hand that is less than the reorder point into a temporary location in main memory.
2. Sort the data into order by inventory number.
3. Present the information on the video display screen (or printer).

The manager now has the information necessary to proceed with reordering certain low-stock items. The important thing to note is that the manager didn't have to specify *how* to get the job done, only *what* needed to be done. In other words, in our example, the user needed only to specify the question, and the system automatically performed each of the three steps listed above.

Figure 8.11 provides an example of a query language, and Table 8.1 lists some of the popular query languages used today. Some query languages also allow the user to add data to and modify database files, which is identical to what database

FIGURE 8.11 Example of a query language statement.

In order to produce a list of certain fields contained in an organization's employee database (called Q.ORG), the SQL instruction, or query, would be:

```
SELECT DEPTNUMB, DEPTNAME, MANAGER, DIVISION, LOCATION FROM Q.ORG
```

The result of the query might be:

DEPTNUMB	DEPTNAME	MANAGER	DIVISION	LOCATION
10	HEAD OFFICE	160	CORPORATE	NEW YORK
15	NEW ENGLAND	50	EASTERN	BOSTON
20	MID ATLANTIC	10	EASTERN	WASHINGTON
38	SOUTH ATLANTIC	30	EASTERN	ATLANTA
42	GREAT LAKES	100	MIDWEST	CHICAGO
51	PLAINS	140	MIDWEST	DALLAS
66	PACIFIC	260	WESTERN	SAN FRANCISCO
84	MOUNTAIN	290	WESTERN	DENVER

management systems software allows you to do. The difference between the definitions for query language and for database management systems software is so slight that most people consider the definitions to be the same.

Report generators are similar to query languages in that they allow users to ask questions of a database and retrieve information from it for a report (the output); however, in the case of a report generator, the user is unable to alter the contents of the database file. And with a report generator, the user has much greater control over what the output (or the result of a query) will look like. The user of a report generator can specify that the software automatically determine how the output should look or can create his or her own customized output reports using special report-generator command instructions. (Ordinary users may need the help of a computer specialist to use a report generator.) In most reports, users require that a total or totals of one or more groups of numbers appear at the bottom. And, if more than one category of information is to be included in the report, the user usually wants subtotals to appear for each category. In the case of a third-generation language, the number of instructions necessary to create totals is about 10 times the number needed in a fourth-generation language because the programmer needs to specify not only what to total but how to total and where to place the total. Report generators have many built-in assumptions that relieve the user from having to make such tedious decisions. Table 8.1 lists the most widely used report generators.

Applications generators, as opposed to query languages and report generators, which allow the user to specify only output-related processing tasks (and some input-related tasks, in the case of query languages), allow the user to reduce the time

TABLE 8.1

Popular Query Languages, Report Generators, and Applications Generators

Category	Package/Language	Vendor
Query language	INTELLECT	Artificial Intelligence Corp.
	On-Line English	Culliname
	Query-By-Example	IBM
	Quick Query	Caci
	SQL	IBM
	Ingress/Star	Relational Technology
	Oracle	Oracle
Report generators	Easytrieve Plus	Pansophic
	GIS	IBM
	Mark IV	Informatics
	NOMAD	NCSS
Applications generators	ADS	Cullinet
	Application Factory	Cortex Corporation
	FOCUS	Information Builders
	MAPPER	Sperry
	MANTIS	CINCOM
	NATURAL	Software AG
	RAMIS	Mathematica, Inc.

it takes to *design* an entire software application that accepts input, ensures data has been input accurately, performs complex calculations and processing logic, and outputs information in the form of reports. Applications generators basically consist of prewritten modules—or program "building blocks"—that comprise fundamental routines that most programs use—such as read, write, compare records, and so on. These modules, usually written in a high-level language, constitute a "library" of routines to choose from. The user must key into computer-usable form the specifications for *what* the program is supposed to do. The resulting specification file is input to the applications generator, which determines *how* to perform the tasks and which then produces the necessary instructions for the software program.

For example, a user like yourself could use an applications generator to design payroll runs—to calculate each employee's pay for a certain period and to output printed checks. Again, as with query languages and report generators, the user doesn't have to specify *how* to get the processing tasks performed. Table 8.1 lists some of the more popular applications generators used today.

Decision support systems and **financial planning languages** combine special interactive computer programs and some special hardware to allow high-level managers to bring data and information together from different sources and manipulate it in new ways—for example, to make projections, do "what if" analyses, and make long-term planning decisions. We cover these fourth-generation software tools in more detail in Chapter 12, Management Information Systems.

Some *microcomputer applications software* can also be used to create specialized applications—in other words, to create new software. Microcomputer software packages that fall into this category include many spreadsheet programs (such as Lotus 1-2-3), database managers (such as dBASE IV), and integrated packages (such as Symphony). For example, in a business without computers, to "age" accounts receivable (to penalize people with overdue account balances), someone has to manually calculate how many days have passed between the invoice date and the current date and then calculate the appropriate penalty based on the balance due. This can take hours of work. However, with an electronic spreadsheet package, in less than half an hour the user can create an application that will calculate accounts receivables automatically. And the application can be used over and over.

Another example of microcomputer software that is used to create new programs is HyperCard for the Macintosh, created by Bill Atkinson of Apple (discussed in Chapter 7). In general, this package is a database management program that allows users to store, organize, and manipulate text and graphics, but it is also a "programmable program" that uses the programming language called *HyperTalk* to allow ordinary users to create customized software by following the "authoring" instructions that come with the package.

Figure 8.12 provides a diagram showing where many fourth-generation software tools appear on the scale of difficulty for the ordinary user.

FIFTH GENERATION

Natural languages represent the next step in the development of programming languages—**fifth-generation languages.** Natural language is similar to query language, with one difference: It eliminates the need for the user or programmer to learn a specific vocabulary, grammar, or syntax. The text of a natural-language statement very closely resembles human speech. In fact, one could word a statement in several ways — perhaps even misspelling some words or changing the order of the words — and get the same result. Natural language takes the user one step farther away from having to deal directly and in detail with computer hardware and software. These languages are also designed to make the computer "smarter" — that is, to simulate the human learning process. Natural languages already available for microcomputers include Clout, Q&A, and Savvy Retriever (for use with databases) and HAL (Human Access Language) for use with Lotus 1-2-3.

The use of natural language touches on *expert systems*, computerized collections of the knowledge of many human experts in a given field, and *artificial intelligence*, independently smart computer systems — two topics that are receiving much attention and development and will continue to do so in the future (covered in more detail in Chapter 12).

Now that you have been introduced to the basics about the *tools* used in developing software, it's time to turn to programming *methods* — the principles and procedures according to which the tools are used.

FIGURE 8.12

Complexity of software development tools. This chart will give you an idea of how relatively easy or difficult many available software development tools are to use. (Adapted from K. C. Laudon and J. P. Laudon, *Management Information Systems: A Contemporary Perspective* [New York: Macmillan, 1988], p. 476.)

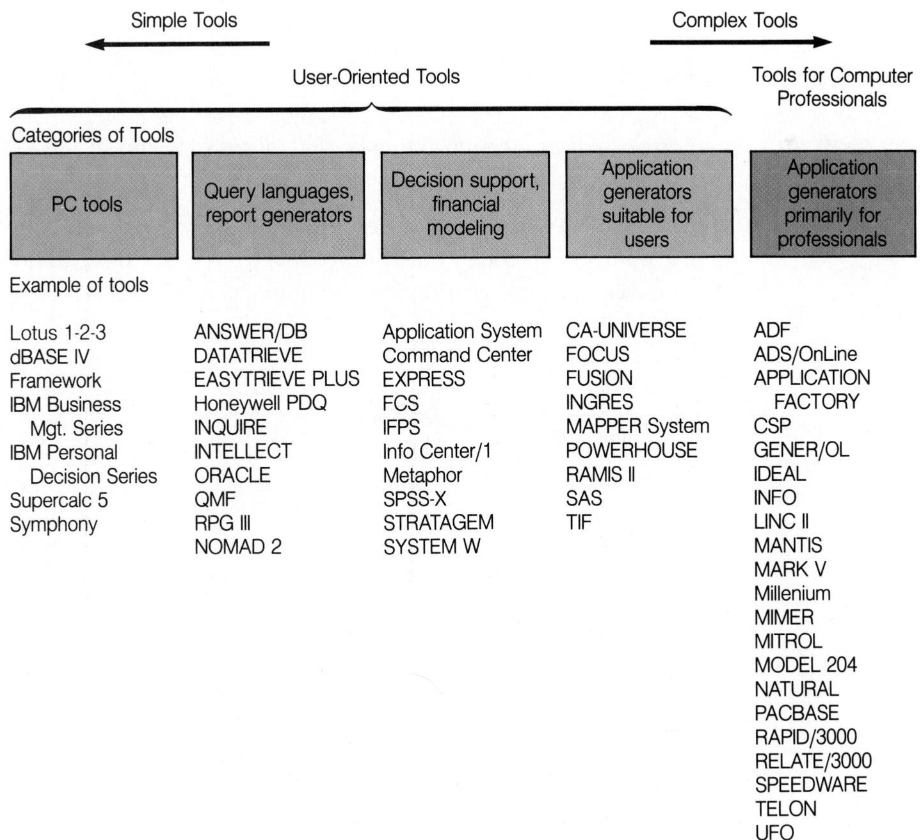

PROGRAMMING: WHAT THE USER NEEDS TO KNOW

For a number of important reasons, the user should understand how a computer programmer develops software using a high-level language. For example, the user may have to evaluate software vendors' claims about what their programs can do. More important, if the user fails to communicate clearly and precisely to the programmer the processing procedures and logic to be incorporated into a program, the programmer will have to make assumptions about what exactly should be done. If the assumptions are wrong, the user will probably end up with reports that contain erroneous information or reports that simply do not *have* the necessary information.

In addition, as we mentioned earlier, some users today are using existing software packages such as electronic spreadsheets to customize their own software applications. If you are one of these people, you should be aware of a few facts. First, no matter how easy a software development tool is to use, you must understand the principal steps you must take to "custom-tailor" an application. Second, the processing logic required for the procedures to be performed must be carefully mapped out. Third, you must understand the importance of testing and documenting the software to ensure it is doing exactly what is expected. Many users do not take this third step seriously, and, as a result, the software they develop often produces erroneous information.

Suppose your boss asks you to create an electronic spreadsheet that will produce information to be considered in making a multimillion-dollar bid for a new project. If you do not proceed carefully, you may end up with problems such as:

- A formula for computing costs that does not include all the required values; as a result, the cost estimate will be too low.
- An estimate of the expected revenues from the project that is incorrectly specified; as a result, the cash flow during the life of the project will be overestimated.

With millions of dollars at stake, you may quickly find yourself out of a job. An infinite number of problems can be created if you are not careful when using software. Many people assume that the numbers in a computer report are always correct. *They are correct only if the processing procedures have been carefully specified and thoroughly tested.*

The orderly process that an organization goes through when identifying its applications software program requirements is referred to as the *Systems Development Life Cycle (SDLC)*, which is discussed in detail in Chapter 10. This section focuses on just a small *part* of the SDLC—namely, the steps involved in developing an applications software program once the requirements for the program have been identified. As mentioned earlier, you need to understand these steps so that you will be able to tell a programmer, in terms he or she can understand, exactly what your programming requirements are. Although this section on programming is not detailed enough to allow you to communicate on the level of a programmer, it will tell you the basics about what you, as a user, need to understand about programming.

Step 1—Define the problem (Figure 8.13).

- "Think first and program later." Consider all possible ways of solving a problem and specify the objectives of the intended program, including who (which departments) will use the information produced.

- Specify output requirements.
- Specify input requirements.
- Specify processing requirements.
- Study the feasibility of the program.
- Document the analysis and objective specification process—this may involve using flowcharts, flow diagrams, data dictionaries that catalog and identify the data elements that will be used, sketches of display screen formats and report layouts, and so on.

Step 1 usually involves meetings that include the programmer(s), users, and the systems analyst/designer who designed the system of which the program to be written will be a part.

Step 2—Map out the program logic and design a solution.

After the problem has been defined, the program must be logically designed. This process is not unlike outlining a long term paper's organization before you actually begin to write it. The programmer must work out **algorithms,** or diagrams of the solutions, before the program is written. The programmer may use a variety of tools to do this, including systems flowcharts (covered in Chapter 10), program flowcharts, pseudocode, and structure charts (discussed later in this chapter). You probably won't ever need to use any of these tools, because they are used mostly by programmers mapping out complex logic or by those using third-generation languages. However, you should have a basic idea of how they are used in order to appreciate the detail that is necessary for a programmer to create a program. The more detail you can give the programmer about your processing requirements, the better the resulting program will be.

After the program has been designed, programmers, systems designers, and users check its logic and documentation by means of a "structured walkthrough."

The five basic steps of program development. **FIGURE 8.13**

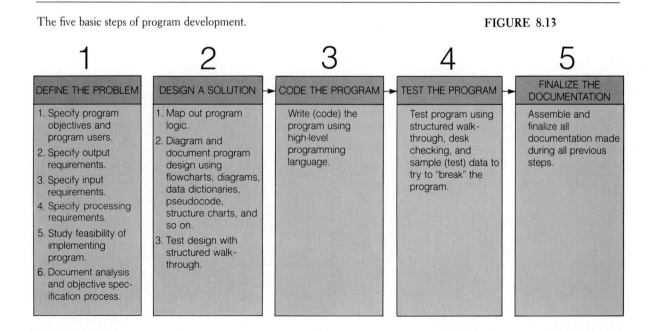

1	2	3	4	5
DEFINE THE PROBLEM	DESIGN A SOLUTION →	CODE THE PROGRAM →	TEST THE PROGRAM →	FINALIZE THE DOCUMENTATION
1. Specify program objectives and program users. 2. Specify output requirements. 3. Specify input requirements. 4. Specify processing requirements. 5. Study feasibility of implementing program. 6. Document analysis and objective specification process.	1. Map out program logic. 2. Diagram and document program design using flowcharts, diagrams, data dictionaries, pseudocode, structure charts, and so on. 3. Test design with structured walk-through.	Write (code) the program using high-level programming language.	Test program using structured walk-through, desk checking, and sample (test) data to try to "break" the program.	Assemble and finalize all documentation made during all previous steps.

Step 3—Write (code) the program.

Translate the processing requirements of the program into the necessary programming (high-level) language statements and then enter the coded instructions into the computer. (This is usually done on a terminal, with the instructions stored on disk. The programmer can modify the instructions as necessary.)

Step 4—Test the program.

Review the program carefully to ensure that it is doing exactly what it is supposed to. Repeat structured walkthoughs, conduct **desk checking** by proofreading a printout of the program, and, using test ("flake") data, and review output reports to determine that they are in the correct format and contain all the required information (logic testing). The user can play an important role in identifying the problem areas, or "bugs," in a program by participating in tests to see how it handles the types of tasks it was asked to do—including trying to "break" the program by inputting unusual test data. The programmer can then fix the problems, or "debug" the program (see Figure 8.14).

Step 5—Collate and finalize the documentation.

Clearly document all the steps, procedures, logic tools, and testing results, as well as the goals of the program and other specific facts. Although listed as Step 5, the activity of *documenting the program actually goes on all the way through the design and coding process*. This documentation, or manual, will tell future program operators, users, managers, and even programmers who may later have to modify the program exactly what the program does and how it does it and what they need to do to use it. Documentation also helps programmers track down errors.

The following sections discuss these steps in more detail.

FIGURE 8.14

Moth found in Mark I components (1945). The origin of word "bug" meaning "program error," dates to the discovery of this moth lodged in the computer's wiring. The moth disrupted the execution of the program.

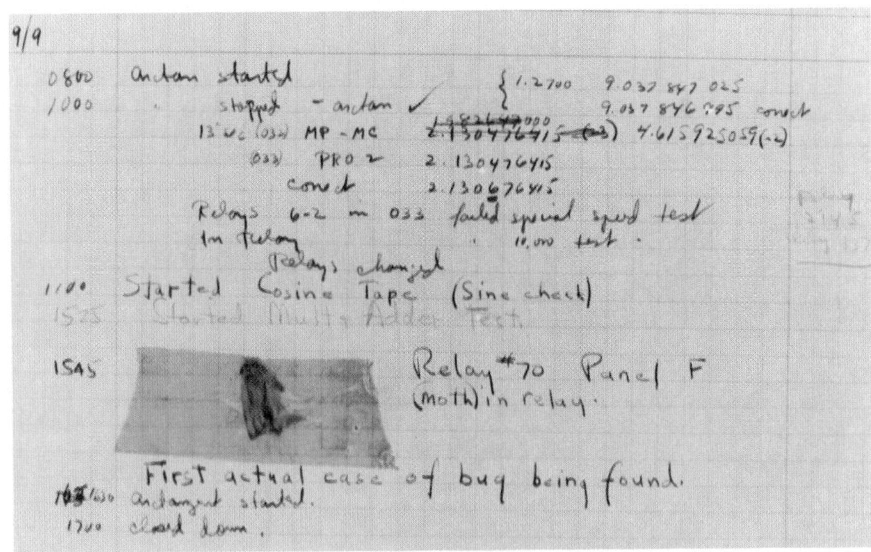

Computers and Careers

Science and Scholarship

You like the outdoors and you're looking forward to a career in environmental science or wildlife management. It's a good thing, then, that we live in an age of computer technology.

Scientists in Idaho, looking for ways to preserve the nation's diversity of plants and animals, have combined satellite images of topography and vegetation with electronic data on land ownership. The result is a mapping system that identifies habitats rich in wild species that have been poorly managed by state and federal governments. The computerized maps help natural resource administrators save money by determining which tracts of land are highest in biological richness and should be acquired before they become targets of development.

At the University of Rhode Island and Brown University, researchers have used computers to recreate the flying patterns of birds. The work has caught the interest of Federal Aviation Administration officials, who are looking into whether the research might help produce a more efficient air traffic control system.

Using computers and aerial photographs taken over five-year intervals since the 1960s, scientists are attempting to track the past movement of coastal erosion and predict yearly movements of shorelines. With this data, suggests a panel of the National Academy of Sciences, government officials could delineate beach areas with imminent, intermediate, and long-term erosion risk and limit building in those areas.

Long used to help with research in the sciences, computers have also become tools of scholarship in other fields. A few years ago, a computer researcher at New Jersey's Bell Laboratories made a discovery that may be one of the most important in the history of art. Lillian Schwartz juxtaposed a self-portrait painted by Leonardo da Vinci with his world-famous painting of the Mona Lisa and found that the eyes, hairline, cheeks, and nose were identical. From this some scholars concluded that the Mona Lisa was in fact a self-portrait by da Vinci.

An exhibition at the I.B.M. Gallery of Science and Art in New York showed that computer technology could be used to reveal new archeological insights from old ruins and artifacts. The ancient Roman port of Pompeii was buried in A.D. 79 in the volcanic eruption of Mount Vesuvius, preserving many details of everyday life. Recently, computer enhancement techniques were used to resurrect texts from charred papyrus documents found in Pompeii. Computers were also used to restore colors and background images to partially destroyed paintings. From a huge database, experts constructed a large computer-generated map of Pompeii that includes positions and shapes of buildings, baths, and other features.

Finally, computer research has been used to bring the maddeningly complex Chinese writing system into the modern world. With more than 50,000 characters, each composed of at least 1 of 214 root parts plus additional strokes, Chinese ideograms have not been adaptable to typewriters and other office technology. In the last decade, however, researchers have succeeded in designing systems that allow word processors to accommodate characters at speeds averaging 60 per minute. ■

STEP 1 — DEFINE THE PROBLEM

Sporting Life needs a computer-based payroll processing program. That's the problem. In specifying the objectives of the program you and your employees would list in great detail everything you want the program to do, which means specifying output, input, and processing requirements. For example, do you want both hardcopy and softcopy output? How often? What information must reports and checks include? Do you want to input employee data on-line and process it on-line, or will batch input and processing work better? What will be the source and format of input data? You would also specify who in your company needs to see reports, in what form, and how often.

After you have defined the problem and listed the output, input, and processing requirements, you should determine if the project is feasible; in other words, do the apparent benefits of the program outweigh the costs of preparing it? Should you proceed? And, of course, don't forget to continually document everything you do in Step 1, as well as in all subsequent steps.

STEP 2 — MAP OUT THE PROGRAM LOGIC AND DESIGN A SOLUTION

During the programming process, users must know how to express their processing requirements in the detailed terms necessary for the computer specialist to convert them into program logic. It may be easy to describe what you want accomplished to someone who is at least slightly familiar with the workings of your department. However, you would be amazed at how much detail is required to communicate to a person unfamiliar with your work exactly what to do, when to do it, and how it is to be done. And exceptions must always be accounted for — a program has to be able to take care of the rare cases as well as the routine ones.

A number of tools and techniques have been developed to assist in documenting the logic to be built into programs. We will discuss only program flowcharts, pseudocode, and top-down design, because it's unlikely that, as a general business user, you would come into direct contact with any other programming tools or techniques.

FLOWCHARTS

A **program flowchart** is a diagram that uses standard ANSI symbols to show the step-by-step processing activities and decision logic needed to solve a problem (Figure 8.15). (A *systems flowchart* maps the flow of data and information throughout an entire organization. This type of flowchart is drawn up as part of the systems development life cycle, which we will discuss in Chapter 10.) Figure 8.16 displays how a program flowchart could show the processing logic used to calculate a sales clerk's bonus at Sporting Life. The flow of logic in a flowchart normally goes from top to bottom and left to right. Arrows are used to show a change from those directions.

Although program flowcharts have some disadvantages — their preparation may be time-consuming and they can be many pages long — they are considered to be a good tool for documenting the procedures to be used in the program, and they are often included in a program's documentation package.

Pseudocode

The prefix *pseudo* means *fake*; **pseudocode,** therefore, literally means *fake code* — that is, not the code that is actually entered into the computer. Pseudocode uses normal language statements instead of symbols (such as flowchart symbols) to represent program logic. It is more precise in representing logic than regular,

Standard flowchart symbols. Programmers use plastic templates (a) to trace standard ANSI flowchart symbols when preparing plans for program design (b). **FIGURE 8.15**

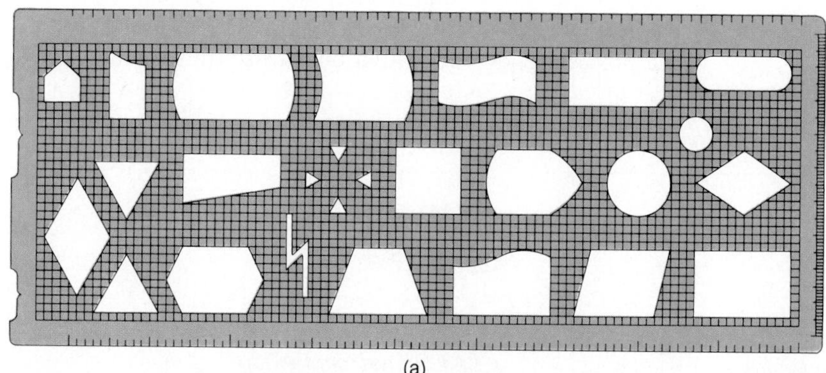

(a)

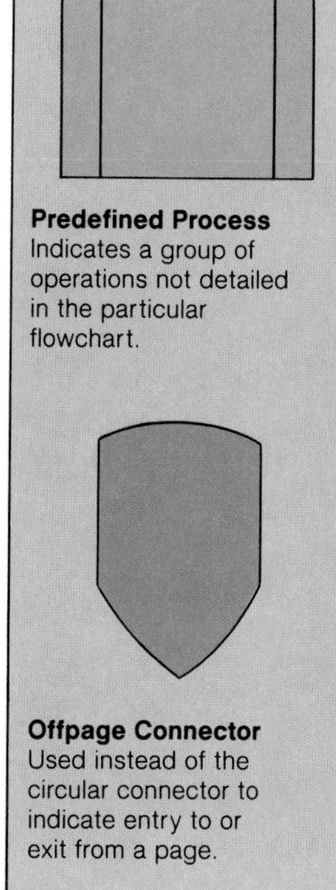
Predefined Process
Indicates a group of operations not detailed in the particular flowchart.
Offpage Connector
Used instead of the circular connector to indicate entry to or exit from a page.

Input/Output
Shows where data is input from a storage device into main memory and where information is output.
Terminal
Marks the beginning, end, or a point of interruption in a program.

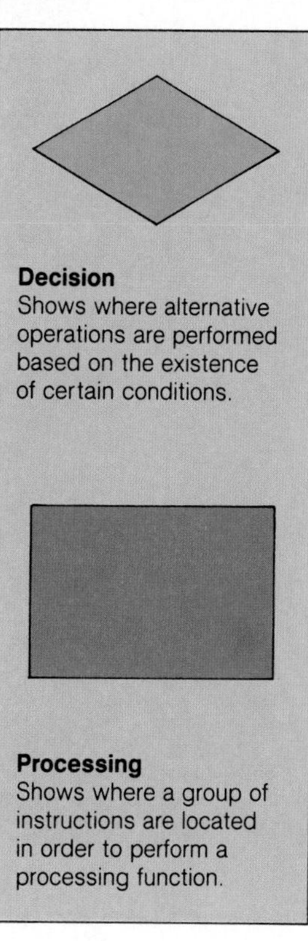
Decision
Shows where alternative operations are performed based on the existence of certain conditions.
Processing
Shows where a group of instructions are located in order to perform a processing function.

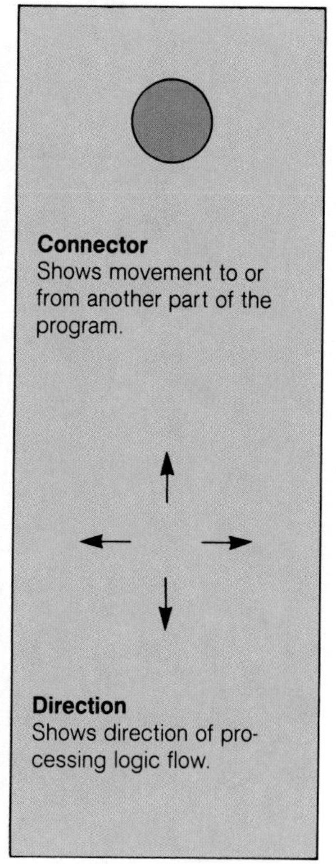
Connector
Shows movement to or from another part of the program.
Direction
Shows direction of processing logic flow.

(b)

idiomatic English but does not follow a specific programming language's syntax. Using pseudocode to document program logic is much less time consuming than flowcharting because the programmer doesn't have to spend time drawing symbols or boxes. Instead, the pseudocode statements can be composed and edited by hand or by using a typical off-the-shelf word processing program. Some people would argue further that pseudocode is much closer to actual code than are flowcharts, which makes pseudocode more productive than flowcharting. However, some programmers don't like to use pseudocode because it doesn't depict the program logic visually like a flowchart does.

Pseudocode uses four statement keywords to portray logic: IF, THEN, ELSE, and DO. Repetitive processing logic is portrayed using the statements DO WHILE (repeat an activity as long as a certain condition exists), DO UNTIL (repeat an activity until a certain condition is met), and END DO (stop repeating the activity). The processing logic is written out in narrative sentences. The logic statement

FIGURE 8.16

Logical Sporting Life bonus. This shows the processing logic necessary to calculate a clerk's bonus depending on whether actual sales exceed goals by more than 20 percent (T = true, F = false).

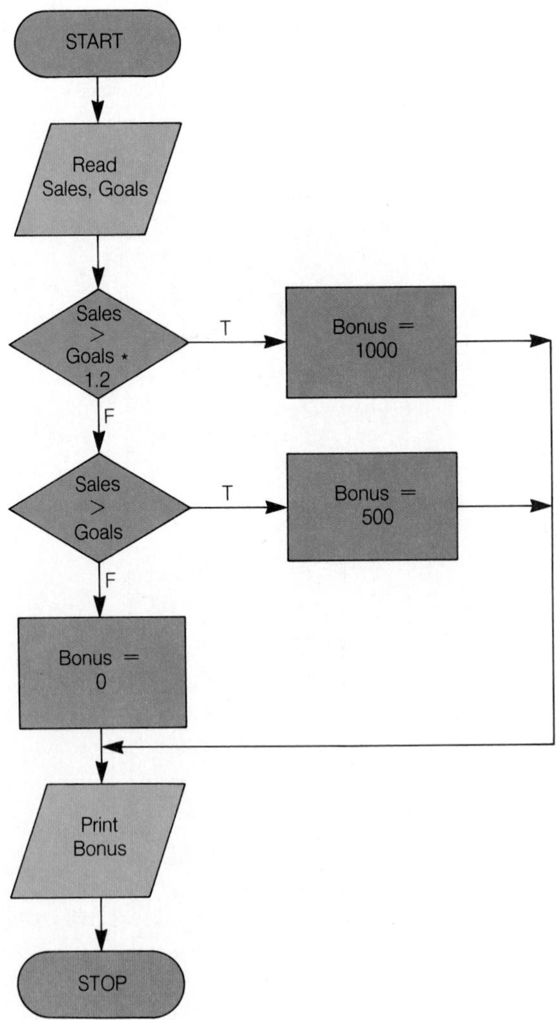

keywords are capitalized, and several levels of standard indentation are used to show decision processes and subprocesses. Figure 8.17 gives you an idea of how the keywords, statements, and indentation are used.

TOP-DOWN DESIGN

Program flowcharts, pseudocode, and the rules of a high-level language enable a programmer to design and write software that leads to predictable results that solve a problem. However, for a long time many computer scientists felt that more structure and control were needed to standardize programming and make it more exact — to change it from an art to a science. Thus, in the mid-1960s, the concept of **structured programming** was developed. Structured programming uses top-down design to "decompose" (break down) main functions into smaller ones (modules) for coding purposes.

The objective of **top-down design** is to identify the main processing steps of the program, called **modules.** (In some programming languages, modules are often referred to as **subroutines.**) If possible, each module should have only a single function, just as an English paragraph should have a single, complete thought; this forces a limit to a module's size and complexity. **Structure charts,** also called **hierarchy charts** (Figure 8.18), are often used to picture the organization and

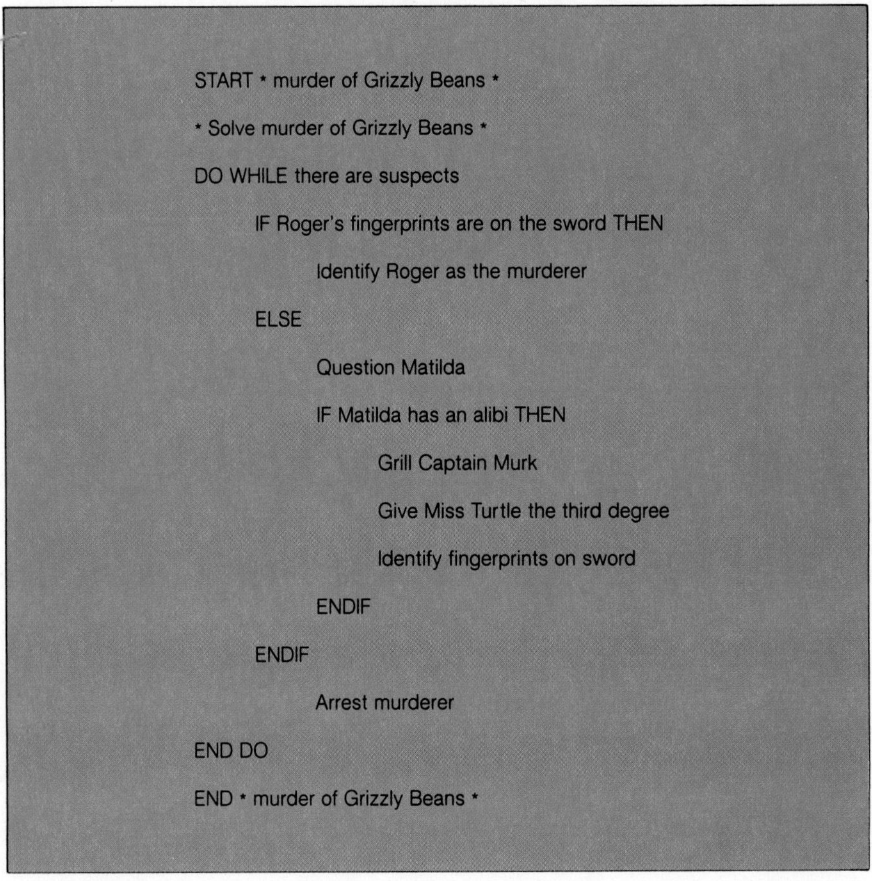

```
START * murder of Grizzly Beans *
* Solve murder of Grizzly Beans *
DO WHILE there are suspects
    IF Roger's fingerprints are on the sword THEN
        Identify Roger as the murderer
    ELSE
        Question Matilda
        IF Matilda has an alibi THEN
            Grill Captain Murk
            Give Miss Turtle the third degree
            Identify fingerprints on sword
        ENDIF
    ENDIF
        Arrest murderer
END DO
END * murder of Grizzly Beans *
```

FIGURE 8.17

Using pseudocode to solve a crime.

FIGURE 8.18 Structure chart for top-down design. In a structure chart, to perform the task given in the top of module (1.0), all substructured tasks must be performed first (for example, 2.1 and 2.2 to perform 2.0). Only one task is given each module, which represents a logical processing step.

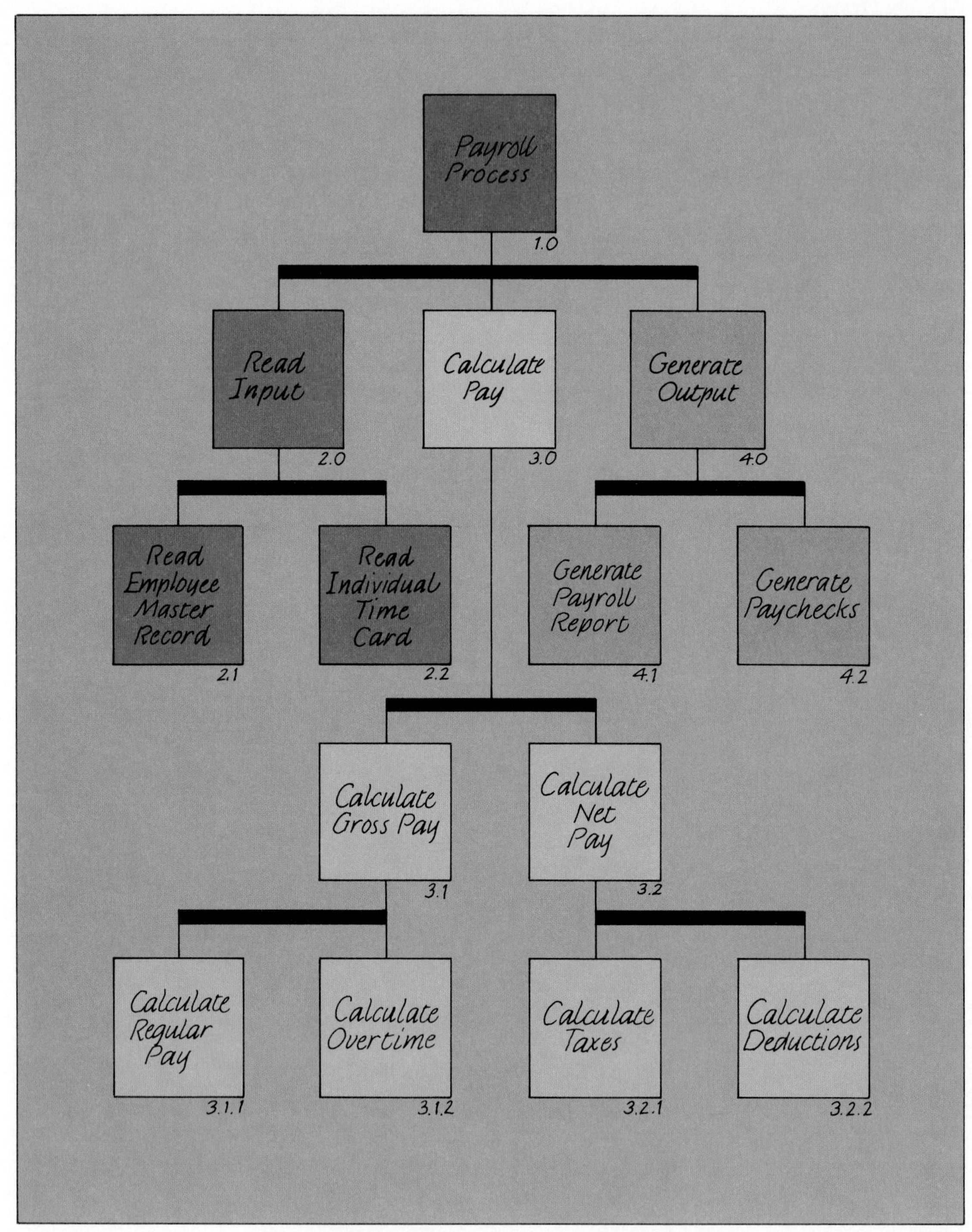

breakdown of modules. A program that is considered modular in design has the following characteristics:

1. Each module must be of manageable size; it should have less than 50 program instructions.
2. Each module should be independent and have a single function.
3. The functions of input and output are clearly defined in separate modules.
4. Each module has a single entry point (execution of the program module always starts at the same place) and a single exit point (control always leaves the module at the same place). (See Figure 8.19.)
5. If one module refers to or transfers control to another module, the latter module returns control to the point from which it was "called" by the first module.

The advantages of a modular program are:

- Complex programs can be organized into smaller and more manageable pieces in a relatively standard way.
- Programs can be modified with less effort than nonmodular programs because, when modular programming guidelines are followed carefully, each module is relatively independent and can be changed without affecting all the other parts of the program.
- A collection or library of standardized modules can be created that can be used in other programs (which saves the user money because similar processing tasks don't have to be programmed redundantly and which helps ensure accuracy because the same task is always accomplished in the same way).
- Errors in logic can be quickly isolated and fixed.

A structure chart can be used as part of a **hierarchy plus input-process-output package,** also called **HIPO**. The HIPO concept was developed by IBM as a tool for program design and documentation. It includes a visual table of contents, an overview diagram, and a detail diagram.

The **visual table of contents (VTOC)** (Figure 8.20a) includes a structure chart, a short description of the contents of the program, and a legend that provides any necessary explanations of symbols used in the overview diagram and the detail diagram.

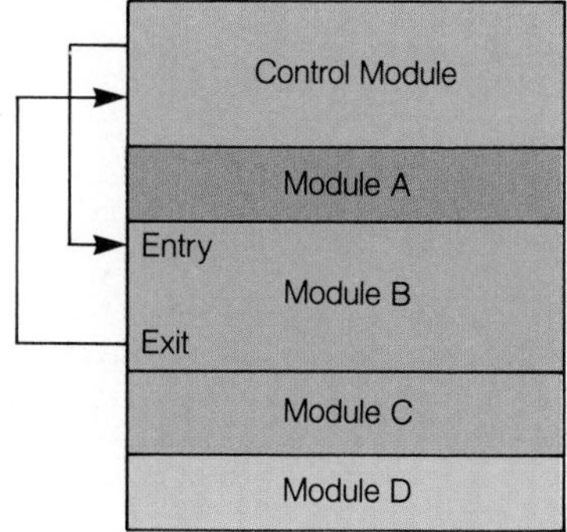

FIGURE 8.19

One way in and one way out. Each module in a top-down design has only one entry point and one exit point in the logical progression.

FIGURE 8.20

HIPOactive. A HIPO package contains a visual table of contents (a) whose module numbers are cross-referenced in the overview diagram (b) and the detail diagram (c). The overview diagram documents the input/processing/output steps of a module and the detail diagram documents the input/processing/output parts of each step.

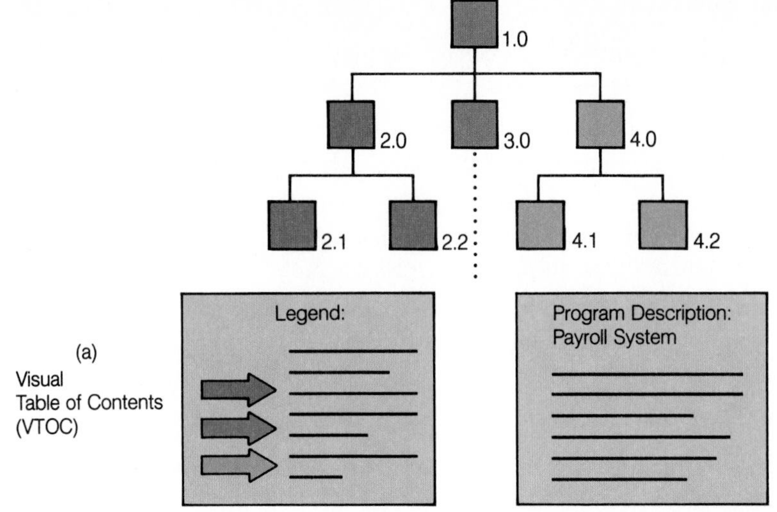

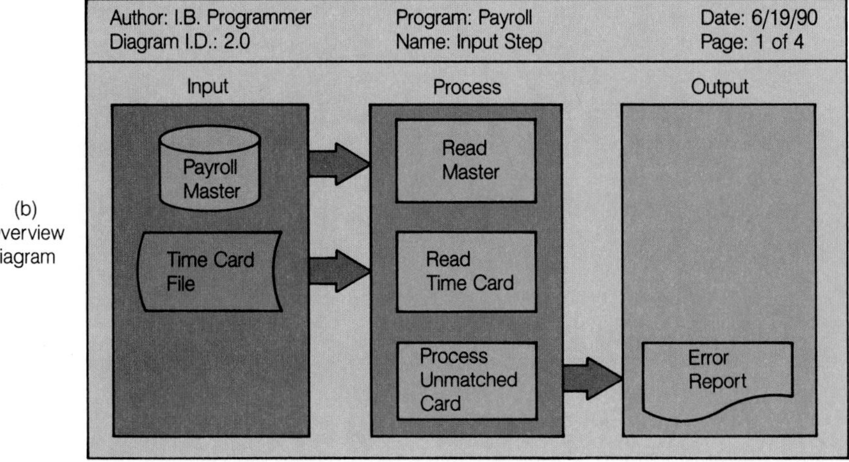

(c)
Detail
Diagram

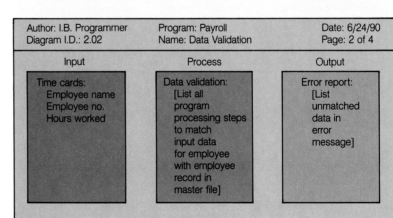

Author: I.B. Programmer
Diagram I.D.: 2.02

Program: Payroll
Name: Data Validation

Date: 6/24/90
Page: 2 of 4

Input	Process	Output
Time cards: Employee name Employee no. Hours worked	Data validation: [List all program processing steps to match input data for employee with employee record in master file]	Error report: [List unmatched data in error message]

The **overview diagram** (Figure 8.20b) shows, from left to right, the inputs, processes, and outputs for the entire program. The steps in this diagram are cross-referenced to the module numbers in the structure chart.

The **detail diagram** (Figure 8.20c) describes in detail what is done within each module.

NEATNESS COUNTS

Whether using flowcharts, pseudocode, or structure charts alone or as part of a HIPO package, programmers must be careful to make their logical maps and documentation understandable to other programmers and involved users. Figure 8.21 lists the rules to remember.

CHECK WORK IN PROGRESS

Before the program is written, or coded (Step 3), it should be subjected to initial testing to avoid costly and time-consuming changes "after the fact." This is usually done by a **structured walkthrough** — a group of programmers meets to review the logic and documentation of a program designed by another programmer in order to identify what is not clear or workable and to verify code. Systems designers and users often also attend such meetings.

STEP 3 — CODE THE PROGRAM

In this step, the programmer actually writes out the program designed in Step 2, using a high-level language. The programmer may write the program out first, using pencil and paper, or he or she may key it in directly. The programmer will follow

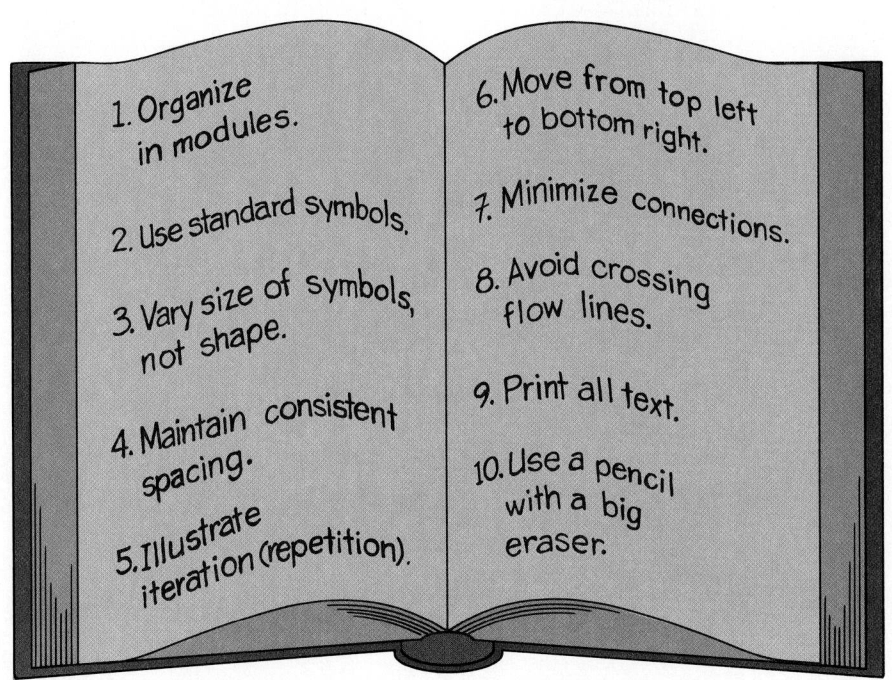

1. Organize in modules.
2. Use standard symbols.
3. Vary size of symbols, not shape.
4. Maintain consistent spacing.
5. Illustrate iteration (repetition).
6. Move from top left to bottom right.
7. Minimize connections.
8. Avoid crossing flow lines.
9. Print all text.
10. Use a pencil with a big eraser.

FIGURE 8.21

Engraved in concrete. Programmers follow these rules in order to produce clear, readable program logic documentation when they are designing a program.

FIGURE 8.22

Sequencing to get net pay. This example shows the computation of net pay using sequencing. The steps are repeated until the end of the file (EOF) is reached.

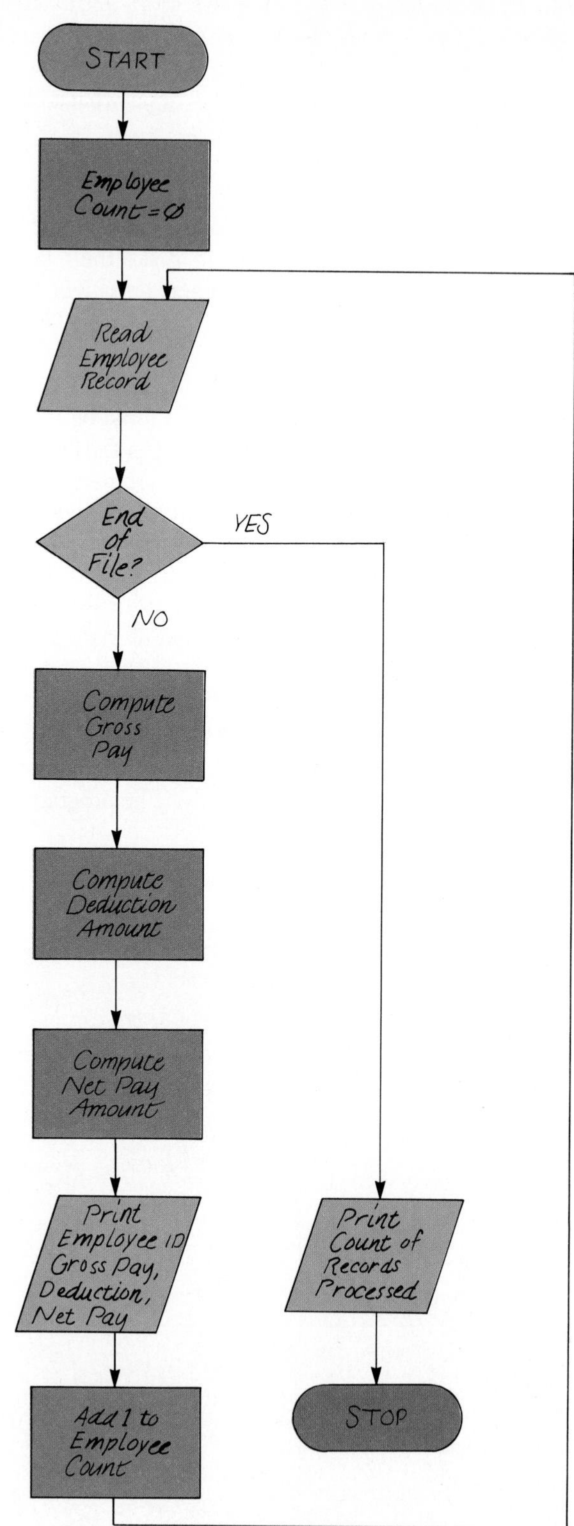

certain rigid rules and use three logic structures that are part of structured programming: sequence, selection, and iteration.

SEQUENCE

According to the **sequence control structure,** when processing begins on any program, each instruction is executed in sequence, one after the other. For example, consider the logic necessary to compute net pay (Figure 8.22). The first step is to input the number of hours worked, the pay rate, and the deduction percentage (taxes, insurance, and so on). The second step is to compute gross pay by multiplying the number of hours worked by the pay rate. The third step is to compute the deduction amount by multiplying the gross pay amount by the deduction percentage. The fourth and final step is to compute the net pay amount by subtracting the deduction amount from the gross pay amount. These events take place in sequence, one after the other, as specified.

SELECTION: IF-THEN-ELSE

The **selection (if-then-else) control structure** (Figure 8.23) allows a condition to be tested to determine which instruction(s) will be performed next; it allows the sequence control to be shifted depending on the outcome of the test. Thus, the programmer can alter the basic sequence control structure when certain conditions apply. The intent of if-then-else is to determine which of two activities is to be performed—or *selected*—as the result of testing the condition. If the condition exists—that is, if it is true—a specified event takes place. If the condition does not exist—if it is false—then the event does not take place. In other words, *if* a condition is true, *then* do a particular processing function, [or] *else* do not do it.

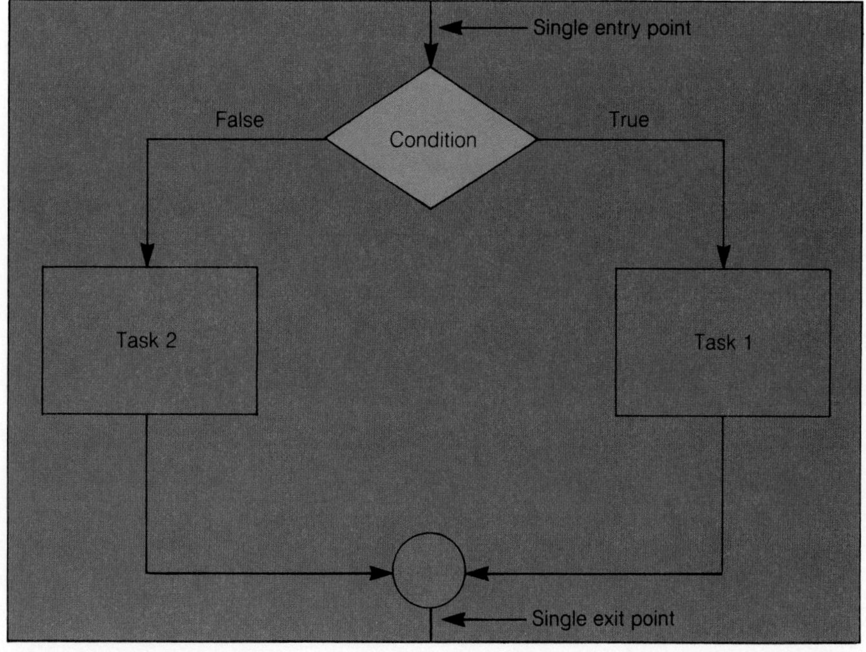

FIGURE 8.23

If-then-else control structure. If a condition is true, then one event takes place; if the event is false—that is, if it does not exist—then the event does not take place.

ITERATION: DO WHILE

The **iteration (do while) control structure** allows an activity to be repeated (iterated) as long as a certain condition remains true (Figure 8.24). Iteration is often referred to as a **loop,** because the program will keep repeating the activity until the condition becomes false. Loops simplify programming because they enable the programmer to specify certain instructions only once and have the computer execute them many times.

STEP 4—TEST THE PROGRAM: GETTING THE BUGS OUT

Even though a program is carefully designed and coded, it cannot be relied on to produce accurate information until it has been thoroughly tested. The object of testing is to "break" the program. If the program can be made to *not* work—that is, if it can be fed data that either halts the program prematurely or gives unexpected

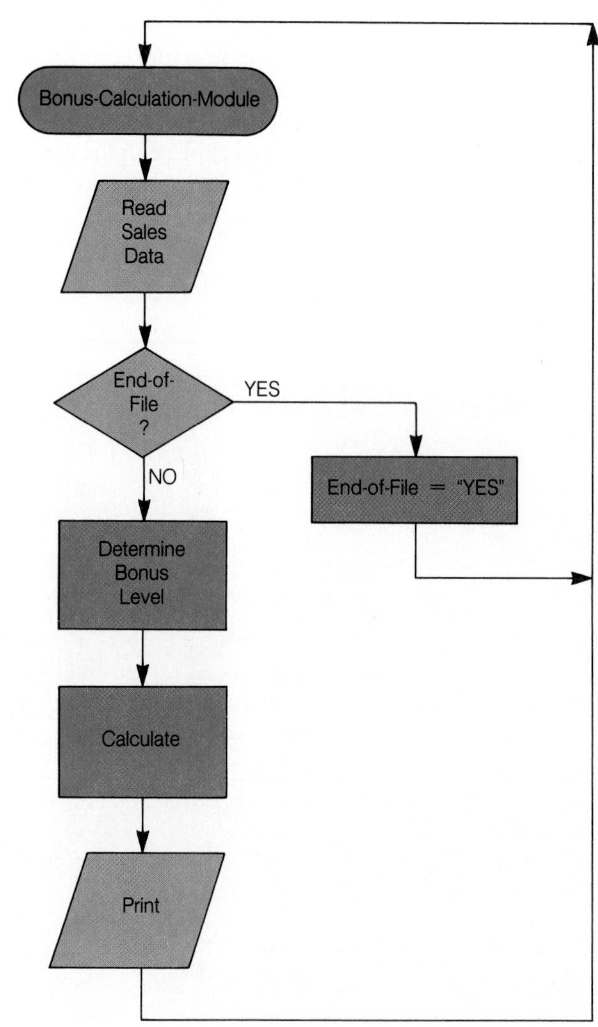

FIGURE 8.24

Iteration. As long as salespeople are listed for whom bonuses must be calculated, the program repeats the activity—the "loop" shown in the drawing. The Bonus-Calculation Module will be performed only *while* the end-of-file marker is set to "No." Before performing this module, the program sets the marker to "No." Once the module sets the marker to "Yes," the module is no longer performed.

answers—that means it has "bugs" that must be eliminated. When a program has passed all the necessary tests, the user can rely on the continued integrity of the results produced by the program.

The tests that the program must pass include the following:

- Structured walkthrough.
- Desk checking—A programmer proofreads a printout of the program line by line looking for syntax and logic errors. A **syntax error** is caused by typographical errors and incorrect use of the programming language. A **logic error** is caused by not using the correct control structures (sequencing, selection, and iteration) in the proper manner.
- Translation attempt—The program is run through the computer using a language processor. Before the program will run, it must be free of syntax errors. Any syntax errors will be identified by the translator.
- Sample data test—After all syntax errors have been corrected, sample data is run through the program to test each program statement.

Of course, all testing procedures and results should be documented.

STEP 5—COLLATE THE DOCUMENTATION

Program documentation should have been going on since the very beginning of program development. The importance of this step cannot be overemphasized. Without documentation, programmers may not be able to update the program in the future; diagnosis of problems will be difficult; identifying and eliminating any remaining bugs will be nightmarish; and users will have no instructions for using the program.

Program documentation should provide the following:

- A permanent record of what the program does.
- Instructions for program users on how to interact with the program.
- Instructions for computer operators on how to organize and control the processing of the program.
- Detailed documentation required to modify the program to meet new requirements.

As you can see, program documentation is required at several levels: user documentation, technical documentation, and operator's instructions.

User documentation is required for programs that have the user interacting directly with the computer during operation—such as entering data into the system, directing the processing, and requesting reports. User documentation usually consists of simple step-by-step procedures that describe what the user is to do and how to do it plus report descriptions and sample output.

Technical documentation consists of a number of items prepared during the development of the program, including:

- A narrative overview of what the program does.
- A series of flowcharts or paragraphs of pseudocode depicting processing logic. (Sometimes a combination of both are used.)

- Examples of all reports produced by the program.
- Examples of any display screen activity such as menus or softcopy reports.
- A listing of the program language statements.

Operator's instructions are required for programs that are run on large computer systems. These instructions identify exactly what is required for the computer operator to prepare the program to process, and they explain what steps are to be followed during processing, including what to do about error messages. (For microcomputers, such instructions are included in the user documentation.)

As we have stated, the absence of good program documentation can create problems. Users can become frustrated when they try to work with the program. Programmers can have a very difficult time modifying programs they did not create if the documentation is inadequate. If a program is lost, it cannot be reconstructed without good documentation. And the need for good documentation doesn't apply just to custom-written programs: Be sure your microcomputer software comes with adequate documentation manuals!

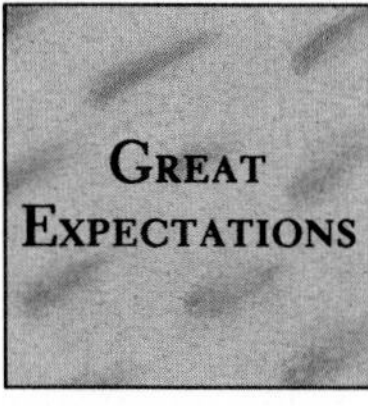

Some programmers and other types of computer professionals believe that programming is best left to the professionals and that businesspeople are better at managing and operating businesses. However, other programmers today think that the direction of the future is veering away from procedural language programming so sharply that, except for program updating and maintenance, the need will clearly decrease for programmers in today's sense. In other words, fourth- and fifth-generation programming languages, with their human language interfaces, will allow more and more nonprofessional programmers to write programs that will do just what they want them to do.

Also, more and more of the third-generation procedural programming languages will have improved speed and flexibility and, like Turbo Pascal, QuickBASIC, and Turbo C 2.0, will combine the best features of interpreters and compilers. This combination means that a program can be run all at once after it has been written (compiler's speed), but the user/programmers can stop the program when a bug appears, correct the bug, and then proceed with the program (interpreter's line-by-line correction feature). Even today, many microcomputer users are using improved versions of third-generation languages to create their own software. Whether or not you choose to do it yourself will be dictated not by how much programming knowledge and experience you acquire but by your budgets for time and money—or by the supportiveness of the company you work for.

ONWARD: SPREADING THE WORD

Now that you have an idea of how computer software programs are created, we will examine how special types of programs are used to support the use of certain hardware for connectivity—that is, for data communications.

SUMMARY

Users need to know what software development tools, or programming languages, are used to create software. If you need additional processing capabilities that can't be satisfied by an off-the-shelf applications software program, you should know how to choose — or help a computer specialist to choose — the software development tool that can most efficiently and effectively satisfy your requirements.

Programming languages can be divided into five generations. Machine language, the only language the computer's processor can understand, is first-generation language — the digits 0 and 1. Assembly language, easier to work with than machine language because it allows the programmer to use abbreviations, is a second-generation language. (Both machine and assembly language are low-level languages.) High-level, or third-generation, languages were developed to make writing software programs even easier by using human-language (for example, English-like) statements. Of the hundreds of high-level languages used today, the following are some of the more popular:

- FORTRAN (FORmula TRANslator): the first high-level language, which was formulated for scientific and mathematical applications; this language does not handle the input and output of large volumes of data efficiently. It is not as structured as COBOL.
- COBOL (COmmon Business Oriented Language): its development as a common programming language for business applications was funded by the U.S. government; this language is noted for its machine independence and its data processing and file-handling capabilities.
- PL/1 (Programming Language 1): designed to combine the computational capabilities of FORTRAN and the data processing and file-handling capabilities of COBOL. Although flexible, it is harder to learn than COBOL and requires a great deal of main storage.
- BASIC (Beginner's All-purpose Symbolic Instruction Code): developed at Dartmouth College for instructional purposes, but now used on microcomputers and certain business systems to solve a variety of relatively simple problems.
- RPG (Report Program Generator): introduced by IBM as a program geared to deal with clear-cut problems and produce reports; users can produce reports by filling out special coding forms and then entering the recorded data.
- C: developed by Bell Laboratories as a tool for writing systems software such as UNIX. It works on a variety of different computers, including microcomputers. However, it is not good for checking types of data, and it has no input/output routines.
- Pascal: named for 17th-century French mathematician Blaise Pascal. Developed to teach structured programming, it has strong mathematical, scientific, and graphics processing capabilities and can be used on large and small computer systems; not used extensively in business.
- Modula-2: an improved version of Pascal; better suited for business; used primarily to write systems software.

- Ada: named for Augusta Ada, Countess of Lovelace (the first programmer), and developed by the U.S. Department of Defense for use as an embedded system in computer-based weapons systems.

Fourth-generation languages do not rely on a long list of detailed procedures that tell the computer *how* to do something. They just use human-language statements to tell the computer *what* to do. The five basic types of fourth-generation language tools are (1) query languages, (2) report generators, (3) applications generators, (4) decision support systems and financial planning languages, and (5) some microcomputer applications software.

Natural languages, which some people refer to as fifth-generation languages, allow users and programmers to interact with the computer by using human-language patterns, including misspellings and mistakes.

The advantages and disadvantages of each programming language relative to the information and systems needs of a company should be analyzed before a programmer begins a programming project.

Most of the foregoing software development tools are commonly used by computer specialists—programmers—to write software programs. However, users have some relatively new microcomputer software packages, including electronic spreadsheets and database management systems, at their fingertips to help them create customized programs to solve unique needs. These packages are so much easier to use than typical programming languages and procedures that often users who have used a computer for just a few hours can develop their own simple applications software.

Regardless of whether a software program is being developed using a high-level programming language or an integrated microcomputer software package, the same steps should be taken once the program requirements have been established: (1) define the problem; (2) map out the program logic—that is, work out the necessary algorithms; (3) code the program; (4) test the program; and (5) document the program.

Many tools and techniques are used to document program logic, including program flowcharts, pseudocode, structure charts, and HIPO packages.

Program flowcharts use standard symbols to represent the step-by-step activities and decision logic needed to solve a processing problem. Logic flow normally goes from top to bottom and left to right.

Pseudocode is a "fake" code—that is, human-language statements that use the structure of the programming language statements to describe instructions but without being hard to understand. Pseudocode uses four keywords to portray logic: IF, THEN, ELSE, and DO. Repetitive processing logic is represented by DO WHILE, DO UNTIL, and END DO.

Structure charts diagram the hierarchy of program modules, each of which represents one processing step. HIPO (hierarchy plus input-processing-output) packages include a structure chart of the program in its visual table of contents along with a program description and a legend. The HIPO package also includes an overview diagram, which shows the input-processing-output activities of the program modules, and a detail diagram, which shows the steps of each activity in a module.

Programmers use structured programming techniques. Structured programming relies heavily on the concept of modularity (top-down design) and uses three basic control structures to form the program code: (1) sequence, (2) selection (if-then-else), and (3) iteration, or looping (do while).

The sequence control structure determines that each program instruction is executed in sequence unless a particular instruction is intended to alter that sequence.

The selection control structure allows a condition to be tested (IF) to determine which instruction(s) will be performed next (THEN or ELSE). Using this structure, the programmer can alter the basic sequence structure.

The iteration control structure (looping) allows an activity to be repeated as long as a certain condition remains true. Loops simplify programming because they enable the programmer to specify instructions only once to have the computer execute them many times.

After a program has been designed, it is tested by a structured walkthrough (formal review of a programmer's work by other programmers, systems designers, and users before it is coded). Then, after the program is coded, it must be tested by structured walkthrough, desk checking (programmer proofreads a printout of the program), translation attempt, and sample data test. Testing is done to weed out syntax errors, caused by typographical mistakes and incorrect use of the programming language, and logic errors, caused by incorrect use of control structures (sequencing, selection, iteration).

Program documentation should be done throughout the five steps of program development. User documentation, technical documentation, and operator's instructions provide guidance for all those who must use, maintain, and modify the program.

KEY TERMS

Ada, p. 307
algorithm, p. 315
American National Standards Institute (ANSI), p. 301
applications generator, p. 311
assembly language, p. 299
BASIC (Beginner's All-purpose Symbolic Instruction Code), p. 304
C, p. 306
COBOL (COmmon Business Oriented Language), p. 302
decision support system, p. 312
desk checking, p. 316
detail diagram, p. 325
fifth-generation language, p. 312
financial planning language, p. 312
first-generation language, p. 299
FORTRAN (FORmula TRANslator), p. 301
fourth-generation language (4GL), p. 309
hierarchy chart, p. 321
hierarchy plus input-process-output (HIPO) package, p. 323
International Standards Organization (ISO), p. 301
iteration (do while) control structure, p. 328
logic error, p. 329
loop, p. 328
Modula-2, p. 307
module, p. 321
natural language, p. 312
nonprocedural language, p. 309
overview diagram, p. 325
Pascal, p. 306
PL/1 (Programming Language 1), p. 303
procedural language, p. 300
program flowchart, p. 318

pseudocode, p. 319
query language, p. 310
report generator, p. 311
RPG (Report Program Generator), p. 305
second-generation language, p. 299
selection (if-then-else) control structure, p. 327
sequence control structure, p. 327
structure chart, p. 321
structured programming, p. 321
structured walkthrough, p. 325
subroutine, p. 321
syntax, p. 297
syntax error, p. 329
third-generation language, p. 300
top-down design, p. 321
visual table of contents (VTOC), p. 323

EXERCISES

MATCHING

Match each of the following terms to the phrase that is the most closely related.

1. _____ syntax
2. _____ third-generation language
3. _____ query language
4. _____ ANSI
5. _____ natural language
6. _____ COBOL
7. _____ fourth-generation languages
8. _____ program flowchart
9. _____ report generator
10. _____ applications generator
11. _____ first-generation language
12. _____ pseudocode
13. _____ BASIC
14. _____ Pascal
15. _____ nonprocedural language

a. High-level language used for creating business applications software
b. Rules for using a language
c. Use of this type of software greatly reduces the time it takes to produce an entire software application.
d. Machine language
e. High-level language that was developed for instructional purposes
f. This type of code isn't actually input to the computer but is used for documenting program logic.
g. High-level language that was developed to teach structured programming
h. Query languages, report generators, applications generators, decision support systems, and financial planning languages
i. This generation of languages was the first to use English-like statements.
j. Fifth-generation language
k. This type of software gives the user greater control of the output format of information retrieved from a database.
l. This type of language allows the user to retrieve information from a database using English-like statements.
m. American National Standards Institute
n. This type of language allows users to specify what the computer is supposed to do without having to specify how the computer is supposed to do it.
o. Diagram that uses ANSI symbols to document a program's processing activities and logic

MULTIPLE CHOICE

1. Which of the following generations of languages will likely include the languages of the future?
   a. first generation
   b. second generation
   c. third generation
   d. fourth generation
   e. fifth generation
2. Which of the following uses English-like statements to represent program logic?
   a. flowcharts
   b. ANSI symbols
   c. pseudocode
   d. algorithms
   e. assembly language
3. Which of the following generations does natural language fall into?
   a. first generation
   b. second generation
   c. third generation
   d. fourth generation
   e. fifth generation
4. Which of the following relates to machine language?
   a. difficult to learn
   b. first-generation language
   c. machine-dependent
   d. instructions and data are represented by binary digits
   e. all the above
5. Which of the following might prevent a program from being modified in the future?
   a. logic errors
   b. pseudocode
   c. lack of program documentation
   d. syntax errors
   e. language processor
6. Which of the following is used to speed up the process of designing the initial version of a software program?
   a. ANSI
   b. BASIC
   c. compiler
   d. applications generator
   e. all the above
7. Which of the following helped develop standards for high-level programming languages?
   a. ANSI
   b. BASIC
   c. compiler
   d. applications generator
   e. ASCII

8. The language that doesn't require the user to learn a specific vocabulary or syntax is:
   a. RPG
   b. FORTRAN
   c. COBOL
   d. BASIC
   e. Pascal
9. Which of the following is a high-level language?
   a. Ada
   b. BASIC
   c. COBOL
   d. FORTRAN
   e. all the above
10. Which of the following allows users to specify what the computer is supposed to do rather than how the computer is supposed to do it?
    a. nonprocedural language
    b. FORTRAN
    c. BASIC
    d. COBOL
    e. procedural language

SHORT ANSWER

1. How do third-generation languages differ from first- and second-generation languages?
2. What is natural language?
3. Why is it relevant to users to know what software development tools, or programming languages, are used to create software?
4. What are the main characteristics of machine language?
5. What are the five main types of fourth-generation language tools?
6. What were the reasons behind the development of high-level programming languages?
7. How does a programmer decide what language should be used to write a particular program?
8. What is the difference between procedural and nonprocedural languages?
9. What is the purpose of a report generator?
10. Why should the user understand how a computer programmer develops software using a high-level language?

PROJECTS

1. Visit the computer laboratory at your school.
   a. Identify which high-level languages are available.
   b. Determine if each language processor identified is a compiler or an interpreter.

c. Determine if the language processors are available for microcomputers, larger computers, or both.
d. Identify any microcomputer-based electronic spreadsheet software and database management system software available.

2. Scan the employment ads in a few major newspapers and report on the procedural programming languages most in demand. For what types of jobs?

Chapter 9

Data Communications

Getting from here to there has always fascinated human beings, going farther and doing it faster. Aside from the thrills associated with speed, going places quickly means being able to stay connected with other people, to spread news and information and receive them in return—in other words, to *communicate*. Obviously, technology reached the point some time ago of allowing communication to occur without having to transport people from one place to another. But what about more recent developments? And what do they have to do with computers in business and the management of data and information? This chapter will explain how electronic data communications affects the business user.

Preview

When you have completed this chapter, you will be able to:

- Identify the basic characteristics of data transmission.
- Describe basic communications hardware in general terms.
- Explain what a communications network is and describe the typical network configurations.
- List some of the communications services available to personal computer users.
- Describe the basic operation and uses of a fax machine.
- Briefly explain what computer viruses are and what can be done about them.

The User Perspective

The wheel, which is thought to have been invented around 3500 B.C., was a tremendous technological advancement; without it or a similar invention, information probably would still be transported by people on foot or horseback, by smoke signals or drum sounds, or by carrier pigeon. By now, however, people have refined the technology of motion to the point where mobility has become a way of life.

The invention of the computer and its introduction into the business environment in the early 1950s marked a similar technological achievement. By the early 1960s, some information needed for business was available in computer-usable form "somewhere"; however, it may have been impractical for one to get it if the information needed was only available in a computer 1,000 miles away. Modern **electronic communications**—the movement of voice and data over long distances through the use of computers and telecommunications channels and equipment—has solved this problem.

You will encounter innumerable situations in the business environment that require data to be sent to, retrieved from, or shared among different locations. For example, you might:

- Send electronic "mail" to another user in the company or to a business contact anywhere in the world, and receive electronic mail on your own computer.
- Share the same database management software and database with other users.
- Share hardware such as printers and secondary storage devices with other users.
- Share processing power, such as a company mainframe, with other users.
- Access data in a huge commercial subscription database with data on almost any subject, using your own computer equipment and telephone lines.
- Participate in teleconferences with people scattered around the world.
- Order equipment or travel services simply by using your computer.
- Deal with banks and suppliers by using your computer.
- Schedule meetings automatically by instructing your computer to consult with other users' computers.
- Participate in decisions about establishing or expanding local area networks that your company or business will use.

What Does It Take to Communicate?

To transmit or receive data, you must have special hardware—that is, a transmission method, which we will discuss shortly—as well as access to a telephone line or other transmission medium and special communications software on-line at both the sending and receiving locations. Learning to use the hardware and software involved in data communications in normal business situations is not difficult; in this chapter we will explain what they do.

CHARACTERISTICS OF DATA TRANSMISSION

When you are talking on the phone with another person who is a few houses away, you can probably hear that person clearly and do not need to speak loudly. However, sometimes the farther away you are from the person, the harder it is to hear clearly what is being said because of static and other noise. A lot of noise increases the chance that parts of your message will be garbled or misinterpreted. This same problem can exist when data is transmitted over phone lines from computer to computer. To overcome this problem, alternative types of computer-based data transmission have been developed, including satellite and microwave—although they are not without their own limitations, as you will see later on. But before we discuss the various methods of data communications, we need to discuss their common characteristics.

ANALOG AND DIGITAL SIGNALS

When we speak, we transmit continuous sound waves, or **analog signals,** that form what we call our "voice" (Figure 9.1). Analog signals could be compared to a steady stream of water coming out of a garden hose. These signals repeat a certain number of times over a certain time period; this is called their **frequency,** which is measured in cycles per second, or *hertz*. Sometimes our voices sound high (composed of high-frequency sound waves) and sometimes our voices sound low (composed of low-frequency sound waves). Analog signals can also differ in **amplitude,** or loudness; a soft voice is at low amplitude. Telephone lines are currently an analog communications medium.

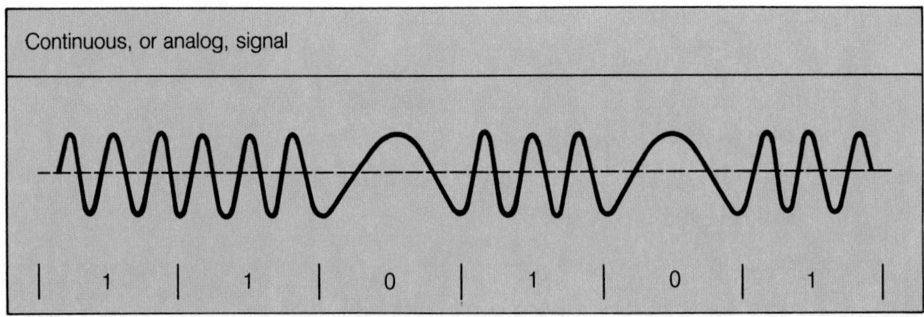

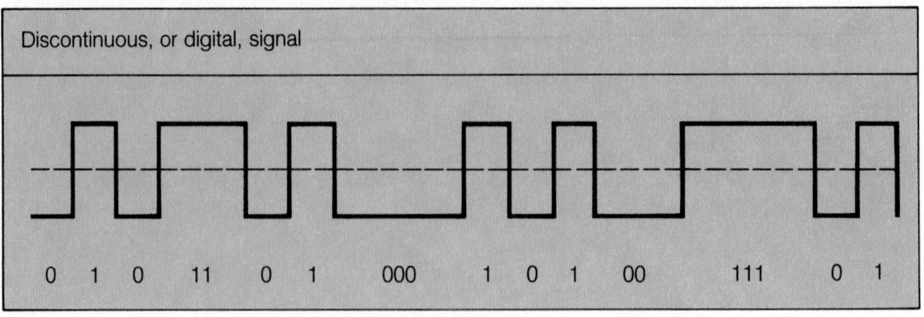

FIGURE 9.1

Analog and digital signals. Analog signals are continuous waves whose patterns vary to represent the message being transmitted; digital signals are discontinuous, or discrete, bursts that form a transmission pattern. In this figure, the horizontal axis represents time, and the vertical axis represents amplitude.

Digital signals, in contrast, can be compared to the short bursts of water that shoot out of a timed garden sprinkler. These signals are discontinuous (discrete) pulses over a transmission medium (Figure 9.1). Computers communicate with each other in streams of binary digits (bits) transmitted in patterns of digital signals —a series of on and off electrical pulses. For data to travel from one computer to another across the phone lines, the sending computer's digital data must be converted into analog form and then reconverted into digital form at the receiving end—modulation and demodulation.

Modulation refers to the process of converting digital signals into analog form so that data can be sent over the phone lines. **Demodulation** is the process of converting the analog signals back into digital form so that they can be processed by the receiving computer. The hardware that performs modulation and demodulation is called a **modem** (*mo*dulate/*dem*odulate); we'll describe modems in more detail later in the chapter. The sending computer must be connected to a modem that modulates the transmitted data, while the receiving computer must be connected to a modem to demodulate the data (Figure 9.2). Both modems are also connected to the telephone line.

MODE OF TRANSMISSION: ASYNCHRONOUS AND SYNCHRONOUS

When signals are transmitted through modems from one computer to another, patterns of bits coded to represent data (Chapter 4) are sent one bit at a time at irregular intervals, as the user inputs data. How does the receiving device know where one character ends and another starts? In **asynchronous transmission,** also called *start-stop transmission*, each string of bits that make up a character is bracketed by control bits (Figure 9.3a). In effect, each group of digital or analog signals making up the code for one character is individually "wrapped" in an electronic

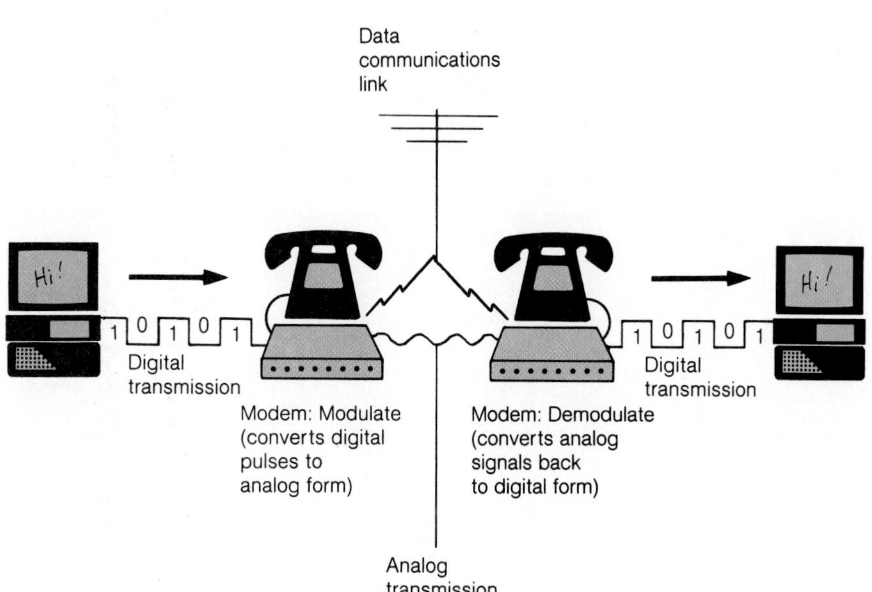

FIGURE 9.2

Helping computers wave to each other. Modems are hardware devices that translate digital signals into analog waves for transmission over phone lines and then back into digital signals for processing.

"envelope" made of a start bit, one or two stop bits, and an error check bit (or parity bit). The error check bit is set according to a parity scheme that can be odd or even. (Chapter 5 explains that this means that the total number of bits representing a character must always be odd or always be even.)

For example, an ASCII "G" would be represented as 00100011100, which has an even number of data bits in the on position (symbolized by a 1). If an odd parity scheme is being used, then the start, stop, and error check bits would be set so that the overall total of bits in the on position would be odd—00100011101, per Figure 9.3a.

Because asynchronous communication is inexpensive, it is widely used; however, it is also relatively slow, because of the number of parity and error check bits that must be transmitted with the data bits.

In **synchronous transmission** (Figure 9.3b), characters can be sent much faster because they are sent as blocks. Header and trailer bytes, called **synch bytes,** are inserted as identifiers at the beginnings and the ends of blocks. Synchronous transmission is used by large computers to transmit huge volumes of data at high speeds. Expensive and complex timing devices must be used to keep the transmission activities synchronized.

Most microcomputers are not equipped to handle synchronous data transmission without the use of special hardware and software. However, users recognize that synchronous transmission allows them to quickly download files from the

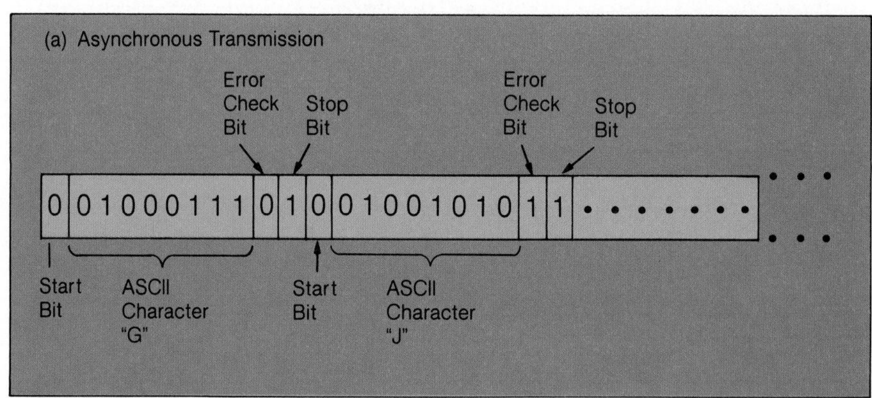

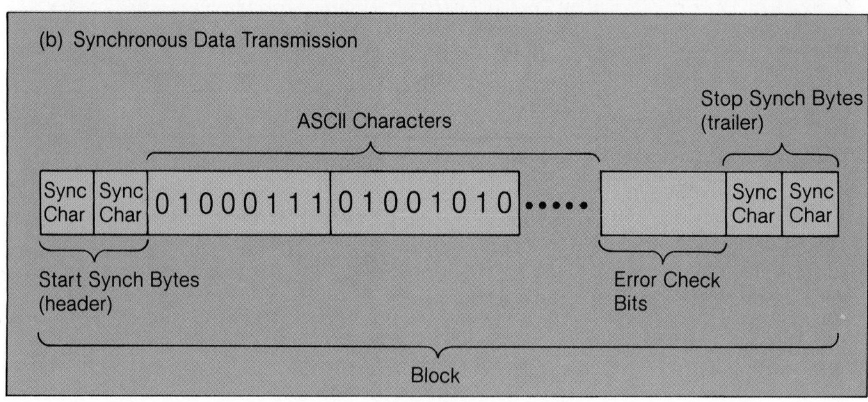

FIGURE 9.3

Asynchronous and synchronous transmission. So that devices receiving data transmission can decode the beginnings and ends of data strings and check for transmission errors, the character strings are transmitted asynchronously (a) or synchronously (b). Synchronous transmission takes less time because groups of characters are transmitted as blocks with no start and stop bits between characters.

company's main computer system into their microcomputers and to upload data that has been initially captured on these microcomputers to the company's main computer system, thus avoiding duplication of data entry on both systems. As a result, microcomputer users often purchase add-on boards—for example, the IRMA 3 board (Figure 9.4) manufactured by Digital Communications Associates—that provide the microcomputer user with the hardware capabilities necessary for synchronous transmission (PC hookups to minis and mainframes). The necessary software to use the board is usually packaged separately; it facilitates the file conversions from mainframe to microcomputer format. Once converted, a microcomputer applications software program can be used to retrieve the file.

Direction of Transmission: Simplex, Half-Duplex, and Full-Duplex

Besides signal type (analog or digital) and manner of data transmission (synchronous or asynchronous), data communications technology must also consider the *direction* of data traffic flow supported by communications links such as modems. In the **simplex** mode, data can travel in only one direction at all times (Figure 9.5). For example, in some museum settings, environmental devices send information about temperature, humidity, and other conditions to a computer that monitors and adjusts office environmental settings automatically. However, the computer does not send information back to the devices. The simplex mode is also used occasionally in some local area networks, which we will discuss later.

A **half-duplex** communications link can support two-way traffic, but data can travel in only one direction at one time (Figure 9.5). This mode of transmission is similar to using a walkie-talkie. When you press the transmit button you can talk, but you cannot receive. After you release the transmit button, you can receive, but you cannot transmit. Transmission of data in this mode over long distances can greatly

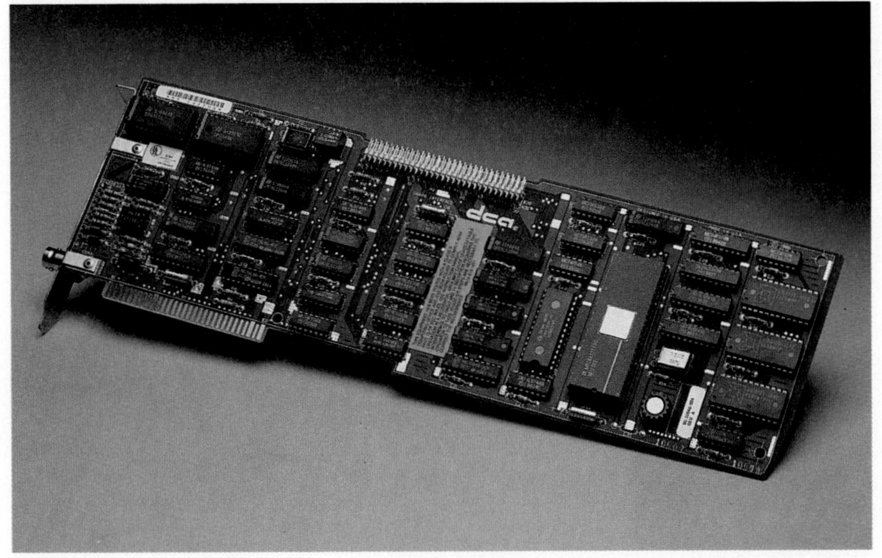

FIGURE 9.4

My friend IRMA. An IRMA 3 add-on board, inserted into an expansion slot inside the microcomputer cabinet, allows the user to download files from and send files (upload) to minis and mainframes, using synchronous transmission.

increase the time it takes to communicate data. This delay is due to three factors: (1) the time needed for device A (at the receiving end) to change from receive mode to transmit mode, (2) the time required for device A to transmit a message to device B requesting confirmation that all is ready for transmission, and (3) the time required for device A to receive the confirmation that device B is ready to receive. The half-duplex transmission mode is most commonly used between a central computer system and the terminals connected to it.

Full-duplex transmission sends data in both directions simultaneously, similar to two trains passing each other in different directions on side-by-side tracks (Figure 9.5). This transmission mode eliminates the problem of transmission delay, but it is more expensive than the other two modes. However, when high-speed communication between computers and peripherals is necessary, the expense may be worthwhile.

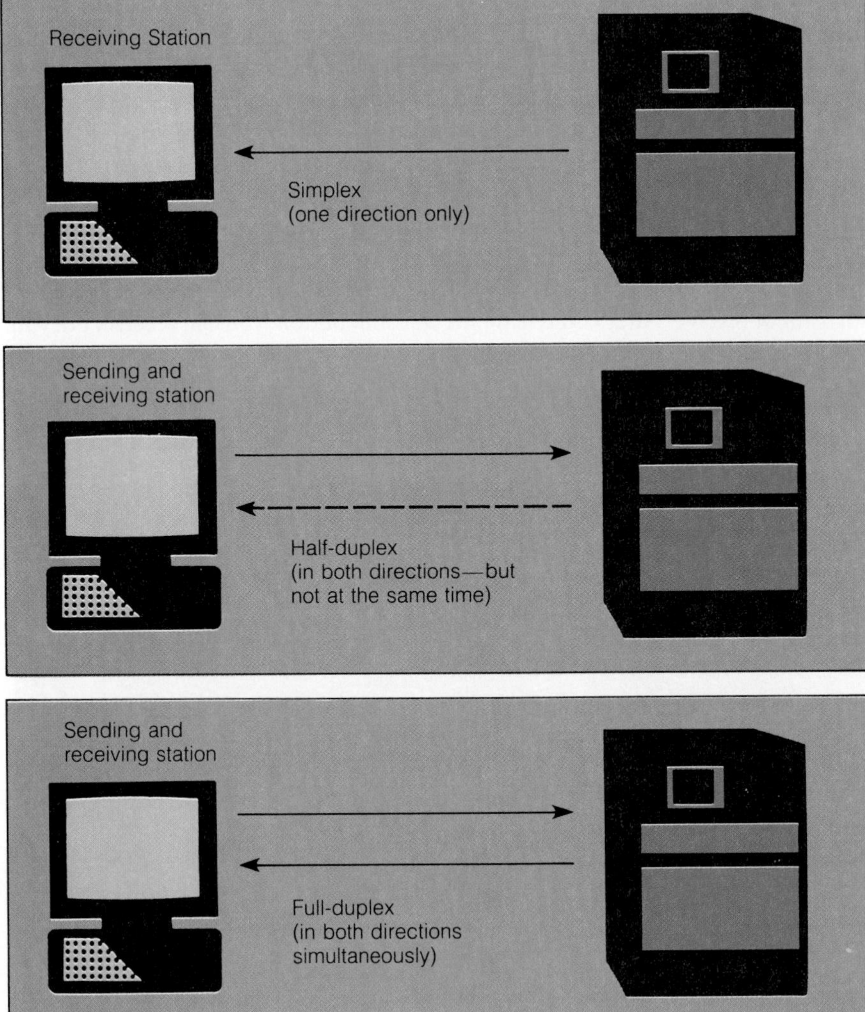

FIGURE 9.5

Two-way, one-way, or the only way. Data traffic moves in simplex, half-duplex, or full-duplex modes.

DATA TRANSMISSION MEDIA

To get from here to there, data must move *through* something. A telephone line, a cable, or the atmosphere are all transmission *media*, or *channels*. But before the data can be communicated, it must be converted into a form suitable for communication. The three basic forms into which data can be converted for communication are:

1. Electrical pulses or charges (used to transmit voice and data over telephone lines).
2. Electromagnetic waves (similar to radio waves).
3. Pulses of light.

The form or method of communications affects the maximum rate at which data can be moved through the channel and the level of noise that will exist—for example, light pulses travel faster than electromagnetic waves, and some types of satellite transmission systems are less noisy than transmission over telephone wires. Obviously, some situations require that data be moved as fast as possible; others don't. Channels that move data relatively slowly, like telegraph lines, are *narrowband* channels. Most telephone lines are *voiceband* channels, and they have a wider bandwidth than narrowband channels. *Broadband* channels (like coaxial cable, fiber optic cable, microwave circuits, and satellite systems) transmit large volumes of data at high speeds.

The transmission media used to support data transmission are telephone lines, coaxial cables, microwave systems, satellite systems, and fiber optic cables. Understanding how these media function will help you sort out the various rates and charges for them and determine which is the most appropriate in a given situation.

TELEPHONE LINES

The earliest type of telephone line was referred to as *open wire*—unsheathed copper wires strung on telephone poles and secured by glass insulators. Because it was uninsulated, this type of telephone line was highly susceptible to electromagnetic interference; the wires had to be spaced about 12 inches apart to minimize the problem. Although open wire can still be found in a few places, it has almost entirely been replaced with cable and other types of communications media. *Cable* is insulated wire. Insulated pairs of wires twisted around each other—called *twisted-pair wire* or *cable* (Figure 9.6)—can be packed into bundles of a thousand or more pairs. These wide-diameter cables are commonly used as telephone lines today and are often found in large buildings and under city streets. Even though this type of line is a major improvement over open wire, it still has many limitations. Twisted-pair cable is susceptible to a variety of types of electrical interference (noise), which limits the practical distance that data can be transmitted without being garbled. (To be received intact, digital signals must be "refreshed" every one to two miles through the use of an amplifier and related circuits, which together are called *repeaters*. Although repeaters do increase the signal strength, which tends to weaken over long distances, they can be very expensive.) Twisted-pair cable has been used for years for voice and data transmission; however, newer, more advanced media are replacing it.

COAXIAL CABLE

More expensive than twisted-pair wire, **coaxial cable** (also called *shielded cable*) (Figure 9.6) is a type of thickly insulated copper wire that can carry a larger volume of data—about 100 million bits per second, or about 1,800 to 3,600 voice calls at once. The insulation is composed of a nonconductive material covered by a layer of woven wire mesh and heavy-duty rubber or plastic. Coaxial cable, which is laid underground and underwater, is similar to the cable used to connect your TV set to

FIGURE 9.6 Twisted wire (d) is being phased out as a communications medium by coaxial cable (b, c) and even more sophisticated media such as microwave and fiber optics.

(a)

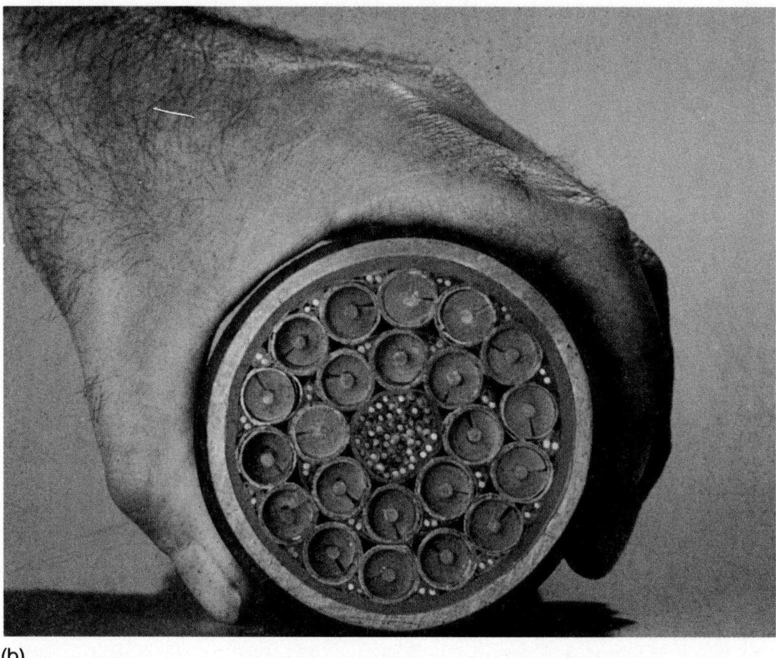

(b)

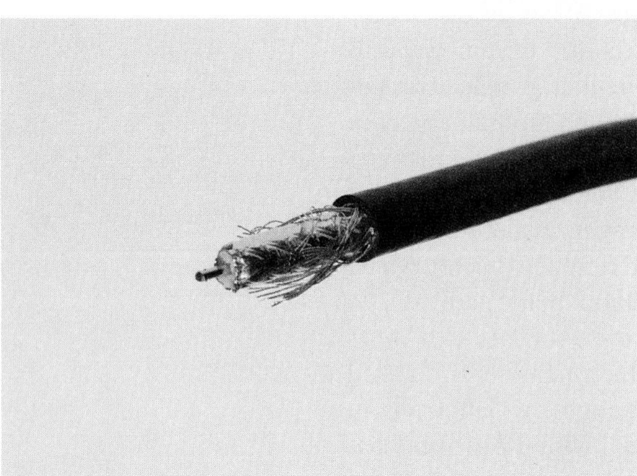

(c)

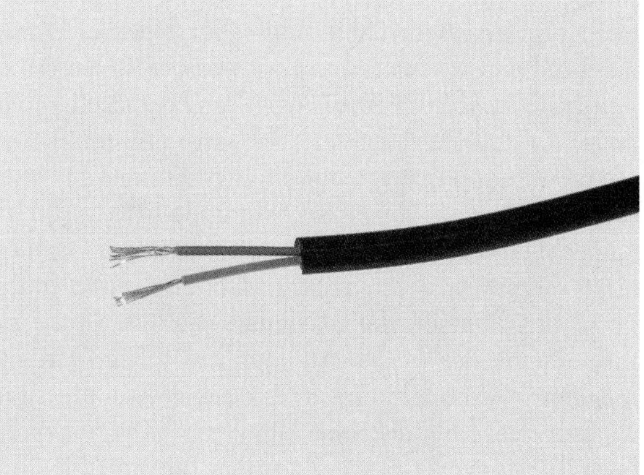

(d)

a cable TV service. Coaxial cables can also be bundled together into a much larger cable; this type of communications line has become very popular because of its capacity and reduced need for signals to be "refreshed," or strengthened, every two to four miles. Coaxial cables are most often used as the primary communications medium for locally connected networks in which all computer communication is within a limited geographic area, such as in the same building. Coaxial cable is also used for undersea telephone lines.

MICROWAVE SYSTEMS

Instead of using wire or cable, **microwave systems** use the atmosphere as the medium through which to transmit signals. These systems are extensively used for high-volume as well as long-distance communication of both data and voice in the form of electromagnetic waves similar to radio waves but in a higher frequency range. Microwave signals are often referred to as "line of sight" signals because they cannot bend around the curvature of the earth; instead, they must be relayed from point to point by microwave towers, or relay stations, placed 20 to 30 miles apart (Figure 9.7). The distance between the towers depends on the curvature of the surface terrain in the vicinity. The surface of the earth typically curves about 8 inches every mile. The towers have either a dish- or a horn-shaped antenna. The size of the antenna varies according to the distance the signals must cover. A long-distance antenna could easily be 10 feet or larger in size; a dish of 2 to 4 feet in diameter, which you often see on city buildings, is large enough for small distances.

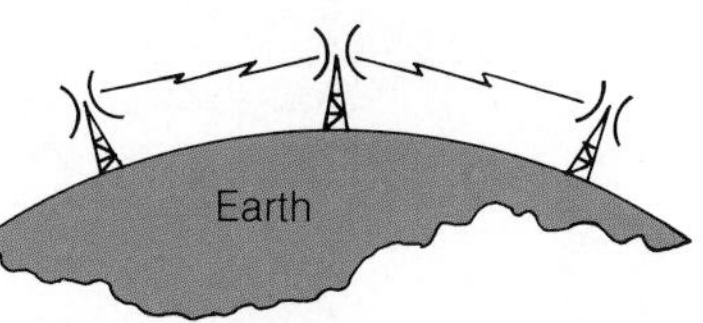

Microwave line-of-sight links

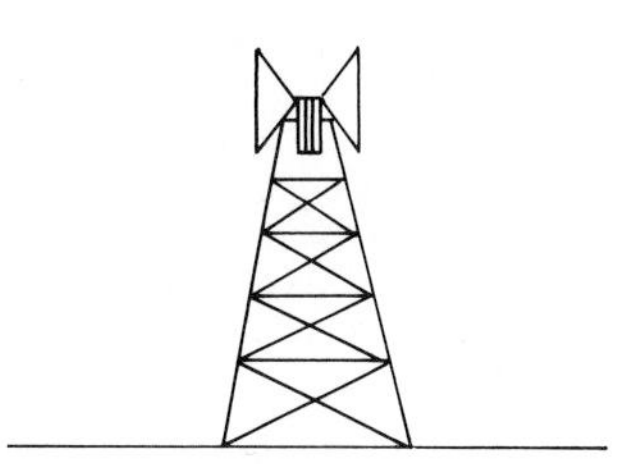

Microwave tower

FIGURE 9.7

Microwave relay station. Microwaves must be relayed from point to point along the earth's surface because they cannot bend.

FIGURE 9.8

Satellite communications. The satellite (a) orbiting the earth has solar-powered transponders that receive microwave signals, amplify the signals, and retransmit them to the earth's surface (b). (c) illustrates how the various communications media can work together as communications links. (d) The AT&T long-distance communications center.

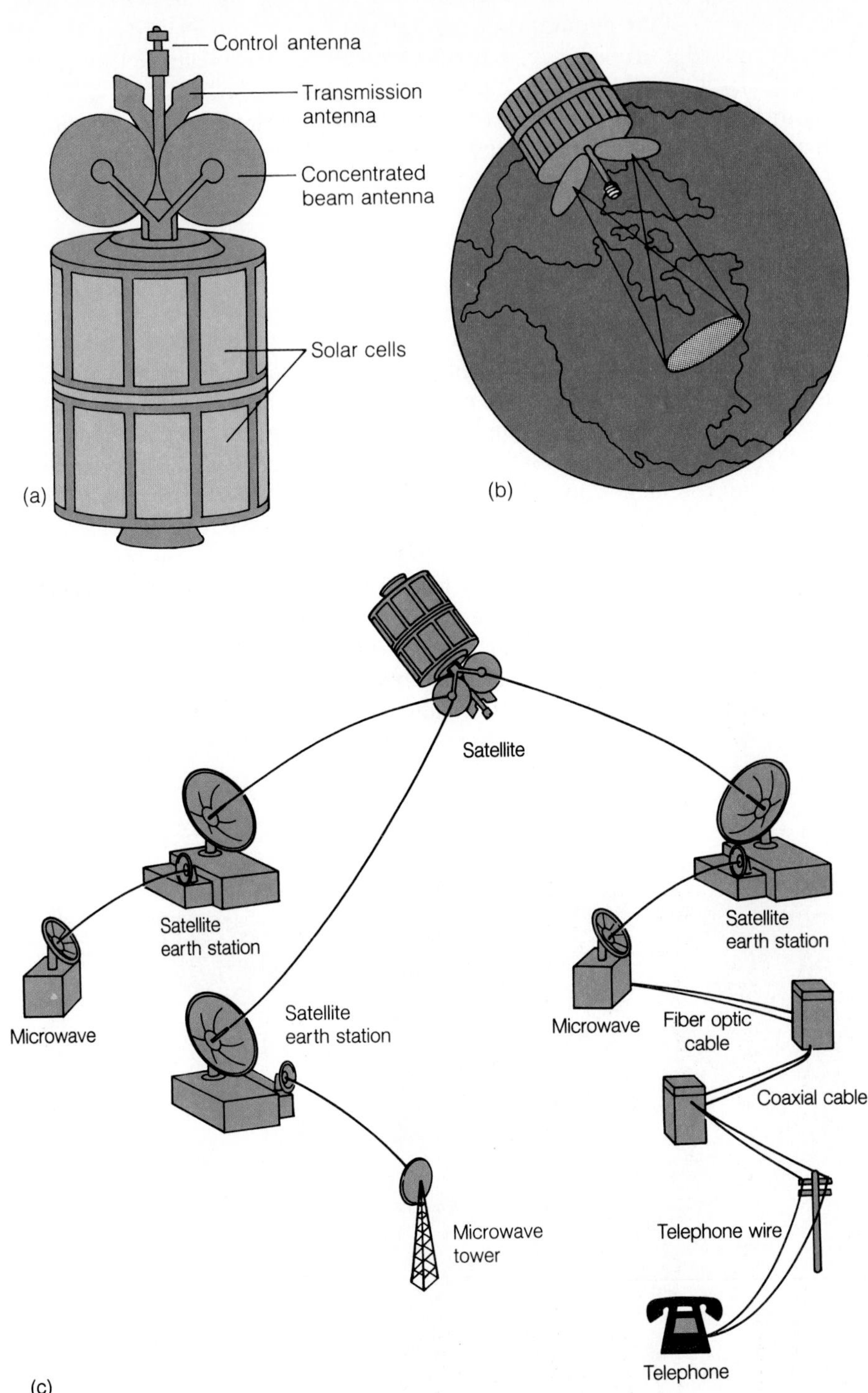

Each tower facility receives incoming traffic, boosts the signal strength, and sends the signal to the next station.

The primary advantage of using microwave systems for voice and data communications is that direct cabling is not required. (Obviously, telephone lines and coaxial cable must physically connect all points in a communications system.) More than one half of the telephone system now uses microwave transmission. However, the saturation of the airwaves with microwave transmissions has reached the point where future needs will have to be satisfied by other communications methods, such as fiber optic cables or satellite systems.

SATELLITE SYSTEMS

Satellite communications systems transmit signals in the gigahertz range—billions of cycles per second. The satellite must be placed in a geosynchronous orbit, 22,300 miles above the earth's surface, so it revolves once a day with the earth (Figure 9.8). To an observer, it appears to be fixed over one region at all times. A **satellite** is a solar-powered electronic device that has up to 100 transponders (a *transponder* is a small, specialized radio) that receive, amplify, and retransmit signals; the satellite acts as a relay station between satellite transmissions stations on the ground (called *earth stations*).

Although establishing satellite systems is costly (owing to the cost of a satellite and the problems associated with getting it into orbit above the earth's surface and compensating for failures), satellite communications systems have become the most popular and cost-effective method for moving large quantities of data over long distances. The primary advantage of satellite communications is the amount of area

(d)

FIGURE 9.8

(continued)

that can be covered by a single satellite. Three satellites placed in particular orbits can cover the entire surface of the earth, with some overlap.

However, satellite transmission does have some problems:

1. The signals can weaken over the long distances, and weather conditions and solar activity can cause noise interference.
2. A satellite is useful for only 7 to 10 years, after which it loses its orbit.
3. Anyone can listen in on satellite signals, so sensitive data must be sent in a secret, or encrypted, form.
4. Depending on the satellite's transmission frequency, microwave stations on earth can "jam," or prevent, transmission by operating at the same frequency.
5. Signal transmission may be slow if the signals must travel over very long distances.

Companies must lease satellite communications time from suppliers such as Westar (Western Union), Telstar (AT&T), Satellite Business Systems (partially owned by IBM), Galaxy (Hughes Aircraft), RCA, Comstar, the American Satellite Company, and the International Telecommunications Satellite Consortium (Intelsat), which is owned by 114 governments. Large companies with offices around the world benefit the most from satellite communications.

FIBER OPTICS

Although satellite systems are expected to be the dominant communications medium for long distances during this decade, fiber optics technology is expected to revolutionize the communications industry because of its low cost, high transmission volume, low error rate, and message security. Fiber optic cables are replacing copper wire as the major communications medium in buildings and cities; major communications companies are currently investing huge sums of money in fiber optics communications networks that can carry *digital* signals, thus increasing communications and capacity.

In **fiber optics** communications, signals are converted to light form and fired by laser in bursts through insulated, very thin (1/2,000 of an inch) glass or plastic fibers (Figure 9.9). The pulses of light represent the "on" state in electronic data representation and can occur nearly 1 billion times per second—nearly 1 billion bits can be communicated through a fiber optic cable per second. Equally important, fiber optic cables aren't cumbersome in size: A fiber optic cable (insulated fibers bound together) that is only ½-inch thick is capable of supporting nearly 250,000 voice conversations at the same time (soon to be doubled to 500,000). However, since the data is communicated in the form of pulses of light, specialized communications equipment must be used.

Fiber optic cables are not susceptible to electronic noise and so have much lower error rates than normal telephone wire and cable. In addition, their potential speed for data communications is up to 10,000 times faster than that of microwave and satellite systems. Fiber optics communications is also very resistant to illegal data theft, because taps into it to listen to or change the data being transmitted can be easily detected; in fact, it is currently being used by the U.S. Central Intelligence Agency.

AT&T has developed undersea optical fiber cables for transatlantic use in the belief that fiber optics will eventually replace satellite communications in terms of cost effectiveness and efficiency. The Japanese have already laid an underwater fiber optic cable. Sprint uses a fiber optics communications network laid along railroad rights-of-way in the United States that carries digital signals (analog voice signals are converted to digital signals at company switching stations).

Point-to-Point and Multidrop Lines

Data communications lines can be connected in two types of configurations: point-to-point and multidrop.

A **point-to-point line** directly connects the sending and the receiving devices. If the point-to-point line is a **switched line,** it is a regular telephone line—the telephone company switching stations direct the call on the line they select, just as they do all the other calls they process. After transmission is completed, the line is disconnected. If the point-to-point line is a **dedicated line,** it is always established—that is, it is never disconnected. The dedicated line is available only to the organization that creates it *(private line)* or leases it *(leased line)* from another organization—for example, from the phone company.

A **multidrop line** connects many devices, not just one sending device and one receiving device. The number of devices or terminals that use the line is determined by the experts who design the communications, or network, system. Multidrop lines are usually leased.

FIGURE 9.9

Fiber optics. Laser-fired light pulses (representing the "on" state in the binary system of data representation) are fired through very thin glass or plastic fibers.

DATA COMMUNICATIONS HARDWARE

Much hardware used in data communications is operated by technical professionals and is rarely of immediate consequence to the user unless it stops working—when you're calling from New York and can't reach your division office in London, for example. However, you should become familiar with certain types of common business communications hardware: modems, which were mentioned briefly in the section on analog and digital signals, multiplexers, concentrators, controllers, front-end processors, and protocol converters.

MODEMS

Modems are probably the most widely used data communications hardware in business. They are certainly the most familiar to microcomputer users who communicate with one another or with a larger computer. As you learned earlier in this chapter, the word *modem* is actually a contraction of *mo*dulate and *dem*odulate; a modem's basic purpose is to convert digital computer signals to analog signals for transmission over phone lines, then to receive these signals and convert them back to digital signals.

Old-fashioned modems called *acoustic couplers* did not directly connect the computer to the telephone line. However, today most modems directly connect the computer to the telephone line (Figure 9.10). These **direct-connect modems** transmit and receive data at speeds from 300 to 2,400 bits per second (bps) (figuring 7 data bits, 1 start bit, 1 stop bit, and 1 parity bit per character, 2,400 bps = 240 characters per second). Some modems run at 9,600 to 38,400 bps, but these modems, used with minicomputers and mainframe computers, are often more expensive than many microcomputers.

Direct-connect modems are either internal or external. An **internal modem** (Figure 9.10) is located on a circuit board that is placed inside a microcomputer (actually plugged into an expansion slot). The internal modem draws its power directly from the computer's power supply. No special cable is required to connect the modem to the computer.

An **external** direct-connect **modem** is an independent hardware component —that is, it is outside the computer—and uses its own power supply (Figure 9.10). The modem is connected to the computer via a cable designed for that purpose. A simple external modem designed to be used with a microcomputer costs less than $500; very fast, more complex modems can cost over several thousand dollars.

Business users who deal with modems and data communications must be sure they are communicating with compatible equipment; like other types of computer hardware and software, not all modems work with other modems, and not all modems work with the same type of software. In addition, microcomputer communications software packages—such as ProComm, Smartcom II and III, and Crosstalk XVI—require users to set their systems at specific "parameters" so that their microcomputer can "talk" to another computer using the same parameters. (Parameters, also called *protocol*, include speed of data transmission, parity scheme, direction of traffic, and so forth. The microcomputer communications software package manual tells users how to set software parameters and how to use a small screwdriver to set certain switches, called DIP [dual in-line package] switches, in the external modem cabinet.) These software packages allow "smart" modems (with certain types of chips) to do more than simply transmit and receive; for example, you can arrange for automatic dialing and transmission, printing of incoming text, and storage of incoming data on disk.

Serial Ports

Microcomputers have two types of interfaces, or *ports*. A *serial interface*, or *serial port*, is used to plug in devices such as modems that transmit data serially—bit by bit in a continuous stream; *parallel interfaces*, or *parallel ports*, are used to connect devices that transmit data in parallel—along eight separate lines simultaneously (Figure 9.11). Parallel transmission is used between the computer and the printer.

FIGURE 9.10

Direct-connect modems. An internal modem (a) is placed inside the computer; an external modem (b) remains outside the computer. In both cases, the phone remains connected for voice communication when the computer is not transmitting.

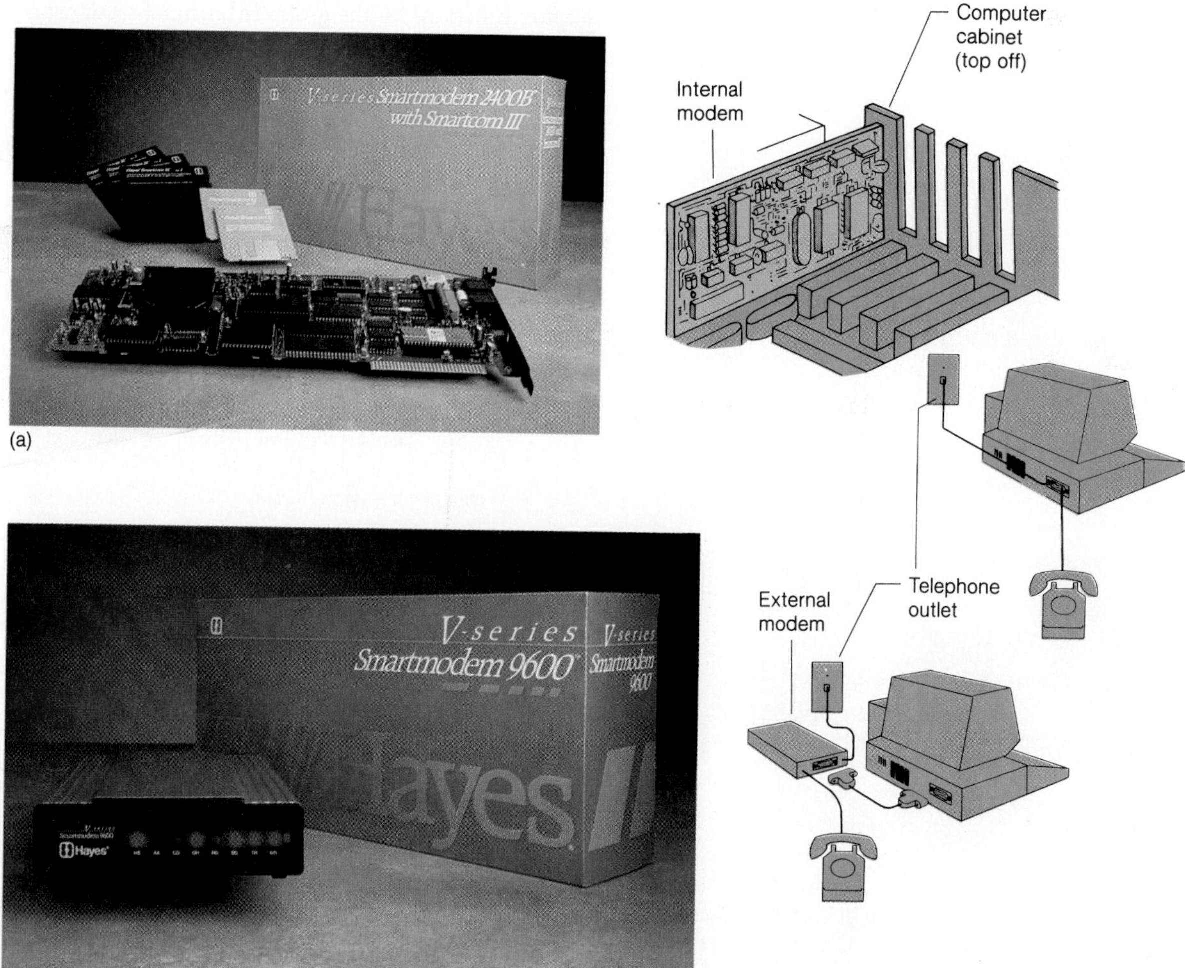

MULTIPLEXERS, CONCENTRATORS, AND CONTROLLERS

When an organization's data communications needs grow, the number of lines available for that purpose often become overtaxed, even if the company has leased one or more dedicated lines, used only for data communications. *Multiplexing* optimizes the use of communications lines by allowing multiple users or devices to share one high-speed line (Figure 9.12), thereby reducing communications costs. Multiplexing can be done by multiplexers, concentrators, or controllers.

Briefly, a **multiplexer** is a data communications hardware device that allows 8, 16, 32, or more devices (depending on the model) to share a single communications line. Messages sent by a multiplexer must be received by a multiplexer of the same type that splits the messages and directs them to their recipients. A **concentrator,** which also allows many devices to share a single communications line, is more "intelligent" than a multiplexer because it can be programmed to temporarily store some transmissions and forward them later. It is also used to multiplex low-speed communications lines onto one high-speed line. A **controller** also supports a group of devices (terminals and printers) connected to a computer. It is used in place of a multiplexer and acts to control and route transmissions, do error checking and retransmission, and perform other functions for the group of terminals. You won't

FIGURE 9.11

Serial and parallel transmission/ports and cables.

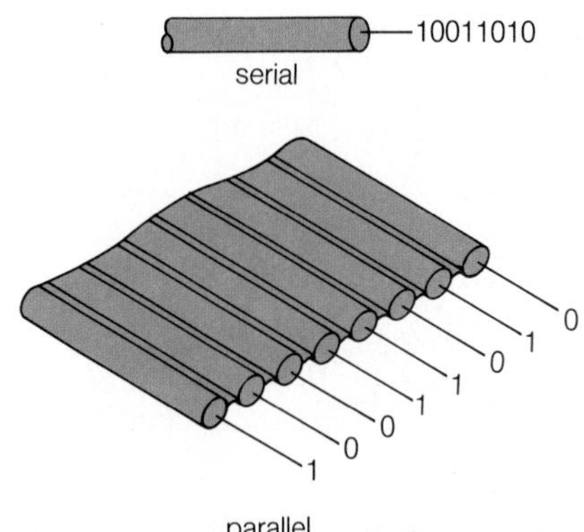

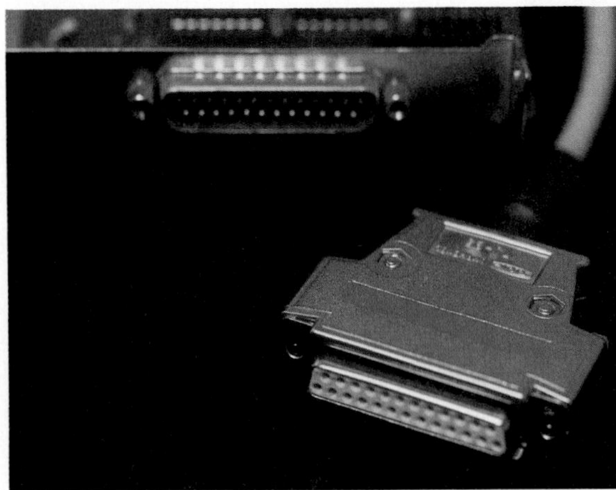

Serial

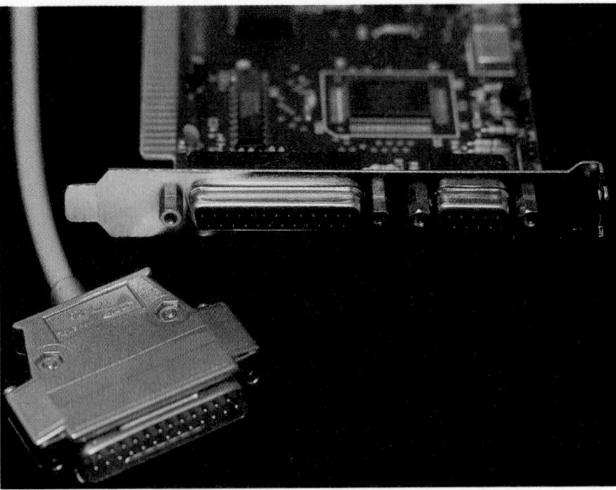

Parallel

need to get involved with many complex aspects of multiplexing unless you choose to take a high-level data communications course. If the computer in your office is connected to a multiplexer that is connected to a modem that is connected to a phone line that is connected to another modem that is connected to . . . , you won't have to learn more than the relatively simple steps involved to get data from one place to another.

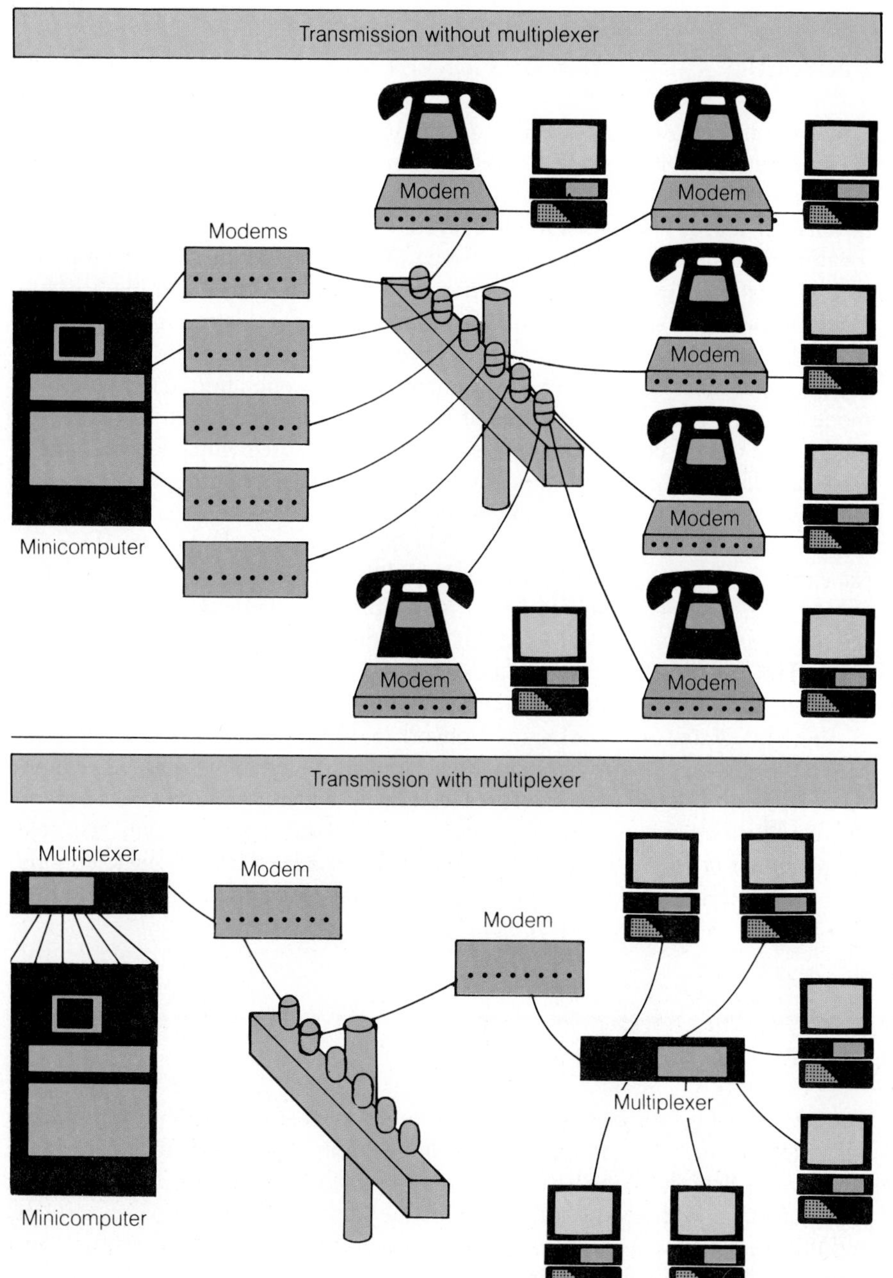

FIGURE 9.12

To multiplex or not to multiplex . . . This figure shows the basic difference between communicating with and without the use of a multiplexer.

FRONT-END PROCESSORS

In some computer systems, the main computer is connected directly into the multiplexer, controller, or concentrator. In other systems, it is first hooked to a **front-end processor,** a smaller computer that relieves the larger one of many data traffic management and communications functions (Figure 9.13). In effect, the front-end processor acts as a "mediator" between the network and the main computer, allowing the main computer to concentrate on processing and improving the responsiveness of the system to the user.

PROTOCOLS AND PROTOCOL CONVERTERS

One of the most frustrating aspects of data communications between different types of computers, especially between a microcomputer and a larger computer system, is that they often use different communications protocols. As we mentioned earlier in the chapter, a **protocol** is the formal set of rules for communicating, including rules for timing of message exchanges, the type of electrical connections used by the communications devices, error detection techniques, means of gaining access to communications channels, and so on. To overcome this problem, a specialized type of intelligent multiplexer called a **protocol converter** can be used. Protocol converters are available that even allow a microcomputer operating in asynchronous mode to talk with a large IBM mainframe computer operating in synchronous mode. This type of device is being used by more and more companies that want to establish effective communications between personal computers and the main computer system and with printing devices.

Some groups are working on the establishment of a standard protocol for data transmission. For example, IBM has released the Systems Network Architecture (SNA) for its own machines, and the International Standards Organization (ISO) has released its set of protocol standards called the Open Systems Interconnection (OSI). However, just because standards exist does not mean that they will be used by everyone or that they can be enforced.

The Integrated Services Digital Network (ISDN) is a set of standards issued by the Consultative Committee of International Telegraphy and Telephony (CCITT) and designed to set rules for a worldwide digital communications network that could simultaneously support voice, data, and video transmission over telephone lines. For ISDN to work, users will have to replace their existing telephones with ISDN telephones (which cost about $200) and insert an ISDN board in their PCs (which costs between $1,500 and $2,000).

COMMUNICATIONS SOFTWARE

Even with the best communications hardware, you won't be able to communicate with another computer without software. Most communications software packages enable users to perform the basic functions of sending files between computers and communicating with a communications service (communications services, systems, and utilities are described shortly). In addition to these functions, however, most users have business requirements that extend beyond basic communications tasks.

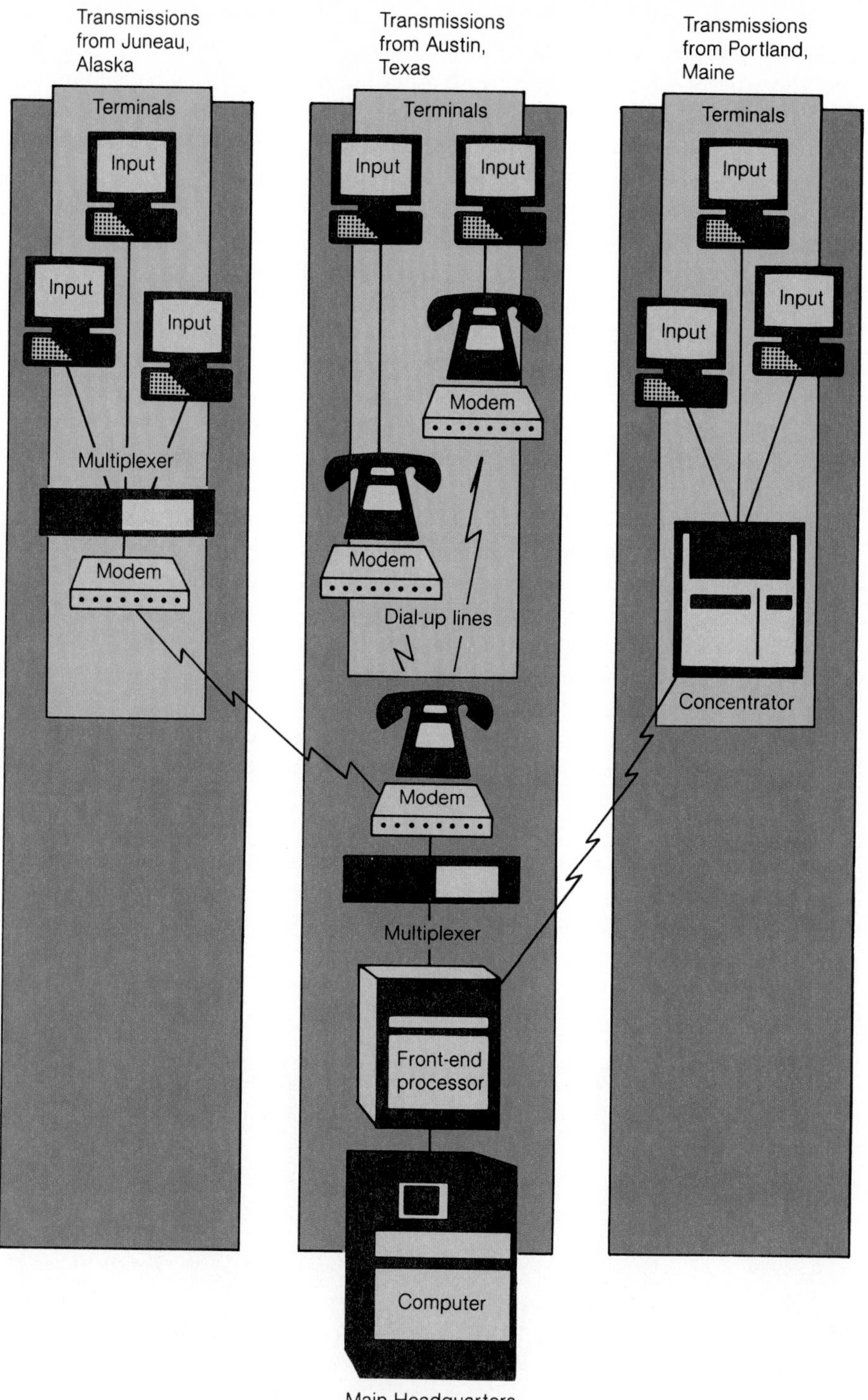

FIGURE 9.13

Help up front. A smaller computer, called a *front-end processor*, is often used to relieve the main computer of many communications functions.

For example, if you work days but want to transmit data only at night to take advantage of low phone rates, your communications software must provide a strong *script language*, similar to a programming language, that will enable you to automate this process. The most popular communications packages for microcomputers include Crosstalk, DynaComm, HyperAccess 5, Mirror III, Procomm Plus, Relay Gold, and Smartcom III (Figure 9.14 shows some of these packages). (Communications software for large computer systems is usually custom written.)

A useful communications package provides a wide range of communications protocols that govern the meaningful transfer of data between two or more computers or services. Most communications programs include protocols for communications with popular information services such as CompuServe. In addition, some communications programs offer protocols that automatically compress a file, or reduce the space it takes up on a storage device, before it is sent, so that the amount of time needed for data transmission is lessened. If you often need to send and retrieve complex data such as spreadsheets and programs, make sure your software includes an efficient error-checking protocol.

If you're concerned with speed, make sure your communications software can support sending data at a rate of more than 9,600 bps. In addition, if you want to perform operations on a remote computer, such as downloading a file to another computer, make sure the communications software supports remote control of communications.

Of all the features of communications software, the capabilities and ease of use of the script language can be the most critical to users. The script language enables you to save time when performing tasks specific to your needs. For example, before a vacation, you can use the script language to instruct your computer to send data to specific locations at specified times while you're gone. You can also program a script language to simplify the task of establishing communication with complex information systems.

Fortunately, much attention has been given in recent years to improving the user interface of most communications packages so that they are easier to use. Now most include easy-to-use menu systems. In addition, the documentation that accompanies communications software has improved.

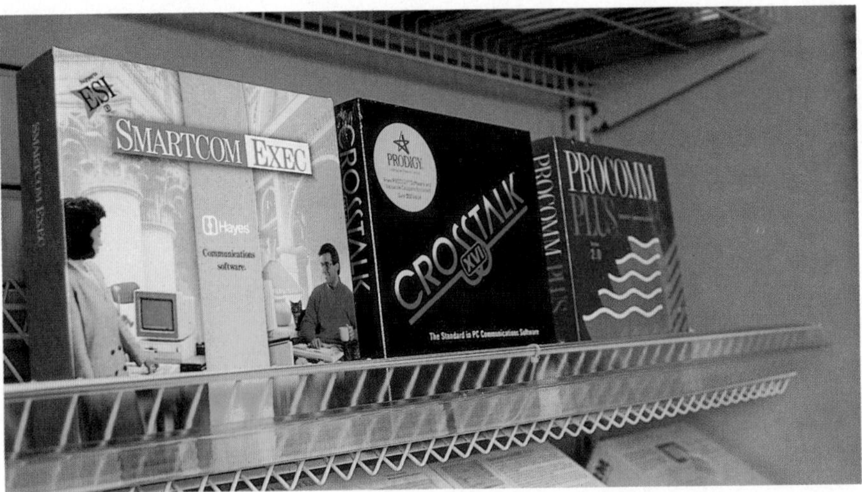

FIGURE 9.14

Microcomputer communications software packages.

Communications Networks: Connectivity

As we have talked about communications media and hardware, we have occasionally referred to communications *networks*. Networks are often used by business workers, and chances are good that you will become acquainted with one or more types of communications networks in your job.

Information and resources gain in value if they can be shared. A **network** is simply a collection of data communications hardware, computers, communications software, and communications media connected in a meaningful group to allow users to share information and equipment. The three most common types of networks are private, public, and international.

A **private network** is specifically designed to support the communications needs of a particular business organization. Many organizations with geographically separated facilities and a need for a large volume of data and voice communications implement or install their own private communications networks. The Southern Pacific Railroad was one of the first organizations to develop its own comprehensive microwave communications network to facilitate communication along all its railways. Its microwave towers can be seen along any of the major rail lines.

A **public network,** in contrast, is a comprehensive communications facility designed to provide subscribers (users who pay a fee) with voice and/or data communications over a large geographical area (in some cases coast to coast). Public networks such as Bell Telephone and AT&T Communications are sometimes referred to as *common carriers*. Some public communications networks offer **teleconferencing** services — electronically linking several people by phone, computer, and video (Figure 9.15).

The term **international network** is used to describe a communications network specifically designed to provide users with intercontinental voice and data

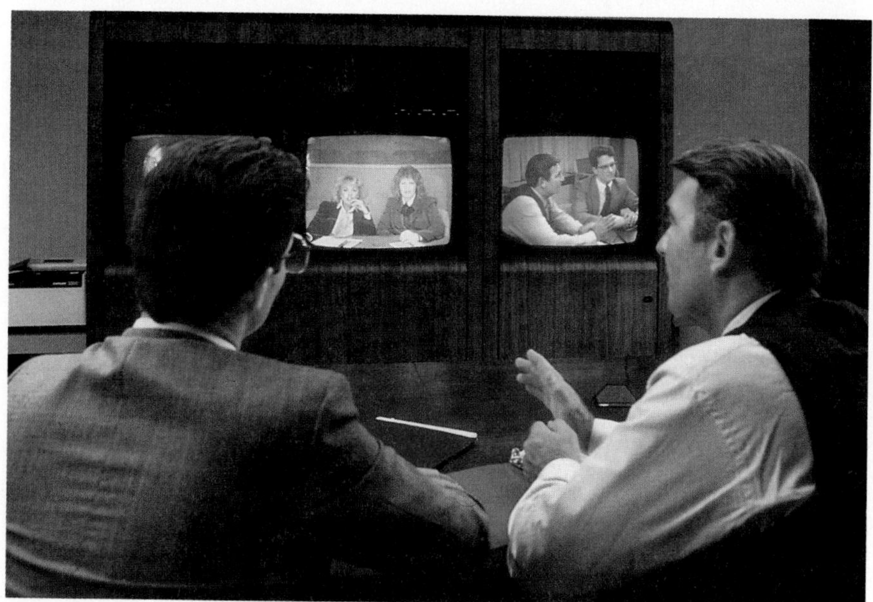

FIGURE 9.15

Teleconferencing. These people are participating in a teleconferencing session. They are connected by voice, video, and computer through public network communications facilities.

communications facilities. The majority of these networks use undersea cable or satellite communications. Western Union and RCA provide international networks.

NETWORK CONFIGURATIONS

A number of different network configurations, or shapes, are used to satisfy the needs of users in different situations. The basic types of configurations are star (and hierarchical) network, bus network, and ring (and token ring) network. Although each network configuration is actively used today by private, public, and international communications networks, you will most likely come into contact with one in the context of a local area network.

A **local area network (LAN)** is a private communications network, connected by a length of wire, cable, or optical fiber, and run by special networking software that serves a company or part of a company that is located on one floor or in a single building (Figure 9.16). A LAN is similar to a telephone system in that any telephone connected to the system can send and receive data. The LAN is generally owned by the company that is using it. It is estimated that, by 1993, more than 20 million PCs in North America will be attached to LANs. Chances are that the microcomputer you will be using in your office will be part of a local area network. LANs allow office workers to share hardware (such as a laser printer or storage hardware), to share software and data, and to essentially make incompatible units compatible. The LAN also provides a communications link to outside communications systems, and it can be connected to other local area networks in different locations, either by public communications lines or by leased dedicated lines. Note that modems are not always needed *within* a local area network; special hardware and software are used instead.

FIGURE 9.16

LAN. One of the world's busiest local area networks is at the Hong Kong Stock Exchange. Of course, such a local network can use communications lines to hook up to networks in other parts of the world.

Metropolitan area networks (MANs) link computer resources that are more widely scattered—such as among office buildings in a city. *Wide area networks (WANs)* link resources scattered around the country and the world. The communications hardware discussed earlier—modems, multiplexers, and so on—would be used to link various LANs together and to link parts of a MAN or a WAN.

STAR NETWORK

The **star network,** a popular network configuration, involves a central unit that has a number of terminals tied into it (Figure 9.17). These terminals are often referred to as *nodes*. Both point-to-point and multidrop lines are used to connect nodes to the central computer. This type of network configuration is well suited to companies with one large data processing facility shared by a number of smaller departments, and it is often used by airline reservation systems. The central unit in the star

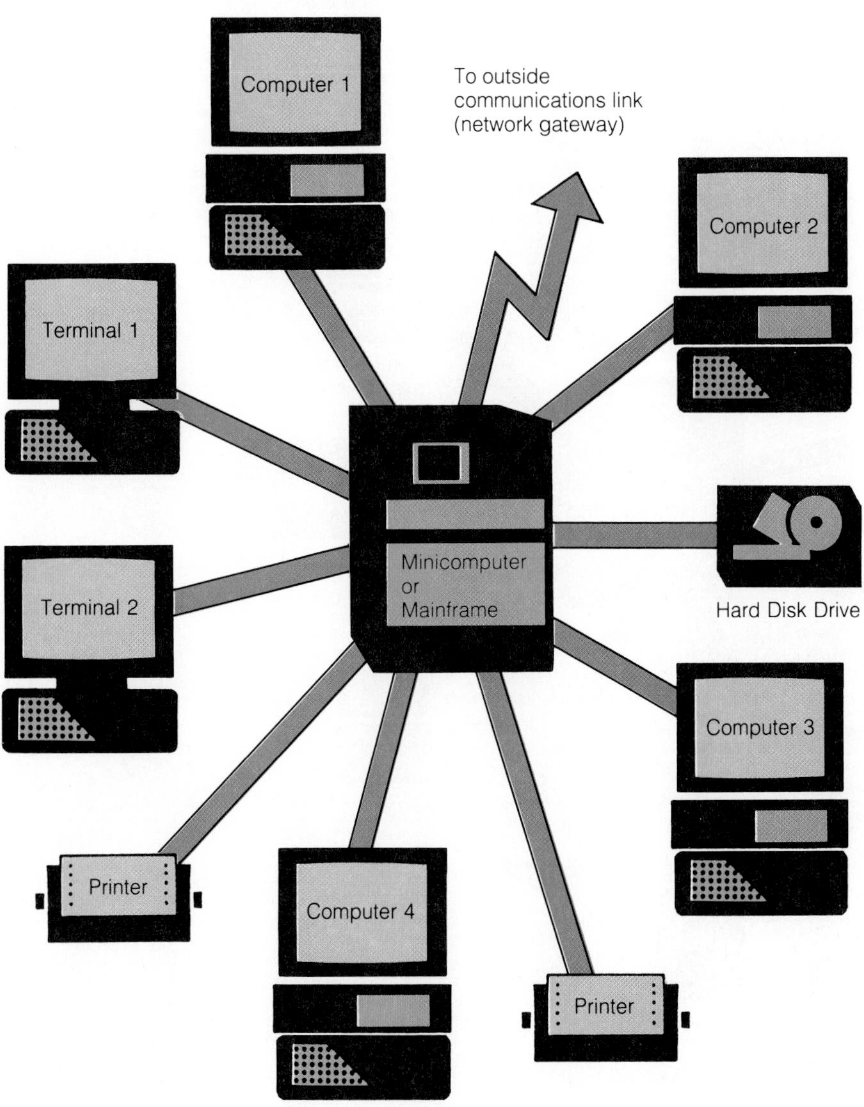

FIGURE 9.17

Star network. In this network configuration, a central computer controls all the data traffic between smaller computers, terminals, and other peripherals (like printers and disk drives) hooked up to it. It also controls communications to locations outside the LAN.

network acts as the traffic controller between all the nodes in the system. The central unit is usually a host computer or a **file server.** The host computer is a large computer, usually a mainframe. A file server is usually a microcomputer with a large-capacity hard disk storage device that stores shared data and programs.

The primary advantage of the star network is that several users can use the central unit at the same time — the star is sometimes used to link microcomputers to a central database. However, its main limitation is that the whole network is affected if the main unit "goes down" (fails to function). Since the nodes in the system are not designed to communicate directly with one another, all communication stops. Also, the cost of cabling the central system and the points of the star together can be very high.

FIGURE 9.18 Hierarchical network. This type of network configuration is basically a star network with smaller star networks attached to some of the nodes.

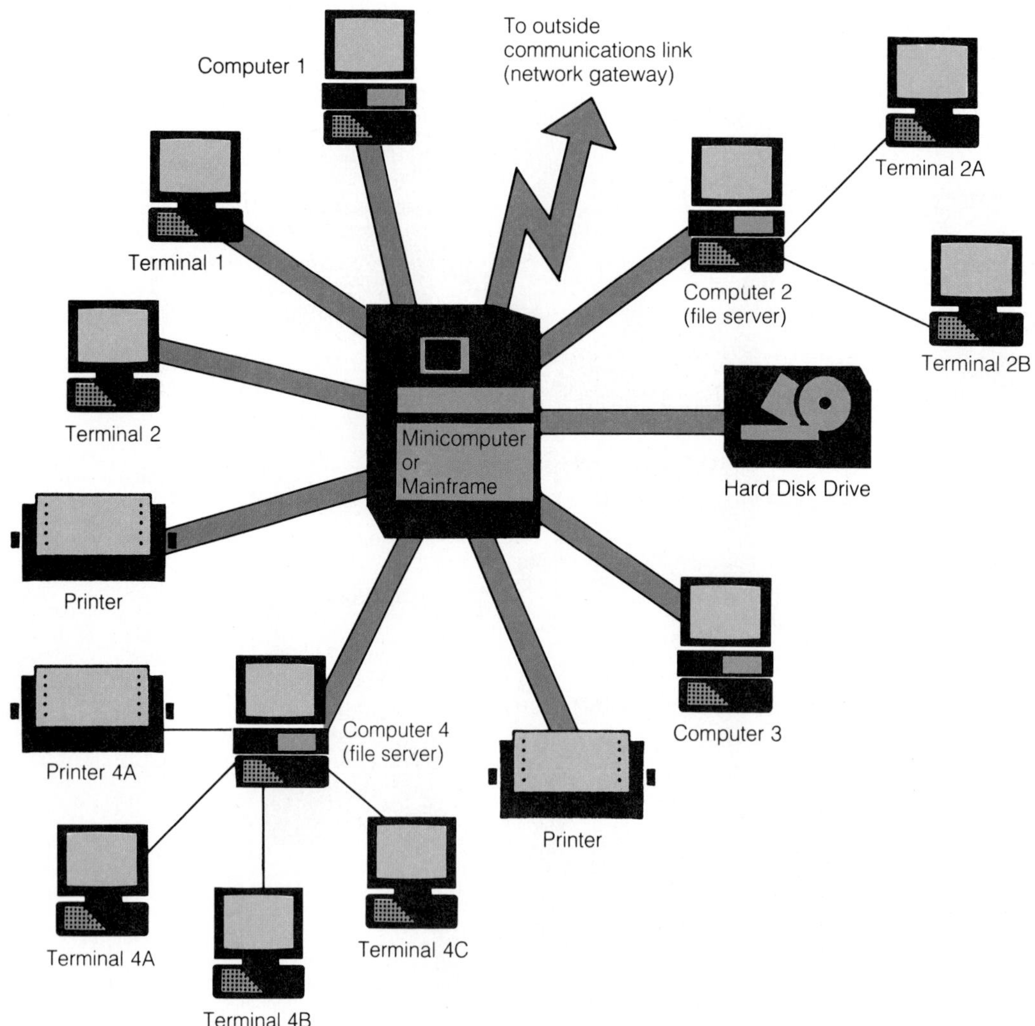

When a number of star networks are configured into a single multilevel system, the resulting network is often referred to as a **hierarchical,** or **tree, network** (Figure 9.18). In this type of network a single host computer still controls all network activity. However, each (or some) of the computers connected into the main computer in the first level of the star has a star network of devices connected to it in turn.

Hierarchical network configuration is often used by large companies with a main communications center linked to regional processing centers. Each regional processing facility acts as a host computer to smaller offices or branch computer facilities within the region. The lowest-level computer facilities allow the users to do some stand-alone applications processing. The regional computer facilities are used to manage large business information resources (usually in the form of regional databases) and to provide processing support that the smaller computers cannot handle efficiently.

BUS NETWORK

In a **bus network,** a number of computers are connected by a single length of wire, cable, or optical fiber (Figure 9.19). All communications travel along this cable, which is called a *bus* (not the same as the CPU buses we discussed in Chapter 5). There is no host computer or file server. The bus network is often used to hook up a small group of microcomputers that share data. The microcomputers are programmed to "check" the communications that travel along the bus to see if they are the intended recipients. The bus network is not as expensive as the star network, and, if one of the microcomputers fails, it does not affect the entire network. However, the bus network is not as efficient as the star network.

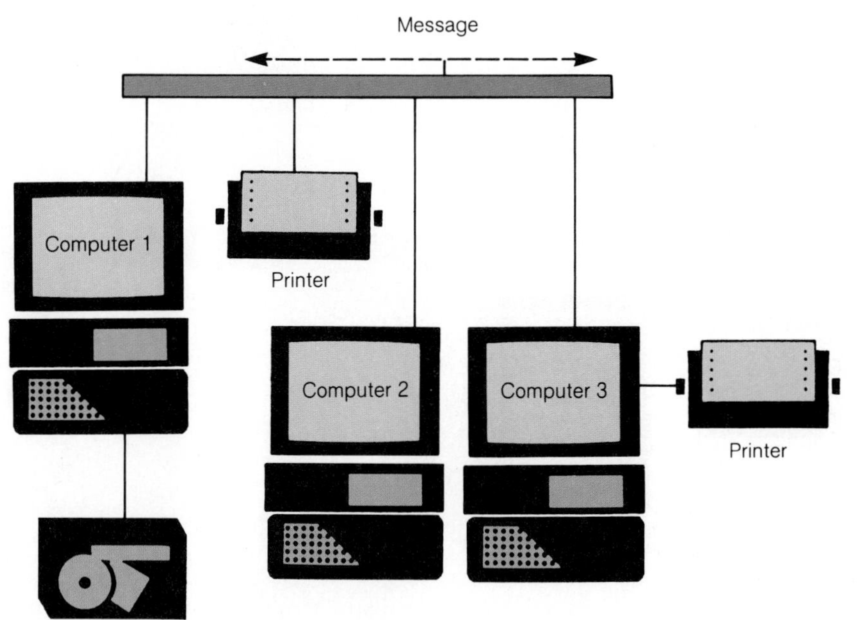

FIGURE 9.19

Bus network. All messages are transmitted to the entire network, traveling from the sender in both directions along the cable. Each microcomputer or device is programmed to sense uniquely directed messages (one signal out of many). The bus network does not necessarily have to be in a straight line; for example, it can be U-shaped.

Ring Network

A **ring network** is much like a bus network, except the length of wire, cable, or optical fiber connects to form a loop (Figure 9.20); each device is connected to two other devices. This type of configuration does not require a central computer to control activity nor does it use a file server. Each computer connected to the network can communicate directly with the other computers in the network by using the common communications channel, and each computer does its own independent applications processing. When one computer needs data from another computer, the data is passed along the ring. The ring network is not as susceptible to

FIGURE 9.20

Ring network. In this type of network configuration, messages flow in one direction from a source on the loop to a destination on the loop. Computers in between act as relay stations. If one computer fails, it can be bypassed, and the network can keep operating.

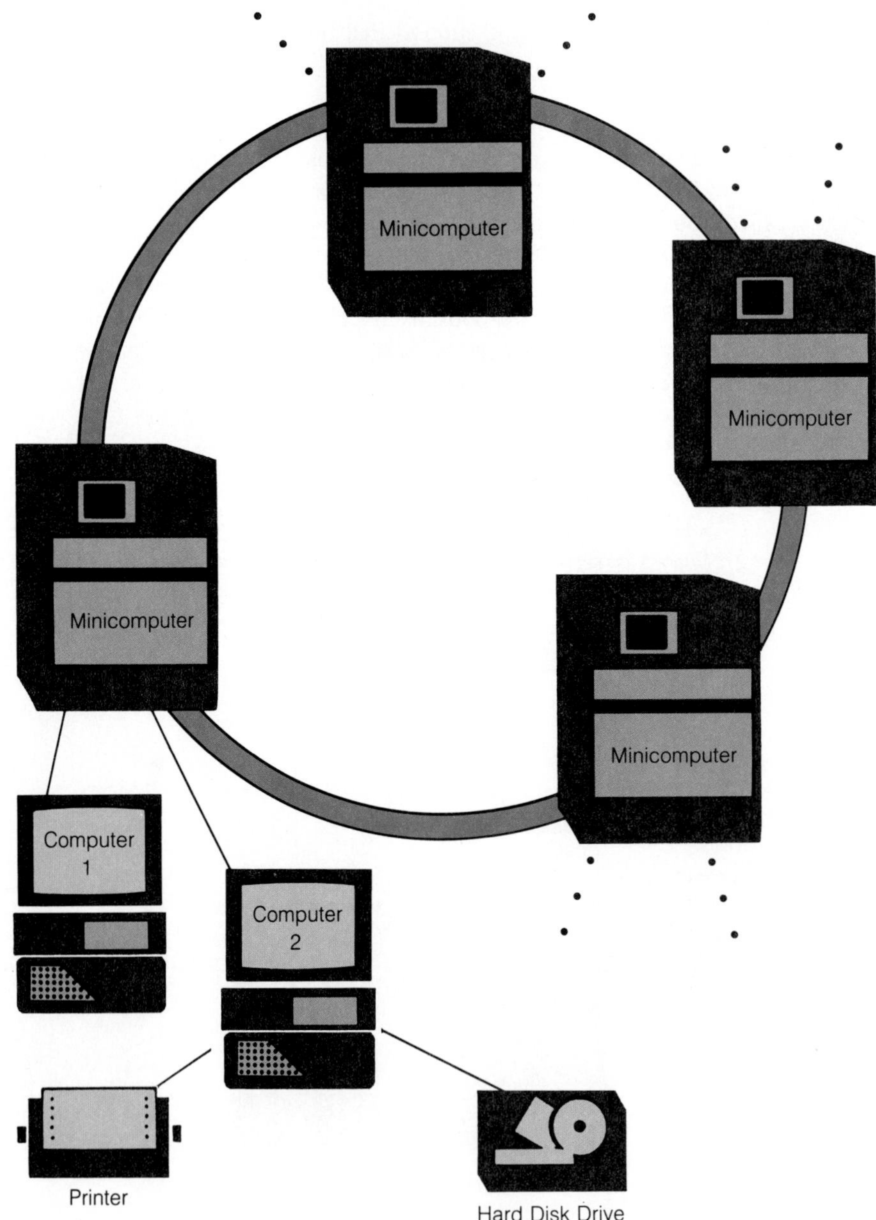

breakdown as the star network, because when one computer in the ring fails, it does not necessarily affect the processing or communications capabilities of the other computers in the ring. The ring configuration is not used as frequently as the other configurations; however, it is often used to link mainframes over wide distances.

TOKEN RING NETWORK

In early 1986, IBM announced a new local area network for personal computers using the ring network configuration called the **token ring network** (Figure 9.21). Before the token system was established, existing ring networks used the following approach:

- A computer with a message to transmit monitored network activity, waited for a lull, and then transmitted the message.
- This computer then checked to determine if other computers in the network were trying to transmit a message at the same time, which might have garbled its message.
- If two or more computers did try to send messages at the same time, then both waited a different random period of time and tried to retransmit their messages.

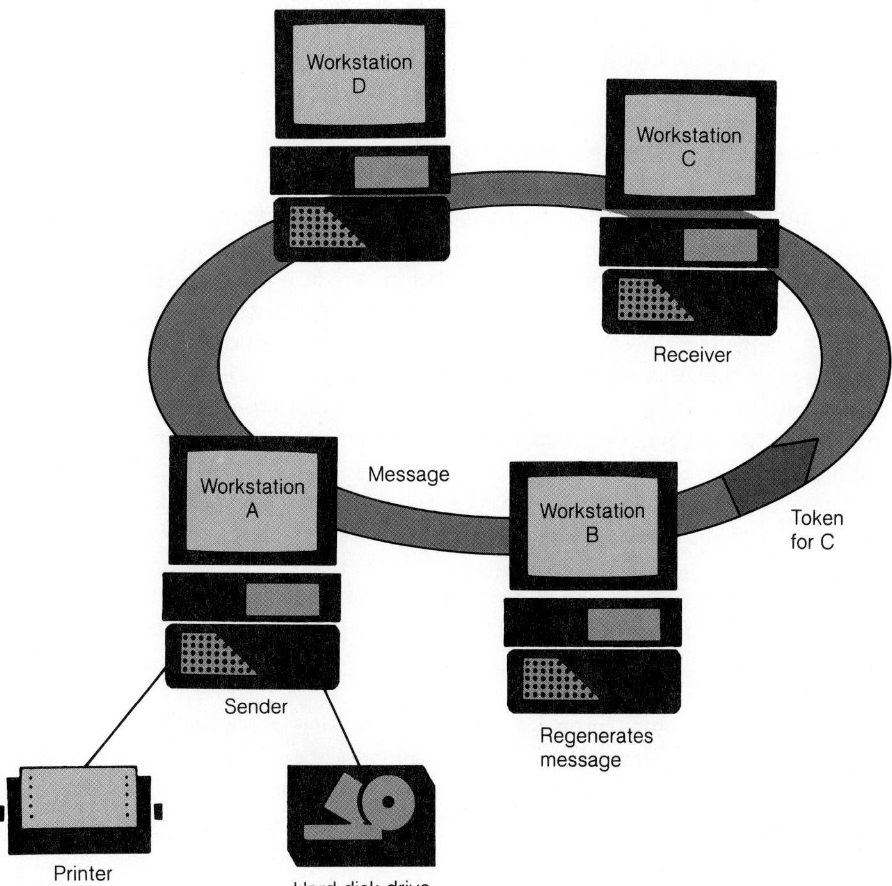

FIGURE 9.21

Token ring network. In this type of ring network, each computer can get exclusive access to the communications channel by "grabbing" a "token" (a predefined pattern of bits) and altering it before attaching a message. The altered token acts as a message indicator for the receiving computer, which in turn generates a new token, freeing up the channel for another computer. Computers in between the sender and the receiver examine the token and regenerate the message if the token isn't theirs. Thus, only one computer can transmit a message at one time.

Obviously, this procedure led to some message garbling and loss of time and productivity. In the token ring network, which was designed to eliminate these problems, a predefined pattern of bits, or *token*, is passed from computer to computer in the network. When a computer receives the token, it is allowed to transmit its message. Then the token is passed on. This method of transmitting messages (which can also be used in the bus network) prevents two computers from transmitting at the same time. The IBM token ring network is expensive but efficient. It can link up to 250 stations per ring over distances of about 770 yards, and separate rings can be linked to form larger networks.

COMMUNICATIONS SERVICES, SYSTEMS, AND UTILITIES

If you have a microcomputer, a modem, a telephone, and data communications software, you can hook up to public networks and sell a printer, buy new software, play a game with one or more people, solve a complex problem by researching information in a database or having a conference with several experts, buy stock, book a plane reservation, send flowers, receive mail — all without leaving your desk. The introduction of the personal computer dramatically broadened the appeal of these networks to the business user and the general user. These networks provide users with the vast resources of (among other things) databases, teleconferencing services, information services, electronic bulletin boards, electronic mail, voice mail, electronic stock trading, shopping, and banking.

PUBLIC DATABANKS/INFORMATION SERVICES

Many industries and professions require access to large volumes of specialized information to conduct business. For example, a law firm must have access to a law library and other specialized legal information. Medical professionals must have access to a tremendous volume of patient histories and research-related information. To serve such needs, **public databanks,** or **information services,** were created by a number of organizations to provide users with access, for a fee, to large databases. (In addition to the fee, the user pays regular phone rates for hook-up time.) The user accesses the databank with a terminal or personal computer through one of the major common carrier networks, like AT&T (telephone lines). The databases contain information in text form and cover a wide range of topics, such as health, education, law, humanities, science, government, and many others.

Some of the largest organizations providing public databases are Mead Data Central, Lockheed Information Systems, Systems Development Corporation, Data Resources, Inc., Interactive Data Corporation, Dow Jones Information Service, G.E. Information Service, PRODIGY, and CompuServe, Inc. (see Table 9.1 for some of these services).

Mead Data Central provides two very extensive public database services: LEXIS and NEXIS. The LEXIS database provides users with access to a tremendous pool of legal information for use in research. It incorporates data from a varicty of sources, including federal, state, and municipal court opinions, federal regulations, and a broad collection of recent publications in legal periodicals. The NEXIS database provides users with access to a huge amount of bibliographic data that has been collected from hundreds of magazines, newspapers, specialized newsletters, and other sources. In addition, NEXIS offers access to the complete text of the *Encyclopedia Britannica*. Students working on term papers and theses can make extensive bibliographic resource searches by using an information service like NEXIS.

Lockheed Information Systems provides a public database service through its Dialog Information Services subsidiary. The DIALOG system provides users with access to close to 100 separate databanks covering a variety of areas, including science, business, agriculture, economics, energy, and engineering. DIALOG is regarded as the largest supplier of bibliographic data to computer users. To promote the use of the system after normal business hours, a special personal computer-oriented service (called *Knowledge Index*) is made available at reduced rates.

Systems Development Corporation offers an information service called Orbit Search Service. This service allows users access to over 70 specialized databases. Many of the databases available can also be accessed through the DIALOG system.

Data Resources, Inc. and Interactive Data Corporation both offer users access to a variety of statistical databanks covering such industries as banking, economics, insurance, transportation, and agriculture. The sources for their data include Chase Econometric Associates, Value Line, Standard & Poor's, and their own staff of economists.

TABLE 9.1

Public Information Services*

Title and Provider	Number	Cost
CompuServe CompuServe, Inc.	800-848-8199	$6–12 per hour
DIALOG Dialog Information Services, Inc.	800-334-2564	$30–300 per hour
Dow Jones Information Service Dow Jones & Co.	800-225-3170	$60–174 per hour
GEnie G.E. Information Service	800-638-9636	$6–18 per hour
LEXIS Mead Data Central	800-543-6862	$39 per hour
NEXIS Mead Data Central	800-229-9597	$39 per hour
PRODIGY Prodigy Services Co. A partnership of IBM and Sears	800-PRO-DIGY	$12.95 per month

* This table provides a partial list of available information services. Each information service provides access to many different databases. With most information services, hourly rates vary depending on when you use the service (hour and day), the speed of your modem, and the database you use. In addition to hourly fees, many information services require you to pay an initial membership fee (approximately $50).

Computers and Careers

Computers for White-Collar Workers

If you're a white-collar worker who sits behind a desk — or even sits behind a steering wheel making sales calls on your mobile phone — it's fairly certain you'll be using computer technology.

Consider real estate sales. Century 21, an international organization of independent real estate agents, developed a system called Century Net that helps agents move away from slips of paper and lists in notebooks. Listing agents enter names and properties for sale from several directories. Sales agents list likely prospects. This database can then be used to generate lists of prospective buyers and generate personalized form letters. It can also be used to make telephone contacts: the sales agent enters a name, the computer dials the contact's telephone, and the date and time of the call are displayed on the screen. The system can also be used to generate reminders for important dates or follow-up calls. The use of modem-equipped laptops only expands the possibilities. When calling on prospective clients, agents can use the machines to do investment analysis for customers, comparing loan interest rates and showing how buying a home compares with other forms of investment.

Small investors themselves have also turned to computers for assistance. The old-time way of playing the stock market was to get stock prices from the newspapers, read investment newsletters, and place orders by phone to one's stockbroker. Now, using a computer in his or her home office, an investor can obtain up-to-the-minute stock quotes and, through modem and telephone links, press a button to transmit buy and sell orders to a broker. Some investors use their computers to do complex stock analysis. For instance, AIQ systems distilled the knowledge of several investment experts to devise a series of rules that rate up to 500 stocks on a 1 – 100, up-or-down scale. When there is a 100 rating on the up side, an investor should definitely buy a stock; the same number on the down side indicates one should sell.

Making money means paying taxes, of course. Many taxpayers turn to tax professionals to prepare their tax returns. Most accountants, however, turn to outside computer services for help with calculations and paperwork. Each year, about 20 service bureaus across the country, such as Computax and Accutax, process millions of tax forms. Accountants collect information from their clients, work out the tax strategy, and then send the numbers to the service bureau, which eliminates a lot of the accountant's most labor-intensive work.

Outside auditors — those analysts who go over company accounts to make sure that accounting principles are being followed, that supplies arrive when ordered, and that vendors' bills are accurate — have found that they are no longer "bean counters." With portable computers they become helpful business advisors, able to spot areas for cutting costs, gathering financial data in hours instead of days, and making essential business decisions by supplying important financial projections, such as those spotting deadbeat customers. For instance, a Peat Marwick auditor performing an annual look at the books for a chain store operator was able to print out 15 different financing scenarios in one day from microcomputers to provide a means for ensuring future operations. ■

The Dow Jones Information Service provides users with access to one of the largest statistical databanks and a news retrieval service. The statistical databanks cover stock market activity from the New York and American stock exchanges. In addition, a substantial amount of financial data covering all of the corporations listed on both exchanges, as well as nearly a thousand others, is maintained. The Dow Jones News/Retrieval system allows users to search bibliographic data on individual businesses and broad financial news compiled from a variety of sources, including *Barron's* and *The Wall Street Journal*.

Other public information services include Baseline, which provides weekly box office receipts of 35,000 films, biographies of 300,000 people in the entertainment industry, and contacts for 10,000 celebrities; Billcast Legislative Forecasts, which provides information on bills recently passed in the U.S. House and Senate; Coffeeline, which provides access to 20,000 abstracts about coffee—anything from growing the plants to health-related issues; Dun's Electronic Yellow Pages, which provides names, addresses, and phone numbers of 8 million companies in the United States; Horse, which provides pedigrees, breeding records, race records, and earnings of thoroughbreds in North America since 1922; National Adoption Network, which has information on 1,500 children with special needs available for adoption and 1,200 families seeking to adopt children; and Philosopher's Index, which provides abstracts of 136,000 philosophical citations.

Since the early 1980s, several new information services have been created for use by personal computer users at home. The most popular of these are PRODIGY and CompuServe.

To access PRODIGY, you need a microcomputer and a keyboard, a modem, a telephone line, and PRODIGY software (which includes documentation for using the service). The PRODIGY software includes communications functions that enable you to communicate with the PRODIGY service. If you want to store or print out the information you download from the information service, you also need a secondary storage device (disk drive) and a printer. For about $10 a month, you have access to a wide variety of services, including electronic banking and shopping. In addition, you can obtain the latest news, weather forecast, and stock quotes, or choose from the many educational and entertaining games that are offered by the PRODIGY service (Figure 9.22). Up to six family members can obtain a password to the system—their own unique sequence of keystrokes to type in.

Many people would say that PRODIGY's greatest attraction is its low cost. Most other on-line services assess hourly fees, whereas PRODIGY charges one monthly fee (which is usually lower than one hour using another on-line service). The major disadvantage of PRODIGY is its inability to download financial data into another program, such as a spreadsheet program. PRODIGY treats financial data graphically; you can print a graph, but you can't download the data that PRODIGY used to generate the graph. In addition, PRODIGY keeps track of current data only—from the last two trading days on the New York and American stock exchanges and the past ten business days on the Dow Jones Industrials.

CompuServe provides more in-depth and extensive capabilities than does PRODIGY. Among its services, CompuServe keeps track of company and market performance for the past 16 years, and it enables users to download financial data to another software program. It is also more expensive—between $6 and $12 per hour. Using CompuServe is similar to using PRODIGY; you would buy a microcomputer communications software package such as Smartcom or Crosstalk XVI and then contact the service through its 800 number and arrange to become a subscriber. As a subscriber (you pay a service fee as well as the fee for phone use) you are assigned two codes, or passwords, to type in when you want to log on to the information service. Like most information services, CompuServe provides written instructions for using its system's commands.

FIGURE 9.22

PRODIGY screens. (a) Opening screen for logging in. (b) A screen with a menu—8 choices for the user.

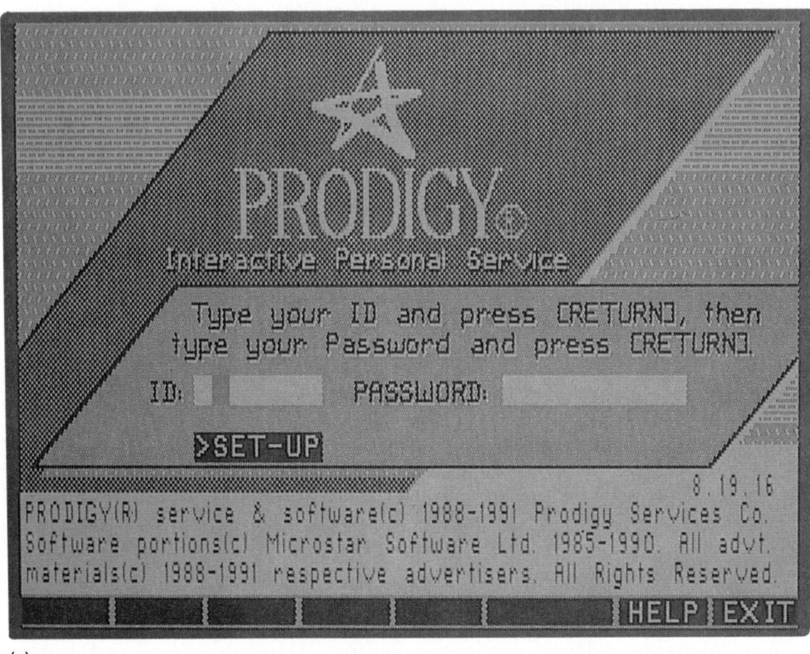

(a)

(b)

ELECTRONIC SHOPPING

One type of public network service provided to users is **electronic shopping** (Figure 9.23). To use this service, you dial into a network such as PRODIGY or CompuServe (by using your computer keyboard) and select the electronic shopping mode desired. A menu of major categories of items available is presented and you select one. You can then browse through the catalog — shown on the screen — looking for the desired item. When the item is found, you indicate that an order is to be placed and enter a previously assigned identification number and perhaps a credit card number (sometimes the credit card number is included in the user I.D. information). You can even get cost comparison information for several items before ordering one.

The variety of goods available through electronic shopping has grown rapidly over the past four years and now includes a wide range of name-brand goods at discount prices from nationally known stores and businesses. In fact, users now not only buy products but send flowers and other gifts and make travel reservations.

ELECTRONIC BULLETIN BOARDS

The **electronic bulletin board service (BBS)** (Figure 9.24) is a popular information service that allows users to either place a message or advertisement into the system or scan the messages placed by others in the system. For example, suppose you have an item you would like to sell or trade — an automobile, a bicycle, a motorcycle, sports equipment, or even a personal computer or some software. After setting up your computer and modem with your communications software, you would dial the information service and select the electronic bulletin board mode.

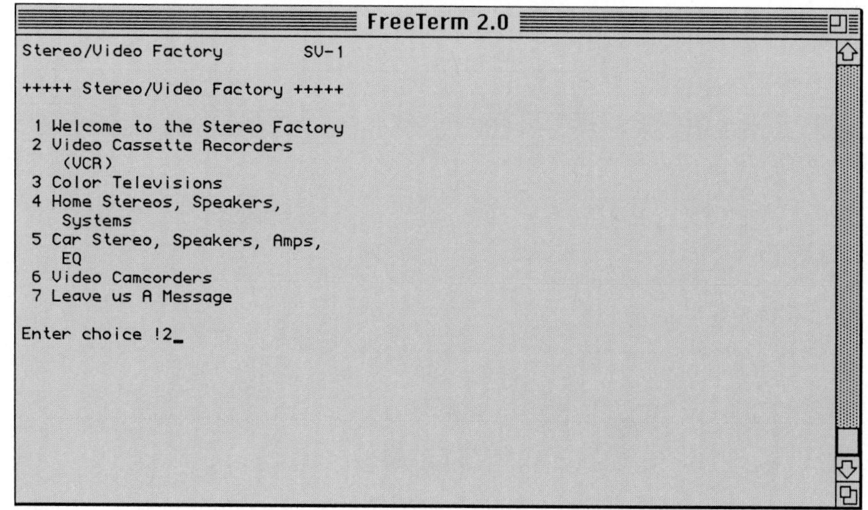

FIGURE 9.23

Spend money faster. Modems and communications software allow the user who subscribes to certain public network services to shop at home. In this example, if you want to buy a car stereo, you would press the 5 key to see a list of brand names and types. You would then press the numbers of the ones for which you want to see a full description, including price. If you wish to purchase one, you would press the numbers for the appropriate options and then type in the answers to the information service's questions about credit card information, delivery address, and so on.

Next, you would compose an electronic 3 × 5-inch card describing the item(s) for sale and include an electronic mailbox number to which inquiries can be directed. You can check back for responses over a period of days, or whenever appropriate.

Electronic bulletin boards are also used simply to exchange information between computers in remote locations, such as offices in different parts of the country, or even within a company at one location. As long as the sending and the receiving computers have modems attached and have established accounts with the same BBS, one user can upload data to the BBS for the other to download. Since data on a BBS is stored in a basic text format, any microcomputer can read it. This is one method many companies use to avoid moving data between machines that store data in incompatible formats. For example, to convert an IBM file into an Apple Macintosh format (IBMs and Macintoshes use different machine languages), the IBM file could be sent to the BBS, at which point the Macintosh user could retrieve it.

The procedure for scanning the bulletin board is very straightforward. Once you have entered the electronic bulletin board mode, you simply identify the type of item you would like to search for and let the computer do the work for you. You can also scan *all* the messages.

ELECTRONIC MAIL

Many public information services provide an **electronic mail** (E-mail) service (Figure 9.25) for fast and inexpensive business and personal communications. Electronic mail is also used internally, within companies, to send and receive text messages. Each user in the system is assigned a unique electronic mail address code. (This code is not tied to a specific location, as a ZIP code is.) When a message has been sent to a specific electronic mailbox, the user is automatically notified when he or she next logs onto the system. The user can then retrieve the message, print it, and send a response, as necessary. Once a message has been placed into the

FIGURE 9.24

Electronic bulletin board screen. Electronic bulletin boards allow users to "post" messages on particular topics, read messages from other people, and reply to messages.

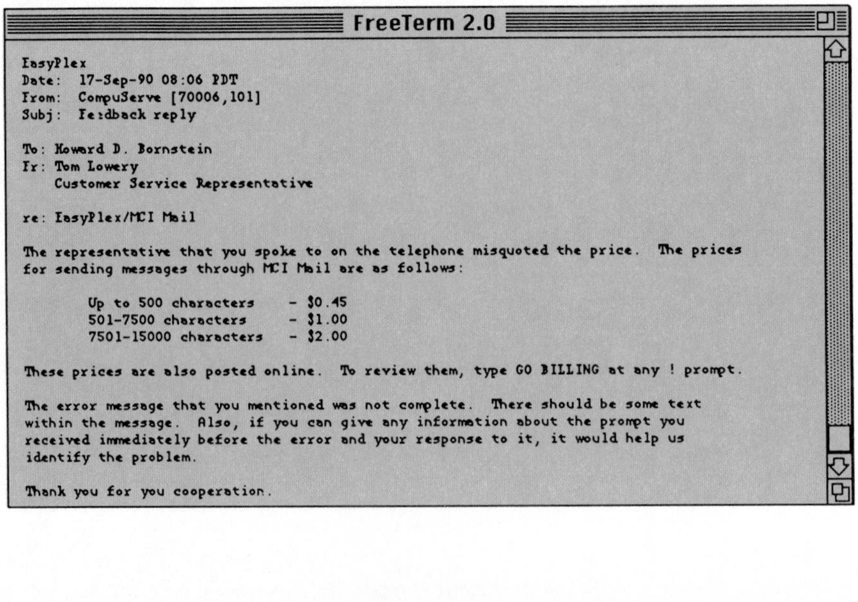

```
FreeTerm 2.0

EasyPlex
Date:  17-Sep-90 08:06 PDT
From:  CompuServe [70006,101]
Subj:  Feedback reply

To: Howard D. Bornstein
Fr: Tom Lowery
    Customer Service Representative

re: EasyPlex/MCI Mail

The representative that you spoke to on the telephone misquoted the price.  The prices
for sending messages through MCI Mail are as follows:

        Up to 500 characters     - $0.45
        501-7500 characters      - $1.00
        7501-15000 characters    - $2.00

These prices are also posted online.  To review them, type GO BILLING at any ! prompt.

The error message that you mentioned was not complete.  There should be some text
within the message.  Also, if you can give any information about the prompt you
received immediately before the error and your response to it, it would help us
identify the problem.

Thank you for you cooperation.
```

electronic system, it can be retrieved by the recipient from any location where the information service has established communications. Business users on the road often use their laptop computers to check their electronic mailboxes for messages (the computer can be hooked up to the hotel telephone).

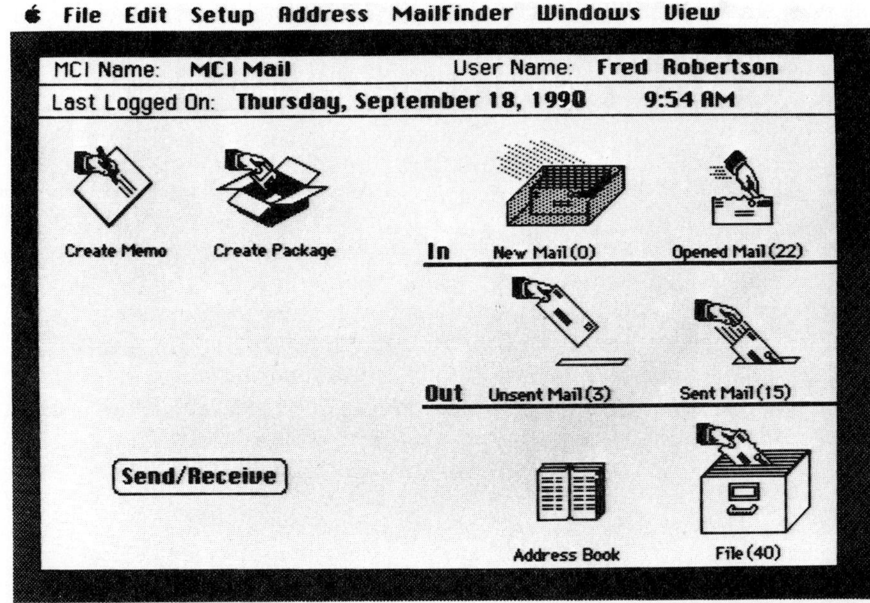

(a)

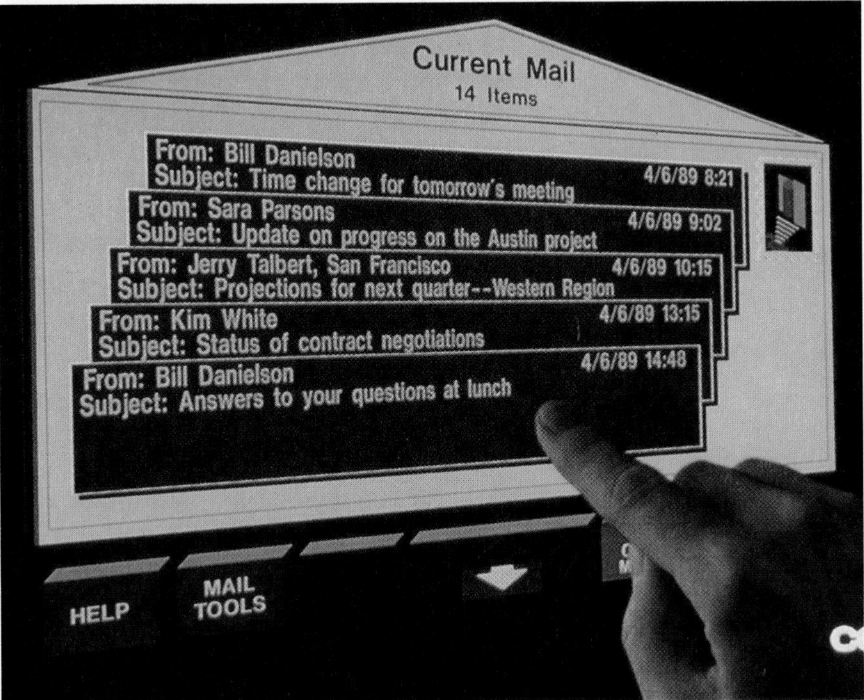

(b)

FIGURE 9.25

Electronic mail screen. No stamps necessary. Computer users can send and receive mail electronically, person to person. (a) This Macintosh screen shows that Fred has no new mail to "open," 15 messages have been sent, and 3 messages remain to be sent. Fred's software also maintains an address book and a file for storing messages. (b) Comshare screen showing messages waiting (E-mail).

VOICE MAIL

Voice mail systems, or voice-messaging systems, are essentially computer-based answering machines. A recording of the user's voice speaks to callers who then leave messages for the user to retrieve later. Voice mail capabilities are provided by computer systems, linked to user's phones, that convert the human voice to digital bits. These systems can also forward calls to wherever the user is—hotel, home, business, etc. He or she can dictate answers that are recorded and sent out to the appropriate people. Voice mail systems can be set up within a company or within a geographical area. Many users can obtain voice mail services by calling their local telephone company.

ELECTRONIC BANKING

In the past few years, many major financial institutions have begun to offer customers a new service referred to as **electronic banking.** This service allows customers to access banking services via a terminal or personal computer from the comfort of their offices or homes. The user just dials into the electronic banking service using the local access telephone number. When the communications link has been established, the user is prompted to enter an identification code. If the code is accepted, the user can request a number of electronic banking services, including:

- Viewing the balances in checking and savings accounts.
- Transferring funds between checking and savings accounts.
- Directing that certain utility bills be paid directly by the bank.
- Verifying the latest rates available on certificates of deposit, passbook savings accounts, and other investment options.

FAX

Today, asking "What is your fax number?" is almost as common as requesting someone's telephone number. In fact, most business cards today include both a telephone number and a fax number. In what seems like a very short time, many businesses and individuals have adopted the **fax machine** (short for *facsimile machine*) as a standard communications medium. A **fax** is a copy of a document that is sent using fax hardware through the phone lines to another location that has fax hardware. The process of sending or receiving a fax is called *faxing*. Faxing a document is obviously faster than sending it through the mail or via an overnight service—and it often is cheaper, too. If you are in the market for fax capabilities, you can purchase either a stand-alone fax machine or a fax board (also called *virtual fax*) that fits into an expansion slot in your microcomputer's system unit. Each method has its advantages.

A stand-alone fax machine (Figure 9.26) comprises a scanner (Chapter 4) for input, a thermal printer (Chapter 6) for output, and a modem, so that text and graphics can be sent across phone lines. The fax machine is plugged into its own phone jack and given its own fax number (essentially, its own telephone number), or it is attached to an existing phone line. (Special equipment is available for users whose fax machine must share the same line as their telephone. For example, if your telephone has "call waiting," a call could disrupt a fax transmission.) To send a fax, the user puts the document(s) to be faxed into the fax machine, punches in the number of the receiving fax machine, and then presses the start button. The machine scans the document(s), converts the data to analog signals, and transmits it. Some fax machines can also transmit photos, and some have many options, such as draft, medium, and fine quality of transmission; number storage and automatic dialing; security checking; printouts of each transaction record; and voice communication before or after the fax is transmitted. The more options it has, the more expensive the fax machine will be. Current prices range from $400 to $2,500.

A fax card, or board (Figure 9.26), is essentially an internal fax modem that can send and receive both text and graphics—and at a faster rate (9,600 bps versus 2,400 bps for stand-alone fax machines). Since fax cards don't provide users with all the options of stand-alone fax machines, they typically cost less. Because the incoming and outgoing faxes skip at least one pass through a fax machine's scanner or thermal printer, fax boards offer users better quality faxes when they are printed out.

Stand-alone fax machine (a) and fax board (b). **FIGURE 9.26**

(a)

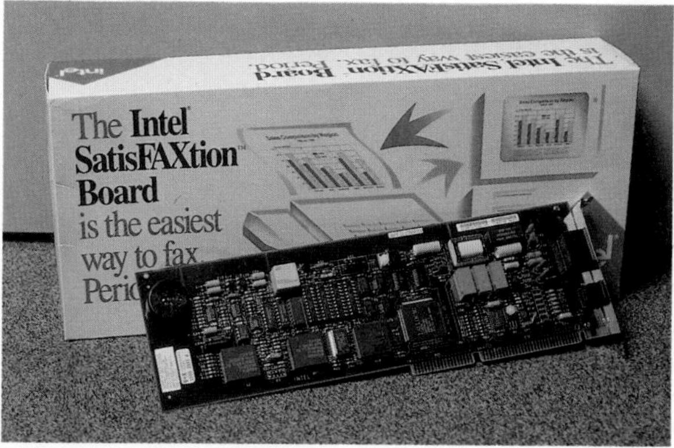

(b)

Users who are using a fax card have to purchase a scanner if they want to fax documents, such as newspaper clippings, that don't originate in the computer. The scanner converts the paper images into computer-usable files that the fax board can then fax to a receiving machine or board. The scanner must be compatible with the fax board. Also, to print a board-faxed document, the user's fax board must be compatible with the printer.

COMPUTER VIRUSES: THE BUGS THAT ARE GOING AROUND

We've indicated in other sections of this book that controls must be designed into a computer-based information system to protect the accuracy, completeness, and security of its data and information. However, the proliferation of relatively low-cost, high-tech communications devices and powerful microcomputers has created a breeding ground for a new kind of computer bug—the computer virus.

Normal bugs are accidental programmer's errors that are weeded out of a system's software during testing. **Viruses** are *intentional* bugs created by sophisticated, obsessive computer users (often called *hackers* or *crackers*) and some programmers. These viruses consist of pieces of computer code (either hidden or posing as legitimate program code) that, when downloaded or run, attach themselves to other programs and files and cause them to malfunction. Sometimes the viruses are programmed to lie dormant for a while before they become active; thus, they can be spread from disk to disk and system to system before they are detected (Figure 9.27). The viruses are transmitted by downloading through modems from

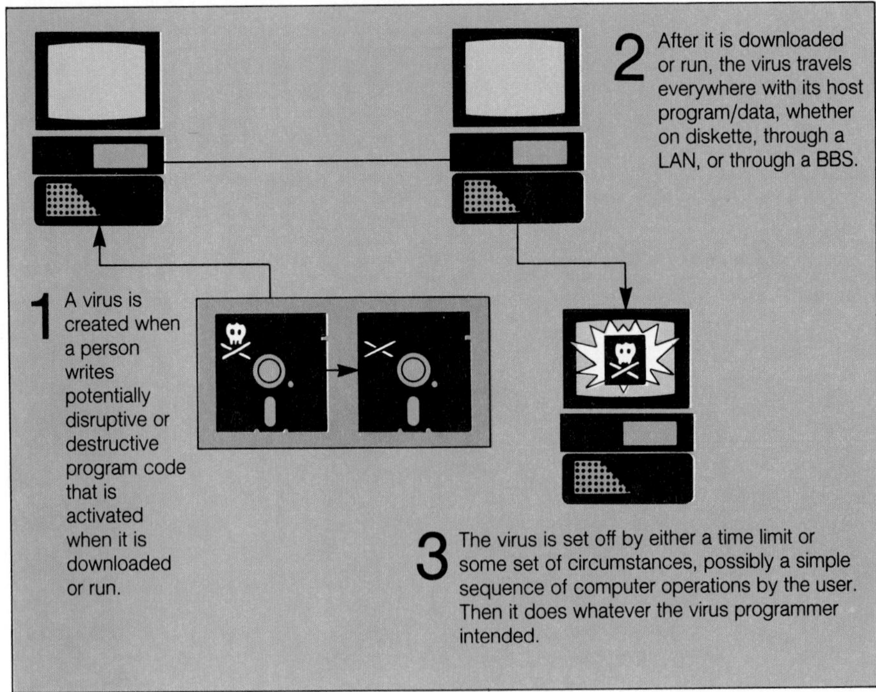

2 After it is downloaded or run, the virus travels everywhere with its host program/data, whether on diskette, through a LAN, or through a BBS.
1 A virus is created when a person writes potentially disruptive or destructive program code that is activated when it is downloaded or run.
3 The virus is set off by either a time limit or some set of circumstances, possibly a simple sequence of computer operations by the user. Then it does whatever the virus programmer intended.

FIGURE 9.27

How a computer virus can spread. Just as a biological virus disrupts living cells to cause disease, a computer virus—introduced maliciously—invades the inner workings of computers and disrupts normal operations of the machines. (Adapted from Knight-Ridder Tribune News/Stephen Cvengros, *Chicago Tribune*, October 6, 1989, Section 1, p. 2.)

electronic bulletin boards and networks, and through shared disks and pirated software. They reproduce themselves over and over again. In recent years, some major companies, universities, and government agencies have had their systems disabled by computer viruses. More than 110 different viruses have been detected to date. Because so many critical aspects of life depend on computer programs, the destructive potential of viruses has become a threat to all of us.

What exactly do viruses do? Among other things, they can rename programs, alter numeric data, erase files, scramble memory, turn off the power, reverse the effect of a command, or simply display a message without damaging the system. (Table 9.2 provides a list of common virus-related items.) For example, in 1988 the so-called *Meta-Virus* was unleashed on users of a particular software system. This virus did not actually damage the system; rather, it was intended to create anxiety on the part of the users. The message that popped up on the user's screen said:

> WARNING! A serious virus is on the loose. It was hidden in the program called 1987 TAXFORM that was on this bulletin board last year. . . . By now, it is possible that your system is infected even if you didn't download this program, since you could easily have been infected indirectly. The only safe way to protect yourself against this virus is to print all your files onto paper, erase all the disks on your system, buy fresh software disks from the manufacturer, and type in all your data again. FIRST! Send this message to everyone you know, so that they will also protect themselves.

TABLE 9.2

Virus-Related Terms

ANTIDOTES—programs that help remove viruses.

BUG—programmer error.

COUNTERHACKER—one who is in the business of identifying hackers.

CRASHING—a term used to describe a computer system that is being halted by a virus.

FINGER HACKER—one who obtains access codes from a service like U.S. Sprint Telephone using a programmable memory telephone.

HACKER (CRACKER)—a sophisticated, obsessive computer programmer who creates computer code that can cause a computer system to malfunction.

PASSWORD—a code used to gain entrance into a computer system so that data can be accessed.

REPLICATE—to copy or rewrite.

SCAN PROGRAMS—used to detect viruses.

VIRUS—an intentional bug created by a computer user (usually a programmer) that can cause harm to data stored in a computer system and cause a computer system to malfunction.

VIRUS STRAIN—a particular virus with its own unique characteristics.

VACCINES—programs that prevent machines from being infected.

WORM—a type of virus that rewrites (replicates) itself on a disk, thus destroying critical data and computer code.

Trojan horses, which act like viruses, except that they don't reproduce themselves, and *worms*, which use up available space by rewriting themselves repeatedly throughout the computer's memory, also create problems for users. What can users do to protect themselves? First, they can obtain free or low-cost software programs (called *freeware* or *shareware*) that detect and cure common viruses — for example, Virus RX, Virus Detective®, VirusCheck, Vaccine, and Interferon. These programs (sometimes called virus stompers) come with instructions for use. Also, personal computer users should:

- Back up their data on a regular basis.
- Increase the use of the write-protect tabs on their diskettes. With 5¼-inch diskettes, this involves putting a plastic sticker (included in every box of diskettes) over the write-protect notch. With 3½-inch diskettes, this involves moving a plastic tab on the back of the diskette.
- Avoid use of computer games from bulletin board services.
- Be cautious with whom they share operations or applications software programs or avoid sharing at all.
- In networks with file servers or host computers, substitute node microcomputers with new diskless PCs; such PCs cannot introduce a virus from an infected disk (nor can they be used to steal company software or data).

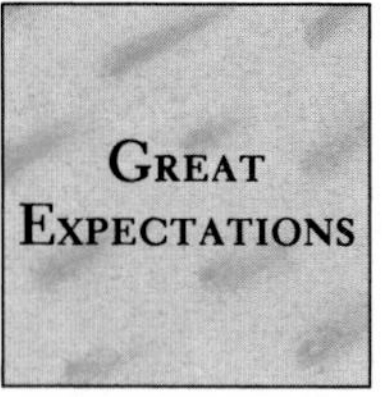

The key principles that data communications offers are *connectivity* and *integration*. As we've mentioned, connectivity expresses the idea that all kinds of hardware can be connected to other kinds of hardware. A microcomputer can be connected by communications networks to a file server, a mainframe, or other microcomputers. Integration seems to suggest that existing information processing systems are reorganized or unified so that all the systems of operating departments or companies are able to pass information back and forth and support common organizational strategies.

Already we can begin to see the promises offered by these concepts. Information may be sent over networks in text or numerical form, as images, or as sound. It may be downloaded from mainframes or large databases to microcomputers. It may be sent through the air to cellular phones. It may be transmitted between fax machines. It may be sent to voice-messaging systems and stored in voice mailboxes.

Experts predict that, by the end of this decade, the entire U.S. phone system will be digital, using the new ISDN technologies and standards. This means that users will be able to hook their computers directly to one phone line without using a modem or a fax machine and transmit data, as well as voice and video, at speeds of up to 64 kilobits per second. The data on an entire floppy disk will be transmitted in just a few seconds. And you'll be able to fax and speak at the same time.

And, even as experts are working to improve the capabilities of phone lines, networks that use light or radio waves to transmit data are being introduced to the business market. These "instant networks," which require no cabling or wiring to connect their components, are attracting a great deal of interest from companies that are growing rapidly, that reconfigure their office/headquarter designs frequently, or that find extensive cabling and wiring to be inconvenient or even dangerous. NCR's Wavelan connects standard AT-class computers (with antennas and special expansion cards) by spread-spectrum radio transmission, which works with DOS and Novell Netware 286, allowing users to share files, programs, electronic mail, printers, and other resources. Other new wireless network systems use infrared light to transmit data and instructions. IBM and Motorola have introduced a handheld terminal that uses radio waves to tap into a central computer from almost anywhere in the field.

What will be the effect of this widespread availability of information? For one thing, offices will become more portable, and "telecommuters" will become more common. Perhaps the greatest result will be the democratization of information. This is seen in one of the most recent applications known as *groupware*—computer-assisted group processes. Groupware allows two or more people on a network to work on the same document at the same time. Communication between microcomputer-equipped group members can be by means of correspondence or voice (including voice mail) but can also include pictorial information. All such shared information can be scanned, searched, stored, and annotated, facilitating the rapid exchange of ideas and dialogue in highly efficient form.

Ultimately, perhaps, information linked in enormous networks could create a pluralistic world in which, according to some seers, all information is available to everyone. Billions of people would be attached to a worldwide electronic network simultaneously over phone lines or satellite connections. Or, conversely, the possession of data and information and control of their dissemination could become the new arbiter of power. Infocrats would control the technopeasants, whose access to information would be limited by those in charge of vast data banks and networking capabilities.

ONWARD: SYSTEMS DEVELOPMENT LIFE CYCLE

Now that you have an idea of how software is created and used and why communications and networking technologies are important, we'll discuss how program and system requirements are determined. How does an organization identify its information needs and data processing requirements? It goes through the systems development life cycle, or SDLC, to be discussed in Chapter 10. First, however, we'll check to see what Sporting Life is doing about communications and purchasing its microcomputer system.

SUMMARY

With the development of modern telecommunications and electronic communications, business users and decision makers have been able to retrieve and send data quickly to and from widely scattered sources through the use of computers and communications hardware, software, and media.

To understand the basics of electronic data communications, one must know something about the characteristics of data transmission. When people speak, the sound travels as analog signals—continuous signals that repeat a certain number of times over a certain period (frequency) at certain amplitudes (degrees of loudness).

Telephone lines carry analog signals. Computers, in contrast, use digital signals—discontinuous (discrete) pulses of electricity (on) separated by pauses (off).

When they communicate, the sending and receiving computers must use modems (*mo*dulate/*dem*odulate) to convert the digital signals into analog signals for transmission and then back again into digital signals for reception. Direct-connect modems connect directly to the computer and can be internal (built into the computer or inserted on an add-on card or board) or external (connected to the computer and the telephone by cable).

When signals are transmitted from computer to computer, patterns of bits coded to represent data are sent one bit at a time. For the receiving computer to be able to determine where one character of data ends and another starts, data is sent either asynchronously or synchronously. In asynchronous transmission, each string of bits that make up a character is bracketed by control bits—a start bit, one or two stop bits, and an error check bit, or parity bit. Most microcomputers use asynchronous transmission.

In synchronous transmission, characters are sent as blocks with synch bits inserted as identifiers at the beginning and end of the blocks. This type of transmission is used by large computers to transmit huge volumes of data at high speeds.

Data communications technology must also consider the direction of data traffic: simplex (one way only), half-duplex (two-way traffic but only one direction at a time), or full-duplex (two-way traffic passing at the same time).

The media most commonly used for communication are telephone wires (open and twisted-wire), coaxial cables, atmosphere (microwave and satellite systems), and fiber optic cables. Each of these media differs in terms of the form of the transmitted data (electrical pulses, electromagnetic waves, or light pulses), the rate at which data moves through it, and its susceptibility to noise and "eavesdropping."

Data communications lines can be connected in two types of configurations: point-to-point and multidrop. A point-to-point line directly connects the sending and the receiving devices. A point-to-point switched line is a regular telephone line; a point-to-point dedicated line is never disconnected—it is either owned or leased by the company that is using it. A multidrop line connects many devices, not just one sending device and one receiving device.

The hardware typically used to communicate between computers includes modems, multiplexers, concentrators, controllers, front-end processors, and protocol converters. Multiplexers, concentrators, controllers, and front-end processors all allow multiplexing—the sharing of one high-speed communications line by multiple users or devices. A concentrator, which is like a multiplexer, is more "intelligent" because it can store and forward transmissions. A controller performs more functions than a multiplexer or a concentrator. A front-end processor, a smaller computer connected to the main computer, not only allows multiplexing but also relieves the main computer of many routine data traffic management and communications functions.

To communicate, the sending and receiving computers must follow the same rules, or protocols. In the case of microcomputer communications, the software parameters can be set on both ends to agree. In other cases, protocol converters must be used. For example, a protocol converter could be used to allow a microcomputer in asynchronous mode to communicate with a mainframe operating in synchronous mode.

Companies often set up communications networks, which are collections of data communications hardware, computers, communications software, and communications media connected in a meaningful group to allow users to share data and information. Three basic types of networks are private, public, and international. Private networks support the communications needs of particular business organizations. Public networks provide paying subscribers with voice or data communications over a large geographical area. International networks provide users with intercontinental voice and data communications facilities. Networks can be set up in different "shapes": star (and hierarchical) network, bus network, and ring (and token ring) network. The normal business user may encounter one of these network shapes in the context of a local area network (LAN), which is a private network that serves a company or a part of a company that is located on one floor, in a single building, or in offices within approximately two miles of one another.

The star network uses a host computer or a file server connected to a number of smaller computers and/or terminals, called nodes. The nodes are not designed to communicate directly with one another, so if the main computer fails, the whole network "goes down."

In a more complicated star network called a hierarchical, or tree, network, some nodes have devices connected to them in smaller star networks.

In a bus network, a number of computers are connected to a single communications line. In this network, if one computer fails, the others can continue to operate.

A ring network is much like a bus network, except that the communications line forms a loop. This network has no central computer, and each computer connected to the network can communicate directly with the others.

In the token ring network, predefined patterns of bits, or tokens, are passed from computer to computer. The computer with the token can transmit; the others cannot. This setup prevents the garbling of messages that occurs when more than one computer tries to transmit at the same time.

More and more offices are using fax machines and fax boards to send and receive documents quickly and cheaply over the phone lines. A fax machine comprises a scanner (input), a thermal printer (output), and a modem; a fax board, or card, is inserted into the computer's system unit, in an expansion slot, to transmit images that originate in the computer. In both cases, text and graphics can be faxed to receiving machines/boards.

The business user can benefit from computer-to-computer communications using a number of public services and utilities to access data and information. Public databanks provide information about such topics as health, education, law, the humanities, science, and government. To use these databanks, the user pays a fee plus the regular phone charges. Public information services also provide the user with such convenience as electronic shopping and banking, electronic bulletin boards, voice mail, and electronic mail.

KEY TERMS

amplitude, p. 340
analog signal, p. 340
asynchronous transmission, p. 341
bus network, p. 363
coaxial cable, p. 346
concentrator, p. 354
controller, p. 354
dedicated line, p. 351
demodulation, p. 341
digital signal, p. 341
direct-connect modem, p. 352
electronic banking, p. 374

electronic bulletin board service (BBS), p. 371
electronic communications, p. 339
electronic mail, p. 372
electronic shopping, p. 371
external modem, p. 352
fax (facsimile) machine, p. 374
fax, p. 374
fiber optics, p. 350
file server, p. 362
frequency, p. 340
front-end processor, p. 356
full-duplex, p. 344
half-duplex, p. 343
hierarchical network, p. 363
information service, p. 366
internal modem, p. 352
international network, p. 359
local area network (LAN), p. 360
microwave system, p. 347
modem, p. 341
modulation, p. 341
multidrop line, p. 351
multiplexer, p. 354
network, p. 359
point-to-point line, p. 351
private network, p. 359
protocol, p. 356
protocol converter, p. 356
public databank, p. 366
public network, p. 359
ring network, p. 364
satellite, p. 349
simplex, p. 343
star network, p. 361
switched line, p. 351
synch byte, p. 342
synchronous transmission, p. 342
teleconferencing, p. 359
token ring network, p. 365
tree network, p. 363
virus, p. 376
voice mail, p. 374

EXERCISES

MATCHING

Match each of the following terms to the phrase that is the most closely related.

1. ____ protocol converter
2. ____ fax board
3. ____ digital signals
4. ____ asynchronous mode
5. ____ half-duplex
6. ____ electronic communications
7. ____ analog signals
8. ____ full-duplex
9. ____ synchronous mode
10. ____ modulation
11. ____ network
12. ____ file server
13. ____ multiplexer
14. ____ fiber optic cable
15. ____ direct-connect modem

a. The movement of voice and data over long distances through the use of computers
b. Signals that are composed of continuous waves
c. Each character is transmitted one at a time—bracketed by start, stop, and parity bits—to the receiving computer.
d. Can be the center of a star network
e. Communications mode in which data can move in two directions, but in only one direction at one time
f. Signals that are composed of discontinuous (discrete) electrical pulses
g. Characters communicated in blocks with identifying synch bits to the receiving computer

h. Modulator/demodulator—internal or external—that connects directly to the phone line and the computer
i. Communications medium that transmits data as pulses of light through strands of glass
j. Collection of data communications hardware, computers, communications software, and communications media connected in a meaningful group to allow users to share information and equipment
k. Expansion card that transmits computer-generated text and graphics over the phone line
l. Communications mode in which data is transmitted in two directions simultaneously
m. Data communications hardware component designed to allow two or more data transmissions to share a single communications line
n. Process of converting a digital signal into analog form so that data can be sent over the phone lines
o. Device that allows a microcomputer to communicate with a mainframe computer

Multiple Choice

1. Which of the following performs modulation and demodulation?
   a. fiber optic
   b. satellite
   c. coaxial cable
   d. modem
   e. protocol converter
2. The process of converting analog signals into digital signals so they can be processed by a receiving computer is referred to as:
   a. modulation
   b. demodulation
   c. synchronizing
   d. asynchronizing
   e. frequency
3. Which of the following communications modes supports two-way traffic but in only one direction at a time?
   a. simplex
   b. half-duplex
   c. three-quarters duplex
   d. full-duplex
   e. asynchronous
4. Which of the following might be used by a company to satisfy its growing communications needs?
   a. front-end processor
   b. multiplexer
   c. controller
   d. concentrator
   e. all the above
5. Which of the following is considered a broadband communications channel?
   a. coaxial cable

   b. fiber optic cable
   c. microwave circuits
   d. satellite systems
   e. all the above

6. Which of the following is not a transmission medium?
   a. telephone line
   b. coaxial cable
   c. modem
   d. microwave system
   e. satellite system.

7. Which of the following can a stand-alone fax machine do?
   a. transmit text and graphics over the phone line
   b. dial up other fax machines automatically
   c. scan documents for transmission
   d. receive text and graphics over the phone line and print them out
   e. all the above

8. Which of the following is an advantage to using fiber optics data transmission?
   a. resistance to data theft
   b. fast data transmission rate
   c. low noise level
   d. few transmission errors
   e. all the above

9. Which of the following types of telephone lines is always established (connected) for one company's data communications only?
   a. multidrop
   b. dedicated
   c. direct
   d. leased
   e. twisted pair

10. What type of network would most likely be found in a company that occupies a single building?
    a. WAN
    b. WIDE
    c. LAN
    d. MAN
    e. WAVE

SHORT ANSWER

1. When might you encounter electronic communications in the business environment?
2. What are modems used for?
3. What is the function of a multiplexer?
4. Explain the difference between analog and digital signals.
5. What does a microcomputer user need to do in order to communicate synchronously?
6. What is the main function of a front-end processor?

7. What is meant by the term *protocol* as it relates to communicating between two computers?
8. Explain why some people think the biggest disadvantage of microwave systems is their popularity.
9. Describe the difference between synchronous and asynchronous transmission modes and how they affect the speed with which data can be communicated.
10. What is a communications network? What are networks used for?

PROJECTS

1. Are the computers at your school or work connected to a network? If so, what are the characteristics of the network? What advantages does the network provide in terms of hardware and software support? What types of computers are connected to the network (microcomputers, minicomputers, and/or mainframes)? Specifically, what software/hardware is allowing the network to function?
2. You need to purchase a computer to use at home to perform business-related/school-related tasks. You want to be able to communicate with the network at work/school so that you can use its software and access its data. Include the following in a report:
   a. A description of the types of tasks you will want to perform at home.
   b. The name of the computer you would buy (include a detailed description of the computer, such as the main memory capacity and disk storage capacity).
   c. The communications hardware/software you would need to purchase.
   d. A cost estimate.
3. Check a local microcomputer publication for information about local electronic bulletin boards. Whom do they serve? What are the primary areas of interest they focus on? What hardware/software must a user have to use the services? Are they free? Do they give each user an ID name or number? Which bulletin board(s) would you use? Why?
4. Many articles and books have appeared lately that discuss the problem of hackers, crackers, and viruses and what individuals, companies, and countries should do to protect themselves and to establish laws and penalties for disruption, destruction, and theft in the area of data processing. Research this issue and report on the penalties and the protective measures you think are appropriate. How far may a government or a company go in protecting its data and information before it infringes on the rights of the individual? What is the Freedom of Information Act, and how does it play a role in this issue?
5. Are you aware of any computer viruses infecting a system or systems on your campus? What kind of virus? How was the virus spread? What damage did it do?

EPISODE 3

SPORTING LIFE

WHAT ARE THE GUIDELINES FOR BUYING A MICROCOMPUTER SYSTEM?

THE STORY CONTINUES . . .

By now things have gotten even wilder at Sporting Life. Two months ago your sales were $4.2 million and climbing—good news, of course, but Luis is still struggling with his problem of trying to keep inventory records up to date, and Kim is hard pressed to keep up with the accounting workload. Now that you have offered a discount to schools in your area (10 percent off all products bought by schools, and larger discounts for individual orders over $500), business is doing even better.

SIZING UP THE SITUATION

In the meeting described in Episode 2, Luis and Kim gave you their "wish lists"—descriptions of what they would like the computer to do. However, because most experts advise that you not buy hardware until you understand what software you will want to run, you have made no moves to install a computer system until you became familiar with software. Now you know something about both hardware and software, and you are in a position to buy.

What follows is a list of some important questions that you or *anyone*—student, businessperson, or hobbyist—can ask salespeople when shopping for computer hardware and software. The questions themselves are general; the examples we give, of course, are those that have grown out of the specific problems you're trying to solve at Sporting Life. (Readers who want more detailed information on purchasing a microcomputer system and installing software will find it in the appendix entitled "Purchasing and Maintaining a Microcomputer System.")

HOW MUCH MONEY DO YOU HAVE TO SPEND? The salesperson may well ask this question (albeit more politely, perhaps wondering what is "in your price range"). You need not state your budget, but you should probably have your top figure in mind. The best strategy is to tell the salesperson the problems you are trying to solve, and then see if you can get the best hardware and software combination that will solve them for the least amount of money.

Note: The word to keep in mind is *upgrade*. You can often start out with an inexpensive computer and then upgrade it by adding parts later. It is not necessary to buy an expensive system to take care of all your *future* needs—especially if you aren't sure what those needs will be. With Sporting Life, for instance, you might end up with 20 stores in five years, but you certainly don't want to buy a system for that now.

HOW SOPHISTICATED DO YOU WANT YOUR COMPUTER TO BE? A microcomputer can be anything from a video game machine to an executive workstation. Sporting Life may be in the business of games, but you don't want a computer that just *plays* games. Here, then, are some matters to consider regarding sophistication:

1. Will the computer remain in your office (a desktop computer) or should it be portable (a laptop) so that you, Luis, and Kim can share it?
2. Should it be the same as, or compatible with, other computers — such as one at home or others linked by telephone?
3. Should it be able to use software you may already have?
4. Do you want it to show images in more than one color?
5. Should it be capable of holding a lot of information or large software programs?
6. Should it be upgradable and expandable? Will you be able to buy add-ons for it later that will make it faster, more powerful, more versatile, and so on?
7. Do you have any special communications needs?

The answers to some of these questions depend on the kind of software you will need, as we shall discuss. At Sporting Life, right now it looks as though you don't need a portable computer or one that runs the same software you have at home. You may, however, want Luis to use a different one than Kim uses — but be sure their equipment is compatible, so that the same software can run on both.

WHAT KIND OF SOFTWARE WILL YOU WANT TO RUN? The answer to this question lies in the answer to another question: What kind of tasks do you want the computer to do for you? You can get a computer and software that will enable you to play games, create art, compose electronic music, and track the stock market, but those are mainly home activities. Microcomputers used for work are another matter. Here are the most common questions to ask yourself — and the salesperson — about what you will use the computer for and, hence, what kind of software you will require:

1. *Word processing:* Will the computer be used for writing — such as letters, memos, reports, papers?
2. *Spreadsheets:* Will the computer be used to compute "what if" types of financial possibilities — such as estimating costs, constructing bids, pricing products, calculating budgets, doing sales forecasts, and other forms of money management?
3. *File or database manager:* Will the computer be used to create mailing lists, address lists, lists of possessions or products, or other forms of recordkeeping?
4. *Telecommunications:* Will the computer need to exchange messages with other computer users and to access computer data banks?
5. *Graphics:* Will the computer be used to create charts and graphs?

6. *Integrated packages:* Will the computer have to mix any of the tasks listed above? For example, will sales figures be extracted from a file, manipulated on a spreadsheet, shown in graph form, put into a report, and/or transmitted by phone to another computer user?
7. *Special requirements:* Will the computer be used for desktop publishing (for, say, publishing a newsletter for Sporting Life employees)? Will it be used to do accounting tasks? Plan business strategy? Do stock market analysis? Special-purpose or industry-specific software is available for all kinds of tasks.

At Sporting Life, Luis needs a program to keep track of inventory; a database management program, such as dBASE IV or R:base for DOS, would be helpful to him. Kim needs software for accounting—a specific accounting program, perhaps, but she might be able to use an integrated package that can retrieve information from a file, display it in spreadsheet or graph form, and print out reports and purchase orders. Symphony, Framework, or Microsoft Works might be the best solution; however, such programs will run only on certain machines (such as IBM PS/2 models) with a minimum required amount of memory (for instance, 640 K to 1 MB).

WHAT KIND OF HARDWARE SHOULD YOU BUY? Because the software is available only for certain brands of computers, your choice automatically rules out some makes. Programs available for a Mac II, for example, will not run on an IBM PS/2 without special equipment. In addition, certain programs will run only on certain *models* of a particular make; some software will run on the AT model of an IBM computer but not on the original PC model. Moreover, if the software requires certain kinds of disk drives, availability of color video display, or access to a printer, those factors will also determine the kind of computer you buy.

The following are basic questions to ask:

1. *Processor:* Does the software require a machine with an 8-, 16-, or 32-bit processor?
2. *Memory:* How much memory (in kilobytes) does the software need?
3. *Expandability:* Is the computer that you are considering expandable in memory capacity? That is, can you add plug-in circuit boards or otherwise increase the memory capacity? Are there limits?
4. *Secondary storage:* Does the software run on 3½-inch or 5¼-inch diskettes? Does it require a hard disk drive?
5. *Video display:* What kind of monitor or video display screen is standard with the computer being considered? Is it adequate to run the software? Will it display 80 columns (usually necessary with most software)? Is a monochrome (one-color) monitor sufficient and, if so, is it green or amber (colors that are less eye-fatiguing than white-on-black)? Is a color monitor warranted with the software you're considering? Is the screen resolution high enough for your purposes?
6. *Interfaces:* Will the computer interface (connect with) the devices such as printers and telecommunications devices that you need to run your software? Note that printers, for instance, may have either serial or parallel interfaces. Parallel transmission is used between the computer and most printers.

7. *Printer:* What kind of printer will you need to take advantage of the software? Do you need a dot-matrix printer in order to print out draft-quality and near-letter-quality text, as well as graphics (pictures)? Do you need a laser printer (which will print higher-quality text and graphics and is quieter, but which may be expensive)? Is the printer fast enough for your needs? Will it have the kind of paper-feed device (friction feed, pin feed, or tractor feed) that will enable you to print with the kinds of paper or forms you want to use? Can you use just a printer for normal width (8½-inch-wide) paper, or do you need a wider printer for accounting or financial planning?
8. *Modem:* With one exception — telecommunications — most software can be run on the equipment we have discussed above. To communicate with another computer over a telephone line, however, you need a modem to connect your computer with a telephone. If you need one, how fast should it be? Faster modems, although they are more expensive, may be easier on the phone bills if you're sending a lot of information. Can the modem both originate and receive messages?
9. *Fax:* Will you need a fax machine to facilitate ordering items that are low in stock? To receive emergency orders from customers? Do you need an internal fax board, or would a stand-alone fax machine do? Do you need to have an additional phone line installed for the fax machine?
10. *Other peripheral devices:* Does your software require a mouse to manipulate images on the screen? Do you need sound effects (for music or speech output), optical scanner, bar code reader, voice-recognition device, or a chip-mounted real-time clock inside the computer?

An analysis of Kim's present needs at Sporting Life suggests that, to keep track of the accounting records (part of which involves analyzing accounts payable and accounts receivable in graphic form) and the personnel/payroll records, she needs the following hardware and software configuration:

1. Spreadsheet, database, and word processing software (or an integrated package).
2. A microcomputer of at least 16 bits, with at least 640 K and expandable memory.
3. A 60 MB (or larger) hard disk drive.
4. A color monitor to display graphics.
5. A laser printer capable of printing out wide accounting reports, with a special paper tray for forms such as invoices and purchase orders, and an envelope feeder.

Kim, her accounting assistant, and her personnel/payroll assistant are the three people who will be using this microcomputer system; they will make up a schedule showing the times each will be using it.

As the controller of accounting, Kim is also in charge of Sporting Life's two cashiers. To track sales, each cashier requires the following microcomputer configuration:

1. A software program that prompts the cashier to enter the item number and number of items purchased and that then prints out a list of the items and their prices, including a total, for the customer.

2. A microcomputer of at least 16 bits, with at least 640 K and expandable memory.
3. A 60 MB (or larger) hard disk drive that stores an inventory file containing the item numbers and prices of every item in stock, as well as one or more transaction files (depending on the day's activities) that contain data about the number of items sold and returned each day. (*Note:* A transaction file can't be larger than the storage capacity of a floppy diskette because the disks later need to be transferred to Luis, who will update the master inventory file.)
4. A monochrome monitor.
5. A small dot-matrix printer that will print out sales receipts (with carbons).

At the end of each day, the cashiers make two copies of the transaction file(s) onto one or more diskettes; one copy goes to Luis so that he can update the master transaction file and determine the status of inventory, and the other copy goes to Kim so that she can keep the accounting records current. (If you can afford it, you can avoid this manual activity by purchasing a communications software package such as Crosstalk XVI and the appropriate length of cable to enable the cashiers to communicate directly with Luis's and Kim's computers. (You'll need modems only if you are communicating over the phone lines.)

The main function of Luis's computer is to keep track of inventory. He requires a microcomputer system similar to Kim's, although he should have at least a 80 MB hard disk drive to accommodate all the data that relates to the more than 1,300 different items that are carried in stock. Luis doesn't need a color monitor; a monochrome monitor would be fine. He should have a laser printer capable of printing out wide inventory reports, although it doesn't need a special paper tray or an envelope feeder. Luis will be the only one using this microcomputer system, unless he hires someone to update the master inventory file at the end of each day.

Of course, you—because you're the boss—get to use the computers almost any time you want!

WHAT KIND OF SUPPORT COMES WITH THE COMPUTER SYSTEM? Before you move on to Part 4 and Episode 4, which deal with systems design, databases, and information management, you need to consider your support system. The purpose of a computer is to save time. But if you have to figure everything out by yourself or fix it yourself, the time your computer saves may be minimal. Thus, questions about support should include the following:

1. Is the computer and software retailer able to give you advice and assistance—either by virtue of being close by or, if a mail order house, by technical support over the telephone?
2. Does the seller offer training classes?
3. Does the seller offer any help in financing your purchases?
4. Can a maintenance contract be purchased to cover parts and labor in case of breakdowns?
5. Is the documentation accompanying each piece of hardware and software clear?

PART IV

SYSTEMS CONCEPTS AND APPLICATIONS

If you choose a descriptive word at random—*nervous*, *planetary*, *educational*—and put it in front of the word *system*, you immediately suggest something powerful: a collection of items forming a whole or serving some purpose more important than the items themselves. Systems are an important concept of computers in business. In the following three chapters, we will see how you can use the concept as a way of solving problems, organizing databases, and managing information.

10

Chapter 10

Systems Development Life Cycle

No matter what your position in an organization, you will undoubtedly come in contact with a systems development life cycle (SDLC)—the process of setting up an *information system*. Regardless of the circumstances, the user has a definite role in a systems development life cycle. And if you, the user, understand its principles, you will be able to apply them to solving *any* type of problem, not just business- and/or computer-related ones.

Preview

When you have completed this chapter, you will be able to:

- Explain why some systems fail.
- Identify six phases of a systems development life cycle.
- List the techniques for gathering and analyzing data describing the current system.
- Describe the extent to which the requirements for a new information system must be defined before it is designed.
- Identify the major factors to consider in designing the input, output, and processing procedures and storage requirements of a new system.
- Describe the role of the user in the systems development life cycle.
- Describe four basic approaches to implementing a new computer-based information system.

The User Perspective

An information system is an arrangement of interdependent human and machine components and procedures that interact to support the information needs of a business and its users. However, such a system does not come prepackaged like some software applications programs; it must be developed by people.

How might you have to deal with systems development? You may be a manager whose staff is unable to handle the current workload and who has requested a study to see if a computer will improve the situation. Or you may be a staff member faced with the task of learning how to use and evaluate a new sales order entry system. Perhaps the division vice president has decided that some departments need computers, and you are asked to submit a report on your department's need for one. And, as you will see, you may be involved with the systems development life cycle process in even more ways.

The extent to which your job brings you in contact with your company's **systems development life cycle (SDLC)**—the formal process by which companies build computer-based information systems—will vary depending on a number of factors, including the size of the organization, your job description, your relevant experience, and your educational background in information-processing concepts, tools, and techniques. In large companies, the SDLC is usually a formal process with clearly defined standards and procedures. Although the technical aspects of each phase of the cycle will undoubtedly be handled by computer specialists, you will likely interface with these specialists. For example:

- It may be necessary for you to explain how the current system works in your department—the manual procedures you use or what you do to support an existing computer-based system.
- You could easily find yourself in a meeting discussing the nature of problems with the current system and how it can be improved.
- You may be required to provide to systems analysts and designers the departmental objectives and requirements that the system must meet. For instance, if you expect to have the new system produce useful reports, then you should plan to assist the computer specialists in designing them.
- As the development of a new system nears completion, you may help in testing it to ensure that it works as expected.
- You may attend briefings and training sessions to learn how the new system will affect your job and what its new operating procedures will be.
- And last, but certainly not least, you will end up using the new system. This may involve preparing data for input or using information produced by the system.

In addition:

- If your company doesn't have a data processing staff or department, you may have to develop a system yourself, using the same steps that systems analysts and designers use.
- With the ever-increasing use of fourth-generation languages and other microcomputer development tools, you will likely become more involved in developing systems themselves (through prototyping—the building of a small, simple model of the system, which we will discuss later).

- You may often be involved in the approval of projects and budgets as a member of a special steering committee (which we also discuss in more detail later).

In a sizable company, the SDLC may seem like a large and complex process to which you are only peripherally related; however, your role in it is still important. Although in a small organization you are likely to be involved in more phases of the SDLC, and your role in each phase will tend to be more detailed, you shouldn't assume that the principles of an SDLC apply only to large computer systems and applications. Users often believe that they can purchase a microcomputer and a payroll software package on Monday and have a staff member produce paychecks on Friday. Unfortunately, it just isn't that simple. The basic principles of an SDLC should be followed even at the microcomputer level.

Remember, in the past, many systems (and often the businesses that set up the systems) have failed because the components and the functions of the system were never clearly defined in terms of specific objectives and were not controlled tightly enough, allowing costs to greatly exceed estimates. These problems can be avoided through user participation—*your* participation—in and control of the systems development process.

THE SYSTEMS DEVELOPMENT LIFE CYCLE

Businesses are made up of many systems and subsystems, including many manual and mechanized procedures. Some systems are very simple; an order entry system could be just a set of procedures for taking down a telephone order from a customer and seeing that the appropriate catalog item is delivered. Other systems are very complicated; a large company's payroll system involves a number of subsystems for tracking employee turnover, pay rate changes, tax exemption status, types of insurance deductions, overtime rates and bonuses, and so on.

You learned earlier that a system for which a computer is used to perform some of the procedures is called a *computer-based information system*. No computer-based system can stand on its own. As we discussed in Chapters 1 and 2, people must interact with the system and perform the manual procedures required to feed it raw data, review the information produced, and take appropriate actions.

The scope of an SDLC can vary. In some cases, the effort will be so large that dozens of people will be involved for a year or more. In other cases, the scope will be much smaller—for example, the owner of a two-person graphic design business would not take long to set up an invoice and payment system. In both extremes, however, it is equally important to follow a clearly defined process. The degree of complexity of an SDLC and the amount of effort that goes into each of its phases will vary according to the scope of the project.

WHY DO SYSTEMS DEVELOPMENT PROJECTS FAIL?

The chances are great that a systems development project will fail if a clearly defined SDLC isn't followed. Sometimes, however, even when companies go to the trouble of establishing a formal and comprehensive SDLC, projects still fail to achieve their objectives. Why? Most failures can be traced to a breakdown in communications between the users and the data processing group or among the computer specialists. The reasons for failure often include:

- *Inadequate user involvement.* Users must assume responsibility for educating the analyst about business applications, requirements, and policies. (For example, a system may fail because major functions weren't anticipated in the design—because users didn't make their needs known.)
- *Continuation of a project that should have been canceled.* Often it's tempting to *not* cancel a project because of the investment already made. Analysts should reevaluate the project at various phases to determine if it remains feasible.
- *The failure of two or more portions of the new system to fit together properly* (called *systems integration*). This often results when major portions of the systems are worked on by different groups of technical specialists who do not communicate well.

Responses to systems failure vary. Project leaders may be fired; usually the systems requirements are reassessed, and the highest-priority requirements are identified to be satisfied by a smaller system that can be more easily controlled.

WANTED: ORDERLY DEVELOPMENT PROCESS

In most sizable companies, a great deal of money is allocated for information processing functions (hardware, software, and staff support). In such companies, a systems development project that costs more than $1 million is not uncommon. Hundreds, even thousands, of individual tasks may need to be performed as part of the development effort (Figure 10.1). These tasks may involve many people within an organization, often in several different organizational units. This multiplicity of effort can lead to conflicting objectives and result in a project that is difficult to coordinate. If the process of developing a system bogs down, the final product can be delayed, and the final cost can be more than double the original estimate. To avoid such difficulties, the SDLC is used as a guideline to direct and administer the activities and to control the financial resources expended—in other words, to impose order on the development process. In a small company, the amount of money spent on project development may not be much; however, following the steps of the SDLC is no less significant. Some, but by no means all, risks of ignoring these steps include the following:

- *The new system does not meet the user's needs.* Inaccurate or incomplete information given by users to systems analysts and designers may result in the development of software that does not do what the user needs.
- *The acquisition of unnecessary hardware or too much hardware.* If personal computers and printers are sitting idle most of the time, then probably far too much money has been invested without a clear definition of how much processing power is needed.
- *The acquisition of insufficient hardware.* The system may be inefficient.
- *Software may be inadequately tested and thus may not perform as expected.* Users tend to rely heavily on the accuracy and the completeness of the

information provided by the computer. However, if software is not adequately tested before it is given to users, undetected programming logic errors may produce inaccurate or incomplete information.

Different organizations may refer to the systems development life cycle by different names—such as Systems Development Cycle (SDC) or Systems Life Cycle (SLC); however, the general objectives will always be the same. The number of steps necessary to complete the cycle may also vary from one company to another, depending on the level of detail necessary to effectively administer and control the development of systems. One way to look at systems development is to divide it into six phases:

FIGURE 10.1 This job description for a typical systems analyst provides an example of some of the many tasks the analyst must perform and the people and departments he or she must serve. (J. Whitten, L. Bentley, and V. Barlow, *Systems Analysis and Design Methods*, 2nd ed. [Homewood, Ill.: Richard D. Irwin, 1989], p. 7.)

JOB DESCRIPTION

JOB TITLE Systems Analyst REPORTS TO Development Center Manager

DESCRIPTION Gathers and analyzes data for developing information systems. A systems analyst shall be responsible for studying the problems and needs set forth by this organization to determine how computer equipment, business procedures, and people can best solve these problems and accomplish improvements. Designs and specifies systems and methods for installing computer-based information systems and guides their installation. Makes formal presentations of findings, recommendations, and specifications in formal reports and in oral presentations.

RESPONSIBILITIES

1. Evaluates projects for feasibility.
2. Analyzes current business systems for problems and opportunities.
3. Defines requirements for improving or replacing systems.
4. Evaluates alternative solutions for feasibility.
5. Selects hardware and software products (subject to approval).
6. Designs system interfaces, flow, and procedures.
7. Supervises system implementation.

DUTIES

1. Estimates personnel requirements, budgets, and schedules for systems projects.
2. Develops and implements systems development plans according to CIS standards.
3. Performs interviews and other data gathering.
4. Documents and analyzes current system operations.
5. Formulates applications of current technology to business problems.
6. Educates user management on capabilities and use of current technology.
7. Evaluates technological possibilities for technical, operational, and economic feasibility.
8. Reviews and presents proposed systems solutions for approval.
9. Designs and tests system prototypes.
10. Designs file and database structures.
11. Designs user interfaces (input, output, and dialogue) to computer systems.
12. Designs data collection forms and techniques.
13. Designs systems security and controls.
14. Prepares specifications for applications programs.
15. Writes, tests, and integrates applications programs.
16. Supervises applications programming.
17. Develops and guides systems testing and conversion plans.

Phase 1—Analyze current system.

Phase 2—Define new systems requirements.

Phase 3—Design new system.

Phase 4—Develop new system.

Phase 5—Implement new system.

Phase 6—Evaluate performance of new system and maintain system.

Figure 10.2 diagrams the six phases of the SDLC. Keep in mind that, although we speak of six separate SDLC phases, one phase does not necessarily have to be completed before the next one is started. In other words, the phases often overlap. The degree of overlap usually depends on the project's size and the amount of resources committed to the project. However, work done on a subsequent phase is subject to change until the work of the preceding phase is completed.

FIGURE 10.1 *(continued)*

JOB DESCRIPTION *(continued)*

EXTERNAL CONTACTS	1. Users of computing services. 2. User management. 3. Technical support personnel. 4. Data administration personnel. 5. Systems and programming personnel. 6. CIS operations personnel. 7. Applications programmers. 8. Computer hardware and software vendors. 9. Other systems analysts (on project teams).
QUALIFYING EXPERIENCE	1. A bachelor's or master's degree in computing, business, statistics, or industrial engineering is required. 2. Programming experience is mandatory. 3. Training or experience in business functions is desirable. 4. Training in systems analysis, especially structured methods, is desirable. 5. Good communications skills—oral and written—are mandatory.
TRAINING REQUIREMENTS	1. Systems development standards. 2. Database methods. 3. Data communications methods. 4. Structured systems development methods. 5. Prototyping methods. 6. Feasibility and cost-benefit methods.
CAREER PATH	Promotion based on time in rank and performance. Job levels are: 1. Systems Analyst 1: 30% analysis and design, 70% programming and implementation. 2. Systems Analyst 2: 50% analysis and design, 50% programming. 3. Systems Analyst 3: 70% analysis and design, 30% programming (mostly prototyping). 4. Senior Analyst: 30% project management, 60% analysis and design, 10% programming (mostly prototyping). 5. Lead Analyst: 75% management of several project managers, 25% analysis and design.

WANTED: PARTICIPANTS

Three groups of personnel are usually involved in an SDLC project: the user group staff members (users), representatives of user management and information processing management (management), and a technical staff consisting of systems analysts and programmers (computer specialists). The users could come from a number of different departments, particularly in large systems. In smaller systems, the user may be a single individual or department. The analysts function as a bridge between the business users and the computer programmers and technicians.

Management participation in systems development is important because it lends support to the efforts underway. The cooperation of all staff members is much easier to obtain when all levels of management have indicated their support for the project. Users must know that management will work with them to minimize any disruption caused by the project. In addition, management needs to review and approve progress as a project proceeds through each phase of the cycle. User management focuses on getting what is required; that is, it makes sure that the system fills all the stated requirements, and it evaluates the system's effect on staff and budget. Certain users, management representatives, and computer specialists form a systems development project management team, which is led by a project leader, a systems analysis specialist.

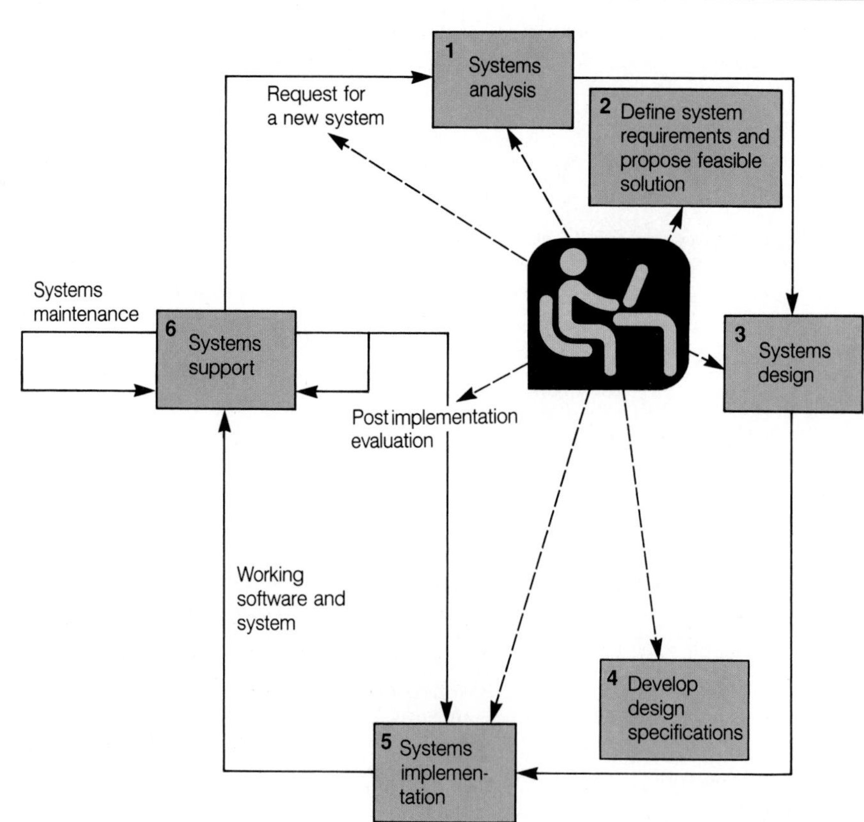

FIGURE 10.2

Typical Systems Development Life Cycle. An SDLC commonly includes six phases. After each of the first four phases, management must decide whether or not to proceed to the next phase. User input and review is a critical part of each phase. (Adapted from J. Whitten, L. Bentley, and V. Barlow, *Systems Analysis and Design Methods*, 2nd ed. [Homewood, Ill.: Richard D. Irwin, 1989], p. 82.)

Occasionally *steering committees* are formed to help decide how to get started—that is, which systems development projects to work on first. A steering committee is a group of individuals from each department in an organization. It may hear reports from experts about the advantages, disadvantages, and costs of a particular project, after which it must decide whether it is in the organization's interest to implement the project. If it decides to go ahead, the systems development life cycle begins.

GETTING STARTED

The development of a system can be initiated in a number of ways. As we have indicated, a project request can come from a steering committee, which has already evaluated the project's potential benefits. In a large organization, a user department (for example, payroll department, personnel department, or marketing department) may fill out a project request and submit it to management. Or top management may decide on its own to replace an archaic system—for instance, the manual accounting system—with a more modern and efficient one. Project requests may also originate from computer professionals or government. The requests are forwarded to the information processing department for review. Then the first phase of the SDLC begins.

PHASE 1: ANALYZE THE CURRENT SYSTEM

As we mentioned, the steering committee may request experts to report on a proposed project. This report, often called a *feasibility study*, is an optional step, but it can be considered part of the first phase of systems development. The goal of a feasibility study is to identify as quickly as possible whether the benefits of a proposed project appear to outweigh its expected cost and disruption. The analyst who conducts the study usually presents the findings to the steering committee along with a recommendation of how much priority should be assigned to the project. Because early feasibility estimates may be overly optimistic, it's usually a good idea to conduct feasibility studies at various times *throughout all phases* of the SDLC to determine whether to continue the project.

PURPOSE OF PHASE 1

The objective of Phase 1 is to gain a clear understanding of the existing system and its shortcomings and to determine where improvements can be made; an analysis of the current system takes place regardless of whether it is manual or computer-based. Figure 10.3 shows how you might have identified the problems in Sporting Life's manual accounting system, as well as areas in which a computer-based system could make improvements. The participants in this phase are usually the systems analyst, who must gain an understanding of the current system, and the users, who must educate the systems analyst about the current system.

Note: Users should keep in mind that, although systems analysts may be experts about computers and their applications, they are not necessarily knowledgeable about the business functions performed by the user. It is the user's responsibility to make sure the analyst is well informed about the current system.

Some aspects of the current system that are studied include:

- Inputs (transactions).
- Outputs.

FIGURE 10.3

Phase I analysis of Sporting Life's current accounting system. These are only a few of the general problems and objectives that may be identified.

```
Sporting Life Problem Definition--Current
Accounting System

The following problems have been detected in
the current accounting system:

1. Because files are spread among many
   filing cabinets in different locations,
   it takes too long to locate the required
   accounting files in order to update them.
   Often a file has been misplaced, or the
   file contains information that belongs
   somewhere else.

2. The procedures for updating all
   accounting files are not clearly defined.
   Mistakes are often made when entering
   accounting data.

3. The files that need to be updated daily
   include the General Ledger, Accounts
   Receivable, Accounts Payable, and the
   payroll files. Because it takes so much
   time to access the files, there is never
   enough time to get the job done;
   consequently, the job is often done
   haphazardly and updated only weekly.

4. Because data is filed in several places
   but under different labels, it is
   difficult to obtain information from the
   accounting files to generate the
   following types of reports:
      Summary reports about the financial
      status of the company (daily, weekly,
      monthly, yearly)
      Reports about the projected growth of
      the company.

Objectives

The new computer-based accounting system
should:

1. Reduce by 50% the amount of time required
   to locate the files that have to be
   updated.

2. Include built-in procedures for the user
   to follow when updating the accounting
   files.

3. Establish built-in controls to reduce
   data input errors.

4. Make it easy to update the accounting
   files daily.

5. Make it easy to obtain information from
   the accounting files to generate reports.
```

- Files.
- Users' interaction.
- Methods and procedures.
- Data storage.
- Controls.
- Existing hardware and software.

The systems analyst studies not only these components individually but also how they interact and how people *use* them. Users can assist the analyst by expanding their own thinking about the components being studied. For example, if you were helping a systems analyst study the existing filing system, you would have to describe *everything* used as a file, including not only files in file cabinets or on disk but also index card boxes, in/out boxes on your desk, the telephone book, notebook, log sheets, materials on your shelf—in other words, anything that is used as reference for obtaining data to help you make decisions. The analyst will also need to know *how* and *when* you use these references/files.

GATHERING DATA

As you can see, the principal activities in this phase involve gathering data about the current system and then analyzing the data. The analyst can use a number of techniques, including:

- Conducting interviews.
- Reviewing policies and procedures.
- Collecting sample forms, documents, memos, reports, and so on.
- Observing operations.
- Using questionnaires to conduct surveys.

Needless to say, the systems analyst does not necessarily do these alone; users themselves can collect data on a current system using these techniques, perhaps in concert with the analyst.

INTERVIEWS

Interviews are probably the most widely used data-gathering technique. The analyst can learn a great deal about what is going on by interviewing the staff members who actually perform the work. Interviewing supervisory and management personnel allows the analyst to get comparative information on what is being done and how, so that he or she can identify any differences between how the supervisors and management believe the work is being done and how the staff is actually doing it. Eliciting feedback from more than one source is one way to avoid getting inaccurate information.

Interviews are usually conducted using an outline form that allows the person being interviewed to talk about what he or she feels comfortable with while still covering all the points the interviewer is interested in. (This is called a *structured interview*; if the questions deviate from the predetermined outline, it is called an *unstructured interview*.) Here are examples of questions and requests an analyst might ask of a user (in this case, a payroll department supervisor):

- How many staff workers are currently in the department?
- Does your company have a formal organization chart? If so, may I obtain a copy?
- What are the responsibilities of each staff member? (The analyst would obtain copies of any formal job descriptions.)
- Please explain the company policies that affect the department. (The analyst would obtain any copies.)
- Please describe the daily processing activities in the department. (The analyst would obtain a copy of the procedures manual.)
- Please describe the current workload, including the times when it is heaviest and lightest.
- Please describe the operating procedure cycles—daily, weekly, monthly, and yearly.
- Which activities are the most labor intensive?
- Please discuss any problems, shortcomings, and inefficiencies.

REVIEWING POLICIES AND PROCEDURES

The extent to which the policies and the procedures have been documented can give the analyst valuable insight into what is going on (see Chapter 8 for a review of the importance of documentation). A lack of formal documentation on current policies and procedures may indicate problems within the current system. The analyst should look over what documentation exists, thereby obtaining a picture of how current system activities were expected to operate. However, all documentation should be compared with the information obtained during interviews to determine if the documentation is up to date. Also, remember that continual documentation of processes and decisions is as important throughout the SDLC as it was during the program development steps described in Chapter 8.

COLLECTING SAMPLE DOCUMENTS

Collecting samples of operating documents can also help the analyst to assemble an accurate picture of current systems activities. The term *document* refers to paper on which data has been recorded, including preprinted forms, handwritten forms, and computer-produced forms. The user must be sure to give the analyst copies of *all* documents used for data recording. A bill received in the mail or a customer purchase order are both examples of documents. Picture the system or organizational unit being studied as a box into which documents flow from outside the company or from other departments and from which documents flow outward to other departments or other companies. To help analyze the current system, the analyst should ask the user the following questions about both inward- and outward-bound documents.

- Why and from whom is each document received?
- What action is taken with each document received?
- Why is the document created?
- When is the document produced?
- For whom is each document intended and how is it used?

OBSERVING CURRENT OPERATIONS

The existing descriptions of procedures (if any) answer the question, What should be done and how? The information gathered during interviews, which represents the consensus of what people say they are doing, answers the question, What do users say is being done? Observing operations will confirm the analyst's understanding of what actually exists and answers the question, What are the users *actually* doing?

SURVEY QUESTIONNAIRES

Analysts find that using questionnaires to take a survey can be useful when information must be collected from a large group of individuals. Although questionnaires take less time than personal interviews, and many responses can be collected, they must be used with care. The questions must be precisely worded so that the user completing the questionnaire understands the instruction and does not need to interpret the questions. The principal drawbacks of using a questionnaire are that responses may be highly biased (intentionally or unintentionally), some users are reluctant to take the time to complete a questionnaire, and many people are cautious about expressing an opinion in writing. Questionnaires can use multiple-choice questions, questions that require the users to rate items or areas of concern according to their relative importance, or questions that are open-ended.

One expert on systems analysis, James Wetherbe, has developed a practical framework for identifying problems and opportunities for improvement in a system. This framework is called PIECES (Figure 10.4), after the first letter of each of the six main categories.

- Need to improve Performance.
- Need to improve and control Information.
- Need to improve Economics and control costs.
- Need to improve Control and security.
- Need to improve Efficiency.
- Need to improve Service to users and customers.

ANALYZING DATA

After the analyst has gathered data on the current system, he or she must analyze the facts to identify problems—including their causes and effects—and opportunities for improvement. Some things that the analyst determines are:

- *Minimum, average, and maximum levels of activity:* for example, when do most sales orders come in?
- *Relative importance of the various activities:* this means prioritizing the activities.
- *Redundancy of procedures:* for example, are two users entering the same sales order data at different times?
- *Unusually labor-intensive and/or tedious activities:* manual activities that could be computerized, such as filling out forms to record sales data.

FIGURE 10.4 PIECES problem-solving framework and checklist. This checklist can be used to identify problems and areas for improvement in a system. Note that the categories can overlap. (J. Wetherbe, *Systems Analysis and Design: Traditional, Structured, and Advanced Concepts and Techniques*, 2nd ed. [St. Paul, Minn.: West Publishing, 1984].)

The following checklist for problem, opportunity, and directive identification uses Wetherbe's PIECES framework. Note that the categories of PIECES are not mutually exclusive; some possible problems show up in multiple lists. Also, the list of possible problems is not exhaustive. The PIECES framework is equally applicable to both computerized and manual aspects of a system.

I. The need to improve performance.
- A. Improve throughput, the amount of work performed over some period of time.
- B. Improve response time: the average delay between a transaction and a response to that transaction.
- C. Throughput and response time should be evaluated separately and collectively.

II. The need to improve information and data.
- A. Improve information (the outputs of the system—used for planning, control, and decision making).
  1. Lack of any information.
  2. Lack of needed information.
  3. Lack of relevant information.
  4. Too much information.
  5. Information that is not in a useful form.
  6. Information that is not accurate.
  7. Information that is difficult to produce.
  8. Information that is not timely.
  9. Illegal information.
- B. Data (the inputs to the system).
  1. Data is not captured.
  2. Data is captured but not in a timely fashion.
  3. Data is not accurately captured.
  4. Data is difficult to capture.
  5. Data is captured redundantly.
  6. Too much data is captured.
  7. Illegal data is captured.
- C. Stored data.
  1. Data is stored redundantly.
  2. Data is not accurate.
  3. Data is not consistent in multiple stores.
  4. Data is not secure against accident.
  5. Data is not secure against sabotage.
  6. Data is not well organized.
  7. Data organization is too inflexible to meet information needs.
  8. Data cannot be easily accessed to produce information.

III. Economics: The need to reduce costs.
- A. Costs are unknown or untraceable to source.
- B. Costs are excessive.

IV. The need to improve control and security.
- A. There is too little control.
  1. Input data is not adequately edited.
  2. Crimes are committed against data.
     - a. Fraud.
     - b. Embezzlement.
  3. Ethics are breached based on data or information.
  4. Redundantly stored data is inconsistent in different files.
  5. Privacy of data is being violated.
  6. Processing errors are occurring.
  7. Decision-making errors are occurring.
  8. System is deviating from planned performance.
- B. Too little security.
  1. People get unauthorized access to space or facilities.
  2. People get unauthorized access to computers.
  3. People get unauthorized access to data or information (manual or computer).
  4. People execute unauthorized updates of data.
- C. Too much control or security.
  1. Bureaucratic red tape slows the system.
  2. Controls inconvenience end-users or customers.
  3. Controls cause excessive processing delays.
  4. Controls result in lost transactions.

V. The need to improve efficiency.
- A. People or machines waste time.
  1. Data is redundantly input or copied.
  2. Data is redundantly processed.
  3. Information is redundantly generated.
- B. Machines or processes waste materials and supplies.
- C. Effort required for tasks is excessive.
- D. Materials required for tasks are excessive.

VI. The need to improve service.
- A. The system produces inaccurate results.
- B. The system produces inconsistent and, hence, unreliable results.
- C. The system is not easy to learn.
- D. The system is not easy to use.
- E. The system is too complex.
- F. The system is awkward.
- G. The system is inflexible to situations and exceptions.
- H. The system is inflexible to change (new needs or requirements).
- I. The system does not interface well to other systems.
- J. The system does not work with other systems.
- K. The system is not coordinated ("left hand does not know what right hand is doing").

- *Activities that require extensive (complex and/or repetitive) mathematical computation:* such as updating customer charge account balances and interest charges.
- *Procedures that have become obsolete:* perhaps your company's licensing requirements have changed, rendering the old procedures useless.

The analyst can use several tools to assist in the analysis, including **data flow diagrams (DFDs)** and special software packages, such as Excelerator, a computer-aided software engineering (CASE) tool that, among other things, automates the production of data flow diagrams (more on this later). Data flow diagrams show the flow of data through a system—where it originates and where it goes. Data flowcharts can be used for clarification in any phase of the systems development life cycle. Figure 10.5 shows the standard symbols used in data flow diagrams. The *process* symbol shows what is done to data in the current system—whether it is filed, printed out and forwarded, checked and discarded, and so on. The *source* symbol indicates where data has come from—that is, from which departments or individuals; a *sink* symbol indicates where data is going to—that is, it indicates the recipient. For example, a customer order record may be sent by Customer Services *(source)* to Inventory *(sink)*. The *file* symbol indicates that data is deposited or stored, whether in an index card file or on magnetic tape, in a filing cabinet or on a desk notepad. *Vectors* (arrows, or flowlines) show the direction of the data flow. To give you an

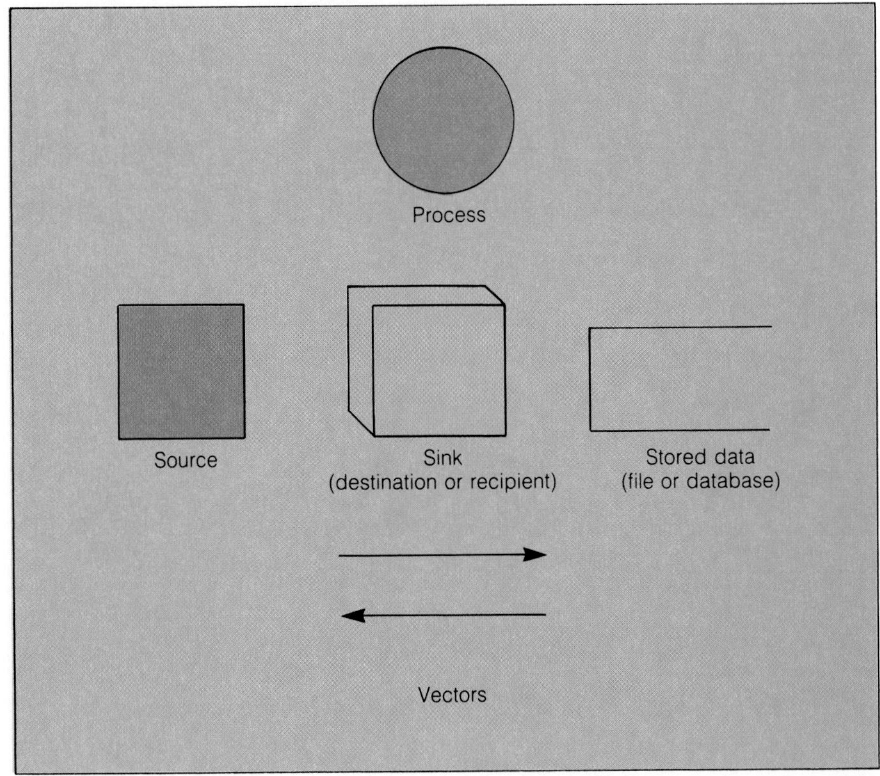

FIGURE 10.5

Data flow diagram symbols. Systems analysts use these symbols to make data flow diagrams throughout the systems development life cycle.

example of how data flow symbols are used, Figure 10.6 diagrams how Sporting Life processes customer orders.

Special types of data flow diagrams can be used to document structured development of real-time systems (discussed in Chapter 4). These data flow diagrams also show the system's interface with devices and machines the system employs and controls, as well as the processes that use and control the devices. Structured development for real-time systems is used to develop, for example, environmental control systems, air traffic control systems, spacecraft control systems, missile tracking and guidance systems, and robots.

The first phase of the SDLC usually concludes with a report to management. The objectives of the Phase 1 report are to provide management personnel in affected departments and in the information processing department with a clear

FIGURE 10.6

General data flow diagram of Sporting Life's system of processing orders. When an order is received, the inventory file is checked to make sure enough items are in stock to satisfy the order (1). If there aren't, an out-of-stock notice (5) is given to the customer; otherwise, a credit check is performed (2). If the credit status is poor, the customer's order is not approved; otherwise, an invoice is prepared (3) and the goods and the invoice are given to the customer (4). (Some details are omitted from this diagram for the purpose of simplification.)

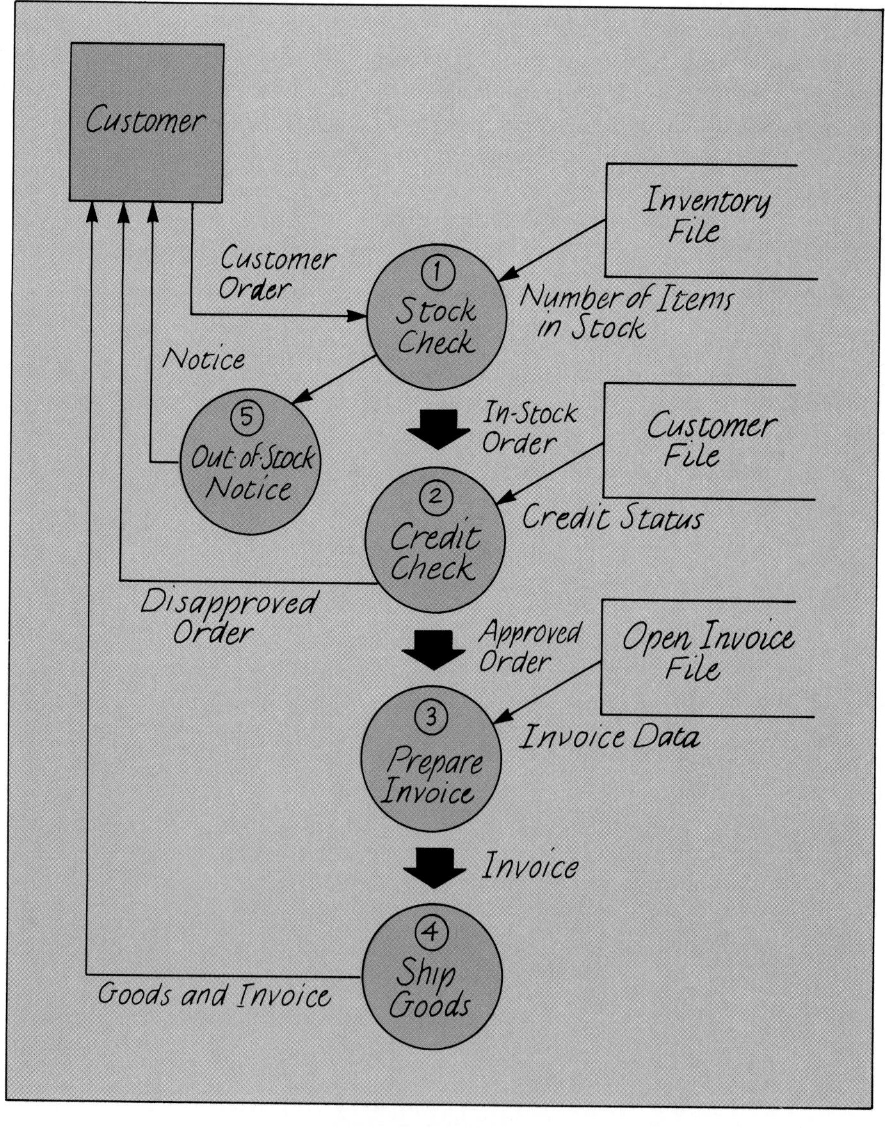

picture of what the system does, how it does it, and what the analysis identified as problems, causes and effects of problems, and areas where improvements can be made. After reading the report, management must be given an opportunity to ask for specific clarification of the points raised in the report and to request a final recommendation from the analyst about whether or not to proceed.

PHASE 2: DEFINE NEW SYSTEMS REQUIREMENTS

In Phase 2 the analyst focuses attention on what he or she—and the users—want the new system to do. But before the analyst can design it, he or she has to define the requirements that the new system must satisfy. And the requirements must be defined very carefully; otherwise, the new system might not end up doing what the users hope it will do.

PURPOSE OF PHASE 2

In the second phase of the SDLC, the analyst defines the requirements for the new system in enough detail so that both computer professionals and users know exactly what the new system is going to do and how the system is going to do it. Needless to say, these requirements should solve the problems identified in the first phase.

The first requirements to be defined should be the *business* requirements—input, storage, processing, and output—that the system is able to accommodate. For example, do the personnel who fill customer orders find that certain inventory items are often out of stock and therefore want inventory reports to be issued more frequently? Has the number of files required by the current system grown so much that users spend too much time searching for customer account information? The requirement of the new system in this instance is to make the finding of file information quick and easy. Figure 10.7 shows some of the requirements identified for Sporting Life's payroll processing system. Computerization is not necessarily

```
Sporting Life: Requirements

The requirements for the Sporting Life payroll
processing system are as follows:

1. Increase the number of time cards that can be
   processed once a week by 20% and decrease the
   time it takes to generate paychecks by 15%.

2. Automatically update the personnel file with
   gross pay information when time cards are
   processed.

3. Automatically calculate regular and overtime
   hourly amounts when time cards are processed.

4. Automatically generate weekly-to-date and
   year-to-date personnel income figures when
   time cards are processed.
```

FIGURE 10.7

Phase 2 requirements of Sporting Life's payroll portion of the new accounting system. These are only a few of the requirements that may be identified by the analyst.

the answer to everything; manual as well as computerized procedures are often required. In some cases, a new manual system may fill a user's or a department's requirements.

Once the requirements of a system are known, then both manual and computer-based alternatives are evaluated for new and improved systems. Among the factors affecting what alternatives should be implemented are the availability of computer hardware that is technologically suited to the business's requirements and that fits within the budget of the proposed system. Cost becomes a major factor if software must be created from scratch by a professional programmer, instead of being bought off the shelf (the "make or buy" decision).

TOOLS FOR DEFINING REQUIREMENTS AND ALTERNATIVES

The systems analyst can use several common tools to define the new system's requirements and suggest ways of fulfilling these requirements. These tools generally fall into one of two categories: modeling tools and prototyping tools.

Modeling tools are the same design tools you read about in Chapter 8—pseudocode, structure charts using top-down design and a modular approach, HIPO packages, and so on. These tools are used to document the program modules necessary to the system, using a structured approach. (Chapter 8 referred to *structured programming*; during systems design and analysis, one refers to *structured design*.) One additional systems development modeling tool is the **systems flowchart.** Like the program flowcharts discussed in Chapter 8, systems flowcharts use their own special set of ANSI symbols (Figure 10.8). They document the design of a new system, including the flow of data (points of input, output, and storage) and

FIGURE 10.8

ANSI systems flowchart symbols. Systems flowcharts use symbols standardized by the American National Standards Institute, just as program flowcharts do (however, not all the symbols are the same).

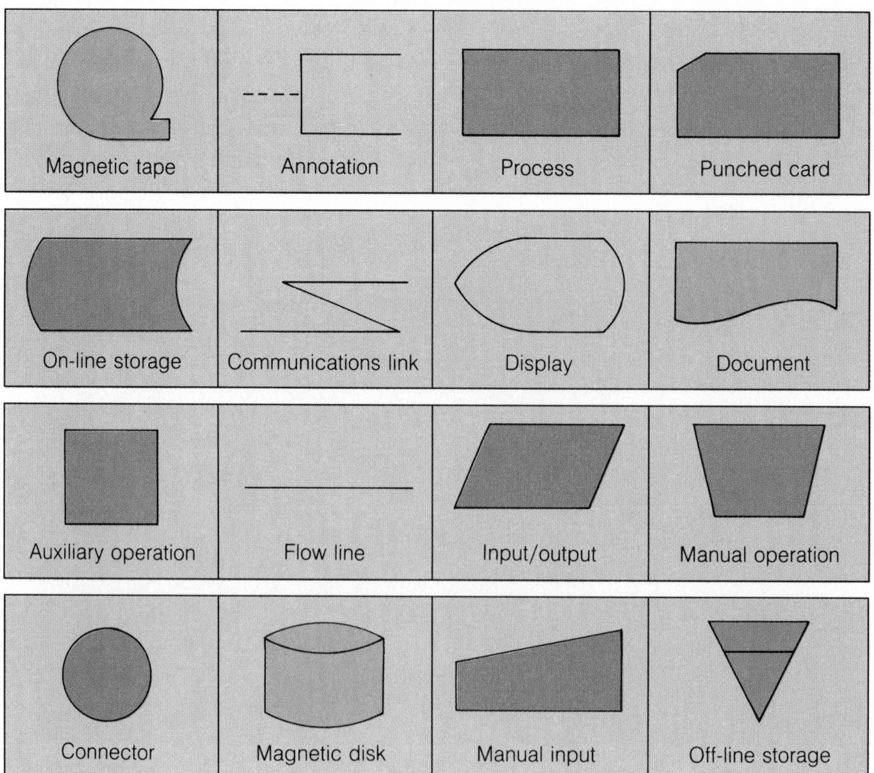

processing activities. The systems flowchart for the accounts receivable portion of Sporting Life's accounting system is shown in Figure 10.9. The activity flows from top to bottom.

Prototyping tools document the systems modules. A prototype is a small-scale working model of the new system module (or of a small system). Analysts use fourth-generation languages and applications generators to quickly generate working models of files, databases, screens, reports, and so on. Figure 10.10 shows a screen from the prototyping language FOCUS. The objective of prototyping is to get feedback from users as soon as possible. Prototyping also encourages more active participation of users in systems development. However, prototyping should not be used as an excuse to skip through detailed analysis and design too quickly. Structured analysis and design techniques should be used *together* with prototyping.

Although we mention modeling and prototyping tools in Phase 2 of the SDLC, keep in mind that these tools will be used throughout the life cycle to continually document design and development progress and to try out program and systems modules.

REQUIREMENTS THAT AFFECT SOFTWARE

Once the business requirements have been defined, most systems analysts and designers focus on the *output* the system must produce. The output requirements

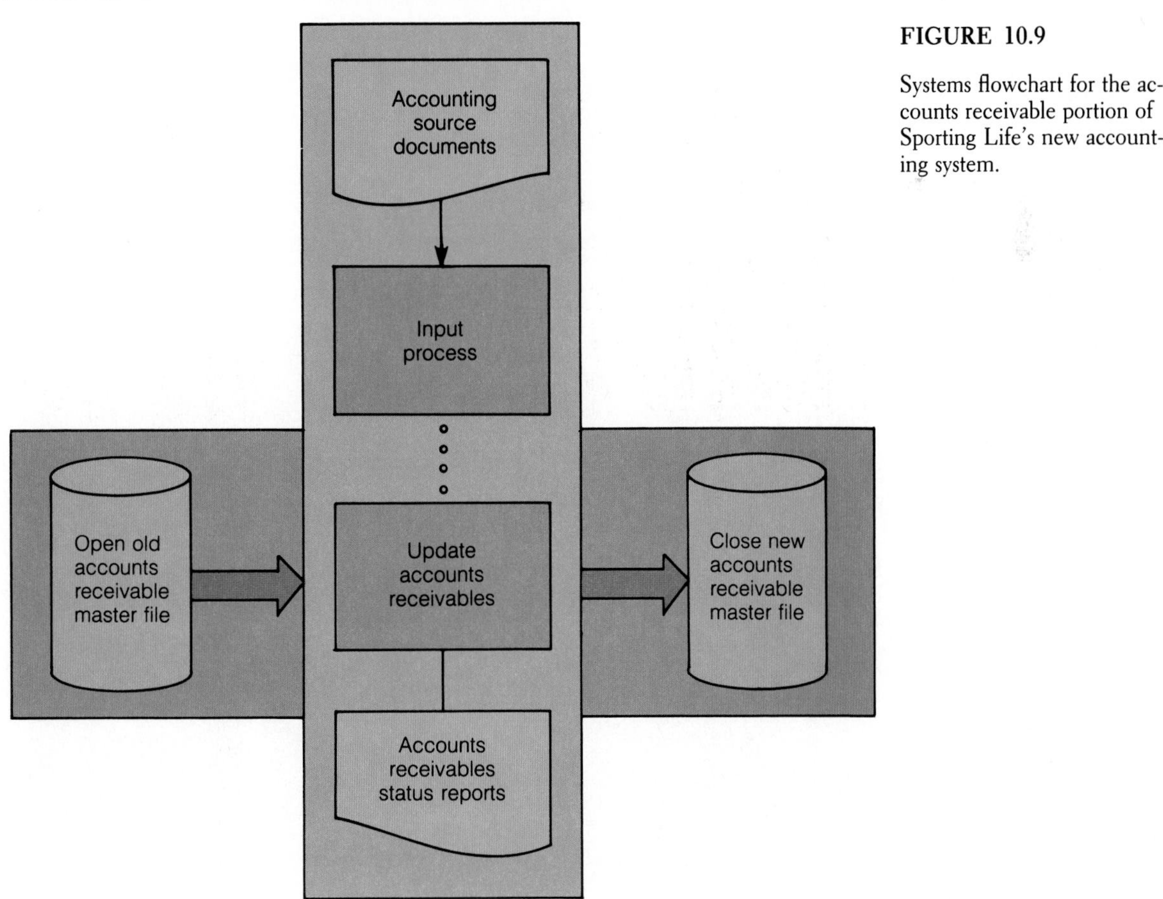

FIGURE 10.9

Systems flowchart for the accounts receivable portion of Sporting Life's new accounting system.

fall into three general categories: hardcopy output (reports, special forms, and so on), softcopy output (displayed on video screen), and computer-usable output (a computer file created during processing for output in one system that is also used as input to another system — for example, a file produced by the payroll system that is later used in the general ledger system). To define the requirements for hardcopy and softcopy outputs, the analyst usually meets with each user who will be using each type of output and carefully identifies:

- The purpose of the output.
- The elements of information it will contain.
- How each element will be used.
- How often and how fast the output will need to be produced.

In some cases, the analyst will model forms for the user to approve (Figures 10.11 and 10.12).

The storage, processing, and input requirements are closely related to the output requirements. They are determined largely on the basis of where the information in an output is going to come from. The input requirements are formulated in terms of:

- Who will be performing the input procedure.
- The elements of data that will be entered.
- The input screens (the information displayed on the screen that tells the user what data elements to enter).
- The control procedures to be exercised over the data entry process.

Figure 10.13 shows the model of an input screen.

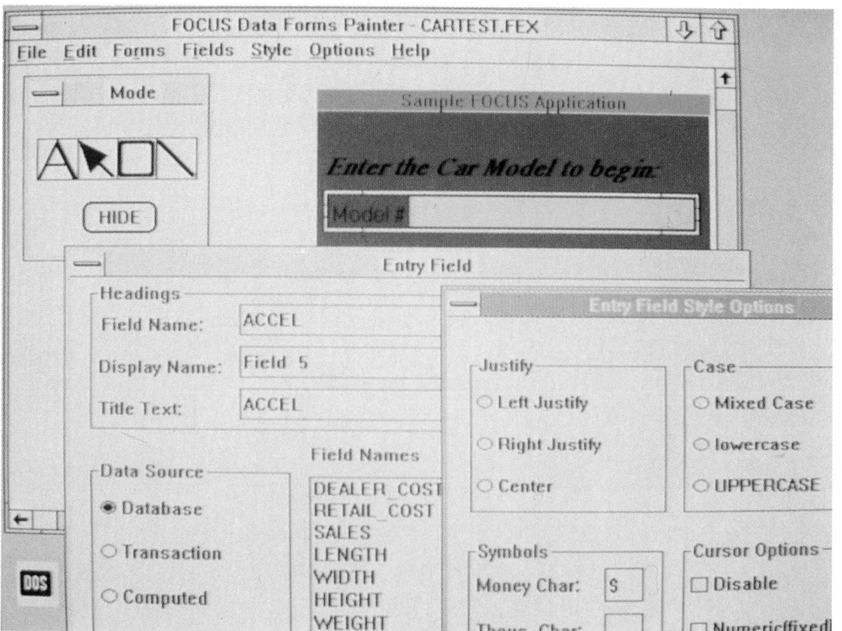

FIGURE 10.10

In FOCUS. Prototyping software allows analysts (or users) to quickly generate working models of data forms (here: car model test forms) using a prototype database with sample data.

```
                         REPORT LAYOUT CHART
   1-10  |  11-20  |  21-30  |  31-40  |  41-50  |  51-60  |  61-70  |  71-80
12345678901234567890123456789012345678901234567890123456789012345678901234567890123456789

                                  ABC

                              CORPORATION

                          PARTS MOVE REPORT
                         -----------------------

     PART-ID   MGR   APPR     LOCATION    QTY-STOCK   QTY-REQUEST   STATUS
    ---------  ----- -------  ----------- ----------  ------------  -------
  1) 999999    XXX    XX     9,999.99    9,999.99     99/99/99       XXX

  2) 999999    XXX    XX     9,999.99    9,999.99     99/99/99       XXX

  3) 999999    XXX    XX     9,999.99    9,999.99     99/99/99       XXX

  4) 999999    XXX    XX     9,999.99    9,999.99     99/99/99       XXX
```

FIGURE 10.11

Specifying the requirements of one type of hardcopy output. This example shows the model of a report form designed with DESIGNAID (Nastec Corp.), a CASE tool. After the form and the system are finalized, the user can call the form up on the screen, insert the appropriate data where the 9s and the Xs appear, and then output the finished report. (X = alphanumeric data; 9 = numeric data.)

```
PANEL DEFINITION MENU ********** ********** END PROCESSING PERFORMED
COMMAND ==>
FUNCTION: UP   CR-CREATE    UP-UPDATE    PU-PURGE    SH-SHOW    LI-LIST

ITEM      PI   PI-IMAGE     PD-DEFIN
                                 FD-FIELD     CE-CONSIS     SL-SEGLOOP
                                   (UP)        (CR,UP)       (CR,UP,PU)

MEMBER NAME:
      HEADER TR____
      ID     XXAD_ PRE-CLASS ASSIGN, STUDENT NAME
      DESC   __________________________________________

ENTER VALUE FOR SPECIFIC ITEM TO BE PROCESSED:
     1. IMAGE   < > + | \ (INPUT OUTPUT OUTIN SELECT LIT-BREAK CHARACTERS)
                24 080    (LINE-COLUMN IMAGE SIZE)
                U         (UPPER/LOWER CASE LITERALS)
     2. DEFIN   Y Y Y Y N (INPUT OUTPUT OUTIN SELECT LITERAL FIELDS LISTED)
     3. FIELD   _________ (NAME OR LINE, COLUMN OR "*PANEL")
     4. CONSIS  _________ (TYPE - "XFEDIT", "SEGEDIT", OR BLANK FOR LIST)
                _________ (NAME - IF TYPE SPECIFIED)
     5. SEGLOOP _________ (TYPE - "FILE" OR "TABLE")
                _______   (FROM NAME OR LINE,COLUMN)
                _______     (TO NAME OR LINE,COLUMN)
```

FIGURE 10.12

Specifying the contents of one type of softcopy output. This screen example was produced using the "screen painter" in TELON DOM Pansophic, a CASE tool. This prototype provides the user with a model of how a particular screen will look when the system is operative.

Storage requirements are defined in terms of the different files that will need to be created to satisfy the processing and output requirements. For instance, we already know that Sporting Life will be using (among other types of files) a master file, an inventory file, an accounts receivable file, an accounts payable file, input transaction and output/report files, and different backup files.

Processing requirements deal with processing schedules — that is, when data is to be input, when output is to be produced, and when files are to be updated — and the identification of logical and computational processing activities. For example, in Sporting Life's accounting system, payroll processing might include such activities as sorting lists of employee names alphabetically for certain reports; calculating deductions, sick pay, overtime pay, and final pay rates; calculating withheld taxes for output on special tax forms; and making sales projections for coming years. The requirements for computational and logical processing procedures are usually documented in narrative or graphic form, or in a mathematical formula. If the processing logic is complex, pseudocode, data flow diagrams, flowcharts, and other tools may be used.

When all of the software-related requirements have been defined, they are usually summarized as a part of the New Systems Requirements Report (described later in this section). The detailed specifications are used as a basis for proceeding (or not) with the next phase of activity: design of the new system.

REQUIREMENTS THAT AFFECT HARDWARE

The new system's software requirements must be defined first to determine what type of computer hardware is needed. This may involve modifying equipment

FIGURE 10.13

Model of an input screen. This model was created with Information Engineering Facility™ from Texas Instruments, Inc.

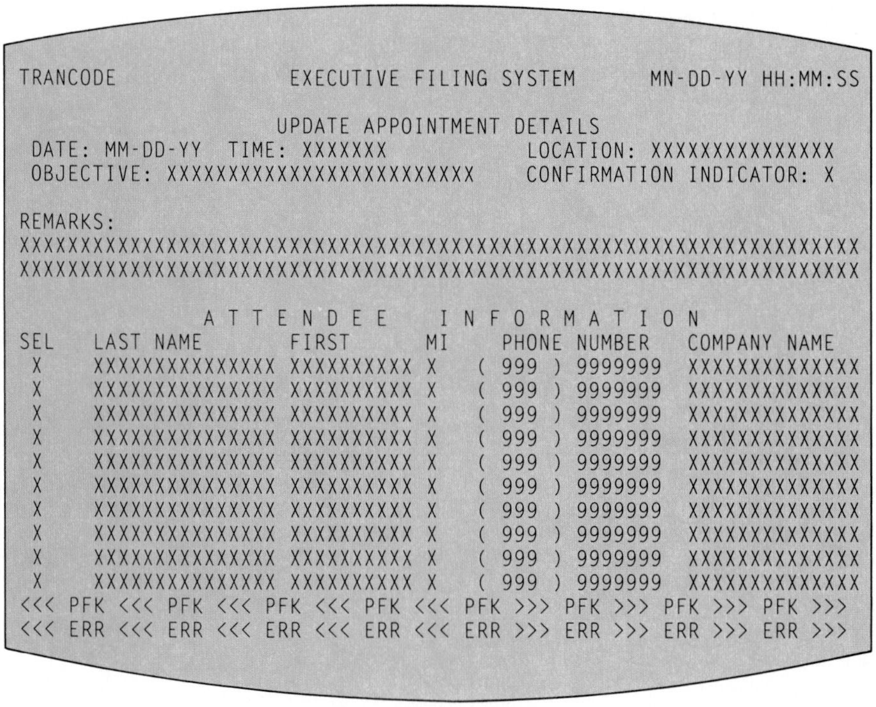

```
TRANCODE                EXECUTIVE FILING SYSTEM       MN-DD-YY HH:MM:SS

                        UPDATE APPOINTMENT DETAILS
 DATE: MM-DD-YY  TIME: XXXXXXX                LOCATION: XXXXXXXXXXXXXXX
 OBJECTIVE: XXXXXXXXXXXXXXXXXXXXXXXXX    CONFIRMATION INDICATOR: X

REMARKS:
XXXXXXXXXXXXXXXXXXXXXXXXXXXXXXXXXXXXXXXXXXXXXXXXXXXXXXXXXXXXXXXXXXXXXX
XXXXXXXXXXXXXXXXXXXXXXXXXXXXXXXXXXXXXXXXXXXXXXXXXXXXXXXXXXXXXXXXXXXXXX

               A T T E N D E E    I N F O R M A T I O N
SEL   LAST NAME        FIRST      MI    PHONE NUMBER    COMPANY NAME
 X    XXXXXXXXXXXXXXX XXXXXXXXXX X    ( 999 ) 9999999  XXXXXXXXXXXXXX
 X    XXXXXXXXXXXXXXX XXXXXXXXXX X    ( 999 ) 9999999  XXXXXXXXXXXXXX
 X    XXXXXXXXXXXXXXX XXXXXXXXXX X    ( 999 ) 9999999  XXXXXXXXXXXXXX
 X    XXXXXXXXXXXXXXX XXXXXXXXXX X    ( 999 ) 9999999  XXXXXXXXXXXXXX
 X    XXXXXXXXXXXXXXX XXXXXXXXXX X    ( 999 ) 9999999  XXXXXXXXXXXXXX
 X    XXXXXXXXXXXXXXX XXXXXXXXXX X    ( 999 ) 9999999  XXXXXXXXXXXXXX
 X    XXXXXXXXXXXXXXX XXXXXXXXXX X    ( 999 ) 9999999  XXXXXXXXXXXXXX
 X    XXXXXXXXXXXXXXX XXXXXXXXXX X    ( 999 ) 9999999  XXXXXXXXXXXXXX
 X    XXXXXXXXXXXXXXX XXXXXXXXXX X    ( 999 ) 9999999  XXXXXXXXXXXXXX
 X    XXXXXXXXXXXXXXX XXXXXXXXXX X    ( 999 ) 9999999  XXXXXXXXXXXXXX
<<< PFK <<< PFK <<< PFK <<< PFK <<< PFK >>> PFK >>> PFK >>> PFK >>>
<<< ERR <<< ERR <<< ERR <<< ERR <<< ERR >>> ERR >>> ERR >>> ERR >>>
```

Computers and Careers

Manufacturing

Use of computers in manufacturing is not just for the mammoth Fortune 500 companies. For his daughter who wanted to open a clothing store, a University of Dayton electrical engineering professor devised a computer-based dressmaking program for tailors. An optical scanner "reads" someone's body, producing figures that can be translated into a personalized dress pattern.

Still, the most dramatic uses of computers have been those employed by large organizations. Once, taking inventory at computer-maker Hewlett-Packard's New Jersey division required the equivalent of 120 hours of a person's time, plus an additional two to three weeks to get the information keypunched and tabulated. Today, two people using electronic wands to scan bar codes on each product finish in less than six hours, and the data is ready immediately.

Moving bar codes from supermarkets to warehouses and factories has produced dramatic productivity gains. Indeed, companies now need entirely too much information in their computer systems for it to be keyed in manually. On an assembly line, laser scanners can read bar codes of up to 360 objects per second. The codes enable a company to keep track of individual lots or products, to track production rates, and do quality control and inventory, all without the need for paper.

Another form of computer technology becoming more frequently used in factories and warehouses is the industrial robot. A Reynolds Metals plastics plant in Virginia uses a robot that stacks a pallet with boxes, then moves it to an automatic pallet wrapper, where it is shrinkwrapped in plastic film. Employees are happier because they are less fatigued at the end of a shift compared to earlier times, when this work had to be done by hand.

Nowadays the factory is being reinvented from the top down. Computer simulations are used to recreate the factory floor on a computer screen, including machine tools, robots, and materials-handling vehicles. Manufacturing processes can then be tried out before a single machine is put in place. With computer-integrated manufacturing (CIM), a product that is ordered may be available the next day. Using computer-aided design (CAD), the part is designed on a video screen. Then, with computer-aided engineering (CAE), it is analyzed for performance. Finally, with computer-aided manufacturing (CAM), the part is produced by an automated system on the shop floor.

Some of the lessons of ideas developed for the factory floor are now being used in other areas. Unlike factory robots, so-called *field*, or *service*, *robots* are mobile and are able to work in nonmanufacturing environments that are hazardous or inaccessible to humans. Field robots equipped with wheels, tracks, legs, and fins are being used to clean up hazardous-waste sites, inspect nuclear power plants, do bomb disposal, and perform maintenance on offshore oil rigs. ■

already owned or buying new equipment. Hardware requirements will be discussed in more detail in Phase 3.

EVALUATING ALTERNATIVES

Once the new system's requirements have been defined and ways to satisfy them have been suggested, the analyst should examine *alternative* approaches to satisfying the requirements. This step keeps people from jumping to conclusions. For example, perhaps an expensive conversion to a computer-based system from a manual one is not really necessary. The analyst carefully weighs the advantages and disadvantages of each alternative, including how each might affect the time required to get the new system in place and its estimated cost. As we discussed in Chapter 8, a company can modify existing software, hire computer specialists to develop it from scratch, or buy software packages off the shelf and perhaps modify them, if necessary. Hardware and software to support the new systems should be selected, but they do not have to be purchased and in use before design begins.

SYSTEMS REQUIREMENTS REPORT

Phase 2 concludes with the analyst's preparation of a **systems requirements report** and a presentation to the steering committee, user department(s) management, and information processing management. The report provides the basis for the final determination of the completeness and accuracy of the new systems requirements, as well as the economic and practical feasibility of the new system. Information processing management reviews the report to determine if the alternatives have been adequately considered from a technical standpoint. After everyone has reviewed and discussed the report, a final decision is made about whether to proceed and, if so, which alternatives to adopt. A schedule for project completion is also worked out. Figure 10.14 shows what a systems requirements report might look like for the order entry portion of Sporting Life's new accounting system.

FIGURE 10.14

Sporting Life's systems requirements report for order entry.

```
Statement of Systems Requirements
Pg. 5 of 20

3.1    Order Handling
       Information Required: customer name,
       product #, quantity ordered
       System Requirement: Produce information
       about quantity-on-hand for product ordered.
       Return order status of either "in-stock" or
       "out-of-stock."
       System Requirement: Produce information
       about customer credit status. Return status
       of either "approved" or disapproved"
       System Requirement: Produce necessary
       out-of-stock or disapproved order reports.
       Produce necessary invoice.
       System Requirement: Update open invoice file.
3.2    Accounts Receivable Status Reports
        .
        .
        .
```

If the company is going outside its organization to develop a new system, its systems requirements report may also contain a document called a **request for proposal (RFP).** This document is used when a company wants to get bids from vendors for prices of software, hardware, programs, supplies, or service. It lists the systems requirements and any limitations.

PHASE 3: DESIGN THE NEW SYSTEM

The third phase of the SDLC focuses on the design of the new system. To determine how the new system will be constructed, the analyst analyzes the requirements defined in Phase 2. The activities in this phase are carried out primarily by computer specialists—that is, programmers. Users may have little direct involvement in the design phase; however, their responses are critical when a programmer needs clarification of logical or computational processing requirements. Users should also continue to be involved in the final approval of procedures that provide for user interface with the system—such as what type of dialog will show up on the terminal—and of proposed report forms, both hardcopy and softcopy. After all, the analysts can leave when their job is done; the users must live with the system!

PURPOSE OF PHASE 3

Phase 3 involves two main objectives: to design the new system and to establish a sound framework of controls within which the new system should operate. The tools and methods used to document the development of the design and the controls vary according to the preferences of the computer specialists and, if there is one, the standards and procedures of the information processing department. Systems flowcharts, program flowcharts, hierarchy-input-processing-output (HIPO) packages, structured design and programming, and prototyping are commonly used tools.

The **CASE (computer-assigned software engineering) tools** mentioned earlier are also used in Phase 3. CASE tools provide computer-automated support for structured design techniques; they speed up the design process and improve the quality of systems development and documentation. CASE tools are built around the concept of a **project dictionary** (Figure 10.15), which stores all the requirements and specifications for all elements of data to be used in the new system. (The term *project dictionary* is replacing the term *data dictionary*, which is now being used in a database management context; see Chapter 11.)

Among other outputs, CASE tools can generate:

- Graphics tools such as data flow diagrams, flowcharts, structure charts, and data models.
- Reports on file contents, properties of data elements, and rules of logic.
- Prototypes.
- Quality analysis reports.
- Programming code for writing software programs.
- Project management tools.
- Cost/benefit analyses.

Figure 10.16 gives you an idea of how these capabilities relate to one another. In addition to Excelerator, CASE tools include Excelerator/RTS (for real-time systems), Design Aid, Information Engineering Workbench, and Analyst/Designer Toolkit.

DESIGNING NEW SYSTEMS CONTROLS

New systems must be designed to operate within a framework of controls, a system of safeguards that protect a computer system and data from accidental or intentional damage, from input and output inaccuracies, and from access by unauthorized persons. As computer systems become easier and easier to use, and as software becomes more and more user friendly, the importance grows of designing adequate security controls into an information system. Controls involve the physical environment of the system (the buildings, rooms, doors, and computer hardware), the manual procedures performed by users and computer specialists, and the computerized processing procedures.

Physical security controls include the use of:

- *Passes and passwords*. Employees and authorized visitors may be required to wear badges or carry passes or cards in order to gain access to the computer building or room.
- *Encryption devices*. Data sent over telecommunications lines is put into secret code by equipment known as "encryption devices." This code can be decoded only by an authorized person using similar equipment at the other end of the line.
- *Safeguards against environmental disasters*. As far as possible, the system should be protected against disasters such as fire, flood, earthquake, electrical surges, power failures, and so on. Backup procedures must also be designed to protect the system's files.

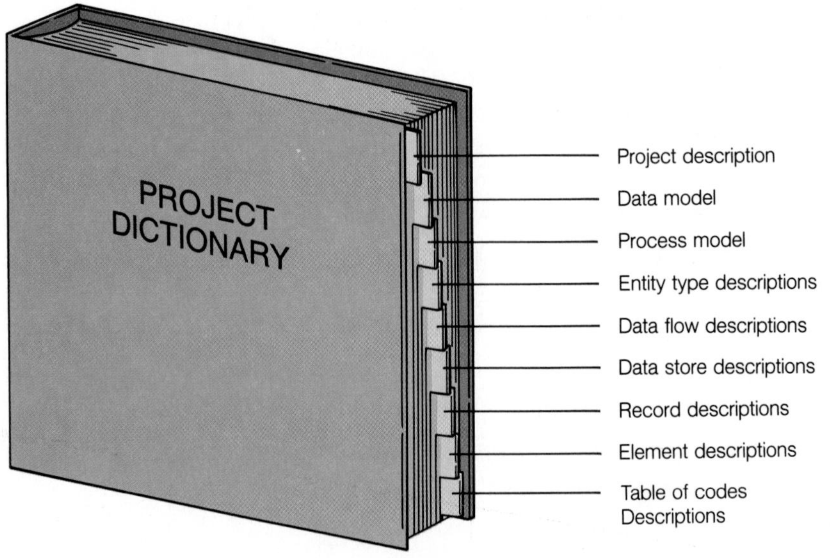

FIGURE 10.15

Project dictionary organization. A project dictionary forms the base of a CASE tool. The dictionary is maintained on the computer and then ultimately output as documentation.

- *Documentation library and file library*. Documentation and storage media should be kept in special rooms and checked out only to personnel who have a current assignment for use.
- *Locks*. Machines not in use should be locked up.

Manual procedures controls include:

- *Keeping a log*. All users of the company's system should sign in and sign out in a log book.
- *Separate employee functions*. If possible, employees' jobs should not overlap; for example, a computer operator should not also be a programmer, and users and computer operators should have access only to those parts of the system and documentation that directly involve their particular routine activities.
- *Creating a disaster plan*. Procedures should be established for all users (and other employees) to follow in case of a disaster.
- *Documented procedures for distributing output*. For example, reports may be kept in a secured area until distribution; users may be asked to sign a

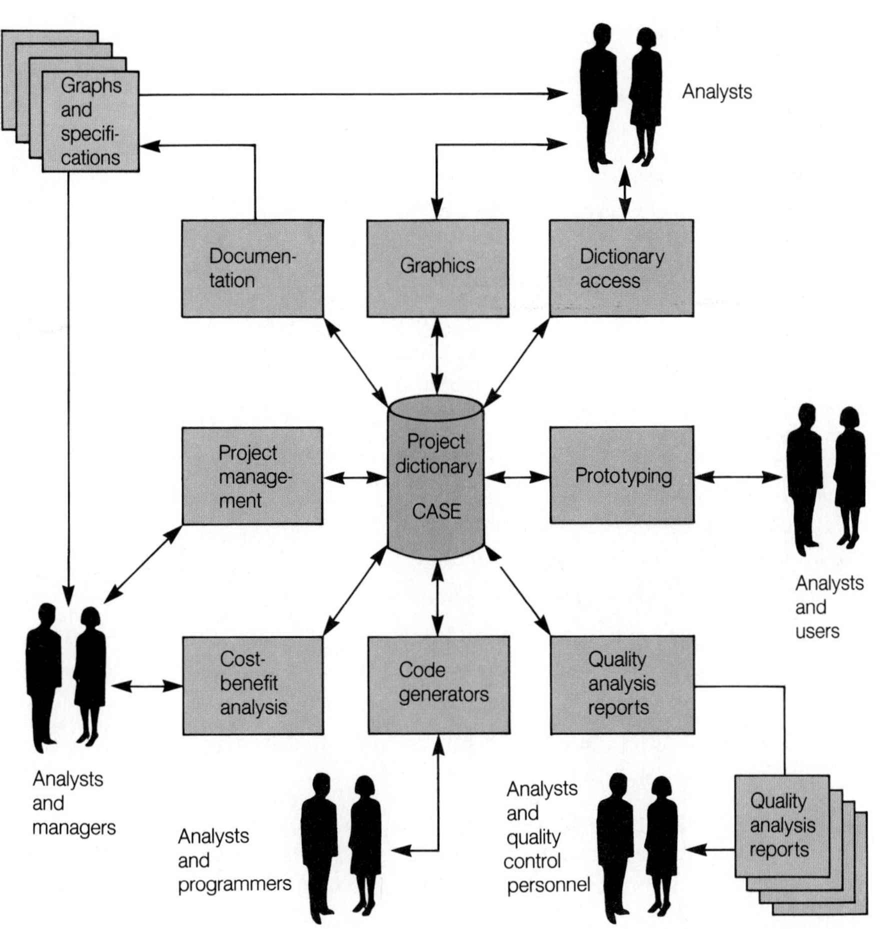

FIGURE 10.16

Some computer-assisted software engineering (CASE) capabilities. This figure shows how the capabilities relate to one another and to the people involved in the systems development process. (Adapted from J. Whitten, L. Bentley, and V. Barlow, *Systems Analysis and Design Methods*, 2nd ed. [Homewood, Ill.: Richard D. Irwin, 1989], p. 127.)

delivery sheet when they receive a report; reports may be shredded after use instead of being thrown away.

Computerized processing security controls include the use of:

- *Passwords*. Users must type in passwords to gain access to the computer system. These passwords should be changed frequently by the computer information department and should not be logically obvious.
- *Software restrictions*. The software program can be written to include user profiles to be activated when a person logs in to authorize that person as a user.
- *Dial-back routines*. When a person dials up a computer (with a Touch-Tone® phone), the computer asks him or her for a password. After the person gives the password, the computer disconnects the line and checks to see if the caller's phone number matches an authorized phone number in its files. If a match is found, the computer calls the person back; if no match is found, the computer alerts an authorized user that an attempt at unauthorized entry to the system was made.
- *Standards for input data and data verification*. The system should include a program for verifying accuracy of input.

This list of controls is not complete; you may be able to think of additional ways systems analysts and designers and users can write security measures into their systems design. However, you can see that systems controls are an important consideration during the design phase.

CONCLUDING THE DESIGN PHASE

The completion of the design phase of the SDLC is marked by three events. First, the analyst/designer completes, organizes, and assembles the new systems design documentation, including records of the general and applications controls, by using a combination of the tools and techniques discussed earlier in the chapter. The documentation should include:

- A complete overview of the new system as a whole.
- A description (narrative or graphic) of the major processing modules into which the system has been divided for design purposes.
- Detailed documentation describing the input, processing, and output activities in each module and submodule.
- Specifications of the storage requirements for the new system; a description of each file to be maintained in the system, including anticipated size and organization scheme/access method to be used.
- A narrative description of the general and applications controls to be used with the new system.

Second, the systems analyst(s) and information processing management meet to review the technical soundness of the design. Third, systems designer(s), user management, and information processing management meet to present and review the design. The outcome of the last meeting is a decision either to approve the design and proceed to the next phase of the SDLC (systems development) or to revise the design before continuing. Although most organizations would decide to discard a project entirely at an earlier phase, it is still possible to terminate the project at this time.

PHASE 4: DEVELOP THE NEW SYSTEM

A company that is changing from a manual to a computer-based system (or modifying an existing computer-based system) cannot run out and buy hardware in Phase 1 because it doesn't yet know what the new system is supposed to do. The company shouldn't make purchases during Phase 2 either because, although its requirements have been established, the new system has not yet been designed. During Phase 3, the system has been designed but not yet accepted. It's not until Phase 4 that the system is accepted and development begins. Now the company can acquire software and hardware.

PURPOSE OF PHASE 4

During Phase 4, four major activities occur:

1. Acquire software.
2. Acquire hardware.
3. Train the users.
4. Test the new system.

ACQUIRE SOFTWARE

If the software is not purchased off the shelf, it must be written by programmers. These programmers use the logic-development tools, coding procedures, and testing and documentation methods discussed in Chapter 8.

ACQUIRE HARDWARE

Here are some points company representatives should keep in mind when buying (or leasing) hardware:

- If some computers have already been acquired, additional units need to be compatible.
- The minimum amount of main memory to satisfy the processing requirements must be established. Some software products require a minimum of 640 K, whereas others require at least 1 MB.
- If processing will involve extensive mathematical calculations, special math coprocessor chips may need to be installed in some computers.
- The video display units will need to be high resolution for certain applications like graphics. If graphics are required, graphics adapter cards and RGB monitors may be required for certain computers.
- The storage requirements should be carefully analyzed to help determine what size system to purchase.

- The quality, volume, and type of printed output to be produced must be considered in determining the types of printers required.
- Determine the delivery schedules for all equipment.
- Determine where the hardware should be installed.
- Determine how many users the system will need to support now—and in a year or two.
- Determine the amount of multiusing and multitasking required.
- Determine the type of operating system that will ensure program compatibility and efficiency.
- Determine computer communications needs.

If using existing hardware, the new system design must be reviewed to determine if additional hardware (more personal computers, additional disk storage capacity, faster printers, more terminals, fax machines, and so on) is required.

Once hardware needs have been identified, the company must determine which vendor to choose. Here are some considerations to keep in mind when deciding on the vendor:

- The financial stability of the vendor should be strong. You want the vendor to be in business when you call for assistance.
- The vendor should have a qualified technical support staff for ongoing maintenance and repair (toll-free lines are invaluable).
- The vendor should have staff available to assist in setting up the equipment and making sure it is ready to operate.
- The vendor should have staff available to provide training in the use of the equipment.

TRAIN THE USERS

The users (and the computer operators) must be trained to use the new hardware and software. This can often be started before the equipment is delivered; for example, the vendor may give training seminars on its own premises or provide temporary training equipment.

TEST THE NEW SYSTEM

Several methods may be used to test the new system, including the methods discussed for testing programs in Chapter 8. Sample data will be fed into the system to see that it performs correctly. Testing may take several months. Of course, any bugs must be eliminated.

PHASE 5: IMPLEMENT THE NEW SYSTEM

The process of developing a new system costs a great deal of time, energy, and money. However, even a beautifully designed and developed system can fail to meet its objectives it if is not carefully implemented. In this phase, the company converts from the old system to the new system.

Purpose of Phase 5

The implementation phase, which gets the new system up and running, involves creating the final operating documentation and procedures, converting files, and using the new system.

Final Operating Documentation and Procedures

In the first step in getting ready to implement a new system, the analyst prepares the final operating documentation and procedures that the users will need to perform regular processing activities. The procedures covered include entering data, making inquiries, directing processing activities, and distributing reports.

In a large system, the operating documentation and procedures must include the information needed by the information processing department for operating the system on a day-to-day basis and for future reference when the system must be modified. The computer operators must have operating documentation that identifies the processing schedule, files to be used, and programs to be run. The data entry group must have procedures on how the input data is to be entered. The control group must have procedures for monitoring system controls and coordinating the distribution of reports. Figure 10.17 shows some elements of a documentation package.

Converting Files

A new computer-based system cannot be used until all the data files are converted into computer-usable form. When a manual system is computerized, file conversion can become a monumental task. The time and effort required to sort through and key in the data—and the corresponding cost of doing it—are great. Outside assistance may be required for large file conversion tasks. If an existing computer-based system is being changed to a new system, the files can be converted by a computer program.

Using the New System

There are four basic approaches to implementing a new system: direct implementation, parallel implementation, phased implementation, and pilot implementation. The concepts behind the four approaches are diagrammed in Figure 10.18.

In **direct implementation,** the change is made all at once. The old system is halted on a planned date and the new system is activated. This approach is most often used for small systems or larger systems for which a systems model was previously developed and thoroughly tested. Simply halting the old system and starting up the new system is a very simple approach; however, this method carries some risks. For example, in most large systems, there are far too many variables to be adequately tested. As a result, a few unexpected errors are almost always found during the initial implementation period. These errors are much more disruptive and difficult to correct when the old system has been halted, because normal processing cannot continue until they are fixed.

Parallel implementation involves running the old system and the new system at the same time for a specified period. The results of using the new system are compared to those of the old system. If the performance of the new system is satisfactory, use of the old system is discontinued. This approach is the safest because operations do not have to be shut down if the new system has problems; however, it is by far the most expensive and difficult approach to coordinate.

Operating two systems instead of one takes much more time and effort. And, in addition to operating both systems, it is still necessary to compare the output from the new system to the old system and evaluate the results.

When the parallel implementation approach is used, a formal meeting of the project development team and the users is held at the end of the trial period. The performance of the new system is discussed and a decision is reached as to whether the findings are positive enough to warrant discontinuing the operation of the old system.

Some systems are just too broad in scope or are so large that they must be implemented in phases to avoid the traumatic effect of trying to implement all the

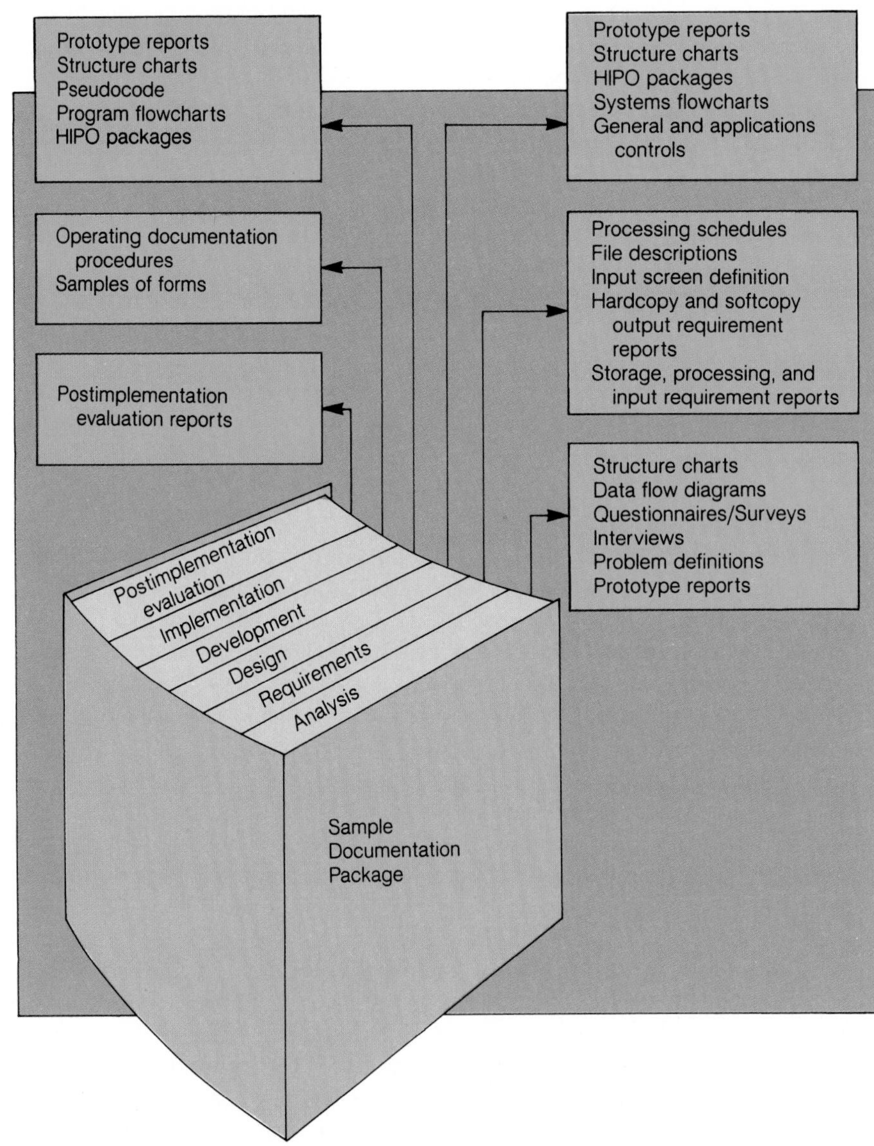

FIGURE 10.17

Sample documentation package.

components at once. Implementation is more easily handled one phase at a time—**phased implementation.** For example, in an accounting system like Sporting Life's, the general ledger components could be implemented first. Once they are running, the accounts payable and accounts receivable components could be implemented.

If a system is to be implemented at many locations in a widely dispersed company, the task can be very difficult to manage all at once. To implement the system at one location at a time—and ensure that it is working correctly before moving on to other locations—is safer. This is called **pilot implementation.**

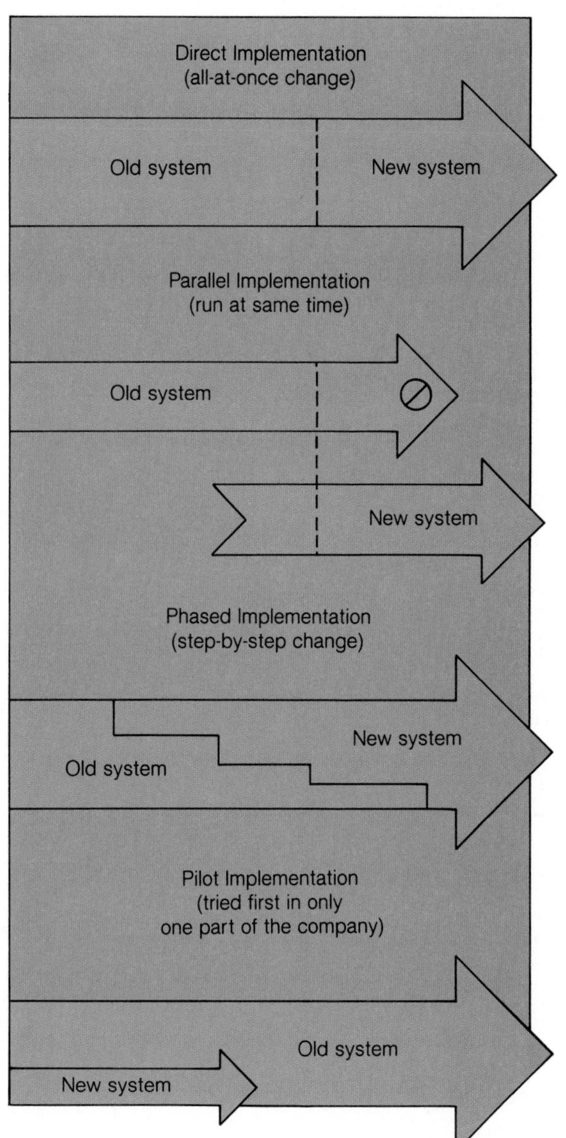

FIGURE 10.18

Four approaches to systems implementation.

PHASE 6: POSTIMPLEMENTATION EVALUATION AND MAINTENANCE

Two very important activities take place after the new system has been implemented: postimplementation evaluation and systems maintenance. **Systems maintenance** is not actually part of the systems *development* life cycle; it refers to adjust-

FIGURE 10.19 User interaction with the systems analysis and design life cycle. This diagram reviews the points at which you, the user, may interact with systems analysts and designers.

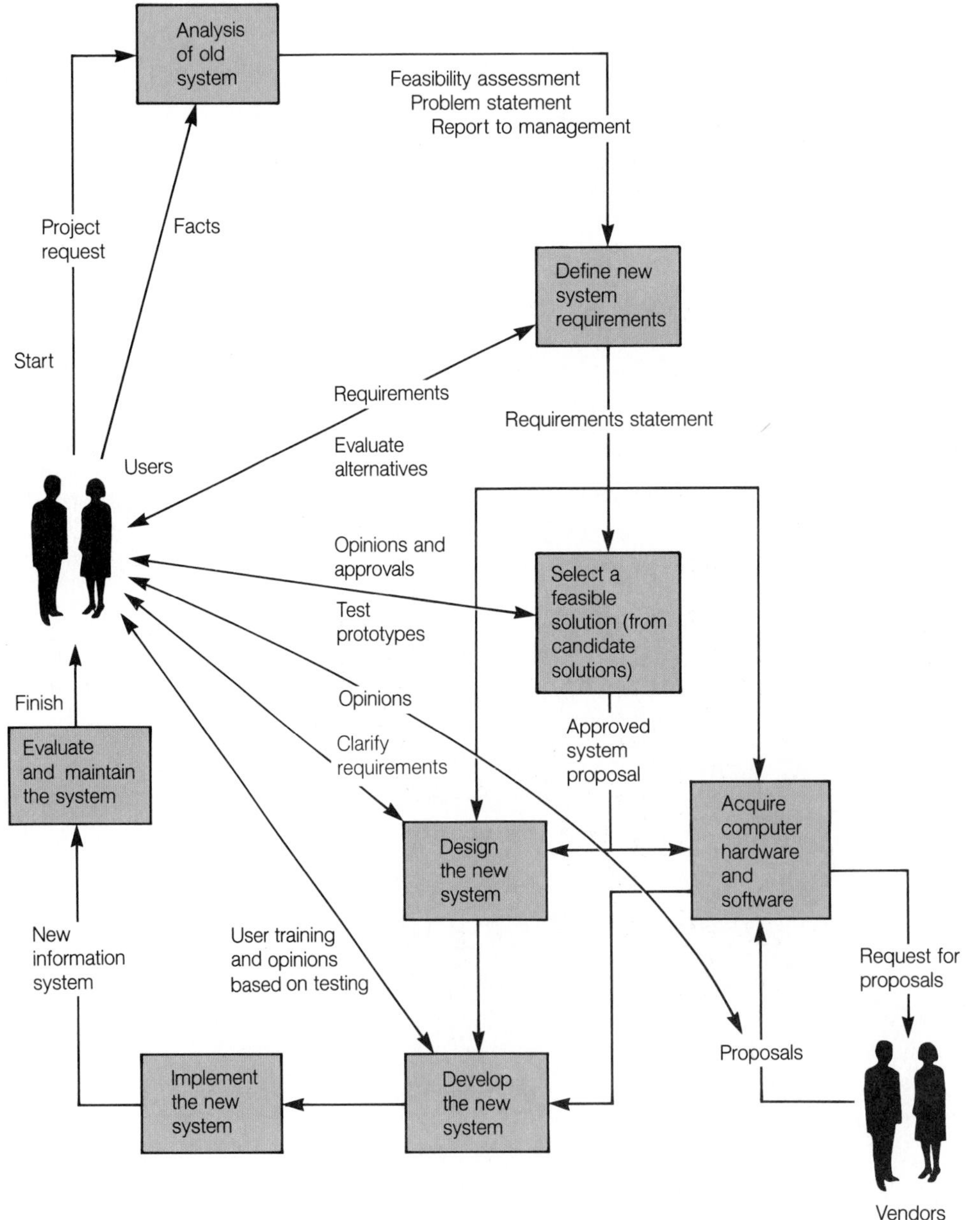

ments and enhancements, or additions, that need to be made to the system after it has been implemented. Adjustments may be needed because, as users gain experience in using the new system, they may discover minor processing errors. Or government reporting regulations may change, creating new requirements for a system to satisfy. Companies must remember to budget funds to pay for maintenance.

PURPOSE OF PHASE 6

After a new system has been in operation for several months and any necessary systems maintenance has been done, a formal evaluation—called a **postimplementation evaluation**—of the new system takes place. This evaluation determines either that the new system is meeting its objectives or that certain things need to be done so that it will.

The end of the final step in the SDLC is marked by the preparation of a new systems evaluation report. The report summarizes the extent to which the system meets the original objectives and includes a list of enhancements to be considered for future development and implementation.

WHAT SKILLS DOES THE USER NEED?

Now that you have learned a bit about systems analysis and design, you're probably wondering what you will have to know in a typical business situation. Figure 10.19 reviews the points at which you, the user, may interact with the systems development life cycle. Whether or not you will need to use any of the tools and techniques for analyzing and documenting systems and their development depends on the type of organization you're with and the level of expertise you have gained. But, in most cases, you will need only a basic understanding of the life cycle used at your place of business and the objectives of each phase. You will need to develop your ability to communicate effectively with computer specialists to help your company operate efficiently and profitably. If you can't communicate your business needs clearly, your requirements may not be met by the new system.

DEALING WITH THE NEXT GENERATION OF COMPUTER-LITERATE USERS*

It used to be that information systems professionals could get away with almost any proposal. The users didn't understand enough about computing to seriously question technical recommendations, schedules, costs, and alternatives. But times are rapidly changing.

Few graduates from higher education are without computing backgrounds. Many (if not most) high school graduates have also been exposed to computers and

* J. Whitten, L. Bentley, and V. Barlow, *Systems Analysis and Design Methods*, 2nd ed. (Homewood, Ill.: Richard D. Irwin, 1989), p. 36. Reprinted with permission.

programming. And even elementary school students are learning about computers. Much of this trend is fueled by the explosion of microcomputers.

Consider now, if you will, the probable computing backgrounds of those students currently going through the school system. What types of users are these people going to be?

These users will be less threatened by the pace of computer technology. They very well may be more receptive to technological change. They will probably be more participative than today's average user. Sounds like utopia at first glance, right? Don't be too hasty.

These same users are going to expect more from their systems analysts and consultants. They are going to be less inclined to accept answers like, "We can't do that" or "That's not possible." They are going to expect much higher quality systems (fewer errors and greater adaptability) than today's user. Instead of just complaining about computer types, they'll try to do something about it. They will probably expect [systems analysts] to be more engineering-like in . . . methods (greater rigor) and more business-like in . . . attitude (proving economic feasibility). In other words, the next generation of users will be more demanding because they are more computer literate.

We are already seeing evidence of this trend, beyond the fact that the new generation has simply had more exposure to computers in school. Users, through information centers, are building a greater and greater number of their own applications. . . . Within the next decade, users will directly fulfill more than half of their own computing requests, although most of those requests will simply involve extracting data from existing files and databases.

As further evidence, look at the microcomputer industry. Hardware and software sales have been more influenced by the buying habits of users than by computer professionals. In virtually all businesses, users are buying micros and software in great volumes.

The potential for superior analyst/user relationships and cooperation will likely result from this computer literacy revolution. Stated more simply, there will be less of a communications gap between technical and nontechnical workers.

Also, the analyst should become liberated from the more mundane work such as generating new reports against existing systems. Instead, the analyst will be called on to develop sophisticated databases and data networks on which the more sophisticated users can draw.

Finally, the applications will probably become much more interesting as users look for new ways to exploit technology to gain some competitive advantage in their marketplace. The fundamental business systems will already be done!

For some analysts it may prove intimidating. To [others], it will be exciting!

ONWARD: DATABASICS

Neatly designed information systems would be useless if there were no organized way of handling all the data that makes up the information. Indeed, the information systems we just discussed would not run without databases and database management systems, which we will cover in the next chapter.

Summary

The systems development life cycle (SDLC) is the formal process by which organizations build computer-based information systems. Systems development life cycles may be known by different names and comprise varying numbers of phases, but their principles are basically the same. The participants in the SDLC are users, information processing staff, management of all departments, and computer specialists (programmers and analysts). Your role in the SDLC will depend on the size of the company you are involved with and your job description, educational background, and past experience. In any case, you will have to participate in the systems analysis and design process because you will have to explain to analysts and designers how you use the current system and what you think is wrong with it. In other words, you will have to help define the new systems requirements. You will also have to be able to follow the charts, diagrams, and written procedures in the new systems documentation so that you will be able to use the new system effectively.

An SDLC is used as a guideline in directing and administering the activities involved in establishing business system requirements, developing the system, acquiring hardware and software, and controlling development costs. Without a reasoned approach to systems analysis and design, systems development can result in disruption of normal working procedures, acquisition of too much or too little computer hardware, development of inadequate software, misunderstood user needs and requirements, new system problems resulting from inadequate testing, and inadequate documentation for system maintenance and future modification.

An SDLC can be divided into six phases:

Phase 1—Analyze current system.

Phase 2—Define new systems requirements.

Phase 3—Design new system.

Phase 4—Develop new system.

Phase 5—Implement new system.

Phase 6—Evaluate performance of new system and maintain new system.

Table 10.1 summarizes the phases and their activities.

In Phase 1, the objective is to gain a clear understanding of the existing system, including its shortcomings, and determine where improvements can be made. Aspects of the system that are studied in Phase 1 include: inputs (transactions), outputs, files, users' interaction, methods and procedures, data storage, controls, and existing hardware and software.

To analyze the current system, analysts and users must gather data about the existing system using such techniques as interviews; reviewing written policies and procedures; collecting sample forms, reports, and other documents; observing operations, and using questionnaires to conduct surveys. After the data has been gathered, it must be analyzed. Problems and opportunities to improve the system are identified. Systems analysts use several tools and techniques to study the system and document the analysis, including data flow diagrams, systems flowcharts, structure charts, HIPO packages, prototyping, and computer-assisted software engineering (CASE) tools. Phase 1 concludes with a report and presentation to management that summarizes the current systems analysis and gives a recommendation about whether or not to proceed.

TABLE 10.1 The SDLC's Six Phases

1. ANALYSIS. Gain a clear understanding of the current system. Summarize to management and recommend whether to proceed with the next phases in the SDLC.

   Study the inputs, outputs, files, users' interaction, methods and procedures, data storage, controls, and existing hardware and software

   Gather data
   - conduct interviews (structured and unstructured)
   - review written policies and procedures
   - collect sample forms
   - observe operations
   - distribute questionnaires

   Analyze data
   - data flow diagrams
   - CASE

   Identify problems

2. REQUIREMENTS. Define the business requirements (software) for the new system. Hardware requirements will be finalized during and after the design phase. Prepare systems requirements report. Evaluate alternatives. Prepare request for proposal (RFP). Use modeling tools to document system modules, using structured approach.

   Output
   - hardcopy
   - softcopy
   - computer-usable

   Input
   - Input screens
   - Input controls

   Storage
   - files

   Processing
   - schedules

   Start to build new system prototype using modeling and prototyping tools
   - pseudocode
   - structure charts
   - HIPO packages
   - systems flowchart
   - 4GLs
   - applications generators
   - CASE

3. DESIGN. Define the technical design of the new system using various programming methods and techniques. Establish a sound framework of controls within which the new system should operate. Continue to assemble documentation about the design of the new system. Continued use of CASE tools. Build project dictionary.

   Systems flowcharts
   - Provide an overview of the entire system

   Program flowcharts

   Prototyping

   HIPO packages
   - Provide an overview of the system in numbered modules (VTOC); include overview diagrams and detail diagrams

   Structured design and programming
   - Design from the top down to ensure simplicity, refinement, and modularity

4. DEVELOPMENT. Create or select the software required by the new system design. Choose vendors. Acquire hardware. Train users and operators. Test new system.

   Design programs
   - flowcharts
   - pseudocode
   - HIPO
   - structure charts
   - applications generators

   Review designs
   - in a design walkthrough

   Write programs
   - using programming languages

   Test programs

   Assemble documentation
   - from each of the development stages (and from prior stages)

5. IMPLEMENTATION. Get the new system running.

   Create final operating documentation and procedures

   Convert files

   Use the system
   - direct, parallel, phased, or pilot implementation

6. POSTIMPLEMENTATION EVALUATION AND SYSTEMS MAINTENANCE. Determine whether the new system is meeting its objectives and make necessary adjustments.

Phase 2 of the SDLC involves defining the business requirements for the new system — manual as well as computer-based procedures. Requirements should be defined in the areas of input, storage, processing, and output. Defining software requirements focuses first on the output that the users will need. Phase 2 concludes with a systems requirements report.

Phase 3 of the SDLC focuses on the technical design of the new system, using programming techniques and methods described in Chapter 8 plus CASE tools and continued prototyping. Designing the new systems controls for both manual and computerized procedures is also an important part of Phase 3.

Phase 4 of the SDLC, developing the new system, involves acquiring software and hardware, training users and operators, and testing the new system.

Hardware must be selected that is compatible with any existing hardware that is to be retained. The need for main memory, mathematical processing, graphics, storage, types and quantity of output, number of users, need for multitasking and multiusing, and the type of existing operating system must be considered before hardware is purchased or leased.

Phase 5 of the SDLC involves implementing the new system. This phase includes three steps: (1) creating final operating documentation and procedures, (2) converting files, and (3) using the system. New systems can be implemented (1) all at once (direct implementation), (2) while the old system is still running (parallel implementation), (3) step-by-step (phased implementation), or (4) in one section of the company at a time (pilot implementation).

Phase 6 of the SDLC involves postimplementation evaluation and systems maintenance. This evaluation determines whether or not the new system is meeting its objectives.

In general, a new system fails because of a lack of communication somewhere along the line. That is the main reason why you should understand the basics of the systems development life cycle — so that you can intelligently communicate to the computer specialists the problems with the current system as it affects your job and your requirements for the new system.

KEY TERMS

computer-assisted software engineering (CASE) tools, p. 415
data flow diagram (DFD), p. 405
direct implementation, p. 421
modeling tools, p. 408
parallel implementation, p. 421
phased implementation, p. 423
pilot implementation, p. 423
postimplementation evaluation, p. 425
project dictionary, p. 415
prototyping tools, p. 409
request for proposal (RFP), p. 415
systems development life cycle (SDLC), p. 393
systems flowchart, p. 408
systems maintenance, p. 424
systems requirements report, p. 414

EXERCISES

MATCHING

Match each of the following terms to the phrase that is the most closely related.

1. ____ pilot implementation
2. ____ computer-assisted software engineering (CASE) tools
3. ____ project dictionary
4. ____ data flow diagram
5. ____ direct implementation
6. ____ modeling tools
7. ____ parallel implementation
8. ____ phased implementation
9. ____ prototyping
10. ____ request for proposal (RFP)
11. ____ systems flowcharts
12. ____ systems requirements report
13. ____ systems maintenance
14. ____ systems development life cycle
15. ____ postimplementation evaluation

a. This marks the completion of the requirements phase of the SDLC, when the economic and practical feasibility of the new system is determined.
b. Situation in which the old system is halted on a planned date and the new system is activated
c. Design tool used by the systems analyst to show the flow of data through a system
d. Process of building a small, simple model of the new system that can be prepared with a minimum of effort
e. Situation in which the old system and the new system are running at the same time for a specified period
f. Charts used to diagram and document the design of a new system
g. Method for implementing a new system used when the system is very broad in scope
h. Adjustments that need to be made to the system after it has been implemented
i. Formal evaluation of the new system
j. This method involves implementing a new system at one location at a time to ensure that it is working correctly before moving on to another location.
k. Document used by a company when it goes outside its organization to develop a new system or purchase parts of a new system
l. Process of setting up an information system
m. Pseudocode, structure charts, systems flowcharts
n. This stores all the requirements and specifications for all elements of data to be used in a new system.

o. These provide computer-automated support for structured design techniques.

MULTIPLE CHOICE

1. Which of the following is done in order to gather data in Phase 1 of the SDLC?
   a. conducting interviews
   b. observing operations
   c. using questionnaires to conduct surveys
   d. reviewing policies and procedures
   e. all the above
2. In Phase 1 of the SDLC, which of the following aspects are usually analyzed?
   a. outputs
   b. inputs (transactions)
   c. controls
   d. existing hardware and software
   e. all the above
3. Which of the following is used when a company goes outside its organization to develop a new system?
   a. project dictionary
   b. request for proposal
   c. systems flowchart
   d. data flow diagram
   e. none of the above
4. Which of the following might be output as a result of using a CASE tool?
   a. prototypes
   b. cost/benefit analysis
   c. programming code
   d. flowcharts, data flow diagrams
   e. all the above
5. Which of the following does not occur in Phase 4 of the SDLC?
   a. acquire hardware
   b. train users
   c. acquire software
   d. test the new system
   e. conduct interviews
6. Which of the following systems implementation approaches should be used if you want to run the old system and the new system at the same time for a specified period?
   a. direct
   b. pilot
   c. phased
   d. parallel
   e. none of the above
7. Which of the following affects the extent to which you're involved with the SDLC in your company?
   a. size of the organization

   b. your job description
   c. your relevant experience
   d. your educational background in information processing concepts
   e. all the above
8. Which of the following is not a factor in the failure of a systems development project?
   a. size of the company
   b. inadequate user involvement
   c. continuation of a project that should have been canceled
   d. failure of systems integration
   e. failure to evaluate the project at various phases of development
9. Which of the following is not a phase in the SDLC?
   a. analyze current system
   b. define the latest technology
   c. design new system
   d. develop and implement new system
   e. hire users
10. Which of the following decides which systems development projects to work on first?
   a. project dictionary
   b. systems flowcharts
   c. data diagram
   d. steering committee
   e. all the above

SHORT ANSWER

1. What is the importance of first defining the output requirements of a proposed system?
2. Briefly describe the six phases of the SDLC.
3. What are some of the techniques used to gather data in the analysis phase of the SDLC?
4. What determines the extent to which your job brings you in contact with your company's SDLC?
5. Why is it important for users to understand the principles of the SDLC?
6. Describe the four basic approaches to implementing a new system.
7. What is the significance of computer-assisted software engineering tools?
8. Several common tools are used for defining a new system's requirements, including modeling tools and prototyping tools. What is the difference between these two types of tools?
9. Why is it important for a company to follow an orderly SDLC?
10. Describe a few different types of security controls that can be used by an organization to protect a computer system and data from accidental or intentional damage.

PROJECTS

1. Using recent computer publications, research the state of the art of computer-assisted software engineering (CASE) tools. What capabilities do these tools have? What do you think the future holds for CASE tools?
2. Designing system controls. Your company is just beginning the process of computerizing its sales order entry activities. Currently, orders are received by mail, over the phone, and at the counter when customers stop by. The plan is to key the phone orders and counter orders into the computer immediately. The orders received in the mail will be entered into the computer in groups. A typical order contains customer information (such as number, name, and address) and product information (such as product number, description, quantity ordered, and unit price).
   a. Identify possible control techniques that could be designed into the system to ensure that all sales orders are input in their entirety to the computer.
   b. Identify possible control techniques to help ensure that all sales order data is accurately entered into the system.
   c. How would the control techniques for phone orders and counter orders differ from those for orders received in the mail?
3. Design a system that would handle the input, processing, and output of a simple form of your choice. Use a data flow diagram to illustrate the system.

Chapter 11

Database Management Systems

Where does the power come from in a computer-based information system? Although your first answer may be "hardware and the speed with which it can process data," if you think about it a bit longer you will probably realize that the *real* power comes from the data. From data comes information, and access to information offers power. But the amounts of data being handled by companies in computer-based systems have grown so large in recent years that managing data properly has become a sophisticated operation.

Preview

When you have completed this chapter, you will be able to:

- Explain what a database is.
- Describe the difference between file management systems and database management systems.
- Describe how database management systems software relates to hardware and the user.
- Identify the advantages and disadvantages of the three database models and of database management systems in general.
- Explain the importance of database administration within an organization.
- Distinguish between the logical and the physical design of a database.

THE USER PERSPECTIVE

Managers need information to make effective decisions. The more accurate, relevant, and timely the information, the better informed management will be when making decisions. Now we turn our attention to the *organization* of the data that makes up the information. In many companies data was (and certainly still is) collected on a grand scale, even redundantly; that is, the same element of data was entered more than once and appeared in more than one file—computerized or not. Nevertheless, data needed for a report was often unavailable or at least not available in a form appropriate to the situation. And to extract data from uncoordinated files was difficult.

By the early 1970s it was apparent that traditional file-handling concepts were often no longer adequate to handle the large amounts of data and the sophisticated and complex informational needs of a business's computer-based information system. To improve the quality of management information—and information for users in general—as well as the ease with which it could be produced, a new tool was developed: the database management system.

In general, database management concepts are the same for large computer systems and for microcomputers. As a general business user, you will most likely be using a microcomputer or a terminal to access data stored in a **database**—a large group of stored, integrated (cross-referenced) data elements that can be retrieved (usually from a minicomputer or a mainframe) and manipulated with great flexibility to produce information. It is therefore important for you to understand not only what a database is but also what a database management system is, so that you can put them to effective use in your job.

WHAT IS A DATABASE MANAGEMENT SYSTEM?

A database is a large group of stored, integrated (cross-referenced) data—usually organized in files—that can be retrieved and manipulated to produce information. A **database management system (DBMS)** is a comprehensive software tool that allows users to create, maintain, and manipulate the database to produce relevant management information. By *integrated* we mean that the file records are logically related to one another so that *all* data on a topic can be retrieved by simple requests. The database management systems software represents the interface between the user and the computer's operating system and database (Figure 11.1).

Picture a typical corporate office with a desk, chairs, telephones, and a row of file cabinets along the wall. A wide variety of business data is stored in these cabinets. If the files have been carefully organized and maintained, then any piece of data that

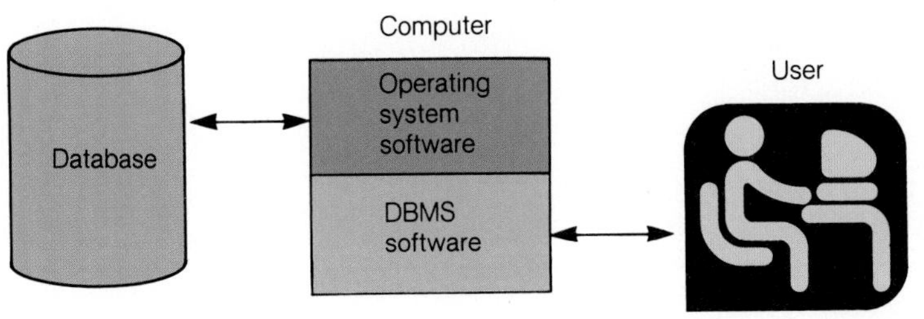

FIGURE 11.1

DBMS software as interface. The database management system is the facilitator that allows the user to access and manipulate integrated data elements in a database.

needs to be retrieved can quickly be located and removed. However, if the data has not been properly filed, some time and effort will be expended to find it. And, regardless of how carefully the files have been organized and maintained, you will always need to retrieve related pieces of data. For example, suppose you need to review the customer files for all invoices for payments due in excess of $2,500 and prepare a simple report. How would you accomplish this task? First, you would probably go through the customer files in alphabetical order, folder by folder. You would examine each invoice in the folders to determine if the amount is in excess of $2,500 and remove and copy each invoice that meets the criterion. You would then have to refile the copies you removed (and risk misfiling them). When you had examined all the customer folders and copied all the appropriate invoices, you would then review the copies and put together your report. Imagine how much time this could take. If there are a lot of customers, you would need to spend hours, if not days.

Now let's look at the situation in a different way. The environment is the same, except that, instead of file cabinets, you have a microcomputer or a terminal and DBMS software that has access to a customer database file (Figure 11.2). In this file a row of customer data is referred to as a *record*, and an individual piece of data within a record, such as a name, is referred to as a *field*. (See Table 11.1 and Figure 11.3 for a review of the filing and database terminology introduced in Chapter 4.) To get the invoice data you need, you would do something like this:

- Turn on the computer and the printer.
- Start up the DBMS software.
- Give the command to "open up" the customer database file stored on your disk, which is similar in concept to manually opening up the customer drawer in a filing cabinet.
- Give the command to search all the records in the database file and display copies of the records that meet your criterion (that is, the names of people with unpaid invoices greater than $2,500). If you were using dBASE IV, a popular microcomputer DBMS, the command would look something like:

FIGURE 11.2

Customer database file. This figure illustrates only a small section of our hypothetical customer file. Data stored electronically in a DBMS can be much more easily retrieved than data stored in filing cabinets.

Customer Name	Date	Item Ordered	Quantity Ordered	Invoice Amount
Arthene Ng	02/12/92	4065	6	2510.67
Pamela Robert	02/13/92	4128	7	1510.62
Jeff Arguello	02/13/92	4111	1	1905.00
Sylvia Arnold	02/14/92	4007	6	2950.93
Richard Mall	02/14/92	4019	1	63.55
Alan Steinberg	02/14/92	4021	3	1393.00
Harry Filbert	02/14/92	4106	2	940.56
Frances Chung	02/15/92	4008	5	2717.00
Bruce Chaney	02/15/92	4007	8	1720.00

```
LIST FOR INV_AMOUNT > 2500
```

If you were using SQL (Structured Query Language), the command would look like this:

```
SELECT NAME FROM CUSTOMER
     WHERE INV_AMOUNT > 2500
     ORDER BY NAME
```

In response to this command, all the records in the file that have an invoice amount greater than $2,500 will be listed on the screen. (The SQL command would also sort the listing into order by name.) This whole procedure would take perhaps only five minutes or less.

The DBMS is a software tool designed to manage a large number of integrated, shared electronic "file cabinets." You describe the type of data you wish to store, and the DBMS is responsible for creating the database file(s) and providing an easy-to-use mechanism for storing, retrieving, and manipulating the data.

WHY SHOULD YOU CARE ABOUT DATABASES?

In small businesses, databases may be both created and operated by the user. In moderate- to large-sized businesses with extensive computer systems, the corporate database is usually created by technical information specialists such as the database

TABLE 11.1

Short Glossary of Database Terminology

Alphanumeric (character) data: data composed of a combination of letters, numbers, and other symbols (like punctuation marks) that are not used for mathematical calculations.

Bit: contraction of binary digit, which is either 1 ("on") or 0 ("off") in computerized data representation.

Character: the lowest level in the data hierarchy; usually one letter or numerical digit; also called **byte** (8 bits).

Data: the raw facts that make up information.

Database: a large collection of stored, integrated (cross-referenced) records that can be maintained and manipulated with great flexibility; the top level in the data hierarchy.

Entity: any tangible or intangible object or concept on which an organization wishes to store data; entities have attributes, such as name, color, and price.

Field, or **attribute,** or **data element:** a group of related characters (*attribute* is also a column of a relation in a relational database, discussed later); the second lowest level in the data hierarchy.

File: a group of related records; the fourth level from the bottom in the data hierarchy.

Information: data that has value to, or that has been interpreted by, the user.

Key: a unique field within a record that uniquely identifies the record.

Numeric data: data composed of numeric digits (numbers) used for mathematical calculations.

Record: a group of related fields; the third level from the bottom in the data hierarchy (analogous to a *tuple*, or *row*, in a relational database, as described later).

FIGURE 11.3

Data hierarchy. The figures show how most of the data terms in Table 11.1 fit into the data hierarchy (first introduced in Chapter 4).

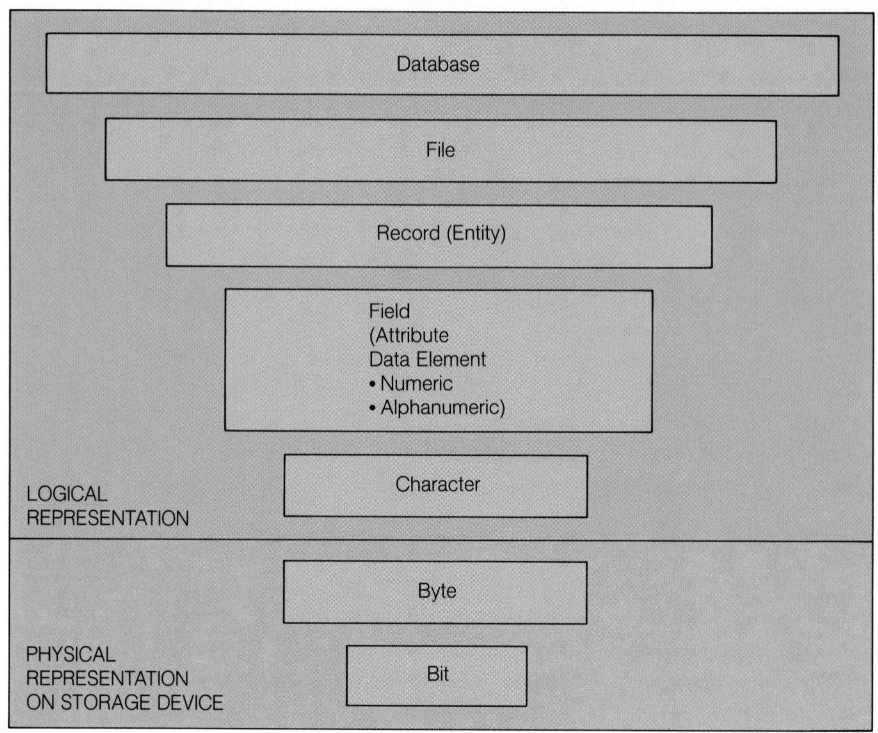

(a)

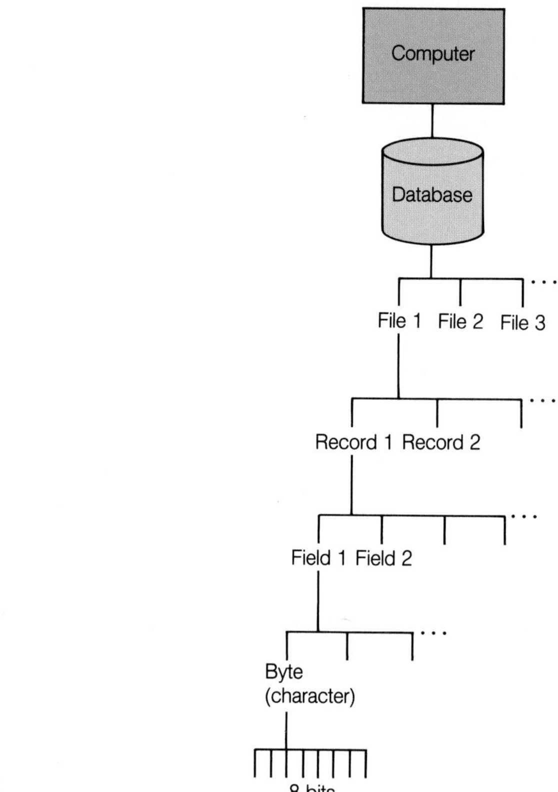

(b)

administrator, but the database management system is acquired by the information systems department. Users generate and extract data stored by the database management system. As with systems analysis and design, which we discussed in Chapter 10, to design a database the organization must describe its informational needs to the designers and specify the type of data needed. Users participate heavily in this process of defining what information needs to be stored in the database.

Since the early 1980s, tremendous advances have been made in developing database management systems for microcomputers. They are now easy enough for users to learn to operate without assistance and powerful enough to produce valuable management information. Regardless of whether you're in a large or a small business, you cannot afford to do without the capabilities that a DBMS can provide. It is one of the most powerful tools available for use as an information resource.

Data Management Concepts

Chapter 4 discussed three methods for storing and retrieving data: sequential; direct, or relative; and indexed. Each method stores records differently within a file, and each method is suited to particular applications and processing requirements. In Chapter 4, we assumed that all data needed for processing is contained in a single file on a storage device. But what appears if needed data elements are spread among many files? For example, student records may be in one file, course and grade records in a second file, and billing records in a third file. The DBMS approach for storing and retrieving data in computer-usable form has evolved to allow users to easily retrieve and update data that is in more than one file. But before we describe why the DBMS approach is significant, and to facilitate your understanding of it, we will first describe in more detail the traditional system it evolved from—the file management system.

File Management Systems

Computers were placed in commercial use in 1954, when General Electric Company purchased a UNIVAC (Universal Automatic Computer) for its research division. At first, the processing performed was straightforward. Applications software programs tended to be sequentially organized and stored in a single file on magnetic tape that contained all the elements of data required for processing. The term **file management system** was coined to describe this traditional approach to managing business data and information (Figure 11.4). However, file management systems did not provide the user with an easy way to group records within a file or to establish relationships among the records in different files. As disk storage became more cost-effective and its capacity grew, new software applications were developed to access disk-based files. The need to access data stored in more than one file was quickly recognized and posed increasingly complex programming requirements.

The most serious problems of file management systems involve:

- Data redundancy.
- Updating files and maintaining data integrity.
- Lack of program and data independence.

In the case of **data redundancy,** the same data elements appear in many different files and often in different formats, which makes updating files difficult, time consuming, and prone to errors. For example, a payroll file and a personnel file may both contain an employee's ID number, name, address, and telephone number. Obviously, having many copies of the same data elements takes up unnecessary storage space.

In addition to wasted space, data redundancy creates a problem when it comes to **file updating.** When an element of data needs to be changed—for example, employee address—it must be updated in *all* the files, a tedious procedure. If some files are missed, data will be inconsistent—that is, **data integrity** is not maintained—and reports will be produced with erroneous information. (Data integrity generally refers to the quality of the data—that is, to its accuracy, reliability, and timeliness. If data integrity is not maintained, data is no longer accurate, reliable, and/or timely.)

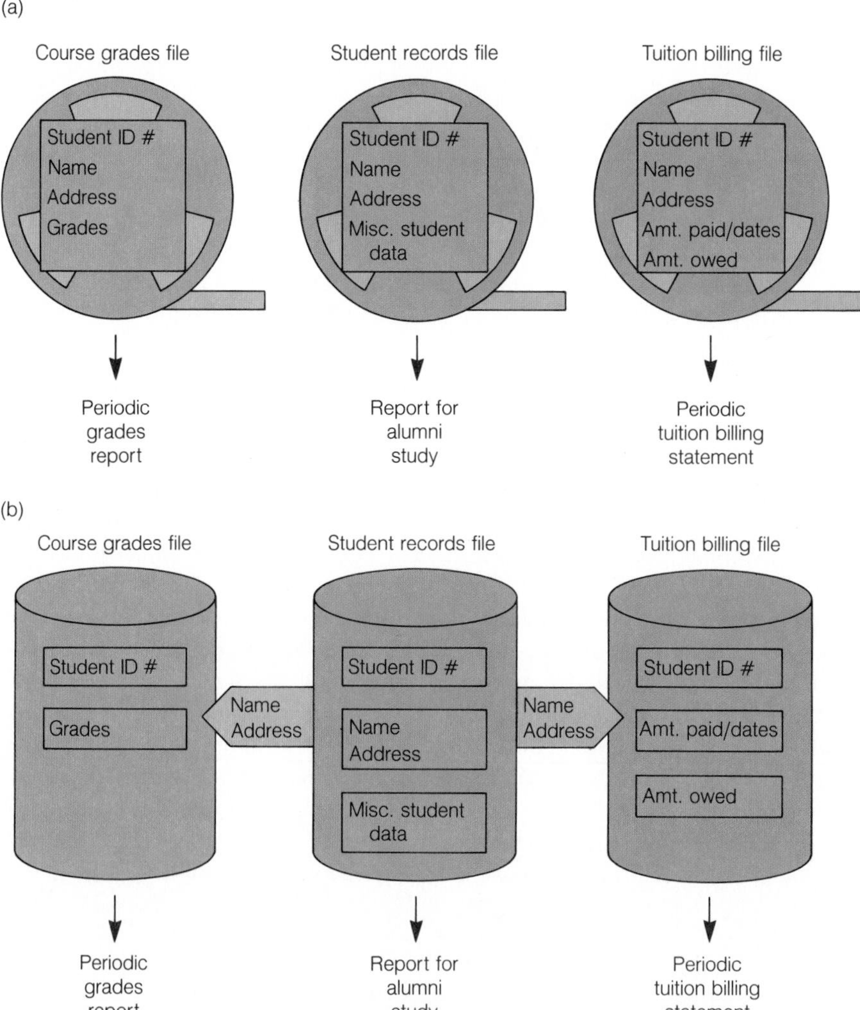

FIGURE 11.4

(a) Single file: Traditional file management approach. In old file management systems, some of the same data elements were repeated in different files. (b) In database management systems, data elements are integrated, thus eliminating data redundancy.

Another limitation of file management systems has to do with the lack of **program independence** and **data independence.** This lack of independence means that different files established in different arrangements, such as some with the date first and expense items second and others vice versa, cannot be used by the same program. Programs must be written by programmers to use a specific file format. This process takes a programmer a large amount of time and costs a company a great deal of money.

To deal with these problems and the ever-growing demands for a flexible, easy-to-use mechanism for managing data, the concept of a database was developed.

Database Management Systems

As mentioned earlier, the term *database* describes a collection of related records that forms an integral base of data, which can be accessed by a wide variety of applications programs and user requests. In a database management system, data needs to be entered into the system only once. When the user instructs the program to sort data or compile a list, the program searches quickly through the data in memory (or in storage), copying needed data into a new file for the purpose at hand. However, the user's instructions do not change the original set of data in any way. (Database administrators may change the data later when they update the database.)

How is this done? Through software—the database management system (DBMS). However, the software must be considered together with the hardware and the database because the type and capacity of certain hardware components and the size of the database will affect both the sophistication and the efficiency of the DBMS software.

Hardware: Storage Counts

Storage capacity is crucial to the operation of a database management system. Even the many megabytes of hard disk storage in an efficient, modern microcomputer can't handle the many gigabytes of data that move through large corporations. To manage these databases, large-scale database management systems need to use very high-capacity and high-speed disks for storage. It is not uncommon for database files in a comprehensive corporate information system to be so large that they use more than one disk storage device (plus additional backup devices).

Recent advances in the speed and the capacity of hard disk drives for microcomputers have made them the main storage resource for microcomputer-based database management systems. Early microcomputer systems relied on diskette-based storage devices with capacities ranging from 150 K to 1.2 MB. Although these capacities allowed small database files to be established, many business applications required files too large to be stored on diskettes. The first hard disks introduced for microcomputers had 10 MB of storage capacity and an average access time of 90 milliseconds (ms). (Recall from Chapter 4 that *access time* refers to the average amount of time required to move the read/write mechanism to the appropriate disk-surface location and begin the process of retrieving data.) Recent hard disk units have cut this access time to less than 10 ms. The increase in speed improves both processing and response time for database applications.

Managers and other users in large organizations usually interact directly with the DBMS via a video display terminal connected to a large computer. The terminal allows users to communicate their requests for information to the system and view the results immediately. In the past, most information was displayed in the form of text. However, because many new terminals have color graphics capability, users can now view information in picture form, which may make it easier to understand (Figure 11.5).

Because database files represent a significant (in many organizations the most important) business resource, they must be protected from damage, loss, and unauthorized use. The most common way to protect the corporate database from loss or damage is to periodically make backup copies of it. In large database systems, backup copies are usually made on one or more reels of standard ½-inch magnetic tape. The backup process for large corporate databases requires the involvement of computer operations specialists. The most popular form of backup for microcomputer hard disks is the tape streamer, or streaming tape unit (Chapter 4). These devices are small, fast, and so easy to use that the user can perform the backup operation unassisted.

Software: In Control

A database management system is an integrated set of software programs that provides all the necessary capabilities for building and maintaining database files, extracting the information required for making decisions, and formatting the information into structured reports. It is intended to:

- *Make data independent of the applications programs being used, so that it is easy to access and change.* Say, for example, you have created a student

FIGURE 11.5

Color graphics display of information being retrieved and manipulated by a graphics-oriented DBMS. Users often find graphic displays (left monitor) to be more helpful than textual displays (right monitor).

database with many student records. After some time, you decide to change the structure of the student database to include phone numbers. With a DBMS you can do this and still use the applications program you were using before you changed the database structure, because the data's organization is independent of the program being used.

- *Establish relationships among records in different files*. The user can obtain *all* data related to important data elements. For example, the user can obtain student course and address information from the student database at the same time as viewing the student's payment status from the billing database.
- *Eliminate data redundancy*. Because data is independent of the applications program being used, it can be stored a single time in a file that can be accessed, for example, by the student billing applications program or the grade averaging program.
- *Define the characteristics of the data*. The user can create a database that has data stored in it based on particular informational needs.
- *Manage file access*. For example, the DBMS can "examine" user requests and clear them for access to retrieve data, thus keeping data safe from unauthorized access.
- *Maintain data integrity*. Because data is not stored redundantly, it needs to be updated only in one place.

Using DBMS software, personnel can request that a program be run to produce information in a predefined format or extract information in a specific way. For example, if you are the manager of a school's registration department, you may want to review a report of the classes that currently have space available; however, the manager of the school's finance division may want to use the same data to generate a report on courses that had low enrollment over the past two years to determine whether to continue offering these courses.

The easiest way to view a DBMS is to think of it as a layer of software that surrounds the database files (Figure 11.6). The DBMS software usually includes a query language, report writers, utilities, and an applications program language interface (usually called the *data manipulation language [DML]*). Each of these will be described in the following sections.

QUERY LANGUAGE

Most managers and other users find a query language for data retrieval (see also Chapter 8) to be the most valuable aspect of DBMS software. Traditionally, many managers rely on the information provided by periodic reports. However, this creates a problem when a decision must be made *now* and the information required to make it will not be produced until the end of the week. The objective of a query language is to allow managers to use simple English (or the language of the company they're working with) to produce information on demand that is also in simple English. To be effective, a query language must allow the user to phrase requests for information in a very flexible fashion. For example, take a request for inventory information. Here are some examples of questions that the user could ask using a query language when a single file is involved:

- List all items in the inventory database for which the quantity on hand equals zero. (Immediate orders would have to be placed to restock these items.)

- List all items in the database for which the quantity on hand is less than or equal to the reorder point. (This information would be used to process regular orders for restocking inventory.)
- List all items in the database for which the unit cost times the quantity on hand exceeds $10,000. (This would show the highest dollar volume items in inventory.)

Here are examples of questions that the user could ask using a query language when more than one file is involved:

- List the names and addresses of all customers who ordered items that were out of stock and that are now in stock. (This would involve using both the customer file and the inventory file and would show a listing of all customers who should be notified by mail that the items they ordered are now available for pickup.)
- List the phone numbers of customers who ordered items that were out of stock and that aren't going to be restocked. (This would also involve using both the customer file and the inventory file and would show a listing of all customers who should be notified by phone that the item they ordered will no longer be carried in inventory.)

You, the user, can learn to use a typical query language effectively with about eight hours of instruction and practice. Once armed with this skill, you can prepare a special report in a few minutes instead of several days or weeks. Several powerful

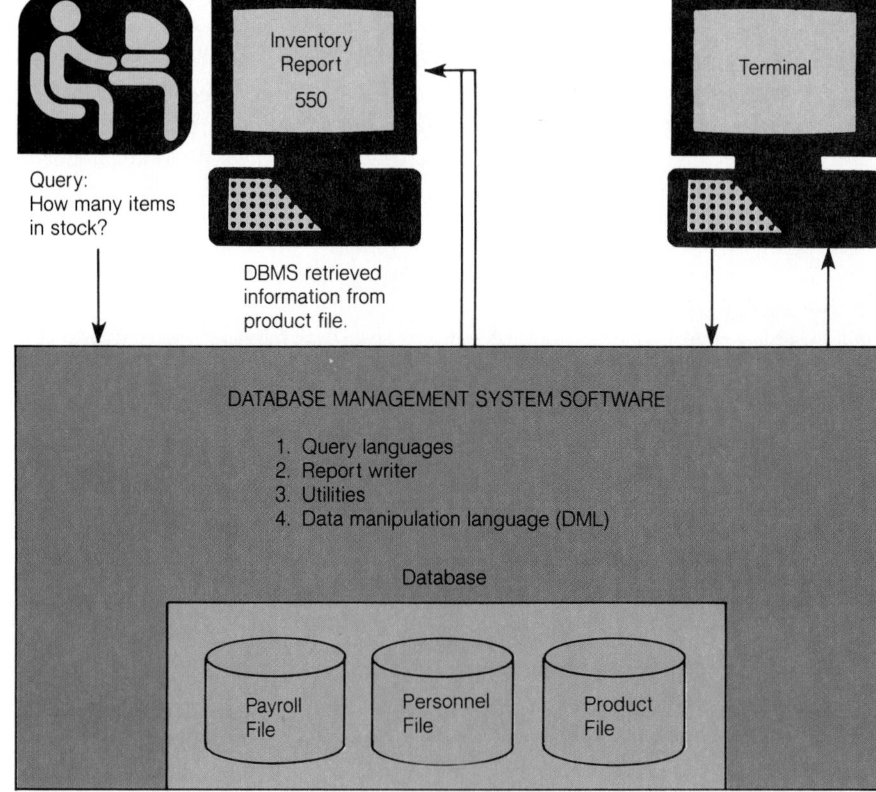

FIGURE 11.6

DBMS software. The software that comprises the functions of a database management system can be thought of as a layer that surrounds the database files. Among other things, this software provides the user interface, which allows the user to interact easily with the system.

query languages, including SQL (IBM), dBASE IV (Ashton-Tate), Oracle (Oracle), and R:base System V, exist for use with microcomputers. About 20 different query languages are available for use with larger computer systems; three of the most widely used are NOMAD2, INTELLECT, and SQL.

To further illustrate how you might use a query language, let's use an inventory database as an example again. The structure of the database is illustrated in the following table.

Field Description	Name	Data Type	Size	Decimals
Part number	PNUM	Numeric	5	
Group code	GROUP	Character	1	
Description	DESCRIPT	Character	20	
Quantity-on-hand	QTYOH	Numeric	3	
Reorder point	ORDERPT	Numeric	3	
Unit cost	COST	Numeric	9	2
Supplier	SUPPLIER	Character	1	

Defining the size of a field tells the applications program how wide the field must be to store the numbers or characters in it; defining the decimals of a field applies only to numeric fields and refers to how many decimal places you want to retain on the right side of the decimal point, with rounding of the rightmost digit.

Let's suppose you are the inventory manager for a small company and will be attending a management meeting this afternoon to discuss the current budget. To prepare for the meeting you need to be able to discuss the status of inventory. You formulate some questions about inventory that you would like answered, including:

1. Which items in inventory are out of stock?
2. Which items in inventory are below the reorder point?
3. Which items to be ordered have a unit cost in excess of $25?
4. From which supplier will the company be ordering the most items?

If we assume that the database has been implemented on a microcomputer using a popular DBMS package such as dBASE IV, you would use the following query language statements:

```
1. LIST FOR QTYOH = 0
2. LIST FOR QTYOH < ORDERPT
3. LIST FOR COST > 25 .AND. QTYOH < ORDERPT
4. LIST FOR QTYOH < ORDERPT .AND. SUPPLIER = "A"
   LIST FOR QTYOH < ORDERPT .AND. SUPPLIER = "B"
   LIST FOR QTYOH < ORDERPT .AND. SUPPLIER = "C"
```

The contents of the database and the results of the queries shown above are displayed in Figure 11.7.

REPORT WRITER

The report writer aspect of DBMS software simplifies the process of generating reports. If we use our inventory file as an example, we might want to generate a

FIGURE 11.7 Results of database queries. These are the types of responses a DBMS would give you based on the queries listed in the text.

Inventory Database Listing

Record#	PNUM	GROUP	DESCRIPT	QTYOH	ORDERPT	COST	SUPPLIER
1	202	2	HAMMERS	23	30	5.75	A
2	207	2	NAILS	14	25	2.75	B
3	211	2	PLIERS	30	25	8.65	A
4	213	2	WRENCHES	0	10	18.00	C
5	202	2	SCREW DRIVERS	13	15	4.80	B
6	218	2	SAW	8	5	15.60	A
7	309	1	BROOM	0	10	9.99	C
8	310	1	MOPS	4	10	11.00	A
9	308	1	SPONGES	19	15	0.80	A
10	308	3	LIGHT BULBS	10	8	7.80	B
11	315	3	POWER CABLES	12	20	15.60	C
12	300	3	EXTENSION CORDS	0	15	8.99	A

Quantity-on-hand is equal to zero.

Record#	PNUM	GROUP	DESCRIPT	QTYOH	ORDERPT	COST	SUPPLIER
4	213	2	WRENCHES	0	10	18.00	C
7	309	1	BROOM	0	10	9.99	C
12	300	3	EXTENSION CORDS	0	15	8.99	A

Quantity-on-hand is less than the reorder point.

Record#	PNUM	GROUP	DESCRIPT	QTYOH	ORDERPT	COST	SUPPLIER
1	202	2	HAMMERS	23	30	5.75	A
2	207	2	NAILS	14	25	2.75	B
4	213	2	WRENCHES	0	10	18.00	C
5	202	2	SCREW DRIVERS	13	15	4.80	B
7	309	1	BROOM	0	10	9.99	C
8	310	1	MOPS	4	10	11.00	A
11	315	3	POWER CABLES	12	20	15.60	C
12	300	3	EXTENSION CORDS	0	15	8.99	A

Cost is greater than 25 and quantity-on-hand is less than reorder point.

No records found.

Quantity-on-hand is less than the reorder point and supplier is equal to "A"

Record#	PNUM	GROUP	DESCRIPT	QTYOH	ORDERPT	COST	SUPPLIER
1	202	2	HAMMERS	23	30	5.75	A
8	310	1	MOPS	4	10	11.00	A
12	300	3	EXTENSION CORDS	0	15	8.99	A

Quantity-on-hand is less than the reorder point and supplier is equal to "B"

Record#	PNUM	GROUP	DESCRIPT	QTYOH	ORDERPT	COST	SUPPLIER
2	207	2	NAILS	14	25	2.75	B
5	202	2	SCREW DRIVERS	13	15	4.80	B

Quantity-on-hand is less than the reorder point and supplier is equal to "C"

Record#	PNUM	GROUP	DESCRIPT	QTYOH	ORDERPT	COST	SUPPLIER
4	213	2	WRENCHES	0	10	18.00	C
7	309	1	BROOM	0	10	9.99	C
11	315	3	POWER CABLES	12	20	15.60	C

report to be handed out at the afternoon meeting that shows the results of the queries given in Figure 11.7 in a polished format (Figure 11.8). The procedure is usually fairly easy and involves specifying column headings for the items to be included in the report, as well as any totals, subtotals, or other calculations.

UTILITIES

The utilities part of the DBMS software is used to maintain the database on an ongoing basis. This includes such tasks as:

- Creating and maintaining the data dictionary (described in more detail later in the chapter).
- Removing records flagged for deletion. (Most DBMSs have built-in protection schemes to prevent users from accidentally deleting records. To delete unwanted records from the database, the user must first mark, or "flag," them for deletion and then give the command to actually remove the flagged records.)
- Establishing control of access to portions of the database (protecting the database against unauthorized use). (Chapter 8 describes some of the ways of designing controls into the system.)
- Providing an easy way to back up the database and recover data if the database is damaged.
- Monitoring performance.
- Preventing data corruption when multiple users attempt to access the same database simultaneously.

DATA MANIPULATION LANGUAGE (DML)

The user needs the **data manipulation language (DML)** software in the DBMS to effect input to and output from the database files; in other words, all programs, including the query language, must go through the DML, which comprises the technical instructions that make up the input/output routines in the DBMS. Each applications program that is written needs certain data elements to process to

```
Page No.        1
01/01/92

                 INVENTORY ITEMS
      QUANTITY-ON-HAND < REORDER POINT

PRODUCT NUMBER DESCRIPTION          SUPPLIER

           202 HAMMERS              A
           207 NAILS                B
           213 WRENCHES             C
           202 SCREW DRIVERS        B
           309 BROOM                C
           310 MOPS                 A
           315 POWER CABLES         C
           300 EXTENSION CORDS      A
```

FIGURE 11.8

DBMS-generated report. This is a more polished report based on the third listing in Figure 11.7.

produce particular types of information. A list of required elements of data is contained within each applications program. The DML uses these lists, identifies the elements of data required, and provides the link necessary to the database to supply the data to the program. (In some cases, the data manipulation language is embedded in the query language.)

DATA DICTIONARIES AND TRANSACTION LOGS

Once a DBMS has been implemented, two types of files are constantly in use besides the database files—the **data dictionary** and a transaction log.

The information in the data dictionary varies from one DBMS to another. In general, the data dictionary contains information about:*

- What data is available.
- Where the data is located.
- Data attributes (descriptions).
- Who owns or is responsible for the data.
- How the data is used.
- Who is allowed to access the data for retrieval.
- Who is allowed to update or change the data.
- Relationships to other data items.
- Security and privacy limitations.

The dictionary is used constantly by the DBMS as a reference tool (Figure 11.9). When an applications program requests elements of data as part of a query, the DBMS refers to the data dictionary for guidance in retrieving them. The database administrator, whose job we'll discuss in more detail later, determines what the data dictionary contains.

The **transaction log** (Figure 11.9) contains a complete record of all activity that affected the contents of a database during the course of a transaction period. This log aids in backup and in rebuilding database files (recovery) if they are accidentally destroyed or damaged. If a backup copy is made each time a database file is updated and a transaction log is created to document the current transaction period's activity, then recovery from the loss of the current copy of the database file(s) is simple. In this case, the previous day's copy of the database is considered to be the current copy, which is then updated by using the most current transaction log. Database management systems for microcomputers do not automatically create a transaction log file. Special provisions must be made in the program design to accommodate this requirement. Database management systems for minicomputers and mainframes usually build the transaction log automatically.

DATABASE MODELS

Three popular models are used to organize a database: (1) hierarchical, (2) network, and (3) relational. These three models have evolved gradually as users and com-

* K. C. Laudon and J. P. Laudon, *Management Information Systems* (New York: Macmillan, 1988), p. 656.

puter specialists gained experience in using database management systems. They differ in terms of the cost of implementation, speed, degree of data redundancy, ease with which they can satisfy information requirements, and ease with which they can be updated.

In use since the late 1960s, the hierarchical and network database models were first developed and used principally on mainframe computers. The concepts behind

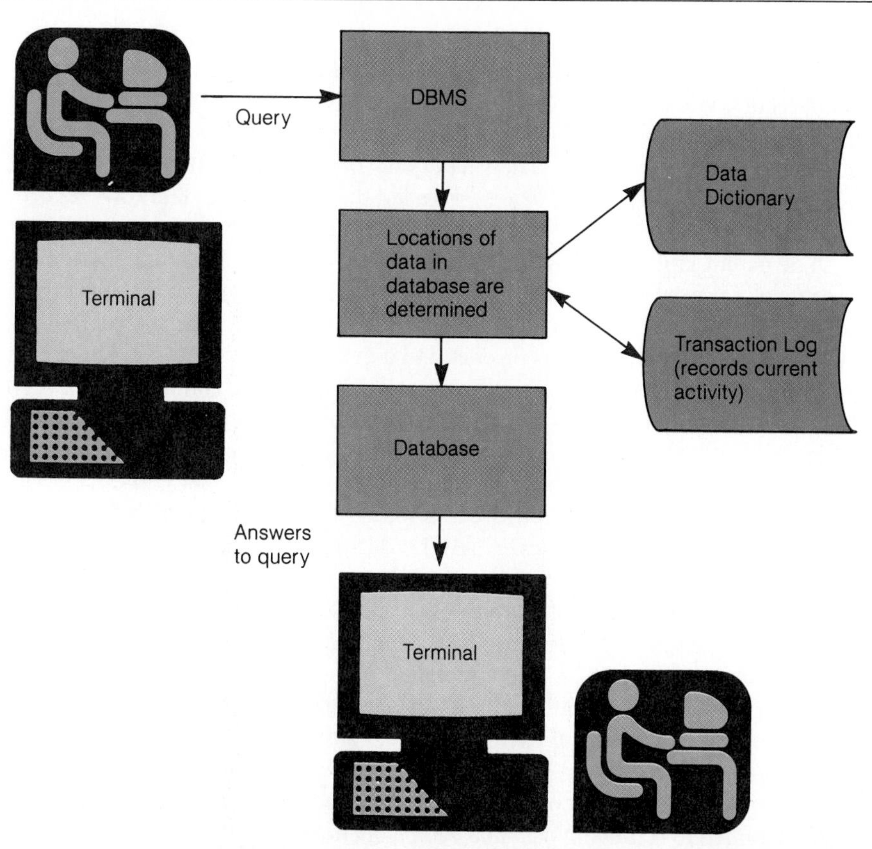

Layout Organize Append Go To Exit 7:25:45 am

Bytes remaining: 3908

Num	Field Name	Field Type	Width	Dec	Index
1	TITLE	Character	4		N
2	FIRSTNAME	Character	10		N
3	LASTNAME	Character	15		N
4	ADDRESS	Character	20		N
5	CITY	Character	15		N
6	STATE	Character	2		N
7	ZIP	Character	10		N
8	HIREDATE	Date	8		N
9	HRLYWAGE	Numeric	5	2	N
10	DEPENDENTS	Numeric	2	0	N
11	DEPT	Character	1		N

Database A:\EMPLOYEE Field 1/11

Enter the field name. Insert/Delete field:Ctrl-N/Ctrl-U

Field names begin with a letter and may contain letters, digits and underscores

FIGURE 11.9

Data dictionary and transaction log. The bottom of the figure shows dBASE IV's data dictionary for an EMPLOYEE database.

the relational database model were pioneered in the early 1970s by E. F. Codd and developed throughout the 1970s. This database model, which takes advantage of large-capacity direct-access storage devices, has been used extensively on microcomputers and is also being used more and more on larger computers for large-scale applications.

HIERARCHICAL MODEL

In the **hierarchical database model,** data is organized into related groups much like a family tree (Figure 11.10). The model comprises two types of records—parent records and child records. **Parent records** are higher in the structure of the model than **child records.** Each "child" can have only one "parent"; that is, each record may have many records below it but only one record above it. The record at the highest level, or top of the "tree," is called the root record. The **root record,** which is the key to the model, connects the various branches.

The parent-child relationship between two record types in a hierarchical database model is also called a **one-to-many relationship,** which means that one parent record has many child records. To store or retrieve a record in a hierarchical model, the DBMS begins at the root occurrence and moves downward through each of the occurrences until the correct record is located. There is no connection between separate branches in this type of model. See, for example, the route that is followed in Figure 11.10 to locate the record of travel expenses for the second week in April.

The primary advantage of the hierarchical database model is the ease with which data can be stored and retrieved, as well as the ease with which data can be extracted for reporting purposes. A few DBMS packages using this model have been available for some time and thus have been refined for continued use.

The main disadvantage of this type of database model is that records in separate groups—in Figure 11.10, for example, medical, travel, and life insurance are separate groups—cannot be directly related without a great deal of effort. For example, the Moser Corporation might want to compare by month and by year the different expense amounts of each category to answer such questions as: "What percentage is each yearly expense amount of the total of all expenses for the year?" or "What is the average expense amount for each month and for the year?" But the user is confined to retrieving data that can be obtained from the established hierarchical links among records. Also, if you delete a parent from the model, you automatically delete all the child records. In addition, modifying a hierarchical database structure is complex and requires a trained and experienced programmer who knows all the physical connections that exist between records. Another restriction is the inability to implement hierarchical models without a great deal of redundancy.

NETWORK MODEL

The **network database model** (Figure 11.11) is somewhat similar to the hierarchical model, but each record can have more than one parent. This model overcomes the principal limitation of the hierarchical model because it establishes relationships between records in different groups. Any record can be related to any other data element.

Figure 11.11 shows the expense types and expense periods for the first quarter of a year for the Moser Corporation as part of a network database model. With this type of model, it would be easy to compare weekly or monthly expense amounts or to determine what percentage travel expenses are of all expenses for the first quarter.

The primary advantage of the network database model is its ability to provide sophisticated logical relationships among the records. However, as in the hierarchi-

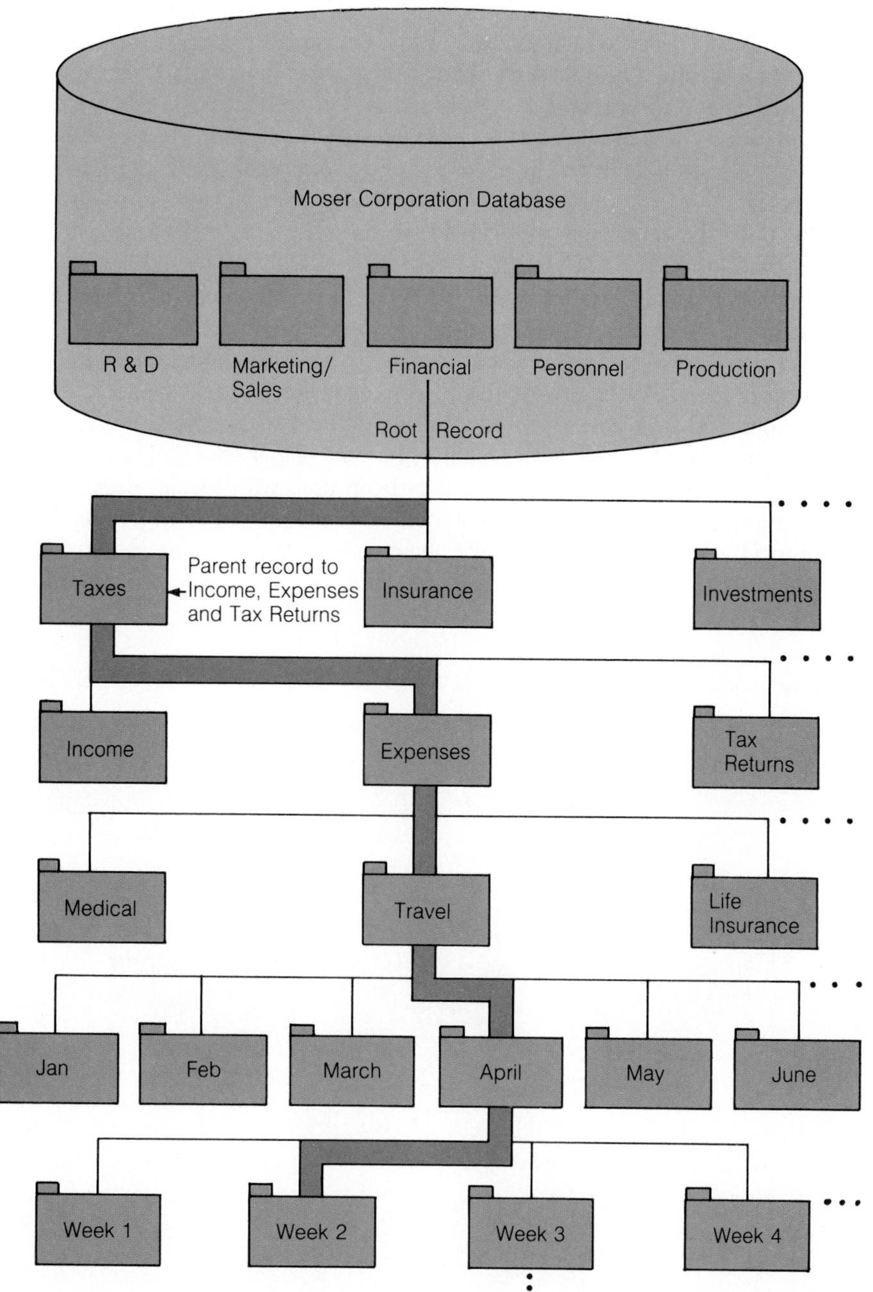

FIGURE 11.10

Hierarchical database model for the Moser Corporation. In this database model, which looks somewhat like a family tree, a parent record can have many child records, but each child record can have only one parent record. The root record is the topmost record.

cal model, the user is limited to retrieving data that can be accessed using the established links between records.

RELATIONAL DATABASE MODEL

The **relational database model** (Figure 11.12) is made up of many tables, called *relations*, in which related data elements are stored. The relations—similar in concept to files—are made up of rows and columns, and they provide data to the user about an *entity* class. A row (similar to a record) is called a *tuple*, and a column (similar to a field) is called an *attribute*. For example, in Figure 11.12, Division Number, Department Number, and Department Name are attributes of the Department Table; the row that contains the values 1, 1, and Accounting is one tuple.

The data content of a relation is determined by the relationship that the parts have to the whole. The main objective of the relational database model is to allow complex logical relationships between records to be expressed in a simple fashion.

Relational databases are useful because they can cross-reference data and retrieve data automatically. Users do not have to be aware of any "structure" to use a relational database, and they can use it with little effort or training. (The installation and use of hierarchical and network database models require the knowledge of a programming language such as Pascal or a particular query language.) Also, data can be easily added, deleted, or modified, and it can be accessed by content, instead of by address (as is the case with hierarchical and network models).

The main disadvantage of the relational model is that searching the database can be time consuming, so it has primarily been used with smaller databases on microcomputers. Indeed, the relational model has become the most popular database model for microcomputer-based database management systems. However, the relational model is finding more and more applications on mini- and mainframe

FIGURE 11.11

Network database model for the Moser Corporation.

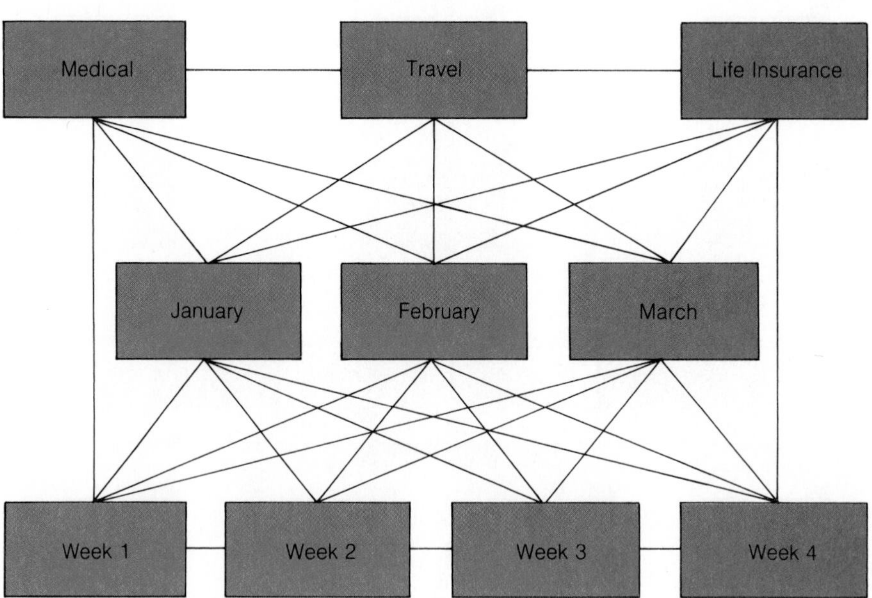

Division Table

Division Number	Division Name
1	East Coast
2	West Coast
3	Europe

Department Table

Division Number	Dept. Number	Dept. Name
1	1	Accounting
1	2	Sales
3	1	Accounting
2	2	Sales
2	3	Personnel
	etc.	

Employee Personnel Table

Employee Number	Name	Address	Phone	Hire Date	Position Description	Date Eval.	Pref. Rating
501	Mary Adams						
502	Frank Sonter						
503	John Jones						
504	Susie Fischer						
505	Juan Valdez						

Employee Salary Table

Employee Number	Salary	YTD Pay	YTD Deductions	Number of Dependents
501	21000	3500	1225	2
502	31000	5166.66	2066.66	0
503	20000	3333	1166.55	2
504	28000	4666.66	1866.66	1
505	35000	5833.33	2624.99	0

FIGURE 11.12

Relational database model.

Computers and Careers

Information

There is a new business breed: "infopreneurs," specialized entrepreneurs moving to exploit opportunities for products and services provided by advances in computers and communications. The real value of information, it has been pointed out, is when it becomes knowledge. This is where the infopreneurs come in.

Infopreneurs transform existing information into new uses. They identify and create new markets by developing new information services and products. Examples are those who have bought the electronic rights to printed lists of names. The telephone Yellow Pages, for instance, appear not only in book form but also in computer form, giving rise to databases that can create different kinds of lists or be sent over communications lines.

Two examples of how the information business works are as follows: Dow Jones News/Retrieval takes information collected by the company's news organizations, such as *The Wall Street Journal*, splits it into news, financial data, and stock prices, and sells them separately. An organization that tracks commercial ocean-going ships, Lloyd's Maritime Data Network, sells the information to shippers, who can use it to negotiate better deals with carriers.

Half the electronic information sold in the United States is financial, used for stock trading and the like. However, there are other uses for databases and communications. For instance, instead of using advertisements and personnel agencies, some companies searching for the right person for the right job use computerized files of résumés offered by industry associations, alumni groups, and entrepreneurs such as Computer Assisted Recruitment International of Schaumberg, Illinois. Comp-U-Card is a merchandise broker that takes orders from home shoppers—either by telephone or modem-linked computer—for thousands of products. CheckFree, of Columbus, Ohio, offers home-computer users an automatic bill-paying service, working with any bank you choose.

Nearly all occupations now have their own specialized information services. Most major law firms, for example, use Mead Data Central's LEXIS service, a computer-based research system for lawyers. Mead also owns Micromedex, which sells information on poisons, drugs, and emergency care to several hospitals and poison centers. Many catalog mailers pay Claritas Corp., a marketing consulting firm, to tell them how to reach certain kinds of prospective buyers, whose lifestyles can be identified according to the ZIP codes they live in.

As computer-based information has become more a part of every industry and occupation, investigative journalists have found that being able to sift through electronic databases is as important as a notepad and good shoes. Indeed, some journalists feel that the only way that reporters can monitor enormous organizations such as government agencies is to get access to computer-based files.

Where will all this deluge of information end? Reportedly the Library of Congress alone doubles its volume every 10 years. As the Information Society continues to increase, more and more people will specialize in the creating and selling of information. ■

computers. Some experts estimate that 60–90 percent of all databases in the early 1990s will be relational as a result of IBM's release of DB2, a relational database management system for mainframes, and Data Manager, a relational database management system for microcomputers. SQL provides the user interface for both systems. Also, the relational model is the new ANSI standard (SQL) and is included in OS/2 (extended) on IBM PS/2 microcomputers.

Designing a Database

Many users in the microcomputer environment will design a database and will actually build and implement it; however, users are less involved in database design and development when the database management system is intended to be used in minicomputer and mainframe computer environments. (Users are highly involved in defining what data needs to be stored in the database, though.) In these situations, design and development are carried out by trained and experienced information system specialists.

Matching the Design to the Organization

Most users working with microcomputer-based DBMS software focus on a very specific set of objectives and information processing needs—that is, their own. For many small applications this is a satisfactory approach. However, the objectives must be broader when working with a large corporation, a large computer system, and more complex and sophisticated DBMS software. And the plans for the use of the database management system must be integrated with the long-range plans for the company's total information system. The information processing needs of the entire corporation must be considered and viewed in terms of a corporate database that facilitates the collection, maintenance, and sharing of data among all the company's organizational units.

The design of a corporatewide database is an enormous task. Tackling this task is often made easier by taking a modular approach—that is, proceeding department by department and identifying the information needs of each, then defining general information needs as they relate to the establishment of a database. Once the general information needs have been established, the design process can proceed. This process usually comprises two distinct phases of activity—the logical design phase and the physical design phase.

Logical Design

Logical database design refers to *what* the database is as opposed to *how* it operates; in other words, the logical design is a detailed description of the database model from the business perspective rather than the technical perspective. The logical design of a database involves defining user information needs, analyzing data element requirements and logical groupings, finalizing the design, and creating the data dictionary. The major focus is on identifying every element of data necessary to produce the required management information systems reports and on the relationship among the records. This process involves defining two distinct views of the database — the schema and the subschema.

Schema refers to the organization of the database in its entirety, including the names of all the data elements and how the records are linked in useful ways. A **subschema** is part of the schema; it refers to the manner in which certain records are linked in ways useful to a *particular* user — perhaps to produce a report or satisfy certain queries (often called *user-views*). In other words, because the data in a database should *not* be accessible to all the employees of a company, subschemas are designed into a DBMS that limit users in certain functional areas within the company — such as accounting and marketing — to certain files and records in the database.

DEFINING DATABASE USER INFORMATION NEEDS

The objective of the first step in logical design is *information requirements analysis* — to identify specific user information needs and to group them logically. For example, let's assume that the personnel and payroll departments of a company have indicated that the following elements of data must be collected about each employee:

PERSONNEL DEPARTMENT	PAYROLL DEPARTMENT
Employee name	Employee name
Home address	Home address
Phone	Pay rate
Hire date	Number of dependents
Department	Deductions
Job title	Year-to-date (YTD) pay
Salary level	
Date of last review	
Date of next review	
Performance rating	
Number of dependents	
Office location	
Extension	

During this step in database design, the data elements required for each user department would be similarly identified and logically grouped by the database designer.

ANALYZING DATA ELEMENTS AND LOGICAL GROUPS

This step in logical design involves composing subschemas. First, the list of data elements that users have identified as necessary is analyzed to:

- Identify redundant data elements.
- Identify the natural groups into which data elements can be organized.
- Identify groups of data elements needed for specific applications programs.

You'll note that there are three redundant elements of data in the items listed above for the personnel and payroll departments: employee name, home address, and number of dependents. And the items can be organized into at least four natural groups: employee data, position data, performance data, and salary data. The elements of data could be grouped as follows:

Employee Data

Employee number
Name
Home address
Home phone

Position Data

Employee number (needed as identifier)
Department
Job title
Office location
Extension

Performance Data

Employee number
Hire date
Date of last review
Performance rating
Date of next review

Salary Data

Employee number
Pay rate
YTD pay
Deductions
Number of dependents

Second, the major output reports to be produced from the database are identified along with the elements of data that will be required for each report. For example, if we know that we will need reports on the dates when a manager's employees are due for their next performance evaluations, we would include the following data elements: employee number, name, hire date, date of last review, performance rating, date of next review, and pay rate. This grouping of data elements would be considered a subschema.

Finalizing the Design

The final step in the logical design of a database is to combine and refine the logical subsets of data — the subschemas — into an overall logical view of the relationships among all elements to be stored in the database — the schema. The schema includes a description of all the data elements to be stored, the logical records into which the data elements will be grouped, and the number of individual database files or relations to be maintained within the framework of the DBMS. In addition, the schema describes the relationships among the data elements and the structure of the database (that is, hierarchical, network, or relational model).

Physical Design

Once the logical design of the database has been defined, the next step is to proceed with the physical design. The **physical database design** involves the specification of exactly *how* the data will be arranged and stored on the direct access storage devices allocated for use by the DBMS. The objective of the physical design is to store data so that it can be updated and retrieved in the quickest and most efficient way possible.

One of the main considerations in the development of the physical design is the users' data-access patterns. In other words, how often will certain data elements need to be retrieved by the users? Knowing the patterns can improve speed and efficiency. Information about them is gathered during the logical design stage, often by counting the number of times users will access data elements by manual methods (such as opening a file drawer for a specific folder). Users' access patterns often change, so whatever physical design is developed must be continually reviewed and updated when necessary to conform to actual access patterns.

DATABASE ADMINISTRATION

The effective use of a database within an organization requires a great deal of cooperation and coordination. User requirements and needs throughout an organization need to be frequently reviewed, and the overall security and integrity of the database must be ensured. Organizations working with DBMSs quickly recognized the need for an individual or a group of individuals to coordinate all related activities and needs and to control the database. A **database administrator (DBA)** undertakes this function.

WHY ADMINISTER?

As we mentioned earlier, the development and implementation of a corporatewide database is a major task that requires the complete support of management, a substantial amount of human resources and user involvement, and often the expenditure of large sums of money. This task needs to be coordinated. In addition, the data in the database often represents the company's most precious asset: It must be managed well, so that it is not misused or damaged.

THE JOB OF THE DATABASE ADMINISTRATOR

The responsibilities for administering the database activities within an organization are usually assigned to an individual or a small group of individuals, depending on the size of the organization and the scope and complexity of the database. The database administrator has six major responsibilities.

1. *Database design*. The DBA plays a key role in both the logical and the physical design phases. He or she guides the definition of the database content and the creation of the database dictionary, as well as setting data classification and coding procedures and backup and restart/recovery procedures.
2. *Database implementation and operation*. The DBA guides the use of the DBMS on a daily basis. Among other things, this includes adding and deleting data, controlling access to data, detecting and repairing losses,

instituting restart/recovery procedures when necessary, and assigning space used on secondary storage devices.

3. *Coordination with user.* The DBA receives and reviews all user requests for additional DBMS support. The administrator establishes feasibility, resolves redundant or conflicting requests, and assists in the process of establishing priorities for the requests. In addition, the DBA is responsible for establishing and enforcing organizationwide DBMS standards for such things as techniques for accessing data, formats in which data elements will be stored, and data element names.
4. *Backup and recovery.* The DBA is responsible for preparing a plan for periodically backing up the database(s) and for establishing procedures for recovering from the failure of the DBMS software or related hardware components.
5. *Performance monitoring.* The DBA constantly monitors the performance of the DBMS using specialized software to calculate and record operating statistics. If a problem occurs, such as slowdown in responsiveness, the DBA must identify the problem and take steps to improve the performance.
6. *System security.* The DBA is responsible for designing and implementing a system of DBMS security that controls who has access to the database files, which DBMS operations can be performed, and which applications programs can be accessed. This system often involves the assignment of user identification codes and passwords.

Experience has shown that organizations that have a well-organized and well-staffed database administration department achieve a much higher degree of success in the use of the database management system to manage business information resources than organizations without such a department.

Advantages and Limitations of the DBMS

The principal advantages of the DBMS approach include:

- *Elimination of data redundancy.* More storage becomes available when maintenance of redundant data elements among traditionally separate application files is rendered unnecessary.
- *Easy file updating.* Because there is only one copy of each data element, all applications have access to the most current data. In traditional systems in which the same element of data was kept on several different files, ensuring that all copies of the data element were updated when changes were made was a problem.
- *Data independence and simplification of program maintenance.* In a DBMS the programs are much more independent of the data than in traditional file processing systems. Previously, programs had to include a substantial amount of information about the format and structure of the fields and records in each file accessed. In a DBMS, this information is contained in the data dictionary; the programs do not need to contain these details. In traditional systems, when a change in format of one or more data elements was necessary,

each program that used the data element had to be modified. In a DBMS only the data dictionary needs to be updated.

- *Increased user productivity*. The ability of a DBMS to respond quickly to user requests for additional information without involving the user in technical language manipulation encourages faster and more efficient work. The report generators and query languages associated with database management systems make them easy to use.
- *Increased security*. Centralized control of access to and use of the database is easily established. With traditional file processing systems, the data was too fragmented for effective security to be exercised.
- *Standardization of data definitions*. Before database management systems, each applications program could define similar elements of data with different names. However, the use of data dictionaries standardizes the names and descriptions of data elements.

Some disadvantages to using a database management system include:

- Database management systems are complex; extensive planning and a substantial amount of technical expertise are needed to implement and maintain a system.
- The costs associated with the development and operation of a corporatewide DBMS can be substantial in terms of software and hardware acquisition, technical support personnel, and operations personnel.
- The consolidation of an entire business's information resources into a DBMS can create a high level of vulnerability. A natural disaster, a fire, or even a hardware- or software-related problem can cause the loss of the current version of the database files. This could be fatal for a business unless proper precautions are taken. A very thorough framework of policies and procedures must be established to ensure that backup copies of the database files are made on a regular basis, that a transaction log is maintained, and that documentation exists for recovery procedures.

WHO OWNS THE DATABASE?

Before ending this chapter we need to say a few words about who owns a given type of database. Small and large databases can all be classified as individual, company, distributed, or proprietary.

The *individual database* is basically a microcomputer database used by one person. The data is usually stored on a large-capacity hard disk. A sales representative, for example, who is on the road a lot, may build and maintain an individual database of customer and sales information. In this case, the individual user owns the database.

The *company database*, or *shared database*, is shared by the users of one company, which owns the database. The data is usually stored on a mini or a mainframe and managed by a DBA. Users are linked via a LAN (local area network, discussed in Chapter 9) to the database through terminals or microcomputer workstations.

The *distributed database* is shared by the users of one company, which owns the database, but the data is not stored where the users are, as it is with a company database. Instead, the data is made accessible to users through a variety of communications networks. For example, users with microcomputers and hard disks could be linked by a WAN (wide area network, discussed in Chapter 9) that is linked to a mainframe.

The *proprietary database* is a huge database that functions as an information service, such as CompuServe, Prodigy, and Dow Jones News/Retrieval (which were discussed in Chapter 9). The proprietor owns the database in this case.

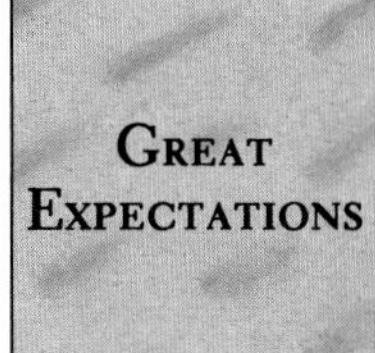

Database management systems can produce nearly infinite possibilities for manipulating information. One result is that, for Americans, the Social Security number, assigned to individuals in order to keep track of their contributions to the national retirement system, has now become the means—the key field—by which their lives are tied to all kinds of databases. This offers many conveniences, for it allows various agencies to pull together different kinds of records. However, it also poses the danger that records that should *not* be connected will be. For instance, someone who is a good worker but has a poor credit background might be denied a job solely because a prospective employer is able to look at credit histories.

The direction of database management is suggested by the development of the *executive information system (EIS)* or *executive support system (ESS)*. This system consists of software that draws together data from an organization's databases and presents it in condensed form, using colorful graphics so that not much effort is required to understand it. An EIS may also be organized to retrieve information from databases outside the company.

Another important development is *hypertext* (discussed in Chapter 8)—microcomputer software that allows any file to be connected with any other file. Although the term was coined by computer visionary Ted Nelson in 1963, it was 20 years before the software began to catch on, first as HyperCard from Apple. Now hypertext is being used in multimedia, which links not only different items of text with other text or pictures but also connects video, music, voice, and animation. Hypertext is designed "to work the way people think." They can pinpoint ideas, bits of information, and experience and link them into whatever sequences of information one wishes. Nelson himself eventually visualizes a "Xanadu system," a distributed rather than centralized publishing medium with millions of simultaneous users adding millions of documents per hour to the system.

ONWARD: WHO'S MINDING THE STORE?

By now you may be wondering how anyone can keep control of all the functions and parts of the computer-based information cycle—input, storage, processing, output—and all the hardware and software that go along with it, let alone the tasks of designing and developing programs, databases, and information systems. Who is put in charge of all this, and how do those in charge manage? How do they make sure what's produced is relevant to the needs of the business? How do they make decisions? The next chapter, on management information systems, will answer these questions.

SUMMARY

Database management systems (DBMS)—comprehensive software tools that allow users to create, maintain, and manipulate an integrated base of business data—have become very popular in the business community. In an integrated database, the records are logically keyed to one another so that all data on a topic can be retrieved by simple requests. Users will probably not get involved in designing databases (except for supplying job information needs to designers), but they will likely be involved in using a DBMS, either on a workstation or a terminal, or on a stand-alone microcomputer.

File management systems used to be the only way of managing data and files. In these systems, data was stored in a series of unrelated files on tape or disk. The major problems associated with file management systems are (1) data redundancy—the same data appears in more than one file; (2) tedious updating procedures—because the same data appeared in many places, updating files was time consuming; (3) poor data integrity—if some redundant data elements were missed during file updating, they were no longer current and could cause inaccurate information to be produced; and (4) lack of data and program independence—programmers could not use the data file to develop new programs because the data and the programs were restricted by existing formats. To update either the applications program or the data file became a major task.

Database management systems were developed to (1) make data independent of the programs, so that it is easy to access and change; (2) eliminate data redundancy; (3) establish relationships among records in different files; (4) define data characteristics; (5) manage file directories; (6) maintain data integrity; and (7) provide a means of securing access to the database.

DBMS software often uses a query language as an interface between the user and the system. This interface allows users to easily ask questions of the DBMS and obtain information to answer the questions and produce reports. DBMS software also includes capabilities to simplify report writing and maintain the database (utili-

FIGURE 11.13

This photo shows several popular DBMS software packages for microcomputers.

ties) as well as to allow different applications programs to use the database (data manipulation language, or DML). During the design of the database, a data dictionary is constructed that contains all the data descriptions used by the DBMS to locate and retrieve data. The DBMS also can include a transaction log of current activity. This log can be used to update necessary backup copies of the database in case of failure of or damage to the operating database system.

A DBMS is usually modeled after one of three structures: (1) hierarchical, (2) network, or (3) relational. These models differ in terms of the cost of implementation, speed, degree of data redundancy, ease with which they can satisfy information requirements, and ease with which they can be updated.

The hierarchical database model resembles a family tree; the records are organized in a one-to-many relationship, meaning that one parent record can have many child records. Records are retrieved from a hierarchical model by starting at the root record at the top and moving down through the structure. There is no connection between separate branches.

The network database model is similar to the hierarchical model, but it allows multiple one-to-many relationships (each child can have more than one parent) and relationships between records in different groups. Also, access to the database can be made from a number of points—not just from the top.

The relational database model is made up of many tables, called *relations*, in which related data elements are stored. The data elements are in rows, called *tuples*, and columns, called *attributes*. The main objective of the relational database model is to allow complex logical relationships between records to be expressed in a simple fashion.

In general, the hierarchical and network models are less expensive to implement and allow faster access to data. However, they are more difficult to update and aren't as effective at satisfying information requirements as the relational model can be. Because the hierarchical and network models are older than the relational model, they are used most often on large computers. The newer relational model is used extensively on microcomputers; however, because relational models are so flexible in satisfying information requests, and because they aren't difficult to update, relational models are being used more and more on large computers.

The process of database design is usually carried out exclusively by specialists; however, users may have occasion to set up small databases for microcomputers. First, the logical design is set up; then the physical design. The logical design, which has to do with *what* the database is, from the business users' perspective, involves defining user information needs; analyzing data element requirements and logical groupings; finalizing the design; and creating the data dictionary. During the logical design the schema (the organization of the entire database, including the structure type) and the subschema (the way *certain* data elements are linked) are defined.

The physical design involves *how* the data will be physically arranged and stored on the storage devices used by the DBMS. During this design phase the database is actually set up, and the data is stored.

Databases are important business resources, and DBMS software is sophisticated; both the database and the DBMS software must be carefully operated and controlled. For this purpose, the job of database administrator (DBA) has been created. The main responsibilities of a database administrator are (1) guiding database design; (2) overseeing database implementation and operation; (3) user coordination; (4) backup and recovery; (5) performance monitoring; and (6) system security.

In general, the main advantages of database management systems are (1) elimination of data redundancy; (2) increased ease of file updating; (3) increased data independence and simplification of program and maintenance; (4) increased user productivity and efficiency; (5) increased security; and (6) standardization of data definitions.

The main disadvantages are (1) complexity; (2) high cost of implementation; and (3) vulnerability of consolidated business data in a central database.

KEY TERMS

child record, p. 450
database, p. 435
database administrator (DBA), p. 458
database management system (DBMS), p. 435
data dictionary, p. 448
data independence, p. 441
data integrity, p. 440
data manipulation language (DML), p. 447
data redundancy, p. 440
file management system, p. 439
file updating, p. 440
hierarchical database model, p. 450
logical database design, p. 455
network database model, p. 450
one-to-many relationship, p. 450
parent record, p. 450
physical database design, p. 457
program independence, p. 441
relational database model, p. 452
root record, p. 450
schema, p. 456
subschema, p. 456
transaction log, p. 448

EXERCISES

MATCHING

Match each of the following terms to the phrase that is the most closely related.

1. ____ hierarchical database model
2. ____ database management system
3. ____ record
4. ____ network database model
5. ____ database administrator
6. ____ one-to-many relationship
7. ____ schema
8. ____ physical database design
9. ____ transaction log
10. ____ data independence
11. ____ database
12. ____ relational database model
13. ____ data redundancy
14. ____ file management system
15. ____ data dictionary

a. Organization of a database in its entirety
b. Major limitation of file management systems
c. Contains all the information about elements of data stored in a database
d. In this database model, each record can have more than one parent.
e. Record of all activity that has affected a database during a period of time
f. Hierarchical database model

g. Using this approach means that applications software programs can access data from only a single file at a time.
h. Specifies exactly how data will be arranged and stored on a storage device for use by the DBMS
i. Collection of related files and records
j. A major advantage to using a database management system
k. This person or group coordinates all related activities to control a database in an organization.
l. Group of related fields
m. This model is composed of parent and child records (one parent to more than one child)
n. Software tool that facilitates the creation and maintenance of databases
o. The most popular type of database model used on microcomputers

Multiple Choice

1. Which of the following hardware components is the most important to the operation of a database management system?
   a. high-resolution video display
   b. printer
   c. high-speed, large-capacity disk
   d. plotter
   e. mouse
2. Database management systems are intended to:
   a. eliminate data redundancy
   b. establish relationships among records in different files
   c. manage file access
   d. maintain data integrity
   e. all the above
3. Which of the following is not characteristic of a relational database model?
   a. tables
   b. tree-like structure
   c. complex logical relationships
   d. records
   e. fields
4. Which of the following is not the responsibility of the utilities component of DBMS software?
   a. creating the physical and logical designs
   b. removing flagged records for deletion
   c. creating and maintaining the data dictionary
   d. monitoring performance
   e. establishing control of access to portions of the database
5. Which of the following is a type of DBMS software?
   a. database manipulation language (DML)
   b. query language
   c. utilities
   d. report writer
   e. all the above

6. Which of the following is a database administrator's function?
   a. database design
   b. backing up the database
   c. performance monitoring
   d. user coordination
   e. all the above
7. A data dictionary does not provide data about:
   a. where data is located
   b. the size of the disk storage device
   c. who owns or is responsible for the data
   d. how the data is used
   e. security and privacy limitations
8. Which two files are used during operation of the DBMS?
   a. query language and utilities
   b. data manipulation language and query language
   c. data dictionary and transaction log
   d. data dictionary and query language
   e. all the above
9. Which of the following is a serious problem of file management systems?
   a. difficult to update
   b. lack of data redundancy
   c. data redundancy
   d. program dependence
   e. all the above
10. Which of the following contains a complete record of all activity that affected the contents of a database during a certain period of time?
    a. report writer
    b. query language
    c. data manipulation language
    d. transaction log
    e. file management system

SHORT ANSWER

1. What is query language and why is it a valuable aspect of DBMS software?
2. Why is it important to administer a company database?
3. Define *database*. Why is it relevant for users to understand the fundamentals of database management systems?
4. Why do you think microcomputer users are more likely than mainframe users to be involved with the design of a database?
5. What is a database management system?
6. What are the main advantages of database management systems?
7. What are the differences between the logical and the physical designs of a database structure?
8. What are data dictionaries and transaction logs? What are their uses?
9. What is the role of software in a DBMS?

10. What are the advantages of organizing a database according to a relational model as opposed to a network model?

PROJECTS

1. Interview someone who works with or manages a database at your school or university. What types of records make up the database, and which departments use it? What types of transactions do these departments enact? Which database structure is used? What are the types and sizes of the storage devices?
2. Research the pros and cons of governmental attempts to establish a database on all its citizens. Based on your research, do you think such a database should be allowed? Has any country done this yet? Are any countries close to doing it?
3. What types of databases do you think would include information about yourself? Prepare a brief summary.
4. Contact TRW Credit, P.O. Box 14008, Orange, CA 92613, and ask for a credit report in your name (the report comes from their huge database). If you are in their database, are there any mistakes in the report? If so, how do you think the incorrect data came to be in your file?

12

Chapter 12

Management Information Systems

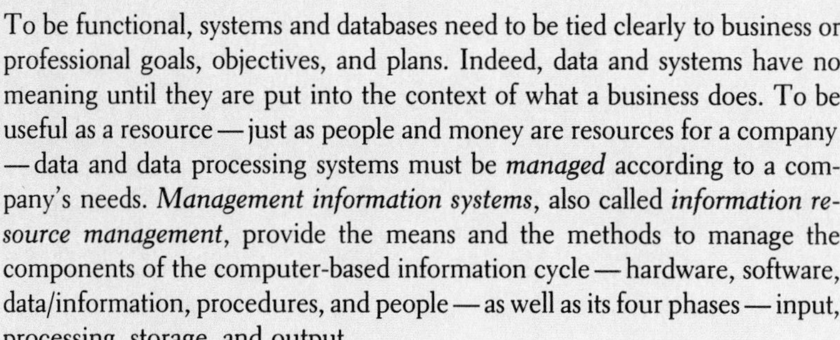

To be functional, systems and databases need to be tied clearly to business or professional goals, objectives, and plans. Indeed, data and systems have no meaning until they are put into the context of what a business does. To be useful as a resource — just as people and money are resources for a company — data and data processing systems must be *managed* according to a company's needs. *Management information systems*, also called *information resource management*, provide the means and the methods to manage the components of the computer-based information cycle — hardware, software, data/information, procedures, and people — as well as its four phases — input, processing, storage, and output.

Preview

When you have completed this chapter, you will be able to:

- Describe a basic management information system and explain its role in the organization.
- Describe the levels of management, the five basic functions of managers, and the types of decisions typically made at each level.
- Distinguish among transaction processing systems, management information systems for middle management, and decision support systems.
- Describe artificial intelligence and expert systems.
- Briefly explain the functions of an information center.

THE USER PERSPECTIVE

Information technology can ruin our lives unless we think of ways to get it under control. Without an organized approach to managing information, we may drown in an ocean of available information, unable to make decisions. Do these statements sound farfetched? They may have seemed so only a few years ago, but today, because of the fast pace of computer hardware and software development, they sound ominously accurate. Although knowledge may be power, we must remember that information does not equal knowledge.

What should managers do to change an information technology into an intelligence technology to assist with decision making and efficient, productive, and high-quality business operation? In other words, how can users of an information system do their jobs better and not just shuffle overwhelming amounts of data and information from input to storage, from storage to processing and back to storage, from processing to output? The answer is, through management information systems. By understanding the principles of information management, users can help exploit technology to accomplish business and professional goals. As more and more hardware, software, and data are shared by multiple users, users are becoming more and more involved in the on-line functioning and management of the entire information system.

INFORMATION SYSTEMS: WHAT THEY ARE, HOW THEY WORK

Chapter 2 described the computer-based information system as comprising five parts—hardware, software, data/information, procedures, and people. The fourth component includes manual and computerized procedures and standards for processing data into usable information. A *procedure* is a specific sequence of steps performed to complete one or more information processing activities. In some organizations, these processing procedures are carried out only by the staff; in others they are carried out by a combination of the staff and the computer specialists.

If you walk into a busy discount consumer-products showroom, stand in a corner, and observe the activities taking place, you will probably see the following kinds of activities: Customers come in and browse around, looking at the display cases. Some customers decide to buy items and begin to fill out order forms. If they are completed properly, the order forms are taken at the counter by a clerk and placed into a *queue*—that is, in line to be processed. If an order form is not complete, the clerk asks the customer questions and completes it. Then a stock person takes the completed order forms into the stockroom or warehouse and returns with the goods. A clerk takes each order form, marks it "Filled," and rings up the sale on the cash register. All these activities form a procedure that is part of the *sales order entry system* (Figure 12.1).

A business is made up of many procedures, grouped logically into systems. The types of information systems found in companies vary according to the nature and the structure of the business; however, the systems commonly found in many businesses include payroll, personnel, accounting, and inventory.

Businesses receive data from a variety of sources, including customers who purchase products or services, vendors from whom supplies are ordered, banks, government agencies, and insurance companies—just to name a few. Information systems help organizations process all this data into *useful* information. One of the most important purposes of a business's information system, then, is to satisfy the knowledge requirements of management.

WHAT IS MANAGEMENT?

You know what an information system is. After we consider what *management* consists of, we will see how the two concepts can be put together as a management information system.

Management often refers to those individuals in an organization who are responsible for providing leadership and direction in the areas of planning, organizing, staffing, supervising, and controlling business activities. These five functions, which are the primary tasks of management, may be defined as follows:

1. *Planning* activities require the manager to formulate goals and objectives and develop short- and long-term plans to achieve these goals. For example, an office manager must work with top management to formulate a plan that satisfies the short- and long-term needs of the organization for office space; the vice president of marketing must take many factors into account when planning short-term advertising campaigns and activities aimed at opening up new long-term markets.
2. Management's responsibility for *organizing* includes the development of an organizational structure and a framework of standards, procedures, and policies designed to carry out ongoing business activities. For instance, top

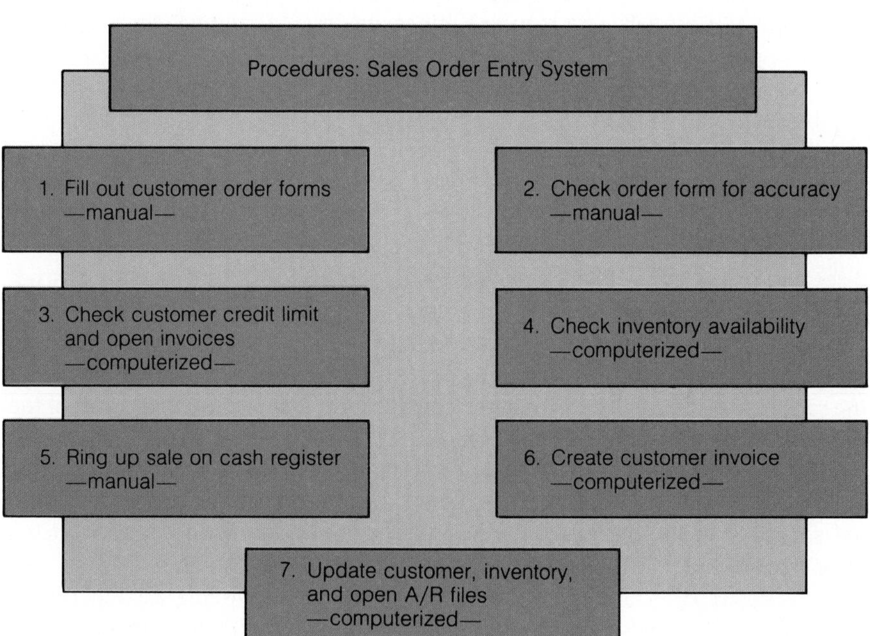

FIGURE 12.1

This group of related procedures makes up a simple sales order entry system.

management must decide on the type and number of divisions and departments in the company and evaluate the effectiveness of the structure; it may decide to combine the personnel and the payroll departments to save money. Office managers establish working procedures, such as "Working overtime must be approved by the department supervisor in advance."

3. *Staffing* refers to management's responsibility for identifying the personnel needs of the organization and selecting the personnel, as well as training staff. Many companies have personnel managers to take charge of these activities.
4. *Supervising* refers to management's responsibility to provide employees with the supervision, guidance, and counseling necessary to keep them highly motivated and working productively toward the achievement of company objectives. This includes the recognition of good work, perhaps through certificates or bonuses, and concrete suggestions about how to improve performance. Companywide educational seminars may also be held to upgrade employees' knowledge of the company in general or perhaps to help them deal with stress and improve their health.
5. *Controlling* refers to management's responsibility to monitor organizational performance and the business environment so that steps can be taken to improve performance and modify plans as necessary in response to the marketplace. This includes keeping alert to new opportunities in the marketplace and recognizing new business opportunities. Many new computer software products, for example, have been developed because software companies are ever watchful for potential markets.

Each primary management function involves making decisions, and information is required to make good decisions. Thus, to fulfill its responsibilities, management must set up information systems and subsystems.

What Is a Management Information System?

A **management information system (MIS)** comprises computer-based processing and/or manual procedures to provide useful and timely information to support management decision making in a rapidly changing business environment. MIS systems enable *information resource management (IRM)*. The MIS system must supply managers with information quickly, accurately, and completely.

The approaches that companies take to develop information systems for management differ depending on the structure and management style of the organization. However, the scope of an MIS is generally companywide, and it services management personnel at all three traditional organizational levels:

1. Low-level, or operating, management.
2. Middle management.
3. Upper, or top, management.

The primary objective of the MIS is to satisfy the need that managers have for information that is *more summarized and relevant to the specific decisions that need to be made* than the information normally produced in an organization and that is *available soon enough to be of value in the decision-making process*. The information flows up and down through the three levels of management and is made available in various types of reports.

LEVELS OF MANAGEMENT: WHAT KINDS OF DECISIONS ARE MADE?

Each level of management (Figure 12.2) can be distinguished by the types of decisions made, the time frame considered in the decisions, and the types of report information needed to make decisions.

OPERATING MANAGEMENT

The lowest—and the largest—level of management, **operating management**, deals mostly with decisions that cover a relatively narrow time frame. Operating management, also called *supervisory management*, actualizes the plans of middle management and controls daily operations—the day-to-day activities that keep the organization humming. Examples of operating managers are the warehouse manager in charge of inventory restocking and the materials manager responsible for seeing that all necessary materials are on hand in a manufacturing firm to produce the product being manufactured. Most decisions at this level require easily defined

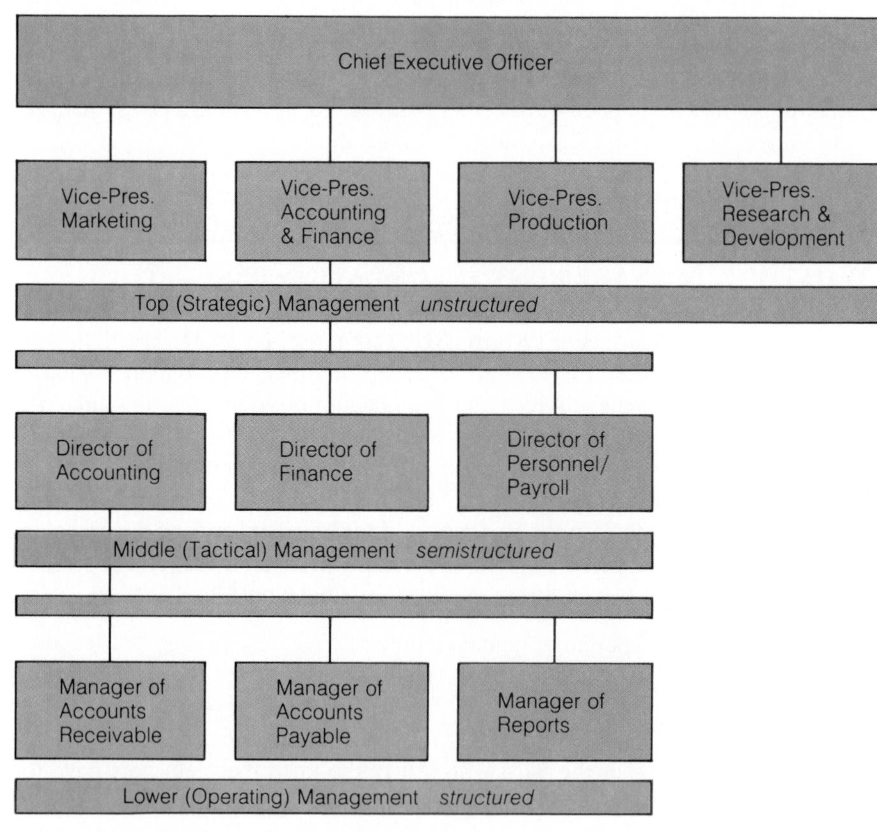

FIGURE 12.2

Three levels of management, three kinds of decisions. Different types of decisions are made depending on the level of management. The higher a manager is in an organization's hierarchy, the more decisions he or she must make from unstructured information. The four basic business functions or departments that top managers control are marketing, accounting and finance, production, and research and development. (a) This part of the figure shows the organizational hierarchy from a vertical perspective, focusing on the department of accounting and finance; (b) this part of the figure shows the hierarchy as a pyramid to indicate that there are fewer managers at higher levels of management.

information that relates to the current status and activities within the basic business functions — for example, the information needed to decide whether to restock inventory. This information is generally given to low-level managers in **detail reports** that contain specific information about routine activities (Figure 12.3a). Because these reports are structured — that is, their form is predetermined — and daily business operations data is readily available, their processing can be easily computerized.

Managers at this level, often referred to as **operational decision makers,** typically make structured decisions (Figure 12.4a). A **structured decision** is a predictable decision that can be made by following a well-defined set of routine procedures. For instance, a manager may not know exactly when inventory will need to be restocked, but he or she knows that a decision to restock must be made soon. This type of decision can easily be programmed as a part of computer-based data processing — for example, identifying the reorder point for a particular part or when to apply a discount to a customer's invoice. A clothing store floor manager's decision to accept your credit card to pay for some new clothes is a structured decision based on several well-defined criteria: (1) Does the customer have satisfactory identification? (2) Is the card current or expired? (3) Is the card number on the store's list of stolen or lost cards? (4) Is the amount of purchase under the cardholder's credit limit?

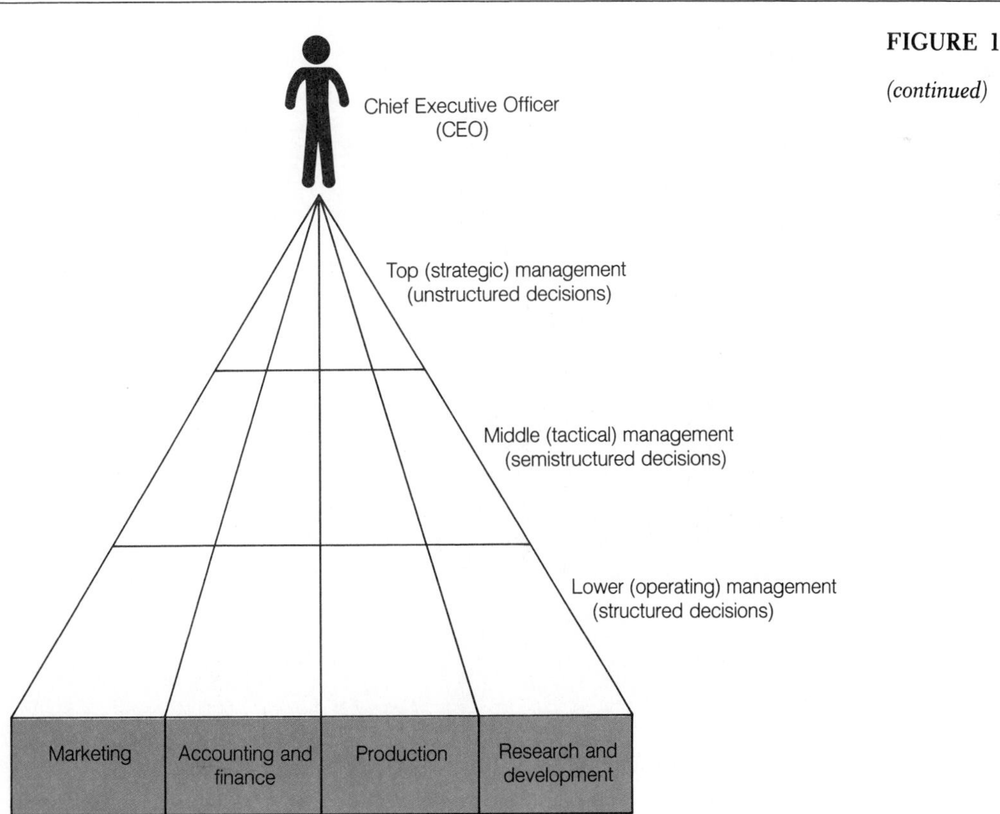

FIGURE 12.2

(continued)

MIDDLE MANAGEMENT

The **middle** level of **management** deals with decisions that cover a somewhat broader range of time and involve more experience. Some common titles of middle managers are plant manager, division manager, sales manager, branch manager, and director of personnel. The information that middle managers need involves review, summarization, and analysis of historical data to help plan and control operations and implement policy that has been formulated by upper management. This information is usually given to middle managers in the form of **summary reports,** which show totals and trends—for example, total sales by office, by product, by salesperson, or total overall sales—and **exception reports,** which show out-of-the-ordinary data—for example, inventory reports that list only those items that number fewer than 10 in stock (see Figure 12.3d). These reports may be

FIGURE 12.3

On report. (a) Low-level managers need information in the form of detail reports; (b) (c) (d) middle managers and top managers use summary reports and exception reports. Reports can be issued on demand, on a regularly scheduled basis (periodic), or on the occurrence of a specific event (event-initiated).

(a)

Low-Level Manager Report
Inventory Listing: Department A

Item Number	Description	Quantity On-Hand
2053	Visors	25
1925	Running shorts	30
2105	Tennis balls	45
3200	Baseball bats	51
2165	Tennis rackets	19

(b)

Middle Manager Report
Reorder Summary: All Departments

Dept	Item Number	Quantity On-Hand	Reorder Point	Reorder Status
A	2053	25	23	Reorder 30
A	1925	30	30	Reorder 60
B	1005	25	25	Reorder 50
B	1128	22	25	Reorder 33
A	2165	19	15	Reorder 21
C	1569	23	24	Reorder 35

(c)

Top-Level Manager Report
Inventory Sales Summary

D = Discontinue
C = Continue

Item Number	Quarter 1	Quarter 2	Quarter 3	Quarter 4	Total	Status
3200	10	8	4	2	25	D
1925	30	35	42	29	136	C
1005	25	50	49	38	162	C
2165	32	3	2	1	38	D
.	.	.	.	.	.	.
.	.	.	.	.	.	.
.	.	.	.	.	.	.

(d)

Exception Report: Department A—List of Items
Quantity On-Hand Less Than 10

Dept	Item Number	Quantity On-Hand	Reorder Point	Reorder Status
A	1105	8	—	—
A	1203	5	—	—
A	1302	7	—	—
A	1315	2	—	—
A	1372	6	—	—

regularly scheduled (periodic reports), requested on a case-by-case basis (on-demand reports), or generated only when certain conditions exist (event-initiated reports).

Periodic reports are produced at predetermined times—daily, weekly, monthly, quarterly, or annually—and commonly include payroll reports, inventory status reports, sales reports, income statements, and balance sheets (we will discuss the last two in a bit more detail later). **On-demand reports** are usually requested by a manager when information is needed that focuses on a particular problem. For example, if a customer wants to establish a large charge account, a manager might request a special report on the customer's payment and order history. **Event-initiated reports** usually deal with a change in conditions that requires immediate attention, such as an out-of-stock report or a report on an equipment breakdown.

Managers at the middle level of management are often referred to as *tactical decision makers* who generally deal with semistructured decisions. A **semistruc-**

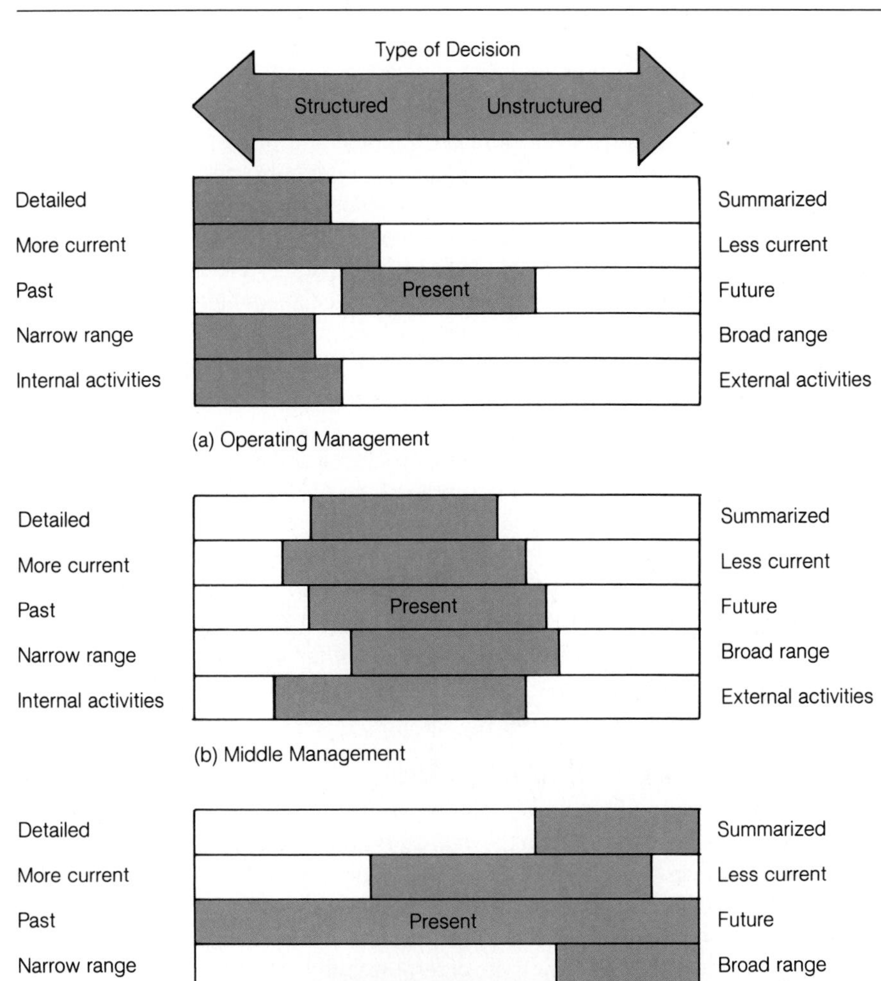

FIGURE 12.4

(a) Structured decisions are typically made at the operating level of management by following clearly defined routine procedures. Operating managers need information that is detailed, focused on the present, and concerned with daily business activities. (b) Semistructured decisions, typically made at the middle-management level, involve information that does not necessarily result from clearly defined, routine procedures. Middle managers need information that is detailed and more summarized than information for operating managers and that compares the present with the recent past. (c) Unstructured decisions, typically made at the upper level of management, are supported by the management information system in the form of highly summarized reports. The information should cover large time periods and survey activities outside (as well as inside) the company.

tured decision is a decision that, unlike a structured decision, must be made without a base of clearly defined informational procedures. In most cases, a semistructured decision (Figure 12.4b) is complex, requiring detailed analysis and extensive computations. Examples of semistructured decisions include deciding how many units of a specific product should be kept in inventory, whether or not to purchase a larger computer system, from what source to purchase personal computers, and whether to purchase a multiuser minicomputer system. At least some of the information requirements at this level can be met through computer-based data processing.

UPPER MANAGEMENT

The **upper** level of **management** deals with decisions that are the broadest in scope and cover the widest time frame. Typical titles of managers at this level are chief executive officer (CEO), president, treasurer, controller, executive vice president, and senior partner. Top managers include only a few powerful people who are in charge of the four basic functions of a business—marketing, accounting and finance, production, and research and development. Decisions made at this level are unpredictable, long-range, and related to the future—not just past and/or current activities; therefore, they demand the most experience and judgment.

A company's MIS must be able to supply information to upper management as needed in periodic reports, event-initiated reports, and on-demand reports. The information must show how all the company's operations and departments are related to and affected by one another. The major decisions made at this level tend to be directed toward (1) strategic planning—for example, how growth should be financed and which new markets should be tackled first; (2) allocation of resources, such as deciding whether to build or lease office space and whether to spend more money on advertising or the hiring of new staff members; and (3) policy formulation, such as determining the company's policy on hiring minorities and providing employee incentives. Managers at this level are often referred to as **strategic decision makers.**

Upper management typically makes unstructured decisions (Figure 12.4c). An **unstructured decision** is the most complex type of decision that managers are faced with. Because these decisions are rarely based on predetermined routine procedures, they involve the subjective judgment of the decision maker. As a result, this type of decision is the hardest to support from a computer-based data processing standpoint. Examples of unstructured decisions include deciding five-year goals for the company, evaluating future financial resources, and deciding how to react to the actions of competitors.

THE ROLE OF THE MIS IN A BUSINESS

Now that you know what we mean by *managers* and understand their need for the right kinds of information, we can go on to describe in more detail the role of the management information system. First, as we have already pointed out, an MIS must provide managers with information (reports) to help them perform activities that directly relate to their specific areas of responsibility. For example, to effectively manage marketing responsibilities, the vice president of marketing needs information about sales, competitors, and consumers. The head of the personnel department needs information about employee performance, work history, and job descriptions, among other things.

Second, a management information system must provide managers with information about other functional areas of the business—accounting and finance, marketing and sales, production, and research and development—so that they can coordinate their departmental activities with activities in these areas. For example, suppose that the accounting department (one functional area), by maintaining an invoice history file, has kept track of all customer invoices produced so far this year. The file contains such information as (1) customer name, (2) customer address, (3) invoice date, (4) products sold, and (5) invoice amount. To better coordinate marketing activities, the vice president of marketing (another functional area) can use this data to produce a variety of information, such as the year-to-date sales by month, a ranking of customers to whom the largest amounts of sales have been made, and an analysis of the months of highest sales. This same information could be passed along to the materials manager in production (another functional area), who can make informed decisions about when inventory levels should be raised or lowered to meet consumer demand.

But *how* do managers use information to make decisions? To understand how an MIS works, you must know something about the decision-making process.

HOW DOES MANAGEMENT MAKE DECISIONS?

Management styles vary. Some managers follow their instincts and deal with situations on a case-by-case basis. Other managers use a more systematic and structured approach to making decisions. If we approach decision making systematically, we can view it as a process involving five basic steps, as shown in Figure 12.5 and described below. Bear in mind that feedback, or review of the gathered information, is analyzed at each step, which may necessitate revisions or a return to a previous step. For example, suppose a company decides in Step 2 to purchase one of two software packages to help with in-house publishing; at Step 3 the company discovers that one of the two software manufacturers has gone out of business. The process must return to Step 2 to evaluate other software alternatives.

STEP 1—PROBLEM RECOGNITION AND IDENTIFICATION

In the first step of the decision-making process, the manager acknowledges a problem that affects the business. Take, for example, a small business like Bowman, Henderson, and Associates (BH&A), which provides training in the use of microcomputer hardware and software. The demand for training has grown so fast that the staff cannot handle it, and the facilities cannot support an increase in the number of students that can be taught per session. The fact that a problem exists becomes obvious when management notices that the staff is too busy to take a day off and everyone is always running around trying to take care of last-minute details. The seriousness of the problem becomes evident when staff morale begins to drop and potential customers are turned away.

STEP 2—IDENTIFICATION AND EVALUATION OF ALTERNATIVES

In the second step of the decision-making process, management considers various alternatives to solving the problem. In the case of BH&A, alternatives include (1) adding more staff and offering training in the existing facilities during expanded

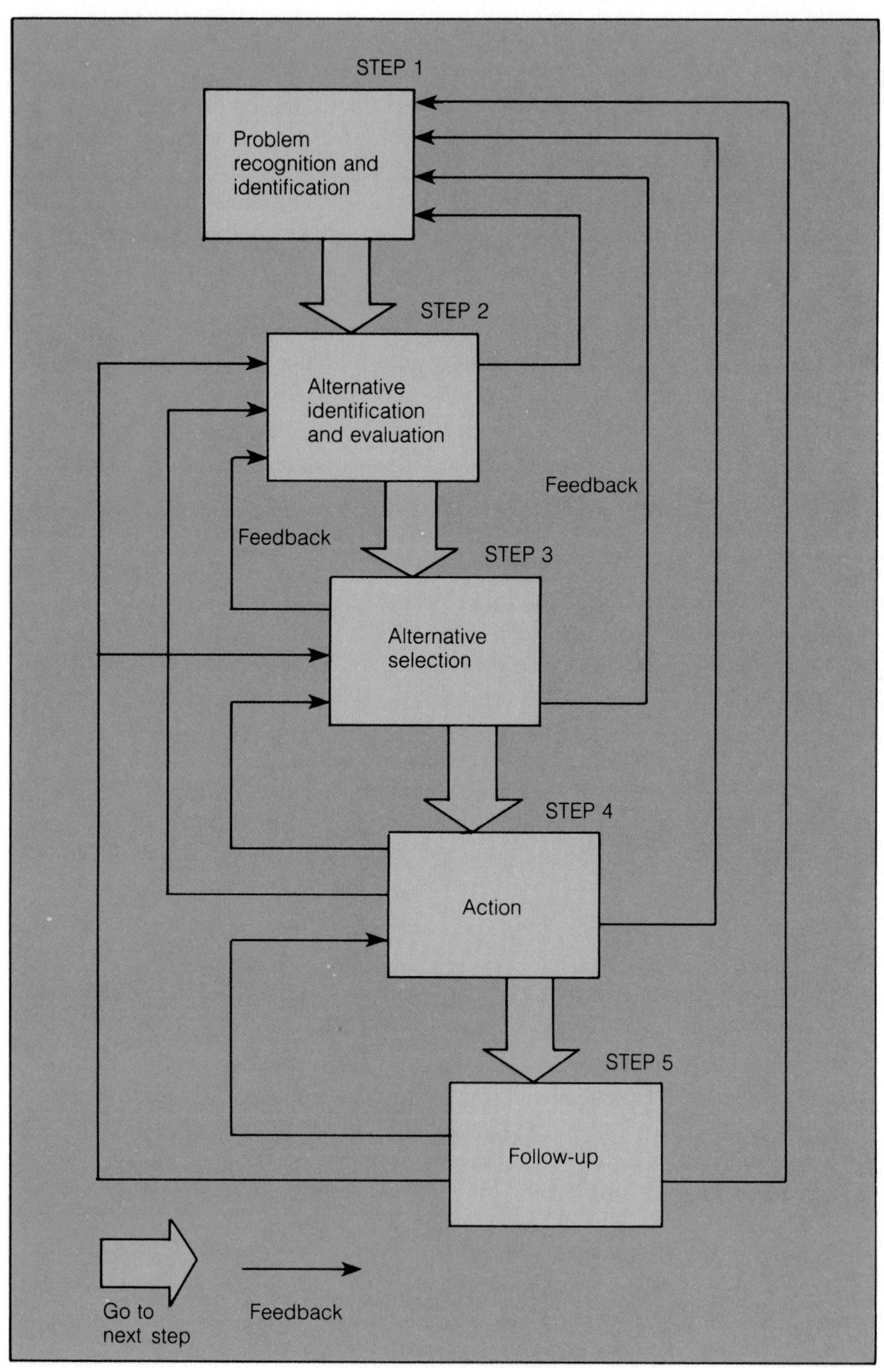

FIGURE 12.5

Five steps of the decision-making process. At any step, feedback—a review of gathered information—may require the return to any of the previous steps.

training hours (perhaps evenings and weekends) and (2) adding more staff, purchasing additional equipment, and leasing additional training facilities. Once the alternative courses of action have been identified, they must be examined and compared in terms of anticipated costs and benefits.

STEP 3—ALTERNATIVE SELECTION

When each alternative has been carefully explored, the next step is to select the one that appears to best meet the manager's objectives. The logical choice would be the alternative that offers the most benefits for the least cost. However, the manager must ensure that the chosen action is not in conflict with other activities or organizational objectives.

STEP 4—ACTION

Once management has decided how to solve the problem, it must act on the decision. Suppose BH&A management selected the alternative that involved adding more staff and scheduling the use of existing facilities for additional hours. Implementing this decision would probably involve (1) defining specific staff requirements and skills, (2) advertising for additional staff, (3) interviewing prospective staff members, (4) selecting the best candidates, (5) notifying existing customers of the additional staff and expanded hours, and (6) scheduling the use of the facility during the new hours of operation.

STEP 5—FOLLOW-UP

In the final step of the decision-making process, management follows up on its choice of action to determine if it has been successful. Management assesses the degree to which original objectives and anticipated benefits are being achieved and takes corrective action when necessary. If the solution to the original problem has created a new problem, a new decision-making process begins to solve it.

WHAT KIND OF INFORMATION DOES MANAGEMENT USE TO MAKE DECISIONS?

Because decisions are made on the basis of information, the decision-making process is greatly affected by the scope and quality of the information provided by the MIS. This information is produced by processing data from three sources:

1. Internally generated data (produced by normal data processing systems of the business).
2. Data provided by higher or lower levels of management.
3. Externally generated data (produced by sources outside the company).

Information, as required by management, has three distinct properties that vary in significance depending on the organizational level and type of decision being made:

1. Level of summarization.
2. Degree of accuracy.
3. Timeliness.

As we mentioned in the discussion of the three management levels, the degree to which information needs to be *summarized* increases as the level of management goes up. Conversely, the lower the level of management, the more detailed the information needs to be. Top managers do not want to wade through mountains of details to make a decision. They want to be able to identify problems and trends at a glance in summary reports and exception reports; that is, they need only essential information, not nonessential details. Operational managers, however, need details on daily operations to make decisions regarding scheduling, inventory, payroll, and so on.

Of course, information must be *accurate* for wise decisions to be made. (Remember: garbage in, garbage out.) The higher the accuracy of the information, the higher the cost of the processing system, because more controls — both manual and computer-based — must be installed to increase the accuracy of output information. Some areas such as inventory may be able to live with an accuracy rate of 90–95 percent, but this rate is probably too low for the accounting department.

The *timeliness* of management information involves how soon the information is needed and whether it needs to relate to the past, the present, or the future. When decisions are time-sensitive (they must be made quickly), the information system must accommodate this need. For example, whether a system is designed to use batch processing or on-line processing might be determined by how fast the information is needed by management. On the one hand, the kind of planning done by top management covers a broad time frame and requires reports that contain information covering past years as well as current performance. This type of decision making is not highly time sensitive, so batch processing would probably be adequate. On the other hand, decisions related to banking activities may be highly time sensitive and require on-line processing to provide up-to-date information.

In general, to support the making of intelligent and knowledgeable decisions, information generated at all levels of management must be:

- Correct (be accurate).
- Complete (include all relevant data).
- Current (be timely).
- Concise (include only the relevant data).
- Clear (be understandable).
- Cost-effective (be efficiently obtained).
- Time sensitive (be based on historical, current, and/or future information and needs as required).

TYPES OF MANAGEMENT INFORMATION SYSTEMS

The more structured the problem, the easier it is to develop computer-based processing support to produce the information needed to solve it. As an organization matures in its use of the computer, the extent to which it uses computers to produce information for decision making grows.

TRANSACTION PROCESSING SYSTEM (TPS)

The support of day-to-day business operating activities, or *transactions*, is usually the first and most important objective of an information system. These activities involve the processing of data received from external sources, as well as data generated internally. A computer-based **transaction processing system (TPS),** also called an *operations information system (OIS)* or an *electronic data processing (EDP) system*, is focused at the operating level of a business (Figure 12.6). The management information produced by transaction processing systems usually consists of detail reports of daily transactions (such as a list of items sold or all the accounting transactions that have been recorded in various ledgers and registers) or future transactions (such as lists of items that need to be ordered).

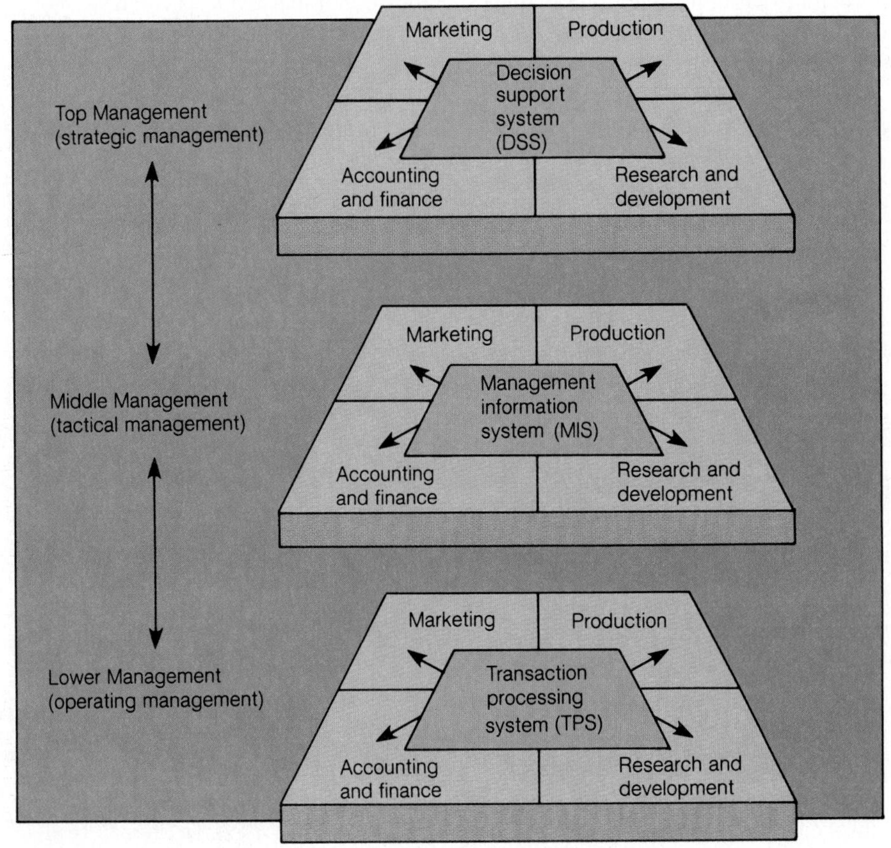

FIGURE 12.6

Three information systems for three levels of management.

A TPS usually operates only within one functional area of a business — in other words, marketing, accounting and finance, production, and research and development each has its own transaction processing system. Database management systems (covered in Chapter 11) were designed to solve the problems involved with sharing computer-based files among the four functional areas. Although the reports generated by a TPS are useful to lower-level managers, they are not helpful to middle managers, who need more summarized information with a wider perspective. Thus, management information systems were developed to take care of middle management's information needs.

Management Information System (MIS)

Management information systems (MIS), also called *information reporting systems*, provide middle management with reports that summarize and categorize information derived from all the company databases. The purpose of the reports is to allow management to spot trends and to get an overview of current business activities, as well as to monitor and control operational-level activities. (Although the term *management information system* is used to refer to *any* type of information system for managers, it is also used to refer specifically to *middle* management information systems.)

The scope of the reports and the characteristics of their information vary according to their purpose. In general, there is less need at the middle-management level for instant information than there is at the operational level. As you have seen, the reports can be periodic (such as income statements and balance sheets [Figure 12.7]), on demand, or event initiated, and they can summarize information or report on exceptional events or conditions. Examples of reports generated by an MIS are sales region analyses, cost analyses, annual budgeting reports, capital investment analyses, and production schedules.

Decision Support System (DSS)

The **decision support system (DSS),** a set of special computer programs and particular hardware, establishes a sophisticated system to produce information not regularly supplied by transaction processing or middle management information systems. This information is analyzed by the DSS and used for unstructured decision making. (TPSs and MISs do not analyze the information they produce.) DSSs are generally used by top management (although they support all levels of management), combine sophisticated analysis programs with traditional data access and retrieval functions, can be used by people who are not computer specialists, and emphasize flexibility in decision making. They are used to analyze unexpected problems and integrate information flow and decision-making activities. A DSS may use database management systems (covered in Chapter 11), query languages, financial modeling or spreadsheet programs, statistical analysis programs, report generators, and graphics programs to provide information.

To reach the DSS level of sophistication in information technology, an organization must have established a transaction processing system and a management information system. But these two types of systems are not designed to handle unpredictable information and decisions well. Decision support systems *are* designed to handle the unstructured types of decisions—the "what if" types of decisions—that traditional management information systems were not designed to support (Figure 12.8). Moreover, decision support systems provide managers with tools to help them better model, analyze, and make decisions about the information they have. Indeed, some people regard decision support systems as a separate type of information system altogether, not just a management information system for top management.

Although most DSSs are designed for large computer systems, electronic spreadsheet packages and database management packages are used by many businesspeople as tools for building a DSS for microcomputers. As microcomputers become more and more powerful, more and more microcomputer-based MISs will include a DSS using a database management system. The popularity of spreadsheet software among managers is due to the fact that it allows managers to examine a variety of business situations—that is, to "see what would happen" if business conditions changed—and to make projections, or guesses, about future developments based on sophisticated computer-based data analysis. Decision support systems designed for large computer systems collect large amounts of data and analyze it in more ways and with greater efficiency than a microcomputer spreadsheet does.

Sporting Life		
Income Statement for Year 1988		
Sales Revenue		$5,109
Cost of Goods Sold		2,208
Gross Profit		$2,901
Operating Expenses	$1525	
Depreciation Expense	119	1,644
Operating Earnings		$1,257
Interest Expense		105
Earnings Before Tax		$1,152
Income Tax Expense		550
Net Income		$ 602

Balance Sheet at End of Year 1988		
Cash		$ 190
Accounts Receivable		557
Inventory		806
Prepaid Expenses		111
Machinery, Equipment,		
Furniture, and Fixtures	$ 435	
Accumulated Depreciation	(105)	
Undepreciated Cost		330
Total Assets		$1,994
Accounts Payable:		
Inventory	$ 313	
Operating Expenses	52	$ 365
Accrued Expenses:		
Operations	$ 109	
Interest	17	126
Income Tax Payable		45
Short-Term Notes Payable		235
Long-Terms Notes Payable		300
Paid-in Capital		750
Retained Earnings		173
Total Liabilities and Stockholders' Equity		$1,994

FIGURE 12.7

Common periodic business reports. The income statement describes the business's income and expenses, plus any profit or loss, for a given period. The balance sheet reports on the business's financial condition on a specific date. These MIS reports are intended for middle management.

Decision support systems generally fall into two distinct categories: general and institutional. A general DSS produces information that can be used in making a wide variety of management decisions. The electronic spreadsheet is an ideal tool for the development of general decision support systems for microcomputers. Large database management systems (Chapter 11) and natural languages or query languages are used to develop decision support systems for large computer systems. An institutional DSS is much more industry- and function-specific. Examples include a DSS for the medical profession (including hospitals), which supports decision making in the areas of administration, patient diagnosis, determination and monitoring of drug dosages, medical records, and so on; a DSS for the advertising profession, which supports strategy in presenting products; and a DSS for the transportation industry, which supports traffic pattern analysis.

DSS HARDWARE

In most cases, the computer hardware in a DSS is used mainly by management personnel. It is not uncommon to find a high-level manager sitting in front of a computer terminal or a personal computer to take advantage of the company's DSS. The terminal would be connected to a large multiuser computer system; the personal computer would have some processing capabilities of its own, but it would also need to be able to connect with the larger computer system for data exchange. In addition, personal printers and hardcopy graphics output devices (such as a plotter or a color ink-jet printer) are often available to the manager. The manager's collection of computer hardware is often called an *executive workstation* (see Chapter 3).

PEOPLE

The users of a DSS must be reasonably comfortable working with the hardware and DSS software to be effective. Many managers develop substantial skills in using some of the microcomputer-based packages, such as electronic spreadsheets, that provide decision support processing capabilities. The software used for DSSs on large computer systems is generally too complex for people who are not computer specialists to handle; the manager would use it only on a simple level—to ask questions and obtain reports. (Executive information systems, or EISs, are becoming available; they provide executives with all the capabilities of a DSS but that are designed specifically to be easy to use.)

FIGURE 12.8

Decision support system. These processing questions represent the types of questions a top manager might ask a DSS. (These questions would not be keyed in to the computer word by word exactly as you see here; the manager would use a query language, such as SQL.)

1. If we discontinue selling baseball bats, will fewer people come into our stores?
2. If we add a new clothing line, will more people come into our stores?
3. How will offering the customer a 10% discount for all purchases totaling over $35 affect next year's net income?
4. What effect will hiring 50 additional sales employees have on the company's overall performance (i.e., profit)?
5. What effect will modernizing our stores have on sales?

Because a DSS is tailored to meet specific management information requirements, the nonmanagement user would not likely be directly involved with it. However, this type of user might be involved in gathering data to be processed by the DSS and then used as information for management.

DSS SOFTWARE

DSS applications software is usually very complex in terms of the instructions of which it is composed. As mentioned earlier, many different types of programs can make up a DSS. In most cases, it can be divided into three levels: database management systems software, query language, and specialized software or languages.

Database management software provides managers with the ability to collect, maintain, manipulate, and retrieve huge amounts of data.

A query language, as you learned in Chapter 8, allows people to use software easily without having to learn countless lists of codes and procedures. This "layer" of DSS software helps managers use the database with less difficulty and perform a variety of activities; for example, basic mathematical operations on fields of data contained in the database; calculation of ratios and various statistical measures; search of the database for records of a certain type; and extraction of records for the preparation of hardcopy reports and graphic representation of data.

Specialized software or languages are used to develop decision-making models. Some organizations purchase industry-specific modeling software for such common activities as financial risk analysis and forecasting (predicting future performance and conditions). However, the most sophisticated DSS users develop their own custom-made business activity and decision-making models.

The following list identifies some of the major differences between a management information system (MIS) and a decision support system (DSS):

- MIS users *receive* reports or information from the system, whereas DSS users interact with the system.
- MIS users can't direct the system to support a specific decision in a specific way, whereas DSS users can.
- MISs generate information based on the past, whereas DSSs use information from the past to create scenarios for the future.
- MIS activity is initiated by middle management, whereas DSS activity is usually initiated by top management.

Although MISs and DSSs effectively process information to support managerial activities, the quantity of available information continues to grow at an alarming rate and threatens to overwhelm the users. Thus, the search for more efficient information management tools continues. What is the next step in turning information into knowledge? The *replacement* of the manager by the computer? Will this be a result of the development of artificial intelligence?

ARTIFICIAL INTELLIGENCE

For years, researchers have been exploring the way people think in hopes of creating a computer that thinks like a person. And little doubt exists that **artificial intelligence (AI)** has the complete attention of computer scientists; indeed, it is their main focus for the present and the future. However, no agreement exists about what artificial intelligence *is*. Existing definitions are contradictory. Some experts say that AI is the science of making machines do things that would require intelligence if done by a person. Others state that if we can imagine a computer that can collect, assemble, choose among, understand, perceive, and know, then we have *artificial intelligence*. Still others believe that there is no such thing as intelligence that is "artificial" and that, therefore, the term *knowledge-based system* should be used.

Why do the definitions differ? First of all, there is not—and never has been—a single agreed-on definition of *human* intelligence. Second, consensus on the point at which a machine exhibits intelligence is difficult to achieve. For example, years ago when a computer could play tic-tac-toe, some researchers considered it to be intelligent because it could choose the next best possible move and could beat its human opponents. Today, most researchers no longer think that a machine's ability to play tic-tac-toe is enough to reflect intelligence. Other characteristics have been added to our definition of intelligent behavior—for example, the ability to reason logically and respond creatively to problems.

WHAT IS AI SUPPOSED TO DO?

The aim of AI is to produce a generation of systems that will be able to communicate with us by speech and hearing, use "vision" (scanning) that approximates the way people see, and be capable of intelligent problem solving. Some of the primary areas of research within AI of particular interest to business users are robotics, natural language processing, artificial reality, and expert systems.

ROBOTICS

According to *Webster's Ninth New Collegiate Dictionary*, a **robot** is an automatic device that performs functions ordinarily ascribed to human beings or that operates with what appears to be almost human intelligence. In the field of artificial intelligence, there are intelligent robots (also called *perception robots*) and unintelligent robots. Most robots are unintelligent; that is, they are programmed to do specific tasks, and they are incapable of showing initiative (Figure 12.9a). An unintelligent robot cannot respond to a situation for which it has not been specifically programmed. Intelligence is provided either by a direct link to a computer or by on-board computers that reside in the robot. Robotic intelligence is primarily a question of extending the sensory (for example, vision) and mobility competence of robots in a working environment.

In the future, reasoning ability will be incorporated into robots, thus improving their ability to behave "intelligently." Robot vision has already been successfully implemented in many manufacturing systems (Figure 12.9b). To "see," a computer measures varying intensities of light of a shape; each intensity has a numerical value that is compared to a template of intensity patterns stored in memory. One of the main reasons for the importance of vision is that production-line robots must be able to discriminate among parts. General Electric, for example, has Bin Vision Systems, which allow a robot to identify and pick up specific parts in an assembly-line format.

Another area of interest is the "personal" robot, familiar to us from science fiction. Existing personal robots exhibit relatively limited abilities, and whether a sophisticated home robot can be made cost-effective is debatable. B.O.B. (Brains On Board) is a device sold by Visual Machines that can speak (using prerecorded phrases), follow people around using infrared sensors, and avoid obstacles using ultrasonic sound. Software will allow the robot to bring its owner something to drink from the refrigerator. The performance limitations of personal robots reflect the difficulties in designing and programming intelligent robots. In fact, we have just begun to appreciate how complicated such mundane tasks as recognizing a can of Pepsi in the refrigerator can be.

NATURAL LANGUAGE PROCESSING

As mentioned in Chapter 8, the goal of natural language processing is to enable the computer to communicate with the user in the user's native language, for example, English. The primary difficulty in implementing this kind of communication is the sheer complexity of everyday conversation. For example, we readily understand the sentence "The spirit is willing, but the flesh is weak." One natural language processing system, however, understood this sentence to mean "The wine is agreeable, but the meat has spoiled." It turns out that the system must have access to a much larger body of knowledge than just a dictionary of terms. People use their world knowledge to help them understand what another person is saying. For

FIGURE 12.9 (a) Unintelligent laboratory robot; (b) intelligent robot feeding a patient in a Japanese hospital; (c) robot vision.

(a)

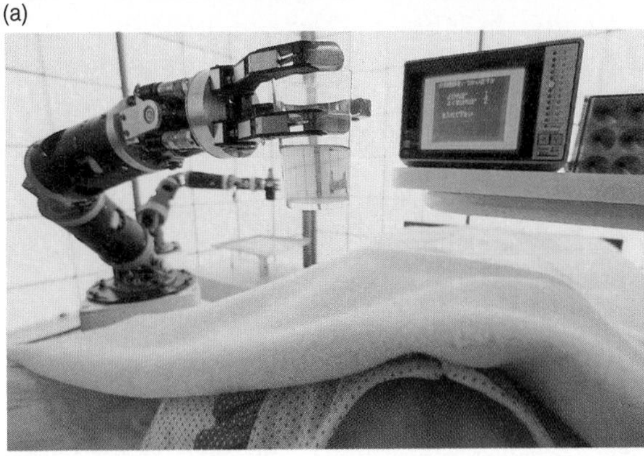
(b)

(c)

Computers and Careers

Transportation

Dashboards that talk to you? Instrument panels that look like video games? These are the more surface uses of computers in automobiles. By now there are electronic systems for engine controls, smart windshield wipers, suspension control, antilock braking, and fuel regulation. And that is only the beginning.

A computer-based navigation system recently available in Japan uses satellites to plot a vehicle's location, then displays it to the driver on a computer map. The car's location is indicated on color maps, which appear on compact disks; the maps are displayed on a 4-inch flat color screen. A driver can choose from five levels of detail, with some maps including the names of thousands of restaurants, hotels, and entertainment facilities and the services they provide. The navigation system can also be used by trucks and helicopters; the vehicles can be moving or standing still.

The reverse is also true; managers of fleets of vehicles— trucks, taxis, ambulances, police cars, armored cars, utility repair trucks, and so on — can keep track of vehicles (and even boats and off-road vehicles) through the use of satellite or ground-based navigation transmitters — locally or anywhere in the country. With such position-finding technologies, dispatchers can monitor drivers and give directions whenever they are needed.

Computer sensor systems are also used to control the roadways. For instance, wire sensors are buried every half mile along the Long Island Expressway and convey to a central computer information on traffic flow. Engineers monitoring this information are able to tap out messages on their keyboards that are displayed on electric signs at various points over the expressway, warning motorists about possible delays.

Fiber optic sensors are also being applied in "smart skin" technology, in which networks of fiber-optic sensors embedded in the fuselages of airplanes can alert pilots to small stresses and microscopic cracks.

Air transportation has long been a major user of computer technology. If you fly United Airlines into Chicago's O'Hare airport, for instance, your luggage will be moved through an underground baggage area that is the size of three football fields and processes up to 480 bags a minute. Whereas once baggage handlers had to read each luggage tag individually, now laser scanning sorters read bar codes and route bags down the appropriate conveyor belts. The airport receiving a planeload of luggage knows exactly which flights each bag is being transferred to even before the jet lands.

United also uses a computer-based Gate Assignment Display System (GADS) to reduce flight delays. This software, which runs on Texas Instruments workstations, uses an artificial intelligence program that captured the experience and knowledge of United Airlines operations experts. GADS replaces a system whereby gate assignments were handled by airline experts relying on memory and wall-sized scheduling boards to chart arrivals and departures.

Airlines also use computers to make fare adjustments. TWA, for instance, has software that can monitor the fares of competitors and can create pricing scenarios flight by flight and determine the profitability of various fares. Continental Airlines can measure bookings against expectations on nearly a half million future flights and can then revise fares and advertising accordingly.

Even ordinary computer users can take advantage of computers to save on fares. With a microcomputer, modem, communications software, and access to CompuServe or similar "gateway" network, you can link with different airline-reservations services and scan lists of available seats for the best deal. ■

example, we know the question "Coffee?" means "Do you want a cup of coffee?" But a computer would have difficulty understanding this one-word question.

Most existing natural language systems run on large computers; however, scaled-down versions are now available for microcomputers. Intellect, for example, is the name of a commercial product that uses a limited English vocabulary to help users query databases on both mainframes and microcomputers. One of the most successful natural language systems is LUNAR, developed to help users analyze the rocks brought back from the moon. It has access to detailed extensive knowledge about geology in its knowledge database and answers users' questions.

The use of natural language on microcomputers isn't limited to database programs. In 1985 GNP Corporation introduced a product called HAL to the users of the Lotus 1-2-3 electronic spreadsheet package. HAL interprets all the user's typed requests and then instructs the 1-2-3 program to execute the appropriate commands. HAL contains a limited amount of artificial intelligence that interprets sentences the user types in colloquial English. HAL understands more than just 1-2-3 terms; it knows quite a bit about microcomputer processing in general.

Artificial intelligence has the potential to solve many problems; however, it may create some as well. For example, some people think that AI is dangerous because it does not address the ethics of using machines to make decisions nor does it require machines to use ethics as part of the decision-making process. However, in spite of these concerns, AI has been used to develop yet another system—the expert system—to support decision making in many areas, including the business environment.

ARTIFICIAL REALITY

Want to take a trip to the moon? Be a racing car driver? See the world through the eyes of an ocean-bottom creature or your cat? Soon, without leaving your chair, you will be able to experience almost anything you want through the form of AI called *artificial reality* (Figure 12.10), also known as *virtual reality* and *virtual environments*. In virtual reality, the user experiences a computer-generated environment called *cyberspace*; he or she is "inside" a world instead of just observing an image on the screen. To put yourself into artificial reality, you need special hardware—a headset called *Eyephones* with 3-D screens and earphones, and gloves called *DataGloves*, which collect data about your hand movements and recognize commands from hand gestures. The headset includes a head-tracking device to enable the viewpoint to change as you move your head. The hardware uses software, such as Body Electric, that translates data into images and sound. Aside from entertainment, artificial reality can provide instructional simulation situations to help people learn to exercise skills under varying conditions—skills such as surgery, driving, flying, outerspace operations, police work, and disaster management, to name but a few.

EXPERT SYSTEMS: HUMAN EXPERTISE IN A COMPUTER

Beginning in the mid-1960s, a new type of system, called an *expert system*, began to be developed to support management in the decision-making process. This new type of system, which represents one of the first practical applications of artificial intelligence, is an exciting addition to the kinds of computer systems available to businesses. And, to answer the question posed earlier, expert systems are designed to be users' *assistants*, not replacements.

An **expert system** solves problems that require substantial expertise to understand. The system's performance depends on the *body of facts* (knowledge) and the *heuristics* (rules of thumb) that are fed into the computer. The expert knowledge and the heuristics are gathered by knowledge engineers—largely through interviews—from human experts in the field for which the computer-based system is being designed to support decisions—fields such as medicine, engineering, or geology. (For example, in the field of medicine, one question that might be asked of an expert system is whether one treatment is better for a patient than another one.) An expert system has the capacity to store the collection of knowledge and manipulate it in response to user inquiries; in some cases, it can even explain responses to the user.

An expert system has four major program components:

1. Natural (software) language interface for the user.

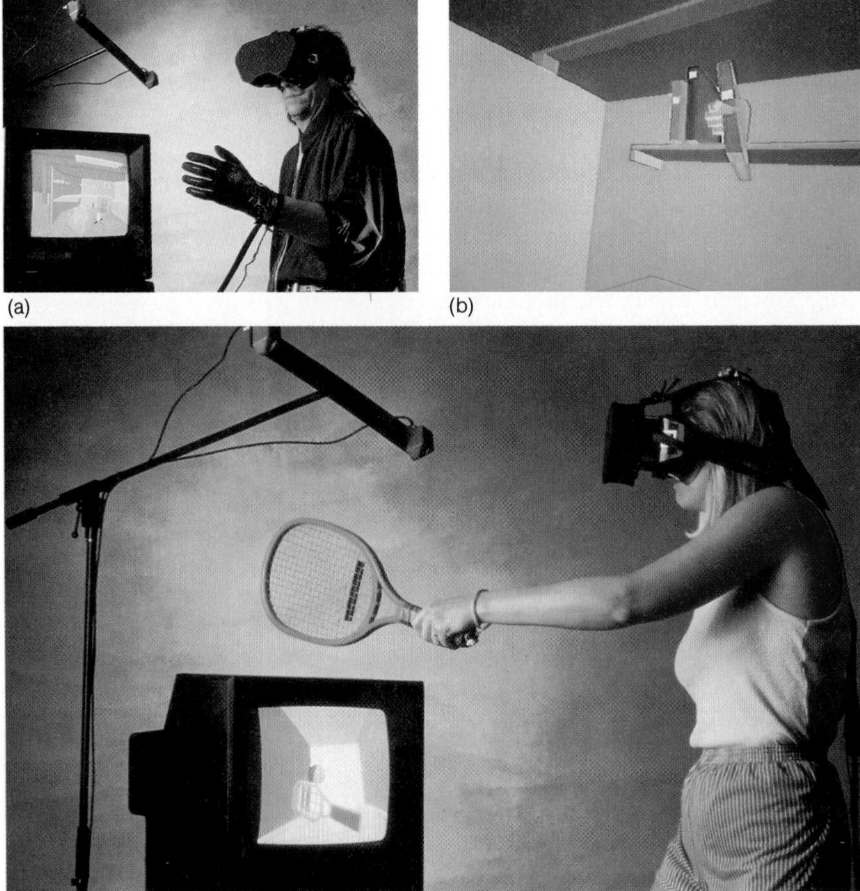

FIGURE 12.10

Artificial reality. (a) An artificial-reality user in an "office"; (b) The user takes a book from the shelf. (c) This person is using artificial reality to practice racquetball strokes.

2. Knowledge base (like a database, where the facts are stored).
3. Inference machine (software that solves problems and makes logical inferences).
4. Explanation module (which explains its conclusions to the user).

One of the most famous expert systems—an older system now being replaced by updated ones—is MYCIN, a system that diagnoses infectious diseases and recommends appropriate drugs. For example, bacteremia can be a fatal disease if it is not treated quickly. Unfortunately, traditional tests for it require 24 to 48 hours to verify a diagnosis. However, MYCIN provides physicians with a diagnosis and recommended therapy within minutes. To use MYCIN, the physician enters data on a patient; as the data is being entered, MYCIN asks questions (for example, "Is patient a burn patient?"). As the questions are answered, MYCIN's inference machine "reasons" out a diagnosis: "IF the infection is primary bacteria, AND the site of the culture is the gastrointestinal tract, THEN there is evidence (0.7) that the identity of the organism causing the disease is *Bacteroides*." The "0.7" means that MYCIN "thinks" there is a 7 out of 10 chance that this diagnosis is correct. This pattern closely follows that of human thought; much of our knowledge is inexact and incomplete, and we often reason using odds (such as "There's a 40 percent chance it's going to rain") when we don't have access to complete and accurate information.

Examples of other expert systems are XCON (a system that puts together the best arrangement of Digital Equipment Corporation [DEC] computer system components for a given company), DENDRAL (a system that identifies chemical compounds), PROSPECTOR (a system that evaluates potential geological sites of oil, natural gas, and so on), and DRILLING ADVISOR (a system that assists in diagnosing and resolving oil rig problems).

Capturing human expertise for the computer is a difficult and time-consuming task. "Knowledge engineers" are trained to elicit knowledge (for example, by interview) from experts and build the expert system. The knowledge engineer may program the system in an artificial intelligence programming language, such as LISP or PROLOG, or may use system-building tools that provide a structure. Tools allow faster design but are less flexible than languages. An example of such a tool is EMYCIN, which is MYCIN without any of MYCIN's knowledge. A knowledge engineer can theoretically enter any knowledge (as long as it is describable in rules) into this empty shell and create a new system. The completed new system will solve problems as MYCIN does, but the subject matter in the knowledge base may be completely different (for example, car repair).

Expert systems are usually run on large computers—often dedicated artificial intelligence computers—because of these systems' gigantic appetites for memory; however, some scaled-down expert systems (such as the OS/2 version of KBMS, Knowledge Base Management System) run on microcomputers. Scaled-down systems generally do not have all the capabilities of large expert systems, and most have limited reasoning abilities. LISP and PROLOG compilers are available for microcomputers, as are some system-building tools such as EXPERT-EASE, NEXPERT, and VP-Expert (Figure 12.11), which allow relatively unsophisticated users to build their own expert system. Such expert-system building software tools are called *shells*.

IMPLICATIONS FOR BUSINESS

Expert systems are becoming increasingly important to business and manufacturing firms. However, it is difficult to define what constitutes "expertise" in business. Defining expertise in business (unlike in some other areas, notably math, medicine, and chemistry) is a formidable task because of its general and "soft" nature; that is, "business" is not made up of a specific set of inflexible facts and rules. Some business activities, however, do lend themselves to expert system development. DEC has developed several in-house expert systems, including ILPRS (which assists in long-range planning) and IPPMS (which assists in project management). Other examples are TAXMAN, which evaluates the tax consequences of various proposed business reorganization schemes; AUDITOR, which helps auditors assess a company's allowance for bad debts; and TAXADVISOR, which makes tax planning recommendations.

Another issue that inhibits the use of expert systems in business is that businesses want systems that can be integrated into their existing computer systems. Many existing expert systems are designed to run in a stand-alone mode. Furthermore, who will use the expert system? Who will be responsible for its maintenance? Who will have authority to add and/or delete knowledge in the expert system? What are the legal ramifications of decisions made by an expert system? These and other questions will have to be answered before expert systems are fully accepted in the business environment.

Cost is also a factor. Large expert systems are still too expensive to build on a scale large enough to satisfy the needs of management across a wide spectrum of business and industry. However, less expensive micro-based tools are becoming increasingly powerful and available to businesses, and the lines of definition between DSSs and expert systems are beginning to blur. As products are developed that incorporate the best aspects of both types of systems, the computer system can address a wider range of problems.

FIGURE 12.11

VP-Expert software package and screen.

Developing and Implementing a Management Information System

The task of developing and implementing any type of management information system is a formidable one, requiring a great deal of planning. Business environments change rapidly, so unless management has great foresight (and the support of good specialists and user input), an information system may be obsolete by the time it is implemented.

The successful development of a management information system requires:

- A long- and a short-range plan for the company; a company must have plans for the future to be able to decide what to do tomorrow, next week, and next month.
- A commitment from management to allocate the personnel and resources necessary to get the job done.
- A staff of technical specialists with the skills necessary to develop the computer-based parts of the system based on user input.

The most important step in undertaking the development of an MIS is the formation of a project development team (which would follow the steps of systems analysis, design, and development discussed in Chapter 10). The team should be made up of managers, information system users, and technical computer specialists. All the team members should be familiar with the company's business objectives, current activities, and problems. And all the members must come to a general understanding of how the business operates. This task is not easy because many managers understand only how their own departments work but little, if anything, about other departments; many managers have difficulty explaining how their own departments work; and many managers, users, and computer specialists use jargon—special vocabulary and expressions—to explain what they do. Jargon is not generally understood by everyone. Modeling, or prototyping (discussed in Chapter 10), is often useful in a situation like this.

The development of a comprehensive MIS is a massive undertaking that may take years to carefully plan and coordinate. However, the organizations that plan to survive the 1990s will have efficient management information systems—including expert systems—to feed management the information it needs to be competitive.

Information Centers

In an effort to further support management decision making, many large organizations have established **information centers** as part of their management information system. The person in charge of the information center is called the chief information officer (CIO). The people who staff an information center are technical experts on the hardware, software, and procedures that the company is using. The staff acts as "troubleshooters"—consultants and problem solvers. However, they focus not only on technology, as they did in the earlier years of computer-based information systems, but also on the goals, productivity, and quality of the business.

The user is the person the information center was created for; the user is the only customer. If the user wants to request a computer, the information center staff will assist in identifying what kind of computer is appropriate. A user with an operating problem with hardware or software would call the information center for help, or for service requests and replacement parts. Information center staff also show users how to use available software to create their own customized applications and provide general training sessions for hardware and software use. In large systems with a mainframe computer, the information center will also assist users in accessing and storing data.

The information center may be a separate department that services the entire company, or each functional area—such as marketing or production—may have its own information center. (The current trend is toward integrating information resource management into all the functional departments of a company.) In their book *Management Information Systems* (New York: Macmillan, 1988), Kenneth C. Laudon and Jane Price Laudon list the following typical activities of an information center:

- Education in high-level languages and development tools.
- Assistance in accessing data.
- Assistance in debugging programs.
- Assistance with applications, queries, and reports employing high-level languages.
- Consultation on appropriate tools and methodologies for developing applications.
- Generation and modification of prototypes.
- Providing reference materials on information center resources.
- Liaison with other information processing groups (such as database specialists) that support information center resources.
- Maintaining a catalog of available applications and databases.

Information center hardware may consist of mainframes, minicomputers, PCs, or a combination of these machines. Typical software tools include the following:

- Graphics software.
- Word processing software.
- Modeling or planning software, including spreadsheets.
- User-friendly fourth-generation languages for queries or simple applications.
- High-level programming languages for user-based applications development.

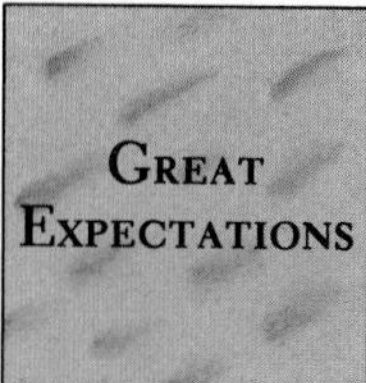

The field of artificial intelligence is still an emerging discipline, with contributions needed from a variety of other disciplines (for example, linguistics). These disciplines will shape the character of AI in the years ahead.

We can expect more AI software products to be available in the commercial marketplace, particularly in business and manufacturing. Carnegie Mellon University and Westinghouse Corporation are developing the factory of the future, which will include the use of intelligent robots and expert systems. With the migration of AI systems to microcomputers, more powerful AI programs will soon be available to the general user. Imagine, for example, a system that can teach you math — one that adjusts itself to your learning behavior and that can analyze and discuss with you your pattern of mistakes.

Expert systems will be available for most subject areas. Wherever human expertise exists, it may be possible to develop a computer model of this expertise. One consequence of this may be increased automation of specialized tasks (for example, credit scoring for loans), changing the nature of the jobs held by such specialists. Artificial intelligence is having, and will continue to have, a social impact that will require our thoughtful attention.

Traditionally, the MIS function has been highly structured, following well-defined procedures to respond to clearly defined departmental needs. In other words, the management information systems established by a company — and the information administrator's duties — were set up to fulfill identified information needs of departments on the operational, middle-management, and top-management (strategic) levels. However, as computer hardware has become smaller and cheaper (and thus more available to more users within various departments), the users and departments have started to generate and manipulate their own information in response to rapidly changing situations, without needing to meet many of an MIS's highly structured requirements. As a result, MIS professionals are becoming business administrators, not just technical administrators, and users are becoming, to varying degrees, technical MIS administrators.

As the business environment on all levels of operation becomes more unstructured and the processing of information becomes less centralized, the roles and responsibilities of the people who develop and control management information systems must also change. Also, the proliferation of the microcomputer — used both as a terminal hooked up to a larger computer system and as an independent processing unit — on all levels of the business environment means that the user is becoming much more involved in the daily operations of information management than just telling software programmers what they want the management information system to accomplish. Computing in companies has become increasingly complex and integrated, and the dividing lines between departments in a company are becoming so blurred that professionals are rejecting the word *department* in favor of *work group* — a group of people who share the same or very similar processing functions and information needs, no matter where these people are located individually.

As the result of the increase in computing complexity, flexibility, and integration, MIS professionals will have to focus more on communications, connectivity, and long-term business goals than they have in the past. Ease of use will continue to be emphasized, so that users without technical backgrounds can use MIS technology effectively in business. The responsibility for applications software development will be transferred to work groups to help resolve the problems of programmer shortages and backlogs of applications requests. Many experts think that MIS departments will have to give up the idea of doing and managing everything. MIS professionals will have to develop partnerships with work groups, with all roles and responsibilities redefined along lines less structured than most people have been used to. In most businesses, the trend is toward decentralization: Decision making is moving down the organization.

Onward: Applications Software Features and Functions

The next part of this book provides detailed information about some popular types of applications software packages, as well as additional information about the keyboard, handling disks, and working with computer files. But before you proceed to Part V, let's see what Sporting Life is doing about setting up a database and using it.

Summary

Every business needs accurate, complete, and timely information to make decisions and survive in today's competitive business environment. Management information systems—organized standards and procedures, both computer-based and manual, for processing data into useful information—help fulfill this need. They are used by three levels of management—(1) operating management, (2) middle management, and (3) upper management—in the areas of planning, organizing, staffing, supervising, and controlling business activities in the departments of marketing, accounting and finance, production, and research and development.

The types of decisions made will differ according to the level of management. Operating management typically makes structured, short-term decisions. Middle management, or tactical management, generally makes semistructured decisions based on information that is less detailed (summarized to some degree). These types of decisions have some nonquantifiable aspects to them and require some subjective judgment on the part of the decision maker. Upper management, or strategic management, typically makes unstructured decisions, which are the most difficult to computerize because they are made with the most subjective judgment. Unstructured decisions are broad in scope, long range, and often unpredictable and future oriented.

Information must be made available to management in the form of reports. Operating management generally uses detail reports that are issued on a regular, or periodic, basis. Middle and top management use summary and exception reports that are issued periodically or on demand or that are initiated by an event.

Managers generally follow five steps when making decisions: (1) problem recognition and identification, (2) identification and evaluation of alternatives, (3) selection of alternative, (4) action, and (5) follow-up. The data they use is generated internally (by normal data processing systems), externally (by sources outside the company), or by other levels of management. The information generated by processing the data into reports differs in level of summarization, degree of accuracy, and degree of time sensitivity, according to the management level.

A business can use three general types of management information systems to satisfy management's need for information. (1) A transaction processing system (TPS) supports the day-to-day operating activities and is used mostly by operating management. (2) A middle management information system (MIS) (or simply a management information system) supports the decision making of middle management with reports that summarize and categorize information derived from data generated on the transaction level. (3) A decision support system (DSS) supports the decision making of top management through a sophisticated software setup designed to answer "what if" questions and aid in making projections. Most DSSs are designed for large computer systems, although electronic spreadsheets and database management systems software can be used to build a type of DSS for microcomputers. General decision support systems produce information that can be used to make a wide variety of management decisions. Institutional decision support systems are much more industry- and function-specific. Managers using a DSS are usually provided with hardware at an executive workstation. DSS software generally uses a query language to make its use easy and specialized software languages to develop decision-making models; it also provides the manager with the ability to retrieve and manipulate huge amounts of data.

Expert systems, an application of artificial intelligence, are also used in the business world to aid in the support of decision making. An expert system is a collection of knowledge (and rules for using it) gathered by knowledge engineers from human experts and fed into a computer system. Artificial intelligence (AI) basically is the science of making machines do what humans can do. In addition to expert systems, areas of AI include robotics, natural language processing, and artificial reality.

Information centers, staffed by experts on a company's hardware, software, and business procedures, are also being used to help managers and users in general to satisfy their ever-growing need for training and information.

KEY TERMS

artificial intelligence (AI), p. 485
decision support system (DSS), p. 482
detail report, p. 473
event-initiated report, p. 475
exception report, p. 474
expert system, p. 490
information center, p. 493
management, p. 470
management information system (MIS), p. 471, 482
middle management, p. 474
on-demand report, p. 475
operating management, p. 472
operational decision maker, p. 473
periodic report, p. 475
robot, p. 486
semistructured decision, p. 475
strategic decision maker, p. 476
structured decision, p. 473
summary report, p. 474
transaction processing system (TPS), p. 481
unstructured decision, p. 476
upper management, p. 476

EXERCISES

MATCHING

Match each of the following terms to the phrase that is the most closely related.

1. ____ unstructured decision
2. ____ natural language
3. ____ on-demand report
4. ____ exception report
5. ____ management
6. ____ upper management

7. ____ decision support system
8. ____ robot
9. ____ structured decision
10. ____ management information system
11. ____ information center
12. ____ periodic report
13. ____ event-initiated report
14. ____ operating management
15. ____ transaction processing system

a. Automatic device that performs functions ordinarily ascribed to human beings
b. These reports usually deal with a change in conditions that requires immediate attention.
c. Individuals in an organization who are responsible for providing leadership and direction
d. Predictable decision made by following a well-defined set of routine procedures
e. Enables the computer to communicate with the user in the user's native language
f. Report requested by a manager when information that focuses on a particular problem is needed
g. Set of special computer programs designed to help all levels of management by providing information for unstructured decision making
h. Level of management that deals with decisions that are the broadest in scope
i. These reports show out-of-the-ordinary data.
j. Electronic data processing (EDP) system
k. The most complex type of decision that management will have to face
l. Report produced at predetermined times such as daily or weekly
m. Computer-based processing and/or manual procedures that provide information to support management decision making
n. Department that can help managers and users by acting as consultants and problem solvers
o. Lowest level of management

MULTIPLE CHOICE

1. Which of the following is generally true about management reports?
   a. Low-level managers need information in the form of detail reports.
   b. Reports can be issued on demand, periodically, or on the occurrence of a specific event.
   c. Middle managers use exception reports.
   d. Middle managers use summary reports.
   e. All the above
2. Which of the following is not an area of artificial intelligence?
   a. expert systems
   b. robotics
   c. natural language processing
   d. transaction processing system
   e. artificial reality

3. Which of the following is not true of expert systems?
   a. Expert systems are collections of human knowledge.
   b. Expert systems are expensive to design.
   c. Expert systems are usually designed to run on small general-purpose computers.
   d. An inference machine is a component of an expert system.
   e. Expert systems solve problems that require substantial expertise to understand.
4. Information is produced by processing data from which of the following sources?
   a. data provided by higher levels of management
   b. data provided by lower levels of management
   c. internally generated data
   d. externally generated data
   e. all the above
5. Which of the following is true of a transaction processing system?
   a. It is used by managers to spot trends.
   b. It supports unstructured decision making.
   c. It usually consists of detailed reports on daily transactions.
   d. It is used by the highest level of management.
   e. It analyzes information.
6. Distinguishing among the different levels of management can be accomplished by analyzing:
   a. types of decisions made
   b. frequency with which decisions are made
   c. time frame considered in making decisions
   d. types of report information needed to make decisions
   e. all the above
7. Which of the following is not one of the components of an expert system?
   a. natural language interface
   b. robotics
   c. knowledge base
   d. inference machine
   e. explanation module
8. Which of the following is not usually characteristic of upper management decisions?
   a. Decisions require judgment.
   b. Decisions are structured.
   c. Decisions are long range.
   d. Decisions are unpredictable.
   e. Decisions require experience.
9. Which of the following statements is the most accurate?
   a. The degree to which information needs to be summarized increases as one moves up through the management levels.
   b. Low-level managers make unstructured decisions.
   c. Upper-level managers make structured decisions.
   d. Low-level managers need general information about operating activities.
   e. Middle managers make unstructured decisions.

10. Which of the following is not a function of an information center?
    a. generation and modification of prototypes
    b. assistance in accessing data
    c. processing payroll
    d. providing reference materials on information center resources
    e. providing hardware and software training

SHORT ANSWER

1. What steps should management follow to make decisions?
2. What is a decision support system?
3. What is the primary function of an information center?
4. What inhibits some companies from using expert systems?
5. Why is it so difficult to define *artificial intelligence?*
6. What is a management information system, and what is its role in an organization?
7. What are transaction processing systems typically used for?
8. Describe some differences between a management information system and a decision support system.
9. What is required to develop a successful management information system?
10. What is the difference between a structured decision and a semistructured decision, and which type of decision is easier to support from a computer-based data processing standpoint?

PROJECTS

1. Decision support systems often take years to develop. Given this long development period, some experts argue that the system will be obsolete by the time it is complete and that information needs will have changed. Other experts argue that no alternatives exist. By reviewing current computer publications that describe management information systems, formulate an opinion about this issue.
2. Research *artificial reality* (or *virtual reality*) in current computer magazines and other popular periodicals such as *Time* and *Newsweek*. What do you think of this new technology? What would you use it for? How could it be applied in educational settings?
3. Does your university or college have an information center? If so, interview the chief information officer and report on the services and functions of the center. Can the CIO identify the various levels of management within the departments that use the center? To whom does the CIO report? What kinds of user input were requested when the center was being set up? Does the center use any sophisticated decision support software? Whom does the center serve, and what kind of reports does it provide? What kinds of services does the center offer to students?

   If your school does not have an information center, interview the CIO of a local company that does have one.

EPISODE 4

SPORTING LIFE

BUILDING A DATABASE AND MANAGING THE SYSTEM

THE STORY CONTINUES . . .

Two months have passed since we last checked on the progress of Sporting Life. You have since purchased a complement of hardware and software that will help Luis with inventory, Kim with accounting, and the cashiers with sales transactions. A total of four computers was purchased.

Although the plan, or logistics, for how the new microcomputer systems will be used was determined in the last episode, the physical implementation of the new system has yet to take place. In other words, Luis and Kim are still performing their inventory and accounting activities manually, and the cashiers are still tracking sales on multipart forms. Sporting Life has hired a consultant from Micro Mentor to help set up the new system. The consultant has noted that the following tasks need to be performed (these represent the types of tasks and training sessions that you may encounter in many jobs):

1. Tracking inventory on Luis's computer.
   a. Using dBASE IV, design the structure for a database to be stored on Luis's computer that will keep track of inventory. Luis would like to be able to find answers to the following questions:
      - Which items in each store have fallen below the reorder point and need to be purchased?
      - Are any items in either store completely out of stock?
      - How many of each item have been sold so far this year?
      - What is the dollar investment in inventory, both overall and for specific product lines?

   b. Train Luis how to use dBASE IV to add records to (update) the database, manipulate the database, and generate reports from the database about the status of inventory.
2. Tracking accounting on Kim's computer.
   a. Design an electronic spreadsheet using Lotus 1-2-3 to maintain the accounting ledgers and to process payroll.
   b. Train Kim and her two assistants to use Lotus 1-2-3 to perform the activities listed above and to produce business graphs such as pie charts and bar charts that will show the status of accounts receivable and accounts payable.

c. Design the structure for a database using dBASE IV to maintain customer records. Kim would like to be able to find answers to the following questions:
   - How many customers have shopped here more than once?
   - Do most of our customers live in town?
   - How many customers have been late on their payments more than once?

d. Train Kim and her two assistants to use dBASE IV.
e. Train Kim to use WordPerfect to generate letters advertising upcoming sales.

3. Tracking sales on the cashiers' computers.
   a. Using dBASE IV, design the structure for a database that contains item number and price information that the cashiers can retrieve when processing a sale.
   b. Using dBASE IV, design the structure for a database that will allow the cashiers to track customer number if the customer has already established an account, customer name and address if the customer is a new customer, item purchased, quantity purchased, and method of payment (cash, check, or credit).
   c. Train cashiers to use dBASE IV to enter sales data into the database and to retrieve information from it.
4. In addition, sometime soon you are going to purchase the necessary hardware and software (Crosstalk XVI) to allow the cashiers to communicate directly with both Luis's and Kim's computers so that the cashiers don't have to hand-deliver daily transaction files to them on diskettes. Luis, Kim, and the cashiers will have to be trained to use the communications software to perform this activity.

Given the information available (user input) about what Luis, Kim, and the cashiers currently do when performing their respective activities—and what they would each *like* to do—the consultant will write structures for the databases and spreadsheets and then conduct workshops to ensure correct usage. Included in the consultant's services will be an evaluation of the feasibility of establishing communications between the cashier's computers and Luis's and Kim's computers.

TOPICS FOR DISCUSSION

The consultant used dBASE IV to design the following data dictionaries.

A data dictionary to be used on Luis's computer for storing inventory data:

FIELD DESCRIPTION	FIELD NAME	FIELD TYPE	FIELD WIDTH	DECIMALS
Item Number	Itemno	Character	4	
Description	Desc	Character	15	
# in Stock	Instock	Numeric	3	0
Reorder Point	Reorder	Numeric	3	0
Vendor I.D.	Vendor	Character	10	

A data dictionary to be used on Kim's computer for storing customer credit data:

FIELD DESCRIPTION	FIELD NAME	FIELD TYPE	FIELD WIDTH	DECIMALS
Customer #	Custno	Character	4	
Customer Name	Name	Character	20	
Address	Address	Character	20	
City	City	Character	20	
State	State	Character	2	
Zip	Zip	Character	10	
New Customer?	Type	Character	2	
Credit Status	Credit	Character	2	

1. If you had to create a data dictionary to be used on the cashiers' computers for tracking sales data, what fields would you include? (Keep in mind that the sales data is also used to update Luis's files and Kim's files. In addition, provision must be made for the different means of payment—cash, check, or credit.)
2. What do you think the advantages would be if the cashiers' computers could act like terminals connected to Luis's computer? Could the inventory database on Luis's computer be automatically updated? Would time be saved? Are there any disadvantages? What type of network might be the most efficient?
3. What basic types of hardware and software would be required to set up the network in Question 2?

Part V

Microcomputer Laboratory

Throughout this book we have tried to emphasize the point that, in most modern societies, we all will become, or are already, computer *users*. Although many of us will not become professional computer technicians, programmers, or analysts, we will use computer technology to achieve something we want to do or have to do in our jobs or in our private lives. Regardless of what business or profession you want to go into — from accounting or choreography to radiology or zookeeping — you will generally find that, if you understand basic software applications concepts, you will be better able to compete for the job you want and function smoothly in the job you get. The following modules give you hands-on instruction in three of the most popular microcomputer applications software packages available, as well as practice using the most popular microcomputer systems software. However, keep in mind that information technology changes rapidly; popular software may be forced into retirement at any time by a dazzling new package. For that reason, it's important for you to concentrate on the basic *concepts* of systems software (DOS) and word processing (WordPerfect), database management (dBASE IV), and spreadsheet (Lotus 1-2-3) software, as well as on the keystrokes.

Introduction to the Modules

Preview

When you have completed this introduction, you will be able to:

- Explain the basic functions of the microcomputer keyboard.
- Explain how main memory and read-only-memory function in the microcomputer system.
- Describe the disk drive-naming conventions used on most microcomputers.
- Describe the conventions for naming the files you create when using a microcomputer.
- Boot a microcomputer.

Microcomputer Hardware Review

Chapters 3–6 described input, storage, processing, and output hardware used on mainframe computers, minicomputers, and microcomputers. In the modules you will use a microcomputer to manage disks and disk files (Module A) and to create documents (Module B), spreadsheets (Module C), databases (Module D), and business graphs (Module E). This section reviews the microcomputer hardware components and conventions you should be familiar with to work through Modules A–E.

Input Hardware: The Keyboard

In the modules, the keyboard is your principal input device. We would therefore like to make you more familiar with it now. As mentioned in Chapter 3, keyboards come in a variety of sizes and shapes (determined by the computer manufacturer), but most keyboards used with computer systems have a certain number of features in common (Figure I.1):

1. Standard typewriter keys.
2. Function keys.
3. Special-purpose keys.
4. Cursor-movement keys.
5. Numeric keys.

You need to understand the purpose of these keys so that you can use the keyboard effectively.

The typewriter-like keys are used to type in text and special characters such as $, *, and #. In general, these keys are positioned in much the same location as the keys on a typewriter. People often refer to the common layout as the **QWERTY** layout, because the first six characters on the top row of alphabetic keys spell QWERTY.

The **function keys,** labeled F1, F2, F3, and so on, are used to issue commands. (Function keys are also called **programmable keys.**) Most keyboards are configured with between 10 and 12 function keys. The software program you are using determines how the function keys are used. For example, using one software program, you would press the F2 key to print your document. However, in a different software program, you would use the F2 key to save your work to disk. The user's manual that comes with the software tells you how to use the function keys.

Computer keyboards also have some special-purpose keys such as Ctrl (Control), Alt (Alternate), Shift, Del (Delete), Ins (Insert), Caps Lock, and Enter. The **Ctrl key,** the **Alt key,** and the **Shift key** are modifier keys. By themselves they do nothing. But pressed along with another key, they modify the function of the other key. For example, in one word processing package (WordStar), when you hold the Ctrl key down and tap the letter G, a character is deleted; thus, the Ctrl key modifies the function of the G key. In another package (WordPerfect), when you hold the Alt key down and then tap the F4 key, you begin marking a whole portion of text to be moved to another place in your document. In this example, the Alt key has modified the function of the F4 key. The software application you are using determines how the Ctrl key and the Alt key are used. When the Shift key is pressed with an alphabetic key, the character becomes a capital letter. When the Shift key is pressed with a numbered key across the top of the keyboard, the character *above* the number is typed—for example, a dollar sign ($) or a percent sign (%).

The **Ins key** and the **Del key** are used for editing what you type: Word processing software uses them frequently to insert and delete text.

The **Caps Lock** key is used to place all the alphabetic keys into an uppercase position (that is, capital letters only). This key is similar to the shift lock key on a typewriter, with one difference. The shift lock key allows you to type the upper character on any typewriter key, whereas the Caps Lock key affects *only* the

FIGURE I.1 Ninety words per minute? These are two kinds of microcomputer keyboards: an IBM PC keyboard on the left and an enhanced IBM PC keyboard on the right (the keyboard on the right has a numeric keypad separate from the cursor-movement keys).

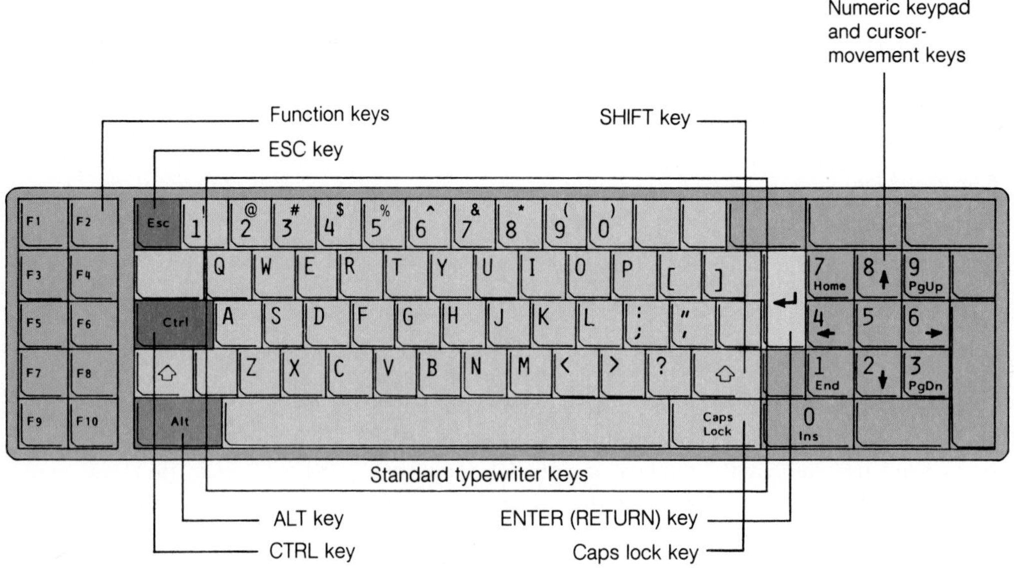

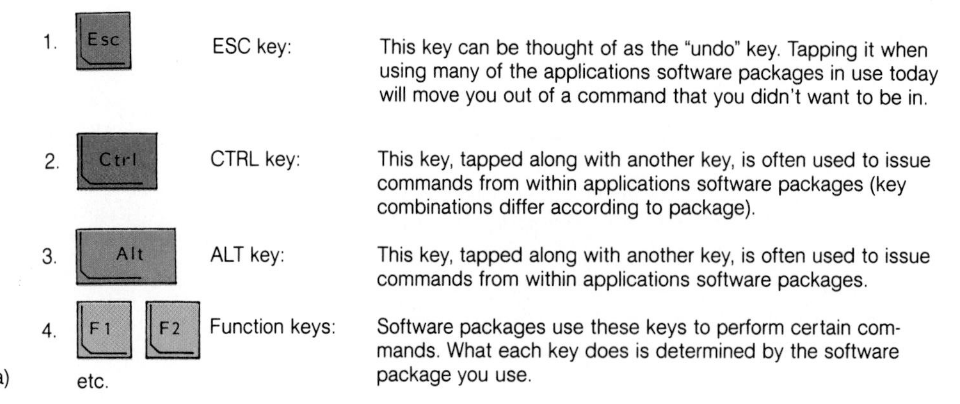

alphabetic keys on the computer keyboard. For example, the * is the upper character on the number 8 key on the keyboard shown in Figure I.1. Pressing the Shift Lock key on a typewriter would allow you to then press the number 8 key to make * appear. However, if you press the Caps Lock key on the computer keyboard and then press 8, an 8 appears unless you also hold down the regular Shift key.

The **Enter** key is usually pressed to tell the computer to execute a command entered by first tapping other keys.

Cursor-movement keys are used to move the cursor around the screen. (The **cursor** is the symbol, or indicator, on the video display screen that shows where the next character or space that is input will be positioned.) On the keyboards used with the early IBM PC–compatible microcomputers (which are still used in many

FIGURE I.1 *(continued)*

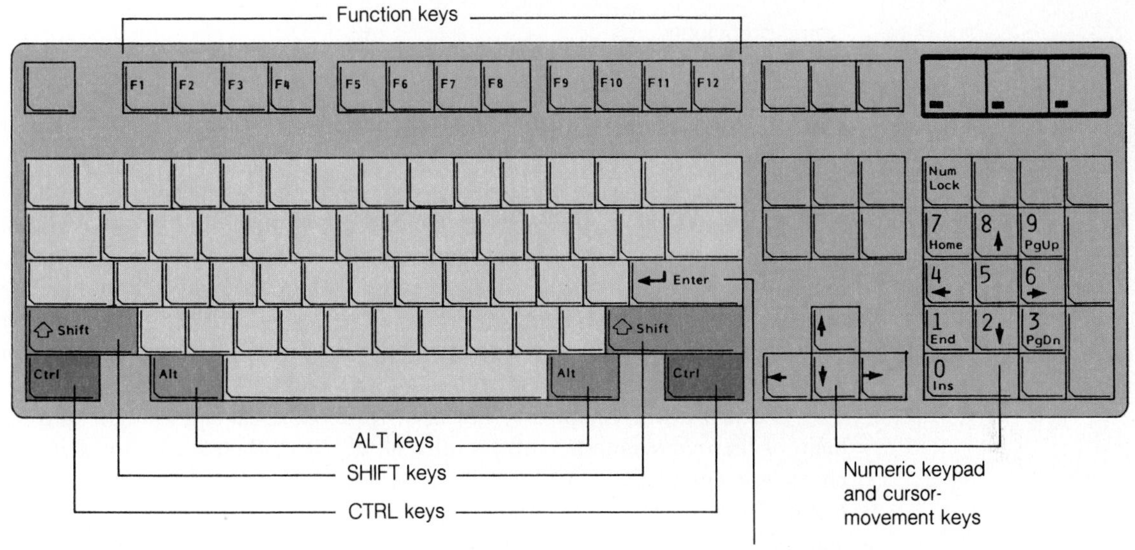

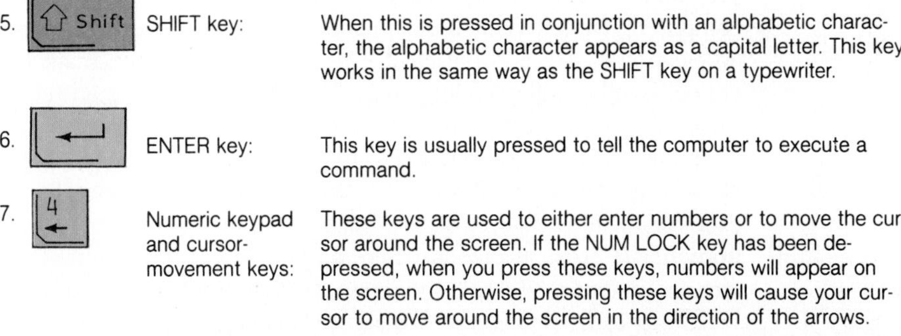

5. SHIFT key: When this is pressed in conjunction with an alphabetic character, the alphabetic character appears as a capital letter. This key works in the same way as the SHIFT key on a typewriter.

6. ENTER key: This key is usually pressed to tell the computer to execute a command.

7. Numeric keypad and cursor-movement keys: These keys are used to either enter numbers or to move the cursor around the screen. If the NUM LOCK key has been depressed, when you press these keys, numbers will appear on the screen. Otherwise, pressing these keys will cause your cursor to move around the screen in the direction of the arrows.

(b)

businesses today), the keys for cursor movement were combined with the **numeric keypad**— the keys used to enter numbers (Figure I.1a). When you turn it on, your microcomputer system "assumes" that the numeric keypad keys will be used for cursor movement. Therefore, you have to remember to press the **Num Lock key** or a Shift key before using these keys to enter numbers. On these older keyboards, it's easier to enter numbers using the numbers across the top of the keyboard.

Most of today's keyboards have cursor-movement keys that are separate from the numeric keypad keys (Figure I.1b). These keyboards are often referred to as the "101-key enhanced" keyboards. When a microcomputer system is turned on that uses an enhanced keyboard, the assumption made by your computer system is that the Num Lock key is active— that is, the numeric keypad will be used for entering numbers.

As mentioned in Chapter 3, if you have used a typewriter keyboard, you should find it easy to learn to work with a computer keyboard. However, because the two types of keyboards are slightly different, you may want to experiment with some of the keyboard familiarization and typing tutorial software on the market today. With these programs you learn to use your keyboard at the same time you improve your typing proficiency.

PROCESSING HARDWARE: RAM AND ROM

The processing hardware components you should be familiar with in order to proceed with Modules A–E are the microprocessor, main memory (RAM), and read-only memory (ROM). These hardware components were described in detail in Chapters 3–6. So that you can proceed with Modules A–E without having to read Chapters 3–6 in their entirety, this section provides a brief overview of these components. As indicated in this section, refer to Chapters 3–6 if you want more detailed information about a particular hardware component.

As described in Chapter 5, the **microprocessor** can be thought of as the brain of the microcomputer. It performs all of the mathematical processing and character manipulation. The microprocessor can work only with data and software instructions that are stored in **main memory**— also referred to as **primary storage** and **random access memory (RAM).** Main memory is an electronic state (often referred to as a "desktop") where data and software instructions reside during processing (that is, when your computer is on). When your computer is off, main memory is empty. Let's say you are creating a document using a word processing program. You are working on page 2 of the document. Suddenly, the power to your computer is cut off. What has happened to your document? Since main memory is an electronic state and the electrical power source is off, main memory will be erased— and so will your document. For this reason, cautious users save their work frequently onto a more permanent (secondary) storage device such as a diskette or a hard disk. Data on these devices is stored magnetically (see Chapter 4) rather than electrically. Therefore, it doesn't matter whether the computer is on or off— the data will still remain stored on the disk. For this reason, disk devices are referred to as **nonvolatile storage** media, whereas main memory is referred to as a **volatile storage** medium. We describe microcomputer disk devices in the next section.

Storage in main memory is measured in **bytes.** Think of a byte as approximately equal to a character. Therefore, the letter A stored in main memory takes up approximately 1 byte of space. Many of today's microcomputers can store a maximum of 655,360 bytes, or 640 kilobytes (640 K) in main memory. Some can store a maximum of 2,048,000 bytes, or 2 megabytes (2 MB), and others can store a maximum of 16,384,000 bytes, or 16 MB. These upper limits are determined by: (1) the sophistication of the microprocessor in your computer, and (2) the amount of main memory the systems software will recognize.

Why should it matter how much main memory you can use in your computer? The reason is simple. As mentioned earlier, during processing, software instructions and data are stored in main memory. If, for example, you have only 256 K of main memory in your computer, do you think you can use a software program that takes up 320 K of space? The answer, of course, is no. The more main memory you have in your computer, the better. Fortunately, main memory is a physical hardware component (composed of chips) that you can buy in a computer store. If you don't have enough main memory in your computer, you can usually upgrade to 640 K and beyond.

Another processing hardware component you should be familiar with is the **ROM chip.** Stored on the ROM chip are some permanent instructions installed by the computer manufacturer that tell your computer what to do when you turn it on. (Also see Chapter 4 for more detailed information on RAM, ROM, and byte measurement.)

SECONDARY STORAGE HARDWARE: DISKETTES AND HARD DISKS

For microcomputers, the typical nonvolatile secondary storage media are diskettes and hard disks (see Chapter 4). Bytes are also used to measure storage capacity on these devices.

Most of the diskettes in use today are one of two sizes: (1) 5¼ inches and (2) 3½ inches. The 5¼-inch diskette has the following characteristics:

1. This diskette can store between 360 K and 1.2 MB. The broad range of storage capacity is determined by the sophistication of the diskette. Chapter 4 describes in more detail the factors affecting the storage capacity of disk devices.
2. The diskette is covered by a flexible plastic cover. The actual surface of the diskette can be viewed through a hole that is referred to as the *data access area*. Do not touch the surface of the diskette through this hole. Touching the disk surface will very likely damage the data stored on the diskette.

The 3½-inch diskette has the following characteristics:

1. Although this diskette is smaller, it can store more; it stores between 720 K and 1.44 MB. Again, the broad range of storage capacity is determined by the sophistication of the diskette.
2. The 3½-inch diskette is covered by a hard protective case. There is no hole in the protective case through which you can touch the disk. Therefore, the chances of damaging the surface of the diskette are less than when using a 5¼-inch diskette.

Before you proceed, read the information in Figure I.2 about taking proper care of diskettes. Users who don't know how to treat their diskettes will probably lose some of their valuable work!

Many computer manufacturers have switched from configuring their computers with 5¼-inch disk drives to 3½-inch disk drives for the obvious reason that the 3½-inch diskette is superior to the 5¼-inch.

In addition to storing data on diskettes, most users also store their data on hard disks. In fact, most computers in the business environment are configured with one

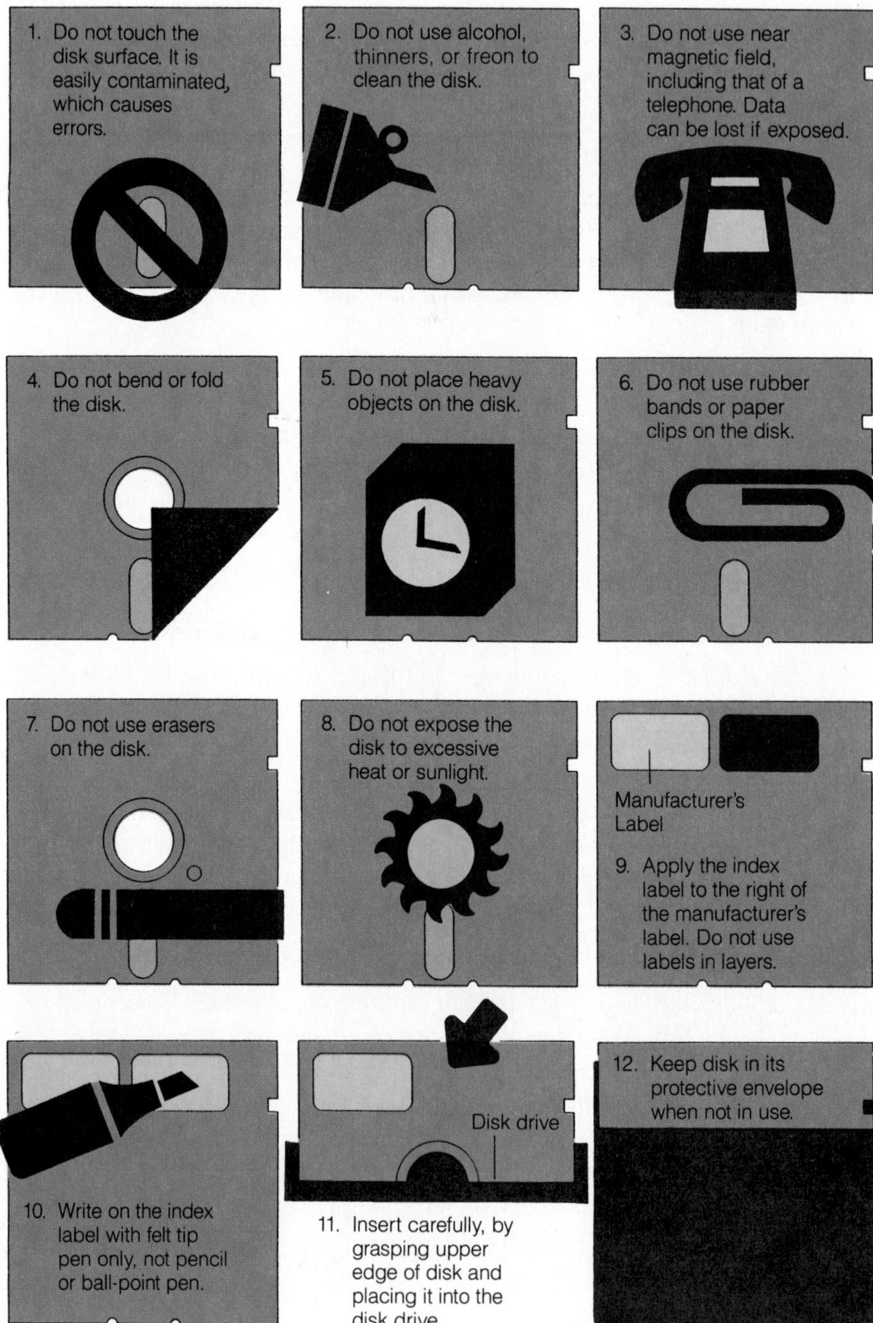
1. Do not touch the disk surface. It is easily contaminated, which causes errors.
2. Do not use alcohol, thinners, or freon to clean the disk.
3. Do not use near magnetic field, including that of a telephone. Data can be lost if exposed.
4. Do not bend or fold the disk.
5. Do not place heavy objects on the disk.
6. Do not use rubber bands or paper clips on the disk.
7. Do not use erasers on the disk.
8. Do not expose the disk to excessive heat or sunlight.
Manufacturer's Label
9. Apply the index label to the right of the manufacturer's label. Do not use labels in layers.
10. Write on the index label with felt tip pen only, not pencil or ball-point pen.
Disk drive
11. Insert carefully, by grasping upper edge of disk and placing it into the disk drive.
12. Keep disk in its protective envelope when not in use.

FIGURE I.2

Handle with care! This illustration shows how to avoid disk damage.

or more diskette drives and a hard disk. Hard disks are substantially superior to diskettes for data storage for the following reasons:

1. They can store much more data. Hard disks typically store between 20 MB to over 300 MB. Therefore, the maximum size of a file that can be stored on a hard disk is much larger than that stored on a diskette.
2. Accessing data doesn't take as long.
3. Hard disks are virtually wear-free. The device for storing and retrieving data from hard disks (the read/write head) is suspended a few millionths of a meter (microns) from the surface of the hard disk. In contrast, a diskette drive's read/write head directly contacts the disk's surface when retrieving or recording data, wearing it out after 25–40 hours of use.

However, hard disks won't take the place of diskettes. First of all, hard disks are much more expensive than diskettes. Hard disks range in price from $100 to well over $1,000. Diskettes range in price from $.50 to $4.00. In addition, once installed, many hard disks aren't meant to be removed from the computer they are in, whereas diskettes are portable. Diskettes enable you to move data from one computer to another. You can even carry a 3½-inch diskette in your pocket.

DISK DRIVE-NAMING CONVENTIONS

Most microcomputers have one of the following disk drive configurations: (1) two diskette drives, (2) one diskette drive and one hard disk, or (3) two diskette drives and one hard disk. (Diskettes and hard disks were described in detail in Chapter 4.) When you are working with applications software and want to save the work you've done, you need to tell the software which disk drive to use to save the work. This is similar in concept to telling someone what drawer to put a folder in. To do this, you must follow certain disk drive-naming conventions.

With DOS (a popular type of systems software that you will learn to use in Module A), the first diskette drive, which is usually located to the left or above the second disk drive (if one is present), is referred to as **drive A.** The second diskette drive is referred to as **drive B.** A hard disk is typically referred to as **drive C** (Figure I.3). When you are using DOS or applications software, the drive letter is always followed by a colon (:) to represent the drive designation—that is, the colon is an essential part of the drive name. For example, when you are using DOS to copy a

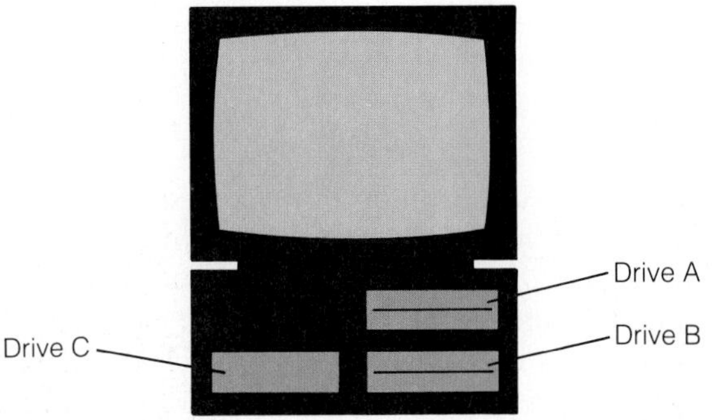

FIGURE I.3

Disk drives. The diskette drives are drives A and B; if you have a hard disk drive, it is drive C.

file from the hard disk to the first diskette drive, your command will include the instruction to copy from C: to A:. The computers you use in your school will have either two diskette drives (drives A and B), one diskette drive and one hard disk (drives A and C), or two diskette drives and one hard disk (drives A, B, and C).

In Modules A–E, we assume you will use either a diskette-based or a hard disk microcomputer system. When the procedures are different for the two types of system, we provide separate instructions; the diskette system instructions are accompanied by a design resembling a diskette, and the hard disk system instructions show a design that looks like a hard disk. The descriptions of these two types are as follows:

- *Diskette system*. This computer configuration consists of two diskette drives. The first diskette drive is referred to as drive A and the second diskette drive is referred to as drive B.
- *Hard disk system*. This computer configuration consists of one or more diskette drives and one hard disk. The first diskette drive is referred to as drive A, the second diskette drive (if one is present) is referred to as drive B, and the hard disk is referred to as drive C.

OUTPUT HARDWARE: MONITORS AND PRINTERS

The typical output hardware components used in a computer system are the video display screen, or monitor, and the printer. (Output hardware was described in Chapter 6.) If your system has a monochrome monitor, it will be turned on when you turn your computer on. However, if you have a color monitor, you typically have to turn the monitor on separately from the computer system unit. In addition, the printer must be turned on separately. Most users turn the system unit on first and then the peripheral devices. For a more detailed description of the different types of monitors and printers used with computers, refer to Chapter 6.

MICROCOMPUTER SOFTWARE OVERVIEW

Chapter 7 described systems and applications software used on mainframe computers, minicomputers, and microcomputers. This section reviews some basic concepts relating to these two types of software that you should be familiar with in order to complete Modules A–E.

SYSTEMS SOFTWARE

Systems software is as important to running your computer as gasoline is to a car. No matter what types of applications software programs you are using, your computer *must* have certain systems software instructions in main memory before it can carry out any applications software instructions.

Think of systems software as a layer that surrounds your computer, and more specifically, the microprocessor (Figure I.4). You "talk," or issue commands, to the systems software and the systems software "talks" to the microprocessor. You can't talk with the microprocessor directly. When you are using applications software, such as word processing or spreadsheet software, you "talk" to the applications software, which talks to the systems software, which in turn talks to the microprocessor. In other words, applications software also needs systems software in order to work with the microprocessor. Because systems software is fundamental to your computer system and must be stored in RAM at all times in order for you to use your computer, you must load it into main memory when you turn on your computer. (You learn how to load DOS, a type of systems software, shortly.)

Applications Software

In Chapter 7, we described the different types of applications software programs typically found in use in business today, including word processing, spreadsheet, and database software. In Modules B–E, you will practice using these types of applications programs. As we mentioned in the preceding section, certain systems software instructions must be present in main memory for your computer to be of use to you. These instructions are loaded into memory when the computer is turned on and act as a layer between you and the microprocessor. Think of an applications software program as another layer surrounding your computer (Figure I.4). When you use word processing software, for example, you "talk" with the word processing software, which talks to the systems software, which talks to the microprocessor. No matter what types of applications software programs you are using, your computer must have certain systems software instructions in main memory before it can carry out any applications software instructions.

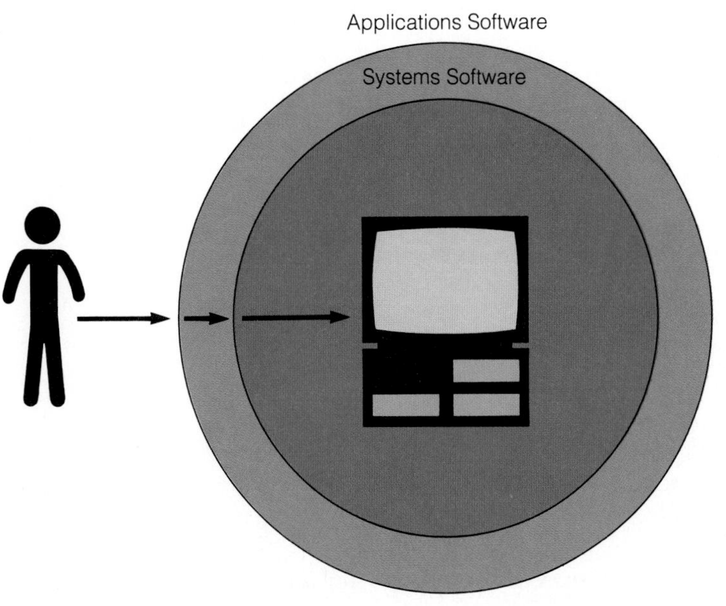

FIGURE I.4

For the user to be able to use applications software, certain systems software instructions must be stored in main memory at all times.

NAMING THE FILES YOU CREATE

When you are using applications software, to save your work (such as a document you have created) into a file stored on a disk, you must tell the program where the data file should be saved (for example, disk drive A:, B:, or C:), and what you want to name the file you wish to save.

To name a file using DOS (the systems software covered in Module A), you must use the following naming conventions.

1. The **filename length** can be between one and eight characters.
2. A file must have a name, but it doesn't have to have a **filename extension** —characters added to the name to aid in file identification.
3. An extension can be between one and three characters.
4. The filename and the extension are separated by a dot (.). Both of the following are valid filenames: BUDGET and BUDGET.JAN ("Jan," in this case, is used to stand for January).
5. If a filename has an extension, you must reference both parts of the name when telling DOS about the file.
6. Not all characters can be used when naming files. The following characters can be used:
   A–Z (upper- or lowercase)
   0–9
   ! @ # $ & ( ) ~ { } ' ' - _
7. Spaces are not allowed in filenames or filename extensions. Often, users designate a space by using an underline. For example, to name a report file and a data file that describe the January budget, you might use the following names: (1) BUD_JAN.RPT and (2) BUD_JAN.DAT.
8. To save a file onto a certain disk, preface the name of the file with the appropriate drive designation. (Make sure not to include any spaces between the drive designation and the name of the file.) For example, to name your work BUDGET and save it onto the diskette in drive A, you would type A:BUDGET when using the SAVE command. It you want to save BUDGET onto the hard disk, you would type C:BUDGET when using the SAVE command.

Figure I.5 shows some valid and invalid filenames.

FIGURE I.5

File-naming conventions. These are some of the valid and invalid filenames that relate to the DOS operating system.

Filename and Extension	Status	Reason
1. QUARTER1	Valid	Contains 8 characters in filename
2. QUARTER1.BUD	Valid	Contains 8 characters in filename and 3 in extension
3. SAMPLEBUD	Invalid	Contains more than 8 characters in the filename
4. QUARTER1.BUD2	Invalid	Contains more than 3 characters in extension
5. A	Valid	Contains 1 character in filename

Filename extensions allow users to distinguish between types of files. For example, you may want to end all your report files with the extension RPT (for "report") and all your data files with the extension DAT (for "data"). Some software programs assign a particular extension to files so that its files can be differentiated from files created by other programs. As an example, Lotus 1-2-3 automatically assigns the extension WK1 to all electronic spreadsheet files. It's important to assign meaningful filenames and filename extensions to your files so you will recognize what the file contains when you see the name a few months later.

LOADING DOS: GIVE IT A BOOT

As we mentioned earlier, for you to be able to use your computer, certain systems software instructions must be stored in main memory (RAM) at all times when the computer is on. To use Modules A–E, you must know how to load MS-DOS/PC-DOS into RAM. (MS-DOS = Microsoft Disk Operating System; PC-DOS = IBM PC Disk Operating System. These two microcomputer operating systems are essentially the same.) To load DOS into your computer, you must turn your computer on, which is often referred to as **booting.** All computers that use DOS go through the following steps (in order) when the computer is turned on, or booted:

1. The computer performs a hardware diagnostic check to make sure the hardware peripherals (keyboard, video display, and so on) are connected properly and the banks of RAM chips (main memory chips) inside the system unit are functioning properly. If you have turned a computer on before, you may have noticed a number counting upward in an upper corner of the screen (not all computers display this number). At that point during the booting process, your computer is checking out the amount of RAM in your computer and whether any bad (unusable) RAM chips exist. A message on the screen will identify any problem that is discovered.
2. Drive A is then checked to see if a diskette containing the DOS system files—that is, COMMAND.COM and two hidden files (IBMBIO.COM and IBMDOS.COM)—is present. You can tell drive A is being checked when the light next to the drive goes on. The light indicates that the read/write heads are clamped down on the diskette. *Note: Never try to remove a diskette when the light is on. You can damage the diskette.* If the disk drive gate for drive A is closed and the DOS system files are present, the instructions in these files will be loaded into RAM. If the disk drive gate is closed but the DOS system files aren't present, a message such as "Non-system disk" or "Missing or bad command interpreter" will appear on the screen. If one of these messages appears (and your intention is to load DOS from the diskette in drive A), (a) replace the current disk in drive A with a DOS disk and then (b) hold the Ctrl and Alt keys down while pressing the Del key once. This will cause your computer to reboot without having to turn it off and then on again. (Turning a computer on and off, because of the resulting changes in temperature, is stressful for a computer system.) This method of booting a computer after it has been turned on is referred to as a **warm boot.**
3. If the computer is a hard disk system and the disk drive gate is left open in step 2, drive C will be checked to see if DOS is stored there. If it is, the

instructions in the DOS system files will be loaded into RAM. Because hard disks usually have the DOS system files stored on them, if you are using a hard disk system, you should always leave the gate open for drive A so that DOS will be loaded from the hard disk. If you leave the gate for drive A closed accidentally, simply open the gate and press any key to load DOS.

To load DOS into RAM, perform the following steps:

FOR DISKETTE SYSTEM USERS

1. Put your DOS diskette in drive A. *Note:* When you put a diskette into a disk drive, use the "rule of thumb." In other words, as shown in Figure I.6, put your thumb on the label and then slide the diskette into the disk drive.
2. Depending on the type of disk you are using, close the disk drive gate or push the disk in the drive until it clicks in place (no gate).
3. Turn the computer on. After DOS has been loaded into RAM, you will be prompted to enter the current date. If an error message appears on the screen instead, try the following before you ask for help:
   a. If you are using 5¼-inch diskettes, check to see that the diskette is seated all the way in the drive. Take the diskette out of the drive and then put it back in.
   b. Perform a warm boot by holding the Ctrl and Alt keys down while pressing the Del key once.
4. Date and time information is stored with a file when you save it. Therefore it is important to keep your computer's clock set with the current date and time. Most systems will prompt you first to type in the current date (Figure I.7) and then the current time when you boot the computer. To prepare for when you save a file during the current work session, type in the date using the following format: MM-DD-YY. For example, if today's date is March 14, 1992, you would type:

FIGURE I.6 Putting a (a) 5¼-inch or (b) 3½-inch diskette in a disk drive.

(a)

(b)

3-14-92. *Note:* If the computer is configured with an internal battery-powered clock, the monitor may already be displaying the current date. If so, simply press the Enter key and proceed with Step 6.

5. After typing in the date:
   PRESS: Enter
   If an error message appears, you typed the date incorrectly. You will be prompted to enter the current date again.
6. You should now be prompted to enter the current time (Figure I.8). Most microcomputers keep track of the current time with the military, or 24-hour, time clock. If the current time is 11:40 in the morning, type 11:40. If it's 2:20 P.M., type 14:20. Type in the current time. *Note:* If the monitor is already displaying the correct current time, simply press the Enter key and proceed with Step 8.
7. After typing in the time:
   PRESS: Enter
   If an error message appears, you typed the time incorrectly. You will be prompted to enter the current time again.
8. The **system prompt**—which designates the disk you booted from—should now be displaying on the screen. It should look like this:
   A> ■

FOR HARD DISK SYSTEM USERS

1. Make sure the disk drive gate for drive A is open and that a diskette isn't clicked in place.
2. Turn the computer on.
3. The computer will look for DOS on the hard disk. Depending on what you see on the screen, perform one of the following two procedures:
   a. If you are prompted to enter the current date, follow Steps 4–7 above (in the

---

```
Current date is Wed 3-14-1992
Enter new date (mm-dd-yy):
```

FIGURE I.7

Date prompt. When you turn your computer on and boot DOS, you will either be prompted to enter the current date or a menu will be displayed.

```
Current date is Wed 3-14-1992
Enter new date (mm-dd-yy):
Current time is 10:11:36.93
Enter new time:
```

FIGURE I.8

Time prompt. If after booting DOS you are prompted to enter the current date, you will then be prompted to enter the current time.

For Diskette System Users section). The system prompt, which looks similar to the following, should now be displaying on the screen:
C>

b. Special instructions are often stored on a hard disk that cause a menu to display after the computer has been turned on. These menus make it easy to start applications software programs because the user can simply choose the option to start a particular program from a menu. If you are viewing a menu, you will need to exit the menu to the system prompt (C>). The menu should include an option for exiting to DOS. If it doesn't, ask your instructor or lab assistant. If a menu is displaying, choose the menu option that exits you to the system prompt. ■

Your computer is now waiting for you to issue a command.

SUMMARY

The computer keyboard will most likely be your principal input hardware component. You will find the following types of keys on the keyboard: (1) standard typewriter keys, (2) function keys, (3) special-purpose keys, (4) cursor-movement keys, and (5) numeric keys.

RAM (random access memory, or main memory) and ROM (read-only memory) are very important processing hardware components. Data and software instructions are stored in RAM during processing. You should configure your computer with the maximum amount of RAM it is capable of supporting; you will then be able to use most microcomputer applications software packages. The ROM chip functions to tell your computer what to do when you turn it on. One of the instructions stored on the ROM chip tells the computer how to locate a copy of DOS in either drive A or drive C.

During processing, your data (for example, a document) is stored in RAM, an electronic state. When you turn your computer off, or cut the electrical current to your computer, you lose the contents of RAM. Therefore, you must save your work onto a nonvolatile magnetic storage medium before you turn your computer off or begin working with a different data file. Diskettes and hard disks are the principal magnetic storage devices used with microcomputers.

The typical output hardware components used in a microcomputer system are the video display screen, or monitor, and the printer.

To use your computer, you must have a copy of certain systems software instructions in main memory (RAM). Without these instructions, your computer and your applications software are useless. Loading these instructions (called *booting*) into main memory is usually accomplished when you turn your computer on.

When you save your work using applications software, you must use certain disk drive-naming conventions to save your work onto the disk of your choice. You also need to know the rules for naming files. In the DOS operating system, a filename can't be longer than eight characters, and an extension can't be longer than three characters. Spaces can't be used in filenames.

KEY TERMS

Alt key, p. 507
booting, p. 517
byte, p. 510
Caps Lock key, p. 508
Ctrl key, p. 507
cursor, p. 509
cursor-movement keys, p. 509
Del key, p. 508
drive A (A:), p. 513
drive B (B:), p. 513
drive C (C:), p. 513
Enter key, p. 509
filename extension, p. 516
filename length, p. 516
function keys, p. 507
Ins key, p. 508
main memory, p. 510
microprocessor, p. 510
nonvolatile storage, p. 510
numeric keypad, p. 510
Num Lock key, p. 510
primary storage, p. 510
programmable keys, p. 507
QWERTY, p. 507
random access memory (RAM), p. 510
ROM chip, p. 511
Shift key, p. 507
system prompt, p. 519
volatile storage, p. 510
warm boot, p. 517

EXERCISES

1. Identify the function keys on your keyboard.
2. What is the main memory (RAM) capacity of the computer you are using?
3. Is the monitor you are using color or monochrome?
4. Is the computer you are using a hard disk system? If so, what is the storage capacity of the hard disk?
5. How many disk drives does the computer system you will be using in your school computer lab have?
6. Boot your computer system so that you can see the DOS system prompt. What does the system prompt look like?
7. What size diskette are you using with your computer system? 3½-inch? 5¼-inch? What is its storage capacity?
8. If you are using a hard disk system, describe what you see when you turn the computer on.
9. If you are using a diskette system (one that doesn't use a hard disk), describe what you see when you turn the computer on.
10. Does your keyboard have a separate numeric keypad and cursor-movement keypad, or are they combined?

Module A

Using DOS

This module helps to put into perspective the importance of operating systems software to your microcomputer system. You must understand how to use some fundamental operating systems commands to effectively manage the files you create and your disk storage devices. This module covers the fundamentals of operating systems software and the use of some important operating systems commands.

Preview

When you have completed this module, you will be able to use MS-DOS/PC-DOS to:

- Format a diskette.
- List, copy, rename, and erase files.
- Check the status of main memory and of a diskette.
- Create and use subdirectories.

Operating Systems Software Fundamentals

In this section, we further define the role of DOS in the microcomputer processing environment. This operating systems software allows you to perform many different file-management tasks (such as listing, erasing, copying, and renaming files) and enables the peripherals (for example, keyboard, monitor, and printer) in your computer system to communicate with one another. No matter what type of applications software you plan to use, you must first become familiar with your operating systems software.

DOS Files

As described in the Introduction to the Modules, to load DOS into your computer, you must turn your computer on. This process is often referred to as **booting** (which is a derivation of *bootstrap loading,* or pulling someone up by the bootstraps). Your computer "looks" in drive A or drive C (depending on whether your computer is configured with a hard disk) for some *special* DOS files. Once found, the instructions in these files are loaded into RAM.

Specifically, your computer looks for a file called **COMMAND.COM** and two hidden files, called **IBMBIO.COM** and **IBMDOS.COM.** These three files are often referred to collectively as the DOS **system files.** Because most of the instructions in these files remain in RAM at all times when your computer is on, these files are referred to as **internal command files,** and the instructions in them are referred to as **internal command instructions.** Most of the instructions in these three files remain in RAM at all times because they are used frequently by DOS and your applications software programs. The instructions in the COMMAND.COM file enable you to perform common disk and file management tasks such as erasing and copying files. The instructions in the IBMBIO.COM file help to manage all the input to and output from the computer. The IBMDOS.COM file contains file-related information that helps DOS keep track of where files have been stored on disk and where to store additional files.

DOS is also composed of other files that are stored on the disk until needed to perform specialized tasks. These files are referred to as **external command files,** and the instructions in them are referred to as **external command instructions.** Because these instructions aren't used often, they aren't loaded into RAM as part of the booting process. If they were loaded into RAM, there might not be enough space available in RAM for your software application instructions and your data. External command files have one of three extensions (COM, EXE, and BAT).

The main difference between internal and external commands is the location of the command instructions. When you use an internal command, DOS finds the command instructions in RAM. When you use an external command, DOS finds the command instructions on the current disk. This module focuses on the internal and external DOS commands that you will find the most useful. Table A.1 lists the DOS commands we describe in this module, as well as the file the command instructions are stored in.

Two additional files, AUTOEXEC.BAT and CONFIG.SYS, are created by the user so that the computer will execute certain commands automatically when your computer boots. The two files must be located on the same disk as the COMMAND.COM file used to boot your computer. The user creates these files and decides what instructions they should contain. (Sometimes the documentation that accompanies your applications software tells you what instructions should be contained in these files and how to get them there.) They can be created using a word processing program or using one of two special DOS commands (COPY CON or EDLIN).

The **AUTOEXEC.BAT** file is used to load certain programs into RAM when the computer is booted. For example, if you want a menu to display automatically on the screen after you turn the computer on or a word processing program to load automatically, you would store the appropriate program load command in an AUTOEXEC.BAT file. The reason many users' computer screens look different after booting is due to the different instructions that were executed in the AUTOEXEC.BAT file when the computer was booted. The **CONFIG.SYS** file, which is also created by the user, stores special configuration information that is required to run certain software applications. For example, to use some database packages, you must have a command stored in this file that designates how many files can be "open," or accessed, at once during processing.

THE CURRENT DISK DRIVE

The **current disk drive,** often referred to as the **default disk drive,** is the drive that DOS will search for files unless you tell DOS otherwise. If you boot DOS from a diskette in drive A, drive A is the current disk drive. Likewise, if you boot DOS from

TABLE A.1 Listing of Commands Described in Module A

Command	File Used	Purpose
DATE	COMMAND.COM	Sets the system date.
TIME	COMMAND.COM	Sets the system time.
VER	COMMAND.COM	Displays the version of DOS being used.
FORMAT	FORMAT.COM	Prepares a disk so it can store data and information.
DIR	COMMAND.COM	Lists the contents of a disk.
COPY CON	COMMAND.COM	Creates a text file.
COPY	COMMAND.COM	Copies files.
RENAME	COMMAND.COM	Renames files.
TYPE	COMMAND.COM	Displays the contents of a file.
ERASE	COMMAND.COM	Erases files.
DEL	COMMAND.COM	Erases files.
CHKDSK	CHKDSK.COM	Checks the status of RAM and disks.
MKDIR (MD)	COMMAND.COM	Makes a subdirectory.
CHDIR (CD)	COMMAND.COM	Changes to another subdirectory and makes it current.
RMDIR (RD)	COMMAND.COM	Removes a subdirectory.
TREE	TREE.COM	Lists subdirectories.

the hard disk, drive C is the current disk drive. DOS will assume that you want all commands to affect the current disk drive unless you specify otherwise. When using DOS, we often make references to the current, or default, disk drive.

Applications software programs make assumptions about what the current disk drive is; this is apparent when you try to save your work. For example, the applications software might assume you want to save your work onto drive C. If you want to save your work onto a different disk, you must specify otherwise by issuing a command.

Operating System Command Hierarchy

In the Introduction to the Modules, you learned how to boot your microcomputer and how to display the system prompt on the screen. Once the system prompt appears, the operating system waits for you to issue a command. DOS does the following when you type a command after the system prompt:

1. Checks to see if you typed an *internal command*. DOS looks in RAM for the instructions. If it finds them, they are executed. If not, DOS proceeds with the next step.
2. Checks to see if you typed a *program load command*. DOS looks on the current disk drive for the external file that corresponds to the command you typed. The command you typed might correspond to either an external DOS command or an applications software command. (For example, if you type TREE after the system prompt, DOS will look on the disk for a file called TREE.COM. Or if you type LOTUS after the system prompt, DOS will look on the disk for a file called LOTUS.COM.) If the file is found, the instructions are loaded into RAM and executed. If not, DOS proceeds with the next step.
3. Checks to see if you typed a *batch file command*. If you did, it is executed. All batch files have an extension of BAT. Batch commands are created by the user to customize a computer system to particular needs and to automate repetitive procedures.
4. If the command you give isn't an internal command, a program load command, or a batch command, an error will appear on the screen and DOS will redisplay the system prompt. At this point, you would try typing the command again. Figure A.1 diagrams the steps the operating system goes through when interpreting commands.

Command Syntax

The operating system software interprets the commands you type on the keyboard and communicates to the computer what you want accomplished. For the operating system software to understand what you want accomplished, your commands must be issued using the correct **syntax.** This can be equated to using correct grammar when speaking or writing. When describing a DOS command, we always provide you with the syntax for the command.

Most of DOS's commands can be used with a number of different options, which are often referred to as command **switches.** These switches are identified with a slash (/). For each command introduced in this module, we also show you the switch that can be used with it.

When you make a mistake typing a command, DOS will display something like "Bad command or filename" and will again display the system prompt. At this point, you can try typing the command again. Although DOS signals any errors you make, it rarely tells you what you did wrong, so to solve complex command problems, you may have to consult your operating system software manual.

ROOT DIRECTORY AND DIRECTORY STRUCTURES

Operating systems software offers the user many useful capabilities, including the capability to create directory structures on a disk storage device. Just as office filing cabinets can become full, so can disk storage devices. What if two different departments are using the same filing cabinet to store business-related documents? Department A and Department B both store accounting, payroll, and inventory-related information in the cabinet. If each department's information is put into the drawer in no particular location or order, it would be difficult for either department to retrieve its information and easy to mix up Department A's and Department B's business information. For this reason, filing cabinets usually contain dividers and subdividers (folders) that store documentation that relates to a common category, such as accounting or payroll.

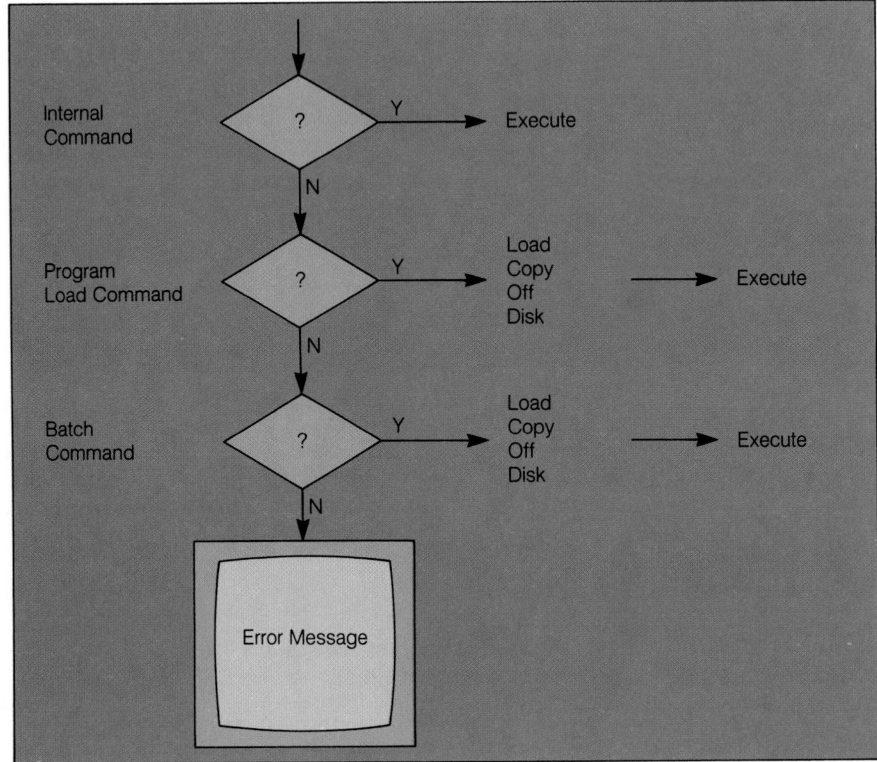

FIGURE A.1

The operating system goes through specific steps when executing commands. If the user tries to issue a command that doesn't fall into any of these categories, an error message will appear on the screen.

When storing files on storage devices that are capable of holding large numbers of files, such as a hard disk, the user must be able to put files that pertain to the same category into the same folder, or subdirectory. A **subdirectory** is a file that contains other files and other subdirectories. The term **directory structure** refers to how a disk is organized into subdirectories.

When you first boot your computer and see the operating system prompt, you are in the **root directory** of your storage device. The root directory is similar in concept to the frame of a file cabinet. Just as file cabinets are composed of drawers that contain folders that in turn contain other folders or files, the root directory can contain subdirectories (drawers) that can contain other subdirectories and other files. In this module, you will use many of the commands necessary to create and maintain a directory structure on a disk. You will be surprised at how easy it is to maintain orderly disk storage.

IN THE LAB

GETTING STARTED WITH DOS

A big problem that new users face when first using operating systems software is how to decide which commands are the most important to master. This tutorial will help you solve this problem by showing you how to use the most common DOS commands. (DOS is the operating system used on many, if not most, of the microcomputers in business today.) The full name of the operating systems software used on your computer will usually reflect the name of the manufacturer of your computer. For example, IBM's version of DOS is called Personal Computer DOS (PC-DOS). Microsoft's version of DOS is called MS-DOS. Compaq Computer's version of DOS is called Compaq DOS, and Digital Research's version of DOS is called Digital Research DOS (DR-DOS). The commands available with each version of DOS are almost identical.

USING THIS TUTORIAL

To make the steps in this module easier to follow, we have adopted the following conventions in the hands-on sections:

1. All characters we want you to type are preceded by the word TYPE (for example, TYPE: copy con). All keys—such as Caps Lock or Enter—are preceded by the word PRESS (for example, PRESS: Enter).
2. When a drive designation appears in a command, such as A:, it will be uppercase. When a filename is included in a command, it will also be uppercase (for example, TEXT1.DOC). All other characters in the command will be lowercase. We've adopted this convention so you can differentiate DOS commands from drive designations and filenames (for example, TYPE: copy con TEXT1.DOC). *Note:* In normal practice, you can type filenames using lowercase.

While you're working through this module, you may decide to take a break and turn your computer system off. After taking a break, to proceed with the tutorial, make sure to (1) boot your system with DOS, (2) display the system prompt, and (3) have your data diskette available.

In the Introduction to the Modules, we described the difference between a diskette system and a hard disk system. For each command described in this tutorial, when necessary, we provide separate instructions for users of diskette systems and hard disk systems. If you aren't sure which instructions to follow, ask your instructor.

NOTE You must have a new data diskette to work through this tutorial. Make sure your data diskette doesn't have any data on it because you will be erasing it in the formatting section. If you don't know what type of diskette to purchase, ask your instructor or lab assistant.

USING DOS COMMANDS

As we described earlier, you issue DOS commands by typing them in after the system prompt, using either upper- or lowercase letters. You must type them in according to specific rules, which are referred to as the *command syntax*. If you type a command incorrectly, a message such as "Bad command or filename" will display on the screen, and the system prompt will reappear. Simply retype the command correctly after the system prompt.

DATE AND TIME COMMANDS

In the Introduction to the Modules, we explained that when you save a file, the current date and time are saved along with the file. This information helps you to identify a file at a later date and determine when it was last modified. Also, we explained that if your computer prompts you to type the current date and time when you boot the computer, you should type them in. Some computers are configured with a battery-powered internal clock that keeps track of the current date and time automatically. In this case, you don't have to type in the current date and time. Some other computers don't prompt you to type the current date and time when you boot your computer. If this is the case with the computer you are using, and if your computer isn't configured with an internal clock (ask your instructor or lab assistant), then you will need to use the DATE and TIME commands. Figure A.2 displays the syntax for the DATE and TIME commands.

To set the current date:

1. The system prompt (A> or C>) should be displaying on the screen.
2. TYPE: date
   PRESS: Enter

FIGURE A.2

Syntax of the DATE and TIME commands. These commands enable you to update your computer with the current date and time.

DATE and TIME syntax

```
date
time
```

3. The date should be displaying on the screen. If this date is the current date, then press Enter. Otherwise, type in the current date using the following format: MM-DD-YY. Once you have typed in the correct date, press Enter.

   To set the current time:

1. The system prompt should again be displaying on the screen.
2. TYPE: time
   PRESS: Enter
3. As described in the Introduction to the Modules, many computers keep track of the current time using the military time clock. If it's 10:15 in the morning, type 10:15. If it is 1:20 in the afternoon, type 13:20. If the current time is already displaying, press Enter.

Once you have typed in the current date and time, press Enter.

VER COMMAND

The **VER** command allows you to easily determine what version of DOS you are using. Before purchasing a software application, you must make sure it is compatible with the version of DOS being used on your computer. To see what version of DOS you are using, perform the following steps:

1. The system prompt should be displaying on the screen.
2. TYPE: ver
   PRESS: Enter

You should now see on the screen information relating to the name and the version of DOS you are using. Figure A.3 displays the syntax for the VER command.

FORMAT COMMAND

Because it prepares new disks so they can store data, the **FORMAT** command is probably the most important DOS command. Since most new disks are packaged unformatted, they must be *formatted* so they can store data. This process, which is also referred to as *initializing*, serves to put a kind of "table of contents" on a disk into which files are organized.

CAUTION If you format a disk that already contains data, all the data will be erased. For this reason, the FORMAT command shouldn't be accessible (on a disk) to the casual user who might accidentally format the hard disk and lose millions of

VER command syntax

```
ver
```

FIGURE A.3

Syntax of the VER command. This command tells you what version of DOS you are using.

characters of data. For the most part, unless you have purchased a hard disk for your own computer, the FORMAT command should be used only on diskettes.

The FORMAT command is an external command. When you use it, the computer looks on the disk in the current drive — in your case, the disk you loaded DOS from — for a file called FORMAT.COM. *If DOS's external files aren't located on the current drive, the FORMAT command won't work*. Specifically, the FORMAT command does the following:

1. Writes a test pattern onto the disk.
2. Reads the test pattern back to see if there are any problems with the disk.
3. Places an organization scheme (or table of contents) on the disk on which you can store data. This scheme prevents you from storing data in "bad" (that is, malfunctioning) areas on the disk.
4. Displays information relating to how many bytes "should" be able to be stored on the diskette (bytes of total disk space) and how many bytes are actually available (bytes available on disk). Right after formatting, the two numbers should be identical. If they aren't, the disk contains some bad spots — just like a scratch on a record. Fortunately, DOS won't allow you to store data in a bad spot. During diskette formatting, bad spots sometimes result from a speck of dust on the disk. Formatting the disk again will sometimes get rid of the bad spots, making the total disk space and the bytes-available numbers the same.
5. Displays a message asking if you want to format another diskette. If you want to format another, you would type Y (for Yes) at this point and then press Enter. The FORMAT command would then prompt you to insert another new diskette into the disk drive and then repeat the formatting process. If you don't want to format another, type N (for No) and then press Enter. At this point, the system prompt will display on the screen.

Figure A.4 displays the syntax of the FORMAT command. The following steps lead you through formatting your data diskette.

FOR DISKETTE SYSTEM USERS

1. Make sure the DOS diskette is in drive A.
2. Place the data diskette in drive B.
3. The system prompt (A>) should be displaying on the screen.
   TYPE: format B:
   PRESS: Enter

(continued)

FIGURE A.4

Syntax of the FORMAT command. Remember to tell the format program the location of the disk you want formatted.

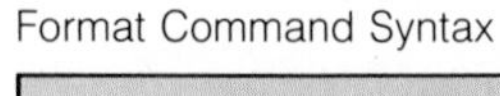

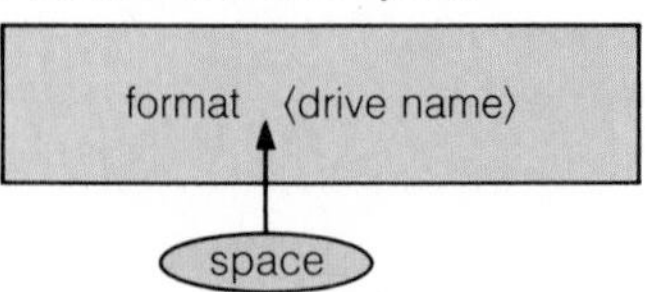

4. Your computer should be prompting you to insert a new diskette in drive B. Since you have already done this:
   PRESS: Enter
5. The light for drive B should be on. When the light goes off and a message queries if you want to format another diskette:
   TYPE: n
   PRESS: Enter
6. The system prompt should be displaying on the screen. ■

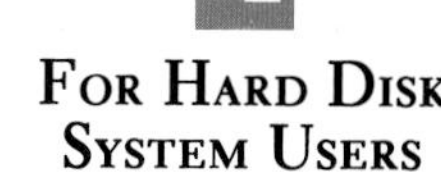

FOR HARD DISK SYSTEM USERS

1. It is likely that DOS's external files are stored in a subdirectory on the hard disk. To make the DOS subdirectory current (we describe subdirectories later in this module), you need to use the CHANGE DIRECTORY (CD) command. For example, if the subdirectory is named DOS, you would type CD\DOS. If you don't know the name of the subdirectory, ask your instructor or lab assistant.
2. Place the data diskette in drive A.
3. The system prompt (C>) should be displaying on the screen.
   TYPE: format A:
   PRESS: Enter
4. Your computer should be prompting you to insert a new diskette in drive A. Since you have already done this:
   PRESS: Enter
5. The disk drive light for drive A should be on. When the light goes off and you are queried if you want to format another diskette:
   TYPE: n
   PRESS: Enter
6. The system prompt should be displaying on the screen. ■

Your data diskette is now ready to store data.

DIR COMMAND

Probably the most widely used command, **DIR** (DIRECTORY) allows you to see what files are stored on a disk and gives you descriptive information about each file (Figure A.5). For every file listed on the screen, the following information is displayed: (1) the filename, (2) the filename extension, (3) the size of the file in

---

COMMAND	COM	23210	3-07-92	1:43p
filename	extension	size in bytes	date created or last changed	time created or last changed

FIGURE A.5

Typical directory listing. The DIRECTORY command shows you what files you have on your disk, the size of each file, and the date and time that the file was created or last changed.

bytes, (4) the date the file was created or last changed, and (5) the time the file was created or last changed. Using the DIR command is like looking in a file drawer to see what folders are stored there. Figure A.6 displays the syntax of the DIRECTORY command. The following steps lead you through using it.

DIR: ALL FILES

The current disk drive for diskette users is drive A; for hard disk system users, the current drive is drive C.

To display information about the files stored on the current disk:
TYPE: dir
PRESS: Enter
A list of all files on the current disk should have scrolled quickly up the screen—too quickly. Shortly, you will learn how to slow down the screen's scroll. Note that, at the bottom of the directory listing, a message is displayed relating to the number of bytes free, or still available, on the disk.

DIR/p: PAUSE

The **DIR/p** command allows you to list all the files stored on the current disk drive using the PAUSE switch (/p). This option causes the screen to pause when it becomes full. Pressing any key will cause the screen to continue its scroll.

1. To display the names of the files on the current disk using the PAUSE switch:
   TYPE: dir/p
   PRESS: Enter
   If you have many files on your disk, the screen should be full of information and a message saying "Press any key when ready" should display at the bottom of the screen.
2. To continue the screen's scroll, press any key.

DIR/w: WIDE

The **DIR/w** command allows you to list all the files stored on the current disk drive using the WIDE switch (/w). This option causes the computer to list all the files on the disk across the width of the screen. With this switch, only filename and filename extension information is displayed.

To display the names of the files on the current disk using the WIDE switch:
TYPE: dir/w
PRESS: Enter
The files should be listed across the width of the screen (Figure A.7).

FIGURE A.6

Syntax of the DIRECTORY command. You have the option of seeing the listing one screenful at a time (/p) or in a wide display (/w).

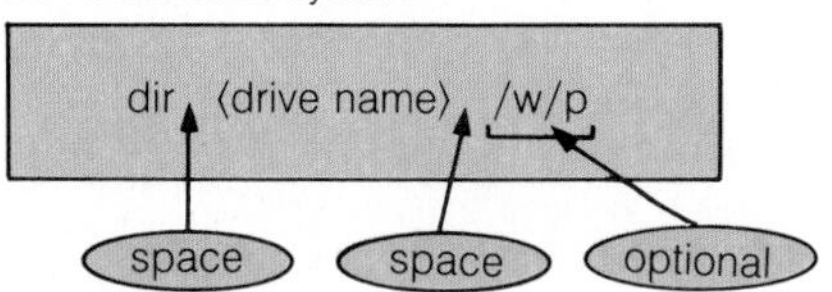

DIR [drive name]

To display the files on a drive other than the current drive, the following procedure is used:

For Diskette System Users

To see if any files are stored on the data diskette in drive B:
TYPE: dir B:
PRESS: Enter
Since the data diskette in drive B has just recently been formatted, it doesn't contain any files. The screen should look similar to Figure A.8. The message "File not found" should be displaying. In addition, you should see a message saying "Volume in drive B has no label." This message simply indicates that you didn't give the diskette an internal label when you formatted it. (The /v switch enables you to label diskettes internally when you format them.) ■

Directory listing using the wide display (/w) option.

FIGURE A.7

```
C>dir/w

 Volume in drive C has no label
 Directory of  C:\DOS

.                .                APPEND   EXE    ASSIGN   COM    ATTRIB   EXE
BACKUP   COM     CHKDSK   COM     COMMAND  COM    COMP     COM    DEBUG    COM
DISKCOMP COM     DISKCOPY COM     EDLIN    COM    EXE2BIN  EXE    FIND     EXE
FORMAT   COM     GRAFTABL COM     GRAPHICS COM    JOIN     EXE    LABEL    COM
LINK     EXE     MORE     COM     PRINT    COM    RECOVER  COM    RESTORE  COM
SHARE    EXE     SORT     EXE     SUBST    EXE    TREE     COM    XCOPY    EXE
WORDS            BASIC    COM     BASICA   COM    BASICA   EXE    NLSFUNC  EXE
REPLACE  EXE     SELECT   COM     SETCLOCK COM    INTEREST BAS    4201     CPI
5202     CPI     EGA      CPI
       42 File(s)   4210688 bytes free

C>
```

```
C>dir A:

 Volume in drive A has no label
 Directory of  A:\

File not found

C>
```

FIGURE A.8

Directory listing of a newly formatted data disk. Since the diskette was just formatted, no files exist on it.

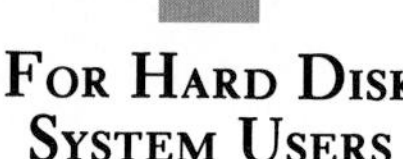

FOR HARD DISK SYSTEM USERS

To see if any files are stored on the data diskette in drive A:
TYPE: dir A:
PRESS: Enter
Since the data diskette in drive A has just recently been formatted, it doesn't contain any files. The screen should look similar to Figure A.8. The message "File not found" should be displaying. In addition, you should see a message saying "Volume in drive B has no label." This message simply indicates that you didn't give the diskette an internal label when you formatted it. (The /V switch enables you to label diskettes internally when you format them.) ■

DIR [WILDCARD CHARACTER]

What if you want to see a list of a group of files stored on a disk? When a disk becomes cluttered with files, you might, for example, want to list only the files that you created with a certain applications program or that relate to a common task (such as a budget you are working on). With what you know now, you can only list *all* the files stored on a disk. DOS's **global, or wildcard, characters**—the asterisk (*) and the question mark (?)—allow you to list selected files on the screen. You can think of these characters as the jokers in a deck of cards. They represent whatever you want them to. The * can be used to represent more than one character, whereas the ? is used to represent one character. Figure A.9 provides additional examples of using the DIR command with these wildcard characters. As you will learn shortly, wildcard characters are especially useful when you are copying files.

1. To list only those files that have an extension of EXE that are stored on the current disk (drive A for diskette users and drive C for hard disk system users):
   TYPE: dir *.EXE
   With this command you are instructing DOS to do the following: "List on the

FIGURE A.9

Examples of using the DIRECTORY (DIR) command.

Command	Purpose
DIR	List the contents of the current disk.
DIR/p	List the contents of the current disk using the PAUSE switch. When the screen becomes full, press any key to view the rest of the directory listing.
DIR/w	List the contents of the current disk using the WIDE switch. Filenames and filename extensions are listed across the width of the screen.
DIR A:	List the contents of the disk in drive A.
DIR B:/w	List the contents of the disk in drive B using the WIDE switch.
DIR *.EXE	List all the files on the current disk that have an extension of EXE.
DIR A:T*.*	List all the files on the diskette in drive A that begin with T.
DIR B:*.DOC	List all the files on the diskette in drive B that have an extension of DOC.

screen all the files that have an extension of EXE. I don't care what the filename is."
PRESS: Enter
If you have files stored on the current disk that have an extension of EXE, they should be listed on the screen now (Figure A.10). If you don't have any such files, you should see the message "File not found."

2. To list all the files on the current disk that begin with the letter C, perform the following steps:
TYPE: dir C*.*
With this command you are instructing DOS to do the following: "List on the screen all the files that begin with the letter C. I don't care what the rest of the filename is or what the filename extension is."
PRESS: Enter
If you don't have any such files, you should see the message "File not found."

CHANGING THE CURRENT DISK DRIVE

Often you will find that you need to issue a series of commands on a drive other than the current one, which would require that you keep specifying the drive designation (A: or B:) in your commands. So you won't have to type in the drive designation each time you issue a series of commands on another disk, DOS lets you change the current drive. You will find more uses for this command in the next section and as you proceed with this module.

```
C>dir *.EXE

 Volume in drive C has no label
 Directory of  C:\DOS

APPEND    EXE     5794   5-27-88  12:00p
ATTRIB    EXE    10656   5-27-88  12:00p
EXE2BIN   EXE     3050   5-27-88  12:00p
FIND      EXE     6403   5-27-88  12:00p
JOIN      EXE     9612   5-27-88  12:00p
LINK      EXE    39076   5-27-88  12:00p
SHARE     EXE     8664   5-27-88  12:00p
SORT      EXE     1946   5-27-88  12:00p
SUBST     EXE    10552   5-27-88  12:00p
XCOPY     EXE    11216   5-27-88  12:00p
BASICA    EXE    79304   5-27-88  12:00p
NLSFUNC   EXE     3029   5-27-88  12:00p
REPLACE   EXE    13886   5-27-88  12:00p
       13 File(s)   4210688 bytes free

C>
```

FIGURE A.10

Directory listing of all the files that have the extension EXE (*.EXE).

FOR DISKETTE SYSTEM USERS

1. The data diskette should be in drive B.
2. TYPE: B:
   PRESS: Enter
   The system prompt should now indicate that drive B is current.
3. To change the current disk drive back to drive A:
   TYPE: A:
   PRESS: Enter ■

FOR HARD DISK SYSTEM USERS

1. The data diskette should be in drive A.
2. TYPE: A:
   PRESS: Enter
   The system prompt should now indicate that drive A is current.
3. To change the current disk drive back to drive C:
   TYPE: C:
   PRESS: Enter ■

GETTING READY TO PRACTICE MORE DOS COMMANDS: COPY CON COMMAND

To practice some more DOS commands, such as the COPY, RENAME, and ERASE commands, you need to have files to work with. Therefore, we are going to lead you through a procedure for creating a very short text file using the **COPY CON** command. CON is the name DOS gives to the keyboard. With the COPY CON command, you can copy your keyboard input into a file. Once you have created a file, you will make copies of it using DOS's COPY command so that you will have more than one file to work with.

Because you will issue a series of commands on the drive that contains your data diskette, you will first change the current disk drive. Then you will instruct DOS to open up a new file on your data disk so that you can key something into it.

FOR DISKETTE SYSTEM USERS

In the following steps, you will change the current drive to the drive that contains your data diskette:

1. Make sure the data diskette is in drive B.
2. If you didn't change the current drive to drive B in the last section:
   TYPE: B:
   PRESS: Enter
   Drive B is now the current drive. ■

FOR HARD DISK SYSTEM USERS

In the following steps you will change the current drive to the drive that contains your data diskette:

1. Make sure the data diskette is in drive A.
2. If you didn't change the current drive to drive A in the last section:
   TYPE: A:
   PRESS: Enter
   Drive A is now the current drive. ■

To create a file named TEXT1.DOC on your data diskette:

1. TYPE: copy con TEXT1.DOC
   PRESS: Enter
   The cursor should be blinking at the left side of the screen. DOS is waiting to accept your keyboard input.
2. TYPE: This is a sample text file for my DOS exercise.
   PRESS: Enter
3. To enter the save code into this text file:
   PRESS: F6
   You should now see ^Z on the screen. The ^ symbol indicates that the Ctrl key was pressed.
4. To save the text file:
   PRESS: Enter
   The message "1 file(s) copied" should be displaying above the system prompt. You have just created a file called TEXT1.DOC on the data diskette.
5. Just to check that the file is on the data diskette:
   TYPE: dir
   PRESS: Enter
   Your screen should look similar to Figure A.11.

COPY COMMAND

Smart users make frequent copies of the data files they work with. The reason is that if the original data file is damaged, all is not lost—a backup copy of the original file can be retrieved to work with. The **COPY** command, an internal command, allows you to make copies of files onto the same disk (but under different names) or onto another disk. Figure A.12 shows the syntax of the COPY command. Figure A.13 provides examples of the COPY command.

```
C>A:

A>copy con TEXT1.DOC
This is a sample text file for my DOS exercise.
^Z
        1 File(s) copied

A>dir

 Volume in drive A has no label
 Directory of  A:\

TEXT1    DOC        49   3-25-92   8:09a
        1 File(s)   1457152 bytes free

A>
```

FIGURE A.11

New directory listing. Your data diskette should have only one file on it now called TEXT1.DOC.

TO COPY A FILE ONTO THE SAME DISK

The following steps will lead you through making five copies of the file you created earlier on the data diskette called TEXT1.DOC. The copies will be made onto the data diskette. *Because you will copy onto the same disk, you must give the copies different names.* To copy the file onto the data diskette under the names TEXT2.DOC, TEXT3.DOC, REPORT.JAN, REPORT.FEB, and REPORT.MAR, follow the steps listed below:

1. Drive B should be the current drive for diskette system users, and drive A should be the current drive for hard disk system users.
2. TYPE: copy TEXT1.DOC TEXT2.DOC
   PRESS: Enter
   A copy of TEXT1.DOC is now stored on the data disk under the name TEXT2.DOC.
3. To see that the copy was made:
   TYPE: dir
   PRESS: Enter
4. TYPE: copy TEXT1.DOC TEXT3.DOC
   PRESS: Enter

FIGURE A.12

Syntax of the COPY command.

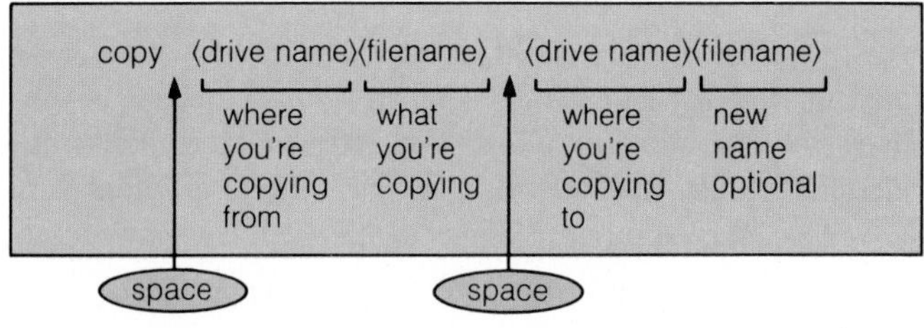

FIGURE A.13

Examples of using the COPY command.

Command	Purpose
COPY TEXT1.DOC BUDGET	Copy the file named TEXT1.DOC that is stored on the current disk onto the same disk; the copy is given the name BUDGET
COPY C:DATA A:	Copy the file named DATA from the hard disk onto the diskette in drive A; the copy is given the name DATA
COPY A:*.WK1 B:	Copy all the files stored on the diskette in drive A that have an extension of WK1 onto the diskette in drive B
COPY C:C*.* A:	Copy all the files stored on the hard disk that begin with C onto the diskette in drive A
COPY REPORT.MAR B:	Copy the file named REPORT.MAR from the current disk onto the diskette in drive B

A copy of TEXT1.DOC is now stored on the data disk under the name TEXT3.DOC.

5. TYPE: copy TEXT1.DOC REPORT.JAN
   PRESS: Enter
   A copy of TEXT1.DOC is now stored on the data disk under the name REPORT.JAN.
6. TYPE: copy TEXT1.DOC REPORT.FEB
   PRESS: Enter
   A copy of TEXT1.DOC is now stored on the data disk under the name REPORT.FEB.
7. TYPE: copy TEXT1.DOC REPORT.MAR
   PRESS: Enter
   A copy of TEXT1.DOC is now stored on the data disk under the name REPORT.MAR.
8. To determine that the copies have indeed been made:
   TYPE: dir
   PRESS: Enter
   The listing should look like Figure A.14.

TO COPY A FILE ONTO A DIFFERENT DISK

You should now be relatively comfortable with copying a file onto the same disk and giving the copy a different name. Another task that is performed more often with the COPY command is to copy a file onto a different disk. In this case, the user has the option of giving the copy another name or keeping the same name.

When copying from one diskette to another, check first to see if you have a file with the same name on both disks. For example, what if you have a file named EMPLOYEES on the diskette in drive A and a file named EMPLOYEES on the diskette in drive B? Although the names of the files are the same, their contents are different. If you copy EMPLOYEES from drive A to drive B, the contents of the EMPLOYEES file on the diskette in drive A will replace the contents of the

```
A>dir

 Volume in drive A has no label
 Directory of  A:\

TEXT1     DOC        49   3-25-92   8:09a
TEXT2     DOC        49   3-25-92   8:09a
TEXT3     DOC        49   3-25-92   8:09a
REPORT    JAN        49   3-25-92   8:09a
REPORT    FEB        49   3-25-92   8:09a
REPORT    MAR        49   3-25-92   8:09a
        6 File(s)    1454592 bytes free

A>
```

FIGURE A.14

Directory listing. Your data disk should now have six files on it. They should all contain the same number of bytes.

EMPLOYEES file on the diskette in drive B, and you will have lost the contents of the file in drive B. Figure A.15 illustrates this concept.

> **CAUTION** If you have a file with the same name on the disk you're copying from and the disk you're copying to, the file you are copying will erase the file on the target disk because they both have the same name. If you are updating a backup file, this may be your intention. However, if it isn't, you will want to rename one of the files before you use the COPY command.

RENAME COMMAND

The **RENAME** command, an internal command, allows you to change the name of a file stored on a disk. Renaming a file might be useful when you have two files (with different contents) with the same name stored on different diskettes. As described above, if you want to copy one of these files from one disk to the other, the

FIGURE A.15

Copying files. If you have two files with the same names on different disks and copy the file on one disk (A:) to the second disk (B:), the contents of the second file will be replaced with the contents of the first file. To avoid losing the contents of the second file, rename the file before copying from disk to disk.

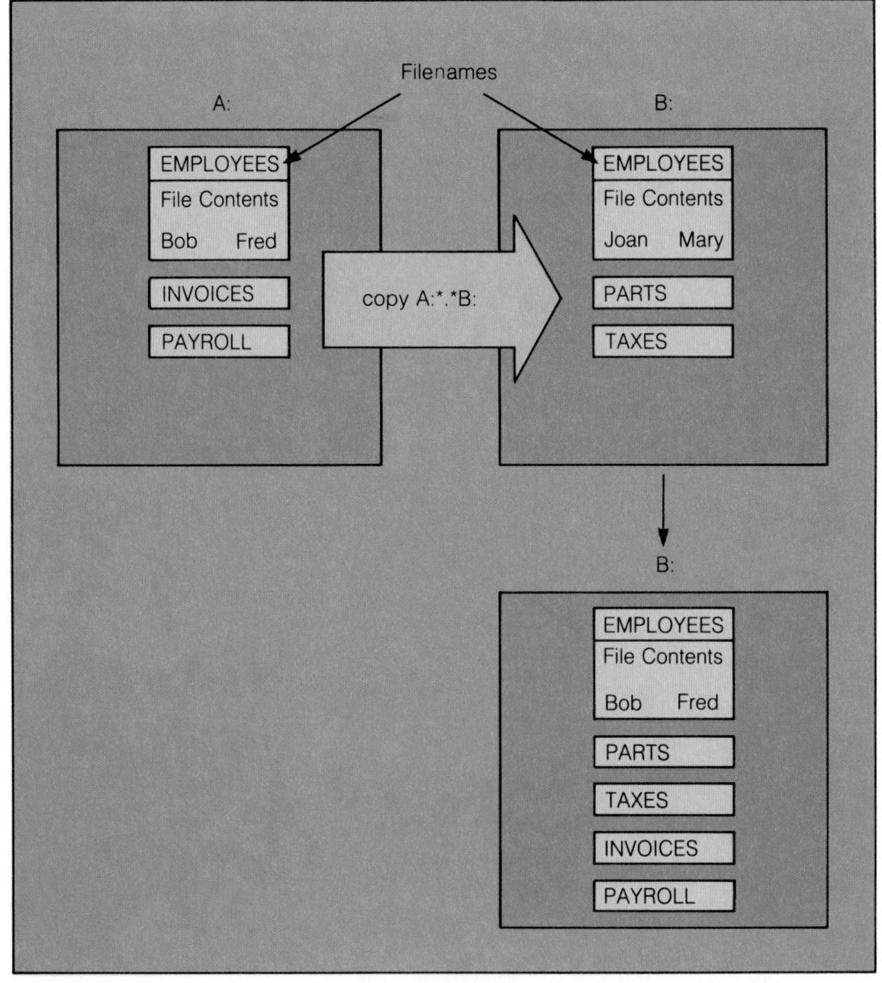

first file will erase the contents of the second file if both files have the same name. If your intent isn't to overwrite the second file, rename the file you are copying before you issue the COPY command. Figure A.16 displays the syntax for using the RENAME command.

In the following steps you will rename the TEXT1.DOC file stored on your data diskette SAMPLE1.DOC.

FOR DISKETTE SYSTEM USERS

1. The data diskette should be in drive B. Drive B should be the current disk drive. If it isn't:
   TYPE: B:
   PRESS: Enter
2. TYPE: rename TEXT1.DOC SAMPLE1.DOC
   PRESS: Enter
3. To determine if the name was actually changed:
   TYPE: dir
   PRESS: Enter
   You should see that one of the files stored on your data disk is called SAMPLE1.DOC and that there is no longer a file named TEXT1.DOC (Figure A.17). ■

RENAME command syntax

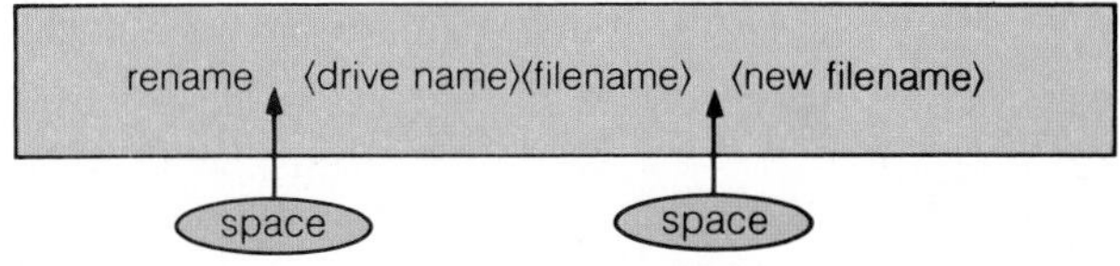

FIGURE A.16

Syntax of the RENAME command. Specify the disk drive where the file you want to rename is located, the name of the file you want to rename, and the new filename.

```
A>rename  TEXT1.DOC  SAMPLE1.DOC

A>dir

 Volume in drive A has no label
 Directory of  A:\

SAMPLE1  DOC        49   3-25-92    8:09a
TEXT2    DOC        49   3-25-92    8:09a
TEXT3    DOC        49   3-25-92    8:09a
REPORT   JAN        49   3-25-92    8:09a
REPORT   FEB        49   3-25-92    8:09a
REPORT   MAR        49   3-25-92    8:09a
        6 File(s)   1454592 bytes free

A>
```

FIGURE A.17

Directory listing after TEXT1.DOC was renamed SAMPLE1.DOC.

FOR HARD DISK SYSTEM USERS

1. The data diskette should be in drive A. Drive A should be the current disk drive. If it isn't:
   TYPE: A:
   PRESS: Enter
2. TYPE: rename TEXT1.DOC SAMPLE1.DOC
   PRESS: Enter
3. To determine if the name was actually changed:
   TYPE: dir
   PRESS: Enter
   You should see that one of the files stored on your data disk is called SAMPLE1.DOC and that there is no longer a file named TEXT1.DOC (Figure A.17). ■

In the preceding commands, if the DOS disk is the current disk, you would have to specify the drive designation before the old filename. For example, if drive A is the current disk drive and you want to rename a file stored on the diskette in drive B, you would type the following:

rename B:TEXT1.DOC SAMPLE1.DOC

A drive designation before the new name (SAMPLE1.DOC) will cause an error because the RENAME command won't allow you to put a renamed file on a different disk. To rename a file and copy it to another disk, use the COPY command.

TYPE COMMAND

The **TYPE** command, an internal command, is especially helpful when you can't remember what the contents of a file are, because it allows you to "take a peek" at the file without having to actually retrieve it using an applications software program. When the TYPE command is used, the contents of the file quickly scroll up the screen. Text files (containing standard keyboard characters) appear in a legible format; however, other files may appear unreadable because of nonstandard characters. Figure A.18 displays the syntax of the TYPE command.

The steps that follow show you how to type the contents of a file that contains text and one that doesn't.

FOR DISKETTE SYSTEM USERS

1. To type the contents of the text file named TEXT2.DOC that is stored on the data diskette:
   TYPE: type B:TEXT2.DOC *(continued)*

FIGURE A.18

Syntax of the TYPE command. Specify the disk drive where the file is located and the filename.

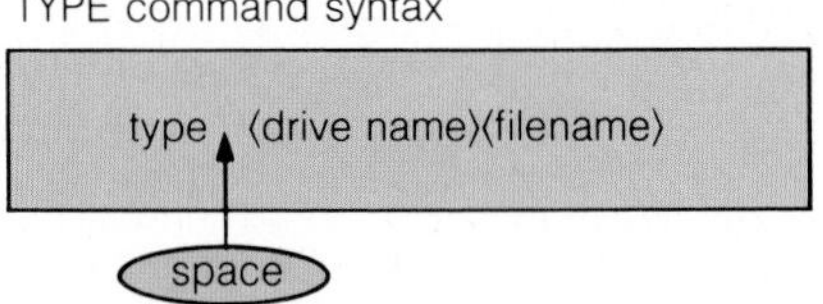

PRESS: Enter
The contents of the TEXT2.DOC file should be displaying on the screen (Figure A.19).

2. To type the contents of a nontext file named COMMAND.COM that should be stored on the disk in drive A:
   TYPE: type A:COMMAND.COM
   PRESS: Enter
   You should see some very strange-looking characters on the screen. Although we can't make any sense of those characters, the computer knows exactly what they mean. ■

FOR HARD DISK SYSTEM USERS

1. To type the contents of the text file named TEXT2.DOC that is stored on the data diskette:
   TYPE: type A:TEXT2.DOC
   PRESS: Enter
   The contents of the TEXT2.DOC file should be displaying on the screen (Figure A.19).
2. To type the contents of a nontext file named COMMAND.COM that should be stored on the disk in drive C:
   TYPE: type C:COMMAND.COM
   PRESS: Enter
   You should see some very strange-looking characters on the screen. Although we can't make any sense of those characters, the computer knows exactly what they mean. ■

ERASE COMMAND

Just as it's sometimes necessary to unclutter your desk and discard notes and papers, it's occasionally necessary to discard old files stored on your data disks. The **ERASE,** or **DEL,** command, an internal command, is used for this purpose. Figure A.20 shows the syntax of the ERASE command. Figure A.21 provides examples of using the ERASE command.

CAUTION Be sure to make current the disk drive containing the file(s) you want to erase. Then you won't accidentally erase files off the wrong disk.

To erase the file named REPORT.MAR from the data diskette, perform the following steps:

1. The disk drive containing the data diskette should be the current drive (drive B

```
C>type A:TEXT2.DOC
This is a sample text file for my DOS exercise.

C>
```

FIGURE A.19

Using the TYPE command to display the contents of the TEXT2.DOC file.

for diskette users and drive A for hard disk users). If not, change the current disk drive to the one that contains your data diskette.

2. TYPE: erase REPORT.MAR
   PRESS: Enter
   Although DOS didn't display a message indicating that the file is erased, if you see the system prompt again on the screen, the file should be gone. Although DOS rarely tells you when you've done something correctly, it usually tells you when you've done something wrong.
3. To confirm that the file named REPORT.MAR no longer exists on the data diskette:
   TYPE: dir
   PRESS: Enter
   The REPORT.MAR filename shouldn't be displaying on the screen.

CAUTION Be careful with wildcard characters when erasing files. You might reference—and thus, erase—a file you actually want to keep. If you want to use a wildcard character in the ERASE command, first use the DIR command to list on the screen the files you will erase. Once you have erased a file, there is only a very small chance that you will get it back (some special utility programs are available that enable you to restore lost files).

CHKDSK COMMAND

The **CHKDSK** command, an external command, is used to analyze the directories on a disk to make sure all files have been recorded correctly. This command also gives the user information about the amount of memory available for use, as well as

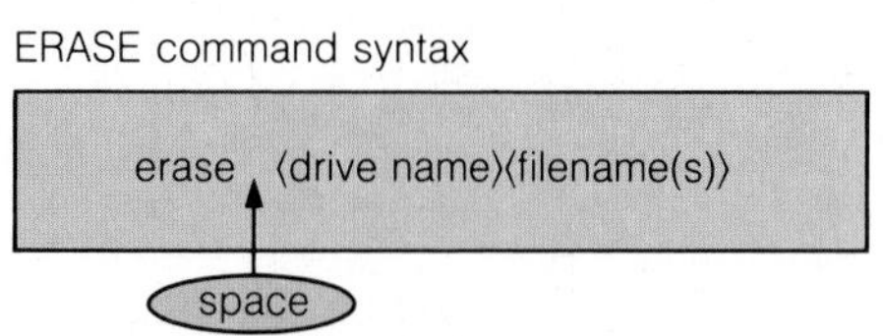

FIGURE A.20

Syntax of the ERASE command. Specify which disk drive contains the file(s) you want to erase and the filename(s).

FIGURE A.21

Examples of using the ERASE command.

Command	Purpose
ERASE BUDGET	Erase BUDGET from the current diskette.
ERASE B:BUDGET	Erase BUDGET from the diskette in drive B.
ERASE A:*.WK1	Erase all the files with an extension of WK1 from the diskette in drive A.
ERASE A:W*.*	Erase all the files that begin with the letter W from the diskette in drive A.

the amount of storage space available on disk. When you work with large files and software products, periodically check the status of RAM and disk storage space. Figure A.22 displays the syntax of the CHKDSK command.

FOR DISKETTE SYSTEM USERS

1. Make drive A the current disk drive.
2. To determine how much RAM is in your computer and the status of the diskette in drive B:
   TYPE: chkdsk B:
   PRESS: Enter
   Your screen should provide information similar to that displayed in Figure A.23. ■

FOR HARD DISK SYSTEM USERS

1. Make drive C the current disk drive.
2. To determine how much RAM is in your computer and the status of the diskette in drive A:
   TYPE: chkdsk A:
   PRESS: Enter
   Your screen should provide information similar to that displayed in Figure A.23. ■

CREATING DIRECTORY STRUCTURES WITH DOS

The following sections will teach you how to use some special DOS commands to create and use subdirectories on a hard disk. (We described what subdirectories are in the Operating Systems Software Fundamentals section at the beginning of this

CHKDSK command syntax

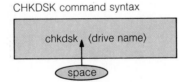

```
chkdsk (drive name)
      ^
    space
```

FIGURE A.22

Syntax of the CHKDSK command. When using the CHKDSK command, if you want to check the status of a disk drive other than the current drive, you must specify it in the command.

```
362496 bytes total disk space
  6144 bytes in 6 user files
356352 bytes available on disk

655360 bytes total memory
597840 bytes free
```

FIGURE A.23

Output of the CHKDSK command. The first three lines of the display describe the characteristics of your disk device, and the last two lines refer to main memory.

module.) The directory structure you create will be the same as the hierarchical structure shown in Figure A.24.

Directory structures are usually created and used only on hard disks because such disks can store a great number of files. However, because we don't know if you have a hard disk in your computer, we will pretend your data diskette is a hard disk and will create a directory structure on it. In the next few sections, the commands will be the same even if your computer is configured with a hard disk because you will be working with your data diskette. You will be using the MKDIR, CHDIR, and RMDIR commands. Although the names are different, the syntax for these three commands is identical (Figure A.25).

MKDIR (MD) COMMAND

The **MKDIR** (**MD**) command is used to make a directory. To create the structure shown in Figure A.24, you will be issuing a number of commands on your data disk. Before beginning, you will change the current drive to the drive that contains your data disk.

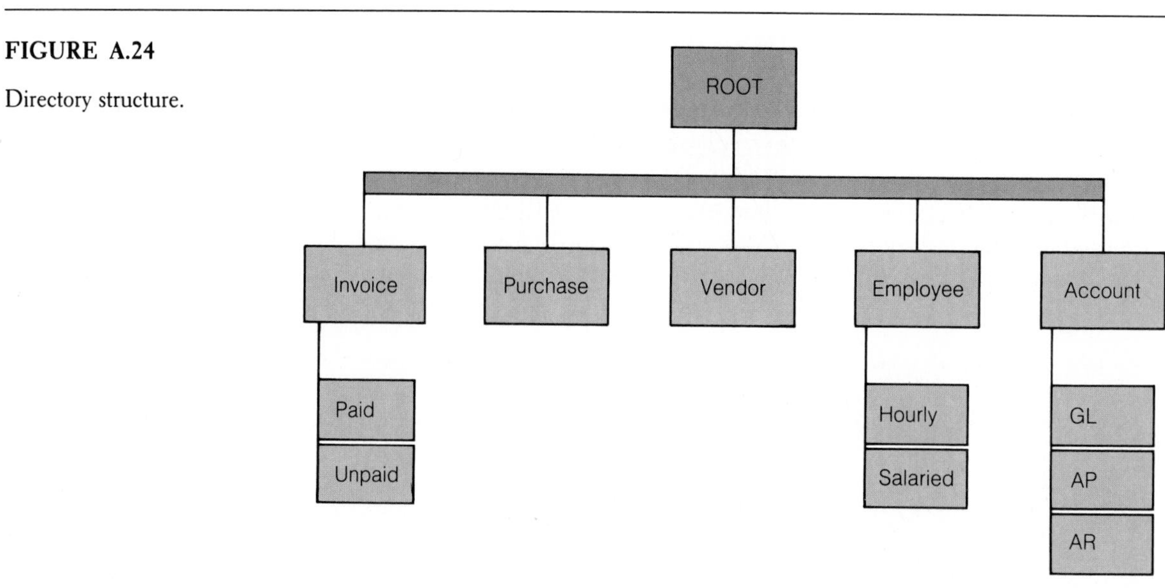

FIGURE A.24

Directory structure.

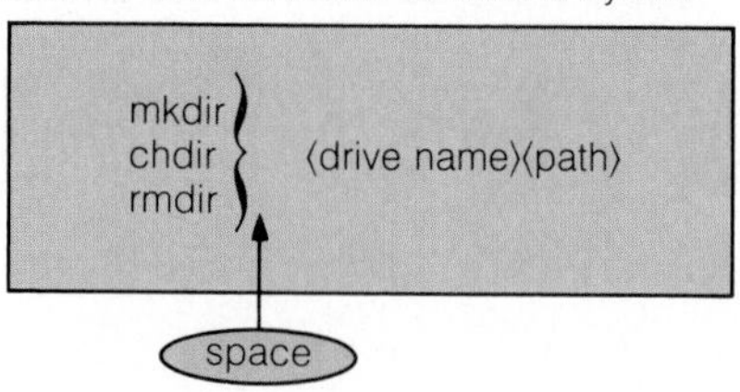

FIGURE A.25

Syntax of MKDIR, CHDIR, and RMDIR commands.

To make the drive containing your data diskette the current drive:

TYPE: B:
PRESS: Enter ■

FOR DISKETTE SYSTEM USERS

To make the drive containing your data diskette the current drive:

TYPE: A:
PRESS: Enter ■

FOR HARD DISK SYSTEM USERS

To create the directory structure pictured in Figure A.24, perform the commands listed below. The first subdirectory you will be creating is called INVOICE.

1. TYPE: md \INVOICE
   PRESS: Enter
   The system prompt should again be displaying on the screen. The backslash (\) that you typed above symbolizes the root directory, which is always at the top of the directory structure. The root directory is created when you format a disk.
2. You have just created a subdirectory right below the root directory, called INVOICE, where you will store your invoice files. To see if the subdirectory in fact exists:
   TYPE: dir
   PRESS: Enter
   The screen should look like Figure A.26. In addition, you should see the subdirectory you just created. It has an extension of <DIR>.
3. To create a subdirectory called PURCHASE:
   TYPE: md \PURCHASE
   PRESS: Enter

```
A>md \INVOICE

A>dir

 Volume in drive A has no label
 Directory of  A:\

SAMPLE1   DOC        49    3-25-92    8:09a
TEXT2     DOC        49    3-25-92    8:09a
TEXT3     DOC        49    3-25-92    8:09a
REPORT    JAN        49    3-25-92    8:09a
REPORT    FEB        49    3-25-92    8:09a
INVOICE        <DIR>       3-25-92    8:20a
        6 File(s)   1454592 bytes free

A>
```

FIGURE A.26

Directory listing after creating the INVOICE subdirectory.

The PURCHASE subdirectory was just created and is located directly below the root directory.

4. To create the VENDOR, EMPLOYEE, and ACCOUNT subdirectories, press the Enter key after typing in each of the following commands after the system prompt.

   md \VENDOR
   md \EMPLOYEE
   md \ACCOUNT

5. Use the directory command (DIR) to see what the listing of your data diskette looks like now (Figure A.27). You should see that you've just created five subdirectories. Think of what you are looking at as the outside of a filing cabinet. We haven't yet shown you how to look inside the subdirectories (you will learn how to use the CD command to look inside subdirectories shortly). Now we are going to lead you through creating the lower-level subdirectories.

6. To create a subdirectory called PAID located directly below the INVOICE subdirectory:
   TYPE: md \INVOICE\PAID
   PRESS: Enter
   If you use the directory command now to list the contents of your data disk, you won't be able to see that you just created the PAID subdirectory. That is because right now the current directory is the root directory, and the DIR command only works to show you the first level of subdirectories below the current directory.

7. To create a subdirectory called UNPAID located directly below the INVOICE subdirectory:
   TYPE: md \INVOICE\UNPAID
   PRESS: Enter

FIGURE A.27

Directory listing of five newly created subdirectories.

```
A>dir

 Volume in drive A has no label
 Directory of  A:\

SAMPLE1  DOC          49   3-25-92   8:09a
TEXT2    DOC          49   3-25-92   8:09a
TEXT3    DOC          49   3-25-92   8:09a
REPORT   JAN          49   3-25-92   8:09a
REPORT   FEB          49   3-25-92   8:09a
INVOICE       <DIR>        3-25-92   8:20a
PURCHASE      <DIR>        3-25-92   8:22a
VENDOR        <DIR>        3-25-92   8:22a
EMPLOYEE      <DIR>        3-25-92   8:22a
ACCOUNT       <DIR>        3-25-92   8:22a
       10 File(s)    1452544 bytes free

A>
```

8. To create the rest of the lower-level subdirectories pictured in Figure A.24, key in the following commands after the system prompt and press the Enter key after each command. Don't type the material in parentheses. That's just for your information.

   md \EMPLOYEE\HOURLY
   md \EMPLOYEE\SALARIED
   md \ACCOUNT\GL (to store general ledger files)
   md \ACCOUNT\AP (to store accounts payable files)
   md \ACCOUNT\AR (to store accounts receivable files)

Again, if you use the directory command (DIR) at this point, you won't see a listing of the lower-level subdirectories you have just created. In the next section, we show you how to "open up" a subdirectory so that it is the current subdirectory; you can then easily view its contents.

CHDIR (CD) Command

The **CHDIR (CD)** command allows you to change the current directory. To practice moving around in the directory structure you've just created, perform the following commands:

1. To make the INVOICE drawer the current drawer (subdirectory):
   TYPE: cd \INVOICE
   PRESS: Enter
   You've now moved into the INVOICE file drawer or subdirectory, which is similar to pulling open a filing cabinet drawer so you can do something to the file folders inside. When you use the DIR command at this point, you'll see a listing of the INVOICE subdirectory's contents, not the contents of the root directory (Figure A.28). DOS automatically places ". <DIR>" and ". . <DIR>" in all of the subdirectories you create. In recent versions of DOS, ". <DIR>"

```
A>cd  \INVOICE

A>dir

 Volume in drive A has no label
 Directory of  A:\INVOICE

.            <DIR>        3-25-92   8:20a
..           <DIR>        3-25-92   8:20a
PAID         <DIR>        3-25-92   8:23a
UNPAID       <DIR>        3-25-92   8:23a
        4 File(s)   1448960 bytes free

A>
```

FIGURE A.28

Directory listing of the INVOICE subdirectory.

provides the user with little or no functional purpose. However, ". . <DIR>", when used in conjunction with the CHDIR command, allows you to move up one level in a directory structure, which is similar to closing one filing cabinet drawer and opening the drawer above.

2. To illustrate the use of the ". ." in conjunction with the CD command:
   TYPE: cd ..
   PRESS: Enter
   If you list the contents of your data diskette now using the DIR command, you should see a listing of the root directory.
3. To make the PAID subdirectory the current subdirectory:
   TYPE: cd \INVOICE\PAID
   PRESS: Enter
   Now that the PAID subdirectory is the current directory, use the DIR command to see a listing of the PAID subdirectory. Note that, as in the case of the INVOICE subdirectory, there are no data or program files in this subdirectory.
4. To make the ACCOUNT subdirectory the current subdirectory:
   TYPE: cd \ACCOUNT
   PRESS: Enter
   If you use the DIR command, you will see that you have three folders (or subdirectories) in it. Your directory listing should look like the one pictured in Figure A.29.
5. Practice moving around in the directory structure a few more times until you feel comfortable with the procedure. After you are finished, move up to the root directory by issuing the following command:
   TYPE: cd \
   PRESS: Enter

FIGURE A.29

Directory listing of the ACCOUNT subdirectory, which contains three subdirectories.

```
A>cd  \ACCOUNT

A>dir

 Volume in drive A has no label
 Directory of  A:\ACCOUNT

.              <DIR>        3-25-92    8:22a
..             <DIR>        3-25-92    8:22a
GL             <DIR>        3-25-92    8:23a
AP             <DIR>        3-25-92    8:23a
AR             <DIR>        3-25-92    8:23a
        5 File(s)    1448960 bytes free

A>
```

Copying Files into a Directory Structure

So far, no subdirectory on your data disk contains any user or program files. Copying files from one directory structure to another really isn't any different from copying files not in a directory structure. However, you must remember to specify the path—one or more directory names, each separated from the previous one by a backslash—from where you are copying and to where you are copying. In the next few steps, you will use the COPY command to copy files from the root directory on your data disk into the drawers (subdirectories) on your data disk.

Perform the following steps:

1. Change the current drive to the drive that contains your data disk (drive B for diskette users and drive A for hard disk users).
2. To copy all the files from the root directory of your data disk that begin with the letters REP into the VENDOR subdirectory:
   TYPE: copy \REP*.* \VENDOR
   PRESS: Enter
3. To make sure the files were actually copied into the correct drawer:
   TYPE: dir \VENDOR
   PRESS: Enter
   The screen should look like Figure A.30. Note that you didn't have to actually change directories to see the files in the VENDOR subdirectory; you just took a peek into it. You should still be in the root directory.
4. To copy all the files that have an extension of DOC from the root directory of your data diskette into the UNPAID subdirectory:
   TYPE: copy *.DOC \INVOICE\UNPAID
   PRESS: Enter
5. To make sure the files were actually copied into the correct drawer:
   TYPE: dir \INVOICE\UNPAID
   PRESS: Enter
   The files in the UNPAID subdirectory should be listing on the screen.

```
A>dir  \VENDOR

 Volume in drive A has no label
 Directory of  A:\VENDOR

.            <DIR>        3-25-92    8:22a
..           <DIR>        3-25-92    8:22a
REPORT   JAN          49  3-25-92    8:09a
REPORT   FEB          49  3-25-92    8:09a
        4 File(s)    1447936 bytes free

A>
```

FIGURE A.30

Listing of the VENDOR subdirectory after files have been copied into it.

6. To copy the file named REPORT.FEB from the root directory of your data diskette into the PURCHASE subdirectory:
   TYPE: copy \REPORT.FEB \PURCHASE
   PRESS: Enter

RMDIR (RD) COMMAND

Sometimes you'll create subdirectories that you never use. The **RMDIR (RD)** command will allow you to remove them. But remember, DOS allows only empty subdirectories to be removed. To illustrate this, we first lead you through trying to remove a subdirectory that isn't empty.

Perform the following steps:

1. Change the current drive to the drive that contains your data diskette (drive B for diskette users and drive A for hard disk users).
2. To remove the UNPAID subdirectory:
   TYPE: rd \INVOICE\UNPAID
   PRESS: Enter
   You should see an error message that looks similar to Figure A.31. To remove a subdirectory, you must first remove the files that are stored in it.
3. To erase the files from the UNPAID subdirectory:
   TYPE: erase \INVOICE\UNPAID
   PRESS: Enter
   DOS should now be asking if you are "sure" that you want to erase the files from this subdirectory.
   TYPE: Y
4. To remove the UNPAID subdirectory:
   TYPE: rd \INVOICE\UNPAID
   PRESS: Enter
   If the system prompt is displaying on the screen, the command was probably successful.
5. To make sure the UNPAID subdirectory has been removed:
   TYPE: dir \INVOICE
   PRESS: Enter
   The UNPAID subdirectory shouldn't be listed on the screen.

TREE COMMAND

Business users often share computers. If the shared computer is configured with a hard disk, it probably also contains a directory structure that was created by the individual who uses the machine the most. What if you want to use the accounting

FIGURE A.31

Error message. You can't remove a subdirectory that isn't empty.

```
Invalid path, not directory,
or directory not empty
```

files, but you don't know where to find them on the hard disk because they're hidden in a subdirectory? The **TREE** command, an external command, allows you to see subdirectories and the files they contain. The syntax for the TREE command is given in Figure A.32.

To use the TREE command, perform the following steps:

For Diskette System Users

1. Make sure the DOS diskette is in drive A. Change the current drive to drive A so that you have access to the DOS files in the current drive.
2. TYPE: tree B:/f
   PRESS: Enter
   You should see a listing of all the subdirectories on your data diskette and the files they contain. ■

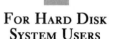

For Hard Disk System Users

1. Change the current drive to drive C so that you have access to the DOS files in the current drive.
2. TYPE: tree A:/f
   PRESS: Enter
   You should see a listing of all the subdirectories on your data diskette and the files they contain. ■

Summary

To effectively and efficiently use computers and applications software, users need to understand some fundamentals about a microcomputer's operating system. Operating systems software provides many commands with which to manage disk storage.

The FORMAT command allows you to prepare a disk so that it is capable of storing data. Use this command with care because it erases any data that existed on a disk *before* it was formatted. The COPY command should also be used with care—especially when the disk you're copying from (source disk) and the disk you're copying onto (target disk) contain a file with the same name. When you copy the first file, its contents replace the contents of the second file. If this isn't your intention, rename the source file before you copy it.

TREE command syntax

tree (drive name)

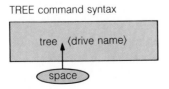

space

FIGURE A.32

Syntax of the TREE command. When using the TREE command to see a listing of all subdirectories on a disk, you must specify the disk drive where the directory is located.

Directory commands are also very important to know about because the chances are great that the computer you use at school or work is configured with a hard disk that contains subdirectories. With a basic understanding of subdirectories, you will be able to use your hard disk effectively. To make a subdirectory, use the MKDIR (MD) command. To change the current subdirectory, use the CHDIR (CD) command, and to remove a subdirectory, use the RMDIR (RD) command. To display a listing of all the subdirectories on a disk, use the TREE command.

DOS is the most widely used microcomputer operating system in the business environment today. To use it effectively, you must follow its rules, referred to as the *command syntax*, carefully.

KEY TERMS

AUTOEXEC.BAT, p. 524
booting, p. 523
CHDIR (CD), p. 549
CHKDSK, p. 544
COMMAND.COM, p. 523
CONFIG.SYS, p. 524
COPY, p. 537
COPY CON, p. 536
current disk drive, p. 524
default disk drive, p. 524
DEL, p. 543
DIR, p. 531
DIR/P, p. 532
DIR/W, p. 532
directory structure, p. 527
ERASE, p. 543
external command files, p. 523
external command instructions, p. 523
FORMAT, p. 529
global (wildcard) characters (*,?), p. 534
IBMBIO.COM, p. 523
IBMDOS.COM, p. 523
internal command files, p. 523
internal command instructions, p. 523
MKDIR (MD), p. 546
RENAME, p. 540
RMDIR (RD), p. 552
root directory, p. 527
subdirectory, p. 527
switches, p. 525
syntax, p. 525
system files, p. 523
TREE, p. 553
TYPE, p. 542
VER, p. 529

EXERCISES

SHORT ANSWER

1. Give an example of when it would be valuable to create a directory structure on your storage device.
2. Why is it significant to know whether the command you want to use is an internal or an external command?
3. When might you find it necessary to rename files?
4. What might the reason(s) be for a computer not to boot when it is turned on?
5. If your computer has a hard disk, why might it be disastrous to reformat it?
6. How would you find out how much main memory (RAM) you have in your computer and what the total storage capacity of your data disk is?
7. How might you determine what version of DOS you are using?
8. Why must you have a copy of DOS in main memory before you can use your computer?

9. How do you know if your computer has booted or not?
10. Why is it important to know the disk drive-naming and file-naming conventions of the operating system you are using? What are DOS's disk drive-naming and file-naming conventions?

HANDS ON

The following exercises should be completed in order.

1. Boot your computer.
2. Check the status of your data diskette and main memory (for diskette users, the data diskette should be in drive B; for hard disk users, the data diskette should be in drive A).
3. Format your data diskette.
4. Determine what version of DOS you are using.
5. Perform the steps to create the text files in the section called "Getting Ready to Practice More DOS Commands" so that you can work with them in some of the next few exercises.
6. List the files present on your data diskette.
7. List the files present on your DOS disk. Now list them using (a) the wide-display option and (b) the page-display option.
8. Copy all the files from your DOS disk that have an extension of .SYS onto your data diskette. How much space do you have left on your data diskette?
9. On your data diskette, make a copy of the file called TEXT3.DOC. Give the new copy your name (such as SARAH or STACEY).
10. Rename the file TEXT2.DOC on your data disk NEWNAME.DOC. Erase the file called TEXT1.DOC from your data diskette.
11. Perform the following steps to practice working with subdirectories:
    a. Create on the data diskette the directory structure pictured in Figure A.33.

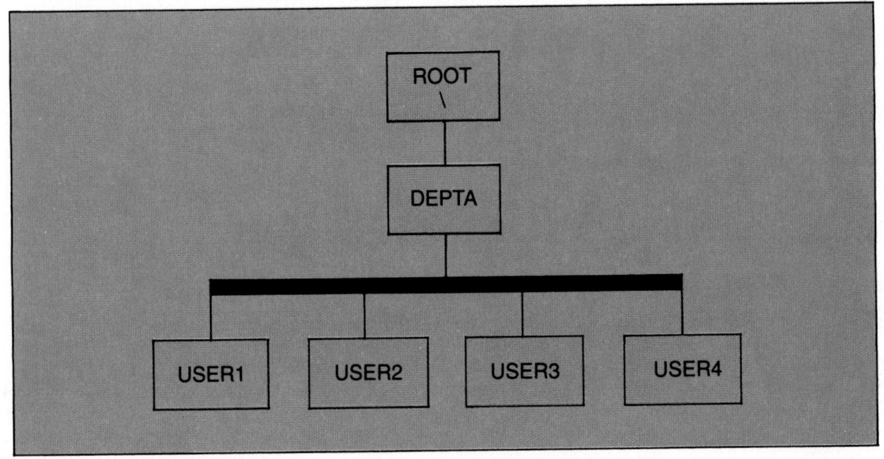

FIGURE A.33

Directory structure for Department A.

This directory structure is intended to be used by "Department A" (DEPTA) to keep track of data files for four users.

b. Copy all the files that have an extension of DOC from the root directory of the data diskette into the USER1 subdirectory.
c. Make the USER2 subdirectory the current subdirectory. Copy the REPORT.FEB file from the root directory of the data diskette into the current subdirectory.
d. Copy the REPORT.FEB file from the current subdirectory into the USER3 subdirectory.
e. Make the USER4 subdirectory the current subdirectory. Copy all the files from the USER1 subdirectory into the current subdirectory.
f. Remove the USER4 subdirectory.
g. Make the root directory the current directory. Copy all the files in the current directory into the USER2 subdirectory.
h. List on the screen all the subdirectories stored on the data diskette.

MODULE B

WORD PROCESSING: WORDPERFECT

B

This module will familiarize you with word processing and demonstrate how useful word processing software can be for you—both personally and professionally. We provide you with a list of the most useful features available in word processing software. We recommend you read the Introduction to the Modules before you proceed with this module.

PREVIEW

When you have completed this module, you will be able to:

- Describe the document cycle.
- Load WordPerfect and use the function keys.
- Create a document.
- Save a document.
- Retrieve a document.
- Use fundamental editing procedures.
- Reveal codes.
- Print a document.

WORD PROCESSING SOFTWARE OVERVIEW

For those of us who are not trained typists, the thought of typing a letter can quickly turn a good mood into a bad one—that is, if we are using a typewriter instead of a computer and word processing software. The process of using a typewriter is familiar to most of us. You begin typing your letter, paying close attention to pressing the correct keys. You finish typing the letter. You reread it, hoping you won't come across any mistakes—but you do. Or you omitted a critical sentence in the middle of your letter. So you have to start all over again.

With the help of word processing software programs, computers give us the ability to avoid such trying situations. This module focuses on using the different features of WordPerfect—a word processing program that is commonly used on microcomputers.

WHAT IS WORD PROCESSING?

Word processing is nothing new; people have been processing words for hundreds of years. For our purposes, **word processing** refers to the preparation of text (words, sentences, paragraphs) for creating, editing, and printing documents (for example, memos, letters, and manuscripts). **Word processing software** allows us to create, edit, format, store and retrieve, and print documents using a computer. This module covers the fundamentals of word processing. You will have the opportunity to create a document using WordPerfect, a very popular word processing software package.

When a user presses a key on a typewriter, a character is immediately printed out on paper in hardcopy form. However, when a user of a computer loaded with word processing software presses a key, the character is stored electronically in main memory, "printed" only on the screen. This innovation gives the computer user one major advantage over the typewriter user: Characters stored electronically can be manipulated easily by the tools made available through the word processing program. The user can change text again and again without having to start over; he or she can correct mistakes without disturbing the rest of the document. Only after the document is "perfect" is it printed out in hardcopy form.

Before using an applications software package, make sure that your computer meets all the necessary hardware requirements to run the software—these **system requirements** are usually listed on the front of the applications package. To use WordPerfect on your computer, you must have at least 384 K of RAM. In addition, it is recommended that your computer be configured with a hard disk, because all the WordPerfect program files and tutorial files take up 4.5 MB of disk storage (if necessary, you can install WordPerfect so that it takes only 2.5 MB of disk storage: See Appendix A for information on software installation). However, you can use WordPerfect on a system configured with two diskette drives as long as each drive has a minimum capacity of 720 K.

WORD PROCESSING FEATURES

As more and more microcomputers are being used in the business workplace, more and more word processing software programs are being written for use with microcomputers. Bookstore and computer store shelves are full of books on different microcomputer word processing software packages. In this section, we provide an overview of the different features that word processing software provides.

Each of the features of word processing involves one or more parts of the document cycle. The **document cycle** involves using word processing software to perform the following activities: (1) entering, (2) editing, (3) spell-checking and using a thesaurus, (4) formatting, (5) saving and retrieving, and (6) printing a document. A seventh feature—merging text from separate documents into a single document—may also be part of the cycle. Each step in the document cycle involves using a number of different word processing features.

ENTERING TEXT

After you have loaded your word processing software into RAM (which you will do shortly in this module), the next step is to enter, or key in, your text. When entering text, you will deal with (1) cursor movement, (2) word wrap and the Enter key, and (3) scrolling.

In most word processing programs, the **cursor** is a blinking or highlighted line (or block), about as wide as a character, that marks where the next character will be entered or the starting point of the next command operation. As you type a character, the cursor moves to the right. When you are editing text, you can control where the cursor is positioned by using the cursor-movement keys on your keyboard.

Another important feature of computer-based word processing is **word wrap.** When you are writing on a typewriter, to begin typing another line, you hit the carriage return or press the Enter key when the print mechanism hits the right-hand margin so that it will return to the left-hand margin. When using a computer and word processing software, you don't have to do anything at the end of a line. When the cursor reaches the right-hand margin, it automatically returns to the left-hand margin of the line below. In other words, the cursor wraps around to start a new line when it reaches the right margin. If a word is being typed in that is too big to fit on the current line, the cursor will automatically take the word down to the next line.

Entering text almost always involves **scrolling**—the automatic movement of blocks of text up or down the screen. Many, if not most, of the documents you create will be too large to see all at once on the screen. The most you can view on your monitor is 24 to 25 lines of text. What happens when you're entering a document that is longer than 25 lines? Your document will move up, or scroll, off the top of the screen. As shown in Figure B.1, your screen acts like a window through which you see portions of the text you have entered. To see the portions of text that have scrolled off the screen, you need to move the cursor to the portions of text you want to see (you will learn how to do this shortly). To see a document that is longer than 25 lines in its entirety, you must print it out.

When you are using WordPerfect, you will use the cursor-movement keys (up, down, left, right) to move the cursor through your document on the screen. In addition, you can use the PgUp key to move the cursor to the first line on the previous page, and the PgDn key to move the cursor to the first line on the next page. These methods for moving the cursor efficiently through a document can save you time, especially when you're working on long documents.

EDITING TEXT

Let's say you've used WordPerfect to create a letter to send to a potential employer. After reviewing it, you decide to improve the letter by making changes to, or **editing,** it. A number of features can be used to edit a document. Two of the most important editing features involve inserting and deleting text. With word processing software, all you have to do to insert text in or delete text from a document is move the cursor to the location where you want to start the operation and then press the appropriate keys. In this way, for example, you could position the cursor in the middle of a paragraph, and then insert a sentence. Once you've performed the desired operation, WordPerfect will automatically reformat your text to fit within the margins. In this module, you will practice inserting and deleting text.

Another convenient editing feature of word processing programs is the ability to perform **block operations.** For example, what if you decide to move the first paragraph in your document to the end of your document? By using block operations, you can move, delete, and copy sentences, paragraphs, and pages by telling the software where the beginning and end points are of the block of text you want to move. Once you have defined the block of text, you issue the appropriate command to either move, delete, or copy it. Word processing software also offers you the capability of creating a separate file out of a block of text. This feature allows you to save parts of documents you will use again and again and incorporate them into new documents.

FIGURE B.1

The window. Most screens allow you to see only 24 to 25 lines of text at one time—through a "window." The text moves (scrolls) up and down the screen so you can view a long document.

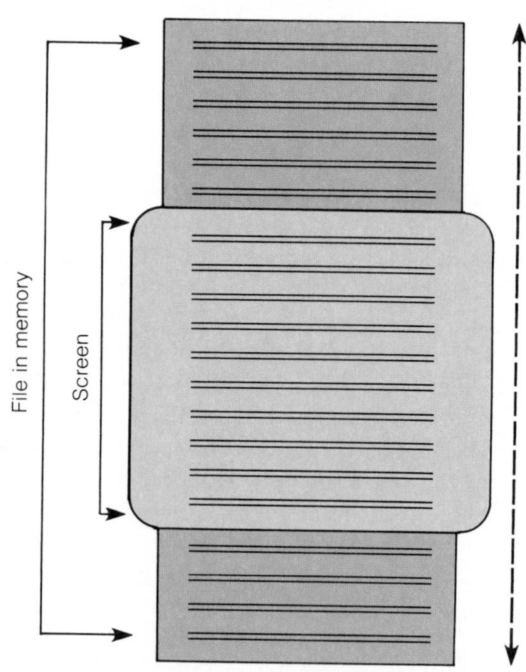

Word processing software also enables you to search for and replace text in a document. For instance, perhaps you used the name John instead of Jack in many places throughout your document. If your document is 20 pages long, it would take a long time to find each occurrence of "John," delete it, and type "Jack." With the **search and replace** capability, you tell the software what word or phrase you want to search for and what word or phrase you would like to replace it with. Then say goodbye to John and hello to Jack.

SPELL-CHECKING AND THE THESAURUS

Word processing packages provide you with the capability to check for spelling errors in a document. It's amazing how many errors the spelling checker finds after you've looked for spelling errors yourself. When you choose the menu option to check the spelling of your document, the spelling dictionary (which accompanies WordPerfect) is loaded into RAM. The words in your document are then compared to the words in the dictionary. The **spelling checker** flags each word in your document that it can't find a match for in the dictionary. For most flagged words, WordPerfect provides a list of suggested correct spellings—you have the option of choosing one to be inserted into your document in place of the incorrectly spelled word.

For example, in Figure B.2, the WordPerfect spelling checker is highlighting the word *becuase* since it considers it to be misspelled. On the bottom half of the screen is a list of suggested correct spellings. In this case, you would type A to replace the incorrect spelling (becuase) with the correct spelling (because). If the speller doesn't come up with any suggested spellings, you have the option of editing the word directly. Sometimes, if the dictionary doesn't contain a word like the one you typed—for instance, someone's last name—WordPerfect will flag it even though it may be spelled correctly; WordPerfect allows you to skip these. WordPerfect also lets you add words to the dictionary, which is very useful if your profession uses special terminology or if you must often use proper names in your documents. If

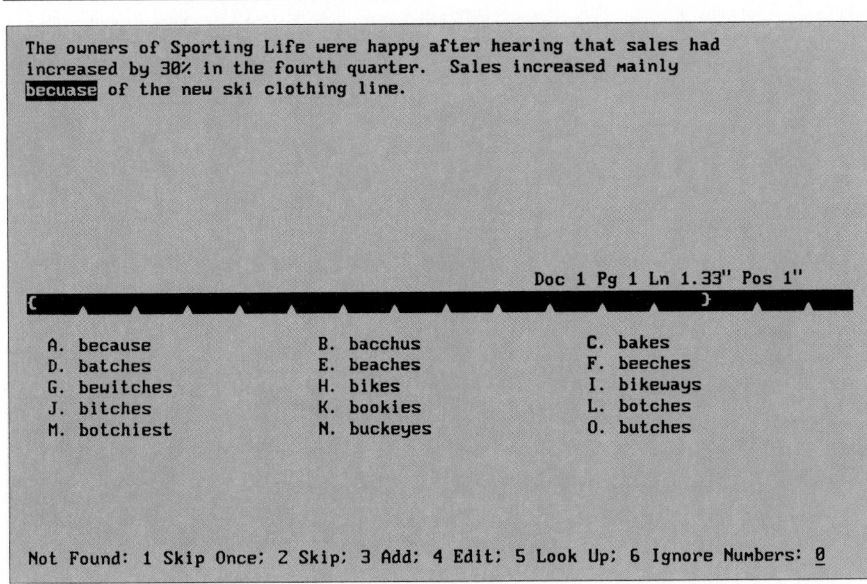

FIGURE B.2

Spelling checker. On the bottom half of the screen, WordPerfect displays a list of suggested correct spellings for the incorrectly spelled word *becuase*.

you don't add these words to the dictionary, it will flag them as misspelled every time you spell-check your document.

Most word processing packages also enable you to identify words with similar meanings through use of a computer-based **thesaurus.** The user simply highlights a word to be looked up and then activates the thesaurus. Words of similar meaning in the thesaurus dictionary will then be listed on the screen. For example, in Figure B.3, the WordPerfect thesaurus is highlighting the word *happy*. On the bottom of the screen, the thesaurus has listed words that have similar meaning. This feature is useful when you know what you want to say but can't find the right words, or when you find you're using the same word over and over in a document.

FORMATTING

What if you want to underline a sentence or a phrase in your document? What if you want certain parts of your text to appear darker, or bolder, when printed out? For example, you may want certain parts of your document, such as your name and address in a resume, to be underlined or set in boldface type for emphasis. Most word processing software can send codes to the printer to tell it to print underlines or print a string of text twice to make it darker. What if you want to center text in your document? These are all **formatting** tasks and are easy to accomplish using word processing software.

In addition, you may want to change the **justification** of your document; in other words, you may want all text to be evenly aligned along the left margin and ragged on the right margin (left-justified), even along both the left and right margins, or centered between both margins (ragged on both the left and right margins) (Figure B.4). Or you may want to change the size of the margins that will appear on the printed page (Figure B.5); when a document is printed, the software

FIGURE B.3

Thesaurus. A list of words that have similar meaning to the highlighted word *(happy)* are displayed on the screen.

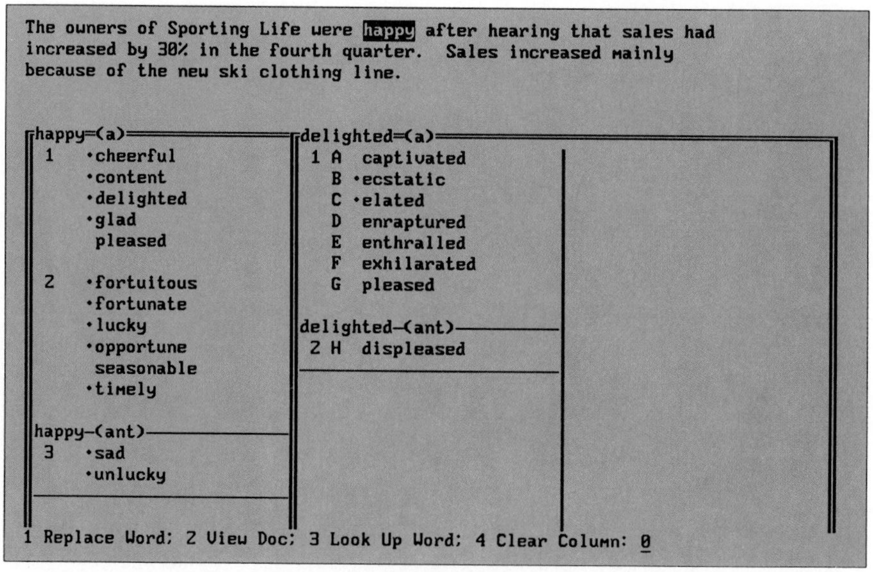

```
The owners of Sporting Life were happy after hearing that sales had
increased by 30% in the fourth quarter.  Sales increased mainly
because of the new ski clothing line.

happy=(a)                      delighted=(a)
 1   •cheerful                   1 A  captivated
     •content                      B •ecstatic
     •delighted                    C •elated
     •glad                         D  enraptured
      pleased                      E  enthralled
                                   F  exhilarated
 2   •fortuitous                   G  pleased
     •fortunate
     •lucky                    delighted-(ant)
     •opportune                  2 H  displeased
      seasonable
     •timely

happy-(ant)
 3   •sad
     •unlucky

1 Replace Word; 2 View Doc; 3 Look Up Word; 4 Clear Column: 0
```

tells the printer to skip lines at the top of the page for the top (or head) margin and at the bottom of the page for the bottom margin, and to skip a few spaces at the left and right sides of the page. You may also want to change the line spacing of your document from single-spaced to double- or triple-spaced.

Word processing software also can put headers or footers on a page (Figure B.5). **Headers** and **footers** are descriptive information that appear at the top or bottom of every page. Headers and footers generally contain such information as page number, date, and document title. Although defined from within the program, headers and footers appear only on your printed output, not on the screen.

You may choose to wait to format your document until after you have edited the document and have finalized the text you want to include in it.

Saving and Retrieving

All software packages, including word processing software, provide ways to save and retrieve your work. Because RAM is an electronic state, created by electricity, if someone accidentally trips on the power cord connected to your computer and pulls it out, you lose your document. When working with applications software, you should periodically save your work onto a permanent nonvolatile storage device such as a diskette or a hard disk. During the saving process, you must give your document a name. Once the document is saved, if you want to change it, you must

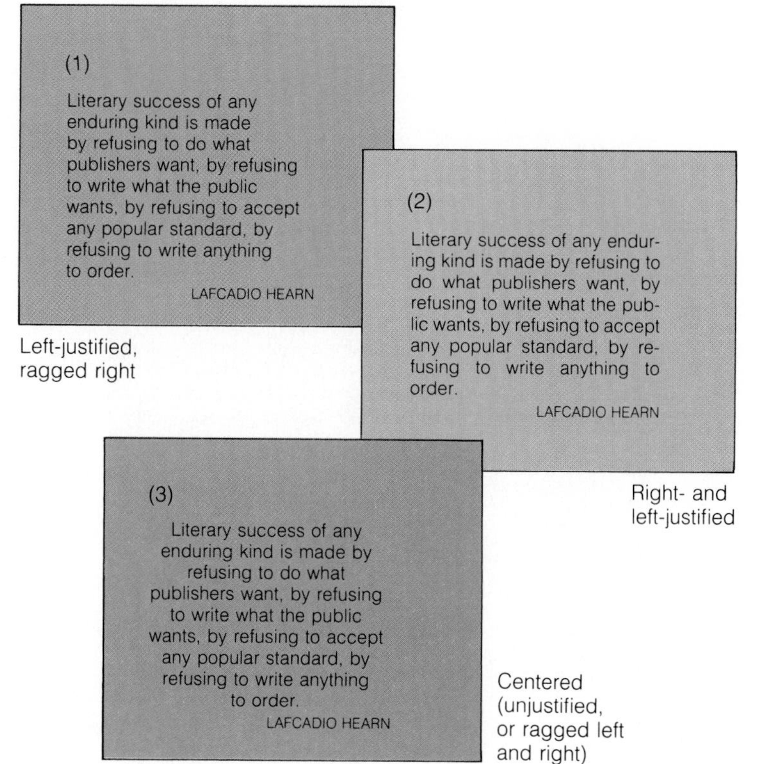

FIGURE B.4

Unjustified (ragged right), justified, and centered text. Changing the justification of your document affects how text is aligned along the margins of the page.

retrieve a copy of it from your storage device and reference the name you used when you saved it.

PRINTING

Once you've created a document and are pleased with it, you'll probably want to print the document out on a printer. Printing a document involves connecting your printer to your computer, turning the printer on, and then issuing the command to print your document. However, before you actually print your document, you may want to enhance the final appearance of the printed page (as described in the next to the last section)—that is, to change the formatting.

Most word processing packages provide you with a number of print options. For example, when you initiate the print command, you can specify whether to print the entire document, or just the page that the cursor is positioned on. In addition, you can specify that you want to print more than one copy of your document. Many word processing packages also enable you to view your document on the screen as it will appear when printed. This feature makes it possible to see the overall effect of your formatting changes (for example, margin changes) without having to print the document out.

FIGURE B.5

Margins. Word processing software allows you to change the size of the margins that will appear on the printed page and to insert a header or a footer. Here, the footer is B.3.

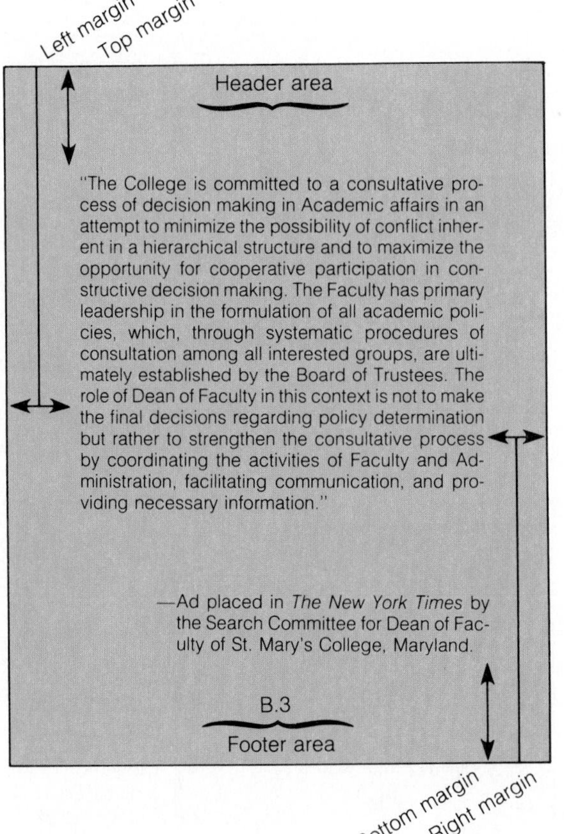

MERGING

Think of how much time you would save if you could send out 50 personalized letters to potential employers in less than an hour! Word processing software can help you do this by enabling you to bring information from two files together, which is referred to as **merging** (Figure B.6).

In this case, the first file that is used in the merging process is the stored form letter—the document. WordPerfect refers to this file as the **primary file.** The second file, called the **secondary file,** or the **data file,** contains the names and addresses of the potential employers. Secondary files must be set up according to a specific format depending on the word processing program you are using.

IN THE LAB

WORD PROCESSING USING WORDPERFECT

In this tutorial, you will create a document using WordPerfect. You will learn how to use most of the word processing features discussed in this module. Because WordPerfect's features are similar to those of most word processing programs, experience with WordPerfect will help you learn how to use another word processing software package. The concepts and procedures are similar.

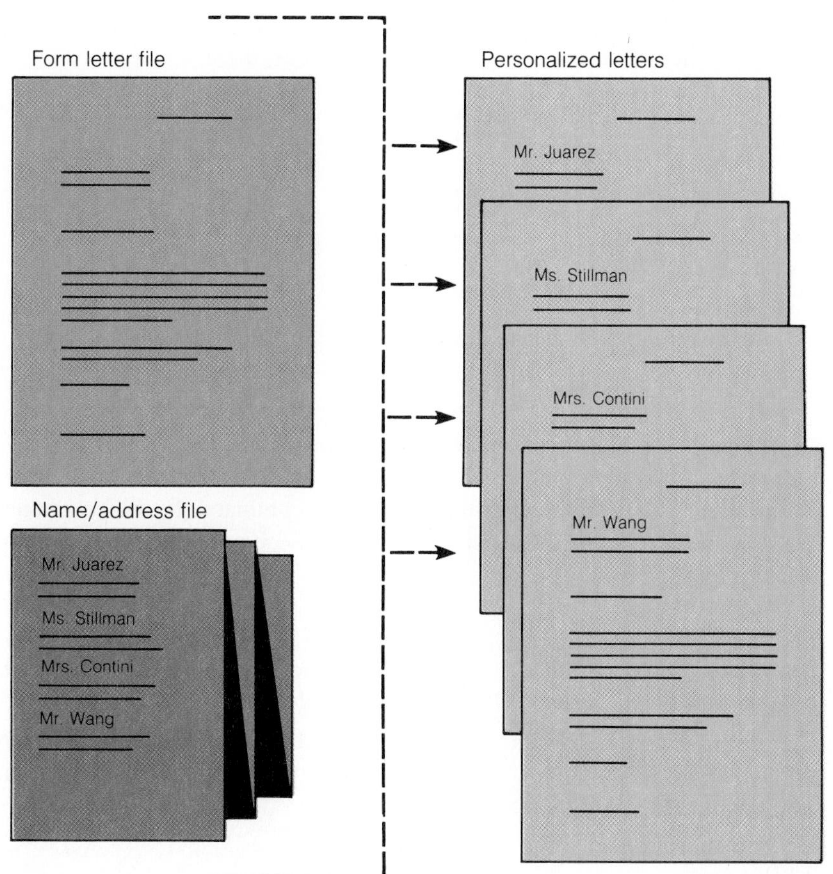

FIGURE B.6

Merging. This editing feature of word processing software allows the user to bring together information from two separate files.

USING THIS TUTORIAL

In this tutorial, we assume you have a formatted data diskette available onto which you can store the documents you create. In addition, we assume you will be using either a diskette system or a hard disk system. The descriptions for these two types of systems can be found in the Introduction to the Modules. When the procedures differ depending on the configuration of your computer, they will be listed beneath one of the two following headings: (1) For Diskette System Users or (2) For Hard Disk System Users. If you're not sure which instructions to follow, ask your instructor.

This tutorial will lead you through the document cycle and help you create some document files. If at any time during this tutorial you have questions about a term, refer to the previous section on Word Processing Features.

LOADING WORDPERFECT

We assume that you have booted your computer with DOS using the procedure described in the Introduction to the Modules. The procedure you use to load WordPerfect differs according to whether you are using a diskette-based system or a hard disk system. *Note*: If you are using a hard disk system but don't have WordPerfect stored on the hard disk (ask your instructor), follow the instructions below for diskette system users.

FOR DISKETTE SYSTEM USERS

1. To load WordPerfect from a diskette drive, put the WordPerfect program diskette in drive A.
2. TYPE: wp
   PRESS: Enter
   Follow the screen messages to display a blank document page. ■

FOR HARD DISK SYSTEM USERS

1. WordPerfect is probably loaded in a subdirectory (named something like WP) on the hard disk. You may be able to load WordPerfect without making the WordPerfect subdirectory current using the CD command (the CD command was described in Module A). To see if this is the case, type the following after the system prompt:
   TYPE: wp
   PRESS: Enter
   If a message such as "Bad Command or Filename" is displaying on the screen, proceed with Steps 2 and 3. Otherwise, skip Steps 2 and 3.
2. Use the CD command to make the WordPerfect subdirectory the current subdirectory. For example, if the WordPerfect subdirectory is called WP, you would type CD \WP to accomplish this.
3. To load WordPerfect:
   TYPE: wp
   PRESS: Enter ■

What do you see? In the upper left-hand corner of the page, the cursor is blinking and waiting for you to enter text. In the bottom right-hand corner of the page, status information appears that (among other things that we'll cover later) tells what position ("Pos") the cursor is in. Note that your cursor is on line (Ln) 1″ (1 inch) and in position (Pos) 1″. Unless you issue a command to change the margins in your document, WordPerfect will print your document with 1-inch margins on all sides of your document (top, bottom, left, and right). By default, WordPerfect sets 1-inch margins on all sides of your document. (The term *default* refers to the assumptions made by a software program; in other words, default values are what you get unless you enter specific values of your own choosing.)

But before we actually exercise your typing skills, we'd like to familiarize you with how to access WordPerfect's commands.

USING THE FUNCTION KEYS

WordPerfect's commands are accessed by holding down the Alternate (Alt), the Shift, or the Control (Ctrl) key while tapping a function key (function keys have the letter F and a number). Figure B.7 shows the WordPerfect 5.1 template, which indicates what each function key will do for you. This template is used with the F1–F10 function keys that are located on the left side of the keyboard. Templates are also available from WordPerfect that are designed to work with function keys that are positioned horizontally across the top of the keyboard.

Note that there are four different commands listed for each function key, each in a different color.

- To perform commands printed in black, press the function key corresponding to your choice.
- To perform commands printed in green, hold the Shift key down and press the appropriate function key.
- To perform commands printed in blue, hold the Alt key down and press the appropriate function key.
- To perform commands printed in red, hold the Ctrl key down and press the appropriate function key.

What keys would you press to center a title on a page? The word *center* is your hint. As you have probably figured out, you would hold the Shift key down and press the F6 key. What keys would you press to use the thesaurus? The spell-checker?

It's now time to exercise your typing skills. *Note:* In this module, don't press any keys unless we instruct you to do so.

Quick Reference

Using the Function Keys

To use the commands shown in:

1. **BLACK** press the function key alone.
2. **BLUE** press the Alt key and the function key.
3. **GREEN** press the Shift key and the function key.
4. **RED** press the Ctrl key and the function key.

CANCEL KEY (F1)

The **Cancel key** (**F1**) is used for two purposes. First, it enables you to cancel a command. If you have initiated a command and then decide you don't want to use it, you can cancel the command by pressing the F1 key. Second, it enables you to restore deleted text. If you are viewing your document on the screen (that is, you aren't viewing a menu) and then press the F1 key, WordPerfect displays on the screen the text you last deleted and provides you with the option of restoring to your document the deleted text. In addition, WordPerfect provides you with the option of viewing your second-to-last deletion and restoring it to your document.

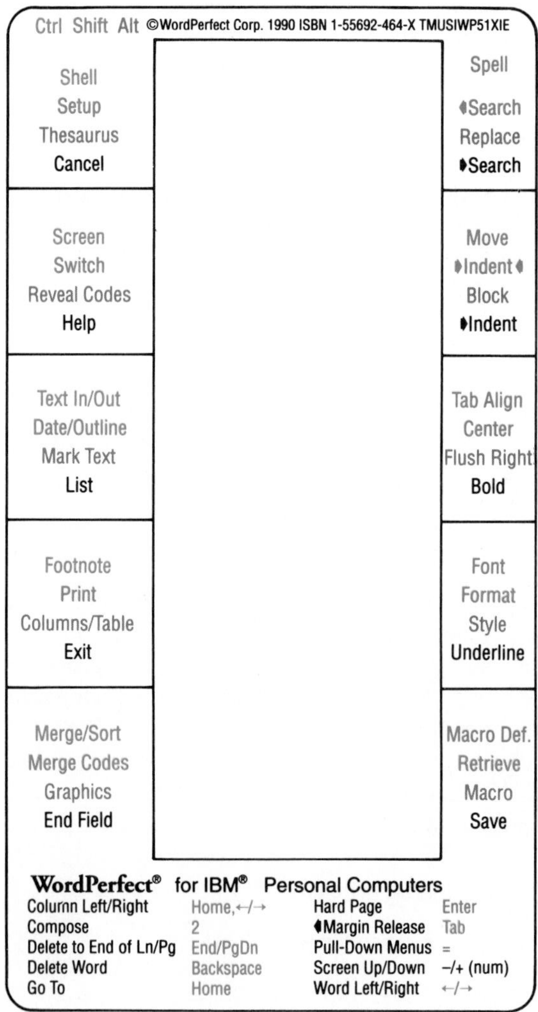

FIGURE B.7

WordPerfect 5.1 template. This template fits around the function keys and tells the user what command each function key controls by itself and in combination with another key (Alt, Ctrl, Shift).

If you are viewing a menu on the screen, this command cancels the current command. If you are viewing a document on the screen, this command enables you to restore text you have previously deleted.

Quick Reference ■ Cancel (F1)

Using Help (F3)

The **Help key (F3)** provides information about any WordPerfect command. To initiate the HELP command, simply press the F3 key. Information about how to use Help will display on the screen (Figure B.8). To obtain information about a particular function key, simply press the appropriate function key (Figure B.9). Or, if you want to determine what keystrokes will enable you to change margins, for example, simply type M, and the keystroke information will appear on the screen (Figure B.10); or type I to obtain keystroke information about indenting. Pressing the Enter key or the space bar exits you out of the HELP command.

Use the Help key (F3) to obtain information about a particular function key or about how to execute a particular command.

1. To initiate the HELP command, press the Help key (F3).
2. Press either a function key or a letter that corresponds to a command.
3. To exit the HELP command, press the Enter key or space bar.

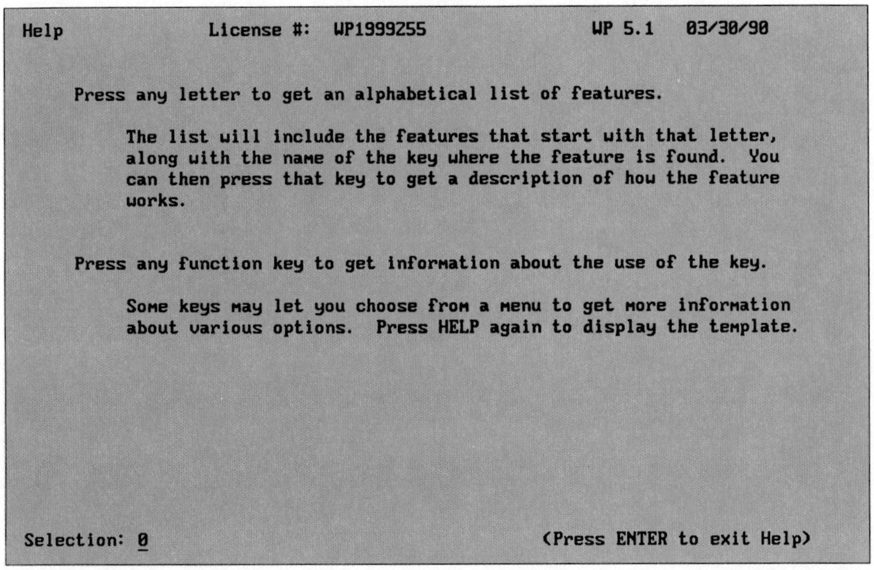

Quick Reference ■ Help (F3)

```
Help              License #:  WP1999255              WP 5.1   03/30/90

    Press any letter to get an alphabetical list of features.

         The list will include the features that start with that letter,
         along with the name of the key where the feature is found.  You
         can then press that key to get a description of how the feature
         works.

    Press any function key to get information about the use of the key.

         Some keys may let you choose from a menu to get more information
         about various options.  Press HELP again to display the template.

Selection: 0                                   (Press ENTER to exit Help)
```

FIGURE B.8

Help! These instructions will display on the screen when you press the F3 (Help) key.

BEGINNING A DOCUMENT: CURSOR MOVEMENT AND INSERTING TEXT

Your cursor should still be blinking in the upper left-hand corner of your screen. This marks where the first character you type will appear. We will now lead you through typing the text pictured in Figure B.11.

FIGURE B.9

Help information about the F2 key.

```
Search

     Searches forward (F2) or backward (Shift-F2) through your text for a
     specific combination of characters and/or codes.  After entering the
     search text, press Search again to start the search.  If the text is
     found, the cursor will be positioned just after (to the right of) it.
     Lowercase letters in the search text match both lowercase and uppercase.
     Uppercase letters match only uppercase.

     Extended Search
     Pressing Home before pressing Search extends the search into headers,
     footers, footnotes, endnotes, graphics box captions, and text boxes.  To
     continue the extended search, press Home, Search.

Selection: 0                                          (Press ENTER to exit Help)
```

FIGURE B.10

Help information about *mar*gins and other commands that begin with M.

```
Features [M]                           WordPerfect Key   Keystrokes

Macro Editor                           Macro Define      Ctrl-F10
Macro Commands                         Macro Commands    Ctrl-PgUp
Macro Commands, Help On                Macro Define      Ctrl-F10
Macros, Define                         Macro Define      Ctrl-F10
Macros, Execute                        Macro             Alt-F10
Macros, Keyboard Definition            Setup             Shft-F1,5
Mail Merge                             Merge/Sort        Ctrl-F9,1
Main Dictionary Location               Setup             Shft-F1,6,3
Manual Hyphenation                     Format            Shft-F8,1,1
Map, Keyboard                          Setup             Shft-F1,5,8
Map Special Characters                 Setup             Shft-F1,5
Margin Release                         Margin Release    Shft-Tab
Margins - Left and Right               Format            Shft-F8,1,7
Margins - Top and Bottom               Format            Shft-F8,2,5
Mark Text For Index (Block On)         Mark Text         Alt-F5,3
Mark Text For List (Block On)          Mark Text         Alt-F5,2
Mark Text For ToA (Block On)           Mark Text         Alt-F5,4
Mark Text For ToC (Block On)           Mark Text         Alt-F5,1
Master Document                        Mark Text         Alt-F5,2
Math                                   Columns/Table     Alt-F7,3
More... Press m to continue.

Selection: 0                                          (Press ENTER to exit Help)
```

INSERTING TEXT: INSERT VERSUS TYPEOVER

To illustrate the fundamentals of inserting text, this section leads you through editing the words "Practice Paragraph."

1. The first item of information you will type is the word "Paragraph." You will insert the word "Practice" shortly.
   TYPE: Paragraph
2. The cursor should be positioned one character to the right of the word "Paragraph."
   PRESS: the cursor-movement key (left-arrow key) to move the cursor to the left nine times
3. The cursor should be positioned beneath the "P" of "Paragraph." WordPerfect operates in **Insert mode.** Therefore anything you type right now—numbers, letters, and other characters—will be inserted at the current cursor location. In addition, pressing the space bar inserts spaces; pressing the Enter key inserts blank lines. *The only keys you can use to move the cursor within a document without affecting the text are the cursor-movement keys.*
   TYPE: Practice
   PRESS: space bar
4. Note that the word "Practice" (followed by a space) was inserted before the word "Paragraph." If you don't want to operate in Insert mode, you can press the Ins key, and WordPerfect will go into **Typeover mode** (most WordPerfect users stay in Insert mode 90 percent of the time). To illustrate Typeover mode:
   PRESS: the cursor-movement key to position the cursor beneath the "P" of "Practice"
   PRESS: Ins key
   The text "Typeover" should be displaying in the bottom-left corner.
   TYPE: My

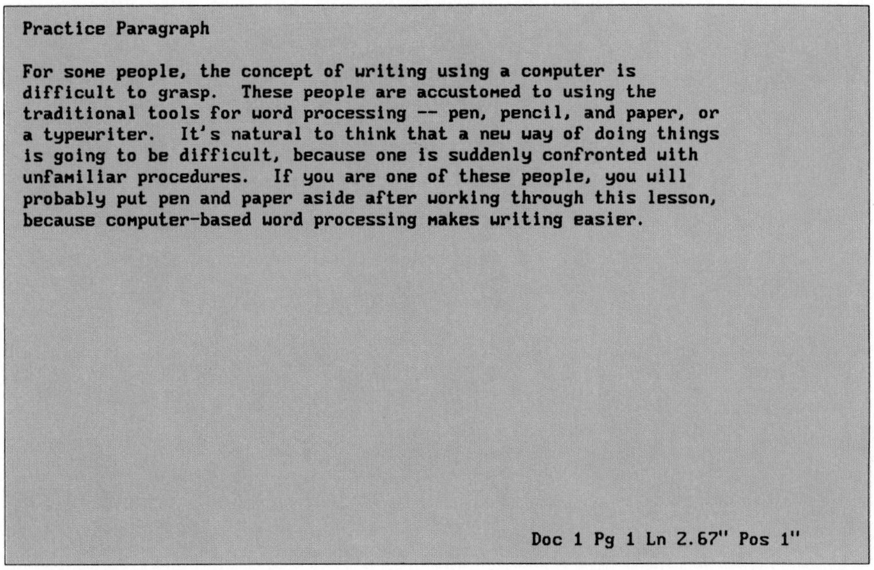

```
Practice Paragraph

For some people, the concept of writing using a computer is
difficult to grasp.  These people are accustomed to using the
traditional tools for word processing -- pen, pencil, and paper, or
a typewriter.  It's natural to think that a new way of doing things
is going to be difficult, because one is suddenly confronted with
unfamiliar procedures.  If you are one of these people, you will
probably put pen and paper aside after working through this lesson,
because computer-based word processing makes writing easier.

                                        Doc 1 Pg 1 Ln 2.67" Pos 1"
```

FIGURE B.11

Practice paragraph.

The screen should look similar to Figure B.12. The word "My" should have overwritten the first two characters of "Practice."

5. To insert a space and "Pr" in the correct position:
   PRESS: Ins key
   WordPerfect is back in Insert mode.
   PRESS: space bar
   TYPE: Pr
   The screen should look like Figure B.13.

FIGURE B.12

Typeover. In Typeover mode, what you type will type over and replace any text that is positioned at the current cursor location.

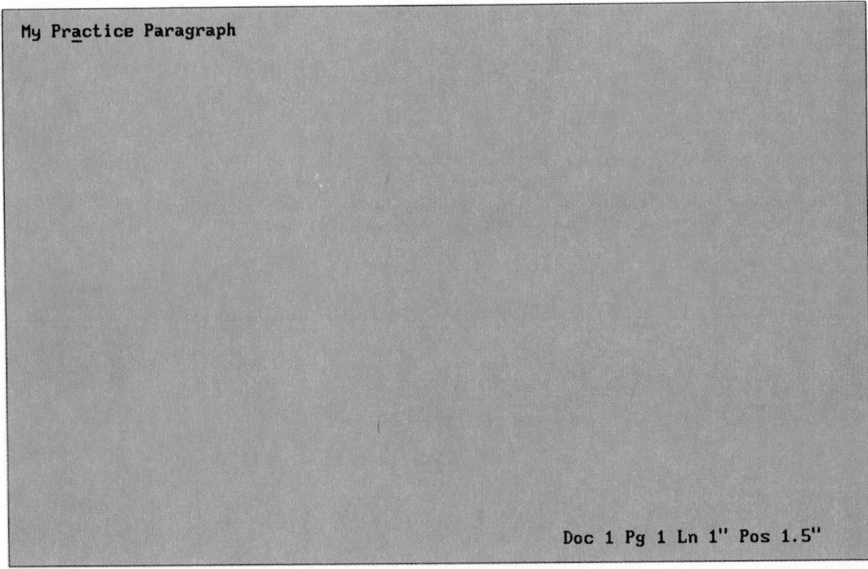

FIGURE B.13

Corrected heading.

6. When the Enter key is pressed, blank lines are inserted in your document. To illustrate:
   PRESS: the cursor-movement keys to position the cursor beneath the letter "P" of "Paragraph."
   PRESS: Enter four times
   The word "Paragraph" was brought down *with* the cursor, and blank lines were inserted. In the next section, you learn how to get the word "Paragraph" back to its original position.

Quick Reference
Inserting Text

Insert text, spaces, or blank lines by using the arrow keys to position the cursor where you want the new items to appear and then by typing in the text (for inserted text), pressing the space bar or Tab key (for inserted spaces), or pressing the Enter key (for blank lines).

DELETING TEXT: DELETE VERSUS BACKSPACE

The two keys that are commonly used to delete text are the **Del key** and the Backspace key. Whereas the Del key deletes the character the cursor is positioned on, the Backspace key deletes the character to the left of the cursor.

1. To get the word "Paragraph" back to its original position using the Del key:
   PRESS: the cursor-movement keys to move the cursor to where the "P" of "Paragraph" was positioned originally (Figure B.14). (In this case, you will need to press the up-arrow key three times and the left-arrow key once. Pressing the left-arrow key moved the cursor to the end of the previous line.)

FIGURE B.14

Before pressing the Del key, make sure to position the cursor in the appropriate location.

2. The cursor should be positioned where "Paragraph" was originally positioned. Do the following to move "Paragraph" back to its original position.
   PRESS: Del four times
   "Paragraph" should have moved back to its original position.
3. To illustrate the use of the Backspace key:
   PRESS: the cursor-movement keys until the cursor is positioned beneath the "P" of "Practice"
   PRESS: Backspace key three times
   The word "My" and the following space have now been deleted.
4. To move the cursor down two lines without moving "Paragraph" down also, you must move the cursor to the end of the current line.
   PRESS: the right-arrow cursor-movement key so that the cursor is positioned one character to the right of "Paragraph"
   PRESS: Enter twice
   The cursor should have moved down two lines, and "Paragraph" should have stayed in its original position. The cursor is now in the appropriate position to begin typing the practice paragraph.

Quick Reference
■
Deleting Text: Delete and Backspace

- Delete text, spaces, or blank lines by using the arrow keys to position the cursor on the text, space, or blank line that you want to delete and then pressing the Delete (Del) key until the item you're deleting is gone.
- Use the Backspace key to delete text or spaces that are to the left of the cursor.

Table B.1 lists a few additional methods for deleting text in a document.

WORD WRAP

When typing the practice paragraph, you will press the Enter key only once — that is, at the end of the paragraph. *Don't press the Enter key at the end of every line.* The words you type will automatically wrap around to the next line when WordPerfect reaches the right margin.

TABLE B.1

Methods for Deleting Text

Key(s)	Description
Delete	Deletes the character the cursor is positioned on.
Backspace	Deletes the character to the left of the cursor.
Ctrl-Backspace	Deletes the word the cursor is positioned on.
Ctrl-End	Deletes to the end of the current line.
Ctrl-PgDn	Deletes to the end of the page.

1. TYPE: For some people, the concept of writing using a computer is difficult to grasp. These people are accustomed to using the traditional tools for word processing -- pen, pencil, and paper, or a typewriter. It's natural to think that a new way of doing things is going to be difficult, because one is suddenly confronted with unfamiliar procedures. If you are one of these people, you will probably put pen and paper aside after working through this lesson, because computer-based word processing makes writing much easier.
2. PRESS: Enter

The screen should now look like Figure B.11.

Quick Reference ■ Word Wrap

When typing in a paragraph, don't press the Enter key at the end of every line. Press the Enter key *only* at the end of the paragraph.

SAVING A DOCUMENT (F10)

Right now, your document is stored in RAM. In WordPerfect, to save your work, use the **Save key (F10).** You will save this document as WPDOC1 onto your data diskette.

FOR DISKETTE SYSTEM USERS

1. Your data diskette should be in drive B of your computer.
2. When you are saving using WordPerfect, it doesn't matter where the cursor is positioned.
   PRESS: F10
3. The text "Document to be saved:" should appear on the bottom left of the screen.
   WordPerfect is waiting for you to tell it where you want to save this document (B:) and what you want to name it (WPDOC1). To save the document onto the diskette in drive B (it doesn't matter whether you use upper- or lowercase letters):
   TYPE: B:WPDOC1
   PRESS: Enter ■

FOR HARD DISK SYSTEM USERS

1. Make sure that your data diskette is in drive A of your computer.
2. When saving using WordPerfect, it doesn't matter where the cursor is positioned.
   PRESS: F10
3. The text "Document to be saved:" should appear on the bottom left of the screen. WordPerfect is waiting for you to tell it where you want to save this document (A:) and what you want to name it (WPDOC1). To save the docu-

ment onto the diskette in drive A (it doesn't matter whether you use upper- or lowercase letters):
TYPE: A:WPDOC1
PRESS: Enter ■

The WPDOC1 document has now been saved onto your data diskette.

Quick Reference
■
Save (F10)

1. PRESS: F10
2. Key in the disk drive designation followed by a filename (for example, B:FILENAME).
3. PRESS: Enter

SAVING A DOCUMENT MORE THAN ONCE (F10)

What if you make some new changes to the current document (the one you just saved)? You should save your work again so that the updated document in RAM will replace the older version of the document on the disk.

1. PRESS: F10
2. The correct disk drive (A: or B:) and filename (WPDOC1) should automatically appear after the text "Document to be saved:".
   PRESS: Enter
3. The message "Replace WPDOC1? (Y/N)" should appear. WordPerfect is asking you whether you want to replace the old, or last saved, version of your document on disk with the updated contents of RAM. Since you do want to update the document stored on disk:
   TYPE: Y

Again, because your documents are stored in RAM (volatile storage) while you're creating them, you should save your work periodically onto either a diskette or a hard disk (nonvolatile storage).

Quick Reference
■
Saving (F10) a Document More Than Once

1. PRESS: F10
2. The correct disk drive and filename should appear after the text "Document to be saved:".
   PRESS: Enter
3. To replace the contents on disk with the updated contents of RAM:
   TYPE: Y

BEGINNING A NEW DOCUMENT (F7)

The procedure to begin work on a new or different document usually involves using the **Exit key (F7)**. Because it is likely you will want, at some point, to begin work on a new document, we will show you the procedure now. We will then walk you through retrieving WPDOC1 from the data diskette.

1. PRESS: F7
2. When prompted by WordPerfect on whether you want to save your document:
   PRESS: N
   (*Note:* You type N because you have already saved your document. However, if you haven't yet saved your work, you can save it at this point by typing Y, the name of the document, and pressing Enter.)
3. When prompted by WordPerfect if you want to exit WordPerfect:
   PRESS: N
   You pressed N because you are not exiting WordPerfect entirely; you are only clearing one document from RAM in order to begin a new one.

Your screen should now be cleared of your document and look like it did after you first loaded WordPerfect.

Quick Reference ■ Clearing RAM (F7) after You Have Used the SAVE Command

1. To initiate the EXIT command:
   PRESS: F7
2. TYPE: N
   TYPE: N

RETRIEVING A DOCUMENT: YOU KNOW THE FILENAME (SHIFT-F10)

Retrieving a document when you know the filename can be accomplished by using the **Retrieve key (Shift-F10).** To retrieve the document called WPDOC1 from your data diskette, perform the following procedure:

FOR DISKETTE SYSTEM USERS

1. To initiate the RETRIEVE command:
   PRESS: Shift-F10
2. WordPerfect is waiting for you to specify the disk drive designation and filename of the file you want to retrieve:
   TYPE: B:WPDOC1
   PRESS: Enter ■

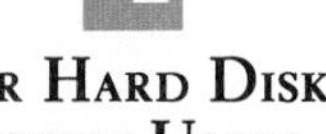

FOR HARD DISK SYSTEM USERS

1. To initiate the RETRIEVE command:
   PRESS: Shift-F10
2. WordPerfect is waiting for you to specify the disk drive designation and filename of the file you want to retrieve:
   TYPE: A:WPDOC1
   PRESS: Enter ■

The document named WPDOC1 should be displaying on the screen.

NOTE If you retrieve a document without clearing RAM first (F7, N, N), WordPerfect will ask if you want to retrieve the document into the current document. If this isn't your intention, save your work, clear RAM, and then retrieve the new document.

Quick Reference
■
Retrieve (Shift-F10)

1. PRESS: Shift-F10
2. Key in the disk drive designation and the name of the file you want to retrieve (for example, B:FILENAME).
3. PRESS: Enter

RETRIEVING A DOCUMENT: YOU'VE FORGOTTEN THE FILENAME (F5)

Unfortunately, it's very easy to forget what names you have given to stored files—especially if you are working with a large number of files. The **List Files key (F5)** provides a means of retrieving a file if you have forgotten its name because it will list the files stored on a disk.

FOR DISKETTE SYSTEM USERS

1. PRESS: F5
2. To list the files stored on the diskette in drive B:
   TYPE: B:
   PRESS: Enter
3. A list of the files stored on the diskette in drive B should be displaying on the screen. The screen should look similar to Figure B.15. Note that one of the

---

FIGURE B.15

The List Files menu (F5).

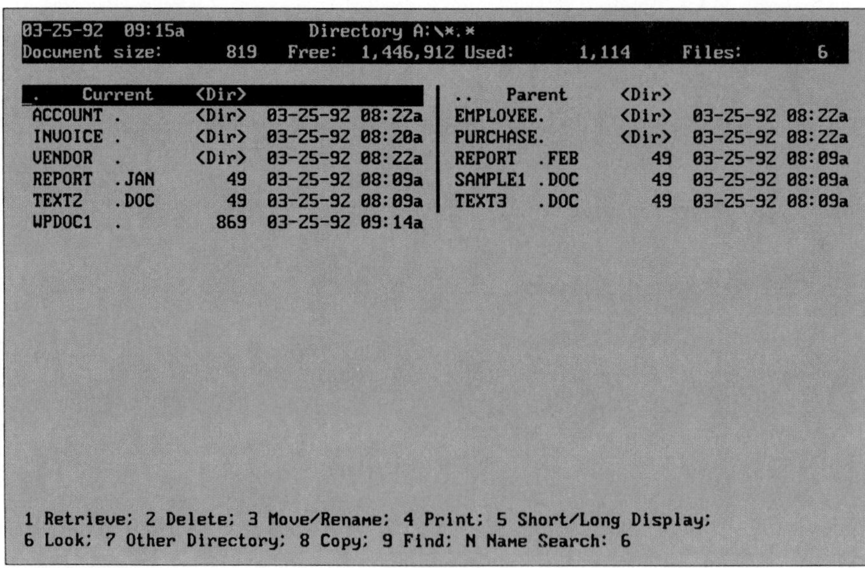

options on the bottom of the screen is "Retrieve." Because you retrieved the WPDOC1 file in the last section, you don't need to retrieve the file again. To exit to the typing area, press the Cancel key (F1). WPDOC1 should be on the screen again. ■

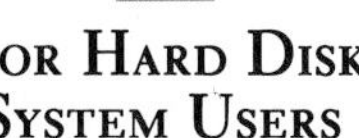

For Hard Disk System Users

1. PRESS: F5
2. To list the files stored on the diskette in drive A:
   TYPE: A:
   PRESS: Enter
3. A list of the files stored on the diskette in drive A should be displaying on the screen. The screen should look similar to Figure B.15. Note that one of the options on the bottom of the screen is "Retrieve." Because you retrieved the WPDOC1 file in the last section, you don't need to retrieve the file again. To exit to the typing area, press the Cancel key (F1). WPDOC1 should be on the screen again. ■

Quick Reference

■

List Files (F5): Retrieving a File

1. PRESS: F5
2. Type in the disk drive designation of the disk with the stored files (for example, B:).
3. PRESS: Enter
4. Use the cursor-movement keys to highlight the file you want to retrieve.
5. TYPE: 1

Editing a Document

In this section, you will edit WPDOC1 so that it looks like the document pictured in Figure B.16. You will perform the following editing tasks:

1. Break the paragraph into two paragraphs.
2. Insert and delete text.
3. Add text to the bottom of the document.

Breaking One Paragraph into Two

Because WordPerfect operates in Insert mode, if you press the Enter key on a line that contains text, the text will move down to the next line. This procedure can be used to break one paragraph into two.

1. Position the cursor beneath the "I" of "It's" at the beginning of the third sentence.
2. PRESS: Enter
   PRESS: Tab

(The Tab key moves the cursor to the right five spaces.)

INSERTING TEXT AND DELETING TEXT

Perform the following steps:

1. Position the cursor at the beginning of the second sentence in the second paragraph (beneath the "I" of "If").
2. TYPE: But word processing software offers users so many advantages that even if
3. To delete the second "If":
   PRESS: Del three times
4. To end the sentence after the word "lesson":
   a. Position the cursor on the comma that follows the word "lesson"
   b. PRESS: Del once
   c. TYPE: .
5. To delete the rest of the sentence:
   a. Position the cursor beneath the "b" of "because"
   b. PRESS: Del until the rest of the sentence has been deleted

ADDING TEXT TO THE BOTTOM OF THE DOCUMENT

Perform the following steps to add text to this document.

1. The cursor should be positioned two spaces to the right of the word "lesson."
   TYPE: The following includes a partial list of what you can do with word processing software to edit a document:
   PRESS: Enter
2. PRESS: Tab

FIGURE B.16

The edited WPDOC1 document.

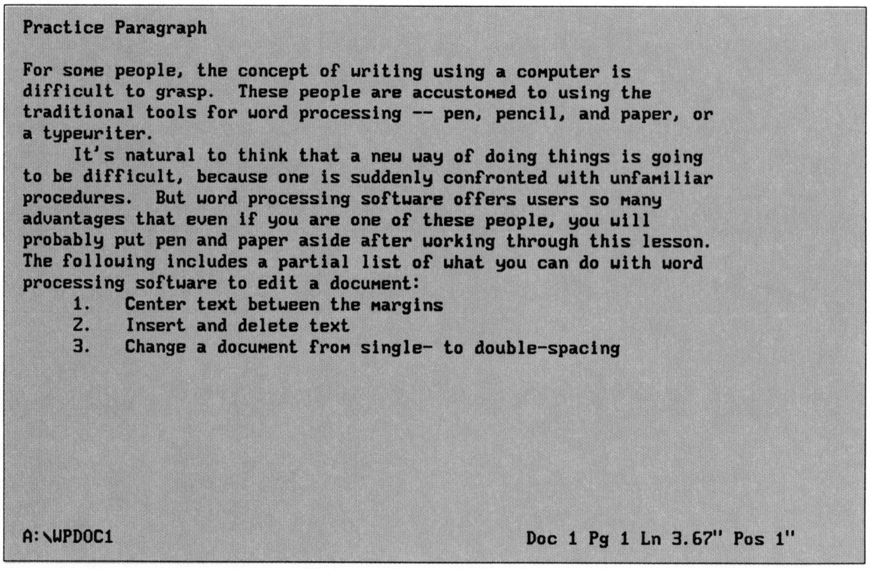

```
Practice Paragraph

For some people, the concept of writing using a computer is
difficult to grasp.  These people are accustomed to using the
traditional tools for word processing -- pen, pencil, and paper, or
a typewriter.
     It's natural to think that a new way of doing things is going
to be difficult, because one is suddenly confronted with unfamiliar
procedures.  But word processing software offers users so many
advantages that even if you are one of these people, you will
probably put pen and paper aside after working through this lesson.
The following includes a partial list of what you can do with word
processing software to edit a document:
     1.    Center text between the margins
     2.    Insert and delete text
     3.    Change a document from single- to double-spacing







A:\WPDOC1                                   Doc 1 Pg 1 Ln 3.67" Pos 1"
```

TYPE: 1.
PRESS: Tab
TYPE: Center text between the margins
PRESS: Enter

3. PRESS: Tab
TYPE: 2.
PRESS: Tab
TYPE: Insert and delete text
PRESS: Enter

4. PRESS: Tab
TYPE: 3.
PRESS: Tab
TYPE: Change a document from single- to double-spacing
PRESS: Enter

Your document should look like Figure B.16.

FORMATTING A DOCUMENT

In this section, you will perform the following formatting tasks:

1. Center the title using the CENTER command (Shift-F6).
2. Change the line spacing from single- to double-spacing.

When printed, your document will look like Figure B.17.

```
                    Practice Paragraph
For some people, the concept of writing using a computer is
difficult to grasp.  These people are accustomed to using the
traditional tools for word processing -- pen, pencil, and paper, or
a typewriter.
     It's natural to think that a new way of doing things is going
to be difficult, because one is suddenly confronted with unfamiliar
procedures.  But word processing software offers users so many
advantages that even if you are one of these people, you will
probably put pen and paper aside after working through this lesson.
The following includes a partial list of what you can do with word
processing software to edit a document:
     1.   Center text between the margins
     2.   Insert and delete text
     3.   Change a document from single- to double-spacing
```

FIGURE B.17

The printed WPDOC2 document.

CENTERING A TITLE (SHIFT-F6)

The **Center key (Shift-F6)** can be used to center text between the margins. Perform the following steps to center the title "Practice Paragraph" between the margins.

1. Position the cursor beneath the "P" of "Practice"
2. To center the title:
   PRESS: Shift-F6
   PRESS: Down cursor-movement key
   The title should appear centered on the screen.

Quick Reference ■ Center (Shift-F6)

1. Position the cursor at the beginning of the line that you want to center.
2. PRESS: Shift-F6
3. TYPE: the text you want to center, or if text was already on the current line, it should now appear centered

---

CHANGING LINE SPACING (SHIFT-F8)

To change the line spacing of the document from single- to double-spaced, you must use the **Format key (Shift-F8).** Perform the following steps:

1. Position the cursor at the beginning of the first paragraph. The document will be affected by the following command from the current cursor position downward.
2. PRESS: Shift-F8
   To choose the Line option:
   PRESS: 1
   To choose the Line Spacing option:
   PRESS: 6
   To specify double-spacing:
   PRESS: 2
   PRESS: Enter
3. To exit the Format menu:
   PRESS: F7

Your document should look like Figure B.17 (when printed).

Quick Reference ■ Changing Line Spacing (Shift-F8)

1. Position the cursor where you want the line spacing command to take effect.
2. PRESS: Shift-F8
3. To choose the Line option:
   TYPE: 1
4. Choose the Line Spacing option:
   TYPE: 6
5. TYPE: [the new line spacing specification—for example, 2 for double-spacing]
6. PRESS: Enter

PRINTING A DOCUMENT TO THE SCREEN (SHIFT-F7)

What if you want to see how a document will look when printed, but you don't want to actually print the document? You can check the formatting of your documents on the screen: What you see is what the document will look like when printed.

1. PRESS: Shift-F7
2. To choose the View Document option:
   TYPE: V
   Although you can't read the text, you can see where the document text will appear on the printed page. The document should look like Figure B.18.
3. To return to your document:
   PRESS: F7

Quick Reference

Viewing a Document (Shift-F7)

1. PRESS: Shift-F7
2. TYPE: V
   The current page should be displaying on the screen.
3. To cancel the current display and return to your document:
   PRESS: F7

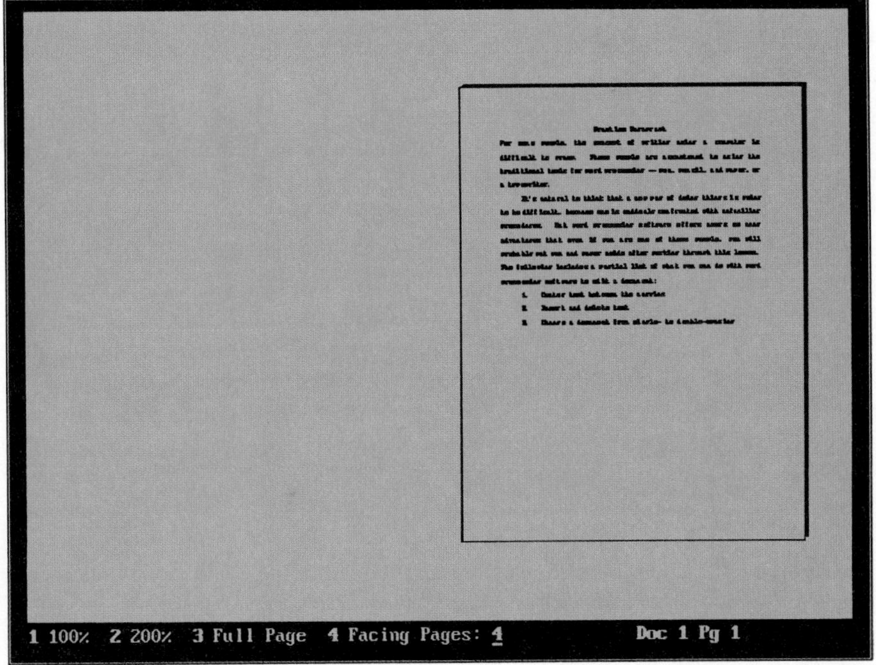

FIGURE B.18

Viewing the WPDOC2 document on the screen.

SAVING THE REVISED DOCUMENT UNDER A DIFFERENT NAME

In this section, you will save the revised document in RAM onto your data disk. However, you will give the revised document the name of WPDOC2.

FOR DISKETTE SYSTEM USERS

1. As we mentioned earlier, when you save a document using WordPerfect, it doesn't matter where the cursor is positioned.
   PRESS: F10
2. The text "Document to be saved:" should appear on the bottom left of the screen followed by the old filename. WordPerfect is waiting for you to tell it where you want to save this document and what you want to name it. To save the document onto your data diskette in drive B with a new filename:
   TYPE: B:WPDOC2
   PRESS: Enter ■

FOR HARD DISK SYSTEM USERS

1. As we mentioned earlier, when you save a document using WordPerfect, it doesn't matter where the cursor is positioned.
   PRESS: F10
2. The text "Document to be saved:" should appear on the bottom left of the screen. WordPerfect is waiting for you to tell it where you want to save this document and what you want to name it. To save the document onto your data diskette in drive A with a new filename:
   TYPE: A:WPDOC2
   PRESS: Enter ■

The document has now been saved onto your data diskette under the name WPDOC2.

REVEALING CODES (ALT-F3) (F11)

When you type characters such as the letters A through Z, they appear on the screen. However, WordPerfect embeds some "invisible" characters, or codes, into the document as you're working on it. Revealing these invisible codes with the **Reveal Codes key (Alt-F3)** (or **F11**) can be quite helpful, especially after you've pressed a few keys accidentally and discover that some of your editing functions don't work because you inadvertently inserted an unwanted code. Once the embedded codes are revealed, you can delete an unwanted code by positioning the cursor on it and pressing the Delete (Del) key. The REVEAL CODES command can be accessed by holding the Alt key down and pressing the F3 key, or by pressing only the F11 key, if you have one on your keyboard.

To see what codes WordPerfect has embedded in the WPDOC2 document, perform the following four steps:

1. Position the cursor at the top of the document.

2. PRESS: Alt-F3 (or F11)
3. The screen should look like Figure B.19. Many people find this display confusing at first. The top half of the screen displays the document without the embedded codes, and the bottom half of the screen displays the document with the embedded codes revealed. When the cursor is moved through the document, it is simultaneously moved through both the top and bottom document screens. The [SRt] codes at the end of many of the lines represent WordPerfect's way of symbolizing word wrap, or a soft return. The [HRt] code at the end of each paragraph is the symbol for pressing the Enter key (hard return). Table B.2 includes a partial list of the codes that WordPerfect embeds in your documents.
4. To turn the Reveal Codes option off:
   PRESS: Alt-F3 (or F11)

Quick Reference

Reveal Codes (Alt-F3) (F11)

1. PRESS: Alt-F3 (or F11)
2. To return to your document:
   PRESS: Alt-F3 (or F11)

Printing a Document (Shift-F7)

When you print a document using the **Print key (Shift-F7),** WordPerfect makes many different assumptions (default values) about what the printed output will look like, including (1) the width of the margins and (2) whether the right margin will appear lined up (even-justified) or jagged (left-justified). Because these assumptions

---

```
                         Practice Paragraph

For some people, the concept of writing using a computer is

difficult to grasp.  These people are accustomed to using the

traditional tools for word processing -- pen, pencil, and paper, or

a typewriter.

    It's natural to think that a new way of doing things is going
A:\WPDOC2                                   Doc 1 Pg 1 Ln 1" Pos 1"
[Center]Practice Paragraph[HRt]
[HRt]
[Ln Spacing:2]For some people, the concept of writing using a computer is[SRt]
difficult to grasp.  These people are accustomed to using the[SRt]
traditional tools for word processing [-][-] pen, pencil, and paper, or[SRt]
a typewriter.  [HRt]
[Tab]It's natural to think that a new way of doing things is going[SRt]
to be difficult, because one is suddenly confronted with unfamiliar[SRt]
procedures.  But word processing software offers users so many[SRt]
advantages that even if you are one of these people, you will[SRt]

Press Reveal Codes to restore screen
```

FIGURE B.19

Revealing Codes (Alt-F3).

TABLE B.2

Partial List of the Codes WordPerfect 5.1 Embeds in a Document.

Code	Description
[Flsh Rt]	Flush right.
[BOLD] [bold]	Begin and end boldfacing.
[Center]	Centering.
[Header N:type;text]	Header definition.
[Footer N;type;text]	Footer definition.
[HPg]	Hard page break inserted by the user.
[HRt]	Hard return inserted by pressing the Enter key.
[~RA Indent]	Beginning of left indent.
[~RA Indent ~LA]	Beginning of left and right indent.
[L/R Mar:*n*,*n*]	Left and right margin settings.
[Pg Num:n]	Page number set to *n*.
[Pg Numbering: position]	Position of page number.
[SPg]	Soft page break inserted by WordPerfect.
[SRt]	Soft return inserted by WordPerfect (word wrap).
[TAB]	Tab.
[UND] [und]	Begin and end underlining.

are based on how most users want their documents formatted, you will probably find that more often than not, WordPerfect's default values are fine for your purposes. However, by using WordPerfect's Format menu (Shift-F8), you can change any defaults. To print the document without changing any of WordPerfect's default values.

1. PRESS: Shift-F7
   The screen should look similar to Figure B.20.
2. To print the entire document:
   PRESS: 1

Quick Reference
■
Print (Shift-F7)

1. PRESS: Shift-F7
2. To print the entire document:
   TYPE: 1

SUMMARY

Word processing software is used to enable users to easily create, edit, store and retrieve, and print documents. Word processing involves one or more activities of the document cycle: (1) entering, (2) editing, (3) spell-checking and using the thesaurus, (4) formatting, (5) saving and retrieving, and (6) printing a document.

When entering text, you will typically deal with the following:

- Cursor movement: the cursor marks where the next character of text will be entered. You can control where the cursor is positioned using the cursor-movement keys on your keyboard.
- Word wrap and the Enter key: you don't have to press the Enter key at the end of every line — only at the end of paragraphs. When you are typing text and hit the end of a line, the word processing software will automatically bring a word for which there wasn't enough space down to the next line.
- Scrolling: the automatic movement of text up or down the screen.

One feature of word processing software that makes editing text easy is its ability to perform commands on more than one character at a time, or to perform block operations. With a block operation, you can use many different commands on a block of text, including copying, moving, saving, printing, and spell-checking.

When editing, users commonly insert and delete text. After text has been inserted or deleted, word processing software automatically makes the document conform to the margin settings.

Before printing a document, you may want to format the document by changing some of the default assumptions made by your word processing program. For example, you may want to underline or boldface text, change the margins, and/or change the line spacing. In addition, you may want to change the justification of the document, or include a header or a footer.

If you want to send the same letter out to a number of different people, you may want to merge a primary file, or letter, with a secondary file, containing the variable data (such as names and addresses).

To load WordPerfect, type WP after the system prompt. WordPerfect's commands are initiated by using the function keys. Each function key provides four different menu options that are shown on the WordPerfect template, which fits around the keys.

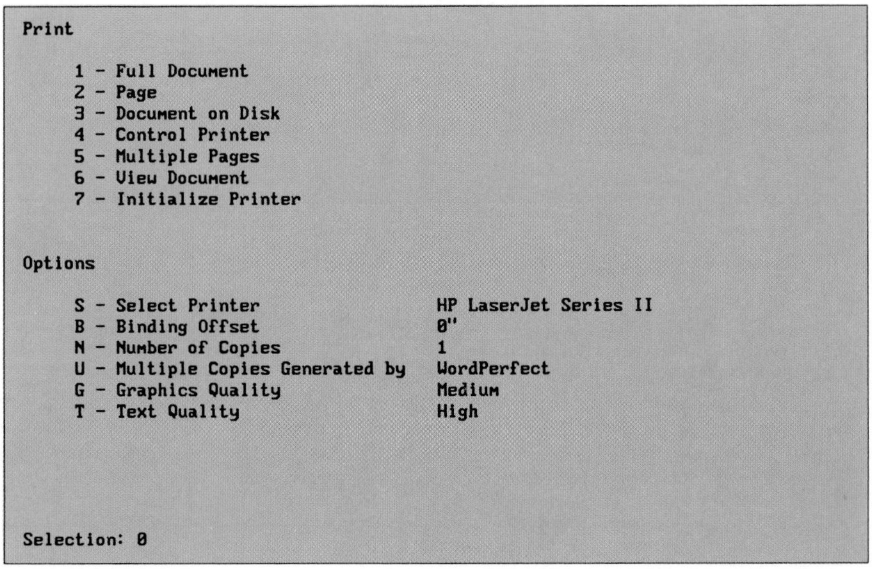

```
Print

     1 - Full Document
     2 - Page
     3 - Document on Disk
     4 - Control Printer
     5 - Multiple Pages
     6 - View Document
     7 - Initialize Printer

Options

     S - Select Printer                  HP LaserJet Series II
     B - Binding Offset                  0"
     N - Number of Copies                1
     U - Multiple Copies Generated by    WordPerfect
     G - Graphics Quality                Medium
     T - Text Quality                    High

Selection: 0
```

FIGURE B.20

The WordPerfect Print menu (Shift-F7).

- To perform commands printed in black, press the function key corresponding to your choice.
- To perform commands printed in green, hold the Shift key down and press the corresponding function key.
- To perform commands printed in blue, hold the Alt key down and press the corresponding function key.
- To perform commands printed in red, hold the Ctrl key down and press the corresponding function key.

WordPerfect operates in Insert mode. Except for when you use the cursor-movement keys, any key you press inserts a code or a character in your document.

The Del key deletes the character the cursor is positioned beneath, whereas the Backspace key deletes the character to the left of the cursor.

To save a document using WordPerfect, you can use either the Exit (F7) key or the Save (F10) key. The Exit key gives you the option of saving your work and then either beginning a new document or exiting WordPerfect. The F10 key saves your work and then keeps the document you saved on the screen. If you save a document more than once, WordPerfect asks if you want to replace the file contents on the disk with the contents of RAM.

The REVEAL CODES command (Alt-F3) (or F11, if your keyboard has it) enables you to see all the codes WordPerfect embeds in your documents. If you can't understand why your document looks a certain way, perhaps a code was inserted in your document accidentally. You can determine if this is true by revealing the hidden codes.

Table B.3 summarizes the commands covered in this module.

TABLE B.3

WordPerfect Command Summary

Task	Command	Keystrokes
Cancel the current command or restore deleted text.	CANCEL	(F1)
Obtain help information.	HELP	(F3)
Save a file.	SAVE	(F10)
Begin a new document or exit WordPerfect.	EXIT	(F7)
Retrieve a file when you know the filename.	RETRIEVE	(Shift-F10)
Retrieve a file when you've forgotten the filename.	LIST FILES	(F5)
Center.	CENTER	(Shift-F6)
Change line spacing.	FORMAT	(Shift-F8)(1)(6)
View a document.	PRINT	(Shift-F8)(V)
Print a document.	PRINT	(Shift-F7)(1)
Reveal codes.	REVEAL CODES	(Alt-F3) (or F11)

KEY TERMS

block operations, p. 560
Cancel key (F1), p. 568
Center key (Shift-F6), p. 582
cursor, p. 559
data file, p. 565
Del key, p. 573
document cycle, p. 559
editing, p. 560
Exit key (F7), p. 576
footer, p. 563
Format key (Shift-F8), p. 582
formatting, p. 562
header, p. 563
Help key (F3), p. 569
Insert mode, p. 571
justification, p. 562
List Files key (F5), p. 578
merging, p. 565
primary file, p. 565
Print key (Shift-F7), p. 585
Retrieve key (Shift-F10), p. 577
Reveal Codes key (Alt-F3) or (F11), p. 584
Save key (F10), p. 575
scrolling, p. 559
search and replace, p. 561
secondary file, p. 565
spelling checker, p. 561
system requirements, p. 558
thesaurus, p. 562
Typeover mode, p. 571
word processing, p. 558
word processing software, p. 558
word wrap, p. 559

EXERCISES

SHORT ANSWER

1. Why is the REVEAL CODES (Alt-F3) command an important command?
2. What does the term *merging* refer to?
3. What is the document cycle?
4. Why is it significant to know that WordPerfect operates in Insert mode?
5. When you are using WordPerfect, why is it important to clear RAM before retrieving another file?
6. What happens if you press the Enter key when the cursor is in the middle of a paragraph?
7. What are headers and footers used for?
8. What is a block operation?
9. What is the function of the Cancel (F1) key?
10. If you are working with a three-paragraph single-spaced document, what procedure would you use to change the line spacing of the second paragraph to double?

HANDS ON

(*Note:* Complete the following exercises in order, and always save your data onto your data diskette.)

1. a. Create the document pictured in Figure B.21. Make sure to include your name and job position (real or made up) in the closing of the letter. Save this document onto your data diskette as WPLETTER.
   b. Print WPLETTER.

2. a. Insert the following text between the second and third paragraphs in the WPLETTER document:

   Specifically, word processing software makes it much easier to make changes to a document by allowing you to:
   1. Insert text.
   2. Move text.
   3. Copy text.
   4. Delete text.
   5. Perform block operations.
   6. Spell-check.
   7. Include special format enhancements (bolding, underlining, centering).

   b. Save this updated document as WPLETTER (you will need to replace the first version of WPLETTER). Print WPLETTER again.

3. Write a 1½-page document describing some of the useful features of word processing software. When finished, save this letter onto your data diskette as FEATURES, and then print the document. Include the following in the document:
   a. Your name and the current date.
   b. Centered title.
   c. Double-spacing.

FIGURE B.21

WPLETTER.

```
March 24, 1992


Mr. Andrew San Martino
210 Spruce Way
San Jose, CA 94063

Dear Mr. San Martino:

I received your letter the other day regarding the upcoming event.
I am in total agreement with you about limiting to 150 the number
of persons who can attend.  In addition, your idea of having the
event catered sounds great.

And now to move onto a different subject.  I noticed that the
letter you wrote me was typed using a typewriter.  You sure do use
correction fluid well!  Or I should say, you sure do use quite a
bit of it!  I'm just teasing... but with the number of letters you
write, you really should think of purchasing a microcomputer and
word processing software.  I am sure you will save time.

If you are interested, come over to my office, and I will show you
some of the fundamentals that relate to word processing.  We could
even use my word processing software to design and print all the
invitations to the upcoming event!

     With best regards,


     [your name]
     [your job position]
```

MODULE C

ELECTRONIC SPREADSHEETS: LOTUS 1-2-3

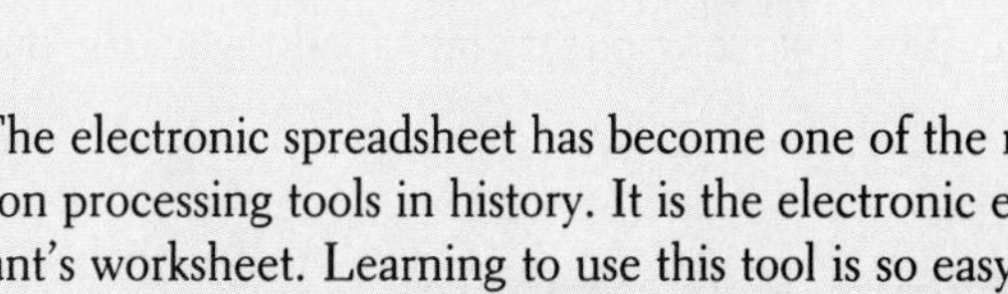

The electronic spreadsheet has become one of the most significant information processing tools in history. It is the electronic equivalent of the accountant's worksheet. Learning to use this tool is so easy that in a short time, the user can master the basics well enough to produce a simple spreadsheet. To help you gain a practical understanding of spreadsheet software, this module provides an overview of the features of electronic spreadsheet processing, followed by a tutorial using Lotus 1-2-3.

PREVIEW

When you have completed this module, you will be able to:

- Describe the general procedures required to create a reliable spreadsheet.
- Describe the features that are common to most electronic spreadsheet packages.
- Load Lotus 1-2-3 and move the cursor.
- Use Lotus 1-2-3's menu system.
- Use Lotus 1-2-3's help facility.
- Enter text, numbers, and formulas.
- Explain the procedure involved with correcting errors.
- Copy and format formulas.
- Widen columns.
- Describe the UNDO command.
- Print a spreadsheet.

ELECTRONIC SPREADSHEET OVERVIEW

A spreadsheet is essentially a grid of rows and columns with headings determined by the situation. Headings used by an accountant who is projecting company taxes over the next five years would differ from the heads used by the inventory manager in an automobile factory who is trying to calculate the need for certain parts over the next two years. But in both cases, the users would put numbers into rows and columns and then perform calculations on them. Until fairly recently, spreadsheets (or worksheets) were done by hand. It often took days or weeks to complete a spreadsheet: If one number had to be changed, the whole spreadsheet had to be recalculated and corrected by hand!

Electronic spreadsheet software, which eliminates this tedious and time-consuming activity, is now being used on approximately one out of every two microcomputers in the business community. Spreadsheet software is indispensable to the business professional who does tax planning or prepares financial statements such as cash projections or budgets. Engineers, scientists, teachers, accountants, architects, graphic designers, and many other professionals also find useful applications for spreadsheet software. The following pages will explain what the business user needs to know about this tool.

MANUAL VERSUS ELECTRONIC SPREADSHEETS

A manual spreadsheet (Figure C.1) is composed of rows and columns. The intersection of a row and column is called a **cell.** The spreadsheet is used to accumulate financial data that is later used in calculations to derive totals or percentages. Spreadsheet organization helps the user produce nicely aligned and organized reports. However, to do this manually, the user needs pencils, erasers, a calculator, and lots of time. Everything in manual spreadsheets, except the lines that form the rows and columns, must be done by hand.

For many people, making the text and numbers legible is more painstaking than deriving the spreadsheet's data! However, real frustration is experienced when a number that affects other numbers in a spreadsheet must be changed. All affected numbers must be erased, recalculated, and reentered.

FIGURE C.1

Manual spreadsheet. This manual spreadsheet is used to keep track of expenses. The intersection of a column and a row is called a *cell*. If a mistake is made entering an expense amount in any one cell, three other cells in the spreadsheet are affected.

	A	B	C	D	E
1	EXPENSE	JAN	FEB	MAR	TOTAL
2	TYPE				
3					
4	Telephone	85	79	82	246
5	Rent	600	600	600	1 800
6	Utilities	35	42	70	147
7	Auto	50	45	196	291
8	Other	121	135	140	396
9					
10	Total	891	901	1 088	2 880

Electronic spreadsheet software and the microcomputer have made it much easier to produce accurate spreadsheets quickly. Specifically, electronic spreadsheets provide users with the following advantages over manual spreadsheets:

1. *Electronic spreadsheets can be larger than manual ones.* A manual spreadsheet is typically no larger than 20 columns by 20 rows. (In effect, the sheet of paper you use should be no larger than the desktop on which you will work.) However, an electronic spreadsheet ranges in size from 128 to more than 256 columns and from 2,048 rows to 10,000 rows. With an electronic spreadsheet, the user can develop larger reports than is possible using a manual spreadsheet. Of course, it's impossible to see an entire electronic spreadsheet on the screen at once. Your screen acts as a window through which you see only a small portion of the spreadsheet (Figure C.2). You must print the spreadsheet to see it in its entirety.
2. *Electronic spreadsheets can perform mathematical calculations, including adding, subtracting, multiplying, and dividing.* The user puts the specifications for a calculation in a cell in the form of a formula, and the spreadsheet automatically performs the calculation and displays the answer in the cell. A **formula** is a mathematical expression that performs a calculation on values

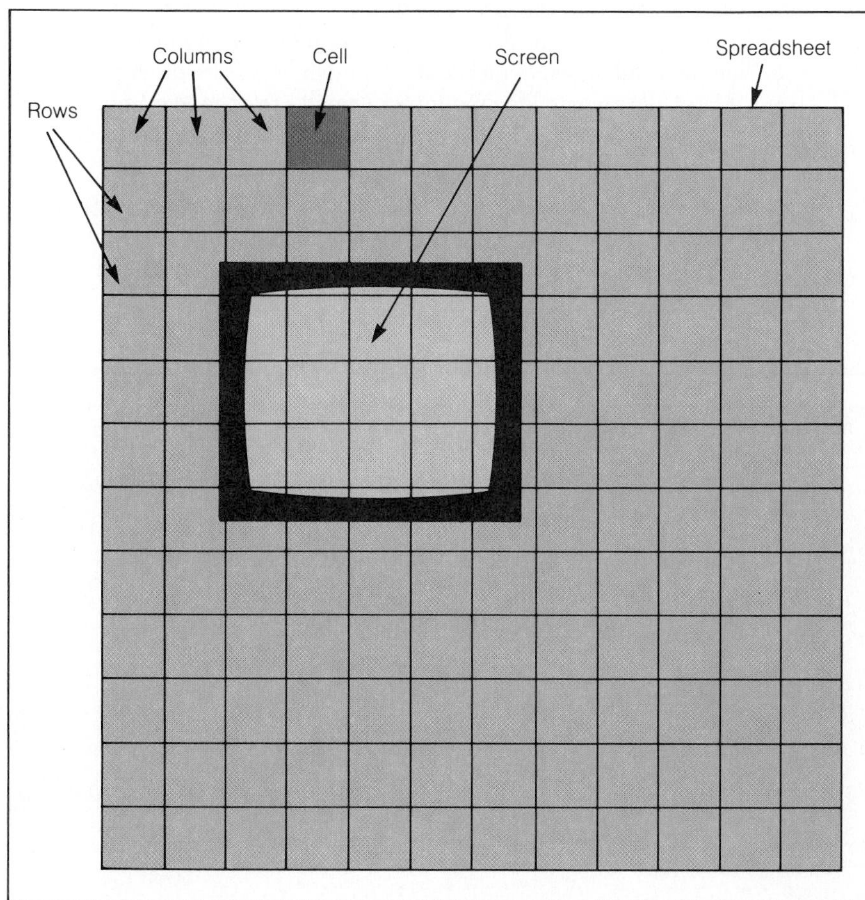

FIGURE C.2

Spreadsheet window. Your screen acts as a window through which you see only a portion of a large electronic spreadsheet. Spreadsheet software packages provide a variety of ways to move around the spreadsheet.

in a spreadsheet (that is, cells that don't contain text). In a manual spreadsheet, to perform calculations the user must have a calculator, a pencil, and a piece of paper. And the user must manually record the result of the calculation in the appropriate cell in the spreadsheet. However, with an electronic spreadsheet, to divide 365 by 24,000, for example, the user need enter only the following data into the appropriate cell: 365/24000. The answer will automatically be displayed in the cell.

3. *Cells in electronic spreadsheets can contain formulas.* In an electronic spreadsheet, cells hold not only text and numbers but also formulas that allow the user to refer to certain cells. For example, instead of putting 365/24000 in a cell, you could put a formula into it that will divide 365 by the number in a certain cell location in the spreadsheet. *After you type a formula into a cell, the cell displays the answer that results from the calculation.* In other words, it does not display the formula itself.
4. *In electronic spreadsheets, calculations are immediate.* In the manual spreadsheet in Figure C.1, data has been entered into columns B through D (JAN, FEB, and MAR), and the results of calculations have been placed into the bottom row of the spreadsheet and in column E (TOTAL). In this spreadsheet, if you need to change March's telephone expense from 82 to 92, you'll need to change three additional cells in the spreadsheet, all of which involve calculations. Figure C.3 shows this same spreadsheet as it would appear on the screen in electronic form if you were using Lotus 1-2-3. The electronic spreadsheet contains formulas in column E and in row 10. These formulas, described later in this module, refer to other cells in the spreadsheet. To change the amount for March's telephone expense in the electronic spreadsheet, you rekey it, and the formulas that refer to that cell location *automatically* recalculate changes.
5. *Electronic spreadsheets can be stored and retrieved.* Business professionals often produce the same report over and over again, updating each report with the current date and data. For example, if you want to change the

FIGURE C.3

Immediate calculations. In this electronic spreadsheet, column E and row 10 contain formulas that automatically recalculate amounts when the monthly expense data is changed.

A1: 'EXPENSE READY

	A	B	C	D	E	F	G
1	EXPENSE						
2	TYPE	JAN	FEB	MAR	TOTAL		
3							
4	TELEPHONE	85	79	82	246		
5	RENT	600	600	600	1800		
6	UTILITIES	35	42	70	147		
7	AUTO	50	45	196	291		
8	OTHER	121	135	140	396		
9							
10	TOTAL	891	901	1088	2880		
11							
12							
13							
14							
15							
16							
17							
18							
19							
20							

27-Feb-92 01:36 PM UNDO CAPS

electronic spreadsheet in Figure C.3 to reflect expenses for April through June, retrieve from disk storage a copy of the old spreadsheet (saved under the name QTR1), change the text for the month headings, and then change the data. The TOTAL formula will automatically recalculate the locations affected by the changes. You don't need to rekey any other text. You can then save this spreadsheet under a new name (QTR2). In this way, reports can be updated easily.

ELECTRONIC SPREADSHEET DEVELOPMENT PROCEDURES

Specific guidelines have evolved for developing electronic spreadsheets on the basis of the collective experience of the many people who have built them. *If you take shortcuts instead of following these procedures, you will develop spreadsheets that aren't reliable.* Recent studies done by several major universities found that 90 percent of all spreadsheets developed by nonprogramming professionals contained at least one error. And business decisions are being made on the basis of spreadsheets like these!

The steps for consistently developing a reliable spreadsheet are as follows:

1. *Establish your objectives.* It's easy to build a spreadsheet that doesn't save you any time at all. However, if you clearly formulate objectives for the spreadsheet before you start building it, you will know whether or not your particular needs will be met by an electronic spreadsheet, as well as what direction to take if you decide to proceed.
2. *Define your requirements.* Once you've decided to build a spreadsheet, you're ready to define your requirements—in other words, redefine your objectives more precisely. For instance, you must determine where data will be entered into the spreadsheet, the type of processing that will take place, and the kind of output you want.
3. *Build the spreadsheet.* If Steps 1 and 2 were completed in sufficient detail, Step 3 should be relatively simple—that is, keying the necessary text and formulas into the cells.
4. *Test the spreadsheet.* The biggest mistake you can make when using electronic spreadsheets is to assume that they automatically produce correct information and that they will inform you of any serious problems. After you have finished building your spreadsheet, you must test it carefully to ensure that it works exactly as you intended. One way to perform the test is by entering sample data into the spreadsheet and having it perform a few calculations; then perform the same calculations manually to see if you get the same results as the electronic spreadsheet. If you do get the same results, you can rely on the accuracy of the information produced by the electronic spreadsheet.
5. *Use the spreadsheet.* After you have tested it, you should write down a list of procedures for using the spreadsheet, so that someone who hasn't seen your spreadsheet before will understand how to use it. It's also a good idea to make a backup copy of your spreadsheet, in case someone accidentally erases it from your disk storage device.

ELECTRONIC SPREADSHEET FEATURES

This section focuses on the features of electronic spreadsheet processing that are common to most electronic spreadsheet packages. Familiarizing yourself with these features will help you to use electronic spreadsheet software effectively.

LOADING THE SPREADSHEET SOFTWARE: WHAT DO YOU SEE?

Once you load the software into main memory, you will be looking at the upper-left corner of a huge electronic spreadsheet. Specifically, you will see the spreadsheet area, the command/data entry area, and the indicator area (Figure C.4).

The **spreadsheet area** of the screen display comprises rows and columns that are labeled with letters and numbers that allow you to identify cells in the spreadsheet. As mentioned earlier, a cell is the intersection of a row and a column. In Figure C.4, cell A1 contains the text EXPENSE, and cell B4 contains the number 85.

At the top of your screen, you see the **command/data entry area.** Most spreadsheet programs display the following types of information in this area: status information telling you what cell the cursor is in, what the format of the cells is (we'll discuss formatting options later), and what the actual contents of the cell are. In Figure C.4, for example, the command/data entry area indicates that the cursor is currently positioned on cell A1 (A1:) and that the text EXPENSE is in the cell ('Expense). In addition, when you instruct the spreadsheet program to issue a command, the list of available commands appears in the command/data entry area along with a description of what a specific command will do for you. Also, characters

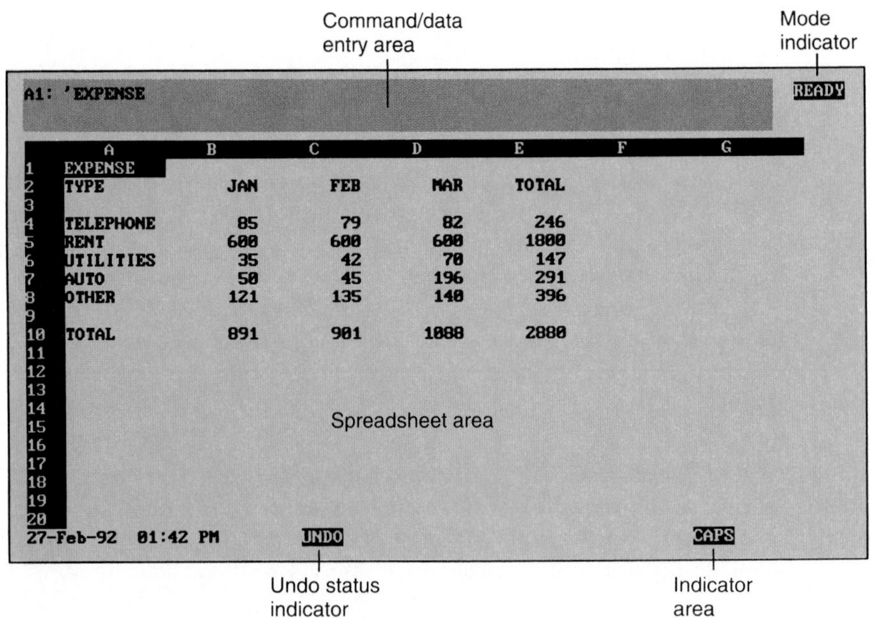

FIGURE C.4

Electronic spreadsheet. A cell in an electronic spreadsheet is identified by column letter and row number—for example, cell A1 contains EXPENSE. The command/data entry area indicates what cell the cursor is in and what the content of the cell is; it also gives you command options and descriptions. The indicator area displays any error messages or messages about certain keys that have been pressed (such as the Num Lock key).

that you're entering into specific cells in the spreadsheet are displayed here until you press the Enter key. To the right of the command/data entry area is a message that tells you what mode of operation you're currently working in (modes of operation will be described in the next section).

Most electronic spreadsheet programs also have an **indicator area,** which is usually positioned in the bottom-right corner of the screen. This area indicates, for example, whether the Caps Lock or Num Lock key has been pressed.

Modes of Operation

Electronic spreadsheet programs often operate in one of four modes: Ready mode, Label mode, Value mode, or Menu mode. When using Lotus 1-2-3, you can always tell what mode the spreadsheet is in by looking in the top right-hand corner of the screen. (In the tutorial section of this module, which leads you through using Lotus 1-2-3, Table C.1 lists some additional modes of operation.)

If you are operating in **Ready mode,** you can move the cursor around the spreadsheet. You need to be able to move the cursor for two reasons. First, to put data into a specific cell, such as cell D8, you need to move the cursor to that cell before you key in the data. When you build a spreadsheet, you will enter data into many cells. Second, to view a spreadsheet that is larger than the screen, you need to move the cursor.

The second mode of operation is called **Label mode.** You are in this mode *after* you have positioned the cursor in the cell into which you want to enter text and have typed one alphabetic key. Once you type that key, the mode indicator will tell you that the spreadsheet is in Label mode.

The spreadsheet is in **Value mode** after you begin typing a number or formula into a cell. Once you have pressed the Enter key to complete the entry of data into a cell, the spreadsheet will again be back in Ready mode.

The fourth mode of operation is **Menu mode.** The commands in most electronic spreadsheets are organized hierarchically — meaning that subselections exist under main command headings. Figure C.5a shows the command hierarchy for Lotus 1-2-3's RANGE group of commands. Menu mode is invoked by pressing the slash key (/). A list of the main command options appears in the command/data entry area. Once you prepare to choose a command option by moving the cursor to it (and thus highlight it), the choices available under that option are then displayed in this area (Figure C.5b). To choose a command option, press the Enter key when the option is highlighted. By proceeding in this fashion, you go deeper and deeper into the hierarchical command structure of the electronic spreadsheet. When you have reached the "bottom" of a command (the lowest level of the command hierarchy), the electronic spreadsheet returns to Ready mode.

Entering Text, Numbers, and Formulas

No matter whether you want to enter text, numbers, or formulas into a cell, you must remember to first move the cursor to the appropriate cell and then key in the data. Keying in the text and numbers is simple — until the text or number becomes wider than the column. The default column width for most electronic spreadsheet programs is nine characters. (The term *default* refers to the assumptions the elec-

FIGURE C.5 Command hierarchy structure. (a) The command hierarchy for Lotus 1-2-3's RANGE group of commands. As you can see, there are many different options to choose from under the RANGE command; (b) what the screen looks like after the / key has been pressed and the cursor is highlighting the RANGE command.

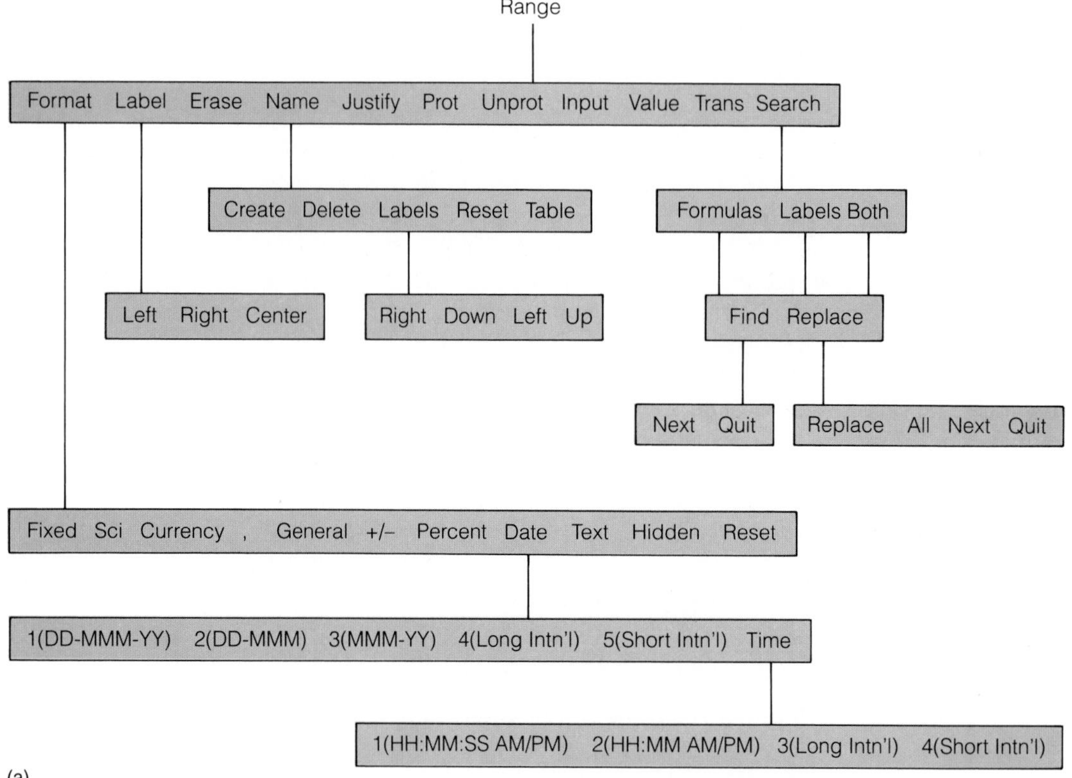

(a)

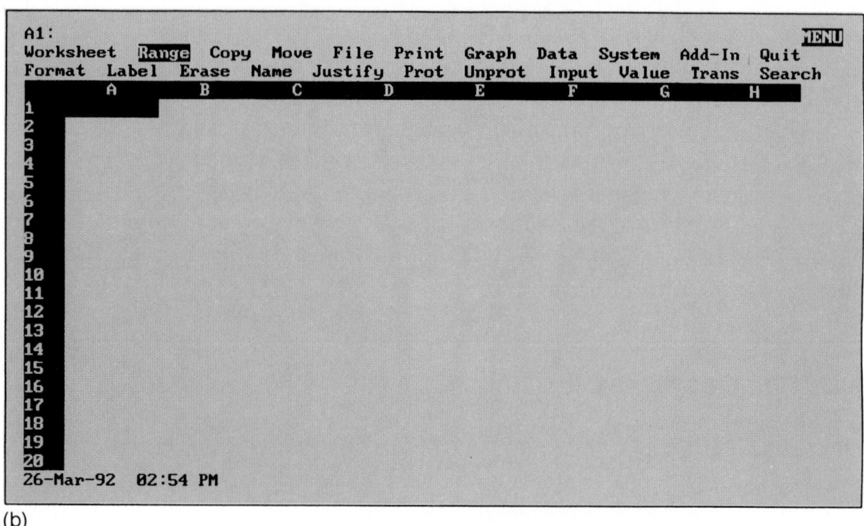

(b)

tronic spreadsheet program makes about a spreadsheet until the user tells it otherwise.) Because users often have to change column width, spreadsheet programs provide the user with a command that performs this task.

Entering formulas is also simple; we'll show you how later. Figure C.6 shows the logical and arithmetic operators that can be used in Lotus 1-2-3 formulas. These operators are similar to those found in most electronic spreadsheet programs.

USING FUNCTIONS

An electronic spreadsheet program provides many powerful **functions,** or electronic shortcuts, that can be used in formulas. Functions can save the user a tremendous amount of time. For example, in Figure C.7, there is a column of numbers in column B. In cell B19, a formula is needed to add the contents of all cells from B5 to B17. Without the use of a function, the formula in cell B19 could be written as follows:

(B5 + B6 + B7 + B8 + B9 + B10 + B11 + B12 + B13 . . .)

Think about the amount of time it would take to add a column of 100 numbers! To save time when adding ranges of numbers — a **range** is one or more cells that form a rectangle (Figure C.8) — electronic spreadsheet programs use a function often referred to as the **@SUM function** to simplify the process. In Lotus 1-2-3, the @SUM function in cell B19 would be:

@SUM(B5 . . B17)

Logical Operators	
=	Equal
<	Less than
<=	Less than or equal to
>	Greater than
>=	Greater than or equal to
<>	Not equal
#NOT#	Not
#AND#	And
#OR#	Or

Arithmetic (Mathematical) operators		**Example**
+	Addition	+A1 + A2
−	Subtraction	+A1 − A2
*	Multiplication	+A1 * A2
/	Divide	+A1 / A2

FIGURE C.6

Formula operators. The logical and arithmetic operators used in Lotus 1-2-3 formulas.

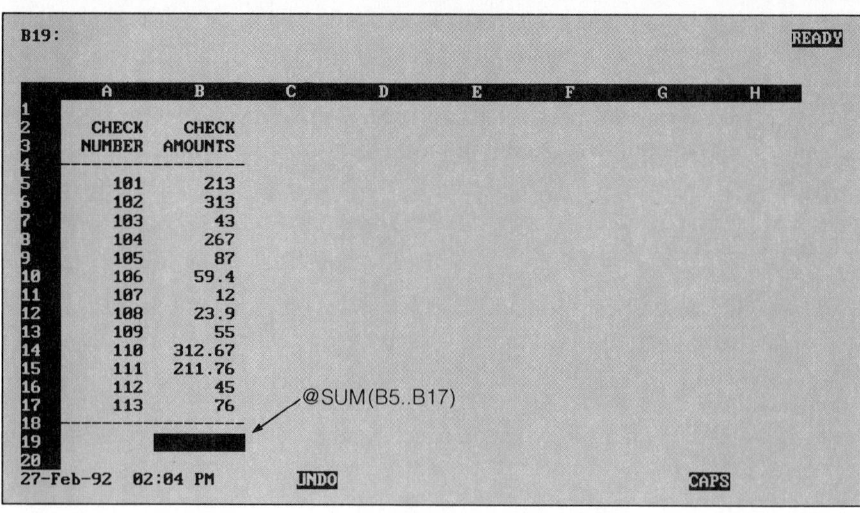

FIGURE C.7

Functions. The user can save time by using the @SUM function in cell B19 to calculate the total amount of the checks. Spreadsheet programs provide a number of different functions.

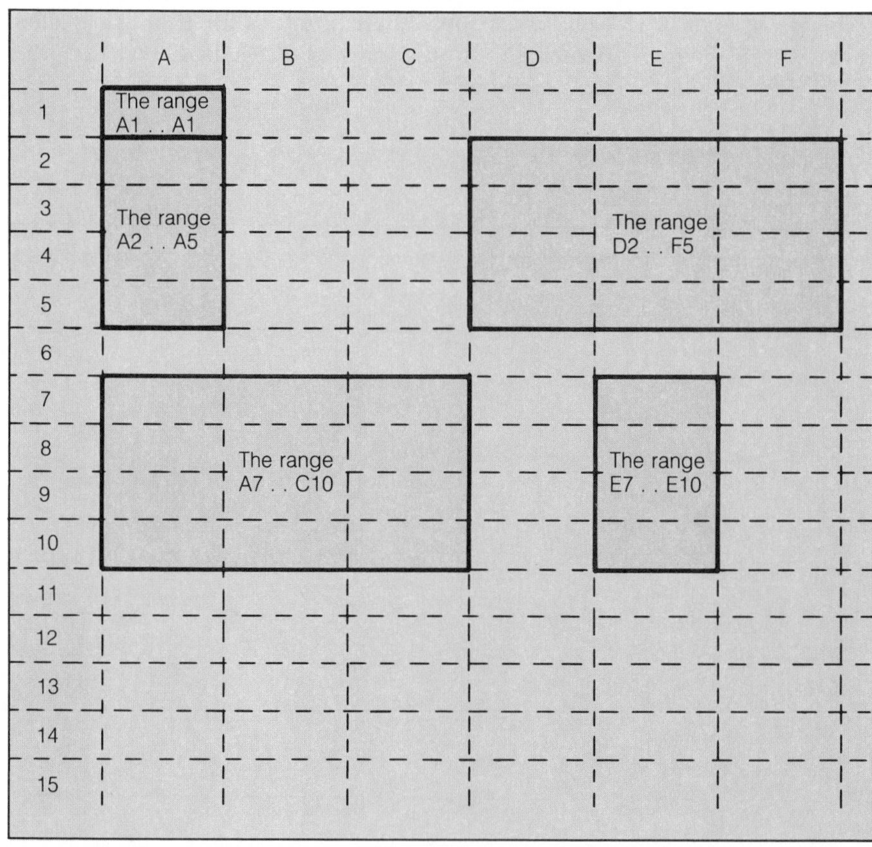

FIGURE C.8

Spreadsheet ranges.

With this function, the user simply specifies the beginning and the end of the range of cells to be added, encloses the range in parentheses, and keys in the text @SUM (all of Lotus 1-2-3's functions are preceded by @) in front of the first parenthesis.

Different types of functions can be used as mathematical shortcuts in formulas. In fact, most spreadsheet programs provide the user with over 80 functions to use. Some functions allow the user to determine the minimum, maximum, and average of a range of cells. In Lotus 1-2-3, these functions would be expressed using the @MIN, @MAX, and @AVG functions (these functions are almost identical to the @SUM function).

COPYING

The text and formulas in cells can be quite long. What happens if you want to place a text string that is 30 characters long in 25 places in the spreadsheet? Do you have to key in 750 characters? No. The process of getting text and formulas into a large number of cells is really quite simple. It involves using a spreadsheet command that allows you to copy. Generally speaking, the steps for copying text and formulas from one cell into many other cells are as follows:

1. Initiate the COPY command.
2. Tell the software where the text or formula is that you want to copy—the column letter and row number.
3. Tell the software what cell or cells you want the text or formula copied into.

When a formula is copied into one or more cells, the spreadsheet analyzes the cell from which the formula is being copied and the cell(s) the formula is being copied into. It then adjusts the cell references in the copied formulas to reflect their new locations in the spreadsheet. This saves the user from typing a number of formulas (that essentially do the same thing, such as adding together a range of cells) into the spreadsheet. This also saves the user a tremendous amount of time. You will use Lotus 1-2-3 to copy a formula later in this module.

FORMATTING

Figure C.9 shows the spreadsheet in Figure C.3 after it has been formatted. As you might have guessed, **formatting** commands allow the user to improve the appearance of a spreadsheet—that is, to make it easier to read. You can choose from a number of formatting commands.

The first command used in Figure C.9 formatted the numbers in columns B through E in the **currency format.** Numbers that are formatted this way are displayed with a dollar sign and a specified number of decimal places. In this figure, the numbers were formatted to two decimal places. In addition, the columns were widened in Figure C.9 to provide more space between the numbers in the columns.

SAVING

While you are working with a spreadsheet program, the spreadsheet specifications reside in main memory. If you want a permanent copy of the specifications that you can retrieve later, you must issue a spreadsheet command that will save your specifications onto disk. The spreadsheet specifications you save consist of all the text, numbers, and formulas you have entered into the spreadsheet. If you want to update the spreadsheet later, simply retrieve a copy of it from disk, add new data, and then save it again.

PRINTING

You have the option of printing a spreadsheet in one of two forms: (1) as a report or (2) as a list of specifications. Figure C.9 shows an example of a printed spreadsheet report. In Lotus 1-2-3, this form is called the **as-displayed format,** which is what you see on the screen. To see what formulas you have in each cell of the spreadsheet and how each cell is formatted, you need to print out the report specifications. In Lotus 1-2-3, this form is called the **cell-formulas format.** It's a good idea to print out a cell-formulas format for every spreadsheet you create, so that you can recreate the spreadsheet's specifications if the spreadsheet is accidentally erased. Figure C.10 shows the cell specifications for the report in Figure C.9.

IN THE LAB USING LOTUS 1-2-3

Lotus 1-2-3 provides users with a variety of capabilities that can be viewed as falling into four categories.

1. Lotus's *spreadsheet capabilities* enable you to enter text and numbers and to then perform calculations—using formulas—on the data you have typed in. When a number is changed in the spreadsheet, the formulas calculate the correct results automatically. Lotus's spreadsheet capabilities are described in this module.

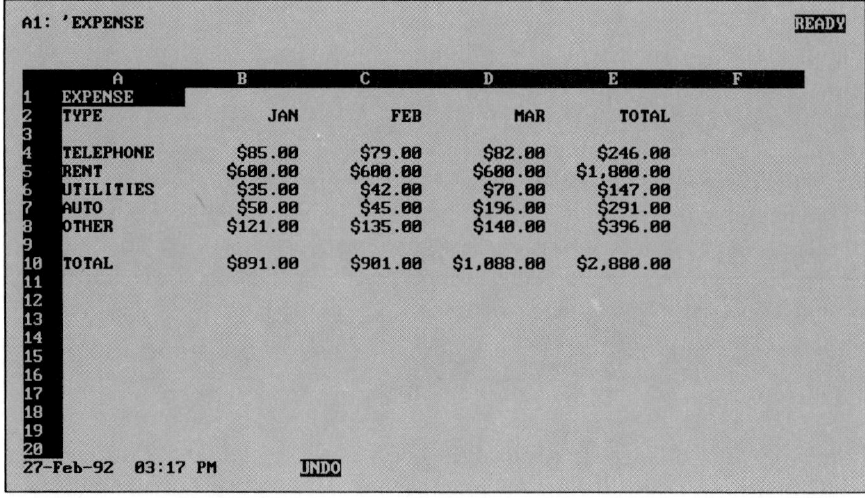

FIGURE C.9

To improve the appearance of the spreadsheet pictured in Figure C.3, a number of different formatting commands were used.

2. With Lotus's *database capabilities*, you can sort data into order and retrieve information from a base of data. Compared with other types of database programs, manipulating data with an electronic spreadsheet program is faster because the entire database is stored in RAM during processing. With other programs, portions of the database are stored on disk, which can slow processing down.
3. Lotus's *graphics capabilities* enable you to present data in the form of business charts, including pie charts, bar charts, stacked bar charts, and area charts. It is often easier to understand data when it is presented in graphic form. Lotus's graphics capabilities are described in Module E.
4. In addition, Lotus provides you with two **add-ins,** which are RAM-resident software instructions, loaded after the applications software is loaded, that provide users with additional capabilities. Allways, a Lotus add-in, enables you to output spreadsheets with presentation-quality graphics and to merge text and graphics on a single page. The Macro Library Manager add-in enables you to store the macros you create in a file that can be accessed from all your spreadsheets, which can ultimately save you time.

```
A1: 'EXPENSE
A2: 'TYPE
B2: "JAN
C2: "FEB
D2: "MAR
E2: "TOTAL
A4: 'TELEPHONE
B4: (C2) 85
C4: (C2) 79
D4: (C2) 82
E4: (C2) @SUM(B4..D4)
A5: 'RENT
B5: (C2) 600
C5: (C2) 600
D5: (C2) 600
E5: (C2) @SUM(B5..D5)
A6: 'UTILITIES
B6: (C2) 35
C6: (C2) 42
D6: (C2) 70
E6: (C2) @SUM(B6..D6)
A7: 'AUTO
B7: (C2) 50
C7: (C2) 45
D7: (C2) 196
E7: (C2) @SUM(B7..D7)
A8: 'OTHER
B8: (C2) 121
C8: (C2) 135
D8: (C2) 140
E8: (C2) @SUM(B8..D8)
A10: 'TOTAL
B10: (C2) @SUM(B4..B8)
C10: (C2) @SUM(C4..C8)
D10: (C2) @SUM(D4..D8)
E10: (C2) @SUM(E4..E8)
```

FIGURE C.10

List of specifications. This printout shows the characteristics of every cell that contains data in the spreadsheet in Figure C.9.

USING THIS TUTORIAL

In this tutorial, you will have the opportunity to create a spreadsheet using the Lotus 1-2-3 spreadsheet package. In this section, you will practice most of the electronic spreadsheet features described thus far. Because all spreadsheet packages are similar in concept and organization, having experience using Lotus 1-2-3 will help you to learn another spreadsheet package if the need arises.

In this tutorial, we assume you will use either a diskette system or a hard disk system. The descriptions for these two types of systems can be found in the Introduction to the Modules. When the procedures differ according to the configuration of your computer, they will be listed beneath one of the two following headings: (1) For Diskette System Users or (2) For Hard Disk System Users. If you're not sure which instructions to follow, ask your instructor.

THE BUSINESS SITUATION

You are the owner of Sporting Life, a sporting goods store that carries a full line of sports equipment and clothing. Over the last few years, sales have increased to more than $900,000. Recently you acquired a computer and had a lesson in how to use operating systems software. You also acquired electronic spreadsheet software because you were told that many activities performed manually at Sporting Life can be performed more quickly and easily using this type of software. One activity that your staff finds time-consuming is keeping track of expenses.

In the following pages, you will build the spreadsheet pictured in Figure C.9 to keep track of Sporting Life's monthly expenses. This spreadsheet will make use of the @ SUM function to add expense amounts.

LOADING LOTUS 1-2-3

We assume that you have booted your computer with DOS using the procedure described in the Introduction to the Modules. The procedure you use to load Lotus 1-2-3 is different depending on whether you are using a diskette-based system or a hard disk system. *Note:* If you are using a hard disk system but don't have Lotus 1-2-3 stored on the hard disk, follow the instructions for diskette system users.

FOR DISKETTE SYSTEM USERS

1. To load Lotus 1-2-3 from a 5¼-inch or 3½-inch diskette drive, put the Lotus 1-2-3 diskette in drive A.
2. TYPE: lotus
   PRESS: Enter
   The screen should look like Figure C.11. You are looking at the Lotus 1-2-3 Access System. The cursor is currently highlighting the 1-2-3 option, and a description of this option is on the second line. *Two methods can be used to choose an option from a Lotus menu. You can either highlight the option (using the cursor-movement keys) and then press the Enter key, or press the first character of the option.* *(continued)*

The PrintGraph option is used for printing the graphs you create (you will create graphs using Lotus 1-2-3 in Module E). The Translate option enables you to transfer data from another software application into Lotus 1-2-3 so that it can be manipulated using Lotus 1-2-3's commands. When you first purchase Lotus 1-2-3, you use the Install option to tell the program about the characteristics of your hardware. (For example, will you use Lotus 1-2-3 on a microcomputer configured with a color monitor? Hard disk? What kind of printer will you use?) By choosing the Exit option, you exit the Lotus 1-2-3 Access System.

3. The cursor should still be highlighting the 1-2-3 option. To choose this option:
   PRESS: Enter ■

FOR HARD DISK SYSTEM USERS

1. Lotus 1-2-3 is probably loaded in a subdirectory (named something like LOTUS or 123) on the hard disk. You may be able to load Lotus 1-2-3 without making the Lotus subdirectory current (using the CD command that was described in the Introduction to the Modules). To see if this is the case, type the following after the system prompt:
   TYPE: lotus
   PRESS: Enter
   The screen should look like Figure C.11. *If a message such as "Bad Command or Filename" is displaying on the screen, proceed with Step 2. Otherwise, skip Step 2 and proceed to Step 3.*
2. Use the CD command to make the Lotus subdirectory the current subdirectory. For example, if the Lotus subdirectory is called LOTUS, you would type CD \LOTUS.
3. To load Lotus 1-2-3, follow Steps 2 and 3 in the instructions for diskette system users. ■

The screen should look like Figure C.12.

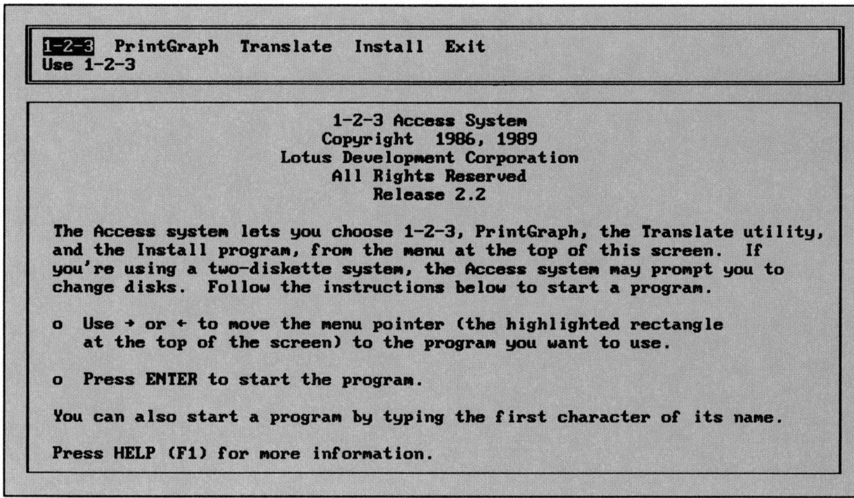

FIGURE C.11

The Lotus Access System.

Quick Reference

■

Loading Lotus 1-2-3

1. After the system prompt:
   TYPE: LOTUS
2. To choose the 1-2-3 option:
   PRESS: Enter

What do you see? Across the top of your screen you should see the letters A – H, and down the left side of the screen you should see the numbers 1 – 20. These are the column and row references you will use to identify a cell. In the upper-right corner of the screen is a mode indicator that says READY. As described earlier, when Lotus is in Ready mode, it is ready for you to move the cursor and then type data into the cells in the spreadsheet. Table C.1 describes the different modes that Lotus operates in.

MOVING THE CURSOR

The cursor is now positioned in cell A1. To create spreadsheets, you need to know how to move the cursor using the cursor-movement keys. Therefore, this is the first procedure we will cover. Figure C.13 lists a few different ways of moving the cursor.

Perform the following five steps:

1. To move the cursor to cell G1, press the Right cursor-movement key six times.
2. To move the cursor to cell J1, press the Right cursor-movement key three more times. You can always tell what cell the cursor is in by looking in the upper-left corner of the screen.

   What has happened to columns A and B? They have scrolled off the screen to the left. Think of your screen as a window through which you are viewing

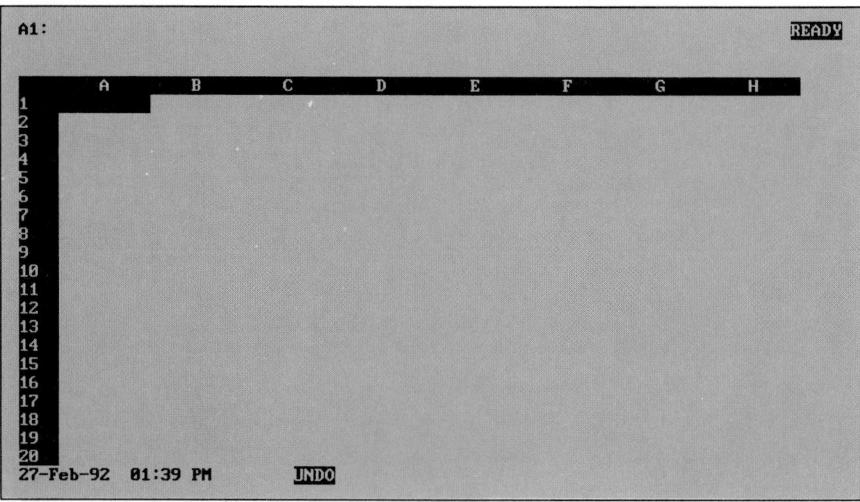

FIGURE C.12

The Lotus 1-2-3 spreadsheet. This is what you see when you first load Lotus 1-2-3.

portions of a very large spreadsheet (this concept was described earlier in Figure C.2).

3. To move the cursor to cell J21, press the Down cursor-movement key 20 times. Note that row 1 has now scrolled off the top of the screen.

TABLE C.1

Modes of Operation

Mode	Description
Edit	You are changing the contents of a cell after either making a mistake in a formula or using the F2 key.
Files	You are displaying a list of files on the screen.
Help	You have pressed the F1 key.
Mem	Lotus warns you with this indicator when the amount of available main memory in your computer has dropped below 4,096 bytes.
Ovr	You have pressed the Ins key, which toggles Insert mode off. As a result, what you type will overwrite existing data rather than be inserted at the current cursor location.
Ready	You can move the cursor around the spreadsheet. Lotus 1-2-3 is "ready" for you to type something into a cell or issue a command.
Label	You are in the process of typing text into a cell.
Menu	You have pressed the slash (/) key to display the Lotus 1-2-3 menu.
Point	You are in the process of using a Lotus 1-2-3 command and are highlighting a range of cells.
Undo	You have activated the Undo feature of Lotus 1-2-3.
Value	You are in the process of typing a number or formula into a cell.

FIGURE C.13

Moving the cursor. These methods of moving the cursor are common to most spreadsheet packages.

Keys	Purpose
Home	Moves cursor to cell A1 from anywhere in the spreadsheet.
End	When used prior to any of the arrow keys, it will move you to the last cell in an empty or filled space.
Left ← Right →	Used to position the cursor either left or right one column.
Up ↑ Down ↓	Used to position the cursor either up or down one row.
PgUp	Used to move the cursor up an entire screen.
PgDn	Used to move the cursor down an entire screen.
Tab	Used to move the cursor an entire screen to the right.
Shift-Tab	Used to move the cursor an entire screen to the left.
F5	Used to move the cursor to a specific cell.

4. Fortunately, there is an easier way to move the cursor up and down 20 rows at a time — using the PgUp and PgDn keys. Press the PgDn key twice. The cursor should now be in cell J61. Press the PgUp key once. The cursor should now be in cell J41.
5. The Home key allows you to easily move to cell A1. Press the Home key. The cursor should again be in cell A1.

As you can see, moving the cursor around the spreadsheet is simple. To create a spreadsheet, you must move the cursor to the appropriate cell before typing anything.

EDITING A CELL

Even though you haven't yet typed anything into a cell, we want to familiarize you with editing procedures in case you make a mistake in any of the following sections. First we'll lead you through typing some text into cell A1. Then we'll lead you through editing it.

Perform the following steps:

1. The cursor should be positioned in cell A1.
   TYPE: xyz
   PRESS: Enter
   The text "xyz" should be displaying in cell A1. (If you look in the upper-left corner of the screen, note that Lotus 1-2-3 automatically inserted an apostrophe before the text. The apostrophe stands for left-alignment. In the next section, you will learn more about entering and aligning text in a cell.)

What if you type text, a number, or a formula into a cell and then decide it needs to be changed? Two methods can be used to edit the contents of a cell in a spreadsheet.

> *Method 1*. Position the cursor on the cell that needs to be changed. Retype the contents. Press the Enter key. Once you press the Enter key, what you typed will replace what was formerly in the cell. This method is best if you need to completely replace the contents of a cell.
>
> *Method 2*. Position the cursor on the cell that needs to be changed. Press the F2 (Edit) key. The contents of the cell the cursor is positioned on will appear above the spreadsheet area so that you can edit it. Make your changes, and then press the Enter key. This method is best if you need to make only a few changes to the contents of a cell.

2. What if you don't want "xyz" in cell A1? Instead you want "abc"? Using the first editing method:
   TYPE: abc
   PRESS: Enter
   The text "abc" should now be displaying in cell A1.
3. What if you don't want "abc" in cell A1? Instead you want "abc company"? Using the second editing method:
   PRESS: F2
4. A copy of the contents of A1 should be displaying on the top of the screen.

PRESS: space bar
TYPE: company
PRESS: Enter
The text "abc company" should now be displaying in the cell. The F2 key can save you a lot of time when you are editing a cell that contains many characters.

Quick Reference

■

Editing a Cell

Method 1. Position the cursor on the cell that needs to be changed. Retype the contents. Press the Enter key, and what you typed replaces what was formerly in the cell.

Method 2. Position the cursor on the cell that needs to be changed. Press the F2 (Edit) key. The contents of the cell the cursor is positioned on appears above the spreadsheet area so that you can edit it. After you edit the contents, press the Enter key.

ENTERING TEXT (LABELS)

When you type the characters A–Z, Lotus goes into Label mode and displays LABEL in the upper-right corner of the spreadsheet. Lotus automatically places the text you type on the left side of the cell and inserts an apostrophe (') before the text. If you want text to appear on the right side of a cell, you must type quotation marks (") before the text. If you want the text to appear centered in a cell, you must type a caret (^) before the text (Figure C.14).

In this section, you will type the descriptive text into the spreadsheet. *As you proceed, refer to the section called "Editing a Cell" (p. 608) if you make a mistake.*

Perform the following steps:

1. So that the letters appear in capitals:
   PRESS: Caps Lock
2. The message CAPS should appear highlighted in the bottom-right corner of the screen. Now all the letters you type will appear in capital letters. Make sure the cursor is positioned in cell A1.
   TYPE: EXPENSE
   PRESS: Enter
3. The text EXPENSE should be in cell A1. As described earlier, if you misspelled EXPENSE, either type it correctly and press the Enter key, or use the Edit key (F2).
   PRESS: Down cursor-movement key once

'	Left-alignment	'hello
"	Right-alignment	"hello
^	Center-alignment	^hello

FIGURE C.14

Label alignment. The ', ", and ^ are used to align labels in a cell.

4. The cursor should have moved to cell A2.
   TYPE: TYPE
   PRESS: Enter
5. The text TYPE should be in cell A2.
   PRESS: Down cursor-movement key twice
6. The cursor should be in cell A4. Position the cursor in the following cells and type in the corresponding text:

CELL LOCATION	YOU TYPE
A4	TELEPHONE
A5	RENT
A6	UTILITIES
A7	AUTO
A8	OTHER
A10	TOTAL

7. In the next few steps, you will type the headings into the range B2 . . E2. So that the text will appear on the right side of the cell (lined up above the numbers you will enter in a later step), you will begin the text with a quotation marks. *Note*: If you omit the quotation marks, the text you type will appear on the left side of the cell—numbers (values), however, always appear on the right side of a cell. Position the cursor in the following cells and type in the corresponding text:

CELL LOCATION	YOU TYPE
B2	"JAN
C2	"FEB
D2	"MAR
E2	"TOTAL

All the text has now been entered into this spreadsheet. The cursor should be positioned in cell E2. Your spreadsheet should now look like Figure C.15.

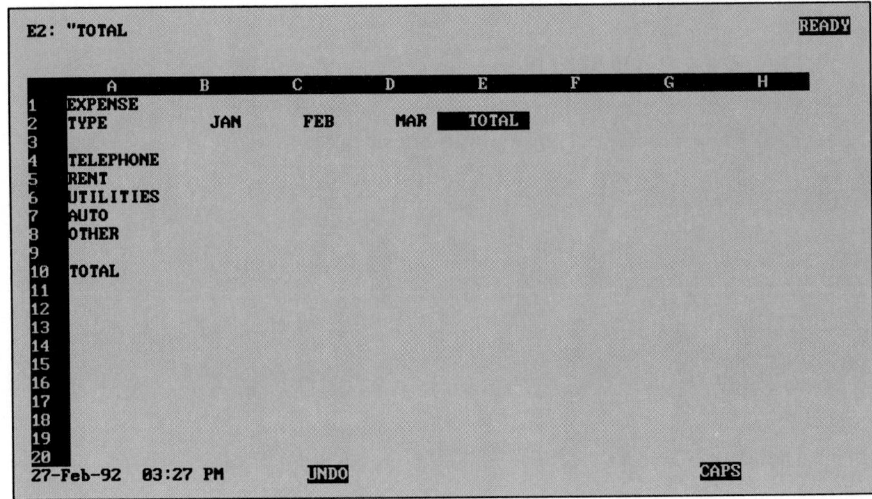

FIGURE C.15

The text has been entered in the spreadsheet.

Entering Numbers (Values)

When you type a number or the plus sign, minus sign, open parentheses, period, pound sign, or "at" sign (@), Lotus goes into Value mode and displays VALUE in the upper-right corner of the spreadsheet. Numbers are keyed into cells in the same way text is.

Perform the following steps *(as you proceed, refer to the section on Editing a Cell, p. 608, if you make a mistake)*:

1. Move the cursor to cell B4 so that the expense data can be entered.
2. In this step, you will enter the expense data for January. Position the cursor in the following cells and type in the corresponding number:

Cell Location	You Type
B4	85
B5	600
B6	35
B7	50
B8	121

3. In this step, you will enter the expense data for February. Position the cursor in the following cells and type in the corresponding number:

Cell Location	You Type
C4	79
C5	600
C6	42
C7	45
C8	135

4. In this step, you will enter the expense data for March. Position the cursor in the following cells and type in the corresponding number:

Cell Location	Number
D4	82
D5	600
D6	70
D7	196
D8	140

All the expense data has now been entered into this spreadsheet. Your spreadsheet should look like Figure C.16.

Entering Formulas

This spreadsheet will contain the following formulas:

1. Row 10 will contain formulas that add the five expense amounts you just entered.

2. Column E will contain formulas that add the three monthly expense amounts for each expense type (telephone, rent, and so on).

Each of these formulas will use the @SUM function, because it simplifies adding a range of numbers (the @SUM function was described earlier in this module).

Perform the following steps *(as you proceed, refer to the section on Editing a Cell if you make a mistake)*:

1. Position the cursor in cell B10 so that a formula can be entered.
2. To add the expenses in column B (*note: do not type spaces between dots in ranges*):
   TYPE: @SUM(B4 . . B8)
   PRESS: Right cursor-movement key
   The total 891 should be displaying in cell B10. If the correct answer isn't displaying, check to see that you entered the formula correctly (position the cursor on cell B10 and then look at the top-left corner of the screen). If the formula is incorrect, retype it, and then press Enter. If your total is wrong but the formula is correct, check to see that the numbers you typed into cells B4, B5, B6, B7, and B8 are the same as in Figure C.9.
3. Position the cursor in the following cells and type in the corresponding formula:

CURSOR POSITION	YOU TYPE
C10	@SUM(C4 . . C8)
D10	@SUM(D4 . . D8)
E10	@SUM(E4 . . E8)

4. The number 0 should appear in cell E10 because no data is in the cells above. As soon as a formula is entered into one of the cells above E10, a total will appear in cell E10.
5. Position the cursor in the following cells and type in the corresponding formula:

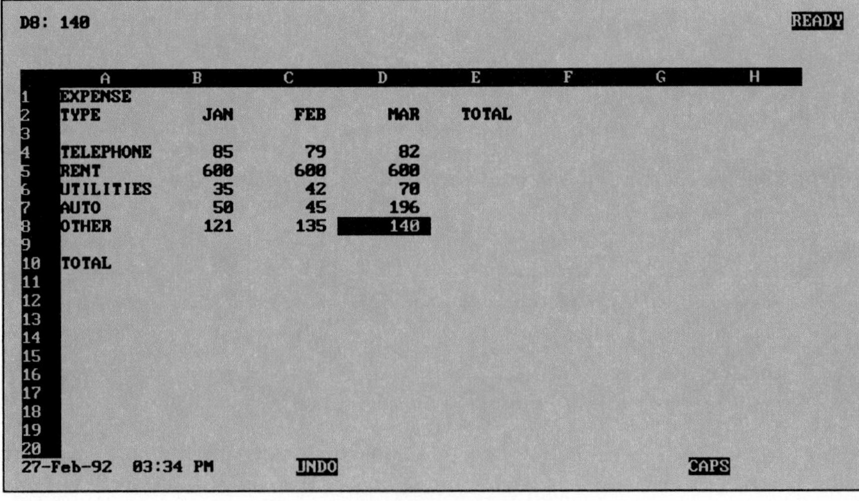

FIGURE C.16

The data has been entered in the spreadsheet.

Cell Location	You Type
E4	@SUM(B4 . . D4)
E5	@SUM(B5 . . D5)
E6	@SUM(B6 . . D6)
E7	@SUM(B7 . . D7)
E8	@SUM(B8 . . D8)

All the formulas have now been entered into this spreadsheet (Figure C.17).

Using Menu Mode

As described earlier, Lotus 1-2-3's commands are organized hierarchically, which means that subselections exist under main command headings. To enter Menu mode, you must press the slash (/) key: MENU appears in the upper-right corner of the spreadsheet. To practice using Lotus 1-2-3's menus, perform the following steps:

1. To enter Menu mode:
   TYPE: /
2. The cursor is highlighting the Worksheet option. On the second line is a list of the Worksheet group of commands.
   PRESS: Right cursor-movement key
3. The cursor is now highlighting the Range option, and a list of the range group of commands is on the line below. As you highlight a menu option, a description of that option appears on the line below. To choose an option, press the Enter key when an option is highlighted. By proceeding in this fashion, you go deeper and deeper into Lotus's hierarchical command structure.

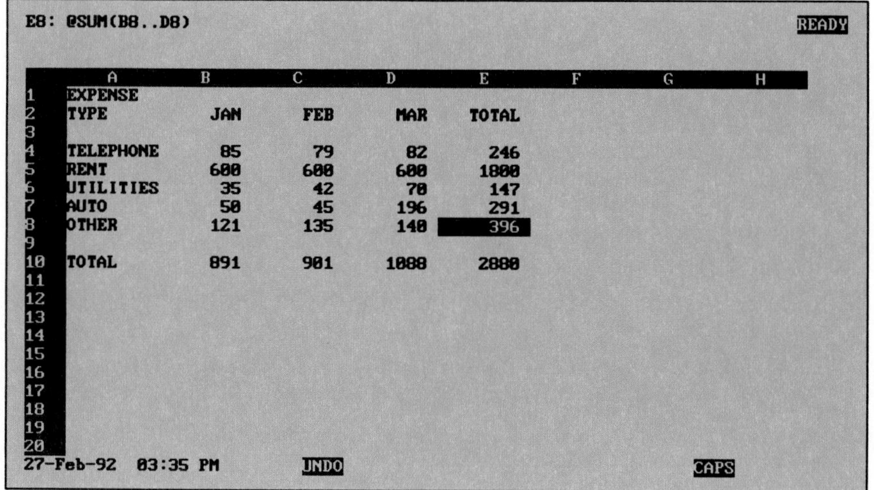

FIGURE C.17

The formulas have been entered in the spreadsheet.

4. To choose the Worksheet group of commands, highlight Worksheet and press Enter. The cursor should now be highlighting the Global option. To choose this option, press Enter. The cursor should be highlighting the Format option. To choose this option, press Enter. Note that you are moving deeper into the command hierarchy. If for some reason you don't want to complete a command, press the Escape key (Esc) to move back up the command structure until the spreadsheet is again in Ready mode.
   PRESS: Esc until the mode indicator says READY
5. You can also choose command options by pressing the first character of the option. To illustrate:
   TYPE: /
6. To choose the File option:
   TYPE: F
7. To choose the Directory option:
   TYPE: D
8. To return to Ready mode:
   PRESS: Esc until the mode indicator says READY

In this module, you will choose commands by pressing the first letter of the option.

Quick Reference

■

Using Menu Mode

1. PRESS: /
2. To choose an option, either highlight the option and then press Enter, or type the first character of the option.
3. To back out of an option:
   PRESS: Esc

GETTING HELP

Since Lotus 1-2-3 provides over 115 commands for you to use, you probably won't be able to remember how to use all of them. If you find yourself in the middle of a command but aren't sure how to use it, use the **help facility,** which provides information about each of Lotus's commands. The help facility is accessed by pressing the Help key (F1).

Perform the following steps to use the help facility:

1. The spreadsheet should be in Ready mode (check the mode indicator in the upper-right corner).
2. PRESS: F1
   If you press the F1 key while the spreadsheet is in Ready mode, the screen pictured in Figure C.18 will display. To retrieve information about a particular command, you can highlight the command using the cursor-movement keys; then press the Enter key. To return to Ready mode, press the Esc key.
3. PRESS: Esc until the spreadsheet is again in Ready mode
4. To illustrate what happens when you press the F1 key while in Menu mode:
   PRESS: /

PRESS: F1
Because the cursor is highlighting the Worksheet group of commands, pressing the F1 key provides information about the Worksheet group of commands (Figure C.19).

5. To exit the help facility:
PRESS: Esc

Quick Reference

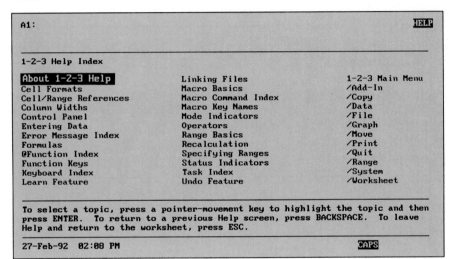

Using Help (F1)

1. When you are in Ready mode, pressing F1 causes a list of commands to display on the screen. Press Enter to display additional information about a highlighted command.
2. When you are in Menu mode, pressing F1 causes information about the highlighted command to display on the screen.

```
A1:                                                              HELP

1-2-3 Help Index

About 1-2-3 Help          Linking Files             1-2-3 Main Menu
Cell Formats              Macro Basics              /Add-In
Cell/Range References     Macro Command Index       /Copy
Column Widths             Macro Key Names           /Data
Control Panel             Mode Indicators           /File
Entering Data             Operators                 /Graph
Error Message Index       Range Basics              /Move
Formulas                  Recalculation             /Print
@Function Index           Specifying Ranges         /Quit
Function Keys             Status Indicators         /Range
Keyboard Index            Task Index                /System
Learn Feature             Undo Feature              /Worksheet

To select a topic, press a pointer-movement key to highlight the topic and then
press ENTER.  To return to a previous Help screen, press BACKSPACE.  To leave
Help and return to the worksheet, press ESC.

27-Feb-92  02:08 PM                                        CAPS
```

FIGURE C.18

The Lotus 1-2-3 Help screen can be accessed from Ready mode by pressing the F1 key.

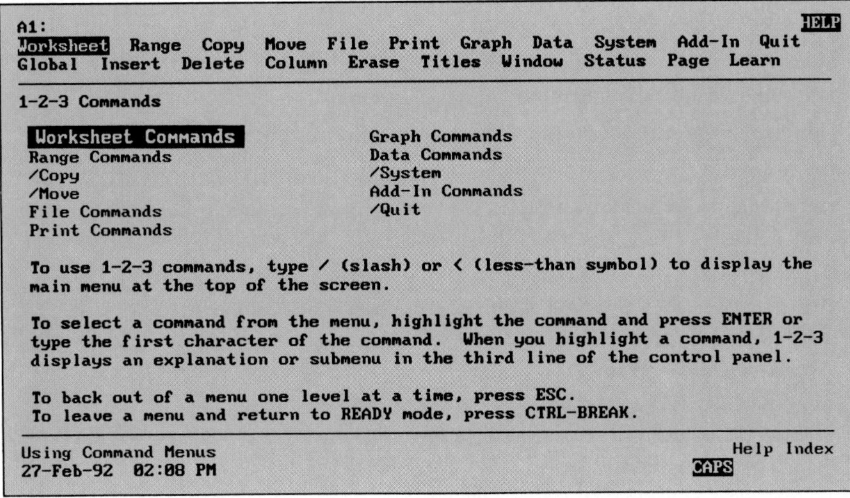

FIGURE C.19

This Lotus 1-2-3 Help screen can be accessed by pressing the F1 key after highlighting the WORKSHEET command.

COPYING

Using the Lotus 1-2-3 COPY command involves the following steps:

1. Position the cursor on the beginning of the range you're copying from.
2. Initiate Menu mode, and then choose the Copy option.
3. Use the cursor-movement keys to highlight the range you're copying from and then press the Enter key.
4. Position the cursor on the first cell in the range you're copying *to*.
5. If you're copying into more than one cell, you must first anchor the beginning of the range you are copying into by pressing the Period (.) key.
6. Once the beginning of the range you're copying into is anchored, use the cursor-movement keys to highlight the cell(s) you're copying into, and then press Enter.

Quick Reference ■ Copying

1. Position the cursor on the cell you want to copy.
2. Initiate Menu mode.
3. Choose the Copy option.
4. Highlight the cell(s) you're copying from, and then press Enter.
5. Position the cursor on the first cell in the range you're copying *to*.
6. To anchor the beginning of the range:
   TYPE: .
7. Highlight the cell(s) you're copying into, and then press Enter.

MOVING

Moving text, data, and formulas involves the same procedure as does copying. The only difference between moving and copying is that the cell(s) you move items from are left blank. Using the MOVE command involves the following steps:

1. Position the cursor on the beginning of the range you're moving from.
2. Initiate the MOVE command.
3. Highlight the range you're moving from and then press the Enter key.
4. Position the cursor on the cell where you want the text, data, and/or formulas to be moved to, and then press Enter.

Quick Reference ■ Moving

1. Position the cursor on the first cell in the range you want to move.
2. Initiate Menu mode.
3. Choose the Move option.
4. Highlight the cell(s) you're moving, and then press Enter.
5. Position the cursor where you want the moved text, numbers, or formulas to be positioned, and then press Enter.

FORMATTING NUMBERS: CURRENCY

Formatting commands allow the user to improve the appearance of a spreadsheet. In this section, you are going to change the way the numbers in columns B through E (specifically, the range of cells B4 . . E10) appear so they are displayed in the currency format with a leading dollar sign and two trailing decimal places. It is always a good idea to position the cursor in the cell at the beginning of the range you're going to format. (Table C.2 describes the different options available when you are formatting numbers.)

Perform the following steps:

1. Position the cursor in cell B4 (the beginning of the range you will format).
2. To enter Menu mode:
   TYPE: /
3. To choose the Range option:
   TYPE: R
4. To choose the Format option:
   TYPE: F
5. To choose the Currency option:
   TYPE: C
6. Lotus 1-2-3 is now prompting you to enter the number of decimal places you want the numbers to be formatted to. To accept two decimal places:
   PRESS: Enter
7. Lotus 1-2-3 is now prompting you to enter the range of cells you want to format. In this step, you will highlight the range to format.
   PRESS: Down cursor-movement key until you've highlighted through row 10, and then
   PRESS: Right cursor-movement key until you've highlighted through column E.
   PRESS: Enter

   Don't be alarmed if you see asterisks in a few cells (Figure C.20). This is Lotus 1-2-3's way of telling you to widen columns because the numbers are too big to fit in the cells. Lotus 1-2-3 won't display a partial number in a cell.

Quick Reference

Formatting a Range of Numbers

1. To initiate Menu mode:
   TYPE: /
2. Choose the RANGE command.
3. Choose the Format option.
4. Choose an option that corresponds to how you want the number to be displayed (Currency, Percent, and so on).
5. Highlight the range to be formatted, and then press Enter.

WIDENING COLUMNS

In this section, you will use a command to widen the columns in the spreadsheet so there is more space between them and so you can see all the numbers in columns D and E. Thus you will provide enough space for all the numbers in each cell, and the asterisks will disappear. Lotus 1-2-3 provides you with a command to widen individual columns in a spreadsheet (the WORKSHEET COLUMN SET-WIDTH command), a range of columns (the WORKSHEET COLUMN

TABLE C.2 Formatting Numbers

After choosing the RANGE FORMAT command or the WORKSHEET GLOBAL FORMAT command, the following options are available:

Option	Purpose	Before Formatting	After Formatting
Fixed	Displays a minus sign for negative numbers, and up to 15 decimal places. For decimal values, the Fixed format will display a leading zero.	1526.346 −415	To zero decimals (F0): 1526 To two decimals (F2): 1526.35 To two decimals (F2): −415.00
Sci(entific)	Displays numbers in scientific (exponential) notation, with up to 15 decimal places in the mantissa and an exponent from −99 to +99.	−4.3 12.245 124600000000	To zero decimals (S0): −4E + 00 To one decimal (S1): 1.2E + 01 To two decimals (S2): 1.25E + 11
Currency	Displays numbers with a leading dollar sign and thousands separated by a comma. In addition, you can specify up to 15 decimal places. Negative numbers are displayed with either a leading minus sign or parentheses (depending on the Worksheet Global Default Other International setting for negatives).	1526.346 −.322	To zero decimals (C0): $1,526 To one decimal (C1): ($0.3) To two decimals (C2): $1,526.35
, (Comma)	Displays numbers with thousands separated by a comma. In addition, you can specify up to 15 decimal places. The Comma format is the same as the Currency format without a dollar sign. Negative numbers are displayed with either a leading minus sign or parentheses (depending on the Worksheet Global Default Other International setting for negatives).	1526.346 −.322	To zero decimals (,0): 1,526 To one decimal (,1): (0.3) To two decimals (,2): 1,526.35

COLUMN-RANGE command), or every column in a spreadsheet (the WORKSHEET GLOBAL COLUMN-WIDTH command). Because you just want to widen columns B through E, we lead you through widening a range of columns.

1. Position the cursor anywhere in column B.
2. To bring up the menu:
   TYPE: /

TABLE C.2 *(continued)*

Option	Purpose	Before Formatting	After Formatting
General	Displays numbers without a comma and no trailing zeros to the right of the decimal point. Negative numbers are displayed with a leading minus sign.	1526.00 −415.5600	(G) 1526 (G) −415.56
+/−	Displays a bar of minus (−) signs, plus (+) signs, or a period (.) that equal the number in the entry. Plus signs indicate a positive value; minus signs indicate a negative value. A period indicates that the value is between −1 and 1.	4.3 −.322 −5.7	(+) ++++ (+) . (+) ++++++
Percent	Displays numbers as percentages (that is, multiplied by 100), with up to 15 decimal places and a trailing percent sign.	.3456	To zero decimals (P0): 35% To one decimal (P1): 34.6% To two decimals (P2): 34.56%
Date	Displays a Julian date (a number between 1 and 73050) as a date in the format you select. The number 1 represents January 1, 1900; the number 73050 represents December 31, 2099.	33778	(D1) 23-Jun-92 (D2) 23-Jun (D3) Jun-92 (D4) 06/23/92
Text	Displays formulas as they appear when you type them in rather than their computed values. After formatting, the cell still contains a value (not a label).	@SUM(A5 . . A10) +B5+B6	(T) @SUM(A5 . . A10) (T) +B5+B6
Hidden	Displays data in a range as invisible; the data still exists in the range, however.	@SUM(A5 . . A10) +B5+B6 1526.00 −415.5600	(H) (H) (H) (H)
Reset	Resets a range to the global cell format, as specified with the WORKSHEET GLOBAL FORMAT command.		

3. To choose the Worksheet option:
   TYPE: W
4. To choose the Column option:
   TYPE: C
5. To choose the Column-Range option:
   TYPE: C
6. To choose the Set-Width option:
   TYPE: S
7. To specify the range of columns you want to widen:
   PRESS: Right cursor-movement key three times
   PRESS: Enter
8. Lotus 1-2-3 is now prompting you to enter a column width for the range of columns.
   TYPE: 12
   PRESS: Enter

Columns B through E should now be widened to 12 characters. Your spreadsheet should look like Figure C.21.

Quick Reference

Widening a Range of Columns

1. Position the cursor in the first column of the range to be widened.
2. To initiate Menu mode:
   TYPE: /
3. Choose the Worksheet option and then the Column option.
4. Choose the Column-Range option and then the Set-Width option.
5. Highlight the range of columns and then press Enter.
6. Type in a column width and press Enter.

FIGURE C.20

Formatted spreadsheet. Columns D and E have to be widened to get rid of the asterisks in cells D10, E5, and E10—the formatted numbers are too wide to fit in those cells.

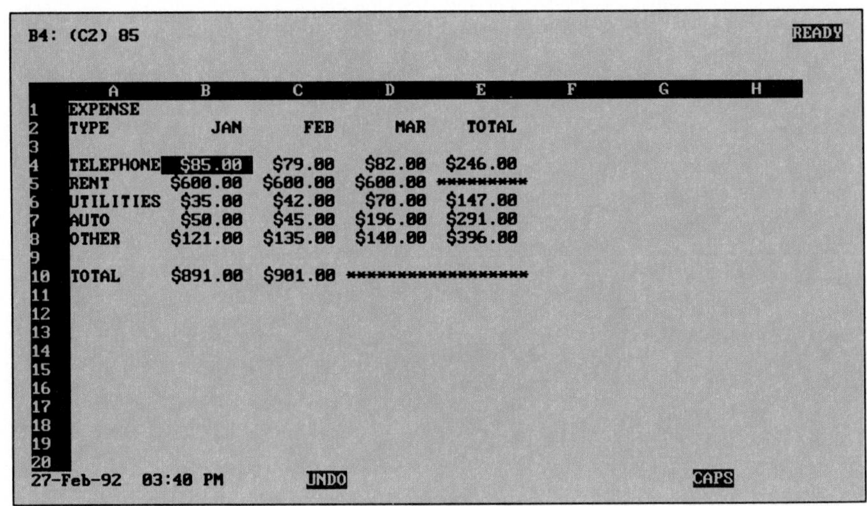

Changing the Current Directory

When you load Lotus 1-2-3, it makes an assumption about where it will save your files. Lotus typically assumes your files will be saved where the Lotus program files are stored. To change the assumption made by Lotus so that it will know where you want your data files to be stored *during the current work session*, perform the following steps:

For Diskette System Users

1. Put your data diskette in drive B.
2. To enter Menu mode:
   TYPE: /
3. To choose the File option:
   TYPE: F
4. To choose the Directory option:
   TYPE: D
5. To tell Lotus 1-2-3 that your data diskette is in drive B:
   TYPE: B:
   PRESS: Enter

   When you save your work, it will automatically be saved onto your data diskette in drive B. ■

For Hard Disk System Users

1. Put your data diskette in drive A.
2. To enter Menu mode:
   TYPE: /

(continued)

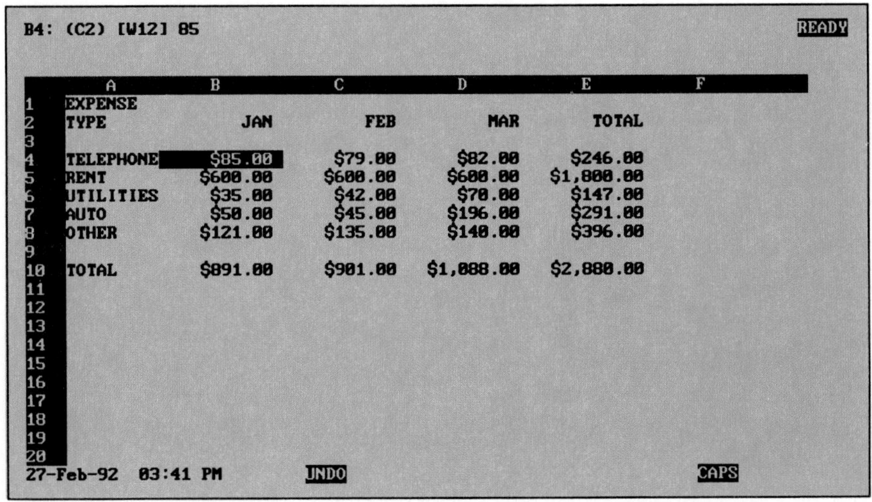

FIGURE C.21

Widened columns. Now all the numbers can be seen in the spreadsheet.

3. To choose the File option:
   TYPE: F
4. To choose the Directory option:
   TYPE: D
5. To tell Lotus 1-2-3 that your data diskette is in drive A:
   TYPE: A:
   PRESS: Enter

   When you save your work, it will automatically be saved onto your data diskette in drive A. ■

Quick Reference
■
Changing the Default Directory

1. To enter Menu mode:
   TYPE: /
2. Choose the File option.
3. Choose the Directory option.
4. Type the new disk drive designation and press Enter.

SAVING THE SPREADSHEET

If you turn the computer off right now or if someone accidentally trips on the power cord to your computer, what do you think will happen? If you guessed you would lose your spreadsheet, you're right. To maintain a permanent copy of your spreadsheet, you should save it periodically onto the disk you have designated. Lotus 1-2-3 automatically supplies an extension of WK1 to all of your spreadsheet files (some of the previous versions of Lotus 1-2-3 supply the extension of WKS). Before saving this spreadsheet, you will type your name into cell B1 so that this spreadsheet can be identified as yours when it is printed.

Perform the following steps:

1. Position the cursor in cell B1.
2. The cursor should now be positioned in cell B1.
   TYPE: [your name]
   PRESS: Enter
3. Before saving, it is a good idea (but not required) to move the cursor to cell A1; when you later retrieve a spreadsheet, the cursor will then be in the cell it was in when you saved it. First move the cursor to cell A1, and then:
   TYPE: /
4. To choose the File option:
   TYPE: F
5. Some additional options should appear on the top of the screen. You will choose the Save option:
   TYPE: S
6. Lotus 1-2-3 is now prompting you to type the name (QTR1) you want to assign to the file.

TYPE: QTR1
PRESS: Enter

A permanent copy of the spreadsheet you have created has now been saved onto the data disk.

Quick Reference

Saving (for the first time)

1. To initiate Menu mode:
   TYPE: /
2. Choose the File option.
3. Choose the Save option.
4. Type the name (QTR1) you want to assign to the file and then press Enter.

THE SYSTEM COMMAND

If you don't want to exit Lotus 1-2-3 but want to issue a DOS command (DOS commands were described in Module A) such as the FORMAT command, use the SYSTEM command. Once you have used the SYSTEM command to exit to the DOS prompt, simply type EXIT to return to the spreadsheet. To use this command, perform the following steps:

1. To initiate Menu mode:
   TYPE: /
2. To choose the System option:
   TYPE: S
   Note that the screen has cleared and the system prompt is displaying on the screen. It looks as if you have exited Lotus 1-2-3. In addition, it seems as if you may have lost the worksheet you were working on. Fortunately, this isn't the case.
3. If you wanted to issue some DOS commands right now, you would type them in after the DOS prompt and then press Enter. To return to the Lotus 1-2-3 display:
   TYPE: exit
   PRESS: Enter

Many users issue the SYSTEM command accidentally when trying to save the spreadsheet. If this happens to you, simply type EXIT and press the Enter key to return to the Lotus 1-2-3 display.

Quick Reference

The SYSTEM Command

1. To initiate Menu mode:
   TYPE: /
2. Choose the System option.
3. To return to the Lotus 1-2-3 display after using the DOS commands of your choice:
   TYPE: exit
   PRESS: Enter

CHANGING A FEW NUMBERS

In this step, you will change a few numbers in the spreadsheet. As you change them, note how the formulas automatically recalculate when new data is entered. To change a number in a spreadsheet, simply move the cursor to the cell you want to change, retype the contents, and then press the Enter key. As mentioned earlier, what you type will replace the old contents.

Perform the following steps:

1. The cursor should be positioned in cell A1. Position the cursor in cell B4.
2. TYPE: 95
   PRESS: Enter
3. The number 95 should be displaying in cell B4. Note that the formulas in cells B10 and E4 automatically recalculated the correct totals.
4. Position the cursor in cell C6.
5. TYPE: 62
   PRESS: Enter

SAVING THE SPREADSHEET MORE THAN ONCE

The procedure to save this updated spreadsheet is almost identical to that described in the section called "Saving the Spreadsheet"; however, you will need to choose one of the following options:

Cancel. By choosing this option, you can save the spreadsheet using a different name.

Replace. By choosing this option, you are replacing the spreadsheet file on disk with the updated spreadsheet in RAM. Lotus automatically gives the spreadsheet file the extension of WK1.

Backup. This option saves the updated spreadsheet in RAM onto the disk and gives this file the extension of WK1. In addition, this option gives the previous version (stored on disk) of the spreadsheet the extension of BAK.

In this section, you will choose the Replace option.

Perform the following steps:

1. To position the cursor in cell A1 and to then initiate the SAVE command:
   PRESS: Home
   TYPE: /
2. You will choose the File option.
   TYPE: F
3. Some additional options should appear on the top of the screen. You will choose the Save option.
   TYPE: S
4. Lotus 1-2-3 is now prompting you to designate the disk drive you want to save the file onto and the name (QTR1) you want to assign to the file. Since Lotus 1-2-3 is assuming you will save it onto the same disk and with the same name as

before, you can simply press the Enter key to accept Lotus 1-2-3's assumption.
PRESS: Enter

5. To choose the Replace option:
   TYPE: R

The updated QTR1 file has been saved onto the data disk, replacing the old QTR1 file.

Quick Reference

Saving a Spreadsheet More Than Once

1. To initiate Menu mode:
   TYPE: /
2. Choose the File option.
3. Choose the Save option.
4. Since Lotus 1-2-3 is assuming you will save the file onto the same disk and with the same name as before, press the Enter key to accept Lotus 1-2-3's assumption.
5. Choose the Replace or Backup option.

ERASING THE SPREADSHEET AREA

If you want to erase the entire contents of your spreadsheet and start again from scratch, you will use the WORKSHEET ERASE command. In this step, you will erase the spreadsheet area.

Perform the following steps:

1. To enter Menu mode:
   TYPE: /
2. To choose the Worksheet option:
   TYPE: W
3. To choose the Erase option:
   TYPE: E
4. To choose the Yes option:
   TYPE: Y

Your screen should look like it did when you first loaded Lotus.

Quick Reference

Erasing the Spreadsheet Area

1. To enter Menu mode:
   TYPE: /
2. Choose the Worksheet option.
3. Choose the Erase option.
4. Choose the Yes option.

RETRIEVING THE SPREADSHEET

What if you want to retrieve a spreadsheet off a disk? This is often the case when you first load Lotus. To retrieve the QTR1 file from your data diskette:

1. To enter Menu mode:
   TYPE: /
2. To choose the File option:
   TYPE: F
3. To choose the Retrieve option:
   TYPE: R
4. The QTR1 file should be listed at the top of the screen on the second line. The cursor should be highlighting the file — if it isn't, use the cursor-movement keys to highlight the QTR1 file.
5. If the cursor is highlighting the QTR1 file:
   PRESS: Enter

The data stored in the QTR1 file should be displaying on the screen.

Quick Reference ■ Retrieving

1. To enter Menu mode:
   TYPE: /
2. Choose the File option.
3. Choose the Retrieve option.
4. Highlight the file you want to retrieve and press Enter.

USING THE UNDO COMMAND

The **UNDO command** enables you to cancel any changes you have made to a spreadsheet since you were last in Ready mode. To use this command, put your spreadsheet in Ready mode. Then hold the Alt key down and press the F4 key. The following provides an example of when the UNDO command would be useful.

1. The cursor is positioned on a cell that contains a formula.
2. You accidentally type some text into the current cell and press the Enter key. The text you typed replaces the formula that was previously in the cell.
3. If you use the UNDO command at this point, the spreadsheet will undo your mistake and look the same as it did before Step 2. In other words, the cell would again contain the formula.

To illustrate, perform the following steps:

1. Position the cursor in cell B10, which contains the @SUM function.
2. TYPE: hello
   PRESS: Enter

3. Note that the word "hello" now appears in cell B10. To bring the formula back, use the UNDO command by holding the Alt key down and pressing the F4 key. Note that the formula again appears in the cell. If you use the UNDO command again, the word "hello" will appear in the cell. Use the UNDO command again so that the @SUM function appears in the cell.

To see what your spreadsheet looked like when it was last in Ready mode:
PRESS: Alt-F4

Quick Reference
■
Undo (Alt-F4)

PRINTING THE SPREADSHEET

You have the option of printing a spreadsheet in one of two forms: (1) as a report or (2) as a list of specifications. As described earlier, the report form is called the *as-displayed format*, which is what you see on the screen. To see what formulas you have in each cell of the spreadsheet and how each cell is formatted, you need to use the specifications form. This form is called the *cell-formulas format*. It's a good idea to print out a cell-formulas format for every spreadsheet you create, so that you can recreate the spreadsheet's specifications (formulas) if the spreadsheet is accidentally erased off the disk. Figure C.22 shows Lotus's Print menu hierarchy and describes some of the options available when you are printing.

In this section, you will print the spreadsheet in both the as-displayed and cell-formulas formats. Before initiating the PRINT command, make sure your computer is attached to a printer (that contains paper) and that the printer is on. Printing the spreadsheet involves specifying the range of cells (A1 . . E10) to be printed.

Perform the following steps to print the spreadsheet in the as-displayed format:

1. To enter Menu mode:
   TYPE: /
2. To choose the Print option:
   TYPE: P
3. Lotus now wants to know whether to direct the output of the PRINT command to a file or to the printer. You will choose the Printer option.
   TYPE: P
4. Some additional options should appear on the top of the screen. You will choose the Range option.
   TYPE: R
5. Lotus 1-2-3 is now waiting for you to specify the range of cells to print.
   TYPE: A1 . . E10
   PRESS: Enter
6. To choose the OPTIONS command:
   TYPE: O

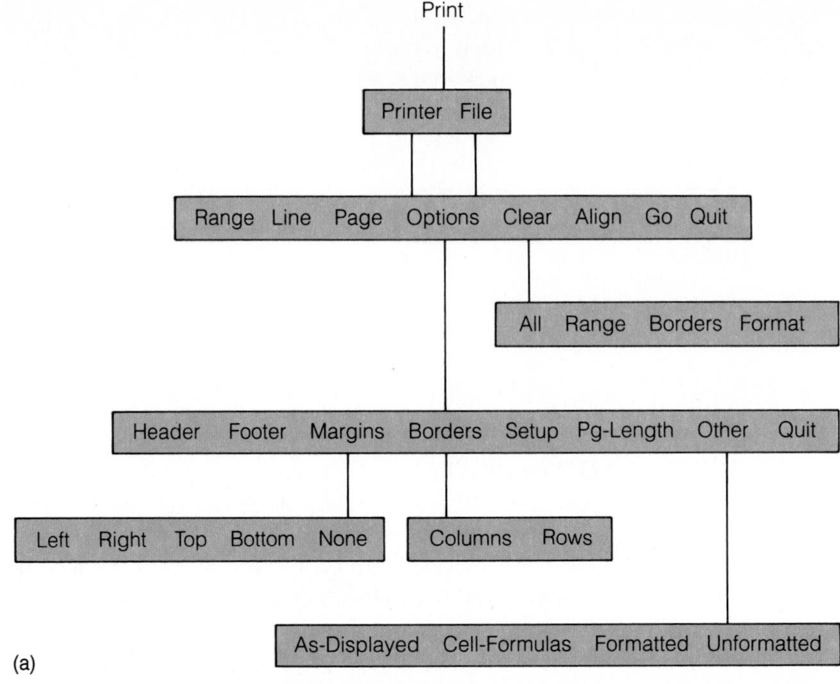

After choosing the Print Printer Options command, you are provided with the following options:

Option	Description
Borders	Prints descriptive information (such as headings) from specific rows and columns in your spreadsheet, to the left and top of every page of print output. Borders are often used as a frame of reference for spreadsheets that are longer than a page.
Footer	Prints a line of text just above the bottom margin of every page. Lotus 1-2-3 automatically leaves two blank lines above the footer.
Header	Prints a line of text just above the top margin of every page. Lotus 1-2-3 automatically leaves two blank lines below the header.
Margins	Sets the left, right, top, and bottom margins, or clears all margins. This command is useful if you need to print your spreadsheet on paper that is larger or smaller than 8 1/2 by 11″.
Other	Determines whether your spreadsheet is printed in the As-Displayed or Cell-Formulas format, or whether headers, footers, and page breaks are included in your spreadsheet.
Pg-Length	Sets the number of lines to be included in the printed page.
Quit	Exits you to the Print menu.
Setup	Enables you to control your printer by sending special codes, in the form of a setup string, to it. For example, depending on the type of printer you're using, you can send a setup string to your printer that will cause it to print in landscape mode (from the top of the page to the bottom rather from the left to right).

(b)

FIGURE C.22

(a) Lotus 1-2-3's Print menu hierarchy. (b) These are some of the options you have to control the appearance of your printed spreadsheet.

7. To choose the OTHER command:
   TYPE: O
8. To choose the AS-DISPLAYED command:
   TYPE: A
9. To move up one level so that you can access the GO command:
   PRESS: Esc once
10. Before printing the spreadsheet, choose the Align option so that Lotus knows where the top of the page is. After choosing this option, Lotus knows to space down a few lines before printing your spreadsheet (for a top margin) and shouldn't print your spreadsheet over the paper's perforation (if you are using continuous-form paper).
    TYPE: A
11. To print:
    TYPE: G
    The spreadsheet should be printing out on the printer.
12. If you are using a printer with continuous-form paper, to move the paper up until the next perforation, use the Page option:
    TYPE: P
13. To exit the PRINT command:
    PRESS: Q

Quick Reference

Printing (As-Displayed)

1. To enter Menu mode:
   TYPE: /
2. Choose the Print option.
3. Choose the Printer option.
4. Choose the Range option.
5. Type the range of cells you want to print and press Enter.
6. Choose the OPTIONS command.
7. Choose the OTHER command.
8. Choose the AS-DISPLAYED command.
9. To move up one level in the print hierarchy:
   PRESS: Esc
10. Choose the Align option.
11. To print, choose the Go option.
12. If you are using a printer with continuous-form paper, to move the paper up until the next perforation, choose the Page option.
13. To exit the PRINT command, choose the Quit option.

Perform the following steps to print the spreadsheet in the cell-formulas format:

1. To enter Menu mode:
   TYPE: /
2. To choose the Print option:
   TYPE: P

3. Lotus now wants to know whether to direct the output of the PRINT command to a file or to the printer. You will choose the Printer option.
   TYPE: P
4. Since you already specified the range of cells to print, you don't need to specify it again. To tell Lotus 1-2-3 you want to print in the cell-formulas format, you will choose the OPTIONS OTHER CELL-FORMULAS command:
   To choose the OPTIONS command:
   TYPE: O
5. To choose the OTHER command:
   TYPE: O
6. To choose the CELL-FORMULAS command:
   TYPE: C
7. To move up one level so that you can access the GO command:
   PRESS: Esc once
8. Before actually printing the spreadsheet, choose the Align option to tell Lotus where the top of the page is:
   TYPE: A
9. To print:
   TYPE: G
   The spreadsheet should be printing out on the printer. The printout should look similar to Figure C.10.
10. If you are using a printer with continuous-form paper, to move the paper up to the next perforation, use the Page option:
    TYPE: P
11. To exit the PRINT command:
    PRESS: Q
12. At this point, it would be a good idea to save the QTR1 spreadsheet, because Lotus saves with the file the print range you specified.

Quick Reference

■

Printing (Cell-Formulas)

1. To enter Menu mode:
   TYPE: /
2. Choose the Print option.
3. Choose the Printer option.
4. Choose the Range option.
5. Type the range of cells you want to print and press Enter.
6. Choose the OPTIONS command.
7. Choose the OTHER command.
8. Choose the CELL-FORMULAS command.
9. To move up one level in the print hierarchy:
   PRESS: Esc
10. Choose the Align option.
11. To print, choose the Go option.
12. If you are using a printer with continuous-form paper, to move the paper up until the next perforation, choose the Page option.
13. To exit the PRINT command, choose the Quit option.

Printing Options

Lotus 1-2-3 includes a number of default settings. You can change any of these assumptions by selecting the OPTIONS command in the Print menu. (Lotus 1-2-3's Print options are described in Figure C.22). Specifically, Lotus assumes the following:

Left margin: 4 spaces from the left side of the page.

Right margin: 76 spaces from the left side of the page.

Top margin: 2 lines from the top of the page.

Bottom margin: 2 lines from the bottom of the page.

Page length: 66 lines.

Exiting

Before exiting Lotus 1-2-3, you should save your work.

Perform the following steps:

1. To enter Menu mode:
   TYPE: /
2. To choose the Quit option:
   TYPE: Q
3. To choose the Yes option:
   TYPE: Y
4. The Lotus 1-2-3 Access System menu should appear. To exit this menu:
   TYPE: E

Quick Reference

■

Exiting Lotus 1-2-3

1. TYPE: /
2. Choose the Quit option.
3. Choose the Yes option.
4. To exit the Lotus Access System, choose the Exit option.

Summary

Electronic spreadsheets provide the business professional with an extremely valuable way to produce information and update reports easily. Electronic spreadsheets are composed of rows and columns; the intersection of a row and column is called a *cell*. Electronic spreadsheets provide the user with a number of advantages over manual spreadsheets including:

- Electronic spreadsheets can be larger than manual ones.
- Electronic spreadsheets can automatically perform mathematical calculations, including adding, subtracting, multiplying, and dividing.

- Cells in electronic spreadsheets can contain formulas and functions. A formula is a mathematical expression that enables you to perform calculations on values in a spreadsheet. Electronic spreadsheets provide many powerful functions that can be used in formulas. Because functions save so much time, they can be thought of as electronic shortcuts.
- In electronic spreadsheets, calculations are immediate.
- Electronic spreadsheets can be stored and retrieved.

When creating a spreadsheet, users must pay attention to the recommended spreadsheet development procedures. These procedures involve:

1. Establishing your objectives.
2. Defining your requirements.
3. Building the spreadsheet.
4. Testing the spreadsheet.
5. Using the spreadsheet.

If these procedures are not followed, the likelihood is great that the spreadsheet will contain errors.

Most spreadsheets typically operate in one of four modes:

1. Ready mode.
2. Label mode.
3. Value mode.
4. Menu mode.

Knowing which mode the spreadsheet is in is important so that you can answer a question such as "Why can't I move the cursor around the spreadsheet?"

After 1-2-3 has been loaded, you will view an empty electronic spreadsheet. Alphabet characters designating the columns in the spreadsheet are displayed across the top of the spreadsheet and numbers designating the rows in the spreadsheet are displayed vertically along the left side of the spreadsheet. The blank area above the column references is referred to as the *command/data entry area*, because this is where Lotus's menus display and where the information you type appears before you press Enter (data entry).

One of the first tasks you should learn to perform using a spreadsheet program is how to move the cursor. Lotus provides a number of methods for moving the cursor around a spreadsheet including:

- Cursor-movement keys.
- PgUp and PgDn keys.
- Home key.
- F5 (Goto) key.

A variety of features are common to almost all spreadsheet programs, including the ability to enter text, numbers, and formulas into cells. Before typing anything into a spreadsheet, remember to move the cursor to the appropriate cell. When numbers are entered into a spreadsheet, Lotus goes into Value mode. Lotus also goes into Value mode when you type +, –, (, @, ., and #. When text is entered into a spreadsheet, Lotus goes into Label mode.

Electronic spreadsheet programs also allow the user to execute many powerful commands that will perform such tasks as copying, formatting, and saving. In addition, spreadsheet programs provide you with commands that enable you to print a spreadsheet in one of two formats. The as-displayed format is a printout of what you see on the screen—namely, your report. The cell-formulas printout is a listing of the contents of every cell in the spreadsheet—including formulas. It is a good idea to have a cell-formulas printout for every spreadsheet you create so that you can recreate the spreadsheet if you need to.

The best way to learn about the power available within an electronic spreadsheet program is to use one. In this tutorial, you practiced using Lotus 1-2-3 (Table C.3 provides a command summary for Lotus 1-2-3). As a result, you should be prepared to tackle any other spreadsheet program, because the basic concepts and procedures are similar from one spreadsheet program to another.

Key Terms

add-in, p. 603
as-displayed format, p. 602
cell, p. 592
cell-formulas format, p. 602
command/data entry area, p. 596
currency format, p. 601
electronic spreadsheet, p. 592
formatting, p. 601
formatting commands, p. 617
formula, p. 593
function, p. 599
help facility, p. 614
indicator area, p. 597
Label mode, p. 597
Menu mode, p. 597
range, p. 599
Ready mode, p. 597
spreadsheet area, p. 596
@SUM function, p. 599
UNDO command, p. 626
Value mode, p. 597

Exercises

Short Answer

1. What does it mean when asterisks appear in a spreadsheet cell? What should you do to get rid of them?
2. Describe the four different modes of spreadsheet operation. How can you tell what mode the spreadsheet is in?
3. What is the purpose of formatting a spreadsheet?
4. Why is it important to use the SAVE command before turning the computer off?
5. Describe what you see when you first load your spreadsheet program into main memory. If you want to make changes to a spreadsheet that is stored on the disk, what should you do?
6. What is a *range* of cells? Why is it relevant for you to understand what a range is?

7. Describe the procedures for developing an electronic spreadsheet.
8. What are two different forms in which an electronic spreadsheet can be printed?
9. What are some of the advantages of using an electronic spreadsheet compared with using a manual spreadsheet?
10. Describe the procedure for putting the number 8 into cell A3.

TABLE C.3

Lotus 1-2-3 Command Summary

Load Lotus 1-2-3	Type LOTUS after the system prompt and press Enter; press Enter to choose the 1-2-3 option.
Move the cursor	Use the cursor-movement keys, PgUp and PgDn keys, Home key, End key, Tab key, and F5 key to move the cursor.
Enter numbers and text	Position the cursor in the appropriate cell, type in the text or number, and press Enter; or use a cursor-movement key to put the data in the cell.
Enter formulas and functions	Position the cursor in the appropriate cell, type in the formula or function, and press Enter; or use a cursor-movement key to put the data in the cell. If you type an invalid formula, Lotus will beep and change the mode indicator to Edit. You must correct the mistake before entering the formula in the cell.
Edit a cell	*Method One:* Position the cursor on the cell that needs to be changed; retype the contents, and then press Enter. *Method Two:* Position the cursor on the cell that needs to be changed; press F2 (Edit); make your changes to the cell contents that appear in the data entry area, and then press Enter.
Use the UNDO command	To see what your spreadsheet looks like when the spreadsheet was last in Ready mode, use the UNDO command by pressing Alt-F4.
Use Menu mode	Press /, highlight a command option, press Enter. To back out of a command, press Esc.
Display Help information	Press F1 (Help) to display help information about the current command.
Copy a range of cells	Press /, press C[opy], highlight the cell(s) you're copying from, press Enter, highlight the cell(s) you're copying to, press Enter.
Move a range of cells	Press /, press M[ove], highlight the cell(s) you're moving, press Enter, move the cursor to where you want the moved data to be positioned, press Enter.

HANDS ON

1. To practice retrieving a file, editing it, and then saving it onto the disk under a different name, perform the following steps:
   a. Retrieve QTR1.WK1 from your data disk.
   b. Edit the QTR1.WK1 spreadsheet by changing the cells listed below to

TABLE C.3

(continued)

Globally format a spreadsheet	Press /, press W[orksheet], press G[lobal], press F[ormat], choose a formatting option, specify the number of decimal places, press Enter.
Format a range of numbers	Press /, press R[ange], press F[ormat], choose a formatting option, press Enter, highlight the range of cells to be formatted, press Enter.
Widen a range of columns	Press /, press W[orksheet], press C[olumn], press C[olumn-Range], press S[et-Width], press Enter, highlight the range of columns to be widened, press Enter, type in the new column width, press Enter.
Change the current directory (temporary change)	Press /, press F[ile], press D[irectory], type in the new disk drive designation, press Enter.
Change the current directory (change is recorded in Lotus 1-2-3's setup file)	Press /, press W[orksheet], press G[lobal], press D[efault], press D[irectory], type in the new disk drive designation, press Enter, press U[pdate], press Q[uit].
Save a spreadsheet for the first time	Press /, Press F[ile], press S[ave], type the spreadsheet name, press Enter.
Using a DOS command without exiting Lotus 1-2-3 permanently	Press /, press S[ystem], to return to Lotus, type Exit, then press Enter.
Save a spreadsheet more than once	Press /, press F[ile], press S[ave], type the spreadsheet name, press Enter, press R[eplace].
Erase the spreadsheet area	Press /, press W[orksheet], press E[rase], press Y[es].
Retrieve a spreadsheet	Press /, press F[ile], press R[etrieve], type the spreadsheet name or highlight it, press Enter.
Print a spreadsheet (as-displayed)	Press /, press P[rint], press P[rinter], press R[ange], type or highlight the range to be printed, press Enter, press O[ptions], press O[ther], press A[s-displayed], press Esc, press A[lign], press G[o], press P[age], press Q[uit].
Print a spreadsheet (cell-formulas)	Press /, press P[rint], press P[rinter], press R[ange], type or highlight the range to be printed, press Enter, press O[ptions], press O[ther], press C[ell-Formulas], press Esc, press A[lign], press G[o], press P[age], press Q[uit].
Exit Lotus 1-2-3	Press /, press Q[uit], press Y[es], press Exit.

reflect the second quarter's expenses. Remember that you can simply position the cursor on the cell you want to edit and retype the contents.

B2	"APR
C2	"MAY
D2	"JUNE
B6	43.44
C4	39.65
C7	119
D6	83.91
D8	98.60

c. Save this spreadsheet onto your data diskette as QTR2.
d. Print the spreadsheet in both the as-displayed and cell-formulas formats.

2. Create the spreadsheet pictured in Figure C.23. Make sure to do the following:
   a. Type a formula into cell E6 that adds the GROSS RECEIPTS amounts for JAN, FEB, and MAR.
   b. Type formulas into row 15 that add the four expense amounts above. These two formulas should use the @SUM function.
   c. Type formulas into the range E10 . . E13 to add the amounts for each expense.
   d. Type formulas into row 18 that calculate NET INCOME by subtracting each monthly expense total from the monthly GROSS RECEIPTS amount.
   e. Format all the cells that contain numbers in the currency format to two decimal places. If necessary, widen columns to accommodate the numbers.
   f. Save this spreadsheet onto your data diskette as INCOME.
   g. Print this spreadsheet in both the as-displayed and cell-formulas formats.
3. Create a spreadsheet that you can use for the month of January to keep track of your weekly expenses and available cash. Make sure to do the following:
   a. Calculate a column total for each type of expense.

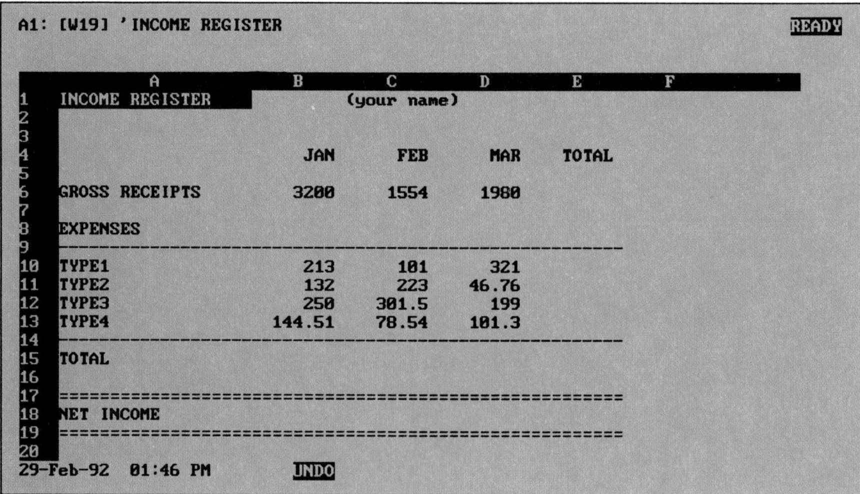

FIGURE C.23

The INCOME.WK1 spreadsheet.

b. Calculate the difference between cash and expenses. The difference might be called EXTRA CASH.
c. Type JANUARY into cell A1 and type your name into cell C1.
d. Decide how to best set up this spreadsheet. (However, make sure to satisfy all the preceding requirements.)
e. Save the spreadsheet onto your data diskette as JAN.
f. Print the spreadsheet in both the as-displayed and cell-formulas formats.

4. Retrieve JAN.WK1 from the data diskette (this spreadsheet was created in the Exercise 3). Edit the spreadsheet to reflect February's expenses by changing some of the amounts. Save the updated spreadsheet onto the data diskette as FEB. Print the spreadsheet in the as-displayed format.

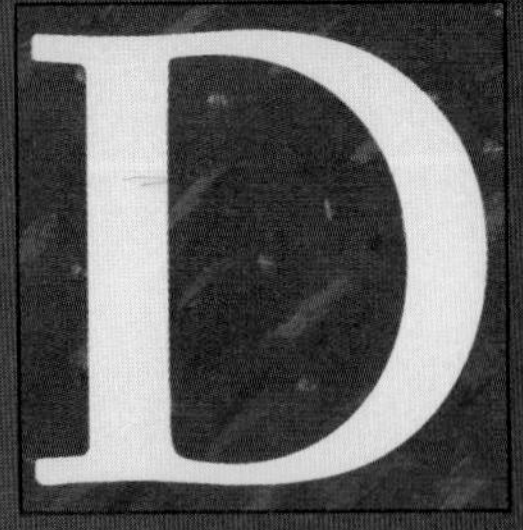

MODULE D

DATABASE MANAGEMENT: dBASE IV

Modern database management systems for microcomputers provide the business user with the means of managing and manipulating large amounts of data. They were introduced to the business community for use on microcomputers at about the same time as electronic spreadsheets. Received with great enthusiasm, both types of software packages are powerful, easy to use, and often used together. This module introduces you to the fundamentals of using the popular database management system (DBMS) software package, dBASE IV.

PREVIEW

When you have completed this module, you will be able to:

- Describe what a database management system is.
- Describe DBMS features that are important to know about when you are:
  - Creating and adding data.
  - Searching a database.
  - Sorting and indexing a database.
  - Modifying the database structure.
  - Creating and printing reports.
- Use dBASE IV to create and manage a database.
- Use dBASE IV to create and print a report.

DATABASE MANAGEMENT SYSTEM (DBMS) OVERVIEW

Picture an office with a row of file cabinets that extends as far as you can see — and you're responsible for them! You use your filing system mainly to track customer-related information, and everything is perfectly organized in alphabetical order by last name. Not even one customer name is out of place! You know exactly where to look to find information on each customer. Great. But what if you need to pull out all folders that contain information on customers who live in a particular area? Your alphabetical organization scheme would no longer be useful. Your manual filing system has become a problem. You need a microcomputer database management system! A **database management system (DBMS)** is a software tool designed to facilitate the creation and maintenance of an information database in order to produce reports. The term **database** describes a collection of data stored for a variety of business purposes.

Let's look at another example. You are a salesperson whose territory covers Indiana and Ohio. You have over a hundred clients to keep track of and are thinking of using a computer-based database management system to handle all the data. Once you have entered all the data pertaining to each client into your computer, then for only the cost of keeping the data current you will have a very valuable tool at your fingertips. You're making a trip through northern Ohio? In a few minutes, you can produce a report showing all the customers in that area prioritized by annual sales and the date of the most recent sales call. You can't remember why a client wasn't interested in your product during the last visit? In a few seconds, you can display on your screen any memo text that pertains to that client.

This module explains the features of a microcomputer-based DBMS and teaches you the fundamentals of using dBASE IV to create, add data to, and retrieve data from a database.

DBMS FEATURES

As with any software package, you must be familiar with the concepts and features of a DBMS before you can start to use it. This section introduces you to these concepts and features so that when you begin using dBASE IV later in this module, you will understand the whys and whats of DBMS processing.

CREATING A DATABASE

After you have loaded dBASE IV into RAM, you can begin using its commands to create or manage a database. Creating a database is often referred to as creating the **database structure** — defining exactly what you want each field in a database record to look like. (*Note:* If you don't understand the meaning of terms like *field*, *record*, and *file*, refer to Table 11.1, reproduced here for your convenience.) Think of this activity as defining how many folders you want in a file drawer and what kind of information each folder should contain. For example, how many clients will you need to keep track of? For each client, do you want to keep track of the client's name and business address? Phone number? Names of products purchased? Value of products purchased?

Figure D.1 shows a database file structure that was defined using dBASE IV. This file structure was saved onto a data disk under the name EMPLOYEE. To create a structure using dBASE IV, the following items must be defined:

TABLE 11.1

Short Glossary of Database Terminology

Alphanumeric (character) data: data composed of a combination of letters, numbers, and other symbols (like punctuation marks) that are not used for mathematical calculations.

Bit: contraction of binary digit, which is either 1 ("on") or 0 ("off") in computerized data representation.

Character: the lowest level in the data hierarchy; usually one letter or numerical digit; also called **byte** (8 bits).

Data: the raw facts that make up information.

Database: a large collection of stored, integrated (cross-referenced) records that can be maintained and manipulated with great flexibility; the top level in the data hierarchy.

Entity: any tangible or intangible object or concept on which an organization wishes to store data; entities have attributes, such as name, color, and price.

Field, or **attribute,** or **data element:** a group of related characters (*attribute* is also a column of a relation in a relational database); the second lowest level in the data hierarchy.

File: a group of related records; the fourth level from the bottom in the data hierarchy.

Information: data that has value to, or that has been interpreted by, the user.

Key: a unique field within a record that uniquely identifies the record.

Numeric data: data composed of numeric digits (numbers) used for mathematical calculations.

Record: a group of related fields; the third level from the bottom in the data hierarchy (analogous to a *tuple*, or *row*, in a relational database).

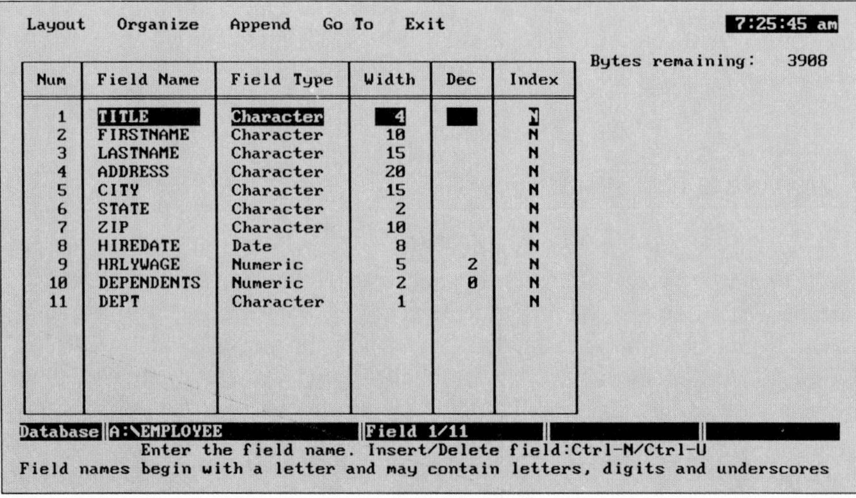

Layout Organize Append Go To Exit
7:25:45 am
Bytes remaining: 3908
Num Field Name Field Type Width Dec Index
1 TITLE Character 4 N
2 FIRSTNAME Character 10 N
3 LASTNAME Character 15 N
4 ADDRESS Character 20 N
5 CITY Character 15 N
6 STATE Character 2 N
7 ZIP Character 10 N
8 HIREDATE Date 8 N
9 HRLYWAGE Numeric 5 2 N
10 DEPENDENTS Numeric 2 0 N
11 DEPT Character 1 N
Database A:\EMPLOYEE Field 1/11
Enter the field name. Insert/Delete field:Ctrl-N/Ctrl-U
Field names begin with a letter and may contain letters, digits and underscores

FIGURE D.1

Database structure. What you would see on the screen if you used dBASE IV to create a database structure to store employee data. The following items were defined: (1) field name, (2) field type, (3) field width, (4) number of decimal places, and (5) indexing choice.

1. Field name. You must give a unique name to each field of data you want to store. A **field name** can be no longer than 10 characters. To manipulate the database, you will often be required to refer to one or more elements of data by their field names. Although field names must begin with a letter, you can use letters, numbers, and underscores when naming fields. Blank spaces aren't allowed in field names, nor any other punctuation marks or special characters.
2. Field type. DBMS programs require you to define what type of information will be stored in the field; in other words, you must define the **field type.** With dBASE IV, data can be one of six types: (a) **character**—data that is **nonnumeric,** such as name and address information; (b) **numeric**—data that will be used in calculations, such as dollar amounts; (c) **float**—data that is stored as a *floating point* number, which is typically used in scientific applications. These numbers speed up operations that require extensive multiplying and dividing of very large and very small numbers; (d) **date**—data that must be entered in a specific date format so that calculations can be performed on it; (e) **logical**—data that indicates whether a field is true or false (such as data regarding a person's marital status, where true = married and false = single); and (f) **memo**—data in the form of a long paragraph of text.
3. Field width. You must determine what the maximum size of the field will be—its **field width.** For example, if you are defining the structure for a field that is to contain an employee's last name, what is the longest name you will probably have? Will it be 10, 20, or 30 characters long? You must be sure that enough space is available for all the data you want to enter. You don't have to enter field widths for date (8 positions wide), logical (1 position wide), or memo fields (10 positions wide). The widths for these are set automatically by dBASE IV.
4. Decimal places. For each numeric field, you must determine the number of **decimal places** you want. Most users store numbers to two decimal places (such as $10.00) instead of no decimal places (such as $10). The number of decimal places that you assign to the width of a numeric or floating point field must be at least two less than the width of the field. The decimal places and decimal point take up space in a field.
5. Index. When creating the structure for a database, you can also specify that once you add data to the database, you want it to be displayed in order by a particular field. You can accomplish this by creating an **index file** that will put the database into order. Indexing is described in more detail later in this module.

You must think carefully about these definitions at the start so you won't have to change your database structure later, after you've entered a number of different records. It is possible to modify a database structure, but depending on the changes you make, you may lose data. (Modifying a database structure is described in more detail shortly.) Before the EMPLOYEE database file structure was created, for example, it was decided to have a separate field for TITLE, FIRSTNAME, and LASTNAME because (1) the database can now be sorted into alphabetical order by last name, and (2) the individual name fields can be referenced in a report. For example, you might want to include only TITLE (Mr., Ms., Miss, or Mrs.) and LASTNAME fields in a specific report. When designing the structure for a database, a good rule of thumb is to give every individual piece of data its own field. Otherwise, it is sometimes difficult to search for or access the data you want to work with.

ADDING DATA TO A DATABASE

Once you have defined your database structure, you can add data to it. However, because you will often have more than one database file stored on the same disk, first you must tell dBASE IV to which file you want to add data. We lead you through adding new records to a database file later in this module. Figure D.2 pictures a listing of the database file called EMPLOYEE (see Figure D.1 for the structure for this database) after 12 records have been entered.

SEARCHING A DATABASE

What if you want to see a list — either on your screen or printed out — of only those elements of your database that meet certain criteria? In a manual file system, depending on how the folders are organized, you might need a long time to perform special searches for information such as the following: "Pull out the folders in the employee filing cabinet for every employee who makes more than $15.00 per hour." If the folders are organized in alphabetical order by name, this could take hours! In contrast, performing **searches** with DBMS software and database files stored in computer-usable form is fast and, once you get comfortable with the procedure, easy. As long as you know the field names defined in your database structure (such as TITLE and FIRSTNAME) and are familiar with the types of operations you can perform, you can ask the DBMS for the answer to any number of questions about your database.

There are four categories of database management operations: (1) arithmetic operations, (2) relational operations, (3) logical operations, and (4) string operations.

FIGURE D.2 EMPLOYEE database file. These records were keyed into the EMPLOYEE database structure that was shown in Figure D.1.

TITLE	FIRSTNAME	LASTNAME	ADDRESS	CITY	STATE	ZIP	HIREDATE	HRLYWAGE	DEPENDENTS	DEPT
Mr.	Rod	Bannister	7279 Ridge Drive	San Mateo	CA	94001	05/06/91	17.00	2	A
Ms.	Evelyn	Chabot	2613 Henderson Hiway	San Diego	CA	95609	02/14/91	18.00	1	B
Mr.	Ahmad	Arguello	4 Chestnut Lane	San Mateo	CA	94001	01/04/91	19.00	0	A
Mr.	Michael	Antonucci	4901 101st Place SW	San Francisco	CA	94104	01/05/91	11.00	3	B
Ms.	Rosalie	Gills	1350 Beverly Road	San Francisco	CA	94109	03/16/91	21.00	0	B
Mr.	Bradley	Wachowiak	700 Cumberland Court	San Mateo	CA	94001	05/11/91	19.50	2	A
Ms.	Karen	Shepherd	3107 Peachtree Drive	San Mateo	CA	94001	02/06/90	21.00	0	A
Ms.	Kathleen	Salazar	75 Dorado Terrace	San Francisco	CA	94104	11/13/90	16.50	2	B
Mr.	Arthur	Sotak	1217 Carlisle Road	San Mateo	CA	94001	11/04/90	23.00	0	A
Ms.	Jean	Hurtado	3202 E Dry Creek Rd	San Diego	CA	95609	11/04/90	10.50	1	B
Mr.	Robert	Keller	416 Whittier Drive	San Francisco	CA	94109	01/03/90	17.00	4	A
Mr.	Herbert	Licon	1220 E Barcelona	San Francisco	CA	94001	09/01/91	17.00	0	A

ARITHMETIC OPERATIONS

You can perform **arithmetic operations** on the numeric fields in your database. The arithmetic operators are:

+	Addition
−	Subtraction
*	Multiplication
/	Division
()	Parentheses (used for grouping operations)

RELATIONAL OPERATIONS

Relational operations are used to analyze the contents of fields. For example, you would need to use a relational operator if you want to list the records in your EMPLOYEE database file that have an hourly wage field that contains an amount greater than 15 (Figure D.3), or if you want to list all employees in the database except those who live in San Diego (Figure D.4). With dBASE IV, the following relational operators can be used to perform relational operations:

>	Greater than
<	Less than
=	Equal to
>=	Greater than or equal to
<=	Less than or equal to
<>	Not equal to

The result of relational operations is always a true (T) or a false (F) answer. Another operation is usually performed on the basis of the answer, such as listing the record on the screen.

LOGICAL OPERATIONS

Logical operations allow you to search your database for special information. For example, you might want to list on the screen all the employees who earn more than 15 per hour *and* who work in San Diego. Two logical operators are:

TITLE	FIRSTNAME	LASTNAME	CITY	HRLYWAGE	DEPT
Mr.	Rod	Bannister	San Mateo	17.00	A
Ms.	Evelyn	Chabot	San Diego	18.00	B
Mr.	Ahmad	Arguello	San Mateo	19.00	A
Ms.	Rosalie	Gills	San Francisco	21.00	B
Mr.	Bradley	Wachowiak	San Mateo	19.50	A
Ms.	Karen	Shepherd	San Mateo	21.00	A
Ms.	Kathleen	Salazar	San Francisco	16.50	B
Mr.	Arthur	Sotak	San Mateo	23.00	A
Mr.	Robert	Keller	San Francisco	17.00	A
Mr.	Herbert	Licon	San Francisco	17.00	A

FIGURE D.3

Listing those records in the EMPLOYEE database that have an hourly wage field that is greater than 15. In this case, the relational operation used was HRLYWAGE>15.

1. AND Allows you to specify two conditions that must exist for a specific action to be taken.
2. OR Allows you to specify one of two conditions that must exist for a specific action to be taken. For example, test to determine if CITY = "San Francisco" OR CITY = "San Mateo". This command would allow you to screen out all records except those containing data on residents in San Francisco or San Mateo.

SOUND SEARCHES

The *Sounds like* operator is used to search for a word in a database that you aren't sure how to spell; however, you think you know how it sounds. A mathematical code, called the Soundex code, is used to describe how a particular word sounds and then attempt to match that sound to other words in the database that sound the same but may be spelled differently. For example, if you want to search the FIRST-NAME field for Sarah or Sara, you could search for *Sounds like "sara"*.

PATTERN SEARCHES

The *Like* operator can be used to search for a particular string of characters in a field. The asterisk (*) and the question mark (?) can be used as wildcard characters. For example, to search for all records that include 95 as the first two characters in the ZIP field, you would search for 95*.

SORTING VERSUS INDEXING

When you ask a DBMS to list, or search for, specific records based on certain criteria, the list displays the record data in the order you input it to the database file. How, then, can you list records in chronological order (by date), for example? You can either sort or index a database into order. Note that these two commands offer very different ways to access the data in a file in a particular sequence. As described below, **indexing** files into a particular order is generally preferable to **sorting** files into order.

When the SORT command is used, a copy of the original file is produced in sorted order (the DBMS will prompt you to give the newly sorted file a new name). Therefore, if you don't have at least twice as much space left on your disk as the size of your database file, the SORT command won't work.

FIGURE D.4

Listing all employees except for those who live in San Diego. In this case, the relational operation used was CITY <> "San Diego".

TITLE	FIRSTNAME	LASTNAME	CITY	HRLYWAGE	DEPT
Mr.	Rod	Bannister	San Mateo	17.00	A
Mr.	Ahmad	Arguello	San Mateo	19.00	A
Mr.	Michael	Antonucci	San Francisco	11.00	B
Ms.	Rosalie	Gills	San Francisco	21.00	B
Mr.	Bradley	Wachowiak	San Mateo	19.50	A
Ms.	Karen	Shepherd	San Mateo	21.00	A
Ms.	Kathleen	Salazar	San Francisco	16.50	B
Mr.	Arthur	Sotak	San Mateo	23.00	A
Mr.	Robert	Keller	San Francisco	17.00	A
Mr.	Herbert	Licon	San Francisco	17.00	A

In contrast, the INDEX command does not produce a complete new copy of the file. As a result, the INDEX command takes less time than the SORT command to put a database file into order. The INDEX command creates a small index file that puts the database into order based on the key field (the field name you are using to determine the order). You can have a file indexed into any number of orders (for example, last-name order, chronological order, order of increasing pay rates). When you want to display database files in a certain order, you tell the DBMS which index file to use. These index files don't take up much space on your data disk, so you don't have to worry about indexing your files too often or in too many different ways. The INDEX command is described in more detail later in this module.

Modifying a Database's Structure

What happens if, after you've entered hundreds of records, you realize you need to modify the structure of your database? Perhaps you want to add a field to each record in the EMPLOYEE database—for example, employee number (EMPNUM). In the early days of DBMS software, this procedure would have been difficult. Recent versions of DBMS software make the problem easier to deal with; however, certain database changes are more difficult to accomplish than others.

One of the most common structure changes that users make affects field width—sufficient space was not allotted initially. As you will see later in this module, changing the field width is easy. However, changing the type of the field—for example, from character to numeric—can cause you to lose data.

Creating and Printing Reports

You've learned that you can manipulate a database by sorting, indexing, and/or listing records that meet your specifications or criteria. Frequently you will want the results of these manipulations to be output in a polished form that can be circulated throughout your company for review. Fortunately, database software provides you with the capability to output the results of your processing activities to a report. This report might include totals and subtotals, arithmetic (based on the numeric fields in your database), and stylized headings and subheadings.

For instance, you may want to include in a report for the company's executives (using data from the EMPLOYEE database) a listing containing LASTNAME, FIRSTNAME, HIREDATE, and HRLYWAGE fields for all the employees who work in Department A. Without using the report module—using only a simple LIST command—the listing looks something like Figure D.4. But if you use the report module, the listing might look like Figure D.5.

In the Lab

Using dBASE IV DBMS Software

In this tutorial, you will have the opportunity to create and manage a database using dBASE IV, a powerful DBMS package. You will learn to use many of the features discussed thus far. These features are common to most DBMS packages, so your experience using dBASE IV will help you learn to use other DBMS packages. *Note: Make sure you have a data diskette available onto which you can store the files you create.*

THE BUSINESS SITUATION

You own the sporting goods store called Sporting Life. Over the last few years, the store has grown substantially, doubling the number of employees. You serve nearly 500 regular customers, plus many new customers. You are interested in tracking customer information in the form of a computer-usable database file so that you can easily retrieve information about customers. This tutorial will teach you to create and manage Sporting Life's customer database and retrieve information from it.

(*Note:* Read the section on Saving the Database in this tutorial before you end your working session—if you don't end your working session properly, your database file might be damaged.)

LOADING dBASE IV

Because the dBASE IV package contains so many program instructions, your computer must be configured with a hard disk for you to run it. In other words, you cannot load dBASE from diskettes—dBASE must be loaded from the hard disk. (As mentioned earlier, you will, however, store the files you create on a diskette.) We assume that you have booted your computer with DOS using the procedure described in the Introduction to the Modules.

To load dBASE IV into RAM, perform the following steps:

1. dBASE IV is probably loaded in a subdirectory (named something like DBASE) on the hard disk. You may be able to load dBASE IV without making the dBASE subdirectory the current subdirectory. To see if this is the case, type the following after the system prompt:
   TYPE: dbase
   PRESS: Enter
   If a message such as "Bad Command or Filename" is displaying on the screen, proceed with Steps 2 and 3. Otherwise, skip Steps 2 and 3.
2. Use the CD command to make the dBASE subdirectory the current subdirec-

FIGURE D.5

Using the report module to list database records.

```
Page No.    1
03/10/92

        FIRST      LAST                                   HOURLY
TITLE   NAME       NAME          CITY                       WAGE  DEPARTMENT

Mr.     Rod        Bannister     San Mateo                 17.00  A
Mr.     Ahmad      Arguello      San Mateo                 19.00  A
Mr.     Bradley    Wachowiak     San Mateo                 19.50  A
Ms.     Karen      Shepherd      San Mateo                 21.00  A
Mr.     Arthur     Sotak         San Mateo                 23.00  A
Mr.     Robert     Keller        San Francisco             17.00  A
Mr.     Herbert    Licon         San Francisco             17.00  A

                                                          133.50
```

tory. For example, if the dBASE subdirectory is called DBASE, you would type CD \DBASE to accomplish this. (Ask your instructor or lab assistant what the name of the subdirectory is.)

3. To load dBASE IV:
   TYPE: dbase
   PRESS: Enter
   A brief copyright message should now be displaying on the screen. You can either press Enter at this point to continue to the next screen or wait a few seconds, at which point the screen will automatically change to display the Control Center (Figure D.6).

THE CONTROL CENTER

The **Control Center** is the center of the dBASE IV menu system. You must become familiar with it before performing any database activities. As shown in Figure D.7, the Control Center is composed of the following:

- *Menu bar.* The menu bar is displaying at the very top of the screen. It contains the following three menu options:
  — The *Catalog* menu. This menu provides you with options to create or modify a **catalog,** which is a subdirectory that enables you to group database files that belong together. For example, you would want to group two databases together if you frequently need to retrieve information from them at the same time. (Subdirectories were described in Module A.)
  — The *Tools* menu. This menu provides file management options and options for modifying the appearance of the screen.
  — The *Exit* menu. This menu provides an option for exiting to (1) the dot prompt, which displays when you exit the Control Center (the dot

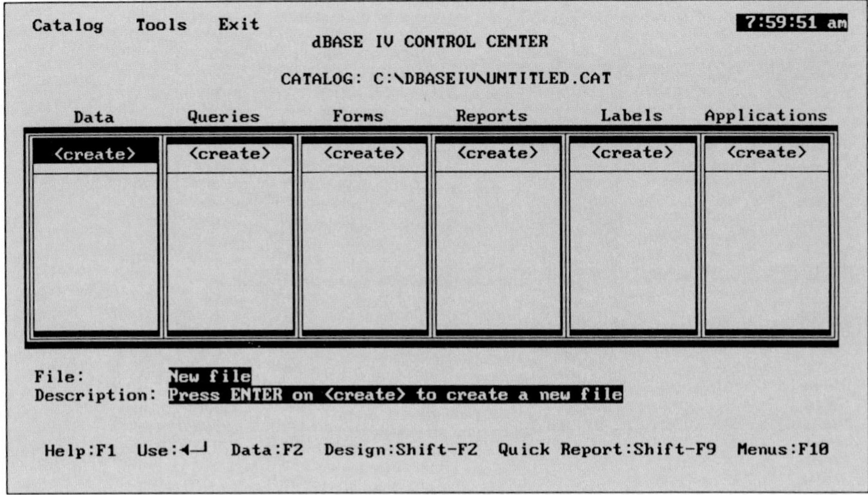

FIGURE D.6

The Control Center. What you see (after the copyright message) when dBASE IV is first loaded into RAM.

prompt is described in the next section) or (2) the DOS prompt, which displays when you exit dBASE.

- *Catalog name*. If you create a catalog name, its name will display near the top of the screen.
- *Panels*. The **panels** in the Control Center are the six vertical sections that make up most of the screen. Each panel enables you to create a different type of file that provides you with specific capabilities. The **<create> marker** in each panel is used to create the file—a different dBASE screen displays for each panel chosen. The following types of files can be created:
  — Choose the Data panel to create database files.
  — Choose the Queries panel to create files that can be used to retrieve information from or update a database.
  — Choose the Forms panel to create files that contain your data entry form specifications. (These files typically make it easier to work with a database because your interface with the database is customized to your particular needs.)
  — Choose the Reports panel to create files that contain your specifications for a stylized report.
  — Choose the Labels panel to create files that contain mailing label specifications.
  — Choose the Applications panel to create program files.

  Once a particular type of file is created, it is displayed in the appropriate panel. Up to 200 filenames can be displayed in a panel.
- *File information*. The two lines near the bottom of the screen display information relating to the currently highlighted file. (At this point, no file is highlighted.)

FIGURE D.7 The different components of the Control Center.

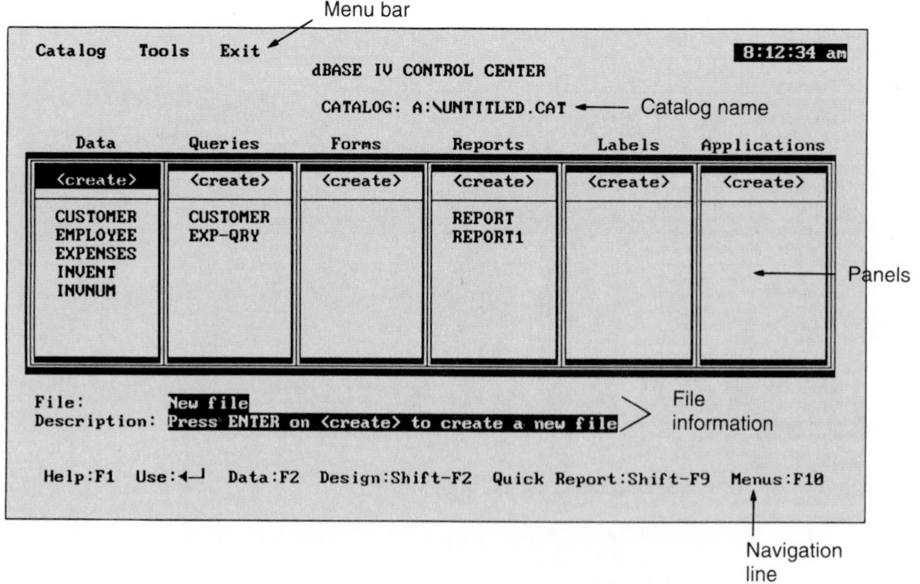

- *Navigation line*. The navigation line at the bottom of the screen contains instructions for using the function keys to perform important commands such as accessing help (F1), displaying the data stored in a file (F2), or activating the options in the menu bar (F10). The function keys are used throughout the dBASE menus to issue commands quickly.

The Dot Prompt

Once dBASE has been loaded into RAM, you can issue commands either from the Control Center (described in the last section) or from the dot prompt. When dBASE II and dBASE III (previous versions of dBASE) were loaded into RAM, all that appeared on the screen was a dot, referred to as the **dot prompt.** All commands had to be typed in after this prompt. To make dBASE easier to use, dBASE III Plus and dBASE IV incorporate a menu system that makes it unnecessary for the user to type in lengthy commands after the dot prompt. (dBASE IV's menu system is the Control Center.) Although all dBASE commands can be executed from the dot prompt, not all dBASE commands can be executed from the Control Center. Therefore, it is sometimes necessary to exit the Control Center to the dot prompt to issue a particular command. Later in this module, we lead you through exiting the Control Center menu to the dot prompt, issuing a command from the dot prompt, and then displaying the Control Center again.

Using the Menus

So that you can become familiar with dBASE's menu system, in this section we lead you through using it to perform some fundamental procedures.

As described in the last section, a menu bar displays at the top of the Control Center screen. In addition, a menu bar displays at the top of most other dBASE screens. To move the highlight up to the menu bar so that you can access the menu options, either press the F10 key (as indicated on the bottom of the screen) or hold the Alt key down and type the letter of the menu option you want to access. Table D.1 lists different methods for using dBASE's menu system. To practice using some of these keys, perform the following steps:

1. To move the highlight to the menu bar:
   PRESS: F10
   The screen should look like Figure D.8, with the Catalog menu displaying.
2. To highlight the Tools menu:
   PRESS: Right cursor-movement key
3. To highlight the Exit menu:
   PRESS: Right cursor-movement key
4. If you decide you don't want to highlight the menu bar:
   PRESS: Esc
5. To again highlight the menu bar:
   PRESS: F10

Note that the Exit menu is now highlighted, whereas the Catalog menu was highlighted when you first activated the menu bar. *No matter what dBASE menu you use, dBASE will always display the last highlighted menu option.*

6. To remove the menu bar from the display:
PRESS: Esc

TABLE D.1

Methods for Using the Control Center

Key	Purpose
F10	Move the highlight to the menu; display the menu that was last used.
Alt and the first letter of a menu name	Move the highlight to the pull-down menu that begins with the typed letter.
← →	Display a pull-down menu to the left/right.
↑ ↓ and then Enter	Highlight and then choose an option displaying in a pull-down menu.
Esc	Back out of a menu or a list of choices.
Ctrl-End	Save your work; accept certain menu assumptions.
Tab	Move cursor to the right when columns are displaying.
Shift-Tab	Move cursor to the left when columns are displaying.
End	Move cursor to the bottom of a list.
Home	Move cursor to the top of a list.
PgDn	Display next group of choices.
PgUp	Display previous group of choices.

FIGURE D.8

The Catalog menu.

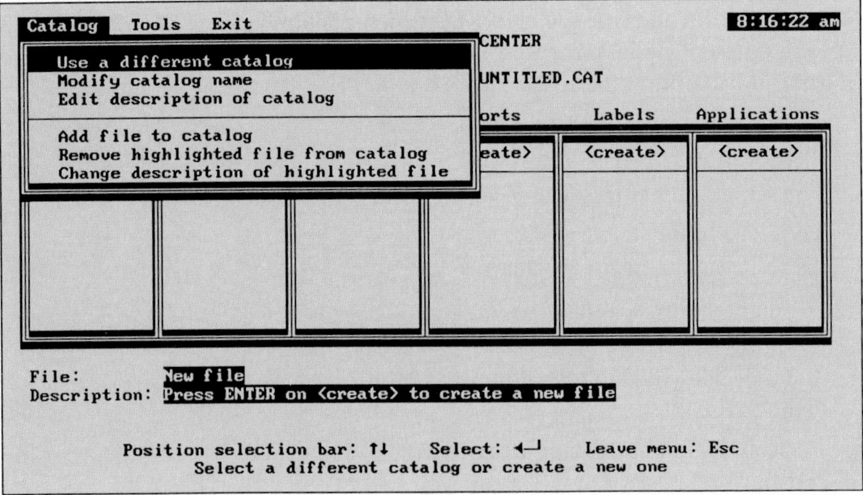

7. If you want to move directly to an option that is displaying in a menu bar, you can hold the Alt key down and type the first letter of the option. For example, to highlight the Tools menu:
   PRESS: Alt-T
   The Tools menu should be displaying on the screen. *To choose a menu option in a menu, you can highlight it using the cursor-movement keys and then press the Enter key.*
8. So that the menu bar isn't displaying:
   PRESS: Esc

Quick Reference

Using the dBASE IV Menus

1. To move the cursor up to the menu bar:
   PRESS: F10
   Note: A pull-down menu can be accessed directly by holding the Alt key down and typing the first letter of the pull-down menu you want to display.
2. Use the Left and Right cursor-movement keys to highlight an adjacent pull-down menu. Use the Up and Down cursor-movement keys to highlight options within a pull-down menu. Press Enter to choose an option.
3. To back out of a menu:
   PRESS: Esc

USING HELP

If you need additional information about how to use a particular command, you can use dBASE's Help system. dBASE provides you with several methods for accessing help information:

- Press F1 from the Control Center.
- Type Help and then press Enter after the dot prompt.
- Choose the Help button when an error box displays on the screen.

In the following steps, you will practice using dBASE's Help system. You will access it by pressing F1 from the Control Center. Perform the following steps:

1. The cursor should be highlighting the <create> marker in the Data panel.
   PRESS: F1
   The screen should look like Figure D.9. Information relating to the current option is displaying in the Help box. At the bottom of the Help box, the following options are displaying:
   a. CONTENTS. Choosing this option displays a Table of Contents that relates to the current panel.
   b. RELATED TOPICS. Choosing this option displays a list of topics that relate to the current one.
   c. PRINT. Choosing this option allows you to print the current Help screen out on the printer.
2. To display the Table of Contents that relates to the current panel, choose the CONTENTS option by highlighting it and then pressing the Enter key. The

screen should look like Figure D.10. Table D.2 lists different cursor-movement methods for using the CONTENTS box.

3. So that this screen no longer displays:
   PRESS: Esc
   The Control Center should again be displaying.
4. To initiate help again so that you can use the RELATED TOPICS option:
   PRESS: F1
5. Choose the RELATED TOPICS option by highlighting it and then pressing the Enter key. The screen should look like Figure D.11. When a new topic is chosen, the Help box displays text relating to the new topic.
6. To exit Help:
   PRESS: Esc twice

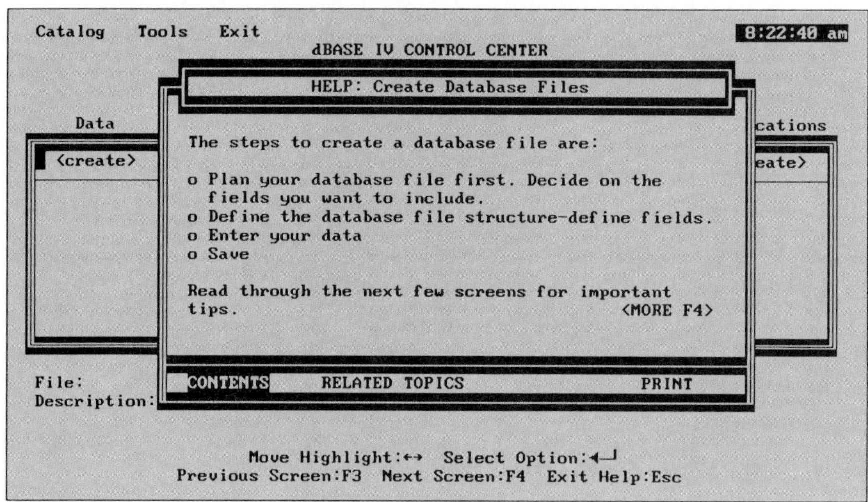

FIGURE D.9

The Help system.

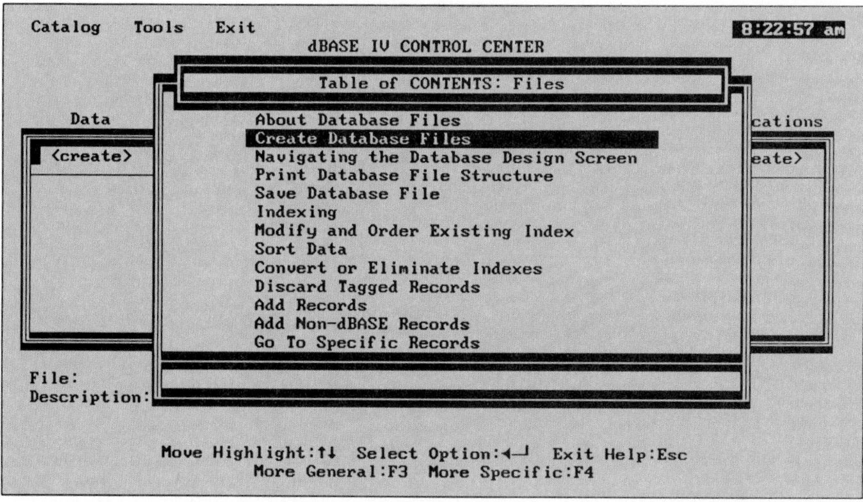

FIGURE D.10

Using the Help system's Table of Contents option.

Pressing the F1 key will display information relating to the currently highlighted dBASE IV menu option. To exit the Help system, press the Esc key to display the last dBASE screen you were working on.

Quick Reference

Using Help

CHANGING THE CURRENT DRIVE

Before creating the structure for a database in the next section, we will lead you through changing the current drive so dBASE knows you will be saving your work onto a data diskette located in drive A. The assumption made by dBASE at this point is to save and retrieve using the hard disk. (Note: If you want to save and retrieve using the hard disk, ignore this section.) Perform the following steps:

1. The Control Center should be displaying on the screen.
2. Insert your formatted data diskette in drive A.

TABLE D.2

Cursor-Movement Methods When Using the Contents Option in dBASE's Help System

Key	Purpose
F3 Previous	Display a broader level of topic detail.
F4 Next	Display a more detailed description of topics.
	Move the cursor up and down in a list of topics.
PgUp and PgDn	Display a list of topics, a box at a time.
Home	Move to the top of a list.
End	Move to the bottom of a list.

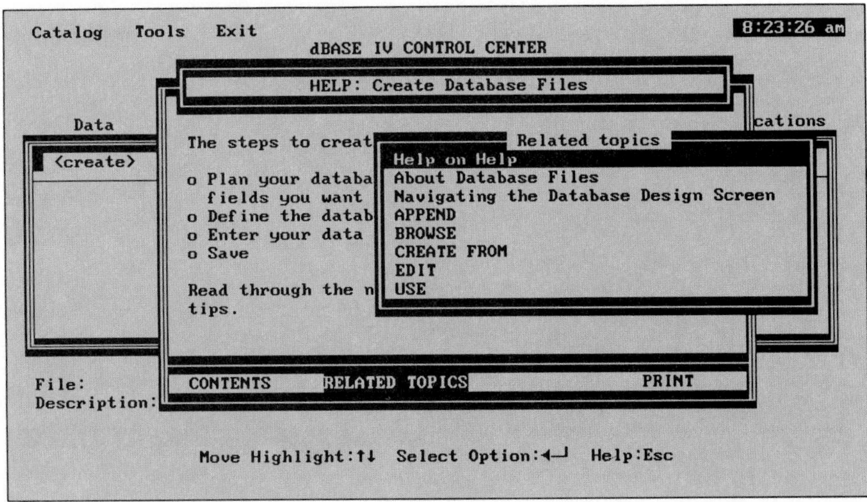

FIGURE D.11

Using the Help system's Related Topics option.

3. To display the dot prompt:
   PRESS: Alt-E
   To choose the Exit to dot prompt option:
   PRESS: Enter
4. The dot prompt should be displaying.
   TYPE: SET DIRECTORY TO A:
   PRESS: Enter
5. The dot prompt should again be displaying on the screen. To display the Control Center:
   TYPE: ASSIST

dBASE now knows it will save and retrieve using the data diskette that is located in drive A.

CREATING THE DATABASE STRUCTURE

In this section, we lead you through creating the structure for the CUSTOMER database—that is, defining the characteristics of each field to be included in the database. The structure of the CUSTOMER database is pictured in Figure D.12. We described what to consider when creating a database in the DBMS Features section earlier in this module. Perform the following steps:

1. The Control Center should be displaying on the screen. Highlight the <create> marker in the Data panel. Press the Enter key.
2. The screen should now look like Figure D.13. When you type in the specifications for the structure of the database, dBASE will convert all your letters to uppercase.
   TYPE: TITLE
   PRESS: Enter

FIGURE D.12

The structure of the CUSTOMER database.

Layout Organize Append Go To Exit 12:02:22 pm

Bytes remaining: 3888

Num	Field Name	Field Type	Width	Dec	Index
1	TITLE	Character	4		N
2	FIRSTNAME	Character	10		N
3	LASTNAME	Character	15		N
4	ADDRESS	Character	30		N
5	CITY	Character	15		N
6	STATE	Character	2		N
7	ZIP	Character	10		N
8	INVNUM	Character	4		N
9	INVAMT	Numeric	7	2	N
10	AMTPAID	Numeric	7	2	N
11	INVDATE	Date	8		N
12		Character			N

Database C:\dbase\<NEW> Field 12/12

Enter the field name. Insert/Delete field:Ctrl-N/Ctrl-U

Field names begin with a letter and may contain letters, digits and underscores

The cursor is now positioned in the Field Type column. Note that dBASE indicates (below the status line on the bottom of the screen) that you can change the field type by pressing the space bar. (Field types were described earlier in the DBMS Features section.) Even though you want this field to be defined as Character, practice changing the field types:
PRESS: space bar
The type should have changed to Numeric.
PRESS: space bar
The type should have changed to Float.
PRESS: space bar until the field type displays "Character" again.
You can also change the field type by typing the first character of the type you want. For example, if you want a field to be numeric, you could type N *while the cursor is positioned in the Type column.*

3. The cursor should be positioned in the Type column, and the text "Character" should be displaying. To move the cursor to the Width column:
   PRESS: Enter
4. To specify a width of 4:
   TYPE: 4
   PRESS: Enter
   Note that dBASE didn't prompt you to enter anything in the Dec column. dBASE prompts you only for the number of decimals for numeric field types.
5. The cursor is now positioned in the Index column. Indexing on a certain field enables you to put the database into order by that field (that is, once data has been added). For now, you will accept dBASE's assumption of N—we will describe indexing in more detail later.
   PRESS: Enter
6. dBASE is now prompting you to enter field information for the second field in the database. By referring to Figure D.12, type in the rest of the structure for the CUSTOMER database.

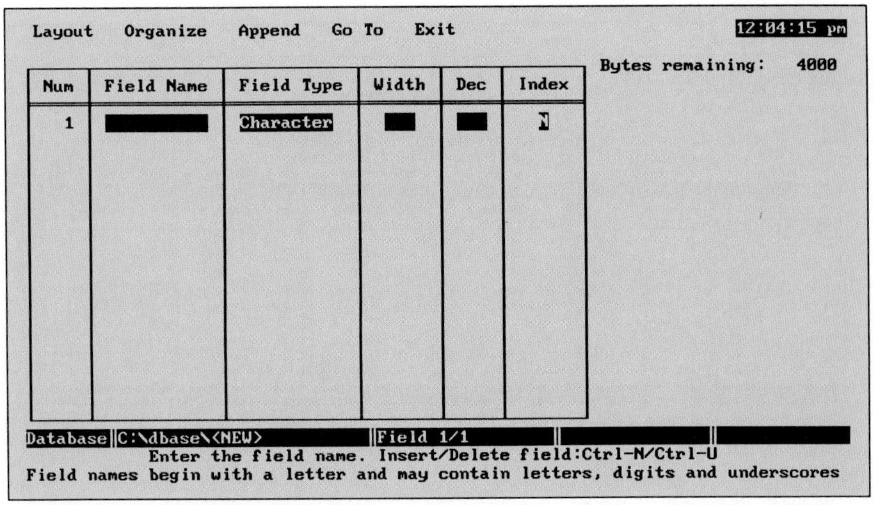

```
Layout   Organize   Append   Go To   Exit                          12:04:15 pm

                                                  Bytes remaining:   4000
 Num | Field Name | Field Type | Width | Dec | Index
  1  |            | Character  |       |     |   N

Database ║C:\dbase\<NEW>          ║Field 1/1  ║
          Enter the field name.  Insert/Delete field:Ctrl-N/Ctrl-U
Field names begin with a letter and may contain letters, digits and underscores
```

FIGURE D.13

To create a database structure, you must type the specifications into this screen.

Note that dBASE automatically put the number 8 into the INVDATE's Width column. Also note that the ZIP and INVNUM fields were defined as Character field types rather than Numeric field types. This is because calculations won't be performed on those fields. For example, you wouldn't want to calculate the average ZIP code or the total of all invoice numbers.

To save the CUSTOMER database structure, perform the following steps:

1. To display the Exit menu:
   PRESS: Alt-E
   The cursor is currently highlighting the option called Save changes and exit. To choose this option:
   PRESS: Enter
2. dBASE is now prompting you to type in a name for the database. It doesn't matter if you use upper- or lowercase letters. In the following steps, you will save the database onto your data diskette:
   a. Make sure your data diskette is in drive A.
   b. TYPE: CUSTOMER
      PRESS: Enter
   The CUSTOMER database structure has now been saved onto your data disk.

The Control Center should be displaying on the screen (Figure D.14). The cursor is highlighting the CUSTOMER filename in the Data panel. Note that the horizontal line is now below the CUSTOMER filename. This indicates that the database is now in use. If other databases were stored on your disk, they would be listed below this horizontal line.

Quick Reference

Creating a Database Structure

1. With the Control Center displaying, highlight the <create> marker in the Data panel, and then press Enter.
2. Type in the specifications for the database structure.
3. To save your specifications, activate the Exit menu, and then choose the Save changes and exit option.

FIGURE D.14

The Control Center. The CUSTOMER database is the active database.

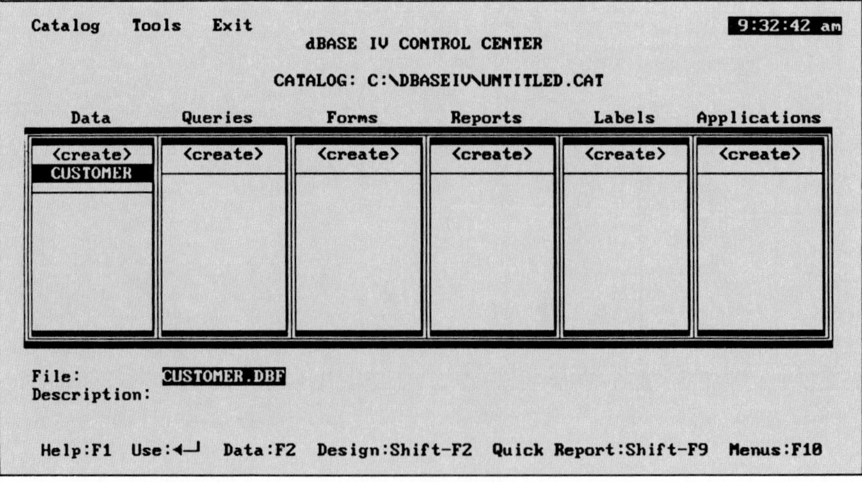

MODIFYING THE DATABASE STRUCTURE

dBASE IV allows you to change the structure of an existing database file by either adding or deleting fields or changing the characteristics of a field (such as field width). When you invoke this command, dBASE makes a temporary backup copy of the database file to be modified. After you've made changes to the structure, dBASE asks you to confirm your changes.

In this section, you will change the width of the FIRSTNAME field from 10 to 12 (to accommodate longer first names). Perform the following steps:

1. Highlight CUSTOMER in the Data panel, and then press Enter. The screen should look like Figure D.15.
2. Choose the Modify structure/order option. The Organize menu should be displaying on the screen; the options in this menu are used when you want to make changes that affect the indexing of the database.
3. Since you don't need to use any of the options in this menu (we describe indexing shortly):
   PRESS: Esc
4. Using the cursor-movement keys, position the cursor in the width column of the FIRSTNAME field.
5. With the cursor in the width column of the FIRSTNAME field:
   TYPE: 12
   PRESS: Enter
6. To activate the Exit menu so you can save the change you made to the structure of the CUSTOMER database:
   PRESS: Alt-E
7. Choose the Save changes and exit option.
8. dBASE now asks if you're sure you want to make changes. To choose the Yes option:
   PRESS: Enter
   The Control Center should be displaying on the screen.

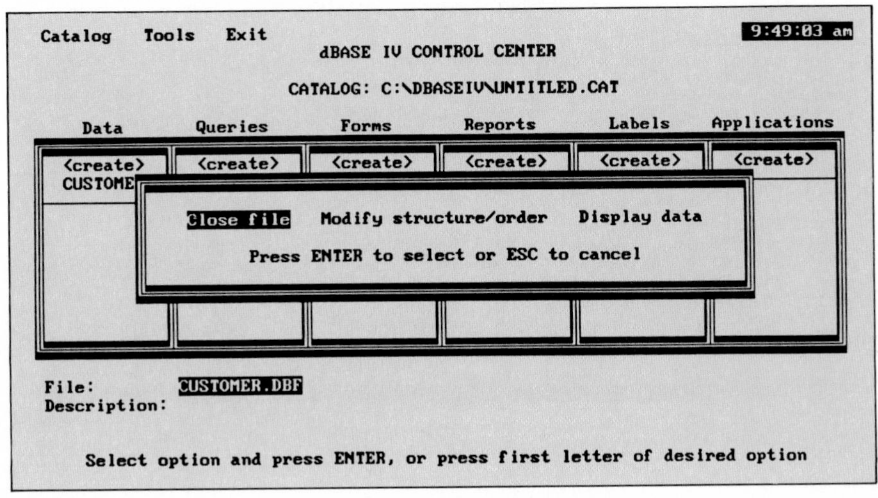

FIGURE D.15

Modifying the structure of the CUSTOMER database.

Quick Reference

■

Modifying the Database Structure

1. From the Control Center, highlight the name of the database you want to modify in the Data panel, and then press Enter.
2. Choose the Modify structure/order option.
3. Make your changes.
4. To save your changes, activate the Exit menu and then choose the Save changes and exit option.

LISTING THE DATABASE STRUCTURE

Once you have modified or created a database structure, you may want to view it on the screen to see its characteristics. To do this, you must exit the Control Center to the dot prompt. To list the CUSTOMER database on the screen, perform the following steps:

1. To activate the Exit menu so you can exit to the dot prompt:
   PRESS: Alt-E
2. Choose the Exit to dot prompt option.
3. The dot prompt should be displaying on the screen.
   TYPE: display structure
   PRESS: Enter
   The screen should look like Figure D.16. Note that the FIRSTNAME field now has a width of 12.
4. To display the Control Center:
   TYPE: assist
   PRESS: Enter
   The Control Center should be displaying on the screen.

FIGURE D.16

Listing the database structure.

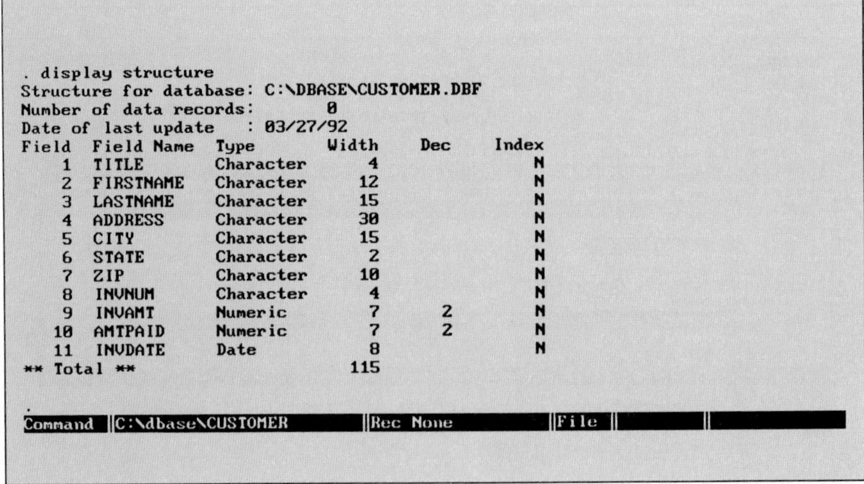

```
. display structure
Structure for database: C:\DBASE\CUSTOMER.DBF
Number of data records:       0
Date of last update   : 03/27/92
Field  Field Name  Type       Width    Dec    Index
    1  TITLE       Character      4               N
    2  FIRSTNAME   Character     12               N
    3  LASTNAME    Character     15               N
    4  ADDRESS     Character     30               N
    5  CITY        Character     15               N
    6  STATE       Character      2               N
    7  ZIP         Character     10               N
    8  INVNUM      Character      4               N
    9  INVAMT      Numeric        7      2        N
   10  AMTPAID     Numeric        7      2        N
   11  INVDATE     Date           8               N
** Total **                     115
.
Command ║C:\dbase\CUSTOMER        ║Rec None          ║File ║
```

Quick Reference
Listing the Database Structure

1. Choose the Exit to dot prompt option from the Exit menu displaying in the Control Center.
2. To display the database structure on the screen:
   TYPE: display structure
   PRESS: Enter
3. To display the Control Center:
   TYPE: assist
   PRESS: Enter

EXITING dBASE IV

One of the most important DBMS functions to learn is how to exit. With dBASE IV, when you exit the program properly, all your database management activities (such as adding or deleting activities) are automatically saved in the database. *If you turn off your computer without exiting dBASE, you may lose data.* Perform the following procedure now and at the end of each working session:

1. To exit dBASE, activate the Exit menu from the Control Center:
   TYPE: Alt-E
2. Choose the Quit to DOS option.
   You should see the DOS prompt on the screen.
3. To load dBASE IV again:
   TYPE: dbase
   PRESS: Enter
   The Control Center should again be displaying on the screen.
4. If you're using a data diskette in drive A, perform the procedure for changing the current drive now (dBASE lost this setting when you exited).

Note that the name CUSTOMER now appears below the line in the Data panel. This is because when you first load the program, dBASE doesn't know what database you're working with. In the next section, we lead you through telling dBASE what database file you want to work with.

Quick Reference
Exiting dBASE IV

Choose the Quit to DOS option from the Exit menu in the Control Center.

USING A DATABASE

You should now be viewing the Control Center. If you completed the last section (Exiting dBASE IV), dBASE doesn't know what database you want to work with. Although you probably have only one database stored on your data diskette, most business tasks involve the use of many databases. Therefore, dBASE requires that you specify what database you want to work with at the beginning of each working session. This is similar in concept to deciding what drawer in a filing cabinet you want to open.

Perform the following steps to use the CUSTOMER database:

1. Highlight CUSTOMER in the Data panel, and then press Enter.
2. Choose the Use file option. The name CUSTOMER now appears above the line in the Data panel. In addition, the name CUSTOMER appears on the bottom of the screen. Any commands you issue right now will pertain to the CUSTOMER database until you either create or use another database file.

Quick Reference
■
Using a Database

1. Highlight the name of the database in the Data panel and then press Enter.
2. Choose the Use file option.

ADDING RECORDS

In this section, you will add the records in Figure D.17 to the CUSTOMER database. At this point, you know you are using the CUSTOMER database because the name CUSTOMER is displaying above the line in the Data panel. If you had just loaded dBASE or had been using another database, you would first need to set the CUSTOMER database up for use (as described in the last section).

Adding records to a database you have *just created* is accomplished by pressing the F2 (Data) key. After records have been added to a database, this key is used to edit, or make changes to, database records. To add *more* records to the database, you will have to activate the Records menu after pressing F2.

Perform the following steps:

1. To add records:
   PRESS: F2
   The screen should look like Figure D.18.

FIGURE D.17 CUSTOMER database listing.

Records Organize Fields Go To Exit

TITLE	FIRSTNAME	LASTNAME	ADDRESS	CITY	STATE	ZIP	INVNUM	INVAMT	AMTPAID	INVDATE
Mr.	Sean	Dennis	132 Walnut Lane	San Francisco	CA	94122	2131	132.11	0.00	07/14/92
Ms.	Veronica	Visentin	90 Spruce Street	San Mateo	CA	94019	2132	245.00	0.00	02/14/92
Mr.	Charles	Cattermole	18 Cameo Road	San Francisco	CA	94102	2133	500.00	200.00	02/27/92
Mr.	Frank	Chihowski	9 Bye Street	San Francisco	CA	94102	2140	1400.00	800.00	04/08/92
Ms.	Heidi	Buehre	3255 S. Parker Road #1-605	San Mateo	CA	94019	2138	350.00	0.00	03/15/92
Ms.	Joellen	Baldwin	2729 Glen Ellen Drive	San Francisco	CA	94102	2136	1400.00	700.00	06/12/92
Ms.	Lynne	Morrow-Tabacchi	11322 Overlook Drive N E	San Mateo	CA	94019	2134	150.00	0.00	06/01/92
Mr.	Samuel	Hussey	23 Linlew Drive, Apt. 15	San Mateo	CA	94102	2149	125.00	0.00	08/03/92
Ms.	Rosalie	Skears	9504 Wellington Street	San Mateo	CA	94102	2145	1000.45	0.00	01/04/92
Ms.	Joan	Vieau	55 Francisco Street	San Francisco	CA	94102	2142	150.00	0.00	06/15/92

Browse ‖C:\dbase\CUSTOMER ‖Rec 1/10 ‖File ‖ ‖

2. The cursor should be blinking in the TITLE field. A note about entering data—if you fill up a field with data, as when you enter STATE information, dBASE will beep and automatically move the cursor to the next field. If you don't fill up a field with data, as when you enter FIRSTNAME data, you will have to press the Enter key to move the cursor to the next field. Key in the following data:

Mr.	Enter
Sean	Enter
Dennis	Enter
132 Walnut Lane	Enter
San Francisco	Enter
CA	
94122	Enter
2131	
132.11	
0	Enter
071492	

   If dBASE asks if you want to add new records, type Y. dBASE should now be waiting for you to enter information into the second record. What if you made a mistake when entering data into the first record? Fortunately, dBASE provides you with a number of methods for moving to records and within records. For practice, perform the following step.

3. To move the cursor to the beginning of the first record:
   PRESS: PgUp
   The cursor should now be positioned beneath the "M" of "Mr."

4. Tap the Down cursor-movement key three times to move the cursor to the ADDRESS field. If you wanted to make changes at this point, you could simply retype the contents of this field. Whereas the Up and Down cursor-movement keys are used to move from field to field, the Right and Left

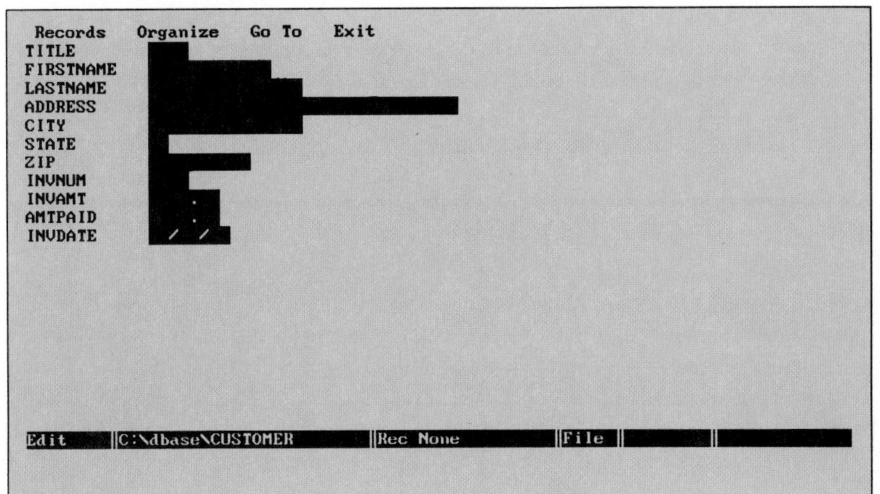

FIGURE D.18

Adding data to the CUSTOMER database.

cursor-movement keys are used to move from character to character within fields. If you want to delete a character, position the cursor on the character and press the Del key. If you want to insert a character or characters, press the Ins key. (Note that when you press the Ins key, your status line indicates that Insert mode has been activated.)

5. To move the cursor to the next record to enter data:
   PRESS: PgDn
   dBASE should now be asking you if you want to add new records:
   TYPE: Y
   After you use what dBASE considers to be an editing command, if your cursor is on the last record of the database, dBASE asks you if you want to add records.
6. Refer to Figure D.17 to enter the rest of the data into the CUSTOMER file. When you have entered the last record and your cursor is on a blank record, proceed with the next step.
7. Since you are finished entering all the data into this database, it is time to return to the Control Center. However, if you exit the CUSTOMER file while your cursor is positioned on a blank record, you will save a blank record along with your database. Before exiting, always press the PgUp key so your cursor is on a record that contains data. (*Note:* Here you are exiting a file to return to the Control Center, you are not exiting dBASE altogether as described on page 659.)
   PRESS: PgUp
8. To exit to the Control Center, you must first activate the menus:
   PRESS: F10
9. Highlight the Exit menu (by pressing the Right cursor-movement key).
10. Choose the Exit option. The Control Center should be displaying on the screen.

Quick Reference ■ Adding Records

1. After activating, or using, a database:
   PRESS: F2
2. Activate the Records menu.
3. Choose the Add new records option.
4. Save the newly added records by first positioning the cursor on a record that contains data and then activating the Exit menu. Choose the Exit option.

DISPLAYING DATA AND EDITING

dBASE provides several methods for displaying and editing the data stored in your database. While viewing the Control Center, you can display all the records easily with the F2 (Data) key. When first pressed, the F2 key will display only the current record on the screen so that you can edit it (Figure D.19). This display mode is referred to as **Edit mode.** Depending on which record is current, display additional records by pressing the PgUp or the PgDn key. If the cursor is on the last record of the database, pressing PgDn will cause dBASE to ask if you want to add additional records. You can respond by typing either Y or N.

Many people prefer to use **Browse mode** when displaying or editing data. This mode enables you to display records horizontally in the form of a table so that you can see more than one record at a time (Figure D.20). To display your data in Browse mode, press the F2 key while viewing your data in Edit mode. *The F2 key is a toggle key that displays your data in either Edit or Browse mode, depending on which mode you used last.* In Browse mode, you can use the Tab key to move the cursor across the screen to the right and the Shift-Tab key combination to move the cursor across the screen to the left. Your Up and Down cursor-movement keys will move the cursor up and down through the database records. As in Edit mode, if you press the Down cursor-movement key while the cursor is on the last record of the database, dBASE will ask if you want to add data.

You can edit your data while in Edit mode or Browse mode by moving the cursor to the record and field you want to edit and then typing in your changes. *If*

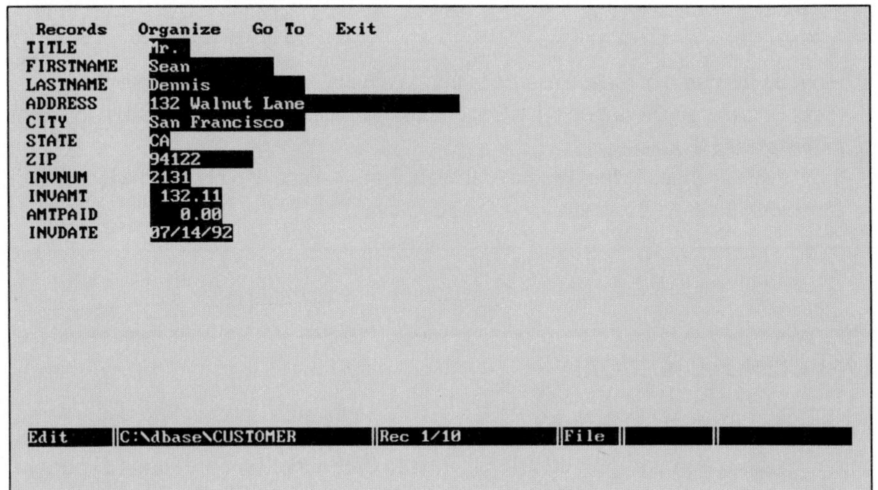

FIGURE D.19

Edit mode.

Records Organize Fields Go To Exit

TITLE	FIRSTNAME	LASTNAME	ADDRESS	CITY
Mr.	Sean	Dennis	132 Walnut Lane	San Francisc
Ms.	Veronica	Visentin	90 Spruce Street	San Mateo
Mr.	Charles	Cattermole	18 Cameo Road	San Francisc
Mr.	Frank	Chihowski	9 Bye Street	San Francisc
Ms.	Heidi	Buehre	3255 S. Parker Road #1-605	San Mateo
Ms.	Joellen	Baldwin	2729 Glen Ellen Drive	San Francisc
Ms.	Lynne	Morrow-Tabacchi	11322 Overlook Drive N E	San Mateo
Mr.	Samuel	Hussey	23 Linlew Drive, Apt. 15	San Mateo
Ms.	Rosalie	Skears	9504 Wellington Street	San Mateo
Ms.	Joan	Vieau	55 Francisco Street	San Francisc

Browse C:\dbase\CUSTOMER Rec 1/10 File

FIGURE D.20

Browse mode.

you do make changes while in Edit or Browse mode, you will need to save your changes by activating the Exit menu and then choosing the Exit option. If you don't make changes, you can simply press the Esc key to exit to the Control Center.

Perform the following steps to practice using the F2 key:

1. To display the data stored in the CUSTOMER database in either Edit or Browse mode:
   PRESS: F2
2. To change the mode of display:
   PRESS: F2
3. Press the F2 key until you are viewing the data in Browse mode. Then practice using the Tab key and the Shift-Tab key combination to move from field to field in the Browse screen.
4. To exit the Control Center without saving (since you haven't made any changes):
   PRESS: Esc

Quick Reference
■
Displaying Data and Editing

1. Highlight the name of a database file in the Data panel of the Control Center.
2. Press F2 to display the data in either Edit or Browse mode. To display the data in a different mode, press F2 again.
3. If you make changes to the database, activate the Exit menu and choose the Exit option. Otherwise, press Esc to display the Control Center.

DELETING A RECORD

Deleting a record from a database requires two steps: (1) mark the record for deletion (this command puts an asterisk next to the marked record) and (2) permanently delete the marked record. One of the main reasons dBASE requires you to perform two steps to permanently delete a record is to protect you from accidentally deleting records with a single command. In this section, we lead you through deleting Joan Vieau's record because she no longer owes any money and has moved away.

MARKING A RECORD FOR DELETION

You must display the record to be deleted in either Edit or Browse mode. To mark the record for deletion, do the following:

1. The Control Center should be displaying on the screen. Press F2 until the data is displaying in Browse mode.
2. Use the cursor-movement keys to position the cursor on Joan Vieau's record.
3. To activate the Records menu:
   PRESS: Alt-R
4. Choose the Mark record for deletion option. "Del" displays on the status line, which indicates that Joan Vieau's record is now marked for deletion.

Quick Reference ■ Marking a Record for Deletion

1. Activate, or use, a database.
2. Press F2 to display the data in either Edit or Browse mode.
3. Position the cursor on the record you want to mark for deletion.
4. Activate the Records menu and choose the Mark record for deletion option.

DELETING MARKED RECORDS

To permanently delete a marked record, you must activate the Organize menu in either Edit or Browse mode. Perform the following steps:

1. You should be viewing the CUSTOMER database in either Edit or Browse mode; Joan Vieau's record has been marked for deletion.
2. To activate the Organize menu:
   TYPE: Alt-O
3. To permanently delete Joan Vieau's record, choose the Erase marked records option.
4. Choose the Yes option.
   Joan Vieau's record has now been permanently deleted from the database.

Quick Reference ■ Deleting Marked Records

1. While displaying data in either Edit or Browse mode, activate the Organize menu.
2. Choose the Erase marked records option.
3. Choose the Yes option.

UNMARKING A RECORD MARKED FOR DELETION

To unmark a record that has been marked for deletion, you must activate the Records menu. The Mark record for deletion option toggles to display the Clear deletion mark option when you press the Enter key. If more than one record has been marked for deletion and you want to unmark them all at once, you must choose the Unmark all records option from the Organize menu.

Quick Reference ■ Unmarking a Record

1. Highlight the record you want to unmark.
2. Activate the Records menu, and then choose the Clear deletion mark option.

Quick Reference ■ Unmarking All Records

Choose the Unmark all records option from the Organize menu.

QUERIES: CREATING VIEWS

What use would a database be if you couldn't ask questions of it? For example, how many customers live in San Francisco? How many customers live in either San Mateo or San Francisco? How many owe us more than $500?

dBASE IV provides a variety of commands that enable you to view specific fields and records of information stored in a database. Each of these commands involves using the Queries panel from the Control Center. In this section, you learn how to create view queries of the data stored in the CUSTOMER database. A **view query** provides the user with a view, or partial picture, of the data stored in database files. The steps typically involved in creating and using view queries are:

1. Use, or activate, a database file.
2. Decide what fields you want to display in the view.
3. Display the data (F2).
4. Name and save the view query (optional).

In the next few sections, we lead you through creating and saving four separate view queries:

1. VIEW1 will enable you to display the LASTNAME, CITY, INVNUM, INVAMT, AMTPAID, and INVDATE fields. In other words, it enables you to list selective fields on the screen.
2. VIEW2 will enable you to view the LASTNAME, CITY, INVNUM, INVAMT, AMTPAID, and INVDATE fields for those records that have invoice amounts (INVAMT) that are greater than 500.
3. VIEW3 will enable you to view the LASTNAME, CITY, INVNUM, INVAMT, AMTPAID, and INVDATE fields for those customers who live in San Francisco (CITY) and who have an invoice amount that is greater than 500.
4. VIEW4 will enable you to view a listing of all customers who live in San Francisco.

THE QUERIES DESIGN SCREEN

In this section, we lead you through using the Queries design screen to view all the fields and records in the CUSTOMER database. We also show you how to be selective about the fields and records that you view on the screen. Before beginning, make sure the CUSTOMER database has been set up for use. Perform the following steps:

1. You should now be viewing the Control Center. Highlight the <create> marker in the Queries panel, and then press Enter.

   The screen should look like Figure D.21. You are now viewing the Queries design screen. Across the top of the screen is the menu bar with options for tailoring a database view to your needs. Below the menu bar is the **file skeleton,** or graphic representation, of the active database (CUSTOMER.DBF), showing the names of all the fields in the database. As you'll learn shortly, you can type selection criteria into the space below each of the field names in order to be selective about the records that are listed on the screen. Note that an arrow automatically precedes each field name. An arrow before a field name causes that field to be displayed when you view the database data. At this point, all fields will be displayed because they are all preceded by arrows. Displaying on the bottom of the screen is the format for the current view of the data, called the **view skeleton.** The right arrow in the bottom right-hand corner of the view box indicates that more fields are included in the view than can currently fit on the screen.

In the following steps we lead you through different methods of moving the cursor around the Queries design screen.

2. Note that you can't see all the fields on the screen.
   PRESS: Tab
   The cursor should be positioned beneath the TITLE field.
3. Press the Tab key until you can see the INVDATE field on the screen. Note that the view on the bottom of the screen stayed the same.
4. To move the cursor to the view skeleton so you can view the fields to the right:
   PRESS: F3
   The cursor should now be highlighting the first field in the view skeleton.
   PRESS: Tab until you see the INVDATE field
   Being able to move the cursor to the view skeleton is important when you want to move view fields.
5. To move the cursor back to the top of the screen, away from the view skeleton:
   PRESS: F3
6. The cursor should be positioned on the top of the screen. To move the cursor back to the Title field:
   PRESS: Shift-Tab until the cursor is beneath the CUSTOMER.DBF file-name
   Table D.3 lists a few different methods for moving the cursor in the Queries design screen.

```
Layout   Fields   Condition   Update   Exit                                12:22:21 pm
Customer.dbf | ↓TITLE | ↓FIRSTNAME | ↓LASTNAME | ↓ADDRESS | ↓CITY | ↓STATE | ↓ZIP | ↓INV

View
<NEW>   Customer->   Customer->   Customer->   Customer->
        TITLE        FIRSTNAME    LASTNAME     ADDRESS

Query  C:\dbase\<NEW>   File 1/1
 Next field:Tab  Add/Remove all fields:F5  Zoom:F9  Prev/Next skeleton:F3/F4
```

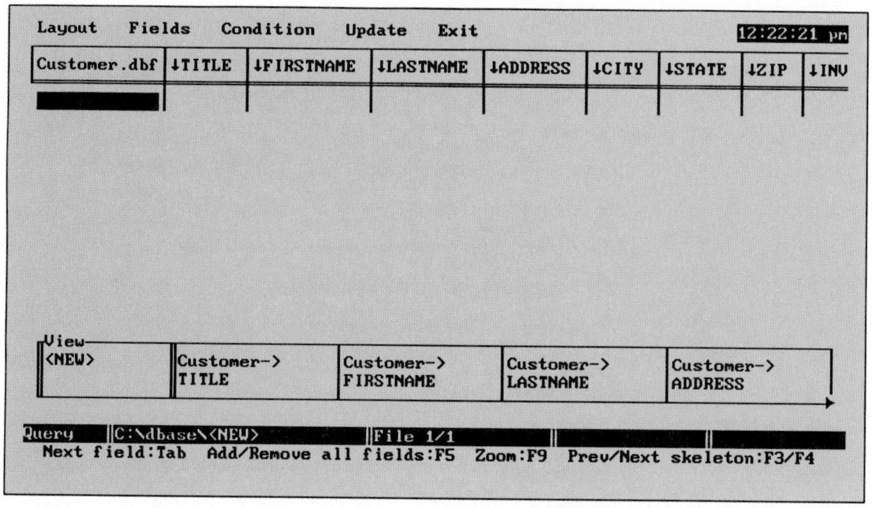

FIGURE D.21

The Queries design screen.

7. With the cursor beneath the database filename:
   PRESS: F5
   Note that all the arrows have disappeared from the display. In addition, since no fields are marked, no view is present on the bottom of the screen. *When viewing only a few fields at a time, it is sometimes easier to unmark all the fields using the F5 key, and to then choose the fields to be viewed.* You'll use this procedure shortly.
8. To re-mark all the fields:
   PRESS: F5
9. The F2 (Data) key is used to view the data.
   PRESS: F2
   The screen should be displaying the data in Edit mode or Browse mode, depending on which mode you last used.
10. Press F2 until you're viewing the data in Browse mode.
11. In Browse mode, note that you can't see all the fields stored in the database.
    PRESS: Tab so that you can display the fields to the right
    Note that the data is listed in the order it was input to the database. Shortly, you learn how to create and use indexes to display data in a different order.
12. To view the Queries design screen again:
    PRESS: Shift-F2

Quick Reference
■
Moving the Cursor in the Queries Design Screen

To move the cursor to fields on the right, press Tab. To move the cursor to fields on the left, press Shift-Tab.

TABLE D.3

Cursor-Movement Methods for Using the Queries Design Screen

Key	Purpose
F3 Prev, F4 Next	Move between the file and view skeletons and the condition boxes.
← →	Move the cursor within a column.
↑ ↓	Move the cursor up and down within the file skeleton.
Tab	Move cursor to the right when columns are displaying.
Shift-Tab	Move cursor to the left when columns are displaying.
End	Move cursor to the right-most column.
Home	Move cursor to the left-most column.
PgDn	Display next group of file skeletons (when you have more than can fit on the screen).
PgUp	Display previous group of file skeletons.

VIEWING SELECTED FIELDS

In the last section, you learned how to use the Queries design screen and how to display all the records in the database. Often, you'll want to view just a few fields present in a database. In this section, you will create a view to display the LASTNAME, CITY, INVNUM, INVAMT, AMTPAID, and INVDATE fields. You will then save the view as VIEW1.QBE (dBASE will automatically supply the extension of QBE to your view filename).

1. You should be viewing the Queries design screen. Position the cursor beneath the filename (CUSTOMER). To unmark all fields (as described earlier):
   PRESS: F5
   No field is currently chosen to be listed. *If a field isn't currently chosen to be included in the view skeleton, to choose it to be included in a view, you must first position the cursor beneath the field name and then activate the Fields menu.* You must then choose the option called Add field to view. To illustrate:
2. Position the cursor (using the Tab key) beneath the LASTNAME field.
3. To activate the Fields menu:
   PRESS: Alt-F
   The screen should look like Figure D.22.
4. To choose the Add field to view option:
   PRESS: Enter
   The screen should look like Figure D.23. Note that the LASTNAME field has now been added to the view skeleton shown on the bottom of the screen. In effect, the view is building on the bottom of the screen.
5. A quick alternative to using the Fields menu to add a field to a view is to use the F5 (Field) key. Position the cursor in the field to be added and then press F5. If you press F5 again, the field will be removed. Use the F5 key to add the CITY,

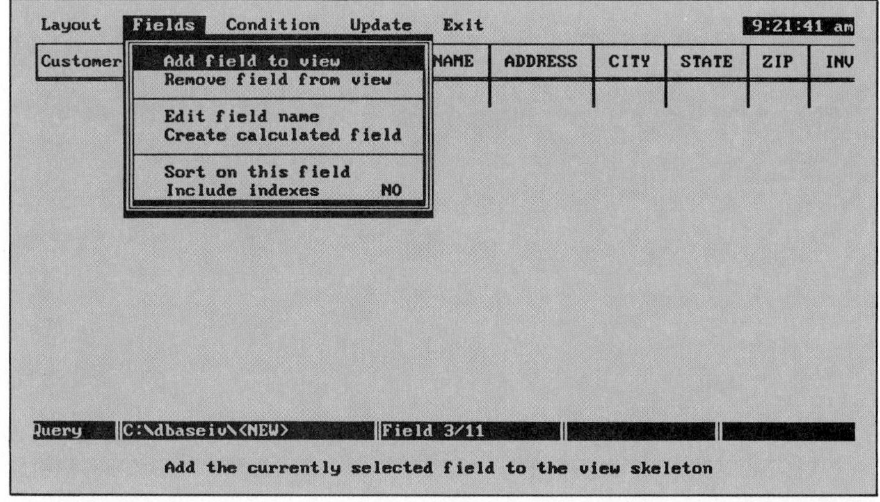

FIGURE D.22

The Fields menu in the Queries design screen.

INVNUM, INVAMT, AMTPAID, and INVDATE fields to the view. Note that as you add a field to the file skeleton, it is also added to the view skeleton.

6. To view the data:
   PRESS: F2
   The screen should look like Figure D.24.
7. To view the Queries design screen:
   PRESS: Shift-F2

Quick Reference
■
Viewing Selected Fields

1. Display the Queries design screen by highlighting the <create> marker in the Queries panel.
2. Unmark all fields by pressing the F5 key.
3. Choose a field to include in the view skeleton by positioning the cursor beneath the field name and then pressing F5.
4. Press F2 to view the data.

To save the view skeleton so you can use it at a later date without having to go through all the steps to create the view, perform the following steps:

1. To activate the Exit menu:
   PRESS: Alt-E
2. Choose the option called Save changes and exit.
3. dBASE is now prompting you to type in a filename for the view skeleton. Perform the following steps:
   a. Make sure your data diskette is in drive A.
   b. TYPE: VIEW1
      PRESS: Enter

   The Control Center should be displaying on the screen.

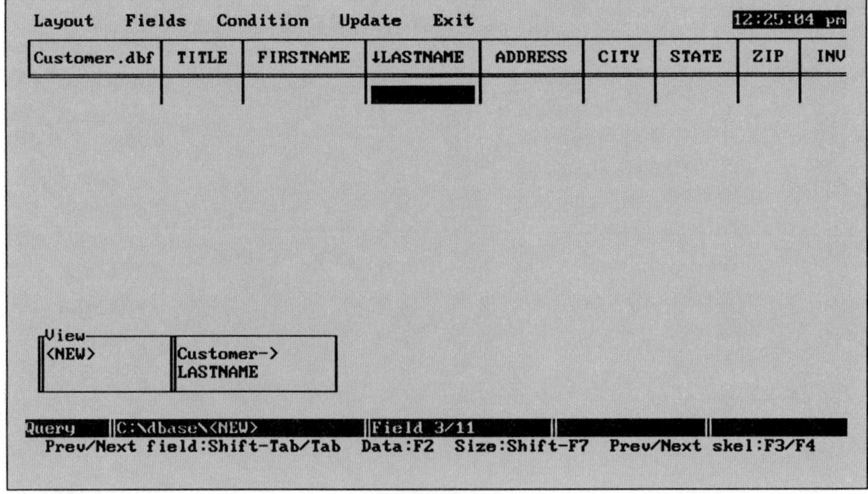

FIGURE D.23

The view skeleton after the LASTNAME field has been added.

Quick Reference

Saving a View Skeleton

1. From the Queries design screen, activate the Exit menu and choose the Save changes and exit option.
2. Type in a filename and then press Enter. dBASE will automatically supply the extension of QBE to the filename.

VIEWING SELECTED RECORDS

In the last section, you learned how to be selective about the fields you list on the screen. In this section, you learn how to be selective about the records that are listed on the screen. For example, what if you want to list only those records that have invoice amounts that are greater than 500? Or invoice dates that are greater than 3/16/92? In this section, you will practice searching for and viewing specific records in the CUSTOMER database.

A. In the next few steps, you will create a view skeleton that will include the LASTNAME, CITY, INVNUM, INVAMT, AMTPAID, and INVDATE fields for those records that have invoice amounts (INVAMT) that are greater than 500. You will then save the view as VIEW2.QBE. Perform the following steps:
   1. The Control Center should be displaying on the screen. Perform Steps 1–5 (p. 669) that lead you through including the LASTNAME, CITY, INVNUM, INVAMT, AMTPAID, and INVDATE fields in the view skeleton.
   2. Position the cursor beneath the INVAMT field.
      TYPE: >500
      The screen should look like Figure D.25.
   3. To view the data:
      PRESS: F2
      The screen should look like Figure D.26.
   4. To display the Queries design screen:
      PRESS: Shift-F2

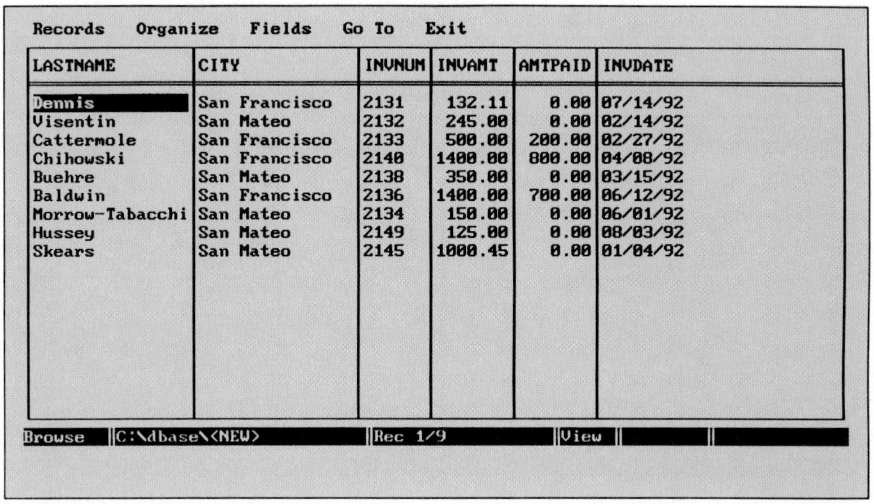

Records Organize Fields Go To Exit

LASTNAME	CITY	INVNUM	INVAMT	AMTPAID	INVDATE
Dennis	San Francisco	2131	132.11	0.00	07/14/92
Visentin	San Mateo	2132	245.00	0.00	02/14/92
Cattermole	San Francisco	2133	500.00	200.00	02/27/92
Chihowski	San Francisco	2140	1400.00	800.00	04/08/92
Buehre	San Mateo	2138	350.00	0.00	03/15/92
Baldwin	San Francisco	2136	1400.00	700.00	06/12/92
Morrow-Tabacchi	San Mateo	2134	150.00	0.00	06/01/92
Hussey	San Mateo	2149	125.00	0.00	08/03/92
Skears	San Mateo	2145	1000.45	0.00	01/04/92

Browse C:\dbase\<NEW> Rec 1/9 View

FIGURE D.24

Viewing the LASTNAME, CITY, INVNUM, INVAMT, AMTPAID, and INVDATE fields.

Quick Reference

■

Viewing Selected Records

1. Display the Queries design screen by highlighting the <create> marker in the Queries panel.
2. Position the cursor beneath the field name that your search is based on.
3. Type in your search condition.
4. Use the F2 key to view the data.

To save the view skeleton so you can use it at a later date without having to go through all the steps to create the view, perform the following steps:

1. To activate the Exit menu:
   PRESS: Alt-E
2. Choose the Save changes and exit option.

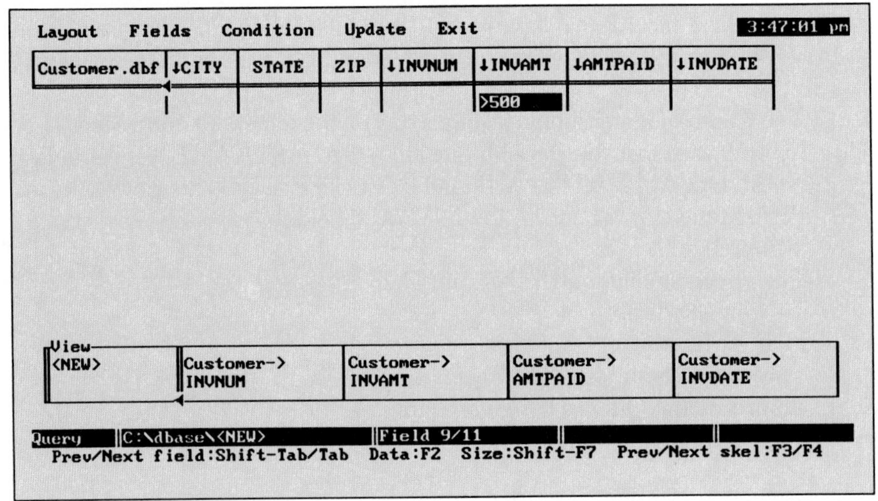

FIGURE D.25

The VIEW2 view skeleton.

Records Organize Fields Go To Exit

LASTNAME	CITY	INVNUM	INVAMT	AMTPAID	INVDATE
Chihowski	San Francisco	2140	1400.00	800.00	04/08/92
Baldwin	San Francisco	2136	1400.00	700.00	06/12/92
Skears	San Mateo	2145	1000.45	0.00	01/04/92

Browse C:\dbase\<NEW> Rec 4/9 View

FIGURE D.26

Viewing the LASTNAME, CITY, INVNUM, INVAMT, AMTPAID, and INVDATE fields for those customers who have an invoice amount that is greater than 500.

3. dBASE is now prompting you to type in a filename for the view skeleton. Perform the following steps:
   a. Make sure your data diskette is in drive A.
   b. TYPE: VIEW2
      PRESS: Enter

   The Control Center should be displaying on the screen.

B. To create a view named VIEW3.QBE that you can use to display the LASTNAME, CITY, INVNUM, INVAMT, AMTPAID, and INVDATE fields for those customers who live in San Francisco (CITY) and who have an invoice amount that is greater than 500, perform the following steps:

   1. The Control Center should be displaying on the screen. Choose the <create> marker in the Queries panel and then include the LASTNAME, CITY, INVNUM, INVAMT, AMTPAID, and INVDATE fields in the view skeleton (these steps were performed earlier).
   2. Position the cursor beneath the CITY field.
      TYPE: "San Francisco"
      Note: The character string "San Francisco" must be typed exactly as you keyed it into the database initially; for example, if you capitalized the S of "San" and the F of "Francisco," you must do so here. Or if you typed San Francisco in all uppercase, you must do so here. In addition, the character string must be enclosed in quotation marks.
   3. Position the cursor beneath the INVAMT field.
      TYPE: >500
   4. To view the data:
      PRESS: F2
      The screen should look like Figure D.27. The records that have an invoice amount that is greater than 500 and a CITY field that is equal to San Francisco are now listed on the screen.
   5. To display the Queries design screen:
      PRESS: Shift-F2

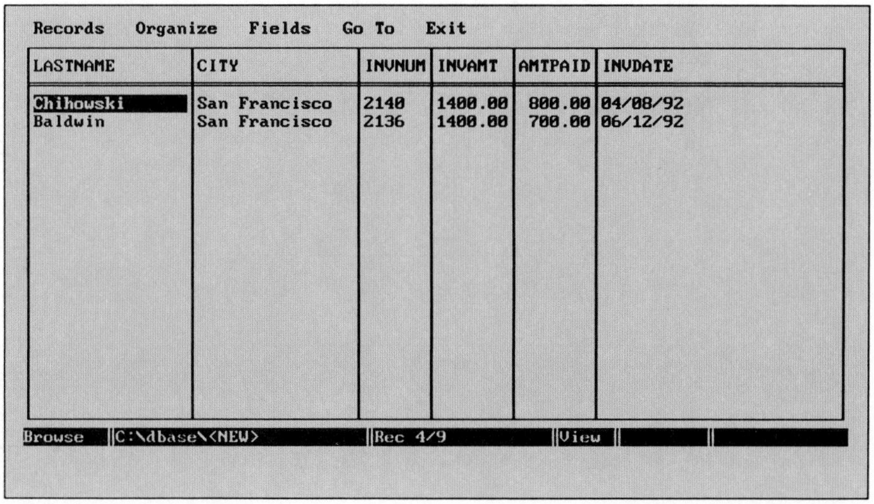

Records Organize Fields Go To Exit

LASTNAME	CITY	INVNUM	INVAMT	AMTPAID	INVDATE
Chihowski	San Francisco	2140	1400.00	800.00	04/08/92
Baldwin	San Francisco	2136	1400.00	700.00	06/12/92

Browse ‖C:\dbase\<NEW> ‖Rec 4/9 ‖View ‖

FIGURE D.27

Viewing the LASTNAME, CITY, INVNUM, INVAMT, AMTPAID, and INVDATE fields for those customers who have an invoice amount that is greater than 500 and who live in San Francisco.

To save the view skeleton so you can use it at a later date without having to go through all the steps to create the view, perform the following steps:

1. To activate the Exit menu:
   PRESS: Alt-E
2. Choose the Save changes and exit option.
3. dBASE is now prompting you to type in a filename for the view skeleton. Perform the following steps:
   a. Make sure your data diskette is in drive A.
   b. TYPE: VIEW3
      PRESS: Enter

   The Control Center should be displaying on the screen.

C. To create a view named VIEW4.QBE that you can use to list just those records for CITY equal to San Francisco, perform the following steps:

   1. The Control Center should be displaying on the screen. Choose the <create> marker in the Queries panel and then include the LASTNAME, CITY, INVNUM, INVAMT, AMTPAID, and INVDATE fields in the view skeleton (these steps were performed earlier).
   2. Position the cursor beneath the CITY field.
      TYPE: "San Francisco"
   3. To view the data:
      PRESS: F2
      The records for customers who live in San Francisco should be displaying on the screen.
   4. To view the Queries design screen:
      PRESS: Shift-F2

   To save the view skeleton so you can use it at a later date without having to go through all the steps to create the view, perform the following steps:

1. To activate the Exit menu:
   PRESS: Alt-E
2. Choose the Save changes and exit option.

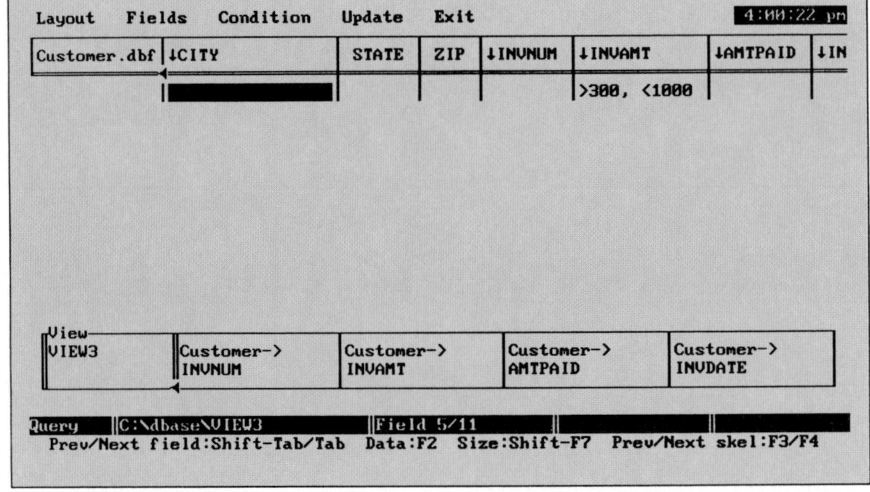

FIGURE D.28

The conditions necessary to view those records with an invoice amount greater than 300 and less than 1,000.

3. dBASE is now prompting you to type in a filename for the view skeleton. Perform the following steps:
   a. Make sure your data diskette is in drive A.
   b. TYPE: A:VIEW4
      PRESS: Enter

The Control Center should be displaying on the screen.

dBASE makes it possible to view almost any information you're interested in. For example, Figure D.28 pictures the conditions necessary to view those records that have an invoice amount that is greater than 300 and less than 1,000. Figure D.29 pictures the conditions necessary to view those records that have an invoice amount that is either less than 300 or greater than 1,000 (to specify an OR condition, you must put the conditions on separate lines). Figure D.30 pictures the conditions necessary to view those records that have a CITY field equal to "San Francisco" and an invoice amount greater than 200.

```
Layout   Fields   Condition   Update   Exit                       4:01:04 pm
Customer.dbf | ↓CITY | STATE | ZIP | ↓INVNUM | ↓INVAMT | ↓AMTPAID | ↓INVDATE
                                              <300
                                              >1000

View
VIEW3    Customer->   Customer->   Customer->   Customer->
         INVNUM       INVAMT       AMTPAID      INVDATE

Query  ||C:\dbase\VIEW3        ||Field 9/11  ||
 Prev/Next field:Shift-Tab/Tab  Data:F2  Size:Shift-F7  Prev/Next skel:F3/F4
```

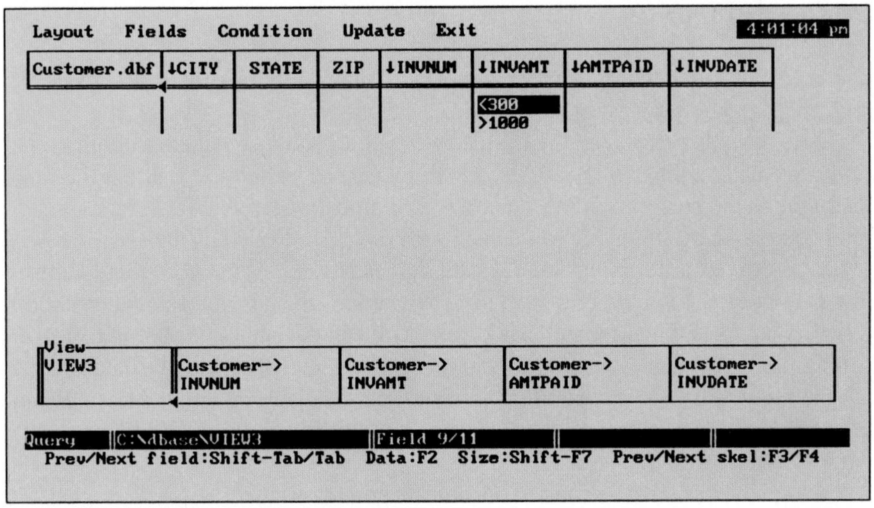

FIGURE D.29

The conditions necessary to view those records with an invoice amount less than 300 or greater than 1,000.

```
Layout   Fields   Condition   Update   Exit                       4:01:55 pm
Customer.dbf | ↓CITY | STATE | ZIP | ↓INVNUM | ↓INVAMT | ↓AMTPAID | ↓INVDAT
               "San Francisco"                 >200

View
VIEW3    Customer->   Customer->   Customer->   Customer->
         INVNUM       INVAMT       AMTPAID      INVDATE

Query  ||C:\dbase\VIEW3        ||Field 5/11  ||
 Prev/Next field:Shift-Tab/Tab  Data:F2  Size:Shift-F7  Prev/Next skel:F3/F4
```

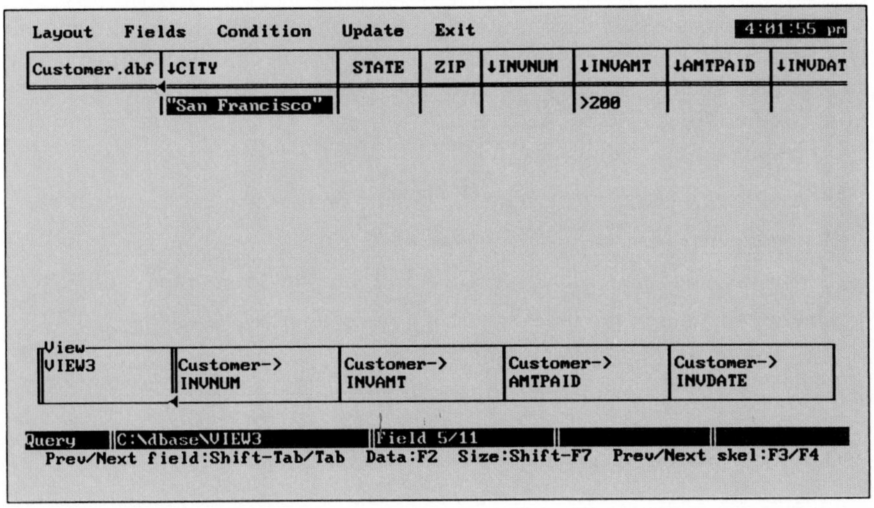

FIGURE D.30

The conditions necessary to view those records with a CITY field equal to "San Francisco" and an invoice amount greater than 200.

INDEXING THE DATABASE

Index files enable you to display database records in a different order without changing the physical location of the records in the database. When compared to *sorting* database records into a particular order, as described in the beginning of the module, indexing provides the user with a number of advantages. The most significant advantage of indexing database records into order over sorting them is that indexing doesn't make an entire copy of the database, which can use up a tremendous amount of disk space if the database is large. Instead, indexing outputs an index file that contains pointers that determine the order of the database records. In addition, when records are added to a file that has been indexed into order, even the newly added records will appear in the correct positions when the database is displayed. However, when you add a record to a file that has been sorted, the record will always appear at the end of the database listing.

ABOUT INDEXING

You can index the records in a database file into many different orders. For example, you might sometimes want to view the database records in order by the LASTNAME field, sometimes by the CITY field. When you *first* initiate a command to index a database into order, dBASE creates a **master index file** that has the same filename as the currently active database, plus an extension of MDX. If, for example, you create an index file to be used with the CUSTOMER database, dBASE would create a master file called CUSTOMER.MDX. When you then create an index to put the database into LASTNAME order, dBASE puts this specification, called a **tag,** into the associated MDX file. You can have any number of tags in an MDX file. Every time you add a record to, or delete a record from, the database file, all the tags in the associated MDX file are automatically updated. After creating more than one index tag, you must use the Organize menu to tell dBASE which tag you want to activate.

Not only does dBASE make it possible for you to create index tags that are based on one field, but you can also create multiple-field indexes. A **single-field index** is an index that puts database records into order by a single field. For example, you could create a single-field index to put the CUSTOMER database in order by the CITY field. But what if you wanted all the records within each city to be in order by another field, such as the LASTNAME field? You could accomplish this using a **multiple-field index.**

The process of creating an index file includes the following steps:

1. Initiate the Organize menu from the Edit or Browse screen.
2. Name the index tag.
3. Define the index expression (that is, the field you want to order the database by).
4. Define the order of the index tag (that is, ascending or descending).
5. Save, and then use, the index tag.

CREATING A SINGLE-FIELD INDEX

The next few steps will show you how to put the CUSTOMER database file into order by the CITY field.

Perform the following steps:

1. Make sure the CUSTOMER database is the active database.
2. The cursor should be highlighting CUSTOMER in the Control Center.
   PRESS: F2
3. To display the Organize menu:
   PRESS: Alt-O
4. Choose the Create new index option. The screen should look like Figure D.31.
5. To specify a name for the index tag, press Enter to choose the Name of index option.
6. Type the following name for the index tag *(it's a good idea to name the tag with the same name as the field(s) you're ordering the database by)*:
   TYPE: CITY
   PRESS: Enter
7. Choose the Index expression option by pressing Enter.
8. Since you want the database to be listed in order by the CITY field:
   TYPE: CITY
   PRESS: Enter
9. Since you're now finished defining the index:
   PRESS: Ctrl-End
10. The screen should now look like Figure D.32. Note that the records are displaying in order by the CITY field.
11. To display the Control Center:
    PRESS: Esc

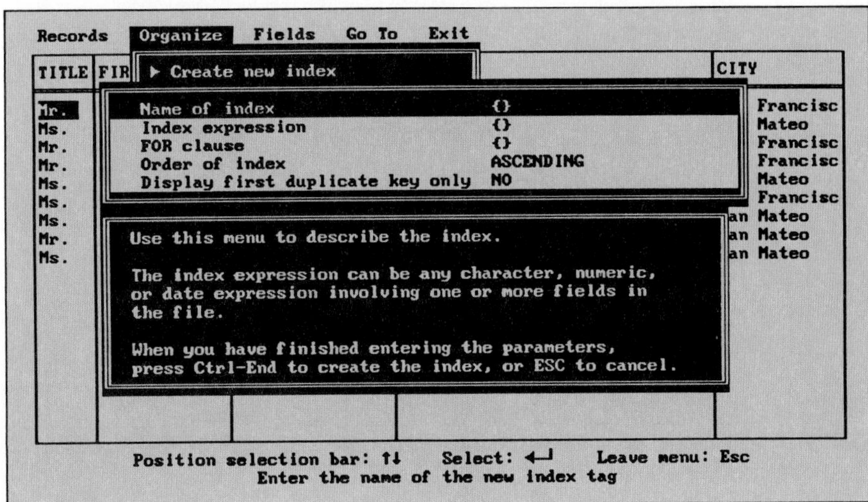

FIGURE D.31

Creating an index—the Organize menu.

As described above, an example of when you might want to create a multiple-field index would be if you want to display the database in CITY order and all the records for each city in LASTNAME order. In this case, the index expression in the index tag would look like the following: CITY + LASTNAME

Quick Reference

■

Creating an Index

1. Activate, or use, a database.
2. Press F2 to display the data in either Edit mode or Browse mode.
3. Activate the Organize menu and choose the Create new index option.
4. Choose the Name of index option, type a name for the index, and then press the Enter key.
5. Choose the Index expression option.
6. Type in the field name you want to index on and then press Enter.
7. To save the index:
   PRESS: Ctrl-End

USING AN INDEX

When you create an index, your data is automatically displayed in order according to the index. To use a different index (if you have more than one index tag in an MDX file), choose the Order records by index option from the Organize menu. A list of the index tags for the current database will display. Choose the index you want, and then display the database with the F2 key.

CREATING AND VIEWING A REPORT

Reports enable you to display the data in your database in a format more stylized than the data display obtained by using the F2 (Data) key or the Queries design screen. dBASE enables you to create two types of reports: quick reports and custom

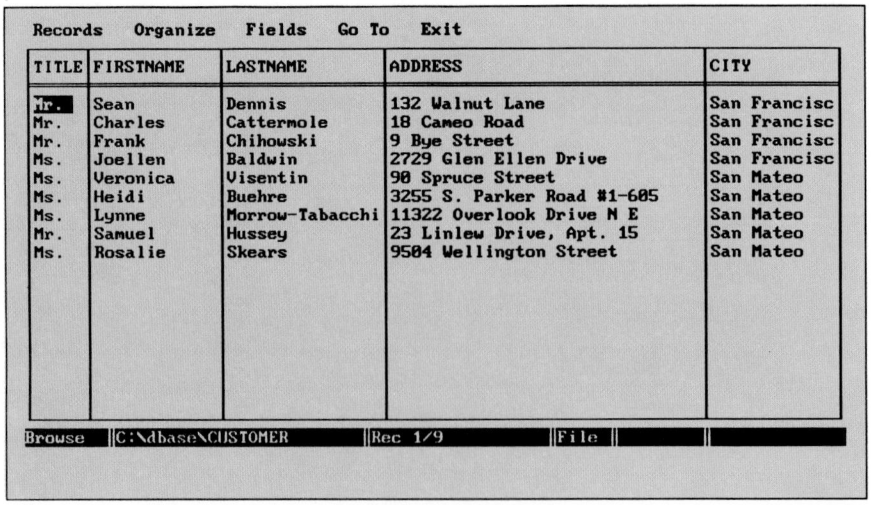

FIGURE D.32

Listing of the CUSTOMER database in order by the CITY index.

Records Organize Fields Go To Exit

TITLE	FIRSTNAME	LASTNAME	ADDRESS	CITY
Mr.	Sean	Dennis	132 Walnut Lane	San Francisc
Mr.	Charles	Cattermole	18 Cameo Road	San Francisc
Mr.	Frank	Chihowski	9 Bye Street	San Francisc
Ms.	Joellen	Baldwin	2729 Glen Ellen Drive	San Francisc
Ms.	Veronica	Visentin	90 Spruce Street	San Mateo
Ms.	Heidi	Buehre	3255 S. Parker Road #1-605	San Mateo
Ms.	Lynne	Morrow-Tabacchi	11322 Overlook Drive N E	San Mateo
Mr.	Samuel	Hussey	23 Linlew Drive, Apt. 15	San Mateo
Ms.	Rosalie	Skears	9504 Wellington Street	San Mateo

Browse ‖C:\dbase\CUSTOMER ‖Rec 1/9 ‖File ‖

reports. The **quick report** option provides a simple means for you to generate a report of your database file or current view. It automatically inserts the current date and page number in the upper-left corner of the screen and automatically totals numeric fields. The headings for each of the columns in the report are the field names you defined in your database. You cannot make any changes to a quick report. Figure D.33 pictures a quick report of the CUSTOMER database.

The **custom report** option provides much greater reporting flexibility, enabling you to design all the features that you want to include in the report. With this command, you can choose the fields that you want to include in the report and change the descriptive text that appears on the top of each column in the report. In addition, you can add graphic elements, such as a line or a box, and add calculated fields that don't exist in your database file or view. You can also include page headers (text that appears on the top of each page) and page footers (text that appears on the bottom of each page) in your report. Once you have created a custom report, you can save it onto your disk so that you can use its specifications again. Figure D.34 pictures a custom report of the CUSTOMER database.

CREATING A QUICK REPORT

In this section, you will create a quick report of the data stored in the CUSTOMER database. Perform the following steps:

1. From the Control Center, highlight the name of the database displaying in the Data panel or the name of the view displaying in the Queries panel that you want to view in the form of a quick report.
2. To display the database or view in the quick report format, as indicated on the bottom of the screen:
   PRESS: Shift-F9

```
Page No.    1
01/14/91

LASTNAME          CITY           INVNUM     INVAMT    AMTPAID  INVDATE

Dennis            San Francisco  2131       132.11       0.00  07/14/92
Visentin          San Mateo      2132       245.00       0.00  02/14/92
Cattermole        San Francisco  2133       500.00     200.00  02/27/92
Chihowski         San Francisco  2140      1400.00     800.00  04/08/92
Buehre            San Mateo      2138       350.00       0.00  03/15/92
Baldwin           San Francisco  2136      1400.00     700.00  06/12/92
Morrow-Tabacchi   San Mateo      2134       150.00       0.00  06/12/92
Hussey            San Mateo      2149       125.00       0.00  08/03/92
Skears            San Mateo      2145      1000.45       0.00  01/04/92
                                           5302.56    1700.00

          Cancel viewing: ESC,  Continue viewing: SPACEBAR
```

FIGURE D.33

A quick report (as viewed on the screen).

Note: Press Shift-F9 while highlighting one of the view filenames; otherwise, too many fields will scroll on the screen.

3. If you want to print the report, choose the Begin printing option. To view it on screen, choose the View report on screen option.

Quick Reference
■
Creating a Quick Report

1. From the Control Center, highlight the name of the database displaying in the Data panel or the name of the view displaying in the Queries panel that you want to view in the form of a quick report.
2. PRESS: Shift-F9
3. To print the report, choose the Begin printing option. To view the report on screen, choose the View report on screen option.

SUMMARY

A database management system (DBMS) is a software tool designed to facilitate the creation and maintenance of an information database used to produce reports. The term *database* describes a collection of data that relates to a common category.

Creating a database is referred to as creating the *database structure*. This process involves defining the following about each field:

1. *Field name*. A field name can't be longer than 10 characters and can't begin with a number.
2. *Field type*. You can store the following types of information in a field: character, numeric, float, date, logical, and memo.

FIGURE D.34

A custom report (as viewed on the screen).

Page No. 1
01/14/91

LASTNAME	CITY	INVOICE NUMBER	INVOICE AMOUNT	AMOUNT PAID	INVOICE DATE
Dennis	San Francisco	2131	132.11	0.00	07/14/92
Visentin	San Mateo	2132	245.00	0.00	02/14/92
Cattermole	San Francisco	2133	500.00	200.00	02/27/92
Chihowski	San Francisco	2140	1400.00	800.00	04/08/92
Buehre	San Mateo	2138	350.00	0.00	03/15/92
Baldwin	San Francisco	2136	1400.00	700.00	06/12/92
Morrow-Tabacchi	San Mateo	2134	150.00	0.00	06/12/92
Hussey	San Mateo	2149	125.00	0.00	08/03/92
Skears	San Mateo	2145	1000.45	0.00	01/04/92

Cancel viewing: ESC, Continue viewing: SPACEBAR

3. *Field width*. You need to determine the width of the field for character and numeric fields. dBASE automatically defines the width for date fields (8), logical fields (1), and memo fields (10).
4. *Decimal places*. For each numeric field, you must determine the number of decimal places you want.
5. *Index*. You have the option of creating an index for the current database.

dBASE IV makes it possible to modify the structure of a database if you need to make changes to it.

Once you've created the structure for the database, you can add data to it. Before adding data, you must make sure dBASE knows which database you're working with. In other words, you must set up the appropriate database for use.

DBMS software makes it easy to perform searches. In other words, you can easily retrieve the information you want from your database. For example, it would be easy to list on the screen all the people in a customer database who live in a particular city. When performing searches, the following types of operations can be performed: arithmetic, relational, logical, sound search, and pattern search.

The SORT and INDEX commands allow you to reorder the data stored in a database file. Indexing is generally preferable to sorting because it doesn't create an entire copy of your database file.

When retrieving information from a database, frequently you will want the results of these manipulations to be output in a polished form that can be circulated throughout your company for review. DBMS software provides you with the tools for creating polished reports.

Saving a database is accomplished by exiting dBASE—always exit dBASE properly to save your database.

Table D.4 provides a summary of the commands used in this module.

KEY TERMS

arithmetic operation, p. 643
Browse mode, p. 663
catalog, p. 647
character, p. 641
Control Center, p. 647
<create> marker, p. 648
custom report, p. 679
database, p. 639
database management system (DBMS), p. 639
database structure, p. 639
date, p. 641
decimal place, p. 641
dot prompt, p. 649
Edit mode, p. 662
field name, p. 641
field type, p. 641
field width, p. 641
file skeleton, p. 666
float, p. 641
index file, p. 641
indexing, p. 644
logical, p. 641
logical operation, p. 643
master index file, p. 676
memo, p. 641
multiple-field index, p. 676
nonnumeric, p. 641
numeric, p. 641
panel, p. 648
quick report, p. 679
relational operation, p. 643
search, p. 642
single-field index, p. 676
sorting, p. 644
tag, p. 676
view query, p. 666
view skeleton, p. 667

EXERCISES

SHORT ANSWER

1. What are the basic components of the dBASE IV Control Center?
2. When you are ready to stop working with dBASE, what must you always do to save your database file(s)?
3. What is a database management system?
4. When you first load dBASE, what must you do before you can begin working on a database?
5. What two methods does dBASE provide for reordering a database?
6. What is involved in modifying a database structure? Why might you want to do this?
7. Being able to create stylized reports of your data is an important capability. How

TABLE D.4

dBASE IV Command Summary

Task	Procedure
Display the menu bar	Press F10
Display a chosen pull-down menu directly	Hold the Alt key down and type the first letter of the pull-down menu you want to display.
Use help	Press F1.
Create a database structure	Highlight the <create> marker in the Data panel (of the Control Center) and press Enter. After defining the structure, choose the Save changes and exit option of the Exit menu.
Change the current drive	From the dot prompt, type SET DIRECTORY TO <drive/directory> and press Enter.
Modify a database structure	From the Control Center, choose the database to be modified. Then choose the Modify structure/order option. Save changes using the Save changes and exit option of the Exit menu.
List the database structure	From the dot prompt, type DISPLAY STRUCTURE and press Enter.
Exit dBASE IV	From the Control Center, choose the Quit to DOS option of the Exit menu.
Use a database	From the Control Center, highlight the database name and press Enter.
Add records	Press F2. From the records menu, choose the Add records option.
Edit data	Press F2 to display the data in either Edit or Browse mode.

does a report listing of your database differ from a "regular" listing of the fields in your database?

8. What is the difference between a quick report and a custom report?
9. What capabilities does the Queries panel provide?
10. What two steps are required to permanently delete a record from a dBASE IV database?

HANDS ON

The following exercises should be completed in order.

1. In this step, you will create the EMPLOYEE database on your data diskette. Perform the following steps:
   a. Create the structure for the EMPLOYEE database. The structure is pictured in Figure D.1 (refer to the beginning of the module).

TABLE D.4

(continued)

Task	Procedure
Mark a record for deletion	Press F2 to display the data in either Edit or Browse mode. After highlighting the record to be marked, choose the Mark record for deletion option on the Records menu.
Delete a marked record	Press F2 to display the data in either Edit or Browse mode. Choose the Erase marked records option on the Organize menu.
Unmark a record marked for deletion	Press F2 to display the data in either Edit or Browse mode. Choose the Clear deletion mark option on the Records menu.
View selected fields	From the Control Center, choose the <create> marker of the Queries panel. Press F5 to add/remove fields from the view. Press F2 to display the data.
Save a view	From the Queries design screen, choose the Save changes and exit option on the Exit menu.
View selected records	From the Control Center, choose the <create> marker of the Queries panel. Position the cursor beneath the field name on which your search is based. Type in a search condition. Press F2 to display the data.
Index a database	Press F2 to display the data in either Edit or Browse mode. Choose the Create new index option on the Organize menu. Choose the Index expression option. Type the field name you want to index on. Press Ctrl-End to save the index.
Create a quick report	From the Control Center, highlight a database or a view. Press Shift-F9, and then choose the Begin printing option or the View report on screen option.

b. Add the records pictured in Figure D.2 to the EMPLOYEE database.
c. Save the database permanently by exiting dBASE.
d. Load dBASE. Use the EMPLOYEE database.
e. Modify the structure for the EMPLOYEE database by changing the width of the STATE field to 3. (Because of this change, dBASE won't beep when you add STATE field data, since the field width (3) is now longer than the data that you put into this field.)
f. Make up data for two more records and then add them to the EMPLOYEE database.

2. Using the EMPLOYEE database that you created in Step 1, perform the following steps:
   a. List all the records.
   b. Use the Queries design screen to:
      — List the following fields on the screen: TITLE, LASTNAME, CITY, and HIREDATE.
      — List the following fields on the screen for those employees who live in San Mateo: TITLE, LASTNAME, CITY, and HIREDATE.
      — List the same fields as in the previous step, except search for those employees who live in San Francisco.
      — List the following fields on the screen for those employees who were hired after January 1, 1992: TITLE, LASTNAME, HRLYWAGE, and HIREDATE.
3. Create the INVENT database on your data diskette. The structure for the database is pictured in Figure D.35. Add the records pictured in Figure D.36 to the INVENT database. Then perform the following steps:
   a. List the INVENT database.
   b. List the ITEMNO, INSTOCK, and REORDER_PT fields.
   c. List those records that have an INSTOCK value that is less than 10.

FIGURE D.35

The INVENT database structure.

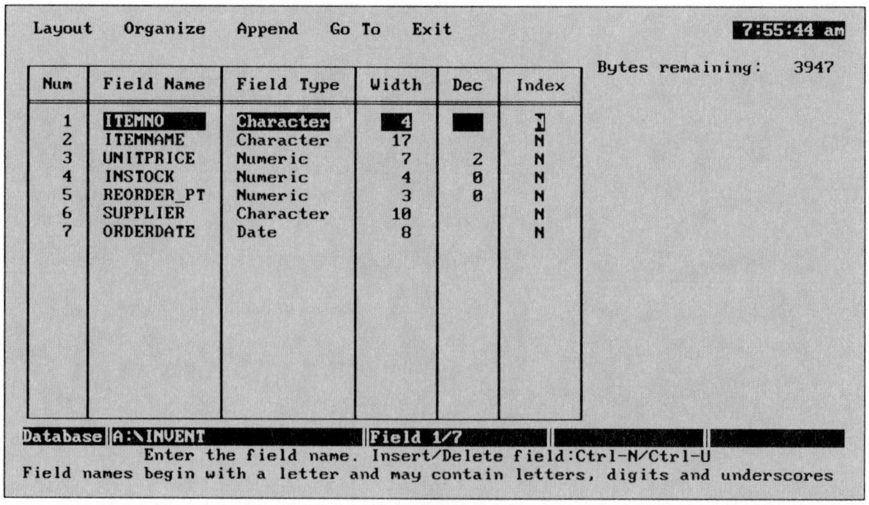

Layout Organize Append Go To Exit 7:55:44 am

Bytes remaining: 3947

Num	Field Name	Field Type	Width	Dec	Index
1	ITEMNO	Character	4		N
2	ITEMNAME	Character	17		N
3	UNITPRICE	Numeric	7	2	N
4	INSTOCK	Numeric	4	0	N
5	REORDER_PT	Numeric	3	0	N
6	SUPPLIER	Character	10		N
7	ORDERDATE	Date	8		N

Database A:\INVENT Field 1/7
Enter the field name. Insert/Delete field:Ctrl-N/Ctrl-U
Field names begin with a letter and may contain letters, digits and underscores

d. List the ITEMNO and DESC fields for those records that have an IN-STOCK value that is less than 15.

4. Create the EXPENSES database on your data diskette. The structure for the database is pictured in Figure D.37. Add the records pictured in Figure D.38 to the INVENT database. Then retrieve the following information:
   a. List all the records and fields in the EXPENSES database.
   b. List all the records but only the ITEM_DESC and EXP_AMOUNT fields.
   c. List all the records and fields in the EXPENSES database that have the word PHONE in the CATEGORY field.
   d. List only the OFFICE expenses.
   e. Quit dBASE IV so that your database is saved.

ITEMNO	ITEMNAME	UNITPRICE	INSTOCK	REORDER_PT	SUPPLIER	ORDERDATE
401	HAMMER	15.68	37	10	ADAMS	05/16/91
209	SHOVEL	19.99	4	5	ADAMS	04/17/91
215	NAILS	4.50	15	20	ZENA	04/25/91
289	BROOM	7.89	22	5	PARNELL	03/15/91
360	SCREW DRIVER	3.99	42	20	ADAMS	06/29/91
300	VACUUM CLEANER	89.99	3	5	PARNELL	05/02/91
299	BATTERIES	3.59	25	20	PARNELL	06/01/91
411	LIGHT BULBS	2.99	55	15	ZENA	07/03/91
399	WRENCH	11.99	12	10	ADAMS	05/15/91
355	MASKING TAPE	1.99	17	10	ZENA	06/01/91
288	HOE	19.99	19	10	ADAMS	05/05/91
366	WOOD STAIN	5.99	35	5	PARNELL	04/21/91
405	CARPET CLEANER	7.99	21	5	ZENA	06/15/91
309	DUST SPRAY	4.21	32	10	ZENA	05/29/91
280	BATHROOM CLEANER	2.99	41	15	PARNELL	06/15/91

FIGURE D.36

The INVENT database records.

Layout Organize Append Go To Exit 7:58:25 am

Bytes remaining: 3951

Num	Field Name	Field Type	Width	Dec	Index
1	ITEMNO	Character	4		N
2	ITEM_DESC	Character	30		N
3	EXP_AMOUNT	Numeric	5	2	N
4	CATEGORY	Character	10		N

Database A:\EXPENSES Field 1/4

Enter the field name. Insert/Delete field:Ctrl-N/Ctrl-U

Field names begin with a letter and may contain letters, digits and underscores

FIGURE D.37

The EXPENSES database structure.

FIGURE D.38

The EXPENSES database records.

ITEMNO	ITEM_DESC	EXP_AMOUNT	CATEGORY
501	PENCILS	13.50	OFFICE
300	FAX TRANSMISSION	3.50	PHONE
119	COMMUNICATION SERVICE	15.00	PHONE
121	LASER PAPER	22.50	OFFICE
149	CALLING CARD	13.00	PHONE
187	PENS	42.00	OFFICE

MODULE E

CREATING GRAPHS: LOTUS 1-2-3

All types of business users recognize that the use of graphics can improve the effectiveness of any informational presentation. The introduction of microcomputer-based graphics software into the business community has made it possible for users to produce professional-looking graphs at very low cost. This module demonstrates how to use Lotus 1-2-3 to create a variety of business charts.

Before you proceed with this module, make sure you have completed Module C.

PREVIEW

When you have completed this module, you will be able to:

- Explain why the user should know how to use graphics and describe the difference between dedicated graphics and spreadsheet-based graphics.
- Describe what pie, line, bar, and XY charts are and what they are used for.
- Use Lotus 1-2-3 to create a pie chart, a line chart, and a bar chart.
- Print charts using PrintGraph.

OVERVIEW OF GRAPHIC REPRESENTATION

Graphic presentation of data is more effective than simple text for the same reason that road maps are easier to follow then written or dictated directions. People seem to remember what they see in the form of images and symbols better than they remember detailed text or speeches. **Graphics,** which are the pictorial representation of words and data, provide us with a superior method of presentation. **Computer graphics** are images that have been generated by a computer; **microcomputer-based business graphics** — the topic of this module — are images that have been generated by a microcomputer to present business-related information. Graphics can be produced in a variety of forms to suit the specific needs of the business professional. Microcomputer images can be displayed on the screen, photographed, plotted on paper in color, or made into transparencies that can be used with an overhead projector.

SPREADSHEET-BASED VERSUS DEDICATED GRAPHICS PACKAGES

The type of software used on microcomputers to generate graphics falls into two categories: (1) spreadsheet-based software packages and (2) dedicated graphics packages. The sole purpose of a **dedicated graphics package** is to provide the user with the capability to produce graphics, whereas a **spreadsheet-based package** (Module C) provides the user with a number of different processing capabilities in addition to the capability to produce graphics.

Compared with spreadsheet-based graphics packages, dedicated graphics packages provide the user with a greater amount of flexibility in presenting data and information in different formats, types, colors, and sizes. When a dedicated graphics package is used, the data to be included in a graph must usually be input directly to the program as the graphic image is created. (Some dedicated packages are able to "import" data from other software packages — such as Lotus 1-2-3 — to be included in the graph.)

Spreadsheet-based graphics are used by the person who has entered data into a spreadsheet and who wants to see the data in graphic form. In this case, the kinds of style choices offered by dedicated graphics packages are not needed; simple graphics will do. Often, if something fancier is needed, the user will use the spreadsheet-based graph to get a general picture of what the data looks like in graphic form and then recreate the graph using a dedicated graphics package. This module's In the Lab section will show you how to create a few different business charts using the Lotus 1-2-3 spreadsheet package.

FORMS OF BUSINESS GRAPHICS PRESENTATION

The most common forms used for presenting business information graphically are (1) pie charts, (2) line charts, (3) bar charts, and (4) XY charts. In the following sections, we refer to the spreadsheet data shown in Figure E.1 — you created this spreadsheet in Module C — when describing each of these types of charts.

PIE CHARTS

A **pie chart,** which is a circle with wedges that look like slices of pie, is the best chart to use when illustrating parts of a whole. For example, you would use a pie chart to show in graphic form what percentage each type of expense in Figure E.1 is of the whole (Figure E.2). To avoid confusion, you should never create a pie chart with more than 12 slices—preferably not more than 8; otherwise, the chart becomes cluttered and loses meaning.

A1: 'EXPENSE READY

	A	B	C	D	E	F
1	EXPENSE					
2	TYPE	JAN	FEB	MAR	TOTAL	
3						
4	TELEPHONE	$85.00	$79.00	$82.00	$246.00	
5	RENT	$600.00	$600.00	$600.00	$1,800.00	
6	UTILITIES	$35.00	$42.00	$70.00	$147.00	
7	AUTO	$50.00	$45.00	$196.00	$291.00	
8	OTHER	$121.00	$135.00	$140.00	$396.00	
9						
10	TOTAL	$891.00	$901.00	$1,088.00	$2,880.00	
11						
12						
13						
14						
15						
16						
17						
18						
19						
20						

02-Mar-92 04:23 PM UNDO CAPS

FIGURE E.1

The QTR1.WK1 spreadsheet. This spreadsheet is used by XYZ Company to calculate its monthly expenses.

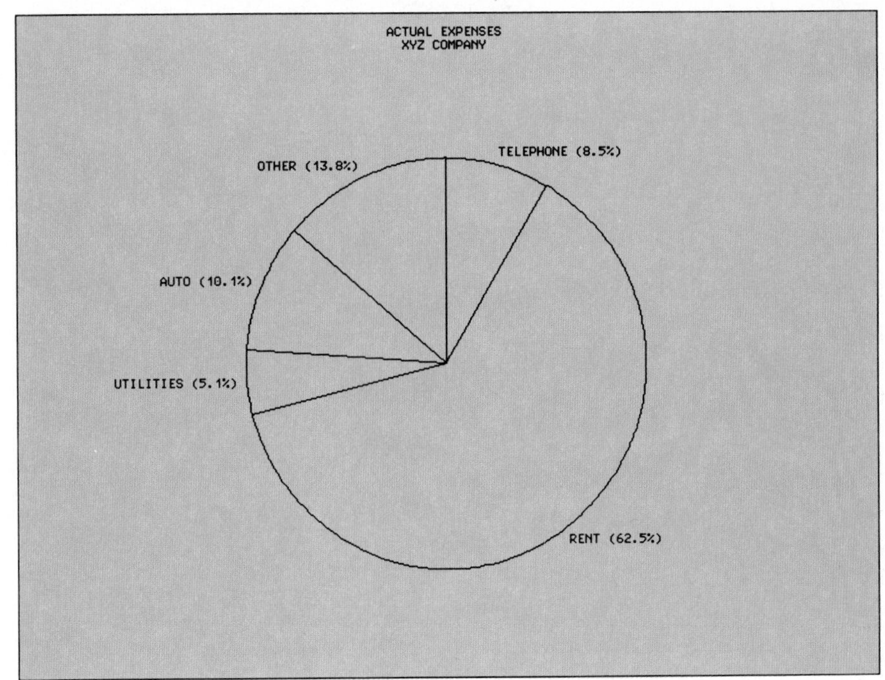

FIGURE E.2

Pie chart. This chart shows what percentage each of XYZ Company's expenses is of total expenses. (Lotus 1-2-3 automatically rounds the percentages up.)

Sometimes, the technique of **exploding** is used in pie charts (Figure E.3). This technique "blows up," or separates, a particular part of the chart for emphasis. For example, if you want to emphasize the fact that the OTHER expense category represents a large percentage of TOTAL expenses, you could enlarge that wedge of the pie chart, or "explode" it so that it appears separate from the rest of the wedges.

LINE CHARTS

When you need to show trends over time, the **line chart** is the appropriate chart form to use. The angles of the line reflect variations in a trend, and the distance of the line from the horizontal axis represents quantity. For example, if you want to show expense trends over the first three months of the year in the form of a line chart, the chart would look like the one in Figure E.4.

When you create a line chart, you must sometimes define the scale for the vertical axis of the chart by specifying the lowest value (zero in Figure E.4) and the highest value (700) on the scale, as well as the number of intervals between the two points (6). Usually, spreadsheet programs will perform this task for you; however, you may want to adjust the scale yourself. Adjusting the scale can change your perception of a chart. For example, the line chart in Figure E.4 has an upper limit of 700, so RENT is shown along the top; however, the line chart in Figure E.5 has an upper limit of 200. The RENT expense isn't graphed because it's off the scale—note that it's now easier to see that AUTO expenses took a big jump in March and that UTILITIES also increased substantially.

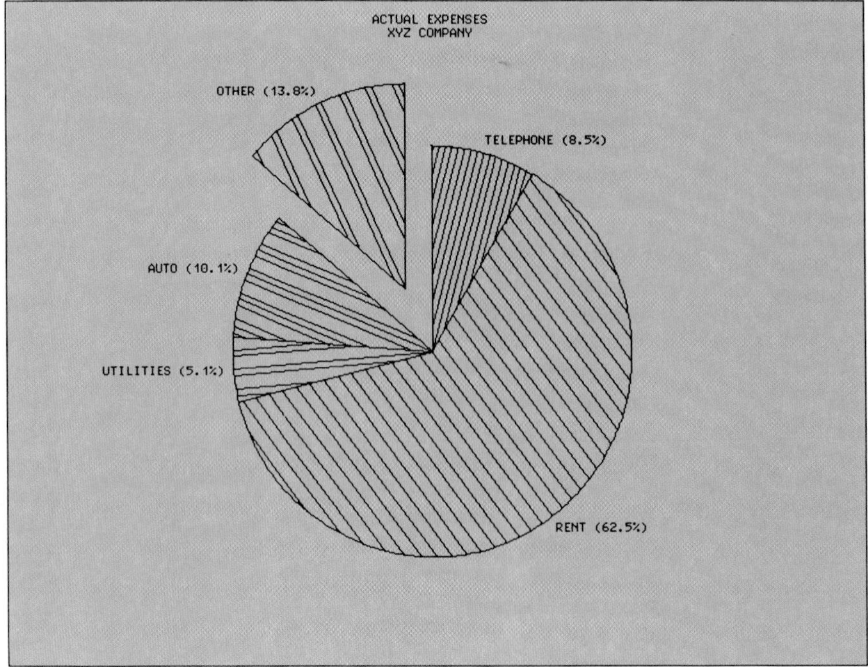

FIGURE E.3

Exploded pie chart. The OTHER pie slice has been separated from the rest of the pie to emphasize that it represents a large percentage of total expenses.

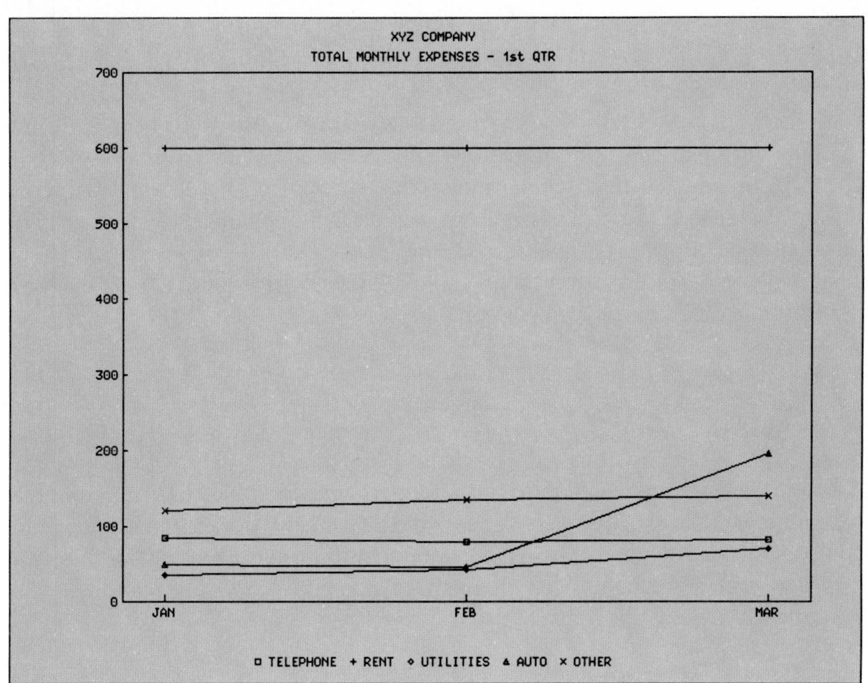

FIGURE E.4

Line chart. This chart shows XYZ Company's expense trends over the first three months of the year. Lotus 1-2-3 set the Y-scale—that is, the lower and upper limits—for this graph automatically.

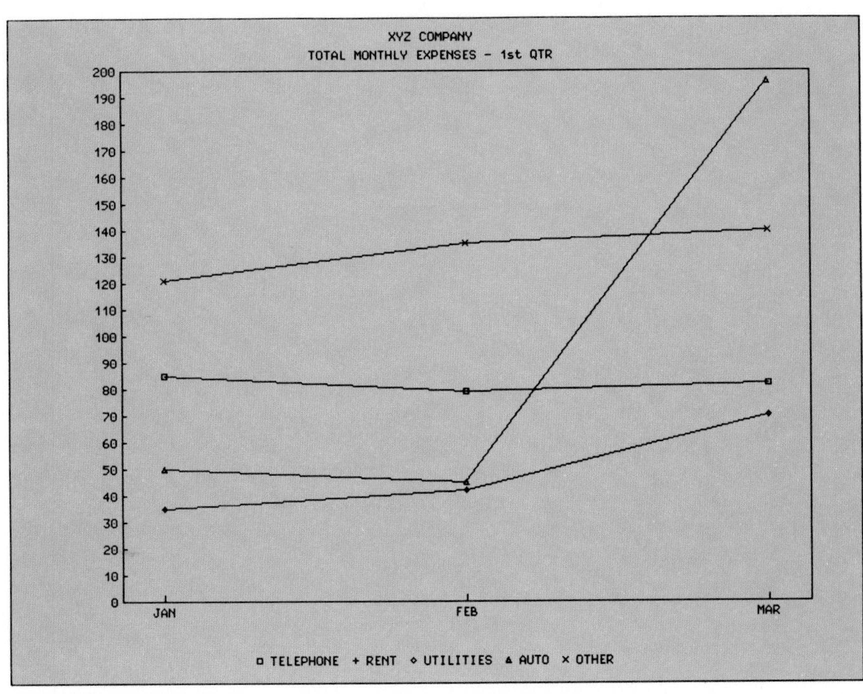

FIGURE E.5

By adjusting the Y-scale manually, the meaning of the graph appears to change.

BAR CHARTS

When the purpose is to compare one data element with another data element, a **bar chart** is the appropriate form to use. Figure E.6 compares the total monthly expense amounts. In this bar chart, it's easy to see that March's expenses were the highest and that January's expenses were the lowest. The chart in Figure E.6 is a simple bar chart. It provides no information about what types of expenses were incurred. Grouped bar charts and stacked bar charts, variations of the simple bar chart, do give information about types of expenses. A **grouped bar chart** (Figure E.7) shows how all data elements compare over time. A **stacked bar chart** (Figure E.8) shows how the components of a data element compare over time.

XY CHARTS

XY charts, which are commonly referred to as *scatter charts*, are used to show how one or more data elements relate to another data element. For example, you could compare sales and profits (Figure E.9), tennis court use and average daily temperature, and so on. Although XY charts look similar to line charts, XY charts include a numeric scale along the X-axis.

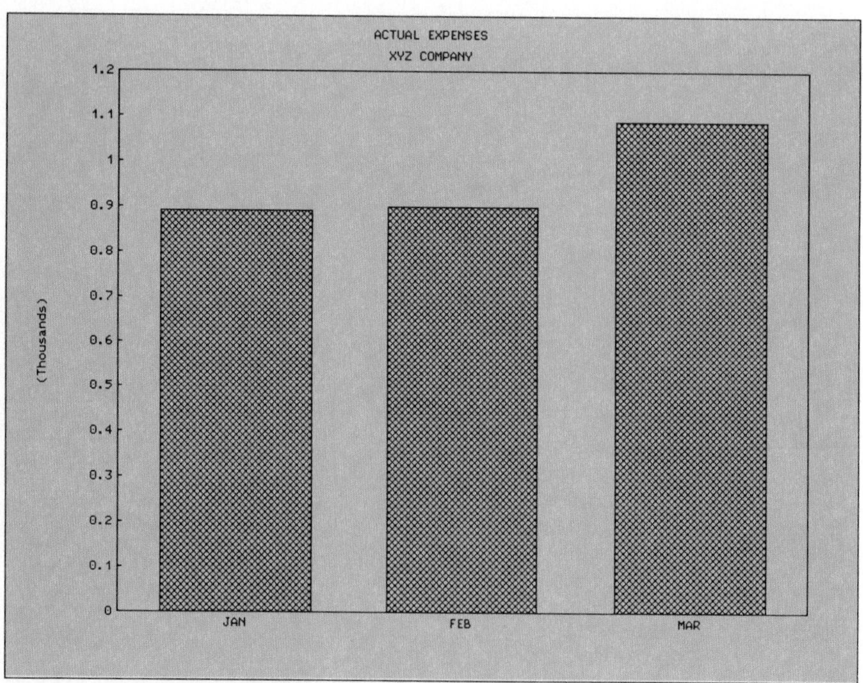

FIGURE E.6

Bar chart. This chart compares the total monthly expense amounts for XYZ Company.

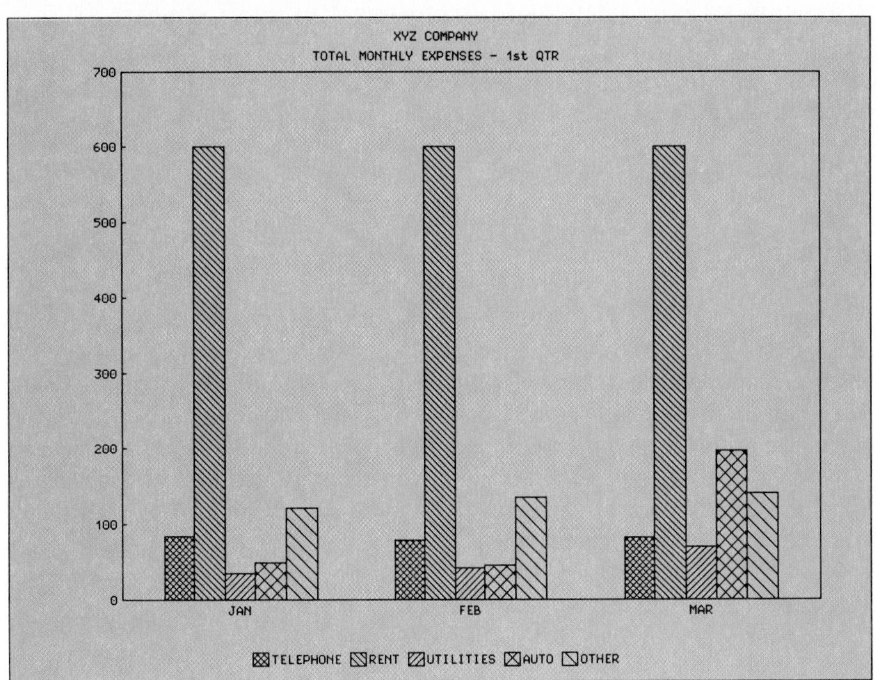

FIGURE E.7

Grouped bar chart.

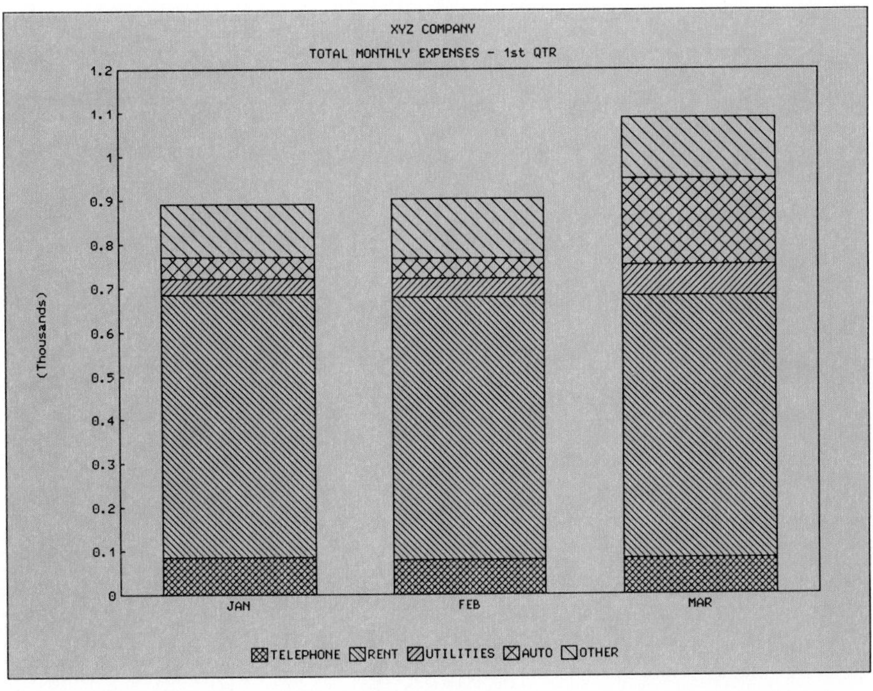

FIGURE E.8

Stacked bar chart.

PRINCIPLES OF BUSINESS GRAPHICS PRESENTATION

No matter how sophisticated your graphics software may be, you would probably be better off using no graphics at all if you don't follow basic principles for creating charts: simplicity, unity, emphasis, and balance. The following sections describe each of these principles.

SIMPLICITY

Many things can cause your chart to look confusing: for example, using too much color, using too much descriptive text, including too many variables (such as too many pie slices in a pie chart). It's natural to try to tell the whole story in one chart, but doing so may defeat the whole purpose of using graphics. You use a chart to symbolize numbers or words because most people tend to find graphics easier to understand than straight text and tables. If you include too much text or detail in a chart, the visual aspects become muddled and the symbols difficult to understand. Always try to keep your charts simple.

UNITY

To be understandable, your graph must clearly relate all the elements of data it contains — that is, it must appear as a unit. For instance, if you use too much space between the variables (such as between bars in a bar chart), you will probably destroy the unity of your chart. Framing, or boxing, a graph can help to unify it.

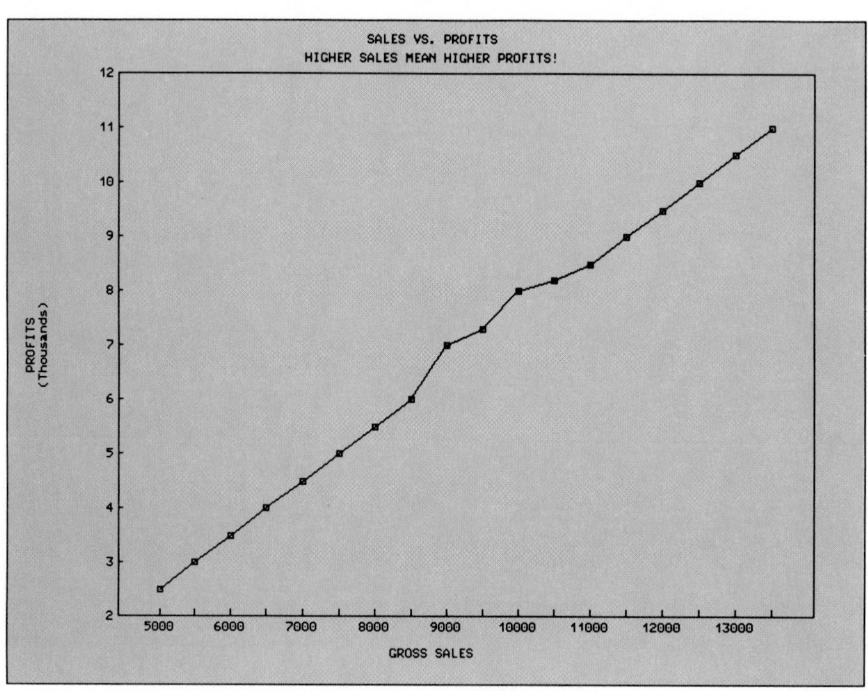

FIGURE E.9

XY chart.

Emphasis

Emphasis is used to make certain data elements stand out. For example, exploding a pie slice emphasizes that piece of a pie chart. No matter what type of chart you create, you can emphasize different parts by using colors and shading.

Balance

Your graph should look balanced—both as a unit and in the context of the rest of the page. One factor that affects balance is the position of descriptive text, including titles and legends. Changing the position of such text affects the balance of the graph. Changing the shading, color, and thickness of the lines used in a graph will also affect balance. For instance, if you create a bar chart made up of eight bars, don't specify a dark color for the four larger bars on the right side of the chart and a light color for the smaller bars on the left. Because dark colors appear heavy, they will make the bar chart look out of balance by "weighing down" the right side.

In the Lab

Business Graphics Using Lotus 1-2-3

In this tutorial, you will create a few charts using Lotus 1-2-3. The general use of this package was covered in Module C. Complete Module C before starting this tutorial, because the graphs you create here are based on the spreadsheet created in Module C.

In this tutorial, we assume you will be using either a diskette system or a hard disk system. The descriptions for these two types of systems can be found in the Introduction to the Modules. When the procedures differ depending on the configuration of your computer, they will be listed beneath one of the two following headings: (1) For Diskette System Users and (2) For Hard Disk System Users. If you're not sure which instructions to follow, ask your instructor.

The Business Situation

As the owner of Sporting Life, for a number of months you've been using a spreadsheet-based program to track expenses. Because in your presentation you prefer to use graphics to present expense trends, you have decided to learn how to use your spreadsheet program to create graphs of the data you enter.

The expense data you will graph is pictured in Figure E.1. In Module C, you created a file called QTR1 and stored it on your data diskette. You will be graphing the data stored in the QTR1 file. (If you haven't completed the In the Lab section in Module C, complete it now.)

Loading Lotus 1-2-3

We assume that you have booted your computer with DOS using the procedure described in the Introduction to the Modules chapter. The procedure you use to load Lotus 1-2-3 is different depending on whether you are using a diskette-based system or a hard disk system. *Note:* If you are using a hard disk system, but don't have Lotus 1-2-3 stored on the hard disk, follow the instructions below for diskette system users.

FOR DISKETTE SYSTEM USERS

1. To load Lotus 1-2-3 from a 5¼-inch or 3½-inch diskette drive, put the Lotus 1-2-3 diskette in drive A.
2. TYPE: lotus
   PRESS: Enter
   You are looking at the Lotus Access System. The cursor is currently highlighting the 1-2-3 option, and a description of this option is on the second line. *Two methods can be used to choose an option from a Lotus menu. You can either highlight the option (using the cursor-movement keys) and then press the Enter key, or press the first character of the option.*
   The PrintGraph option is used for printing the graphs you create (you will use this option at the end of this module). The Translate option enables you to transfer data from another software application into Lotus 1-2-3 so that it can be manipulated using Lotus 1-2-3's commands. When you first purchase Lotus 1-2-3, you use the Install option to tell the program about the characteristics of your hardware. (For example, will you use Lotus 1-2-3 on a microcomputer configured with a color monitor? Hard disk? What kind of printer will you use?) By choosing the Exit option, you exit the Lotus Access System.
3. The cursor should still be highlighting the 1-2-3 option. To choose this option:
   PRESS: Enter ■

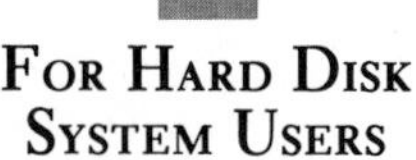

FOR HARD DISK SYSTEM USERS

1. Lotus 1-2-3 is probably loaded in a subdirectory (named something like LOTUS or 123) on the hard disk. You may be able to load Lotus 1-2-3 without making the Lotus subdirectory current (using the CD command that was described in the Introduction to the Modules chapter). To see if this is the case, type the following after the system prompt:
   TYPE: lotus
   PRESS: Enter
   If a message such as "Bad Command or Filename" is displaying on the screen, proceed with Step 2. Otherwise, skip Step 2 and proceed to Step 3.
2. Use the CD command to make the Lotus subdirectory the current subdirectory. For example, if the Lotus subdirectory is called LOTUS, you would type CD \LOTUS.
3. To load Lotus 1-2-3, follow Steps 2 and 3 in the instructions for diskette system users. ■

CHANGING THE CURRENT DIRECTORY

When you load Lotus 1-2-3, it makes an assumption about where it will save your files. Lotus typically assumes your files will be saved where the Lotus program files are stored. To change the assumption made by Lotus so that it will know where you want your data files to be stored *during the current work session*, perform the following steps:

For Diskette System Users

1. Put your data diskette in drive B.
2. To enter Menu mode:
   TYPE: /
3. To choose the File option:
   TYPE: F
4. To choose the Directory option:
   TYPE: D
5. To tell Lotus 1-2-3 that your data diskette is in drive B:
   TYPE: B:
   PRESS: Enter

When you save your work, it will automatically be saved onto your data diskette in drive B. ■

For Hard Disk System Users

1. Put your data diskette in drive A.
2. To enter Menu mode:
   TYPE: /
3. To choose the File option:
   TYPE: F
4. To choose the Directory option:
   TYPE: D
5. To tell Lotus 1-2-3 that your data diskette is in drive A:
   TYPE: A:
   PRESS: Enter

When you save your work, it will automatically be saved onto your data diskette in drive A. ■

Using Lotus 1-2-3 to Create and Print Graphs

No matter what type of graph you are creating, you must follow certain steps. Figure E.10 displays Lotus's graph settings sheet. During the process of creating a graph, you will fill in this settings sheet with your graph specifications. Once you have created a graph, you will probably want to print it. The rest of this module describes in detail the steps involved in creating and printing graphs. The following is an overview of the process. *Note: Don't perform these steps.*

1. Clear any graph specifications from RAM that may have been left over from a previously created graph.
2. Select the graph type.
3. Select the data ranges to be graphed. Lotus lets you define up to six data ranges

(A, B, C, D, E, and F). For example, Figure E.11 labels the data ranges in a spreadsheet and displays a bar graph of the data.

4. Add data labels (if applicable). (A *data label*—usually a number—identifies, for example, each point on a line chart, or the value of each bar in a bar chart.)
5. Add titles and legends (if applicable) or use one or more of the other graph options available after choosing the GRAPH OPTIONS command (Table E.1). (A *legend* is descriptive text, usually a word, that identifies each data range.)

FIGURE E.10

Lotus's graph settings sheet.

```
A1: 'EXPENSE                                                              MENU
Type  X  A  B  C  D  E  F  Reset  View  Save  Options  Name  Group  Quit
Line  Bar  XY  Stack-Bar  Pie
 ------------------------------------ Graph Settings ------------------------
  Type: Line                         Titles: First
                                             Second
  X:                                         X axis
  A:                                         Y axis
  B:
  C:                                                    Y scale:      X scale:
  D:                                         Scaling    Automatic     Automatic
  E:                                         Lower
  F:                                         Upper
                                             Format     (G)           (G)
  Grid: None          Color: No              Indicator  Yes           Yes

     Legend:                       Format:   Data labels:             Skip: 1
  A                                Both
  B                                Both
  C                                Both
  D                                Both
  E                                Both
  F                                Both

02-Mar-92  04:25 PM                                                   CAPS
```

TABLE E.1

Graph Options. These options are available after choosing the GRAPH OPTIONS command.

Option	Purpose
Legend	Used to label the A–F data ranges.
Format	In line and XY graphs, this option enables you to choose whether data points are connected with lines, symbols, lines and symbols, or neither lines nor symbols.
Titles	Used to add First and Second titles, and X-axis and Y-axis titles.
Grid	Adds or removes horizontal or vertical grid lines in a graph.
Scale	Determines axis scaling and the format of the numbers on the axis.
Color	If you are using a color monitor, this option enables you to display your graphs in color.
B&W	Causes Lotus 1-2-3 to display graphs in black and white.
Data-Labels	Uses the cell contents of a data range as labels for the bars or points in a graph.
Quit	Exits you to the Graph menu.

6. Name the graph. This command gives a name to your graph specifications so that you can modify the graph later (you can't modify a graph from within PrintGraph). The output of this command isn't a file; it is simply a name inside the current worksheet that enables you to call up, or reference, the specifications for a particular graph.
7. Save the graph using the GRAPH SAVE command. To print a graph using Lotus, you must exit Lotus 1-2-3 and load Lotus PrintGraph (the procedure is

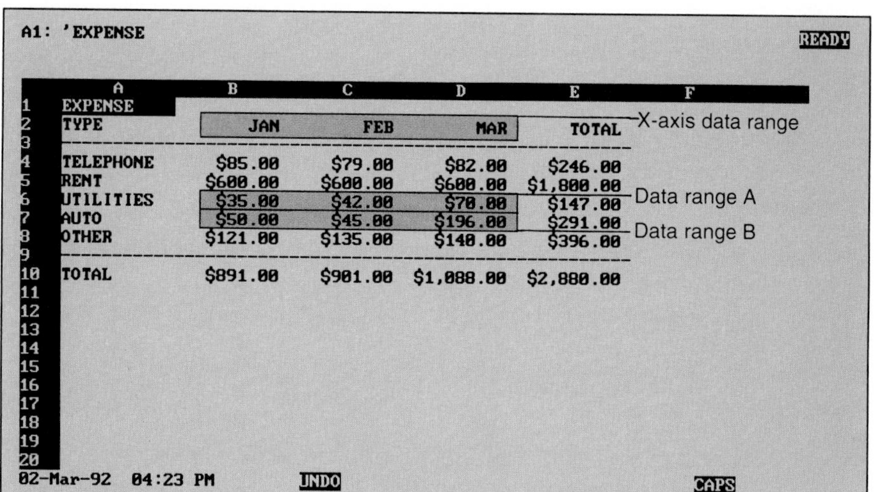

(a)

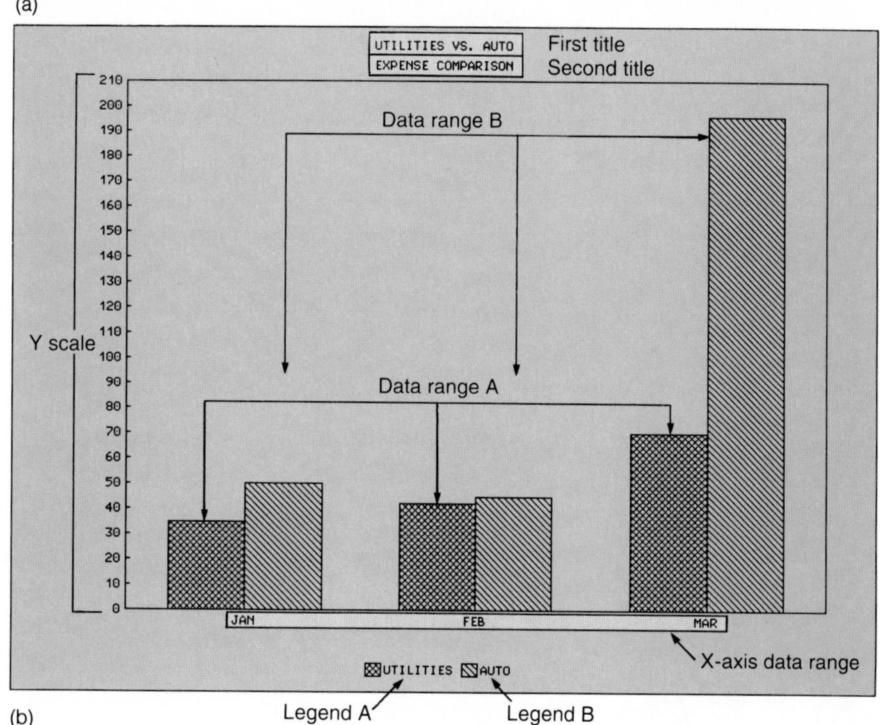

(b)

FIGURE E.11

(a) You must define the data ranges to be graphed, (b) before you can display a graph.

described later in this module). The GRAPH SAVE command saves your graph specifications in a file that the PrintGraph program can understand. These graph files have the extension PIC.

8. Save the spreadsheet file using the FILE SAVE command. This command is used to save any graph names you defined in Step 6.
9. Exit Lotus 1-2-3 and load PrintGraph.
10. Choose the graph(s) you want to print.

CREATING A PIE CHART

In this section, you will create a pie chart that shows what percentage each type of expense is of total expenses. When you are done, the pie chart should look similar to the one pictured in Figure E.2.

Perform the following steps to create the pie chart:

1. Retrieve QTR1.WK1 from your data diskette (the procedure for retrieving is described in Module C).
2. To initiate the GRAPH command:
   TYPE: /
   To choose the Graph option:
   TYPE: G
3. A list of graph options should be displaying on top of the screen (Figure E.12). To specify the type of graph you want to create:
   TYPE: T
4. To choose the Pie option:
   TYPE: P

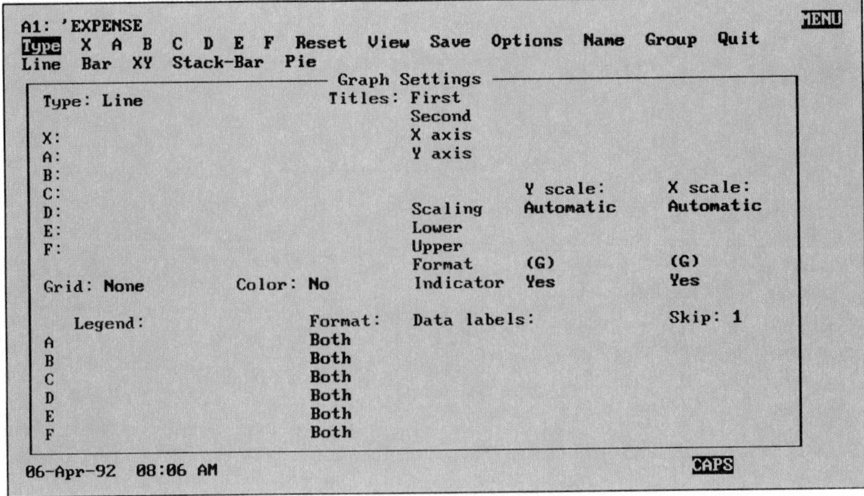

FIGURE E.12

The Graph menu. The cursor is currently highlighting the Type option.

5. Now you need to define where the data to be graphed is stored, which involves identifying the A data range. The data you want to graph is stored in the range of cells E4 . . E8.
   TYPE: A
   TYPE: E4 . . E8
   PRESS: Enter
6. To see what your graph looks like at this point, choose the View option:
   TYPE: V
   Your pie chart should be displaying on the screen (Figure E.13). *Note: The F10 key can be used at any time to view the current graph specifications*. In the next few steps, you will define the title for your chart and the descriptive text for each piece of the pie.
   PRESS: any key to display the Graph menu

Quick Reference

Viewing a Graph (F10)

Two methods are available for viewing the current graph specifications: (1) from within the main Graph menu, you can choose the View option or (2) you can press the F10 key.

---

7. To define the title for the graph, you must first choose the OPTIONS command and then the Titles option. To choose the OPTIONS command:
   TYPE: O
   The screen should look like Figure E.14.

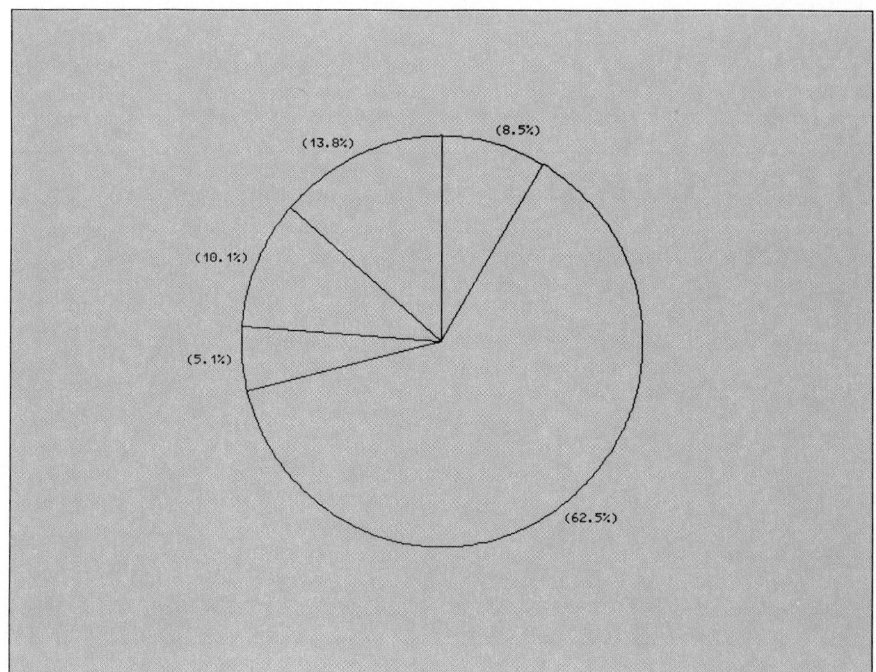

FIGURE E.13

Creating a pie chart. The A data range (E4 . . E8) has been defined.

8. To choose the TITLES command:
   TYPE: T
9. To create the main, or "first," title:
   TYPE: F
   TYPE: ACTUAL EXPENSES
   PRESS: Enter
10. To create the subtitle, or "second," title:
    TYPE: T
    TYPE: S
    TYPE: XYZ COMPANY
    PRESS: Enter
11. Specifying the descriptive text that will identify the different pieces of the pie involves choosing the X option. To move up in the menu hierarchy so you can access the X option, first choose the Quit option.
    PRESS: Q
12. To choose the X option and then specify the range A4 . . A8:
    TYPE: X
    TYPE: A4 . . A8
    PRESS: Enter
13. To view the completed graph on the screen:
    TYPE: V
    The graph should look like Figure E.2. To display the Graph menu:
    PRESS: any key to display the Graph menu

To give a name to the specifications for this pie chart so that you can view this chart at a later date, perform the following steps:

1. To choose the Name option:
   TYPE: N

FIGURE E.14

The choices available after choosing the OPTIONS command.

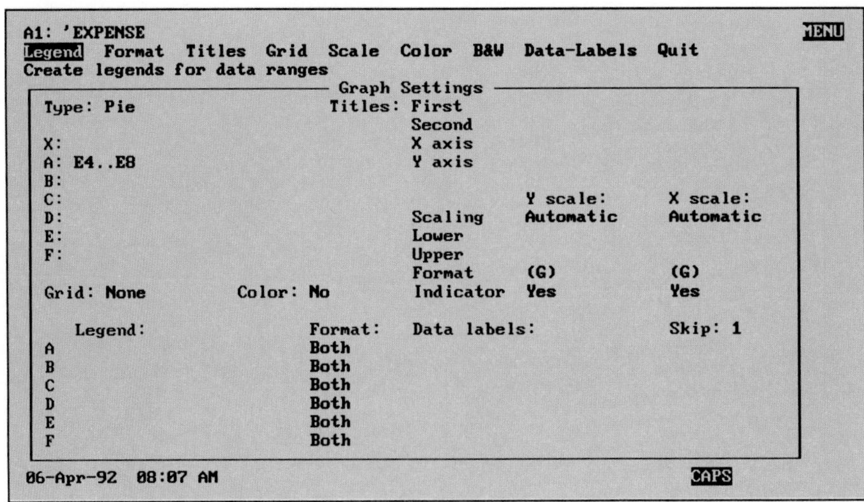

2. To choose the Create option:
   TYPE: C
3. To name the specifications PIE1:
   TYPE: PIE1
   PRESS: Enter

To save the specifications for the pie chart into a file that PrintGraph can understand (a PIC file):

1. The Graph menu should be displaying on the screen. To choose the Save option:
   TYPE: S
2. To save the graph onto your data disk as PIE1.PIC, type either B:PIE1 (for diskette system users) or A:PIE1 (for hard disk system users).
   TYPE: [the appropriate disk drive designation and the name of the file]
   PRESS: Enter

Quick Reference

Naming and Saving Graph

1. Within the Graph menu, choose the Name option.
2. TYPE: [a name for the graph]
   PRESS: Enter
3. To save the graph in the form of a graph file that has the extension of PIC, choose the Save option.
4. TYPE: [a filename for the graph]
   PRESS: Enter

To save the QTR1.WK1 spreadsheet with the named PIE1 specifications:

1. To exit the Graph menu and return to Ready mode:
   PRESS: Q
2. To save the QTR1 spreadsheet:
   TYPE: /
   TYPE: F
   TYPE: S
3. To save the file onto the same disk using the same name (QTR1.WK1):
   PRESS: Enter
4. To replace the copy on disk with the contents of RAM:
   TYPE: R

EXPLODING AND SHADING

To include an exploded pie piece or shading in a graph (Figure E.3), you must specify a B range that is composed of values with specific characteristics (Figure E.15, column F). The numbers in the B range must be numbered consecutively beginning with either the number 0 or 1. If you don't want the chart to include shading, the values in the B range must begin with the number 0 (0, 1, 2, and so on).

If you do, the values in the B range must begin with the number 1 (1, 2, 3, and so on). Each number corresponds directly to a different cell in the A range. If you add 100 to a number in the B range, the corresponding pie slice will appear exploded, or separate from the rest of the pie slices.

In this step, you will modify the QTR1 spreadsheet to include a B range and define the B range in the Graph menu. You will then save the graph specifications.

1. The graph specifications from the pie chart you just created should still be stored in main memory. In other words, if you use the GRAPH VIEW command, the pie chart will appear on the screen. To illustrate:
   TYPE: /
   To choose the Graph option:
   TYPE: G
   To choose the View option:
   TYPE: V
   The pie chart should be displaying on the screen. To display the Graph menu:
   PRESS: any key
   To exit the Graph menu:
   TYPE: Q
2. Position the cursor in the following cells and type in the corresponding numbers:

CELL LOCATION	YOU TYPE
F4	1
F5	2
F6	3
F7	4
F8	105

   (The numbers are displaying in the currency format because the spreadsheet is globally formatted in the currency format to zero decimal places.)

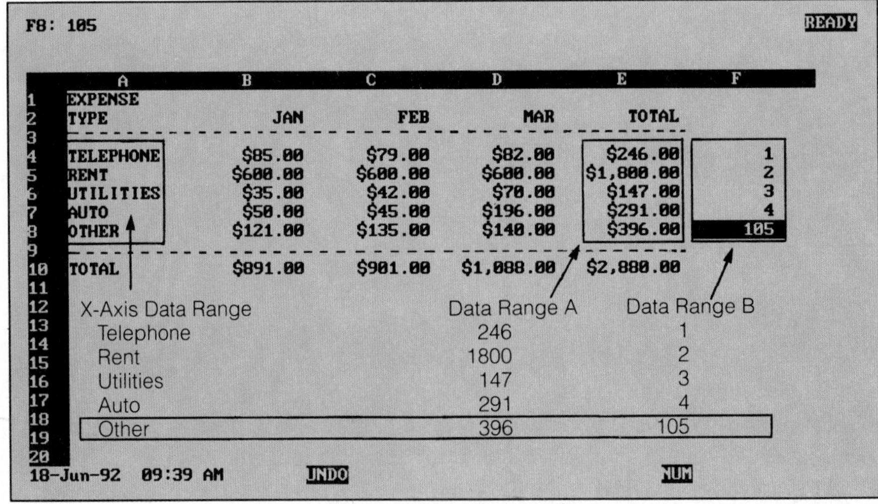

	A	B	C	D	E	F
1	EXPENSE					
2	TYPE	JAN	FEB	MAR	TOTAL	
3						
4	TELEPHONE	$85.00	$79.00	$82.00	$246.00	1
5	RENT	$600.00	$600.00	$600.00	$1,800.00	2
6	UTILITIES	$35.00	$42.00	$70.00	$147.00	3
7	AUTO	$50.00	$45.00	$196.00	$291.00	4
8	OTHER	$121.00	$135.00	$140.00	$396.00	105
9						
10	TOTAL	$891.00	$901.00	$1,088.00	$2,880.00	

FIGURE E.15

Creating an exploded pie chart. The range F4 . . F8 will be defined as the B data range.

3. To define the B range as the range F4 . . F8, first initiate Menu mode and then choose the Graph option:
   TYPE: /
   TYPE: G
4. To choose the B option and then specify the range F4 . . F8:
   TYPE: B
   TYPE: F4 . . F8
   PRESS: Enter
5. To view the graph:
   TYPE: V
   The chart should look similar to Figure E.3.
6. Press any key to display the Graph menu.

Quick Reference

Exploding or Shading a Pie Segment

You must specify a B range that has certain characteristics.

1. If the values in the B range are numbered consecutively beginning with zero (0, 1, 2, and so on), the graph won't include shading.
2. If the values in the B range are numbered consecutively beginning with 1 (1, 2, 3, and so on), the graph will include shading.
3. To explode a pie piece, add 100 to a value in the B range.

To give a name to the specifications for this pie chart so that you can view this chart at a later date, perform the following steps:

1. To choose the Name option:
   TYPE: N
2. To choose the Create option and then name the specifications EXPLODED:
   TYPE: C
   TYPE: EXPLODED
   PRESS: Enter

To save the specifications for the pie chart into a file that PrintGraph can understand (a PIC file):

1. The Graph menu should be displaying on the screen. To choose the Save option:
   TYPE: S
2. To save the graph onto your data disk as EXPLODED.PIC, type either B:EXPLODED (for diskette system users) or A:EXPLODED (for hard disk system users).
   TYPE: [the appropriate disk drive designation and the name of the file]
   PRESS: Enter

To save the QTR1.WK1 spreadsheet with the named EXPLODED specifications:

1. To exit the Graph menu and return to Ready mode:
   TYPE: Q

2. To save the QTR1 spreadsheet:
   TYPE: /
   TYPE: F
   TYPE: S
3. To save the file onto the same disk using the same name (QTR1.WK1):
   PRESS: Enter
4. To replace the copy on disk with the contents of RAM:
   TYPE: R

CREATING A SIMPLE BAR CHART

In this section, you will use the QTR1.WK1 spreadsheet to create a bar chart that compares XYZ Company's monthly expense totals. When you are done, the bar chart should look similar to the one in Figure E.6.

The bar chart you create here will include the same first and second titles as the pie chart you created in the last section. The data you are graphing is in the range B10 . . D10, and the X-axis labels are in the range B2 . . D2. Perform the following steps to create this chart, name it, save the graph specifications, and then save the QTR1.WK1 file. Before you begin however, you will clear the graph specifications from RAM of the previous graph (the exploded pie chart) you created:

To clear the graph specifications from the previous graph:

1. To enter Menu mode and then choose the Graph option:
   TYPE: /
   TYPE: G
2. To choose the Reset option:
   TYPE: R
3. To choose the Graph option:
   TYPE: G

Quick Reference
■
Clearing Graph Specifications

1. Initiate Menu mode.
2. Choose the Graph option.
3. Choose the Reset option.
4. Choose the Graph option.

Perform the following steps to specify the characteristics for the bar chart:

1. A list of graph options should be displaying at the bottom of the screen. To specify the type of graph you want to create:
   TYPE: T
2. To choose the Bar option:
   TYPE: B
3. Now you need to define where the data to be graphed is stored, which involves

identifying the A data range. The data you want to graph is stored in the range of cells B10 . . D10.
TYPE: A
TYPE: B10 . . D10
PRESS: Enter

4. To see what your graph looks like at this point, choose the View option:
TYPE: V
Your bar chart should be displaying on the screen (Figure E.16).
PRESS: any key to display the Graph menu
5. In this step, you need to identify another range. Specifically, you need to define the labels for the X-axis (the horizontal axis) by choosing the X option. The labels for the X-axis are stored in the range B2 . . D2.
TYPE: X
TYPE: B2 . . D2
PRESS: Enter
6. And finally, to define the title for the graph, choose the OPTIONS command and then the TITLES command:
TYPE: O
TYPE: T
7. To create the main, or "first," title:
TYPE: F
TYPE: ACTUAL EXPENSES
PRESS: Enter

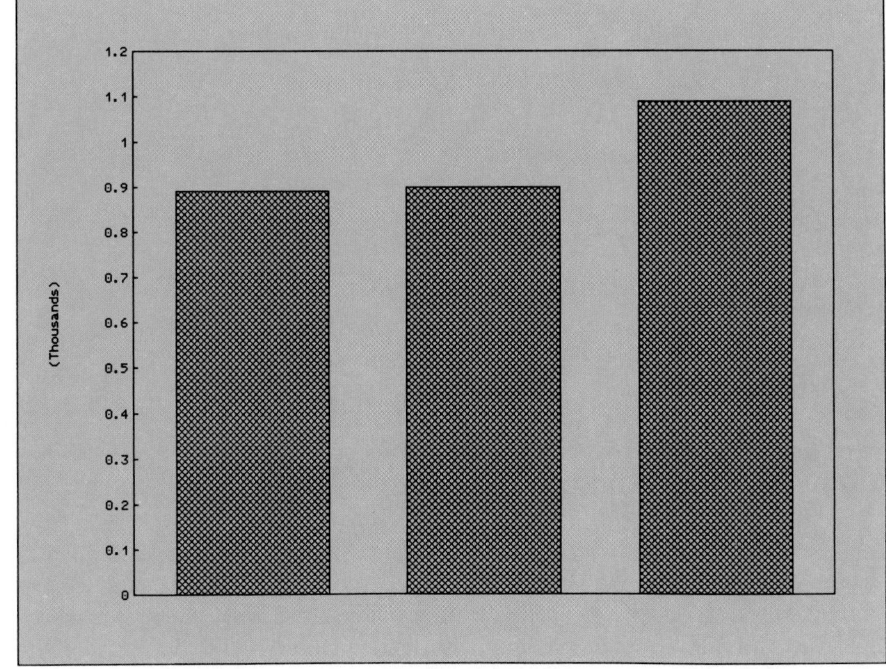

FIGURE E.16

Creating a bar chart. The A data range (B10 . . D10) has been defined.

8. To create the subtitle, or "second," title:
   TYPE: T
   TYPE: S
   TYPE: XYZ COMPANY
   PRESS: Enter
9. To view the completed graph on the screen, you must first move up the menu hierarchy one level.
   PRESS: Esc
   TYPE: V
   The screen should look like Figure E.6.
10. Press any key to display the Graph menu.

To name the graph specifications:

1. To choose the Name option:
   TYPE: N
2. To choose the Create option and then name the specifications BAR1:
   TYPE: C
   TYPE: BAR1
   PRESS: Enter

To save the graph specifications into a file that PrintGraph can understand:

1. The Graph menu should be displaying on the screen. To choose the Save option:
   TYPE: S
2. To save the graph onto your data disk as BAR1.PIC, type either B:BAR1 (for diskette system users) or A:BAR1 (for hard disk system users).
   TYPE: [the appropriate disk drive designation and the name of the file]
   PRESS: Enter

To save the QTR1.WK1 spreadsheet with the named bar chart specifications:

1. To exit the Graph menu and return to Ready mode:
   PRESS: Q
2. To save the QTR1 spreadsheet:
   TYPE: /
   TYPE: F
   TYPE: S
3. To save the file onto the same disk using the same name (QTR1.WK1):
   PRESS: Enter
4. To replace the copy on disk with the contents of RAM:
   TYPE: R

CREATING A STACKED BAR CHART

In this section, you will create a stacked bar chart that compares XYZ Company's monthly expense totals. This chart is similar to the bar chart you created in the last section; however, this chart will provide information about what expenses make up each bar. You will need to identify five data ranges in this chart (A, B, C, D, and E). When you are done, the bar chart should look similar to the one in Figure E.8.

To clear the graph specifications from the previous graph:

1. To enter Menu mode and then choose the Graph option:
   TYPE: /
   TYPE: G
2. To choose the Reset option:
   TYPE: R
3. To choose the Graph option:
   TYPE: G

Perform the following steps to specify the characteristics for the stacked bar chart:

1. To tell Lotus 1-2-3 what type of graph you want to create:
   TYPE: T
2. To choose the Stack Bar option:
   TYPE: S
3. Now you need to define where the data to be graphed is stored, which involves identifying a few different data ranges. The data for the A range (Telephone) is stored in the range of cells B4 . . D4.
   TYPE: A
   TYPE: B4 . . D4
   PRESS: Enter
4. The data for the B range (Rent) is stored in the range of cells B5 . . D5.
   TYPE: B
   TYPE: B5 . . D5
   PRESS: Enter
5. The data for the C range (Utilities) is stored in the range of cells B6 . . D6.
   TYPE: C
   TYPE: B6 . . D6
   PRESS: Enter
6. The data for the D range (Auto) is stored in the range of cells B7 . . D7.
   TYPE: D
   TYPE: B7 . . D7
   PRESS: Enter
7. The data for the E range (Other) is stored in the range of cells B8 . . D8.
   TYPE: E
   TYPE: B8 . . D8
   PRESS: Enter
8. To see what your graph looks like at this point, choose the View option:
   TYPE: V
   The stacked bar chart should be displaying on the screen (Figure E.17).
   PRESS: any key to display the Graph menu

In the next few steps, you will define the labels for the X-axis and then the titles for the graph:

1. To choose the X option and then specify the range B2 . . D2:
   TYPE: X
   TYPE: B2 . . D2
   PRESS: Enter

2. To define the title for the graph, you need to choose the OPTIONS command and then the TITLES command.
   TYPE: O
   TYPE: T
3. To create the main, or "first," title:
   TYPE: F
   TYPE: XYZ COMPANY
   PRESS: Enter
4. To create the subtitle, or "second" title:
   TYPE: T
   TYPE: S
   TYPE: TOTAL MONTHLY EXPENSES--1st QTR
   PRESS: Enter
5. To see what your graph looks like at this point, first choose the Quit option (to move up one level in the Graph menu) and then choose the View option:
   TYPE: Q
   TYPE: V
   The stacked bar chart with added titles should be displaying on the screen.
   PRESS: any key to display the Graph menu

To identify what each bar represents, you need to define the legend for each bar. To accomplish this, perform the following steps:

1. To choose the OPTIONS command:
   TYPE: O
2. To choose the Legend option and then create a legend for the A range:

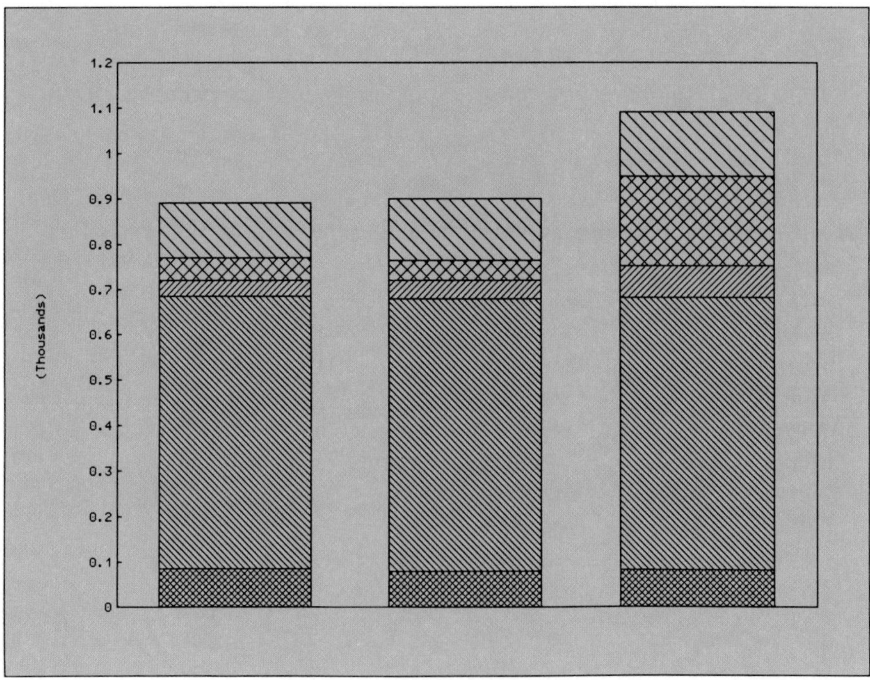

FIGURE E.17

Creating a stacked bar chart. Five data ranges have been defined.

TYPE: L
TYPE: A
TYPE: TELEPHONE
PRESS: Enter

3. To choose the Legend option and then create a legend for the B range:
TYPE: L
TYPE: B
TYPE: RENT
PRESS: Enter

4. To choose the Legend option and then create a legend for the C range:
TYPE: L
TYPE: C
TYPE: UTILITIES
PRESS: Enter

5. To choose the Legend option and then create a legend for the D range:
TYPE: L
TYPE: D
TYPE: AUTO
PRESS: Enter

6. To choose the Legend option and then create a legend for the E range:
TYPE: L
TYPE: E
TYPE: OTHER
PRESS: Enter
The screen (displaying all the current graph settings) should look like Figure E.18.

7. To see what your graph looks like at this point, first choose the Quit option (to move up one level in the Graph menu), and then choose the View option:
TYPE: Q
TYPE: V

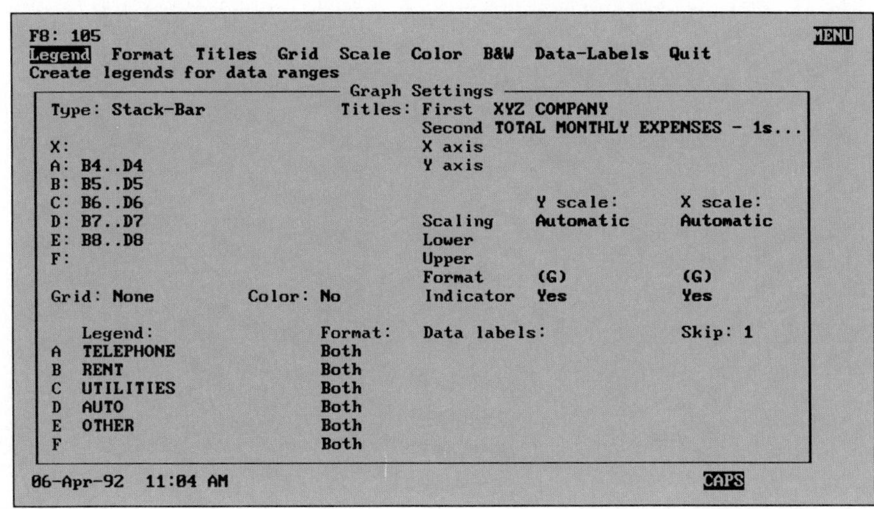

```
F8: 105                                                              MENU
Legend  Format  Titles  Grid  Scale  Color  B&W  Data-Labels  Quit
Create legends for data ranges
                              Graph Settings
 Type: Stack-Bar                 Titles: First   XYZ COMPANY
                                         Second  TOTAL MONTHLY EXPENSES - 1s...
 X:                                      X axis
 A: B4..D4                               Y axis
 B: B5..D5
 C: B6..D6                                         Y scale:        X scale:
 D: B7..D7                               Scaling   Automatic       Automatic
 E: B8..D8                               Lower
 F:                                      Upper
                                         Format    (G)             (G)
 Grid: None          Color: No           Indicator Yes             Yes

    Legend:                     Format:  Data labels:               Skip: 1
 A  TELEPHONE                   Both
 B  RENT                        Both
 C  UTILITIES                   Both
 D  AUTO                        Both
 E  OTHER                       Both
 F                              Both

06-Apr-92  11:04 AM                                            CAPS
```

FIGURE E.18

The graph settings sheet allows you to view all the current graph settings on the screen at once.

The stacked bar chart should be displaying on the screen (Figure E.19).
PRESS: any key to display the Graph menu

To name the graph specifications:

1. To choose the Name option:
TYPE: N
2. To choose the Create option and then name the specifications BAR2:
TYPE: C
TYPE: BAR2
PRESS: Enter

To save the graph specifications into a file that PrintGraph can understand:

1. The Graph menu should be displaying on the screen. To choose the Save option:
TYPE: S
2. To save the graph onto your data disk as BAR2.PIC, type either B:BAR2 (for diskette system users) or A:BAR2 (for hard disk system users).
TYPE: [the appropriate disk drive designation and the name of the file]
PRESS: Enter

To save the QTR1.WK1 spreadsheet with the named stacked bar chart specifications:

1. To exit the Graph menu and return to Ready mode:
TYPE: Q
2. To save the QTR1 spreadsheet:
TYPE: /

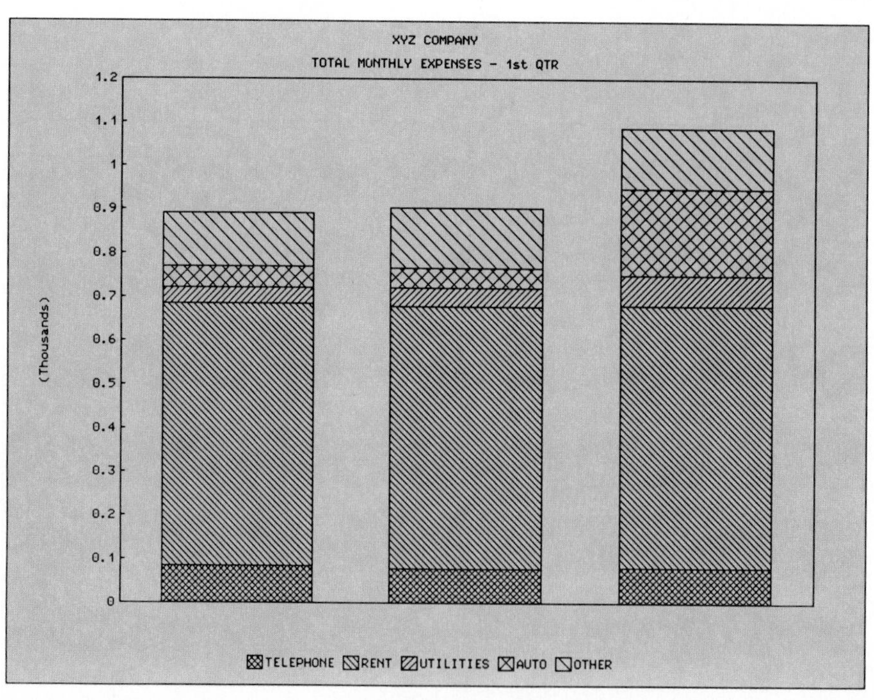

FIGURE E.19

The titles and legends have been defined for the stacked bar chart. The chart still needs X-axis labels.

TYPE: F
TYPE: S

3. To save the file onto the same disk using the same name (QTR1.WK1):
PRESS: Enter
4. To replace the copy on disk with the contents of RAM:
TYPE: R

CREATING A GROUPED BAR CHART

In this section, you will create a grouped bar chart that compares XYZ Company's monthly expense totals. This chart is similar to the stacked bar chart you created in the last section; however, this chart compares the expenses individually over January, February, and March. Because the charts are so similar, you will use the graph specifications you created in the last section, except change the "type" from Stacked Bar to Bar. When you are done, the bar chart should look similar to the one pictured in Figure E.7.

To tell Lotus 1-2-3 you want to use the BAR2 specifications:

1. To enter Menu mode and then choose the Graph option:
TYPE: /
TYPE: G
2. To specify that you want to use the BAR2 specifications:
TYPE: N
TYPE: U
TYPE: BAR2
PRESS: Enter
The stacked bar chart should be displaying on the screen.
PRESS: any key to display the Graph menu

The type of chart you are creating in this section is Bar. Perform the following steps to create this chart:

1. The Graph menu should be displaying on the screen. To choose the Type option:
TYPE: T
2. To choose the Bar option:
TYPE: B
3. To view the completed chart:
TYPE: V
The grouped bar chart should look similar to Figure E.7.
4. Press any key to display the Graph menu.

To name the graph specifications:

1. To choose the Name option:
TYPE: N
2. To choose the Create option and then name the specifications BAR3:
TYPE: C
TYPE: BAR3
PRESS: Enter

To save the graph specifications into a file that PrintGraph can understand:

1. The Graph menu should be displaying on the screen. To choose the Save option:
   TYPE: S
2. To save the graph onto your data disk as BAR3.PIC, type either B:BAR3 (for diskette system users) or A:BAR3 (for hard disk system users).
   TYPE: [the appropriate disk drive designation and the name of the file]
   PRESS: Enter

To save the QTR1.WK1 spreadsheet with the named grouped bar chart specifications:

1. To exit the Graph menu and return to Ready mode:
   TYPE: Q
2. To save the QTR1 spreadsheet:
   TYPE: /
   TYPE: F
   TYPE: S
3. To save the file onto the same disk using the same name (QTR1.WK1):
   PRESS: Enter
4. To replace the copy on disk with the contents of RAM:
   TYPE: R

CREATING A LINE CHART

In this section, you will create a line chart that compares XYZ Company's monthly expense totals over time. When you are done, the line chart should look similar to the one pictured in Figure E.4. To create this chart, all you have to do is change the "type" of the BAR3 chart you created earlier from Bar to Line. All the other graph specifications are correct (such as titles and legends).

To tell Lotus 1-2-3 you want to use the BAR3 specifications:

1. To enter Menu mode and then choose the Graph option:
   TYPE: /
   TYPE: G
2. To specify that you want to use the BAR3 specifications:
   TYPE: N
   TYPE: U
   TYPE: BAR3
   PRESS: Enter
   The grouped bar chart should be displaying on the screen.
   PRESS: any key to display the Graph menu

The type of chart you are creating in this section is Line. Perform the following steps to create this chart:

1. The Graph menu should be displaying on the screen. To choose the Type option:
   TYPE: T

2. To choose the Line option:
   TYPE: L
3. To view the completed chart:
   TYPE: V
   The line chart should be displaying on the screen (Figure E.4).
4. Press any key to display the Graph menu.

To name the graph specifications:

1. To choose the Name option:
   TYPE: N
2. To choose the Create option and then name the specifications LINE1:
   TYPE: C
   TYPE: LINE1
   PRESS: Enter

To save the graph specifications into a file that PrintGraph can understand:

1. The Graph menu should be displaying on the screen. To choose the Save option:
   TYPE: S
2. To save the graph onto your data disk as LINE1.PIC, type either B:LINE1 (for diskette system users) or A:LINE1 (for hard disk system users).
   TYPE: [the appropriate disk drive designation and the name of the file]
   PRESS: Enter

To save the QTR1.WK1 spreadsheet with the named line chart specifications:

1. To exit the Graph menu and return to Ready mode:
   TYPE: Q
2. To save the QTR1 spreadsheet:
   TYPE: /
   TYPE: F
   TYPE: S
3. To save the file onto the same disk using the same name (QTR1.WK1):
   PRESS: Enter
4. To replace the copy on disk with the contents of RAM:
   TYPE: R

Creating a Table of Graph Names

To generate a list of the graph names you have defined, you can use the GRAPH NAME TABLE command. The list of names is placed where the cursor is positioned, so make sure the cursor is in an unused section of your spreadsheet report.

Perform the following steps to generate a list of graph names in cell B14:

1. To initiate Menu mode and choose the Graph option:
   TYPE: /
   TYPE: G

2. To choose the Name option:
   TYPE: N
3. To choose the Table option:
   TYPE: T
4. Position the cursor in cell B14.
5. With the cursor positioned in cell B14:
   PRESS: Enter
6. To choose the Quit option:
   TYPE: Q
   The screen should look like Figure E.20.

Quick Reference

■

Creating a Table of Graph Names

1. Initiate Menu mode.
2. Choose the GRAPH command.
3. Choose the Name option.
4. Choose the Table option.
5. Position the cursor where you want the table to be positioned, and then press Enter.
6. Choose the Quit option.

LOADING PRINTGRAPH

To load PrintGraph, you must exit Lotus 1-2-3 so that the Lotus Access System is displaying on the screen; then choose the PrintGraph option. If you are using a diskette system, once you choose the PrintGraph option from the Lotus Access System menu, you will be prompted to insert the PrintGraph diskette.

FIGURE E.20

A table of graph names. The first column identifies the name of the chart. The second column identifies the type of chart you created. The third column displays the First title.

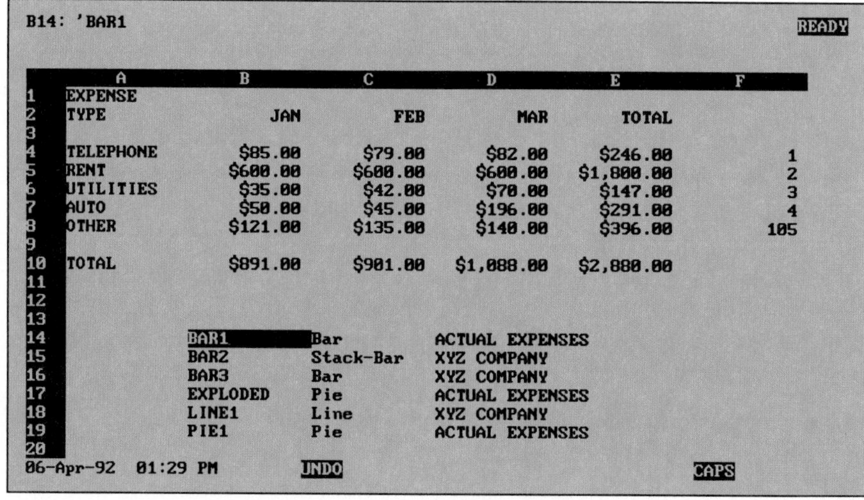

B14: 'BAR1 READY

	A	B	C	D	E	F
1	EXPENSE					
2	TYPE	JAN	FEB	MAR	TOTAL	
3						
4	TELEPHONE	$85.00	$79.00	$82.00	$246.00	1
5	RENT	$600.00	$600.00	$600.00	$1,800.00	2
6	UTILITIES	$35.00	$42.00	$70.00	$147.00	3
7	AUTO	$50.00	$45.00	$196.00	$291.00	4
8	OTHER	$121.00	$135.00	$140.00	$396.00	105
9						
10	TOTAL	$891.00	$901.00	$1,088.00	$2,880.00	
11						
12						
13						
14		BAR1	Bar	ACTUAL EXPENSES		
15		BAR2	Stack-Bar	XYZ COMPANY		
16		BAR3	Bar	XYZ COMPANY		
17		EXPLODED	Pie	ACTUAL EXPENSES		
18		LINE1	Line	XYZ COMPANY		
19		PIE1	Pie	ACTUAL EXPENSES		
20						

06-Apr-92 01:29 PM UNDO CAPS

Perform the following steps to load the PrintGraph program:

1. To exit Lotus 1-2-3 and display the Lotus Access System menu:
   TYPE: /
   TYPE: Q
   TYPE: Y
   The Lotus Access System should be displaying on the screen.
2. To choose the PrintGraph option:
   TYPE: P
   (*Note:* If using a diskette system, you may be prompted to insert a PrintGraph diskette.) The screen should look similar to Figure E.21.

The screen displays the current PrintGraph assumptions—you can change any of these using the Settings command (Figure E.22). For example, PrintGraph assumes your graphs will print in a certain size. In addition, PrintGraph assumes you will retrieve your graph files from a certain disk as indicated below the text "Graphs directory." If your data diskette is in drive A (where the PIC files are stored), PrintGraph should assume that the graphs directory is A:\. Likewise, if your data diskette is in drive B, PrintGraph should assume that the graphs directory is B:\. If your screen isn't displaying the correct graphs directory, follow the steps below:

FOR DISKETTE SYSTEM USERS

1. To choose the System option:
   TYPE: S
2. To choose the Hardware option:
   TYPE: H
3. To choose the Graphs-Directory option:
   TYPE: G
4. To tell PrintGraph that your data diskette is in drive B:
   TYPE: B:
   PRESS: Enter

(continued)

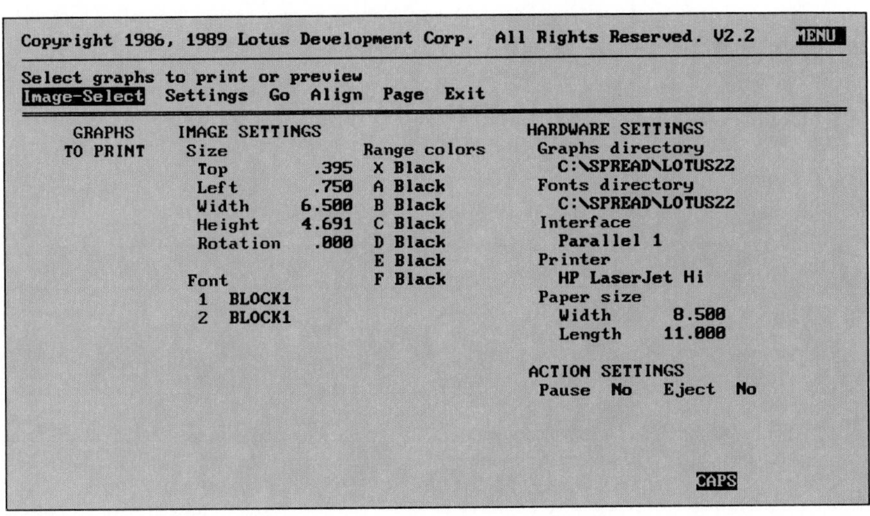

FIGURE E.21

The PrintGraph opening screen.

5. To display the main PrintGraph menu:
   TYPE: Q
   TYPE: Q ■

FOR HARD DISK SYSTEM USERS

1. To choose the System option:
   TYPE: S
2. To choose the Hardware option:
   TYPE: H
3. To choose the Graphs-Directory option:
   TYPE: G
4. To tell PrintGraph that your data diskette is in drive A:
   TYPE: A:
   PRESS: Enter
5. To display the main PrintGraph menu:
   TYPE: Q
   TYPE: Q ■

PrintGraph now knows where your graph files are stored.

FIGURE E.22 The PrintGraph menu structure.

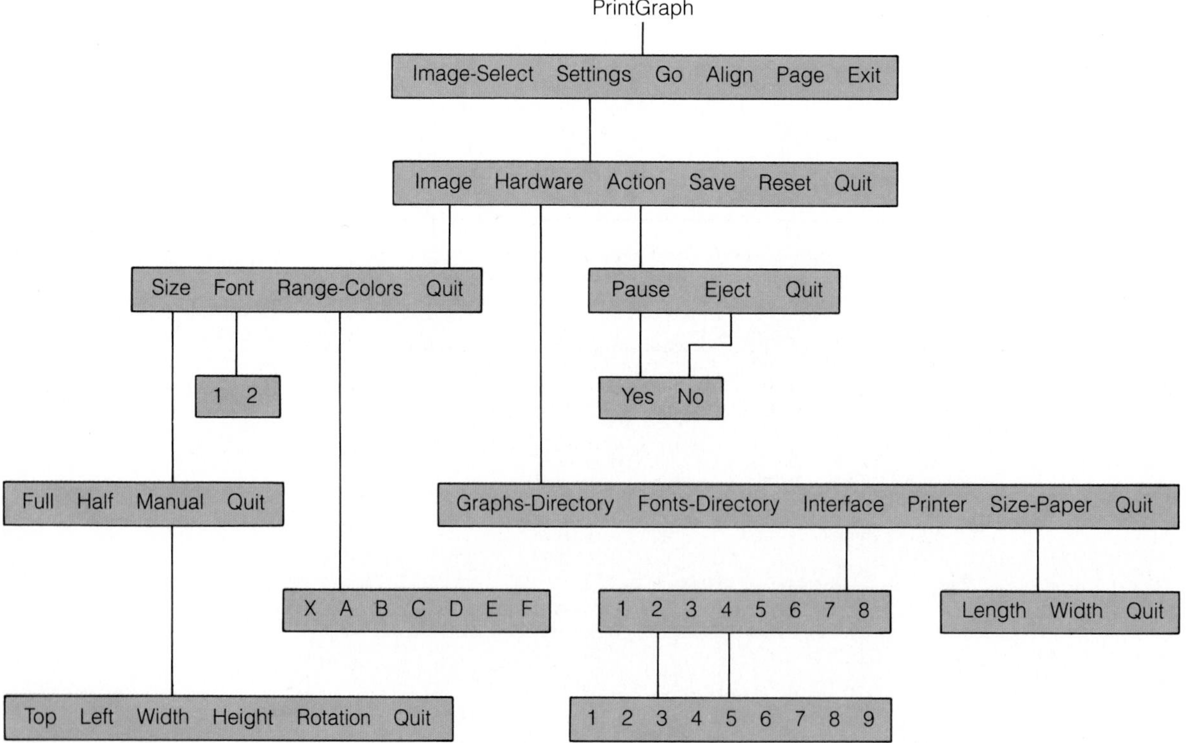

PRINTING A GRAPH

To print a graph, you must perform the following steps:

1. Make sure PrintGraph knows where the diskette that contains your graph files is located (the procedure required to accomplish this was described in the last section).
2. Choose a graph to print. To select an image, simply highlight the image and then press the space bar to choose the image. By pressing the space bar, a pound sign (#) is placed next to the filename. If, after pressing the space bar, you decide you don't want to print the graph, press the space bar again, and the # will disappear.

To print a graph, perform the following steps:

1. The main PrintGraph menu should be displaying on the screen. To choose the Image-Select option:
   TYPE: I
   The screen should look like Figure E.23.
2. To choose one or more graphs to print, highlight the graph(s) and then press the space bar.
3. To View a marked graph, press the F10 key. Then press the space bar to again view the list of graph files.
4. To select the marked pictures, press the Enter key. The main PrintGraph menu should be displaying on the screen.
5. To actually print a marked graph, choose the Align option and then the Go option. (Make sure your printer is on.)

When you are finished using PrintGraph, you will want to exit to the Lotus Access System.

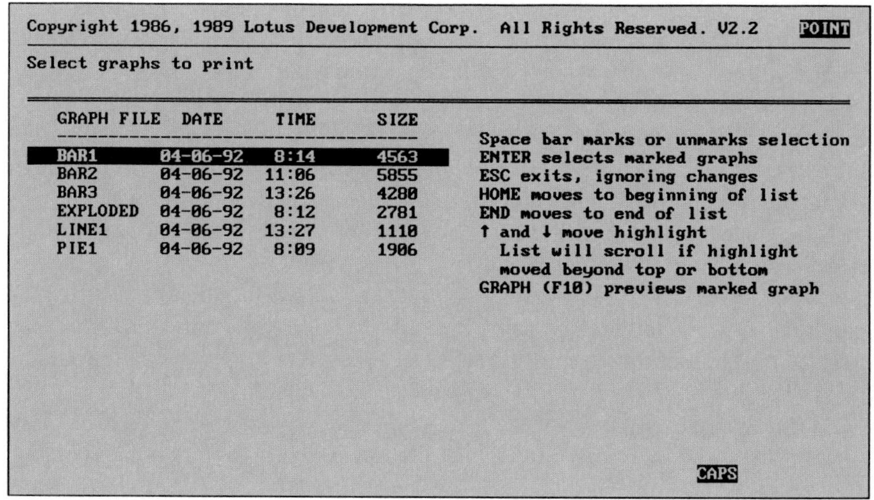

FIGURE E.23

This list of .PIC files appears after you choose the Image-Select option. To choose a graph to print, highlight the graph and then press the space bar.

Perform the following steps:

1. To choose the Exit option:
   TYPE: E
2. To choose the Yes option:
   TYPE: Y
   The Lotus Access System should again be displaying on the screen.

SUMMARY

The most common forms for presenting business information graphically are (1) pie charts, (2) line charts, (3) bar charts, and (4) XY charts. A pie chart is the best chart to use when illustrating parts of a whole. The technique of exploding is often used in pie charts to emphasize a particular piece of the pie. When creating a pie chart, you are required to define only an A data range. However, if you want to explode a piece of a pie, or include cross-hatching in the chart, you must define a B data range.

Line charts are the appropriate charts to use when you need to show trends over time. The angles of the line reflect variations in a trend, and the distance of the line from the horizontal axis represents quantity.

Bar charts are the appropriate chart to use when you need to compare one data element with another data element. A simple bar chart graphs only one data range. A grouped bar chart shows how more than one data element compares over time. A stacked bar chart shows how the components of a data element compare over time.

XY charts, which are commonly referred to as scatter charts, are used to show how one or more data elements relate to another data element. Although XY charts look similar to line charts, XY charts include a numeric scale along the X-axis.

While creating charts, you should keep some principles in mind. First, keep your charts simple. If you clutter them with unnecessary information, their meaning becomes lost. Second, keep your charts unified. Don't, for example, include too much space between the variables (such as between bars in a bar chart). Third, use emphasis to make certain data elements stand out. For example, exploding a pie slice emphasizes that piece of a pie chart. And finally, keep your charts balanced, both as a unit and in the context of the rest of the page.

When you are finished creating a graph with Lotus 1-2-3, perform the following steps: (1) use the GRAPH SAVE command, which creates a picture file (with the extension of .PIC) that PrintGraph understands, (2) use the GRAPH NAME command, which gives a name to your graph specifications so that you can modify the graph later, and (3) use the FILE SAVE command, which saves any graph names you defined in the preceding step.

The GRAPH NAME TABLE command is used to generate a list of the graph names (that you created using the GRAPH NAME command). For each graph, Lotus outputs into a spreadsheet range the type of graph, the name, and the title of the graph.

PrintGraph is used to print the Lotus 1-2-3 graphs you create. To load PrintGraph, you must exit Lotus 1-2-3 so that the Lotus Access System is displaying on the screen. You must then choose the PrintGraph option. To print a graph, choose the Image-Select option and press the space bar while highlighting the graph you want to print.

Figure E.24 displays Lotus 1-2-3's graph menu hierarchy.

The Lotus 1-2-3 graph menu hierarchy.

FIGURE E.24

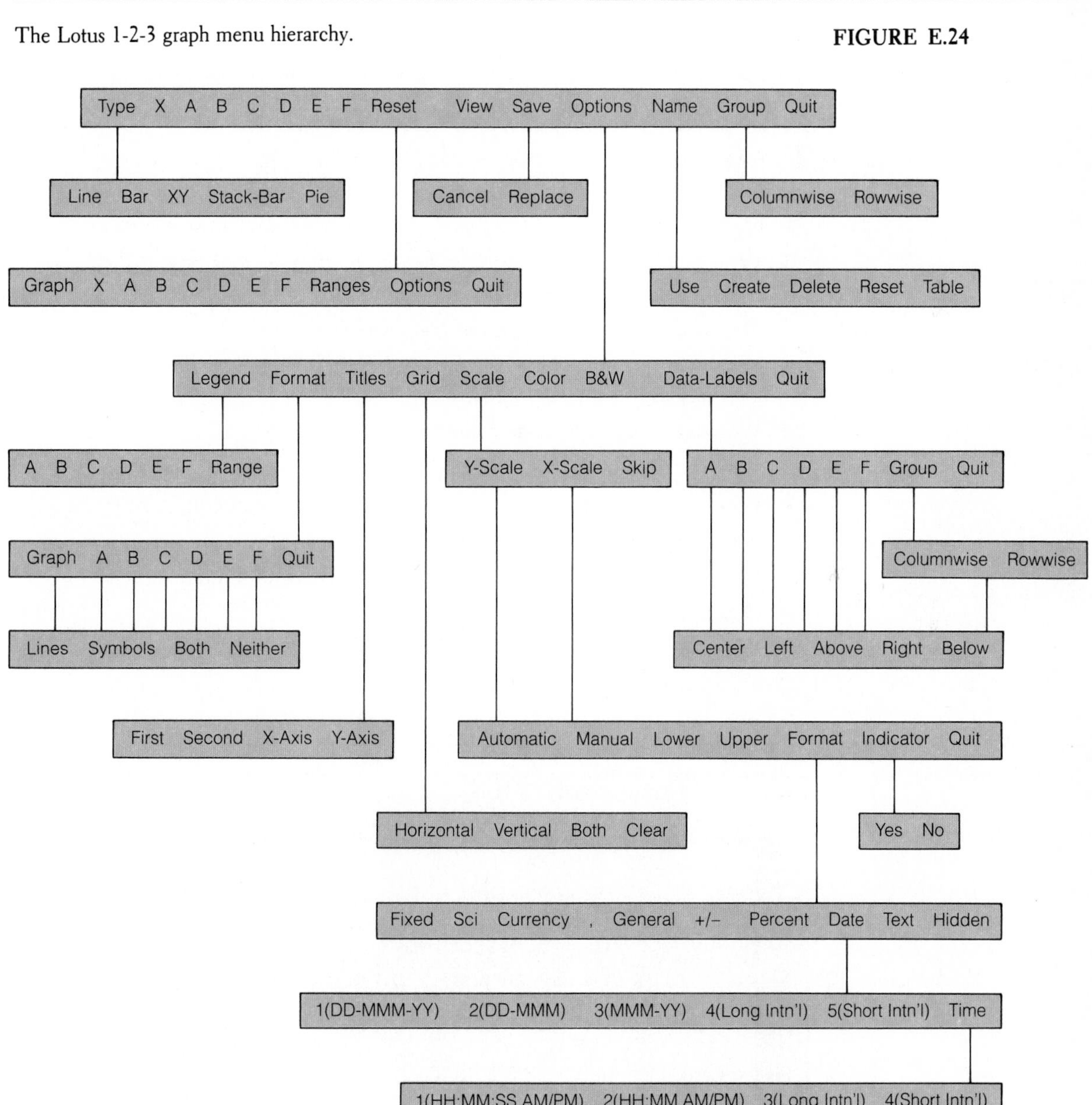

KEY TERMS

bar chart, p. 692
computer graphics, p. 688
dedicated graphics package, p. 688
exploding, p. 690
graphics, p. 688
grouped bar chart, p. 692
line chart, p. 690
microcomputer-based business graphics, p. 688
pie chart, p. 689
spreadsheet-based package, p. 688
stacked bar chart, p. 692
XY chart, p. 692

EXERCISES

SHORT ANSWER

1. Why is it important to name your graph specifications before saving your spreadsheet?
2. Describe the basic principles of graphics presentation.
3. What is the purpose of saving your graph specifications in the form of a graphics file that has the extension of PIC?
4. What basic steps must you follow to create a graph?
5. Why is the GRAPH NAME TABLE command useful?
6. What do you have to do if you want to shade the segments in a pie chart?
7. What are XY charts typically used for?
8. When saving a graph, what three steps should you follow?
9. Describe the procedure for using PrintGraph.
10. What do you have to do if you want to explode a pie chart segment?

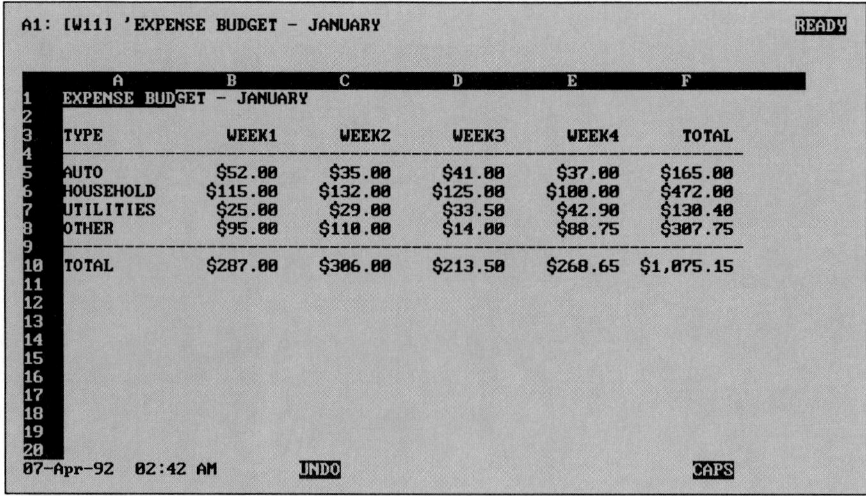

A1: [W11] 'EXPENSE BUDGET - JANUARY READY

	A	B	C	D	E	F
1	EXPENSE BUDGET - JANUARY					
2						
3	TYPE	WEEK1	WEEK2	WEEK3	WEEK4	TOTAL
4						
5	AUTO	$52.00	$35.00	$41.00	$37.00	$165.00
6	HOUSEHOLD	$115.00	$132.00	$125.00	$100.00	$472.00
7	UTILITIES	$25.00	$29.00	$33.50	$42.90	$130.40
8	OTHER	$95.00	$110.00	$14.00	$88.75	$307.75
9						
10	TOTAL	$287.00	$306.00	$213.50	$268.65	$1,075.15
11						
12						
13						
14						
15						
16						
17						
18						
19						
20						

07-Apr-92 02:42 AM UNDO CAPS

FIGURE E.25

The January expense spreadsheet.

HANDS ON

On the basis of the spreadsheet pictured in Figure E.25:

1. Create a bar chart to compare January's weekly expense totals. The data you will graph is in the range B10 . . E10.
2. Create a pie chart using the data in the range B10 . . E10.
3. Create a bar chart to compare each monthly expense total for each type of expense. The data you will be graphing is in the range F5 . . F8.
4. Create a grouped bar chart comparing each expense type over the four weeks of January. The data you will be graphing is in the following ranges:
   a. B5 . . E5
   b. B6 . . E6
   c. B7 . . E7
   d. B8 . . E8
5. Using the graph specifications you defined in Step 4, create a stacked bar chart.

Appendix A

Purchasing and Maintaining a Microcomputer System

Many different microcomputers—with different features and processing capabilities—exist on the market today. If you, or your company, are in the market to purchase a microcomputer, you should consider carefully your processing needs. An afterthought like the following can be quite expensive: "Oh, I should have purchased a printer that can output graphics." Not only should you define your software and hardware requirements clearly before you purchase a microcomputer system, but you should also investigate the company from which you are buying the computer to make sure it will offer support in the long run.

Despite the substantial investment they have made, many users treat their microcomputers with no more respect than a desktop calculator or a telephone. Would you leave a record album in the direct sunlight for long? If so, you would have an unusable record album on your hands because the surface would become wrinkled or warped. Similarly, you shouldn't leave your microcomputer in the direct sunlight, because microcomputers are very sensitive to temperature changes. Temperature is only one factor that will affect the life of your computer. We'll cover others. This appendix provides you with a few simple rules that you should follow before purchasing a microcomputer system and to maintain it over time.

Purchasing a System: What to Consider

"You need an 80 MB hard disk." "You must purchase a laser printer." "By all means, purchase *this* word processing package." Purchasing a microcomputer system involves doing some research, listening to a lot of advice, and ultimately making a number of different purchasing decisions. Many people will buy hardware and software solely at the recommendation of a friend. Although recommendations are helpful, if you don't do additional research, you may find yourself spending more for a system that offers features you will never use. In this section we provide advice on choosing software and hardware to support your processing needs and explain what to consider before you purchase a microcomputer *clone*—a microcomputer that is virtually identical to and compatible with the brand of computer it is copying. In addition, we describe some factors that should affect where you purchase a microcomputer system.

What Software and Hardware Will You Need?

If you are a first-time buyer of a microcomputer, you should choose your applications software *first*, after you identify your processing needs. For example, do you want to generate documents? Budgets? Graphics? In color? Depending on your needs, you will need to purchase one or more applications software packages.

Once your applications software needs have been determined, choose the compatible hardware models and systems software that will allow you to use your applications software efficiently and expand your system if necessary. (Sometimes the systems software is automatically included with the computer.)

The documentation (user's manual) that accompanies the applications software you purchase will list the minimum hardware requirements necessary to run the software. For example, your microcomputer must have a minimum of 640 K RAM to run many software programs on the market today. And if your objective is to output graphics, you must make sure that your printer is compatible with your software and will support graphics. By choosing your applications software first, you will ensure that all your processing requirements will be satisfied: You won't be forced to buy a software package that is your second choice simply because your first software choice wasn't compatible with the hardware or systems software already purchased.

When you go to work in an office, chances are that the computer hardware and systems software will already be in operation, so if you have to choose anything, it will most likely be applications software, to help you do your job. If you do find yourself in a position to choose applications software make sure not only that it will satisfy the processing requirements of your job, but also that it is compatible with your company's hardware and existing software.

Microcomputer Clones: A Good Bet?

It depends. There are good clones and bad clones. But if you ask some important questions before making a purchase, you will end up with a compatible system for a good price.

- Is the microcomputer accompanied by proper and adequate documentation? This is extremely important. If your microcomputer needs to be repaired or upgraded, the computer technician will want to look at the technical documentation that accompanies your system. No matter what the price, if the system comes without documentation, you should not buy it.
- Is the ROM chip a known compatible? If the answer is "yes," then you will be able to run all the software (generally) that is written for the microcomputer your machine is a clone of.
- Are the characteristics of the motherboard—the main circuit board of the microcomputer system—similar to the brand-name machine? If they are, then adapter boards (such as expanded memory or video adapter boards) will work in the clone.

- Is the system covered by a warranty? The system should be covered by a 6–12 month warranty. If something fails in that time, the manufacturer should repair it at no cost.
- If the system fails after the warranty period, will parts be available? The manufacturer should service your computer after the warranty period expires. In other words, watch out for "fly-by-night" manufacturers.

Companies like NCR have conducted studies that prove their computers are 100 percent compatible with the microcomputer they are cloning. This type of information is useful to the microcomputer clone buyer; ask your dealer about such studies.

Because IBM microcomputers are very popular in the business environment, computer makers often manufacture IBM clones and sell them with their own manufacturing label. Don't think that a microcomputer with an IBM label is better than an IBM clone—clones are sometimes more powerful and typically less expensive than the machines they copy. As a result, IBM clones have become extremely popular and have achieved a niche of their own in the marketplace. When IBM makes a change in its microcomputer line, you can be sure that other compatibles, or clones, that incorporate those changes will appear. The microcomputers that have been cloned the most are the IBM PC and IBM XT microcomputers (based on the 8088 microprocessor chip) and the IBM AT microcomputer (based on the Intel 80286 microprocessor chip).

WHERE TO GO

The following three factors should greatly influence where you purchase a microcomputer: (1) the company's reputation, (2) the warranty agreement, and (3) the price. Since each of these factors influences the others, they can't be described independently.

If a local computer store has been in business for a few years, you can be reasonably confident that it has tested the waters and won't go out of business. Purchasing a computer from a local computer store offers a number of advantages, including:

- Manufacturers generally support warranties on computers sold through dealers. Should anything happen to the computer in 6–12 months, parts and labor are covered by the manufacturer's warranty, or agreement between the manufacturer (and sometimes the seller) and purchaser. If a computer has a problem, you will likely experience it in the first 6–12 months anyway, so a 6–12 month warranty is a fair deal. If a computer is sold through someone other than an authorized dealer—computers sold in this way are referred to as *gray-market computers* —many manufacturers ignore the manufacturer's warranty.
- Since the computer store is local, you have a convenient place to take the computer if it needs to be serviced.
- You can establish personal contacts at the computer store should you have questions about your system.

If you are *very* careful you can purchase a microcomputer and peripheral equipment from a mail-order company for a substantial discount. Unfortunately, some computer manufacturers, such as IBM, Compaq, and NEC, don't sell directly to mail-order companies because the mail-order companies don't usually offer support to their customers. Some manufacturers, however, do support their warranties no matter who sells the computer; these manufacturers include AT&T, Everex, Toshiba, and Zenith. *Make sure your microcomputer is supported by a warranty before purchasing it.*

Computer magazines such as *Byte*, *PC World*, *PC Computing*, *Personal Computing*, and *InfoWorld* all contain advertisements for mail-order companies. Although many mail-order companies have solid reputations, some don't. If you don't do the following homework before purchasing through a mail-order company, you may be abandoned with little or no hardware, a computer that doesn't work, or one that has no warranty:

- Check back issues of the magazine to see if the advertisement has been running regularly. If it has, the company has been paying its bills.
- Check the ad for a street address. If no street address exists—only a P.O. box—it is possible that the company may be a temporary operation.
- Compare the prices offered by different mail-order companies. If the price you are eying is more than 25 percent lower than that of the competition, you might be looking at something that is too good to be true.
- Make sure the system's price includes all the features and peripherals that you want. For example, make sure the price includes a monitor and a keyboard.
- Make sure the system you purchase is covered by a manufacturer's warranty. Many major computer manufacturers, including IBM and Compaq, don't honor warranties on computers sold through mail-order companies.
- In addition, you may want to check with the Better Business Bureau or local consumer protection department in the company's area to find out more details about the company.

If everything adds up, you have found yourself a good deal. Of course you still won't have the personalized support that you get when purchasing from a local computer store.

Other Practical Considerations

Following are a few more guidelines that will help you in choosing a microcomputer system:

1. After you decide what you want the system to do for you and have chosen your software, determine what the minimum hardware requirements are to run the software. These requirements are listed in the documentation that accompanies each software program.
2. Determine if any of your hardware needs to be portable.
3. To ensure the possibility of upgrading the computer in the future, choose one designed with open architecture.
4. Determine if your system must be compatible with another system—either in your office or in another context—or with software you or your office is already using. If so, be sure to choose compatible hardware, and make sure that any systems software that comes with the computer is compatible also.

5. If possible, buy everything (computer, keyboard, monitor, printer, and so on) at one place, so you have to make only one phone call to ask questions and solve problems.
6. Consider having someone from the computer store or outlet come to your office to set up the system, install the software, and make sure everything is running properly. (Independent professionals can also do this for you.) It's also a plus if the seller offers training classes.
7. Buy a monitor and a keyboard that are comfortable to use; try them out first.
8. Determine how much storage you will need and buy accordingly.
9. Determine if you need color in either hardcopy or softcopy output.
10. Determine your most common output needs. For example, will you need to print out forms with many carbon layers? Will you be outputting mostly business letters or internal memos? Will you to need to output graphics also?

See the end of the appendix for a portable checklist that you can take with you when you decide to purchase a microcomputer.

INSTALLING APPLICATIONS SOFTWARE

Once you have bought your applications software package, you must install it to work with your microcomputer system. *Software installation* usually involves telling the software what the characteristics are of the hardware you will be using so that the software will run smoothly. When you purchase a software application, check to see that the documentation tells you how to install the software.

To install software, you first insert the applications software diskette as indicated by the package documentation. Then the installation program usually asks a number of different questions about your hardware. For example, the installation program will usually display on your monitor a list of the popular printers on the market. You will be instructed to choose the name of the printer that corresponds to the one you are using. If the printer you are using doesn't appear on the list, and you are given no "generic" choice, you must contact the support staff at the company who developed your software and tell them what printer you are using. (Use the 800 number given in the documentation.) They will respond in one of the following ways:

- Send you the printer driver for the printer you are using. A *printer driver* is a file stored on a disk containing instructions that enable your software program to communicate, or print, on the printer you are using.
- Tell you to choose a different printer from the list. If the printer you are using operates similarly to one on the list, your printer can use the printer driver of the other printer. This is often referred to as *emulating* the characteristics of another printer.

You may also be asked other questions during the installation procedure:

- What is the make and model of the microcomputer you are using?
- Are you using a color monitor? If so, what kind?
- Are you using a monochrome monitor? If so, what kind?

- Are you using 5¼-inch or 3½-inch diskettes?
- Are you using a hard disk?
- Where will you want the working copy of your applications software to be stored? On a diskette? On the hard disk?

Think about the answers to these questions *before* initiating the installation process. Once you have completed the installation procedure, your program will store most of your responses in a special file on the disk, which is referred to by your applications program when you load the software. In addition, if you will be using a hard disk, many installation programs automatically copy the program files to the hard disk for you. (*Note:* If you are using a hard disk, the installation process involves transferring *copies* of the programs that came on the diskettes in the applications package. Keep the original diskettes as backup in case your hard disk crashes. If you are using diskettes, make copies of the original package diskettes and use the copies as your working diskettes. The originals will serve as backups.)

Once the installation procedure is completed, you are ready to roll!

MAINTAINING A SYSTEM

A microcomputer system presents a sizeable investment—from a few hundred to a few thousand dollars. Even so, many users don't take care of this investment, which leads to system abuse and failures. Most microcomputer problems could have been prevented by regular maintenance. Maintaining a system properly—on an ongoing basis—is easy, and will pay for itself many times over by reducing hardware malfunctions and data loss and increasing the life of your computer.

TEMPERATURE

Computer systems should be kept in an environment with as constant a temperature as possible. In cold climates, where office temperatures are controlled by an automatic thermostat causing warmer temperatures during the day and much cooler temperatures at night, microcomputers tend to have the most system failures. The ideal room temperature for microcomputers ranges from 60 to 90 degrees Fahrenheit when the system is on and from 50 to 110 degrees when the system is off. But maintaining a constant temperature in an environment is more important than the number of degrees.

The following problems can eventually occur if a microcomputer system is subjected to substantial changes in temperature in short amounts of time:

- The chips inside the system unit can work their way out of their sockets in the system boards. In addition, the chip connectors can corrode more quickly so that they become brittle and crack.
- Hard disks suffer from dramatic changes in temperature, which can cause read/write problems. If a new hard disk drive has been shipped in a cold environment, manufacturers usually recommend that users wait for at least a few hours and as long as a day before operating the hard disk.

These problems are caused by the expansion and contraction that naturally occur when materials are heated and then cooled. The bottom line is that changes in temperature are stressful for microcomputer systems.

TURNING THE COMPUTER ON/OFF

As described in the last section, sudden changes in temperature can cause lasting damage to a computer system. When a computer system is turned on, it is subjected to the *most* extreme change in temperature — computers are relatively cool when they are off and become quite warm when they are turned on. For this reason, the fewer times a system has to be turned on, the longer it will remain in good working order. Ideally, a microcomputer system should be kept on continuously — 24 hours a day, 7 days a week; however, because of the issue of security during nonbusiness hours and continuous power consumption, it is unlikely that the typical office worker can keep his or her machine running all the time. A better solution is to keep the system on all day so that it is turned on only once each day.

One myth that we would like to dispel is that leaving a microcomputer system on will wear down a hard disk. By running a hard disk continuously, you are greatly reducing any stress on the drive due to temperature variations. This will reduce the potential of any read/write failures that are caused by such variations and improve the life of the drive. If you can't leave your microcomputer system on continuously, at least let the system warm up for 15 minutes or so before reading from or writing to the drive. By remembering this simple rule, you will improve the reliability of the data stored on your disk.

If you do leave your system on all the time, make sure that the screen automatically goes blank after a few minutes if the keyboard or other input device isn't used. Many manufacturers include this feature with their computer systems — if not, special software (screen utility) is available that will do this for you. If your screen doesn't go blank, the phosphors on the screen can burn, leaving a permanent image on the screen (Macintosh computers typically don't show these phosphor burn effects). The monitors in airports that display flight information show these phosphor-burn effects.

PLUGGING IN THE SYSTEM

Many users plug a number of different system components into one power strip that contains a number of different plug outlets. However, certain types of equipment, including coffee makers, laser printers, and copy machines, can cause voltage *spikes* (surges of electricity), which can do damage to a computer that is connected to the same line. Therefore, it's best to keep your computer on a line separate from other equipment. If you must connect peripheral equipment on the same power line, turn on that equipment *before* turning on the computer.

If your computer is in an environment that is susceptible to power surges or power outages, you should plug your system into a surge protector or uninterruptible power supply. *Surge protectors*, the simplest form of power protection, are devices into which you can plug your microcomputer system and which in turn are connected to the power line. Costing between $20 and $200, surge protectors help protect the power supply and other sensitive circuitry in your computer system from voltage spikes. An *uninterruptible power supply (UPS)* is also used to protect your hardware from the damaging effects that a power surge can have on your computer system. In addition, should you lose power, it will keep your system running for around 15 minutes, providing you with plenty of time to save your work and shut the system down. The cost of a UPS system is determined by the amount of time it can continue to provide power to your computer system after the power has been cut off. Prices range from around $400 to many thousands of dollars.

DUST AND POLLUTANTS

As an experiment, when your computer is on, light a match in front of a diskette drive and notice where the smoke goes. The smoke is inhaled by the system unit!

Most IBM and IBM-compatible microcomputers are configured with a fan inside the system unit that is mounted near the power supply. This fan causes air to be drawn into the system unit through any possible opening and then exhausted out. Systems are designed this way to allow for the even cooling of the microcomputer system. Unfortunately, in this process, dust, smoke, and any other pollutants in the air are drawn into the system unit. Over time these particles will insulate the system unit and prevent it from cooling properly. In addition, some of these particles can conduct electricity, causing minor electrical shorts in the system.

Diskette drives are especially susceptible to dust and other pollutants because they provide a large hole through which air flows. The read/write heads in the diskette drive won't work accurately if they are contaminated with foreign particles. (Hard disks aren't at risk because they are stored in air-tight, sterile containers.) For this reason, many companies enforce "No Smoking" policies where computers are present.

If you want to clean the diskette drives in your computer system (the read-write heads can become dusty over time, which reduces the reliability with which they can store and retrieve data), an easy method does exist. You must first purchase a head-cleaning disk from a local computer store. Head-cleaning disks come in two basic styles—wet or dry. The wet cleaning disk uses a liquid cleaning agent that has been squirted onto the disk, and the dry cleaning disk uses an abrasive material that has been put onto the cleaning disk. Most computer professionals recommend using the wet system, because the dry system can actually damage the read-write heads of the disk if it is used too often. To use a cleaning disk, simply put it into the disk drive and run a program (that is stored on the disk) to make the disk spin. When the disk spins in the disk drive, the read-write heads touch the surface of the cleaning disk and are wiped clean. In a clean (smoke-free) office environment, diskette drives should be cleaned once a year. In a smoking environment, diskette drives should be cleaned every three to six months.

The diskette drives aren't the only system components that should be cleaned periodically. If a microcomputer system is operated in a dirty environment, such as on the floor of a lumber shop, it should also be cleaned every three to six months. But in most office environments, the cleaning should be done every one to two years. You can either clean the appropriate components yourself or hire a professional to clean them for you. If you aren't familiar with the process of cleaning a microcomputer, hire a professional.

BACKING UP YOUR MICROCOMPUTER SYSTEM

The scenario: You've stored a year's worth of client information on your hard disk. You are able to retrieve client information easily onto the screen. You have confidence in your computer system . . . until the hard disk crashes. The read/write heads fall onto the surface of the disk making the disk unusable and causing the loss of all the data stored on the disk! Well, at least you have a backup copy of your client files . . . What? You don't?

One of the most important tasks involved in maintaining a microcomputer system is to make copies of—or back up—your data files. A popular rule of thumb is to never let the time between backups go longer than the amount of data it represents that you are willing to lose in a disaster. Depending on the amount of activity on a system, hard disks should be backed up at the end of each day or each week. All managers should make sure that office policies include backup procedures.

PROCEDURES

When making backup copies, you must decide how often you want to back up your data. Do you want to back up the entire hard disk or simply the files that have been changed since the last backup? Perhaps you want to make daily copies of the files that have been changed, and at the end of the week, make a backup copy of the entire disk including software and data files. Whatever the procedures, they should be defined clearly and followed routinely.

Also, remember that backup must be done on *removable media*—storage media that can easily be removed from the system and stored remotely. Some businesses configure microcomputers with two hard disks. The first hard disk is the work disk onto which all the current processing activities and updated files are stored. The second hard disk is used as a backup disk—the contents of the first disk are copied onto the second. This is not advisable. Suppose the microcomputer system is subjected to a massive power surge. The contents of *both* disks will be destroyed. Or suppose the entire microcomputer system is stolen. Once more, you won't have any backup files.

HARDWARE AND SOFTWARE

Diskettes are still used in some cases as backup media. Almost all microcomputer systems come with at least one diskette drive, so without a substantial hardware investment in a *dedicated backup system*—hardware and software used only for backup purposes—the user can back up the contents of a hard disk onto removable media (diskettes). Backup software for diskette systems is available that assists in the backup process, prompting the user to "insert a new diskette, please" when one diskette becomes full. One such program is called FASTBACK, by 5th Generation Systems. However, using diskettes to back up a hard disk is slow.

As described in Chapter 4, magnetic tape is the more commonly used storage media for backing up hard disks. With a hard disk of 20 MB or higher, a reliable tape storage unit is a good investment. Tape backup units can easily support 60 MB or more and are fast and accurate. Once you decide to purchase a tape backup unit, you must decide what software to purchase to run the tape system. Many tape backup manufacturers write their own software. In addition to your specific needs, you should be sure that the software facilitates the following:

- Files can be backed up individually or all at once.
- Several backups can be copied onto a single tape.
- A backup can span more than one tape.
- The backup data can be verified to ensure that it was recorded reliably on the tape.

By paying special attention to the temperature of your system, the number of times you turn it on/off, how it is plugged in, the quality of the air surrounding the system, and routine backup procedures, you will increase the life of your computer system.

PORTABLE CHECKLIST FOR BUYING A MICROCOMPUTER SYSTEM

PRICE RANGE (INCLUDING PERIPHERALS)

______ up to $1,000 ______ up to $3,000 ______ up to $5,000

______ up to $2,000 ______ up to $4,000

USES (SOFTWARE NEEDED)

__________ Writing letters and reports; preparing professional papers (Word Processing Software)

__________ Personal finance; budgeting and planning; taxes (Spreadsheet Software)

__________ Programming (programming language, such as BASIC, COBOL, Pascal, FORTRAN)

__________ Business applications; finance management, accounting, planning, scheduling, inventory and sales management (Spreadsheet, Database Management, and/or Graphics Software)

__________ Entertainment (Software Games)

__________ Education (Tutorial Software)

__________ Mailing lists (Word Processing Software)

__________ Publishing newsletters and brochures (Word Processing, Graphics, Desktop Publishing Software)

__________ Information retrieval from public information services (Communications Software)

__________ Personal record keeping (Desktop Management Software)

__________ Creating art and graphics for use in published materials (Graphics and Desktop Publishing Software)

HARDWARE

(Check your chosen software's documentation for minimum hardware requirements.)

1. ______ System must be compatible with other systems? (Y/N) If yes, what kind:

   ____

2. ______ 640 K RAM; ______ 1 MB RAM; ______ 2 MB RAM; ______ 4 MB RAM (random access memory, primary memory, or main memory)
3. ______ 16-bit processor; ______ 32-bit processor (number of bits that can be handled by the microprocessor once)
4. ______ mHz (clock speed)

5. ______ Must be portable? (Y/N)
6. ______ Monochrome screen; ______ color screen ______ special size screen
7. ______ CGA; ______ EGA; ______ VGA; ______ other (screen resolution, or clarity of image)
8. ______ Screen can tilt and swivel? (Y/N)
9. ______ System cabinet can be put on floor to save desk space? (Y/N)
10. ______ Detachable keyboard
11. ______ QWERTY keyboard; ______ other keyboard
12. ______ Numeric keypad
13. ______ Number of required function keys
14. ______ Voice input
15. ______ Single diskette drive; ______ dual diskette drive
16. ______ 20 MB hard disk; ______ 40 MB hard disk; ______ 60 MB hard disk; ______ 80 MB hard disk
17. ______ Tape backup
18. ______ Surge protector; ______ uninterrupted power supply
19. ______ Mouse
20. ______ Dot matrix printer; ______ daisy wheel printer; ______ laser printer

    ______ color capability; ______ graphics capability

    ______ multiple form capability; ______ font availability

    ______ speed; ______ noise level
21. ______ Modem
22. ______ Fax

SUPPORT
Investigate the following:

1. Manufacturer's reputation and length of time in business.
2. Dealer's reputation and length of time in business.
3. Warranties.
4. Quality of documentation (User's manuals); easy to follow? detailed?
5. Hotline availability to solve problems in emergencies.
6. Location and availability of repair services.
7. Availability of training.

APPENDIX B

BASIC PROGRAMMING FOR THE USER

INTRODUCTION TO BASIC

It's important for users like yourself to have some exposure to traditional programming languages like those described in Chapter 8. First, in the business environment it is likely that you will have to communicate to a professional programmer what you'd like a software program to do to meet your needs. By knowing some of what's involved in creating a program, you can be much more effective at communicating your needs. Second, it is also likely that you will at some point be using one of the newer software development tools for microcomputers described in Chapter 8, such as an electronic spreadsheet package or a database management system. Having some experience with a traditional programming language, no matter how limited, will help you appreciate the power of these newer software development tools.

We have chosen BASIC to demonstrate the use of a traditional programming language because it is considered the easiest of the traditional programming languages to learn. Again, our objective isn't for you to learn everything there is to know about the BASIC programming language, but to give you some "basic" experience using a traditional programming language. We have provided numerous sample programs to demonstrate good programming practice.

A BRIEF HISTORY

BASIC was developed at Dartmouth College in an attempt to improve a system used by scientists doing numeric calculations. Originally the users had to submit cards to a centrally located card reader, which would then instruct the computer to run a program; the output was printed a few hours (or even days) later.

A timesharing system that improved efficiency and ease of use demanded an interactive language — BASIC — that would allow each user to type programs into a terminal (similar to a personal computer) on whose screen the output would be displayed immediately.

Since its invention, BASIC has been adopted by almost all computer and microcomputer manufacturers. However, because the manufacturers found the language to be limited, each manufacturer would change it slightly to make use of enhancements particular to various machines. Thus, different versions (called *dialects*) of BASIC emerged. Your instructor will help you with any differences between your BASIC and the BASIC described in this appendix.

STRUCTURED PROGRAM DEVELOPMENT

Since the mid-1960s, industry has used the concept of *structured program development*, described in detail in Chapter 8. Since that time the structured methodology has gained such acceptance that we introduce it immediately. Each of our sample programs uses the structured techniques described in Chapter 8. Let's summarize the process.

The first and most important step in programming is to define the problem. You may have a perfectly written program but it is useless if it doesn't solve the correct problem. As part of the problem definition, write down exactly what you want the program to do, including a description of the input to the program and the desired output. Until you can do this, you can't begin to write the program.

After defining the problem, the next step is to break the program that is supposed to solve it into logical sections, or *modules*. We can represent these modules graphically using a *structure chart*. An organization chart has many similarities to a structure chart: The top boxes in each represent the modules or people that control the program flow or activity in the boxes under them, and the bottom boxes represent the level at which most of the detail work is done.

The upper modules or "manager modules" of a structure chart direct processing to the proper place at the proper time. The worker modules each perform one simple task.

A program is much easier to write, test, and modify if we break each of the top modules into smaller and smaller modules, much as we would write an outline. The process is called *top-down programming*. For example, if we must calculate pay, we might create submodules to compute regular pay, overtime pay, and deductions.

As we break the problem into submodules, we will get to a point where the module can no longer be decomposed. At this stage we will code the module using *pseudocode*, a human language-like programmer's shorthand that can outline the steps that the module must perform. Pseudocode is BASIC without commas or exact syntax; indeed, the actual translation to BASIC code is quite simple.

Pseudocode is useful both for program design and for program documentation. As you recall from Chapter 8 of this text, another aid to program documentation and design is the *flowchart*. Take a moment to review the symbols and control structures used in flowcharting (found in Chapter 8). Flowcharting provides a highly visual and easily understood way of representing the program's flow of logic.

Once the program is defined and designed, we encode (or code) it in a programming language, again using structured techniques. We have described the logic of each worker module using pseudocode and/or a flowchart. We have recognized that the manager module or modules direct the order in which the worker modules are called on to perform their tasks. At this point, the translation to BASIC is straightforward.

Each worker module becomes what BASIC calls a *subroutine*. Within the subroutines are lines of BASIC code that may be almost line-by-line translations from pseudocode.

The main manager module (at the top of the structure chart) becomes the driver module. In most programs that you write at this stage of your knowledge, the driver module calls subroutines (worker modules) directly, in proper sequence, to perform their tasks. Later we will introduce "middle management"; that is, subroutines called by the driver module that in turn call lower-level subroutines to perform the lowest level tasks.

As an example, see Figure 8.16, reproduced here as Figure 1. In BASIC terms, the Payroll Process module becomes the driver module of the BASIC program. It calls the Read Input subroutine (a middle manager), which in turn calls two more subroutines (worker modules): Read Employee Master Record and Read Individual Time Card. As you can see from the Calculate Pay part of the structure chart, there can be more than one level of middle management! For example, once all this is translated to BASIC, the driver module (Payroll Process) would at the correct time call the subroutine Calculate Pay, which at the correct time would call the subroutine Calculate Gross Pay, which at the right time would (finally!) call the subroutine Calculate Regular Pay.

We will explore these concepts in depth throughout this appendix. At first, modular programming may seem cumbersome to you, especially for simpler programs. Why use a subroutine, some would ask, when you can just write fewer instructions "in line"? The reasons become clear when the programs become lengthy and when each subroutine consists of many lines of code. The modular approach allows the programmer to write in a logical fashion, coding the general outline first and then coding each section separately. In the past, programmers would be almost finished writing a program only to discover a major flaw in their logic, which often required rewriting nearly the entire program. With modular programming the basic logic is written and checked first. Because each set of steps is written as a separate module, changes and corrections made to that section don't require changes to other modules. For these reasons, most companies have standardized on structured program development for all their computer tasks.

TEST YOUR LEARNING

1. Define:
   a. Module.
   b. Pseudocode.
   c. Structure chart.
   d. Top-down programming.

GETTING STARTED IN BASIC

Enough philosophy for now! Let's find out how BASIC works. The best way to learn is to do, and you will learn much quicker if you dare to make mistakes. Don't worry about breaking the computer by mistyping something. The computer can take care of itself. If you have questions about how BASIC will respond to a particular instruction, try it and see.

FIGURE 1 Structure chart for a top-down design.

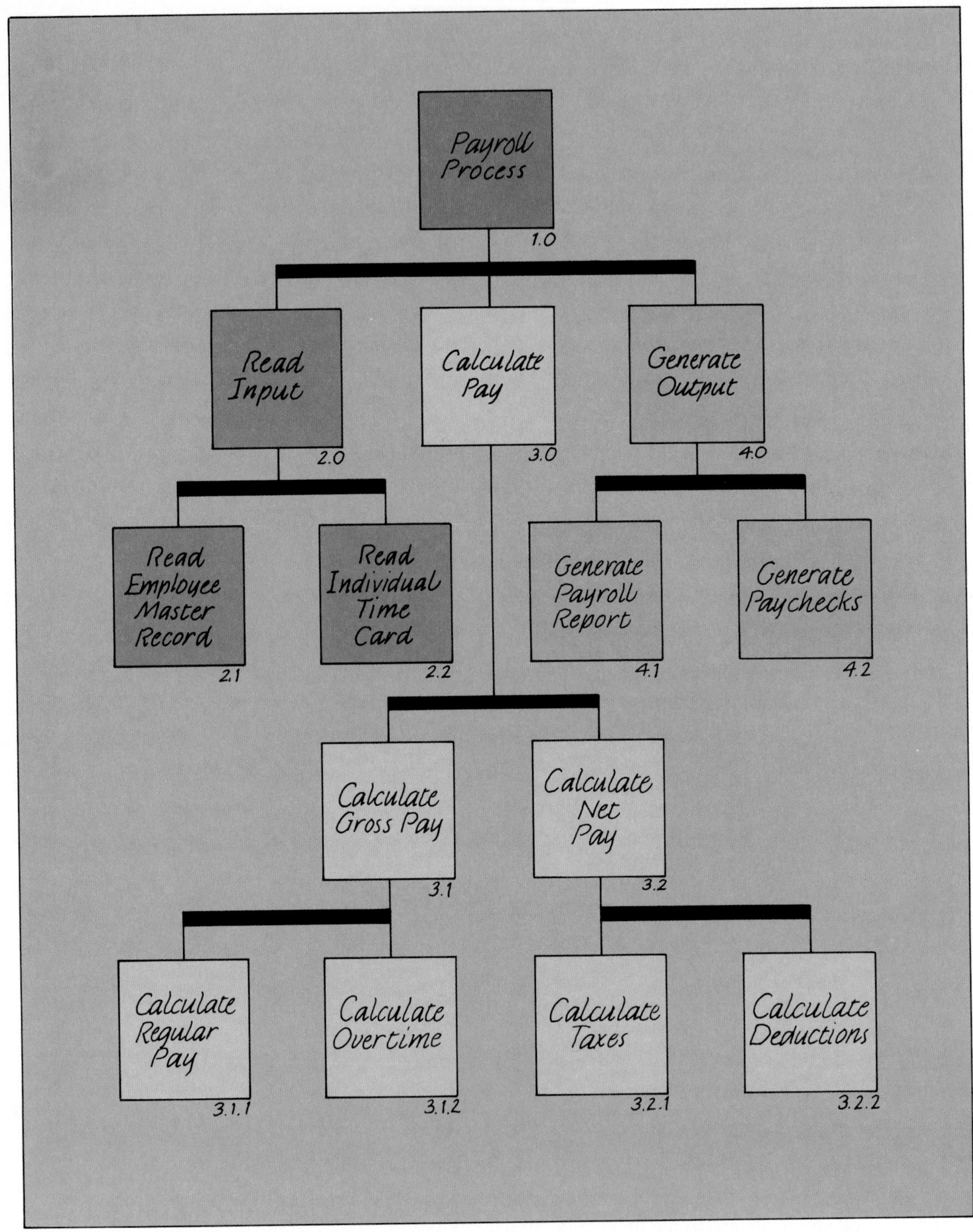

Each instruction has a particular format, or syntax. If you do not follow the correct syntax, BASIC will usually display an error message. You can then reenter the instruction correctly.

First Things First

You'll need to ask your instructor how to access the particular dialect of BASIC at your location. You need to know *both* how to get into BASIC and how to get out. Once you are in (and once you have learned some BASIC) you may begin to type.

Pressing Return

After you type a line, the computer will wait for you to type a signal that you are finished with the line. You give this signal by tapping the Return (or Enter) key. This key is usually a large one located to the right of the alphabetic keyboard. It is similar in purpose and in placement to the carriage return key on a typewriter. (See Figure 1 in the Introduction to Part V for a description of the keyboard.)

The Cursor

As you type, you'll notice a blinking light on the screen that indicates where the next character will appear. This is the *cursor*. When you press Return, the cursor moves to the beginning of the next line. The cursor always lets you know where you are on the screen.

A Simple Example

Let's try using BASIC as a calculator. We will do this by using the PRINT statement. Note: In this and following examples, we will underline everything that you type in and not underline what BASIC displays in reply.

```
PRINT 3 Return
3
```

We typed PRINT followed by a space, the digit 3, and pressed Return. BASIC responded by displaying the digit 3.

```
PRINT 2 + 2 Return
 4
```

We typed PRINT followed by a space and the numeric expression 2 + 2. BASIC evaluated the expression and displayed the result.

Here is another example:

```
PRINT 3, 2 + 2 Return
 3             4
```

Not so hard, is it? But what is it that we are doing? By typing `PRINT 3` we are issuing a command to a program called a BASIC Interpreter. When we tap Return, we tell the BASIC Interpreter (BASIC, for short) to check our command for errors and, if none are found, translate the command into machine language and execute. All that happens at great speed! Let's try a few more examples.

COMMAS AND SEMICOLONS

We can make BASIC type two values on one line by placing a comma between calculations.

```
PRINT 1,2,3,4,5 Return
 1             2             3             4             5
PRINT 1,    2,    3,     4,      5 Return
 1             2             3             4             5
```

Note what happened: BASIC divided the display line into *print zones*. These print zones are commonly spaced 14 columns apart, creating five print zones on an 80-column screen. (The exact number will depend on the dialect.) The comma between the values causes BASIC to skip to the next print zone for each value. By using commas, we can print output in neat columns. The extra spaces between values on the PRINT line, as in the second example, do not affect the spacing of the output.

Numeric values are displayed with a minus sign in front if the value is negative and a space in front if the value is positive. In most dialects they are also followed by a space.

If you want to print values next to one another, you use the semicolon, which suppresses movement to the next print zone. Here is an example:

```
PRINT 1;-2;3 + 3 Return
 1 -2  6
```

Using the semicolon, results are printed next to one another, with the space for the sign in front and a space after.

The comma and the semicolon are used as *delimiters* to separate values. Because of this, no commas should be placed in values over 999. To print 12,345 we must type `PRINT 12345`. If we write `PRINT 12,345`, Electra BASIC will interpret it as the two numbers 12 and 345.

USING THE PRINTER

In our initial discussions we will be printing to the screen; however, the same information can be printed on the printer if your system has one. In most systems, this is done with the LPRINT statement. LPRINT uses the same syntax as PRINT. However, LPRINT directs output to the printer instead of the screen. On some systems, simultaneously pressing the Ctrl and PrtSc keys or the Ctrl and P keys will cause all output that is sent to the screen to be sent to the printer as well. This acts as a toggle; that is, the first Ctrl and PrtSc (for example) will turn *on* the connection between the computer and the printer. The next Ctrl and PrtSc will turn it *off*. Because dialects vary so widely, we will not describe LPRINT in detail.

TEST YOUR LEARNING

1. How do commas and semicolons affect the PRINT command?
2. What will be printed by each of these statements? Try to predict what will happen, then try it on your computer.
   a. `PRINT 1, 2, 3, 1 + 2 + 3`
   b. `PRINT 1,500; 2,567`
   c. `PRINT 1,234,500`
   d. `PRINT 1 2 3`
3. Write a statement to print the following:
   a. The sum of 400 plus 35.
   b. The number 5321.
4. Write a statement that will print the values 3,567,16.2, and −3 in separate print zones. Then write a statement to print the values next to each other.

CONSTANTS AND VARIABLES

CONSTANTS

In the preceding PRINT examples, we used numbers and numbers added to one another. Because the values of numbers do not change, they are called *constants*. All *numeric constants*, such as those displayed in the examples above, consist entirely of numbers. Other examples of numeric constants are as follows:

```
5   3.1416   -739.2   276387
```

Constants consisting of characters (such as letters, punctuation, and other special characters) may be printed by placing quotes around the constant. Consider the following example:

```
PRINT "Hi, I am a string constant!" Return
Hi, I am a string constant!
```

```
PRINT "The interest rate is 5%" Return
The interest rate is 5%
```

Constants of alphanumeric characters (letters or numbers) are called *string constants* or just *strings*. They are often used to prepare report headings and titles and to print names and addresses. In contrast to numeric constants, string constants print without leading or trailing spaces. All characters within the quotes, including spaces, print exactly as they appear. The quotes themselves do not print; they just define the beginning and ending of the string for BASIC.

As with numeric constants, more than one string constant may be printed on the same line. The constants may be separated by commas to cause printing in the next print zone or by semicolons to cause printing in the next available position. In fact, both numeric and string constants may be printed on the same line.

```
PRINT "The sum of 4 and 7 is"; 4 + 7 Return
The sum of 4 and 7 is 11
```

TEST YOUR LEARNING

1. What are constants?
2. What is a string constant?
3. What is a numeric constant?
4. Write a statement that will print your last name, age, and birth date on one line with each item in separate print zones.
5. Write a statement to print the name of your city, your state, and your ZIP code. Use a separate constant for each. Separate the constants with semicolons.

ARITHMETIC EXPRESSIONS

So far we have used only addition in arithmetic expressions. As in arithmetic, BASIC uses the plus sign (+) to represent addition and the minus sign (−) to represent subtraction. However, multiplication is represented by the asterisk (*) and division by the forward slash (/). Be sure not to use the letter "x" when you want to multiply two numbers. BASIC will interpret "x" as a letter and not the multiply operator. To show exponentiation, some versions of BASIC use the up caret (^) while others use the up arrow (↑). These symbols represent the *arithmetic operators*. Here are some examples of printing *arithmetic expressions:*

Statement	Meaning	Result
`PRINT 5 + 2 - 3`	5 plus 2 minus 3	`4`
`PRINT 12.2 * 6`	12.2 times 6	`73.2`
`PRINT 150 / 12`	150 divided by 12	`12.5`
`PRINT 25^3`	25 raised to the third power	`15625`

ORDER OF PRECEDENCE

What is the value of the numeric expression 1 + 2/3*4? Depending on whether we add, divide, or multiply first, we can arrive at different answers. BASIC examines each expression to see what operators are used in it. The order that BASIC uses in solving numeric expressions is called the *order of precedence*. As shown in Table 1, BASIC performs exponentiation first. Next it performs all the multiplication and division. Finally it performs addition and subtraction. At each level BASIC performs the operations moving from left to the right.

PARENTHESES

The order of precedence may not reflect how we want the expression to be evaluated. As in algebra, we can insert parentheses to tell BASIC to solve the enclosed expression first. When solving for the value of an expression that contains parentheses, BASIC looks first at the expression within parentheses and evaluates it as any other numeric expression, following the order of precedence for operators. Then it evaluates the remainder of the expression outside the parentheses. As in algebra, sets of parentheses may be placed within other sets. (Be sure you type the ordinary parentheses symbols. The other special bracket symbols—[ ] or { }—are not valid here.)

Parentheses may also be used to make an expression clear and understandable to users even though BASIC does not require them.

Here are some examples of printing expressions with and without parentheses:

Statement	Order of Evaluation	Result
`PRINT 1 + 2 * 3`	1 + 6	7
`PRINT 2 * 3 + 4 * 5`	6 + 20	26
`PRINT 2 * (3 + 4) * 5`	2 * 7 * 5	70
`PRINT 4 + 7 * (6 - 4) / (2 + 5)`	4 + 7 * 2 / 7 = 4 + 2	6

TEST YOUR LEARNING

1. How does BASIC decide which arithmetic operations to perform first?
2. How can you force BASIC to change this order?
3. What value will be printed by each of these statements? Type each in your system to check your answer.
   a. `PRINT 10 + 4 / 2 - 3`
   b. `PRINT 1 + 2 + 3 + 4 * 5`
   c. `PRINT 5 + 6 * 8 / 4`
   d. `PRINT 4 * 4 - 9 / 3`
4. Write a line in BASIC to perform the following calculation and print the result.
   a. `3(4) + 2(12 + 3(5))`
   b. `5(7 - 10)/5`
5. A painter needs to estimate how much paint will be needed to cover an area of 3,600 square feet. One gallon of paint covers 300 square feet.
   a. Write a program to calculate and display the number of gallons needed.
   b. Paint costs $12 per gallon. Add a line to the program that will print the cost.

TABLE 1

Order of Precedence for Arithmetic Operators

Operator	Meaning	Example
^	Exponentiation	3 ^ 2 = 9
* /	Multiplication and division	3 * 2 = 6 6 / 2 = 3
+ –	Addition and subtraction	3 + 2 = 5 3 - 2 = 1

Expressions in parentheses are evaluated first.

When ties in precedence occur, expressions are evaluated from left to right.

LET AND VARIABLES

We have learned how to do simple computations; however, sometimes we need to store or save values. BASIC allows us to store values in *variables* by using the LET statement. First, we must give the variable a name. Then we specify the value to be stored in the variable. The variable name is placed to the left of an equal sign and the value assigned to it is placed to the right. The following is an example of using the *numeric variable* B4:

```
LET B4 = 45 Return
PRINT B4 Return
45
```

After BASIC executes the above LET statement, B4 will have the value of 45. The PRINT statement displays this value.

BASIC knows that B4 is a variable name and not a constant because it begins with a letter (so it can't be a numeric constant), and it doesn't have quotes around it (so it can't be a string constant).

Most BASIC dialects permit the programmer to omit the command LET. Thus, the following two lines are equivalent in most BASICs:

```
LET B4 = 45 Return
B4 = 45 Return
```

VARIABLE NAME VERSUS VARIABLE VALUE

A variable is like a mailbox—it displays a name, such as A or C7, and has mail (values) inside, such as 12 or −200.3. As with a mailbox, the contents of a variable can change. If we type `LET B4 = 57`, the value of B4 will be changed from 45 to 57 (see Figure 2). We can also place the results of an arithmetic expression in a variable.

```
LET B4 = (10 + 5) / 3 Return
PRINT B4 Return
5
```

GOOD VARIABLE NAMES

The rules for naming variables vary from dialect to dialect; however, all dialects of BASIC require that variable names begin with a letter. Some dialects are limited to two-character names, a letter and (optionally) one digit. Upper- and lowercase letters are considered the same for variables.

With two-letter variable names, it is difficult to make variable names that reflect the use of the variable. Other dialects of BASIC allow for long names that can better describe the variable. Examples of a long name are COST and DISCOUNT. Some dialects allow up to eight characters, some have a maximum of 40, and others allow over 200. Special characters such as periods or dashes may be used in some dialects as separators, as in the name `YEAR.TO.DATE.TOTAL`.

Warning: Although some dialects, such as Apple BASIC and early Radio Shack BASIC, allow the user to enter long variable names, they will recognize only the first two characters of the variable name. In these versions the names CUSTACT and CUSTBAL will be interpreted as the same variable because they both begin with CU.

When possible, *avoid short variable names or abbreviations*. Although they are clear to BASIC, short names confuse the people who work with the program. We will use descriptive names in all of our examples.

MISSPELLING VARIABLE NAMES

Misspelling is a problem with long variable names. Whenever BASIC encounters a numeric variable for the first time, it initializes the variable to zero. If you typed the following, BASIC would print 0:

```
LET COST = 10 Return
PRINT CSOT Return
```

To BASIC, `CSOT` is a new variable to which it assigns an initial value of zero. You must always verify that you have correctly spelled each variable name. BASIC won't say that you have made an error; it will just give you an erroneous result.

STRING VARIABLES AND DOLLAR SIGNS

BASIC also allows us to store names and other character data in variables. To differentiate these from numeric variables, BASIC requires that we name the variables that store strings of characters *(string variables)* with a dollar sign at the end of the name.

For example, to define CUSTNAME$ as a string variable, we can type the following:

```
LET CUSTNAME$ = "Margaret Johansen" Return
PRINT CUSTNAME$ Return
Margaret Johansen
```

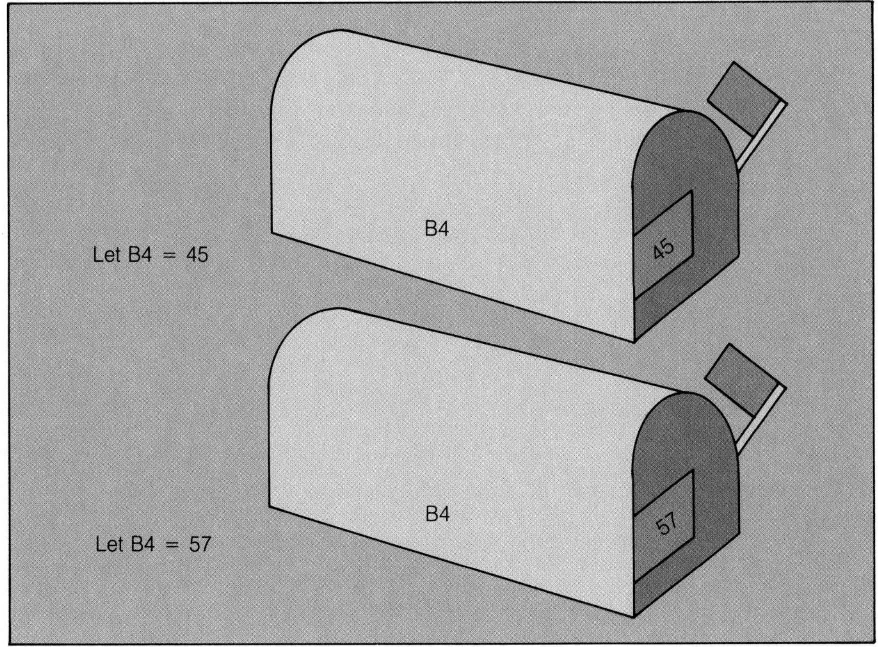

FIGURE 2

Variable name and contents.

RESERVED WORDS

Variables can't have the same names as ***reserved words***, such as the commands PRINT and LIST, which have special meaning to BASIC. The list of reserved words varies from system to system; the Quick Reference at the end of this appendix lists those that we discuss. Check with your instructor for a complete list for your dialect.

FORMATTED OUTPUT

In many cases we would want a number rounded to one or two decimal places. BASIC provides formatting statements to round, to place dollar signs in currency amounts, and to align numeric values on the decimal point. Because these statements vary widely from dialect to dialect, we will not cover them in this generic discussion of BASIC.

A related issue involves how some dialects of BASIC store the fractional parts of numbers. On some versions of BASIC you may get unexpected results from arithmetic operations. Consider the following:

```
PRINT 10 * .0715 Return
.7150001                ← this should be .715
```

This problem occurs because on some machines BASIC uses binary arithmetic, which provides no exact representation for .01. Formatted printing will usually help to solve this problem.

TEST YOUR LEARNING

1. What is a variable?
2. How does BASIC know whether a variable should store numeric or string data?
3. What are the restrictions for naming variables? (Check the rules for your dialect.)
4. Write statements to assign the following values to the variables listed below. If your system allows only two-character names for variables, use just the first two letters of the variables shown below (for example, use CO for COUNTER).

Value	Variable Name
45	COUNTER
34.57	P2
Gross Pay	MESSAGE$
Sacramento	CITY$

5. What is a reserved word? Why should you know the list of reserved words for your dialect?

PROGRAMS AND LINE NUMBERS

So far, as soon as we typed the line and pressed Return, BASIC executed the statement. If BASIC performed only one statement at a time, as in the examples shown so far, its use would be limited. Fortunately, BASIC does much more. We can tell it to follow a series of instructions. Just as a cook can follow a recipe step by step, BASIC can follow the instructions of a program step by step. But, what exactly is a *program?*

WORKSPACE AND NOTECARDS

Imagine that inside your computer's main memory is a workspace consisting of a set of notecards (see Figure 3). On each notecard is a BASIC statement that tells the computer what to do. Each notecard also has a number; the cards are kept in numeric order.

To write a program, we type a series of BASIC program lines. The program lines are like the numbered notecards in the preceding analogy; the computer's memory is the workspace. A program line is composed of a line number (such as 10 or 100 or 1000), a space, and a BASIC statement. The following is a program with the instructions shown in Figure 3.

```
100 PRINT "Student Name", "Score" Return
110 PRINT Return
120 PRINT "Adams, M.", 85 Return
130 PRINT "Jones, K.", 95 Return
140 PRINT "Mitchell, L.", 75 Return
```

This time when you press Return the statement is not executed immediately. The line number indicates to BASIC that the instruction is to be stored in the workspace as a line in a program.

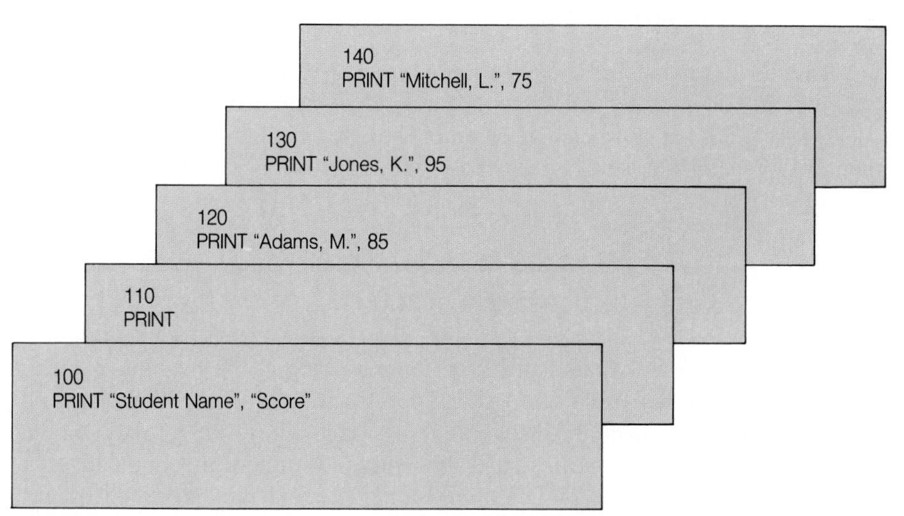

FIGURE 3

A program is like a set of notecards.

You will note that we have numbered the lines in increments of 10. Although you don't need to follow this practice, you'll find it helpful because it will allow you to insert other lines as you develop your program.

Enter this first program into BASIC. *Don't worry* if you make an error. Simply retype the line if you do.

BLANK LINES

A blank line improves readability in reports or screen displays. The PRINT statement used alone, as in Line 110 in our program, will cause a blank line to be printed when the program is run.

END

At the end of the program, we type the BASIC statement END. END tells BASIC to stop executing the program and return control to the user. Some dialects of BASIC require this statement as the last physical line of the program. For others, END may occur anywhere in the listing but should be the last statement executed by the program. For still other dialects, END is optional. We will add an END statement to our program.

```
999 END Return
```

RUN

Typing in all of these BASIC lines is like writing a recipe. Let's see how our recipe (program) "tastes."

Type RUN to instruct BASIC to execute all the lines of the program in its workspace.

```
RUN Return
Student Name Score

Adams, M.     85
Jones, K.     95
Mitchell, L. 75
```

After RUN was entered and Return pressed, BASIC began with the first line of the program and executed each one until the END statement was reached.

To see what happens, change some of the lines in the program by retyping them. RUN again. This kind of trial exercise is invaluable for learning any computer language.

STRUCTURING OUR FIRST PROGRAM

As you recall, we emphasized structured programming at the beginning of this appendix. It is clear that this first program is not structured. For one thing, it has no "manager" or driver module. The whole thing is a low-level worker module! To structure our first program we need to do two things: document and modularize. In this section we will describe how you should document each program. We'll discuss some commands that allow you to view, modify, and make permanent copies of your program. Then we will show you BASIC commands used to create structured programs.

PROGRAM DOCUMENTATION AND REM

If we had followed the entire structured methodology, we would have produced documentation such as a structure chart, pseudocode, and a flow chart. ("For this short program?" you ask. "Ridiculous!" Hang on! We'll get to the longer programs. We've got to walk before we run!) So here we would be with all sorts of preliminary documentation, but with nothing to indicate what in the world this program is for, who wrote it, or when. Programs are written by and for people. Well-written programs are easy to understand. They contain notes to the reader called *documentation* (see Chapters 8 and 10) that tell what the programs do and provide other important information. Business programs tend to be used for 10 years or more. During this time many programmers will be called on to change the program to meet current business needs. Documentation helps these programmers modify existing programs quickly and correctly. Let's look at some types of documentation.

PROGRAM IDENTIFICATION BLOCK

At the very least, every program should contain information that identifies it by giving its name, who wrote it, the date it was written, and a short statement about what the program does. (Your instructor may require more information.) The BASIC statement that allows for making remarks in a program is REM. The REM statement is not executed by BASIC; therefore, we can put any characters or message after REM that we wish. These comments will appear when the program is listed and serve as an explanation to the reader.

The following is a sample program identification block. We use asterisks to make it stand out to the reader of the program.

```
10 REM ************************************ Return
20 REM      Program Name:  SCORES Return
30 REM         Written by EB Cohen Return
40 REM         December 25, 1992 Return
50 REM Return
60 REM     This program prints student scores Return
70 REM          and the average score Return
80 REM ************************************ Return
```

It may seem a waste of line numbers to increment by 10 here. Again, though, we may wish to insert more information later.

DATA DICTIONARY

To make our program usable by others, we also need to tell the reader what the variable names stand for. Variable names like TOT.SCORE and AVG.SCORE may seem self-evident; but if our program is of any length at all, readers will need a specific place in the program listing to help remind them of a variable's meaning. The list of variable names and their meanings is called a *data dictionary*.

Here, then, is the result of our first step of structuring the program. The following program contains a program identification block and a data dictionary. We've added a few new lines as well. In Line 240, the variable TOT.SCORE stores the total of all the scores. In Line 250, AVG.SCORE stores the average.

```
10 REM **********************************
20 REM     Program Name:  SCORES
30 REM        Written by EB Cohen
40 REM        December 25, 1992
50 REM
60 REM    This program prints student scores
70 REM         and the average score
80 REM **********************************
90 REM *          DATA DICTIONARY        *
100 REM
110 REM TOT.SCORE = total score
120 REM AVG.SCORE = average score
130 REM **********************************
140 REM
150 PRINT "Student Name", "Score"
160 PRINT
170 PRINT "Adams, M.", 85
180 PRINT "Bradly, J.", 72
190 PRINT "Duncan, A.", 86
200 PRINT "Franklin, B.", 73
210 PRINT "Jones, K.", 95
220 PRINT "Lopez, M.", 88
230 PRINT "Thompson, F.", 70
240 LET TOT.SCORE = 85 + 72 + 86 + 73 + 95 + 88 + 70
250 LET AVG.SCORE = TOT.SCORE / 7
260 PRINT
270 PRINT "Average Score", AVG.SCORE
280 END
```

Type this in and RUN it. (*Note:* We will now begin to leave out the underlines and RETURNS in longer programs.) Your output should look something like this:

```
Student Name  Score

Adams, M.     85
Bradly, J.    72
Duncan, A.    86
Franklin, B.  73
Jones, K.     95
Lopez, M.     88
Thompson, F.  70

Average Score 81.28571
```

You may want to read on for a few pages before you exit BASIC. We will teach you commands that will allow you to save this program for future use.

MULTISTATEMENT LINE

Often we will want a remark on the same line as another statement to explain its meaning. We can do this by placing a colon (or a backslash, depending on the dialect) between the statements.

```
190 LET AVG.SCORE = TOT.SCORE / 7  :REM Calculate average score
```

Although BASIC allows other statements to be placed on the same line, for ease of reading and understanding we recommend doing so only with a REM statement. Because BASIC ignores all characters after REM, you can't add another statement after it.

Some dialects allow REM to be replaced by an apostrophe (') or exclamation point (!).

WRAP-AROUND

As you write programs, you may find that a line of code is greater than 80 characters. For example, we could have written the line to calculate the average score as follows:

```
240 LET AVG.SCORE = (85 + 72 + 86 + 73 + 95 + 88 + 70) / 7   :REM
Calculate average score
```

As we type the 80th character of this line we reach the end of the screen. No problem. As we continue typing, the 81st character appears in the first column of the next row on the screen. This feature is called *wrap-around*. To BASIC, the program line is not ended until the Return key is pressed. Some dialects have a maximum line length, others do not. A common maximum line length is 254 characters, just over 3 lines on an 80-column terminal.

TEST YOUR LEARNING

1. What is documentation?
2. Why is documentation important?
3. How do you get a line to hold more than a single statement?
4. What happens when a line is greater than 80 characters? What is the maximum line length for your dialect of BASIC?
5. A house measures 75 feet by 50 feet and costs $45 per square foot to build. Write a program that calculates and prints the total number of square feet and then calculates and prints the total cost.
6. Your gross pay is $300.00, from which the following is withheld:

   Social security tax, which is .0715 of the gross.
   Federal withholding tax, which is $45.00.
   Disability insurance, which is .009 of the gross.

   The resulting net pay is $230.85. Write a program that will calculate and print the amount of each tax, then calculate and print net pay.

SOME CRUCIAL COMMANDS

You certainly don't want to retype a program every time you use it! In addition, you may want to view part or all of the program on the screen. The following commands instruct BASIC to do something with the program. Therefore they are not part of the program itself and are not preceded by line numbers.

LIST

LIST instructs BASIC to show us the program that is currently in the workspace. This is what happens when we type LIST and press Return:

```
LIST Return
10 REM **********************************
20 REM     Program Name:  SCORES
30 REM        Written by EB Cohen
40 REM        December 25, 1992
50 REM
60 REM    This program prints student scores
70 REM         and the average score
80 REM **********************************
90 REM *         DATA DICTIONARY        *
100 REM
110 REM TOT.SCORE = total score
120 REM AVG.SCORE = average score
130 REM **********************************
140 REM
150 PRINT "Student Name", "Score"
160 PRINT
170 PRINT "Adams, M.", 85
180 PRINT "Bradly, J.", 72
190 PRINT "Duncan, A.", 86
200 PRINT "Franklin, B.", 73
210 PRINT "Jones, K.", 95
220 PRINT "Lopez, M.", 88
230 PRINT "Thompson, F.", 70
240 LET TOT.SCORE = 85 + 72 + 86 + 73 + 95 + 88 + 70
250 LET AVG.SCORE = TOT.SCORE / 7
260 PRINT
270 PRINT "Average Score", AVG.SCORE
280 END
```

Depending on the size of your screen, the program probably would not all fit. To see selected lines we use a form of LIST. The following statement will list just lines 170 through 190.

```
LIST 170-190 Return
170 PRINT "Adams, M.", 85
180 PRINT "Bradly, J.", 72
190 PRINT "Duncan, A.", 86
```

If you want a printed copy of your program, you can list your program on the printer. Again, each system varies on how to do this. One common way is to use the command LLIST in place of LIST. Check with your instructor regarding the system you are using.

SAVE

When you end your session or turn the computer off, the workspace is cleared, erasing the program (see Figure 4). This sample program is only a few lines long and so would not take too long to retype. However, soon our programs will be much longer and we would not want to retype them each time we want to use them.

Luckily, BASIC provides us with a way to save our program onto permanent storage. To do so, we must first assign a name to the program. The rules for program names vary with each dialect. In our examples, we will use filenames of eight or fewer characters. Let's call our program SCORES and make a copy with the following command:

`SAVE "SCORES"` Return

Some dialects require quotes around the name of the file; others do not.

If you turn your computer off now, the program will disappear from memory. But the copy we saved will remain on the disk (or tape). Note that there is no line number used with SAVE. It is a command that we want BASIC to execute immediately, not part of a program.

LOAD

When we wish to copy our program back into our workspace, we can type the following:

`LOAD "SCORES"` Return

A copy of the program that we saved with the name SCORES is now in the workspace. Again, some dialects require the quotes, others do not. Also, some dialects use the word OLD instead of LOAD:

`OLD SCORES` Return

Some computers may need you to specify the disk drive on which the program is to be saved. One common way to identify disk drives is to give them names such as A, B, or C. On such a system, you may be required to place your personal diskette in the drive named B. To save your file to drive B you will need to prefix the filename with B:. Here is an example that saves the file SCORES on drive B.

`SAVE "B:SCORES"` Return

When you wish to retrieve the program, use the following command:

`LOAD "B:SCORES"` Return

If you were to forget to include the B:, the system may look on the wrong drive and report:

```
File not found.
```

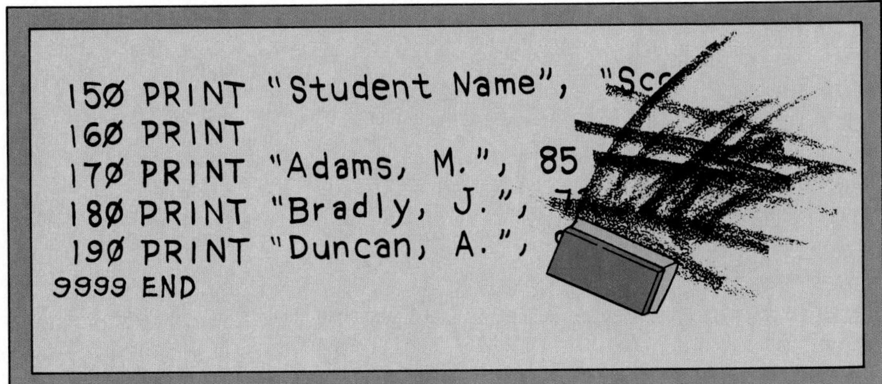

FIGURE 4

The workspace gets erased.

NEW

Let's try typing and running a small sample program segment:

```
10 PRINT "This is a new program." Return
20 PRINT Return
280 END Return
RUN Return
This is a new program.

Student Name  Score
Adams, M.     85
Bradly, J.    72
Duncan, A.    86
Franklin, B.  73
Jones, K.     95
Lopez, M.     88
Thompson, F.  70
Average Score 81.28571
```

What happened? Why did the messages from the previous program appear? Type LIST to find out what program is currently in memory.

```
LIST Return
10 PRINT "This is a new program."
20 PRINT
30 REM          Written by EB Cohen
40 REM          December 25, 1992
50 REM
60 REM      This program prints student scores
70 REM           and the average score
80 REM ***********************************
90 REM *          DATA DICTIONARY        *
100 REM
110 REM TOT.SCORE = total score
120 REM AVG.SCORE = average score
130 REM ***********************************
140 REM
150 PRINT "Student Name", "Score"
160 PRINT
170 PRINT "Adams, M.", 85
180 PRINT "Bradly, J.", 72
190 PRINT "Duncan, A.", 86
200 PRINT "Franklin, B.", 73
210 PRINT "Jones, K.", 95
220 PRINT "Lopez, M.", 88
230 PRINT "Thompson, F.", 70
240 LET TOT.SCORE = 85 + 72 + 86 + 73 + 95 + 88 + 70
250 LET AVG.SCORE = TOT.SCORE / 7
260 PRINT
270 PRINT "Average Score", AVG.SCORE
280 END
```

Because our old program is still in the workspace, the new lines we typed were inserted into the existing program. To get a new clean workspace we must type the BASIC command NEW (without line number).

```
NEW Return
LIST Return
```

Nothing is listed, showing that now we have a new, clean workspace with all old program lines removed. We can now begin to enter a new program.

Correcting Lines

So far, if we are good typists we have typed in all the lines without error. Being human, we won't be able to keep this up for long; luckily, BASIC provides ways for us to correct mistakes.

If we discover an error before we press Return, we can backspace, deleting the error, and retype the remainder of the line. However, if we discover the error only after we have pressed Return, this method won't work. For example, suppose that the score for Jones should be 98, not 95, and we don't realize it until later. To correct the error, we must first load the program back into the workspace.

```
LOAD "SCORES" Return
```

To correct the line we retype it:

```
210 PRINT "Jones, K.", 98 Return
```

When we now list the program we see that the retyped line replaces the former line with that same number:

```
LIST 170-230 Return
170 PRINT "Adams, M.", 85
180 PRINT "Bradly, J.", 72
190 PRINT "Duncan, A.", 86
200 PRINT "Franklin, B.", 73
210 PRINT "Jones, K.", 98
220 PRINT "Lopez, M.", 88
230 PRINT "Thompson, F.", 70
```

At this point the correction has been made only to the copy of the program that is in the workspace. If we wish to correct the permanent copy also, we must save the corrected version.

```
SAVE "SCORES" Return
```

The program currently in the workspace replaces the former program that we stored with the name SCORES.

An alternative possibility is to save similar copies of our programs for use in slightly different situations. In that case we would type:

```
SAVE "SCORES2" Return
```

We now have two different programs saved on disk or tape.

ADDING LINES

At this point we wish to add more students to our program. We can add lines by simply typing more statements and assigning line numbers that will place them in the proper sequence.

```
35 REM          SSN 111-11-1111
275 PRINT "That's all folks!"
```

Let's LIST the program again. Note that BASIC inserted the new lines in the proper sequence.

<u>LIST</u> <u>Return</u>

```
10 REM ************************************
20 REM      Program Name:   SCORES
30 REM          Written by EB Cohen
35 REM          SN 111-11-1111
40 REM          December 25, 1992
50 REM
60 REM     This program prints student scores
70 REM          and the average score
80 REM ************************************
90 REM *          DATA DICTIONARY          *
100 REM
110 REM TOT.SCORE = total score
120 REM AVG.SCORE = average score
130 REM ************************************
140 REM
150 PRINT "Student Name", "Score"
160 PRINT
170 PRINT "Adams, M.", 85
180 PRINT "Bradly, J.", 72
190 PRINT "Duncan, A.", 86
200 PRINT "Franklin, B.", 73
210 PRINT "Jones, K.", 98
220 PRINT "Lopez, M.", 88
230 PRINT "Thompson, F.", 70
240 LET TOT.SCORE = 85 + 72 + 86 + 73 + 98 + 88 + 70
250 LET AVG.SCORE = TOT.SCORE / 7
260 PRINT
270 PRINT "Average Score", AVG.SCORE
275 PRINT "That's all Folks!"
280 END
```

REMOVING LINES

BASIC's DELETE command will delete one or more lines.

`DELETE 10`	will delete just Line 10.
`DELETE 10-100`	will delete all lines from Line 10 to and including Line 100.
`DELETE 10-`	will delete all lines from Line 10 to the end of the file.
`DELETE -10`	will delete all lines from the start of the file up to and including Line 10.

To delete Line 275 that we have added to our demonstration program type, we key:

DELETE 275 Return

When we LIST the program we will see that Line 275 is erased.

LIST 240-280 Return

```
240 LET TOT.SCORE = 85 + 72 + 88 + 73 + 98 + 88 + 70
250 LET AVG.SCORE = TOT.SCORE / 7
260 PRINT
270 PRINT "Average Score", AVG.SCORE
280 END
```

Be careful! In some dialects DELETE typed by itself will delete all the program lines from the workspace!

An alternate way to delete one line is to type just the line number. Typing 140 Return has the same result as DELETE 140 Return.

RENUM

Because we have been adding and deleting lines, the line numbers are no longer in increments of 10. BASIC provides the RENUM command to renumber the lines. There is no common syntax for this command, so you will have to check with your instructor about the options available on your computer.

TEST YOUR LEARNING

1. What is a workspace?
2. What happens if you forget to SAVE your file?
3. What happens if you forget to type NEW?
4. How do you correct a BASIC line?
5. How do you delete a BASIC line?
6. What does RENUM do?
7. Write a program to print a list of the following monthly household expenses.

```
Rent    450
Car     175.85
Food    359
Other   75
```

   a. Save the program using the name EXPENSE.
   b. Load the program and run it again.
8. Make the following changes to the program EXPENSE that you wrote in Exercise 7. Change the car payment to 155.35. Add a new expense category—Pets, 35—and print it after Food. Run the program to test the changes.

MODULARIZATION

In our earlier discussion of structured programming we described the techniques of dividing modules into managers and workers. Three BASIC statements allow us to transform our modules into a driver module and subroutines: STOP, GOSUB, and

RETURN. In this section we will complete the transformation of our sample program into a structured format. In successive sections we will demonstrate further BASIC commands with structured programs.

GOSUB . . . RETURN

In general, the GOSUB statement allows us to branch to another location in the program, perform any number of processing steps until we reach the RETURN statement, and resume processing where we left off. In structured programming this is used to branch out of the driver routine to a subroutine and back.

For example, let's say we have a driver module and three worker modules. To transform the workers into subroutines called from the driver routine, we write the subroutines below the driver module. Here is an otherwise useless program for the purpose of illustration. (We've left out the beginning documentation for brevity.)

```
100 REM Here is the Driver Module
110 GOSUB 1000  :REM Out to the First Subroutine
120 GOSUB 2000  :REM Out to the Second Subroutine
130 GOSUB 3000  :REM Out to the Third Subroutine
140 PRINT "All done."
150 END
1000 REM ***********************************
1010 REM Here's the first subroutine.
1020 PRINT "Here's the first subroutine."
1030 RETURN
2000 REM ***********************************
2010 REM Here's the second subroutine.
2020 PRINT "Here's the second subroutine."
2030 RETURN
3000 REM ***********************************
3010 REM Here's the third subroutine.
3020 PRINT "Here's the third subroutine."
3030 RETURN
```

Let's discuss this, point by point.

If we RUN this program we get the following results.

```
RUN Return
Here's the first subroutine.
Here's the second subroutine.
Here's the third subroutine.
All done.
```

Here is the order in which the lines were executed:

```
100, 110, 1000, 1010, 1020, 1030, 120, 2000, 2010, 2020,
2030, 130, 3000, 3010, 3020, 3030, 140, 150.
```

If the END statement were *not* in Line 150, BASIC would assume you wished to continue processing. BASIC would process Line 140 and then (assuming no Line 150) process 1000, 1010, 1020, and give an error on 1030. Most BASICs give an error that says something like "RETURN without GOSUB." This tells you that because of a logic error on your part, BASIC got into a subroutine by mistake. Careful attention will help you avoid this error.

Note that we addded a large number of REM statements. As we have said, structured programming requires sufficient documentation for the program reader to follow your logic. The conventions we use are: (1) place documentation at the beginning of each routine (driver or subroutine) to describe its purpose; (2) briefly document the purpose for each GOSUB.

STOP

Note the placement of the END statement in the example we have just shown. Line 150 is the last line that the program is to *execute;* therefore, we placed the END statement here to signal that processing is completed and control is to be returned to the user. Some dialects require that END be the last ***physical*** line in the program. What do we do when we actually want processing to stop at Line 150? One solution uses the STOP statement. STOP is similar to END in that it halts processing and returns control to the user; differences between the two statements vary from dialect to dialect. STOP usually displays a message indicating the line at which processing was halted, whereas END does not. The other differences are not significant to our discussion at this point.

To satisfy the requirement of some dialects that END be the last physical statement, we could modify the program, changing Line 150 to read `150 STOP`, and add the line `9000 END`.

PROGRAMMING WITH SUBROUTINES

To achieve desired modularity, we write all (or most) processing instructions in subroutines. Three guidelines for writing subroutines are contained in what is known as the "*One rule,*" which has three parts:

- A *subroutine does but one task.* If we have two tasks to do, we write two subroutines.
- A *subroutine has only one entrance.* A subroutine should be entered only through its first line—the line number indicated by the GOSUB that directed processing to this subroutine. Although a number of different GOSUBs may direct control to the same subroutine, none should branch to a line in the middle of the subroutine.
- A *subroutine has only one exit.* This is the line with RETURN at the end of the subroutine. There should be only one RETURN within the subroutine.

Unfortunately, BASIC allows us to break this rule without warning us of the consequences. If we do break the "One rule," our program will not be truly structured; in addition, it will be prone to error and difficult to follow or modify.

Based on our discussions, we will change the example program we've been using into a fully structured program.

```
10 REM ***********************************
20 REM      Program Name:   SCORES
30 REM         Written by EB Cohen
40 REM         December 25, 1992
50 REM
60 REM     This program prints student scores
70 REM          and the average score
80 REM ***********************************
90 REM *           DATA DICTIONARY          *
100 REM
```

```
110 REM TOT.SCORE = total score
120 REM AVG.SCORE = average score
130 REM **********************************
140 REM
150 REM Driver Module
160 GOSUB 1000  : REM Initialize Variables
170 GOSUB 2000  : REM Print Report Header
180 GOSUB 3000  : REM Print Scores
190 GOSUB 4000  : REM Calculate Total and Average
200 GOSUB 5000  : REM Print Results
210 END
1000 REM **********************************
1010 REM Initialize Variables
1020 LET TOT.SCORE = 0
1030 LET AVG.SCORE = 0
1040 RETURN
2000 REM **********************************
2010 REM Print Report Header
2020 PRINT "Student Name", "Score"
2030 PRINT
2040 RETURN
3000 REM **********************************
3010 REM Print Scores
3020 PRINT "Adams, M.", 85
3030 PRINT "Bradly, J.", 72
3040 PRINT "Duncan, A.", 86
3050 PRINT "Franklin, B.", 73
3060 PRINT "Jones, K.", 98
3070 PRINT "Lopez, M.", 88
3080 PRINT "Thompson, F.", 70
3090 RETURN
4000 REM **********************************
4010 REM Calculate Total and Average
4020 LET TOT.SCORE = 85 + 72 + 86 + 73 + 98 + 88 + 70
4030 LET AVG.SCORE = TOT.SCORE / 7
4040 RETURN
5000 REM **********************************
5010 REM Print Results
5020 PRINT
5030 Print "Average Score", AVG.SCORE
5040 RETURN
```

In the name of structured programming we have turned about a 13-line program into a 51-line program that produces the same output! What's going on here? Remember our earlier discussions. Industry has determined that structured programs are much easier to understand (because of the documentation) and maintain (because of modularity). A very great number of hours have been saved for those who maintain industry's programs at a very small relative cost to those who develop them in a structured way. As a partial demonstration of this, glance at the REM statements associated with the driver module. You can quickly tell what the entire program is about without having to read the details in the subroutines.

One module bears further discussion: the subroutine that begins with Line 1020. It is common to initialize all variables in most programming languages. Most often, numerical variables are set to zero and string variables to blank (" "). Many BASIC dialects take care of this for you, but initialization is a good structured programming technique. Many times a variable will have another logical initial value. Imagine, for example, a variable to be used as a denominator, it must *never* have a value of zero and may logically be initialized to 1.

TEST YOUR LEARNING

1. What does GOSUB do? What other statement is associated with it and what does it do?
2. On your system, what are the differences between END and STOP?
3. What are the three parts to the "One rule"?
4. What is initialization? Why is it necessary?

DATA-ORIENTED COMMANDS

INPUT

Consider a simple program that calculates the markup rate for a given product.

```
NEW Return
10 REM ***********************************
20 REM      Program Name:   MARKUP
30 REM      Written by John Richards
40 REM      June 20, 1992
50 REM
60 REM   This program calculates markup rate for a
70 REM               given product.
80 REM ***********************************
90 REM *          DATA DICTIONARY          *
100 REM
110 REM Price = price of the product
120 REM Cost = Cost to company of the product
130 REM Markup = Markup rate
140 REM ***********************************
150 REM
160 REM Driver Module
170 GOSUB 1000   : REM Initialization
180 GOSUB 2000   : REM Assign Values
190 GOSUB 3000   : REM Figure Markup Rate
200 GOSUB 4000   : REM Print Markup Rate
210 END
1000 REM ***********************************
1010 REM Initialization
1020 LET PRICE = 0
```

```
1030 LET COST = 1   : REM Denominator in Formula
1040 LET MARKUP = 0
1050 RETURN
2000 REM **********************************
2010 REM Assign Values
2020 LET PRICE = 130
2030 LET COST = 100
2040 RETURN
3000 REM **********************************
3010 REM Figure Markup Rate
3020 LET MARKUP = (PRICE - COST) / COST
3030 RETURN
4000 REM **********************************
4010 REM Print Markup
4020 PRINT "Where price = ", PRICE
4030 PRINT "Where cost = ", COST
4040 PRINT "Markup = ", MARKUP
4050 RETURN
```

This program calculates the markup rate for only one value of PRICE and COST. We would like to use this program to compute markup for all sorts of products; do we need to revise our program for each item? No. The INPUT statement allows us to get the values of PRICE and COST from the user. Here's how INPUT works.

WITHOUT PROMPT

When BASIC executes the INPUT statement, it displays a question mark on the screen and waits for the user to enter something and press Return. We could change Line 2020 in the program to read:

```
2020 INPUT PRICE Return
```

Now RUN the program.

```
RUN Return
?
```

BASIC is executing Line 2020 and waiting for us to enter a value and press Return. It will then store the value in variable PRICE and proceed to the next line.

Type the amount 150 and press Return; the program will continue as before.

```
? 150 Return
Where price = 150
Where cost = 100
Markup = .5
```

Now we have the ability to enter any amount as the price. Try running the program and entering different values.

WITH PROMPT

The question mark is cryptic: How does the user know what the program is asking for? We could PRINT a message or *prompt* just before executing the INPUT statement.

```
2015 PRINT "What is the value for PRICE"; Return
2020 INPUT PRICE Return
```

When we run the program, the prompt `"What is the value for PRICE?"` will appear. The semicolon (;) at the end of the PRINT statement keeps the cursor from advancing to the next line.

```
RUN Return
What is the value for PRICE? 130 Return
Where price = 130
Where cost = 100
Markup = .3
```

Note that because the need for a prompt with INPUT is so common, almost all BASIC dialects allow the prompt message to be placed directly in the INPUT statement; therefore, we can replace Lines 2015 and 2020 with one line:

```
DELETE 2015 Return
2020 INPUT "What is the value for PRICE"; PRICE Return
```

The prompt is placed within quotes and followed by a semicolon. Because the syntax for this statement varies, check for the correct format for your system. Some dialects use a colon instead of the semicolon; some automatically place the question mark after the prompt, others don't. Our examples will show a dialect that uses a semicolon and automatically generates a question mark.

Because we've written the program in a modular fashion, it is easy to replace the subroutine that begins with line 2000.

```
2000 REM ***********************************
2010 REM Assign values
2020 INPUT "What is the value for PRICE"; PRICE
2030 INPUT "What is the value for COST"; COST
2040 RETURN
```

Nothing else in the program need be changed.

INPUTTING MORE THAN A SINGLE VARIABLE

We can input more than one value with a single INPUT statement, although this is not typically a recommended practice.

```
DELETE 2020 Return
2030 INPUT "What are the values for COST and PRICE"; COST, PRICE Return
```

In this example of INPUT, we were asked to enter two numbers. We must type one number, a comma, and the other number. The comma separates the numbers. When the line is executed, the first value entered is placed in the variable COST, and the second is placed in the variable PRICE.

```
RUN Return
What are the values for COST and PRICE? 100, 130 Return
Where price = 130
Where cost = 100
```

You must enter the same number of values as variables in the INPUT statement. If you don't, BASIC will display an error message. Here is the message one dialect displays:

```
What are the values for COST and PRICE? 100 Return
?Redo from start
What are the values for COST and PRICE?
```

At this point the user should type the correct number of values and press Return. The program would then continue. An important question is whether the program user will know to separate values with commas and what to do about such a cryptic error message "?Redo from start." For this reason, we do not recommend asking for more than one value in an input statement. Remember, the programmer should write the program with the user's perspective in mind!

INPUTTING STRING VALUES

You may also input string values with the INPUT statement. For example, to have the user enter the customer's last name, we use the following:

```
200 INPUT "Customer last name"; CUST.LAST.NAME$ Return
```

The important thing to remember is that string data must be entered into a string variable. If we used the variable name `CUST.LAST.NAME` (instead of `CUST.LAST.NAME$`), BASIC would display an error message telling us we used the wrong variable type.

TEST YOUR LEARNING

1. What does INPUT do?
2. a. Why would you use a prompt?
   b. Does your system allow a prompt? If so, what punctuation mark is used after the prompt?
   c. If your system does not allow a prompt in the INPUT statement, how can you display a prompt?
3. Write a program segment that asks the user to input his or her name and a number. Use a prompt to tell the user what to do. Then print the number preceded by the message, `"The number you entered is"`.
4. Write a program that uses two INPUT statements to allow the user to enter two numbers. Print the sum and the product of these numbers.
5. The formula for calculating the area of a circle is pi (pi = 3.1416) times the radius squared. Write a program that asks the user to input the radius of the circle and prints the area for that radius.
6. You wish to determine your gas mileage and cost for gas on a trip. Write a program that accepts as input the beginning mileage, the ending mileage, the total number of gallons of gas, and the cost per gallon. The program displays as output the average miles per gallon and cost of gas per mile.

READ AND DATA

Many programs have data that seldom changes. A good example of such data is the tax rates, which usually remain constant for at least a year. We can place the social security and state disability rates in a program in several ways. We could ask the user to enter them each time the program is run, as in the following:

```
1000 INPUT "Please enter social security tax rate: ", SS.RATE
1010 INPUT "Please enter state disability tax rate: ", SDI.RATE
1020 LET SS.AMOUNT = GROSS * SS.RATE
1030 LET SDI.AMOUNT = GROSS * SDI.RATE
```

Or we could code them into the program:

```
1000 LET SS.AMOUNT = GROSS * .0715
1010 LET SDI.AMOUNT = GROSS * .009
```

The disadvantage with the first method is that the program relies on the user to remember and enter the tax rates correctly each time the program is run. The second method eliminates this possibility for error, but when rates change, the programmer must search for each LET statement and change the values. If the rates are also used in other lines, the programmer must be sure to find all places where they are used.

STORING VALUES

The DATA statement offers us a way to store values that rarely need to be changed. We can store the values with this statement:

```
NEW Return
100 DATA .0715, .009 Return
```

The values given in the DATA statement are placed in a data list when the RUN command is given and before any program statements are executed. The values are stored sequentially in the same order as they appear in the program listing.

RETRIEVING VALUES

To retrieve the values we use the READ statement:

```
100 DATA .0715, .009
110 READ SS.RATE
120 READ SDI.RATE
130 LET SS.AMOUNT = GROSS * SS.RATE
140 LET SDI.AMOUNT = GROSS * SDI.RATE
```

When the READ statement is executed, BASIC assigns the next unread value in the data list to the variable named in the READ statement. Thus, the first value of `.0715` is assigned to `SS.RATE`, and the second value of `.009` is assigned to `SDI.RATE`.

Line 100 shows that more than one value may be stored with a single DATA statement. The values are separated by commas. Also, more than one value may be read with a single READ statement. Lines 110 and 120 could be replaced by this single line:

```
110 READ SS.RATE, SDI.RATE
```

Strings as well as numbers can be placed in DATA statements. However, a string DATA value must be read into a string variable. For example, we can store a heading in a DATA statement and print it using the following statements:

```
500 DATA Gross
510 READ TITLE1$
520 PRINT TITLE1$
```

Note that although quotes are not always needed around string constants in DATA statements, they may be used. The following short program uses DATA statements to store headings, tax rates, and gross amounts, which are retrieved for use in the program using READ statements. Note that in this example the DATA statements appear at the end of the program. Remember, the values in DATA statements are placed in the data list *before the program is executed*. Therefore, it doesn't matter where the DATA statements are placed in the program as long as the values appear in the sequence in which they are to be read. Table 2 shows the DATA list for this program and the variables to which the values are assigned by the READ statements.

```
10 REM ************************************
20 REM      Program to demonstrate use of READ and DATA
30 REM
40 REM      Calculate and print taxes for
50 REM         several gross amounts.
60 REM ************************************
70 REM *          DATA DICTIONARY          *
80 REM
90 REM TITLE1$, TITLE2$, TITLE3$ = titles for columns
100 REM SS.RATE = social security rate
110 REM SDI.RATE = state disability insurance rate
120 REM GROSS1, GROSS2, GROSS3 = gross amounts
130 REM ************************************
140 REM
150 REM Driver Module
```

TABLE 2

Data List for Demonstration Program

Value	Assigned to this Variable
Gross	TITLE1$
SS Amount	TITLE2$
SDI Amount	TITLE3$
.0715	SS.RATE
.009	SDI.RATE
100	GROSS1
500	GROSS2
1000	GROSS3

```
160 GOSUB 1000   : REM Read and Print Titles
170 GOSUB 2000   : REM Read rates
180 GOSUB 3000   : REM Process Gross Amounts
190 REM End of Driver Module
200 REM
210 REM DATA Statements
220 DATA Gross, SS Amount, SDI Amount
230 DATA .0715, .009
240 DATA 100, 500, 1000
250 REM End of DATA Statements
260 END
1000 REM ***********************************
1010 REM Read and Print Titles
1020 READ TITLE1$, TITLE2$, TITLE3$
1030 PRINT TITLE1$, TITLE2$, TITLE3$
1040 PRINT
1050 RETURN
2000 REM ***********************************
2010 REM Read Rates
2020 READ SS.RATE, SDI.RATE
2030 RETURN
3000 REM ***********************************
3010 REM Process Gross Amount
3020 READ GROSS1
3030 PRINT GROSS1, GROSS1 * SS.RATE, GROSS1 * SDI.RATE
3040 READ GROSS2
3050 PRINT GROSS2, GROSS2 * SS.RATE, GROSS2 * SDI.RATE
3060 READ GROSS3
3070 PRINT GROSS3, GROSS3 * SS.RATE, GROSS3 * SDI.RATE
3080 RETURN
```

The results of running the program are:

```
GROSS  SS Amount  SDI Amount

100   7.150001   .9
500   35.75      4.5
1000  71.5       9
```

In this example we used DATA statements to store the gross salaries. Normally we would use the INPUT statement to enter these values because they change for each employee. However, when learning programming or when testing programs, DATA statements are frequently used in place of INPUT.

RESTORE

We can reread the same DATA values in the program using the RESTORE statement. RESTORE causes the next READ statement to begin with the first DATA value in the list.

If we try to read more items than the list holds without using RESTORE, BASIC will display an error message such as: `Out of DATA in 170`, in which 170 is the number of the line where the error occurred.

TEST YOUR LEARNING

1. What does the DATA statement do?
2. How are the values stored by DATA statements retrieved?
3. What value will be assigned to each variable and what will be printed by the following sets of program lines? One set has an error; what's wrong with it? Try each on your computer.

```
10 DATA 20, 450, Range 1
20 DATA 50, 900, Range 2
30 READ R1.MIN, R1.MAX, R1.DISC$
40 READ R2.MIN, R2.MAX, R2.DISC$
50 PRINT R1.MIN, R1.MAX, R1.DISC$
60 PRINT R2.MIN, R2.MAX, R2.DISC$
70 END
```

```
10 DATA 20, 450
20 DATA 50, 900
30 DATA Range 1, Range 2
40 READ R1.MIN, R1.MAX
50 READ R2.MIN, R2.MAX
60 READ R1.DISC$, R2.DISC$
70 PRINT R1.MIN, R1.MAX, R1.DISC$
80 PRINT R2.MIN, R2.MAX, R2.DISC$
90 END
```

```
10 DATA Range 1, Range 2
20 DATA 20, 450
30 DATA 50, 900
40 READ R1.MIN, R1.MAX
50 READ R2.MIN, R2.MAX
60 READ R1.DISC$, R2.DISC$
70 PRINT R1.MIN, R1.MAX, R1.DISC$
80 PRINT R2.MIN, R2.MAX, R2.DISC$
90 END
```

4. Write a program segment that reads the names of the days in the week from DATA statements and displays them on the screen.

COMMANDS FOR SELECTION AND ITERATION

In Chapter 8 we discussed control structures for selection and iteration. Selection allows the programmer to determine the flow of program logic depending on conditions. A common example: if one condition exists, call a certain subroutine; if another condition exists, call another subroutine. Iteration allows the programmer to repeat certain program logic until a certain condition is met. An example used every day is, for each person on a payroll, process all payroll steps. The iteration ends when there are no more people to be processed.

In this section we describe the BASIC statements used to implement selection and iteration.

IF . . . THEN

In a simple payroll system we pay people their number of hours worked times their hourly rate. If the hours worked are over 40, we pay the regular rate for 40 hours plus an overtime rate for overtime hours. One way of writing the pseudocode for this problem is:

```
set overtime hours to 0
IF hours worked exceed 40 THEN set overtime hours to hours worked minus 40
set regular hours to hours worked minus overtime hours
set regular pay to regular hours times the pay rate
set overtime pay to overtime hours times the pay rate times 1.5
set total pay to regular pay plus overtime pay
```

BASIC uses IF and THEN just like the example above. The syntax consists of the reserved word IF followed by a logical condition, the reserved word THEN, and a BASIC statement. If the condition is true, the action following THEN is executed. If the action is false, the action is not taken. The flowchart for the IF . . . THEN statement is shown in Figure 5.

Here is a simple payroll program that uses this concept. We will use this program for future examples.

```
10 REM ***********************************
20 REM    Program Name: PAYROLL
30 REM    Written by Sue Williams
40 REM    July 9, 1992
50 REM
60 REM  This program calculates simple payroll
70 REM ***********************************
80 REM *          DATA DICTIONARY         *
90 REM
```

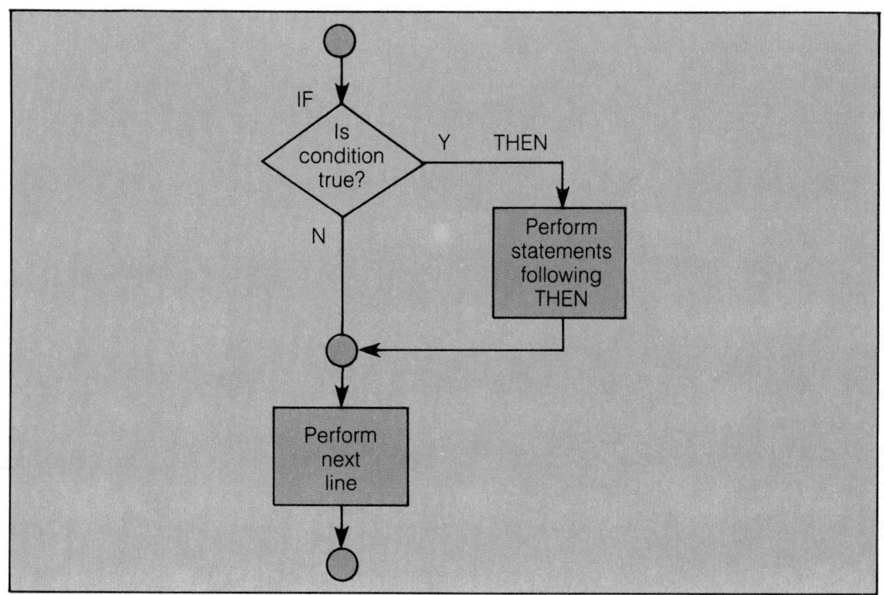

FIGURE 5

Flowchart of IF . . . THEN.

```
100 REM HOURS.WORKED = total hours worked
110 REM REG.HOURS = regular hours
120 REM OT.HOURS = overtime hours
130 REM REG.PAY = pay from regular hours
140 REM OT.PAY = pay from overtime hours
150 REM TOT.PAY = total pay
160 REM RATE = pay rate
170 REM ***********************************
180 REM
190 REM Driver Module
200 GOSUB 1000  : REM Initialize
210 GOSUB 2000  : REM Get input data on hours worked and rate
220 GOSUB 3000  : REM Figure Regular and OT Hours
230 GOSUB 4000  : REM Figure Pay
240 GOSUB 5000  : REM Print Results
250 END
1000 REM ***********************************
1010 REM Initialize variables
1020 HOURS.WORKED = 0
1030 REG.HOURS = 0
1040 OT.HOURS = 0
1050 REG.PAY = 0
1060 OT.PAY = 0
1070 TOT.PAY = 0
1080 RETURN
2000 REM ***********************************
2010 REM Get Input Data on Hours Worked and Rate
2020 INPUT "How many hours worked"; HOURS.WORKED
2030 INPUT "What is the pay rate"; RATE
2040 RETURN
3000 REM ***********************************
3010 REM Figure Regular and Overtime Hours
3020 IF HOURS.WORKED > 40 THEN OT.HOURS = HOURS.WORKED - 40
3030 REG.HOURS = HOURS.WORKED - OT.HOURS
3040 RETURN
4000 REM ***********************************
4010 REM Figure Pay
4020 REG.PAY = REG.HOURS * RATE
4030 OT.PAY = OT.HOURS * RATE * 1.5
4040 TOT.PAY = REG.PAY + OT. PAY
4050 RETURN
5000 REM ***********************************
5010 REM Print Results
5020 PRINT "Regular Hours = ", REG.HOURS
5030 PRINT "Overtime Hours = ", OT.HOURS
5040 PRINT "Regular Pay = ", REG.PAY
5050 PRINT "Overtime Pay = ", OT.PAY
5060 PRINT "Total Hours = ", HOURS.WORKED
5070 PRINT "Total Pay = ", TOT.PAY
5080 RETURN
```

Line 3020 implements the selection specified in the pseudocode. Note that if the value of `HOURS.WORKED` is less than or equal to 40, the value of `OT.HOURS` remains 0, as set in the initialization module.

Conditions

In this example, we used the symbol > to represent "greater than." There are six such symbols, called *relational operators*.

>	greater than
<	less than
=	equal
>=	greater than or equal
<=	less than or equal
<>	not equal

These relational operators can be used to construct *conditions* that can be evaluated as either true or false. Here are some more conditions:

```
AMOUNT <> 99999
HOURS <= 40
ANS$ = "YES"
```

In addition to the relational operators, the *logical operators* AND, OR, and NOT can be used to create more complex conditions.

Suppose we want to perform a module for all males under age 25. We could use the following IF . . . THEN selection:

```
IF SEX$ = "M" AND AGE < 25 THEN GOSUB 2000
```

In this case both conditions `(SEX$ = "M" and AGE < 25)` must be true for the subroutine to be executed. If either condition is false, the entire condition will be evaluated as false. In that case, processing will continue on the line following the IF.

When two conditions are joined with OR, if at least one of them is true, the entire condition is evaluated as true. To select all customers living in the states of California or Arizona we would write:

```
IF STATE$ = "CA" OR STATE$ = "AZ" THEN GOSUB 3000
```

The third logical operator, NOT, reverses true and false. For example, `NOT BALANCE > 0` is true when `BALANCE` is less than or equal to zero and is false when `BALANCE` is greater than zero.

Let us revise the program MARKUP used as an example a few pages ago in the section called Data Oriented Commands. The purpose of that program was to calculate a markup rate for a product, given the price and cost of the product. Now let's say that the store hires a new manager who decrees that no markup shall be less than 10 percent or greater than 50 percent. If the markup is incorrect (less than 10 percent or greater than 50 percent) two things happen. First, an error message is produced. Second, the price and markup are automatically adjusted either up to 10 percent or down to 50 percent. Here is one way of programming the new version of MARKUP:

```
10 REM **********************************
20 REM    Program Name: NEW MARKUP
30 REM    Written by John Richards
40 REM    July 21, 1992
50 REM
60 REM  This program calculates markup rate for a
70 REM  given product. In case of a markup that is
72 REM  too low, the price and markup are adjusted to the
74 REM  minimum allowable. In case of a markup that is
76 REM  too high, the price and markup are adjusted to the
78 REM  maximum allowable.
80 REM **********************************
90 REM *         DATA DICTIONARY         *
100 REM
110 REM PRICE = price of the product
120 REM COST = cost to company of the product
130 REM MARKUP = markup rate
132 REM MAX.MARK = maximum allowable markup rate
134 REM MIN.MARK = minimum allowable markup rate
140 REM **********************************
150 REM
160 REM Driver Module
170 GOSUB 1000  : REM Initialization
180 GOSUB 2000  : REM Assign Values
190 GOSUB 3000  : REM Figure Markup Rate
200 GOSUB 4000  : REM Print Markup Rate
210 END
1000 REM **********************************
1010 REM Initialization
1020 PRICE = 0
1030 COST = 1        : REM Denominator in Formula
1040 MARKUP = 0
1050 MAX.MARK = .5  : REM Change Here for New Maximum
1060 MIN.MARK = .1  : REM Change Here for New Minimum
1070 RETURN
2000 REM **********************************
2010 REM Assign Values
2020 INPUT "What is the value for PRICE"; PRICE
2030 INPUT "What is the value for COST"; COST
2040 RETURN
3000 REM **********************************
3010 REM Figure Markup Rate
3020 MARKUP = (PRICE - COST) / COST
3030 REM Check for Error
3040 IF (MARKUP < MIN.MARK) OR (MARKUP > MAX.MARK) THEN
     PRINT "Markup rate is in error. Price and markup will be adjusted."
3050 IF (MARKUP < MIN.MARK) THEN GOSUB 3500  : REM Adjust to Min
```

```
3060 IF (MARKUP > MAX.MARK) THEN GOSUB 3600  : REM Adjust to Max
3070 RETURN
3500 REM *********************************
3510 REM Adjust to Minimum Allowable Markup. Adjust Price.
3520 PRICE = COST + (COST * MIN.MARK)
3530 MARKUP = MIN.MARK
3540 RETURN
3600 REM *********************************
3610 REM Adjust to Maximum Allowable Markup. Adjust Price.
3620 PRICE = COST + (COST * MAX.MARK)
3630 MARKUP = MAX.MARK
3640 RETURN
4000 REM *********************************
4010 REM Print Markup
4020 PRINT "Where price = "; PRICE
4030 PRINT "Where cost = "; COST
4040 PRINT "Markup ="; MARKUP
4050 RETURN
```

Note Lines 1050 and 1060. This is a programming technique often used in industry. If the manager should change his or her mind about the maximum and/or minimum markups, this is the only place in the program that these values would have to be changed. Throughout the rest of the program the variable names are used: MAX.MARK and MIN.MARK. Their values are whatever they have been assigned in the initialization module.

Let's examine the subroutine that begins at Line 3010. It figures the markup for values of PRICE and COST input in Lines 2020 and 2030. Line 3040 says that if the markup is too small or too large, produce an error message. Line 3050 directs the program to execute a correction module starting at 3500 if the markup rate is too small. Line 3060 directs to 3600 if the markup rate is too large.

There are numerous ways of programming this problem. The programmer would ask the potential user of the program what he or she would like to see, and program it that way. For example, how would you change the logic to produce these error messages when appropriate?

```
Markup rate is too low. Price and Markup will be raised to minimum.
```

or

```
Markup rate is too high. Price and Markup will be lowered to maximum.
```

IF . . . THEN . . . ELSE

We frequently want to perform one action if a condition is true and another if the condition is false. Most dialects of BASIC provide the IF . . . THEN . . . ELSE statement, an extension of the IF . . . THEN statement that allows selection of one action or another.

The syntax of this statement is the reserved word IF followed by a logical condition, the reserved word THEN, a BASIC statement, the reserved word ELSE, and another BASIC statement. If the condition is true, the statement following THEN is executed. If the condition is false, the statement following

ELSE is executed. One and only one of the THEN and ELSE clauses is executed. A flowchart of this statement is shown in Figure 6.

Here's a series of statements that give a 10 percent discount to customers 65 and over.

```
1200 LET TAX = .06
1210 IF AGE < 65 THEN LET PRICE = PRICE + TAX * PRICE ELSE LET PRICE = .9 *
 (PRICE + TAX * PRICE)
```

Note that it took more than one screen width (80 columns) to write the last statement. Rather than accept the spacing that the screen gives us, we'll break the line to improve readability. This may be done by adding appropriate spaces after PRICE. This clearly separates the actions to be taken on the true and false conditions:

```
1210 IF AGE < 65 THEN LET PRICE = PRICE + TAX * PRICE
                 ELSE LET PRICE = .9 * (PRICE + TAX * PRICE)
```

Here's another set of statements that direct processing of products on an assembly line, depending on the value of the variable WEIGHT.

```
4050 REM IF Product Too Light or Heavy, Reject, Else Continue.
4060 IF (WEIGHT < MIN) OR (WEIGHT > MAX) THEN PRINT "Reject" ELSE GOSUB 9000
```

NESTED IF . . . THEN . . . ELSE

Many dialects support a more complex version of the IF statement that allows you to nest one IF statement within another. For reasons that have to do with structured

FIGURE 6

Flowchart of IF . . . THEN . . . ELSE.

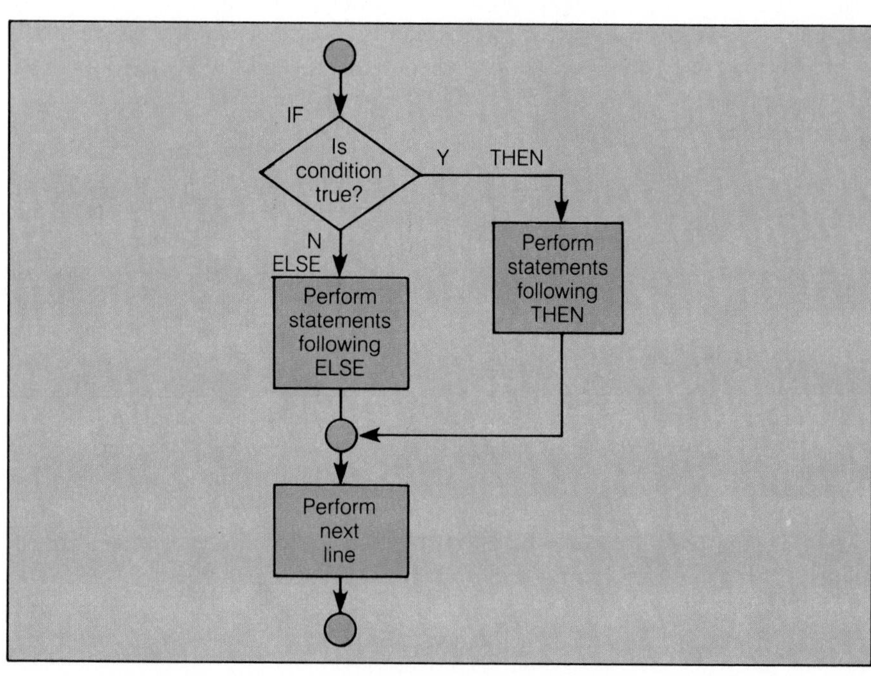

programming (described below) we do not recommend this structure. However, because it is a part of BASIC and to demonstrate further the utility of structured programming, we include the structure here.

To demonstrate, we'll write a statement to select a salesperson's commission factor. Two items determine the commission: the employee's gross sales and the bonus rate assigned to that employee. If the gross sales figure is greater than 20,000, and the bonus rate is 2, the commission factor is to be 4. If gross sales is greater than 20,000, but the bonus rate is not 2, then the commission factor is to be 3. If gross sales is 20,000 or less but greater than 10,000, the commission factor is to be 2. If gross sales is 10,000 or less the commission factor is to be 1.

Before writing the code, let's write this proposal as pseudocode.

```
IF Gross > 20000
   THEN IF bonus = 2
         THEN LET commission factor = 4
         ELSE LET commission factor = 3
   ELSE IF Gross > 10,000
         THEN LET commission factor = 2
         ELSE LET commission factor = 1
```

Now we'll rewrite the pseudocode in BASIC as one nested IF . . . THEN . . . ELSE statement. (See Figure 7 for the flowchart of this statement.)

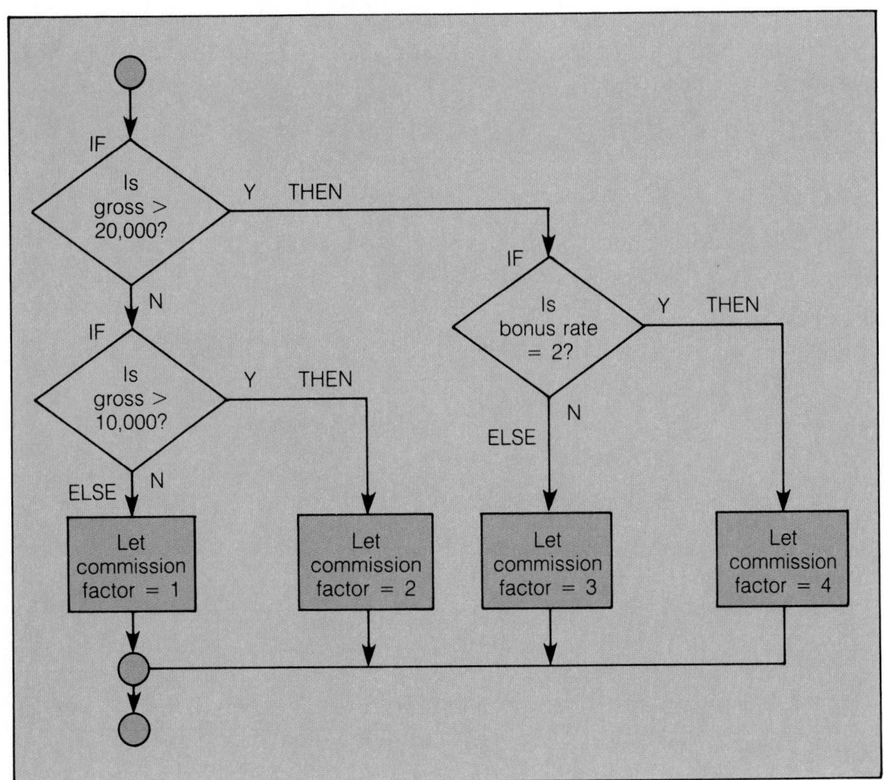

FIGURE 7

Flowchart of nested IF . . . THEN . . . ELSE.

```
50 IF GROSS > 20000 THEN IF BONUS.RATE = 2 THEN LET COMMISSION.FACTOR = 4
     ELSE LET COMMISSION.FACTOR = 3 ELSE IF GROSS > 10000
     THEN LET COMMISSION.FACTOR = 2 ELSE LET COMMISSION.FACTOR = 1
```

If you're using Apple BASIC or another dialect that doesn't support nested IFs, you can write the following statements to replace the one above:

```
50 IF GROSS > 20000 AND BONUS.RATE = 2 THEN LET COMMISSION.FACTOR = 4
60 IF GROSS > 20000 AND BONUS.RATE <> 2 THEN LET COMMISSION.FACTOR = 3
70 IF GROSS =< 20000 AND GROSS > 10000 THEN LET COMMISSION.FACTOR = 2
80 IF GROSS =< 10000 THEN LET COMMISSION.FACTOR = 1
```

Why have we said we don't recommend the use of nested IF . . . THEN . . . ELSE? A simple reason may be found in looking at Line 50 from the viewpoint of a programmer trying to interpret it five years from now. What IFs go with what THENs go with what ELSEs? It is not immediately obvious without studying the code in more depth than one should have to.

For another even more important reason, consider what would happen if we wanted to add to the criteria for determining commission factors, as often happens when programs handle more complex distinctions. In addition, consider what would happen if we wanted not only to determine criteria, but also to report that we had done so. The current code would soon become even more hopelessly muddled than it already is.

A much better method of coding uses the modularization technique of structured programming. Line 50 simply becomes:

```
50 IF GROSS > 20000 THEN GOSUB 1000 ELSE GOSUB 2000
```

In subroutine 1000 we put the code for determining what happens if the bonus rate is equal to 2 or not. We can easily add other code in the subroutine. For example:

```
1010 IF BONUS.RATE = 2 THEN COMMISSION.FACTOR = 4
                       ELSE COMMISSION.FACTOR = 3
1020 PRINT "The Bonus Rate is equal to 2"
```

Further modularization can be carried out if more detail is required.

TEST YOUR LEARNING

1. What is selection?
2. Where is processing directed if the condition following the IF is false?
3. Under what conditions will the following lines print the message "Paid In Full" and under what conditions will it print "Balance Due"?

```
10 LET MESSAGE$ = "Paid In Full"
20 PRINT "Balance";
30 INPUT BALANCE
40 IF BALANCE > 0 THEN LET MESSAGE$ = "Balance Due"
50 PRINT MESSAGE$
```

4. Write a program that asks the user to enter two numbers. If the first number is greater or equal to the second, print the sum of the numbers. If the first number is less than the second, print their product.

5. Depending on its weight and size a package will be sent by a particular shipping service. If the package weighs less than one pound, it will be sent first class no matter what the size. If it weighs less than 25 pounds, and the height times the width times the length (in inches) is not greater than 1,728, then it will be sent third class. Otherwise, it will be sent parcel post. Write a program that asks the user to enter the weight, height, length, and width and prints a message indicating which way the package is to be sent.

Iteration (the loop)

We will find that much of the power of programming comes from our ability to direct program execution to parts of the program other than the next line. You are already familiar with the concept of iteration, or looping. When following the recipe for baking a cake, we are told to mix the batter until it is smooth. The cookbook author does not write 100 or 1,000 lines that say "beat batter one time," because sometimes the batter would be underbeaten and other times overbeaten. In effect, the author tells us to loop. We are told (1) if the batter is smooth, move on to the next instruction; otherwise (2) beat the batter once and go back to (1). In this way, we beat the batter the exact number of times needed.

FOR . . . NEXT

BASIC provides two sets of special instructions to support looping. The first set, FOR and NEXT, executes a set of instructions an exact number of times. Consider the following demonstration program:

```
NEW
10 REM Demonstration program for FOR . . . NEXT
20 FOR COUNTER = 1 TO 5
30      PRINT "The current count is ";COUNTER
40 NEXT COUNTER
50 END
RUN
The current count is 1
The current count is 2
The current count is 3
The current count is 4
The current count is 5
```

The FOR statement in Line 20 begins the loop. The variable COUNTER is used to keep track of the number of times the loop has been executed (see Figure 8). It is called the *counter*, *control variable*, or *loop index*. Any variable name is permitted here. Following COUNTER are the initial and maximum values for the counter.

Line 30 is the *loop body*. Any number of instructions can be included here as part of the loop body. (In this case, only one line forms the loop body.) The loop body will be executed each time the loop is repeated.

The NEXT statement in Line 40 defines the end of the loop. Although not all dialects require it, the counter used in the FOR statement is again listed following the word NEXT.

When this loop is entered, COUNTER is initialized to the first value specified in the FOR statement. At Line 20, COUNTER is initialized to 1. The value of COUNTER is then tested against the ending value specified in the FOR statement (which is 5 in this example). Because it is not greater than the ending value, the loop body (Line 30) is executed. When the NEXT statement in Line 40 is reached, control passes back to the FOR statement in Line 20. The value of COUNTER is incremented by 1. This repetition continues until the value of COUNTER is greater than 5. Then control passes to the line after the NEXT, Line 50. In this manner the loop is repeated a total of five times.

Note that we add spaces before the statements in the body of the loop to indent it. This indentation, which makes the loop body more readable, helps us to make the program easily maintainable and understandable.

FIGURE 8

Flowchart of FOR . . . NEXT loop.

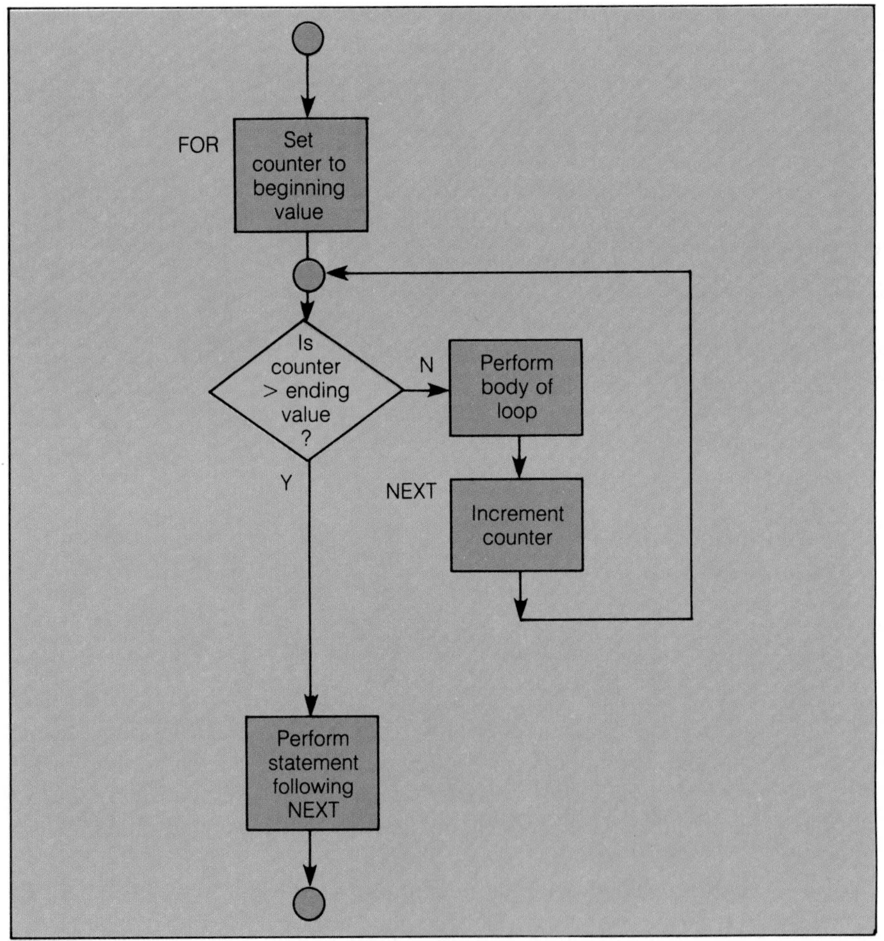

Let's consider a program we have used as a recent example, NEW MARKUP. NEW MARKUP must be run every time a markup is to be calculated. That's tedious if a user has 100 markups to check! Because we have written the program in a structured manner, we can easily change it to loop 100 times. The subroutines stay the same so we won't repeat them. All we have to change is the driver module. We'll add one line to the data dictionary to account for our new looping variable

```
10 REM ***********************************
20 REM      Program Name: NEW MARKUP
30 REM      Written by John Richards
40 REM      July 21, 1992
50 REM      Updated August 5, 1992
60 REM    This program calculates markup rate for a
70 REM    given product. In case of a markup that is
72 REM    too low, the price and markup are adjusted to
74 REM    the minimum allowable. In case of a markup
76 REM    that is too high, the price and markup are
78 REM    adjusted to the maximum allowable.
80 REM ***********************************
90 REM *          DATA DICTIONARY          *
100 REM
110 REM PRICE    = price of the product
120 REM COST     = cost to company of the product
130 REM MARKUP   = markup rate
132 REM MAX.MARK = maximum allowable markup rate
134 REM MIN.MARK = minimum allowable markup rate
136 REM PRODUCT  = counter variable for loop
140 REM ***********************************
150 REM
160 REM Driver Module
165 FOR PRODUCT = 1 to 100
170     GOSUB 1000 : REM Initialization
180     GOSUB 2000 : REM Assign Value
190     GOSUB 3000 : REM Figure Markup Rate
200     GOSUB 4000 : REM Print Markup Rate
205 NEXT PRODUCT
210 END
```

What if the user did not know whether he or she had 1 or 100 markups to count? In that case we may use an input statement to ask the user how many products are to be checked. We will replace the constant (100) with the variable (NUM.PROD).

```
160 REM Driver Module
162 INPUT "How many products are you checking";NUM.PROD
165 FOR PRODUCT = 1 to NUM.PROD
```

Both the starting and ending values in the FOR statement may be variables.

FOR . . . NEXT WITH STEP

We will want the counter for most applications to be incremented by 1; however, using the STEP clause we can increment the counter by a value other than 1. Let's make a change to the program we used to introduce FOR . . . NEXT.

```
NEW
10 REM Demonstration program for FOR . . . NEXT STEP
20 FOR COUNTER = 1 TO 5 STEP 2
30      PRINT "The current count is ";COUNTER
40 NEXT COUNTER
50 END
RUN
```

Changing Line 20 to include `STEP 2` causes the counter to be incremented by 2 each time the loop is executed. The loop will now be executed three times and `COUNTER` will have the values of 1, 3, and 5.

```
RUN
The current count is 1
The current count is 3
The current count is 5
```

NESTED FOR . . . NEXT LOOPS

One FOR . . . NEXT loop may be placed inside another FOR . . . NEXT loop to form *nested loops*, as the following program segment demonstrates. When the outer loop is entered for the first time, the counter `OUTER` has the value of 1. The inner loop is then entered. This loop is repeated twice with `INNER` having the values of 1 and 2. `OUTER` is then incremented by the NEXT statement in Line 130, and the outer loop is executed again. The outer loop is performed a total of three times. The inner loop is performed a total of six times, twice each time the outer loop is performed. Note again that the statements inside each loop are indented.

```
10 REM -- Initialize Accumulators --
20 LET OUT.COUNT = 0
30 LET IN.COUNT = 0
40 REM -- Begin Outer Loop --
50 FOR OUTER = 1 to 3
60      PRINT "Outer Loop Number"; OUTER
70      LET OUT.COUNT = OUT.COUNT + 1      :REM Count Outer Loop
80      REM -- Begin Inner Loop --
90      FOR INNER = 1 TO 2
100          PRINT "    Inner Loop Number"; INNER
110          LET IN.COUNT = IN.COUNT + 1   :REM Count Inner Loop
120      NEXT INNER
130 NEXT OUTER
140 PRINT "Number of times Outer Loop was executed"; OUT.COUNT
150 PRINT "Number of times Inner Loop was executed"; IN.COUNT
160 END
RUN
Outer Loop Number 1
   Inner Loop Number 1
   Inner Loop Number 2
```

```
Outer Loop Number 2
   Inner Loop Number 1
   Inner Loop Number 2
Outer Loop Number 3
   Inner Loop Number 1
   Inner Loop Number 2
Number of times Outer Loop was executed 3
Number of times Inner Loop was executed 6
```

Have you ever wondered just how many gifts were given in the song "The Twelve Days of Christmas"? Here's a structured program that uses nested loops to solve that query.

```
10 REM ***********************************
20 REM          Program Name: TWELVE DAYS OF CHRISTMAS
30 REM          Written by John Truelove
40 REM          December 24, 1992
50 REM
60 REM   This program figures how many gifts I have to give
70 REM      in the next twelve days.
80 REM
90 REM ***********************************
100 REM *         DATA DICTIONARY          *
110 REM
120 REM  TOTAL.GIFTS     =    total gifts to give away
130 REM  DAY             =    counter for per day loop
140 REM  DAY.GIFTS       =    gifts on a given day
150 REM  GIFT            =    counter for gift loop
160 REM
170 REM ***********************************
180 REM  Driver Module
190 GOSUB 1000          : REM Initialization
200 REM  Count Gifts for Each Day
210 FOR DAY = 1 to 12
220     GOSUB 1000            : REM Accumulate Today's Gifts
230     GOSUB 2000            : REM Report Today's Gifts
240     GOSUB 3000            : REM Accumulate Total Gifts
250     NEXT DAY
260 GOSUB 4000                : REM Report Final Total
270 END
1000 REM ***********************************
1010 REM Accumulate Today's Gifts
1020 DAY.GIFTS = 0            : REM Initialize Today's Gifts
1030 FOR GIFT = 1 to DAY
1040     DAY.GIFTS = DAY.GIFTS + GIFT
1050 NEXT GIFT
1060 RETURN
2000 REM ***********************************
2010 REM Report Today's Gifts
2020 PRINT "On Day"; DAY; "the number of gifts is"; DAY,GIFTS
2030 RETURN
```

```
3000 REM ***********************************
3010 REM Accumulate Total Gifts
3020 TOTAL.GIFTS = TOTAL.GIFTS + DAY.GIFTS
3030 RETURN
4000 REM ***********************************
4010 REM Report Final Total
4020 PRINT "Total number of gifts is: "; TOTAL.GIFTS
4030 RETURN
```

When we run the program we obtain these results:

```
On Day 1 the number of gifts is 1
On Day 2 the number of gifts is 3
On Day 3 the number of gifts is 6
On Day 4 the number of gifts is 10
On Day 5 the number of gifts is 15
On Day 6 the number of gifts is 21
On Day 7 the number of gifts is 28
On Day 8 the number of gifts is 36
On Day 9 the number of gifts is 45
On Day 10 the number of gifts is 55
On Day 11 the number of gifts is 66
On Day 12 the number of gifts is 78
Total number of gifts is: 364
```

We've used a number of important constructs in this program. To maintain structure we placed the nested FOR . . . NEXT loop in a subroutine. In Line 1040 we've used what is called an accumulator; that is, the variable DAY.GIFTS accumulates the number of gifts in a day. Think through the loop from Line 1030 to Line 1050 for a moment. When DAY is equal to 1 (that is, we are on the first day determined by the outer loop) the inner loop will be executed one time; GIFT will only get the value 1 in the inner loop. You may read Line 1040 as follows: The new value for DAY.GIFTS may be determined by adding the current value for GIFT to the former value of DAY.GIFTS. The first time through the inner loop (remember, DAY equals 1) the new value of DAY.GIFTS becomes the former value (0) plus the current value of GIFT (1).

We now exit to the main loop at Line 230. We report the number of gifts for a given day at Line 2020. (You may ask, "A whole subroutine for one print statement?" Don't forget, we may wish to lengthen the report for this day later on. That's easy with a module!) Then back to the main loop at 240. In Line 3020 we have another accumulator, TOTAL.GIFTS. A new value for TOTAL.GIFTS may be determined by adding the current value of DAY.GIFTS (we found that in subroutine 1000) to the former value of TOTAL.GIFTS.

Now back around the main loop so that DAY gets the value 2. In order to accumulate the gifts for DAY = 2, we need to reinitialize DAY.GIFTS to 0 in Line 1020. If we did not, we would retain the value of DAY.GIFTS from when DAY = 1. We don't want that! Our module only gets one day's gifts at a time.

The concepts of nested loops, accumulators, and reinitialization are used very often in industry. Take a good look at this program, following the values of the variables closely at each step. To help you, add the following temporary lines of code and run the program again.

```
225 PRINT "This is day "; DAY
1045 PRINT "GIFT = "; GIFT; "and DAY.GIFTS = "; DAY.GIFTS
```

WHILE . . . WEND

WHILE and WEND (Figure 9) are the other set of statements that create loops in BASIC. (WEND is a contraction of W for WHILE and END for end of the WHILE loop.) Although most dialects of BASIC have this set of statements, they may vary slightly; we will discuss the most common version. (*Note:* The WHILE and WEND statements are not available in most Tandy or Apple BASIC. We'll present a way to simulate the WHILE loop when we discuss the GOTO statement. You may wish to read that section at this time. Consult your instructor if you need to simulate the WHILE . . . WEND loop.)

The WHILE statement consists of the word WHILE followed by some condition. If the condition is true, all the statements between the WHILE and

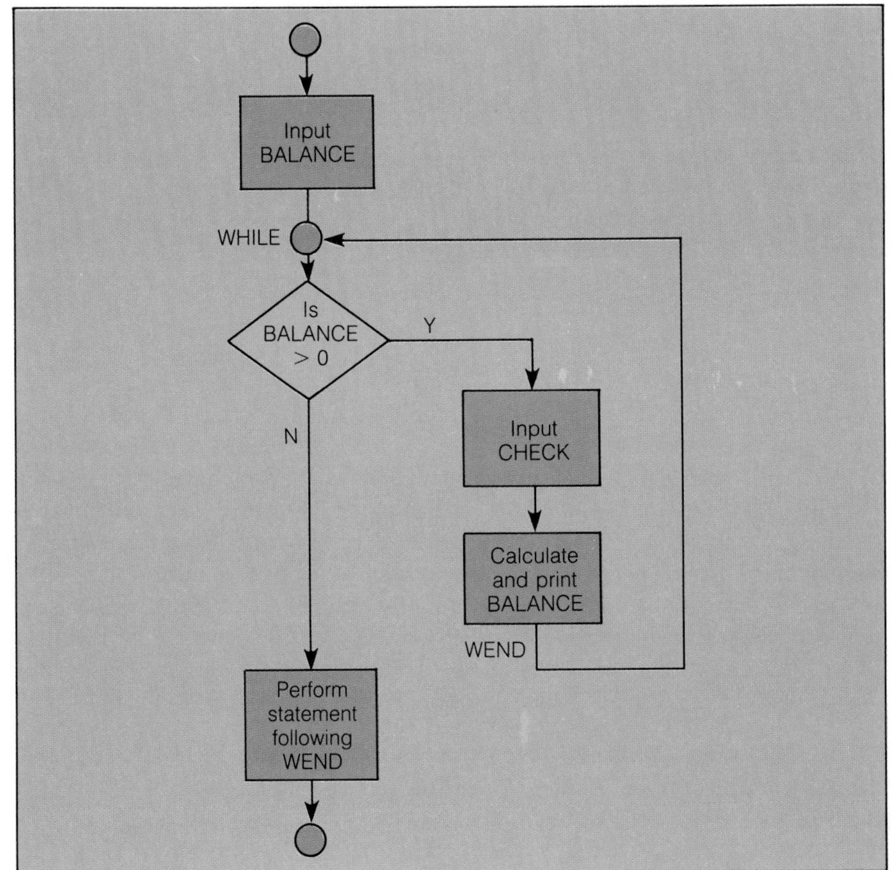

FIGURE 9

Flowchart of WHILE . . . WEND.

WEND statements are executed. Control then returns to the WHILE statement. If the condition is false, processing is directed to the statement following the WEND.

Here is an example of a WHILE . . . WEND loop.

```
10 REM Demo Segment for WHILE . . . WEND
20 INPUT "What is your check balance"; BALANCE
30 WHILE BALANCE > 0
40    INPUT "How much is this check"; CHECK
50    LET BALANCE = BALANCE - CHECK
60    PRINT "Current Balance: "; BALANCE
70 WEND
80 PRINT "Oops, you are overdrawn"
90 END
```

This program segment asks users for their checkbook balance and repeatedly asks for checks until the account is overdrawn. At that point, it prints the message "`Oops, you are overdrawn`".

The loop consists of Lines 30 through 70. It begins with the WHILE statement in Line 30 and ends with the WEND in Line 70. When execution reaches Line 30, it tests the condition after the word WHILE. In this case, the condition is `BALANCE>0`. If the condition is true, control passes to the line after the WHILE. Control then passes sequentially from Line 40 to 50 to 60 to 70, the WEND statement. The WEND statement returns control to its matching WHILE at Line 30 where the condition is checked again. If the condition is false, control passes to the line after the WEND.

Here is the demonstration program in action:

```
RUN
What is your check balance? 100 Return
How much is this check? 50 Return
Current Balance: 50
How much is this check? 51 Return
Current Balance: -1
Oops, you are overdrawn
```

PROCESSING WITHIN A WHILE . . . WEND LOOP

WHILE . . . WEND loops are commonly used to overcome two problems. First, as we did with the FOR . . . NEXT loop, we may use WHILE . . . WEND so that we don't have to rerun the program for each new set of values. Second, what if we have a looping situation that does not involve counting, as the FOR . . . NEXT loop does? For example, what if we wish to stop looping a payroll program when the user answers "No" to the question "Do you wish to enter another employee?" As another example, consider allowing users to enter "DONE" when they wish to stop processing. Let's use the PAYROLL program to demonstrate each of these. Again, our structured programing makes the changes easy. We'll leave out the subroutines since they remain the same.

```
10 REM ************************************
20 REM    Program Name: PAYROLL
30 REM    Written by Sue Williams
```

```
40 REM    July 9, 1992
50 REM    Updated November 2, 1992
60 REM  This program calculates simple payroll
70 REM ***********************************
80 REM *          DATA DICTIONARY         *
90 REM
100 REM HOURS.WORKED =        total hours worked
110 REM REG.HOURS    =        regular hours
120 REM OT.HOURS     =        overtime hours
130 REM REG.PAY      =        pay from regular hours
140 REM OT.PAY       =        pay from overtime hours
150 REM TOT.PAY      =        total pay
160 REM RATE         =        pay rate
165 REM ANS$         =        answer for loop
170 REM ***********************************
180 REM
190 REM Driver Module
194 INPUT "Do you wish to enter another employee (Y/N)";ANS$
196 WHILE (ANS$ = "Y") OR (ANS$ = "y")
200    GOSUB 1000      : REM Initialize
210    GOSUB 2000      : REM Get input data on hours worked and rate
220    GOSUB 3000      : REM Figure Regular and OT Hours
230    GOSUB 4000      : REM Figure Pay
240    GOSUB 5000      : REM Print Results
244    INPUT "Do you wish to enter another employee (Y/N)";ANS$
246 WEND
250 END
```

In Line 194 the user initializes the WHILE loop. If the user answers anything other than Y or y, the program terminates. If the user answers Y or y, the first employee is processed. Once inside the loop the user is asked the continuation question at Line 244.

Another technique that is often used asks the user to enter the word DONE after the last employee has been processed. In that case, the Driver Module would look like this:

```
190 REM Driver Module
194 INPUT "What is the employee's name (enter DONE to quit)";
       EMPNAME$
196 WHILE EMPNAME$ <> "DONE"
200    GOSUB 1000      : REM Initialize
210    GOSUB 2000      : REM Get input data on hours worked and
                         rate
220    GOSUB 3000      : REM Figure Regular and OT Hours
230    GOSUB 4000      : REM Figure Pay
240    GOSUB 5000      : REM Print Results
244    INPUT "What is the employee's name (enter DONE to quit)";
          EMPNAME$
246 WEND
250 END
```

Note again how we prime the loop. The first time, the user is asked to enter EMPNAME$ before the loop is entered. A second INPUT statement appears at the end of the loop. The first statement primes the loop using the first employee. The placement of the second INPUT statement ends the loop immediately after DONE is entered.

DATA VALIDATION

WHILE . . . WEND is commonly used immediately after INPUT to ensure that the value of the data that the user has entered is within the correct range. That is called *data validation* or *input validation*. In the program segment below, we ask the user to enter YES if processing is to continue. What if the user answered NO, or XVCBR, or even yes? In all of these cases, processing would end. (Uppercase characters are not equal to lowercase; therefore, YES does not equal yes.) We want the user to enter either YES or NO. We also want to check that the value of GROSS is greater than zero and less than 5000. To have the program check for this, we can add the following:

```
75 INPUT "Do you wish to enter another employee (YES/NO)"; ANS$
76      WHILE ANS$ <> "YES" AND ANS$ <> "NO"
77           INPUT "Please enter YES or NO", ANS$
78      WEND
100     INPUT "Gross pay; "; GROSS
101     WHILE GROSS < 0 OR GROSS > 5000
102          INPUT "Please enter an amount between 0 and 5000"; GROSS
103     WEND
165     INPUT "Do you wish to enter another employee (YES/NO)"; ANS$
166     WHILE ANS$ <> "YES" AND ANS$ <> "NO"
167          INPUT "Please enter YES or NO"; ANS$
168     WEND
```

As you can see, adding validation increases the length of the program. Most programs are like this. Because users are human, they make mistakes. If a program is to prevent these mistakes from being accepted, as all programs should, a considerable portion of the program will be devoted to data validation.

TEST YOUR LEARNING

1. What is a loop?
2. How can you create loops in BASIC?
3. Name the three parts of the FOR . . . NEXT loop and describe the function of each part.
4. How does the WHILE . . . WEND loop differ from the FOR . . . NEXT loop?
5. What is the difference between AND, OR, and NOT?
6. How can you validate input in BASIC?
7. Using IF . . . THEN, write a program to do the following:
   a. Ask the user to input the salesperson's name and gross sales. If the gross sales is greater than 5000, set the bonus sales to gross minus 5000.

b. Using FOR . . . NEXT, modify the program to input five salespeople. After entry is completed print the total bonus sales.
c. Because the cutoff for the bonus may not always be 5000, place this value in a DATA statement.
d. If WHILE . . . WEND is available on your system, change the loop to allow for any number of salespeople to be entered. Ask the user to enter QUIT as the name when entry is completed.

8. Write a program that asks the user to input the name, hours, and hourly rate for each of five employees. Calculate and print the gross wages (hours times rate) for each employee. After all five have been entered, print a blank line followed by the total gross wages.
   a. If your dialect has WHILE . . . WEND or a similar construct, have the program validate that the hours are within the range 0 to 40.
   b. If your dialect has WHILE . . . WEND, change the program to allow any number of employees to be entered. Instruct the user to enter DONE as the name when entry is complete.
9. Write a program that asks the user for an employee's name, gross monthly pay, and the percentage of the pay he or she wants withheld and deposited in a credit union. Using a FOR . . . NEXT loop, calculate and print the monthly balance for 12 months, assuming an interest rate of 1 percent per month. The output should appear as follows:

```
Employee? Sarah Gentry
Monthly Gross? 500
Percent to credit union (enter 10% as 10)? 10
Month          Balance
 1              50
 2              105
 3              165.5
 4              232.05
 5              305.255
 6              385.7805
 7              474.3585
 8              571.7944
 9              678.9738
 10             796.8712
 11             926.5584
 12             1069.214
```

MENUS

We will frequently write a program that asks the user to select from a number of processing options, which are usually displayed as a numbered list on the screen (such as shown in Figure 10). This list is called a *menu*. The user is asked to enter one of the numbers to indicate the selected option.

Three of the BASIC commands we have learned are generally used to implement menus. With a WHILE . . . WEND loop, we can put the menu back on the screen until the user indicates he or she is finished. With IF . . . THEN we choose between the options offered on the screen. With GOSUB we can direct processing to the desired section of the program and return to the menu when that section has been completed.

Here is a program segment that displays the menu in Figure 10. At this point only a message is displayed when an option is selected. The detailed instructions have not yet been written. This demonstrates another advantage afforded by structured modular programming, called *stubbing*. Because we have divided the program into modules in the design phase we can write subroutine *stubs* for lower-level modules. As we finish coding and testing the manager modules, we can fill in the detailed instructions later.

```
100 REM Driver Module
110 REM
120 FINISH$ = "0"                          : REM Initialize FINISH$
130 WHILE FINISH$<>"5"
140     GOSUB 500                          : REM Menu Display and Input
150     IF FINISH$ = "1" THEN GOSUB 1000 : REM Add a New Client
160     IF FINISH$ = "2" THEN GOSUB 2000 : REM Display Current Client
170     IF FINISH$ = "3" THEN GOSUB 3000 : REM Modify Existing Client
180     IF FINISH$ = "4" THEN GOSUB 4000 : REM Print Report
190 WEND
200 END
500 REM ********************************
510 REM Menu Display and Input
520 CLS : REM Clears Screen in Many BASIC Dialects
530 PRINT
540 PRINT "1 = Add new client"
550 PRINT "2 = Display current client"
560 PRINT "3 = Modify existing client"
570 PRINT "4 = Print report"
580 PRINT "5 = End processing"
590 PRINT
600 INPUT "Please enter your selection (1-5); "; FINISH$
610 RETURN
```

FIGURE 10

Menu presents options to user.

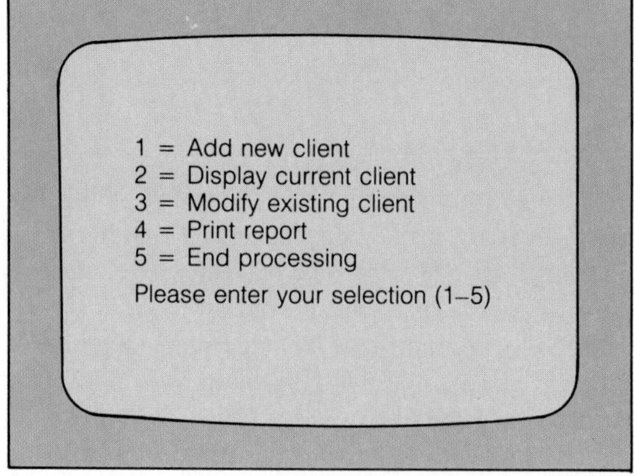

```
1000 REM ***********************************
1010 REM Add a New Client
1020 PRINT "Module to add new client"
1030 INPUT "Press RETURN when ready"; DUMMY$
1040 RETURN
2000 REM ***********************************
2010 REM Display Current Client
2020 PRINT "Module to display current client"
2030 INPUT "Press RETURN when ready"; DUMMY$
2040 RETURN
3000 REM ***********************************
3010 REM Modify Existing Client
3020 PRINT "Module to modify existing client"
3030 INPUT "Press RETURN when ready"; DUMMY$
3040 RETURN
4000 REM ***********************************
4010 REM Print Report
4020 PRINT "Module to print report"
4030 INPUT "Press RETURN when ready"; DUMMY$
4040 RETURN
```

The loop continues until the user chooses 5 on the input. We used the string variable FINISH$ because users often make typos. If the user types 1, 2, 3, or 4, the appropriate subroutine will be called. If he or she types a 5, the ending condition on the WHILE loop is satisfied, ending the program. If the user types anything else the menu screen will refresh. Other codes could be added later to give explicit error messages. If we had used a numeric variable instead of FINISH$ and the user had typed a "Q" by mistake (or any other letter), the generic BASIC data input error message (?Redo from start) would have been given. We want to spare our users this, as we have said.

In the stubs we have repeated an INPUT statement. This freezes the screen before leaving the module, allowing the programmer to look at whatever messages are on the screen. While the program is under development, many messages from partially coded subroutines might be of value to the programmer. When the subroutine is finished, we simply delete the INPUT statement.

As noted in Line 520, CLS clears the screen in many BASIC dialects.

TEST YOUR LEARNING

1. How is a menu used in a program?
2. Write a program that displays the following menu for a payroll program. If the user enters an invalid choice, display a message asking the user to reenter a number within the valid range. Have each module display a message, then return to the menu.

```
Payroll Menu

1 = Enter New Employee
2 = Terminate Employee
3 = Enter Pay Data
```

```
4 = Print Pay Checks
5 = Print Payroll Reports
6 = End Processing

Your Selection?
```

3. The XYZ Company carries four products, numbered 1 through 4. Each has a different price and discount schedule for high-volume customers as shown in the following table:

```
Product #1          Price $100.00
Qty:  0-100  = 0%     101-300 = 10%     301-1000 = 15%   over 1000 = 20%
Product #2          Price $495.00
Qty:  0-10   = 0%     11- 20 = 5%       21 - 50 = 10%    over 50 = 15%
Product #3          Price $5.95
Qty: 0-1000  = 5%     1001-5000 = 10% over 5001 = 12%
Product #4          Price $10,000
Qty: no discounts
```

Write a program that asks the user for the product number and quantity ordered, then computes the total list price and the discounted price. Use a separate subroutine for each product type. Allow the user to enter as many orders as desired. At the end of the program, print for each product the total number ordered, the total list price, and the total discounted price. Also print the preceding totals for all orders.

DEBUGGING BASIC

A program can have various types of errors. A *syntax error* occurs when BASIC tries to execute a line that it doesn't understand. For example, consider the following:

```
1230 PRIMT "This line has PRINT misspelled"
RUN
Syntax error
```

BASIC has not the foggiest idea what `PRIMT` means. BASIC will find syntax errors for us, but only when the line is actually executed. When the line is encountered, BASIC will tell us that it has found a syntax error by displaying a message on the screen.

Another type of error is the *logic error*. Here the program makes perfect sense to BASIC, yet it does not solve our problem. This can occur, for example, when we type `GOSUB 2000` when we meant to type `GOSUB 3000`. Or we meant to pay overtime as time and a half, but our program mistakenly gives double time. The program runs, but the output is wrong.

As you are probably aware, errors in programs are called *bugs*. Therefore, the process of finding and correcting errors in programs is called *debugging*. Because it is inevitable that any program you write will have some bugs, several techniques have been developed to decrease the number of bugs and to quickly correct those that do occur.

INCREMENTAL DEBUGGING

Because BASIC gives error messages when syntax errors occur, one of the easiest ways to find this type of error is to use BASIC. In other words, run your program as you type it in. Then debug any syntax errors. Repeat this process by typing in some more modules, running, and debugging. BASIC will point out any syntax errors.

For example, as part of a payroll program we have a module in which the employee data is entered. We can write just those lines and test them before writing any code that processes the data.

```
3100 REM   ***           Enter Pay Data           ***
3110 REM
3120 INPUT "What is the gross pay"; GROSS
3130 WHILE GROSS < 0 or GROSS > 5000
3140   INPUT "Please enter an amount for gross between 0 and 5000 ", GROSS
3150 WEND
3160 INPUT "Please enter the number of allowances ", NUMALLOWANCES
3170 PRINT "Please enter filing status:"
3180 PRINT " 1 = single"
3190 PRINT " 2 = married"
3200 INPUT " Employee's status"; STATUS
3210 WHILE STATUS < 1 OR STATUS > 2
3220       INPUT "Status must be 1 or 2, please reenter"; STATUS
3230 WEND
9999 END
```

Even though this is just a section of the program, we can RUN these lines to make sure they contain no syntax errors. By stopping to check for errors as we code, we can easily catch and correct most syntax errors as we make them.

TEST DATA

To test logic errors we need to create some *test data* for which we know the correct output. The test lines we have just written contain no output, but we can check that the variables `GROSS`, `NUMALLOWANCES`, and `STATUS` contain the correct values by displaying their values on the screen in two ways. We could run the lines and then type `PRINT` in the immediate mode.

```
PRINT GROSS, NUMALLOWANCES, STATUS
```

Or we can insert temporary lines into the program to display these values. To our sample we can add:

```
3221 PRINT "The values of GROSS, NUMALLOWANCES and STATUS are: ";
           GROSS, NUMALLOWANCES, STATUS
```

We will remove this temporary line only when we are satisfied that the variables are being calculated and stored correctly.

Top–Down Debugging

A more formalized type of incremental debugging is *top-down debugging*, a companion to top-down programming. Like incremental debugging, top-down debugging calls for you to test your program as you code it; but it also calls for you to test the modules in a certain order, from top to bottom.

The essence of top-down debugging is to test each module as you write it, starting with the uppermost modules. In this way you can detect and correct the errors at each level as you go along. An error in an upper module that is not detected until after the minor modules have been written can result in hours or days of rewriting. For this reason the upper modules are tested first and most often. Taking the time to test at each step will actually reduce the total time it takes to produce the final, bug-free product. In this case, taking time saves more time.

How can we test a module that uses other modules that have not yet been written? We write dummy or *stub modules* for the lesser modules. We made use of stub modules in the earlier program segment that displayed the menu. The stub may contain as little as a simple PRINT statement to inform us control has reached that module. Let's say we wish to write a program to calculate withholding taxes. To begin writing this program we would first code the three top modules.

```
NEW
1000 REM ***********************************
1010 REM       Main Module
1020 REM ***********************************
1030 GOSUB 2000          :REM Initialize
1040 WHILE EMPNAME$ <> "DONE"
1050    GOSUB 3000       :REM Process one Employee's Record
1060 WEND
1070 GOSUB 4000          :REM Print Totals
1080 END
2000 REM ***********************************
2010 PRINT "Insert lines to initialize here"
2020 INPUT "What is the Employee's name (enter DONE to quit)"; EMPNAME$
2030 RETURN
3000 REM ***********************************
3010 PRINT "Insert lines to process employee here"
3020 INPUT "What is the Employee's name (enter DONE to quit)"; EMPNAME$
3030 RETURN
4000 REM ***********************************
4010 PRINT "Insert lines to print totals here"
4020 RETURN
```

We can now run the program to ensure this part works correctly. If all is well, we proceed to write and test each submodule.

Using STOP and CONT

The BASIC command STOP is used to halt processing at some location other than the physical end of the program. STOP also displays a message that indicates at which line processing was halted. This function becomes very useful while debugging. We can insert temporary STOP statements to halt processing at a particular spot in the program. When the program encounters the STOP instruction, it passes control back to the user. The program is put in a suspended state with all variables keeping their values. This allows us, using PRINT in the immediate mode, to find out what values different variables have. We can even change the value of variables using LET in immediate mode.

To continue the program at this point, type `CONT`. When you press Return, the program will resume where it left off. This ability to halt processing temporarily, modify the value of variables, and then continue is a major difference between STOP and END.

TEST YOUR LEARNING

1. Compare incremental debugging with top-down debugging.
2. How can STOP and CONT be used for debugging?

GOTO

GOTO is perhaps the most controversial statement in BASIC. Like GOSUB, GOTO directs processing to another line in the program; however, GOTO does not have a statement that returns processing to the point from which it branched. Controversy has arisen because the misuse of GOTO can cause programs that jump from here to there. Indiscriminate use of GOTO creates programs that are very difficult to test or modify. Structured programming was developed as a way of controlling this misuse; indeed, at one time it was called "GOTO-less programming." Programmers don't agree on the use of GOTO: Some believe it should never be used; others believe GOTO should be used only in certain restricted situations. Still others (fewer and fewer) feel that GOTO has many valid uses.

VALID USES

Some programmers believe that GOTO can be used if it does not cause branching that violates the "One rule." Thus, it can be used for *forward branching*—a process that transfers control to a line that follows the GOTO statement. It does not jump processing into or out of a loop, or into or out of a subroutine. The following is an example of forward branching.

```
10 LET PRICE = 75
20 LET DISCOUNT = 0
30 INPUT "Quantity"; QTY
40 IF QTY < 100 THEN GOTO 60
50 LET DISCOUNT = .1         :REM Apply Discount
60 LET SELL.PRICE = QTY * (Price - PRICE * DISCOUNT)
70 PRINT "The selling price is"; SELL.PRICE
80 END
```

The GOTO statement in Line 40 caused branching to Line 60 when the value of QTY is less than 100. This example could also be written using GOSUB.

```
10 LET PRICE = 75
20 LET DISCOUNT = 0
30 INPUT "Quantity"; QTY
40 IF QTY => 100 THEN GOSUB 80        :REM Apply Discount
50 LET SELL.PRICE = QTY * (PRICE - PRICE * DISCOUNT)
60 PRINT "The selling price is"; SELL.PRICE
70 END
80  REM  **     Apply Discount    **
90  LET DISCOUNT = .1
100 PRINT "discount taken"
110 RETURN
```

Because of the advantages of modularity, we recommend the use of GOSUB in place of GOTO wherever possible.

GOTO IN PLACE OF STOP

Some dialects require END to be the last physical line of a program. We have discussed the use of STOP to halt processing at a line other than the last line. However, STOP usually displays the message "Break in line nnn," which can be disconcerting to the user. To avoid this problem, we can replace STOP with a GOTO statement that directs processing to the END statement:

```
10 LET PRICE = 75
20 LET DISCOUNT = 0
30 INPUT "Quantity"; QTY
40 IF QTY => 100 THEN GOSUB 80        :REM Apply Discount
50 LET SELL.PRICE = QTY * (Price - PRICE * DISCOUNT)
60 PRINT "The selling price is"; SELL.PRICE
70 GOTO 120           :REM   Go To End
80  REM  **   Apply Discount**
90  LET DISCOUNT = .1
100 PRINT "discount taken"
110 RETURN
120 END
```

USING GOTO AND IF TO SIMULATE WHILE . . . WEND

Another valid use of GOTO is to simulate the WHILE . . . WEND construct in those dialects that don't have it. Using GOTO, we could write the checkbook balance example that we wrote during the discussion of WHILE . . . WEND like this:

```
10 REM segment to simulate WHILE . . .WEND using GOTO
20 INPUT "What is your check balance"; BALANCE
30 IF BALANCE <= 0 THEN GOTO 80
40    INPUT "How much is this check"; CHECK
50    LET BALANCE = BALANCE - CHECK
60    PRINT "Current Balance: "; BALANCE
```

```
70 GOTO 30
80 PRINT "Oops, you are overdrawn"
90 END
```

BASIC allows us to omit the word GOTO in the IF . . . THEN statement. Line 30 could be written as:

```
30 IF BALANCE <= 0 THEN 80
```

TEST YOUR LEARNING

1. Why should you avoid using GOTO?
2. What is a legitimate use of GOTO?
3. What BASIC statement is best for directing processing elsewhere in the program?
4. How can you correct the problem with the following program?

```
10 LET C3 = 0
20 IF C3 > 20 THEN GOTO 50
30 LET C3 = C3 + 6
40 PRINT C3
50 GOTO 20
60 END
```

5. Write a program that uses GOTO to simulate a FOR . . . NEXT loop. Execute the loop a total of four times. On each pass through the loop, print the value of the counter. (Remember to add 1 to the counter on each pass.)
6. Rewrite the following WHILE . . . WEND loop using GOTO.

```
100 INPUT "Customer Name (or EXIT to end)"; CUST.NAME$
110 WHILE CUST.NAME$ <> "EXIT"
120      PRINT CUST.NAME$
130      INPUT "Customer Name (or EXIT to end)"; CUST.NAME$
140 WEND
```

7. What happens in this program? (*Note:* This "spaghetti code" led to the development of structured programming.)

```
10 INPUT "Enter First Number (9999 to end)"; N1
20 IF N1 > 10 THEN GOTO 90
30 IF N1 > 50 THEN GOTO 110
40 PRINT "First Number is "; N1
50 PRINT "Enter Second Number"; N2
60 PRINT "First times Second is "; N1 * N2
70 IF N1 = 9999 THEN GOTO 130
80 GOTO 10
90 LET N2 = 25
100 GOTO 60
110 LET N1 = 30
120 GOTO 50
130 END
```

ARRAYS

Up to this point, when we have wanted to hold data in a program, we've assigned a separate variable name to each data element. We have used numeric data variables that hold only numeric values and string data variables that hold nonnumeric or character values such as names and addresses.

Data Element	Variable Name
`3`	`COUNT`
`14.56`	`PRICE`
`"BETTY BOYD"`	`EMPNAME$`

SINGLE-DIMENSION ARRAYS

Frequently we need to store a list within a program. Think of a "To-Do" list in which you note various tasks. If there are seven items on your list you could number them and refer to the first as "To-Do #1," the second as "To-Do #2," and so on.

To-Do List

1. Do Laundry
2. Pay Bills
3. Cut Lawn
4. Finish Math Assignment
5. Go to Store
6. Call Jane and Jack
7. Clean Kitchen

Instead of assigning a different variable name to each item, we can place the list in BASIC using an *array*. We assign a name to the array (or list) using the same rules as for ordinary variables. Following the name, in parentheses, is a number or a numeric value. This number is called the *subscript*. The subscript tells BASIC to which item in the list we are referring. For example, if we want to put the preceding "To-Do" list into a BASIC program as an array we could assign it the name `TODO$`. Because this list contains string data, we gave it a string name. To refer to the fifth item, `Go to Store`, we would use `TODO$(5)`. The value of `TODO$(5)` is `Go to Store`. The value of `TODO$(3)` is `Cut Lawn`.

The elements of the array `TODO$` and their values are as follows:

Array Name: `TODO$`

Element Name	Value of Element
`TODO$(1)`	`Do Laundry`
`TODO$(2)`	`Pay Bills`
`TODO$(3)`	`Cut Lawn`

```
TODO$(4)          Finish Math Assignment
TODO$(5)          Go to Store
TODO$(6)          Call Jane and Jack
TODO$(7)          Clean Kitchen
```

Before we can use this array, we must instruct BASIC that `TODO$` refers to an array and that the maximum number of entries or ***elements*** in the array is seven. The DIM (DIMension) statement does this. We use the DIM statement `DIM TODO$(7)` to instruct BASIC to establish the string array `TODO$`, reserving room in its workspace for elements with subscripts up to seven.

Now we can write a short program segment to enter and print this list.

```
100 DIM TODO$(7)
200 PRINT "Enter up to seven things for your To-Do List"
210 FOR ITEM = 1 TO 7
220      INPUT "Enter next item: ", TODO$(ITEM)
230 NEXT ITEM
240 REM
300 PRINT "Current To-Do List"
310 FOR ITEM = 1 TO 7
320      PRINT ITEM, TODO$(ITEM)
330 NEXT ITEM
340 END
```

Note that we use the variable `ITEM` as a subscript in Lines 220 and 320. Much of the power of arrays comes from this use of subscripts.

As a final note, even though we dimensioned the array `TODO$` to seven, in many dialects it will actually have eight elements, with subscripts 0 through 7. In this program we have ignored the element with the subscript of zero. BASIC does not require a DIM statement for single-dimension arrays with 10 or fewer elements; however, good programming practice dictates always dimensioning arrays. A typical place to dimension arrays is in the initialization subroutine.

In the previous program segment we knew how many "things" we wanted in our To-Do list—seven. What if we wanted to make the list more flexible? It is possible to use a numeric variable in the DIM statement to determine the size of the array. Let's transform the previous program segment into a structured program and demonstrate this concept.

```
10 REM ************************************
20 REM     Program Name: TO-DO
30 REM     Written by Sally Roberts
40 REM     January 23, 1992
50 REM
60 REM  This program compiles a simple To-Do list
70 REM ************************************
80 REM *          DATA DICTIONARY         *
90 REM
100 REM TODO$ =array to store To-Do items
110 REM NUMITEMS = number of To-Do items
120 REM ITEM = subscript and counter
```

```
130 REM ***********************************
140 REM Driver Module
150 GOSUB 1000   : REM Initialization
160 GOSUB 2000   : REM Input List
170 GOSUB 3000   : REM Print List
180 END
1000 REM ***********************************
1010 REM Initialization
1020 INPUT "How many items in today's list"; NUMITEMS
1030 DIM TODO$ (NUMITEMS)
1040 ITEM = 0
1050 RETURN
2000 REM ***********************************
2010 REM Input List
2020 PRINT "Enter "; NUMITEMS; "items for your To-Do list."
2030 FOR ITEM = 1 to NUMITEMS
2040      PRINT "Enter item number"; ITEM;
2050      INPUT TODO$ (ITEM)
2060 NEXT ITEM
2070 RETURN
3000 REM ***********************************
3010 REM Print List
3020 PRINT "Current To-Do List"
3030 PRINT "------------------"
3040 FOR ITEM = 1 to NUMITEMS
3050      PRINT ITEM, TODO$ (ITEM)
3060 NEXT ITEM
3070 RETURN
```

The user will be queried "How many items in today's list?" The variable NUMITEMS will accept that value, serve in the DIM statement to determine the size of the array, and serve as the upper boundary of the FOR . . . NEXT loops.

Note that once an array has been dimensioned in a program, it may not be redimensioned. Another way of saying this is that once the DIM statement has been executed for a certain array, another DIM statement for that array may not be executed. One consequence of this is that the DIM statement must not be placed inside a loop.

An array may be filled, blanked, and then filled again. In program TO–DO above, after the array values are printed, the array still contains those values, just as any variable would. If we wished to put new values in the array, we could simply assign new values to any or all array locations. If we wished to completely blank the array (remember, no redimensioning!) we could simply execute the following module:

```
4000 REM Blank String Array
4010 FOR ITEM = 1 to NUMITEMS
4020      TODO$ (ITEM) = " "
4030 NEXT ITEM
4040 RETURN
```

With this code we set each array element to a blank or a space. We could just as easily have filled each location with some other character or characters. For a numerical array we typically "blank" it by setting the value of each element to zero.

Parallel Arrays

To represent some data, we need more than one list. Consider the following tax table that is used for calculating the amount of federal income tax to withhold.

If you earn more than	but not more than	your tax is	plus this percent	of the amount over
$ 0	$ 57	$ 0	—	
57	173	0	12	$ 57
173	385	13.92	15	173
385	605	45.72	19	385
605	913	87.52	25	605
913	1,154	164.52	30	913
1,154	1,373	236.82	34	1,154
1,373		311.28	37	1,373

The table contains five columns of data. For any given earned amount we can use one line of the table to compute our tax. For example, if we earn $500, we use the fourth line. Our tax is $45.72 plus 19 percent of ($500 − $385). These five sets of lists are parallel. Collectively they form a table.

We could program this table by using five arrays, but note the redundancy in the arrays. All the information in the "but not more than" and "amount over" columns is found in the "If you earn" column. We can store all this information in BASIC using just three parallel arrays: one for the lower limit of the range, one for the minimum tax, and one for the rate.

LOWER	AMOUNT	RATE
0	0	.00
57	0	.12
173	13.92	.15
385	45.72	.19
605	87.52	.25
913	164.52	.30
1154	236.82	.34
1373	311.28	.37

The following program segment will READ the values from DATA statements and store them into three parallel arrays. Note that subscripts allow us to use a FOR . . . NEXT loop to read the values from the DATA statements into the arrays.

```
2170 REM ************************************
2180 REM   Read In Withholding Table
2190 REM
2200 DIM LOWER(8), AMOUNT(8), RATE(8)
2205 NUM.IN.TABLE=8
2210 FOR ITEM = 1 to 8
2230     READ LOWER(ITEM), AMOUNT (ITEM), RATE(ITEM)
2250 NEXT ITEM
2270 REM ************************************
2280 REM            Data Statements
2290 REM ************************************
2380 REM ****   1986 Tax Table for Single, Biweekly  ***
2390 REM Lower, Amount, Rate
2400 DATA    0,   0.00, .00
2410 DATA   57,   0.00, .12
2420 DATA  173,  13.92, .15
2430 DATA  385,  45.72, .19
2440 DATA  605,  87.52, .25
2450 DATA  913, 164.52, .30
2460 DATA 1154, 236.82, .34
2470 DATA 1373, 312.76, .37
2480 REM
```

Now that the values are stored in the arrays we can write the code to calculate the tax (amount to withhold for given earnings). To find the proper range, we'll test the earnings against the lower limit. If it is greater than this amount but less than or equal to the next limit, then the amount to withhold is the minimum amount plus the rate times the difference between the limit and the earnings. This method works for all except the last range (because there is no "next limit" for that one). We'll test for that range separately.

In the following code, the FOR . . . NEXT loop checks the amount subject to withholding against the limits for each step except the last. If the amount falls within any of these ranges, the amount to withhold is calculated according to the following formula: Subtract the lower limit from the amount subject to withholding. Multiply the difference times the rate for this range. Add the product to the base amount for this range. For the last range there is no upper limit. Therefore, if the amount subject to withholding is greater than the last limit, we perform the calculation using the data for the last range.

```
3500 REM   ****    Compute Amount to Withhold    ****
3510 LET WITHHOLDING = 0
3520 REM   **            Search Tax Array           **
3530 FOR ITEM = 1 TO NUM.IN.TABLE-1
3540    IF SUBJECT > LOWER(ITEM) AND SUBJECT <= LOWER(ITEM+1)
           THEN LET WITHHOLDING = AMOUNT(ITEM) + RATE(ITEM) *
             (SUBJECT - LOWER(ITEM))
```

```
3550 NEXT ITEM
3560 REM **         Check for Last Range          **
3570 IF SUBJECT > LOWER(NUM.IN.TABLE) THEN LET WITHHOLDING =
        AMOUNT(NUM.IN.TABLE) + RATE(NUM.IN.TABLE)  *
        (SUBJECT - AMOUNT(NUM.IN.TABLE))
3580 REM   **      Calculate Social Security and SDI **
3590 LET SS.AMOUNT = GROSS * SS.RATE
3600 LET SDI.AMOUNT = GROSS * SDI.RATE
3610 REM   **        Calculate Total Withholding     **
3620 LET WITHHOLDING = WITHHOLDING + SS,AMOUNT + SDI.AMOUNT
3630 RETURN
3640 REM
```

Multidimension Arrays

In the previous discussion we learned how to load the tax rates for a single person on a biweekly payroll into three arrays. However, not all employees are single; we also need the tax rates for married employees. We could create a separate set of parallel arrays with separate names for the married rates. Fortunately BASIC provides a simple way of expanding an array to more than one dimension by the use of multiple subscripts. Let's look first at the array `LOWER` that contains the lower limit for each income bracket. Instead of representing the lower limits as a list, we need to represent them as a table as shown below:

	Lower Limit	
	Single	**Married**
Range 1	0	0
Range 2	57	100
Range 3	173	398
Range 4	385	795
Range 5	605	980
Range 6	913	1199
Range 7	1154	1419
Range 8	1373	1859

To identify an element in a list we need only give the row in which it appears. For a table, we need to give both the row and the column. In the single-dimension array, to retrieve the third range for a single person we referenced it as `LOWER(3)`. To reference it from a similarly named table, we use `LOWER(3,1)` (row 3, column 1); to reference the third range for a married person we use `LOWER(3,2)` (row 3, column 2). The first subscript indicates the range; the second subscript indicates the marital status (1 equals single, 2 equals married).

We can now change our subroutine to build two-dimensional arrays for the tax rate tables. Note that the DIM statement in `LINE` 2200 has been changed to reflect the creation of arrays with eight rows and two columns.

```
2170 REM ***********************************
2180 REM    Read In Withholding Table
2190 REM
2200 DIM LOWER(8,2), AMOUNT(8,2), RATE(8,2)
2210 FOR COL = 1 TO 2
2220     FOR ROW = 1 TO 8
2230         READ LOWER(ROW,COL), AMOUNT(ROW,COL), RATE(ROW,COL)
2240     NEXT ROW
2250 NEXT COL
2260 RETURN
2270 REM ***********************************
2280 REM            Data Statements
2290 REM ***********************************
2370 REM
2380 REM     **** 1986 Tax Table for Single, Biweekly  ***
2390 REM Lower, Amount, Rate
2400 DATA    0,   0.00, .00
2410 DATA   57,   0.00, .12
2420 DATA  173,  13.92, .15
2430 DATA  385,  45.72, .19
2440 DATA  605,  87.52, .25
2450 DATA  913, 164.52, .30
2460 DATA 1154, 236.82, .34
2470 DATA 1373, 312.76, .37
2480 REM
2490 REM     **** 1986 Tax Table for Married, Biweekly  ***
2500 REM Lower, Amount, Rate
2510 DATA    0,   0.00, .00
2520 DATA  100,   0.00, .12
2530 DATA  398,  35.76, .17
2540 DATA  795, 103.25, .22
2550 DATA  980, 143.95, .25
2560 DATA 1199, 198.70, .28
2570 DATA 1419, 260.30, .33
2580 DATA 1859, 405.50, .37
2590 REM
```

TEST YOUR LEARNING

1. What is an array? What is an element of an array? What is a subscript?
2. What does DIM do?
3. a. Write a statement to dimension an array with up to 12 elements.
   b. Write a statement to dimension an array that represents the sales in five locations for each of 12 months.
4. Write a program to read the names of each month and the number of days in that month from DATA statements and load them into two arrays: one, a string array containing the names of the months; the other, a numeric array containing the number of days in the month.

5. a. Write a program that prompts the user to enter the description and cost for nine products. Place this data in two single-dimension arrays.
   b. Add a second part of the program that displays the name of each product and asks the user the quantity ordered. Store the response in a third array. When entry is completed, print a report listing the name, price, quantity ordered, and total cost for the items ordered. If zero is ordered for a particular product, do not print it. At the end of the list print the total cost for all items.
6. There are five manufacturing areas in the company. Management wants an analysis of the output of each area over a six-month period. Write a program to do the following:

   Ask the user to enter for each department its name and total output for each of six months. Place the names in a single-dimension array and the output in a two-dimension array (one subscript will be department number and the other, month).

   Total the output for each department and compute the average total output.

   At the end of the program, display a report that shows the department name, the total output, and the amount that the output is over or under the average.

SEQUENTIAL FILES

In Chapter 4 we discuss three major storage and retrieval methods: sequential, direct access, and indexed. Many BASIC dialects include commands to store and access data using files created in all three methods. In this section we describe the use of sequential files and discuss BASIC commands and techniques for their use. As you write more sophisticated programs you will want to investigate the other techniques.

Why use files at all? Recall from our earlier discussions that, as soon as you exit BASIC, the workspace gets erased. We introduced the SAVE command to allow you to save your program into a file. What about data? When the workspace is erased, all variable values are erased, too. Imagine any program with a large amount of data. We may well wish to save the data values to files for future reference.

To introduce the notion of processing with files, picture a storage cabinet with one large file drawer. In order to use the storage, one must first own the storage cabinet! To put a piece of paper in storage, we open the drawer and place the paper in the drawer. We might put the paper in the front of the drawer or the rear. Then we close the drawer. To get a piece of paper we open the drawer, find the paper, and close the drawer. BASIC provides commands for each of these operations on a file.

OPEN

The OPEN command is used to create and open a file if it doesn't already exist, or just open the file if it does exist. The format of the command is:

```
OPEN filename FOR mode AS filenumber
```

The filename is any legal BASIC filename, including the disk designation, if desired.

A file must be opened for one of three modes: INPUT, OUTPUT or APPEND. We open for INPUT when we wish to bring data from the file into the program via a special version of the INPUT command, described later. We cannot open a file for INPUT if the file doesn't exist; there's nothing in a nonexistent file to bring into the program.

We open for OUTPUT when we wish to write to the file and, if needed, create the file. When we write to a file after opening for OUTPUT, we write to the beginning (or front) of the file. If there's any information already in the file, the new information will be written right over it. Sometimes that is desirable.

When we want to add information to the end or back of the file, we can open for APPEND. (This command also creates the file if needed.) Writing to a file opened for APPEND adds all information to the *end* of the file, thus preserving all information already there.

Most BASICs permit you to have more than one file open at once. The file number keeps track of which file you are inputting from or writing to. The number of files permitted to be open depends on the BASIC dialect.

Let's look at some examples:

```
200 OPEN "PAYROLL" FOR APPEND AS #1
```

This opens a file named PAYROLL, creating it if it is not already there. If we were to write to it, all information would be written at the end of the file. Until it is closed, file PAYROLL will be designated as #1.

```
300 CURRENT$ = "A:NAMES"
310 OPEN CURRENT$ FOR INPUT AS #2.
```

Here we see that the filename can be a string variable. This is useful if we want to use a single subroutine to handle multiple files. Since we opened it for INPUT, we will be getting information from the file into the program. The file is on the A drive.

CLOSE

In order to close a file we simply execute the CLOSE instruction with the proper file number.

```
500 CLOSE #1
```

Simply executing CLOSE with no file numbers closes all open files. It is good programming practice to CLOSE a file as soon as the program is finished with it.

KILL

To delete a file under program control, we execute the KILL command with the full filename.

```
100 KILL "PAYROLL"
200 KILL "A:JOBS"
300 KILL "B:MYFILE,TXT"
```

WRITE

As we discussed above, depending on how the file was opened, the WRITE command writes a record onto the beginning (OPEN FOR OUTPUT) or end (OPEN FOR APPEND) of the file. The format for the command is:

`WRITE` filenumber, list of constants and/or variables

Here are some examples.

```
100 WRITE #1, "Hi, Sally"
200 WRITE #1, NUMCUST, TOTAL
300 WRITE #2, "REPORT FOR MONTH =", MONTH$
```

In the first example, the constant string "Hi, Sally" is written to the file opened as #1. In the second, the values associated with NUMCUST and TOTAL are written to the same file. In the third, the constant string and value for MONTH$ are written to the file opened as #2.

INPUT

INPUT reads a single record from the file associated with the file number. The record to be read depends on the processing logic. For example, if the file has just been opened for INPUT, the INPUT statement will read the first record. The format is:

`INPUT` filenumber, list of variables

The type of data read into each variable (string or numeric) must agree with the type of variable (string or constant). As an example, assume that the following data exists in a file called HSINFO.

```
"Joe Smith", 28,78
"Mary Johnson", 38,68
"Sue Richards", 18,88
```

Consider the following program segment.

```
100 OPEN "HSINFO" FOR INPUT AS #1
110 FOR COUNTER = 1 to 2
120      INPUT #1, STUNAME$,AGE,YEAR
130      PRINT STUNAME$,AGE,YEAR
140 NEXT COUNTER
150 INPUT #1, STUNAME,AGE,YEAR
160 PRINT STUNAME$,AGE,YEAR
170 CLOSE #1
```

When run, the code would produce:

```
Joe Smith    28 78
Mary Johnson 38 68
Error - Type Mismatch
```

The first and second records would be input correctly into the variables and then printed. Because the third INPUT had no string variable in the first field of the record (i.e., STUNAME instead of STUNAME$) an error was reported, stopping program execution.

EOF

EOF tests for an end-of-file condition. As we shall see, it is most often used with a WHILE . . . WEND loop. Its format is:

EOF (filenumber)

An example is:

```
EOF(1)
```

A BRIEF EXAMPLE

Because we include file processing in our extensive example at the end of this appendix, we include only a short program segment as illustration here.

```
100 REM A Brief Example
110 REM Open Test File for Append in Case It Already Exists
120 OPEN "TEST" FOR APPEND AS #1
130 INPUT "Add a record (Y,N)"; ADD$
140 WHILE (ADD$ = "Y") OR (ADD$ = "y")
150       REM Get Info from User
160       INPUT "Name"; TESTNAME$
170       INPUT "SSN"; SSN
180       REM Write to End of File
190       WRITE #1, TESTNAME$, SSN
200       INPUT "Add another record"; ADD$
210 WEND
220 CLOSE #1
230 REM Get Old (if any) Plus New Info Out and Print It
240 OPEN "TEST" FOR INPUT AS #1
250 WHILE NOT EOF(1)
260       INPUT #1, YRNAME$ SSN
270 PRINT YRNAME$, SSN
280 WEND
290 CLOSE #1
```

Line 120 opens for APPEND because we're going to write information when we don't know if there is any information already in file TEST. With the WHILE . . . WEND loop we add as many records to TEST as the user wishes. All records are added to the end of TEST, preserving any records previously there if TEST already existed before the OPEN statement. In Line 220 we close the file because we are finished writing. We then open the file for INPUT so we can get information out. The WHILE . . . WEND loop executes until there are no more records, inputting into the variables YRNAME$ and SSN, and printing the values on the screen. If TEST existed prior to this program, many names and SSNs might be printed (the old names and SSNs plus the ones the user just input). If we created the file with Line 120, only those just input by the user will be printed.

TEST YOUR LEARNING

1. What is a file?
2. What is the difference between opening a file for INPUT, OUTPUT, and APPEND?
3. How can we create a file?
4. Write a program to execute the following logic: Create two new files. Receive input from the user, and write those records into both files so that you end up with two identical files. Close the files. Open them again. Copy all information from one file to the end of the other. Close the files. Destroy the shorter file. Open the longer one and print its contents. Close it.

A SAMPLE PROGRAM

In prior sections, we have discussed and coded portions of a payroll withholding program. At this point we will develop a complete program to demonstrate the concepts discussed in this appendix.

These are the steps for calculating the various taxes:

FEDERAL INCOME TAX

1. Calculate the amount subject to withholding by multiplying the number of allowances times the allowance rate for a biweekly payroll and subtracting the result from the gross.
2. Select the table appropriate for the employee's marital status.
3. For this table, select the range appropriate for the employee's amount subject to withholding that was calculated in Step 1.
4. Use the table values to calculate the amount to withhold.

SOCIAL SECURITY (FICA) TAX

1. Multiply the gross pay times the social security tax rate.

STATE DISABILITY INSURANCE (SDI) TAX

1. Multiply the gross pay by the current SDI rate.

Both social security and SDI have a maximum amount to be withheld during the calendar year. This sample program does not check for the limits; to do so would require that the program have access to year-to-date data.

DESIGN

The complete structure chart for this program is shown in Figure 11.

ANNOTATED PROGRAM LISTING

```
100 REM ***      Sample Payroll Program: PAYROLL      ***
110 REM           Written by EB Cohen
120 REM           11/11/92
130 REM This is a sample program for calculating net pay.
140 REM It uses Arrays, READ . . . DATA, and Files
200 REM ********************************
210 REM ****    DATA DICTIONARY        ****
220 REM ALLOWANCE        =  ALLOWANCE.RATE times NUMALLOWANCES
230 REM ALLOWANCE.RATE   =  rate per allowance for biweekly payroll
240 REM AMOUNT           =  base amount of tax on table (array)
250 REM EMPNAME$         =  employee's name
260 REM GROSS            =  gross pay
270 REM ROW              =  counter for loop
280 REM COL              =  counter for loop
290 REM LOWER            =  lower limit on tax table (array)
300 REM NUMALLOWANCES    =  number of allowances for employee
```

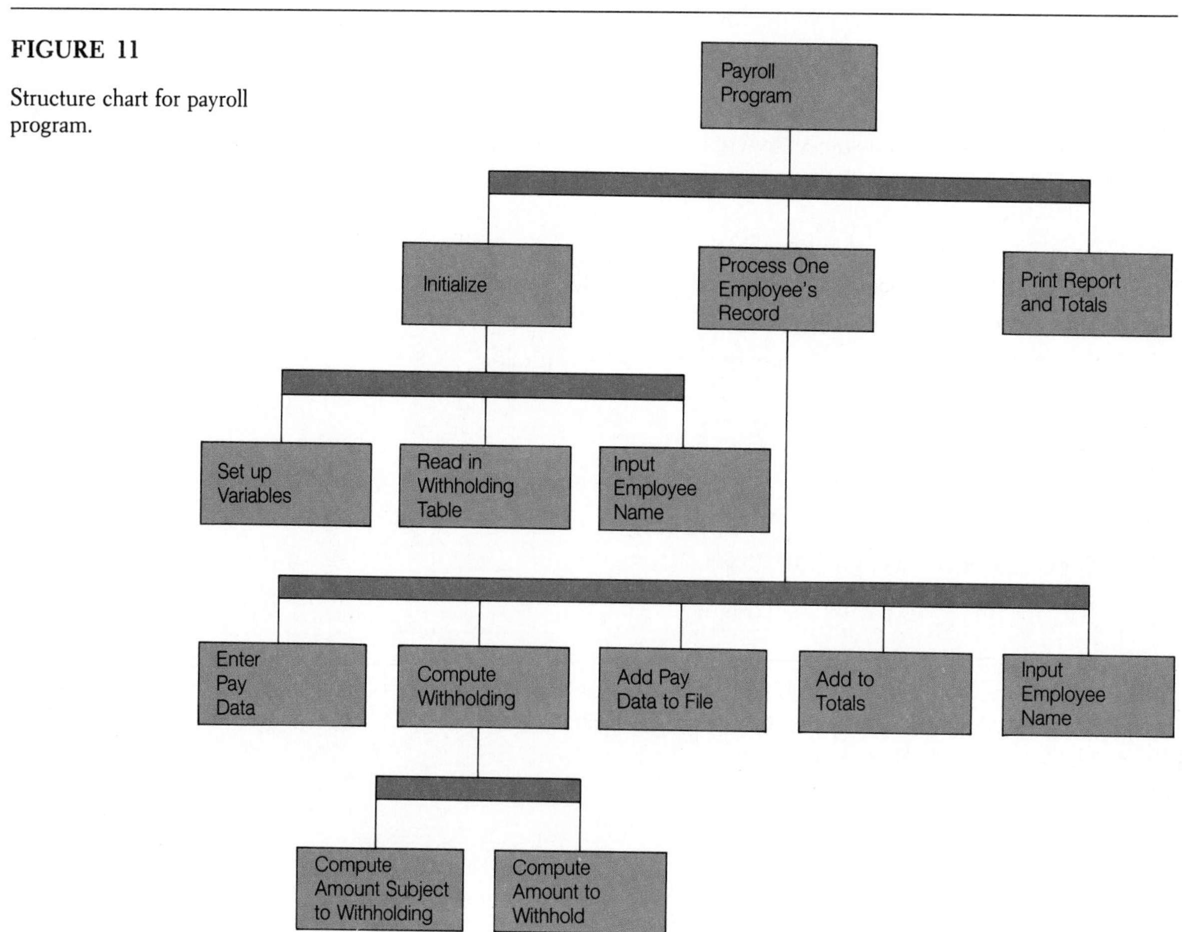

FIGURE 11

Structure chart for payroll program.

```
310 REM NUM.IN.TABLE     =  number of tax rates in table
320 REM NUM.STATUS       =  number of marital status categories
330 REM RATE             =  percentage rate in tax table (array)
340 REM SDI.AMOUNT       =  amount to be withheld for SDI
350 REM SDI.RATE         =  tax rate for State Disability Insurance
360 REM SS.AMOUNT        =  amount to be withheld for Social Security
370 REM SS.RATE          =  tax rate for Social Security
380 REM STATUS           =  marital status for employee
390 REM SUBJECT          =  calculated amount subject to
                            withholding
400 REM TOT.GROSS        =  total gross wages
410 REM TOT.WITHHOLDING  =  total amount withheld
420 REM WITHHOLDING      =  amount to be withheld for this employee
430 REM GRMINWITH        =  Gross-withholding
1000 REM ***********************************
1010 REM ***********************************
1020 REM
1030 GOSUB 2000          :REM  Initialize
1035 OPEN "PAYINFO" FOR OUTPUT AS #1
1040 WHILE EMPNAME$ <> "DONE"
1050    GOSUB 3000       :REM  Process one employee's record
1060 WEND
1065 CLOSE #1
1070 GOSUB 4000          :REM  Print Report and Totals
1080 END
1090 REM ***********************************
1100 REM ***********************************
```

After initializing the tax rate tables and other variables, the program will process one employee at a time. The user will enter DONE as the employee's name to signal that entry is complete. At that point the program will print the final report, final totals, and then end.

```
2000 REM    ****          Initialize        ****
2010 GOSUB 2100          :REM  Set Up Variables
2020 GOSUB 2300          :REM  Read In Withholding Table
2030 GOSUB 2800          :REM  Input Employee Name (Initial Input)
2040 RETURN
2050 REM ***********************************************
2100 REM ***           Set Up Variables               ***
2110 REM              Set Totals to Zero
2120 LET TOT.GROSS = 0              :REM Total Gross
2130 LET TOT.WITHHOLDING = 0        :REM Total Withholding
2140 REM   *******     Read Data Constants     **********
2150 READ NUM.STATUS                :REM Number of Filing Categories
2160 READ NUM.IN.TABLE              :REM Number of Tax Brackets in Table
2170 READ ALLOWANCE.RATE            :REM Allowance per Deduction
2180 READ SS.RATE                   :REM Social Security Rate
2190 READ SDI.RATE                  :REM State Disability Insurance Rate
2200 RETURN
2210 REM ***********************************************
```

To allow for ease of modification when the tax rates change, all the tax data is placed in DATA statements. When any rates change, only the corresponding DATA statements need to be changed.

```
2300 REM ****         Read In Withholding Table          ****
2310 REM          Define Arrays for Withholding Table
2320 DIM LOWER(NUM.IN.TABLE, NUM.STATUS), AMOUNT(NUM.IN.TABLE,
         NUM.STATUS), RATE(NUM.IN.TABLE, NUM.STATUS)
2330 FOR COL = 1 TO NUM.STATUS
2340      FOR ROW = 1 TO NUM.IN.TABLE
2350          READ LOWER(ROW,COL), AMOUNT(ROW, COL), RATE(ROW,COL)
2360      NEXT ROW
2370 NEXT COL
2380 RETURN
```

Note that the variables `NUM.STATUS` and `NUM.IN.TABLE` are used in the DIM and FOR statements in place of actual numbers. This practice allows changes in these criteria to be implemented without rewriting these instructions.

```
2390 REM *******************************************
2400 REM          Data Statements - 1986 Tax Rules
2410 REM *******************************************
2420 REM Number of Filing Status Categories and Entries in Tables
2430 DATA 2, 8
2440 REM Dependent Allowance for Biweekly Payroll
2450 DATA 41.54
2460 REM Social Security and Disability Tax Rates
2470 DATA .0715
2480 DATA .009
2490 REM
2500 REM      ****     Single Biweekly Tax Table    ****
2510 REM Lower, Amount, Rate
2520 DATA    0,   0.00, .00
2530 DATA   57,   0.00, .12
2540 DATA  173,  13.92, .15
2550 DATA  385,  45.72, .19
2560 DATA  605,  87.52, .25
2570 DATA  913, 164.52, .30
2580 DATA 1154, 236.82, .34
2590 DATA 1373, 312.76, .37
2600 REM
2610 REM      ****     Married Biweekly Tax Table     ****
2620 REM Lower, Amount, Rate
2630 DATA    0,   0.00, .00
2640 DATA  100,   0.00, .12
2650 DATA  398,  35.76, .17
2660 DATA  795, 103.25, .22
2670 DATA  980, 143.95, .25
2680 DATA 1199, 198.70, .28
2690 DATA 1419, 260.30, .33
2700 DATA 1859, 405.50, .37
```

```
2710 REM
2800   ********* Input Employee Name ************
2810 PRINT
2820 INPUT "What is the Employee's name (enter DONE to quit)";
         EMPNAME$
2830 RETURN
2840 REM
```

The first employee name is entered as part of the initialization before executing the main WHILE . . . WEND loop. All remaining names will be entered at the end of the loop.

```
3000 REM   ********    Process One Employee Record    *******
3010 REM   ***************************************************
3020 GOSUB 3100          :REM Enter Pay Data
3030 GOSUB 3300          :REM Compute Withholding
3050 GOSUB 3800          :REM Add Pay Data to File
3060 GOSUB 3900          :REM Add to Totals
3070 GOBUS 2800          :REM Input Employee Name
3080 RETURN
3090 REM
3100 REM   ***            Enter Pay Data            ***
3110 REM
3120 INPUT "What is the gross pay"; GROSS
3130 WHILE GROSS < 0 OR GROSS > 5000
3140    INPUT "Please enter an amount for gross between 0 and 5000"; GROSS
3150 WEND
3160 INPUT "Please enter the number of allowances"; NUMALLOWANCES
3170 PRINT "Please enter filing status:"
3180 PRINT " 1 = single"
3190 PRINT " 2 = married"
3200 INPUT "Employee's status"; STATUS
3210 WHILE STATUS < 1 OR STATUS > 2
3220       INPUT "Status must be 1 or 2, please reenter"; STATUS
3230 WEND
3240 RETURN
3250 REM
3300 REM   ***         Compute Withholding        ***
3310 REM
3320 GOSUB 3400          :REM Compute Amount Subject to Withholding
3330 GOSUB 3500          :REM Compute Amount to Withhold
3340 RETURN
3350 REM
3400 REM  ****  Compute Amount Subject to Withholding  ****
3410 LET ALLOWANCE = ALLOWANCE.RATE * NUMALLOWANCES
3420 IF GROSS - ALLOWANCE > 0 THEN LET SUBJECT = GROSS - ALLOWANCE
      ELSE LET SUBJECT = 0
3430 RETURN
3440 REM
```

We call subroutine 2800 from Lines 2030 and 3070. This modularity allows us to revise the subroutine and call it from wherever it is needed.

The amount subject to withholding is the gross less the number of allowances times the rate per allowance. We must handle the possibility that this result could be less than zero.

```
3500 REM    ****     Compute Amount to Withhold     ****
3510 LET WITHHOLDING = 0
3520 REM    **           Search Tax Array           **
3530 FOR ROW = 1 TO NUM.IN.TAB-1
3540    IF SUBJECT > LOWER(ROW,STATUS) AND SUBJECT <= LOWER(ROW+1,STATUS)
          THEN LET WITHHOLDING = AMOUNT(ROW,STATUS) + RATE(ROW,STATUS) *
              (SUBJECT - LOWER(ROW,STATUS))
3550 NEXT ROW
3560 REM    **        Check for Last Range          **
3570 IF SUBJECT > LOWER(NUM.IN.TABLE,STATUS) THEN LET WITHHOLDING =
      AMOUNT(NUM.IN.TABLE,STATUS) + RATE(NUM.IN.TABLE,STATUS) *
      (SUBJECT - AMOUNT(NUM.IN.TABLE,STATUS))
3580 REM    **      Calculate Social Security and SDI **
3590 LET SS.AMOUNT = GROSS * SS.RATE
3600 LET SDI.AMOUNT = GROSS * SDI.RATE
3610 REM    **        Calculate Total Withholding      **
3620 LET WITHHOLDING = WITHHOLDING + SS.AMOUNT + SDI.AMOUNT
3630 RETURN
3640 REM
```

To find the proper range, we must find the one in which the amount subject to withholding is greater than the lower limit but less than or equal to the next limit. The FOR . . . NEXT loop checks the amount subject to withholding against the limits for each step except the last. If the amount falls within any of these ranges, the amount to withhold is calculated according to the following formula: (1) Subtract the lower limit from the amount subject to withholding. (2) Multiply the difference times the rate for this range. (3) Add the product to the base amount for this range. For the last range there is no upper limit; therefore, if the amount subject to withholding is greater than the last limit, we perform the calculation using the data for the last range.

Social security and SDI are calculated by multiplying the gross times the rate for each of these taxes.

The three taxes are added together to give the total amount to be withheld.

```
3700 REM      Print Heading
3710 PRINT
3720 PRINT "Emp Name","Gross","Deductions","Withholding","Pay"
3730 PRINT
3740 RETURN
3800 REM    Add Pay Data to File
3810 REM
3820 WRITE #1, EMPNAME$, GROSS, NUMALLOWANCES, WITHHOLDING, GROSS -
     WITHHOLDING
3830 RETURN
3900 REM        Add to Totals
3910 REM
3920 LET TOT.GROSS = TOT.GROSS + GROSS
3930 LET TOT.WITHHOLDING = TOT.WITHHOLDING + WITHHOLDING
```

```
3940 RETURN
4000 REM Final Report and Totals
4010 OPEN "PAYINFO" FOR INPUT AS #1
4020 REM
4030 REM Print Heading
4040 PRINT
4050 PRINT "Emp Name", "Gross", "Deductions", "Withholding", "Pay"
4060 PRINT
4070 REM Input and Print All Records in the File
4080 WHILE NOT EOF(1)
4090    INPUT #1, EMPNAME$, GROSS, NUMALLOWANCES, WITHHOLDING, GRMINWITH
4100    PRINT EMPNAME$, GROSS, NUMALLOWANCES, WITHHOLDING, GRMINWITH
4110 WEND
4115 PRINT
4120 PRINT "TOTALS", TOT.GROSS, , TOT.WITHHOLDING, TOT.GROSS-TOT.WITHHOLDING
4130 RETURN
4140 REM      *** End of Listing ***
```

SAMPLE OUTPUT

```
What is the Employee's name (enter DONE to quit)? JOE DOE
What is the gross pay? 1300
Please enter the number of allowances? 4
Please enter filing status:
  1 = single
  2 = married
  Employee's status? 2
What is the Employee's name (enter DONE to quit)? BETTY BOYD
What is the gross pay? 1900
Please enter the number of allowances? 1
Please enter filing status:
  1 = single
  2 = married
  Employee's status? 1
What is the Employee's name (enter DONE to quit)? DONE

Emp Name      Gross        Deductions     Withholding     Pay

JOE DOE       1300         4               287.06         1012.94
BETTY BOYD    1900         1              1037.62          862.38

TOTALS        3200                        1324.68         1875.32
```

TEST YOUR LEARNING

1. The ABC Company needs a program to keep track of its inventory. It has 12 products in its inventory. These products are assigned product numbers 1 through 12.

a. Write a program that builds a table that holds the current quantity on hand for each product. Use either INPUT from the user or INPUT from a file to establish the initial quantities, depending on whether inventory already exists.

b. Write a program that displays a menu and asks the user to select one of the following options:

```
1 = Add to existing inventory
2 = Take from existing inventory
3 = Display current quantity for selected product
4 = Print report of current quantity for all products
5 = End processing and update file
```

c. Write separate modules to perform each of these tasks.

Use top-down programming and testing. Validate that the product number entered is 1 through 12 and that the quantity is 999 or less.

When the menu's option 2 is selected, test the quantity remaining after the order is placed. If the quantity is less than 10, display a message directing the user to reorder this product. If the order would result in a quantity less than zero, change the order to the quantity on hand and display a message that says the order has been changed to the number on hand and directs the user to reorder the product.

2. The ABC Company has expanded to two more locations. Modify the program described in Exercise 1 to keep track of the inventory at each of the three locations. (Use two-dimension arrays.) The program should allow the user to add, delete, or inquire about any product at any of the locations. The report produced in the menu's option 4 will show the quantity of each product at each location as well as the total quantity at all locations.

Quick Reference

■

Selected Reserved Words

CLOSE	closes a file
DATA	places value in data list
DELETE	removes one or more lines from BASIC's workspace
DIM	allocates space for array
END	terminates execution
EOF	tests for end of file
FOR . . . NEXT	loops for a given number of times
GOSUB . . . RETURN	temporarily transfers control to a module
GOTO	permanently transfers control
IF . . . THEN . . . ELSE	selects which statements to execute
INPUT	gets values for variables from the user or file
KILL	deletes file
LET	assigns a value to a variable
LIST	displays the program in the workspace
LOAD	copies a program from storage into the workspace
NEW	clears the workspace
ON . . . GOSUB	transfers control based on value
OPEN	opens file
PRINT	displays values

(continued)

READ	retrieves values from DATA list
REM	used for documentation
RENUM	renumbers the lines of a program
RESTORE	restarts at beginning of DATA list
RUN	causes a program to execute
SAVE	copies a program from the workspace to storage
STOP	pauses execution, CONT resumes
WHILE . . . WEND	create a loop
WRITE	writes data to a file

GLOSSARY

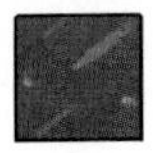

access time Average time to locate instructions or data from secondary (auxiliary) storage device and transfer to computer's main memory (RAM).

acoustic coupler Modem consisting of a cradle formed by two rubber cups to hold telephone receiver and transmit data via sound signals (converted from digital to analog form) over the telephone line. The acoustic coupler is separate from the computer and must be plugged into the computer and a phone jack. *Compare* **direct-connect modem.**

Ada High-level programming language developed by Department of Defense for military systems; supports real-time procedures, automatic error recovery, and flexible input and output operations.

add-ins *See* **add-on utility.**

add-on memory board Circuit board with memory chips plugged into expansion slot on motherboard to increase capacity of microcomputer's main memory.

add-on (add-in) utility **RAM-resident** software used in conjunction with applications software to provide additional capabilities—for example, to print output lengthwise instead of across the width of the paper or to improve the appearance of the output. Add-on software is loaded *after* the initial applications software is loaded.

addressing scheme Computer design feature that determines amount of main memory CPU can control at any one time.

algorithm Well-defined rules or step-by-step procedures for solving a problem; may include diagrams.

alphanumeric data Data that can include letters, digits, and special symbols such as punctuation marks; it cannot be mathematically manipulated. *Compare* **numeric data.**

alphanumeric monitor (terminal) Screen that displays only letters, numbers, and special characters such as $, *, and ? but no graphics.

Alt key Modifier key on the computer **keyboard;** when a modifier key is pressed along with another key, the function of that other key is modified. The applications software program determines how modifier keys are used.

American National Standards Institute (ANSI) Organization that develops standards for all **high-level programming languages.**

American Standard Code for Information Interchange (ASCII) Pronounced "*as*-key." Standard 8-bit code used in data communications, microcomputers, and many minicomputers; 128 valid characters can be formulated with ASCII.

amplitude Size of voltage or magnitude of wave form in data or voice transmission.

analog signal Signal that is continuously varying and represents a range of frequencies; the telephone system is based on analog signals. *See* **digital signal.**

analytical graphics Graphical forms used to make numerical data easier to understand; the most common analytical graphics forms are bar chart, line chart, and pie chart. Analytical graphics are usually *spreadsheet based;* that is, they are created using a **spreadsheet software** package. *Compare* **presentation graphics.**

ANSI *See* **American National Standards Institute.**

Apple DOS Microcomputer disk **operating system** introduced by Apple Computer Corporation in late 1970s.

applications controls Controls to ensure that input and processing of data is accurate, complete, and authorized; they include (1) input controls, (2) processing controls, (3) output controls, and (4) authorization controls.

applications generator Software system that generates computer programs in response to a user's needs. The system consists of precoded modules that perform various functions. The user selects the functions he or she needs, and the applications generator determines how to perform the tasks and produces the necessary instructions for the software program.

applications software Program or programs designed to carry out a specific task to satisfy a user's specific needs—for example, calculate payroll and print out checks. *Compare* **systems software.**

applications software utility Inexpensive program—RAM-resident or retrived from disk—that performs basic "office management" functions for the user. *See* **add-on utility; disk utility; keyboard utility; screen utility.**

arithmetic/logic unit (ALU) Part of the computer's central processing unit (CPU) that performs all arithmetic and logical (comparison) functions.

arithmetic operations The operations of addition, subtraction, multiplication, division, and exponentiation.

artificial intelligence (AI) Field of study concerned with using computer hardware and software to simulate human thought processes such as imagination and intuition.

ASCII *See* **American Standard Code for Information Interchange.**

as-displayed format In Lotus 1-2-3, choosing this format enables you to print your report as it appears on the screen. *Compare* **cell-formulas format.**

assembly language Language using low-level symbolic abbreviations to represent machine-language instructions. Assembly language is specific to different makes and models of computers. Assembly languages are also known as **second-generation languages.** *Compare* **machine language; procedural language.**

asynchronous transmission In data communications, sending one character, or **byte** (8 bits), at a time, each byte preceded by a "start" bit and followed by one or two "stop" bits and an error check bit (or parity bit). An inexpensive and widely used but relatively slow form of data communication. Also called *start-stop transmission*.

AUTOEXEC.BAT This file, when stored in the **root directory** of the disk you load DOS from during the **boot** process, is used to load programs automatically when the computer is turned on.

automated teller machine (ATM) *See* **financial transaction terminal.**

auxiliary storage *See* **secondary storage.**

backup file Copy of file made to ensure data and programs are preserved if original file is damaged or destroyed.

ball printer Letter-quality printer that uses a ball-shaped print mechanism, much like a typewriter ball, to form characters.

band printer *See* **line printer.**

bandwidth (1) Speed at which data can be transmitted on a communications frequency. (2) In determining video screen resolution, the rate at which data can be sent to the electron gun to control its movement, positioning, and firing.

bar chart This chart, which is made up of bars of varying length, compares one data element with another data element. *See also* **analytical graphics.**

bar code *See* **bar code reader.**

bar code reader Input scanning device for reading the light and dark bar codes (stripes) on products that represent their inventory stock numbers or product numbers. The scanner analyzes the bars for width and spacing and translates this data into electrical signals for the computer. Two types of scanners are the handheld wand and the countertop scanner.

BASIC (Beginner's All-Purpose Symbolic Instruction Code) **High-level** (procedural) interactive **programming language** designed to teach users how to program on microcomputers.

batch A group of documents or transactions intended for input to the computer all at once and in a controlled fashion.

batch commands Commands used to create batch command files, which automate frequently used command sequences and make procedures easier for users unfamiliar with the computer's operating system. Batch command files are considered external command files because their instructions are not loaded into main memory (RAM) at the time the computer is booted.

batch entry Technique whereby data is collected over a period of time and then is input at one time for storage or for processing and output.

baud rate The number of times per second that a data communications signal changes; with each change, one or more bits can be transmitted.

belt printer *See* **line printer.**

binary code Scheme for encoding data using **binary digits.**

binary digit (bit) In binary notation, either 1 or 0. The digit 1 represents an "on" electrical (or magnetic) state; the digit 0 represents an "off" state. A group of adjacent bits (usually 8 bits) constitutes a **byte,** or single character.

bit *See* **binary digit.**

bit-mapped display **Cathode-ray tube** screen display system in which each possible dot is controlled by a single character in memory. Also known as *dot-addressable* or *all-points addressable* display.

block Group of contiguous records on magnetic tape. Each block is separated on the tape by a gap (interblock gap) to compensate for the tape's acceleration and deceleration as it moves past the read/write head.

block operations By using block operations, it is possible to move, delete, and copy entire sentences, paragraphs, and pages by issuing commands to the software.

boot To start up the computer and load the necessary software instructions into **RAM.**

bpi Bits per inch; *see* **recording density.**

Browse mode In dBASE IV, this mode enables you to see database **records** in rows on the screen; this mode is used for editing the records in a database. *See also* **edit mode.**

bug Programming error.

bus An "electronic highway," or communications path, linking several devices and parts of the **central processing unit (CPU).**

bus network Communications **network** in which all messages are transmitted to the entire network (whose ends are not connected to form a circle), traveling from the sender in both directions along the cable until a message reaches the computer for which it was intended. A central computer is not required to control activity.

byte A group of contiguous bits, usually 8 bits, that form a character.

C **High-level programming language** introduced by Bell

Laboratories for use in writing systems software. Though complex to learn, C can be used on a variety of machines.

cache memory High-speed temporary storage area for program instructions and data; 10 times faster than **RAM** and about 100 times more expensive.

Cancel key In WordPerfect, if a menu is displaying on the screen, this key enables you to cancel out of a **menu;** if a document is displaying on the screen, this key enables you to restore deleted text to your document.

Caps Lock key Keyboard key used to place all the alphabetic keys into uppercase position—that is, capital letters only.

card dialer *See* **Touch-Tone™ device.**

card reader Device that translates the holes in punched cards into electrical signals, which are input to the computer; it is also another name for a **Touch-Tone™ device,** also known as a *card dialer*.

cartridge tape unit Device that reads **magnetic tape** in cassette form; often used as alternative type of **secondary storage** to **hard disk** and as backup storage for hard disks. The most popular tape cartridges use ¼-inch tape in reels up to 1,000 feet long. *See also* **streaming tape.**

catalog In dBASE IV, catalogs provide a means by which you can group related database **files.**

cathode-ray tube (CRT) Electronic screen used with computer terminals to display data entered into a computer and information available from it (**softcopy** output). Its principal components are an **electron gun,** a **yoke,** a **shadow mask,** and a phosphor-coated screen; also called *video display screen*.

CD-ROM *See* **compact disk/read-only memory.**

cell In a spreadsheet program, this marks the intersection of a column and a row.

cell-formulas format In Lotus 1-2-3, choosing this format enables the user to print the characteristics of every cell in the spreadsheet. *Compare* **as-displayed format.**

Center key In WordPerfect, this key enables the user to center text between the margins.

centralized computer facility A single computer department in a company established to provide sole data processing support to all other departments.

central processing unit (CPU) The "brain" of the computer; the part of the computer composed of electrical circuitry directing most of the computer system's activities. The CPU consists of the **control unit** and the **arithmetic/logic unit (ALU),** connected by a **bus.**

CGA *See* **color graphics adapter.**

chain printer *See* **line printer.**

character *See* **byte.**

character box Fixed location on a video display screen where a standard character can be placed. Most screens can display 80 characters of data horizontally and 25 lines vertically, or 2,000 character boxes (called *character-mapped display*)—the number the electron gun can target. The more pixels that fit into a character box, the higher the resolution of the resulting image. Each character box is "drawn" according to a prerecorded template stored in **read-only memory (ROM).**

character-mapped display *See* **character box.**

character printer *See* **letter-quality printer.**

characters per second (cps) Measure of speed of printers and other output devices.

check bit *See* **parity bit.**

child record In hierarchical database, record subordinate to parent record. *Compare* **parent record.**

chip Integrated circuit made of a semiconductor (silicon) and containing electronic components; can be as little as ¼-inch square.

clock Device in **CPU** that synchronizes all operations in a **machine cycle.**

closed architecture Attribute of computers that cannot be upgraded by the use of expansion cards; the user cannot open the system unit. *Compare* **open architecture.**

coaxial cable Type of thickly insulated copper wire for carrying large volumes of data—about 1,800–3,600 voice calls at once. Often used in local networks connecting computers in a limited geographic area.

COBOL (COmmon Business Oriented Language) **High-level programming language** for business. Its commands and syntax use common human language (for example, English). COBOL is most appropriate for business applications.

code-oriented Refers to **page description software** that displays all the formatting codes on the screen, thus preventing the user from seeing what the page will actually look like when it is printed out. *Compare* **WYSIWYG.**

color graphics adapter (CGA) Expansion card plugged into **expansion slot** in **system unit (cabinet)** that allows compatible **monitor** to display bit-mapped graphics; must be used with appropriate software; monitor displays four colors, as well as monochrome images.

color monitor *See* **RGB monitor.**

COMMAND.COM This **DOS** file must be stored on the **boot** disk. The instructions in the COMMAND.COM file enable the user to perform common disk and file management tests such as erasing and copying files.

command/data entry area In Lotus 1-2-3, the area at the top of the screen where **menus** are displayed and where the data that the user types in is displayed before it is entered into the spreadsheet.

command syntax *See* **syntax.**

common carrier *See* **public network.**

communications software Programs that allow users to access software and data from a computer in a remote location and to transmit data to a computer in a remote location.

compact disk/read-only memory (CD-ROM) **Optical storage** disk whose data is imprinted by the disk manufacturer via a laser process; the user cannot change it or write on the disk—the user can only "read" the data. *Compare* **erasable optical disk; write once, read many (WORM).**

compatibility Capability of operating together; can refer to different models of computers, different types of hardware peripherals, and various systems and applications software—not all software is compatible with all computers and other types of hardware, and not all types of hardware are compatible with one another. Incompatibility can often be overcome with the use of modems and/or special hardware and software.

compiler Computer program that translates **high-level programming language** instructions (**source code**) into **machine-language** instructions (**object code**) all at once. *Compare* **interpreter.**

computer Data processing device made up of electronic and electromechanical components that can perform computations, including arithmetic and logical operations. Also known as **hardware.** By itself, a computer has no intelligence.

computer-aided design (CAD) The use of a computer and special graphics software to design products.

computer-aided engineering (CAE) The use of a computer and special software to simulate situations that test product designs.

computer-aided manufacturing (CAM) The use of computers to control manufacturing equipment; includes robots.

computer-assisted software engineering (CASE) Software tools used in systems design, development, and documentation.

computer-based information system Computer system for collecting data, processing it into information, and storing the information for future reference and output. The system consists of five components: hardware, software, data/information, procedures, and people. (**Connectivity** is sometimes a sixth component.) It has four major phases of activity: input, processing, output, and storage.

computer generation One of four phases of computer development; the term is used to delineate major technological developments in hardware and software.

computer graphics *See* **analytical graphics; presentation graphics.**

computer literacy Basic understanding of what a computer is and how it can be used as a resource; includes some experience with commonly used software packages, such as word processing, spreadsheet, and/or database software.

computer output microfilm/microfiche (COM) system Equipment that captures computer output on microfilm or microfiche.

computer professional Person with formal education in technical aspects of computers—for example, a programmer, a systems analyst, or a computer operator.

computer system System of (1) hardware, (2) software, (3) data/information, (4) procedures, and (5) people.

concentrator Communications device that multiplexes (combines) low-speed communications lines onto one high-speed line; it is more "intelligent" than a **multiplexer** because it can store communications for later transmission.

connectivity When one computer system is set up to communicate with another computer system, connectivity becomes the sixth system element, after (1) hardware, (2) software, (3) data/information, (4) procedures, and (5) people; it describes the manner in which the systems are connected.

Control Center The center of dBASE IV's **menu** system.

controller Device that allows multiple terminals and printers to share a communications link but that also controls and routes transmissions and performs error checks and other functions; used in place of a **multiplexer.**

control program *See* **supervisor.**

control structure Used in structured programming to solve problems in programming logic. There are three control structures: **sequence, selection** (if-then-else), and **iteration** (or looping; do-while).

control unit Part of the **CPU** that reads, interprets, and sees to the execution of software instructions.

coprocessor chip Special integrated circuit designed to speed up numeric processing. It can be added to a computer after manufacture.

COPY **DOS** command that enables the user to copy files onto the same disk (the copy must have a different name) or onto a different disk (the copy can have the same or a different name).

COPY CON **DOS** command that enables the user to create **ASCII** text files by copying the keyboard input into a file.

cps *See* **characters per second.**

CPU *See* **central processing unit.**

<create> marker Part of each dBASE IV **panel** used to create a file; a different dBASE screen displays for each panel chosen.

CRT *See* **cathode-ray tube.**

Ctrl key Modifier key on the computer keyboard; when a modifier key is pressed along with another key, the function of that other key is modified. The specific use of modifier keys is determined by the software program.

currency format Lotus 1-2-3 formatting option that causes numbers to display with a leading dollar sign and up to 15 decimal places.

current disk drive *See* **default disk drive.**

cursor Indicator on video display screen that shows where next character or space that is input will appear.

cursor-movement keys Computer keyboard keys, usually marked with arrows, that are used to move the **cursor** around the video screen.

custom report This dBASE IV report format provides greater reporting flexibility than dBASE's **quick report** format, enabling the user to design all the features to be included in the report. With this command, the user can choose fields to be included in the report and change the descriptive text that appears at the top of each column. Graphic elements can also be added.

cylinder All the tracks in a disk pack with the same **track** number, lined up, one above the other. The **read/write heads** in a disk pack move together and so are always on the same cylinder at the same time.

daisy wheel printer **Impact printer** with plastic or metal disk with typeface impressions of characters on outside tips of spokes; the print character is forced against ribbon and paper.

data Raw, unevaluated facts and figures, concepts, or instructions; after processing, data becomes **information.**

data access area Exposed part of a **disk,** through which the **read/write head** inside the disk drive "reads" and "writes" data from and to a disk.

database Large group of stored, integrated (cross-referenced) data that can be retrieved and manipulated to produce information.

database administrator (DBA) Person who coordinates all related activities and needs for a corporation's **database.** A DBA has six major responsibilities: (1) database implementation, (2) coordination with user, (3) backup, (4) recovery, (5) performance monitoring, and (6) system security.

database management system (DBMS) Comprehensive software tool that allows users to create, maintain, and manipulate an integrated base of business data to produce relevant management information. A DBMS represents the interface between the user and the computer's **operating system** and **database.**

database management system (DBMS) software Program that allows storage of large amounts of data that can be easily cross-indexed, retrieved, and manipulated to produce information for management reports.

database structure The characteristics of every **field** stored in a database.

data bus Electronic communication link that carries data between components of the computer system.

data dictionary Reference file in a **database management system** that stores information about data and information that is essential to the management of that data and information as a resource.

data file *See* **file.**

data flow diagram (DFD) Graphic representation of flow of data through a system; standard **ANSI** symbols are used to represent various activities such as input and processing.

data independence Attribute of data that is stored independent of applications programs being used, so that it is easy to access and change.

data integrity Attribute of data that describes its accuracy, reliability, and timeliness; that is, if data has integrity, then it is accurate, reliable, and timely.

data manipulation language (DML) Program that is part of **database management system** software and that effects input to and output from the **database** files; the technical instructions the make up the input/output routines in the DBMS.

data processing *See* **processing.**

data (information) processing Operations for refining, summarizing, categorizing, and otherwise manipulating data into a useful form for decision making.

data redundancy Attribute of data that describes how often the same data appears in different files, often in different formats; a high degree of data redundancy makes updating files difficult.

data storage hierarchy The levels of data stored in a computer file: (1) **files** (broadest level), (2) **records,** (3) **fields,** (4) **bytes,** and (5) **bits** (narrowest level).

DBMS *See* **database management system.**

decentralized computer facilities Separate computer facilities, established to service the needs of each major department or unit in an organization.

decision support system (DSS) A computer-based information system for assisting managers (usually high-level managers) in planning and decision making. A DSS may use **database management systems, query languages,** financial modeling or **spreadsheet** programs, statistical analysis programs, **report generators,** and/or **graphics** programs to provide information. A DSS may be general or institutional.

dedicated data entry system Specialized single-purpose system used for nothing else but entering data; usually **terminals** connected to a **minicomputer** that do nothing but input and direct the storage of data.

dedicated graphics software package Software application that functions solely to provide the user with the capability of producing graphics.

dedicated line Communication line created or leased by a company for its own transmission purposes. *See also* **point-to-point line.**

default disk drive The disk drive that is automatically affected by commands unless the user specifies another drive.

default values The values, or determinations, that a software assumes are true, unless the user instructs the software otherwise.

Del key Deletes the character the **cursor** is positioned on.

demodulation Process of using communications hardware to convert **analog signals** sent over a telephone line into **digital signals** so that they can be processed by a receiving computer.

desk checking Proofreading a printout of a newly written program; part of testing new programs.

desktop computer *See* **microcomputer.**

desktop management (software) utility Software designed to be available at any time to the user by residing in **main memory** at all times (**RAM-resident**); it provides many routine office support functions such as calendar organization, dictionary, and calculator.

desktop publishing software Programs that enable user to use a **microcomputer,** graphics **scanners,** and a desktop-sized **laser printer** to combine text and graphics files created by different software applications packages to produce high-quality publications.

desktop terminal A **keyboard** and a **video display screen** connected to a central computer but fitting on top of the user's desk.

detail diagram Part of a **hierarchy plus input-process-output (HIPO) package,** it describes in detail what is done within each **module;** used in programming.

detail report Computer-produced report for **operating** (lower-level) **management** that contains specific information about routine activities; such reports are highly structured and their form is predetermined.

digital signal Signal that is discontinuous and discrete; it consists of bursts that form a transmission pattern. Computers communicate with each other in streams of bits transmitted as digital signals—a series of on and off electrical pulses. *See* **analog signal.**

digitizer Input device that can be moved over a drawing or a photograph, thereby converting the picture to computerized data that can be stored, printed out, or shown on a video display screen. The device can also be moved over an electronic tablet in order to communicate data to the computer.

digitizing tablet *See* **digitizer.**

DIR **DOS** command used to display a listing of the files stored on a disk. *Compare* **DIR/p; DIR/w.**

DIR/p **DOS** command used to display a listing, 24 lines at a time, of the files stored on a disk. *Compare* **DIR; DIR/w.**

DIR/w **DOS** command used to display a listing, across the width of the screen, of the files stored on a disk. *Compare* **DIR; DIR/p.**

direct access storage and retrieval Situation in which records are stored and retrieved in any order. Also called *random access.*

direct-connect modem Modem that directly connects computer to telephone line, resulting in less interference and higher data transmission speeds (300–2400 bps or higher). An internal direct-connect modem is placed inside the computer; an external direct-connect modem is outside the computer. *Compare* **acoustic coupler.**

direct entry Data input that uses nonkeyboard input devices such as **card readers** and **scanning devices.** *Compare* **keyboard entry.**

direct file File in which data is recorded and stored according to its disk address or relative position within the file; the data is retrieved by the **direct access storage and retrieval** method. Also called *relative file.*

direct implementation One of four approaches to systems implementation; the change is made all at once, with the old system being halted at the same time the new system is activated. *Compare* **parallel implementation; phased implementation; pilot implementation.**

directory commands **Internal command instructions** used in microcomputers to create **directory structures** on a storage device.

directory structure The way a disk is organized into **subdirectories.**

disk Revolving platter (**secondary storage** medium) on which data and programs are recorded electronically or optically (laser) in the form of spots representing electrical "on" and "off" states.

disk cartridge Form of **secondary storage** consisting of a 5¼- or 3½-inch cartridge containing one or two platters and enclosed in a hard plastic case; the cartridge is inserted into the disk drive much like a music tape cassette.

disk drive Device into which a **diskette** (floppy disk), **hard disk,** or **disk pack** is placed for storing and retrieving data.

disk drive gate Door of disk drive, which must be closed for the read/write operation to be performed. (Not all computers have disk-drive gates—for example, the Apple Macintosh does not.)

diskette Thin plastic (Mylar) disk, enclosed in paper or plastic, that can be magnetically encoded with data; originally 8 inches in diameter, standard diskettes are now 5¼ or 3½ inches. (Diskettes used to be known as *floppy disks,* but now some of them are covered by rigid plastic and are no longer "floppy.")

disk operating system (DOS) **Internal command instructions** for microcomputers; MS-DOS and PC-DOS have become the industry standard for IBM PC microcomputers; **Operating System 2 (OS/2)** is used on IBM's PS/2 Series microcomputers; **Apple DOS** and **Macintosh DOS** are used on the Apple Company's microcomputers; TRS-DOS is used on Tandy/Radio Shack microcomputers. These disk operating systems are not generally mutually compatible.

disk pack Removable direct access storage medium holding 6–12 magnetic platters usually 14 inches in diameter; capacity is 150–250 MB.

disk utility **Applications software** utility stored on disk; used to recover files that were accidentally erased, to make backup copy of a hard disk, and to organize a hard disk by means of a **menu-driven** system.

distributed computer facility **Centralized computer facility** and **decentralized computer facilities** combined; users have own computer equipment, but some computer terminals are connected to a bigger computer in a remote location.

DO *See* **pseudocode.**

documentation Written description of a system's or a software package's parts and procedures; can come in the form of a user's manual that tells the user how to operate a piece of hardware or run a particular software program, or it can be a large collection of volumes and printouts to be used by programmers and computer operators.

document cycle Use of **word processing software** for entering, editing, spell-checking, saving and retrieving, and printing a document. The cycle may also include merging text from separate documents into a single document.

DOS *See* **disk operating system.**

dot-matrix printer **Impact printer** using pin-like hammers to strike a ribbon against paper in computer-determined patterns of dots, making possible a variety of type styles and graphics.

double-density *See* **recording density.**

double-sided disk Disk(ette) that stores data on both sides.

double-sided disk drive Disk drive with **read/write heads** for both top and bottom surfaces of a disk.

do while **Pseudocode** logic statement; directs the computer to repeat an activity as long as a particular condition exists. *See also* **iteration.**

drive A (A:) Designation for the first disk(ette) drive in a microcomputer; the program diskette is usually inserted in this drive, which is often the left-hand or the upper drive.

drive B (B:) Designation for the second disk(ette) drive in a micromputer; the data diskette is usually inserted in this drive, which is often the right-hand or the lower drive.

drive C (C:) Designation for the **hard disk** drive in a microcomputer.

drive gate *See* **disk drive gate.**

drum plotter Special-purpose output device for reproducing computer-generated drawings. Paper is placed on a drum, and stationary pens move across the paper as the drum revolves.

drum printer *See* **line printer.**

DSS *See* **decision support system.**

dumb terminal A **terminal** that is entirely dependent on the computer system to which it is connected; it cannot do any processing on its own and is used only for data input (using the keyboard) and retrieval (data is displayed on the monitor). *Compare* **intelligent terminal; smart terminal.**

EBCDIC *See* **Extended Binary Coded Decimal Interchange Code.**

E-cycle *See* **execution cycle.**

editing Process of changing text—for example, inserting and deleting.

Edit mode In dBASE IV, this mode enables the user to see a database **record** one at a time on the screen; used for editing the records in a database. *See* **Browse mode.**

EGA *See* **enhanced graphics adapter.**

electrically erasable programmable read-only memory (EEPROM) Type of **read-only (ROM) memory** (chip) much the same as **erasable programmable read-only memory** except that changes can be made to an integrated circuit electrically—new instructions can be recorded—byte-by-byte under software control.

electroluminescent (EL) display Type of **video display screen** with light-emitting layer of phosphors and two sets of electrodes surrounding the phosphor layer—one side forming vertical columns (usually 512) and the other side forming horizontal rows (usually 256). To form a **pixel** on the screen, current is sent to a row-column intersection, and the combined voltages cause the phosphor to glow at that point.

electron gun A component of a **cathode-ray tube (CRT);** it creates an image on the screen by firing a beam of electrons at the inside of the screen, which causes the phosphors to glow. The electron beam is directed across the screen horizontally and vertically by the magnetic field produced by the yoke under the control of the computer software.

electronic banking Service enabling customers to access banking activities from home or private office via a terminal or personal computer connected to their telephones.

electronic bulletin board service (BBS) **Information service** that can be reached via computer connected to telephone lines that allows user to place messages and read messages from other users.

electronic communications Movement of voice and data over short and long distances, such as by telephone or microwave, through the use of computers and communications hardware and software.

electronic mail Transmission and storing of messages by computers and telecommunications.

electronic shopping Service through which users can order merchandise by using microcomputers and electronic communications to browse through products listed on remote databases.

electronic spreadsheet software *See* **spreadsheet software.**

electrostatic plotter Special-purpose output device for reproducing computer-produced drawings. The plotter produces images on specially treated paper with small dots of electrostatic charges, and the paper is then run through a developer to make the image appear.

ELSE *See* **pseudocode.**

enhanced graphics adapter (EGA) Expansion card plugged into expansion slot in **system cabinet** that allows compatible monitor for display **bit-mapped graphics.** Must be used with appropriate software: monitor displays 16 colors at a resolution higher than **CGA** does.

Enter key Computer **keyboard** key pressed to execute a command that was entered by pressing other keys first.

erasable optical disk **Optical storage** disk whose data can be changed and erased. *Compare* **compact disk/read-only memory (CD-ROM); write once, read many (WORM).**

erasable programmable read-only memory (EPROM) Type of **read-only memory** in which, with the help of a special device using ultraviolet light, the data or instructions on an integrated circuit (chip) can be erased and new data can be recorded in its place.

erase **DOS** command that enables the user to erase files from a disk storage device.

ergonomics Science of designing products so that they are easy to use by people; also called *human engineering*.

event-initiated report Report generated for **middle management** only when certain conditions exist, such as changes requiring immediate attention (for example, equipment breakdown).

exception report Report generated for **middle management** that shows out-of-the-ordinary data—for example, inventory reports listing only items numbering fewer than 10 in stock.

execution cycle (E-cycle) Activity in CPU that includes execution of instruction and subsequent storing of result in a **register.** *See also* **instruction cycle; machine cycle.**

executive desktop workstation **Intelligent terminal** or **microcomputer** used by a manager to assist in daily activities. Workstations can be operated by themselves or in connection with a mainframe computer; they usually have voice and data communications capabilities and often have built-in software.

expanded memory In a microcomputer, **main memory (RAM)** that has been added to exceed the usual 640 K maximum; it consists of an add-on memory board and special driver software; used only in compatible 8088, 8086, 80286, and 80386 microcomputers.

expansion card *See* **add-on memory board.**

expansion slot In a microcomputer that has **open architecture,** an area within the **system unit (cabinet)** where expansion cards—such as color graphics adapter cards and expanded memory cards—can be inserted and plugged into the computer's circuitry.

expert system Kind of software consisting of knowledge and rules for using it gathered from human experts in a particular occupation. One of the first practical applications of **artificial intelligence,** it consists of (1) a **natural language** interface with the user, (2) a knowledge base, (3) an inference machine to solve problems and make logical inferences, and (4) an explanation module to explain the conclusions to the user.

Extended Binary Coded Decimal Interchange Code (EBCDIC) Pronounced "*eb*-see-dick." The most popular code used for IBM and IBM-compatible mainframe computers.

extended graphics array (XGA) Advanced graphics adapter for IBM PS/2 microcomputers; an XGA monitor can display 256 colors at a resolution of 1024 × 768.

extended memory In a microcomputer, **main memory (RAM)** that has been added to exceed the usual 640 K maximum; it consists of an **add-on memory board** and special driver software; used only in compatible 80286, 80386, and 80486 microcomputers.

external command file **DOS** command instructions that aren't loaded into **RAM** when you **boot** your computer. *See* **external command instructions.**

external command instructions General-purpose instructions kept in **secondary storage** for "housekeeping" tasks on microcomputers, such as the sorting of files and formatting of disks; part of a computer's **systems software.** *See also* **internal command instructions.**

external label Identifying paper label placed on magnetic tape reel.

external modem **Direct-connect modem** that is outside the microcomputer and uses its own power supply; it is connected to the computer by a cable.

fax A faxed item. *See* **fax machine.**

fax board (card) Internal fax machine.

fax machine Short for *facsimile machine*, a type of **scanner** that "reads" text and graphics and transmits them over telephone lines to a computer with a fax board or to another fax machine.

fiber optics Form of communications in which signals are converted to light form and fired by laser in bursts through thin (2,000ths of an inch) insulated glass or plastic fibers. Nearly 1 billion bits per second can be communicated through a fiber optic cable.

field Group of related characters (bytes) of data. *See* **data storage hierarchy.**

field name In a database structure, the unique name given to each **field** of data that is stored. A field name can be no longer than 10 characters.

field type In a **database structure,** the specification of the kind of data that will be stored in a given **field** (character, numeric, date, logical, float, or memo).

field width In a **database structure,** the width of each **field** (must be defined by the user).

fifth-generation language *See* **natural language.**

file Group of related **records.** A file may contain data (data file) or software instructions (program file). *See* **data storage hierarchy.**

file management system *See* **flat-file database management system.**

filename extension One to three characters added to a filename to aid in file identification. The filename and the extension are separated by a dot.

filename length Convention specified by different **operating systems**—for example, DOS specifies one to eight characters in filenames.

file protection ring Plastic ring inserted into back of magnetic tape reel to protect tape from accidentally being written on; a tape can be written on only when the ring is in place.

file server A computer, usually a microcomputer with large-capacity storage, that stores data and programs shared by a network of terminals; often the central unit in a **star network.**

file updating A factor in **data redundancy** and **data integrity;** when an element of data in a **database** needs to be updated (changed), it must be updated in *all* files that contain it.

financial planning language Special **interactive** business software used by high-level managers to make projections, "what if" analyses, and long-term planning decisions.

financial transaction terminal **Terminal** used in banking activities to access a central computer. It may be an automated teller machine (ATM) or specialized terminal used by bank tellers.

first-generation language *See* **machine language.**

fixed disk Magnetic disk for secondary storage that cannot be removed from the disk drive.

flatbed plotter Special-purpose output device for reproducing computer-generated drawings. Paper is placed flat and pens move horizontally and vertically across it.

flat-file database management system **Database management system** software that can deal with data in only one **file** at a time; cannot establish relationships among data elements stored in different files.

flat-screen technology Video display screens for laptop computers; the screens are much thinner than a **cathode-ray tube (CRT).** *See* **electroluminescent display; gas plasma display; liquid crystal display.**

float **Field type** in dBASE IV. Floating point numbers are typically used in scientific applications.

floppy disk *See* **diskette.**

flowchart *See* **program flowchart.**

font All the characters of one size in one particular typeface; includes numbers, punctuation marks, and upper- and lowercase letters.

footer Descriptive information (such as page number and date) that appears at the bottom of each page of a document.

FORMAT **DOS** command that prepares a disk to store data by writing a series of **tracks** and **sectors** on the disk.

Format key Provides options for changing the appearance (**formatting**) of documents.

formatting (1) Directing the computer to put magnetic **track** and **sector** pattern on a disk to enable the disk to store data or information. Also known as *initializing*. (2) In **word processing,** the alteration of text appearance by addition of underlining or boldface, change of margins, centering of headings, and so on.

formatting commands *See* **formatting** (2).

formula In Lotus 1-2-3, a mathematical expression that defines the relationships among various **cells** in an electronic **spreadsheet.**

FORTRAN (FORmula TRANslator) One of the first **high-level programming languages;** used for technical and scientific applications, primarily on minicomputers and mainframes.

fourth-generation language (4GL) **Nonprocedural programming language** that allows nonprofessional computer users to develop software. *See* **applications generator; query language; report generator.** *Compare* **high-level programming language.**

frame Row of magnetic spots and spaces (1s and 0s) recorded across the width of a magnetic tape.

frequency Number of times a signal repeats the same cycle in a second.

front-end processor Computer used in a computer center to handle data transmission and communications from outside terminals and devices to allow the main computer to concentrate solely on processing applications as quickly as possible.

full-duplex transmission mode Communications transmitted in both directions simultaneously.

function keys Specialized keys on a microcomputer **keyboard** for performing specific tasks with applications software; the keys are used differently with each applications package; they are labeled F1, F2, F3, and so on.

functions In Lotus 1-2-3, mathematical shortcuts that can be used in formulas to perform calculations. All of Lotus's functions begin with @.

gas plasma display Used as **video display screen** in some **laptop microcomputers.** Gas plasma display uses three pieces of glass sandwiched together. The inner layer has numerous small holes drilled in it. The outer two layers are placed on both sides of the middle one, and the holes are filled with a gas mixture, usually a mixture of argon and neon. Both outer layers of glass have a thin grid of vertical and horizontal wires. A **pixel** appears at a particular intersection when the appropriate horizontal and vertical wires are electrified.

GB *See* **gigabyte.**

gigabyte (GB) One billion bytes.

global (wildcard) character With **DOS** and **applications software,** the asterisk (*) and the question mark (?) allow the user to list selected files on the screen. The * is used to represent more than one character, whereas the ? is used to represent one character.

graphics monitor (terminal) Screen that can display both **alphanumeric data** and graphics; different types can display one-, two-, or three-dimensional graphics. *Compare* **alphanumeric monitor (terminal).**

graphics software Programs that allow the user to present information in pictorial form, often with text. *See* **analytical graphics, presentation graphics.**

graphic user interface Software feature that allows user to select **menu** options by choosing an **icon** that corresponds to a particular processing function; makes software easier to use, and typically employs a **mouse.** Examples are **Presentation Manager** and **Microsoft Windows.**

grouped bar chart Variation of the simple **bar chart;** shows how all data elements compare over time. *Compare* **stacked bar chart.**

half-duplex transmission mode Two-way data communications in which data travels in only one direction at a time.

handheld scanner Small input device used to scan printed documents on a limited basis to input the documents' contents to a computer.

handheld terminal **Terminal** that is small enough to be carried around in the user's hand; often used in the field.

hardcard Type of **secondary storage** device consisting of a circuit board with a disk that is plugged into a microcomputer **expansion slot.** A hard card can store up to 40 MB of data.

hardcopy Output recorded on a tangible medium (generally meaning that you can touch it) such as paper or microfilm. *Compare* **softcopy.**

hard disk **Secondary storage** device consisting of a rigid metal platter connected to a central spindle; the entire unit, including the **read/write heads,** is enclosed in a permanently sealed container. Hard disks store much more data than do **diskettes**—40 MB and up.

hard-sectored disk **Hard disk** or **diskette** that always has the same number and size of **sectors,** as determined by the manufacturer. *Compare* **soft-sectored disk.**

hardware Four categories of electronic and electromechanical computer components: input, storage, processing, and output hardware. *See also* **computer.** *Compare* **software.**

header Descriptive information (such as page number and date) that appears at the top of each page of a document.

Help key Key used to obtain help information about the current command, a particular function key, or a particular topic.

hierarchical database model Type of **database** organization in which data is arranged into related groups resembling a family tree, with **child records** subordinate to **parent records.** A parent record can have many child records, but each child record can have only one parent record. The record at the highest level, or top of the "tree," is called the *root record.*

hierarchical network Star **networks** configured into a single multilevel system, with a single large computer controlling all network activity. However, a computer connected to the main computer can have a star network of devices connected to it in turn. Also known as a *tree network.*

hierarchy chart *See* **structure chart.**

hierarchy plus input-process-output (HIPO) package Programming and systems design tool that uses three types of diagrams: (1) **visual table of contents (VTOC),** which includes a **structure chart,** a short description of the contents of the program, and a legend that explains the symbols used; (2) **overview diagram,** which shows, from left to right, the inputs, processes, and outputs for the entire program; and (3) **detail diagram,** which describes in detail what is done within each **module.**

high-level programming language Third-generation programming language designed to run on different computers with few changes—for example, **COBOL, FORTRAN,** and **BASIC.** Most high-level languages are considered to be procedure-oriented because the program instructions comprise lists of steps, or procedures, that tell the computer not only what to do but how to do it. Also known as *procedural language.*

HIPO *See* **hierarchy plus input-process-output package.**

history file Data file created to collect data for long-term reporting purposes.

hub Round opening in the center of a diskette, which enables the disk to fit over a spindle in the disk drive.

hypertext Software that links basic file units (text and graphics) with one another in creative ways. The user typically sees index-type "cards" and "card stacks" on the screen as well as other pictorial representations of file units and combination choices; card and stack contents can be determined by the user or supplied in an **off-the-shelf software** package (stackware).

IBMBIO.COM This **DOS** file must be present in the **root directory** of the **boot** disk. The instructions in this file help to manage all the input to and output from the computer. *Compare* **IBMDOS. COM.**

IBMDOS.COM This **DOS** file must be present in the **root directory** of the **boot** disk. The IBMDOS.COM file contains file-related information that helps DOS keep track of where files have been stored on disk and where to store additional files. *Compare* **IBMBIO.COM.**

icon Picture that represents the different application programs and processing procedures the user can execute. Macintosh programs and **Microsoft Windows** uses icons extensively.

I-cycle *See* **instruction cycle.**

IF *See* **pseudocode.**

If-Then-Else *See* **selection control structure.**

impact printer Output device that makes direct contact with paper, forming a print image by pressing an inked ribbon against paper with a hammer-like mechanism. Impact printers are of two types. *See* **letter-quality printer; dot-matrix printer.**

indexed file organization Method of secondary storage file organization whereby records are stored sequentially but with an index that allows both sequential and direct (random) access. Used almost exclusively with random access microcomputer storage devices to provide maximum flexibility for processing. *See also* **direct access storage and retrieval; sequential file organization.**

index file In dBASE IV, this file contains a series of pointers that enable the user to display a database **file** in a different order.

index hole Hole in protective jacket enclosing **diskette** that enables the disk to be positioned over a photoelectric sensing mechanism. Each time the disk revolves, a hole in the disk passes under the index hole in the jacket and activates a timing mechanism that determines which portion of the disk is over or under the **read/write heads.**

indexing Process of creating or using an **index file.**

indicator area In Lotus 1-2-3, this area is positioned at the bottom right of the screen and indicates whether the Caps Lock or the Num Lock key has been pressed.

information Raw data processed into usable form by the computer. It is the basis for decision making.

information center Department staffed by experts on the

hardware, software, and procedures used in the company; the experts help users in all matters relating to computer use. In companies without a mainframe, it is often called a *personal computer support center*.

information reporting system *See* **management information system (MIS).**

information service *See* **public data bank.**

information system An organization's framework of standards and procedures for processing data into usable information; it can be manual or computer-based. *See also* **computer-based information system.**

initializing *See* **formatting.**

initial program load (IPL) Refers to starting up a mainframe computer.

ink-jet printer **Nonimpact printer** that resembles **dot-matrix printer** in that it forms images or characters with dots. The dots are formed not by hammer-like pins but by droplets of ink fired through holes in a plate.

input controls Manual and computerized procedures to safeguard the integrity of input data, ensuring that all such data has been completely and accurately put into computer-usable form.

input/output (I/O) operations Instructions provided by a program for inputting data into **main memory (RAM)** and for outputting information.

input phase First phase of activity in the **computer-based information system,** during which data is captured electronically—for example, via a **keyboard** or a **scanner**—and converted to a form that can be processed by a computer.

input screen On a **video display screen,** a kind of format that is a combination of displayed text and pictorial data that identifies the elements of data to be entered and in which order they are to be entered. Input screens allow data entry operators to verify visually all data being entered.

Insert mode In **word processing,** the editing mode that allows you to insert text at the position of the cursor without typing over existing text. *Compare* **Typeover (Replace) mode.**

Ins key Key used to take the computer in and out of **Insert mode.**

instruction(s) Set of characters (code) directing a data processing system to perform a certain operation. *See also* **software.**

instruction cycle (I-cycle) In the **CPU,** the operation whereby an instruction is retrieved from **main memory (RAM)** and is decoded, alerting the circuits in the CPU to perform the specified operation.

integrated circuit *See* **chip.**

integrated software package Software combining several applications into a single package with a common set of commands. **Word processing,** electronic **spreadsheets, database management systems, graphics,** and **data communications** software have been combined in such packages.

integrated workstation *See* **executive workstation.**

intelligent terminal **Terminal** that can be used to input and retrieve data as well as do its own processing; in addition to the keyboard, monitor, and communications link, an intelligent terminal also includes a processing unit, storage capabilities, and software; microcomputers are often used as intelligent terminals. *Compare* **dumb terminal; smart terminal.**

interactive Describes computer systems or software that actively involve the user in asking and answering on-screen questions and in responding directly to software requests.

interactive processing *See* **on-line processing.**

interblock gaps (IBGs) Blank sections inserted between groups or blocks of records on magnetic tape to allow for the acceleration and deceleration of tape through a tape drive.

internal command files Files that contain **DOS** command instructions that are stored in **RAM** at all times. The instructions in these files are loaded into RAM when the computer is turned on. *See* **internal command instructions.**

internal command instructions **Operating system** software instructions loaded into **main memory (RAM)** when microcomputer is booted, where they direct and control applications software and hardware; they remain in main memory until the computer is turned off. *See also* **external command instructions.**

internal label Label recorded on tape magnetically; it is examined by a program before processing begins to ensure that the tape is the correct one. Also known as *header label.*

internal memory *See* **main memory.**

internal modem **Direct-connect modem** that is inside a microcomputer; it is located on a circuit board plugged into an expansion slot and draws power directly from the computer's power supply. No special cable is required.

international network **Network** providing intercontinental voice and data communications, often using undersea cable or satellites.

International Standards Organization (ISO) Organization working to develop standards for programming languages, communications, and compatibility among computers.

interpreter **Language processor** that converts high-level program instructions into **machine language** one instruction statement at a time. *Compare* **compiler.**

interrecord gaps (IRGs) Spaces left between records when data is written on magnetic tape.

iteration (do-while) control structure In **structured programming,** the structure that allows an activity to be repeated (iterated) as long as a certain condition remains true. Also known as a *loop*.

justification In **word processing,** the activity of evenly aligning words on a margin.

K *See* **kilobyte.**

key *See* **key field.**

keyboard Device resembling typewriter keyboard for entering data and computer-related codes. Besides standard typewriter keys, it has special **function keys, cursor-movement keys, numeric keys,** and other special-purpose keys.

keyboard entry Inputting data using a **keyboard.** *Compare* **direct entry.**

keyboard utility **Applications software utility,** usually **RAM-resident,** used to change the way the **cursor** appears on the screen.

key field (key) Unique element of data contained in each **record** used to identify the record and to determine where on the disk the record should be stored or retrieved using the **direct access storage and retrieval** method.

keypunch machine Device used to transcribe data from a **source document** by punching holes into cards via a keyboard using a special code.

key-to-disk (diskette) data entry System of dedicated high-volume data entry in which keyed-in data is recorded on disks (often in disk packs) or diskettes; the disks/diskettes can be stored separately and transported to a different area where the data is input to the main computer.

key-to-tape data entry System of dedicated data entry in which keyed-in data is recorded as magnetized spots on magnetic tape; the tape can be transported to a tape drive in a different area where the data is read into the main computer.

kilobyte (K) 1,024 bytes.

Label mode Lotus 1-2-3 goes into this mode when an alphabetic character or ', ", ^ are pressed. *Compare* **Value mode.**

language processor Program that translates **high-level programming languages** and **assembly languages** into **machine language.** Also known as *translator*.

laptop microcomputer Microcomputer using **flat-screen technology** that is small enough to be held on a person's lap.

laser printer Output device in which a laser beam is directed across the surface of a light-sensitive drum to record an image as a pattern of tiny dots. As with a photocopying machine, the image is then transferred to the paper a page at a time.

latency period *See* **rotational delay.**

left justification Words at the left margin are evenly aligned.

letter-quality printer **Impact printer** in which, like a typewriter, a hammer presses images of fully formed characters against a ribbon. *See* **daisy wheel printer; thimble printer.**

light pen Pen-shaped input device consisting of a light-sensitive photoelectric cell that, when touched to a video display screen, is used to signal the screen position to the computer.

line chart Shows trends over time; the angles of the line reflect variations in a trend, and the distance of the line from the horizontal axis represents quantity. *See also* **analytical graphics.**

line printer Nonserial impact output device in which a whole line of characters is printed practically at once. Includes band (belt) printers, drum printers, and print-chain printers, in which a printable character is located on a band (belt), drum, or print chain, with a separate print hammer for each print position across the width of the paper guide. As the band, drum, or print chain revolves around the print line, the hammers are activated as the appropriate characters pass in front of them.

liquid crystal display (LCD) Used as a flat **video display screen** in some laptop microcomputers. LCD uses a clear liquid chemical trapped in tiny pockets between two pieces of glass. Each pocket of liquid is covered both front and back by thin wires. When current is applied to the wires, a chemical reaction turns the chemical a dark color, thereby blocking light. The point of blocked light is the **pixel.**

List files key In WordPerfect, this key is used to list on the screen the files stored on the **current disk;** also used to erase, rename, copy, and print files.

local area network (LAN) Communications **network** connected by wire, cable, or fiber optics link that serves parts of a company located close to one another, generally in the same building or within two miles of one another. LANs allow workers to share hardware, software, and data.

logical database design Detailed description of database model from business rather than technical perspective; it involves defining user information needs, analyzing data element requirements and logical groupings, finalizing the design, and creating the **data dictionary.** Every element of data necessary to produce required management information system reports is identified, and the relationship among records is specified. *See also* **schema; subschema.**

logical field type In a database, the data that indicates whether a record contains true or false data, or "yes" or "no" data.

logical operations Operations consisting of three common comparisons: equal to, less than, and greater than. Three words used in basic logical operations are AND, OR, and NOT.

logical record **Record** defined by user according to logic of the program being used; it is independent of the **physical records.**

logic error In programming, an error caused by incorrect use of **control structures,** incorrect calculation, or omission of a procedure.

loop *See* **iteration (do-while) control structure.**

low-level programming language *See* **assembly language.**

machine cycle In the **CPU** during processing, the **instruction cycle** and the **execution cycle** together, as they apply to one instruction.

machine language The language the **CPU** understands; data and instructions are represented as **binary digits.** Each type of computer responds to a unique version of machine language. Also known as *first-generation language*.

Macintosh DOS Disk **operating system** designed by Apple Computers for the Apple Macintosh microcomputer.

magnetic-ink character recognition (MICR) Data entry

technology used in processing checks; it involves the electronic reading of numeric characters and special symbols printed on checks with magnetic ink.

magnetic tape Plastic ribbon coated with material that can be magnetized to record the **bit** patterns that represent data.

mainframe computer After the **supercomputer,** the most powerful type of computer; it is usually housed in a controlled environment and can support many powerful peripheral devices and the processing requirements of hundreds of users.

main memory The primary storage of a computer, where data and instructions are held for immediate access by the **CPU;** main memory is **volatile**—when the power is turned off, all data and instructions in memory are lost unless they have been permanently recorded on a **secondary storage** medium. Also known as *internal memory* and **RAM (random access memory).**

management Individuals responsible for providing leadership and direction in an organization's areas of planning, organizing, staffing, supervising, and controlling of business activities. Management may be low-level (operating or supervisory), middle-level, or upper-level (strategic). *See also* **middle management; operating management; upper management.**

management information system (MIS) Computer-based processing and/or manual procedures within a company to provide useful and timely information to support decision making on all three levels of management; at the **middle management** level, also called *information reporting system.*

margins Space between the right, left, top, and bottom edges of printed text and the edge of the paper.

mass storage system System for storing enormous amounts of data; it may consist of as many as 2,000 honeycomb-like cells that hold data cartridges with magnetic tape, each of which can store 50 MB of data. Each cartridge may be retrieved individually and positioned under a special read/write head for data transfer.

master file File used to store data permanently for access and updating. *Compare* **transaction file.**

master index file In dBASE IV, when the user first initiates a command to index a database into order, dBASE creates this file, which has the same filename as the currently active database, plus an extension of MDX.

MB *See* **megabyte.**

medium (*pl. media*) Type of material on which data is recorded—for example, paper, magnetic tape, magnetic disk, or optical disk.

megabyte (MB) 1,000 K—approximately 1 million characters.

megahertz (MHz) One million hertz; a measure of speed at which computers perform operations; **clock** speed.

memo **Field type** in dBASE IV used for entering up to 64 K of information about a particular **record.**

memory *See* **main memory.**

menu List of options, or choices, offered to the user by the software

menu-driven Describes a software program that offers varying levels of menus, or lists of choices displayed on the screen, to the user to lead him or her through the program function; menus may also include small descriptive pictures, or **icons.**

Menu mode In Lotus 1-2-3, the mode that displays **menu** options; accessed by pressing the slash (/) key.

merging Bringing together information from two different files.

microcomputer Small, general-purpose computer system that uses a microprocessor chip as its **CPU.** It can usually be used by only one person at one time; can be used independently or as a **terminal.** Also known as *personal computer, desktop computer.*

microcomputer terminal *See* **microcomputer.**

microprocessor **Integrated circuit** (**chip**) containing the **CPU** circuitry for a microcomputer.

Microsoft Windows **Graphic user interface** software similar to **Presentation Manager,** used with **Operating System 2 (OS/2).**

microwave system Communications technology using the atmosphere above the earth for transmitting signals point to point from tower to tower. Such systems are extensively used for high-volume as well as long-distance communication of both data and voice in the form of electromagnetic waves similar to radio waves but in a higher frequency range. Microwave signals are said to be "line-of-sight" because they cannot bend around the curvature of the earth.

middle management Level of management dealing with decisions that cover a broader range of time and are less structured than decisions made by **operating management.** However, middle management deals with decisions that are more time specific and more structured than decisions made by **upper-level,** or strategic, **management.**

millions of instructions per second (mips) Unit of measure for speed at which a computer processes software instructions.

minicomputer Computer that is similar to but less powerful than a **mainframe computer;** it can support 2–50 users and computer professionals.

mips *See* **millions of instructions per second.**

MIS *See* **management information system.**

MKDIR (MD) **DOS** command used to make a **subdirectory.**

modeling tools Program and systems design tools such as **computer-assisted software engineering (CASE), pseudocode, structure chart, data flow diagram, systems flowchart, HIPO,** and so on.

modem Device for translating **digital signals** from a computer into **analog signals** for transmission over telephone lines and then back into digital signals again for processing (a modem must be hooked up at each end of the transmission). Modem stands for MOdulate/DEModulate., *See also* **acoustic coupler; direct-connect modem.**

Modula-2 **High-level programming language** that is an improvement of **Pascal;** it is better suited for business use than Pascal and can be used as an applications software development tool.

modulation Process of converting **digital signals** from a computer into **analog signals** so that data can be sent over a telephone line.

module In **top-down programming design,** a small, easy-to-work-with unit in a program that has only a single function, a single entry, and a single exit point. Also known as *subroutine*.

monitor Device for viewing computer output. Also known as *cathode-ray tube (CRT), screen, video display screen*.

monochrome monitor Device for viewing text and, in some cases, graphics in a single color, commonly green or amber. It has only one electron gun. *Compare* **RGB monitor.**

motherboard Main circuit board in a microcomputer system. It normally includes the **microprocessor chip** (or **CPU**), **main memory (RAM)** chips, all related support circuitry, and the **expansion slots** for plugging in additional components. Also known as *system board*.

mouse Handheld input device connected to a microcomputer by a cable; when the mouse is rolled across the desktop, the **cursor** moves across the screen. A button on the mouse allows users to make **menu** selections and issue commands.

MS-DOS *See* **disk operating system.**

multidrop line Communications line that connects many devices; usually leased. *Compare* **point-to-point line.**

multimedia Sophisticated software that combines basic text and graphics along with animation, video, music, and voice.

multiple-field index dBASE IV index that is based on more than one **field.**

multiplexer Device that allows several terminals to share a single communications line.

multiprocessing Activity in which an **operating system** manages simultaneous execution of programs with two or more **CPUs.** This can entail processing instructions from different programs or different instructions from the same program. *Compare* **multitasking.**

multiprogramming *See* **multitasking.**

multitasking Activity in which more than one task or program is executed at a time. A small amount of each program is processed, and then the **CPU** moves to the remaining programs, one at a time, processing small parts of each. Also known as **multiprogramming.**

natural language Programming language designed to resemble human speech. Similar to **query language,** it eliminates the need for user to learn specific vocabulary, grammar, or **syntax.** Examples of natural languages are Clout for microcomputers and Intellect for mainframes. Also known as *fifth-generation language*.

network Collection of data communications hardware, computers, communications software, communications media, and applications software connected so that users can share information and equipment. *See also* **international network; private network; public network; ring network; star network; token ring network.**

network database model Type of **database** organization similar to **hierarchical database model** but allowing multiple **one-to-many relationships;** each **child record** can have more than one **parent record.** Access to the database can be from a number of points, not just the top.

nonimpact printer Output device that does not make direct contact with paper when it prints. *See* **ink-jet printer; laser printer; thermal printer.** *Compare* **impact printer.**

nonnumeric *See* **alphanumeric data.**

nonprocedural language Programming language that allows programmers and users to specify what the computer is supposed to do without having to specity *how* the computer is supposed to do it. *See also* **fourth-generation language.** *Compare* **procedural language.**

nonvolatile storage Type of storage that is relatively permanent—such as data saved to disk or tape; that is, computer instructions and data are not lost when the power is turned off. *Compare* **volatile storage.**

numeric data Data that can be mathematically manipulated *Compare* **alphanumeric data.**

numeric field type **Field type** in dBASE IV. *See* **numeric data.**

numeric keys (keypad) The keys labeled 0–9 on the computer **keyboard;** used to enter numbers for mathematical manipulation.

Num Lock key When a computer **keyboard** combines the **numeric keys** with the **cursor-movement keys,** the Num Lock key must be pressed before numbers can be entered via the numeric keys. Then the Num Lock key is pressed again to restore the function of the cursor-movement keys.

object code Program consisting entirely of **machine-language** instructions. *Compare* **source code.**

off-the-shelf software **Applications software** that can be purchased in a computer store, as opposed to software that is custom written by a programmer.

on-demand report Report requested by **middle management** on a case-by-case basis.

one-to-many relationship In a **hierarchical database model,** the parent-child relationship between two record types; one **parent record** has many **child records.**

on-line processing Input data processed immediately, not stored temporarily in a **transaction file** for later processing; anything in a computer system that is on-line is linked up to current processing operations.

open architecture Attribute of computers that can be upgraded by the use of expansion cards, such as **expanded memory;** the user can open the **system unit (cabinet)** and insert the expansion cards in the computer's **expansion slots.** *Compare* **closed architecture.**

open wire Earliest type of telephone line, composed of unsheathed, uninsulated copper wires strung on telephone poles.

operating management The lowest level of management in an organization; operating managers deal mostly with **structured decisions** covering a relatively narrow time frame, actualizing the plans of **middle management** and controlling daily operations. Also known as *supervisory management*.

operating system Set of **internal command instructions** or programs to allow computer to direct its own resources and operations; in microcomputers, called a *disk operating system*.

Operating System/2 (OS/2) IBM and Microsoft microcomputer **systems software** intended to take advantage of 80286 and 80386 microprocessors (such as in the IBM PS/2 Series of microcomputers) and support multitasking and software applications requiring up to 16 MB of main memory (RAM); used in conjunction with **Presentation Manager** and **Microsoft Windows.**

operating system command Internal or external command that allows users to manage disks and disk files. *See* **external command instructions; internal command instructions.**

operating systems software Program that starts up the computer and functions as the principal coordinator of all hardware components and applications software programs. *See* **internal command instructions.**

operational decision maker Low-level manager who typically makes structured decisions regarding daily business operations.

optical character recognition (OCR) Input system whereby input device reads hardcopy data from source documents into computer-usable form; such devices use light-sensitive equipment to read bar codes, optical marks, typewritten characters, and handwriting.

optical mark Mark made by special pencil on form meant to be read by an **optical mark reader.**

optical mark reader (OMR) Device that reads data recorded with special pencil on preprinted sheets and converts it into computer-usable form.

optical storage **Secondary storage** technology using a high-power laser beam to burn microscopic spots in a disk's surface coating. Data is represented by the presence and the absence of holes in the storage locations (1s and 0s). A much lower-power laser beam is used to retrieve the data. Much more data can be stored in this way than with traditional storage media, and it is faster and cheaper.

output Computer-produced text, graphics, or sound in **hardcopy** or **softcopy** form that can be used immediately by people, or computer-produced data stored in computer-usable form for later use by computers and people.

output file Data that is processed and then output in the form of a **file** to be used by another person or program at a later time.

output phase A phase of activity in the **computer-based information system** during which the user is provided with all the necessary information to perform and manage day-to-day business activities and make decisions. Output can be provided for immediate use or for storage by the computer for future use.

overview diagram Part of a **hierarchy plus input-process-output (HIPO) package,** used as a tool for program design and **documentation;** the overview diagram shows from left to right the inputs, processes, and outputs for the entire program, and the steps in the diagram are cross-referenced to the module numbers in the corresponding **structure chart.**

page description language (PDL) *See* **page description software.**

page description software Part of **desktop publishing software;** it allows the **laser printer** to combine text and graphics from different files on a single page.

page printer *See* **laser printer.**

panel One of six vertical sections (panels) in dBASE IV's **Control Center** that make up most of the screen. Each panel enables the user to create a different type of file with specific capabilities.

parallel implementation One of four approaches to systems implementation; the old system and new system are run at the same time for a specified period, then the old system is discontinued when the new system is judged satisfactory. *Compare* **direct implementation; phased implementation; pilot implementation.**

parallel processing Using many processors (**CPUs**) to process data simultaneously, thus speeding up processing.

parent record In **hierarchical database model,** the **record** higher in the structure than a **child record.** Each child can have only one parent—that is, each record may have many records below it but only one record above it, which is a **one-to-many ralationship.** Deletion of a parent record automatically deletes all child records.

parity bit An extra (ninth) **bit** attached to the end of a **byte;** it is used as part of an error-checking scheme. Computers are designed to use either an odd-parity scheme or an even-parity scheme, in which the total number of 1s in each byte, including the parity bit, must add up to an odd number or an even number.

Pascal **High-level programming language** for large and small computer systems; developed to teach programming as a systematic and structured activity. It has strong mathematical and scientific processing capabilities.

PC-DOS *See* **disk operating system.**

periodic report Report for **middle management** produced at predetermined times—for example, payroll report, inventory status report.

personal computer *See* **microcomputer.**

phased implementation One of four approaches to systems implementation; a system is so large it is implemented one phase at a time. *Compare* **direct implementation; parallel implementation; pilot implementation.**

physical database design In design of a **database,** the stage following the **logical design.** Physical design involves specifying how best to store data on the **direct access storage and retrieval devices** so that it can be updated and retrieved quickly and efficiently.

physical records *See* **block.**

pie chart Circle with wedges that look like pie slices; best chart to use for illustrating parts of a whole. *See* **analytical graphics.**

pilot implementation One of four approaches to system implementation in which, in a widely dispersed company, the system is introduced at one location at a time. *Compare* **direct implementation; parallel implementation; phased implementation.**

pixel Picture element; a glowing phosphor on a **cathode-ray tube (CRT) screen.** Small pixels provide greatest image clarity (**resolution**).

PL/1 (Programming Language 1) High-level, general-purpose programming language for computation and heavy-duty file handling. Primarily used on minicomputers and mainframes.

plotter Output device used to create **hardcopy** drawings on paper in a variety of colors. *See also* **drum plotter; electrostatic plotter; flatbed plotter.**

pointing device Nonkeyboard data entry device that moves **cursor** and sends command messages to computer—such as **digitizing tablet, mouse, light pen,** and **touch screen.**

point-of-sale (POS) terminal Input/output device (**smart terminal**) used like a cash register to print sales transaction receipt and to send sales and inventory data to a central computer for processing.

point-to-point line Communications line that directly connects the sending and the receiving devices; if it is a *switched line*, it is disconnected when transmission is finished; if it is a *dedicated line*, it is always established. *Compare* **multidrop line.**

port Electrical interconnection—for example, on a microcomputer, the point where the printer is plugged into the computer.

portable printer Printer that is compact and typically weighs less than 5 lbs.

portable terminal Input/output device that users can carry with them to remote locations and connect via telecommunications lines to a central computer. **Dumb terminals** can send and receive data to and from the main computer; **smart terminals** permit some data to be entered and edited before they are connected to the main computer.

postimplementation evaluation In systems design, a formal evaluation of a new system after operation for several months and after systems maintenance has been done to determine if the system is meeting its objectives.

power supply Source of electrical power to components housed in the **system unit** of a microcomputer.

presentation graphics Graphical forms that go beyond simple **analytical graphics** (bar charts, line charts, pie charts); sophisticated presentation graphics software allows the user to function as an artist and combine free-form shapes and text.

Presentation Manager **Graphic user interface** similar to **Microsoft Windows,** used with **Operating System/2 (OS/2).**

primary file When **merging** using WordPerfect, data from the **secondary file** is merged with data from this file to form a customized document.

primary storage *See* **main memory.**

print-chain printer *See* **line printer.**

printer Output device that prints characters, symbols, and sometimes graphics on paper. *See also* **impact printer; nonimpact printer.**

Print key Key used to print documents out on the printer.

private network **Network** supporting the voice and data communications needs of a particular organization.

procedural language *See* **high-level programming language.**

procedure In an information system, specific sequence of steps performed to complete one or more information processing activities.

procedures manual Written **documentation** of noncomputerized and computerized procedures used in a **computer-based information system.**

processing The computer-based manipulation of **data** into information.

processing phase The second phase of activity in the **computer-based information system,** during which all the number and character manipulation activities are done that are necessary to convert the **data** into an appropriate form of **information.**

program Group of related instructions that perform specific processing tasks.

program files Programs stored on magnetic disk or tape.

program flowchart Diagram using standard **ANSI** symbols to show step-by-step processing activities and decision logic needed to solve a programming problem.

program independence Attribute of programs that can be used with data files arranged in different ways—for example, some with the date first and expense items second and others with expense items first and date second. Program dependence means that a separate program has to be written to use each differently arranged data file.

programmable keys *See* **function keys.**

programmable read-only memory (PROM) Type of **read-only memory (ROM)** chip in which data or program instructions are not prerecorded when it is manufactured; thus, users can record their own data or instructions, but once the data has been recorded, it cannot always be changed.

project dictionary Stores all the requirements and specifications for all elements of data to be used in a new system.

proprietary operating system **Operating system** developed for only one brand of computer.

protocol In electronic communications, formal rules for communicating, including those for timing of message exchanges, the type of electrical connections used by the communications devices, error detection techniques, methods required to gain access to communications channels, and so on.

protocol converter Specialized intelligent **multiplexer** that facilitates effective communications between microcomputers and the main computer system.

prototyping In systems analysis and design, the process of building a small-scale working model of a new system, or part of a new system, in order to get feedback from users as quickly as possible. **Report generators, applications generators, DBMS (database management) software,** and **CASE (computer-assisted software engineering)** software may be used as prototyping tools.

pseudocode "Fake" code; programming code, not actually entered into the computer, that uses modified human language statements (instead of flowchart symbols) to represent program logic. It is more precise in representing logic than regular, idiomatic human language but does not follow a specific syntax. It uses four statement keywords to portray logic: IF, THEN, ELSE, and DO.

public databank Information service providing users with access, for a fee, to large databases.

public network **Network** providing subscribers with voice and data communications over a large geographical area. Also known as *common carrier, specialized common carrier.*

quad-density *See* **recording density.**

query language **Fourth-generation** programming **language** that allows users to ask questions about, or retrieve information from, database files by forming requests in normal human language statements. Learning the specific grammar, vocabulary, and **syntax** is usually a simple task. The definitions for query language and for **database management systems software** are so similar that they are usually considered to be the same.

quick report dBASE IV reporting option that provides means to generate a report of database file or current view; automatically inserts column headings and current date and page number in the upper-left corner of the screen; automatically totals numeric fields. *Compare* **custom report.**

QWERTY Term that designates the common computer **keyboard** layout, whereby the first six letters of the first row of lettered keys spell "QWERTY".

RAM *See* **random access memory.**

RAM-resident software (utility) In a microcomputer, software always available to the user because it resides in **main memory (RAM)** at all times.

random access *See* **direct access storage and retrieval.**

random access memory (RAM) The name given to the integrated circuits **(chips)** that make up main memory, which provides **volatile** temporary storage of data and program instructions that the **CPU** is using; data and instructions can be retrieved at random, no matter where they are located in main memory. RAM is used for storing **operating system** software instructions and for temporary storage of **applications software** instructions, input data, and output data. *See also* **internal command instructions.**

range One or more **cells** in a **spreadsheet** that together form a rectangle.

raster scan rate Measure of number of times per second the image on a video display screen can be refreshed—that is, "lit up" again. Because the phosphors hit by the electron beam do not glow very long, the beam must continuously sweep the screen. With a low raster scan rate, the screen will seem to flicker.

read-only memory (ROM) Type of memory in which instructions to perform operations critical to a computer are stored on integrated circuits (chips) in permanent, **nonvolatile** form. The instructions are usually recorded on the chips by the manufacturer. *Compare* **electrically erasable programmable read-only memory; erasable programmable read-only memory; programmable read-only memory; random access memory (RAM).**

read/write head Recording mechanism in magnetic storage devices that "reads" (accepts) the magnetic spots of data and converts them to electrical impulses and that "writes" (enters) the spots on the magnetic tape or disk. Most disk drives have two read/write heads to access the top and bottom surfaces of a disk simultaneously.

Ready mode In Lotus 1-2-3, the **spreadsheet** is in this mode when the user can move the **cursor** from **cell** to cell.

real-time processing Immediate processing; each transaction is fully processed when input, and there is immediate feedback (action can be taken right away). All related computer files affected by the transaction are updated immediately, and printed output can be produced on the spot. *Compare* **batch entry.**

record Collection of related fields. *See also* **data storage hierarchy.**

recording density Number of **bits** per inch (bpi) that can be written onto the surface of a magnetic disk. Disks and drives have three kinds of recording densities: (1) single-density, (2) double-density, or (3) quad-density. The higher the density number, the more data a disk can hold.

Reduced Instruction Set Computing (RISC) Simplified chip architecture and instruction sets, enabling faster processing.

register Temporary storage location within the **CPU** that quickly accepts, stores, and transfers data and instructions being used immediately. An instruction that needs to be executed must be retrieved from **main memory (RAM)** and placed in a register for access by the **ALU (arithmetic/logic unit).** The larger the register (the more **bits** it can carry at once), the greater the processing power.

relational database model Type of database organization in which many tables (called *relations*) store related data elements in rows (called *tuples*) and columns (called *attributes*). The structure allows complex logical relationships between records to be expressed in a simple fashion. Relational databases can cross-reference data and retrieve data automatically, and data can be easily added, deleted, or modified. Data can be accessed by content, instead of address, which is the case with **hierarchical database** and **network database models.**

relational operation Operation comparing two elements of data to determine if one element is greater than, less than, or equal to the other.

report file Data file in a small computer system that stores information for reports for later transfer to a special computer system for printing.

report generator **Fourth-generation language** similar to **query language,** which allows users to ask questions of a **database** and retrieve information from it for a report. The user cannot alter the contents of the database file but has great control over the appearance of the output.

request for proposal Part of the systems requirement report of phase 2 of the **systems development life cycle;** companies going outside their own organizations for help in developing a new system use it to request bids from vendors for prices of software, hardware, programs, supplies, and/or services.

resolution Clarity of the image on the **video display screen.** Three factors measuring resolution are number of lines of resolution (vertical and horizontal), **raster scan rate,** and **bandwidth.**

Retrieve key Enables user to retrieve into **RAM** a copy of a file that is stored on disk.

retrieving Obtaining previously created documents from a storage device and placing them in **main memory (RAM).**

Reveal codes key Enables the user to display all the codes that WordPerfect has included (embedded) in a document.

RGB (red/green/blue) monitor Device for viewing text and graphics in various colors. It has three **electron guns,** and the screen is coated with three types of phosphors: red, green, and blue. Each **pixel** is made up of three dots of phosphors, one of each color, and is capable of producing a wide range of colors. *Compare* **monochrome monitor.**

right justification Words at the right margin of a document are evenly aligned.

ring network Electronic communications **network** in which messages flow in one direction from a source on the loop to a destination on the loop. Computers in between act as relay stations, but if a computer fails, it can be bypassed.

RISC *See* **Reduced Instruction Set Computing.**

robot Automatic device that performs functions ordinarily ascribed to humans or that operates with what appears to be almost human intelligence; in the field of **artificial intelligence (AI),** produced to assist in industrial applications, such as **computer-aided manufacturing (CAM).**

ROM *See* **read-only memory.**

root directory In the hierarchy of the MS-**DOS** directory structure, when a microcomputer program is **booted,** the first directory displayed is the root directory. This contains subdirectories, which can in turn contain sub-subdirectories. The root directory is similar in concept to the filing cabinet.

root record In a **hierarchical database model,** the record at the highest level or top of the "tree." Root records, which are the key to the structure, connect the various branches.

rotational delay In a disk drive, the time required for the disk to revolve until the correct **sector** is under or over the **read/write head(s).**

RPG (report program generator) **High-level programming language** designed to help small businesses generate reports and update files easily. It can be used to solve clear-cut and relatively simple problems.

satellite system In electronic communications, a system that uses solar-powered satellites in stationary orbit above the earth to receive, amplify, and retransmit signals. The satellite acts as a relay station for microwave stations on the ground (called *earth stations*).

Save key Enables the user to save his/her work; after pressing this key, the user must supply a name for the file being saved.

saving Activity of permanently storing data from a microcomputer's **main memory (RAM)** (primary storage) on disk or tape **(secondary storage).**

scanner (scanning device) Hardware device that "reads" text and graphics and converts them to computer-usable form; scanners "read" copy on paper and transmit it to the user's computer screen for manipulation, output, and/or storage.

scatter chart *See* **XY chart.**

schema Describes organization of **relational database** in its entirety, including names of all data elements and ways records are linked. A **subschema** is part of the schema.

screen *See* **monitor.**

screen utility **Applications software utility, RAM-resident,** used to increase the life of the computer video screen.

scrolling Activity of moving text up or down on the video display screen.

search and replace In **word processing,** the activity of automatically searching for and replacing text in a document.

search operation Using **database management system software,** the activity of using arithmetic, relational, logical, and string operations to search for information stored in a database.

secondary file Data file used during the **merging** process; is combined with data in the **primary file** to create a customized document.

secondary storage Any storage device designed to retain data and instructions in permanent form. Secondary storage is **nonvolatile;** data and instructions remain intact when the computer is turned off. Also called *auxiliary storage*. *Compare* **primary storage.**

second-generation language *See* **assembly language.**

sector One of several wedge-shaped areas on a hard disk or diskette used for storage reference purposes. The point at which a sector intersects a **track** is used to reference the data location. *See* **hard-sectored disk; soft-sectored disk.**

seek time In a disk drive, the time required for the drive to position the **read/write heads** over the proper **track.**

selection (if-then-else) control structure In **structured programming,** the **control structure** that allows a condition to be tested to determine which instruction(s) will be performed next.

semiconductor Material (often silicon) that conducts electricity with only a little ("semi") resistance; impurities are added to it to form electrical circuits. Today, the integrated circuits (**chips**) in the **main memory (RAM)** of almost all computers are based on this technology.

semistructured decision Decision typically made at the **middle-management** level that, unlike **structured decisions,** must be made without a base of clearly defined informational procedures.

sequence control structure In **structured programming,** the **control structure** that specifies that all events take place in sequence, one after the other.

sequential file organization Method of file recording and storage in which data is retrieved one record at a time in the sequence in which it was recorded on the storage medium.

setting time In a disk drive, the time required to place the **read/write heads** in contact with the disks.

shadow mask In a **CRT (cathode-ray tube),** a shield with holes to prevent dispersion of the beam from the **electron gun** so that only a small, precise portion of the beam is allowed to reach the screen. The distance between any two adjacent holes in the shadow mask is referred to as *dot pitch*.

Shift key Computer **keyboard** key that works in the same way that a typewriter Shift key works: when pressed in conjunction with an alphabetic key, the letter appears uppercase.

simplex transmission mode Communications transmission in which data travels only in one direction at all times.

single-density disk *See* **recording density.**

single-field index dBASE IV index that is based on one **field.**

single-sided disk Diskette that stores data on one side only.

smart card Credit card-sized personal transaction computer that can be inserted into special card-reading **point-of-sale terminals.** Smart cards have memory chips containing permanent records that are easily updated each time the card is used. The transaction data stored on the card can later be read into the computer to update the user's bank records.

smart terminal **Terminal** that can be used to input and retrieve data and also do some limited processing on its own, such as editing or verifying data. *Compare* **dumb terminal; intelligent terminal.**

softcopy Output produced in a seemingly intangible form such as on a video display screen or provided in voice form. *Compare* **hardcopy.**

soft-sectored disk Disk that is marked magnetically by the user's computer system during **formatting,** which determines the size and number of **sectors** on the disk. *Compare* **hard-sectored disk.**

software Electronic instructions given to the computer to tell it what to do and when and how to do it. Frequently made up of a group of related programs. The two main types of software are **applications software** and **systems software.**

software installation Process of telling an applications software package what the characteristics are of the hardware you will be using so that the software will run smoothly.

software package **Applications software** and **documentation** usually created by professional software writers to perform general business functions.

sorting Process of reorganizing a **database** into a different order.

source code Program written in **high-level programming language.** Source code must be translated by a **language processor** into **object code** before the program instructions can be executed by the computer.

source document Document such as an order form on which data is manually recorded for later entry in computer-usable form.

specialized common carrier *See* **public network.**

spelling checker In **word processing,** program that checks a document for spelling errors.

spreadsheet area The **spreadsheet** cells that are visible on the screen.

spreadsheet-based graphics *See* **analytical graphics.** *Compare* **presentation graphics.**

spreadsheet software Software program enabling user to create, manipulate, and analyze numerical data and develop personalized reports involving the use of extensive mathematical, financial, statistical, and logical processing. The user works with an electronic version of the accountant's traditional worksheet, with rows and columns, called a *spreadsheet*.

stacked bar chart Variation of the simple **bar chart;** shows how the components of a data element compare over time. *Compare* **grouped bar chart.** *See also* **analytical graphics.**

star network Electronic communications **network** with a central unit (computer or **file server**) linked to a number of smaller computers and/or terminals (called *nodes*). The central unit acts as traffic controller for all nodes and controls communications to locations outside the network.

start-stop transmission *See* **asynchronous transmission.**

status report Management report used to supply data and information on the state of something, such as the number of items in inventory; it is a form of output.

storage devices (hardware) Devices that accept and hold computer instructions and data in a form that is relatively permanent, commonly on magnetic disk or tape or on optical disk.

storage phase Phase of activity in the **computer-based information system** during which data, information, and processing instructions are stored in computer-usable form, commonly on magnetic disk or tape or on optical disk; stored data can be processed further at a later date or output for the user in **softcopy** and **hardcopy** form.

strategic decision maker Manager in **upper-level management** who makes **unstructured decisions**—unpredictable and long-range, not just about past and/or current activities. Such decisions tend to be directed toward strategic planning, allocation of resources, and policy formulation.

streaming tape Storage method in which data is written onto a tape in one continuous stream, with no starting or stopping, no **IBGs (interblock gaps)** or **IRGs (interrecord gaps)**. Streaming tape cassettes are often used as backup storage for hard disks.

string Designated sequence, or group, of text characters.

string operations Commands that enable the user to search for the occurrence of a specific **string** in a database.

structure chart In systems analysis, a chart for diagramming the breakdown of **modules** in a program. Also known as *hierarchy chart*.

structured decision Predictable decision that can be made about daily business activities by following a well-defined set of routine procedures; typically made by **operating management.**

structured design A **top-down design** system to ensure that agreement is reached as early as possible on major program design decisions. Its goals are simplicity, refinement by level, and modularity. *See also* **module.**

structured programming Method of programming using **top-down design** and three **control structures** (that is, **sequence, selection, iteration**) to break down main functions into smaller **modules** for coding purposes.

structured walkthrough In programming, the method whereby a group of programmers meet to review a program designed by another programmer in order to identify what is not clear or not workable.

stub testing Process by which several high-level **modules** in a program are tested before the program is designed for the rest of the lower-level modules; the objective is to eliminate as many errors as possible without having to write the whole program first. A stub is an unprogrammed module.

subdirectory Second level in the MS-**DOS** directory hierarchy; equivalent to a file drawer in a file cabinet (root directory), it can contain sub-subdirectories.

subroutine *See* **module.**

subschema Part of the **schema** of a relational database; it refers to the way certain records are linked to be useful to the user.

sub-subdirectory Low in the hierarchy of the MS-**DOS** directory structure, it is contained within a subdirectory of the **root directory.** A sub-subdirectory resembles a file folder.

@SUM function Lotus 1-2-3 **function** used to determine the total amount of values stored in a **range** of spreadsheet **cells.**

summary report Report for **middle management** that reviews, summarizes, and analyzes historical data to help plan and control operations and implement policy formulated by **upper management.** Summary reports show totals and trends.

supercomputer The largest and most powerful computer; it is about 50,000 times faster than a **microcomputer** and may cost as much as $20 million. Supercomputers are housed in special rooms; the next most powerful computer is the **mainframe.**

superconductor A not-yet-developed material to be used for integrated circuits (**chips**); this material would conduct electricity faster (with less or no resistance) and with less heat output than semiconductors.

supermicro A very powerful **microcomputer.**

super video graphics array (Super VGA) Expansion card plugged into **expansion slot** in **system unit (cabinet)** that allows compatible monitor to display **bit-mapped graphics** in color; must be used with appropriate software; displays up to 256 colors at a very high **resolution.**

supervisor The "captain" of the **operating system,** it remains in a microcomputer's **main memory** and calls in other parts of the operating system as needed from **secondary storage** and controls all other programs in the computer. In a **multitasking** environment, a supervisor coordinates the execution of each program. Also known as *control program*.

supervisory management *See* **operating management.**

switched line **Point-to-point communications line** that is disconnected when transmission is finished.

switches **DOS** command options.

synch bytes Header and trailer **bytes** inserted as identifiers at beginnings and ends of blocks of coded data; used in **synchronous transmission.**

synchronous transmission Form of transmitting groups of characters as blocks with no start and stop bits between characters. Characters are sent as blocks with header and trailer bytes (called **synch bytes**) inserted as identifiers at the beginnings and ends of blocks. Synchronous transmission is used by large computers to transmit huge volumes of data at high speeds. *Compare* **asynchronous transmission.**

syntax Rules and patterns required for forming programming language sentences or statements that tell the computer what to do and how to do it.

syntax error In programming, an error resulting from incorrect use of the rules of the language the program is being written in.

system board *See* **motherboard.**

system cabinet *See* **system unit.**

system prompt Characters that display on the screen to indicate what disk drive is current and what subdirectory is current.

system requirements Refers to the hardware and software that is required to use a particular software application.

systems development life cycle (SDLC) Formal process by which organizations build **computer-based information systems.** Participants are users, information processing staff, management of all departments, and computer specialists. The SDLC is used as a guide in establishing a business system's requirements, developing the system, acquiring hardware and software, and controlling development costs. It is generally divided into six phases: (1) analyze current system; (2) define new system requirements; (3) design new system; (4) develop new system; (5) implement new system; and (6) evaluate performance of and maintain new system.

systems files Files that must be stored on the disk that **DOS** is loaded from.

systems flowchart Systems development modeling tool used to diagram and document design of a new system and present an overview of the entire system, including data flow (points of input, output, and storage) and processing activities.

systems maintenance The phase after a new system has been implemented when adjustments must be made (correction of minor processing errors).

systems requirements report Report concluding the second phase of the **systems development life cycle;** it enables managers to determine the completeness and accuracy of the new system requirements, as well as the economic and practical feasibility of the new system; it may also include a **request for proposal** for prices of software, hardware, supplies, and/or services from vendors.

systems software Programs that are the principal interface between all hardware, the user, and applications software; comprise **internal command instructions, external command instructions,** and **language processor.** *Compare* **applications software.**

system unit Main computer system cabinet in a microcomputer, which usually houses the power supply, the **motherboard,** and some storage devices.

tactical decision maker **Middle-level manager** who generally deals with **semistructured decisions.**

tag Specification stored in a **master index file** that specifies the order of **database.**

TB *See* **terabyte.**

teleconferencing Electronic linkage of several people who participate in a conversation and share displayed data at the same time.

terabyte (TB) One trillion bytes.

terminal Input/output device; it typically consists of a **video display screen,** a **keyboard,** and a connecting cable. A dumb terminal is entirely dependent for all its capabilities on the computer system to which it is connected; it cannot do any processing of its own. A smart terminal is able to do some editing and storage of data without interacting with the central computer system, but it cannot be used for programming. An intelligent terminal can input and receive data, as well as allow users to edit and program.

THEN *See* **pseudocode.**

thermal printer **Nonimpact printer** that uses heat to produce an image. The print mechanism heats the surface of chemically treated paper, producing dots as characters. No ribbon or ink is used.

thesaurus Lists of words that have similar meaning to a given word; word processing programs often include a thesaurus to help users pick just the right word.

thimble printer Letter-quality **impact printer** similar to a **daisy wheel printer,** except that the spokes curve upward instead of lying flat.

third-generation language *See* **high-level programming language.**

timesharing System that supports many user stations or terminals simultaneously. A **front-end processor** may be used to schedule and control all user requests entering the system from the **terminals,** enabling the main computer to concentrate solely on processing.

token ring network Electronic communications **network** in which each computer obtains exclusive access to the communications channel by "grabbing" a "token" (predetermined pattern of bits) and altering it before attaching a message. This altered token acts as a message indicator for the receiving computer, which in turn generates a new token, freeing up the channel for another computer. Computers in between the sender and the receiver examine the token and regenerate the message if the token is not theirs. Thus, only one computer can transmit a message at one time.

top-down design In **structured programming** and systems design, the act of identifying the main functions of a program and then breaking them into smaller units (**modules**).

touch screen **Video display screen** sensitized to receive input from touch of a finger.

Touch-Tone™ device Input device hooked up to the telephone line for the purpose of running credit card checks; the device sends data to a central computer, which then checks the data against its files and reports credit information back to the store. Also called *card dialer* or *card reader*.

track (1) On magnetic tape a channel of magnetic spots and spaces (1s and 0s) running the length of the tape. (2) On disks, a track is one of the circular bands.

trackball Input hardware device that functions like a **mouse** except that it doesn't need to be rolled around on the desktop; the ball is held in a socket on the top of the stationary device.

track density Number of **tracks** on magnetic storage medium. Common track densities are 48 tracks per inch (tpi) and 96 tpi. Track density affects capacity.

transaction file Temporary storage file in which data is stored in computer-usable form until needed for processing. *Compare* **master file.**

transaction log Complete record of activity affecting contents of a **database** during transaction period. This log aids in rebuilding database files if they are damaged.

transaction processing system (TPS) Information system supporting day-to-day business operating activities or transactions; usually the first and most important objective of an information system. A computer-based transaction processing system operates at the lowest level of a business and usually within only one functional area of a business—marketing, accounting and finance, production, or research and development. Also called an *operations information system (OIS)* or an *electronic data processing (EDP) system.*

translator *See* **language processor.**

TREE **DOS** command used to display a listing of all **subdirectories** stored on a disk.

tree network *See* **hierarchical network.**

TRS-DOS **Disk operating system** for some Tandy/Radio Shack microcomputers.

turnaround document Computer-produced output document forwarded to a recipient, who records any additional data on it and returns it to the sender.

twisted-pair cable Insulated pairs of wires twisted around each other; they are often packed into bundles of a thousand or more pairs, as in telephone lines.

TYPE **DOS** command used to display the contents of a file that contains text.

Typeover (Replace) mode In **word processing,** the mode of inserting text in which existing text is typed over as new text is typed in. *Compare* **Insert mode.**

UNDO In Lotus 1-2-3, command that makes it possible to view a spreadsheet as it appeared when it was last in **Ready mode.**

UNIX **Operating system** initially created for **minicomputers;** it provides a wide range of capabilities, including **virtual storage, multiprogramming,** and **timesharing.**

unjustified text Text with an unaligned (ragged) margin.

unstructured decision Decision rarely based on predetermined routine procedures; involves the subjective judgment of the decision maker and is mainly the kind of decision made by **upper management.** Unstructured decisions are supported by management information systems in the form of highly summarized reports covering information over long time periods and surveying activities outside as well as inside the company.

upload To transfer programs or data from a small computer to a larger one, or from a computer to a **network** or an **electronic bulletin board.**

upper management The level of management dealing with decisions that are broadest in scope and cover the longest time frame. Top managers include only a few powerful people who are in charge of the four basic functions of a business: (1) marketing, (2) accounting and finance, (3) production, and (4) research and development. A manager at this level is also known as a *strategic decision maker. Compare* **middle management; operating management.**

user Person receiving the computer's services; generally someone without much technical knowledge who makes decisions based on reports and other results that computers produce. *Compare* **computer professional.**

utility *See* **applications software utility.**

Value mode Lotus 1-2-3 goes into this mode when a numeric character or +, −, @, $, or (is pressed. *Compare* **Label mode.**

video display screen Device for viewing computer output. Two main types are **cathode-ray tube (CRT)** and **flat screen.**

video graphics array (VGA) Expansion card plugged into **expansion slot** in **system unit (cabinet)** that allows compatible monitors to display **bit-mapped graphics** in color; must be used with appropriate software; displays 16 colors at a resolution higher than **EGA.**

view query In dBASE IV, refers to a picture of the data stored in a **database** file.

view skeleton Format for the current **view query.**

virtual memory **Operating system** element that enables the computer to process as if it contained an almost unlimited supply of **main memory.** It enables a program to be broken into modules, or small sections, that can be loaded into main memory when needed. Modules not currently in use are stored on high-speed disk and retrieved one at a time when the operating system determines that the current module has completed executing. Also known as *virtual storage.*

virtual storage *See* **virtual memory.**

virus Bugs (programming errors) created intentionally by some programmers, usually "hackers," that consist of pieces of computer code (either hidden or posing as legitimate code) that, when downloaded or run, attach themselves to other programs or files and cause them to malfunction.

visual table of contents (VTOC) Part of a **hierarchy plus input-process-output (HIPO) package,** it includes a **structure chart,** a short description of the contents of the program, and a legend that provides any necessary explanations of symbols used in the **overview diagram** and the **detail diagram,** also parts of the HIPO package.

voice input device Input device that converts spoken words into electrical signals by comparing the electrical patterns produced by the speaker's voice to a set of prerecorded patterns. If a matching pattern is found, the computer accepts it as a part of its standard "vocabulary" and then activates and manipulates displays by spoken command. Also known as *voice recognition system.*

voice mail Electronic voice-messaging system that answers callers with a recording of the user's voice and records messages. Messages can be forwarded to various locations; local telephone companies provide voice mail services; voice mail systems are also used within companies.

voice output Synthesized or taped sound; computer output used in situations where other **softcopy** output is inappropriate, as in automotive systems.

voice recognition system *See* **voice input device.**

volatile storage Form of memory storage in which data and instructions are lost when the computer is turned off. *Compare* **nonvolatile storage.** *See also* **random access memory (RAM).**

wand *See* **bar code reader.**

warm boot Loading **DOS** into **RAM** *after* the computer has been turned on.

window Most **video display screens** allow 24–25 lines of text to be viewed at one time; this portion is called a *window*. By moving (scrolling) text up and down the screen, other text becomes available.

Windows *See* **Microsoft Windows.**

word processing Preparation of text for creating, editing, or printing documents.

word processing software Program enabling user to create and edit documents by inserting, deleting, and moving text. Some programs also offer **formatting** features such as variable margins and different type sizes and styles, as well as more advanced features that border on **desktop publishing.**

word wrap In **word processing,** when the **cursor** reaches the right-hand margin of a line it automatically returns (wraps around) to the left-hand margin of the line below and continues the text; the user does not have to hit a key to make the cursor move down to the next line.

write once, read many (WORM) **Optical disk** whose data and instructions are imprinted by the disk manufacturer but whose content is determined by the buyer; after the data is imprinted, it cannot be changed. *Compare* **compact disk/read-only memory (CD-ROM); erasable optical disk.**

write/protect notch On a diskette, a notch in the protective cover that can be covered to prevent the **read/write head** from touching the disk surface so that no data can be recorded or erased.

WYSIWYG (what you see is what you get) **Page description software** that allows the user to see the final version of a **desktop publishing** document on the screen before it is printed out. *Compare* **code-oriented.**

XY chart Used to show how one or more data elements relate to another data element; also called *scatter chart*. *See also* **analytical graphics.**

yoke In a **cathode-ray tube (CRT),** the cylinder placed in front of the **electron gun** that can generate a controlled magnetic field (like a directional magnet). The yoke directs the electron beam of the electron gun across the screen horizontally and vertically.

INDEX

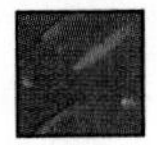

G

H

L

M

N

O

W–X

Photo Credits

This page constitutes a continuation of the copyright page.

We are grateful to the following organizations for providing us with photographs:

Chapter 1

Figure 1.1a Jon Feingersh/Stock Imagery; **Figure 1.1b** Courtesy of General Signal Corporation; **Figure 1.1c** Courtesy of Walgreen Company; **Figure 1.1d** Mark Joseph Photography; **Figure 1.4** Courtesy of Egghead Discount Software; **Figure 1.5** Courtesy of Martin Marietta Corporation; **Figure 1.6** Steve Niedorf/The Image Bank; **Figure 1.7** Courtesy of Hewlett-Packard Company; **Figure 1.8** Courtesy of International Business Machines Corporation; **Figure 1.9** Walter Bibikon/Image Bank; **Figure 1.10a** Courtesy of Apple Computer, Inc.; **Figure 1.11a** John Thoeming/Richard D. Irwin; **Figure 1.12a-f** Courtesy of International Business Machines Corporation; **Figure 1.13** Bettmann Newsphotos; **Figure 1.15a** Chris Gilbert; **Figure 1.15b** Courtesy of Apple Computers, Inc.; **Figure 1.18** Michael Grecco/Stock Boston; **Figure 1.19a** Stacy Pick/Stock Boston; **Figure 1.19b** Stacy Pick/Stock Boston; **Figure 1.20a** Larry Keenan/Image Back; **Figure 1.20b** James Wilson/Woodfin Camp; **Figure 1.21a** Courtesy of Borden, Inc.; **Figure 1.21b** Courtesy of Boeing; **Figure 1.22** Fredrich Cantor/Onyx Enterprises, Inc.; **Figure 1.23** Michael Abramson/Woodfin Camp

Chapter 2

Figure 2.1a Courtesy of Hewlett-Packard Company; **Figure 2.1b** John Thoeming/Richard D. Irwin, Inc.; **Figure 2.1c** Courtesy of Hewlett-Packard Company

Chapter 3

Figure 3.2a Courtesy of International Business Machines, Corporation; **Figure 3.2b** Courtesy of Northgate Computer Systems, Inc.; **Figure 3.3** Fred Bodin; **Figure 3.4** John Thoeming/Richard D. Irwin; **Figure 3.5a** Bill Varie/The Image Bank; **Figure 3.6a** David Dempster; **Figure 3.7** Courtesy of NCR Corporation; **Figure 3.8** Courtesy of Data General Corporation; **Figure 3.9** Reprinted with permission of Bell South/Bud Hunter; **Figure 3.10** Courtesy of Hewlett-Packard Company; **Figure 3.13a** CARDMATION Company; **Figure 3.13b** Courtesy of International Business Machines Corporation; **Figure 3.14** Courtesy of CARDMATION Company, Inc.; **Figure 3.16a** Courtesy of Radio Shack, a division of Tandy Corporation; **Figure 3.16b** Courtesy of Hand Held Products; **Figure 3.16c** Gale Zucker/Stock Boston; **Figure 3.18** Courtesy of SCRANTON Corporation; **Figure 3.19b** Spencer Grant/The Picture Cube; **Figure 3.20a** Courtesy of Apple Computers, Inc.; **Figure 3.20b** Courtesy of Soricon Corporation; **Figure 3.21** James Aronovsky/Picture Group; **Figure 3.22a** Courtesy of International Business Machines Corporation; **Figure 3.23** Courtesy of SmartCard International; **Figure 3.24a** Courtesy of Texas Instruments; **Figure 3.24b** Fred Bodin; **Figure 3.26** Lou Jones/Image Bank; **Figure 3.27a** John Thoeming/Richard D. Irwin; **Figure 3.27b** Courtesy of Kensington; **Figure 3.28** Michael Abramson/Woodfin Camp; **Figure 3.29a** Billy E. Barnes/TSW; **Figure 3.29b** Hank Morgan/Rainbow; **Figure 3.30** Michael Melford/The Image Bank; **Figure 3.32** Andreas Stephan/Black Star

Chapter 4

Figure 4.15a Michael Salas/The Image Bank; **Figure 4.16** Jon Riley/TSW; **Figure 4.19b** Dan McCoy/Rainbow; **Figure 4.19c** Courtesy of International Business Machines Corporation; **Figure 4.21a** Courtesy of Seagate Technology; **Figure 4.21b** Courtesy of International Business Machines Corporation; **Figure 4.22** Courtesy of Apple Computer, Inc.; **Figure 4.24a** Courtesy of Plus Development Corporation; **Figure 4.25** Courtesy of Tandon Corporation; **Figure 4.26** Courtesy of Irwin Magnetic Systems, Inc.; **Figure 4.27a** Courtesy of Unisys Corporation; **Figure 4.28** Courtesy of International Business Machines Corporation; **Figure 4.29** Courtesy of International Business Machines Corporation; **Figure 4.30b** Courtesy of Maxtor Corporation; **Figure 4.31** Fred Bodin

Chapter 5

Figure 5.4a Courtesy of International Business Machines Corporation; **Figure 5.4b** Courtesy of Thomas A. Way/International Business Machines Corporation; **Figure 5.4c** Courtesy of Intel Corporation; **Figure 5.4d** Courtesy of Motorola, Inc.; **Figure 5.4e** Courtesy of AT&T Archives; **Figure 5.5a** Dan McCoy/Rainbow; **Figure 5.5b** Dan McCoy/Rainbow; **Figure 5.6** Courtesy of Advanced Transducer, Inc.; **Figure 5.9** John Thoeming/Richard D. Irwin, Inc.; **Figure 5.10** Chris Gilbert; **Figure 5.11** Courtesy of Intel Corporation; **Figure 5.12** Courtesy of Thinking Machines Corporation

Chapter 6

Figure 6.1a Courtesy of Hewlett-Packard Company; **Figure 6.1b** Courtesy of Apple Computer, Inc.; **Figure 6.1c** Courtesy of Hewlett-Packard Company; **Figure 6.2a** Courtesy of Hewlett-Packard; **Figure 6.2b** Lou Jones; **Figure 6.4a** Courtesy of Qume Corporation; **Figure 6.4b** Courtesy of Qume Corporation; **Figure 6.5c** NEC Information Systems; **Figure 6.6b** NEC Information Systems; **Figure 6.8d** Courtesy of Unisys Corporation; **Figure 6.9b** Courtesy of Hewlett-Packard Company; **Figure 6.10** Courtesy of Versatec; **Figure 6.11a** Courtesy of Dataproducts Corporation; **Figure 6.11c** Courtesy of Hewlett-Packard Company; **Figure 6.12a** Courtesy of Versatec; **Figure 6.12b** Courtesy of Versatec; **Figure 6.12c** Courtesy of Hewlett-Packard Company; **Figure 6.13b** Courtesy of Minolta Corporation; **Figure 6.14** Courtesy of Eastman Kodak Company; **Figure 6.18** Fred Bodin; **Figure 6.19a** Fred Bodin; **Figure 6.19b** Fred Bodin; **Figure 6.20** Chris Gilbert; **Figure 6.21a** Courtesy of NEC Home Electronics; **Figure 6.21b** Courtesy of Compaq Computers; **Figure 6.21c** Courtesy of Zenith Data Systems; **Figure 6.22** Courtesy of Hewlett-Packard Company; **Figure 6.23a** Courtesy of GRID Systems Corporation; **Figure 6.23b** Courtesy of Toshiba America Information Systems; **Figure 6.23c** Courtesy of International Business Machines Corporation; **Figure 6.24** Courtesy of Kurzweil Computer Products; **Figure 6.25** James Wilson/Woodfin Camp & Associates; **Figure 6.26** Courtesy of QMS, Inc.

Chapter 7

Figure 7.1a Courtesy of International Business Machines Corporation; **Figure 7.1b** Courtesy of Hewlett-Packard Company; **Figure 7.3** © Thom O'Connor; **Figure 7.11a** John Thoeming/Richard D. Irwin, Inc.; **Figure 7.11b** Courtesy of Unisys Corporation; **Figure 7.13a** Courtesy of International Business Machines Corporation; **Figure 7.13b** Fred Bodin; **Figure 7.14** Stan Rowin/The Picture Cube; **Figure 7.19** Charles Gupton/TSW; **Figure 7.20** Courtesy of Martin Marietta Corporation; **Figure 7.21** Courtesy of Unocal/Bob Thomason (TSW); **Figure 7.32a** Courtesy of Microsoft Corporation; **Figure 7.32b** Courtesy of Microsoft Corporation

Chapter 8

Figure 8.14 Courtesy of Naval Surface Warfare Center, Dahlgren, VA

Chapter 9

Figure 9.4 Courtesy of Digital Communications Associates, Inc.; **Figure 9.6a** Courtesy of AT&T Archives; **Figure 9.6b** Fred Bodin; **Figure 9.6c** Fred Bodin; **Figure 9.7c** Jean Pierre Pieuchot/The Image Bank; **Figure 9.8d** Hank Morgan/Rainbow; **Figure 9.9** Antonio Luiz Hamdan; **Figure 9.10a** Courtesy of Hayes Microcomputer Products, Inc.; **Figure 9.10b** Courtesy of Hayes Microcomputer Products; **Figure 9.11b** Fred Bodin; **Figure 9.11c** Fred Bodin; **Figure 9.14** Fred Bodin; **Figure 9.15** Courtesy of AT&T; **Figure 9.16** Romilly Lockyer/The Image Bank; **Figure 9.22b** Fred Bodin; **Figure 9.25b** Courtesy of Comshare, Inc.; **Figure 9.26a** Comstock; **Figure 9.26b** Fred Bodin

Chapter 10

Figure 10.10 Courtesy of Information Builders, Inc.

Chapter 11

Figure 11.5 Courtesy of Zenith Electronics Corporation; **Figure 11.13** Fred Bodin

Chapter 12

Figure 12.9a Richard Wood/The Picture Cube; **Figure 12.9b** Gregory Heisler/The Image Bank; **Figure 12.9c** Dan McCoy/Rainbow; **Figure 12.10a** Courtesy of Autodesk, Inc.; **Figure 12.10b** Courtesy of Autodesk, Inc.; **Figure 12.10c** Courtesy of Autodesk, Inc.; **Figure 12.11** Fred Bodin

Introduction to the Modules

Figure I-6a Dan McCoy/Rainbow; **Figure I-6b** Courtesy of International Business Machines Corporation